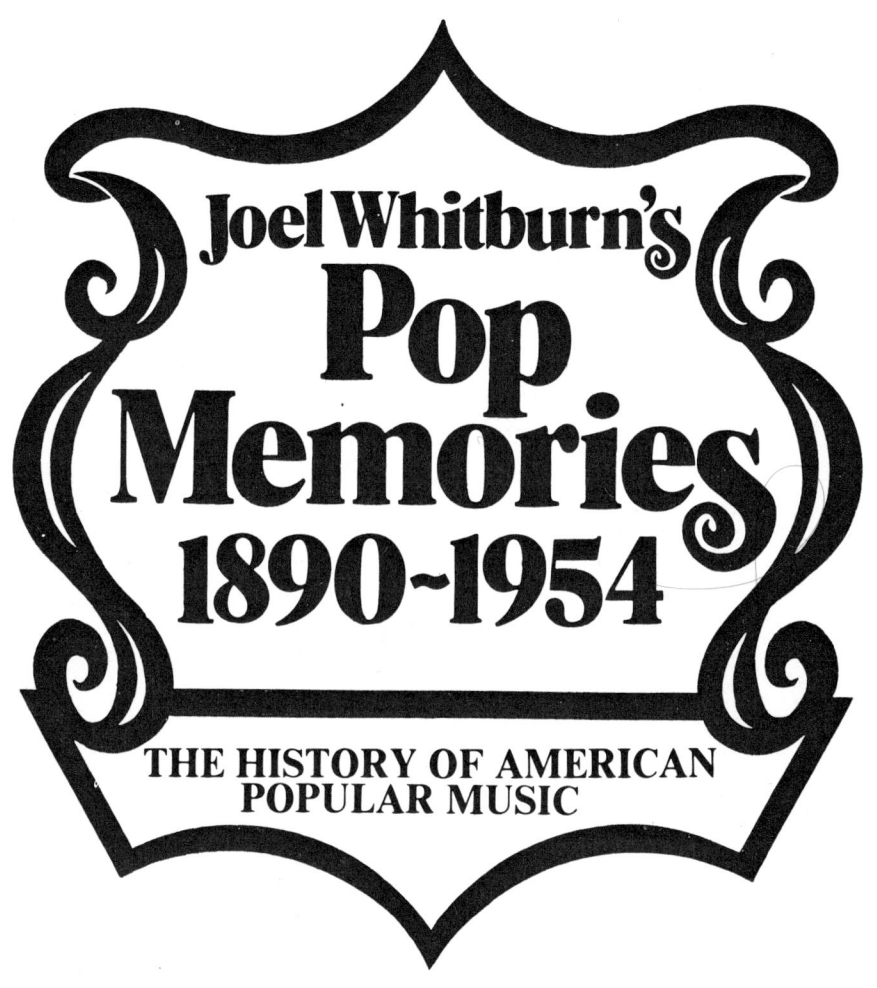

Joel Whitburn's Pop Memories 1890-1954

THE HISTORY OF AMERICAN POPULAR MUSIC

Compiled from America's popular music charts 1890-1954.

Record Research Inc.
P.O. Box 200
Menomonee Falls, Wisconsin 53051

ISBN 0-89820-083-0

Published by Record Research Inc.
P.O. Box 200, Menomonee Falls, Wisconsin 53051

CONTENTS

INTRODUCTION

The birth and early development of an art form is a rare and exciting thing. It is even more exciting when the story of that evolution has been lost in the mists of history to all but a few scholars, and the opportunity arises to uncover and tell it all to the world.

I believe this is what "Pop Memories" represents. It is the history of American popular records from the first stirrings of the industry in the Victorian age to the dawn of the rock era. We can see so much of ourselves in this history: the innocent sentimentality of the 1890s (Dan Quinn's "Daisy Bell"), the clash of personal and national emotions in World War I (the Peerless Quartet's "I Didn't Raise My Boy To Be a Soldier", the American Quartet's "Over There"), the sunny romanticism overlying fear during the Depression (Fred Astaire's "Cheek to Cheek", Bing Crosby's "Brother, Can You Spare a Dime?"). Yet, until now, an astonishing amount of this history has been largely unknown.

Have you ever heard of Len Spencer or Russell Hunting? They were two of the true pioneers of early popular recordings, however, for the last 50 years their names have been almost totally forgotten. How about Billy Murray and Ada Jones? They were the recording superstars of their time, yet even the finest popular music histories give them little more than passing mention. Here, for the first time, all receive the recognition they have so long deserved.

When I started the research on this book, the intention was to carry the popular record charts back to the 1920s. Although I've grown up on and loved the music of the Beatles and Bruce Springsteen, the great artists of the dance band era have been just as meaningful to me since I discovered them through my parents. The music of Ellington, Basie, Goodman, and Miller, and the song stylings of Sinatra and Billie Holiday, are every bit as vital and thrilling to this child of the rock era as they must have been to those who experienced it first hand.

But what I learned about the artists and records of the pre-1920 era came as a revelation to me. The duets of Ada & Billy were absolutely delightful in the innocent sense of flirtatious fun they conveyed. The records of the Haydn, Peerless, and American Quartets conjured up the classic era of barbershop four-part harmonies. Cal Stewart's tales of "Uncle Josh" were often hilarious and revealing slices of life in the great tradition of American storytelling. And all of this is in addition to the already-recognized greatness of Caruso and McCormack.

One of the things I would especially love to see happen as a result of this book would be for RCA Victor and Columbia to open up their mighty archives and reissue some of the priceless recordings they made during the pioneer era. Until then, the best appreciation of the popular records of that age can be found right here.

Steve Sullivan

Editors note: Steve Sullivan spent three years doing intensive research work for this monumental project at the Library of Congress Recorded Sound Reference Center.

RESEARCHING THE CHARTS

Now for some explanation of how the early charts came to be. Billboard's earliest music charts were sheet music listings in 1913. However, from 1896-1899, The Phonoscope, the leading record publication of its time, printed monthly lists of top popular recordings (although not in precise rank or chart form). Going back several years earlier, The Phonogram provided invaluable information on records and artists of the early 1890s. The catalogs of Columbia, Edison, Berliner, and regional labels helped fill the gaps. To compile the charts of that decade I combined this material with data on sheet music sales and other popular song listings from ASCAP and the books of musicologist David Ewen.

The single most important source for the charts and artist information of the 1900-1920s era was Jim Walsh, the world's leading authority on the pioneer recording age, through his remarkable 40 years of regular columns for Hobbies Magazine. (Jim's columns also shed light on the hits of the 1890s.) Nearly as significant was Talking Machine World, a superb periodical which began in 1905 and offered monthly lists of nearly all popular record releases. Record label publications, particularly those of Victor and Edison, also contained valuable information.

From 1914-21, the major record companies provided monthly lists of their best sellers to Talking Machine World. While not always totally reliable, they were carefully factored in. Billboard, in addition to its short-lived sheet music charts, also printed weekly lists of the most popular songs in vaudeville from 1913-18. Both Billboard and Variety provided abundant information on the hit records and songs of the 1920s. All this was again combined with sheet music sales and ASCAP lists to produce the charts of this era.

In late 1929 another invaluable source emerged when Variety began printing monthly rankings of the best-selling records for each of the top labels, a more systematic version of what Talking Machine World had previously done. By 1934 both Billboard and Variety were regularly charting the top songs in radio airplay and sheet music sales. This made it necessary to compile two separate weekly charts: one for best-selling records, and one for the top recordings of the most popular radio and sheet-music songs.

"Your Hit Parade" came along in April 1935 - weekly rankings which were far from definitive, but nonetheless extremely useful. These were incorporated here into the radio airplay charts. In November of that year Billboard picked up the record label best-seller charts. In early 1938 Billboard stopped running these listings, which were then carried by Metronome until the end of the year, when they ceased to exist. Billboard opened up an important new frontier late that same year with weekly surveys of the most popular records in juke boxes around the country - making for a new separate chart.

Finally, on July 20, 1940, Billboard printed its first comprehensive Best Selling Records chart which combined all labels. It was these charts that I chronicled in my "Top Pop Singles 1940-1955" book. On this date, we cut off the Hit Parade/radio airplay charts. From 1940-44 both the best-seller and juke box charts were supplemented by Billboard's information on regional favorites.

In 1945 came the Billboard "Most Played by Disc Jockeys" survey. This compiled the triad of charts - record sellers, juke boxes, and radio airplay -that would continue to the end of the period covered by this book. The few songs which appeared on the Billboard "Honor Roll of Hits" but not on the other surveys were added.

During the 1945-47 and 1952-54 period when Billboard cut down on the size of its charts, the gap was filled by the magazine's listings of "up and coming"and regional hits, supplemented by data from Variety and other sources.

The explanation of the research that went into this book would not be complete without very special thanks to the Library of Congress' Recorded Sound Reference Center. Virtually all of the original materials for the 1890s-1920s era were obtained through its unparalleled resources, including the early periodicals, catalogs, and the Rigler and Deutsch Index of data on 78s.

So there you have it. My intention is for this book to serve as the ultimate, definitive source on American popular records and artists of the pre-1955 era. Therefore its value to collectors, radio programmers and scholars is obvious. But I also think "Pop Memories" will be a delight to every music lover with any curiosity about how we got where we are today. It represents a wonderful legacy we can now share, handed down from generations of musical talent. Enjoy.

Joel Whitburn

CHART SYNOPSIS

Years	Chart Size	Sources
1890-1899	1-3	1. Phonogram (early 1890s record industry periodical) 2. Phonoscope (1896-1899; monthly lists of top records) 3. Sheet music sales 4. ASCAP and other lists of top period songs 5. Record label catalogs: Columbia, Edison, Berliner, & regional labels 6. Jim Walsh columns for Hobbies Magazine on pioneer recording artists
1900-1909	5-10	1. Jim Walsh 2. Talking Machine World (monthly record industry periodical) 3. Sheet music sales 4. ASCAP 5. Record label publications: Victor, Edison, Columbia, Zon-o-Phone 6. Best-selling-records information
1910-1919	10	1. Talking Machine World (published monthly lists of record labels' top sellers from 1914-21) 2. Billboard (sheet music best sellers, 1913; weekly lists of top songs in vaudeville, 1913-18) 3. Jim Walsh 4. Sheet music sales 5. ASCAP 6. Record label publications 7. Best-selling-records information
1920-1926	10-15	1. Billboard 2. Talking Machine World (through 1929) 3. Other trade publications 4. Sheet music sales 5. ASCAP 6. Best-selling-records information
1927-1933	20	1. Record label best-seller rankings (published each month in trade periodicals from 1929-1938) 2. Billboard 3. Other trade publications 4. Sheet music sales 5. ASCAP

CHART SYNOPSIS — Cont'd

Years	Chart Size	Sources
1934-1938	20	**BEST SELLING RECORDS:** 1. Record label best-seller rankings 2. Miscellaneous reference sources (for record labels not listed)
1934-1940	20	**HIT PARADE/RADIO AIRPLAY:** 1. "Your Hit Parade" (April 1935-July 1940) 2. Billboard radio airplay charts 3. ASCAP
1938-1954	15-30	**JUKE BOX CHARTS:** 1. Billboard "Music Box Machine" (1938-44) and "Most Played in Juke Boxes" (1944-54) charts 2. Billboard regional favorites (1940-44) 3. Billboard "up and coming hits" (Nov. 1947-May 1948) 4. Billboard "Best Buys" - regional and up & coming hits - supplemented by other trade publications (used from Nov. 1952-Dec. 1954 for positions #21-30 when Billboard reduced chart size)
1940-1954	15-30	**BEST SELLING RECORDS:** 1. Billboard "Best Sellers in Stores" chart (began July 20, 1940) 2. Billboard regional favorites (1940-44) 3. Miscellaneous reference sources (used to cover gaps in limited 1945-47 charts) 4. Billboard up & coming hits (1947-48) 5. Billboard regional and up & coming hits, with other trade publications (1952-54)
1945-1954	15-30	**DISC JOCKEY CHARTS:** 1. Billboard "Most Played by Disc Jockeys" chart 2. Billboard up & coming hits (1947-48) 3. Billboard regional and up & coming hits, with other trade publications (1952-54)

CHRONOLOGY OF MILESTONES IN POPULAR MUSIC/RECORDING HISTORY 1877-1954

Dec. 24, 1877: Thomas Edison files a patent application for his latest invention, the phonograph. It consists of a metal cylinder with a fine spiral groove, two diaphragm-and-needle units (one for recording and one for playback), and a small horn. The cylinder is rotated by handle while one speaks into the recording horn; the sound collected by the horn causes the diaphragm to vibrate, driving the stylus to form grooves into the tin foil wrapped around the cylinder. Reversing the process causes the playback stylus to reproduce the sounds formed by the grooves, amplified by the horn. The machine is designed at first for office dictation, but its possibilities for recording music, though still crude, soon become evident. In January, the Edison Speaking Phonograph Company is formed.

Sept. 26, 1887: The next crucial step in recording technology is introduced when Emile Berliner (who ten years before invented the microphone) files a patent application for the gramophone, which utilizes zinc discs instead of cylinders.

Nov. 1887: Edison records his first solid-wax cylinders to replace the primitive tinfoil recordings which could be played back one time only. His new cylinder phonograph operates on battery-powered electricity.

June 14, 1888: Edison founds the North American Phonograph Company, originally to produce machines for business dictation. In January 1889 the Columbia Phonograph Company is established as North American's Washington, D.C.-area licensee.

May 24, 1889: The first commercial musical recordings are made by North American for operators of West Coast coin-operated phonographs. These "phonograph parlors", begun in San Francisco, enable customers to sit at a desk, order a selection for a nickel by speaking into a tube, and listen through a separate tube connected to a cylinder phonograph in the room below while the selection is played. By the mid-1890s nearly every American city has at least one phonograph parlor.

October 1890: Columbia issues its first record catalog, consisting solely of recordings by John Philip Sousa's U.S. Marine Band. Within the next year its selection will rapidly expand as the company emerges as a significant rival to Edison.

1890: North American begins using the first crude record duplicating process, with up to ten tubes leading from the master phonograph to blank cylinders in other phonographs; previously each record had to be custom-made. Soon a more refined "pantograph" system makes possible 150 copies of each record. A popular artist such as George Washington Johnson must still record a hit like "The Laughing Song" literally thousands of times.

January 1891: The Phonogram, the first publication devoted to the phonograph and recording industry, begins.

Nov. 9, 1891: The New York debut of "A Trip to Chinatown", the first significant long-running Broadway musical. One song interpolated in the show, "After the Ball", sells five million copies of sheet music.

April 1892: North American begins to produce cylinders for the home market as well as for the coin-slot industry, which is approaching its peak of popularity. Phonograph prices (beginning at $150) are still too high for most. Record demand is increasing beyond the capacity of North American to meet it (a maximum of 2,000 cylinders can now be made from each recording), so its regional member companies - New Jersey, Ohio, and others in addition to Columbia - begin making their own recordings.

1894: Columbia introduces a new spring-motored phonograph which sells for only $40. Before long the phonograph will become a fixture in the American home.

August 1894: Edison, to forestall legal maneuvers against his patents by the American Phonograph Company (which in 1895 will obtain control of Columbia), puts North American into bankruptcy. For the next two years Columbia and the regional companies will have the cylinder record business to themselves. By decade's end, Columbia will effectively drive the smaller companies out of business.

November 1894: Billboard begins publication as the authoritative trade weekly of the amusement industries.

Fall 1895: The Berliner Gramophone Company is established to market the first commercial flat disc recordings. Under the Berliner system, sound cuts lateral grooves into the surfaces of wax-coated zinc discs, which were then immersed in chromic acid. An electrotyping process using metal "stampers" reproduced the zinc originals. Mass production would carry the recording industry into a new era.

January 1896: Edison, once again in legal control of his patents, organizes the National Phonograph Company, which quickly moves into even competition with Columbia for the cylinder record business.

March 1898: The debut of the Edison Standard Phonograph, priced at $20 to compete with Columbia. The average price of the 1890s' standard two-minute cylinders is 50 cents.

1899: Ragtime, a dynamic new style of music, is symbolized by composer-pianist Scott Joplin. Len Spencer, Arthur Collins, and banjoist Vess Ossman are the most popular ragtime-styled recording artists.

May 1900: The new century brings a major new force into the recording industry, Eldridge Johnson's Consolidated Talking Machine Company. Johnson's "Improved Gram-o-phone Records" are laterally-cut wax discs similar to those of his former employer, Berliner, but with improved sound quality. The company's symbol is the famous image of a dog peering into a gramophone horn and listening to "His Master's Voice".

June 1900: Berliner, pressured in part by legal challenges made by another disc record company, Zon-o-Phone, issues his last recordings.

October 1901: Victor Talking Machine Company is formed out of Consolidated, with Johnson as 60% owner and Berliner as 40% shareholder.

January 1902: Edison begins producing moulded metallic wax cyliners, phasing out the old brown wax cylinders. As many as 150 cylinders can be turned out daily from a single mould, vastly increasing total production. Record prices are cut to 35 cents.

March 18, 1902: Enrico Caruso's first recordings for Victor are perhaps the first musically satisfactory records ever made, and for the first time recordings come to be seen as an acceptable vehicle for serious music. The vast popularity of Caruso's records - despite their intimidating price of five dollars (equal to a week's pay for many) - launches Victor's prestigious Red Seal label.

1903: This is the golden age of barbershop quartets, and the most famous one of all, the Empire City Quartet, introduces the classic "Sweet Adeline". Male vocal groups - particularly the Haydn, Peerless, and American Quartets - will be enormously popular on records until the early 20s.

November 1904: "Little Johnny Jones" helps make George M. Cohan the dominant force in Broadway musicals. Billy Murray becomes the nation's most popular recording artist in large part because of his hit recordings of many Cohan classics.

January 1905: Talking Machine World begins publication as the leading journal of the recording industry. In December, Variety begins as the professional show business weekly.

June 1905: Arthur Collins' "The Preacher and the Bear" is the first generally-recognized million-selling record, although Len Spencer's 1902 hit "Arkansaw Traveler" may have previously achieved that level.

1906: Eldridge Johnson introduces the Victrola, the first record player to remove the famous tin horn from atop the phonograph and fold it into the wooden cabinet beneath. Also, during 1906, Victor cuts standard record prices to 35 cents, eliminating the competitive advantage of Edison cylinders.

August 1907: Enrico Caruso's "Vesti la Giubba" from "I Pagliacci" is the first million-selling classical record. Thanks in large part to Caruso, Victor is now established as the #1 record company in both sales and prestige.

November 1907: Ada Jones and Billy Murray, the most popular of all female-male vocal pairings, have their first #1 record. Up until now nearly all vocal records have been in one of two styles, minstrel-styled comedy (such as Collins & Harlan), or formal European-influenced ballad singing (led by Henry Burr). Ada & Billy introduce a more casual, natural style.

October 1908: Columbia advertises America's first two-sided records, and the appeal of "two songs for the price of one" proves irresistible. Within a few months Victor quietly begins producing double-sided discs, although Red Seals will not be doubled until 1923.

November 1908: Edison begins producing four-minute wax Amberol cylinders, nearly doubling the previous maximum length.

1910: Sheet music sales achieve an all-time high of two billion, led by two six-million sellers - "Let Me Call You Sweetheart" and "Down by the Old Mill Stream".

1912: Columbia stops all production of cylinders, leaving Edison as the only major cylinder company; they will remain popular in rural areas into the 1920s, but the disc vs. cylinder battle is effectively over.

October 1912: Edison responds to the expanding dominance of discs by introducing the Diamond Disc Phonograph and records. Their sound quality is widely hailed, but since the phonograph will play only "hill-and-dale"-grooved records, and not the laterally-cut discs made by Victor and Columbia, their popular impact is limited. At the same time, Edison begins production of "unbreakable" four-minute Blue Amberol cylinders, far more durable than their predecessors.

July 1913: Billboard briefly prints weekly sheet music best-seller charts, then in August begins regular surveys of the most popular songs in vaudeville.

1913: Ballroom dancing, symbolized by Vernon & Irene Castle, is at its peak. 1913 also sees the introduction of the decade's biggest dance craze, the fox-trot.

1914: ASCAP, the American Society of Composers, Authors, & Publishers, is formed as the first organization to protect the work of songwriters, later serving as a recognized licensing agency.

September 1914: Talking Machine World prints its first monthly list of the best-selling records for each major record company, information furnished by the companies themselves.

1914: W.C. Handy's "Memphis Blues" and "St. Louis Blues" are the first "blues" songs to be published and achieve wide popularity. "St. Louis Blues" will ultimately become the song recorded by more artists than any other song in American history.

Jan. 30, 1917: "Darktown Strutters' Ball" by the Original Dixieland Jazz Band is the first commercial jazz recording, and the music which began in the 1890s as the native folk sound of New Orleans begins to transform American popular music.

1917: As the exclusive patent rights held by Victor, Columbia and Edison begin to expire, the record industry opens up to new companies, including Okeh, Brunswick, Vocalion and Emerson. The longtime European company Pathe' also enters the American market.

1918: Vaudeville is at its peak with 25,000 performers touring in some 4,000 theaters nationwide.

January 1920: "Dardanella" by Ben Selvin's Novelty Orchestra hits #1, and becomes the first record to sell more than three million copies.

August 10, 1920: "Crazy Blues" by Mamie Smith is the first authentic blues recording, and is an immediate sensation.

1921: Radio explodes from a novelty into a nationwide phenomenon, with some 500 stations established by 1922 and over 1,000 by 1925. Broadcasts of dance band performances become a mainstay of the new medium, and singers such as Billy Jones & Ernest Hare and Vaughn DeLeath become stars primarily through their radio programs.

July 1922: Louis Armstrong, the young cornet genius soon to become the single most important figure in the early evolution of jazz, comes from New Orleans to Chicago to join the band of King Oliver.

December 1922: "Three O'Clock In The Morning" is the three-million-selling #1 record for the decade's dominant dance band, Paul Whiteman's orchestra. The balance of power on the charts has now shifted decisively from vocalists to bands.

Feb. 16, 1923: Bessie Smith, the world's greatest blues singer, records "Down Hearted Blues", which becomes an extraordinary million-seller almost totally in the "race" market.

1923: Columbia Records, burdened by a large inventory of unsold phonographs, goes into receivership before reorganization in 1924; sales of Bessie Smith's records are credited in part with its recovery.

1923: The Charleston is the biggest dance craze of the decade, and its theme song hits #1 in January 1924.

Feb. 12, 1924: George Gershwin, best known as composer of the Al Jolson smash "Swanee", stuns the music world with the New York premiere of his jazz concerto, "Rhapsody In Blue".

1924: Victor produces its first line of radio receivers. But all the record companies are slow in responding to competition from the new medium, and the result is an industry-wide slump.

1924-25: A year of experiments by engineers at Bell Laboratories results in the historic breakthrough of electrical recording. Instead of the acoustic process of singers and musicians performing directly into a recording horn, they are now able to record with a condenser microphone in a spacious studio. With the use of a vacuum tube amplifier and an electromagnetically-powered cutting stylus, the frequency range of recorded music expands by two and a half octaves. Within a year, every major recording studio converts to the new system.

May 1925: "The Prisoner's Song" by Vernon Dalhart hits #1, on its way to selling more than seven million copies.

1925: "Adeste Fidelis" and "John Peel" by the 850-voice Associated Glee Clubs of America is the double-sided Columbia choral hit which dramatically demonstates the vastly improved sound quality of electrical recordings. In November, Brunswick's "Panatrope" and Victor's "Electrola" are introduced as the first electrical phonographs.

November 1925: The first Nashville radio broadcast of the "Grand Ole Opry".

Nov. 15, 1926: NBC Radio goes on the air; CBS follows on Sept. 18, 1927.

1927: Total record sales reach a peak of 140 million; at year's end Gene Austin's "My Blue Heaven" begins its run toward sales of five million. But darkness lies just ahead.

Oct. 6, 1927: "The Jazz Singer", starring Broadway's greatest star of the last decade, Al Jolson, is the first motion picture with singing, and its premiere creates an immediate sensation. ("Don Juan" a year earlier was the first sound film). Within two years, movies will become the predominant source of popular song hits.

December 1927: Duke Ellington, destined to be the greatest of all jazz composers, begins a five-year run with his orchestra at Harlem's famous Cotton Club.

Dec. 27, 1927: After more than 40 years of Broadway musicals that were basically spectacle with little story line or substance, "Show Boat", by Jerome Kern and Oscar Hammerstein II, ushers the American musical into a new age.

1928: Country music has its first all-time great recording stars in Jimmie Rodgers and the Carter Family.

February 1929: "Broadway Melody" is the first "all talking, all singing, all dancing" motion picture.

October 1929: The stock market collapses, and the Great Depression begins. Also, this month is the final Edison recording session as he leaves the business to concentrate on radio production.

November 1929: Variety prints its first monthly best-selling record chart, consisting, like the previous Talking Machine World, of lists of information supplied by the major record companies.

February 1931: Having served his apprenticeship with Paul Whiteman, Bing Crosby steps out to become the nation's most popular singer, a distinction the "crooner" will retain for most of the next 20 years.

1931: Victor makes a first abortive attempt at long-playing records to go beyond the three-to-four-minute limit on 78 rpm records; the idea is right, but the timing and the economy are not.

1932: "Brother, Can You Spare a Dime?" is the classic hit symbolizing the Great Depression. It is also the tune being sung by the record industry, which has undergone an almost total collapse to only six million records sold for the year. Beyond the obvious impact of the desolate national economy, the opportunity to hear all popular songs on the radio for free, and general disenchantment with "canned music", are other factors in the desperate slump.

Early 1933: "42nd Street" dramatically revitalizes the Hollywood musical.

End 1933: "Flying Down To Rio" introduces the motion picture dance team that will captivate America: Broadway star Fred Astaire and Ginger Rogers.

December 1933: The repeal of Prohibition stimulates the opening of thousands of bars and cocktail lounges throughout the country. Many are equipped with juke boxes, which, like the phonograph parlors of the 1890s, create a significant new market for records.

June 1934: Billboard prints its first weekly survey of the most-played songs on network radio.

September 1934: Decca Records, a European company newly expanded into America, launches an energetic promotional campaign built around its stable of top stars (led by Bing Crosby) and its 35-cent record prices. For the first time in nearly five years, the slowly recuperating record industry begins to see daylight.

November 1934: Cole Porter's "Anything Goes" is the decade's most acclaimed Broadway musical.

April 20, 1935: The first radio broadcast of "Your Hit Parade" - ranking the week's most popular songs according to sheet music sales and radio airplay; the show quickly achieves wide influence.

Sept. 25-Oct. 1, 1935: The sensational success of Benny Goodman and his band at the Los Angeles Palomar ballroom marks the beginning of the "swing era" in popular music, and a new national musical vitality.

Oct. 11, 1935: George Gershwin's masterwork, the folk opera "Porgy And Bess", premieres on Broadway.

November 1935: Billboard begins weekly coverage of the major record companies' best-seller charts.

1936: The jukebox becomes a nationwide phenomenon, present wherever people gather to listen to music or dance, with some 225,000 in operation by 1939. Wurlitzer and Rock-ola set the industry standards, and the jukebox will be at the heart of the record business' recovery through World War II.

1937: "Jitterbugging" is the swing-era dance craze.

Jan. 16, 1938: Jazz comes of age with the historic Carnegie Hall concert of Benny Goodman and his band.

February 1938: The original-soundtrack recordings from the first full-length animated movie, "Snow White and the Seven Dwarfs", sweep the country.

April 1938: Billboard initiates the "Record Buying Guide", a weekly survey of the most popular records in jukeboxes around the country.

1938: Ella Fitzgerald's "A-Tisket, A-Tasket", Will Glahe's "Beer Barrel Polka", and Artie Shaw's "Begin the Beguine" are the first records in nearly ten years to sell more than 300,000 copies, all eventually reaching the million mark.

February 1940: As "In the Mood" hits #1 for 12 weeks, Glenn Miller is confirmed as the most popular bandleader of the big band era.

1940: Walt Disney's classic "Fantasia" is the first significant effort at motion picture stereo sound.

July 1940: Billboard begins its "Best-Selling Retail Records" weekly chart, the first published independent national record survey.

1940: A breakdown in contract negotiations between ASCAP and radio broadcasters leads to a nine-month blackout of ASCAP-licensed songs, and the formation of a rival licensing agency, Broadcast Music Incorporated (BMI).

November 1941: Glenn Miller's "Chattanooga Choo Choo" reaches #1, and will be honored with the first "gold record", officially certifying it as a million-seller.

August 1, 1942: It is a dark day for the record industry as the American Federation of Musicians precipitates a ban on recording by all bands following a dispute over musicians' royalties. Singers may continue to record, and they step into the vacuum and alter popular musical tastes with acappella vocal records. On Sept. 18, 1943 agreement is reached with all the record companies except Victor and Columbia, who finally come to terms November 11, 1944.

October 1942: Bing Crosby's recording of Irving Berlin's "White Christmas" soars to #1, and will become the biggest-selling record in popular music history, with total sales through the years of more than thirty million.

November 1942: The Mosque Theater in Newark, N.J. is the scene for the first public demonstration of "Sinatra mania" as Frank Sinatra, solo after three years of stardom with Tommy Dorsey, electrifies female fans like no one before him.

March 31, 1943: "Oklahoma!", the first collaboration by Richard Rodgers (after nearly 20 years of enduring hits with Lorenz Hart) and Oscar Hammerstein II, premieres and is the greatest breakthrough in Broadway musical history. Honored with the Pulitzer Prize, the show has unprecedented unity of story, music, and choreography, and its original-cast album makes recording history.

1944: Louis Jordan is the first true rhythm-and-blues performer to achieve great crossover chart success.

1946: The success of "The Jolson Story", and the even greater success of its soundtrack album, enables Al Jolson to achieve the most remarkable comeback in popular music history. Also during 1946, RCA Victor issues its one billionth record - John Philip Sousa's "The Stars and Stripes Forever".

December 1946: In the space of a few weeks, eight of the country's most popular bands, including those of Benny Goodman and Tommy Dorsey, break up. Although most later re-form, it effectively marks the end of the fabled big band era.

June 21, 1948: The Columbia Broadcasting System demonstrates the long-playing microgroove recording, playing like the 1931 Victor experiment at thirty three and a third revolutions per minute. The albums of old, consisting of several 10-or-12-inch 78s, can now be replaced with a single record. In short order Victor comes out with its own innovation, the seven-inch 45 rpm record. After two years of confusion and competition, 45s become the standard for single releases and 78s are phased out by the late-50s.

Fall 1948: Regular network television programming begins.

April 7, 1949: "South Pacific" by Rodgers & Hammerstein debuts on Broadway. It will ultimately run even longer than "Oklahoma!", and its original-cast album will reign as #1 for an astonishing 69 weeks.

1949: Hank Williams emerges as the first modern country music superstar.

August 1950: "Goodnight, Irene" is the two-million-selling #1 record launching The Weavers, who bring American folk music to its widest audience ever.

June 1951: The Dominoes' giant rhythm & blues hit "Sixty Minute Man" is a major precursor to rock and roll.

1951-52: Gene Kelly's "An American in Paris" and "Singin' In the Rain" are the most acclaimed and popular movie musicals since the initial heyday of Fred Astaire.

1954: The motion picture "From Here to Eternity" and the record "Young at Heart" re-establish Frank Sinatra as America's pre-eminent popular singer.

August 1954: "That's All Right" is the first Sun Records release by a young man named Elvis Presley.

THE ARTISTS

This section lists, alphabetically by artist name, every single that made America's popular music charts from 1890 through 1954.

Each artist's charted hits are listed in chronological order. A sequential record count is shown in front of each song title to indicate the number of charted hits by each artist. All #1 hits are highlighted in dark type.

Headings & Symbols

DATE CHARTED: Date record first charted.

PEAK POS: Record's highest charted position (in dark type).

WKS CHRT'D: Total weeks charted.

LABEL & NUMBER: Original record label and number.

(): Number in parenthesis after #1 and #2 records indicates total weeks record held that position.

+: Indicates record peaked in the year after which it first charted.

●: Million Seller

Symbols in brackets after titles indicate the following:

[C] Comedy
[F] Foreign Language
[I] Instrumental
[N] Novelty
[R] Reissue or Re-release
[T] Talking
[X] Christmas

If both sides of a record made the charts, a diagonal symbol (/) separates the two titles. The label and number are shown only once - after the second title.

Directly under the artist's name are notes about the artist and/or orchestra that may be of interest.

Directly under a majority of the song titles are notes of special interest, such as the vocalist, accompaning orchestra or backing musicians. If a song is featured in a Broadway musical or film, the title of that show is given under the record title.

DATE CHARTED	PEAK POS	WKS CHRT'D	ARTIST — Record Title	Label & Number

A

IRVING AARONSON & HIS COMMANDERS
Artie Shaw, Tony Pastor and Gene Krupa were briefly members of this band between 1929 and 1933. Irving later became musical supervisor for MGM movies; he died on 5/10/63 (68).

DATE CHARTED	PEAK POS	WKS CHRT'D	ARTIST — Record Title	Label & Number
6/04/27	13	3	1. I Never See Maggie Alone .... vocal by Phil Saxe	Victor 20473
7/28/28	17	1	2. Evening Star	Victor 21451
1/05/29	5	6	3. Let's Do It, Let's Fall In Love .... from the Broadway musical "Paris"; vocal: Phil Saxe & Jack Armstrong	Victor 21745
6/29/29	19	1	4. All By Yourself In The Moonlight	Victor 21867
9/15/34	5	6	5. Pardon My Southern Accent .... vocal by Ernie Mathias	Columbia 2946

ROY ACUFF
One of country music's most beloved figures, Roy made his debut on Nashville's Grand Ole Opry in 1938, and has been an enduring favorite there ever since.

DATE CHARTED	PEAK POS	WKS CHRT'D	ARTIST — Record Title	Label & Number
9/24/38	13	3	1. Great Speckle Bird .... with the Crazy Tennesseeans	Vocalion 4252
12/24/38	12	2	● 2. Wabash Cannon Ball	Vocalion 4466
2/12/44	19	1	3. The Prodigal Son	Okeh 6716
12/30/44	26	1	4. I'll Forgive You, But I Can't Forget..............	Okeh 6723

CHARLES ADAMS
celesta player

DATE CHARTED	PEAK POS	WKS CHRT'D	ARTIST — Record Title	Label & Number
10/30/15	10	1	1. Silver Threads Among The Gold .... [I]	Columbia 1796

FAYE ADAMS
Rhythm & Blues singer - real name: Faye Scruggs

DATE CHARTED	PEAK POS	WKS CHRT'D	ARTIST — Record Title	Label & Number
10/03/53	22	2	● 1. Shake A Hand	Herald 416

CHARLES AGNEW & HIS STEVENS HOTEL ORCHESTRA
Chicago-based dance band

DATE CHARTED	PEAK POS	WKS CHRT'D	ARTIST — Record Title	Label & Number
8/19/33	13	2	1. Don't Blame Me	Columbia 2793

AIR LANE TRIO

DATE CHARTED	PEAK POS	WKS CHRT'D	ARTIST — Record Title	Label & Number
11/22/47	23	1	1. My Guitar Is My Sweetheart........................ vocal by Ted Martin	DeLuxe 1120

TONY ALAMO
Baritone singer with the Sammy Kaye band, 1949-51

FRANCES ALDA
New Zealand-born soprano with the New York Metropolitan Opera; died on 9/18/52 (67)

DATE CHARTED	PEAK POS	WKS CHRT'D	ARTIST — Record Title	Label & Number
5/14/10	9	1	1. Il Trovatore - Miserere (I Have Sighed To Rest Me) .... [F] ENRICO CARUSO & FRANCES ALDA	Victor 89030
6/04/10	9	1	2. Ave Maria .... [F]	Victor 88213
8/03/12	10	1	3. Martha - Quartetto Nocturno (Good Night Quartet, Act II, Part III) .... [F] ENRICO CARUSO, FRANCES ALDA, JOSEPHINE JACOBY, & MARCEL JOURNET	Victor 95210
9/22/17	9	1	4. For Your Country And My Country	Victor 64689
9/29/17	8	2	5. La Marseillaise.................................... [F] the French National Anthem; backed by the Metropolitan Opera Chorus	Victor 64693
3/13/20	7	2	6. The Bells Of St. Mary's	Victor 64844

ALEXANDER BROTHERS

DATE CHARTED	PEAK POS	WKS CHRT'D	ARTIST — Record Title	Label & Number
9/02/50	26	1	1. Goodnight Irene..	Mercury 5465

DATE CHARTED	PEAK POS	WKS CHRT'D	ARTIST — Record Title	Label & Number
			GEORGE ALEXANDER Baritone balladeer, real name Clifford Alexander Wiley; died on 3/2/13 (45).	
12/19/03	**3**	5	1. Mighty Like A Rose.................................. *also released on Columbia cylinder 32295*	Columbia 1585
5/27/05	**7**	1	2. America...	Columbia 3099
7/28/06	**10**	1	3. Dearie .... *also released on Columbia cylinder 32928*	Columbia 3378
			VAN ALEXANDER & HIS ORCHESTRA Arranger for Chick Webb's band, scored background music for TV and movies in 1950s	
11/18/39	**13**	3	1. Hot Dog Joe.. *vocal by Butch Stone*	Variety 8082
			ALL-STAR TRIO Victor Arden (piano), F. Wheeler Wadsworth (alto sax), and George Hamilton Green (xylophone)	
4/05/19	**6**	3	1. I'll Say She Does.................................... [I] *from the Broadway musical "Sinbad"*	Victor 18527
1/14/20	**5**	2	2. I Want A Daddy Who Will Rock Me To Sleep.. [I] *from the Broadway musical "Greenwich Village Follies of 1919"*	Victor 18626
3/06/20	**8**	2	3. Poor Little Butterfly Is A Fly Gal Now .... [I]	Victor 18641
4/03/20	**8**	2	4. You'd Be Surprised .... [I] *from the Broadway musical "Ziegfeld Follies of 1919"*	Victor 18643
4/24/20	**11**	1	5. Swanee .... [I] *from the Broadway musical "Sinbad"*	Victor 18651
5/14/21	**5**	4	6. Moonbeams .... [I]	Victor 35708
			BOB ALLEN Singer with the Hal Kemp band, 1934-40	
			EDWARD ALLEN Real name Arthur Middleton; died on 2/16/29 (48).	
1/03/20	**10**	1	1. Oh! What A Pal Was Mary	Edison 50594
			HENRY ALLEN & HIS ORCHESTRA Leading jazz trumpeter who started in New Orleans with King Oliver and later played with Luis Russell, Fletcher Henderson, Mills Blue Rhythm Band, and Louis Armstrong. His own band featured tenor sax great Coleman Hawkins (1933), J.C. Higginbotham (trombone), and Cozy Cole (drums). All vocals by Allen.	
6/09/34	**20**	1	1. I Wish I Were Twins	Perfect 15948
6/15/35	**17**	2	2. Body And Soul .... *from the Broadway musical "Three's a Crowd"*	Vocalion 2965
8/08/36	**18**	1	3. On The Beach At Bali Bali.........................	Vocalion 3261
11/21/36	**15**	2	4. Midnight Blue .... *from the Broadway musical "Ziegfeld Follies of 1936"*	Vocalion 3339
12/05/36	**16**	2	5. When Did You Leave Heaven?..................... *from the movie "Sing, Baby, Sing"*	Vocalion 3302
1/16/37	**10**	5	6. When My Dream Boat Comes Home/	
1/16/37	**17**	1	7. Here's Love In Your Eyes .... *from the movie "Big Broadcast of 1937"*	Vocalion 3389
7/03/37	**16**	2	8. Meet Me In The Moonlight	Vocalion 3574
10/02/37	**13**	3	9. Can I Forget You?.................................... *from the movie "High, Wide and Handsome"*	Vocalion 3690
			REX ALLEN Known as "The Arizona Cowboy", Rex made over thirty movie Westerns in the 1950s, and was the familiar voice of many Walt Disney programs in later years.	
2/10/51	**20**	4	1. The Roving Kind....................................... *with orchestra & chorus directed by Lew Douglas*	Mercury 5573
4/28/51	**28**	2	2. Sparrow In The Tree Top............................ *orchestra directed by Harry Geller*	Mercury 5597
8/01/53	**8**	15	● 3. Crying In The Chapel................................	Decca 28758

DATE CHARTED	PEAK POS	WKS CHRT'D	ARTIST — Record Title	Label & Number
			STEVE ALLEN Comedian/actor/composer/author; original star of the 'Tonight Show". (see Al (Jazzbo) Collins)	
			STUART ALLEN Singer with the Richard Himber Band, 1935-39.	
			TERRY ALLEN Singer with Red Norvo (1939), Larry Clinton (1939-40), Will Bradley (1940-41), and Claude Thornhill (1942) bands.	
			FRAN ALLISON Co-star of the famous children's TV series "Kukla, Fran, and Ollie" (1954-57, 1961-62)	
4/22/50	26	1	1. Peter Cottontail	RCA Victor 3727
7/14/51	20	2	2. Too Young	RCA Victor 4105
			above two with orchestra conducted by Jack Fascinato	
			MICKEY ALPERT Pseudonym for Ben Selvin	
			AMBROSE & HIS ORCHESTRA London-born Bert Ambrose was one of England's top bandleaders from 1927-1950. Among the major talents he led were Ted Heath, Lew Stone, pianists George Shearing and Eddie Calvert, and vocalist Vera Lynn. He died at the age of 76 in 1973.	
1/20/34	9	8	1. Without That Certain Thing/	
2/17/34	10	4	2. Love Locked Out	Brunswick 6755
3/02/35	20	1	3. London On A Rainy Night	Decca 360
8/17/35	3	12	4. I'm On A See-Saw	Decca 467
			from the British musical "Jill Darling"	
9/07/35	6	10	5. Hors D'oeurves [I]	Decca 500
10/12/35	18	2	6. Embassy Stomp [I]	Decca 551
12/19/36	16	1	7. I'm In A Dancing Mood	Decca 971
			from the British musical "This'll Make You Whistle"	
12/02/39+	8	7	8. South Of The Border (Down Mexico Way)	Decca 2732
			vocal by Denny Dennis	
			LOLA AMECHE (also see Al Trace)	
7/28/51	24	3	1. Hitsity Hotsity [N]	Mercury 5675
			LOLA AMECHE with AL TRACE & HIS ORCHESTRA	
			AMERICAN QUARTET Three-quarters different from the famous American Quartet: William F. Hooley, S.H. Dudley, Albert Campbell, and W.T. Leahy.	
9/08/00	3	3	1. A Night Trip To Buffalo [C]	Gram-o-Phone 43
			AMERICAN QUARTET Hugely popular vocal group led by Billy Murray (tenor, featured soloist), originally with tenor John Bieling, baritone Steve Porter, and bass William F. Hooley. Group was known on Edison as Premier Quartet. Bieling left in 1914 to be replaced by John Young; Hooley died in late 1918, succeeded by Donald Chalmers. In 1920, a revamped American Quartet featured Murray, Albert Campbell, John Meyer, and Frank Croxton; the group disbanded in 1925. (also see Heidelberg Quintet)	
2/05/10	8	2	1. Wedding Bells	Edison 10294
			shown as Premier Quartet	
6/18/10	1(11)	17	● 2. **Casey Jones**	Victor 16483
			orchestra leader Walter B. Rogers replaced Steve Porter on this famous record, which may have sold 2 million copies; also recorded by Murray & chorus on Edison Amberol 450 song based on the 1900 Illinois "Cannon Ball Express" train wreck	
7/30/10	4	4	3. He's A College Boy	Victor 16492
			also recorded by Murray & chorus on Edison 10354	
9/03/10	1(4)	10	4. **Call Me Up Some Rainy Afternoon**	Victor 16508
			ADA JONES & AMERICAN QUARTET	
11/05/10	5	4	5. Any Little Girl That's A Nice Girl Is The Right Little Girl For Me	Victor 16560

DATE CHARTED	PEAK POS	WKS CHRT'D	ARTIST — Record Title	Label & Number
12/24/10+	**2(1)**	6	6. Play That Barber-Shop Chord...................... from Broadway's "Ziegfeld Follies of 1910" 2, 3, 5, & 6: BILLY MURRAY & AMERICAN QUARTET	Victor 5799
1/07/11	**5**	3	7. In The Gloaming........................... WILL OAKLAND & AMERICAN QUARTET flip side of "Silver Bell" by the Peerless Quartet	Victor 16646
3/18/11	**4**	4	8. The Grizzly Bear	Victor 16681
3/18/11	**5**	3	9. I'm Looking For A Nice Young Fellow Who Is	Victor 5811
			Looking For A Nice Young Girl	
3/25/11	**10**	1	10. Tickle Toes... above two: ADA JONES & AMERICAN QUARTET	Victor 16683
5/13/11	**1(3)**	11	11. **Come, Josephine, In My Flying Machine**..... ADA JONES, BILLY MURRAY & AMERICAN QUARTET	Victor 16844
5/13/11	**3**	6	12. Some Of These Days.................................	Victor 16834
5/20/11	**8**	1	13. I Love It	Victor 16837
9/09/11	**5**	2	14. Baby Shoes...	Victor 16859
10/07/11	**9**	1	15. Dance Of The Grizzly Bear .... from Broadway's "Ziegfeld Follies of 1910"	Victor 16881
10/28/11	**9**	1	16. In The Land Of Harmony............................	Victor 16896
11/11/11	**2(2)**	10	17. I Want A Girl (Just Like The Girl That	
			Married Dear Old Dad)........................ WALTER VAN BRUNT & AMERICAN QUARTET	Victor 16962
12/16/11+	**1(1)**	12	18. **Oh, You Beautiful Doll**............................ 8, 15, 18 & 20: BILLY MURRAY & AMERICAN QUARTET	Victor 16979
1/20/12	**6**	2	19. That Mysterious Rag .... recorded as Premier Quartet for Edison 10539	Victor 16982
2/03/12	**9**	1	20. Oh That Navajo Rag .... Premier Quartet: Edison Amberol 917	Victor 17000
2/24/12	**3**	5	21. Ragtime Violin .... Premier Quartet: Edison 10560 & Edison Amberol 966	Victor 17025
3/09/12	**1(8)**	16	22. **Moonlight Bay**.. Premier Quartet: Edison 10550 & Edison Amberol 962	Victor 17034
4/20/12	**8**	2	23. Another Rag (A Raggy Rag)........................ Premier Quartet: Edison Amberol 937	Victor 17027
5/18/12	**6**	2	24. The Skeleton Rag .... [C] Premier Quartet: Edison 10575 & Edison Amberol 1064	Victor 17041
6/01/12	**3**	7	25. When I Was Twenty-One And You Were	
			Sweet Sixteen .... HARRY MACDONOUGH & AMERICAN QUARTET	Victor 17057
9/14/12	**6**	2	26. You're My Baby .... Premier Quartet: Edison Amberol 1119	Victor 17114
10/05/12	**5**	4	27. When You're Away .... "EDNA BROWN" (Elsie Baker) & AMERICAN QUARTET from the Broadway musical "The Winsome Widow"	Victor 17139
11/02/12	**10**	1	28. Mary Was My Mother's Name	Victor 17130
11/09/12	**1(1)**	10	29. **Everybody Two-Step**................................	Victor 17171
12/28/12+	**5**	4	30. Hitchy-Koo	Victor 17196
2/08/13	**3**	6	31. On The Mississippi .... from the Broadway musical "Hanky Panky"	Victor 17237
2/15/13	**3**	6	32. Parisienne	Victor 17239
3/15/13	**2(1)**	6	33. That Old Girl Of Mine	Victor 17264
3/29/13	**7**	2	34. Beautiful Doll, Good-Bye	Victor 17244
4/26/13	**8**	1	35. Row, Row, Row... from Broadway's "Ziegfeld Follies of 1912"	Victor 17295
10/18/13	**5**	5	36. On The Banks Of The Wabash.................... HARRY MACDONOUGH & AMERICAN QUARTET	Victor 17397
12/06/13	**5**	7	37. Sailing Down The Chesapeake Bay.............. Premier Quartet: Edison Amberol 2039	Victor 17411
3/21/14	**1(6)**	11	38. **Rebecca Of Sunny-brook Farm**.................	Victor 17534
3/28/14	**5**	4	39. All Aboard For Dixieland/ from the Broadway musical "High-Jinks"	
4/25/14	**9**	1	40. The Ragtime Dream	Victor 17535

DATE CHARTED	PEAK POS	WKS CHRT'D	ARTIST — Record Title	Label & Number
5/09/14	2(3)	7	41. Do You Take This Woman For Your Lawful Wife? - "I Do, I Do".......................... [C]	Victor 17554
11/28/14	1(7)	13	42. **It's A Long, Long Way To Tipperary** .... British song, featured in the Broadway musicals "Chin-Chin" & "Dancing Around"	Victor 17639
12/26/14+	3	8	43. When You Wore A Tulip And I Wore A Big Red Rose	Victor 17652
1/09/15	6	4	44. At The Mississippi Cabaret	Victor 17650
2/20/15	1(2)	11	45. **Chinatown, My Chinatown**........................ from the 1910 Broadway musical "Up and Down Broadway"	Victor 17684
3/20/15	2(1)	6	46. On The 5:15/	
4/10/15	9	1	47. They All Had A Finger In The Pie	Victor 17704
12/25/15+	5	4	48. America, I Love You!	Victor 17902
1/22/16	3	6	49. Along The Rocky Road To Dublin .... Premier Quartet: Edison 50328	Victor 17900
6/24/16	9	1	50. Siam..	Victor 17993
3/10/17	9	1	51. Rolling Stones (All Come Rolling Home Again)	Victor 18215
3/31/17	5	3	52. How's Every Little Thing In Dixie?.............. Premier Quartet: Edison Amberol 3143	Victor 18225
5/19/17	6	2	53. Let's All Be Americans Now	Victor 18256
6/23/17	1(3)	9	54. **Oh Johnny, Oh Johnny, Oh!**..................... from the Broadway musical "Follow Me"; also recorded for Edison Amberol 3237 & Edison 50442	Victor 18279
9/29/17	1(9)	18	55. **Over There** .... George M. Cohan's World War I classic Billy Murray also recorded song for Edison Amberol 3275	Victor 18333
9/29/17	1(1)	8	56. **Good-Bye Broadway, Hello France**............. from the Broadway musical "The Passing Show of 1917"	Victor 18335
12/08/17	3	5	57. Sailin' Away On The Henry Clay.................	Victor 18353
11/09/18	5	3	58. Everything Is Peaches Down In Georgia	Victor 18497
9/13/19	9	1	59. Anything Is Nice If It Comes From Dixie........ Premier Quartet: Edison 50537	Victor 18589
11/01/19	10	1	60. Breeze (Blow My Baby Back To Me)............. Premier Quartet: Edison 50584	Victor 18605
11/26/21	5	4	61. Strut, Miss Lizzie....................................	Victor 18799
2/25/22	12	1	62. Mandy'n Me	Victor 18832
7/22/22	5	3	63. In The Little Red School House	Victor 18904
1/13/23	7	3	64. Nellie Kelly I Love You .... from the Broadway musical "Little Nellie Kelly"	Victor 18957
4/11/23	8	1	65. Carolina In The Morning	Victor 19006
3/29/24	14	1	66. What Do You Do Sunday, Mary? .... from the Broadway musical "Poppy"	Victor 19188

AMES BROTHERS

Ed, Gene, Joe and Vic Ames (real name: Urick) got their professional start in Boston; Ed became a solo star in the 60s. (also see Russ Morgan)

DATE CHARTED	PEAK POS	WKS CHRT'D	ARTIST — Record Title	Label & Number
8/21/48	21	3	1. A Tree In The Meadow.............................. MONICA LEWIS with the AMES BROTHERS	Signature 15078
2/26/49	23	4	2. You, You, You Are The One .... adapted from a popular German song	Coral 60015
4/16/49	29	1	3. Cruising Down The River...........................	Coral 60035
1/14/50	1(2)	14	● 4. **Rag Mop/** also issued on Coral 60173	
1/28/50	1(1)	27	5. **Sentimental Me**...................................	Coral 60140
3/18/50	14	6	6. (Put Another Nickel In) Music! Music! Music!	Coral 60153
6/24/50	17	4	7. Stars Are The Windows Of Heaven..............	Coral 60209
8/12/50	5	19	8. Can Anyone Explain? (No, No, No!)..............	Coral 60253
11/11/50	26	2	9. Thirsty For Your Kisses............................	Coral 60300
11/25/50	20	6	10. Oh Babe!	Coral 60327

DATE CHARTED	PEAK POS	WKS CHRT'D	ARTIST — Record Title	Label & Number
12/23/50	**29**	1	11. The Thing .... [N]	Coral 60333
6/23/51	**16**	3	12. Wang Wang Blues.....................................	Coral 60489
			above records backed by the Roy Ross Orchestra	
9/08/51	**21**	4	13. Hawaiian War Chant (Ta-Hu-Wa-Hu-Wai)	Coral 60510
			with Roy Smeck and the Serenaders	
9/29/51	**2(1)**	21	● 14. Undecided/	
10/06/51	**23**	4	15. Sentimental Journey..............................	Coral 60566
			above two with Les Brown & His Band of Renown	
1/19/52	**19**	4	16. I Wanna Love You/	
3/29/52	**29**	1	17. I'll Still Love You.....................................	Coral 60617
			above two with orchestra directed by Marty Manning	
8/16/52	**13**	8	18. Auf Wiederseh'n Sweetheart	Coral 60773
			with The Ray Bloch Orchestra and The Sweetland Singers	
8/23/52	**18**	7	19. String Along	Coral 60804
10/18/52	**15**	5	20. My Favorite Song.....................................	Coral 60846
			above two & 22 backed by The Ray Bloch Orchestra	
1/17/53	**21**	4	21. No Moon At All...	Coral 60870
			with Les Brown & His Band of Renown	
3/14/53	**23**	1	22. Can't I?...	Coral 60926
6/27/53	**1(8)**	31	● 23. **You You You**	RCA Victor 5325
10/24/53	**29**	1	24. My Love, My Life, My Happiness..................	RCA Victor 5404
12/12/53	**22**	3	25. I Can't Believe That You're In Love With Me..	RCA Victor 5530
3/20/54	**6**	18	26. The Man With The Banjo/	RCA Victor 5644
4/17/54	**30**	1	27. Man, Man, Is For The Woman Made...........	
6/19/54	**29**	1	28. Leave It To Your Heart	RCA Victor 5764
10/09/54	**25**	2	29. Hopelessly...	RCA Victor 5840
			backed on all Victor records by Hugo Winterhalter & His Orchestra	

GENE AMMONS
Renowned jazz tenor saxophonist, with Billy Eckstine (1944-47) and Woody Herman (1949) bands; son of great boogie-woogie pianist Albert Ammons.

AMOS 'N ANDY
Charles Correll and Freeman Gosden created this famous comedy act, popular for years on radio.

12/14/29	**16**	1	1. Is Everybody In Your Family As Dumb As You Is?.. [C]	Victor 22119

LAURIE ANDERS
Comic "glamour cowboy" on the Ken Murray TV show.

5/19/51	**13**	6	1. I Like The Wide Open Spaces......................	Columbia 39404
			ARTHUR GODFREY & LAURIE ANDERS	

CAT ANDERSON
William Alonzo Anderson - trumpet star with Lucky Millinder, Erskine Hawkins. Lionel Hampton (1942), and Duke Ellington (1944-47), 1950-59; died on 4/30/81 (64).

IVIE ANDERSON
Became famous as Duke Ellington's featured vocalist from 1931-42 ("I Got It Bad and That Ain't Good" her most memorable record); appeared in the Marx Brothers film "A Day at the Races". Ivy died on 12/28/49 (45).

4/08/44	**16**	1	1. Mexico Joe	Exclusive 3113
			accompanied by Ceele Burke's Orchestra	

LEROY ANDERSON & HIS "POPS" CONCERT ORCHESTRA
Composer of the Christmas standard "Sleigh Ride" and each of his charted hits; Leroy served as arranger for the Boston Pops Orchestra and in 1958 wrote the score for the Broadway musical "Goldilocks".

3/31/51	**12**	14	● 1. The Syncopated Clock .... [I]	Decca 16005
			famous as the theme of TV's "Late Show"	
12/29/51+	**1(5)**	38	● 2. **Blue Tango**.. [I]	Decca 27875
			sold two million copies	
1/03/53	**22**	1	3. A Christmas Festival............................ [I-X]	Decca 16041

DATE CHARTED	PEAK POS	WKS CHRT'D	ARTIST — Record Title	Label & Number
11/07/53	**21**	4	4. The Typewriter .... [I]	Decca 28881

MARIAN ANDERSON
Famed black American contralto who made her New York Philharmonic debut in 1925; performed throughout Europe, and in 1939 sang before 75,000 at the Lincoln Memorial.

8/29/25	**15**	1	1. Nobody Knows The Trouble I've Seen..........	Victor 19560

FABIAN ANDRE & HIS ORCHESTRA
Co-writer of "Dream a Little Dream of Me"

7/27/40	**25**	1	1. Dance Of An Ear Of Corn .... [I]	Columbia 35476

ANDREWS SISTERS
Patty, Maxene and LaVerne Andrews emerged from Minneapolis to become the most popular female vocal group of the entire pre-1955 era. Led by Patty, the trio appeared in many 40s movies, and their unmistakable sound helped define the wartime era. LaVerne died on 5/8/67 (52); the nostalgia wave led Patty and Maxene to star in a 1974 Broadway musical, "Over There". Accompanied by Vic Schoen & His Orchestra, except as noted. (also see Bing Crosby)

1/01/38	**1(5)**	10	1. **Bei Mir Bist Du Schoen**/ [N] from the 1933 Yiddish musical "I Would If I Could"	
1/08/38	**12**	3	2. Nice Work If You Can Get It	Decca 1562
			from the movie "A Damsel in Distress"; band on above two includes Bobby Hackett (trumpet)	
3/19/38	**18**	1	3. Joseph, Joseph .... [N] adaptation of a Yiddish song	Decca 1691
3/26/38	**12**	4	4. Ti-Pi-Pin..	Decca 1703
3/26/38	**16**	2	5. Shortenin' Bread .... [N]	Decca 1734
7/16/38	**10**	5	6. Says My Heart...................................	Decca 1875
9/10/38	**9**	4	7. Tu-Li-Tulip Time/	
11/12/38	**17**	1	8. Sha-Sha .... [N] above two & 11 accompanied by Jimmy Dorsey & His Orchestra	Decca 1974
12/10/38	**10**	3	9. Lullaby To A Jitterbug/	
5/20/39	**15**	1	10. Pross-Tchai (Goodbye)	Decca 2082
			"Pross-Tchai" is Russian for "Goodbye"	
1/14/39	**2(1)**	11	11. Hold Tight, Hold Tight	Decca 2214
5/13/39	**14**	1	12. You Don't Know How Much You Can Suffer ...	Decca 2414
5/27/39	**4**	7	13. Beer Barrel Polka (Roll Out The Barrel)/ popular Czechoslovakian song; English lyrics added in 1934	
6/17/39	**5**	15	14. Well All Right (Tonight's The Night)	Decca 2462
11/25/39	**11**	5	15. Chico's Love Song...............................	Decca 2756
3/16/40	**4**	10	16. Say "Si, Si" (Para Vigo Me Voy)	Decca 3013
			adaptation of a Latin American tango	
4/06/40	**6**	12	17. The Woodpecker Song/ based on Italian song "Reginella Campagnola"	
4/20/40	**21**	1	18. Down By The O-HI-O..............................	Decca 3065
5/18/40	**11**	9	19. Rhumboogie.....................................	Decca 3097
10/12/40	**1(3)**	14	20. **Ferryboat Serenade**/	
10/26/40	**27**	1	21. Hit The Road	Decca 3328
			19 & 21 from the film "Argentine Nights"	
11/02/40+	**2(3)**	14	22. Beat Me, Daddy, Eight To The Bar	Decca 3375
2/01/41	**10**	7	23. Scrub Me, Mama, With A Boogie Beat .... [N]	Decca 3553
3/01/41	**6**	8	24. Boogie Woogie Bugle Boy	Decca 3598
			revived in 1973 by Bette Midler	
4/12/41	**11**	6	25. I, Yi, Yi, Yi, Yi (I Like You Very Much)/ [N] from the film "That Night in Rio"	
4/26/41	**5**	17	26. (I'll Be With You) In Apple Blossom Time ...	Decca 3622
			24 & 26 from the film "Buck Privates"	
5/31/41	**10**	11	27. Aurora..	Decca 3732
8/30/41	**22**	1	28. Sonny Boy .... [N]	Decca 3871
9/27/41	**22**	1	29. The Nickel Serenade	Decca 3960
10/04/41	**22**	1	30. Sleepy Serenade	Decca 3821
			27 & 30 from the film "Hold That Ghost"	

DATE CHARTED	PEAK POS	WKS CHRT'D	ARTIST — Record Title	Label & Number
11/01/41	20	2	31. I Wish I Had A Dime (For Ev'ry Time I Missed You)..	Decca 3966
11/15/41	12	9	32. Jealous..	Decca 4019
1/10/42+	3	7	33. The Shrine Of St. Cecelia	Decca 4097
3/07/42	22	1	34. I'll Pray For You	Decca 4153
5/23/42	8	17	35. Three Little Sisters	Decca 18319
5/23/42	16	1	36. Don't Sit Under The Apple Tree....................	Decca 18312
8/08/42	17	3	37. Pennsylvania Polka/ from the film "Give Out, Sisters"	
8/29/42	18	2	38. That's The Moon, My Son .... [N] 35, 36 & 38 from the film "Private Buckaroo"	Decca 18398
9/26/42	14	2	39. Mister Five By Five/ from the film "Behind The Eight Ball"	
10/10/42	6	9	40. Strip Polka .... [N]	Decca 18470
10/24/42	17	2	41. Here Comes The Navy.............................. uses same melody as "Beer Barrel Polka"	Decca 18497
6/05/43	18	1	42. East Of The Rockies	Decca 18533
12/25/43+	1(9)	21	43. **Shoo-Shoo Baby/** from the film "Three Cheers For The Boys"	
1/29/44	20	1	44. Down In The Valley............................... from the film "Moonlight and Cactus"	Decca 18572
6/17/44	8	13	45. Straighten Up And Fly Right/ [N]	
7/08/44	24	1	46. Tico Tico.................................... [N] from the film "Bathing Beauty"	Decca 18606
7/01/44	24	1	47. Sing A Tropical Song............................. from the film "Happy-Go-Lucky"	Decca 18581
1/06/45	1(10)	20	● 48. **Rum And Coca-Cola/** uses calypso melody from Trinidad ("L'Anee' Passee'", 1906)	
2/17/45	15	1	49. One Meat Ball .... [N] based on 1855 song "The Lone Fish Ball"	Decca 18636
1/13/45	21	1	50. Corns For My Country .... [N] from the film "Hollywood Canteen"	Decca 18628
9/29/45	8	8	51. The Blond Sailor.................................	Decca 18700
2/02/46	9	5	52. Money Is The Root Of All Evil	Decca 23474
3/16/46	12	1	53. Patience And Prudence.............................	Decca 18780
6/01/46	24	1	54. Coax Me A Little Bit..............................	Decca 18833
8/31/46	17	1	55. I Don't Know Why.................................	Decca 18899
9/28/46	15	5	56. House Of Blue Lights.............................	Decca 23641
10/19/46	4	13	57. Rumors Are Flying............................... ANDREWS SISTERS with LES PAUL	Decca 23656
12/14/46	22	4	58. Winter Wonderland/ [X]	
12/21/46+	7	4	● 59. Christmas Island .... [X] above two with Guy Lombardo & His Royal Canadians	Decca 23722
9/06/47	21	4	60. On The Avenue .... accompanied by Carmen Cavallaro & His Orchestra	Decca 24102
9/27/47	2(1)	17	61. Near You..	Decca 24171
10/18/47	7	2	62. The Lady From 29 Palms	Decca 23976
11/22/47+	3	1	63. Civilization (Bongo, Bongo, Bongo).............. DANNY KAYE/ANDREWS SISTERS from the Broadway musical "Angel In the Wings"	Decca 23940
12/20/47	20	2	64. Christmas Island .... [X-R]	Decca 23722
12/20/47+	24	3	65. Your Red Wagon.................................	Decca 24268
12/27/47	22	1	66. How Lucky You Are	Decca 24171
3/20/48	21	1	67. Teresa .... DICK HAYMES & ANDREWS SISTERS	Decca 24320
4/17/48	3	17	68. Toolie Oolie Doolie (The Yodel Polka)/ Swiss polka melody	
6/12/48	14	7	69. I Hate To Lose You	Decca 24380
5/15/48	21	5	70. Heartbreaker/	
5/22/48	20	3	71. Sabre Dance .... based on Khachaturian's "Gayne Ballet Suite"	Decca 24427

DATE CHARTED	PEAK POS	WKS CHRT'D	ARTIST — Record Title	Label & Number
7/19/48	**18**	6	72. Woody Woodpecker.......................... [N] ANDREWS SISTERS & DANNY KAYE	Decca 24462
7/31/48	**24**	1	73. Blue Tail Fly.. BURL IVES & ANDREWS SISTERS	Decca 24463
9/04/48	**5**	12	74. Underneath The Arches/	
9/04/48	**8**	12	75. You Call Everybody Darling..................... above two recorded in England and accompanied by Billy Ternant's Orchestra	Decca 24490
10/09/48	**12**	14	76. Cuanto La Gusta .... CARMEN MIRANDA & THE ANDREWS SISTERS from the film "A Date With Judy"	Decca 24479
11/20/48	**23**	2	77. Bella Bella Marie .... from the film "Music Man"	Decca 24499
1/08/49	**26**	1	78. Christmas Island .... [X-R]	Decca 23722
1/29/49	**30**	3	79. More Beer!..	Decca 24548
5/07/49	**30**	1	80. I'm Bitin' My Fingernails And Thinking Of You... ERNEST TUBB & ANDREWS SISTERS	Decca 24592
9/24/49+	**1(5)**	25	● 81. **I Can Dream, Can't I?**/ from the Broadway musical "Right This Way"	
10/01/49	**20**	2	82. The Wedding Of Lili Marlene.................. above two with Gordon Jenkins & His Orchestra	Decca 24705
12/10/49	**22**	2	83. She Wore A Yellow Ribbon/	
12/17/49+	**15**	4	84. Charley My Boy...................................... above two: ANDREWS SISTERS/RUSS MORGAN & HIS ORCHESTRA	Decca 24812
1/07/50	**18**	1	85. Merry Christmas Polka .... [X] with Guy Lombardo & His Royal Canadians	Decca 24748
1/28/50	**23**	3	86. The Wedding Samba............................... CARMEN MIRANDA & THE ANDREWS SISTERS	Decca 24841
5/13/50	**1(2)**	21	87. **I Wanna Be Loved**................................. 81 & 87: Patty Andrews solo, backed by sisters	Decca 27007
9/27/50	**22**	1	88. Can't We Talk It Over? .... above two accompanied by Gordon Jenkins & His Orchestra	Decca 27115
12/09/50	**22**	4	89. A Bushel And A Peck .... from the Broadway musical "Guys and Dolls"	Decca 27252
3/03/51	**17**	7	90. A Penny A Kiss - A Penny A Hug................	Decca 27414

PATTY ANDREWS
Lead singer of the Andrews Sisters

1/22/49	**12**	6	1. The Pussy Cat Song (Nyow! Nyot! Nyow!)....... PATTY ANDREWS & BOB CROSBY	Decca 24533
6/16/51	**19**	6	2. Too Young... accompanied by Victor Young & His Orchestra	Decca 27569

HARRY ANTHONY
After recording for over a decade under this pseudonym, in 1914 he joined the American Quartet under his real name, John Young; also sang tenor in the Criterion Quartet. Died in 1954 (84).

7/29/05	**10**	1	1. Excelsior... HARRY ANTHONY & JAMES F. HARRISON	Edison 8985
10/28/05	**7**	1	2. Down Where The Silv'ry Mohawk Flows........	Edison 9075
11/04/05	**5**	2	3. When The Mists Have Rolled Away	Edison 9105
8/11/06	**5**	1	4. Let The Lower Lights Be Burning .... above two: HARRY ANTHONY & JAMES F. HARRISON	Edison 9272
10/27/06	**6**	1	5. Love Me And The World Is Mine	Edison 9371
11/28/08	**9**	1	6. Beautiful Isle Of Somewhere	Edison 9959
2/12/10	**4**	5	7. Meet Me Tonight In Dreamland.................... ELIZABETH WHEELER & HARRY ANTHONY "Dreamland" said to refer to original amusement section of Coney Island	Edison 10290
10/15/10	**10**	1	8. See The Pale Moon.................................. 6 & 8: HARRY ANTHONY & JAMES F. HARRISON	Victor 5780
2/18/11	**10**	1	9. Alma .... HARRY ANTHONY & INEZ BARBOUR from the Broadway musical "Alma, Where Do You Live?"	Victor 5805

DATE CHARTED	PEAK POS	WKS CHRT'D	ARTIST — Record Title	Label & Number
5/25/12	**5**	3	10. Love Never Dies .... Victor 17042 HARRY ANTHONY & INEZ BARBOUR from the Broadway musical "Little Boy Blue"	Victor 17042

RAY ANTHONY

Ray (born Raymond Antonini) played trumpet briefly with Glenn Miller and Jimmy Dorsey before starting his own successful band. He was married for a time to movie actress Mamie Van Doren.

DATE CHARTED	PEAK POS	WKS CHRT'D	ARTIST — Record Title	Label & Number
11/19/49+	**11**	10	1. A Dreamer's Holiday .... [I]	Capitol 761
1/28/50	**21**	1	2. Sitting By The Window	Capitol 794
4/22/50	**7**	15	3. Sentimental Me	Capitol 923
5/27/50	**4**	21	4. Count Every Star .... vocal: Dick Noel	Capitol 979
7/29/50	**19**	2	5. Roses	Capitol 1001
9/02/50	**5**	13	6. Can Anyone Explain.......................... vocals on 2 & 6: Ronnie Deauville & the Skyliners	Capitol 1131
9/30/50	**4**	17	7. Harbor Lights/ vocals on 3, 5 & 7: Ronnie Deauville	
10/21/50	**9**	14	8. Nevertheless (I'm In Love With You).......... vocal: Ronnie Deauville & the Skyliners featured in the movie "Three Little Words"	Capitol 1190
1/13/51	**26**	1	9. The Night Is Young And You're So Beautiful..	Capitol 1310
1/27/51	**13**	16	10. Be My Love................................. from the movie "Toast of New Orleans"	Capitol 1352
6/02/51	**17**	7	11. These Things I Offer You (For A Lifetime)...... vocal: Tommy Mercer & the Skyliners	Capitol 1522
7/28/51	**28**	2	12. My Truly, Truly Fair................................	Capitol 1583
11/10/51	**10**	11	13. Undecided .... vocals: Tommy Mercer, Gloria Craig, & The Skyliners	Capitol 1824
2/09/52	**2(1)**	15	14. At Last .... vocals on 10, 12 & 14: Tommy Mercer	Capitol 1912
2/23/52	**24**	2	15. Bermuda	Capitol 1956
6/28/52	**10**	4	16. As Time Goes By .... vocal: Tommy Mercer; originally from the Broadway musical "Everybody's Welcome"	Capitol 2104
7/26/52	**21**	4	17. Slaughter On 10th Avenue .... [I] ballet theme from the Broadway musical "On Your Toes"	Capitol 2085
10/11/52	**20**	1	18. Marilyn... vocals: Tommy Mercer & The Skyliners; song dedicated to Marilyn Monroe	Capitol 2207
11/01/52	**13**	5	19. Bunny Hop .... vocals on 15 & 19: Tommy Mercer & Marcie Miller	Capitol 2251
1/17/53	**26**	4	20. On The Trail .... [I] from the second movement of Ferde Grofe's "Grand Canyon Suite"	Capitol 2327
4/04/53	**28**	2	21. Wild Horses .... vocal: Jo Ann Greer	Capitol 2349
6/06/53	**26**	2	22. Thunderbird .... vocal: Leo Anthony	Capitol 2451
8/29/53	**2(1)**	13	23. Dragnet .... [I] theme from the TV series	Capitol 2562
12/26/53+	**15**	4	24. O Mein Papa (Oh! My Papa)/ from the 1948 Swiss musical "Fireworks"	
2/06/54	**29**	1	25. Secret Love .... from the movie "Calamity Jane"; vocal: Tommy Mercer	Capitol 2678
9/25/54	**18**	5	26. Skokiaan.. [I]	Capitol 2896

CHARLIE APPLEWHITE

Discovered by Milton Berle, who featured Charlie on his TV show in 1953.

DATE CHARTED	PEAK POS	WKS CHRT'D	ARTIST — Record Title	Label & Number
2/27/54	**28**	2	1. Cabbages And Kings	Decca 29001
4/10/54	**21**	4	2. This Is You..	Decca 29055
6/05/54	**26**	1	3. No One But You .... from the movie "Flame and the Flesh" accompanied on all three by the Jack Pleis Orchestra	Decca 29125

DATE CHARTED	PEAK POS	WKS CHRT'D	ARTIST — Record Title	Label & Number
			### HARRY ARCHER & HIS ORCHESTRA	
			Composer of the 1923 hit "I Love You" and scores for six Broadway musicals; died on 4/23/60 (72)	
5/29/26	**10**	1	1. Sweet And Low-Down .... [I]	Brunswick 3096
4/02/27	**14**	2	2. When Day Is Done	Brunswick 3399
3/03/28	**20**	1	3. Thinking Of You	Brunswick 3704
			vocals on above two: Franklyn Baur	
			### VERNON ARCHIBALD	
			Baritone, began as a member of the Archibald Brothers Quartet; in the late 20s he helped form the American Singers.	
7/25/14	**7**	2	1. In The Valley Of The Moon	Edison Amb. 2300
			he also recorded this song with Helen Clark (Edison 80162)	
11/28/14	**10**	1	2. Somewhere A Voice Is Calling	Edison Amb. 2453
			also on Edison Diamond Disc 80125 above two: ELIZABETH SPENCER & VERNON ARCHIBALD	
			### ARDEN-OHMAN ORCHESTRA	
			Victor Arden and Phil Ohman, piano duo which appeared in several 20s Broadway musicals	
2/13/26	**5**	3	1. Sentimental Me .... [I]	Brunswick 2984
			Regent Club Orchestra; song from Broadway's "Garrick Gaieties"	
4/24/26	**12**	1	2. Looking For A Boy................................. [I]	Brunswick 3035
			from the Broadway musical "Tip Toes"	
6/25/27	**12**	3	3. At Sundown (When Love Is Calling Me Home).	Brunswick 3481
10/22/27	**14**	2	4. Broken Hearted	Brunswick 3592
4/07/28	**14**	3	5. Funny Face	Victor 21114
			vocal: Johnny Marvin; title song of Broadway musical	
1/26/29	**6**	6	6. Lover, Come Back To Me!/	
1/26/29	**15**	2	7. Marianne	Victor 21776
			above two vocals by The Revelers above two songs from the Broadway musical "The New Moon"	
10/19/29	**9**	3	8. How Am I To Know?................................	Victor 22111
2/15/30	**3**	11	9. Should I?	Victor 22255
			from the movie "Lord Byron of Broadway" above two vocals: Scrappy Lambert	
3/29/30	**12**	3	10. Strike Up The Band................................	Victor 22308
			vocal: The Revelers; title song of Broadway musical	
11/29/30	**11**	3	11. Can This Be Love?/	
12/06/30	**10**	3	12. Fine And Dandy	Victor 22552
			above two from the Broadway musical "Fine and Dandy"	
11/21/31	**10**	6	13. You're My Everything/	
			above three vocals by Frank Luther	
12/12/31	**10**	3	14. Ooh! That Kiss.......................................	Victor 22818
			vocal: Sylvia Froos and Frank Luther above two songs from Broadway musical "The Laugh Parade"	
2/13/32	**3**	7	15. When We're Alone (Penthouse Serenade)	Victor 22910
2/27/32	**13**	3	16. I Love A Parade......................................	Victor 22892
			from the Broadway musical "George White's Music Hall Varieties"; above two by Frank Luther	
			### TONI ARDEN	
			Former vocalist with Al Trace and Joe Reichman in the 1940s	
11/19/49+	**7**	14	1. I Can Dream, Can't I?	Columbia 38612
			accompanied by Hugo Winterhalter's Orchestra	
6/02/51	**15**	9	2. Too Young...	Columbia 39271
5/24/52	**14**	8	3. Kiss Of Fire/	
6/21/52	**24**	2	4. I'm Yours	Columbia 39737
			accompanied on above three by Percy Faith's Orchestra	
			### HAROLD ARLEN	
			Harold Arlen, one of America's greatest popular composers, was born Hyman Arluck in Buffalo, N.Y. on 2/15/05. "Get Happy" in 1930 was the first of more than twenty Top Ten songs written by Arlen over the next three decades, including "Stormy Weather", "Over the Rainbow", and "Blues In the Night". He died on 4/23/86 (81).	
7/18/31	**4**	6	1. Little Girl	Columbia 2488
			Joe Venuti's Blue Four, vocal by Harold Arlen	

DATE CHARTED	PEAK POS	WKS CHRT'D	ARTIST — Record Title	Label & Number
3/25/33	1(8)	19	2. **Stormy Weather** .... Leo Reisman Orchestra, vocal by Harold Arlen	Victor 24262
2/10/34	19	1	3. Let's Fall In Love............................ accompanied by Ray Sinatra's Orchestra; movie title song	Victor 24467
4/04/34	3	6	4. Ill Wind.. Eddy Duchin Orchestra, vocal by Harold Arlen; from the Cotton Club revue "Parade in Harlem"	Victor 24579
8/25/34	6	6	5. You're A Builder Upper........................... Leo Reisman Orchestra, vocal: Harold Arlen; from the Broadway musical "Life Begins at 8:40"	Brunswick 6941

KAY ARMEN
Popular 1940s radio singer, appeared in the 1955 movie musical "Hit The Deck".

DATE CHARTED	PEAK POS	WKS CHRT'D	ARTIST — Record Title	Label & Number
11/20/43+	7	10	1. The Dreamer/	
11/20/43+	10	10	2. How Sweet You Are............................... above two from the movie "Thank Your Lucky Stars"	Decca 18566
12/04/43	19	1	3. Later Tonight/ from the movie "Wintertime"	
12/18/43	19	1	4. Cuddle Up A Little Closer, Lovey Mine .... featured in the movie "Coney Island" above four with The Balladiers	Decca 18568

LOUIS ARMSTRONG
Louis Armstrong, one of the towering giants in 20th century American music, was born in New Orleans on July 4, 1900. He learned to play cornet at a waifs' home, and by 1918 was a protege of King Oliver. Four years later he came to Chicago to join Oliver's band; a new jazz age was dawning, and Louis' astonishing virtuosity was its herald. By the time he formed his own band in 1926, young "Satchmo" was already a legend, and the records that group made the next few years helped create a new international audience for jazz. Louis' greatest popularity came with his uniquely raspy, scat-tinged vocals starting in 1929. In years to come frequent movie appearances as well as concerts and records made him one of the world's best-known and most beloved entertainers, and so he remained at his death on 7/6/71. (also see Fletcher Henderson, King Oliver, Bessie Smith, Clara Smith, and Clarence Williams). All vocals by Louis except as noted.

DATE CHARTED	PEAK POS	WKS CHRT'D	ARTIST — Record Title	Label & Number
7/17/26	8	2	1. Muskrat Ramble .... [I]	Okeh 8300
4/09/27	13	3	2. Big Butter And Egg Man........................... vocal: May Alix and Louis above two by Louis Armstrong and His Hot Five: Louis (cornet), Kid Ory (trombone), Johnny Dodds (clarinet), Lil Armstrong (Louis' wife, piano), Johnny St. Cyr (banjo)	Okeh 8423
10/29/27	16	2	3. Keyhole Blues...................................... Louis and Hot Seven: Louis, Lil, Dodds, St. Cyr, plus John Thomas (trombone), Pete Briggs (brass bass), Baby Dodds (drums)	Okeh 8496
12/10/27	12	3	4. Potato Head Blues .... [I]	Okeh 8503
			larger band, including Earl Hines (piano)	
5/12/28	10	3	5. Hotter Than That....................................	Okeh 8535
7/14/28	14	3	6. Struttin' With Some Barbecue.................. [I]	Okeh 8566
9/15/28	8	6	7. West End Blues .... jazz classic selected for the NARAS Hall of Fame	Okeh 8597
12/01/28	19	1	8. A Monday Date.. vocal: Louis & Earl Hines above four: Louis & His Hot Five, including Hines (piano), Fred Robinson (trombone), Jimmy Strong (clarinet), & Zutty Singleton (drums)	Okeh 8609
5/04/29	15	3	9. St. James' Infirmary............................... "Louis Armstrong & His Savoy Ballroom Five" song eventually banned from network radio	Okeh 8657
9/28/29	7	4	10. Ain't Misbehavin'..................................... from the Broadway musical "Hot Chocolates"	Okeh 8714
12/07/29	15	2	11. When You're Smiling................................ also released on Okeh 41298. Band on above three includes Robinson, Strong, and Singleton	Okeh 8729
2/08/30	11	3	12. St. Louis Blues....................................... also see Bessie Smith	Okeh 41350
8/30/30	19	1	13. I'm A Ding Dong Daddy (From Dumas)	Okeh 41442

DATE CHARTED	PEAK POS	WKS CHRT'D	ARTIST — Record Title	Label & Number
9/20/30	13	2	14. If I Could Be With You One Hour Tonight ...... featured in the film "Ladies They Talk"	Okeh 41448
11/29/30	18	1	15. Memories Of You .... from the Broadway musical "Blackbirds of 1930"	Okeh 41463
2/28/31	15	2	16. The Peanut Vendor .... above four listed as "Louis Armstrong & His Sebastian New Cotton Club Orchestra" Lionel Hampton (drums, vibraphone) on above four	Okeh 41478
11/14/31	13	3	17. I'll Be Glad When You're Dead, You Rascal You..	Okeh 41504
12/19/31	16	2	18. Star Dust/ also released on Okeh 41530	
1/16/32	5	7	19. Chinatown, My Chinatown........................ also released on Okeh 41534; from the Broadway musical "Up And Down Broadway"	Columbia 2574
1/23/32	4	16	20. You Can Depend On Me............................ also on Okeh 41538	Columbia 2590
2/20/32	1(2)	18	21. All Of Me/ from the film "Careless Lady"	
3/05/32	18	1	22. Home .... above two also released on Okeh 41552	Columbia 2606
3/12/32	12	2	23. Between The Devil And The Deep Blue Sea/	
4/02/32	11	3	24. Kickin' The Gong Around........................ above two also released on Okeh 41550	Columbia 2600
3/26/32	4	6	25. Love, You Funny Thing............................ also released on Okeh 41557	Columbia 2631
4/02/32	17	2	26. I Got Rhythm .... from the Broadway musical "Girl Crazy"; also released on Okeh 41534	Columbia 2590
5/28/32	15	2	27. Lawd, You Made The Night Too Long/	
6/04/32	17	2	28. Keepin' Out Of Mischief Now.................... above two also on Okeh 41560	Columbia 2646
8/06/32	14	3	29. Rockin' Chair/ vocal: Louis and Hoagy Carmichael; recorded 12/13/29, issued on Okeh 8756	
8/20/32	6	9	30. Sweethearts On Parade............................ recorded 12/23/30	Columbia 2688
10/01/32	7	5	31. Body And Soul/ from the Broadway musical "Three's a Crowd" recorded 10/9/30, released on Okeh 41468	
10/01/32	17	1	32. Shine.. recorded 3/9/31, released on Okeh 41486 Lionel Hampton plays on above two	Columbia 2707
12/17/32	15	2	33. After You've Gone .... recorded 11/26/29, released on Okeh 41350	Columbia 2727
1/14/33	10	4	34. Hobo, You Can't Ride On This Train/	
3/11/33	17	2	35. That's My Home .... Chick Webb drummer on above two	Victor 24200
2/25/33	18	1	36. I Gotta Right To Sing The Blues .... from Broadway's "Earl Carroll's Vanities of 1932"	Victor 24233
10/26/35	3	7	37. I'm In The Mood For Love/ from the movie "Every Night at Eight"	
11/02/35	6	5	38. You Are My Lucky Star .... from the movie "Broadway Melody of 1935"	Decca 580
1/04/36	15	2	39. Red Sails In The Sunset............................ from the Broadway musical "Provincetown Follies"	Decca 648
2/15/36	17	1	40. Thanks A Million.................................... movie title song	Decca 666
2/22/36	13	2	41. I Hope Gabriel Likes My Music	Decca 672
6/20/36	19	1	42. Keyhole Blues....................................[R] reissue of earlier hit (recorded 5/13/27)	Vocalion 3110
7/25/36	10	3	43. Lyin' To Myself	Decca 835
10/31/36	17	1	44. On A Cocoanut Island................................ with The Polynesians; vocal: Louis, Andy Iona, George Archer, Harry Baty	Decca 914

DATE CHARTED	PEAK POS	WKS CHRT'D	ARTIST — Record Title	Label & Number
6/12/37	**19**	1	45. Darling Nelly Gray .... LOUIS ARMSTRONG & THE MILLS BROTHERS	Decca 1245
8/14/37	**7**	3	46. Public Melody Number One........................	Decca 1347
10/09/37	**12**	2	47. Alexander's Ragtime Band .... Henry "Red" Allen (trumpet) on above two	Decca 1408
1/08/38	**15**	2	48. Once In A While	Decca 1560
2/26/38	**18**	1	49. I Double Dare You................................	Decca 1636
6/18/38	**19**	1	50. Love Walked In .... from the movie "Goldwyn Follies"	Decca 1842
10/29/38	**20**	1	51. Basin Street Blues ....[R] recorded 12/4/28, released on Okeh 8690 & 41241; vocal: Louis, Earl Hines & Mancy Cara	Vocalion 3008
12/17/38	**16**	2	52. Going To Shout All Over God's Heaven .... with Decca Mixed Chorus	Decca 2085
2/04/39	**12**	5	53. Jeepers Creepers .... from the movie "Going Places"	Decca 2267
4/01/39	**10**	4	54. When The Saints Go Marching In...............	Decca 2230
6/17/39	**13**	1	55. West End Blues .... new version of his 1928 hit Henry "Red" Allen (trumpet) and J.C. Higginbotham (trombone) in band on 53 & 55	Decca 2480
7/13/40	**26**	1	56. W.P.A. .... LOUIS ARMSTRONG & THE MILLS BROTHERS	Decca 3151
6/28/41	**25**	1	57. The Peanut Vendor ....[R] return of his 1931 hit	Okeh 41478
4/06/46	**10**	2	58. You Won't Be Satisfied (Until You Break My Heart)....................................... ELLA FITZGERALD & LOUIS ARMSTRONG accompanied by Bob Haggart's Orchestra	Decca 23496
10/22/49	**19**	3	59. That Lucky Old Sun .... accompanied by Gordon Jenkins & His Orchestra Billy Butterfield (trumpet) on above two; Cozy Cole (drums) on 58	Decca 24752
10/14/50	**28**	1	60. La Vie En Rose... with Earl Hines (piano)	Decca 27113
11/18/50	**30**	1	61. Can Anyone Explain? (No! No! No!)............... ELLA FITZGERALD & LOUIS ARMSTRONG above two with Sy Oliver's Orchestra; Paul Webster (trumpet) on above two; Ray Brown (bass) on 61	Decca 27209
6/30/51	**19**	2	62. Gone Fishin' .... BING CROSBY & LOUIS ARMSTRONG band includes Red Nichols & Ziggy Elman (trumpets), Matty Matlock (tenor sax), Buddy Cole (piano), Perry Botkin (guitar)	Decca 27623
9/01/51	**10**	16	63. (When We Are Dancing) I Get Ideas/	
11/24/51+	**16**	11	64. A Kiss To Build A Dream On .... from the film "The Strip" accompanied on above two by Sy Oliver's Orchestra, including Al Klink (tenor sax) & Cutty Cutshall (trombone)	Decca 27720
1/12/52	**19**	3	65. When It's Sleepy Time Down South .... accompanied by Gordon Jenkins Orchestra, including Eddie Miller (tenor sax) Louis' longtime theme song; he originally recorded it in 1931 (Okeh 41504)	Decca 27899
6/07/52	**20**	2	66. Kiss Of Fire .... adapted from the Argentine tango, "El Choclo", published in 1913	Decca 28177
10/18/52	**19**	2	67. Takes Two To Tango	Decca 28394
1/31/53	**26**	1	68. Chloe.. accompanied by Gordon Jenkins Orchestra	Decca 28524
8/22/53	**30**	1	69. The Dummy Song/	
9/12/53	**30**	1	70. Sittin' In The Sun (Countin' My Money)....... above two accompanied by Jack Pleis' Orchestra	Decca 28803
10/02/54	**29**	1	71. Skokiaan (South African Song) .... orchestra on 67 & 71 directed by Sy Oliver	Decca 29256

DATE CHARTED	PEAK POS	WKS CHRT'D	ARTIST — Record Title	Label & Number
10/30/54	28	1	72. Muskrat Ramble	Decca 29280
			"Louis Armstrong & His All-Stars"; new version of Louis' 1926 hit Barney Bigard (clarinet) plays on 66, 69-72; Cozy Cole (drums) on 68-70; Charlie Shavers & Taft Jordan (trumpets) on 71	

GUS ARNHEIM & HIS ORCHESTRA

West Coast-based bandleader who also composed "I Cried for You" and his own #1 "Sweet and Lovely"; in addition to Gus on piano the band featured saxophonist Jimmie Grier and future movie actor Fred MacMurray (clarinet/tenor sax), and in the mid-30s Woody Herman and Stan Kenton. Gus died on 1/19/55 (57).

DATE CHARTED	PEAK POS	WKS CHRT'D	ARTIST — Record Title	Label & Number
3/02/29	6	7	1. Avalon Town	Okeh 41174
7/13/29	2(2)	9	2. Sleepy Valley...	Victor 21986
			vocal: Buster Dees	
8/24/29	9	7	3. Singin' In The Rain .... [I]	Victor 22012
			from the movie "Hollywood Revue of 1929"	
9/27/30	3	7	4. Go Home And Tell Your Mother..................	Victor 22505
			vocal: Bobby Burns	
11/22/30	4	6	5. It Must Be True	Victor 22561
12/27/30+	7	5	6. Them There Eyes/	
			vocal: Bing Crosby & The Rhythm Boys	
1/03/31	4	5	7. The Little Things In Life	Victor 22580
2/21/31	3	10	8. I Surrender, Dear....................................	Victor 22618
			this record helped earn Bing Crosby a CBS radio contract	
4/25/31	5	6	9. One More Time.......................................	Victor 22700
			Bing Crosby: vocals on 5 & above three	
6/06/31	6	4	10. Ho Hum!...	Victor 22691
			vocal: Bing Crosby and Loyce Whiteman	
6/27/31	8	3	11. Why Shouldn't I?...................................	Victor 22702
			vocal: Loyce Whiteman	
7/25/31	1(6)	14	12. **Sweet And Lovely**..................................	Victor 22770
			vocal: Donald Novis	
7/23/32	5	5	13. You're Blase	Victor 24054
			vocal: Meri Bell	
7/30/32	7	4	14. You've Got Me In The Palm Of Your Hand	Victor 24061
			vocal: Three Rhythm Rascals	
2/25/33	10	4	15. Love In The Moonlight	Victor 24235
			vocal: Loyce Whiteman	
3/04/33	17	1	16. Love Is A Dream....................................	Victor 24234
			8-16: "Gus Arnheim & His Cocoanut Grove Orchestra"	
11/25/33	15	2	17. I'm No Angel...	Brunswick 6683
			vocal: Shirley Ross; motion picture title song	
7/24/37	2(1)	8	18. So Rare..	Brunswick 7919
9/18/37	11	3	19. Have You Got Any Castles, Baby?..............	Brunswick 7937
			from the film "Varsity Show"	
9/18/37	11	2	20. My Cabin Of Dreams.............................	Brunswick 7933
			above three: Jimmy Farrell (vocals); Stan Kenton (piano) & Irving Fazola (clarinet)	

EDDY ARNOLD

"The Tennessee Ploughboy" dominated the country music charts from 1947 to 1955, often with his own compositions, and ever since his 1960s comeback has remained a Nashville giant.

DATE CHARTED	PEAK POS	WKS CHRT'D	ARTIST — Record Title	Label & Number
11/01/47	22	3	● 1. I'll Hold You In My Heart (Till I Can Hold You In My Arms)	RCA Victor 2332
5/15/48	17	1	● 2. Anytime/	
5/15/48	29	1	3. What A Fool I Was.............................	RCA Victor 2700
6/19/48	13	27	● 4. Bouquet Of Roses/	
7/03/48	18	1	5. Texarkana Baby	RCA Victor 2806
			above records: "Eddy Arnold & His Tennessee Plowboys"	
9/11/48	13	9	● 6. Just A Little Lovin' (Will Go A Long, Long Way)	RCA Victor 3013
12/11/48	23	2	7. A Heart Full Of Love (For A Handful Of Kisses)/	
1/08/49	30	1	8. Then I Turned And Walked Slowly Away	RCA Victor 3174

35

DATE CHARTED	PEAK POS	WKS CHRT'D	ARTIST — Record Title	Label & Number
3/19/49	**23**	2	9. Don't Rob Another Man's Castle.................	RCA Victor 0002
5/28/49	**23**	1	10. One Kiss Too Many	RCA Victor 0051
8/20/49	**18**	2	11. I'm Throwing Rice (At The Girl I Love).........	RCA Vic. 78-0083

PAUL ASH & HIS ORCHESTRA
Dance band leader born in Germany (U.S.-raised), wrote several 1920s hits (the Kay Kyser theme "Thinking of You"); died on 7/13/58 (67).

DATE CHARTED	PEAK POS	WKS CHRT'D	ARTIST — Record Title	Label & Number
1/12/24	**5**	4	1. Rememb'ring .... [I]	Brunswick 2498
			"Paul Ash & His Granada Orchestra"	
7/07/28	**18**	1	2. My Pet	Columbia 1349
			vocal: Milton Watson	
8/26/33	**17**	2	3. Shadows On The Swanee...........................	Columbia 2796

SAM ASH
Popular tenor who appeared in the 1916 Broadway operetta "Katinka", and later acted in several movies; died on 10/21/51 (67). (listed on some records as Samuel Ash)

DATE CHARTED	PEAK POS	WKS CHRT'D	ARTIST — Record Title	Label & Number
9/11/15	**9**	1	1. When I Leave The World Behind.................	Columbia 1772
10/09/15	**3**	5	2. Hello, Frisco!	Columbia 1801
			ELIDA MORRIS & SAM ASH	
			from the Broadway musical "Follies of 1915"	
11/20/15	**7**	2	3. Floating Down The Old Green River	Columbia 1825
			from the Broadway musical "Maid in America"	
1/08/16	**4**	5	4. America, I Love You................................	Columbia 1842
2/16/18	**10**	1	5. Give Me The Moonlight, Give Me The Girl (And Leave The Rest To Me).................	Columbia 2415
3/16/18	**10**	1	6. Smile And Show Your Dimple.....................	Columbia 2425
			in 1933, Irving Berlin used this same melody for "Easter Parade"	
8/17/18	**9**	2	7. I'm Always Chasing Rainbows.....................	Emerson 930
			from the Broadway musical "Oh, Look!"	
4/19/19	**8**	1	8. Beautiful Ohio...	Emerson 9132
5/31/19	**6**	2	9. Tears..	Columbia 2700
12/20/19	**7**	2	10. A Pretty Girl Is Like A Melody	Okeh 4025
			from Broadway's "Ziegfeld Follies of 1919" also recorded for Pathe 22219	
6/25/21	**8**	2	11. I Found A Rose In The Devil's Garden	Columbia 3374
10/22/21	**9**	1	12. They Needed A Song Bird In Heaven (So God Took Caruso Away)...........................	Grey Gull 2067
6/02/23	**10**	1	13. Love Sends A Little Gift Of Roses	Vocalion 14534
			Sam previously recorded this song in 1921 for Okeh 4387	

VIRGINIA ASHER - see HOMER RODEHEAVER

PERRY ASKAM

DATE CHARTED	PEAK POS	WKS CHRT'D	ARTIST — Record Title	Label & Number
3/22/30	**20**	1	1. Lover, Come Back To Me/	
			from the Broadway musical "The New Moon"	
4/05/30	**20**	1	2. Stout-Hearted Men	Victor 22317
			above two with the chorus of the "New Moon" Company from the Broadway musical "The New Moon"	

ASSOCIATED GLEE CLUBS OF AMERICA
This historic record was the first electrically-recorded disc to create a popular impact, and featured the largest choir popular music has ever known: some 4,800 voices (according to Columbia Records)

DATE CHARTED	PEAK POS	WKS CHRT'D	ARTIST — Record Title	Label & Number
7/25/25	**5**	2	1. Adeste Fideles/	
8/22/25	**9**	1	2. John Peel...	Columbia 50013
			traditional English song, published in 1820	

DATE CHARTED	PEAK POS	WKS CHRT'D	ARTIST — Record Title	Label & Number
			FRED ASTAIRE	
			America's greatest song and dance man was born Frederick Austerlitz in Omaha, Neb. 5/10/1899. He and sister Adele were featured in ten major Broadway musicals from 1917-31. Fred then stepped out on his own, and proceeded to make movie history with some thirty unforgettable musicals over the next four decades, most notably the ten with Ginger Rogers. In later years a respected dramatic actor, Fred Astaire remains the epitome of unassuming class in popular entertainment.	
4/20/29	**18**	1	1. My One And Only................ from the Broadway musical "Funny Face"	Columbia 5173
8/01/31	**4**	7	2. I Love Louisa/	
8/01/31	**10**	4	3. New Sun In The Sky .... above two from the Broadway musical "The Band Wagon"	Victor 22755
12/17/32	**1(10)**	18	4. **Night And Day/** song inspired by a Mohammedan religious chant in Morocco	
2/11/33	**17**	2	5. I've Got You On My Mind............ above two from the Broadway musical "Gay Divorce" above four: Leo Reisman & His Orchestra, vocals by Fred Astaire	Victor 24193
4/04/34	**6**	4	6. Flying Down To Rio/	
4/04/34	**14**	2	7. Music Makes Me .... above two from the movie "Flying Down to Rio"	Columbia 2912
8/03/35	**1(11)**	18	8. **Cheek To Cheek/**	
9/07/35	**9**	6	9. No Strings	Brunswick 7486
8/10/35	**2(2)**	13	10. Top Hat, White Tie, And Tails/	
8/24/35	**3**	11	11. Isn't This A Lovely Day?............ accompanied on above two by Johnny Green's Orchestra	Brunswick 7487
8/31/35	**10**	6	12. The Piccolino .... accompanied on 8-9 & 12 by the Leo Reisman Orchestra above five from the movie "Top Hat"	Brunswick 7488
2/22/36	**1(1)**	10	13. **I'm Putting All My Eggs In One Basket/**	
3/07/36	**15**	3	14. We Saw The Sea	Brunswick 7609
2/22/36	**4**	8	15. I'm Building Up To An Awful Letdown/	
3/07/36	**12**	4	16. I'd Rather Lead A Band	Brunswick 7610
3/07/36	**2(2)**	12	17. Let Yourself Go/	
3/07/36	**5**	11	18. Let's Face The Music And Dance .... above six from the movie "Follow the Fleet"	Brunswick 7608
8/29/36	**1(6)**	17	19. **The Way You Look To-night/**	
9/12/36	**7**	6	20. Pick Yourself Up............	Brunswick 7717
8/29/36	**1(5)**	12	21. **A Fine Romance**	Brunswick 7716
8/29/36	**5**	6	22. Never Gonna Dance/	
9/19/36	**17**	2	23. Bojangles Of Harlem............ above five from the movie "Swing Time", all with Johnny Green & His Orchestra	Brunswick 7718
4/17/37	**1(1)**	11	24. **They Can't Take That Away From Me/**	
5/01/37	**13**	2	25. (I've Got) Beginner's Luck	Brunswick 7855
4/17/37	**3**	6	26. Shall We Dance?/	
4/24/37	**5**	9	27. Let's Call The Whole Thing Off............	Brunswick 7857
4/17/37	**6**	11	28. They All Laughed .... above five from the movie "Shall We Dance?" accompanied on 13-28 by Johnny Green & His Orchestra	Brunswick 7856
11/13/37+	**1(1)**	15	29. **Nice Work If You Can Get It/**	
12/18/37	**19**	1	30. Things Are Looking Up............	Brunswick 7983
11/13/37	**3**	10	31. A Foggy Day .... above three from the movie "A Damsel in Distress"	Brunswick 7982
8/27/38	**1(2)**	8	32. **Change Partners/**	
9/10/38	**8**	3	33. I Used To Be Color Blind............	Brunswick 8189
8/27/38	**10**	10	34. The Yam .... above three from the movie "Carefree" accompanied on above six by Ray Noble's Orchestra	Brunswick 8190
3/20/43	**23**	1	35. I'm Old-Fashioned .... from the film "You Were Never Lovelier" orchestra directed by John Scott Trotter	Decca 18489

DATE CHARTED	PEAK POS	WKS CHRT'D	ARTIST — Record Title	Label & Number
4/21/51	30	1	36. How Could You Believe Me When I Said I Loved You When You Know I've Been A .	
			36. Liar All My Life .... MGM 30316	
			FRED ASTAIRE & JANE POWELL from the film "Royal Wedding"	

BOB ATCHER & BONNIE BLUE EYES
Country vocal duo

7/31/43	19	1	1. Pins And Needles (In My Heart)	Okeh 6689

JOHN YORKE ATLEE
"Artistic whistler" who was one of the very first popular recording artists; died on 4/1/10 (68).

8/22/91	1(6)	6	1. The Mocking Bird............................ Columbia	
			song best known as "Listen to the Mocking Bird"	
10/17/91	2(3)	3	2. Home, Sweet Home	Columbia
7/08/93	2(3)	3	3. After The Ball	Columbia
			song featured in Broadway musical "A Trip to Chinatown" accompanied on piano by Fred Gaisberg	

JAN AUGUST
Real name Jan Augustoff; former pianist for Paul Specht and xylophonist for Paul Whiteman. (also see Roberta Quinlan)

12/28/46	7	6	1. Misirlou .... [I]	Diamond 2009
5/20/50	8	12	2. Bewitched .... [I]	Mercury 5399
			JAN AUGUST & JERRY MURAD'S HARMONICATS from the Broadway musical "Pal Joey"	

GEORGE AULD
Acclaimed tenor saxophonist with Bunny Berigan (1937-38), Artie Shaw (1938-39, 1941-42), and Benny Goodman (1940-41).

GENE AUSTIN
The most popular singer of the late 1920s, Gene Austin was born on 6/24/1900 in Gainesville, Tex. Gene started in vaudeville, and in 1925 his amiable vocal and piano style launched him on radio and records as "The Voice the Southland". His recording of "My Blue Heaven" was the second biggest non-holiday record seller of the entire pre-1955 era. A gifted songwriter as well as entertainer, Gene died on 1/24/72 (71).

5/02/25	3	6	1. When My Sugar Walks Down The Street........	Victor 19585
			AILEEN STANLEY & GENE AUSTIN	
6/27/25	2(4)	8	2. Yearning (Just For You)	Victor 19625
7/25/25	5	4	3. The Flapper Wife	Victor 19638
7/25/25	9	1	4. Way Down Home	Victor 19637
			GENE AUSTIN & CARSON ROBISON	
7/25/25	11	1	5. The Only, Only One For Me........................	Victor 19599
8/01/25	1(7)	17	6. Yes Sir! That's My Baby/	
9/12/25	9	1	7. Everything Is Hotsy Totsy Now	Victor 19656
			above two accompanied by Billy Carpenter (ukelele)	
9/26/25	6	2	8. Let It Rain, Let It Pour	Victor 19677
3/06/26	8	2	9. I Never Knew	Victor 19864
3/27/26	1(1)	11	10. Five Foot Two, Eyes Of Blue/	
3/27/26	3	5	11. Sleepy Time Gal	Victor 19899
3/27/26	13	1	12. Save Your Sorrow (for Tomorrow)	Victor 19857
5/29/26	13	1	13. Sweet Child (I'm Wild About You)	Victor 19928
7/31/26	1(3)	12	14. Bye Bye, Blackbird/	
9/04/26	8	2	15. Ya Gotta Know How To Love	Victor 20044
2/26/27	1(3)	13	16. Tonight You Belong To Me	Victor 20371
3/26/27	11	3	17. Sunday/	
			from Broadway musical "The Merry World"	
4/02/27	16	1	18. I've Grown So Lonesome, Thinking Of You ..	Victor 20411
4/02/27	9	4	19. I've Got The Girl.....................................	Victor 20397
6/25/27	1(1)	11	20. Forgive Me/	
6/25/27	5	6	21. Someday, Sweetheart	Victor 20561
6/25/27	4	6	22. Ain't She Sweet?	Victor 20568

DATE CHARTED	PEAK POS	WKS CHRT'D	ARTIST — Record Title	Label & Number
9/24/27	**13**	2	23. One Sweet Letter From You .... 17-19, 21 & 23 accompanied by Abel Baer (piano)	Victor 20730
12/03/27	**1(13)**	26	● 24. **My Blue Heaven** .... sold over five million copies	Victor 20964
12/24/27+	**8**	4	25. The Sweetheart Of Sigma Chi.....................	Victor 20977
1/07/28	**3**	8	26. My Melancholy Baby/ first major hit record of the classic song published in 1912	
1/07/28	**8**	4	27. There's A Cradle In Caroline....................	Victor 21015
3/24/28	**10**	4	28. The Lonesome Road .... featured in 1929 movie version of "Show Boat"	Victor 21098
5/19/28	**1(8)**	17	● 29. **Ramona/** accompanied by Nat Shilkret Orchestra; song written to promote silent film of the same name	
5/26/28	**2(3)**	13	30. Girl Of My Dreams .... with whistling by Bob McGimsey above two accompanied by Viola Klaiss (pipe organ)	Victor 21334
6/23/28	**5**	6	31. Without You, Sweetheart/	
7/07/28	**14**	2	32. In My Bouquet Of Memories	Victor 21374
6/30/28	**9**	4	33. So Tired..	Victor 21329
8/18/28	**5**	6	34. Just Like A Melody Out Of The Sky	Victor 21454
9/08/28	**1(5)**	15	35. **Jeannine (I Dream Of Lilac Time)**.............. song written to accompany the silent film "Lilac Time"	Victor 21564
9/22/28	**6**	6	36. Memories Of France/	
10/27/28	**10**	3	37. Old Pals Are The Best Pals After All	Victor 21545
1/12/29	**3**	7	38. She's Funny That Way/	
1/12/29	**12**	2	39. Sonny Boy... from the movie "The Singing Fool"	Victor 21779
2/09/29	**1(7)**	14	40. **Carolina Moon**.......................................	Victor 21833
2/16/29	**12**	2	41. I Can't Give You Anything But Love............ from the Broadway musical "Blackbirds of 1928"	Victor 21798
4/13/29	**5**	7	42. Weary River.....................................	Victor 21856
5/04/29	**8**	5	43. Wedding Bells Are Breaking Up That Old Gang Of Mine/ with Ed Smalle and Dick Robertson	
7/27/29	**20**	1	44. That's What I Call Heaven......................	Victor 21893
6/29/29	**12**	2	45. Dream Mother/	
7/06/29	**15**	2	46. A Garden In The Rain.............................	Victor 21915
7/27/29	**7**	5	47. Little Pal.. from the movie "Say It With Songs" accompanied by Nat Shilkret & His Orchestra on 1, 3, 5, 9, 10, 12, 16, 20, 22, 24-32, 34-42, & 45-47	Victor 21952
8/17/29	**10**	3	48. I've Got A Feeling I'm Falling..................... from the movie "Applause"	Victor 22033
9/28/29	**9**	3	49. Ain't Misbehavin'....................................... from Broadway musical "Hot Chocolates"	Victor 22068
12/28/29	**20**	1	50. My Fate Is In Your Hands .... 48 & 50 with Fats Waller on piano	Victor 22223
5/02/31	**3**	5	51. Please Don't Talk About Me When I'm Gone/	
5/09/31	**10**	4	52. When Your Lover Has Gone..................... accompanied by Leonard Joy & His Orchestra on 43-44 & above five	Victor 22635
12/26/31	**20**	1	53. Lies.. accompanied by Ben Pollack's Orchestra also released on Banner 32325	Perfect 15542
12/10/32	**15**	3	54. Just A Little Street Where Old Friends Meet.. accompanied by members of Dorsey Brothers Orchestra	Melotone 12529
7/07/34	**17**	3	55. Ridin' Around In The Rain.........................	Victor 24663

DATE CHARTED	PEAK POS	WKS CHRT'D	ARTIST — Record Title	Label & Number
			GENE AUTRY	
			Hollywood's first "singing cowboy", Gene Autry was born 9/29/1907 in Texas, began on Oklahoma radio in the late 1920s before launching his movie career in 1934. Gene made more than 100 films, hosted his own radio and TV shows, and became a prosperous businessman, including ownership of baseball's California Angels.	
11/18/33	12	2	1. The Last Round-Up .... also on Perfect 12952; featured in "Ziegfeld Follies of 1934"	Melotone 12832
2/09/35	10	7	2. Ole Faithful	Melotone 13354
2/16/35	10	5	3. Tumbling Tumbleweeds	Melotone 13315
8/24/35	7	5	● 4. That Silver-Haired Daddy Of Mine .... GENE AUTRY & JIMMY LONG originally recorded on 10/29/31	Vocalion 2991
11/25/39	12	4	5. South Of The Border (Down Mexico Way).......	Vocalion 5122
7/20/40	20	2	6. Goodbye Little Darlin' Goodbye.................... above two from the film "South Of The Border"	Vocalion 5463
5/03/41	23	1	7. Be Honest With Me...................................	Okeh 5980
8/30/41	23	1	8. You Are My Sunshine	Okeh 06274
8/25/42	14	1	9. Jingle Jangle Jingle .... from the film "The Forest Ranger"	Okeh 6690
1/15/44	20	1	10. Tweedle O'Twill.....................................	Columbia 36587
12/27/47	9	2	● 11. Here Comes Santa Claus (Down Santa Claus Lane) .... [X]	Columbia 37942
11/20/48	17	3	12. Buttons And Bows .... from the movie "Paleface"	Columbia 20469
12/08/48+	8	5	13. Here Comes Santa Claus (Down Santa Claus Lane) .... [X-R]	Columbia 20377
12/03/49+	1(1)	6	● 14. **Rudolph, The Red-Nosed Reindeer** .... [X] with the Pinafores; eventually sold over eight million copies, second in the pre-1955 era only to "White Christmas"	Columbia 38610
1/07/50	24	1	15. Here Comes Santa Claus (Down Santa Claus Lane) .... [X-R]	Columbia 20377
4/01/50	5	5	16. Peter Cottontail....................................	Columbia 38750
12/02/50	3	7	17. Rudolph, The Red-Nosed Reindeer .... [X-R]	Columbia 38610
12/09/50+	7	6	● 18. Frosty The Snow Man.......................... [X] with the Cass County Boys & Carl Cotner's Orchestra	Columbia 38907
3/31/51	19	2	19. Peter Cottontail................................... [R]	Columbia 38750
12/22/51	16	3	20. Rudolph, The Red-Nosed Reindeer .... [X-R]	Columbia 38610
12/20/52	9	2	21. The Night Before Christmas Song .... [X] GENE AUTRY & ROSEMARY CLOONEY with Carl Cotner's Orchestra	Columbia 39876
12/20/52	23	3	22. Frosty The Snow Man........................ [X-R]	Columbia 38907
12/27/52	12	1	23. Rudolph, The Red-Nosed Reindeer .... [X-R]	Columbia 38610
12/19/53	26	3	24. Rudolph, The Red-Nosed Reindeer .... [X-R]	Columbia 38610
			AVON COMEDY FOUR	
			Group very popular in vaudeville: Irving Kaufman, Harry Goodwin, and the famous comedy duo of Joe Smith and Charles Dale	
1/13/17+	10	1	1. Way Out Yonder In The Golden West...........	Victor 18133
2/16/18	8	1	2. I'm Crazy Over Every Girl In France............	Columbia 2399
4/05/19	7	2	3. Come On, Papa......................................	Columbia 2692
			MITCHELL AYRES & HIS FASHIONS IN MUSIC	
			Mitchell (real surname Agress), formerly with Little Jack Little's band, featured alto saxophonist Harry Terrell in his own organization. In the late 1940s he began a long association as musical director for Perry Como; died 9/5/69 (58).	
3/02/40	15	2	1. Row, Row, Row....................................... vocal: Mary Ann Mercer	Bluebird 10541
4/13/40	20	1	2. Little Girl.. vocal: Tommy Taylor	Bluebird 10627
5/04/40	18	2	3. How High The Moon .... from Broadway musical "Two for the Show"	Bluebird 10609

DATE CHARTED	PEAK POS	WKS CHRT'D	ARTIST — Record Title	Label & Number
5/25/40	1(2)	13	4. **Make-Believe Island**.................................... vocals on above two: Mary Ann Mercer	Bluebird 10687
7/13/40	12	3	5. Playmates	Bluebird 10585
7/20/40	14	3	6. Blue Lovebird .... from the film "Lillian Russell"	Bluebird 10738
7/20/40	16	1	7. I Can't Love You Any More (Any More Than I Do)	Bluebird 10653
11/16/40	27	1	8. I Just Wanna Play With You .... vocals on 5 & 8: Mary Ann Mercer & Tommy Taylor	Bluebird 10884
11/23/40	7	4	9. I Give You My Word .... vocals on 7 & 9: Tommy Taylor	Bluebird 10895
11/23/40	9	9	10. Two Dreams Met.. from the movie "Down Argentine Way"	Bluebird 10877
6/28/41	11	1	11. Just A Little Bit South Of North Carolina...... vocals on 6, 10 & 11: Mary Ann Mercer	Bluebird 11101
10/11/41	18	1	12. I Don't Want To Set The World On Fire......... vocal: Johnny Bond	Bluebird 11275
10/31/42	22	1	13. Under A Strawberry Moon .... vocal: Meredith Blake	Bluebird 11588

DON AZPIAZU & HIS HAVANA CASINO ORCHESTRA
Cuban bandleader who also recorded the original version of "Green Eyes" in 1931 (Victor 22729)

DATE CHARTED	PEAK POS	WKS CHRT'D	ARTIST — Record Title	Label & Number
11/08/30+	1(7)	28	1. **The Peanut Vendor**................................. vocal: Arturo Machin adapted from "El Manisero"; featured in 1931 film "Cuban Love Song"	Victor 22483

B

HARRY BABBITT
Extremely popular singer with Kay Kyser band (1937-44,47-49); biggest hit "Who Wouldn't Love You?".

BOB BACHELDER & HIS ORCHESTRA
Boston-based band

DATE CHARTED	PEAK POS	WKS CHRT'D	ARTIST — Record Title	Label & Number
7/18/53	22	3	1. TV Rhumba .... [I] medley of ten TV theme songs	Mood 1011

MILDRED BAILEY
Few jazz singers were so widely admired as Mildred Bailey, who started her career on Los Angeles radio, and through her brother Al Rinker was hired in 1929 by Paul Whiteman. She and husband Red Norvo became known as "Mr. and Mrs. Swing". Mildred died on 12/12/51 (44). (also see Glen Gray & the Casa Loma Orchestra, Benny Goodman, and Red Norvo)

DATE CHARTED	PEAK POS	WKS CHRT'D	ARTIST — Record Title	Label & Number
1/30/32	19	1	1. Georgia On My Mind .... accompanied by Matt Malneck's Orchestra	Victor 22891
8/05/33	9	5	2. Lazy Bones... accompanied by Dorsey Brothers Orchestra, including Bunny Berigan (trumpet) with Glenn Miller (arranger)	Brunswick 6587
12/19/36	18	1	3. For Sentimental Reasons	Vocalion 3367
12/26/36+	15	2	4. More Than You Know .... from the Broadway musical "Great Day"; band on above two includes Ziggy Elman (trumpet), Artie Shaw (clarinet), Teddy Wilson (piano), & Cozy Cole (drums)	Vocalion 3378
3/06/37	4	8	5. Trust In Me/	
3/13/37	10	4	6. My Last Affair..................................... from Broadway musical "New Faces of 1934"	Vocalion 3449
4/10/37	5	12	7. Where Are You? .... from the movie "Top of the Town". Band on above three features Roy Eldridge (trumpet)	Vocalion 3456
5/08/37	8	4	8. Never In A Million Years .... from the movie "Wake Up and Live"	Vocalion 3508
6/12/37	13	2	9. Rockin' Chair.. band on above two with Eddie Sauter (trumpet and arranger)	Vocalion 3553

DATE CHARTED	PEAK POS	WKS CHRT'D	ARTIST — Record Title	Label & Number
8/28/37	**14**	2	10. It's The Natural Thing To Do .... from the movie "Double or Nothing"; band features Buck Clayton (trumpet)	Vocalion 3626
11/06/37	**14**	2	11. Bob White (Whatcha Gonna Swing Tonight) ...	Vocalion 3712
12/04/37	**19**	1	12. Right Or Wrong .... from the movie "Something to Sing About" Red Norvo (xylophone) director on 8, 9, 11, & 12	Vocalion 3758
3/05/38	**11**	3	13. Thanks For The Memory .... from the movie "The Big Broadcast of 1938". Band features Chu Berry (tenor sax) and Teddy Wilson (piano)	Vocalion 3931
3/26/38	**9**	7	14. Don't Be That Way...................................	Vocalion 4016
5/21/38	**8**	6	15. I Let A Song Go Out Of My Heart	Vocalion 4083
8/06/38	**9**	4	16. Small Fry .... from the movie "Sing You Sinners"	Vocalion 4224
8/27/38	**2(2)**	11	17. So Help Me	Vocalion 4253
11/05/38	**10**	4	18. My Reverie .... based on Debussy's "Reverie"	Vocalion 4408
2/25/39	**13**	1	19. Blame It On My Last Affair .... different than song 6	Vocalion 4632
8/05/39	**14**	2	20. Moon Love... based on theme from Tchaikovsky's 5th Symphony, 2nd Movement Red Norvo bandleader on above seven	Vocalion 4939
8/03/40	**24**	1	21. It's So Peaceful In The Country	Decca 3953
8/02/47	**21**	1	22. Almost Like Being In Love .... orchestra directed by Julian Work from the Broadway musical "Brigadoon"	Majestic 1140

PEARL BAILEY

Pearl, a former singer with Cootie Williams' band, became widely known on Broadway with "St. Louis Woman" in 1946, leading to a successful movie, TV, and concert career. She married jazz drummer Louis Bellson.

9/27/52	**7**	17	1. Takes Two To Tango .... accompanied by Don Redman's Orchestra, featuring Taft Jordan (trumpet)	Coral 60817

EUGENIE BAIRD

Former vocalist with the Casa Loma and Tony Pastor orchestras

10/27/45	**20**	1	1. I Fall In Love Too Easily .... EUGENE BAIRD with MEL TORME'S MEL-TONES from the movie "Anchors Aweigh"	Decca 18707
5/23/53	**26**	1	2. Say "Si Si"	Vinrob 3

BELLE BAKER

Longtime vaudeville star who also appeared on Broadway and in two movies; died in 1957

12/13/19	**8**	2	1. Poor Little Butterfly Is A Fly Gal Now	Pathe 22208
12/29/23	**11**	1	2. I've Got The Yes! We Have No Bananas Blues .... [C] with the Virginians	Victor 19135
12/27/24	**13**	1	3. Hard-Hearted Hannah..............................	Victor 19436
3/09/29	**20**	1	4. My Man... featured in 1929 movie "My Man"	Brunswick 4086
8/24/29	**19**	1	5. My Sin	Brunswick 4343

BONNIE BAKER

'Wee Bonnie Baker' (real name Evelyn Nelson), sang with Orrin Tucker band 1939-42, voted most popular female band vocalist in 1940 Billboard college poll.

ELSIE BAKER

Contralto who frequently recorded under pseudonym "Edna Brown"; also a member of the Victor Light Co. Died on 4/28/58 (71).

7/20/12	**3**	5	1. Please Don't Take My Lovin' Man Away........	Victor 17102
8/31/12	**1(2)**	11	2. **I Love You Truly**	Victor 17121
10/05/12	**5**	2	3. When You're Away .... "EDNA BROWN" & AMERICAN QUARTET from Broadway musical "The Winsome Widow"	Victor 17139
12/21/12	**6**	2	4. Silent Night, Hallowed Night .... [X]	Victor 17164

DATE CHARTED	PEAK POS	WKS CHRT'D	ARTIST — Record Title	Label & Number
5/17/13	2(1)	7	5. Daddy Has A Sweetheart And Mother Is Her Name .... from "Ziegfeld Follies of 1912"	Victor 17320
7/05/13	5	4	6. The Land Of Golden Dreams .... ELSIE BAKER & FREDERICK WHEELER	Victor 17334
8/09/13	9	1	7. The Trail Of The Lonesome Pine.................	Victor 17338
8/16/13	4	4	8. Sunshine And Roses...................... above two: "EDNA BROWN" & JAMES F. HARRISON	Victor 17359
10/25/13	6	2	9. A Perfect Day......................	Victor 17387
11/29/13	5	4	10. When It's Apple Blossom Time In Normandy.. from the Broadway musical "Roly Poly"; song based on Beethoven's "Minuet in G"	Columbia 1383
1/31/14	9	1	11. If We Were On Our Honeymoon .... above two & 13: "EDNA BROWN" & JAMES F. HARRISON	Columbia 1423
2/06/15	10	1	12. Home, Sweet Home	Victor 35398
8/07/15	9	1	13. The Flame Of Love...................... from the Broadway musical "The Peasant Girl"	Victor 17762
3/04/16	3	5	14. Go To Sleep, My Dusky Baby .... ELSIE BAKER, OLIVE KLINE, & MARGUERITE DUNLAP melody based on Dvorak's "Humoresque"	Victor 17918
5/06/16	6	3	15. There's A Broken Heart For Every Light On Broadway .... flip side of #1 hit "The Lights of My Home Town" by the Peerless Quartet	Victor 17943
6/17/16	10	1	16. Some Sort Of Somebody........................... BILLY MURRAY & "EDNA BROWN" from the Broadway musical "Very Good, Eddie"	Victor 17992
7/01/16	5	3	17. Fair Hawaii........................... "EDNA BROWN & JAMES REED" (Reed Miller)	Victor 18032
8/19/16	4	6	18. Simple Melody........................... BILLY MURRAY & "EDNA BROWN" from the Broadway musical "Watch Your Step"	Victor 18051
3/10/17	1(4)	11	19. **Hush-A-Bye Ma Baby (The Missouri Waltz)**.	Victor 18214
8/18/17	5	3	20. For You A Rose	Victor 18301
2/22/19	4	4	21. A Little Birch Canoe And You.....................	Victor 45156
4/24/20	14	1	22. Sweet And Low	Victor 45174
5/14/21	7	3	23. Look For The Silver Lining........................ CHARLES HARRISON & "EDNA BROWN" from the Broadway musical "Sally"	Victor 18731
11/12/21	6	2	24. Where The Lazy Mississippi Flows	Victor 45252
4/01/22	3	6	25. Ka-Lu-A .... "EDNA BROWN" & ELLIOTT SHAW from the Broadway musical "Good Morning, Dearie"	Victor 18854
7/01/22	5	3	26. Marcheta (A Love Song of Old Mexico) .... 24 & 26: OLIVE KLINE & ELSIE BAKER	Victor 45309

KENNY BAKER

Sang on Jack Benny's radio show in 1930s, hosted his own show several years later; Kenny also stared in the 1943 Broadway musical "One Touch of Venus".

DATE CHARTED	PEAK POS	WKS CHRT'D	ARTIST — Record Title	Label & Number
5/21/38	14	3	1. Love Walked In .... from the movie "Goldwyn Follies"	Decca 1795
11/18/39+	15	2	2. Two Blind Loves...................... from the movie "The Marx Brothers At The Circus" accompanied by Nat Finston's Orchestra	Victor 26413
12/28/40	20	1	3. There I Go	Victor 27207
2/08/41	12	5	4. You Walk By........................... accompanied on above two by Leonard Joy's Orchestra	Victor 27250
5/30/42	21	1	5. Whisper That You Love Me........................	Decca 18313
6/27/42	11	6	6. Johnny Doughboy Found A Rose In Ireland ...	Decca 18274
7/25/42	14	1	7. Always In My Heart................... accompanied on 1, 5, 6, & 7 by the Harry Sosnik Orchestra	Decca 18262
2/08/47	11	2	8. The Old Lamplighter	Decca 23781
5/24/47	16	1	9. My Adobe Hacienda................... accompanied on above two by Russ Morgan's Orchestra	Decca 23846

DATE CHARTED	PEAK POS	WKS CHRT'D	ARTIST — Record Title	Label & Number
			TWO-TON BAKER & HIS MUSIC MAKERS	
			Dick Baker, novelty band leader	
10/11/47	12	5	1. Near You/	
11/29/47	21	1	2. I'm A Lonely Little Petunia (In An Onion Patch) .... [N] Mercury 5066	
			ERNEST BALL	
			One of the great popular songwriters of the pre-1920 era ("Love Me and the World Is Mine", "Mother Machree"); died on 5/7/27 (48).	
7/01/16	8	2	1. Good-Bye, Good Luck, God Bless You .... Columbia 1978	
			accompanied by Charles Prince & His Orchestra	
			GEORGE WILTON BALLARD	
			Tenor who recorded for 15 years with Edison; died 4/6/50 (72)	
1/23/15	9	1	1. You're More Than The World To Me .... Victor 17654	
3/25/16	7	2	2. M-O-T-H-E-R (A Word That Means The World To Me) .... Edison 50325	
9/13/19	10	1	3. I'm Forever Blowing Bubbles...................... Edison Amb. 3798	
			HELEN CLARK & GEORGE WILTON BALLARD also on Edison 50534	
			SMITH BALLEW & HIS ORCHESTRA	
			Popular singer whose band sometimes included Tommy and Jimmy Dorsey, Jack Teagarden, and Bunny Berigan, with arrangements by Glenn Miller. (also see Emil Coleman, Dorsey Brothers Orchestra, Ben Pollack, & Ben Selvin)	
6/29/29	12	3	1. I Kiss Your Hand, Madame .... Okeh 41226	
3/15/30	18	2	2. Sing, You Sinners .... Okeh 41384	
			from the movie "Honey"	
5/16/31	15	2	3. Say A Little Prayer For Me .... Columbia 2430	
10/17/31	17	2	4. What Is It? .... Columbia 2503	
10/31/31	6	6	5. Time On My Hands (You In My Arms)/	
			from the Broadway musical "Smiles"	
11/07/31	12	4	6. You Call It Madness (But I Call It Love)....... Columbia 2544	
			above three: "Smith Ballew & His Piping Rock Orchestra"	
3/02/35	17	2	7. The Night Is Young .... Perfect 16059	
			movie title song	
10/12/35	10	7	8. Roll Along, Prairie Moon .... Melotone 351006	
			from the movie "Here Comes the Band"	
			D.C. BANGS	
			comedian	
12/02/93	2(2)	2	1. Rastus And The Watermillion ....[T-C] Columbia	
			BAR HARBOR SOCIETY ORCHESTRA	
			Irving Kaufman sang on many of this band's records	
11/25/22	13	1	1. Chicago (That Toddlin' Town) .... [I] Vocalion 14412	
5/05/23	7	2	2. Love Sends A Little Gift Of Roses .... [I] Vocalion 14500	
			RAY BARBER	
			Baritone ballad singer	
9/29/51	23	1	1. Because Of You .... Mercury 5643	
			accompanied by Russ Case Orchestra	
			DAVE BARBOUR	
			Guitarist with Red Norvo, Hal Kemp, Artie Shaw, and Benny Goodman; married Peggy Lee, and co-wrote several of her biggest hits; died on 12/11/65 (53).	
9/09/50	27	1	1. The Mambo (Que Rico El Mambo)............. [I] Capitol 973	
			INEZ BARBOUR	
2/18/11	10	1	1. Alma .... Victor 5805	
			from the Broadway musical "Alma, Where Do You Live?"	
5/25/12	5	3	2. Love Never Dies .... Victor 17042	
			from the Broadway musical "Little Boy Blue" above two: HARRY ANTHONY & INEZ BARBOUR	
1/09/15	9	1	3. Same Sort Of Girl.................................... Columbia 1609	
			INEZ BARBOUR & JOHN BARNES WELLS from the Broadway musical "The Girl from Utah"	

DATE CHARTED	PEAK POS	WKS CHRT'D	ARTIST — Record Title	Label & Number
			ROY BARGY & RAMONA Roy Bargy was early-1920s musical director of the Benson Orchestra of Chicago, and served as Paul Whiteman's pianist/arranger from 1928-38; died on 1/15/74.	
4/15/33	**13**	2	1. What Have We Got To Lose?........................ vocal: Ramona	Victor 24268
			BLU LU BARKER R&B singer (Louisa Barker) married to New Orleans jazz guitarist/banjo player Danny Barker.	
11/05/38	**15**	2	1. Don't You Make Me High .... with Danny Barker's Fly Cats, including Benny Carter (trumpet) & Buster Bailey (clarinet)	Decca 7506
12/18/48+	**4**	14	2. A Little Bird Told Me................................	Capitol 15308
			CHARLIE BARNET & HIS ORCHESTRA Tenor saxophonist whose popular swing band featured such top musicians as Billy May and Neal Hefti (trumpets) and Buddy DeFranco (clarinet), and in later years guitarist Barney Kessel and trumpet stars Clark Terry and Doc Severinsen. Lena Horne sang briefly with the band in 1941.	
9/19/36	**16**	2	1. Bye Bye Baby.. vocal: Barnet Modernaires	Bluebird 6504
10/24/36	**6**	5	2. Sing, Baby, Sing .... movie title song	Bluebird 6593
12/05/36	**10**	4	3. Did You Mean It?...................................... vocals on above two: Charlie Barnet	Bluebird 6605
3/11/39	**15**	1	4. Knockin' At The Famous Door .... [I]	Bluebird 10131
3/18/39	**13**	3	5. The Gal From Joe's................................. [I]	Bluebird 10153
9/16/39	**15**	3	6. For Tonight .... vocal: Larry Taylor	Bluebird 10361
10/14/39	**15**	3	7. Cherokee .... [I] Charlie's theme song	Bluebird 10373
11/04/39	**8**	5	8. Lilacs In The Rain .... vocal: Del Casino	Bluebird 10439
2/24/40	**16**	2	9. Between 18th And 19th On Chestnut Street ..	Bluebird 10543
5/25/40	**1(2)**	10	10. **Where Was I?**.................................... from the film "'Til We Meet Again"	Bluebird 10669
5/25/40	**8**	4	11. It's A Wonderful World	Bluebird 10610
5/25/40	**14**	1	12. From Another World .... from the Broadway musical "Higher and Higher" vocals on above four: Mary Ann McCall	Bluebird 10637
8/03/40	**14**	3	13. All This And Heaven Too .... vocal: Larry Taylor	Bluebird 10751
9/07/40	**11**	1	14. Six Lessons From Madame La Zonga .... [N] vocal: Mary Ann McCall	Bluebird 10743
10/19/40	**3**	13	15. Pompton Turnpike .... [I] Billy May featured on trumpet	Bluebird 10825
11/23/40	**24**	1	16. Night And Day .... [I] from the Broadway musical "Gay Divorce"	Bluebird 10888
12/28/40	**18**	2	17. Redskin Rhumba .... [I]	Bluebird 10944
1/11/41	**2(5)**	16	18. I Hear A Rhapsody................................. vocal: Bob Carroll	Bluebird 10934
2/08/41	**20**	1	19. Southern Fried..................................... [I]	Bluebird 10944
3/15/41	**19**	1	20. Whatcha Know, Joe?.............................. vocal: Ford Leary & Three Moaxes	Bluebird 10918
4/19/41	**24**	1	21. Charleston Alley .... [I]	Bluebird 11037
6/07/41	**23**	1	22. Afraid To Say "Hello" .... vocal: Bob Carroll	Bluebird 11051
6/26/43	**20**	1	23. Washington Whirligig .... [I]	Decca 18547
12/09/44	**27**	1	24. I Don't Want Anybody At All .... vocal: Huck Andrews	Decca 18541
3/31/45	**19**	1	25. Skyliner.. [I] one of the band's most famous instrumentals	Decca 18659
6/08/46	**13**	2	26. Cement Mixer (Put-Ti, Put-Ti)................. [N] vocal: Art Robey	Decca 18862

DATE CHARTED	PEAK POS	WKS CHRT'D	ARTIST — Record Title	Label & Number
			JENNY BARRETT	
6/13/53	**21**	4	1. He Loves Me	Vogue 1024
			accompanied by Hall Daniels Orchestra	
			DICK BARRIE & HIS ORCHESTRA	
9/03/38	**19**	1	1. Tu-Li Tulip Time...........................	Vocalion 4285
			BLUE BARRON & HIS ORCHESTRA	
			Born Harry Friedland; Cleveland-based sweet-band leader.	
3/12/38	**13**	3	1. At A Perfume Counter	Bluebird 7419
2/17/40	**14**	4	2. Darn That Dream...........................	Bluebird 10525
			from the Broadway musical "Swingin' the Dream"	
1/25/41	**7**	6	3. You Walk By................................	Bluebird 10894
			vocalist on above three: Russ Carlyle	
5/24/47	**14**	3	4. Chi-Baba, Chi-Baba	MGM 10027
7/03/48	**9**	17	5. You Were Only Fooling	MGM 10185
			vocal: Clyde Burke	
11/27/48	**20**	2	6. A Strawberry Moon (In A Blueberry Sky).......	MGM 10297
			vocal: Clyde Burke & Dolores Hopkins	
1/29/49	**1(7)**	20	● 7. **Cruising Down The River/**	
2/26/49	**18**	6	8. Powder Your Face With Sunshine	MGM 10346
			above two: vocal by ensemble	
7/02/49	**25**	1	9. Whose Girl Are You	MGM 10412
4/01/50	**19**	8	10. Are You Lonesome Tonight?......................	MGM 10628
			vocal: Bobby Beers & The Blue Notes; narration by John McCormick (disc jockey)	
4/07/51	**26**	1	11. Let Me In....................................	MGM 10923
			vocal: Johnny Goodfellow & The Blue Notes	
			EILEEN BARTON	
			Started in late 1930s as child performer with Milton Berle	
3/11/50	**1(10)**	16	● 1. **If I Knew You Were Comin' I'd've Baked A Cake**...............................	National 9103
			with the New Yorkers	
7/15/50	**25**	3	2. May I Take Two Giant Steps	National 9112
12/08/51+	**10**	11	3. Cry.......................................	Coral 60592
			accompanied by Neal Hefti's Orchestra	
3/22/52	**30**	1	4. Wishin'....................................	Coral 60651
			accompanied by Paul Nelson's Orchestra	
2/28/53	**17**	3	5. Pretend...................................	Coral 60927
			orchestra directed by Jack Pleis	
3/14/53	**24**	1	6. Don't Let The Stars Get In Your Eyes..........	Coral 60882
8/01/53	**21**	5	7. Toys......................................	Coral 61019
2/06/54	**25**	2	8. Don't Ask Me Why	Coral 61109
			accompanied on above two by Jack Pleis Orchestra	
4/03/54	**26**	1	9. Pine Tree, Pine Over Me......................	Coral 61126
			JOHNNY DESMOND, EILEEN BARTON & McGUIRE SISTERS with Dick Jacobs Orchestra	
7/03/54	**21**	4	10. Sway (Quien Sera)............................	Coral 61185
			accompanied by Terry Gibbs Sextet	
			COUNT BASIE & HIS ORCHESTRA	
			William (Count) Basie, widely regarded as second only to Duke Ellington among all jazz band leaders, was born 8/21/1904 in Red Bank, N.J. After several years as accompanist to vaudeville performers, he played with Walter Page's Blue Devils, then Bennie Moten's famous Kansas City band from 1929-35. After Moten's death, Basie took its best musicians for his own band, which within two years became one of the jazz world's most acclaimed. Its extraordinary soloists (led by tenor saxman Lester Young), singer Jimmy Rushing, and Count's own simple but swinging piano style, created an enduring international reputation. For more than four decades thereafter, the name 'Basie' would remain synonymous with the best in big-band musicianship. Count died on 4/26/84 (79). (also see Benny Goodman, and Metronome All-Star Band)	
9/18/37	**15**	3	1. One O'Clock Jump .... [I]	Decca 1363
			the classic Basie theme song; selected for NARAS Hall of Fame; Lester Young-2nd tenor sax solo	

DATE CHARTED	PEAK POS	WKS CHRT'D	ARTIST — Record Title	Label & Number
7/30/38	18	1	2. Sent For You Yesterday And Here You Come Today	Decca 1880
9/24/38	19	1	3. Doggin' Around [I]	Decca 1965
10/08/38	6	4	4. Stop Beatin' Round The Mulberry Bush	Decca 2004
11/05/38	17	1	5. Mama Don't Want No Peas An' Rice An' Coconut Oil	Decca 2030
			vocals on 2, 4 & 5: Jimmy Rushing	
12/17/38+	11	4	6. Jumpin' At The Woodside [I]	Decca 2212
			featuring Lester Young (tenor sax) & Buck Clayton (trumpet)	
5/20/39	16	2	7. And The Angels Sing	Vocalion 4784
			vocal: Helen Humes	
5/18/40	28	1	8. Easy Does It [I]	Columbia 35448
5/25/40	26	1	9. Red Wagon [I]	Decca 3071
			Basie Orchestra, 1937-40: Basie (piano, director), Buck Clayton, Harry Edison, Ed Lewis, Shad Collins (trumpets), Dicky Wells, Benny Morton, Dan Minor (trombones), Earl Warren (alto sax), Jack Washington (alto & baritone sax), Lester Young, Herschel Evans (tenor sax), Freddy Green (guitar), Walter Page (bass), Jo Jones (drums), Young left in late 1940, most of others continued	
9/27/41	25	1	10. Goin' To Chicago Blues	Okeh 6244
5/29/43	18	1	11. Rusty Dusty Blues/	
			vocalist on above two: Jimmy Rushing	
7/03/43	14	1	12. All Of Me	Columbia 36675
			vocal: Lynne Sherman	
1/22/44	21	1	13. For The Good Of Your Country	Columbia 36685
			Don Byas (tenor sax) on above four	
2/17/45	21	1	14. I Didn't Know About You	Columbia 36766
			vocal: Thelma Carpenter	
10/06/45	10	1	15. Jimmy's Blues	Columbia 36831
			vocalist on 13 & 15: Jimmy Rushing	
1/26/46	12	1	16. Jivin' Joe Jackson	Columbia 36889
			vocal: Ann Moore	
3/23/46	14	2	17. Patience And Fortitude/ [I]	
4/06/46	10	10	18. The Mad Boogie [I]	Columbia 36946
9/14/46	8	4	19. Blue Skies	Columbia 37070
			vocal: Jimmy Rushing; featured in the movie "Blue Skies" Illinois Jacquet (tenor sax) plays on above two	
2/08/47	1(1)	7	20. **Open The Door, Richard!** [N]	Victor 2127
			vocal: Harry Edison and Bill Johnson	
4/19/47	7	3	21. Free Eats [I]	Victor 2148
6/14/47	12	2	22. One O'Clock Jump [I-R]	Decca 25056
			reissue of original hit, recorded 7/7/37	
6/28/47	8	4	23. One O'Clock Boogie [I]	Victor 2262
8/02/47	7	4	24. I Ain't Mad At You (You Ain't Mad At Me)	Victor 2314
			vocal: Taps Miller	
1/10/48	21	2	25. Blue And Sentimental	Victor 2602
			vocal: Bob Bailey	
3/20/48	22	1	26. Robbin's Nest [I]	Victor 2677
			above three featuring Paul Gonsalves (tenor sax)	
5/01/54	29	1	27. Softly With Feeling [I]	Clef 89112
10/16/54	29	1	28. 16 Men Swinging [I]	Clef 89147
			featuring Thad Jones (trumpet)	

FRANKLYN BAUR

First tenor of the Revelers during the late 1920s; the original "Voice of Firestone" on radio; died on 2/24/50 (46). (also see Ipana Troubadors & Ben Selvin)

DATE CHARTED	PEAK POS	WKS CHRT'D	ARTIST — Record Title	Label & Number
11/15/24	5	4	1. Deep In My Heart	Victor 19378
			from the Broadway musical "The Desert Song"	
1/30/26	11	1	2. Brown Eyes, Why Are You Blue?	Victor 19806
2/27/26	9	1	3. Just A Cottage Small	Columbia 499
9/25/26	12	1	4. At Peace With The World	Victor 20057
			LEWIS JAMES & FRANKLYN BAUR	
12/25/26+	5	6	5. Tonight You Belong To Me	Brunswick 3319

DATE CHARTED	PEAK POS	WKS CHRT'D	ARTIST — Record Title	Label & Number
6/25/27	**19**	1	6. At Sundown (When Love Is Calling Me Home).	Victor 20504
8/13/27	**12**	3	7. Russian Lullaby	Victor 20613
10/29/27	**15**	2	8. Just A Memory..................................	Brunswick 3590
1/21/28	**20**	1	9. Diane (I'm In Heaven When I See You Smile)..	Victor 21019
3/02/29	**15**	3	10. Marie..	Victor 21787
8/31/29	**19**	1	11. Where Is The Song Of Songs For Me?...........	Victor 21904

LES BAXTER & HIS ORCHESTRA
Les was a member of Mel Torme's vocal group the Mel-Tones before becoming an orchestra leader and arranger for various radio shows and such artists as Nat King Cole and Margaret Whiting.

DATE CHARTED	PEAK POS	WKS CHRT'D	ARTIST — Record Title	Label & Number
7/14/51	**4**	21	1. Because Of You	Capitol 1760
3/15/52	**10**	17	2. Blue Tango................................... [I]	Capitol 1966
6/28/52	**26**	3	3. Lonely Wine	Capitol 2106
7/26/52	**20**	6	4. Auf Wiederseh'n Sweetheart	Capitol 2143
4/04/53	**2(3)**	22	5. April In Portugal .... [I] Portugese song originally published as "Coimbra"	Capitol 2374
5/23/53	**7**	12	6. Ruby .... [I] theme from the movie "Ruby Gentry"; harmonica solo: Danny Welton	Capitol 2457
6/13/53	**23**	2	7. Gigi/ [I]	
7/18/53	**13**	10	8. I Love Paris .... above two from the Broadway musical "Can Can"	Capitol 2479
7/31/54	**4**	13	9. The High And The Mighty .... [I] movie title song	Capitol 2845

NORA BAYES
Nora (real name Dora Goldberg) made her Broadway debut at 21 in 1901, and rose to stardom in shows with husband Jack Norworth; together they also wrote many popular songs, most notably the classic "Shine On, Harvest Moon". She died on 3/19/28; the 1944 movie "Shine On, Harvest Moon" profiled Nora and Jack.

DATE CHARTED	PEAK POS	WKS CHRT'D	ARTIST — Record Title	Label & Number
5/14/10	**2(1)**	7	1. Has Anybody Here Seen Kelly?	Victor 60013
6/18/10	**3**	6	2. Come Along, My Mandy.......................... NORA BAYES & JACK NORWORTH above two from Broadway musical "The Jolly Bachelors"	Victor 70016
8/06/10	**7**	2	3. Young America	Victor 70015
10/22/10	**8**	1	4. Rosa Rosetta	Victor 70019
11/19/10	**8**	1	5. That Lovin' Rag..............................	Victor 60023
8/12/11	**7**	3	6. Turn Off Your Light, Mr. Moon Man............. from the Broadway musical "Little Miss Fix-It" 4 & 6: NORA BAYES & JACK NORWORTH	Victor 70038
4/18/14	**2(1)**	7	7. The Good Ship Mary Ann	Victor 60113
8/05/16	**7**	2	8. Hello, Hawaii, How Are You?	Victor 45099
10/07/16	**4**	4	9. For Dixie And Uncle Sam .... accompanied on above two by Rosario Bourdon & His Orchestra	Victor 45100
11/03/17	**1(3)**	10	10. **Over There/** George M. Cohan's World War I classic	
12/01/17	**5**	3	11. (Goodbye, And Luck Be With You) Laddie Boy...................................... accompanied on above two by Joseph Pasternach & His Orchestra	Victor 45130
5/18/18	**7**	2	12. Some Day They're Coming Home Again .... accompanied on most Columbia records by Charles Prince's Orchestra	Columbia 6030
6/08/18	**5**	4	13. Regretful Blues	Columbia 6038
8/31/18	**7**	3	14. The Man Who Put The Germ In Germany	Columbia 6051
3/01/19	**3**	5	15. Goodbye, France..............................	Columbia 2678
3/15/19	**2(3)**	7	16. How Ya Gonna Keep 'Em Down On The Farm (After They've Seen Paree)	Columbia 2687
11/15/19	**5**	5	17. You Can't Get Lovin' Where There Ain't No Love	Columbia 2771
1/24/20	**7**	3	18. Everybody Calls Me Honey	Columbia 2816
2/28/20	**7**	3	19. Prohibition Blues......................................	Columbia 2823

DATE CHARTED	PEAK POS	WKS CHRT'D	ARTIST — Record Title	Label & Number
4/24/20	**3**	5	20. Just Like A Gypsy .... from Broadway musical "Ladies First"	Columbia 6138
5/01/20	**6**	3	21. Oh! How I Laugh When I Think That I Cried 　　Over You	Columbia 2852
7/03/20	**8**	2	22. Patches...	Columbia 2921
12/18/20	**9**	2	23. The Argentines, The Portugese, And The 　　Greeks .... [N]	Columbia 2980
1/08/21	**7**	2	24. The Japanese Sandman	Columbia 2997
1/29/21	**10**	1	25. Broadway Blues	Columbia 3311
4/30/21	**10**	1	26. Why Worry?	Columbia 3360
6/11/21	**1(3)**	10	27. **Make Believe**....................................	Columbia 3392
8/27/21	**12**	1	28. In A Little Front Parlor (On An Old 　　Backstreet)......................................	Columbia 3397
9/10/21	**9**	1	29. Tea Leaves	Columbia 3416
10/15/21	**5**	4	30. Cherie	Columbia 3443
12/24/21	**9**	1	31. Saturday..	Columbia 3471
7/29/22	**3**	5	32. All Over Nothing At All...........................	Columbia 3601
7/29/22	**12**	1	33. Sing Song Man	Columbia 3592
10/28/22	**11**	1	34. I Never Had Nobody Crazy Over Me	Columbia 3652
12/09/22	**7**	2	35. Good Mornin' (It's Mighty Good To Be Home) .	Columbia 3669
1/13/23	**5**	4	36. Homesick	Columbia 3711
3/03/23	**4**	4	37. Lovin' Sam (The Sheik Of Alabam')	Columbia 3757
3/31/23	**9**	1	38. Who Did You Fool, After All?.....................	Columbia 3771
6/30/23	**7**	3	39. Dearest (You're The Nearest To My Heart).....	Columbia 3862

SIDNEY BECHET
New Orleans-born jazz great on soprano sax and clarinet; played with King Oliver, Clarence Williams, Mamie Smith, Duke Ellington, and Noble Sissle; his 1949 record "Les Oignons" was a French million-seller. Sidney died 5/14/59 (62).

MOLLY BEE

1/03/53	**19**	2	1. I Saw Mommy Kissing Santa Claus........ [X-N] orchestra directed by Van Alexander	Capitol 2285

BIX BEIDERBECKE
Leon Bismarck "Bix" Beiderbecke, one of the great jazz cornet players as well as a fine pianist, made his reputation with Frankie Trumbauer's band, then played with Jean Goldkette and Paul Whiteman. He died on 8/7/31 (28); the 1950 film "Young Man With A Horn" was loosely based on his life.

2/11/28	**20**	1	1. In A Mist.. [I] piano solo by Bix, selected for NARAS Hall of Fame	Okeh 40916
2/18/28	**15**	2	2. At The Jazz Band Ball........................... [I] "Bix Beiderbecke & His Gang", including Adrian Rollini (baritone sax)	Okeh 40923

HARRY BELAFONTE
Born in New York but partly raised in Jamaica, Harry's folk and calypso songs made him a nationwide sensation in the late 50s; later a successful actor and producer, and one of the primary organizers of USA for Africa.

12/27/52	**30**	1	1. Scarlet Ribbons (For Her Hair)..................... accompanied by Milliard Thomas Orchestra	RCA Victor 5051
3/28/53	**19**	2	2. Gomen Nasai (Forgive Me) .... accompanied by Henri Rene Orchestra; Japanese song	RCA Victor 5210
4/03/54	**30**	1	3. Hold 'Em, Joe .... accompanied by Hugo Winterhalter's Orchestra from the Broadway musical "John Murray Anderson's Almanac"	RCA Victor 5617

BELL SISTERS
16-year-old Cynthia and 11-year-old Kay.

1/05/52	**7**	16	1. Bermuda	RCA Victor 4422
3/01/52	**10**	11	2. Wheel Of Fortune....................................	RCA Victor 4520
3/15/52	**19**	6	3. Hambone... BELL SISTERS & PHIL HARRIS above three accompanied by Henri Rene's Orchestra	RCA Victor 4584

DATE CHARTED	PEAK POS	WKS CHRT'D	ARTIST — Record Title	Label & Number
			### LOUIS BELLSON Leading jazz drummer (born Louis Balassoni) with Benny Goodman (1943, 1946), Tommy Dorsey (1947-49), & Duke Ellington (1951-52); married Pearl Bailey, often performed with her; in TV's "Tonight Show" band in 1970s.	
			### BELLTONES	
9/08/51	30	1	1. Way Up In North Carolina .... record originally released on regional Colonial label in North Carolina	Mercury 5692
			### JOE BELMONT Famous whistling soloist known as "The Human Bird"; real name Joseph Walter Fulton; as a singer, also a member of the Columbia Male Quartet. Joe died on 8/28/49 (73). (also see Ada Jones & Billy Murray)	
7/29/99	3	4	1. The Mocking Bird .... later recorded for Victor 2173	Edison 7169
3/02/01	2(1)	4	2. Whip-Poor-Will Song.............................. later recorded for Victor 1092	Edison 7682
6/22/01	1(3)	6	3. **Tell Me, Pretty Maiden** .... BYRON HARLAN, FRANK STANLEY, JOE BELMONT, & FLORODORA GIRLS from the Broadway musical "Florodora"	Columbia 31604
11/22/02	4	2	4. The Birds .... BYRON HARLAN & JOE BELMONT	Columbia 927
9/05/03	2(1)	6	5. Beautiful Bird, Sing On .... HARRY MACDONOUGH & JOE BELMONT	Victor 2332
8/26/05	7	1	6. The Chirpers...................................... JOE BELMONT with ARTHUR PRYOR'S BAND	Victor 4370
			### TEX BENEKE & HIS ORCHESTRA Gordon "Tex" Beneke was Glenn Miller's featured tenor saxophonist from 1938-42, and after Glenn's death formed a new band to carry on the Miller sound.	
			TEX BENEKE & THE GLENN MILLER ORCHESTRA:	
5/25/46	4	9	1. Hey! Ba-Ba-Re-Bop/	
6/22/46	19	1	2. The Whiffenpoof Song .... song published in 1909, long associated with Yale University	RCA Victor 1859
6/01/46	12	1	3. It Couldn't Be True (Or Could It?)	RCA Victor 1835
6/15/46	15	2	4. Cynthia's In Love .... vocal: Artie Malvin, Lillian Lane & The Crew Chiefs	RCA Victor 1858
8/03/46	9	3	5. I Know..	RCA Victor 1914
8/17/46	4	18	6. Give Me Five Minutes More........................ from the movie "Sweetheart of Sigma Chi"	RCA Victor 1922
10/19/46	4	22	7. The Woodchuck Song/ vocals on 5 & 7 by the Crew Chiefs	
10/19/46	9	5	8. Passe'... vocal: Lillian Lane; adaptation of French song	RCA Victor 1951
12/21/46+	6	8	9. A Gal In Calico/ vocal: The Crew Chiefs & Tex Beneke	
2/01/47	11	3	10. Oh, But I Do................................... vocal: Artie Malvin above two from movie "The Time, Place and the Girl"	RCA Victor 1991
2/22/47	3	11	11. Anniversary Song .... vocal: Garry Stevens & The Mello Larks; from movie "The Jolson Story"; song based on melody from "Danube Waves" (1880)	RCA Victor 2126
6/21/47	22	4	12. My Heart Is A Hobo/ vocal by the Mello Larks	
7/19/47	21	3	13. As Long As I'm Dreaming........................ vocal by Garry Stevens	RCA Victor 2260
			TEX BENEKE & HIS ORCHESTRA:	
2/21/48	26	1	14. Moonlight Whispers.................................	RCA Victor 2667
4/10/48	5	17	15. St. Louis Blues March............................ [I] Glenn Miller's Army Air Force Band made this arrangement famous	RCA Victor 2722
7/10/48	21	2	16. Meadowlands .... [I]	RCA Victor 2898

DATE CHARTED	PEAK POS	WKS CHRT'D	ARTIST — Record Title	Label & Number
11/12/49+	**12**	12	17. I Can Dream, Can't I.................................. RCA 78-3553 vocal: Glenn Douglas; from the Broadway musical "Right This Way"	

LEE BENNETT
Baritone ballad singer with Jan Garber (1933-36, 1938-41).

TONY BENNETT
Tony Bennett, one of the most universally admired singers of the postwar era, was born Anthony Dominick Benedetto on 8/13/26 in Queens, N.Y. Bob Hope gave him his first important concert engagement in 1950, and Tony has remained in the forefront of American jazz and ballad vocalists ever since. (Accompanied on all records by Percy Faith & His Orchestra)

DATE CHARTED	PEAK POS	WKS CHRT'D	ARTIST — Record Title	Label & Number
6/23/51	**1(10)**	32	● 1. **Because Of You**/ song published in 1940; featured in 1951 film "I Was an American Spy"	
6/30/51	**12**	17	2. I Won't Cry Anymore .... Columbia 39362	
7/28/51	**1(6)**	27	● 3. **Cold, Cold Heart** .... Columbia 39449	
10/13/51	**16**	11	4. Blue Velvet/	
10/27/51	**17**	6	5. Solitaire.. Columbia 39555	
5/24/52	**15**	10	6. Here In My Heart .... Columbia 39745	
8/16/52	**16**	5	7. Have A Good Time .... Columbia 39764	
11/22/52	**29**	1	8. Stay Where You Are............................ Columbia 39866	
1/24/53	**20**	7	9. Congratulations To Someone .... Columbia 39910	
4/25/53	**22**	2	10. I'm The King Of Broken Hearts.................. Columbia 39964	
9/19/53	**1(8)**	25	● 11. **Rags To Riches** .... Columbia 40048	
11/28/53+	**2(1)**	19	● 12. Stranger In Paradise/ from the Broadway musical "Kismet"; song based on a theme from "Polovetsian Dances" in the opera "Prince Igor" (1888)	
12/19/53	**26**	1	13. Why Does It Have To Be Me? .... Columbia 40121	
3/13/54	**7**	12	14. There'll Be No Teardrops Tonight .... Columbia 40169	
5/08/54	**29**	1	15. Please Driver (Once Around The Park Again)/	
5/15/54	**25**	3	16. Until Yesterday (Non E La Pioggia)............ Columbia 40213	
8/07/54	**8**	7	17. Cinnamon Sinner.................................. Columbia 40272	
10/23/54	**27**	1	18. Not As A Stranger................................ Columbia 40311	
10/23/54	**29**	1	19. Take Me Back Again .... Columbia 40272	
12/25/54	**24**	2	20. Funny Thing .... Columbia 40376	

BENSON ORCHESTRA OF CHICAGO
Founded by Edgar A. Benson, this band's most notable members were pianist Roy Bargy (1920-21), saxophonist Frankie Trumbauer, clarinetist Art Kassel, and pianist Don Bestor, who served as musical director on most of its later records.

DATE CHARTED	PEAK POS	WKS CHRT'D	ARTIST — Record Title	Label & Number
8/13/21	**9**	2	1. Ain't We Got Fun? .... [I] Victor 18757	
9/03/21	**7**	2	2. Crooning .... [I] Victor 18765	
10/29/21	**5**	4	3. San .... [I] Victor 18779	
1/21/22	**4**	4	4. Bimini Bay .... [I] Victor 18824	
1/28/22	**6**	2	5. Wabash Blues .... [I] Victor 18820	
5/13/22	**7**	2	6. Virginia Blues .... [I] Victor 18868	
11/11/22	**4**	4	7. Say It While Dancing.............................. [I] Victor 18938	
1/27/23	**12**	1	8. Toot Toot Tootsie! (Goo-Bye!).................... [I] Victor 18954 from Broadway musical "Bombo"	
7/14/23	**10**	1	9. Trot Along .... [I] Victor 19044	
11/03/23	**9**	2	10. Dreams Of India .... [I] Victor 19106	
11/17/23	**6**	3	11. That Old Gang Of Mine .... [I] Victor 19136	
1/05/24	**8**	2	12. In A Covered Wagon With You .... [I] Victor 19147	
2/09/24	**4**	5	13. When Lights Are Low .... [I] Victor 19198	
8/23/24	**10**	1	14. Forget-Me-Not (Means Remember Me) .... [I] Victor 19312	
1/03/25	**5**	5	15. Tea For Two .... [I] Victor 19438 from Broadway musical "No, No, Nanette"	
1/24/25	**5**	4	16. Copenhagen... [I] Victor 19470	
10/17/25	**6**	3	17. Oh, How I Miss You Tonight....................... Victor 19685 vocal: Cloyd Griswold	

DATE CHARTED	PEAK POS	WKS CHRT'D	ARTIST — Record Title	Label & Number
10/31/25	15	1	18. Riverboat Shuffle.................................[I]	Victor 19688

BUNNY BERIGAN & HIS ORCHESTRA
Roland Bernard "Bunny" Berigan, one of the top trumpet stars of the dance band era, played with a long succession of bands, including Hal Kemp, the Dorsey Brothers, Paul Whiteman, and Benny Goodman, before leading his own in the late 30s. It is primarily his 1937 recordings with Tommy Dorsey, and his own classic "I Can't Get Started", for which he is best remembered. Bunny died on 6/2/42 (33).

DATE CHARTED	PEAK POS	WKS CHRT'D	ARTIST — Record Title	Label & Number
4/04/36	18	1	1. It's Been So Long....................................	Vocalion 3179
5/23/36	17	3	2. A Melody From The Sky............................ with Artie Shaw on clarinet	Vocalion 3224
7/18/36	19	1	3. If I Had My Way..................................... vocalist on above three: Chick Bullock Eddie Condon, guitarist on above two	Vocalion 3254
4/24/37	4	4	4. Honeysuckle Rose...................................[I] special "jam session" quartet: Fats Waller (piano), Bunny Berigan (trumpet), Tommy Dorsey (trombone), and Dick McDonough (guitar)	Victor 25559
6/19/37	18	1	5. Swanee River ....[I]	Victor 25588
6/26/37	8	7	6. The First Time I Saw You........................... vocal: Ford Leary	Victor 25593
8/28/37	18	1	7. Turn On That Red Hot Heat	Victor 25646
10/02/37	5	5	8. Ebb Tide	Victor 25664
12/04/37	19	1	9. A Strange Loneliness .... vocalist on above three: Gail Reese	Victor 25690
1/29/38	10	3	10. I Can't Get Started.................................. vocal by Bunny Berigan; from the Broadway musical "Ziegfeld Follies of 1936"; Bunny originally recorded it for Vocalion 3225 (with Shaw on clarinet); Victor version also released on 36208; selected for the NARAS Hall of Fame	Victor 25728
5/28/38	18	2	11. It's The Little Things That Count................. vocal: Ruth Gaylor	victor 25868
10/29/38	19	1	12. Russian Lullaby ....[I]	Victor 26001
12/31/38	13	1	13. I Cried For You...................................... vocal: Kathleen Lane 1938 Berigan band included Irving Goodman (trumpet), Ray Conniff (trombone), George Auld (tenor sax), and Buddy Rich (drums)	Victor 26116

IRVING BERLIN
No other songwriter has created more popular hits than the man born Israel Baline in Temun, Russia (5/11/1888). Raised in New York, Irving composed his first best-selling song in 1909, and the next half-century was filled with Berlin classics ranging from "Alexander's Ragtime Band" to "White Christmas".

DATE CHARTED	PEAK POS	WKS CHRT'D	ARTIST — Record Title	Label & Number
6/11/10	10	1	1. Oh, How That German Could Love! ....[N]	Columbia 804

AL BERNARD
Vaudeville comedy singer known as "the boy from Dixie"; died on 3/9/49 (60). (also see Original Dixieland Jazz Band)

DATE CHARTED	PEAK POS	WKS CHRT'D	ARTIST — Record Title	Label & Number
6/14/19	9	1	1. The St. Louis Blues................................. in 1921 Al recorded this again with the Original Dixieland Jazz Band (Victor 18772)	Emerson 9163
10/04/19	4	3	2. I Want To Hold You In My Arms ....[C] AL BERNARD & ERNEST HARE	Edison 50558
3/18/22	10	1	3. I Want My Mammy .... VERNON DALHART & AL BERNARD	Columbia 3520

BEN BERNIE & HIS ORCHESTRA
Born Benjamin Anzelwitz, Ben was a vaudeville performer before starting a dance band; radio performances popularized his expression, "Yow-sah, yow-sah!" as well as his music. Alto saxman Dick Stabile was featured as well as Ben's violin. He died on 10/20/43 (52). (Listed on most 1923-29 records as "Ben Bernie & His Hotel Roosevelt Orchestra").

DATE CHARTED	PEAK POS	WKS CHRT'D	ARTIST — Record Title	Label & Number
4/25/23	11	1	1. My Buddy...[I]	Vocalion 14494
6/16/23	2(2)	8	2. Swinging Down The Lane ....[I]	Vocalion 14537
7/14/23	3	5	3. Wildflower..[I] title song from Broadway musical	Vocalion 14555
10/13/23	7	3	4. Love Tales...[I]	Vocalion 14622

DATE CHARTED	PEAK POS	WKS CHRT'D	ARTIST — Record Title	Label & Number
1/31/25	**10**	1	5. Tea For Two .... [I] from the Broadway musical "No, No, Nanette"	Vocalion 14901
6/27/25	**1(5)**	13	6. **Sweet Georgia Brown**............................ [I] later the famous Harlem Globetrotters theme	Vocalion 15002
9/12/25	**8**	2	7. Cheatin' On Me...................................... [I]	Vocalion 15027
10/03/25	**9**	1	8. Are You Sorry? .... [I]	Vocalion 15036
11/07/25	**8**	2	9. Gigolette .... [I] from Broadway's "Andre Charlot Revue of 1925"	Vocalion 15048
11/14/25	**5**	3	10. Yes Sir, That's My Baby .... [I]	Vocalion 15080
2/20/26	**1(4)**	13	11. **Sleepy Time Gal** .... vocal: Arthur Fields	Brunswick 2992
7/17/26	**2(2)**	6	12. Reaching For The Moon/ vocal: Paul Hagan	
7/31/26	**4**	5	13. Cherie, I Love You .... vocal: Paul Hagan & Jack Pettis	Brunswick 3170
3/26/27	**5**	6	14. Muddy Water/ vocal: Frank Munn	
3/26/27	**6**	5	15. Hello, Swanee, Hello!............................	Brunswick 3414
4/30/27	**1(4)**	12	16. **Ain't She Sweet?/** vocal: Scrappy Lambert & Billy Hillpot	
4/30/27	**3**	8	17. I'm Looking Over A Four-Leaf Clover .... vocal: Scrappy Lambert	Brunswick 3444
7/16/27	**17**	1	18. It All Depends On You .... vocal: Lambert and Hillpot; from Broadway musical "Big Boy"	Brunswick 3464
6/02/28	**18**	1	19. Let's Misbehave.................................... vocal: Scrappy Lambert & Billy Hillpot song written for Broadway musical "Paris", but deleted	Brunswick 3761
6/30/28	**19**	1	20. Can't Help Lovin' Dat Man........................ vocal: Vaughn DeLeath from the Broadway musical "Show Boat"	Brunswick 3808
10/20/28	**10**	4	21. Ten Little Miles From Home....................... vocal: Frank Luther	Brunswick 4020
3/23/29	**16**	2	22. Makin' Whoopee .... vocal: Scrappy Lambert from the Broadway musical "Whoopee"	Brunswick 4142
2/08/30	**13**	2	23. Crying For The Carolines .... from the movie "Spring is Here"	Brunswick 4665
2/22/30	**10**	3	24. What Is This Thing Called Love? .... from the Broadway musical "Wake Up and Dream"	Brunswick 4708
9/06/30	**18**	2	25. The Kiss Waltz......................................	Brunswick 4837
9/20/30	**18**	1	26. F'r Instance	Brunswick 4869
10/18/30	**16**	2	27. I'm Yours	Brunswick 4898
11/15/30	**15**	2	28. Au Revoir, Pleasant Dreams/ vocal: Ben Bernie; the band's closing theme	
12/13/30	**16**	3	29. It's A Lonesome Old Town (When You're Not Around) .... the band's opening theme; vocal by Donald Saxon	Brunswick 4943
1/24/31	**3**	5	30. To Whom It May Concern	Brunswick 6008
1/31/31	**3**	5	31. Just A Gigolo	Brunswick 6023
2/28/31	**7**	7	32. The King's Horses (And The King's Men).......	Brunswick 6024
3/21/31	**13**	3	33. Ninety-Nine Out Of A Hundred (Wanna Be Loved)... vocal: Frank Sylvano	Brunswick 6062
9/19/31	**11**	3	34. Me!/ vocal: Ben Bernie	
9/19/31	**12**	2	35. Sweet And Lovely	Brunswick 6166
10/08/32	**11**	3	36. Let's Put Out The Lights (And Go To Sleep) ... from "George White's Music Hall Varieties" vocal: Ben Bernie	Brunswick 6385
4/15/33	**18**	1	37. Let's All Sing Like The Birdies Sing .... vocals on 35 & 37 by Pat Kennedy	Brunswick 6504
9/16/33	**10**	5	38. Marching Along Together	Columbia 2804

DATE CHARTED	PEAK POS	WKS CHRT'D	ARTIST — Record Title	Label & Number
10/14/33	**10**	4	39. You Gotta Be A Football Hero (To Get Along With The Beautiful Girls)/	
10/21/33	**14**	2	40. This Is Romance......................................	Columbia 2820
10/21/33	**8**	5	41. Who's Afraid Of The Big Bad Wolf?............. from the animated film "The Three Little Pigs"	Columbia 2824
10/03/36	**6**	5	42. When Did You Leave Heaven?/ from the movie "Sing, Baby, Sing"	
9/19/36	**14**	3	43. A Star Fell Out Of Heaven	Decca 878
9/19/36	**20**	1	44. Long Ago And Far Away .... from the movie "Three Cheers for Love" vocalist on above three: Ray Hendricks	Decca 874

CHU BERRY
Important tenor saxophonist with Benny Carter, Teddy Hill, Fletcher Henderson (1935-36), & Cab Calloway (1937-41) bands; died on 10/31/41 (31) after a car accident.

LEON BERRY
Pipe organist

4/11/53	**26**	1	1. Misirlou .... [I]	Dot 15063

DON BESTOR & HIS ORCHESTRA
Don was the mainstay of the Benson Orchestra of Chicago in the 1920s; he became best known as orchestra leader for Jack Benny's radio program.

1/07/33	**9**	5	1. My Darling.................................... from the Broadway musical "Earl Carroll's Vanities of 1932"; vocal: Neil Buckley	Victor 24142
3/18/33	**1(3)**	12	2. **Forty-Second Street/** vocal: Dudley Mecum	
4/01/33	**2(1)**	8	3. Shuffle Off To Buffalo.............................. vocal: Maurice Cross above two from the movie "Forty-Second Street"	Victor 24253
7/22/33	**10**	4	4. Hold Your Man/	
8/05/33	**8**	4	5. Under A Blanket Of Blue......................... vocals on above two: Florence Case	Victor 24345
9/23/33	**2(2)**	10	6. The Last Round-Up .... featured in Broadway's "Ziegfeld Follies of 1934"; vocal: Neil Buckley	Victor 24391
10/07/33	**15**	2	7. Swingy Little Thingy	Victor 24390
10/07/33	**16**	2	8. Beloved...	Victor 24391
10/28/33	**2(2)**	8	9. Who's Afraid Of The Big Bad Wolf?............. from the animated film "The Three Little Pigs" vocal: Florence Case, Charles Yontz, Frank Sherry	Victor 24410
2/24/34	**9**	3	10. Throw Another Log On The Fire .... vocal: The Chanters	Victor 24523
3/18/34	**4**	7	11. A Thousand Goodnights/	
4/18/34	**13**	2	12. Little Dutch Mill.....................................	Victor 24587
5/05/34	**17**	3	13. Waitin' At The Gate For Katy .... from the movie "Bottoms Up"; vocal: Maurice Cross	Victor 24596
7/07/34	**7**	7	14. Thank You For A Lovely Evening	Victor 24667
8/25/34	**5**	8	15. I'll Close My Eyes To Everyone Else .... vocalist on 11, 12, 14, & 15: Neil Buckley	Victor 24694
8/31/35	**14**	4	16. Animal Crackers In My Soup..................... from the Shirley Temple movie "Curly Top"	Brunswick 7495

BEVERLY HILL BILLIES
Country group; Stuart Hamblen was a member.

5/24/30	**7**	14	1. When The Bloom Is On The Sage	Brunswick 421
8/02/30	**15**	5	2. My Pretty Quadroon	Brunswick 441

JOHN BIELING
First tenor of the Manhansett Quartet in the 1890s, later a member of both the Haydn and American Quartets; died on 3/30/48 (79).

12/02/99	**4**	2	1. Just As The Sun Went Down .... records 1-7: HARRY MACDONOUGH & JOHN BIELING	Berliner 0552
5/16/03	**1(4)**	6	2. **In The Sweet Bye And Bye**....................	Victor 1855
7/11/03	**4**	2	3. Tessie...	Victor 2056

DATE CHARTED	PEAK POS	WKS CHRT'D	ARTIST — Record Title	Label & Number
3/18/05	**3**	4	4. Marguerite..	Edison 8938
1/26/07	**8**	1	5. A Flower From Home, Sweet Home	Victor 4877
9/19/08	**2(1)**	5	6. Over The Hills And Far Away......................	Victor 5506
10/31/08	**6**	1	7. When Sweet Marie Was Sweet Sixteen	Victor 5505
1/13/12	**9**	1	8. Her Bright Smile Haunts Me Still	Victor 16970
			WALTER VAN BRUNT & JOHN BIELING	

PAUL BIESE TRIO
Led by tenor saxophonist Paul Biese

4/10/20	**4**	4	1. Mystery .... [I]	Victor 18647
			also recorded for Brunswick 2032	
9/11/20	**4**	4	2. Chili Bean	Columbia 2952
			FRANK CRUMIT with PAUL BIESE TRIO	
4/09/21	**5**	3	3. Rose/ [I]	
4/16/21	**7**	2	4. Timbuctoo..	Columbia 3352
			FRANK CRUMIT with PAUL BIESE TRIO	
6/18/21	**10**	1	5. Toddle .... [I]	Columbia 3383
10/29/21	**10**	1	6. Mimi...	Columbia 3430
11/26/21	**7**	3	7. I Ain't Nobody's Darling............................	Columbia 3459
			above two: FRANK CRUMIT with PAUL BIESE TRIO	

BIG FOUR QUARTET
Arthur Collins, Byron Harlan, Joe Natus, and A.D. Madeira

3/30/01	**1(3)**	8	1. **Good-Bye, Dolly Gray**.............................	Edison 7728

BARNEY BIGARD & HIS JAZZOPATORS
Clarinetist Leon "Barney" Bigard played with Duke Ellington from 1927 to 1942, and after a year with Freddie Slack became a member of Louis Armstrong's postwar jazz band. He died on 6/27/80 (74).

6/19/37	**20**	1	1. Caravan .... [I]	Variety 515
			with Cootie Williams (trumpet), Juan Tizol (trombone), Harry Carney (baritone sax), Duke Ellington (piano), Billy Taylor (bass), & Sonny Greer (drums)	

BUD & JOE BILLINGS
Pseudonyms for Frank Luther and Carson Robison

FRANK BLACK & HIS ORCHESTRA
Pianist-bandleader, later conductor and musical director for NBC Radio from 1932-48.

5/07/27	**15**	2	1. A Tree In The Park	Brunswick 3432
			from the Broadway musical "Peggy-Ann"	
12/24/27	**16**	2	2. The Best Things In Life Are Free	Brunswick 3657
			from the Broadway musical "Good News"	

TED BLACK & HIS ORCHESTRA
Sweet band which did some radio and musical theater

9/19/31	**6**	7	1. Love Letters In The Sand	Victor 22799
			vocal: Ted Black; song loosely based on "The Spanish Cavalier" (1881)	
2/13/32	**19**	1	2. Pagan Moon..	Victor 22878
7/16/32	**2(2)**	7	3. In A Shanty In Old Shanty Town	Victor 20450
			from the movie "The Crooner"	
			above two vocals by Chick Bullock	
7/16/32	**3**	7	4. Masquerade/	
7/23/32	**12**	3	5. Banking On The Weather	Victor 24046
			above two vocals by Dick Robertson	

JERRY BLAINE & HIS STREAMLINE RHYTHM
New York-based bandleader who later established Jubilee Records.

1/08/38	**7**	4	1. Bei Mir Bist Du Schoen	Bluebird 7344
			adapted from Yiddish song	
1/08/38	**17**	1	2. The Snake Charmer .... [I]	Bluebird 7228
3/12/38	**9**	4	3. Ti-Pi-Pin...	Bluebird 7443
			song based on "Espana" and "Symphonie Espagnole"	
			vocals on 1 & 3: Phyllis Kenny	

JANET BLAIR
Beautiful 1940s movie star, born Margaret Janet Lafferty, who first sang with Hal Kemp ("So You're the One").

DATE CHARTED	PEAK POS	WKS CHRT'D	ARTIST — Record Title	Label & Number
			EUBIE BLAKE	
			Eubie, ragtime pianist and composer long associated with Noble Sissle, enjoyed a remarkable comeback in the 1970s, capped by a successful Broadway revue of his songs. He died, still active at age 100, on 2/12/83.	
11/26/21	**8**	2	1. Bandana Days.................................... [I] Victor 18791	
			introduced by "I'm Just Wild About Harry"; both songs from the Sissle-Blake Broadway musical "Shuffle Along"	
1/14/22	**10**	1	2. Arkansas Blues....................................... Emerson 10443	
			NOBLE SISSLE, EUBIE BLAKE, & THEIR SIZZLING SYNCOPATORS	
9/29/23	**13**	1	3. Down-Hearted Blues............................. Victor 19086	
			NOBLE SISSLE (vocals) & EUBIE BLAKE (piano)	
			MEL BLANC	
			Long famous as the voice of Bugs Bunny, Daffy Duck and a host of other Walter Lantz cartoon characters. (also see Spike Jones)	
7/17/48	**2(5)**	9	1. Woody Woodpecker.............................. [N] Capitol 15145	
			THE SPORTSMEN & MEL BLANC	
12/03/49	**26**	1	2. Toot, Toot, Tootsie (Good-Bye) .... [N] Capitol 780	
1/27/51	**9**	11	3. I Taut I Taw A Puddy Tat....................... [C] Capitol 1360	
			music by Billy May	
			JIMMY BLANTON	
			Extremely influential bassist with Duke Ellington from 1939-42; died on 7/30/42 (24) of tuberculosis.	
			ARCHIE BLEYER	
			Arranger, musical director for Arthur Godfrey's TV show; head of Cadence Records.	
5/22/54	**2(2)**	17	1. Hernando's Hideaway .... Cadence 1241	
			from Broadway musical "The Pajama Game"	
			castanet soloist: Maria Alba	
			RAY BLOCH & HIS ORCHESTRA	
			After years of prolific radio work, Ray became orchestra conductor for the Jackie Gleason and Ed Sullivan TV programs in the 1950s and 60s; he died 3/31/82 (79).	
9/20/47	**11**	2	1. Kate (Have I Come Too Early Too Late)........ Signature 15114	
			vocal: Alan Dale	
5/23/53	**22**	3	2. Anna .... Coral 60963	
			movie title song	
			BERT BLOCK & HIS BELL MUSIC	
			Bert's original band featured singer Jack Leonard.	
11/20/37	**9**	3	1. Vieni, Vieni.. Vocalion 3747	
			vocal: Bill Johnson	
			BLUE & WHITE MARIMBA BAND	
4/08/16	**6**	3	1. Marimba March .... [I] Victor 17928	
			BOB & JEANNE	
			Vocal duo	
5/21/49	**21**	1	1. Careless Hands...................................... Decca 24563	
			with Hawaiian guitar and organ backing	
			JOHN BOLES	
			Baritone star of many early Hollywood musicals; died 2/27/69 (70).	
8/09/30	**9**	5	1. For You .... Victor 22373	
			from the film "Captain of the Guard"; accompanied by Leroy Shield's Orchestra	
			RAY BOLGER	
			One of Broadway's best-loved dancers and comedians, Ray was featured in eleven productions from 1926 to 1969 and made his permanent mark on movie history as the Scarecrow in "The Wizard of Oz".	
4/16/49	**16**	7	1. Once In Love With Amy .... Decca 40065	
			from the Broadway musical "Where's Charley"	
			one of the first hit singles over four minutes in length since the Edison Amberols	
3/04/50	**12**	11	2. Dearie/	
			from the "Copacabana Show of 1950"	
3/11/50	**20**	2	3. I Said My Pajamas (And Put On My Prayers). Decca 24873	

DATE CHARTED	PEAK POS	WKS CHRT'D	ARTIST — Record Title	Label & Number
4/29/50	**15**	3	4. If I Knew You Were Comin' I'd've Baked A Cake	Decca 24944
5/05/51	**29**	1	5. Once Upon A Nickel	Decca 27506
			above four: ETHEL MERMAN & RAY BOLGER accompanied on all by Sy Oliver & His Orchestra	

BON BON
Popular singer (born George Tunnell) with Jan Savitt (1937-40), voted #5 male band vocalist in 1940 Billboard college poll; one of the first black singers with a white orchestra.

BETTY JANE BONNEY
Sang with Les Brown ("Joltin' Joe DiMaggio"), later with Jan Savitt & Sammy Kaye.

BEA BOOZE
Baltimore-born blues singer (real name Muriel Nicholls); died in 1975 (approximately 55).

DATE	PEAK	WKS		
6/12/43	**20**	1	1. See See Rider Blues	Decca 8633

IRENE BORDONI
Paris-born performer who achieved success on the Broadway and London musical stage; died 3/19/53 (60).

3/08/24	**4**	5	1. So This Is Love..	Victor 19199
			from the Broadway musical "Little Miss Bluebeard"	
6/19/26	**9**	1	2. This Means Nothing To Me	Victor 19966
			from the Broadway musical "Naughty Cinderella" accompanied by Eddie Ward (piano)	

EARL BOSTIC
Alto saxophonist and arranger, briefly with Cab Calloway and Lionel Hampton; his 1952 R&B hit "Flamingo" (King 4475) was a reported million-seller; died on 10/28/65 (45).

BOSTON POPS ORCHESTRA
Arthur Fiedler joined the Boston Pops Orchestra around 1915 as a viola player. In 1930 he began his long reign as director of the world-famous "Pops", where he remained until his death on 7/10/79 (85).

5/07/38	**13**	3	● 1. Jalousie.. [I]	Victor 12160
			1926 composition first known as "Tango Tzigane"	
12/24/49	**24**	1	2. Sleigh Ride .... [I-X]	RCA Vic. 78-1484
6/09/51	**28**	2	3. Syncopated Clock .... [I]	RCA Victor 3044
			theme from TV's "The Late Show" above two composed by the orchestra's former arranger, Leroy Anderson	

BOSTON SYMPHONY ORCHESTRA
Conducted by Karl Muck; one of the earliest symphonic recordings

12/22/17	**8**	2	1. Lohengrin, Act III Prelude .... [I]	Victor 64744

BOSWELL SISTERS
Connee, Martha, and Helvetia "Vet" Boswell, all born in New Orleans, constituted the most popular female vocal group before the Andrews Sisters. They were frequently accompanied by some of the top musicians in jazz.

4/25/31	**6**	6	1. When I Take My Sugar To Tea	Brunswick 6083
			from the Marx Brothers film "Monkey Business"	
6/20/31	**7**	5	2. Roll On, Mississippi, Roll On	Brunswick 6109
			accompanied on above two by Dorsey Brothers Orchestra	
6/27/31	**3**	5	3. I Found A Million-Dollar Baby	Brunswick 6128
			from the Broadway musical "Billy Rose's Crazy Quilt"; accompanied by Victor Young's Orchestra	
9/05/31	**9**	4	4. It's The Girl	Brunswick 6151
			accompanied by Dorsey Brothers Orchestra, including Tommy (trombone), Jimmy (alto sax), Joe Venuti (violin), & Eddie Lang (guitar)	
10/10/31	**20**	1	5. (With You On My Mind I Find) I Can't Write The Words	Brunswick 6170
			accompanied by the New Yorkers	
11/21/31	**3**	11	6. Gems From "George White's Scandals"	Brunswick 20102
			BING CROSBY, BOSWELL SISTERS, MILLS BROTHERS, & THE VICTOR YOUNG ORCHESTRA medley: The Thrill Is Gone/Life Is Just a Bowl of Cherries	

DATE CHARTED	PEAK POS	WKS CHRT'D	ARTIST — Record Title	Label & Number
12/26/31+	12	3	7. An Evening In Caroline	Brunswick 6218
3/05/32	7	4	8. Was That The Human Thing To Do?	Brunswick 6257
4/09/32	14	3	9. Stop The Sun, Stop The Moon (My Man's Gone)	Brunswick 6271
5/07/32	13	3	10. Between The Devil And The Deep Blue Sea ... accompanied on above four by Dorsey Brothers Orchestra, including Bunny Berigan (trumpet)	Brunswick 6291
2/17/34	13	3	11. Coffee In The Morning (Kisses In The Night)... from the film "Moulin Rouge"; accompanied by Victor Young's Orchestra	Brunswick 6733
4/25/34	17	1	12. You Oughta Be In Pictures (My Star Of Stars). from Broadway's "Ziegfeld Follies of 1934"	Brunswick 6798
11/10/34	7	5	13. Rock And Roll the first popular song to use this phrase in its title; from the film "Transatlantic Merry-Go-Round"	Brunswick 7302
1/05/35	1(2)	10	14. **The Object Of My Affection** featured in the film "Times Square Lady" accompanied on above two by Jimmie Grier's Orchestra	Brunswick 7348
4/20/35	3	6	15. Dinah/ accompanied by Bobby Sherwood (guitar) and piano	
4/20/35	9	5	16. Alexander's Ragtime Band Tommy & Jimmy Dorsey on 11 & 16	Brunswick 7412
7/27/35	15	3	17. St. Louis Blues band includes Manny Klein (trumpet) & Joe Venuti (violin)	Brunswick 7467
11/02/35	10	4	18. Cheek To Cheek from the film "Top Hat"	Decca 574
2/08/36	3	8	19. I'm Gonna Sit Right Down And Write Myself A Letter Artie Shaw (clarinet) on above two; Will Bradley (trombone) on 18	Decca 671
8/06/38	4	5	20. Alexander's Ragtime Band [R] reissue of their 1935 hit, due to the film "Alexander's Ragtime Band"	Vocalion 4239

CONNEE BOSWELL

Connee was one of the most admired and popular female vocalists of her time, overcoming the polio which restricted her to a wheelchair; she died on 10/12/76 (64).

DATE CHARTED	PEAK POS	WKS CHRT'D	ARTIST — Record Title	Label & Number
10/10/32	10	5	1. Say It Isn't So	Brunswick 6393
11/17/34	19	1	2. Isn't It A Shame with Jimmy Grier's Orchestra	Brunswick 7303
2/08/35	19	1	3. Moon Over Miami	Decca 657
7/18/36	3	8	4. On The Beach At Bali-Bali accompanied by Bob Crosby's Orchestra	Decca 829
10/23/37	9	3	5. Whispers In The Dark from the film "Artists and Models"	Decca 1420
11/20/37	1(1)	12	6. **Bob White (Whatcha Gonna Swing Tonight?)/**	
11/27/37	12	3	7. Basin Street Blues above two: BING CROSBY & CONNEE BOSWELL accompanied by John Scott Trotter Orchestra	Decca 1483
6/18/38	11	3	8. Fare Thee, Honey, Fare Thee Well accompanied on 5 & 8 by Ben Pollack's Orchestra including Muggsy Spanier (trumpet)	Decca 1862
7/16/38	5	5	9. I Let A Song Go Out Of My Heart	Decca 1896
8/20/38	1(2)	11	10. **Alexander's Ragtime Band** BING CROSBY & CONNEE BOSWELL with spoken introduction by Eddie Cantor; song featured in film of the same name	Decca 1887
11/05/38	12	9	11. Simple And Sweet from the film "Harold Teen"	Decca 2028
8/05/39	2(2)	14	12. An Apple For The Teacher from the film "The Star Maker"	Decca 2640
9/16/39	12	1	13. (Ho-Dle-Ay) Start The Day Right above two: BING CROSBY & CONNEE BOSWELL	Decca 2626
9/30/39	14	2	14. At Least You Could Say "Hello"	Decca 2613

DATE CHARTED	PEAK POS	WKS CHRT'D	ARTIST — Record Title	Label & Number
1/20/40	12	13	15. Between 18th And 19th On Chestnut Street .... BING CROSBY & CONNEE BOSWELL	Decca 2948
2/17/40	3	11	16. On The Isle Of May.......................... melody based on Andante Cantabile from Tchaikovsky's String Quartet in D Major; accompanied on above five by John Scott Trotter & His Orchestra	Decca 3004
12/28/40	25	1	17. Let's Be Buddies........................... from the Broadway musical "Panama Hattie"; accompanied by Harry Sosnik Orchestra	Decca 3478
9/27/41	24	1	18. Sand In My Shoes	Decca 3893
10/11/41	22	1	19. I'll Keep On Loving You .... accompanied on above two by Victor Young's Orchestra	Decca 3959
9/12/42	21	1	20. South Wind	Decca 18413
11/21/42	22	1	21. Moonlight Mood...........................	Decca 18509
12/26/42	21	1	22. Why Don't You Fall In Love With Me?	Decca 18483
2/02/46	9	5	23. Let It Snow! Let It Snow! Let It Snow!.......... accompanied by Russ Morgan's Orchestra	Decca 18741
8/17/46	22	3	24. Who Told You That Lie? .... with the Paulette Sisters	Decca 18881
11/09/46	14	3	25. Ole Buttermilk Sky .... from the film "Canyon Passage" above two accompanied by Bob Haggart's Orchestra	Decca 18913
4/03/48	19	2	26. You Were Meant For Me.................... accompanied by Victor Young's Orchestra	Decca 25313
11/22/52	25	2	27. My Little Nest Of Heavenly Blue .... accompanied by Artie Shaw & His Gramercy Five; from the operetta "Frasquita"; featured in the film "Rich, Young, and Pretty"	Decca 28377
2/07/53	27	1	28. Singin' The Blues........................... accompanied by the Lawson-Haggart Jazz band, including Yank Lawson (trumpet), Bob Haggart (bass), Lou McGarity (trombone) & Lou Stein (piano)	Decca 28498
4/11/53	29	1	29. Main Street On Saturday Night....................	Decca 28626
11/21/53	29	1	30. I'm Gonna Sit Right Down And Write Myself A Letter.............................. the Boswell Sisters first recorded this song in 1936	Decca 28832
4/24/54	30	1	31. The Philadelphia Waltz........................	Decca 29051
9/11/54	10	11	32. If I Give My Heart To You .... accompanied on above two by George Siravo's Orchestra	Decca 29148

PERRY BOTKIN
Longtime studio musician, orchestra leader and movie composer; died on 10/14/73 (66). (also see Hoagy Carmichael, Bing Crosby, Frankie Laine, Ella Logan & Red Nichols)

THOMAS BOTT
1890s baritone

| 12/03/92 | 1(4) | 4 | 1. **Love's Old Sweet Song**............................
 also recorded for New Jersey 156 | North Amer. 309 |

RICHARD BOWERS

| 3/14/53 | 15 | 2 | 1. Gomen Nasai (Forgive Me) ....
 with the Tokyo Orchestra | Columbia 39954 |
| 7/25/53 | 21 | 2 | 2. Baby Let Me Kindle Your Flame ....
 orchestra directed by George Siravo | Columbia 40016 |

AL BOWLLY
England's #1 singing star of the 1930s, born in Mozambique, who was featured vocalist for bands of Lew Stone and (most memorably) Ray Noble. Al was killed by an air raid bomb in London on 4/17/41 (43). (also see Noble and Stone)

1/12/29	12	4	1. If I Had You .... accompanied by Fred Elizalde's Orchestra	Brunswick 3948
2/02/35	5	6	2. Blue Moon	Victor 24849
5/25/35	20	1	3. My Melancholy Baby .... accompanied on above two by Ray Noble's Orchestra	Victor 25007

JIMMY BOYD
Thirteen years old in 1952

| 12/06/52 | 1(2) | 5 | ● 1. **I Saw Mommy Kissing Santa Claus.....** [X-N] | Columbia 39871 |

59

DATE CHARTED	PEAK POS	WKS CHRT'D	ARTIST — Record Title	Label & Number
3/14/53	4	12	2. Tell Me A Story/	
3/28/53	24	1	3. The Little Boy And The Old Man .... above two: FRANKIE LAINE & JIMMY BOYD	Columbia 39945
6/06/53	25	1	4. Dennis The Menace .... ROSEMARY CLOONEY & JIMMY BOYD based on the Hank Katcham comic strip accompanied on 1 & 4 by Norman Luboff	Columbia 39988

LUCIENNE BOYER
Popular French cabaret performer; died on 12/7/83 (80).

11/24/34	2(1)	10	1. Hands Across The Table .... from the Broadway musical "Continental Varieties"	Columbia 2971
12/08/34	5	5	2. Speak To Me Of Love (Parlez-Moi D'amour) [F] recorded in January, 1930	Columbia DF-61

JANET BRACE
Sang in the early 50s with Johnny Long's Orchestra

10/23/54	23	4	1. Teach Me Tonight .... orchestra directed by Jack Pleis	Decca 28990

BRADFORD & ROMANO
Male vocal duo

2/25/50	17	3	1. Chattanoogie Shoe Shine Boy .... also released on Columbia 78-3685	RCA Victor 3208

OWEN BRADLEY & HIS QUINTET
Organist and combo leader (also see Four Aces, Georgia Gibbs, Mills Brothers)

12/17/49	11	7	1. Blues Stay Away From Me......................... vocal duet: Jack Shook and Dottie Dillard	Coral 60107
5/20/50	23	3	2. The Third Man Theme .... [I] from the film "The Third Man"	Coral 60159

WILL BRADLEY & HIS ORCHESTRA
Born Wilbur Schwichtenberg. Will played trombone with Red Nichols and Ray Noble, among other bands, before starting his own in 1939, featuring boogie-woogie pianist Freddie Slack and drummer-vocalist Ray McKinley. Will later played with the NBC "Tonight Show" band. (also see Bing Crosby)

5/11/40	26	1	1. (What Can I Say) After I Say I'm Sorry .... [I]	Columbia 35543
8/03/40	2(1)	22	2. Beat Me, Daddy, Eight To The Bar	Columbia 35530
11/23/40+	2(1)	10	3. Scrub Me, Mama, With A Boogie Beat/ above two vocals: Ray McKinley	
12/21/40+	5	7	4. There I Go .... vocal: Jimmy Valentine	Columbia 35743
12/21/40	10	6	5. Down The Road A Piece/ vocal: Ray McKinley & Will Bradley	
11/30/40	19	1	6. Celery Stalks At Midnight .... [I]	Columbia 35707
2/08/41	9	3	7. High On A Windy Hill .... vocal: Jimmy Valentine	Columbia 35912
1/29/44	23	1	8. Cryin' The Boogie Blues......................... [I] Will Bradley & His Boogie Woogie Boys, including Billy Butterfield (trumpet)	Beacon 7013

NAT BRANDYWYNNE & HIS STORK CLUB ORCHESTRA
Pianist-society hotel bandleader who also worked with Russ Columbo and Kate Smith.

6/20/36	7	4	1. Take My Heart/	
6/27/36	6	7	2. These Foolish Things (Remind Me Of You)...	Brunswick 7676
8/15/36	14	3	3. Until Today .... above three vocals: Buddy Clark	Brunswick 7712
8/15/36	18	5	4. If We Never Meet Again.......................... [I]	Brunswick 7714

SOPHIE BRASLAU
Contralto with the New York Metropolitan Opera; died on 12/22/35 (43).

7/08/16	2(1)	5	1. Birds In The Night (A Lullaby)....................	Victor 64539

DATE CHARTED	PEAK POS	WKS CHRT'D	ARTIST — Record Title	Label & Number
			BOBBY BREEN Child star (born 1927) who appeared in several period movies	
6/20/36	**14**	3	1. Let's Sing Again .... movie title song	Decca 798
			TERESA BREWER Lovely Ohio-born Teresa was featured on local radio from age five. Her early hits had jazz accompaniment, and she recorded years later with Duke Ellington and other top jazzmen.	
2/04/50	**1(4)**	17	● 1. **Music! Music! Music!**............................. accompanied by The Dixieland All Stars, including Max Kaminsky (trumpet) & Cutty Cutshall (trombone)	London 30023
4/22/50	**17**	5	2. Choo'n Gum... accompanied by Jimmy Lytell & The Dixieland All Stars	London 30100
9/15/51	**23**	1	3. Longing For You......................................	London 1086
5/31/52	**25**	2	4. Gonna Get Along Without Ya Now .... accompanied by Ray Bloch's Orchestra	Coral 60676
9/27/52	**17**	6	5. You'll Never Get Away............................ DON CORNELL & TERESA BREWER accompanied on 3, 5 & all later records by Jack Pleis Orchestra	Coral 60829
12/13/52+	**1(7)**	24	● 6. **Till I Waltz Again With You**	Coral 60873
4/11/53	**17**	2	7. Dancin' With Someone (Longin' For You)	Coral 60953
6/13/53	**23**	3	8. Into Each Life Some Rain Must Fall .... accompanied by Les Brown & His Band of Renown	Coral 60994
10/03/53	**2(2)**	20	● 9. Ricochet (Rick-O-Shay)..............................	Coral 61043
10/31/53	**12**	5	10. Baby Baby Baby .... from the movie "Those Redheads From Seattle"	Coral 61067
1/30/54	**17**	4	11. Bell Bottom Blues/	
1/30/54	**23**	1	12. Our Heartbreaking Waltz	Coral 61066
4/24/54	**6**	9	13. Jilted	Coral 61152
7/03/54	**22**	2	14. Skinnie Minnie (Fish Tail)........................... accompanied on 3, 5-7, & 9-14 by Jack Pleis Orchestra	Coral 61197
			ELIZABETH BRICE Featured in many Broadway musicals from 1906-20; died 1/25/65	
7/29/11	**5**	3	1. Let Me Live And Stay In Dixieland .... from the Broadway musical "The Slim Princess"; orchestra directed by Walter B. Rogers	Victor 5843
7/08/16	**10**	1	2. That Hula Hula... from the Broadway musical "Stop! Look! Listen!"	Columbia 1944
10/28/16	**3**	5	3. My Own Iona...	Columbia 2059
7/07/17	**6**	2	4. Hawaiian Butterfly.................................... above four: CHARLES KING & ELIZABETH BRICE	Columbia 2226
8/11/17	**4**	4	5. Oh, Johnny! Oh, Johnny! Oh!..................... from the Broadway musical "Follow Me"; orchestra directed by Charles Prince	Columbia 2265
12/01/17	**8**	1	6. In Lilac Time (When You Stole This Heart Of Mine).. CHARLES KING & ELIZABETH BRICE	Columbia 2339
			FANNY BRICE Born Fannie Borach 10/29/1891 in New York, Fanny Brice's infectious comedy style and vocals made her a mainstay of nearly all the "Ziegfeld Follies" shows from 1910 to 1923. She starred in several early movie musicals, and extended her fame portraying Baby Snooks on 1940s radio. Fanny died 5/29/51, and was immortal- ized by Barbra Streisand in "Funny Girl".	
2/11/22	**1(1)**	9	1. **My Man/** popular French song ("Mon Homme")	
2/18/22	**3**	7	2. Second Hand Rose .... above two from "Ziegfeld Follies of 1921"	Victor 45263
4/15/22	**9**	1	3. I'm An Indian.. orchestra on above three directed by Rosario Bourdon	Victor 45303
4/07/28	**12**	3	4. My Man... new version of her trademark song	Victor 21168

DATE CHARTED	PEAK POS	WKS CHRT'D	ARTIST — Record Title	Label & Number
3/30/29	**16**	2	5. I'd Rather Be Blue Over You (Than Be Happy With Somebody Else).......................... from the movie "My Man" orchestra on above two directed by Leonard Joy	Victor 21815
			ACE BRIGODE & HIS VIRGINIANS Dance band best known in Midwest; Ace died 2/3/60	
10/24/25	**10**	1	1. Yes Sir! That's My Baby	Columbia 398
			ALFREDO BRITO & HIS SIBONEY ORCHESTRA	
6/20/31	**17**	2	1. Siboney .... [I] Spanish song ("Canto Siboney")	Victor 22685
			PHIL BRITO Real name Philip Colombrito; sang with Al Donohue's band from 1939-42.	
9/02/44	**17**	1	1. You Belong To My Heart/ from the movie "The Three Caballeros"	
9/23/44	**15**	5	2. I Don't Want To Love You (Like I Do) .... accompanied on both by the Paul Lavalle Orchestra	Musicraft 15018
			ELTON BRITT Born James Britt Baker, Elton's first hit was one of the biggest-selling country records ever up to that time; died on 6/23/72 (59).	
9/26/42+	**7**	7	● 1. There's A Star-Spangled Banner Waving Somewhere	Bluebird 9000
3/16/46	**19**	1	2. Wave To Me, My Lady...............................	Victor 1789
			BROADWAY DANCE ORCHESTRA	
8/26/22	**15**	1	1. Stumbling .... [I]	Edison 50989
			BROADWAY NITELITES - see BEN SELVIN	
			BROADWAY QUARTET	
12/31/21	**11**	1	1. My Sunny Tennessee.................................. from Broadway musical "The Midnight Rounders"	Columbia 3465
			NORMAN BROOKS Canadian-born singer (real name: Norman Joseph Arie) best known for his vocal similarity to Al Jolson, whom he portrayed in the 1956 film "The Best Things in Life Are Free".	
2/28/53	**20**	5	1. Hello Sunshine.................................... accompanied by Lou Harold Orchestra	Zodiac 101
5/09/53	**22**	4	2. You Shouldn't Have Kissed Me The First Time/	
5/30/53	**22**	2	3. Somebody Wonderful .... above two accompanied by Burt Farber & His Orchestra	Zodiac 102
			BIG BILL BROONZY Widely acclaimed country blues singer/guitarist; died on 8/14/58 (60).	
11/23/40	**23**	1	1. Romance In The Dark............................... with Lil Green	Bluebird 8524
			BROTHER BONES & HIS SHADOWS "Brother Bones" (knuckle bones and whistling) with group featuring organ and Joe Darensbourg (clarinet). (also see Mr. Goon Bones)	
11/27/48+	**10**	16	1. Sweet Georgia Brown .... the original Harlem Globetrotters "warm-up" theme with its whistling chorus	Tempo 652
			(SIX) BROWN BROTHERS Actually five Brown brothers - Alec, William, Vern, Fred, and Tom - plus Harvey Finkelstein.	
7/10/15	**4**	3	1. That Moaning Saxophone Rag .... [I]	Victor 17677
11/17/17	**10**	1	2. Darktown Strutters' Ball........................ [I]	Victor 18376
			CLEO BROWN R&B pianist/singer from Mississippi	
7/13/35	**13**	2	1. Me And My Wonderful One	Decca 486

DATE CHARTED	PEAK POS	WKS CHRT'D	ARTIST — Record Title	Label & Number
			EDDY BROWN Violin soloist with the New York Philharmonic and other orchestras; later music director of the Mutual Broadcasting System; died on 6/14/74 (78).	
1/27/20	**10**	1	1. That Naughty Waltz .... [I]	Columbia 2989
			EDNA BROWN Pseudonym for Elsie Baker	
			LES BROWN & HIS ORCHESTRA Clarinetist Les Brown worked as an arranger for Jimmy Dorsey, Larry Clinton, and other bands before his own orchestra took off. Brown's leading musicians during the 40s included Billy Butterfield (trumpet, 1942), tenor saxist Ted Nash, and trombonists Si Zentner and Warren Covington. Vocalist Doris Day was the band's biggest star. In the 1950s Les' band was featured on Steve Allen's TV show, and ever since has accompanied Bob Hope on Bob's programs and overseas tours. (also see Ames Brothers, Teresa Brewer)	
12/09/39	**18**	1	1. Make It With The Kisses .... vocal: Herb Muse	Bluebird 10480
9/20/41	**25**	1	2. Lament To Love 	Okeh 6258
10/11/41	**12**	3	3. Joltin' Joe DiMaggio............................... above two vocals: Betty Bonney	Okeh 6377
12/13/41	**11**	2	4. 'Tis Autumn .... vocal: Ralph Young	Okeh 6430
2/24/45	**12**	1	5. Robin Hood... vocal: Butch Stone	Columbia 36763
3/03/45	**1(9)**	28	● 6. **Sentimental Journey/** vocal: Doris Day	
3/17/45	**16**	1	7. Twilight Time .... [I]	Columbia 36769
3/03/45	**18**	1	8. Sleigh Ride In July................................ vocal: Gordon Drake; from the film "Belle of the Yukon"	Columbia 36763
3/17/45	**1(7)**	16	9. **My Dreams Are Getting Better All The Time**.. vocal: Doris Day; from the film "In Society"	Columbia 36779
6/30/45	**10**	1	10. 'Tain't Me..	Columbia 36804
8/18/45	**3**	13	11. Till The End Of Time .... based on Chopin's "Polanaise in A-Flat Major" from the film "A Song to Remember"	Columbia 36828
11/24/45+	**11**	4	12. Aren't You Glad You're You? .... from the film "The Bells of St. Mary's"	Columbia 36875
12/29/45+	**13**	3	13. Come To Baby, Do/	
1/12/46	**4**	15	14. You Won't Be Satisfied (Until You Break My Heart)... Doris Day: vocals on above four	Columbia 36884
3/09/46	**6**	4	15. Doctor, Lawyer, Indian Chief/ vocal: Butch Stone; from film "The Stork Club"	
3/30/46	**15**	2	16. Day By Day	Columbia 36945
6/15/46	**10**	5	17. I Got The Sun In The Morning .... from the Broadway musical "Annie Get Your Gun" above two vocals: Doris Day	Columbia 36977
9/14/46	**11**	2	18. I Guess I'll Get The Papers (And Go Home)/ vocal: Jack Haskel	
10/19/46	**6**	11	19. The Whole World Is Singing My Song.......... vocal: Doris Day	Columbia 37066
12/07/46	**15**	1	20. The Best Man .... vocal: Butch Stone	Columbia 37086
1/04/47	**12**	2	21. The Christmas Song .... [X]	Columbia 37174
1/25/47	**13**	1	22. Sooner Or Later.................................... from the animated film "The Song of the South" above two vocals: Doris Day	Columbia 37153
12/25/48+	**1(1)**	17	● 23. **I've Got My Love To Keep Me Warm**........ [I] the last great instrumental hit of the Big Band Era recorded on 9/16/46; from the 1937 film "On The Avenue"	Columbia 38324
5/13/50	**22**	2	24. It Isn't Fair .... vocal: Four Hits and a Miss	Columbia 38735

DATE CHARTED	PEAK POS	WKS CHRT'D	ARTIST — Record Title	Label & Number
5/02/53	**26**	1	25. I'll Be Hangin' Around .... vocal: The Modernaires	Coral 60946
5/02/53	**29**	1	26. Ruby .... theme from the film "Ruby Gentry" above two: "Les Brown & His Band of Renown"	Coral 60959

ROY BROWN
Best known as writer of the landmark rhythm & blues hit "Good Rockin' Tonight", Roy's own 1950 hit "Hard Luck Blues" (Deluxe 3304) was a reported million-seller.

RUTH BROWN
Major star of 1950s R&B whose 1952 record "5-10-15 Hours" (Atlantic 962) reportedly was an eventual million-seller.

3/14/53	**23**	3	● 1. (Mama) He Treats Your Daughter Mean .... band includes Taft Jordan (trumpet)	Atlantic 986

SAM BROWNE
Singer formerly with the Ambrose Orchestra

4/10/48	**22**	5	1. A Tree In The Meadow .... accompanied by Bert Thompson & His Orchestra	London 123

BROX SISTERS
Kathlyn, Dagmar, and Lorraine Brox launched their careers in Broadway's "Music Box Revue".

8/26/22	**11**	1	1. School House Blues................................ accompanied by Bennie Krueger's Orchestra	Brunswick 2268
7/26/24	**12**	1	2. Lazy..	Victor 19298
8/29/25	**12**	1	3. Who?... from the Broadway musical "Sunny"	Victor 19631
5/22/26	**10**	1	4. Kentucky's Way Of Saying "Good Morning"/	
6/26/26	**15**	1	5. Tie Me To Your Apron Strings Again	Victor 19921

CLIFF BRUNER'S TEXAS WANDERERS
This popular country band, led by fiddler Cliff Bruner, also featured pianist Moon Mullican.

12/03/38	**16**	1	1. It Makes No Difference Now .... vocal: Dickie McBride	Decca 5604

BRUNSWICK QUARTET - see ARTHUR CLOUGH

RUSTY BRYANT & THE CAROLYN CLUB BAND
Tenor saxophonist-bandleader, previously played with Lionel Hampton.

4/03/54	**25**	1	1. All Night Long..	Dot 15134

WILLIE BRYANT & HIS ORCHESTRA
Swing band which originally included Ben Webster (tenor sax), Benny Carter (trumpet), and Teddy Wilson (piano); Willie died on 2/9/64 (55).

5/02/36	**20**	1	1. Moonrise On The Lowlands/	
6/13/36	**14**	2	2. Is It True What They Say About Dixie?....... vocals on above two: Willie Bryant Taft Jordan (trumpet) and Cozy Cole (drums) on above two	Bluebird 6362

JACK BUCHANAN
Scottish-born star of English musical stage and movies for thirty years, best known here as co-star with Fred Astaire in the 1953 film version of "The Band Wagon"; died on 10/13/57 (66).

3/27/26	**5**	4	1. A Cup Of Coffee, A Sandwich, And You......... GERTRUDE LAWRENCE & JACK BUCHANAN from British musical "The Charlot Revue, 1926"	Columbia 512

EUGENE BUCKLEY
Pseudonym for Arthur Fields

BULAWAYO SWEET RHYTHMS BAND
South African group

8/28/54	**17**	8	1. Skokiaan.. [I] "Skokiaan": a drink prepared by African Zulu tribes	London 1491

DATE CHARTED	PEAK POS	WKS CHRT'D	ARTIST — Record Title	Label & Number

CHICK BULLOCK & HIS ORCHESTRA
Band singer who recorded with Bunny Berigan, Ted Black, Duke Ellington, Russ Morgan, Ben Pollack, Nat Shilkret, and Fred Waring, among many others.

DATE CHARTED	PEAK POS	WKS CHRT'D	ARTIST — Record Title	Label & Number
4/26/30	20	1	1. Lazy Lou'siana Moon	Banner 0671
12/10/32	18	1	2. Underneath The Harlem Moon	Perfect 15678
2/25/33	19	1	3. (When It's) Darkness On The Delta	Melotone 12584

band on above three includes Tommy Dorsey (trombone) and Jimmy Dorsey (clarinet/alto sax); Bunny Berigan (trumpet) on above two

DATE CHARTED	PEAK POS	WKS CHRT'D	ARTIST — Record Title	Label & Number
5/04/35	19	1	4. Lullaby Of Broadway	Melotone 13358

from the film "Gold Diggers of 1935"

SONNY BURKE
Arranger for Charlie Spivak, Jimmy Dorsey, & Gene Krupa, composer of several popular songs, orchestra conductor for Billy Eckstine, Dinah Shore, & other singers.

MAURICE BURKHARDT

DATE CHARTED	PEAK POS	WKS CHRT'D	ARTIST — Record Title	Label & Number
10/26/12	6	3	1. The Ragtime Jockey Man	Columbia 1188

MAURICE BURKHARDT & PEERLESS QUARTET
from the Broadway musical "The Passing Show of 1912"

DATE CHARTED	PEAK POS	WKS CHRT'D	ARTIST — Record Title	Label & Number
1/04/13	3	6	2. Ghost Of The Violin	Victor 17195

WALTER VAN BRUNT & MAURICE BURKHARDT

F.F. BURNHAM

DATE CHARTED	PEAK POS	WKS CHRT'D	ARTIST — Record Title	Label & Number
12/03/92	2(3)	3	1. My Sweetheart's The Man In The Moon	Columbia

GEORGE BURNS & GRACIE ALLEN
George and wife Gracie starred together in vaudeville, movies, radio and TV from the 1930s until Gracie's death in 1964. George went on to enjoy a remarkable second career, winning the Academy Award in 1975 for "The Sunshine Boys".

DATE CHARTED	PEAK POS	WKS CHRT'D	ARTIST — Record Title	Label & Number
6/24/33	6	4	1. Burns And Allen Dialog, Parts 1 & 2 ......[T-C]	Columbia 2780

RALPH BURNS
Pianist/composer/arranger formerly with Charlie Barnet, most famous for work with Woody Herman from 1944 through 50s; wrote "Early Autumn".

HENRY BURR
Henry Burr, the #1 ballad singer of recorded music's 1890-1930 pioneer era, was born Harry H. McClaskey on 1/15/1882 in New Brunswick, Canada. The soft-voiced tenor became a major star soon after his first recordings in 1903, and remained so for the next quarter-century - as a solo, in duets with Albert Campbell and many other partners, and as a featured member of the Columbia Male Quartet, Peerless Quartet (1906-28) and Sterling Trio. He frequently used the pseudonym "Irving Gillette", and sometimes his real name. All told, Henry is said to have sung on some twelve thousand recordings - far more than any other vocalist in history. Henry was a regular on NBC's National Barn Dance radio show at the time of his death on 4/6/41. (also see aforementioned groups, Columbia Orchestra, Roger Wolfe Kahn, Art Landry, and Frank Stanley)

DATE CHARTED	PEAK POS	WKS CHRT'D	ARTIST — Record Title	Label & Number
6/13/03	3	3	1. The Rosary	Columbia 1354
7/11/03	1(4)	9	2. **Come Down, Ma Ev'ning Star**	Columbia 1405

also on Columbia cylinder 32174; from Broadway musical "Twirly Whirly"

DATE CHARTED	PEAK POS	WKS CHRT'D	ARTIST — Record Title	Label & Number
11/07/03	5	1	3. To My First Love	Columbia 32246
4/09/04	5	1	4. Sammy	Columbia 1665

from Broadway musical "The Wizard of Oz"

DATE CHARTED	PEAK POS	WKS CHRT'D	ARTIST — Record Title	Label & Number
7/02/04	5	2	5. My Cosey Corner Girl	Columbia 32465

5 & 8 from Broadway musical "The School Girl"

DATE CHARTED	PEAK POS	WKS CHRT'D	ARTIST — Record Title	Label & Number
7/16/04	4	2	6. Blue Bell	Columbia 1813

also on Zon-o-Phone 5808

DATE CHARTED	PEAK POS	WKS CHRT'D	ARTIST — Record Title	Label & Number
8/13/04	3	2	7. Good-Bye, My Lady Love	Columbia 1815
12/24/04+	3	3	8. My Little Canoe	Columbia 1894
2/25/05	8	1	9. Sing Me To Sleep	Edison 8861

also recorded for Zon-o-Phone 7062
all of Henry's Edison records were under pseudonym "Irving Gillette"

DATE CHARTED	PEAK POS	WKS CHRT'D	ARTIST — Record Title	Label & Number
4/22/05	1(7)	12	10. **In The Shade Of The Old Apple Tree** .... later recorded for Victor 4338	Edison 8958
4/29/05	7	1	11. Oh Promise Me .... featured in Broadway musical "Robin Hood"	Edison 8929
11/25/05	6	1	12. In Dear Old Georgia................................	Edison 9099
3/03/06	2(1)	7	13. Good Night, Little Girl, Good Night.............. later issued on Columbia 1133	Columbia 3330
11/03/06	1(7)	11	14. **Love Me And The World Is Mine**.............. also on Columbia cylinder 33184, and Zon-o-Phone 622	Columbia 3499
12/08/06	5	1	15. All Through The Night .... also recorded for Zon-o-Phone 710	Columbia 3498
5/25/07	8	1	16. Won't You Come Over To My House?........... also on Columbia cylinder 33117	Columbia 3603
6/13/08	3	3	17. I Love, And The World Is Mine .... from Broadway musical "A Waltz Dream"; also on Zon-o-Phone 5353	Victor 5418
6/27/08	6	1	18. As Long As The World Rolls On	Columbia 3804
7/25/08	7	1	19. Kiss Duet .... HENRY BURR & "ELISE WOOD" (Elise Stevenson) from the Broadway musical "A Waltz Dream"	Columbia 33225
8/29/08	7	1	20. I Want You .... from Broadway musical "The Talk of New York"	Victor 5463
11/28/08	3	4	21. You Have Always Been The Same Old Pal ..... also recorded for Zon-o-Phone 5072 & Indestructable 883	Columbia 591
1/09/09	4	4	22. Then You'll Remember Me......................... also recorded for Zon-o-Phone 5157	Columbia 615
4/03/09	5	1	23. When You And I Were Young, Maggie	Columbia 5088
5/22/09	1(3)	13	24. **To The End Of The World With You** .... also recorded for Columbia 648 & Indestructable 1003	Victor 16292
9/04/09	1(8)	13	25. **I Wonder Who's Kissing Her Now** .... from the Broadway musical "The Prince of Tonight" flip side of Arthur Collins' #2 hit "I Love, I Love, I Love My Wife, But Oh You Kid!"	Columbia 707
11/06/09	2(2)	5	26. Honey On Our Honeymoon .... flip side of the #1 hit "I've Got Rings on My Fingers" by Ada Jones	Columbia 741
6/04/10	5	4	27. My Southern Rose....................................	Columbia 803
6/25/10	7	2	28. Where The River Shannon Flows .... also recorded for Zon-o-Phone 5662	Columbia 815
11/12/10	1(4)	10	29. **Meet Me To-Night In Dreamland** .... also recorded for Oxford 4658	Columbia 905
12/03/10	2(1)	6	30. All That I Ask Of You Is Love	Columbia/In. 1419
12/24/10	6	2	31. Every Little Movement............................. HENRY BURR & "MARGARET MAYHEW" (believed to be Elise Stevenson) from the Broadway musical "Madame Sherry"	Columbia 894
6/24/11	7	2	32. Day Dreams, Visions Of Bliss .... from the Broadway musical "The Spring Maid"	Victor 5830
8/05/11	7	2	33. Love Is Like A Red, Red Rose .... from Broadway musical "He Came from Milwaukee"	Victor 16854
10/14/11	5	3	34. Save Up Your Kisses For A Rainy Day .... also issued on Zon-o-Phone 5768	Victor 16907
10/14/11	6	2	35. When You're In Town .... also recorded for Columbia 1021, Zon-o-Phone 5747 & U.S. Everlasting 1264 above four: HENRY BURR & ELISE STEVENSON	Victor 16898
4/27/12	6	2	36. I Love Love (I Love You, Dear)..................... HENRY BURR & CAROLINE VAUGHAN from the Broadway musical "The Red Widow"	Columbia 1099
5/04/12	5	3	37. Come To The Ball .... from Broadway musical "The Quaker Girl" also recorded for Zon-o-Phone 5855	Victor 17030
12/16/12	4	4	38. That's How I Need You............................. also recorded for Edison Amberol 1589 & Indestructable 3279	Victor 17173
4/05/13	1(7)	15	39. **When I Lost You**..................................... also recorded for Edison Amberol 1738	Victor 17275

DATE CHARTED	PEAK POS	WKS CHRT'D	ARTIST — Record Title	Label & Number
7/05/13	**4**	4	40. To Have, To Hold, To Love .... from the Broadway musical "The Isle O' Dreams"	Columbia 1319
8/16/13	**1(6)**	22	41. **Last Night Was The End Of The World** ...... also recorded for Columbia 1303	Victor 17339
10/25/13	**4**	6	42. There's A Girl In The Heart Of Maryland....... HENRY BURR & "EDGAR STODDARD" (Andrea Sarto)	Columbia 1360
11/01/13	**10**	1	43. Flow Gently, Sweet Afton	Victor 17386
12/13/13	**2(4)**	11	44. Peg O' My Heart.. from Broadway's "Ziegfeld Follies of 1913" also on Indestructable 3317	Columbia 1404
2/14/14	**9**	1	45. On The Old Front Porch .... ADA JONES & HENRY BURR	Columbia 1443
3/21/14	**8**	1	46. Somewhere A Voice Is Calling .... shown as by Harry McClaskey (Henry's real name)	Victor 17475
4/04/14	**7**	4	47. Rebecca Of Sunny-brook Farm .... "IRVING GILLETTE" & HELEN CLARK Burr & Campbell also recorded song for Edison Amberol 2270	Columbia 1483
5/09/14	**9**	1	48. Where Can I Meet You To-Night? .... ADA JONES & HENRY BURR	Columbia 1495
5/16/14	**1(7)**	14	49. **The Song That Stole My Heart Away**	Columbia 1512
6/13/14	**3**	6	50. In The Heart Of The City That Has No Heart .. also recorded for Columbia 1521; Burr & Ada Jones also recorded song for Edison Amberol 2336	Victor 17544
8/01/14	**2(2)**	8	51. In The Valley Of The Moon .... HENRY BURR & HELEN CLARK also recorded for Columbia 1533	Victor 17587
8/29/14	**3**	6	52. You Planted A Rose In The Garden Of Love ...	Columbia 1549
11/21/14	**2(3)**	10	53. When You're A Long, Long Way From Home.. also recorded for Columbia 1681 & Indestructable 3350	Victor 17632
5/01/15	**9**	1	54. There's A Little Spark Of Love Still Burning..	Victor 17697
5/29/15	**4**	5	55. Maybe A Day, Maybe A Year	Victor 17752
10/23/15	**2(1)**	6	56. There's A Little Lane Without A Turning (On The Way To Home Sweet Home) .... also recorded for Columbia 1791	Victor 17878
12/04/15	**5**	5	57. When I Leave The World Behind/ also recorded for Indestructable 3357	
12/04/15	**5**	2	58. It's Tulip Time In Holland	Victor 17874
1/08/16	**6**	3	59. When You're In Love With Someone Who Is Not In Love With You.......................... HENRY BURR & HELEN CLARK (listed as "Miriam Clark")	Columbia 1800
2/12/16	**1(6)**	11	60. **M-O-T-H-E-R (A Word That Means The** **World To Me)** .... also recorded for Columbia 1899 & Indestructable 3351; later Majestic 108	Victor 17913
3/25/16	**4**	4	61. My Mother's Rosary/ also on Indestructable 3381	
5/06/16	**9**	1	62. Memories .... above two as Harry McClaskey	Columbia 1923
4/22/16	**9**	1	63. What A Wonderful Mother You'd Be	Victor 17953
6/10/16	**1(6)**	10	64. **Good-Bye, Good Luck, God Bless You (Is** **All That I Can Say)** .... also recorded for Indestructable 3372	Victor 17984
7/29/16	**9**	1	65. Baby Shoes...	Columbia 2001
8/04/17	**8**	2	66. Your Eyes, Your Lips, Your Heart	Victor 18283
8/25/17	**4**	3	67. All The World Will Be Jealous Of Me .... also recorded for Emerson 7249 & Imperial 5454	Columbia 2275
9/08/17	**2(2)**	6	68. Joan Of Arc .... also recorded for Imperial 5486	Columbia 2273
1/19/18	**2(2)**	6	69. Somewhere In France Is The Lily.................	Columbia 2408
1/26/18	**10**	1	70. Life In A Trench In Belgium...................... LT. GITZ RICE & HENRY BURR	Columbia 2410
4/06/18	**10**	1	71. I'm Going To Follow The Boys.................... HENRY BURR & ELIZABETH SPENCER	Victor 18433

DATE CHARTED	PEAK POS	WKS CHRT'D	ARTIST — Record Title	Label & Number
4/20/18	1(11)	15	● 72. **Just A Baby's Prayer At Twilight (For Her Daddy Over There)** .... also recorded for Columbia 2490, Emerson 915, Indestructable 3436 & Pathe 20307	Victor 18439
4/20/18	3	4	73. Are You From Heaven? .... also recorded for Columbia 2513 & Pathe 20310 (all Burr records for Pathe as "Harry McClaskey")	Victor 18435
6/15/18	1(2)	9	74. **I'm Sorry I Made You Cry** .... also recorded for Indestructable 3443 & Pathe 20198	Victor 18462
6/29/18	4	6	75. There's A Little Blue Star In The Window (And It Means All The World To Me) .... also recorded for Columbia 2543 & Paramount 30049	Victor 18468
7/06/18	9	1	76. Three Wonderful Letters From Home .... also recorded on Pathe 20366	Columbia 2529
8/31/18	7	3	77. When You Come Home	Columbia 2562
1/04/19	3	5	78. Oh How I Wish I Could Sleep Until My Daddy Comes Back Home .... also recorded for Victor 18506, Okeh 1108, Emerson 997, & Pathe 22004	Columbia 2656
3/01/19	8	1	79. Don't Cry, Little Girl, Don't Cry .... also recorded for Columbia 2681	Victor 18516
3/29/19	2(1)	6	80. Baby's Prayer Will Soon Be Answered	Columbia 2691
5/17/19	1(9)	14	81. **Beautiful Ohio** .... became the official state song of Ohio	Columbia 2701
6/21/19	3	6	82. That Wonderful Mother Of Mine................... also recorded for Okeh 1185	Columbia 2711
10/25/19	1(6)	15	83. **Oh! What A Pal Was Mary** .... also recorded for Pathe 22173, Paramount 33018, & Indestructable 3454	Victor 18606
1/31/20	11	1	84. Weeping Willow Lane .... HENRY BURR & FRANK CROXTON	Victor 18609
1/31/20	13	1	85. Carolina Sunshine...................................	Okeh 4006
2/28/20	11	1	86. Just For Me And Mary	Columbia 2830
2/28/20	12	1	87. I Never Knew .... 85 & 87: HENRY BURR & JOHN MEYER	Okeh 4043
4/17/20	10	1	88. Was There Ever A Pal Like You? .... also recorded for Columbia 2861, Pathe 22303, & Empire 416	Victor 18645
5/29/20	11	1	89. When My Baby Smiles At Me........................ from Broadway musical "Greenwich Village Follies of 1919"	Columbia 2894
6/05/20	9	2	90. Daddy, You've Been A Mother To Me .... also recorded for Vocalion 14037 & Pathe 22333	Victor 18656
7/03/20	5	3	91. Rose Of Washington Square .... from Broadway musical "Ziegfeld Midnight Frolic"	Columbia 2928
11/27/20	12	1	92. I'm In Heaven When I'm In My Mother's Arms	Columbia 2978
12/18/20	9	1	93. You're The Only Girl That Made Me Cry	Columbia 2984
1/15/21	5	4	94. Old Pal, Why Don't You Answer Me?	Columbia 2995
11/19/21	9	1	95. You Made Me Forget How To Cry	Victor 18782
6/24/22	11	1	96. Time After Time	Victor 18875
11/04/22	1(1)	10	97. **My Buddy**	Victor 18930
1/27/23	10	1	98. Mary, Dear	Victor 18955
2/24/23	9	1	99. You Remind Me Of My Mother .... from Broadway musical "Little Nellie Kelly"	Victor 18957
5/12/23	3	5	100. Faded Love Letters	Victor 19015
5/26/23	5	3	101. You Know You Belong To Somebody Else (So Why Don't You Leave Me Alone)	Victor 19026
11/24/23	3	6	102. Just A Girl That Men Forget	Victor 19131
6/28/24	12	1	103. Wonderful One	Victor 19282
7/12/24	4	5	104. What'll I Do?/ HENRY BURR & MARCIA FREER from the Broadway musical "Music Box Revue of 1923"	
9/27/24	15	1	105. She's Everybody's Sweetheart (But Nobody's Gal)...................................	Victor 19301
6/27/25	14	1	106. Honest And Truly	Victor 19597

DATE CHARTED	PEAK POS	WKS CHRT'D	ARTIST — Record Title	Label & Number
9/26/25	**13**	1	107. West Of The Great Divide	Victor 19651
12/26/25+	**5**	3	108. Alone At Last/	
1/30/26	**5**	3	109. You Forgot To Remember........................... Rudy Wiedoeft (alto sax) & Frank Banta (piano) featured on 103, 106, 108 & 109	Victor 19780
3/06/26	**7**	2	110. I Wonder Where My Baby Is To-night? .... HENRY BURR & BILLY MURRAY the only American duet these superstars recorded together	Victor 19864
5/22/26	**3**	5	111. Always..	Victor 19959
9/25/26	**13**	1	112. I Wish I Had My Old Gal Back Again............	Victor 20070
11/27/26	**13**	1	113. The Prisoner's Sweetheart........................	Victor 20098
1/08/27	**12**	3	114. Because I Love You.................................	Victor 20258
11/12/27	**10**	4	115. Are You Lonesome To-night?.....................	Victor 20873
10/13/28	**19**	1	116. Memories Of France	Brunswick 4045

HENRY BURR & ALBERT CAMPBELL
This famous duo also recorded together in the Peerless Quartet and Sterling Trio.

DATE CHARTED	PEAK POS	WKS CHRT'D	ARTIST — Record Title	Label & Number
4/15/11	**3**	5	1. On Mobile Bay...	Columbia 976
2/17/12	**8**	2	2. Down In Sunshine Valley .... previously recorded for Columbia 1034	Victor 17018
5/11/12	**1(4)**	10	3. **When I Was Twenty-One And You Were Sweet Sixteen**...................................	Columbia 1138
6/01/12	**8**	2	4. In A Little While.................................... later recorded for Victor 17237	Columbia 1129
10/05/12	**9**	1	5. Sweetheart Sue .... later recorded for Columbia 1224 as "I Love You, Sweetheart Sue"	Victor 17116
12/21/12	**7**	2	6. I'd Love To Live In Loveland With A Girl Like You..	Columbia 1209
6/21/13	**1(3)**	10	7. **The Trail Of The Lonesome Pine**	Columbia 1315
11/08/13	**2(2)**	10	8. Sailing Down The Chesapeake Bay.............. also on Indestructable 3335	Columbia 1378
2/14/14	**1(6)**	12	9. **I'm On My Way To Mandalay** .... HENRY BURR, ALBERT CAMPBELL, & WILL OAKLAND Burr & Campbell also recorded song for Columbia 1484, Edison Amberol 2233, & Indestructable 3337	Victor 17503
8/15/14	**6**	3	10. Off With The Old Love, On With The New	Victor 17594
10/31/14	**10**	1	11. Dear Love Days .... HENRY BURR, ALBERT CAMPBELL, & WILL OAKLAND known as the "Lyric Trio"; also recorded for Victor 17789	Columbia 1577
11/14/14	**8**	3	12. California And You...................................	Columbia 1601
4/24/15	**4**	6	13. When My Ship Comes In............................ Burr also recorded song with Frances Fisher on Columbia 1698 flip side of the #3 hit "The Little House Upon The Hill" by James F. Harrison & James Reed	Victor 17732
6/26/15	**9**	1	14. In The Land Of Love With The Songbirds ...... with bird songs by Joe Belmont; also recorded for Col. 1726	Victor 17721
8/14/15	**2(1)**	9	15. My Little Girl	Victor 17810
9/25/15	**1(2)**	10	16. **Close To My Heart**	Columbia 1790
10/02/15	**6**	3	17. When It's Peach Picking Time In Delaware .... flip side of the #1 hit "Hello, Frisco!" by Olive Kline & Reinald Werrenrath	Victor 17837
2/12/16	**2(2)**	6	18. Is There Still Room For Me 'Neath The Old Apple Tree?... later recorded for Pathe 30402	Columbia 1900
2/26/16	**4**	4	19. The Wedding Of The Sunshine And The Rose. flip side of Henry Burr's #1 hit "M-O-T-H-E-R"	Victor 17913
7/22/16	**1(3)**	6	20. **There's A Quaker Down In Quaker Town** ... also recorded for Indestructable 3379 & Majestic 162	Victor 18034
9/09/16	**5**	3	21. Through These Wonderful Glasses Of Mine....	Columbia 2019
11/18/16+	**3**	8	22. She Is The Sunshine Of Virginia .... also recorded for Columbia 2067 & Indestructable 3397	Victor 18112
12/16/16+	**2(2)**	6	23. You Were Just Made To Order For Me	Victor 18137

69

DATE CHARTED	PEAK POS	WKS CHRT'D	ARTIST — Record Title	Label & Number
2/24/17	3	4	24. My Hawaiian Sunshine............................ with Helen Louise & Frank Ferera on Hawaiian guitars	Victor 18202
4/21/17	5	4	25. Where The Black-Eyed Susans Grow	Victor 18239
7/21/17	7	2	26. For Me And My Gal	Pathe 20163
7/28/17	1(2)	6	27. **Lookout Mountain** .... also recorded for Columbia 2263	Victor 18295
10/20/17	9	2	28. Shenandoah.. also recorded for Columbia 2300	Victor 18327
11/24/17	3	5	29. Hush-A-Bye Ma Baby (The Missouri Waltz) .... later recorded for Pathe 20293; song became the official state song of Missouri (Burr recorded solo for Emerson 929)	Columbia 2358
7/27/18	2(1)	5	30. Your Lips Are No Man's Land But Mine .... later recorded for Columbia 2580 & Pathe 20393	Victor 18470
7/27/18	8	1	31. One Day In June (It Might Have Been You) .... previously recorded for Columbia 2442; also recorded for Pathe 20198; flip side of Henry's #1 solo hit "I'm Sorry I Made You Cry"	Victor 18462
8/17/18	3	8	32. Belgian Rose.. also recorded for Okeh 1110, Emerson 978, & Pathe 20390	Columbia 2559
10/05/18	2(2)	7	33. After You've Gone .... also recorded for Pathe 20439	Columbia 2582
11/16/18	3	5	34. Smiles .... from Broadway musical "The Passing Show of 1918"	Columbia 2616
1/11/19	10	1	35. They'll Be Mighty Proud In Dixie Of Their Old Black Joe	Columbia 2641
1/25/19	6	3	36. Hindustan	Columbia 2661
2/15/19	1(9)	15	37. **Till We Meet Again** .... also recorded for Emerson 9109 & Paramount 30085; Burr recorded song for Vocalion 12087 as Harry McClaskey	Columbia 2668
5/17/19	1(2)	12	38. **I'm Forever Blowing Bubbles** .... also recorded for Okeh 1195; duo also recorded song with Columbia Saxophone Quartette (Columbia 2784)	Columbia 2701
8/02/19	8	2	39. Somebody's Waiting For Someone................ Burr recorded song for Okeh 1231	Columbia 2729
3/27/20	12	1	40. Dardanella	Pathe 22291
4/17/20	9	1	41. Where The Lanterns Glow	Columbia 2842
10/23/20	5	5	42. I'll Be With You In Apple Blossom Time........	Columbia 2967
1/29/21	2(1)	6	43. Feather Your Nest.................................... Rudy Wiedoeft featured on saxophone; from Broadway musical "Listen Lester"; also recorded for Okeh 4185	Victor 18708
3/26/21	11	1	44. Mandalay	Columbia 3350
8/27/21	11	1	45. Carolina Lullaby....................................	Victor 18762
3/03/23	10	1	46. Carry Me Back To My Carolina Home	Victor 18975
2/09/24	6	3	47. I'm Sitting Pretty In A Pretty Little City........	Victor 19180
4/25/25	11	1	48. At The End Of The Road	Victor 19530

EARL BURTNETT & HIS LOS ANGELES BILTMORE HOTEL ORCHESTRA

Pianist and latter-day director of the Art Hickman band, Earl was
a successful composer ("Canadian Capers", "Mandalay") whose career
as bandleader ended with his death on 1/2/36 (39).

DATE CHARTED	PEAK POS	WKS CHRT'D	ARTIST — Record Title	Label & Number
1/29/27	9	4	1. Song Of The Wanderer (Where Shall I Go?). [I]	Columbia 787
7/23/27	12	2	2. The Doll Dance .... [I]	Columbia 934
6/23/28	3	9	3. Sweet Sue - Just You/	
7/21/28	20	1	4. Stay Out Of The South (If You Want To Miss A Heaven On Earth) .... above two vocals by the Biltmore Trio	Columbia 1361
12/22/28	10	3	5. Sally Of My Dreams................................	Brunswick 4104
6/15/29	10	4	6. The Wedding Of The Painted Doll .... from the movie "Broadway Melody"	Brunswick 4232
8/24/29	4	10	7. Singin' In The Rain .... from the movie "Hollywood Revue of 1929" above two vocals: Paul Gibbons	Brunswick 4375
11/02/29	20	1	8. The Web Of Love .... vocal: Biltmore Trio	Brunswick 4511

DATE CHARTED	PEAK POS	WKS CHRT'D	ARTIST — Record Title	Label & Number
11/16/29	9	7	9. Sunny Side Up/	
12/07/29	9	5	10. If I Had A Talking Picture Of You	Brunswick 4501
11/23/29	7	4	11. Turn On The Heat	Brunswick 4573
			above three from the movie "Sunny Side Up"	
12/21/29	17	3	12. Look What You've Done To Me....................	Brunswick 4605
3/15/30	17	1	13. Puttin' On The Ritz	Brunswick 4679
			movie title song	
4/19/30	11	3	14. 'Leven Thirty Saturday Night.....................	Brunswick 4754
6/28/30	2(2)	9	15. So Beats My Heart For You........................	Brunswick 4830
9/13/30	4	5	16. Little White Lies....................................	Brunswick 4881
12/27/30	13	2	17. It Must Be True	Brunswick 4984
2/21/31	18	1	18. I Surrender, Dear..................................	Brunswick 6034
			vocal: Don Dewey	
3/14/31	15	2	19. Imagine....................................	Brunswick 6059
			vocal: Gene Conklin	
5/26/34	8	4	20. (She Walks Like You, She Talks Like You) She Reminds Me Of You......................	Columbia 2922
			vocal: Stanley Hickman; from movie "We're Not Dressing"	
5/26/34	13	3	21. Ridin' Around In The Rain........................	Columbia 2921
			above two listed as "Earl Burtnett & His Drake Hotel Orchestra"	

BILLY BURTON
Pseudonym for Charles Harrison

HENRY BUSSE & HIS ORCHESTRA
German-born Henry Busse became nationally known as trumpet soloist for Paul Whiteman on such hits as "When Day Is Done" and Henry's theme "Hot Lips" from 1919-28. He died on 4/23/55 (60).

DATE CHARTED	PEAK POS	WKS CHRT'D	ARTIST — Record Title	Label & Number
11/23/29	18	2	1. Satisfied..	Victor 22116
7/04/31	7	4	2. I'm Through With Love	Victor 22677
			vocal: Richard Barry	
7/14/34	3	11	3. Hot Lips .... [I]	Columbia 2937
7/28/34	9	5	4. All I Do Is Dream Of You	Columbia 2932
			from the film "Sadie McKee"	
1/16/37	1(1)	9	5. With Plenty Of Money And You	Decca 1076
			vocal: Bob Hannon; from the film "Gold Diggers of 1937"	
7/30/38	7	4	6. I'm Gonna Lock My Heart..........................	Decca 1924
9/10/38	19	1	7. Tu-Li Tulip Time...............................	Decca 1975
10/08/38	16	2	8. Bambina	Decca 1976
			above three vocals: Don Huston	
6/03/39	6	4	9. My Last Good-Bye.................................	Decca 2454
			vocal: Dick Wharton	
10/19/40	26	1	10. Hot Lips.. [I-R]	Columbia 2937

CHAMP BUTLER

DATE CHARTED	PEAK POS	WKS CHRT'D	ARTIST — Record Title	Label & Number
5/26/51	29	1	1. I Apologize	Columbia 39189
			with the Skippy Martin Orchestra	
9/29/51	17	15	2. Down Yonder	Columbia 39533
5/17/52	26	1	3. Be Anything (But Be Mine)........................	Columbia 39690
			with Percy Faith & his orchestra	

BILLY BUTTERFIELD & HIS ORCHESTRA
Billy's reputation as a trumpet virtuoso was established on such Bob Crosby hits as "What's New?"; he also played with Artie Shaw, Benny Goodman and Les Brown. (also see Frank Sinatra)

DATE CHARTED	PEAK POS	WKS CHRT'D	ARTIST — Record Title	Label & Number
7/24/43	12	19	1. My Ideal..	Capitol 134
			from the 1930 film "Playboy of Paris"	
1/20/45	10	2	2. There Goes That Song Again/	
2/10/45	15	2	● 3. Moonlight In Vermont.............................	Capitol 182
			Margaret Whiting: vocalist on above three Chris Griffin (trumpet), Will Bradley & Cutty Cutshall (trombones), Matty Matlock (clarinet/alto sax), Eddie Miller (tenor sax), & Bob Haggart (guitar) on above two	
10/26/46	6	7	4. Rumors Are Flying.................................	Capitol 282
			vocal: Pat O'Connor	

DATE CHARTED	PEAK POS	WKS CHRT'D	ARTIST — Record Title	Label & Number
			RED BUTTONS Began as vaudeville and TV comic, became a successful screen actor (1957 Oscar as Best Supporting Actor in "Sayonara").	
5/02/53	**9**	9	1. The Ho Ho Song/ [N]	
5/09/53	**15**	4	2. Strange Things Are Happening (Ho Ho, Hee Hee, Ha Ha) .... [N] Columbia 39981 above 2 with Elliot Lawrence & his Orchestra	
			DON BYAS Tenor sax star with Andy Kirk (1939-40), Count Basie (1941), & Dizzy Gillespie; died 8/23/72 (59).	
			JERRY BYRD Country steel guitarist	
9/23/50	**19**	4	1. Harbor Lights .... [I] Mercury 5461 with Jerry Murad & the Harmonicats	
			BOBBY BYRNE & HIS ORCHESTRA Trombonist formerly with Jimmy Dorsey; bandleader for Steve Allen's 1953-54 "Tonight Show".	
4/27/40	**27**	1	1. Easy Does It .... Decca 3020 vocal: Dorothy Claire	
10/19/40	**18**	1	2. Maybe..................................... Decca 3392 vocal: Jimmy Palmer	
3/29/41	**22**	1	3. You Walk By.. Decca 3613 vocal: Jerry Wayne	

C

DATE CHARTED	PEAK POS	WKS CHRT'D	ARTIST — Record Title	Label & Number
			CALIFORNIA RAMBLERS Bass saxophonist Adrian Rollini was a longtime member of this heavily recorded band, which also at times included Tommy and Jimmy Dorsey and Red Nichols; Arthur Hall, Vernon Dalhart, and Irving Kaufman were among its vocalists.	
7/29/22	**10**	1	1. My Honey's Lovin' Arms .... [I] Vocalion 14329	
3/01/24	**10**	1	2. Moonlight Kisses .... [I] Columbia 15	
4/12/24	**10**	1	3. Roamin' To Wyomin' .... [I] Columbia 39	
6/28/24	**10**	1	4. California, Here I Come .... [I] Columbia 67 from the Broadway musical "Bombo"	
9/13/24	**10**	1	5. Shine... [I] Columbia 127	
10/22/27	**14**	3	6. Lazy Weather .... Columbia 1038 vocal: Ed Kirkeby	
6/02/28	**12**	2	7. Singapore Sorrows .... [I] Columbia 1314	
1/17/31	**5**	5	8. The Peanut Vendor .... Columbia 2351 adapted from the Cuban song "El Manisero"	
			CAB CALLOWAY & HIS ORCHESTRA One of the most charismatic showmen in popular music history, Cabell Calloway was born on 12/25/07 in Rochester, New York. It was on the stage of New York's famous Cotton Club that Cab made his reputation during the 1930s. Known to most for his "hi-de-ho" scat singing, he also fronted a superb jazz band, which at various times included tenor saxists Ben Webster & Chu Berry, trumpet stars Dizzy Gillespie & Jonah Jones, and drummer Cozy Cole. During the 50s & 60s Cab was featured in productions of "Porgy and Bess" and "Hello, Dolly!". (All vocals by Cab)	
12/06/30	**16**	2	1. St. Louis Blues...................................... Brunswick 4936 listed as "Jungle Band"	
3/21/31	**1(1)**	17	2. **Minnie The Moocher** .... Brunswick 6074 Cab's famous theme, based on the traditional folk song "Willy the Weeper"	
5/16/31	**3**	8	3. St. James' Infirmary/ song banned from network radio	
6/13/31	**13**	2	4. Nobody's Sweetheart .... Brunswick 6105	
8/22/31	**14**	2	5. Six Or Seven Times .... Brunswick 6141	
10/31/31	**17**	1	6. You Rascal, You .... Brunswick 6196	

DATE CHARTED	PEAK POS	WKS CHRT'D	ARTIST — Record Title	Label & Number
11/14/31	**4**	7	7. Kickin' The Gong Around/	
11/27/31	**15**	3	8. Between The Devil And The Deep Blue Sea..	Brunswick 6209
11/28/31	**8**	4	9. Tickeration..	Brunswick 6214
3/26/32	**17**	1	10. Cabin In The Cotton	Brunswick 6272
			vocal: Cab and Bennie Payne	
5/14/32	**11**	3	11. Strictly Cullud Affair...........................	Brunswick 6292
6/11/32	**8**	8	12. Minnie The Moocher's Wedding Day	Brunswick 6321
7/23/32	**11**	2	13. Reefer Man	Brunswick 6340
10/22/32	**14**	2	14. Hot Toddy .... [I]	Brunswick 6400
11/19/32	**18**	1	15. I've Got The World On A String	Brunswick 6424
1/14/33	**17**	3	16. I Gotta Right To Sing The Blues	Brunswick 6460
			from "Earl Carroll's Vanities of 1932"	
4/18/34	**20**	1	17. Jitter Bug..	Victor 24592
8/18/34	**7**	4	18. Moon Glow .... [I]	Victor 24690
10/20/34	**6**	4	19. Chinese Rhythm	Brunswick 6992
2/23/35	**20**	1	20. Keep That Hi-De-Hi In Your Soul	Brunswick 7386
4/25/36	**20**	1	21. You're The Cure For What Ails Me	Brunswick 7639
			above two featured in movie "The Singing Kid"	
10/24/36	**13**	2	22. Copper Colored Gal	Brunswick 7748
6/05/37	**17**	1	23. Wake Up And Live	Variety 535
			movie title song	
7/24/37	**17**	1	24. Congo/	
			also released on Vocalion 3825	
			above five with Ben Webster (tenor sax); replaced by Chu	
			Berry	
9/04/37	**18**	1	25. Peckin'	Variety 593
			also on Vocalion 3830; from movie "New Faces of 1937"	
10/16/37	**17**	2	26. She's Tall, She's Tan, She's Terrific	Variety 643
			also on Vocalion 3787	
10/16/37	**19**	1	27. Moon At Sea	Variety 651
			also on Vocalion 3789	
10/23/37	**20**	1	28. Mama, I Wanna Make Rhythm......................	Variety 644
			also on Vocalion 3788; from movie "Manhattan Merry-Go-Round"	
1/15/38	**18**	2	29. Every Day's A Holiday	Vocalion 3896
			movie title song	
10/29/38	**19**	1	30. Mister Toscanini, Swing For Minnie......... [N]	Vocalion 4369
12/10/38+	**14**	3	31. F.D.R. Jones/	
			from the Broadway musical "Sing Out the News"	
12/17/38	**3**	4	32. Angels With Dirty Faces	Vocalion 4498
			inspired by, but not written for, movie of same name	
6/03/39	**13**	1	33. The Ghost Of Smokey Joe	Vocalion 4807
7/29/39	**2(4)**	12	● 34. (Hep-Hep!) The Jumpin' Jive	Vocalion 5005
10/12/40	**23**	1	35. Fifteen Minute Intermission......................	Okeh 5644
4/26/41	**24**	1	36. Bye Bye Blues...	Okeh 6084
10/04/41	**23**	1	37. Greechee Joe	Okeh 6147
12/13/41	**23**	1	38. I See A Million People..............................	Okeh 6341
1/31/42	**8**	8	39. Blues In The Night	Okeh 6422
			movie title song	
			above five with Dizzy Gillespie (trumpet)	
3/27/43	**18**	1	40. Ogeechee River Lullaby	Columbia 36662
7/10/43	**18**	1	41. St. Louis Blues.................................. [R]	Brunswick 4936
			reissue of Cab's first hit (recorded 7/24/30)	
11/11/44	**28**	1	42. The Moment I Laid Eyes On You..................	Columbia 36751
3/10/45	**20**	1	43. Let's Take The Long Way Home	Columbia 36786
			from the movie "Here Come the Waves"	

EDDIE CALVERT
British trumpet player - died on 8/7/78

12/05/53+	**6**	14	● 1. Oh, Mein Papa..................................... [I]	Essex 336
			accompanied by Norrie Faramor's Orchestra	
			from the Swiss movie musical "Fireworks"	

DATE CHARTED	PEAK POS	WKS CHRT'D	ARTIST — Record Title	Label & Number

CAMARATA & HIS ORCHESTRA
Salvador Tutti (Toots) Camarata: played trumpet for Charlie Barnet and Jimmy Dorsey, did arrangements for many of the Dorsey band's top hits; later orchestra conductor for Ella Fitzgerald, Bing Crosby, and Dick Haymes, among others, and served as musical director at Walt Disney Studios.

DATE CHARTED	PEAK POS	WKS CHRT'D	ARTIST — Record Title	Label & Number
10/25/52	26	2	1. Veradero .... [I]	Decca 28376
8/08/53	27	1	2. Return To Paradise .... [I]	Decca 28714

movie theme song
both listed as "Music by Camarata"

ALBERT CAMPBELL
Tenor balladeer who made his first recordings in 1897, and achieved his most enduring success in duets with Henry Burr and group recordings with the Columbia Male Quartet, Peerless Quartet, and Sterling Trio between 1904 and 1925; died on 1/25/47 (74).
(also see Henry Burr)

DATE	PEAK	WKS	TITLE	LABEL
9/03/98	2(2)	2	1. She Was Bred In Old Kentucky	Berliner 1859
			also on Berliner 019	
10/01/98	2(1)	3	2. The Moth And The Flame	Columbia 7180
			later recorded for Edison 5719	
1/21/99	4	2	3. My Old New Hampshire Home	Chicago 3074
			also recorded for Berliner 0136	
3/04/99	2(1)	4	4. Because	Edison 5710
			from Broadway musical "The French Maid"	
5/20/99	3	4	5. The Girl I Loved In Sunny Tennessee	Edison 5718
6/17/99	1(6)	14	6. **My Wild Irish Rose**	Berliner 0139
			also recorded for Edison 5720; from Broadway musical "A Romance of Athlone"	
1/20/00	2(4)	5	7. Mandy Lee	Edison 7297
1/20/00	3	2	8. If You Were Only Mine	Edison 7352
12/29/00+	1(7)	11	9. **Ma Blushin' Rosie**	Gram-o-Phone 219
7/02/04	2(3)	8	10. You're The Flower Of My Heart, Sweet Adeline	Edison 8677
			ALBERT CAMPBELL & JAMES F. HARRISON	
5/06/05	2(3)	6	11. In The Shade Of The Old Apple Tree	Columbia 3153
			also recorded for Zon-o-Phone 73 under pseudonym "Frank Howard"	
1/27/06	3	2	12. Will You Love Me In December As You Do In May?	Columbia 3324
10/20/06	1(3)	8	13. **Love Me And The World Is Mine**	Victor 4823
10/26/07	4	2	14. Dreaming	Columbia 3701
3/21/08	3	3	15. School Days	Columbia 3745
1/20/12	5	4	16. That Mysterious Rag	Columbia 1086
			ARTHUR COLLINS & ALBERT CAMPBELL	
			also recorded for Zon-o-Phone 5822	

EDDIE CANTOR
Born Eddie Israel Iskowitz in New York on 1/31/1892, Eddie Cantor became one of the most popular entertainers in vaudeville and musical comedy history. His broad humor and inexhaustable energy catapulted him to stardom in the "Ziegfeld Follies of 1917", and Eddie remained a national figure for four decades - on stage, radio, movies, and even TV in the early 50s. Hollywood celebrated him with "The Eddie Cantor Story" in 1953; he died on 10/10/64.

DATE	PEAK	WKS	TITLE	LABEL
12/08/17	10	1	1. That's The Kind Of A Baby For Me	Victor 18342
			from "Ziegfeld Follies of 1917"; orchestra directed by Rosario Bourdon	
11/15/19	9	1	2. You Don't Need The Wine To Have A Wonderful Time	Pathe 22163
2/14/20	3	7	3. You'd Be Surprised	Emerson 10102
			from "Ziegfeld Follies of 1919"	
3/27/20	9	2	4. When It Comes To Lovin' The Girls, I'm Way Ahead Of The Times	Emerson 10105
5/22/20	9	1	5. All The Boys Love Mary	Emerson 10119
8/28/20	11	1	6. The Argentines, The Portugese, And The Greeks	Emerson 10200

DATE CHARTED	PEAK POS	WKS CHRT'D	ARTIST — Record Title	Label & Number
10/09/20	9	1	7. Snoops, The Lawyer .... [C]	Emerson 10212
2/05/21	1(5)	12	8. **Margie**	Emerson 10301
2/12/21	5	4	9. Palesteena	Emerson 10292
8/12/22	3	5	10. I Love Her-She Loves Me (I'm Her He-She's My She)	Columbia 3624
3/24/23	9	1	11. He Loves It	Columbia 3754
10/06/23	7	3	12. Oh! Gee, Oh! Gosh, Oh! Golly, I'm In Love.. [C] from Broadway's "Ziegfeld Follies of 1922"	Columbia 3934
11/17/23	1(2)	9	13. **No, No, Nora/**	
11/17/23	2(3)	6	14. I've Got The Yes! We Have No Bananas Blues .... [N]	Columbia 3964
11/15/24	3	6	15. Charley, My Boy	Columbia 182
12/20/24+	5	3	16. Doodle-Doo-Doo	Columbia 213
7/18/25	1(5)	12	17. **If You Knew Susie** .... from the Broadway musical "Big Boy"	Columbia 364
10/24/25	9	1	18. Row, Row, Rosie	Columbia 415
1/16/26	9	1	19. Oh Boy! What A Girl	Columbia 457
2/09/29	2(2)	10	20. Makin' Whoopee .... from the Broadway musical "Whoopee"	Victor 21831
4/20/29	15	2	21. I Faw Down And Go Boom .... [N] orchestra on above two directed by Nat Shilkret	Victor 21862
11/26/32	7	5	22. What A Perfect Combination...................... from movie "The Kid from Spain"	Columbia 2723
12/08/34	19	1	23. Okay, Toots .... from movie "Kid Millions"	Melotone 13184
6/24/50	27	1	24. The Old Piano Roll Blues........................... EDDIE CANTOR & LISA KIRK with Sammy Kaye & His Orchestra featuring Stan Freeman (piano)	RCA Victor 3751

FRANKIE CARLE & HIS ORCHESTRA

Pianist and composer of such hits as "Sunrise Serenade" and "Oh What It Seemed to Be", Frankie Carle played four years each with Mal Hallett and Hoarce Heidt before becoming a bandleader. His main singer, billed as Marjorie Hughes, was his daughter.

DATE CHARTED	PEAK POS	WKS CHRT'D	ARTIST — Record Title	Label & Number
10/07/44	25	1	1. Charmaine.. Frankie Carle and His Girl Friends	Columbia 36690
2/03/45	4	14	2. A Little On The Lonely Side...................... vocal: Paul Allen	Columbia 36760
2/10/45	8	1	3. Saturday Night (Is The Loneliest Night In The Week).. vocal: Phyllis Lynne	Columbia 36777
2/24/45	16	1	4. Evelina .... from the Broadway musical "Bloomer Girl"	Columbia 36764
7/14/45	17	1	5. Counting The Days .... above two vocals: Paul Allen	Columbia 36805
1/26/46	1(11)	20	6. **Oh! What It Seemed To Be** .... vocal: Marjorie Hughes	Columbia 36892
6/08/46	10	8	7. One More Tomorrow .... movie title song	Columbia 36978
8/17/46	14	1	8. I'd Be Lost Without You	Columbia 36994
9/14/46	24	1	9. Without You/	
9/21/46	1(9)	18	10. **Rumors Are Flying**	Columbia 37069
11/30/46	6	4	11. It's All Over Now .... above four vocals: Marjorie Hughes	Columbia 37146
4/12/47	9	5	12. Roses In The Rain....................................	Columbia 37252
11/01/47	24	1	13. And Mimi	Columbia 37819
11/22/47	21	2	14. Peggy O'Neil	Columbia 37930
1/17/48	22	1	15. (I'm A-Comin', I'm A-Courtin') Corabelle........	Columbia 37972
2/07/48	5	16	16. Beg Your Pardon .... vocal: Marjorie Hughes	Columbia 38036
3/13/48	25	1	17. Dreamy Lullaby.. vocals on 13-15 & 17: Gregg Lawrence	Columbia 38090
12/04/48	10	1	18. Twelfth Street Rag .... [I]	Columbia 35572

DATE CHARTED	PEAK POS	WKS CHRT'D	ARTIST — Record Title	Label & Number
3/19/49	**8**	12	19. Cruising Down The River (On A Sunday After-Noon) .... Columbia 38411 vocal: Marjorie Hughes & Sunrise Serenaders	

UNA MAE CARLISLE
Pianist-singer discovered by Fats Waller; died in 1956 at 37.

5/17/41	**14**	4	1. Walking By The River .... Bluebird 11033 band includes Benny Carter (trumpet), Slam Stewart (bass), & Zutty Singleton (drums)	

HOAGY CARMICHAEL
Composer of the most-recorded love song of all time, "Stardust", Hoagy Carmichael was born on 11/22/1899 in Bloomington, Indiana. In addition to writing dozens of other major hits and performing in his own amiable style, Hoagy was a successful actor in many films from 1937-55. He died on 12/27/81 (82).

6/18/32	**19**	1	1. Lazy River .... Victor 23034 band includes Tommy and Jimmy Dorsey, Joe Venuti (violin), and Eddie Lang (guitar); recorded 11/20/30	
8/06/32	**14**	3	2. Rockin' Chair .... Columbia 2688 Louis Armstrong & His Orchestra; vocal: Louis and Hoagy; recorded on 12/13/29	
11/12/38	**13**	3	3. Two Sleepy People .... Brunswick 8250 HOAGY CARMICHAEL & ELLA LOGAN from the film "Thanks for the Memory"	
8/25/45	**6**	3	4. Hong Kong Blues .... ARA 123 from the film "To Have and Have Not"	
3/16/46	**18**	1	5. Doctor, Lawyer, Indian Chief .... ARA 126 from the film "Stork Club"	
10/12/46	**2(4)**	19	6. Ole Buttermilk Sky .... ARA 155 from the film "Canyon Passage"	
11/23/46+	**1(2)**	15	7. **Huggin' And Chalkin'** .... Decca 23675 with the Chakadees, and Vic Schoen's Orchestra	
5/13/50	**11**	10	8. The Old Piano Roll Blues .... Decca 24977	
4/14/51	**23**	3	9. The Aba Daba Honeymoon .... Decca 27474 featured in the film "Two Weeks With Love" above two with Cass Daley, and Matty Matlock's All-Stars	

ART CARNEY
Years after becoming famous as Ed Norton in TV's "The Honeymooners", Art won the Academy Award as Best Actor in 1974.

12/18/54	**24**	1	1. Santa And The Doodle-Li-Boop .... [X-N] Columbia 40400	

HARRY CARNEY
Duke Ellington's featured baritone saxophonist from 1926 until Duke's death (also see Lionel Hampton, Billie Holiday, Savannah Churchill)

LILY ANN CAROL
Former vocalist with The Louis Prima Band

3/21/53	**25**	1	1. More Luck Than Money .... RCA Victor 5184	

LESLIE CARON
French dancer and actress best known for the films "An American In Paris" and "Gigi".

5/16/53	**30**	1	1. Hi-Lili, Hi-Lo .... MGM 30759 LESLIE CARON & MEL FERRER with Hans Sommer & the MGM Studio Orchestra from the film "Lili"	

CARLETON CARPENTER
Singer-dancer with Broadway experience

2/03/51	**3**	17	● 1. Aba Daba Honeymoon .... MGM 30282 CARLETON CARPENTER & DEBBIE REYNOLDS accompanied by George Stoll & the MGM Orchestra featured in the film "Two Weeks With Love"	

JOE "FINGERS" CARR
Real name Lou Busch; honkytonk-style pianist who played in the 1930s with the George Olsen and Hal Kemp bands; married singer Margaret Whiting. (also see Kay Starr)

6/17/50	**7**	13	1. Sam's Song .... Capitol 962	
10/20/51	**14**	17	2. Down Yonder .... [I] Capitol 1777	

DATE CHARTED	PEAK POS	WKS CHRT'D	ARTIST — Record Title	Label & Number
4/10/54	**24**	3	3. Until Sunrise	Capitol 2730
			1 & 3 with the Carr-Hops	

BOB CARROLL
Baritone who sang with Charlie Barnet, Jimmy Dorsey, Kay Kyser, and Gordon Jenkins bands.

DATE CHARTED	PEAK POS	WKS CHRT'D	ARTIST — Record Title	Label & Number
2/21/53	**14**	4	1. Say It With Your Heart	Derby 814
			accompanied by Jimmy Leyden's Orchestra	
5/23/53	**28**	1	2. A Little Love	Derby 821

DAVID CARROLL & HIS ORCHESTRA
Orchestra conductor/arranger from Chicago. (also see Crew Cuts, Vic Damone, Rusty Draper)

DATE CHARTED	PEAK POS	WKS CHRT'D	ARTIST — Record Title	Label & Number
10/09/54	**29**	1	1. In A Little Spanish Town	Mercury 70444

HELEN CARROLL

DATE CHARTED	PEAK POS	WKS CHRT'D	ARTIST — Record Title	Label & Number
11/16/46	**7**	6	1. Ole Buttermilk Sky	RCA Victor 1982
			with the Satisfiers & Russ Case Orchestra from the film "Canyon Passage"	
4/02/49	**29**	1	2. Cruising Down The River...........................	Mercury 5249
			with The Carolers	

FIDDLIN' JOHN CARSON
Georgia fiddle player already in his 50s when he became the first nationally popular "hillbilly" recording artist; he helped introduce a wide audience to generations-old folk songs. Died on 12/11/49 (81).

DATE CHARTED	PEAK POS	WKS CHRT'D	ARTIST — Record Title	Label & Number
12/08/23	**9**	2	1. The Little Old Log Cabin In The Lane..........	Okeh 4890
3/29/24	**2(1)**	8	● 2. You Will Never Miss Your Mother Until She Is Gone	Okeh 4994
5/17/24	**2(1)**	8	● 3. Fare You Well, Old Joe Clark	Okeh 40038
9/27/24	**14**	1	4. Arkansas Traveler	Okeh 40108
			with the Virginia Reelers	
11/08/24	**10**	1	5. John Henry Blues	Okeh 7004
4/04/25	**10**	1	6. Old Dan Tucker	Okeh 40263

KEN CARSON
Singer featured on TV's "Garry Moore Show"

DATE CHARTED	PEAK POS	WKS CHRT'D	ARTIST — Record Title	Label & Number
6/30/51	**30**	1	1. Wond'rous Word (Of The Lord)	Silvertone 770
			with the Hal Kanner Chorus & Orchestra	

MARY CARSON

DATE CHARTED	PEAK POS	WKS CHRT'D	ARTIST — Record Title	Label & Number
7/24/15	**8**	2	1. Simple Melody...	Edison Amb. 2607
			WALTER VAN BRUNT & MARY CARSON song better known as "Play A Simple Melody" from the Broadway musical "Watch Your Step"	

MINDY CARSON
Sang on Paul Whiteman's 1940s radio show, hosted her own radio and TV programs, and later appeared on Broadway.

DATE CHARTED	PEAK POS	WKS CHRT'D	ARTIST — Record Title	Label & Number
10/19/46	**12**	2	1. Rumors Are Flying....................................	Signature 15043
			HARRY COOL & MINDY CARSON	
3/11/50	**12**	7	2. Candy And Cake.......................................	RCA Vic. 78-3681
4/29/50	**6**	11	3. My Foolish Heart	RCA Victor 3204
			movie title song; also released on 78-3681 accompanied on above two by Henri Rene's Orchestra	
10/28/50	**24**	1	4. A Rainy Day Refrain	RCA Victor 3921
			accompanied by Andrew Acker's Orchestra	
7/21/51	**25**	1	5. Lonely Little Robin	RCA Victor 4151
			accompanied by Norman Leyden's Orchestra	
11/01/52	**24**	2	6. 'Cause I Love You, That's A-Why.................	Columbia 39879
			GUY MITCHELL & MINDY CARSON	
1/24/53	**22**	4	7. Tell Me You're Mine (Per Un Bacio D'amour)..	Columbia 39914
			accompanied by Jimmy Carroll's Orchestra	
7/18/53	**23**	1	8. Tell Us Where The Good Times Are..............	Columbia 39992
			GUY MITCHELL & MINDY CARSON accompanied on 6 & 8 by Mitch Miller's Orchestra	
6/12/54	**29**	1	9. This Above All	Columbia 40206

DATE CHARTED	PEAK POS	WKS CHRT'D	ARTIST — Record Title	Label & Number
			CARTER FAMILY	
			"The First Family of Country Music", influential for generations to follow: A.P. (Alvin Pleasant) Carter, wife Sarah (lead vocalist and autoharp), and her cousin Maybelle (alto vocalist and guitar), all Virginia-born. Maybelle's daughter June carried on the family tradition singing with husband Johnny Cash.	
4/28/28	**10**	4	1. Bury Me Under The Weeping Willow.............	Victor 21074
8/11/28	**3**	10	● 2. Wildwood Flower	Victor 40000
10/27/28	**9**	5	3. Keep On The Sunny Side...........................	Victor 21434
1/05/29	**14**	2	4. Little Darling, Pal Of Mine	Victor 21638
6/22/29	**10**	4	5. I'm Thinking Tonight Of My Blue Eyes.........	Victor 40089
9/06/30	**14**	3	6. Worried Man Blues..................................	Victor 40317
4/18/31	**15**	2	7. Lonesome Valley	Victor 23541
8/24/35	**17**	1	8. Can The Circle Be Unbroken (Bye and Bye) ...	Banner 33465
			BENNY CARTER & HIS ORCHESTRA	
			Great alto saxophonist who played with Fletcher Henderson, McKinney's Cotton Pickers, and Chick Webb; achieved his greatest fame in Europe. Benny later composed various film background scores.	
5/25/40	**27**	1	1. Sleep.. [I]	Vocalion 5399
			featuring Coleman Hawkins (tenor sax)	
2/05/44	**11**	6	2. Poinciana/ [I]	
3/11/44	**27**	1	3. Hurry, Hurry!...	Capitol 144
			vocal: Savannah Churchill; band includes J.J. Johnson (trombone)	
			ENRICO CARUSO	
			Perhaps the most legendary singer who ever lived, Enrico Caruso was born in Naples, Italy on 2/27/1873. He made his operatic debut in 1894; after being acclaimed throughout Europe, Caruso came to America in 1902 and began his long association with the New York Metropolitan Opera. In 1904 his first recording for Victor created a sensation; no other individual was more responsible for the early growth of the recording industry than Caruso. The great tenor's death on 8/2/21 triggered international mourning.	
5/07/04	**2(1)**	6	1. I Pagliacci - Vesti La Giubba (On With The Play)... [F]	Victor 81032
6/04/04	**3**	3	2. Aida - Celeste Aida (Heavenly Aida) .... [F]	Victor 85022
6/17/05	**4**	2	3. Iris - Serenata .... [F]	Victor 85048
7/29/05	**6**	1	4. Cavalleria Rusticana - Brindisi (Drinking Song) .... [F]	Victor 81062
6/30/06	**2(1)**	6	5. Forza Del Destino - Solenne In Quest 'Ora (Swear In This Hour) .... [F]	Victrola 89001
			ENRICO CARUSO & ANTONIO SCOTTI	
7/28/06	**6**	1	6. La Boheme - Raccantodi Radolfo (Rudolph's Recital, Act I) .... [F]	Victor 88002
4/13/07	**3**	4	7. Ideale (My Ideal!) .... [F]	Victor 88049
7/27/07	**8**	1	8. La Boheme - O Soave Fanciulla (Thou Sweetest Maiden)........................... [F]	Victor 95200
			ENRICO CARUSO & NELLIE MELBA	
8/10/07	**1(4)**	9	● 9. **I Pagliacci - Vesti La Giubba (On With The Play)**... [F]	Victor 88061
			(new version of 1904 hit)	
4/11/08	**4**	3	10. Dorn Sebastian - In Terra Solo (On Earth Alone) .... [F]	Victor 88106
7/18/08	**4**	2	11. Madama Butterfly - Finale Act I: O Quantiocchi Fisi (O Kindly Heavens)	Victor 89017
			CARUSO & JERALDINE FARRAR	
7/25/08	**5**	1	12. Rigoletto - La Donna E' Mobile (Woman Is Fickle)... [F]	Victor 87017
8/29/08	**4**	2	13. La Boheme - Quartetto: "Addio, Dolce Svegliare" (Farewell, Sweet Love) ...... [F]	Victor 96002
			ENRICO CARUSO, GERALDINE FARRAR, ANTONIO SCOTTI & GINA VIAFORA	

DATE CHARTED	PEAK POS	WKS CHRT'D	ARTIST — Record Title	Label & Number
8/29/08	**8**	1	14. Il Trovatore - Ai Nostri Monti (Home To Our Mountains).................................... [F] CARUSO & LOUISE HOMER	Victor 89018
2/12/10	**5**	3	15. Carmen - Air De La Fleur (Flower Song) .... [F]	Victor 88208
4/23/10	**8**	2	16. Faust - "Mon Coeur Est Penetre Depouvante!" (My Heart Is Torn With Grief)............ [F] ENRICO CARUSO & GERALDINE FARRAR	Victor 89033
5/14/10	**9**	1	17. Il Trovatore - Miserere (I Have Sighed To Rest Me) .... [F] ENRICO CARUSO & FRANCES ALDA	Victor 89030
9/24/10	**6**	3	18. Madama Butterfly - Duet, Act I: "Amore Ogrillo" (Love Or Fancy?) .... [F] CARUSO & ANTONIO SCOTTI	Victor 89043
3/18/11	**4**	4	19. For You Alone................................. Caruso's first recording in English	Victor 87070
4/01/11	**6**	2	20. Addio (Good-Bye) .... [F]	Victor 88280
5/20/11	**5**	3	21. Aida - Duet, Act IV: Aida A Me Togliesti (Aida Thou Hast Taken)................... [F] CARUSO & LOUISE HOMER	Victor 89051
3/09/12	**4**	4	22. Canta Pe' Me (Neapolitan Song) .... [F]	Victor 87092
5/18/12	**1(3)**	9	23. **Love Is Mine**	Victor 87095
5/25/12	**5**	4	24. Aida - Celeste Aida .... [F] new version of his 1904 hit	Victor 88127
5/25/12	**9**	1	25. Crucifix .... [F] CARUSO & MARCEL JOURNET	Victor 89054
7/20/12	**3**	5	26. The Lost Chord	Victor 88378
8/03/12	**10**	1	27. Martha - Quartetto Nocturno (Good Night Quartet)................................... [F] CARUSO, FRANCES ALDA, MARCEL JOURNET, & JOSEPHINE JACOBY	Victor 95210
8/17/12	**2(1)**	8	28. Dreams Of Long Ago .... 28 & 36-39 accompanied by Walter Rogers' Orchestra	Victor 88376
2/22/13	**4**	8	29. Because	Victor 87122
4/05/13	**6**	2	30. Rigoletto - Deh! Non Parlare Al Misero (Recall Not The Past)................................. [F] ENRICO CARUSO & GERALDINE FARRAR	Victor 89058
8/09/13	**7**	4	31. Ave Maria .... [F] 31 & 33 accompanied by Mischa Elman (violin)	Victor 89065
8/30/13	**4**	5	32. Your Eyes Have Told Me What I Did Not Know	Victor 87159
11/15/13	**8**	2	33. Elegie - Melodie .... [F]	Victor 89066
5/16/14	**7**	3	34. Amor Mio (My Love) .... [F]	Victor 87176
9/18/15	**8**	2	35. La Mia Canzone (My Song To Thee) .... [F]	Victor 87213
6/17/16	**3**	7	36. O Sole Mio (My Sunshine) .... [F]	Victor 87243
11/25/16	**4**	5	37. Santa Lucia (Neapolitan Folk Song).......... [F]	Victor 88560
12/23/16	**6**	3	38. Chantique De Noel (Holy Night)..............[X-F]	Victor 88561
5/05/17	**9**	2	39. Chanson De Juin (Song Of June).............. [F]	Victor 88579
10/19/18	**1(3)**	6	40. **Over There** .... with choruses in English and French	Victor 87294
2/15/19	**9**	2	41. Garibaldi's Hymn.............................. [F]	Victor 87297
6/07/19	**9**	1	42. Samson Et Dalila - Je Viens Celebrer La Victoire (I Come To Celebrate Victory) [F] CARUSO, LOUISE HOMER, & MARCEL JOURNET	Victor 89088
7/17/20	**9**	1	43. Love Me Or Not	Victor 88616
3/26/21	**13**	1	44. A Dream	Victor 87321
10/08/21	**5**	3	45. Dreams Of Long Ago .... [R] reissue of Caruso's 1912 hit following his death	Victor 88376

MARIAN CARUSO

DATE CHARTED	PEAK POS	WKS CHRT'D	ARTIST — Record Title	Label & Number
10/11/52	**28**	2	1. My Favorite Song................................. with Don Costa's Orchestra & The Overtones	Devon 1001

CASA LOMA ORCHESTRA - see GLEN GRAY

DATE CHARTED	PEAK POS	WKS CHRT'D	ARTIST — Record Title	Label & Number
			PABLO CASALS	
			Puerto Rican-born cello virtuoso, internationally renowned from the early years of the century until his death at 96 in 1973.	
6/26/15	**10**	1	1. Serenade: Spanish Dance No. 2 .... [I]	Columbia 5650
10/16/20	**10**	1	2. The Swan .... [I]	Columbia 49796
			above two accompanied by Charles Albert Baker (piano)	
			RUSS CASE & HIS ORCHESTRA	
			Played trumpet with Frankie Trumbauer, Paul Whiteman, Hal Kemp, and Raymond Scott; orchestra conductor for Perry Como, Dinah Shore, and other singers; died on 10/10/64 (52).	
10/01/49	**26**	1	1. You're Breaking My Heart	MGM 10478
			vocal by the Quintones based on "La Mattinata" (1904)	
			MICHAEL CASEY	
			Pseudonym for Russell Hunting	
			ADRIENNE CASILLOTTI	
2/19/38	**10**	4	1. Someday My Prince Will Come	Victor 25737
			as the voice of Snow White in the animated movie "Snow White and the Seven Dwarfs"	
			CASTILLIAN TROUBADORS	
2/03/34	**4**	9	1. Carioca	Brunswick 6749
			from the movie "Flying Down to Rio"	
5/26/34	**16**	3	2. My Shawl	Brunswick 6893
			CASTILLIANS	
7/28/34	**20**	1	1. Amapola	Columbia 2938
			BOB CAUSER & HIS ORCHESTRA	
4/18/34	**18**	1	1. Why Do I Dream These Dreams?.................	Melotone 12925
			from the movie "Wonder Bar"	
			CAVALIERS - see BEN SELVIN	
			CARMEN CAVALLARO & HIS ORCHESTRA	
			Classically-trained pianist who played in 1930s with Al Kavelin, Rudy Vallee, and Abe Lyman; he provided the 1956 movie soundtrack for "The Eddy Duchin Story". (Also see Bing Crosby)	
6/30/45	**3**	19	● 1. Chopin's Polonaise................................. [I]	Decca 18677
9/17/49	**29**	1	2. There's Yes! Yes! In Your Eyes...................	Decca 24678
3/11/50	**5**	9	3. Music! Music! Music!...............................	Decca 24881
			vocal: Bob Lido & Cavaliers	
9/27/52	**28**	1	4. Meet Mister Callaghan .... [I]	Decca 28373
			British song	
			DAVE CAVANAUGH	
			Tenor saxist with Julia Lee, orchestra conductor/arranger for Kay Starr, other singers.	
			JOSEPH CAWTHORN	
			Longtime musical comedy star who also appeared in many films from 1928-42; died at 82 in 1949.	
8/02/13	**7**	2	1. You Can't Play Every Instrument In The Band	Victor 70098
			from the Broadway musical "The Sunshine Girl"	
8/26/16	**4**	4	2. I Can Dance With Everybody But My Wife	Victor 55074
			from the Broadway musical "Sybil"	
			FRANK CHACKSFIELD & HIS ORCHESTRA	
			British orchestra leader and arranger	
5/30/53	**5**	13	1. Limelight (Terry's Theme) .... [I]	London 1342
			from the movie "Limelight"; song written by Charlie Chaplin	
8/29/53	**2(4)**	23	● 2. Ebb Tide .... [I]	London 1358
			DONALD CHALMERS	
			Bass singer, member of the American Quartet in 1918-19; died on 5/17/39 (58).	
9/07/12	**5**	4	1. Till The Sands Of The Desert Grow Cold	Edison Amb. 1043

DATE CHARTED	PEAK POS	WKS CHRT'D	ARTIST — Record Title	Label & Number
			THOMAS CHALMERS	
			Baritone with the New York Metropolitan Opera; died on 1/12/66 (81).	
3/02/18	**10**	1	1. The Battle Hymn Of The Republic	Edison 28279
			ANNA CHANDLER	
			Popular vaudeville singer; died at 70 in 1957.	
4/22/16	**8**	2	1. When You're Down In Louisville/	
5/06/16	**8**	1	2. Hello, Hawaii, How Are You?	Columbia 1939
6/17/16	**5**	3	3. You Can't Get Along With 'Em Or Without 'Em..	Columbia 1956
			flip side of "Yaaka Hula Hickey Dula" (POS 2) by Al Jolson	
1/13/17	**7**	2	4. Sometimes You Get A Good One And Sometimes You Don't	Columbia 2105
			orchestra on all directed by Charles Prince	
			JEFF CHANDLER	
			Actor featured in "Broken Arrow" and many other films from 1947 until his death in 1961 (33).	
4/17/54	**21**	4	1. I Should Care	Decca 29004
			accompanied by Victor Young's Orchestra	
			KAREN CHANDLER	
			Married to conductor/arranger Jack Pleis; sang with Benny Goodman in 1946 under pseudonym Eve Young. (also see Eve Young)	
10/25/52+	**5**	18	● 1. Hold Me, Thrill Me, Kiss Me	Coral 60831
5/02/53	**27**	1	2. Goodbye, Charlie, Goodbye........................	Coral 60958
12/26/53+	**23**	2	3. Why	Coral 61088
			accompanied on all by Jack Pleis' Orchestra	
			CAROL CHANNING	
			All-time Broadway musical comedy great, became a star in 1949's "Gentlemen Prefer Blondes", later in "Hello, Dolly!".	
			CHARIOTEERS	
			Cincinnati-based vocal group led by William B. Williams. (also see Buddy Clark, Frank Sinatra)	
9/14/40	**23**	1	1. So Long	Columbia 35424
10/12/46	**12**	1	2. On The Boardwalk In Atlantic City	Columbia 37074
			from the film "Three Little Girls in Blue"	
3/08/47	**6**	3	3. Open The Door, Richard........................ [C]	Columbia 37240
7/19/47	**16**	3	4. Chi-Baba, Chi-Baba (My Bambina Go To Sleep).................................	Columbia 37384
1/24/48	**21**	2	5. What Did He Say?/	
2/28/48	**20**	1	6. Ooh! Look-A-There, Ain't She Pretty?........	Columbia 38065
7/02/49	**19**	1	7. A Kiss And A Rose.................................	Columbia 38438
			CHARLESTON CHASERS	
			Jazz band often led by Red Nichols	
5/07/27	**19**	1	1. Someday, Sweetheart .... [I]	Columbia 861
7/02/27	**14**	2	2. One Sweet Letter From You......................	Columbia 911
			vocal: Kate Smith	
10/12/29	**19**	1	3. Moanin' Low	Columbia 1891
			vocal: Eva Taylor; from the Broadway musical "The Little Show" Red Nichols (trumpet) director on above three all with Jimmy Dorsey (clarinet/alto sax)	
3/21/31	**15**	4	4. Walkin' My Baby Back Home	Columbia 2404
			listed as "Johnny Walker & His Orchestra"	
5/09/31	**14**	5	5. Basin Street Blues	Columbia 2415
			vocal: Jack Teagarden (also trombone); Benny Goodman (director & clarinet); Glenn Miller (trombone/arranger), Gene Krupa (drums) on above two	
			KITTY CHEATHAM	
			Died on 1/5/45 (81).	
8/06/10	**6**	3	1. I've Got A Pain In My Sawdust	Columbia 5168

DATE CHARTED	PEAK POS	WKS CHRT'D	ARTIST — Record Title	Label & Number

CHEERS
West Coast vocal group including future TV actor Bert Convy

10/16/54	**15**	11	1. (Bazoom) I Need Your Lovin'	Capitol 2921

DON CHERRY
Sang briefly with postwar Tommy Dorsey and Victor Young Orchestras; left music to become a pro golfer in the late 50s.

9/23/50	**4**	21	1. Thinking Of You .... accompanied by Dave Terry's Orchestra featured in the film "Three Little Words"	Decca 27128
7/28/51	**11**	13	2. Vanity .... accompanied by Sy Oliver's Orchestra	Decca 27618
9/01/51	**25**	1	3. Belle, Belle, My Liberty Belle .... accompanied by Sonny Burke & His Orchestra	Decca 27717

BOB CHESTER & HIS ORCHESTRA
Detroit-based bandleader who previously played tenor sax for Russ Morgan, Ben Pollack, and Ben Bernie, among others; his band included trumpet stars Alec Fila and (later) Louis Mucci.

4/27/40	**18**	1	1. With The Wind And The Rain In Your Hair.... vocal: Dolores O'Neill	Bluebird 10614
9/21/40	**3**	13	2. Practice Makes Perfect .... vocal: Al Stuart	Bluebird 10838
11/09/40	**11**	6	3. Now I Lay Me Down To Dream.....................	Bluebird 10821
2/08/41	**15**	2	4. May I Never Love Again .... above two vocals: Dolores O'Neill	Bluebird 10904
3/01/41	**26**	1	5. Till The Lights Of London Shine Again	Bluebird 10972
5/31/41	**17**	1	6. My Sister And I .... above two vocals: Bill Darnell	Bluebird 11088
1/17/42	**22**	1	7. Madelaine.. vocal: Bob Haymes	Bluebird 11355

MAURICE CHEVALIER
The personification of debonair French charm, Maurice Chevalier was born in Paris on 9/12/1888, and was the most popular entertainer in his country when he made the first of many successful Hollywood musicals in 1929. The 1958 film "Gigi" introduced Chevalier to a new generation; he died on 1/1/72 (83).

6/08/29	**3**	10	1. Louise/	
7/20/29	**9**	4	2. Wait Till You See Ma Cherie .... orchestra directed by Tom Griselle above two from the film "Innocents of Paris"	Victor 21918
2/15/30	**15**	2	3. My Love Parade.................................. from film "The Love Parade"	Victor 22285
5/31/30	**12**	4	4. You Brought A New Kind Of Love To Me .... from film "The Big Pond"	Victor 22405
1/03/31	**12**	4	5. My Ideal.................................... from the film "Playboy of Paris"	Victor 22542
8/29/31	**18**	1	6. Mama Inez.................................... orchestra on 1 & 3-6 directed by Leonard Joy	Victor 22731
8/06/32	**9**	6	7. Mimi....................................... from the film "Love Me Tonight"; orchestra directed by Nat Finston	Victor 24063

CHORDETTES
Jimmy Lochard, Carol Bushman, Nancy Overton, and Lynn Evans; first won national exposure on Arthur Godfrey's TV show

10/30/54	**1(7)**	20	● 1. **Mr. Sandman**	Cadence 1247

CHORDS
R&B quintet from the Bronx, New York · Carl Feaster, lead singer

7/03/54	**5**	16	1. Sh-Boom .... the original version of this rock classic	Cat 104

CHARLIE CHRISTIAN
Before his tragic death at age 22 of pneumonia (3/2/42), Charlie Christian revolutionized jazz guitar while playing with Benny Goodman from 1939-41.

DATE CHARTED	PEAK POS	WKS CHRT'D	ARTIST — Record Title	Label & Number
			JUNE CHRISTY Jazz singer (real name Shirley Luster) who achieved national fame with the Stan Kenton band.	
2/21/53	**22**	3	1. My Heart Belongs To Only You .... accompanied by Pete Rugolo's Orchestra	Capitol 1073
			SAVANNAH CHURCHILL Top jazz/R&B singer who worked with Jimmy Lytell and Benny Carter; died on 4/19/74 (54).	
5/10/47	**21**	1	1. I Want To Be Loved	Manor 1046
5/22/48	**20**	3	2. Time Out For Tears .... with the Four Tunes Harry Carney (baritone sax) & Trummy Young (trombone) on above two	Manor 1116
10/06/51	**5**	17	3. (It's No) Sin	RCA Victor 4280
10/03/53	**22**	2	4. Shake A Hand	Decca 28836
			CINCINNATI SYMPHONY ORCHESTRA	
9/08/17	**10**	1	1. Waltz Of The Hours .... [I]	Columbia 5943
			BUDDY CLARK Buddy (real name Samuel Goldberg) was first widely heard on the 1930s Benny Goodman and Hit Parade radio shows. After receiving his own show several years later, his records and those with Ray Noble ("Linda") made Buddy one of the country's most popular singers before a plane crash took his life on 10/1/49 (37). (also see Nat Brandwynne, Lud Gluskin, Freddy Martin)	
7/23/38	**19**	1	1. Spring Is Here .... from the Broadway musical "I Married An Angel"	Vocalion 4191
2/15/47	**1(2)**	23	2. **Linda** .... with Ray Noble & His Orchestra	Columbia 37215
3/01/47	**6**	8	3. How Are Things In Glocca Mora .... from the Broadway musical "Finian's Rainbow"	Columbia 37223
6/28/47	**1(6)**	15	4. **Peg O' My Heart** .... from the Broadway musical "Ziegfeld Follies of 1913"	Columbia 37392
11/08/47	**14**	1	5. An Apple Blossom Wedding	Columbia 37488
11/15/47	**22**	2	6. Don't You Love Me Anymore? .... accompanied on above four by Mitchell Ayres' Orchestra	Columbia 37920
12/06/47+	**3**	15	7. I'll Dance At Your Wedding/	
12/06/47+	**21**	1	8. Those Things Money Can't Buy .... above two with Ray Noble & His Orchestra	Columbia 37967
1/03/48	**26**	1	9. You Are Never Away .... from the Broadway musical "Allegro"	Columbia 37985
1/10/48	**5**	7	10. Ballerina .... accompanied by Dick Jones' Orchestra	Columbia 38040
1/17/48	**23**	2	11. (The Treasure Of) Sierra Madre....................	Columbia 38026
3/13/48	**22**	1	12. Matinee..	Columbia 38083
3/13/48	**23**	2	13. Serenade (Music Played On A Heartstring)..... 11 & 13 with Ray Noble & His Orchestra	Columbia 38091
3/27/48	**6**	5	14. Now Is The Hour (Maori Farewell Song) .... with the Charioteers based on the traditional New Zealand song "Hearere Ra"	Columbia 38115
5/29/48	**1(5)**	24	● 15. **Love Somebody/**	
6/26/48	**16**	11	16. Confess..	Columbia 38174
7/10/48	**23**	1	17. Where The Apple Blossoms Fall .... with organ accompaniment	Columbia 38241
11/20/48	**7**	13	18. My Darling, My Darling .... from the Broadway musical "Where's Charley?"	Columbia 38353
2/26/49	**16**	3	19. Powder Your Face With Sunshine (Smile! Smile! Smile!)................................ 15, 16, 18 & 19: DORIS DAY & BUDDY CLARK all accompanied by George Siravo's Orchestra	Columbia 38394
3/19/49	**24**	2	20. I Love You So Much It Hurts .... accompanied by Earle Hagen's Orchestra	Columbia 38406
3/19/49	**25**	4	21. It's A Big, Wide, Wonderful World............... from the Broadway musical "All In Fun" 12 & 21 accompanied by Mitchell Ayres' Orchestra	Columbia 38370

DATE CHARTED	PEAK POS	WKS CHRT'D	ARTIST — Record Title	Label & Number
5/07/49	**4**	19	22. **Baby, It's Cold Outside** .... Columbia 38463 DINAH SHORE & BUDDY CLARK from the film "Neptune's Daughter"	
8/20/49	**4**	16	23. **You're Breaking My Heart** .... Columbia 38546 accompanied by Harry Zimmerman's Orchestra; based on "La Mattinata" (1904)	
11/05/49	**12**	11	24. **A Dreamer's Holiday** .... Columbia 38599 22 & 24 accompanied by Ted Dale's Orchestra	

HELEN CLARK
New York-born contralto, a member of the Victor Light Opera Co.

DATE CHARTED	PEAK POS	WKS CHRT'D	ARTIST — Record Title	Label & Number
12/28/12	**9**	1	1. **Rose Of Pyramid Land** .... Victor 17173	
3/22/13	**1(2)**	8	2. **Sympathy** .... Victor 17270 from the Broadway musical "The Firefly" above two: WALTER VAN BRUNT & HELEN CLARK	
5/03/13	**5**	6	3. **When I Waltz With You** .... Victor 17298	
12/20/13	**10**	1	4. **Come On Over Here** .... Victor 17441 BILLY MURRAY & HELEN CLARK from the Broadway musical "The Doll Girl"	
4/04/14	**7**	4	5. **Rebecca Of Sunny-brook Farm** .... Columbia 1483	
8/01/14	**2(3)**	8	6. **In The Valley Of The Moon** .... Victor 17587 above two: HENRY BURR & HELEN CLARK Helen also recorded this song with Vernon Archibald (Edison 80162); 6 also on Columbia 1533	
7/10/15	**9**	1	7. **Don't Take My Darling Boy Away** .... Edison Amb. 2622 HELEN CLARK & JOSEPH PHILLIPS	
1/08/16	**6**	3	8. **When You're In Love With Someone Who Is Not In Love With You** .... Columbia 1800 HENRY BURR & HELEN CLARK (listed as "Miriam Clark")	
5/12/17	**8**	2	9. **Pack Up Your Troubles In Your Old Kit Bag and Smile, Smile, Smile** .... Edison 50419	
5/04/18	**8**	2	10. **The Siren's Song** .... Edison 80382 HELEN CLARK & GLADYS RICE from the Broadway musical "Leave It To Jane"	
10/05/18	**7**	3	11. **One For All And All For One** .... Victor 18488	
9/13/19	**10**	1	12. **I'm Forever Blowing Bubbles** .... Edison Amb. 3798 HELEN CLARK & GEORGE WILTON BALLARD also on Edison 50534	

KATHARINE CLARK
Pseudonym for Grace Kerns.

BUCK CLAYTON
Trumpet star with Count Basie (1936-43), also performed on hits by
Billie Holiday & Teddy Wilson.

CLEVELANDERS
Led by Harry Reser (banjo)

DATE CHARTED	PEAK POS	WKS CHRT'D	ARTIST — Record Title	Label & Number
3/05/27	**17**	2	1. **Take In The Sun, Hang Out The Moon** .... Brunswick 3375 vocal: Tom Stacks; also issued on Vocalion 15486	

CLICQUOT CLUB ESKIMOS
Led by Harry Reser

DATE CHARTED	PEAK POS	WKS CHRT'D	ARTIST — Record Title	Label & Number
6/09/28	**19**	1	1. **Wings** .... Columbia 1322	
1/12/29	**13**	4	2. **Avalon Town** .... Columbia 1592 vocal: Tom Stacks	

LARRY CLINTON & HIS ORCHESTRA
Brooklyn-born composer ("Satan Takes a Holiday", "My Reverie") and
arranger for Isham Jones, Tommy and Jimmy Dorsey, and Casa Loma
orchestras; his own band featured singer Bea Wain and alto saxist
Toots Mondello. He died on 5/2/85 (75).

DATE CHARTED	PEAK POS	WKS CHRT'D	ARTIST — Record Title	Label & Number
11/13/37	**7**	3	1. **The Big Dipper** .... [I] Victor 25697 the band's main theme song	
12/04/37+	**3**	11	2. **True Confession** .... Victor 25706	
12/18/37	**8**	2	3. **The One Rose (That's Left In My Heart)** .... Victor 25724	
1/15/38	**17**	1	4. **Abba Dabba (One Of The Arabian Knights)** . [I] Victor 25707	
1/29/38	**6**	8	5. **I Double Dare You** .... Victor 25740	
2/05/38	**15**	2	6. **Love Is Here To Stay** .... Victor 25761 from the film "Goldwyn Follies"	

DATE CHARTED	PEAK POS	WKS CHRT'D	ARTIST — Record Title	Label & Number
2/12/38	12	3	7. Two Dreams Got Together	Victor 25740
2/26/38	9	7	8. Always And Always	Victor 25768
3/12/38	2(3)	16	9. Martha	Victor 25789
3/12/38	3	12	10. You're An Education	Victor 25794
3/26/38	1(4)	15	11. **Cry, Baby, Cry**	Victor 25819
3/26/38	12	2	12. Romance In The Dark	Victor 25800
6/11/38	4	9	13. I Married An Angel Broadway musical title song	Victor 25837
7/02/38	12	3	14. If It Rains, Who Cares?	Victor 25841
7/23/38	3	12	15. You Go To My Head	Victor 25849
8/13/38	1(8)	19	16. **My Reverie** adapted from the Debussy art song "Reverie" (1895)	Victor 26006
9/17/38	17	1	17. Put Your Heart In A Song from the film "Breaking the Ice"	Victor 25892
10/01/38	1(1)	14	18. **Heart And Soul**	Victor 26046
10/08/38	11	4	19. At Long Last Love from the Broadway musical "You Never Know"	Victor 26014
10/15/38	3	9	20. Summer Souvenirs	Victor 26042
10/22/38	4	6	21. Old Folks	Victor 26056
11/05/38	6	7	22. Who Blew Out The Flame? Bea Wain: all above vocals	Victor 26073
12/10/38	14	5	23. The Devil With The Devil/	
12/30/38+	12	2	24. Jeepers Creepers above two vocals by Ford Leary; from the film "Going Places"	Victor 26108
12/30/38	14	2	25. For Men Only .... [I]	Victor 26118
1/07/39	4	3	26. My Heart Belongs To Daddy from the Broadway musical "Leave It to Me"	Victor 26100
2/04/39	1(9)	13	27. **Deep Purple** written several years earlier as piano solo	Victor 26141
2/11/39	5	8	28. (I'm Afraid) The Masquerade Is Over	Victor 26151
4/08/39	10	5	29. I Want My Share Of Love vocals on above four: Bea Wain	Victor 26158
7/01/39	7	4	30. Comes Love vocal: Ford Leary; from Broadway musical "Yokel Boy"	Victor 26277
7/15/39	12	2	31. In A Persian Market .... [I]	Victor 26283
8/19/39	10	7	32. Over The Rainbow vocal: Bea Wain; from the film "The Wizard of Oz"	Victor 26174
9/02/39	11	6	33. The Little Man Who Wasn't There vocal: Ford Leary	Victor 26308
9/23/39	16	2	34. I'll Remember vocal: Mary Dugan	Victor 26303
1/06/40	16	1	35. Johnson Rag .... [I]	Victor 26414
6/28/41	23	1	36. Because Of You vocal: Peggy Mann	Bluebird 11094
5/29/48	22	2	37. The Dickey-Bird Song from the film "Three Daring Daughters"	Decca 24301
12/04/48	25	1	38. On A Slow Boat To China above two vocals: Helen Lee & Dipsy Doodlers	Decca 24482

BETTY CLOONEY
Younger sister of Rosemary, with whom she sang in the Tony Pastor band in the late 40s.

DATE CHARTED	PEAK POS	WKS CHRT'D	ARTIST — Record Title	Label & Number
10/09/54	30	2	1. Sisters ROSEMARY & BETTY CLOONEY accompanied by Paul Weston & His Orchestra from the movie "White Christmas"	Columbia 40305

DATE CHARTED	PEAK POS	WKS CHRT'D	ARTIST — Record Title	Label & Number
			ROSEMARY CLOONEY	
			One of the most popular singers of the 1950s, Rosemary and sister Betty sang with the Tony Pastor band in late 40s before her solo career was launched. Rosemary was featured in "White Christmas" and several other 50s movies; after a period of personal difficulties she re-emerged in the late 70s as a successful jazz and ballad singer.	
2/24/51	**24**	2	1. You're Just In Love.............................. Columbia 39052	
			ROSEMARY CLOONEY & GUY MITCHELL from the Broadway musical "Call Me Madam"	
3/03/51	**11**	14	2. Beautiful Brown Eyes .... Columbia 39212	
			accompanied by the Mitch Miller Orchestra	
7/07/51	**1(8)**	20	● 3. **Come On-A My House**.............................. Columbia 39467	
			from the off-Broadway musical "The Son" Stan Freeman (harpsichord/piano) featured on 3, 5, 6 & 7	
9/15/51	**22**	1	4. Mixed Emotions.................................... Columbia 39333	
			accompanied by Percy Faith's Orchestra	
9/22/51	**21**	4	5. I'm Waiting Just For You/	
9/22/51	**24**	1	6. If Teardrops Were Pennies .... Columbia 39535	
9/22/51	**27**	2	7. I Wish I Wuz .... Columbia 39536	
			from the film "Slaughter Trail"	
2/09/52	**18**	3	8. Be My Life's Companion............................ Columbia 39631	
3/01/52	**17**	6	● 9. Tenderly .... Columbia 39648	
			"Tenderly" voted the #2 all-time standard song in Billboard disc jockey poll; Rosemary's recording voted the #6 all-time record	
5/03/52	**1(3)**	27	● 10. **Half As Much** .... Columbia 39710	
			above two accompanied by Percy Faith's Orchestra	
6/28/52	**2(3)**	17	● 11. Botch-A-Me (Ba-Ba-Baciami Piccina) .... Columbia 39767	
			from Italian film "Una Famiglia Impossibile"	
8/23/52	**12**	6	12. Too Old To Cut The Mustard .... Columbia 39812	
			ROSEMARY CLOONEY & MARLENE DIETRICH above two featuring Stan Freeman (harpsichord) accompanied on 12 by Frank Carroll (bass), Terry Snyder (drums), Mundell Lowe & Sal Salvador (guitars)	
9/27/52	**17**	3	13. Blues In The Night/	
			movie title song	
2/21/53	**23**	2	14. Who Kissed Me Last Night? .... Columbia 39813	
			above two accompanied by Percy Faith's Orchestra	
12/20/52	**9**	2	15. The Night Before Christmas Song .... [X] Columbia 39876	
			ROSEMARY CLOONEY & GENE AUTRY accompanied by Carl Cotner's Orchestra	
1/10/53	**18**	2	16. You'll Never Know .... Columbia 39905	
			with Harry James & His Orchestra; from the film "Hello, Frisco, Hello"	
1/17/53	**26**	1	17. If I Had A Penny .... Columbia 39910	
			accompanied by Percy Faith's Orchestra	
6/06/53	**25**	1	18. Dennis The Menace................................. Columbia 39988	
			ROSEMARY CLOONEY & JIMMY BOYD accompanied by Norman Luboff	
1/02/54	**30**	1	19. Happy Christmas, Little Friend .... [X] Columbia 40102	
			official 1953 Christmas Seal song; accompanied by Paul Weston & His Orchestra	
7/17/54	**1(6)**	27	● 20. **Hey There/**	
			from the Broadway musical "The Pajama Game"	
8/07/54	**1(3)**	27	21. **This Ole House**.................................... Columbia 40266	
10/09/54	**30**	2	22. Sisters.. Columbia 40305	
			ROSEMARY & BETTY CLOONEY accompanied by Paul Weston & His Orchestra	
11/13/54	**10**	12	23. Mambo Italiano .... Columbia 40361	
12/11/54	**27**	1	24. Count Your Blessings Instead Of Sheep......... Columbia 40370	
			22 & 24: from the film "White Christmas" above two with the Mellomen 20, 21, 23 & 24 accompanied by Buddy Cole & His Orchestra	
			ARTHUR CLOUGH	
			Tenor who frequently appeared in vaudeville and musical comedies	
1/01/10	**9**	1	1. It's Hard To Kiss Your Sweetheart When The Last Kiss Means Good-Bye .... Edison 10251	

DATE CHARTED	PEAK POS	WKS CHRT'D	ARTIST — Record Title	Label & Number
2/19/10	**3**	5	2. Put On Your Old Gray Bonnet	Columbia 778
4/30/10	**5**	3	3. Daisies Won't Tell..................................	Columbia 792
5/06/11	**2(2)**	9	4. Let Me Call You Sweetheart........................	Edison Amb. 637
10/28/11	**1(1)**	9	5. **Down By The Old Mill Stream**	Columbia 1057
			ARTHUR CLOUGH & BRUNSWICK QUARTET Clough solo version recorded for Edison Amberol 796	

CLUB ROYAL ORCHESTRA
Band included saxophonist Clyde Doerr and Harry Reser (banjo)

DATE CHARTED	PEAK POS	WKS CHRT'D	ARTIST — Record Title	Label & Number
3/25/22	**3**	4	1. The Sheik... [I]	Victor 18831
10/14/22	**8**	2	2. Dancing Fool .... [I]	Victor 18923

TOM COAKLEY & HIS PALACE HOTEL ORCHESTRA
California-based hotel band

DATE CHARTED	PEAK POS	WKS CHRT'D	ARTIST — Record Title	Label & Number
12/30/33+	**12**	3	1. Good Morning Glory .... from the film "Sitting Pretty"	Victor 24480
7/07/34	**17**	2	2. I'll String Along With You .... from the film "Twenty Million Sweethearts"	Victor 24600
6/29/35	**1(2)**	15	3. **East Of The Sun (And West Of The Moon)** .. listed as Tom Coakley & His Orchestra all vocals: Carl Ravazza	Victor 25069

JOLLY COBURN & HIS ORCHESTRA
Eastern society band

DATE CHARTED	PEAK POS	WKS CHRT'D	ARTIST — Record Title	Label & Number
10/20/34	**2(3)**	9	1. The Continental (You Kiss While You're Dancing)... vocal: Harold Van Emburgh & Roy Strom from the film "The Gay Divorcee"	Victor 24735

GEORGE M. COHAN
The man who personally created a bold new style of American musical comedy was born on 7/3/1878 in Providence, R.I. He graduated from the Four Cohans family vaudeville act to write, manage, and star in a long series of hit Broadway musicals from the turn of the century to 1937; "Give My Regards to Broadway" and "You're a Grand Old Flag" are but two of many Cohan classic songs. Shortly after he was honored by the film "Yankee Doodle Dandy", George M. Cohan died on 11/5/42 (64).

DATE CHARTED	PEAK POS	WKS CHRT'D	ARTIST — Record Title	Label & Number
8/05/11	**5**	3	1. Life's A Funny Proposition, After All........... from his 1904 musical "Little Johnny Jones"	Victor 60042
12/02/11	**8**	2	2. The Small-Town Gal .... from his 1908 musical "Fifty Miles from Boston" orchestra directed by Walter B. Rogers	Victor 60052

BUDDY COLE
Pianist formerly with Alvino Rey & the King Sisters, then orchestra leader for Bing Crosby, Johnny Ray, & other singers; died on 11/5/64 (47).

COZY COLE
Drummer with long and successful career: with Willie Bryant, Stuff Smith, Teddy Wilson, Cab Calloway, & Louis Armstrong during 1935-53 period; scored with his own 1958 million-seller, "Topsy". He died on 1/29/81 (71).

NAT "KING" COLE
One of the most popular singers in recording history, Nat Cole was born on 3/17/17 in Montgomery, Ala. He began his career as a jazz pianist and with guitarist Oscar Moore and bassist Wesley Prince (later replaced by Johnny Miller) he formed the King Cole Trio in 1939. The trio soon became the hottest small instrumental combo in the country, but once Nat began to sing his future course was clear. Nat appeared in several movies from 1953 on, hosted his own TV series, and remained at the top of his profession when he died on 2/15/65. Daughter Natalie became a star a decade later. (Except as noted, all 1943-49 records with the King Cole Trio)

DATE CHARTED	PEAK POS	WKS CHRT'D	ARTIST — Record Title	Label & Number
11/20/43	**18**	1	1. All For You..	Capitol 139
4/29/44	**9**	7	2. Straighten Up And Fly Right/	
5/06/44	**28**	1	3. I Can't See For Lookin'	Capitol 154
10/21/44	**15**	2	4. Gee, Baby, Ain't I Good To You?.................	Capitol 169
1/05/46	**19**	1	5. The Frim Fram Sauce	Capitol 224

DATE CHARTED	PEAK POS	WKS CHRT'D	ARTIST — Record Title	Label & Number
8/03/46	11	8	6. Get Your Kicks On Route 66 .... Capitol 256 the Trio's most renowned jazz/R&B theme, celebrating the famous westward highway	
9/07/46	10	1	7. You Call It Madness .... Capitol 274	
11/09/46	1(6)	25	8. **(I Love You) For Sentimental Reasons/**	
11/16/46	14	3	9. The Best Man .... Capitol 304	
11/30/46	3	7	● 10. The Christmas Song .... [X] Capitol 311 holiday classic selected for NARAS Hall of Fame	
5/17/47	22	2	11. You Don't Learn That In School .... Capitol 393	
10/25/47	12	1	12. Save The Bones For Henry Jones/	
11/08/47	12	1	13. Harmony .... Capitol 15000 above two: JOHNNY MERCER & THE KING COLE TRIO	
12/06/47	22	3	14. Those Things Money Can't Buy .... Capitol 15011	
12/13/47	23	2	15. The Christmas Song .... [X-R] Capitol 311	
1/17/48	22	1	16. What'll I Do? .... Capitol 15019 from the Broadway musical "Music Box Revue of 1923"	
4/17/48	1(8)	18	● 17. **Nature Boy/** Nat solo, accompanied by Frank DeVol's Orchestra possibly based on the Yiddish song "Schweig Mein Hartz" (Be Calm, My Heart)	
4/17/48	20	4	18. Lost April .... Capitol 15054	
6/05/48	24	1	19. A Boy From Texas .... Capitol 15085	
7/17/48	30	1	20. Put 'Em In A Box, Tie It With A Ribbon .... Capitol 15060 from the film "Romance On the High Seas"	
7/31/48	21	1	21. Don't Blame Me .... Capitol 15110	
11/13/48	25	1	22. Little Girl .... Capitol 15165	
1/08/49	24	1	23. The Christmas Song .... [X-R] Capitol 15201	
4/01/50	26	1	24. I Almost Lost My Mind .... Capitol 889	
6/10/50	1(8)	27	● 25. **Mona Lisa** .... Capitol 1010 accompanied by Les Baxter's Orchestra from the film "Capt. Carey, U.S.A." sold over three million copies	
9/02/50	22	1	26. Home .... Capitol 1133	
9/30/50	5	14	27. Orange Colored Sky .... Capitol 1184 with the Cole Trio, and Stan Kenton & His Orchestra, including Maynard Ferguson & Shorty Rogers (trumpet) & Art Pepper (alto sax) possibly the first hit song introduced on TV	
1/06/51	9	1	28. Frosty The Snowman .... [X] Capitol 1203 with the Pussy Cats	
2/10/51	20	2	29. Jet .... Capitol 1365 with the Ray Charles Singers & Joe Lipman's Orchestra	
4/07/51	28	2	30. Always You .... Capitol 1401 adapted from Tchaikovsky's "Romance"	
4/14/51	1(5)	29	● 31. **Too Young** .... Capitol 1449 above two accompanied by Les Baxter's Orchestra	
5/19/51	24	2	32. Red Sails In The Sunset .... Capitol 1468 from the Broadway musical "Provincetown Follies" 28 & 32 accompanied by Pete Rugolo's Orchestra	
6/09/51	17	4	33. Because Of Rain .... Capitol 1501 accompanied by Les Baxter's Orchestra	
11/03/51+	12	15	34. Unforgettable .... Capitol 1808	
5/31/52	8	25	35. Somewhere Along The Way .... Capitol 2069 above two accompanied by Nelson Riddle's Orchestra	
7/05/52	8	12	36. Walkin' My Baby Back Home/ accompanied by Billy May's Orchestra	
8/16/52	26	1	37. Funny (Not Much) .... Capitol 2130 accompanied by Pete Rugolo's Orchestra	
9/27/52	16	5	38. Because You're Mine/ movie title song	
10/18/52	22	1	39. I'm Never Satisfied .... Capitol 2212	

DATE CHARTED	PEAK POS	WKS CHRT'D	ARTIST — Record Title	Label & Number
10/11/52	23	3	40. The Ruby And The Pearl/ accompanied by Les Baxter's Orchestra from the film "Thunder In the East"	
10/11/52	24	4	41. Faith Can Move Mountains .... accompanied by Nelson Riddle's Orchestra	Capitol 2230
1/03/53	30	1	42. The Christmas Song .... [X-R]	Capitol 15201
1/31/53	20	3	43. Strange	Capitol 2309
2/07/53	2(1)	21	● 44. Pretend/	
2/14/53	23	2	45. Don't Let Your Eyes Go Shopping (For Your Heart) .... above three accompanied by Nelson Riddle's Orchestra	Capitol 2346
3/21/53	16	5	46. Can't I? .... accompanied by Billy May's Orchestra	Capitol 2389
6/06/53	19	4	47. I Am In Love .... from the Broadway musical "Can-Can"	Capitol 2459
7/18/53	15	4	48. Return To Paradise .... movie title song	Capitol 2498
8/22/53	17	4	49. A Fool Was I/	
8/22/53	28	1	50. If Love Is Good To Me	Capitol 2540
11/07/53	16	5	51. Lover, Come Back To Me! .... accompanied by Billy May's Orchestra from the Broadway musical "The New Moon"	Capitol 2610
2/13/54	6	19	● 52. Answer Me, My Love/	
2/27/54	27	1	53. Why	Capitol 2687
5/01/54	16	3	54. It Happens To Be Me/	
6/12/54	25	1	55. Alone Too Long .... from the film "By the Beautiful Sea"	Capitol 2754
7/03/54	19	6	56. Make Her Mine	Capitol 2803
9/18/54	10	11	57. Smile .... music written by Charlie Chaplin for the 1936 film "Modern Times"	Capitol 2897
11/06/54	26	3	58. Unbelievable/	
11/13/54	14	7	59. Haji Baba (Persian Lament) .... from film "The Adventures of Haji Baba"	Capitol 2949
12/25/54	29	1	60. The Christmas Song .... [X] new version of his 1946 hit above nine accompanied by Nelson Riddle's Orchestra	Capitol 2955

EMIL COLEMAN & HIS ORCHESTRA
Popular hotel band long featured at New York's Waldorf Astoria

DATE CHARTED	PEAK POS	WKS CHRT'D	ARTIST — Record Title	Label & Number
1/27/23	13	1	1. Pack Up Your Sins (And Go To The Devil) .. [I] from the Broadway musical "Music Box Revue of 1922"	Vocalion 14462
12/27/30+	6	4	2. Where Have You Been? .... from the Broadway musical "The New Yorkers"	Brunswick 6006
2/21/31	14	2	3. I've Got Five Dollars .... from the Broadway musical "America's Sweetheart"	Brunswick 6036
11/25/33	12	3	4. Mine .... from the Broadway musical "Let 'Em Eat Cake"	Columbia 2831
12/30/33+	12	2	5. What Is There To Say? .... from Broadway musical "Ziegfeld Follies of 1934"	Columbia 2859
1/06/34	4	9	6. (When Your Heart's On Fire) Smoke Gets In Your Eyes .... from the Broadway musical "Roberta" above three listed as Emil Coleman & His Riviera Orchestra	Columbia 2846
3/03/34	14	4	7. In A Shelter From A Shower/	
3/03/34	15	3	8. Music Makes Me .... from the film "Flying Down to Rio"	Columbia 2893
3/17/34	20	2	9. Wonder Bar .... movie title song above three listed as Emil Coleman & His Palais Royal Orchestra	Columbia 2894
6/23/34	2(3)	7	10. Little Man, You've Had A Busy Day/	
6/23/34	13	3	11. So Help Me	Columbia 2930

DATE CHARTED	PEAK POS	WKS CHRT'D	ARTIST — Record Title	Label & Number
7/28/34	**8**	4	12. I Wish I Were Twins (So I Could Love You Twice As Much)................................... most vocals by Jerry Cooper & The Harmonians	Columbia 2933

ROGER COLEMAN

2/28/53	**29**	1	1. You Say It With Your Eyes	Decca 28529

AL (JAZZBO) COLLINS
Former disc jockey

8/08/53	**22**	3	1. Little Red Riding Hood/ [N]	
8/29/53	**22**	1	2. The Three Little Pigs....................... [N] accompanied on both by jazz pianist Lou Stein; "hipster" versions of the fairy tales, originated by Steve Allen	Brunswick 86001

ARTHUR COLLINS
Arthur Collins, the leading minstrel-style dialect-comedy singer of the early 1900s, was born on 2/7/1864 in Philadelphia. His solo hits, led by the famous "Preacher and the Bear", were plentiful, but he was most famous for his many hits with Byron Harlan; Collins was also a member of the Peerless Quartet (1906-18). He died on 8/3/33 (69). (also see Big Four Quartet)

12/24/98	**3**	3	1. Zizzy Ze Zum Zum .... [C]	Edison 5452
1/28/99	**1(4)**	9	2. **Kiss Me, Honey, Do**............................... [C]	Edison 5462
2/25/99	**1(2)**	7	3. **When You Ain't Got No More Money, Well, You Needn't Come Around** .... [C] later recorded on Berliner 0758	Edison 5469
3/18/99	**1(4)**	8	4. **I Guess I'll Have To Telegraph My Baby** .... later recorded for Berliner 0883	Edison 5471
4/15/99	**1(4)**	10	5. **Hello, Ma Baby**................................ later recorded for Berliner 01004	Edison 5470
12/02/99	**1(7)**	10	6. **I'd Leave My Happy Home For You** .... also recorded for Berliner 0758	Edison 7278
2/03/00	**1(6)**	8	7. **Mandy Lee**................................... also recorded for Berliner 01289	Edison 7404
8/04/00	**1(6)**	11	8. **Ma Tiger Lily**.................................... [C] also recorded for Edison 7517 & Gram-o-Phone 156	Berliner 01291
3/16/01	**2(1)**	4	9. Cindy, I Dreams About You .... also recorded for Edison 7740	Gram-o-Phone 409
7/13/01	**3**	3	10. I Never Trouble Trouble Until Trouble Troubles Me .... [C]	Edison 7816
2/08/02	**2(2)**	5	11. Tell Me, Dusky Maiden.............................. from the Broadway musical "Sleeping Beauty and the Beast" above two: ARTHUR COLLINS & JOE NATUS	Edison 8000
7/12/02	**1(8)**	13	12. **Bill Bailey, Won't You Please Come Home** .. .. [C] also recorded for Edison 8112	Columbia 872
12/06/02	**1(3)**	8	13. **Under The Bamboo Tree**...................... [C] also recorded for Victor 1633	Edison 8215
12/20/02+	**3**	3	14. If Money Talks, It Ain't On Speaking Terms With Me.. [C]	Victor 1631
1/31/03	**4**	2	15. Down Where The Wurzburger Flows......... [C] also see Collins & Harlan	Victor 1635
6/27/03	**3**	4	16. I'm A Jonah Man .... [C] also recorded for Edison 8440	Victor 2052
9/19/03	**2(2)**	5	17. You Can't Fool All The People All The Time .. .. [C] also recorded for Edison 8460	Victor 2407
10/31/03	**1(4)**	7	18. **Good-Bye, Eliza Jane**............................	Edison 8515
12/05/03	**1(5)**	8	19. **Any Rags?**...................................... [C] also recorded for Edison 8525 & Zon-o-Phone 5635; later for Columbia 1669 & 32377	Victor 2519
5/28/04	**2(2)**	4	20. I've Got A Feelin' For You	Edison 8661
5/28/04	**4**	2	21. Hannah, Won't You Open That Door? .... [C] later recorded for Columbia 1800 & 32508	Edison 8637

DATE CHARTED	PEAK POS	WKS CHRT'D	ARTIST — Record Title	Label & Number
6/03/05	**1(11)**	14	● 22. **The Preacher And The Bear** .... [C] the first two-million-selling record, and the biggest hit of all time until 1920; also recorded for Columbia 3146 & 32720, Victor 4431, Zon-o-Phone 120, Indestructable 1087, & U.S. Everlasting 1092	Edison 9000
7/22/05	**3**	7	23. My Irish Molly O .... from the Broadway musical "Sargeant Brue"	Victor 4371
10/07/05	**2(2)**	6	24. Nobody .... [C] also recorded for Edison 9084 and Columbia 3264 & 32800	Victor 4391
10/28/05	**2(2)**	5	25. What You Goin' To Do When De Rent Comes 'Round?... [C] also recorded for Victor 4432, Edison 9111 & Zon-o-Phone 298	Columbia 3250
7/28/06	**7**	1	26. The Parson And The Turkey.................. [C]	Columbia 3416
9/01/06	**5**	1	27. Here It Comes Again .... [C] later recorded for Victor 31566	Edison 9302
10/27/06	**4**	2	28. I Don't Know Where I'm Goin', But I'm On My Way .... [C] also recorded for Edison 9357, Columbia 33005, & Zon-o-Phone 540	Victor 4804
11/16/07	**3**	4	29. If I'm Goin' To Die, I'm Goin' To Have Some Fun....................................... [C] from the Broadway musical "The Honeymooners" also recorded for Edison 9684 and Columbia 3715 disc & 33193 cylinder	Victor 5228
1/25/08	**4**	2	30. Dixie Dan .... [C] from the Broadway musical "The Gay White Way" also recorded for Columbia 33211 & Indestructable 642	Victor 5285
11/07/08	**4**	2	31. The Old-Time Rag	Edison 9956
8/21/09	**2(3)**	7	32. I Love, I Love, I Love My Wife, But Oh You Kid! .... [C] flip side of #1 hit "I Wonder Who's Kissing Her Now" by Henry Burr	Columbia 707
9/18/09	**3**	3	33. That's A-Plenty .... [C] also recorded for Columbia 724	Victor 16344
8/20/10	**3**	5	34. If He Comes In, I'm Goin' Out................. [C] also on Indestructable 1381	Columbia 845
9/10/10	**3**	5	35. Oh That Beautiful Rag .... from the Broadway musical "Up and Down Broadway" also recorded for Zon-o-Phone 5653; Collins & Harlan version on Indestructable 1424	Columbia 853
2/11/11	**3**	6	36. I Love It! .... [C] also recorded for Edison Amberol 668, Indestructable 1449, Zon-o-Phone 5690, & U.S. Everlasting 1190; Collins & Harlan version later on Victor 16937	Columbia 940
4/01/11	**10**	1	37. I'm So Tired Of Livin', I Don't Care When I Die .... [C] previously recorded in 1903 for Edison 8309	Victor 16683
4/08/11	**6**	2	38. Grizzly Bear .... [C]	Indestructable 1459
7/01/11	**2(1)**	6	39. Steamboat Bill .... [C] also recorded for Columbia 1005	Victor 16867
8/19/11	**5**	3	40. In The Land Of Harmony.......................... also recorded for U.S. Everlasting 379	Columbia 1010
11/25/11	**6**	2	41. Chicken Reel .... [C] also recorded for Columbia 1044, Zon-o-Phone 5714, & U.S. Everlasting 400	Victor 16897
12/30/11+	**4**	5	42. The Oceana Roll .... also recorded for U.S. Everlasting 433 & Zon-o-Phone 5788	Columbia 1071
1/20/12	**5**	4	43. That Mysterious Rag .... ARTHUR COLLINS & ALBERT CAMPBELL also recorded for Zon-o-Phone 5822	Columbia 1086
9/07/12	**2(1)**	6	44. When Uncle Joe Plays A Rag On His Old Banjo .... also recorded for Zon-o-Phone 5924, later for Columbia 1222; Collins & Harlan version on Edison 1117	Victor 17118
11/02/12	**6**	3	45. In Ragtime Land...................................... above two accompanied by Vess Ossman (banjo)	Victor 17126

DATE CHARTED	PEAK POS	WKS CHRT'D	ARTIST — Record Title	Label & Number
9/06/19	**9**	1	46. It's Nobody's Business But My Own.......... [C] also recorded for Okeh 1213	Emerson 9177
11/27/20	**15**	1	47. The Argentines, The Portugese, And The Greeks .... [C]	Gennett 9065

ARTHUR COLLINS & BYRON HARLAN
The most famous of all comedy singing teams; both fine vocalists, baritone Collins and tenor Harlan would typically offer minstrel-style comedy interludes in the midst of their songs.

DATE CHARTED	PEAK POS	WKS CHRT'D	ARTIST — Record Title	Label & Number
12/21/01	**2(2)**	6	1. The Wedding Of Reuben And The Maid ..... [C] from Broadway musical "Rogers Brothers in Washington"; later on Columbia disc 791	Columbia 31685
12/20/02+	**1(5)**	11	2. **Down Where The Wurzburger Flows** ...... [C] also recorded for Zon-o-Phone 5441	Edison 8238
1/10/03	**4**	2	3. Under The Bamboo Tree .... [C] also on Columbia cylinder 31910 from the Broadway musical "Sally in Our Alley"	Columbia 970
9/05/03	**1(5)**	10	4. **Harrah For Baffin's Bay** .... from the Broadway musical "The Wizard of Oz"; also recorded for Victor 31074, Edison 8447, & Zon-o-Phone 5598	Columbia 1491
10/10/03	**3**	3	5. Parody On "Hiawatha" .... [C] later recorded for Columbia 1616 & Zon-o-Phone 5736	Edison 8475
4/16/04	**2(3)**	4	6. Under The Anhauser Bush .... [C] also recorded for Columbia 1742 disc & 32409 cylinder	Victor 2668
8/20/04	**5**	1	7. Good-Bye, Fedora .... from "The Wizard of Oz"	Columbia 1803
2/25/05	**2(3)**	7	8. Coax Me.. [C] also recorded for Victor 4174, Columbia 3052 & 32621, & Zon-o-Phone 114	Edison 8907
7/15/05	**2(1)**	7	9. Tammany.. [C] from the Broadway musical "Fantana" also recorded for Edison 8979	Victor 4373
8/26/05	**6**	1	10. Come Along, Little Girl, Come Along .... also recorded for Columbia 3241 & 32777; Zon-o-Phone 189	Edison 9028
12/30/05	**7**	1	11. In My Merry Oldsmobile .... inspired by the first transcontinental auto race, won by an Oldsmobile	Zon-o-Phone 290
3/10/06	**5**	1	12. The Leader Of The German Band................. also recorded for Edison 9115	Victor 4555
5/26/06	**8**	1	13. Paddle Your Own Canoe........................ [C] also recorded for Victor 4602	Edison 9184
7/28/06	**4**	1	14. Out In An Automobile .... [C] previously recorded for Columbia 3320 & 32872	Victor 4709
11/03/06	**4**	3	15. I'm Crazy 'Bout It! .... [C] also recorded for Edison 9343 & Columbia 3452	Victor 4850
11/24/06	**7**	1	16. Susan, Kiss Me Good And Hard .... [C] also recorded for Victor 4850, Columbia 3494 & 33010	Edison 9377
12/29/06+	**1(2)**	9	17. **Camp Meetin' Time**............................. [C] later recorded for Victor 4995	Columbia 3513
12/29/06	**7**	1	18. Would You Leave Your Happy Home For Me?.	Columbia 3514
3/16/07	**4**	2	19. Good-A-Bye, John! .... from the Broadway musical "The Red Mill"; also recorded for Columbia 3610 & 33105, & Zon-o-Phone 664	Victor 4941
6/22/07	**4**	2	20. Bake Dat Chicken Pie............................ [C] also recorded for Edison 9499, Columbia 3610 & 33105, Zon-o-Phone 664	Victor 5116
6/29/07	**8**	1	21. That Welcome Mat Ain't Out For Me .... [C] also recorded for Columbia 3650 & 85121	Victor 5092
7/06/07	**4**	2	22. And A Little Bit More .... [C] also on Columbia cylinder 33150; Arthur Collins versions on Edison 9582 & Victor 5233	Columbia 3649
1/25/08	**10**	1	23. Who Do You Love?............................... [C] also recorded for Edison 9727, Columbia 3712 & 33190, U.S. Everlasting 335	Victor 5288
3/28/08	**5**	1	24. Come On And Kiss Yo' Baby .... [C] also recorded for Columbia 3741 & 33209, Zon-o-Phone 5389	Victor 5312
5/16/08	**2(4)**	6	25. My Gal Irene .... [C] also recorded for Edison 9823, Indestructable 742, & U.S. Everlasting 336	Victor 5399

DATE CHARTED	PEAK POS	WKS CHRT'D	ARTIST — Record Title	Label & Number
7/25/08	**8**	1	26. Honey, Won't You Please Come Down? ..... [C] also recorded for Victor 5471, Columbia 85160, & Indestructable 776	Edison 9858
10/24/08	**4**	2	27. Down In Jungle Town .... [C] also recorded for Edison 9941 & Indestructable 816	Victor 5484
11/28/08	**6**	1	28. It Looks Like A Big Night To-Night .... [C]	Edison 9985
1/30/09	**4**	3	29. Alabam' .... [C] also recorded for Columbia 615, Edison 10075, Zon-o-Phone 5192, & Indestructable 954; from the Broadway musical "A Broken Idol"	Victor 5618
1/30/09	**6**	1	30. Honey Lou .... [C] also recorded for Columbia 614, Edison 10037, Zon-o-Phone 5192, & Indestructable 932	Victor 5605
2/06/09	**1(6)**	11	31. **The Right Church, But The Wrong Pew** . [C]	Columbia 621
3/13/09	**2(3)**	5	32. Down Among The Sugar Cane .... [C] also recorded for Edison 10110 & Indestructable 1015	Victor 5670
4/24/09	**4**	2	33. The Sweetest Gal In Town .... [C] also recorded for Columbia 633 & Indestructable 977	Victor 16262
4/24/09	**7**	1	34. Yip-I-Addy-I-Ay! .... [C] from the Broadway musical "The Merry Widow Burlesque"	Edison 10094
10/16/09	**4**	2	35. My Wife's Gone To The Country (Hurrah! Hurrah!) .... [C] also recorded for Columbia 724	Victor 5736
12/25/09	**7**	1	36. Down At The Huskin' Bee .... also recorded for Edison 10234, Indestructable 1096, & U.S. Everlasting 342	Victor 16365
1/22/10	**3**	5	37. On A Monkey Honeymoon .... [C] also recorded for Edison Amberol 162 & Indestructable 1089	Victor 16426
2/24/10+	**10**	1	38. I'm A-Dreamin' Of You	Columbia 3326
3/26/10	**6**	2	39. Down Where The Big Bananas Grow .... [C] also recorded for Columbia 5138, Indestructable 3011, & U.S. Everlasting 1013	Victory 16446
4/23/10	**8**	1	40. Some Day, Melinda .... later recorded for Victor 16489; also on Indestructable 1268 & U.S. Everlasting 219	Edison 10326
4/30/10	**2(3)**	8	41. That Mesmerizing Mendelssohn Tune .... ragtime treatment of Mendelssohn's "Spring Song" also recorded for Columbia 801, Edison 50063, Edison Amberol 395, Zon-o-Phone 5659, & U.S. Everlasting 3065 flip side of Columbia version (Columbia 801): "The Mississippi Stoker" (#4) by Bert Williams	Victor 16472
5/21/10	**3**	5	42. The Cubanola Glide .... [C] also recorded for Edison 10500, Edison Amberol 432, Indestructable 1305, & U.S. Everlasting 1080	Columbia 800
7/02/10	**7**	2	43. Moonlight In Jungle Land .... [C] also recorded for Columbia 814, Edison Amberol 415, Indestructable 3071, & U.S. Everlasting 1034	Victor 16483
9/17/10	**3**	5	44. Sugar Moon .... [C] also recorded for Columbia 853, Edison Amberol 496, Zon-o-Phone 5646, Indestructable 3121, & U.S. Everlasting 1049	Victor 16540
12/03/10	**5**	2	45. Casey Jones .... also recorded for Zon-o-Phone 5677; Collins solo version on Indestructable 3163	Columbia 907
1/28/11	**3**	4	46. The Honeymoon Glide .... [C]	Indestructable 1437
2/04/11	**1(5)**	9	47. **Under The Yum Yum Tree** .... [C] later recorded for Victor 16836; also Edison Amberol 646, Indestructable 3178, & U.S. Everlasting 1100	Columbia 943
3/11/11	**8**	1	48. Oh That Moonlight Glide .... [C] also recorded for Columbia 954 & Indestructable 1497	Victor 5807
3/25/11	**1(5)**	10	49. **Put Your Arms Around Me, Honey** .... [C] also recorded for Columbia 978, Zon-o-Phone 5677, & Indestructable 3186	Victor 16708
8/19/11	**10**	1	50. The Mississippi Dippy Dip .... [C] also recorded for Columbia 1005, Edison Amberol 720, Indestructable 3243, & Zon-o-Phone 5734	Victor 16870

DATE CHARTED	PEAK POS	WKS CHRT'D	ARTIST — Record Title	Label & Number
9/16/11	1(10)	17	51. **Alexander's Ragtime Band** .... also recorded for Columbia 1032, Indestructable 3251, Edison Amberol 720, U.S. Everlasting 399 & Zon-o-Phone 5766 flip side: "The Oceana Roll" (POS #4) by Eddie Morton	Victor 16908
2/03/12	2(5)	10	52. Everybody's Doing It Now..................... also recorded for Columbia 1123 & U.S. Everlasting 445	Victor 17020
5/04/12	8	2	53. I'm Going Back To Dixie............................ also recorded for Zon-o-Phone 5879	Columbia 1112
9/14/12	8	2	54. That Precious Little Thing Called Love (The Riddle Song) .... [C] also recorded for Columbia 1163, U.S. Everlasting 1501, & Zon-o-Phone 5914	Victor 17094
10/05/12	3	6	55. Oh! You Circus Day............................ [C] also recorded for U.S. Everlasting 1545	Columbia 1187
11/16/12	3	5	56. Waiting For The Robert E. Lee	Edison Amb. 1144
11/30/12	9	1	57. Ragtime Soldier Man .... [C] also recorded for Columbia 1201	Victor 17150
1/25/13	7	2	58. Row! Row! Row! .... from the Broadway musical "Ziegfeld Follies of 1912"; also on U.S. Everlasting 1609	Edison Amb. 1529
2/08/13	1(6)	12	59. When The Midnight Choo Choo Leaves For Alabam' .... also recorded for Victor 17246, Edison Amberol 1719, Indestructable 3289, & U.S. Everlasting 1637	Columbia 1246
3/08/13+	5	4	60. Down In Dear Old New Orleans...................	Columbia 1260
4/19/13	2(2)	5	61. Melinda's Wedding Day....................... also recorded for Victor 17295 & Edison Amberol 1844 flip side of "Row, Row, Row" (#8) by the American Quartet	Victor 17295
5/24/13	6	3	62. Here Comes My Daddy Now (Oh Pop-Oh Pop- Oh Pop) .... [C] also recorded for Columbia 1277 flip side of "At the Devil's Ball" (#6) by the Peerless Quartet	Victor 17315
7/12/13	4	4	63. Snookey Ookums.......................... [C] also recorded for Edison Amberol 1796 & Indestructable 3296	Columbia 1317
12/27/13+	3	9	64. The International Rag/ also recorded for Columbia 1406	
12/27/13+	6	2	65. On The Honeymoon Express .... [C] also recorded for Columbia 1420 & Edison Amberol 2130	Victor 17431
1/03/14	5	4	66. On The Old Fall River Line	Columbia 1419
2/07/14	8	2	67. Underneath The Tango Moon .... [C] also recorded for Columbia 1421 & Edison Amberol 2159	Victor 17480
2/21/14	4	5	68. Down In Chattanooga .... [C] also recorded for Columbia 1453 flip side of "When You're All Dressed Up and No Place To Go" (#3) by Billy Murray	Victor 17527
5/16/14	1(3)	8	69. **I Love The Ladies**................................ [C]	Columbia 1513
6/06/14	9	1	70. Camp Meeting Band .... [C] also recorded for Columbia 1496 & Edison Amberol 2268	Victor 17537
6/27/14	3	5	71. Celebratin' Day In Tennessee.................. [C] also recorded for Edison Amberol 2314	Columbia 1525
9/26/14	9	1	72. Eagle Rock .... from the Broadway musical "The Passing Show of 1914"	Victor 17610
10/10/14	1(2)	11	73. **The Aba Daba Honeymoon**.................... [C] also recorded for Columbia 1600 & Edison Amberol 2468	Victor 17620
3/03/15	7	2	74. On The 5:15..	Columbia 1675
8/14/15	9	1	75. Minstrel Parade .... [C] from the Broadway musical "Watch Your Step"	Victor 17783
8/21/15	8	1	76. Auntie Skinner's Chicken Dinner .... [C] flip side of "The Little Ford Rambled Right Along" (#3) by Billy Murray	Victor 17755
9/04/15	8	1	77. Memphis Blues/	
9/11/15	2(2)	6	78. Alabama Jubilee .... also recorded for Victor 17825	Columbia 1721
10/16/15	7	3	79. Just Try To Picture Me Down Home In Tennessee..	Victor 17841

DATE CHARTED	PEAK POS	WKS CHRT'D	ARTIST — Record Title	Label & Number
10/23/15	**10**	1	80. **Those Charlie Chaplin Feet** .... [C] possibly the first popular song about a movie star	Columbia 1780
2/12/16	**9**	1	81. **You'd Never Know That Old Home Town Of** **Mine** .... also recorded for Victor 17911	Columbia 1867
7/08/16	**7**	2	82. **Yaaka Hula Hickey Dula** .... [C] from the Broadway musical "Robinson Crusoe, Jr."; also recorded for Pathe 30426	Victor 18014
10/21/16	**1(2)**	9	83. **Oh How She Could Yacki Hacki Wicki** **Wachi Woo (That's Love In** **Honolulu)** .... [C] also recorded for Columbia 2043, Edison 50372, & Edison Amberol 2965	Victor 18110
2/10/17	**2(2)**	6	84. **They're Wearing 'Em Higher In Hawaii** ..... [C] Arthur Collins version on Emerson 7142	Victor 18210
7/28/17	**8**	1	85. **Night Time In Little Italy** .... [C] also recorded for Emerson 17156	Victor 18262
10/27/17	**5**	4	86. **Lily Of The Valley**............................... [C] later recorded for Victor 18398	Columbia 2296
1/12/18	**3**	4	87. **The Old Grey Mare**............................... [C] also recorded for Columbia 2382, Emerson 7298, & Imperial 5512 derived from 1858 song "Down in Alabam'", which under new title "Old Abe Lincoln" was used in the 1860 presidential campaign	Victor 18387
3/30/18	**1(1)**	5	88. **Dark Town Strutters' Ball** .... also recorded for Indestructable 3447 flip side of Al Jolson's #1 hit "I'm All Bound Round for the Mason Dixon Line" - the second double-sided #1 record	Columbia 2478
11/02/18	**9**	1	89. **When Uncle Joe Steps Into France**.............. also recorded for Columbia 2599	Victor 18492

DOROTHY COLLINS
Born Marjorie Chandler in Canada, Dorothy sang in 1940s with
Raymond Scott, then became famous on TV's "Hit Parade".

COLONIAL CLUB ORCHESTRA
Bob Haring, leader

12/28/29	**19**	1	1. **Find Me A Primitive Man**........................... vocal: Libby Holman from the Broadway musical "Fifty Million Frenchmen"	Brunswick 4666
4/19/30	**4**	5	2. **Stein Song (University Of Maine)**................. written in 1901 as an instrumental march, based on one of Brahms' "Hungarian Dances"; adapted in 1910 with lyrics as University of Maine's theme	Brunswick 4748
7/19/30	**8**	6	3. **I Am Only Human, After All**....................... from the Broadway musical "Garrick Gaieties of 1930"	Brunswick 4848
8/16/30	**8**	4	4. **Hittin' The Bottle**..................................... from the Broadway musical "Earl Carroll's Vanities of 1930" above two vocals: Irving Kaufman	Brunswick 4858

JERRY COLONNA
Popular comedian in vaudeville and radio

7/06/40	**30**	1	1. **Who's Yehoodi?**................................... [C]	Columbia 35512
7/26/45	**9**	2	2. **Bell-Bottom Trousers** .... based on a traditional sea chantey published in 1907	Capitol 204

COLUMBIA COMEDY TRIO
Billy Murray, Byron Harlan, and Steve Porter

11/30/07	**10**	1	1. **At The Village Post Office** .... [C] also released on Columbia cylinder 33182	Columbia 3704

COLUMBIA MALE QUARTET
Henry Burr, Albert Campbell, Steve Porter, and Tom Daniels (latter
two to be replaced by Frank Stanley and Arthur Collins) - all
group hits listed under their subsequent name, the Peerless
Quartet.

COLUMBIA MIXED DOUBLE QUARTET

8/19/16	**1(2)**	6	1. **America/**	
8/19/16	**5**	3	2. The Battle Hymn Of The Republic.............	Columbia 2012

DATE CHARTED	PEAK POS	WKS CHRT'D	ARTIST — Record Title	Label & Number
			COLUMBIA MIXED QUARTET	
			Grace Kerns, Mildred Potter, Charles Harrison, and Frank Croxton	
8/17/12	**6**	2	1. The Battle Hymn Of The Republic..............	Columbia 1155
12/23/16	**5**	2	2. Hark! The Herald Angels Sing .... [X]	Columbia 2104
			COLUMBIA ORCHESTRA	
			Charles A. Prince, director (also see Prince's Orchestra)	
4/11/03	**3**	4	1. Hiawatha .... [I]	Columbia 1155
3/06/20	**9**	1	2. William Tell Overture .... [I]	Columbia 6129
4/24/20	**10**	1	3. That Naughty Waltz .... [I]	Columbia 6139
			vocal: Henry Burr and Albert Campbell	
5/19/23	**10**	1	4. Love Sends A Little Gift Of Roses .... [I]	Columbia 3816
			Columbia Dance Orchestra	
			COLUMBIA SAXOPHONE SEXTETTE	
7/19/19	**2(2)**	5	1. Chong... [I]	Columbia 2730
10/25/19	**10**	1	2. Where The Lanterns Glow .... [I]	Columbia 2759
			COLUMBIA STELLAR QUARTET	
			Original members Charles Harrison, John Barnes Wells, Frank Croxton, and Andrea Sarto; in 1915 Wells was replaced by Henry Burr, who soon left to be succeeded by Reed Miller. Guest vocalists sometimes recorded with the group, as noted.	
5/18/12	**3**	6	1. Take Me Back To The Garden Of Love	Columbia 1141
			CHARLES HARRISON & COLUMBIA STELLAR QUARTET	
1/31/14	**9**	1	2. The Girl I Left Behind Me	Columbia 1440
4/15/16	**9**	1	3. Some Day I'll Wander Back Again................	Columbia 5785
			MARGARET KEYES & COLUMBIA STELLAR QUARTET	
11/24/17	**3**	4	4. Tramp, Tramp, Tramp (The Boys Are Marching)....................................	Columbia 2357
2/09/18	**1(1)**	6	5. **The Battle Hymn Of The Republic**............	Columbia 2367
			above two: CHARLES HARRISON & COLUMBIA STELLAR QUARTET	
2/23/18	**4**	3	6. There's A Long, Long Trail........................	Columbia 2452
5/11/18	**4**	3	7. Pack Up Your Troubles In Your Old Kit Bag...	Columbia 6028
			above two: OSCAR SEAGLE & COLUMBIA STELLAR QUARTET	
10/26/18	**9**	2	8. My Old Kentucky Home	Columbia 6059
			LUCY GATES & COLUMBIA STELLAR QUARTET	
2/08/19	**8**	2	9. The Old Folks At Home...........................	Columbia 6082
			OSCAR SEAGLE & COLUMBIA STELLAR QUARTET	
11/26/21	**11**	1	10. My Gal Sal...	Columbia 3436
3/04/22	**9**	1	11. Swanee River Moon	Columbia 3432
			COLUMBIANS	
			Ben Selvin directed many of the band's 1927-29 recordings	
1/28/22	**12**	1	1. Say It With Music .... [I]	Columbia 3472
			from the Broadway musical "Music Box Revue of 1921"	
3/17/23	**8**	1	2. Sixty Seconds Ev'ry Minute (I Think Of You)..................................... [I]	Columbia 3745
8/25/23	**11**	1	3. Swingin' Down The Lane........................ [I]	Columbia 3874
10/27/23	**14**	1	4. I Cried For You.................................... [I]	Columbia 3917
1/07/28	**11**	3	5. Broken Dreams	Columbia 1135
8/10/29	**5**	5	6. Pagan Love Song	Columbia 1817
			theme from the film "Pagan" above two directed by Ben Selvin	
			RUSS COLUMBO	
			For three years Russ Columbo was one of America's three most popular romantic singers along with Bing Crosby and Rudy Vallee. He previously sang with Gus Arnheim, and co-wrote several of his own hits, including "Prisoner of Love". A tragic pistol accident took his life on 9/2/34 (26).	
9/26/31	**5**	8	1. You Call It Madness (But I Call It Love)/	
			Russ' theme song	
10/03/31	**19**	1	2. Sweet And Lovely	Victor 22802
10/10/31	**13**	3	3. Guilty	Victor 22801
11/07/31	**3**	5	4. Good Night, Sweetheart	Victor 22826
			from Broadway musical "Earl Carroll's Vanities of 1931"	

DATE CHARTED	PEAK POS	WKS CHRT'D	ARTIST — Record Title	Label & Number
12/19/31	**13**	3	5. Where The Blue Of The Night (Meets The Gold Of The Day)/	
1/02/32	**16**	1	6. Prisoner Of Love... accompanied on 1, 2, & 6 by Nat Shilkret's Orchestra	Victor 22867
2/13/32	**12**	2	7. You're My Everything/ from the Broadway musical "The Laugh Parade"	
2/27/32	**14**	3	8. Just Friends .... accompanied on 5, 7, & 8 by Leonard Joy's Orchestra	Victor 22909
5/14/32	**18**	1	9. Paradise..	Victor 22976
8/27/32	**6**	4	10. As You Desire Me	Victor 24076
9/29/34	**18**	1	11. When You're In Love .... accompanied by Jimmie Grier's Orchestra from the film "Wake Up and Dream"	Brunswick 6972

COMMANDERS
(also see Dolores Gray)

6/06/53	**25**	1	1. Swanee River Boogie .... [I]	Decca 28659

PERRY COMO
Born on 5/18/12 in Canonsburg, Pa., Perry left his hometown barber shop to sing with Freddie Carlone's local band in 1933; about four years later Ted Weems hired him as featured vocalist. When the Weems band broke up in 1942 he secured a local CBS radio show, and once he started recording the following year there was no stopping him. Perry's relaxed style and romantic vocals made his TV series a popular favorite from the early 50s to 1963, and he has continued as an enduring musical institution.

8/28/43	**18**	1	1. Goodbye, Sue/	
11/20/43	**18**	1	2. There'll Soon Be A Rainbow	Victor 1538
1/15/44	**19**	2	3. Have I Stayed Away Too Long?	Victor 1548
4/29/44	**8**	7	4. Long Ago (And Far Away)/ from the film "Cover Girl"	
4/29/44	**12**	3	5. I Love You... from Broadway musical "Mexican Hayride"	Victor 1569
8/26/44	**13**	3	6. Lili Marlene	Victor 1592
1/27/45	**10**	2	7. I Dream Of You/	
3/03/45	**12**	1	8. Confessin'	Victor 1629
3/17/45	**14**	2	9. More And More.. from the film "Can't Help Singing"	Victor 1630
6/16/45	**15**	1	10. Temptation... from the film "Going Hollywood" accompanied by Ted Steele's Orchestra	Victor 1658
7/21/45	**4**	17	● 11. I'm Gonna Love That Gal/ records 11-18 accompanied by Russell Case's Orchestra	
7/28/45	**3**	13	12. If I Loved You .... from the Broadway musical "Carousel"	Victor 1676
8/18/45	**1(10)**	19	● 13. **Till The End Of Time**/ sold over two million copies; song based on Chopin's "Polonaise in A-Flat Major"; from the film "A Song to Remember"	
8/25/45	**9**	11	14. (Did You Ever Get) That Feeling In The Moonlight	Victor 1709
12/08/45+	**3**	14	● 15. Dig You Later (A Hubba-Hubba-Hubba)/	
12/29/45	**12**	3	16. Here Comes Heaven Again....................... above two from the film "Doll Face"	Victor 1750
2/02/46+	**5**	8	● 17. I'm Always Chasing Rainbows/ from the Broadway musical "Oh, Look!"; featured in film "The Dolly Sisters"; melody adapted from Chopin's "Fantasie Impromptu in C-Sharp Minor"	
2/09/46	**5**	14	18. You Won't Be Satisfied (Until You Break My Heart).. with the Satisfiers on 14, 17, & 18	Victor 1788
3/30/46	**1(3)**	21	● 19. **Prisoner Of Love**/	
5/11/46	**8**	5	20. All Through The Day.............................. from the film "Centennial Summer" above two accompanied by Andre Kostelanetz Orchestra	RCA Victor 1814

DATE CHARTED	PEAK POS	WKS CHRT'D	ARTIST — Record Title	Label & Number
6/01/46	4	13	21. They Say It's Wonderful/ from the Broadway musical "Annie Get Your Gun"	
6/08/46	14	4	22.　If You Were The Only Girl In The World......	RCA Victor 1857
6/29/46	1(1)	17	23. **Surrender/**	
8/17/46	19	1	24.　More Than You Know............................. from the 1929 Broadway musical "Great Day!"	RCA Victor 1877
10/12/46	21	2	25. Temptation................................[R]	Victor 1658
10/12/46	22	2	26. A Garden In the Rain	RCA Victor 1916
11/16/46+	19	1	27. If I'm Lucky... movie title song	RCA Victor 1945
12/28/46+	9	7	28. Sonata/	
2/01/47	19	1	29.　That's The Beginning Of The End	RCA Victor 2033
12/28/46	10	1	30. Winter Wonderland...............................[X] with the Satisfiers accompanied on 21-27 & 30 by Russ Case & His Orchestra	RCA Victor 1968
3/08/47	21	4	31. I Want To Thank Your Folks/	
5/17/47	21	3	32.　That's Where I Came In	RCA Victor 2117
5/24/47	1(3)	13	● 33. **Chi-Baba, Chi-Baba (My Bambino Go To Sleep)**	Victor 2259
7/12/47	2(1)	19	34. When You Were Sweet Sixteen..................... accompanied on 28-29 & 31-34 by Lloyd Shaffer's Orchestra with the Satisfiers on 30, 33 & 34	RCA Victor 2259
8/02/47	2(5)	17	35. I Wonder Who's Kissing Her Now................. Perry Como with Ted Weems' Orchestra; recorded on 10/5/39; from the Broadway musical "The Prince of Tonight"; title song of the 1947 film	Decca 25078
10/25/47	11	2	36. So Far/	
11/01/47	25	1	37.　A Fellow Needs A Girl .... above two from the Broadway musical "Allegro" with Russ Case's Orchestra	RCA Victor 2402
12/06/47+	21	3	38. Two Loves Have I .... song published in 1931	RCA Victor 2545
12/27/47	23	1	39. White Christmas..................................[X] accompanied by Lloyd Shaffer's Orchestra	RCA Victor 1970
1/24/48	21	4	40. Pianissimo..	RCA Victor 2593
3/13/48	4	18	● 41. Because	RCA Victor 2653
3/13/48	20	6	42. Haunted Heart .... from the Broadway musical "Inside U.S.A."	RCA Victor 2713
4/03/48	20	3	43. Laroo, Laroo, Lilli Bolero	RCA Victor 2734
7/31/48	18	14	44. Rambling Rose .... above four accompanied by Russell Case Orchestra, with the Satisfiers on 44	RCA Victor 2947
1/08/49	4	17	45. Far Away Places................................... accompanied by Henri Rene Orchestra	RCA Victor 3316
1/15/49	20	6	46. N'yot N'yow (The Pussycat Song) .... with the Fontane Sisters	RCA Victor 3288
2/26/49	18	3	47. Blue Room.. from the Broadway musical "The Girl Friend"	RCA Victor 3329
3/19/49	2(1)	25	48. Forever And Ever/ adapted from a Swiss waltz accompanied on nearly all 1949-52 records by Mitchell Ayres' Orchestra	
4/09/49	11	15	49.　I Don't See Me In Your Eyes Anymore	RCA Vic. 78-3347 also released on RCA Victor 45-2892
4/09/49	1(2)	15	50. **"A" - You're Adorable** .... with the Fontane Sisters also released on RCA Victor 45-2899	RCA Vic. 78-3381
4/30/49	1(5)	26	● 51. **Some Enchanted Evening/**	
4/30/49	5	16	52.　Bali Ha'i.. above two from the Broadway musical "South Pacific" also released on RCA Victor 45-2896	RCA Vic. 78-3402
7/09/49	23	2	53. Just One Way To Say I Love You/	
7/16/49	15	10	54.　Let's Take An Old-Fashioned Walk .... above two from the Broadway musical "Miss Liberty" also released on RCA Victor 45-2931	RCA Vic. 78-3469

DATE CHARTED	PEAK POS	WKS CHRT'D	ARTIST — Record Title	Label & Number
9/03/49	**23**	2	55. Give Me Your Hand .... also released on RCA Victor 45-2929	RCA Vic. 78-3521
10/08/49+	**3**	19	56. A Dreamer's Holiday .... also released on RCA Victor 45-3036	RCA Vic. 78-3543
11/26/49	**18**	8	57. I Wanna Go Home .... above two with the Fontane Sisters also released on RCA Victor 45-3082	RCA Vic. 78-3586
12/17/49	**28**	2	58. The Lord's Prayer/ [X]	
12/24/49	**22**	3	59. Ave Maria .... [X] also released on RCA Victor 45-0071 with choir, organ, and Mitchell Ayres' Orchestra	RCA Vic. 78-0436
1/28/50	**14**	6	60. Bibbidi-Bobbidi-Boo.............................. from the animated film "Cinderella"	RCA Vic. 78-3113
4/29/50	**1(2)**	17	61. **Hoop-Dee-Doo/** above two with the Fontane Sisters	
4/29/50	**16**	5	62. On The Outgoing Tide............................	RCA Victor 3747
8/12/50	**25**	2	63. I Cross My Fingers .... with the Fontane Sisters	RCA Victor 3846
9/30/50	**7**	12	64. Patricia.. accompanied by Russell Case's Orchestra	RCA Victor 3905
10/21/50	**3**	18	65. A Bushel And A Peck .... PERRY COMO & BETTY HUTTON from the Broadway musical "Guys and Dolls"	RCA Victor 3930
12/09/50+	**5**	17	66. You're Just In Love............................... with the Fontane Sisters from the Broadway musical "Call Me Madam"	RCA Victor 3945
1/13/51	**1(8)**	24	● 67. **If/** song published in 1934	
1/13/51	**12**	8	68. Zing Zing-Zoom Zoom .... accompanied by Sigmund Romberg Orchestra	RCA Victor 3997
4/28/51	**27**	1	69. Hello, Young Lovers .... from the Broadway musical "The King and I"	RCA Victor 4112
6/23/51	**20**	2	70. There's No Boat Like A Rowboat/	
6/23/51	**25**	2	71. There's A Big Blue Cloud (Next To Heaven)....	RCA Victor 4158
10/13/51	**24**	4	72. Rollin' Stone/	
10/20/51	**28**	1	73. With All My Heart And Soul	RCA Victor 4269
12/15/51+	**19**	3	74. It's Beginning To Look Like Christmas ..... [X] above three with the Fontane Sisters	RCA Victor 4314
1/26/52	**16**	4	75. Tulips And Heather/	
2/16/52	**12**	10	76. Please, Mr. Sun	RCA Victor 4453
3/08/52	**23**	1	77. Noodlin' Rag	RCA Victor 4542
5/03/52	**18**	8	78. One Little Candle	RCA Victor 4631
6/14/52	**3**	18	79. Maybe/	
6/14/52	**19**	6	80. Watermelon Weather............................ above two: PERRY COMO & EDDIE FISHER	RCA Victor 4744
10/04/52	**22**	1	81. My Love And Devotion............................	RCA Victor 4877
11/01/52	**19**	1	82. To Know You (Is To Love You) .... 77, 81 & 82 with the Fontane Sisters	RCA Victor 4959
12/06/52+	**1(5)**	21	● 83. **Don't Let The Stars Get In Your Eyes/**	
12/07/52+	**30**	1	84. Lies .... above two with the Ramblers	RCA Victor 5064
12/27/52	**27**	2	85. Winter Wonderland.......................... [X-R] 67, 69-85 accompanied by Mitchell Ayres' Orchestra	RCA Victor 1968
2/14/53	**6**	12	86. Wild Horses/ adapted from Robert Schumann's "Wilder Reiter" ("Wild Horseman")	
2/21/53	**17**	2	87. I Confess..	RCA Victor 5152
4/25/53	**3**	16	88. Say You're Mine Again/	
5/09/53	**11**	7	89. My One And Only Heart .... above two with the Ramblers	RCA Victor 5277

DATE CHARTED	PEAK POS	WKS CHRT'D	ARTIST — Record Title	Label & Number
6/20/53	1(4)	22	90. **No Other Love/** based on Richard Rodgers' "Beneath the Southern Cross" from the TV documentary series "Victory at Sea"	
9/05/53	30	1	91. Keep It Gay .... accompanied on above two by Henri Rene's Orchestra above two from the Broadway musical "Me and Juliet"	RCA Victor 5317
10/24/53	11	5	92. Pa-Paya Mama/	
10/31/53	9	13	93. You Alone	RCA Victor 5447
3/06/54	1(8)	22	● 94. **Wanted/**	
3/06/54	24	1	95. Look Out The Window (And See How I'm Standing In The Rain)...........................	RCA Victor 5647
6/19/54	15	5	96. Hit And Run Affair/	
6/19/54	21	4	97. There Never Was A Night So Beautiful........ accompanied on 86-89 & 92-97 by Hugo Winterhalter's Orchestra	RCA Victor 5749
10/02/54	4	18	● 98. Papa Loves Mambo/	
10/16/54	22	4	99. The Things I Didn't Do...........................	RCA Victor 5857
12/18/54+	8	4	100. Home For The Holidays........................... [X] accompanied on above three by Mitchell Ayres' Orchestra	RCA Victor 5950

EDDIE CONDON
Renowned jazz guitarist who played with Louis Armstrong, Fats Waller, Riley-Farley band, and many others; died on 8/4/73 (67).

ZEZ CONFREY & HIS ORCHESTRA
Real name Edward Elzear Confrey; his many piano compositions remained popular for years ("Stumbling" in addition to hits below). Zez died in 1972 (77).

6/04/21	5	5	1. Kitten On The Keys............................... [I]	Brunswick 2082
7/15/22	5	4	2. Kitten On The Keys............................... [I] new version	Victor 18900
10/08/27	18	1	3. Dizzy Fingers .... [I]	Victor 20777

RAY CONNIFF
Trombonist-arranger with Bunny Berigan, Bob Crosby, Harry James, Vaughn Monroe, and Artie Shaw bands; later conductor-arranger on many hit albums in the 50s and 60s.

DOLLY CONNOLLY
Wife of composer Percy Wenrich

11/25/11	7	2	1. Red Rose Rag..	Columbia 1028
4/06/12	3	6	2. Moonlight Bay	Columbia 1128
5/11/12	7	2	3. Ragtime Mocking Bird................................	Columbia 1126
10/19/12	4	5	4. Waiting For The Robert E. Lee	Columbia 1197

FLORENCIO CONSTANTINO
Spanish tenor who sang The Metropolitan Opera in 1910-11; died on 11/19/20 (51).

10/26/07	7	1	1. Rigoletto - E Il Sol Dell Prima (Love Is The Sun)... [F] ALICE NIELSEN & FLORENCIO CONSTANTINO	Columbia 3681

DICK CONTINO
Popular accordionist

12/04/54	23	1	1. Yours .... [I]	Mercury 70455

CONWAY'S BAND
Patrick Conway, director of popular concert band

11/23/12	6	3	1. Moonlight Bay Medley .... [I]	Victor 17155
11/06/15	5	3	2. Ragging The Scale .... [I]	Victor 17850
9/30/16	9	1	3. Have A Heart - "Ziegfeld Follies Of 1915" Medley .... [I]	Victor 35571
9/22/17	8	1	4. Indiana .... [I]	Victor 35645
8/09/19	4	5	5. Spirit Of Independence March .... [I]	Victor 18559
3/20/20	9	1	6. Tents Of Arabs..................................... [I]	Okeh 4071

DATE CHARTED	PEAK POS	WKS CHRT'D	ARTIST — Record Title	Label & Number
			LAWRENCE (PIANO ROLL) COOK Boogie-woogie pianist	
4/15/50	**13**	11	1. The Old Piano Roll Blues............................ with the Jim Dandies	Abbey 15003
9/29/51	**22**	2	2. Down Yonder .... [I]	Abbey 15053
			HARRY COOL Sang with Dick Jurgens band from 1939-43	
10/19/46	**12**	2	1. Rumors Are Flying.................................... HARRY COOL & MINDY CARSON	Signature 15043
			FRANK COOMBS Died on 10/31/41 (70).	
1/27/12	**3**	5	1. The Harbor Of Love................................... FRANK COOMBS & WILLIAM H. THOMPSON	Columbia 1087
			COON-SANDERS ORCHESTRA Carleton Coon and Joe Sanders led a Kansas City-based band widely popularized through their NBC radio show; Coon died on 5/3/32 (38) and Sanders on 5/14/65 (70).	
8/20/21	**9**	1	1. Some Little Bird .... [I]	Columbia 3403
9/20/24	**10**	1	2. Night Hawk Blues .... vocal: Sanders & Coon	Victor 19316
11/28/25	**11**	1	3. Yes Sir, That's My Baby .... vocal: Carleton Coon	Victor 19745
5/29/26	**15**	1	4. Flamin' Mamie .... above three: "Coon-Sanders' Original Nighthawk Orchestra"	Victor 19922
4/07/28	**19**	1	5. Is She My Girl Friend?	Victor 21148
9/22/28	**20**	1	6. Ready For The River	Victor 21501
11/17/28	**16**	2	7. Down Where The Sun Goes Down .... above four vocals: Joe Sanders	Victor 21546
7/06/29	**16**	2	8. Little Orphan Annie	Victor 21895
11/16/29	**13**	2	9. I Gotta Great Big Date With A Little Bitta Girl..	Victor 22123
4/30/32	**20**	1	10. Keepin' Out Of Mischief Now .... above three vocals: Joe Sanders	Victor 22969
			COWBOY COPAS Lloyd T. (Cowboy) Copas, Oklahoma-born country singer and guitarist, who recorded one of the first versions of "Tennessee Waltz" (1948); died in an air crash on 3/5/63 (49).	
12/29/51+	**15**	12	1. Don't Leave My Poor Heart Breaking........... with Elliot Lawrence and R. Patton	King 15137
			COPLEY PLAZA ORCHESTRA - see BOB HARING	
			JILL COREY Real name Norma Jean Speranza	
1/16/54	**22**	1	1. Robe Of Calvary .... accompanied by Percy Faith's Orchestra	Columbia 40123
			DON CORNELL Popular singer-guitarist who worked from late 30s with many bands but achieved greatest success with Sammy Kaye ("It Isn't Fair") from 1946-50.	
10/21/50	**28**	1	1. I Need You So .... accompanied by Hugo Winterhalter's Orchestra	RCA Victor 3884
3/22/52	**5**	19	2. I'll Walk Alone .... from the film "With A Song In My Heart"	Coral 60659
4/26/52	**3**	17	● 3. I'm Yours	Coral 60690
7/19/52	**20**	3	4. This Is The Beginning Of The End .... accompanied on 2-4, 6-9, 11 & 13 by Norman Leyden's Orchestra	Coral 60748
9/27/52	**17**	6	5. You'll Never Get Away.............................. TERESA BREWER & DON CORNELL accompanied by Jack Pleis' Orchestra	Coral 60829
11/01/52	**7**	8	6. I .... the shortest song title ever charted	Coral 60860
2/28/53	**28**	1	7. S'posin'..	Coral 60903

DATE CHARTED	PEAK POS	WKS CHRT'D	ARTIST — Record Title	Label & Number
7/11/53	**23**	2	8. She Loves Me..	Coral 61011
9/05/53	**18**	3	9. Please Play Our Song (Mister Record Man).....	Coral 61030
12/05/53+	**10**	10	10. Heart Of My Heart....................................	Coral 61076
			DON CORNELL, ALAN DALE, & JOHNNY DESMOND accompanied by Jack Pleis' Orchestra	
12/12/53	**24**	1	11. You're On Trial	Coral 61068
3/13/54	**23**	3	12. Size 12	Coral 61125
5/08/54	**22**	4	13. Believe In Me	Coral 61171
9/11/54	**2(1)**	18	● 14. Hold My Hand	Coral 61206
			from the film "Susan Slept Here" accompanied on 12 & 14 by Jerry Carr's Orchestra	

EMILE COTE SERENADERS
A capella vocal group; Emile directed Victor choral groups in the early 1940s.

5/08/48	**22**	3	1. Tea Leaves	Columbia 38230
			also issued on Algene 1933	

COTTON PICKERS
Frankie Trumbauer, Tommy and Jimmy Dorsey, and Glenn Miller were among the musicians who passed through this band.

9/23/22	**6**	2	1. Hot Lips.. [I]	Brunswick 2292
			featuring Phil Napoleon (trumpet) & Miff Mole (trombone)	

WALLY COX
Popular TV comedy actor, star of "Mr. Peepers" (1952-55); died on 2/15/73 (48).

5/09/53	**27**	1	1. What A Crazy Guy (Dufo)/ [C]	
5/23/53	**24**	2	2. There Is A Tavern In The Town............. [N]	RCA Victor 5278
			believed to be the first record issued with picture sleeve; accompanied by Bernard Green's Orchestra	

FRANCIS CRAIG & HIS ORCHESTRA
Nashville-based pianist and composer who led bands from the 1920s on; his early band featured Casa Loma vocalist Kenny Sargent and Phil Harris on drums.

8/09/47	**1(17)**	25	● 1. **Near You**..	Bullet 1001
			the first major hit on an independent label; became Milton Berle's theme song	
1/17/48	**3**	20	2. Beg Your Pardon	Bullet 1012
			vocals on above two: Bob Lamm	

FLOYD CRAMER
Played piano on all of Elvis Presley's early RCA Victor recordings

1/16/54	**28**	1	1. Fancy Pants .... [I]	Fabor 146
			with the Louisiana Hayride Band	

JESSE CRAWFORD
First organ soloist at Los Angeles' famous Grauman's Theatre in 1918; in late 20s achieved wide following at New York's Paramount Theatre and on radio, including providing background music for NBC and CBS dramas; died on 5/28/62 (66).

4/25/25	**15**	1	1. Rose Marie .... [I]	Victor 19520
			title song of the Broadway musical	
11/27/26	**14**	1	2. Valencia .... [I]	Victor 20075
12/25/26	**12**	1	3. At Dawning .... [I]	Victor 20110
10/01/27	**13**	2	4. Russian Lullaby .... [I]	Victor 20791

JOAN CRAWFORD
All-time movie great; 1945 Academy Award winner for "Mildred Pierce"; died on 5/10/77 (73).

4/29/39+	**19**	1	1. It's All So New To Me	Victor 26205
			accompanied by Nat Finston & The MGM Studio Orchestra	

CREW-CUTS
Rudi Maugeri, Pat Barrett, Roy Perkins, & Johnnie Perkins - from Toronto, Canada.

5/08/54	**8**	18	1. Crazy 'Bout Ya Baby	Mercury 70341
7/10/54	**1(9)**	20	● 2. **Sh-Boom**/	
			the first #1 rock and roll song	
8/21/54	**24**	1	3. I Spoke Too Soon....................................	Mercury 70404

DATE CHARTED	PEAK POS	WKS CHRT'D	ARTIST — Record Title	Label & Number
9/25/54	**13**	7	4. Oop-Shoop .... Mercury 70443 accompanied on above songs by David Carroll's Orchestra	

BING CROSBY

The most popular entertainer of the 20th century's first 50 years, Harry Lillis Crosby was born on 5/2/01 (or 04) in Tacoma, Wash. He and singing partner Al Rinker were hired in 1926 by Paul Whiteman; with Harry Barris they became the Rhythm Boys and gained an increasing following. The trio split from Whiteman in 1930, and heim, "I Surrender, Dear", which earned Bing a CBS radio contract, and launched an unsurpassed solo career. Over the next three decades the resonant Crosby baritone and breezy persona sold more than 300 million records and was featured in over 50 movies (including the 1944 Academy Award for "Going My Way"). Bing Crosby died on 10/14/77. (also see Whiteman, Arnheim, Dorsey Brothers Orchestra, Duke Ellington, & Frankie Trumbauer)

DATE CHARTED	PEAK POS	WKS CHRT'D	ARTIST — Record Title	Label & Number
3/28/31	**12**	2	1. Just A Gigolo/	
5/23/31	**4**	6	2. Wrap Your Troubles In Dreams .... Victor 22701 above two accompanied by members of Gus Arnheim's Orchestra	
4/25/31	**1(3)**	8	3. **Out Of Nowhere** .... Brunswick 6090 from the film "Dude Ranch"	
6/06/31	**1(2)**	19	4. **Just One More Chance/**	
6/20/31	**12**	3	5. Were You Sincere? .... Brunswick 6120 above two accompanied by Victor Young's Orchestra	
7/11/31	**2(3)**	6	6. I Found A Million-Dollar Baby/ from the Broadway musical "Crazy Quilt"	
7/25/31	**3**	7	7. I'm Through With Love .... Brunswick 6140	
7/25/31	**1(3)**	9	8. **At Your Command/**	
8/01/31	**3**	9	9. Many Happy Returns Of The Day .... Brunswick 6145	
9/12/31	**5**	5	10. Star Dust/	
9/19/31	**3**	6	11. Dancing In The Dark .... Brunswick 6159 from the Broadway musical "The Band Wagon"	
10/10/31	**3**	5	12. I Apologize/	
10/10/31	**9**	4	13. Sweet And Lovely .... Brunswick 6179	
10/31/31	**5**	8	14. Good Night, Sweetheart .... Brunswick 6203 accompanied by Victor Young's Orchestra; from the Broadway musical "Earl Carroll's Vanities of 1931"	
10/31/31	**8**	3	15. A Faded Summer Love .... Brunswick 6200	
11/21/31	**3**	11	16. Gems From "George White's Scandals" .... Brunswick 20102 BING CROSBY, MILLS BROTHERS, BOSWELL SISTERS, & THE VICTOR YOUNG ORCHESTRA medley: The Thrill Is Gone/Life Is Just A Bowl of Cherries	
1/09/32	**1(2)**	9	17. **Dinah/**	
2/20/32	**10**	4	18. Can't We Talk It Over? .... Brunswick 6240 above two: BING CROSBY & THE MILLS BROTHERS	
1/16/32	**4**	7	19. Where The Blue Of The Night (Meets The Gold Of The Day) .... Brunswick 6226 from Bing's first feature film, "The Big Broadcast of 1932"; became his radio theme song; based on "Tit-Willow" from the Gilbert & Sullivan operetta "The Mikado"	
2/13/32	**11**	2	20. Snuggled On Your Shoulder (Cuddled In Your Arms) .... Brunswick 6248	
4/16/32	**7**	5	21. Paradise .... Brunswick 6285	
4/16/32	**7**	5	22. Shine .... Brunswick 6276 BING CROSBY & THE MILLS BROTHERS band on 17, 18, & 21 includes Will Bradley (trombone), Bennie Krueger (alto sax), & Eddie Lang (guitar)	
6/04/32	**4**	5	23. Lazy Day .... Brunswick 6306	
6/11/32	**2(3)**	8	24. Sweet Georgia Brown .... Brunswick 6320 accompanied on above two by Isham Jones' Orchestra, including Woody Herman (clarinet/alto sax), Saxie Mansfield (tenor sax), & Eddie Lang (guitar)	
7/09/32	**11**	4	25. Cabin In The Cotton .... Brunswick 6329	

DATE CHARTED	PEAK POS	WKS CHRT'D	ARTIST — Record Title	Label & Number
8/06/32	**4**	6	26. Love Me Tonight/ movie title song	
9/03/32	**16**	2	27. Some Of These Days............................ accompanied on 25 & 27 by Lennie Hayton's Orchestra, including Frankie Trumbauer (saxophone) & Eddie Lang (guitar)	Brunswick 6351
10/08/32	**1(6)**	16	28. **Please/**	
10/29/32	**6**	11	29. Waltzing In A Dream......................... accompanied on above two by Anson Weeks' Orchestra	Brunswick 6394
11/12/32	**11**	3	30. Here Lies Love .... 28 & 30 from the film "The Big Broadcast of 1932"	Brunswick 6406
11/19/32	**1(2)**	8	31. **Brother, Can You Spare A Dime?** .... the definitive song of the Depression; accompanied by Lennie Hayton's Orchestra; from the Broadway musical "Americana"	Brunswick 6414
1/07/33	**2(2)**	11	32. Just An Echo In The Valley/ from the film "Going Hollywood"	
1/21/33	**5**	6	33. (I Don't Stand) A Ghost Of A Chance With You...	Brunswick 6454
2/04/33	**13**	3	34. Street Of Dreams	Brunswick 6464
2/11/33	**1(4)**	14	35. **You're Getting To Be A Habit With Me/**	
3/04/33	**2(1)**	7	36. Young And Healthy................................ above two from the film "Forty-Second Street"	Brunswick 6472
2/18/33	**12**	2	37. You're Beautiful Tonight, My Dear .... accompanied on above three by Guy Lombardo & His Royal Canadians	Brunswick 6477
3/25/33	**19**	1	38. I've Got The World On A String .... band includes Bunny Berigan (trumpet), Tommy Dorsey (trombone), Benny Goodman (clarinet), & Eddie Lang (guitar)	Brunswick 6491
4/01/33	**12**	3	39. You've Got Me Crying Again	Brunswick 6515
7/01/33	**1(2)**	8	40. **Shadow Waltz/**	
8/08/33	**9**	4	41. I've Got To Sing A Torch Song .... above two from the film "Gold Diggers of 1933"	Brunswick 6599
7/08/33	**3**	6	42. Learn To Croon	Brunswick 6594
7/15/33	**8**	5	43. Down The Old Ox Road/ above two from the film "College Humor"	
7/22/33	**10**	5	44. Blue Prelude.......................................	Brunswick 6601
8/12/33	**4**	5	45. My Love...	Brunswick 6623
9/16/33	**2(2)**	7	46. Thanks	Brunswick 6643
9/30/33	**3**	9	47. The Day You Came Along.................... above two from the film "Too Much Harmony" accompanied on above eight by Jimmie Grier's Orchestra	Brunswick 6644
10/21/33	**2(2)**	5	48. The Last Round-Up/ featured in Broadway's "Ziegfeld Follies of 1934"	
11/04/33	**18**	1	49. Home On The Range.............................	Brunswick 6663
12/09/33	**11**	3	50. Beautiful Girl....................................	Brunswick 6694
12/30/33+	**3**	12	51. Temptation/	
1/20/34	**8**	6	52. We'll Make Hay While The Sun Shines....... above three from the film "Going Hollywood" accompanied on above six by Lennie Hayton's Orchestra	Brunswick 6695
12/30/33	**5**	5	53. Did You Ever See A Dream Walking?........... from the film "Sitting Pretty"	Brunswick 6724
3/31/34	**1(5)**	11	54. **Little Dutch Mill** .... accompanied by Jimmie Grier's Orchestra	Brunswick 6794
4/07/34	**2(3)**	7	55. Good Night, Lovely Little Lady/	
5/05/34	**11**	3	56. Once In A Blue Moon............................	Brunswick 6854
4/14/34	**2(1)**	11	57. Love Thy Neighbor/	
5/26/34	**13**	3	58. Ridin' Around In The Rain	Brunswick 6852
4/14/34	**4**	6	59. May I?/ accompanied on 56, 57, & 59 by Nat Finston's Orchestra	
4/14/34	**10**	5	60. She Reminds Me Of You.......................... 55, 56, 57, 59, & 60 from the film "We're Not Dressing" accompanied on 58 & 60 by Jimmie Grier's Orchestra	Brunswick 6853

DATE CHARTED	PEAK POS	WKS CHRT'D	ARTIST — Record Title	Label & Number
8/04/34	1(6)	15	61. **Love In Bloom/** became most famous as Jack Benny's theme song	
9/29/34	16	2	62. Straight From The Shoulder .... above two from the film "She Loves Me Not"	Brunswick 6936
9/15/34	12	5	63. Give Me A Heart To Sing To........................ accompanied on above three by Irving Aaronson's Orchestra	Brunswick 6953
11/03/34	5	4	64. Two Cigarettes In The Dark .... from the film "Kill That Story"	Decca 245
11/03/34	11	3	65. The Very Thought Of You/	
11/03/34	13	3	66. The Moon Was Yellow (And The Night Was Young)...	Decca 179
11/24/34	1(7)	12	67. **June In January/**	
12/22/34+	8	9	68. Love Is Just Around The Corner	Decca 310
12/15/34+	4	7	69. With Every Breath I Take/ above three from the film "Here Is My Heart"	
12/22/34+	14	3	70. Maybe I'm Wrong Again	Decca 309
3/16/35	1(1)	11	71. **Soon/**	
4/06/35	17	2	72. Down By The River .... above three from the film "Mississippi"	Decca 392
3/16/35	1(2)	9	73. **It's Easy To Remember** .... with the Rhythmettes & Three Shades of Blue 65-73 accompanied by the Georgie Stoll Orchestra	Decca 391
9/14/35	2(2)	7	74. I Wished On The Moon.............................. from the film "The Big Broadcast of 1936"	Decca 543
9/14/35	5	10	75. Without A Word Of Warning .... above three from the film "Two for Tonight" accompanied on above four by Dorsey Brothers Orchestra, including Tommy (trombone), Jimmy (clarinet/alto sax), Charlie Spivak (trumpet), & Ray McKinley (drums)	Decca 548
9/14/35	7	5	76. I Wish I Were Aladdin/	
9/28/35	10	7	77. From The Top Of Your Head	Decca 547
12/14/35	1(2)	7	78. **Red Sails In The Sunset**.......................... from the Broadway musical "Provincetown Follies" Decca 616-870 accompanied by Victor Young's Orchestra	Decca 616
12/21/35+	7	3	● 79. Silent Night, Holy Night .... [X] with the Guardsmen Quartette Bing's recording of this holiday classic proved one of the biggest sellers of all time over the years with estimates running from seven to well over ten million; song written in 1818 in Germany ("Stille Nacht, Hellige Nacht")	Decca 621
12/21/35	8	4	80. On Treasure Island	Decca 617
4/18/36	20	1	81. Would You?... from the film "San Francisco"	Decca 756
4/25/36	4	9	82. The Touch Of Your Lips............................	Decca 757
5/30/36	2(2)	10	83. Robins And Roses...................................	Decca 791
7/11/36	18	1	84. It Ain't Necessarily So .... from the folk opera "Porgy and Bess"	Decca 806
8/29/36	2(4)	13	85. I'm An Old Cowhand/	
8/29/36	7	11	86. I Can't Escape From You.......................... above two with Jimmy Dorsey & His Orchestra	Decca 871
9/19/36	8	3	87. Empty Saddles .... above three from film "Rhythm On the Range"	Decca 870
9/19/36	14	2	88. Song Of The Islands	Decca 880
10/03/36	3	8	89. South Sea Island Magic........................... accompanied on above two by Dick McIntyre & His Harmony Hawaiians	Decca 886
10/24/36	9	5	90. Me And The Moon................................... accompanied by Victor Young & His Orchestra	Decca 912
11/28/36	1(10)	15	91. **Pennies From Heaven/**	
12/19/36+	10	4	92. Let's Call A Heart A Heart	Decca 947
11/28/36	18	1	93. So Do I/	
1/09/37	19	4	94. One, Two, Button Your Shoe.................... above four from the film "Pennies from Heaven"; accompanied on all by Georgie Stoll & His Orchestra	Decca 948

DATE CHARTED	PEAK POS	WKS CHRT'D	ARTIST — Record Title	Label & Number
4/03/37	1(10)	25	● 95. **Sweet Leilani/**	
4/10/37	5	13	96. Blue Hawaii .... Decca 1175	
			accompanied on above two by Lani McIntyre & His Hawaiians	
4/03/37	1(1)	10	97. **Too Marvelous For Words/**	
			from the film "Ready, Willing, and Able"	
4/03/37	5	6	98. What Will I Tell My Heart? .... Decca 1185	
4/03/37	8	7	99. Sweet Is The Word For You...................... Decca 1184	
			accompanied on 99, 101 & 102 by Victor Young's Orchestra	
			95, 96, & 99 from the film "Wakiki Wedding"	
5/01/37	2(3)	12	100. Never In A Million Years .... Decca 1210	
			from the film "Wake Up and Live"	
5/01/37	10	3	101. Moonlight And Shadows............................ Decca 1186	
5/29/37	19	1	102. My Little Buckaroo .... Decca 1234	
7/03/37	9	3	103. Peckin' .... Decca 1301	
			from the film "New Faces of 1937"	
			97, 98, 100, & 103 with Jimmy Dorsey & His Orchestra	
			including Toots Camarata (trumpet), Bobby Byrne (trombone),	
			& Ray McKinley (drums)	
9/11/37	1(4)	11	104. **The Moon Got In My Eyes/**	
9/18/37	18	1	105. (You Know It All) Smarty .... Decca 1375	
9/11/37	2(1)	6	106. It's The Natural Thing To Do...................... Decca 1376	
			above three from the film "Double or Nothing"	
10/30/37	1(3)	6	107. **Remember Me?/**	
			from the film "Mr. Dodd Takes the Air"	
11/13/37	6	8	108. I Still Love To Kiss You Goodnight............. Decca 1451	
			from the film "Fifty-Second Street"	
11/13/37	8	3	109. Can I Forget You?.................................. Decca 1462	
			from the film "High, Wide, and Handsome"	
			accompanied on above six by John Scott Trotter's Orchestra	
11/20/37	1(1)	12	110. **Bob White (Whatcha Gonna Swing Tonight?)/**	
11/27/37	12	3	111. Basin Street Blues .... Decca 1483	
			above two: BING CROSBY & CONNEE BOSWELL	
			accompanied by John Scott Trotter's Orchestra	
11/28/37	8	7	112. The One Rose (That's Left In My Heart)........ Decca 1201	
			accompanied by Victor Young's Orchestra	
12/11/37	4	5	113. Sail Along, Silvery Moon .... Decca 1518	
			accompanied by Lani McIntyre & His Hawaiians	
1/01/38	5	5	114. When The Organ Played "Oh Promise Me" ..... Decca 1554	
1/01/38	6	14	115. There's A Gold Mine In The Sky .... Decca 1565	
			accompanied on above two by Eddie Dunstedter (organ)	
2/26/38	4	10	116. On The Sentimental Side.......................... Decca 1648	
			from the film "Doctor Rhythm"	
2/26/38	10	4	117. Moon Of Manakoora .... Decca 1649	
			from the film "The Hurricane"	
6/04/38	7	7	118. Let Me Whisper I Love You........................ Decca 1819	
			accompanied on above three, and on 120-121 by John	
			Scott Trotter's Orchestra	
7/16/38	3	10	119. When Mother Nature Sings Her Lullaby .... Decca 1874	
			accompanied by Eddie Dunstedter (organ)	
7/30/38	7	8	120. Now It Can Be Told .... Decca 1888	
			120 & 124 from the film "Alexander's Ragtime Band"	
8/06/38	1(4)	17	121. **I've Got A Pocketful Of Dreams**................. Decca 1933	
			121, 123, & 125 from the film "Sing, You Sinners"	
8/27/38	3	13	122. Small Fry/	
8/13/38	7	5	123. Mr. Gallagher And Mr. Shean .... [C] Decca 1960	
			adaptation of the classic with special lyrics by Johnny	
			Mercer	
			above two: BING CROSBY & JOHNNY MERCER	
			accompanied by Victor Young's Small Fryers (including	
			Spike Jones, drums)	
8/20/38	1(2)	11	124. **Alexander's Ragtime Band** .... Decca 1887	
			BING CROSBY & CONNEE BOSWELL	
			with spoken introduction by Eddie Cantor	
9/03/38	19	2	125. Don't Let That Moon Get Away .... Decca 1934	

DATE CHARTED	PEAK POS	WKS CHRT'D	ARTIST — Record Title	Label & Number
10/08/38	**3**	10	126. Mexicali Rose	Decca 2001
			accompanied on above three, and on Decca 2200-2289, by John Scott Trotter's Orchestra	
11/19/38	**3**	5	127. My Reverie	Decca 2123
			song adapted from Debussy's "Reverie"	
12/03/38	**1(2)**	11	128. **You Must Have Been A Beautiful Baby**	Decca 2147
			from the film "Hard to Get" accompanied on above two by Bob Crosby's Orchestra, including Billy Butterfield (trumpet), Irving Fazola (clarinet), & Eddie Miller (tenor sax)	
12/17/38	**10**	2	129. Silent Night .... [X-R]	Decca 621
1/07/39	**3**	5	130. You're A Sweet Little Headache	Decca 2200
1/07/39	**4**	12	131. I Have Eyes/	
1/28/39	**5**	4	132. The Funny Old Hills	Decca 2201
			above three from the film "Paris Honeymoon"	
1/14/39	**14**	2	133. Someone Stole Gabriel's Horn	Brunswick 6533
			recorded 3/14/33 with Dorsey Brothers Orchestra, including Bunny Berigan (trumpet)	
2/04/39	**17**	1	134. It's A Lonely Trail (When You're Travelin' All Alone)	Decca 2237
2/11/39	**12**	2	135. The Lonesome Road	Decca 2257
2/25/39	**13**	4	136. I Cried For You....................................	Decca 2273
3/04/39	**15**	2	137. Between A Kiss And A Sigh/	
3/11/39	**14**	2	138. My Melancholy Baby	Decca 2289
3/18/39	**12**	1	139. Ah! Sweet Mystery Of Life	Decca 2315
			accompanied by Victor Young's Orchestra, from Broadway operetta "Naughty Marietta"	
4/08/39	**6**	6	140. East Side Of Heaven/	
4/09/39	**8**	3	141. Sing A Song Of Sunbeams	Decca 2359
			accompanied on above two, and on Decca 2400-2671, by John Scott Trotter's Orchestra 140, 141, & 144 from the film "East Side of Heaven"	
4/15/39	**14**	2	142. Deep Purple	Decca 2374
			accompanied by Matty Malneck & His Orchestra	
4/15/39	**17**	2	143. God Bless America................................	Decca 2400
			Irving Berlin originally wrote this in 1918 for "Yip Yip Yaphank", but did not use it for 21 years	
4/29/39	**10**	1	144. That Sly Old Gentleman (From Featherbed Lane)...	Decca 2360
5/06/39	**3**	2	145. Little Sir Echo....................................	Decca 2385
			with the Music Maids; song published in 1917	
5/13/39	**10**	4	146. And The Angels Sing	Decca 2413
6/03/39	**6**	10	147. Alla En El Rancho Grande	Decca 2494
			with the Foursome	
6/03/39	**14**	2	148. Whistling In The Wildwood	Decca 2448
8/05/39	**2(2)**	14	149. An Apple For The Teacher	Decca 2640
			149 & 152: BING CROSBY & CONNEE BOSWELL	
8/12/39	**10**	7	150. Go Fly A Kite/	
8/26/39	**4**	9	151. A Man And His Dream	Decca 2641
			above three from the film "The Star Maker"	
9/16/39	**12**	1	152. (Ho-Dle-Ay) Start The Day Right	Decca 2626
10/12/39	**2(2)**	10	153. What's New?.......................................	Decca 2671
11/25/39	**18**	1	154. My Isle Of Golden Dreams	Decca 2775
			accompanied by Dick McIntyre & His Harmony Hawaiians	
1/20/40	**12**	13	155. Between 18th & 19th On Chestnut Street	Decca 2948
			BING CROSBY & CONNEE BOSWELL	
3/02/40	**11**	10	156. Sweet Potato Piper/	
			with the Foursome	
3/16/40	**16**	5	157. Just One More Chance............................	Decca 2999
			new version of his 1931 hit	
3/09/40	**3**	12	158. I'm Too Romantic	Decca 2998
			156 & 158 from film "The Road to Singapore"	
3/16/40	**3**	13	159. The Singing Hills	Decca 3064
4/06/40	**12**	7	160. Tumbling Tumbleweeds	Decca 3024

DATE CHARTED	PEAK POS	WKS CHRT'D	ARTIST — Record Title	Label & Number
6/01/40	**10**	7	161. April Played The Fiddle/	
6/15/40	**13**	1	162. I Haven't Time To Be A Millionare	Decca 3161
6/22/40	**15**	4	163. Meet The Sun Half-Way...............................	Decca 3162
			above three from the film "If I Had My Way"	
7/06/40	**1(4)**	14	164. **Sierra Sue**	Decca 3133
			song published in 1916	
			accompanied on above ten by John Scott Trotter's Orchestra	
7/20/40	**18**	1	165. Mister Meadowlark.....................................	Decca 3182
			BING CROSBY & JOHNNY MERCER	
			accompanied by Victor Young's Orchestra	
9/07/40	**1(4)**	17	166. **Trade Winds**	Decca 3299
			accompanied by Dick McIntyre's Orchestra	
9/07/40	**8**	7	167. Can't Get Indiana Off My Mind	Decca 3321
9/07/40	**9**	7	168. That's For Me..	Decca 3309
9/28/40	**1(9)**	20	169. **Only Forever/**	
9/28/40	**27**	1	170. When The Moon Comes Over Madison Square	Decca 3300
			above three from the film "Rhythm On The River"	
11/09/40	**27**	1	171. Where The Blue Of The Night (Meets The Gold Of The Day)...............................	Decca 3354
			new version of his 1932 hit	
			accompanied by the Paradise Island Trio	
12/21/40	**25**	1	172. You Made Me Love You.............................	Decca 3423
			with the Merry Macs & Victor Young's Orchestra	
1/18/41	**24**	1	173. Please..	Decca 3450
			new version of his 1932 hit	
2/15/41	**4**	3	174. Along The Santa Fe Trail	Decca 3565
2/15/41	**23**	1	175. Lone Star Trail.......................................	Decca 3584
			accompanied on above three by John Scott Trotter's Orchestra	
2/22/41	**7**	11	176. New San Antonio Rose/	
3/01/41	**23**	1	177. It Makes No Difference Now	Decca 3590
			accompanied on above two by Bob Crosby's Orchestra	
3/01/41	**22**	1	178. Does Your Mother Come From Ireland?........	Decca 3609
			with the King's Men & Victor Young's Orchestra	
4/05/41	**2(1)**	15	179. Dolores	Decca 3644
			with Merry Macs and Bob Crosby's Bob Cats, including Muggsy Spanier (cornet) & Eddie Miller (tenor sax); from the film "Las Vegas Nights"	
7/12/41	**23**	1	180. Paradise Isle	Decca 3797
			with Paradise Island Trio	
9/06/41	**5**	12	181. You And I/	
7/26/41	**20**	2	182. Brahms' Lullaby (Cradle Song)	Decca 3840
8/09/41	**6**	11	183. 'Til Reveille	Decca 3886
8/16/41	**19**	1	184. Be Honest With Me...................................	Decca 3856
			accompanied on above four & 188 by John Scott Trotter's Orchestra	
8/30/41	**19**	1	185. You Are My Sunshine	Decca 3952
			accompanied on 185 & 190 by Victor Young's Orchestra	
11/01/41	**9**	14	186. The Whistler's Mother-In-Law	Decca 3971
			BING CROSBY & MURIEL LANE	
			with Woody Herman's Woodchoppers	
11/08/41	**23**	1	187. The Waiter And The Porter And The Upstairs Maid..	Decca 3970
			BING CROSBY, MARY MARTIN, & JACK TEAGARDEN	
			with Jack Teagarden's Orchestra	
11/29/41	**20**	1	188. Clementine	Decca 4033
			with the Music Maids & Hal Hopper	
12/06/41+	**4**	9	189. Shepherd Serenade/	
			European song	
			accompanied by Harry Sosnik's Orchestra	
12/27/41	**24**	1	190. The Anniversary Waltz...........................	Decca 4065
12/27/41+	**11**	2	191. Silent Night ....[X-R]	Decca 621
2/28/42	**3**	9	192. Deep In The Heart Of Texas	Decca 4162
			with Woody Herman's Woodchoppers	
3/14/42	**9**	3	193. I Don't Want To Walk Without You	Decca 4184
			from the film "Sweater Girl"	

DATE CHARTED	PEAK POS	WKS CHRT'D	ARTIST — Record Title	Label & Number
3/21/42	**22**	1	194. Sing Me A Song Of The Islands .... accompanied by Dick McIntyre & His Harmony Hawaiians, from the film "Song of the Islands"	Decca 4173
3/28/42	**9**	8	195. Miss You .... from the film "Strictly In the Groove"	Decca 4183
4/11/42	**23**	1	196. The Lamplighter's Serenade	Decca 4249
7/11/42	**21**	1	197. When The White Azaleas Start Blooming ...... accompanied on above two by Victor Young's Orchestra	Decca 18391
7/18/42	**14**	1	198. Skylark.. accompanied on 193, 195, 198 & 200-203 by John Scott Trotter's Orchestra	Decca 4193
8/15/42	**19**	1	199. The Bombadier Song .... with the Music Maids & Hal Hopper	Decca 18432
8/22/42	**2(6)**	15	200. Be Careful, It's My Heart	Decca 18424
10/03/42	**1(11)**	17	●201. **White Christmas** .... [X] with the Ken Darby Singers above two from the film "Holiday Inn" the biggest-selling record of all time, with total sales through the years of over 30 million; selected for the NARAS Hall of Fame	Decca 18429
12/12/42+	**1(2)**	17	202. **Moonlight Becomes You/**	
2/20/43	**13**	1	203. Constantly .... above two from the film "The Road to Morocco"	Decca 18513
8/21/43	**1(7)**	19	●204. **Sunday, Monday, Or Always/**	
9/18/43	**5**	12	205. If You Please.. above two with Ken Darby Singers; both from the film "Dixie"	Decca 18561
9/11/43	**20**	1	206. Mary's A Grand Old Name .... from the 1906 musical "Forty-Five Minutes from Broadway" featured in the film "Yankee Doodle Dandy"	Decca 18360
10/09/43	**2(1)**	17	207. People Will Say We're In Love/	
10/30/43+	**4**	13	208. Oh, What A Beautiful Mornin' .... above two with Trudy Erwin & the Sportsmen Glee Club above two from the Broadway musical "Oklahoma!"	Decca 18564
12/04/43	**3**	7	●209. I'll Be Home For Christmas..................... [X] accompanied on 206, 209, & 212-222 by John Scott Trotter's Orchestra	Decca 18570
12/04/43+	**6**	6	210. White Christmas/ [X-R]	
12/25/43	**18**	1	211. Let's Start The New Year Right .... accompanied by Bob Crosby's Orchestra from the film "Holiday Inn"	Decca 18429
3/11/44	**1(5)**	22	212. **San Fernando Valley/**	
2/26/44	**3**	15	213. Poinciana	Decca 18586
4/08/44	**1(5)**	18	214. **I Love You** .... from the Broadway musical "Mexican Hayride"	Decca 18597
4/22/44	**1(4)**	24	215. **I'll Be Seeing You**................................... from the 1938 Broadway musical "Right This Way"	Decca 18595
5/13/44	**1(9)**	28	●216. **Swinging On A Star/**	
9/09/44	**15**	1	217. Going My Way...................................... accompanied on above two by John Scott Trotter's Orchestra, & the Williams Brothers Quartet (including Andy Williams, age 7) 216, 217, 220 & 222 from the film "Going My Way"	Decca 18597
7/08/44	**2(2)**	16	218. Amor/ from the film "Broadway Rhythm"	
7/08/44	**5**	9	219. Long Ago (And Far Away)....................... from the film "Cover Girl"	Decca 18608
9/23/44	**15**	2	220. The Day After Forever/	
9/30/44	**18**	2	221. It Could Happen To You .... from the film "And the Angels Sing"	Decca 18580
10/14/44	**4**	12	●222. Too-Ra-Loo-Ra-Loo-Ral .... originally from the 1914 Broadway musical "Shameen Dhu"	Decca 18621
12/02/44	**27**	1	223. Sweet And Lovely .... [R] reissue of his 1931 hit	Brunswick 80057
12/16/44	**5**	3	224. White Christmas................................ [X-R]	Decca 18429
12/23/44	**16**	1	225. I'll Be Home For Christmas................. [X-R]	Decca 18570

DATE CHARTED	PEAK POS	WKS CHRT'D	ARTIST — Record Title	Label & Number
1/27/45	9	5	226. Evelina .... accompanied by Camarata's Orchestra from the Broadway musical "Bloomer Girl"	Decca 18635
2/24/45	14	3	227. Sleigh Ride In July/	
3/03/45	15	1	228. Like Someone In Love .... above two from the film "Belle of the Yukon"	Decca 18640
4/14/45	4	10	229. Just A Prayer Away .... accompanied by Victor Young's Orchestra	Decca 23392
5/05/45	12	1	230. All Of My Life................................... accompanied on 227, 228, 230, 235-236 by John Scott Trotter's Orchestra	Decca 18658
5/12/45	5	7	231. Yah-Ta-Ta, Yah-Ta-Ta (Talk, Talk, Talk)....... BING CROSBY & JUDY GARLAND accompanied by Joseph Lilley's Orchestra	Decca 23410
6/02/45	3	14	232. You Belong To My Heart/	
6/16/45	6	2	233. Baia .... above two with Xavier Cugat's Orchestra both from the film "The Three Caballeros"	Decca 23413
7/21/45	14	1	234. My Baby Said Yes .... BING CROSBY & LOUIS JORDAN with Louis' Tympany Five	Decca 23417
7/28/45	3	15	235. On The Atchison, Topeka, And The Santa Fe. with Six Hits & A Miss; from the film "The Harvey Girls"	Decca 18690
8/18/45	8	6	236. If I Loved You .... from the Broadway musical "Carousel"	Decca 18686
10/13/45	1(2)	16	237. **It's Been A Long, Long Time** .... with the Les Paul Trio	Decca 18708
11/17/45	21	1	238. The Road To Morocco............................. BING CROSBY & BOB HOPE title song of the movie	Decca 40000
11/24/45	1(6)	20	●239. **I Can't Begin To Tell You**....................... with Carmen Cavallaro's Orchestra from the film "The Dolly Sisters"	Decca 23457
12/15/45	1(2)	4	240. **White Christmas** .... [X-R]	Decca 18429
12/22/45+	8	9	241. Aren't You Glad You're You?/	
1/05/46	18	1	242. In The Land Of Beginning Again .... above two from the film "The Bells of St. Mary's accompanied by John Scott Trotter's Orchestra	Decca 18720
1/05/46	3	12	243. Symphony .... accompanied by Victor Young's Orchestra	Decca 18735
1/19/46	16	1	244. Give Me The Simple Life........................... with Jimmy Dorsey's Orchestra from the film "Wake Up And Dream"	Decca 23469
3/02/46	21	3	245. The Bells of St. Mary's........................... title song of the movie	Decca 18721
3/16/46	10	4	●246. McNamara's Band .... song published in 1917	Decca 23405
3/23/46	15	1	247. Day By Day .... BING CROSBY & MEL TORME with the Mel-Tones	Decca 18746
4/06/46	3	16	248. Sioux City Sue..................................... 246 & 248 with The Jesters & Bob Haggart's Orchestra	Decca 23508
4/06/46	9	3	249. Personality .... with Eddie Condon's Orchestra, featuring Wild Bill Davison (cornet) from the film "The Road to Utopia"	Decca 18790
6/08/46	12	4	250. They Say It's Wonderful........................ accompanied by Jay Blackton's Orchestra from the Broadway musical "Annie Get Your Gun"	Decca 18829
9/21/46	21	3	251. Night And Day....................................... from the Broadway musical "Gay Divorce"	Decca 18887
11/16/46	12	6	252. You Keep Coming Back Like A Song .... from the film "Blue Skies"	Decca 23647
12/07/46+	1(1)	6	253. **White Christmas** .... [X-R]	Decca 23778
1/11/47	8	6	254. A Gal In Calico .... with the Calico Kids from the film "The Time, The Place, And The Girl"	Decca 23739

DATE CHARTED	PEAK POS	WKS CHRT'D	ARTIST — Record Title	Label & Number
3/15/47	**22**	3	255. Easter Parade .... Decca 23819 from the Broadway musical "As Thousands Cheer"	
4/26/47	**17**	1	256. That's How Much I Love You....................... Decca 23840 with Bob Crosby's Orchestra	
5/10/47	**20**	2	●257. Alexander's Ragtime Band .... Decca 40038 BING CROSBY & AL JOLSON accompanied by Morris Stoloff's Orchestra	
9/13/47	**9**	4	258. Feudin' And Fightin' .... Decca 23975 accompanied by Bob Haggart's Orchestra, including Yank Lawson (trumpet) & Perry Botkin (guitar) from the Broadway musical "Laffing Room Only"	
11/01/47	**8**	8	259. You Do/ from the film "Mother Wore Tights"	
11/08/47+	**6**	14	260. How Soon (Will I Be Seeing You) .... Decca 24101 above two with Carmen Cavallaro's Orchestra	
11/15/47	**7**	7	●261. Whiffenpoof Song.................................... Decca 23990 with Fred Waring's Glee Club; song published in 1909 as the theme song for a branch of the Yale University Glee Club	
12/06/47+	**3**	5	262. White Christmas............................. [X-R] Decca 23778	
12/20/47	**22**	1	263. Silent Night .... [X-R] Decca 23777 new version of 1935 classic, with John Scott Trotter's Orchestra & Max Terr's Chorus; previously on Decca 18510	
1/17/48	**10**	8	264. Ballerina .... Decca 24278 accompanied on 252-253 & 264 by John Scott Trotter's Orchestra	
1/31/48	**1(3)**	23	●265. **Now Is The Hour** .... Decca 24279 based on the traditional New Zealand song "Hearere Ra" 260 & 262 with the Ken Darby Choir with the Ken Darby Choir	
1/31/48	**21**	1	266. Pass That Peace Pipe................................ Decca 24269 from the film "Good News"	
2/07/48	**20**	3	267. But Beautiful .... Decca 24283 from the film "The Road to Rio"	
3/27/48	**22**	1	268. Easter Parade .... Decca 23819 from the Broadway musical "As Thousands Cheer"	
5/22/48	**23**	2	269. Blue Shadows On The Trail/ above two accompanied by Victor Young's Orchestra	
5/29/48	**23**	1	270. A Fella With An Umbrella .... Decca 24433 from the film "Easter Parade"	
12/11/48+	**6**	6	271. White Christmas............................. [X-R] Decca 23778	
1/08/49	**2(3)**	19	272. Far Away Places...................................... Decca 24532 269 & 272 with the Ken Darby Choir	
1/22/49	**3**	17	●273. Galway Bay .... Decca 24295 British song; accompanied by Victor Young's Orchestra	
4/23/49	**27**	1	274. If You Stub Your Toe On The Moon .... Decca 24524 with the Rhythmaires from the film "A Connecticut Yankee in King Arthur's Court"	
5/07/49	**12**	10	275. Careless Hands.................................... Decca 24616	
5/14/49	**14**	10	276. Riders In The Sky .... Decca 24618 movie title song above two with Ken Darby Singers and Perry Botkin's Orchestra	
5/28/49	**3**	20	277. Some Enchanted Evening/	
6/18/49	**12**	7	278. Bali Ha'i.. Decca 24609 above two from the Broadway musical "South Pacific"	
12/03/49+	**2(4)**	17	●279. Dear Hearts And Gentle People/ with Jud Conlon's Rhythmaires	
11/19/49	**4**	12	280. Mule Train.. Decca 24798 accompanied on above two by Perry Botkin's String Band	
11/19/49	**21**	2	281. Way Back Home .... Decca 24800 accompanied by Fred Waring's Pennsylvanians	
12/17/49+	**5**	4	282. White Christmas............................. [X-R] Decca 23778	
2/04/50	**4**	13	283. Chattanoogie Shoe Shine Boy.................... Decca 24863 accompanied by Vic Schoen's Orchestra	
7/08/50	**22**	2	284. I Didn't Slip - I Wasn't Pushed - I Fell .... Decca 27018 accompanied by Sy Oliver's Orchestra & Aristokats	

DATE CHARTED	PEAK POS	WKS CHRT'D	ARTIST — Record Title	Label & Number
7/29/50	2(2)	19	●285. Play A Simple Melody/ from the Broadway musical "Watch Your Step"	
7/29/50+	3	19	286. Sam's Song................................... above two: BING & (son) GARY CROSBY accompanied by Matty Matlock's Orchestra (billed on label as "Gary Crosby & Friend")	Decca 27112
8/05/50	13	6	287. La Vie En Rose/	
8/05/50	18	4	288. I Cross My Fingers .... accompanied on above two by Axel Stordahl's Orchestra	Decca 27111
10/07/50	11	12	289. All My Love .... accompanied by Victor Young & His Orchestra adapted from the French song "Bolero"	Decca 27117
10/28/50	26	1	290. Beyond The Reef/	
11/11/50	8	13	291. Harbor Lights... accompanied on above two by Lynn Murray's Orchestra, featuring a Hawaiian guitar	Decca 27219
12/16/50	13	4	292. White Christmas................................... [X-R]	Decca 23778
12/16/50	14	4	293. Rudolph, The Red-Nosed Reindeer .... [X] accompanied by John Scott Trotter's Orchestra	Decca 27159
12/23/50	22	2	294. A Crosby Christmas .... [X] BING & (sons) GARY, PHILLIP, DENNIS, & LINDSAY sing 4 new songs	Decca 40181
1/06/51	24	1	295. A Marshmellow World .... [X] accompanied by Sonny Burke's Orchestra	Decca 27230
4/21/51	8	10	296. When You And I Were Young, Maggie, Blues/	
4/21/51	14	6	297. Moonlight Bay...................................... above two: BING CROSBY & GARY CROSBY	Decca 27577
6/30/51	19	2	298. Gone Fishin' .... BING CROSBY & LOUIS ARMSTRONG band includes Red Nichols & Ziggy Elman (trumpets), Matty Matlock (tenor sax), Buddy Cole (piano), & Perry Botkin (guitar)	Decca 27623
8/04/51	11	6	299. In The Cool, Cool, Cool Of The Evening........ BING CROSBY & JANE WYMAN from the film "Here Comes the Groom"	Decca 27678
9/08/51	21	1	300. Shanghai..	Decca 27653
11/03/51	15	6	301. Domino .... accompanied by John Scott Trotter's Orchestra	Decca 27830
12/22/51+	13	3	302. White Christmas................................... [X-R]	Decca 23778
7/26/52	28	2	303. Watermelon Weather............................... BING CROSBY & PEGGY LEE	Decca 28238
8/02/52	16	6	304. Till The End Of The World......................... accompanied by Grady Martin & His Slew Foot Five	Decca 28265
8/09/52	18	6	305. Zing A Little Zong................................. BING CROSBY & JANE WYMAN from the film "Just for You"	Decca 28255
12/27/52+	20	2	306. Silver Bells .... [X] BING CROSBY & CAROL RICHARDS from the film "The Lemon Drop Kid"	Decca 27229
12/27/52	28	1	307. Keep It A Secret	Decca 28511
1/24/53	23	2	308. You Don't Know What Lonesome Is/	
1/31/53	22	3	309. Open Up Your Heart	Decca 28470
3/07/53	24	2	310. Hush-A-Bye	Decca 28581
12/26/53	21	2	311. White Christmas................................... [X-R]	Decca 23778
1/30/54	13	3	312. Changing Partners/ 307 & 312 with Jud Conlon's Rhythmaires	
1/30/54	20	3	313. Y'all Come..	Decca 28969
1/30/54	28	1	314. Down By The Riverside .... BING & GARY CROSBY	Decca 28955
5/08/54	24	2	315. Young At Heart .... with Guy Lombardo & His Royal Canadians; movie title song	Decca 29054
12/04/54	27	3	316. Count Your Blessings (Instead Of Sheep) .... accompanied by Joseph Lilley's Orchestra from the film "White Christmas"	Decca 29251
12/25/54	21	3	317. White Christmas................................... [X-R]	Decca 23778

112

DATE CHARTED	PEAK POS	WKS CHRT'D	ARTIST — Record Title	Label & Number
			BING CROSBY & ANDREWS SISTERS	
11/04/39	13	3	1. Ciribiribin (They're So In Love)/	
11/18/39+	4	12	2. Yodelin' Jive..	Decca 2800
			accompanied on above two by Joe Ventuti's Orchestra, including Bobby Hackett (trumpet)	
11/06/43	2(4)	11	● 3. Pistol Packin' Mama/	
11/13/43+	5	13	4. Victory Polka..	Decca 23277
			accompanied on all subsequent records by Vic Schoen's Orchestra	
12/25/43	19	1	5. Jingle Bells .... [X]	Decca 23281
9/09/44	2(1)	12	6. Is You Is Or Is You Ain't (Ma' Baby)/	
			from the film "Follow the Boys"	
9/23/44	1(6)	14	7. **A Hot Time In The Town Of Berlin**..........	Decca 23350
11/25/44	1(8)	21	● 8. **Don't Fence Me In**	Decca 23364
			from the film "Hollywood Canteen"	
2/03/45	2(1)	9	9. Ac-Cent-Tchu-Ate The Positive....................	Decca 23379
			from the film "Here Come the Waves"	
2/03/45	8	5	10. The Three Caballeros	Decca 23364
			movie title song	
9/15/45	2(1)	11	11. Along The Navajo Trail	Decca 23437
8/03/46	2(1)	19	12. South America, Take It Away/	
			from the Broadway musical "Call Me Mister"	
8/10/46	14	2	13. Get Your Kicks On Route 66.....................	Decca 23569
7/05/47	10	10	14. Tallahassee	Decca 23885
			from the film "Variety Girl"	
7/19/47	25	1	15. There's No Business Like Show Business	Decca 40039
			BING CROSBY, THE ANDREWS SISTERS, & DICK HAYMES from the Broadway musical "Annie Get Your Gun"	
10/25/47	21	1	16. The Freedom Train	Decca 23999
12/13/47	21	2	17. Jingle Bells/	[X-R]
12/27/47	22	1	18. Santa Claus Is Comin' To Town.......... [X-R]	Decca 23281
1/31/48	21	2	19. You Don't Have To Know The Language	Decca 24282
			from film "The Road to Rio"	
11/06/48	23	2	20. 160 Acres..	Decca 24481
1/21/50	24	4	21. Have I Told You Lately That I Love You?......	Decca 2482
1/28/50	6	17	22. Quicksilver	Decca 24827
3/10/51	8	15	23. Sparrow In The Tree Top.........................	Decca 27477
			BOB CROSBY & HIS ORCHESTRA	
			Bing's younger brother fronted one of the era's top dance bands, specializing in Dixieland jazz. Tenor saxophonist Gil Rodin was effective leader of the band, which also featured trumpet stars Billy Butterfield and Muggsy Spanier, clarinet virtuoso Irving Fazola, Eddie Miller (tenor sax), trombonists Buddy Morrow and Ray Conniff (both briefly), pianists Bob Zurke and Jess Stacy, and bassist Bobby Haggart. (also see Dorsey Brothers Orchestra, Georgia Gibbs)	
6/22/35	12	2	1. Flowers For Madame/	
6/29/35	1(3)	13	2. **In A Little Gypsy Tea Room**	Decca 478
			above two vocals: Frank Tennille (father of 1970s singing star Toni Tennille)	
12/28/35+	8	6	3. A Little Bit Independent	Decca 629
4/04/36	7	5	4. Goody Goody	Decca 727
			above two vocals: Bob Crosby	
8/07/37	1(4)	13	5. **Whispers In The Dark**............................	Decca 1346
			from the film "Artists and Models"	
1/15/38	16	2	6. A Foggy Day	Decca 1539
			from the film "A Damsel in Distress"	
4/30/38	12	3	7. Please Be Kind	Decca 1693
			above three vocals: Kay Weber	
11/05/38	18	1	8. Louise, Louise......................................	Decca 2032
			vocal: Eddie Miller (Decca 2123 & 2147: Bing Crosby with Bob Crosby & His Orchestra)	
11/12/38	10	4	9. Deep In A Dream	Decca 2151
			vocal: Marian Mann	

DATE CHARTED	PEAK POS	WKS CHRT'D	ARTIST — Record Title	Label & Number
11/12/38	**11**	3	10. Two Sleepy People .... vocal: Bob Crosby & Marian Mann from the film "Thanks for the Memory"	Decca 2150
1/28/39	**11**	1	11. Loopin' The Loop.................................... Bob Crosby's Bob Cats, vocal by band Eddie Miller & Irving Fazola featured	Decca 2209
2/04/39	**16**	1	12. Swingin' At The Sugar Bowl....................... vocal: Nappy Lamare	Decca 2210
5/06/39	**14**	3	13. At A Little Hot Dog Stand .... vocal: Bob Crosby & Marian Mann	Decca 2401
6/03/39	**15**	2	14. I Never Knew Heaven Could Speak.............. vocal: Marian Mann from the film "Rose of Washington Square"	Decca 2464
6/24/39	**13**	2	15. The Lady's In Love With You...................... vocal: Bob Crosby; from the film "Some Like It Hot"	Decca 2465
9/02/39	**1(1)**	13	16. **Day In, Day Out** .... vocal: Helen Ward	Decca 2703
9/02/39	**10**	8	17. What's New?.. [I] recorded 10/19/38 as "I'm Free" Billy Butterfield (trumpet) featured	Decca 2205
9/16/39	**2(2)**	8	18. Over The Rainbow .... from the film "The Wizard of Oz"	Decca 2657
10/07/39	**8**	3	19. Blue Orchids.. above two vocals: Teddy Grace	Decca 2734
10/21/39	**3**	12	20. Lilacs In The Rain	Decca 2763
11/18/39	**8**	7	21. Can I Help It?.......................................	Decca 2776
12/09/39	**16**	3	22. (Why Couldn't It Last) Last Night................ above three vocals: Bob Crosby	Decca 2812
12/16/39	**15**	1	23. Between 18th And 19th On Chestnut Street .. vocal: Nappy Lamare & Eddie Miller	Decca 2935
3/09/40	**2(3)**	14	24. With The Wind And The Rain In Your Hair.... vocal: Marion Mann	Decca 3018
3/09/40	**7**	11	25. Leanin' On The Ole Top Rail .... vocal: Bob Crosby	Decca 3027
4/06/40	**8**	5	26. I've Got My Eyes On You........................... from the film "Broadway Melody of 1940"	Decca 2991
4/13/40	**10**	4	27. So Far, So Good.....................................	Decca 3055
6/08/40	**12**	1	28. Believing..	Decca 3103
6/22/40	**28**	1	29. You, You, Darlin' .... above four vocals: Marion Mann	Decca 3018
11/16/40+	**2(1)**	13	30. Down Argentina Way................................ vocal: Bonnie King; movie title song	Decca 3404
11/23/40+	**14**	7	31. You Forgot About Me .... vocals on 31 & 33: Bob Crosby & Bob-o-Links	Decca 3417
5/17/41	**23**	1	32. Cow Cow Blues.................................... [I] Mugsy Spanier (trumpet) featured (Decca 3590: Bing Crosby with Bob Crosby & His Orchestra; Decca 3644: Bing with Bob Crosby's Bob Cats)	Decca 3488
10/25/41	**18**	1	33. Do You Care?..	Decca 3860
6/06/42	**23**	1	34. Barrelhouse Bessie From Basin Street.......... vocal: Eddie Miller	Decca 4169
7/03/43	**20**	2	35. Blue Surreal .... [I] recorded 9/17/41; Eddie Miller (tenor sax) featured (Decca 18429 B-side & Decca 23840: Bing Crosby with Bob Crosby & His Orchestra)	Decca 4415
2/16/46	**14**	1	36. Let It Snow! Let It Snow! Let It Snow!...........	ARA 129
9/28/46	**12**	5	37. Five Minutes More .... from the film "Sweetheart of Sigma Chi"	Decca 18909
1/22/49	**12**	6	38. The Pussy Cat Song (Nyow! Nyot Nyow!)........ PATTY ANDREWS & BOB CROSBY	Decca 24533
10/09/49	**22**	3	39. Maybe It's Because .... vocal: Marion Morgan	Columbia 38504
8/26/50	**25**	2	40. Play A Simple Melody .... vocal: Georgia Gibbs; from the Broadway musical "Watch Your Step"	Coral 60227
7/21/51	**22**	1	41. Shanghai.. vocal by Bob Crosby	Capitol 1525

DATE CHARTED	PEAK POS	WKS CHRT'D	ARTIST — Record Title	Label & Number
			GARY CROSBY Bing's son	
7/29/50	**2(2)**	19	● 1. Play A Simple Melody................................. from the Broadway musical "Watch Your Step"	Decca 2711
7/29/50+	**3**	19	2. Sam's Song.. shown as Gary Crosby & Friend	Decca 27112
4/21/51	**8**	10	3. When You And I Were Young, Maggie, Blues..	Decca 2757
4/21/51	**14**	6	4. Moonlight Bay..	Decca 27577
1/30/54	**28**	1	5. Down By The Riverside................................ above five: BING CROSBY & GARY CROSBY	Decca 28955
			CROWS R&B quartet from New York City; Daniel "Sonny" Norton, lead singer	
3/06/54	**14**	6	1. Gee	Rama 5
			FRANK CROXTON Sang bass for Columbia Stellar Quartet and (from 1919-25) Peerless Quartet; died on 9/3/49 (71).	
3/08/13	**9**	1	1. Till The Sands Of The Desert Grow Cold	Columbia 1247
3/15/13	**3**	6	2. On The Road To Mandalay	Columbia 5441
1/31/20	**11**	1	3. Weeping Willow Lane .... HENRY BURR & FRANK CROXTON	Victor 18609
			FRANK CRUMIT Extremely popular entertainer who appeared in 1920s Broadway musicals and hosted radio show with wife Julia Sanderson from 1929-43; composed several of his hits. Frank died on 9/7/43 (53).	
7/24/20	**3**	5	1. Oh! By Jingo! Oh! By Gee!/ from the Broadway musical "Linger Longer Letty"	
8/21/20	**7**	2	2. So Long, Oo-Long (How Long You Gonna Be Gone)	Columbia 2935
9/11/20	**4**	4	3. Chili Bean .... with Paul Biese Trio	Columbia 2952
11/20/20	**6**	4	4. My Little Bimbo Down On The Bimbo Isle...... from the Broadway musical "Silks and Satins"	Columbia 2981
2/12/21	**7**	2	5. Margie/	
2/26/21	**4**	4	6. I'm A Lonesome Little Raindrop................ from the Broadway musical "Greenwich Village Follies of 1920"	Columbia 3332
2/26/21	**11**	1	7. Palesteena..	Columbia 3324
4/16/21	**7**	2	8. Timbuctoo... 8, 13, & 14 with the Paul Biese Trio	Columbia 3352
5/28/21	**10**	1	9. Home Again Blues	Columbia 3375
7/30/21	**7**	2	10. I Used To Love You, But It's All Over Now.....	Columbia 3388
8/27/21	**5**	4	11. All By Myself	Columbia 3415
10/29/21	**5**	3	12. Three O'Clock In The Morning.................... from the Broadway musical "Greenwich Village Follies of 1921"	Columbia 3431
10/29/21	**10**	1	13. Mimi/	
11/19/21	**14**	1	14. Oh Me! Oh My!..................................... FRANK CRUMIT & PAUL BIESE TRIO	Columbia 3430
11/26/21	**7**	3	15. I Ain't Nobody's Darling...........................	Columbia 3459
12/17/21+	**3**	6	16. Sweet Lady.. from the Broadway musical "Tangerine"	Columbia 3475
12/31/21+	**5**	4	17. Dapper Dan	Columbia 3477
8/26/22	**6**	2	18. Stumbling..	Columbia 3626
10/27/23	**10**	1	19. When You Walked Out, Someone Else Walked Right In	Columbia 3933
1/12/24	**4**	4	20. Old-Fashioned Love/ from the Broadway musical "Running Wild"	
1/26/24	**9**	2	21. My Home Town In Kansas .... from the Broadway musical "Little Jessie James"	Columbia 3997
3/15/24	**8**	1	22. Say It With A Ukelele	Columbia 26
5/24/24	**8**	2	23. Mindin' My Business .... accompanied by the Virginians	Victor 19259

DATE CHARTED	PEAK POS	WKS CHRT'D	ARTIST — Record Title	Label & Number
10/25/24	**15**	1	24. Ida (Sweet As Apple Cider)............................ accompanied by Phil Ohman (piano); featured in the Broadway musical "Roly Boly Eyes"	Victor 19365
11/28/25	**13**	1	25. I Married The Bootlegger's Daughter .... [C]	Victor 19739
5/29/26	**12**	1	26. I'm Sitting On Top Of The World..................	Victor 19928
5/28/27	**9**	4	27. Crazy Words-Crazy Tune............................ accompanied by Frank Banta (piano) on above three	Victor 20462
9/10/27	**18**	1	28. Frankie And Johnny	Victor 20715
1/14/28	**5**	8	29. 'S Wonderful.. accompanied by Jack Shilkret (pipe organ) from the Broadway musical "Funny Face"	Victor 21029
12/15/28+	**2(1)**	10	30. A Gay Caballero	Victor 21735
11/30/29	**19**	1	31. Return Of The Gay Caballero .... above two accompanied by Leonard Joy's Orchestra	Victor 22154

XAVIER CUGAT & HIS WALDORF-ASTORIA ORCHESTRA

The Spanish-born showman who became the most famous exponent of Latin-American dance music began as a classical violinist in the 1920s. A successful composer as well as bandleader, he attracted as much publicity in later years through his beautiful wives (including Abbe Lane and Charo) as through his music. (Also see Bing Crosby)

DATE CHARTED	PEAK POS	WKS CHRT'D	ARTIST — Record Title	Label & Number
5/18/35	**3**	12	1. The Lady In Red .... vocal: Don Reid; from the film "In Caliente"	Victor 25012
8/03/35	**20**	1	2. The Cocoanut Pudding Vendor .... vocal: Pedro Berrios & Faust Delgado	Victor 25071
11/09/35	**13**	2	3. Begin The Beguine .... vocal: Don Reid; from the Broadway musical "Jubilee"	Victor 25133
11/21/36	**19**	1	4. Para Vigo Me Voy (Say "Si Si")..................... vocal by Perdo Berrios & band; reissue of Victor 25237	Victor 25407
4/22/39	**9**	4	5. Night Must Fall .... [I]	Victor 26074
3/16/40	**17**	1	6. Quiero A Mi Mama (I Want My Mama) .... [F] vocal: Carmen Castillo from the Broadway musical "Earl Carroll's Vanities"	Victor 26522
8/10/40	**13**	1	7. The Breeze And I.................................... adapted from Spanish song "Andalucia"	Victor 26641
10/12/40	**22**	1	8. Whatever Happened To You?/	
12/14/40+	**19**	2	9. The Rumba-Cardi.................................... Dinah Shore: above three vocals	Victor 26665
1/25/41	**3**	16	10. Perfidia (Tonight)................................... [I] recorded 6/12/39	Victor 26334
4/12/41	**26**	1	11. Chica, Chica, Boom, Chic .... vocal: Lena Romay; from the film "That Night In Río"	Columbia 35995
7/05/41	**23**	1	12. Intermezzo (A Love Story)........................ [I]	Columbia 36041
9/06/41	**16**	1	13. Quierme Mucho (Yours)............................ vocal: Dinah Shore; recorded 6/12/39	Victor 26384
9/20/41	**16**	1	14. Green Eyes .... recorded 9/6/40, originally issued on Victor 26794 Cuban song "Acuellos Ojos Verdes"	Victor 27443
1/23/43	**2(7)**	24	15. Brazil .... Brazilian samba ("Aquarelo do Brasil") from the animated film "Saludos Amigos" above two vocals by band	Columbia 36651
10/16/43	**18**	1	16. Thanks For The Dream .... vocal: Carmen Castillo	Columbia 36681
4/29/44	**27**	1	17. Babalu... [F] vocal: Miguelito Valdes; recorded 3/14/41; song later associated with Desi Arnaz	Columbia 36068
7/15/44	**10**	9	18. Amor... vocal: Carmen Castillo; from the film "Broadway Rhythm"	Columbia 36718
6/02/45	**6**	7	19. Good, Good, Good (That's You-That's You) .... vocal: Del Campo	Columbia 36793
8/17/46	**6**	13	20. South America, Take It Away .... vocal: Buddy Clark from the Broadway musical "Call Me Mister"	Columbia 37051
1/01/49	**27**	1	21. Cuanto Le Gusta .... [I] from the film "A Date With Judy"	Columbia 38239

116

DATE CHARTED	PEAK POS	WKS CHRT'D	ARTIST — Record Title	Label & Number
			BERNIE CUMMINS & HIS ORCHESTRA Akron-based bandleader, former boxer	
3/03/28	**14**	2	1. Where The Cot-Cot-Cotton Grows................ vocal trio	Brunswick 3722
6/28/30	**7**	8	2. Absence Makes The Heart Grow Fonder (For Somebody Else)................................ vocal: Paul Small flip side of #1 hit "Dancing With Tears in My Eyes" by Nat Shilkret & His Orchestra	Victor 22425
7/05/30	**20**	1	3. Livin' In The Sunlight, Lovin' In The Moonlight .... from the film "The Big Pond" 2 & 3: Bernie Cummins & His Hotel New Yorker Orchestra	Victor 22409
11/11/33	**18**	1	4. I'll Be Faithful..	Columbia 2827
11/13/37	**16**	1	5. The Lady Is A Tramp............................ vocal: Connie Barleau; from the Broadway musical "Babes in Arms"	Vocalion 3714
			SONNY CURTIS Played lead guitar on Buddy Holly's earliest recordings; later sang the TV theme song for "The Mary Tyler Moore Show".	
9/26/53	**28**	1	1. The Best Way To Hold A Girl	Coral 61023

D

DATE CHARTED	PEAK POS	WKS CHRT'D	ARTIST — Record Title	Label & Number
			ROYAL DADMUN Baritone; died in 1964 (age about 78).	
4/15/22	**2(1)**	8	1. The Song Of Love .... LUCY ISABELLE MARSH & ROYAL DADMUN from the Broadway musical "Blossom Time" melody adapted from Schubert's "Unfinished" Symphony	Victor 45304
			TED DAFFAN & HIS TEXANS One of the 1940s' best country-western songwriters, steel guitarist Ted Daffan composed both his hits plus the standard "Worried Mind".	
7/17/43	**9**	17	● 1. No Letter Today/ vocal by Chuck Keeshan & Leon Seago	
8/28/43	**19**	3	2. Born To Lose .... vocal: Leon Seago	Okeh 6706
			DAGMAR Statuesque blonde (real name Jennie Lewis) who was featured on TV's "Broadway Open House" (1950-51)	
6/23/51	**21**	5	1. Mama Will Bark................................ [N] FRANK SINATRA & DAGMAR accompanied by Axel Stordahl's Orchestra	Columbia 39425
			FRANK DAILEY & HIS ORCHESTRA Sweet-band leader, later owner of famous Meadowbrook Club in New Jersey; died on 2/27/56 (54).	
7/10/37	**20**	1	1. Good Mornin' .... from the film "Mountain Music"	Variety 568
			ALAN DALE Baritone singer formerly with Carmen Cavallaro; hosted his own TV show in 1951. (also see Ray Bloch)	
8/28/48	**29**	1	1. At The Darktown Strutters' Ball................. CONNIE HAINES & ALAN DALE with Ray Bloch's Swing Eight	Signature 15197
12/05/53+	**10**	10	2. Heart Of My Heart.................................... DON CORNELL, JOHNNY DESMOND, & ALAN DALE accompanied by Jack Pleis' Orchestra song published in 1899 as "The Story of the Rose"	Coral 61076
5/22/54	**28**	1	3. East Side, West Side.............................. JOHNNY DESMOND, ALAN DALE & BUDDY GRECO, with Dick Jacobs Orchestra remake of "The Sidewalks of New York"	Coral 61176

DATE CHARTED	PEAK POS	WKS CHRT'D	ARTIST — Record Title	Label & Number
			EDWIN DALE	
12/03/21+	**9**	3	1. If You Only Knew..	Columbia 3463
2/25/22	**14**	1	2. Love Will Find A Way..............................	Columbia 3496
			from the Broadway musical "Shuffle Along"	
3/18/22	**5**	3	3. The Song Of Love	Columbia 3517
			from the Broadway musical "Blossom Time"	
9/02/22	**2(3)**	8	4. In May Time (I Learned To Love)/	
9/16/22	**4**	5	5. Song Of Persia	Columbia 3638
			CASS DALEY	
			Movie and radio singer/comedienne, started in vaudeville	
5/13/50	**11**	10	1. The Old Piano Roll Blues...........................	Decca 24977
4/14/51	**23**	3	2. The Aba Daba Honeymoon	Decca 27474
			featured in the film "Two Weeks With Love" above two: HOAGY CARMICHAEL & CASS DALEY both accompanied by Matty Matlock's All-Stars	
			VERNON DALHART	
			Born Marion Try Slaughter on 4/6/1883 in Jefferson, Texas, Vernon Dalhart was a light opera tenor before starting his recording career in 1916. It was his transformation to hillbilly singer of mournful story songs that enabled Dalhart to make music history with monumental sales on some thirty record labels and under dozens of pseudonymns ("Al Craver" and "Mack Allen" the most-used). He died on 9/15/48.	
8/11/17	**10**	1	1. Till The Clouds Roll By.............................	Emerson 7192
			from the Broadway musical "Oh, Boy!"	
3/29/19	**9**	2	2. Till We Meet Again.................................	Edison Amb. 3670
			VERNON DALHART & GLADYS RICE	
12/10/21+	**2(1)**	7	3. Tuck Me To Sleep (In My Old 'Tucky Home) ...	Victor 18807
			with Criterion Trio	
3/04/22	**5**	3	4. Weep No More, My Mammy	Columbia 3500
			flip side of #1 classic "April Showers" by Al Jolson	
3/18/22	**10**	1	5. I Want My Mammy	Columbia 3520
			VERNON DALHART & AL BERNARD	
5/27/22	**12**	1	6. Dear Old Southland.................................	Edison Amb. 4508
			also recorded for Gennett 4827 & Emerson 10511	
12/13/24+	**4**	5	7. The Pal That I Loved (Stole The Gal I Loved) .	Okeh 40177
			also recorded for Pathe 032072	
3/21/25	**1(5)**	20	● 8. **The Prisoner's Song/**	
			the biggest-selling non-holiday record of the pre-1955 era, with total sales over seven million; also recorded for Columbia 257, Edison 51459, Edison Amberol 4954, Vocalion 10850, Gennett 5588, Pathe 032085, Banner 1496, Domino 3466, Regal 9795; later recorded for Brunswick 2900 & Emerson 3013; also sang on versions by Ross Gorman Orchestra (Columbia 563) and by the Yellow Jackets (Okeh 40549)	
5/16/25	**4**	8	9. The Wreck Of The Old 97	Victor 19427
			also recorded for Edison Amberol 4898, Gennett 5588, Banner 1531 & Regal 9829	
7/25/25	**14**	1	10. In The Baggage Coach Ahead......................	Victor 19627
			also recorded for Edison 51557, Banner 1549, Cameo 766, Domino 3519, & Regal 9847	
10/24/25	**10**	1	11. The Letter Edged In Black..........................	Brunswick 2900
			also recorded for Edison Amberol 5088, Banner 1653, Cameo 809, & Regal 9959; later on Victor 19837 & Edison 51649	
12/05/25+	**1(7)**	12	● 12. **The Prisoner's Song** .... [R]	Victor 19427
			original hit returns to #1 position	
12/26/25+	**3**	7	13. The Death Of Floyd Collins/	
			also recorded for Edison Amberol 5049; later for Columbia 15064	
1/02/26	**6**	3	14. The Wreck Of The Shenandoah	Victor 19779
			also recorded for Columbia 15041, Edison 51620, Edison Amberol 5078, Gennett 3158, Banner 1652, Cameo 809, Domino 3623, & Regal 9958	
1/02/26	**9**	2	15. The Convict And The Rose	Victor 19770
			also recorded for Okeh 40506, Edison 51643, Edison Amberol 5081, Gennett 3158, Pathe 32150, Perfect 12229, Banner 1652, Cameo 810, Domino 3624, & Regal 9959	

DATE CHARTED	PEAK POS	WKS CHRT'D	ARTIST — Record Title	Label & Number
6/26/26	**8**	2	16. The Governor's Pardon .... Victor 19983 known on some labels as "The Prison Clock"; also recorded for Columbia 15066, Okeh 40608, Edison 51729, Edison Amberol 5151, Banner 1724, Domino 3694, & Regal 8032	
11/27/26	**4**	6	17. There's A New Star In Heaven Tonight - 　　Rudolph Valentino............................. Columbia 718 also recorded for Victor 20193, Edison 51827, Edison Amberol 5239, Gennett 3370, Path 32203, & Champion 15139	
1/15/27	**14**	2	18. The Miami Storm .... Columbia 15100 also recorded for Okeh 40692, Edison 51856, Edison Amberol 5237, Gennett 3378, Pathe 32209, & Champion 15165	
5/28/27	**16**	2	19. The Wreck Of The Number Nine .... Columbia 15121 also recorded for Okeh 45086, Vocalion 5138, Edison 52088, Edison Amberol 5394, Gennett 6051, Banner 1990, Domino 3959, & Regal 8322	
8/13/27	**17**	2	20. The Mississippi Flood .... Victor 20611 also recorded for Columbia 15146, Okeh 45107, Edison 52088, Edison Amberol 5395, Banner 1990, Domino 3959, Harmony 417, & Regal 8322	
8/20/27	**4**	5	21. Lindbergh (The Eagle Of The U.S.A.)/ also recorded for Victor 20674, Edison 52029, Edison Amberol 5362, & Gennett 6169	
8/27/27	**11**	2	22. 　Lucky Lindy .... Columbia 1000 also recorded for Brunswick 3572, Vocalion 5168, Edison 52029, & Edison Amberol 5356	
10/08/27	**7**	4	23. My Carolina Home .... Victor 20795 previously recorded for Okeh 45085	
1/21/28	**7**	8	24. My Blue Ridge Mountain Home.................... Victor 20539 also recorded for Okeh 45190; Dalhart & Charlie Wells recorded it for Columbia	
3/31/28	**19**	1	25. A Memory That Time Cannot Erase............. Victor 21094 above three: VERNON DALHART & CARSON ROBISON also recorded for Edison 52229, Edison Amberol 5495, Banner 7099, Domino 4140, & Regal 8544	
11/17/28	**6**	5	26. Hallelujah, I'm A Bum .... Columbia 1488 based on the traditional hymn "Revive Us Again"	
10/12/29	**7**	4	27. Farm Relief Song .... Columbia 15449 as "Al Craver"	

CHARLES D'ALMAINE
British-born first violinist for the New York Metropolitan
Opera, best known as accompanist on some of Len Spencer's biggest
hits; died on 6/17/43 (72). (also see Harry Macdonough)

9/20/02	**3**	3	1. Shepherd's Dance .... [I]　Edison 8070	
3/31/06	**9**	1	2. Medley Of Old-Time Reels........................ [I]　Victor 31480	

VIC DAMONE
Born Vito Farinola, Vic is among the most popular of postwar
ballad singers; he also appeared in several movies and hosted a TV
series (1956-57).

8/30/47	**7**	7	1. I Have But One Heart ("O Marinariello")........ Mercury 5053 Vic sings English & Italian verses on 1 & 8	
11/01/47	**7**	9	2. You Do .... Mercury 5056 from the film "Mother Wore Tights" accompanied on above two by Jerry Gray's Orchestra	
2/21/48	**22**	1	3. Thoughtless.. Mercury 5104 accompanied by Camarata's Orchestra	
6/05/48	**27**	1	4. My Fair Lady .... Mercury 5121 accompanied by Glen Osser's Orchestra	
9/18/48	**24**	1	5. It's Magic .... Mercury 5138 from the film "Romance On the High Seas"	
10/30/48	**23**	4	6. Say Something Sweet To Your Sweetheart..... Mercury 5192 VIC DAMONE & PATTI PAGE accompanied by Eric Robinson's Orchestra	
4/09/49	**6**	21	● 7. Again .... Mercury 5261 from the film "Road House"	
6/18/49	**1(4)**	26	● 8. **You're Breaking My Heart/** based on Italian art song "Mattinata" ('Tis the Day)	
7/23/49	**16**	3	9. 　The Four Winds And The Seven Seas .... Mercury 5271	
8/27/49	**10**	6	10. My Bolero... Mercury 5313	

DATE CHARTED	PEAK POS	WKS CHRT'D	ARTIST — Record Title	Label & Number
10/29/49	**20**	7	11. Why Was I Born? .... from the Broadway musical "Sweet Adeline"	Mercury 5326
1/28/50	**29**	1	12. Sitting By The Window	Mercury 5343
3/18/50	**27**	1	13. God's Country .... accompanied on 6-13 by Glenn Osser's Orchestra	Mercury 5374
7/01/50	**17**	13	14. Vagabond Shoes	Mercury 5429
7/22/50	**6**	11	15. Tzena, Tzena, Tzena .... adaptation of Israeli popular song	Mercury 5454
8/26/50	**13**	2	16. Just Say I Love Her/ above two accompanied by Ronnie Selby's Orchestra & Chorus	
10/14/50	**25**	1	17. Can Anyone Explain? (No! No! No!)............. accompanied by Ralph Martiere's Orchestra	Mercury 5474
9/16/50	**11**	3	18. Cincinnati Dancing Pig .... accompanied by Ralph Martiere's Orchestra & the Meadowlarks	Mercury 5477
12/30/50+	**4**	15	19. My Heart Cries For You/ adapted from French folk song "Chanson de Marie Antoinette"	
12/30/50+	**18**	2	20. Music By The Angels..............................	Mercury 5563
2/03/51	**21**	4	21. Tell Me You Love Me .... adapted from an aria in the opera "I Pagliacci"	Mercury 5572
2/17/51	**28**	3	22. If .... above four accompanied by George Siravo's Orchestra	Mercury 5565
6/02/51	**4**	17	23. My Truly, Truly Fair..............................	Mercury 5646
8/04/51	**12**	11	24. Longing For You....................................	Mercury 5655
10/06/51	**13**	3	25. Calla Calla...	Mercury 5698
5/10/52	**22**	1	26. Jump Through The Ring .... above four accompanied by George Bassman's Orchestra	Mercury 5785
6/14/52+	**8**	9	27. Here In My Heart	Mercury 5858
7/12/52	**30**	3	28. Take My Heart/	
7/26/52	**23**	2	29. Rosanne.. above two accompanied by Norman Leyden's Orchestra	Mercury 5877
1/17/53	**13**	3	30. Sugar	Mercury 70054
5/16/53	**10**	7	31. April In Portugal................................... Portugese song originally published as "Coimbra" above two accompanied by David Carroll's Orchestra	Mercury 70128
8/08/53	**12**	5	32. Eternally.. theme from the film "Limelight", composed by Charlie Chaplin	Mercury 70186
10/17/53	**10**	11	33. Ebb Tide	Mercury 70216
12/26/53	**30**	1	34. A Village In Peru .... above three accompanied by Richard Hayman's Orchestra	Mercury 70269
1/23/54	**21**	4	35. The Breeze And I................................... adapted from the Spanish song "Andalucia"	Mercury 70287
4/03/54	**27**	1	36. The Sparrow Sings .... above two accompanied by David Carroll's Orchestra & the Jack Halloran Singers	Mercury 70326

DARDANELLE TRIO
Dardanelle: talented pianist-vibraphonist-singer

12/14/46	**11**	2	1. September Song.. from the Broadway musical "Knickerbocker Holiday"	RCA Victor 1993

BILL DARNEL
Singer formerly with the Red Nichols, Bob Chester, and Al Kavelin bands.

2/25/50	**18**	2	1. Chattanoogie Shoe Shine Boy	Coral 60147
7/08/50	**26**	1	2. M-I-S-S-I-S-S-I-P-P-I .... with the Heathertones accompanied on above two by Roy Ross' Orchestra	Coral 60220
8/08/53	**21**	5	3. Tonight, Love... accompanied by Bob Austin's Orchestra melody based on Liszt's "Second Hungarian Rhapsody"	Decca 28706

DAVIS SISTERS
Skeeter Davis (real name Mary Frances Penick) and Betty Davis (died in a 1953 car accident).

10/10/53	**18**	2	1. I Forgot More Than You'll Ever Know..........	RCA Victor 5345

DATE CHARTED	PEAK POS	WKS CHRT'D	ARTIST — Record Title	Label & Number
			JANETTE DAVIS	
			Featured on Arthur Godfrey's TV show. (see Jerry Wayne)	
			JIMMIE DAVIS	
			Country-western star who wrote such standards as "You Are My Sunshine" (his version on Decca 5813); twice elected governor of Louisiana, 1944-48 and 1960-64.	
12/11/37	19	1	1. Nobody's Darling But Mine	Decca 1504
12/17/38	13	1	2. Meet Me Tonight In Dreamland....................	Decca 5616
			with Charles Mitchell & His Texans	
			LILLIAN DAVIS	
			Pseudonym for Marguerite Dunlap	
			MEYER DAVIS & HIS ORCHESTRA	
			Bandleader best known for booking dance bands for the White House and other prestige affairs; Claude Thornhill was his 1933 pianist.	
5/30/25	15	1	1. Washington And Lee Swing .... [I]	Victor 19526
			introduction: Sweetheart of Sigma Chi; listed as "Meyer Davis' Le Paradis Band"	
11/18/33	17	1	2. Heat Wave..	Columbia 2821
			vocal: Charlotte Murray; from the Broadway musical "As Thousands Cheer"	
12/16/33	6	4	3. Did You Ever See A Dream Walking?...........	Columbia 2852
			from the film "Sitting Pretty"	
			MILES DAVIS	
			All-time jazz trumpet great; played in 1940s with Charlie Parker and Benny Carter bands. (also see Billy Eckstine)	
			SAMMY DAVIS, JR.	
			Dynamic singer/dancer/actor, a polished entertainer from childhood, successful on Broadway, movies, and TV.	
8/21/54	16	10	1. Hey There	Decca 29199
			from the Broadway musical "The Pajama Game"	
12/18/54	28	1	2. The Red Grapes.......................................	Decca 29310
			accompanied on both by Sy Oliver's Orchestra	
			DOLLY DAWN & HER DAWN PATROL	
			Dolly, born Theresa Maria Stabile, was George Hall's popular singer and after several years his adopted daughter; all 1936-42 records under her name were with the Hall band.	
6/06/36	20	1	1. I'll Stand By	Bluebird 6381
3/20/37	17	1	2. What Will I Tell My Heart?	Bluebird 6796
7/10/37	7	5	3. The You And Me That Used To Be	Variety 557
9/25/37	8	4	4. Have You Got Any Castles, Baby?...............	Variety 621
			from the film "Varsity Show"	
12/04/37	4	4	5. Blossoms On Broadway............................	Vocalion 3790
1/01/38	1(1)	11	6. **You're A Sweetheart**...............................	Vocalion 3874
			movie title song	
4/16/38	17	3	7. How'd Ja Like To Love Me?........................	Vocalion 4018
			from the film "College Swing"	
11/05/38	8	5	8. Who Blew Out The Flame?	Vocalion 4383
1/21/39	14	3	9. Where Has My Little Dog Gone?	Vocalion 4509
11/11/39	9	10	10. Goody Goodbye	Vocalion 5160
2/07/42	22	1	11. Pig Foot Pete	Bluebird 11402
			from the film "Keep 'Em Flying"	
4/03/48	23	1	12. The Same Old Cry....................................	Regent 112
			with Danny Mendelsohn Orchestra	
			DENNIS DAY	
			New York-born tenor (real name Eugene McNulty) who sang and performed in comedy sketches on Jack Benny's radio and TV shows from 1939 to the 1960s; also in several movies.	
5/03/47	8	5	1. Mam'selle..	RCA Victor 2211
			from the film "The Razor's Edge"	
3/26/49	23	1	2. Clancy Lowered The Boom	RCA Victor 2810
1/14/50	14	4	3. Dear Hearts And Gentle People	RCA Victor 3102
			with the Rhythmaires	
			also released on RCA Victor 78-3596	
			above three accompanied by Charles Dant's Orchestra	

DATE CHARTED	PEAK POS	WKS CHRT'D	ARTIST — Record Title	Label & Number
8/26/50	17	8	4. Goodnight Irene...	RCA Victor 3870
8/26/50	29	1	5. Mona Lisa .... with the Ray Charles Choir & Henri Rene's Orchestra from the film "Captain Carey, U.S.A."	RCA Victor 3753
10/14/50	22	4	6. All My Love .... based on the French song "Bolero" above two accompanied by Charles Dant Orchestra	RCA Victor 3870
6/09/51	13	7	7. Mister And Mississippi................................ with Norman Luboff Choir	RCA Victor 4140

DORIS DAY

Born Doris Kappelhoff on 4/3/22 in Cincinnati. Doris sang briefly with Bob Crosby in 1940 and shortly thereafter became a major star with the Les Brown band ("Sentimental Journey"). Her great solo recording success was soon transcended by Hollywood as Doris became the #1 box office star of the late 50s and early 60s; her 1968-73 TV series was also popular.

DATE CHARTED	PEAK POS	WKS CHRT'D	ARTIST — Record Title	Label & Number
11/08/47	21	3	1. Papa, Won't You Dance With Me? .... accompanied by Lou Bring's Orchestra; from the Broadway musical "High Button Shoes"	Columbia 37931
2/28/48	24	2	2. Thoughtless.. with the Modernaires	Columbia 38079
5/29/48	1(5)	24	● 3. **Love Somebody/**	
5/29/48	16	11	4. Confess... above two: DORIS DAY & BUDDY CLARK	Columbia 38174
5/29/48	27	1	5. Put 'Em In A Box, Tie It With A Ribbon (And Throw 'Em In The Deep Blue Sea)/	
7/17/48	2(1)	21	● 6. It's Magic .... above two from the film "Romance on The High Seas"	Columbia 38188
11/20/48	7	13	7. My Darling, My Darling .... from the Broadway musical "Where's Charley"	Columbia 38353
2/26/49	16	3	8. Powder Your Face With Sunshine (Smile! Smile! Smile!)....................................... above two: DORIS DAY & BUDDY CLARK above five accompanied by George Siravo's Orchestra	Columbia 38394
5/21/49	2(2)	19	9. Again/ from the film "Roadhouse"	
6/11/49	22	1	10. Everywhere You Go.............................. above two with the Mellomen	Columbia 38467
8/06/49	17	6	11. Let's Take An Old-Fashioned Walk .... FRANK SINATRA & DORIS DAY accompanied by Axel Stordahl's Orchestra from the Broadway musical "Miss Liberty"	Columbia 38513
8/27/49	20	7	12. Now That I Need You................................ from the Broadway musical "Red, Hot, and Blue"	Columbia 38507
10/22/49	15	10	13. Canadian Capers (Cuttin' Capers)................ featured in the film "My Dream Is Yours" 9, 10, 12 & 13 accompanied by John Rarig's Orchestra	Columbia 38595
11/05/49	19	2	14. Bluebird On Your Windowsill .... accompanied by George Siravo's Orchestra	Columbia 38611
1/21/50	20	3	15. Quicksilver .... with the Country Cousins	Columbia 38638
3/04/50	21	6	16. I Said My Pajamas (And Put On My Prayers)...	Columbia 38709
3/04/50	24	3	17. Enjoy Yourself (It's Later Than You Think)....	Columbia 38650
5/06/50	17	12	18. Hoop-Dee-Doo .... above two and 20 accompanied by George Wyle's Orchestra 18 & 20 with the Mellomen	Columbia 38771
5/13/50	9	15	19. Bewitched .... with the Mellomen & John Rarig's Orchestra "Bewitched, Bothered, and Bewildered" from the Broadway musical "Pal Joey"	Columbia 38698
6/24/50	19	4	20. I Didn't Slip-I Wasn't Pushed-I Fell..............	Columbia 38818
11/04/50	16	8	21. A Bushel And A Peck .... from the Broadway musical "Guys and Dolls" also released on Columbia 45-838	Columbia 39008
1/13/51	30	1	22. It's A Lovely Day Today............................ accompanied by George Siravo & His Orchestra from the Broadway musical "Call Me Madam"	Columbia 39055

DATE CHARTED	PEAK POS	WKS CHRT'D	ARTIST — Record Title	Label & Number
3/10/51	**10**	10	23. Would I Love You (Love You, Love You)........ with Harry James & His Orchestra	Columbia 39159
6/30/51	**7**	17	24. Shanghai...	Columbia 39423
11/17/51	**21**	4	25. Domino... adaptation of a French popular song	Columbia 39596
3/15/52	**1(1)**	19	● 26. **A Guy Is A Guy** .... adapted from the World War II soldiers' song "A Gob is a Slob", which in turn was based on 1719 British "I Went to the Alehouse (A Knave Is A Knave)" above three accompanied by Paul Weston's Orchestra	Columbia 39673
6/21/52	**7**	14	27. Sugarbush... DORIS DAY & FRANKIE LAINE with the Norman Luboff Choir accompanied by Carl Fischer's Orchestra	Columbia 39693
8/02/52	**20**	3	28. When I Fall In Love................................... with the Norman Luboff Choir & Percy Faith's Orchestra from the film "One Minute to Zero"	Columbia 39786
10/25/52	**25**	2	29. No Two People .... DORIS DAY & DONALD O'CONNOR from the film "Hans Christian Andersen"	Columbia 39863
12/13/52	**20**	2	30. A Full Time Job/	
12/27/52	**23**	1	31. Ma Says, Pa Says.................................... South African song above two: DORIS DAY & JOHNNIE RAY	Columbia 39898
1/17/53	**10**	7	32. Mister Tap Toe .... with the Norman Luboff Choir	Columbia 39906
4/25/53	**29**	1	33. When The Red Red Robin Comes Bob-Bob- Bobbin' Along....................................	Columbia 39970
6/13/53	**17**	2	34. Candy Lips .... DORIS DAY & JOHNNIE RAY	Columbia 40001
8/15/53	**30**	1	35. Kiss Me Again, Stranger/	
8/29/53	**25**	1	36. A Purple Cow..	Columbia 40020
9/19/53	**20**	2	37. Choo Choo Train (Ch-Ch-Foo) .... [N] adapted from the French popular song "Le Petit Train" above nine accompanied by Paul Weston's Orchestra	Columbia 40063
1/09/54	**1(4)**	22	● 38. **Secret Love** .... from the film "Calamity Jane"	Columbia 40108
4/24/54	**16**	4	39. I Speak To The Stars................................ from the film "Lucky Me" above two accompanied by Ray Heindorf's Orchestra	Columbia 40210
9/11/54	**3**	17	40. If I Give My Heart To You/ with the Mellomen	
10/02/54	**27**	1	41. Anyone Can Fall In Love.......................... accompanied by Frank DeVol's Orchestra	Columbia 40300

EDITH DAY
Minneapolis-born star of Broadway and London musical stage, most noteably "Irene", "Orange Blossoms", and "Wildflower"; died on 5/1/71 (75).

4/17/20	**1(1)**	9	1. **Alice Blue Gown**	Victor 45173
5/15/20	**3**	4	2. Irene .... above two from the Broadway musical "Irene"	Victor 45176

IRENE DAYE
Sang with Mal Hallett, Gene Krupa (1938-41), & Charlie Spivak bands, later married Spivak; died on 11/1/71 (53).

ALAN DEAN

8/23/52	**26**	4	1. Luna Rossa (Blushing Moon) .... accompanied by the Joe Lipman Orchestra	MGM 11269

DE CASTRO SISTERS
Peggy, Babette & Cherie, raised in Cuba

10/09/54+	**2(1)**	20	1. Teach Me Tonight	Abbott 3001

LOLA DEE WITH STUBBY & THE BUCCANEERS

5/08/54	**25**	2	1. Padre	Mercury 70342

DATE CHARTED	PEAK POS	WKS CHRT'D	ARTIST — Record Title	Label & Number
			DEEP RIVER BOYS	
			R&B group; made some recordings with Count Basie	
11/20/48	18	5	1. Recess In Heaven...................................	RCA Victor 3203
			BUDDY DeFRANCO	
			Great jazz clarinetist who played with Gene Krupa (1941-42), Charlie Barnet (1943-44), Tommy Dorsey (1944-46,47-48), and Count Basie (1950).	
			EMILIO DeGOGORZA	
			Brooklyn-born baritone, of Spanish parents; never performed on opera stage, but said to have one of the great voices of his time. Died on 5/10/49 (74).	
8/31/01	4	3	1. In The Shade Of The Palm..........................	Victor 780
			under pseudonym Herbert Goddard; from the Broadway musical "Floradora"; based on a Nocturne by Chopin	
2/25/05	6	1	2. Carmen: Toreador Song .... [F]	Victor 4074
			as "Sig. Francisco"	
11/30/07	6	1	3. Drink To Me Only With Thine Eyes	Victor 74077
8/08/08	3	3	4. O Sole Mio.. [F]	Victor 74105
1/08/16	7	1	5. Noche Serena (Calm Night) .... [F]	Victor 64480
7/22/16	9	1	6. Non E Ver ('tis Not True) .... [F]	Victor 74421
7/12/19	6	3	7. Juanita..	Victor 64812
			GLORIA DeHAVEN	
			Star of many Hollywood musicals, started as band singer with Bob Crosby and Jan Savitt.	
9/08/51	11	12	1. Because Of You	Decca 27666
			GLORIA DeHAVEN with GUY LOMBARDO & HIS ROYAL CANADIANS featured in the film "I Was An American Spy"	
			GUIDO DEIRO	
			Guido and Pietro Deiro, Italian-born brothers, long-popular accordionists; Guido died on 7/26/50 (64).	
7/15/11	6	2	1. Sharpshooters' March............................ [I]	Columbia 984
			PIETRO DEIRO	
			Died on 11/3/54 (66).	
4/04/14	7	2	1. Broadway Medley .... [I]	Victor 17486
7/15/16	8	1	2. Over The Waves Waltz............................ [I]	Victor 17950
			DE JOHN SISTERS	
			Julie & Dux DeGiovanni	
12/25/54	26	1	1. No More	Epic 9085
			orchestra directed by O.B. Masingill	
			EDDIE DeLANGE	
			Co-leader of the Hudson-DeLange Orchestra, wrote lyrics to the hit songs "Moonglow" and "Solitude"; died on 7/13/49 (45).	
11/12/38	11	5	1. Button, Button (Who's Got The Button?).......	Bluebird 7837
11/19/38	17	3	2. My Kid's Singing Swing Songs....................	Bluebird 10003
1/21/39	11	3	3. What This Country Needs Is Foo'............. [N]	Bluebird 10074
4/15/39	13	4	4. Beer Barrel Polka	Bluebird 10199
			adaptation of a popular Czechoslovakian song all vocals: Elisse Cooper	
			VAUGHN DELEATH	
			Renowned as the first woman to sing on radio, Vaughn (real name: Leonore Vonderleath) was said to have performed over 15,000 songs on 2,000 broadcasts from early 20s to mid-30s. Credited by some as the first "crooner", she also co-wrote a number of songs; died on 5/28/43 (46). (Also see Ben Bernie, Sam Lanin, Fred Rich, Ben Selvin, and Paul Whiteman)	
8/27/21	13	1	1. All By Myself	Okeh 4355
9/23/22	10	1	2. I'm Just Wild About Harry	Gennett 4905
			from the Broadway musical "Shuffle Along"	
8/22/25	6	4	3. Ukelele Lady..	Columbia 361
10/23/26	10	1	4. Where'd You Get Those Eyes?....................	Gennett 3347

DATE CHARTED	PEAK POS	WKS CHRT'D	ARTIST — Record Title	Label & Number
12/25/26	**12**	1	5. Cross Your Heart .... VAUGHN DELEATH & ED SMALLE from the Broadway musical "Queen High"	Columbia 711
4/30/27	**15**	2	6. Blue Skies .... from the Broadway musical "Betsy"	Okeh 40750
8/06/27	**17**	1	7. The Whisper Song .... also recorded for Edison 52018	Okeh 40814
10/01/27	**4**	7	8. Are You Lonesome Tonight?	Edison 52044
11/19/27	**18**	1	9. Baby Your Mother (Like She Babied You)	Victor 20873
1/28/28	**20**	1	10. Here Comes The Showboat	Edison 52104
2/04/28	**13**	3	11. Together, We Two .... VAUGHN DELEATH & ED SMALLE	Victor 21042
6/30/28	**11**	3	12. Little Mother	Brunswick 3893
11/10/28	**16**	2	13. Do I Hear You Saying "I Love You"? .... VAUGHN DELEATH & "FRANK HARRIS" (Irving Kaufman) from the Broadway musical "Present Arms"	Columbia 1470
			DELTA RHYTHM BOYS Gospel-styled vocal group; in some minor 40s movies. (Also see Ella Fitzgerald)	
2/23/46	**17**	1	1. Just A-Sittin' And A-Rockin'	Decca 18739
			CLARK DENNIS Tenor ballad singer and pianist, briefly with Ben Pollack and Paul Whiteman bands.	
6/21/47	**8**	10	1. Peg O' My Heart .... accompanied by Billy May's Orchestra from the Broadway musical "Ziegfeld Follies of 1913"	Capitol 346
3/26/49	**23**	1	2. Galway Bay .... accompanied by Buddy Cole's Orchestra	Capitol 15403
10/10/54	**24**	2	3. Grenada	Tiffany 1302
			JACK DENNY & HIS ORCHESTRA Sweet-band leader, born in Canada; died on 9/15/50 (56).	
12/07/29	**12**	4	1. Congratulations	Brunswick 4604
6/13/31	**5**	5	2. Nevertheless (I'm In Love With You) .... vocal: Rob May	Brunswick 6114
2/20/32	**3**	9	3. Auf Wiedersehen, My Dear .... listed as "Jack Denny & His Mount Royal Hotel Orchestra"	Victor 22917
5/28/32	**17**	1	4. Night .... vocal: Frank Luther	Victor 22995
12/24/32+	**10**	5	5. I've Told Ev'ry Little Star/	
12/31/32+	**12**	4	6. The Song Is You .... above two from the Broadway musical "Music in the Air"	Victor 24183
1/28/33	**5**	6	7. Moon Song .... from the film "Hello, Everybody" above three vocals: Paul Small	Victor 24217
			WILL DENNY Boston-born pioneer recording artist; died on 10/2/08 (48).	
9/24/92	**1(2)**	2	1. **The Pretty Red Rose**	New England
12/14/01	**1(4)**	7	2. **Any Old Place I Hang My Hat Is "Home, Sweet Home" To Me** .... also recorded for Edison 7901 & 3564	Gram-o-Phone 956
5/26/06	**7**	1	3. Nothing Like That In Our Family .... [C] also on Columbia cylinder 32919	Columbia 3368
			HAL DERWIN Baritone singer previously with Shep Fields and Les Brown bands	
11/30/46	**5**	10	1. The Old Lamplighter .... accompanied by Frank DeVol's Orchestra	Capitol 288
11/08/47	**25**	2	2. My, How The Time Goes By .... with the Hi-Liters	Capitol 409
3/27/48	**23**	1	3. Worry, Worry, Worry	Capitol 498

DATE CHARTED	PEAK POS	WKS CHRT'D	ARTIST — Record Title	Label & Number
			JOHNNY DESMOND	
			Born Giovanni Desimons in Detroit, Johnny sang with Bob Crosby, Gene Krupa, and Glenn Miller's military band, and throughout the 50s was featured on the "Breakfast Club" radio show. Johnny died on 9/6/85 (65).	
3/16/46	**21**	4	1. Don't You Remember Me? .... Victor 1796	
			accompanied by Russ Case & His Orchestra	
3/22/47	**12**	3	2. Guilty .... RCA Victor 2109	
			with the Page Cavanaugh Trio	
12/24/49	**22**	1	3. Don't Cry, Joe (Let Her Go, Let Her Go) .... MGM 10518	
			featuring trumpet solo by Bobby Hackett	
3/25/50	**25**	2	4. C'est Si Bon (It's So Good) .... MGM 10613	
			adaptation of a French popular song	
7/01/50	**20**	1	5. The Picnic Song.................................. MGM 10703	
8/26/50	**24**	1	6. Just Say I Love Her.............................. MGM 10758	
12/09/50	**29**	1	7. A Bushel And A Peck .... MGM 10800	
			from the Broadway musical "Guys and Dolls"	
9/08/51	**17**	8	8. Because Of You .... MGM 10947	
9/22/51	**30**	1	9. I Want To Be Near You .... MGM 11027	
11/01/52	**19**	3	10. Nina Never Knew/	
12/06/52	**26**	1	11. Stay Where You Are........................... Coral 60848	
1/31/53	**23**	3	12. Trying .... Coral 60823	
			5, 7, 8, 9 & 12 with Ray Charles Singers	
			above nine accompanied by Tony Mottola's Orchestra	
11/07/53+	**9**	7	13. Woman .... Coral 61069	
12/05/53+	**10**	10	14. Heart Of My Heart............................ Coral 61076	
			DON CORNELL, JOHNNY DESMOND, & ALAN DALE accompanied by Jack Pleis' Orchestra; song published in 1899 as "The Story of the Rose"	
4/03/54	**26**	1	15. Pine Tree, Pine Over Me........................ Coral 61126	
			JOHNNY DESMOND, EILEEN BARTON & McGUIRE SISTERS	
5/22/54	**28**	1	16. East Side, West Side............................ Coral 61176	
			JOHNNY DESMOND, ALAN DALE & BUDDY GRECO revival of "The Sidewalks of New York" above two accompanied by Dick Jacobs Orchestra	
7/17/54	**17**	5	17. The High And The Mighty....................... Coral 61204	
			accompanied by George Cates' Orchestra; movie title song	
12/25/54	**23**	2	18. My Own True Love (Tara's Theme) .... Coral 61301	
			vocal version of the "Gone With the Wind" theme; accompanied by Richard Shores' Orchestra	
			EMERY DEUTSCH & HIS ORCHESTRA	
			Hungarian-born violinist-bandleader who wrote "Play, Fiddle, Play" and "Stardust on the Moon", among other popular songs.	
10/30/37	**18**	1	1. Vieni, Vieni.................................... Brunswick 7972	
			popular Corsican song with English lyrics	
11/06/37	**19**	1	2. When The Organ Played "Oh Promise Me" ..... Brunswick 7979	
			above two vocals: Barry McKinley	
9/16/39	**13**	5	3. Vas Vilst Du Gaily Star .... Bluebird 10340	
			vocal: Mildred Craig	
			FRANK DeVOL & HIS ORCHESTRA	
			Lead alto saxophonist and arranger for the Hoarce Heidt band in the late 30s, arranger for Alvino Rey; orchestra conductor for Doris Day, Nat King Cole, Gordon MacRae, Kay Starr, Margaret Whiting, and other singers. Frank later composed background scores for many films, and the TV theme for "My Three Sons".	
9/23/50	**28**	1	1. Dream Awhile .... Capitol 1143	
			vocal by choir	
			EMIL DEWAN QUARTONES	
			Piano, vibes, guitar and bass	
8/11/51	**22**	1	1. Aeluna Mezzumare (Butcher Boy) .... Mercury 5537	
			AL DEXTER & HIS TROOPERS	
			Born Albert Poindexter, a top country singer/songwriter/guitarist; died on 1/31/84 (81).	
6/19/43	**1(8)**	34	● 1. **Pistol Packin' Mama**............................. Okeh 6708	
4/01/44	**23**	1	2. Too Late To Worry, Too Blue To Cry .... Okeh 6718	

DATE CHARTED	PEAK POS	WKS CHRT'D	ARTIST — Record Title	Label & Number
4/22/44	**29**	1	3. Rosalita	Okeh 6708
3/02/46	**16**	1	4. Guitar Polka	Columbia 36898

LEO DIAMOND
Harmonica virtuoso

10/03/53	**14**	5	1. Off Shore.. [I]	Ambassador 1005

MARLENE DIETRICH
All-time great movie star and glamour symbol, born Maria Magdalene Dietrich Von Losch in Weimar, Germany; in her first American-released film, "The Blue Angel" (1931), she popularized the song "Falling in Love Again".

8/23/52	**12**	6	1. Too Old To Cut The Mustard	Columbia 39812

ROSEMARY CLOONEY & MARLENE DIETRICH
accompanying band led by Stan Freeman (harpsichord)

BOB DINI
Singer from Boston

8/22/53	**22**	3	1. Too Long..	Derby 826

accompanied by Norman Leyden's Orchestra

10/17/53	**22**	4	2. Goodbye My Love	Derby 833

accompanied by Paul Werrick's Orchestra

DINNING SISTERS
Ginger, Lou and Jean Dinning from Chicago

5/03/47	**9**	4	1. My Adobe Hacienda.................................	Capitol 389
10/11/47	**12**	1	2. I Wonder Who's Kissing Her Now	Capitol 433

movie title song; originally from the Broadway musical "The Prince of Tonight"

2/28/48	**12**	3	3. Beg Your Pardon	Capitol 490

accompanied by Jack Fascinato's Orchestra

10/30/48	**5**	16	● 4. Buttons And Bows	Capitol 15184

from film "The Paleface"
2 & 4 accompanied by Art Van Damme Quintet

HELENE DIXON

6/13/53	**21**	2	1. The Breeze (That's Bringin' My Honey Back To Me/	

accompanied by Norman Leyden's Orchestra
song published in 1934

7/04/53	**27**	2	2. Don't Call My Name	Okeh 6964

accompanied by George Siravo's Orchestra

RAYMOND DIXON
Pseudonym for Lambert Murphy

WILLIE DIXON
Important Chicago blues bassist and songwriter, long associated with Muddy Waters. (see Rosetta Howard)

LEW DOCKSTADER
Popular vaudeville and minstrel show comedy star from the late 1870s to the early 1900s; died on 10/26/24 (68).

12/23/05	**4**	2	1. Everybody Works But Father .... [C]	Columbia 3251

also on Columbia cylinder 32927

JOHNNY DODDS' BLACK BOTTOM STOMPERS
Leading New Orleans-born jazz clarinetist, played with King Oliver, Louis Armstrong, and Jelly Roll Morton; died on 8/8/40 (48).

10/08/27	**15**	2	1. Wild Man Blues .... [I]	Brunswick 3567

band includes Louis Armstrong (cornet), Barney Bigard (tenor sax), and Earl Hines (piano)

CLYDE DOERR & HIS ORCHESTRA
Alto saxophonist-bandleader; sidemen included Harry Reser (banjo)

1/13/23	**5**	3	1. Suez... [I]	Victor 18947

BILL DOGGETT
Jazz organist who played with Lucky Millinder, Ink Spots (1942-44), Louis Jordan; his "Honky Tonk" was a 1956 million-seller. (also see Ella Fitzgerald)

DATE CHARTED	PEAK POS	WKS CHRT'D	ARTIST — Record Title	Label & Number
			FATS DOMINO New Orleans' immortal contribution to rock and roll, Antoine Domino ultimately sold some 60 million records.	
6/14/52	**30**	1	● 1. Goin' Home.. #1 R&B hit	Imperial 5180
6/13/53	**24**	2	● 2. Goin' To The River....................................	Imperial 5231
			DOMINOES Landmark R&B group, led by Clyde McPhatter and pianist Billy Ward	
8/25/51	**17**	9	● 1. Sixty Minute Man..................................... 14 weeks at #1 on R&B charts	Federal 12022
			DON, DICK, N' JIMMY	
3/06/54	**23**	2	1. Angela Mia	Crown 104
10/23/54	**14**	6	2. That's What I Like	Crown 125
			AL DONOHUE & HIS ORCHESTRA Boston-born bandleader, also a songwriter and arranger; singer Paula Kelly was band's brightest star. Al died on 2/20/83 (80).	
2/01/36	**11**	3	1. Alone .... vocal: Barry McKinley; from the Marx Brothers film "A Night at the Opera"	Decca 626
8/27/38	**14**	1	2. Stop Beating 'Round The Mulberry Bush/	
9/17/38	**7**	6	3. Lambeth Walk .... from the British musical "Me and My Girl"	Vocalion 4318
11/05/38	**16**	2	4. Heart And Soul	Vocalion 4398
12/10/38+	**1(5)**	13	5. **Jeepers Creepers**.................................. from the film "Going Places"	Vocalion 4513
7/15/39	**7**	6	6. Moon Love... based on a theme from Tchaikovsky's 5th Symphony, 2nd movement	Vocalion 4888
7/15/39	**12**	3	7. Stairway To The Stars .... adaptation of the instrumental "Park Avenue Fantasy"	Vocalion 4846
7/22/39	**14**	2	8. South American Way................................ from the Broadway musical "The Streets of Paris" Paula Kelly: above seven vocals	Vocalion 4902
3/01/41	**22**	1	9. I Hear A Rhapsody	Okeh 5888
4/05/41	**3**	9	10. The Wise Old Owl .... vocal: Dee Keating	Okeh 6037
6/07/41	**24**	1	11. With A Twist Of The Wrist......................... from the Broadway musical "Crazy With the Heat" vocals on 9 & 11: Phil Brito	Okeh 6012
			SAM DONOHUE & HIS ORCHESTRA Widely admired tenor saxophonist who played with Gene Krupa and (more briefly) with Harry James and Benny Goodman, and took over Artie Shaw's Navy band after Shaw's discharge. Later he led the Billy May Orchestra, played with Stan Kenton, and in 1960s became leader of the late Tommy Dorsey's band. Sam died on 3/22/74 (56).	
9/13/41	**17**	1	1. Do You Care?.. vocal: Irene Day	Bluebird 11198
7/13/46	**9**	6	2. Dinah	Capitol 260
8/03/46	**8**	7	3. Just The Other Day................................. vocal: Mynell Allen	Capitol 275
10/26/46	**8**	2	4. Put That Kiss Back Where You Found It .... vocal: Bill Lockwood	Capitol 293
12/14/46+	**7**	7	5. A Rainy Night In Rio .... from the film "The Time, The Place, And The Girl"	Capitol 325
4/19/47	**5**	7	6. My Melancholy Baby .... [I]	Capitol 357
5/10/47	**2(1)**	23	7. I Never Knew .... vocal: Bill Lockwood & Blue Hues	Capitol 405
11/01/47	**9**	2	8. Red Wing/	
11/08/47	**6**	7	9. The Whistler....................................	Capitol 472
2/21/48	**21**	2	10. Tacos, Enchiladas, & Beans/ above three vocals: Shirley Lloyd	
3/13/48	**23**	1	11. Robbins Nest .... [I]	Capitol 493
8/21/48	**24**	1	12. Saxa-Boogie..................................... [I]	Capitol 1508

DATE CHARTED	PEAK POS	WKS CHRT'D	ARTIST — Record Title	Label & Number
10/16/48	**26**	3	13. I'll Get Along Somehow............................ Capitol 15081 vocal: Bill Lockwood	
12/11/48	**26**	1	14. September In The Rain .... Capitol 15172 vocal: Bob DuRant, Tak Takvorian, & Ralph Osborn; from the film "Melody for Two"	

HUGH DONOVAN
Pseudonym for Charles Harrison

RAY DOREY
Sang with Larry Green's Orchestra

DATE CHARTED	PEAK POS	WKS CHRT'D	ARTIST — Record Title	Label & Number
5/03/47	**7**	8	1. Mam'selle...................................... Majestic 7217 accompanied by Paul Baron's Orchestra from the film "The Razor's Edge"	

DORSEY BROTHERS ORCHESTRA
Tommy and Jimmy Dorsey were two of the hottest session musicians in the country during the 1928-33 period, and the records under their name during these years featured some of the era's other top sidemen. In 1934 they formed a permanent band with arrangements by Glenn Miller. Both went on to individual glory after splitting in 1935, but the brothers were reunited in 1953 when Jimmy joined Tommy's band. Together they hosted summer TV shows in 1954 and 1955-56. (also see Boswell Sisters and Bing Crosby)

DATE CHARTED	PEAK POS	WKS CHRT'D	ARTIST — Record Title	Label & Number
6/23/28	**20**	1	1. Coquette .... Okeh 41007	
9/22/28	**19**	1	2. Dixie Dawn................................... Okeh 41050 one of the few records on which Tommy played trumpet above two vocals: Bill Dutton	
2/02/29	**17**	2	3. Sally Of My Dreams............................ Okeh 41151 vocal: Smith Ballew	
3/23/29	**9**	4	4. Let's Do It (Let's Fall In Love) .... Okeh 41181 vocal by Bing Crosby; from the Broadway musical "Paris"	
12/27/30	**18**	1	5. Fine And Dandy .... Okeh 41471 as "The Travelers"; vocal: Scrappy Lambert; Broadway musical title song	
1/16/32	**18**	1	6. Ooh! That Kiss .... Columbia 2581 vocal: Tony Starr; from Broadway musical "The Laugh Parade" Glenn Miller (trombone) on above four; Eddie Lang (guitar) on 3-5; Bunny Berigan (trumpet) on 6 (Brunswick 6533: Bing Crosby with Dorsey Brothers Orchestra)	
9/16/33	**20**	1	7. Old Man Harlem .... [I] Brunswick 6624	
11/03/34	**15**	2	8. Lost In A Fog............................... Decca 195 originally written as the Dorseys' radio theme from the film "Have A Heart" first hit by the permanent Dorsey band, featuring Tommy and Glenn Miller (trombones), Jimmy (clarinet/alto sax), Charlie Spivak (trumpet), and Ray McKinley (drums)	
11/17/34	**20**	1	9. I'm Gettin' Sentimental Over You .... Decca 115 Tommy's theme song, previously recorded for Columbia 36065	
11/24/34	**5**	7	10. What A Diff'rence A Day Made .... Decca 283 from the popular Spanish song "Cuando Vuelva a tu Lado" above three vocals: Bob Crosby	
12/22/34	**17**	2	11. You're The Top .... Decca 319 vocal: Ray McKinley; from the Broadway musical "Anything Goes"	
1/19/35	**16**	3	12. It's Dark On Observatory Hill...................... Decca 314	
1/19/35	**19**	1	13. Honeysuckle Rose.................................. Decca 296 vocals: Don Mattison, Skeets Herfurt & Roc Hillman	
2/02/35	**3**	7	14. I Believe In Miracles................................. Decca 335	
2/16/35	**18**	1	15. If It's Love .... Decca 321 from the Broadway musical "Calling All Stars" vocals on above two & 12: Bob Crosby	
2/23/35	**10**	4	16. Tiny Little Fingerprints .... Decca 367 vocal: Kay Weber	
3/02/35	**10**	4	17. Night Wind .... Decca 376	
4/06/35	**1(2)**	11	18. **Lullaby Of Broadway** .... Decca 370 from the film "Gold Diggers of 1935" above two vocals: Bob Crosby	
6/22/35	**1(3)**	9	19. **Chasing Shadows** .... Decca 476 vocal: Bob Eberle	

DATE CHARTED	PEAK POS	WKS CHRT'D	ARTIST — Record Title	Label & Number
7/06/35	10	7	20. Every Little Movement/	
7/13/35	14	2	21. I'll Never Say "Never Again" Again............ Decca 480 vocal: same trio as 13 (Decca 543, 547, & 548: Bing Crosby with Dorsey Brothers Orchestra)	Decca 480
7/27/35	17	1	22. Every Single Little Tingle Of My Heart.......... Decca 476 vocals on 20 & 22: Kay Weber	Decca 476
10/12/35	2(1)	5	23. You Are My Lucky Star .... Decca 559	Decca 559
10/12/35	3	11	24. I've Got A Feelin' You're Foolin'................ Decca 560 above two vocals: Bob Eberle; both from the film "Broadway Melody of 1936"	Decca 560
10/26/35	17	1	25. The Gentlemen Obviously Doesn't Believe (In Love).. Decca 561 vocal: Kay Weber above three without Tommy Dorsey	Decca 561
4/10/54	30	1	26. My Friend The Ghost................................ Bell 1029 vocal: Gordon Polk; listed as "Tommy Dorsey & His Orchestra with Jimmy Dorsey"	Bell 1029

JIMMY DORSEY & HIS ORCHESTRA

Jimmy Dorsey, born on 2/29/04 in Shanandoah, Pa., used his vast skills as alto saxophonist and clarinetist with a multitude of bands during the late 20s and early 30s: both he and Tommy played with the California Ramblers, Charleston Chasers, Jean Goldkette, Red Nichols, and Paul Whiteman, among others; Jimmy also recorded with Ted Lewis and Ben Selvin. When Tommy walked out on the brothers' band in 1935, most of the members stayed with Jimmy. It was the vocals of Bob Eberly and Helen O'Connell which swept the band onto a remarkable wave of popularity in the early 40s. Jimmy died on 6/12/57 just as his million-seller "So Rare" was climbing the charts. (also see Andrews Sisters, Bing Crosby & Francis Langford)

DATE CHARTED	PEAK POS	WKS CHRT'D	ARTIST — Record Title	Label & Number
12/14/35	19	2	1. You Let Me Down...................................... Decca 602 from the film "Stars Over Broadway"	Decca 602
5/23/36	5	6	2. You .... Decca 764 from the film "The Great Ziegfeld"	Decca 764
5/30/36	1(4)	10	3. Is It True What They Say About Dixie?/ above three vocals: Bob Eberle	
5/30/36	18	1	4. Welcome, Stranger.................................. Decca 768 vocal: Kay Weber	Decca 768
6/06/36	19	1	5. What's The Reason (I'm Not Pleasin' You) .. [I] Decca 762 mainstays of late-30s Jimmy Dorsey band: Bobby Byrne (trombone), Toots Camarata (trumpet/arranger), Ray McKinley (drums) (Decca 871: Bing Crosby with Jimmy Dorsey & His Orchestra) (Decca 940: Frances Langford with Jimmy Dorsey & His Orchestra)	Decca 762
12/19/36	19	1	6. Pennies From Heaven .... Decca 951 vocal: Bob Eberle; movie title song (Decca 1185 & 1210: Bing Crosby with Jimmy Dorsey & His Orchestra)	Decca 951
5/01/37	6	8	7. The Love Bug Will Bite You .... Decca 1187 vocal: Ray McKinley	Decca 1187
3/19/38	4	12	8. How'd Ja Like To Love Me?/ [H-R] vocal: Don Mattison	
3/26/38	3	7	9. I Fall In Love With You Every Day .... Decca 1671 above two from the film "College Swing"	Decca 1671
3/26/38	7	7	10. Love Walked In/ from the film "Goldwyn Follies"	
4/16/38	9	4	11. At A Perfume Counter .... Decca 1724 above three vocals: Bob Eberle	Decca 1724
5/14/38	10	3	12. At Your Beck And Call .... Decca 1784 vocal: Don Mattison	Decca 1784
6/18/38	13	2	13. John Silver.. [I] Decca 1860	Decca 1860
8/13/38	16	4	14. There's A Faraway Look In Your Eye .... Decca 1834 (Decca 1974 & 2214: Andrews Sisters with Jimmy Dorsey & His Orchestra)	Decca 1834
10/08/38	1(2)	12	15. Change Partners .... Decca 2002 from the film "Carefree" above two vocals: Bob Eberle	Decca 2002

DATE CHARTED	PEAK POS	WKS CHRT'D	ARTIST — Record Title	Label & Number
10/22/38	**12**	8	16. I Haven't Changed A Thing .... vocal: June Richmond	Decca 1961
3/04/39	**4**	12	17. The Masquerade Is Over	Decca 2293
3/11/39	**2(2)**	7	18. Deep Purple .... written several years earlier for solo piano	Decca 2295
3/18/39	**9**	5	19. I Get Along Without You Very Well	Decca 2322
5/06/39	**4**	2	20. Our Love .... melody adapted from a theme in Tchaikovsky's "Romeo and Juliet"	Decca 2352
7/22/39	**13**	2	21. I Poured My Heart Into A Song .... from the film "Second Fiddle" above five vocals: Bob Eberly	Decca 2553
7/29/39	**10**	7	22. Especially For You .... vocal: Helen O'Connell	Decca 2554
8/05/39	**8**	5	23. Stairway To The Stars .... adapted from instrumental "Park Avenue Fantasy"	Decca 2567
11/25/39	**20**	1	24. So Many Times......................................	Decca 2727
12/23/39	**13**	2	25. I Didn't Know What Time It Was................. from the Broadway musical "Too Many Girls" Freddy Slack: pianist on Decca 1724-2813	Decca 2813
1/13/40	**13**	3	26. On A Little Street In Singapore	Decca 2838
5/25/40	**1(1)**	14	27. **The Breeze And I/** adapted from the Spanish song "Andalucia" above five vocals: Bob Eberly	
6/01/40	**16**	3	28. Little Curly Hair In A High Chair .... [N] from the film "Forty Little Mothers"	Decca 3150
6/29/40	**4**	14	29. Six Lessons From Madame La Zonga .... above two vocals: Helen O'Connell	Decca 3152
7/20/40	**9**	6	30. All This And Heaven Too .... movie title song	Decca 3259
9/07/40	**24**	1	31. Where Do You Keep Your Heart?	Decca 3270
12/07/40	**25**	1	32. And So Do I .... above vocals: Bob Eberly	Decca 3311
12/14/40+	**23**	2	33. The Bad Humor Man/ [N]	
1/11/41	**19**	1	34. You've Got Me This Way .... above two vocals: Helen O'Connell; both from the film "You'll Find Out" top sidemen in early-40s Dorsey band: Shorty Sherlock (trumpet, 1938-40), Sonny Lee (trombone), Herbie Haymer (tenor sax), and Joe Lippman (piano)	Decca 3435
1/18/41	**1(2)**	10	35. **I Hear A Rhapsody**	Decca 3570
2/08/41	**1(2)**	10	36. **High On A Windy Hill**	Decca 3585
3/15/41	**1(10)**	17	● 37. **Amapola**... vocal: Bob & Helen; adaptation of a Spanish song featured in the film "First Love"	Decca 3629
3/22/41	**9**	8	38. Tonight (Perfidia)............................... [I]	Decca 3198
4/12/41	**11**	13	39. I Understand.......................................	Decca 3585
4/19/41	**22**	1	40. Turn Left .... [I]	Decca 3647
5/10/41	**1(2)**	12	41. **My Sister And I**................................... vocals on 35-36, 39 & 41: Bob Eberly	Decca 3710
5/17/41	**1(4)**	24	● 42. **Green Eyes/** vocal: Bob & Helen; Cuban song published in 1931 ("Aquellos Ojos Verdes")	
5/17/41	**1(6)**	18	43. **Maria Elena**....................................... vocal: Bob Eberly; Mexican song with English lyrics	Decca 3698
5/31/41	**2(2)**	18	44. Yours .... vocal: Bob & Helen; Spanish popular song ("Quierme Mucho")	Decca 3657
6/07/41	**7**	11	45. The Things I Love	Decca 3737
7/05/41	**1(1)**	20	46. **Blue Champagne/**	
7/19/41	**22**	1	47. All Alone And Lonely............................. above three vocals: Bob Eberly	Decca 3775
8/16/41	**10**	13	48. Time Was	Decca 3859
8/30/41	**23**	1	49. Embraceable You................................... vocal: Helen O'Connell; from the Broadway musical "Girl Crazy"	Decca 3928

DATE CHARTED	PEAK POS	WKS CHRT'D	ARTIST — Record Title	Label & Number
9/27/41	2(1)	14	50. Jim .... vocals on 48 & 50: Bob & Helen	Decca 3963
11/15/41	23	1	51. Wasn't It You?/	

11/29/41	25	1	52. Moonlight Masquerade ....
			    based on Isaac Albeniz' "Tango" in D-Minor
			    vocals on above two & 54: Bob Eberly
				Decca 3991

1/17/42	10	3	53. I Said No!/ featured in the film "Sweater Girl"	
2/07/42	20	1	54. This Is No Laughing Matter	Decca 4102
2/07/42	15	2	55. (There'll Be Bluebirds Over) The White Cliffs Of Dover	Decca 4103
3/28/42	18	1	56. Arthur Murray Taught Me Dancing In A Hurry/ vocal: Helen O'Connell	
5/02/42	22	1	57. Not Mine	Decca 4122

4/18/42	1(6)	16	58. **Tangerine**........................
			    vocals on 53, 57 & 58: Bob & Helen
			    56, 58, 60 & 63 from the film "The Fleet's In"
				Decca 4123

4/18/42	24	1	59. When The Roses Bloom Again........................	Decca 4165
4/25/42	9	10	60. I Remember You........................	Decca 4132
5/09/42	9	9	61. Jersey Bounce .... [I]	Decca 4288
5/09/42	16	1	62. Always In My Heart........................ vocals on 59-60 & 62: Bob Eberly	Decca 4277
5/16/42	23	1	63. If You Build A Better Mousetrap........................ vocal: Bob & Helen	Decca 4132
6/06/42	12	2	64. I Threw A Kiss In The Ocean	Decca 4304
6/06/42	22	1	65. Heavenly Hideaway........................	Decca 4207
6/20/42	22	1	66. Wonder When My Baby's Coming Home .... vocals on 64 & 66: Helen O'Connell	Decca 18362
6/27/42	20	1	67. If You Are But A Dream/	
7/04/42	19	1	68. Full Moon........................	Decca 4312

7/18/42	13	5	69. This Is Worth Fighting For/
			    from the film "When Johnny Comes Marching Home"
			    vocals on 65, 67-69 & 71: Bob Eberly	

7/25/42	7	13	70. Take Me........................ vocal: Helen O'Connell	Decca 18376
8/22/42	3	11	71. My Devotion/	
9/19/42	21	1	72. Sorghum Switch .... [I]	Decca 18372
10/03/42	19	1	73. Manhattan Serenade/ published in 1928 as an instrumental	
10/10/42	21	1	74. At The Cross-Roads	Decca 18467
10/31/42	18	1	75. Daybreak .... based on Ferde Grofe's "Mississippi Suite"	Decca 18460
10/31/42	20	1	76. Ev'ry Night About This Time/	
3/06/43	19	1	77. I'm Getting Tired So I Can Sleep........................ from the Broadway musical "This is the Army"	Decca 18462

12/26/42+	14	3	78. Brazil ....
			    vocal: Bob & Helen; Brazilian samba ("Aquarelo do Brasil"),
			    featured in the film "Saludos Amigos"
				Decca 18460

5/29/43	11	4	79. Let's Get Lost .... from the film "Happy-Go-Lucky"	Decca 18532

7/24/43	20	1	80. I'll Find You........................
			    above two recorded on 7/14/42
			    vocals on 73-77 & 79-80: Bob Eberly
				Decca 18545

12/04/43+	2(1)	12	81. They're Either Too Young Or Too Old/ vocal: Kitty Kallen; from the film "Thank Your Lucky Stars"	
12/25/43+	3	16	82. Star Eyes .... vocal: Bob Eberly & Kitty Kallen; from the film "I Dood It"	Decca 18571
1/01/44	1(7)	23	● 83. **Besame Mucho**/ vocal: Bob & Kitty; Mexican song	
1/08/44	5	11	84. My Ideal........................ from the film "Playboy of Paris"	Decca 18574

DATE CHARTED	PEAK POS	WKS CHRT'D	ARTIST — Record Title	Label & Number
2/05/44	**4**	14	85. **When They Ask About You/** vocal: Kitty Kallen; from the film "Stars on Parade"	
2/26/44	**27**	1	86.　My First Love... vocals on 84 & 86: Bob Eberly	Decca 18582
4/08/44	**13**	2	87. Holiday For Strings .... [I] featuring Si Zentner (trombone)	Decca 18593
9/23/44	**20**	2	88. An Hour Never Passes .... [I]	Decca 18616
12/23/44	**29**	1	89. The Moon On My Pillow........................... above two with Buddy Morrow (trombone)	Decca 18627
4/21/45	**13**	2	90. I Should Care .... from the film "Thrill of a Romance"	Decca 18656
6/02/45	**15**	2	91. Dream/	
6/16/45	**8**	6	92.　There! I've Said It Again .... above four vocals: Teddy Walters	Decca 18670
6/30/45	**8**	1	93. Can't You Read Between The Lines? .... vocal: Jean Cromwell (Decca 23469, Jan. 1946: Bing Crosby with Jimmy Dorsey & His Orchestra)	Decca 18676
6/15/46	**8**	10	94. Doin' What Comes Natur'lly....................... vocal: Dee Parker; from the Broadway musical "Annie Get Your Gun"	Decca 18872
12/07/46	**12**	1	95. The Whole World Is Singing My Song........... vocals on 95 & 97: Bob Carroll	Decca 18917
3/29/47	**11**	1	96. Heartaches .... vocal: Bob Carroll & Dee Parker	MGM 10001
1/17/48	**10**	1	97. Ballerina	MGM 10035
1/31/48	**25**	1	98. On Green Dolphin Street .... vocal: Bill Lawrence theme from the film "Green Dolphin Street"	MGM 10098
1/14/50	**13**	11	99. Johnson Rag.. [I]	Columbia 38649
3/11/50	**15**	5	100. Rag Mop... vocal: Claire Hogan & band above two with Charlie Teagarden (trumpet) & Cutty Cutshall (trombone)	Columbia 38710

THOMAS A. DORSEY

Gospel music's greatest songwriter ('Precious Lord, Take My Hand') began in the 1920s as a blues pianist/singer who accompanied Ma Rainey and Tampa Red.

TOMMY DORSEY & HIS ORCHESTRA

Among the greatest trombonists in jazz history, Tommy Dorsey was born on 11/19/05 in Shenandoah, Pa. He played with the same wide range of bands as Jimmy, and with Vincent Lopez and Rudy Vallee, as well. Tommy started his band in 1935 with the heart of the Joe Haymes ensemble, and over the years led an extraordinary array of top musicians. The jazz arrangements of Sy Oliver were among the most acclaimed of the era, and during the early 40s the band got a sensational new star in Frank Sinatra. Tommy died on 11/26/56 (51)

DATE CHARTED	PEAK POS	WKS CHRT'D	ARTIST — Record Title	Label & Number
10/26/35	**1(1)**	14	1. **On Treasure Island/** vocal: Edythe Wright	
11/09/35	**4**	11	2.　Take Me Back To My Boots And Saddle ...... vocal: Cliff Weston	Victor 25144
11/09/35	**10**	6	3. You Are My Lucky Star............................... vocal by Eleanor Powell; from the film "Broadway Melody of 1936"	Victor 25158
11/30/35	**9**	5	4. Don't Give Up The Ship/ from the film "Shipmates Forever"	
11/30/35	**20**	2	5.　At A Little Church Affair .... above two vocals: Cliff Weston	Victor 25183
12/21/35+	**1(5)**	9	6. **The Music Goes Round And Round/**　　[N] vocal: Edythe Wright, plus dialogue with Tommy; featured in film "The Music Goes 'Round"	
1/18/36	**10**	6	7.　(If I Had) Rhythm In My Nursery Rhymes..... vocal: Edythe Wright; above two: Tommy's Clambake Seven	Victor 25201
1/11/36	**1(6)**	14	8. **Alone** .... vocal: Cliff Weston; from the Marx Brothers film "A Night At the Opera"	Victor 25191
2/22/36	**13**	3	9. A Little Rendezvous In Hawaii .... vocal: Jack Leonard	Victor 25246

DATE CHARTED	PEAK POS	WKS CHRT'D	ARTIST — Record Title	Label & Number
2/29/36	**8**	4	10. I'm Getting Sentimental Over You............ [I] Tommy's famous theme song	Victor 25236
3/21/36	**12**	3	11. Lovely Lady.. vocal: Buddy Gately; from the film "King of Burlesque"	Victor 25216
4/25/36	**5**	9	12. You Started Me Dreaming........................... vocal: Joe Dixon top sidemen in 1936 Dorsey band: Max Kaminsky (trumpet) and Joe Dixon (clarinet); most early Dorsey arrangements by Paul Weston	Victor 25284
5/02/36	**1(1)**	10	13. **You**... from the film "The Great Ziegfeld"	Victor 25291
6/06/36	**8**	5	14. Star Dust .... flip side of record: Benny Goodman's hit version of same song	Victor 25320
6/27/36	**9**	5	15. On The Beach At Bali Bali/ above three vocals: Edythe Wright	
7/18/36	**4**	9	16. No Regrets .... vocal: Jack Leonard	Victor 25349
7/25/36	**10**	5	17. San Francisco .... movie title song	Victor 25352
8/29/36	**7**	4	18. Did I Remember? .... from the film "Suzy" vocals on above two & 21: Edythe Wright	Victor 25341
11/21/36	**11**	3	19. Close To Me	Victor 25447
1/02/37	**5**	6	20. I'm In A Dancing Mood .... from London musical "This'll Make You Whistle" above two vocals: Jack Leonard	Victor 25476
1/02/37	**12**	4	21. There's Frost On The Moon	Victor 25482
1/23/37	**17**	2	22. If My Heart Could Only Talk .... first hit with Bunny Berigan (trumpet) in band	Victor 25508
3/13/37	**1(2)**	8	● 23. **Marie/** vocal on 22-23, & 25: Jack Leonard	
3/27/37	**5**	5	24. Song Of India..................................... [I] Rimsky-Korsakov's "Chanson Indoue" from the 1897 opera "Sadko"; Bunny Berigan featured on above two	Victor 25523
3/13/37	**11**	3	25. May I Have The Next Romance With You? ..... from the British film "Head Over Heels In Love"	Victor 25487
4/24/37	**4**	4	26. Honeysuckle Rose................................. [I] special jam session: Tommy, Bunny, Fats Waller (piano), and Dick McDonough (guitar)	Victor 25559
5/01/37	**11**	2	27. They Can't Take That Away From Me.......... vocal: Jack Leonard; from the film "Shall We Dance?"	Victor 25549
5/08/37	**15**	3	28. That Foolish Feeling................................. vocal: Edythe Wright; from the film "Top of the Town"	Victor 25474
5/22/37	**18**	1	29. Twilight In Turkey .... [I] featured in the film "Ali Baby Goes to Town"	Victor 25568
7/24/37	**1(3)**	11	30. **Satan Takes A Holiday/** [I]	
5/29/37	**4**	11	31. Nola .... [I]	Victor 25570
5/29/37	**11**	2	32. Dark Eyes .... [I] traditional Russian folk song Bud Freeman (tenor sax) featured on 29 & 32	Victor 25556
6/12/37	**4**	5	33. Alibi Baby	Victor 25577
7/10/37	**6**	4	34. 'Posin' .... above two & 29: Tommy Dorsey & His Clambake Seven	Victor 25605
7/31/37	**9**	9	35. Stardust On The Moon..............................	Victor 25630
8/07/37	**3**	15	36. My Cabin Of Dreams................................ above four vocals & 40: Edythe Wright	Victor 25620
8/28/37	**2(1)**	12	37. Have You Got Any Castles, Baby?............... from the film "Varsity Show"	Victor 25635
9/04/37	**1(2)**	7	38. **The Big Apple**...................................... 36 & 38: Tommy & Clambake Seven	Victor 25652
10/09/37	**3**	5	39. Josephine... vocals on 37 & 39: Jack Leonard	Victor 25676
10/09/37	**11**	7	40. You And I Know .... from the film "Virginia"; vocal by Edythe Wright	Victor 25648
10/16/37	**3**	5	41. In The Still Of The Night .... vocal: Jack Leonard; from the film "Rosalie"	Victor 25663

DATE CHARTED	PEAK POS	WKS CHRT'D	ARTIST — Record Title	Label & Number
10/23/37	1(7)	14	42. **Once In A While/** vocal quartet	
10/23/37	4	11	43. If It's The Last Thing I Do	Victor 25686
11/06/37	15	2	44. The Lady Is A Tramp................................ from the Broadway musical "Babes in Arms"	Victor 25673
11/06/37	20	1	45. An Old Flame Never Dies.................... from the film "Virginia"; above two vocals: Jack Leonard	Victor 25649
11/13/37	1(6)	15	46. **The Dipsy Doodle/** [N] vocals on 44 & 46: Edythe Wright	
11/20/37	5	10	47. Who?....................................... from the Broadway musical "Sunny"	Victor 25693
1/15/38	19	1	48. A Little White Lighthouse	Victor 25733
2/05/38	5	11	49. I Can Dream, Can't I?/ from the Broadway musical "Right This Way"	
2/26/38	16	3	50. The One I Love.................................... above four vocals: Jack Leonard	Victor 25741
2/26/38	6	4	51. More Than Ever....................................	Victor 25774
2/26/38	15	1	52. Just A Simple Melody...........................[I]	Victor 25750
4/02/38	3	8	53. Yearning (Just For You) .... vocals on 51, 53, 59 & 60: Jack Leonard	Victor 25815
4/09/38	3	11	54. You Couldn't Be Cuter .... vocal: Edythe Wright; from the film "Joy of Living"	Victor 25768
4/16/38	9	8	55. Bewildered	Victor 25795
5/21/38	4	16	56. You Leave Me Breathless/	
5/21/38	7	7	57. Says My Heart................................ above two from the film "Cocoanut Grove"	Victor 25828
6/18/38	1(6)	20	58. **Music, Maestro, Please**........................... above two vocals & 60: Edythe Wright	Victor 25866
7/02/38	2(1)	15	59. Now It Can Be Told/	
8/13/38	8	1	60. My Walking Stick .... above two from the film "Alexander's Ragtime Band"	Victor 25856
7/16/38	10	5	61. I Hadn't Anyone Till You..........................	Victor 25848
7/23/38	14	4	62. I'll Dream Tonight.................................... from the film "Cowboy from Brooklyn" vocals on 59 & above two: Jack Leonard	Victor 25832
8/20/38	2(1)	12	63. Stop Beatin' Around The Mulberry Bush .... vocal: Edythe Wright & Skeets Herfurt	Victor 26012
8/20/38	12	2	64. A-Tisket, A-Tasket..............................	Victor 25899
10/01/38	5	11	65. My Own.................................... vocals on 64 & 65: Edythe Wright; 65 from the film "That Certain Age"	Victor 26005
10/22/38	3	9	● 66. Boogie Woogie................................ [I] Tommy's most famous instrumental, featuring pianist Howard Smith; originally "Pinetop's Boogie Woogie" (Clarence "Pinetop" Smith, from 1928)	Victor 26054
10/22/38	16	2	67. Marie................................ [R]	Victor 25523
10/29/38	17	1	68. Stompin' At The Stadium .... vocal: Edythe Wright & Skeets Herfurt	Victor 26062
11/19/38	8	4	69. You Must Have Been A Beautiful Baby .... from the film "Hard To Get"	Victor 26066
12/31/38+	7	7	70. Thanks For Everything .... movie title song vocals on 69-70, & 75: Edythe Wright	Victor 26119
12/31/38+	13	5	71. A Room With A View...........................	Victor 26097
1/07/39	13	1	72. Sweet Sue	Victor 26105
3/11/39	8	9	73. This Is It .... from the Broadway musical "Stars In Your Eyes"	Victor 26149
3/11/39	16	2	74. This Night/ vocals on 71-74 & 76-80: Jack Leonard	
4/29/39	20	1	75. Honolulu................................. above two from the film "Honolulu"	Victor 26172
4/08/39	1(1)	11	76. **Our Love** .... melody adapted from theme in Tchaikovsky's "Romeo and Juliet"	Victor 26202
4/08/39	4	8	77. Little Skipper.....................................	Victor 26195

DATE CHARTED	PEAK POS	WKS CHRT'D	ARTIST — Record Title	Label & Number
5/06/39	**5**	9	78. A New Moon And An Old Serenade.............. Victor 26181 top sidemen in 1938-39 Dorsey band: Lee Castle, Yank Lawson, & Pee Wee Erwin (trumpets), Skeets Herfurt (tenor & alto sax), & Dave Tough (drums)	
6/10/39	**7**	10	79. In The Middle Of A Dream .... Victor 26226	
6/24/39	**11**	6	80. All I Remember Is You................................ Victor 26281	
6/24/39	**13**	1	81. Dawn On The Desert ....[I] Victor 26246	
7/01/39	**9**	2	82. Rendezvous Time In Paree....................... Victor 26264 from the Broadway musical "Streets of Paris"	
7/08/39	**9**	7	83. This Is No Dream/	
7/08/39	**10**	7	84. To You.. Victor 26234	
7/15/39	**13**	1	85. How Am I To Know?................................ Victor 26294	
7/22/39	**3**	11	86. The Lamp Is Low .... Victor 26259 melody adapted from Maurice Revel's "Pavanne for a Dead Infanta"	
8/05/39	**2(3)**	12	87. Oh, You Crazy Moon................................ Victor 26287	
8/26/39	**11**	4	88. Running Through My Mind .... Victor 26325 above seven vocals: Jack Leonard	
9/02/39	**6**	12	89. Are You Having Any Fun?/ vocal: Edythe Wright	
10/28/39	**18**	1	90. Goodnight, My Beautiful .... Victor 26335 above two from the Broadway musical "George White's Scandals of 1939"	
10/21/39	**14**	4	91. March Of The Toys................................[I] Victor 26346 from the Broadway musical "Babes in Toyland"	
12/09/39+	**1(1)**	16	92. **Indian Summer** .... Victor 26390 song published in 1919	
12/16/39+	**1(2)**	13	93. **All The Things You Are** .... Victor 26401 from the Broadway musical "Very Warm for May"	
12/16/39	**15**	3	94. After All... Victor 26418	
2/03/40	**13**	2	95. The Starlit Hour .... Victor 26445 vocals on 90-95: Jack Leonard	
2/10/40	**18**	1	96. Angel.. Victor 26465 above two from Broadway musical "Earl Carroll's Vanities" first hit with Buddy Rich (drums)	
2/17/40	**6**	7	97. I've Got My Eyes On You/ above two vocals: Alan DeWitt	
4/06/40	**20**	1	98. I Concentrate On You .... Victor 26470 above two from the film "Broadway Melody of 1940"	
3/16/40	**16**	2	99. Darn That Dream..................................... Victor 26433 from the Broadway musical "Swingin' the Dream" above two vocals: Anita Boyer	
4/27/40	**18**	1	100. Polka Dots And Moonbeams...................... Victor 26539 first hit vocal by Frank Sinatra, who also sings on 102 & 104	
5/18/40	**9**	6	101. You're Lonely And I'm Lonely.................... Victor 26596 from the Broadway musical "Louisiana Purchase"	
5/25/40	**12**	3	102. Say It/ Bunny Berigan rejoins band through 113	
6/08/40	**13**	5	103. My! My!... Victor 26535 vocal: Pied Pipers; above two from the film "Buck Benny Rides Again"	
6/22/40	**8**	6	104. Imagination .... Victor 26581	
6/29/40	**1(12)**	20	●105. **I'll Never Smile Again**.............................. Victor 26628 vocal: Frank Sinatra & Pied Pipers	
8/10/40	**12**	2	106. All This And Heaven Too .... Victor 26653 movie title song	
8/10/40	**12**	2	107. Fools Rush In (Where Angels Fear To Tread).. Victor 26593	
8/31/40	**11**	5	108. The One I Love Belongs To Somebody Else.... Victor 26660 vocal: Frank Sinatra & Pied Pipers	
8/31/40	**14**	3	109. The Call Of The Canyon/ movie title song	
8/31/40	**17**	1	110. Love Lies .... Victor 26678	

DATE CHARTED	PEAK POS	WKS CHRT'D	ARTIST — Record Title	Label & Number
9/14/40	**10**	11	111. Trade Winds/ vocals on 106-107 and above three: Frank Sinatra	
9/28/40	**7**	9	112. Only Forever .... Victor 26666 vocal: Alan Starr; from the film "Rhythm On the River"	Victor 26666
10/12/40	**17**	1	113. I Could Make You Care	Victor 26717
11/02/40	**5**	5	114. Our Love Affair .... Victor 26736 from the film "Strike Up the Band"	Victor 26736
11/09/40	**3**	10	115. We Three (My Echo, My Shadow, And Me)...... Victor 26747 above three vocals: Frank Sinatra	Victor 26747
11/16/40	**12**	3	116. Two Dreams Met..................................... Victor 26764 vocal: Connie Haines; from the film "Down Argentine Way" the most famous Dorsey band, featuring Tommy (trombone), Ziggy Elman & Ray Linn (trumpets), Johnny Mince (clarinet/alto sax), Heinie Beau (tenor sax/ clarinet), & Buddy Rich (drums)	Victor 26764
1/04/41	**7**	5	117. Star Dust .... Victor 27233 vocal: Frank Sinatra & Pied Pipers; new version of band's 1936 hit	Victor 27233
1/04/41+	**14**	1	118. You've Got Me This Way .... Victor 26770 vocal: Pied Pipers; from the film "You'll Find Out"	Victor 26770
3/01/41	**2(6)**	14	119. Oh, Look At Me Now/	
3/22/41	**14**	1	120. You Might Have Belonged To Another .... Victor 27274 above two vocals: Frank Sinatra, Connie Haines, & Pied Pipers	Victor 27274
4/05/41	**1(1)**	13	121. **Dolores**/ from the film "Las Vegas Nights"	
8/23/41	**21**	1	122. I Tried .... Victor 27317	Victor 27317
4/12/41	**4**	7	123. Do I Worry? .... Victor 27338 vocals on 121 & 123: Frank Sinatra & the Pied Pipers	Victor 27338
4/19/41	**9**	10	124. Everything Happens To Me .... Victor 27359 vocals on 122 & 124: Frank Sinatra	Victor 27359
5/03/41	**7**	5	125. Let's Get Away From It All .... Victor 27377 vocal: Pied Pipers	Victor 27377
7/05/41	**4**	23	126. Yes, Indeed! .... Victor 27421 vocal: Jo Stafford & Sy Oliver	Victor 27421
8/30/41	**3**	24	127. This Love Of Mine.................................. Victor 27508	Victor 27508
8/30/41	**8**	5	128. Kiss The Boys Goodbye............................ Victor 27461 vocal: Connie Haines; movie title song	Victor 27461
8/30/41	**11**	5	129. You And I.. Victor 27532 vocals on 127, 129 & 131-132: Frank Sinatra	Victor 27532
10/04/41	**12**	3	130. I Guess I'll Have To Dream The Rest .... Victor 27526 vocal: Frank Sinatra & Pied Pipers	Victor 27526
12/20/41	**9**	7	131. Two In Love/	
12/20/41	**15**	1	132. A Sinner Kissed An Angel .... Victor 27611	Victor 27611
1/03/42	**21**	1	133. The Skunk Song .... [N] Victor 27621 vocal: Charlie Peterson; narration: Tommy	Victor 27621
2/28/42	**8**	7	134. How About You?.................................... Victor 27749 from the film "Babes on Broadway"	Victor 27749
3/21/42	**20**	1	135. I Think Of You .... Victor 27701 above two vocals: Frank Sinatra	Victor 27701
3/28/42	**13**	1	136. What Is This Thing Called Love? .... Victor 27782 vocal: Connie Haines; from the Broadway musical "Wake Up and Dream"	Victor 27782
6/20/42	**17**	1	137. The Last Call For Love .... Victor 27849 vocal: Frank Sinatra & Pied Pipers; from the film "Ship Ahoy"	Victor 27849
7/04/42	**18**	1	138. Well, Git It!................................... [I] Victor 27887 Ziggy Elman (trumpet) featured	Victor 27887
7/18/42	**6**	10	139. Just As Though You Were Here/	
7/25/42	**17**	2	140. Street Of Dreams .... Victor 27903	Victor 27903
8/08/42	**5**	10	141. Take Me/	
8/09/42	**13**	6	142. Be Careful, It's My Heart .... Victor 27923 from the film "Holiday Inn"	Victor 27923
8/08/42	**15**	1	143. I'll Take Tallulah .... Victor 27869 from the film "Ship Ahoy" vocals on 139-140 & 143: Frank Sinatra & the Pied Pipers	Victor 27869

DATE CHARTED	PEAK POS	WKS CHRT'D	ARTIST — Record Title	Label & Number
8/22/42+	21	1	144. Light A Candle In The Chapel .... vocals on 141-142, & 144: Frank Sinatra	Victor 27941
10/17/42+	4	14	145. Manhattan Serenade/ vocal: Jo Stafford; song published in 1928 as an instrumental	
10/17/42	20	1	146. Blue Blazes .... [I] Ziggy Elman featured	Victor 27962
10/24/42	10	5	147. Daybreak/ vocal: Frank Sinatra; based on a theme from Ferde Grofe's "Mississippi Suite"	
11/07/42+	1(6)	26	●148. **There Are Such Things** .... vocals on 148 & 150: Frank Sinatra & the Pied Pipers	Victor 27974
1/16/43+	5	30	●149. Boogie Woogie.................................. [I-R] reissue of the 1938 hit, on and off the charts for over a year	Victor 26054
2/06/43	4	17	150. It Started All Over Again/	
3/13/43	16	2	151. Mandy, Make Up Your Mind .... [I] from the Broadway musical "Dixie to Broadway"	Victor 1522
6/19/43	20	1	152. Song Of India/ [I-R]	
9/18/43	23	1	153. Star Dust .... [R] reissue of the 1941 hit under a new number	Victor 27520
7/03/43	1(3)	19	154. **In The Blue Of The Evening**...................... recorded 6/17/42	Victor 27947
7/10/43	3	13	155. It's Always You .... recorded 1/15/41; originally released on Victor 27345 from the film "The Road to Zanibar" above two vocals: Frank Sinatra	Victor 1530
9/25/43	19	1	156. You Took My Love .... vocal: Jo Stafford; recorded 7/2/42	Victor 1539
10/23/43	21	1	157. The Dipsy Doodle............................. [N-R]	Victor 25693
3/25/44	26	1	158. Another One Of Them Things.................. [I] recorded 8/29/40, originally released on Victor 27208	Victor 1553
5/20/44	4	17	159. I'll Be Seeing You.................................. vocal: Frank Sinatra; recorded 2/26/40, released on Victor 26539; from the Broadway musical "Right This Way"	Victor 1574
8/12/44	21	1	160. Boogie Woogie................................. [I-R]	Victor 26054
11/25/44	29	1	161. Will You Still Be Mine? .... vocal: Connie Haines; recorded 2/17/41, released on Victor 27421	Victor 1576
1/06/45	4	9	●162. I Dream Of You/ vocal: Freddy Stewart	
3/03/45	12	3	163. Opus No. 1 .... [I] famous instrumental voted the #12 all-time record in the Billboard disc jockey poll; Buddy DeFranco (clarinet) featured with Nelson Riddle (trombone)	Victor 1608
2/10/45	15	2	164. Sleigh Ride In July................................. from the film "Belle of the Yukon"	Victor 1622
3/03/45	10	3	165. More And More...................................... from the film "Can't Help Singing" above two vocals: Bonnie Lou Williams	Victor 1614
4/28/45	11	3	166. I Should Care .... vocal: Bonnie Lou Williams & Sentimentalists; from the film "Thrill of a Romance"	Victor 1625
6/16/45	16	1	167. On The Sunny Side Of The Street................ vocal by the Sentimentalists	Victor 1648
7/21/45	12	1	168. Out Of This World .... movie title song	Victor 1669
7/28/45	9	1	169. A Friend Of Yours .... above two vocals: Stuart Foster	Victor 1657
8/11/45	6	6	170. On The Atchison, Topeka, And The Santa Fe . vocal: The Sentimentalists; from the film "The Harvey Girls"	Victor 1682
9/15/45	4	4	171. Boogie Woogie................................. [I-R] reissue of Victor 26054	Victor 1715
9/22/45	20	6	172. You Came Along (From Out Of Nowhere)/	
10/06/45	8	3	173. Hong Kong Blues .... vocal: Skeets Herfurt; from the film "To Have and Have Not"	Victor 1722

DATE CHARTED	PEAK POS	WKS CHRT'D	ARTIST — Record Title	Label & Number
12/01/45	15	4	174. A Door Will Open/ vocal: Stuart Foster & Sentimentalists	
1/19/46	14	1	175. Aren't You Glad You're You?.................... from the film "The Bells of St. Mary's"	Victor 1728
1/26/46	11	3	176. The Moment I Met You............................... vocal: The Sentimentalists	Victor 1761
5/04/46	25	1	177. We'll Gather Lilacs .... vocals on 172, 175 & 177: Stuart Foster	Victor 1809
6/08/46	23	3	178. There's Good Blues Tonight........................ vocal by Sy Oliver	Victor 1842
7/20/46	16	5	179. I Don't Know Why (I Just Do)......................	Victor 1901
3/15/47	9	5	180. How Are Things In Glocca Mora?................. from the Broadway musical "Finian's Rainbow"	Victor 2121
6/07/47	21	5	181. It's The Same Old Dream............................. above three vocals by Stuart Foster from the film "It Happened in Brooklyn"	Victor 2210
9/11/48	4	21	182. Until... vocal: Harry Prime; Ziggy Elman & Buddy DeFranco featured	Victor 3061
1/29/49	11	9	183. Down By The Station............................... vocal: Denny Dennis, Lucy Ann Polk, & Sentimentalists	Victor 3317
6/04/49	5	21	184. The Hucklebuck/ vocal: Charlie Shavers (also featured on trumpet); based on the Charlie Parker jazz instrumental "Now's the Time"	
6/04/49	6	15	185. Again .... [I] from the film "Roadhouse" Louis Bellson (drummer) on above four (1950 Tommy Dorsey band with Billy Butterfield & Doc Severinsen, trumpets)	Victor 3427
8/01/53	21	5	186. The Most Beautiful Girl In The World .... [I] from the Broadway musical "Jumbo" featuring Lee Castle (trumpet)	Decca 5449

LARRY DOUGLAS
Sang with Carmen Cavallaro and later appeared in the original
Broadway cast of "The King & I"

5/03/47	14	1	1. Linda... from the film "The Story of G.I. Joe" accompanied by Ray Bloch's Radio Seven	Signature 15106

LEW DOUGLAS & HIS ORCHESTRA

2/27/54	27	3	1. Turn Around Boy.................................... vocal: Bill Bailey	MGM 11654

MIKE DOUGLAS
The longtime syndicated TV talk show host (real name: Michael
Dowd) was Kay Kyser's featured singer from 1945-50; "Ole
Buttermilk Sky" and "The Old Lamplighter" were his biggest hits.

MORTON DOWNEY
Popular tenor balladeer who sang in the early 20s with Paul
Whiteman and hosted various radio shows from 1931 through the
1940s; died in October, 1985 (83).

1/30/26	12	1	1. The Lonesomest Girl In Town	Brunswick 2975
5/25/29	9	5	2. I'll Always Be In Love With You .... from the film "Syncopation"; orchestra directed by Nat Shilkret	Victor 21860
6/07/31	18	1	3. Wabash Moon...	Victor 22673
3/26/32	17	2	4. Auf Weiderseh'n, My Dear	Melotone 12319
10/13/34	15	2	5. They Didn't Believe Me .... from the Broadway musical "The Girl from Utah"	Melotone 13197
10/21/44	25	1	6. Spring Will Be A Little Late This Year	Decca 18607
12/14/46	16	1	7. The Old Lamplighter .... above two accompanied by Jimmy Lytell & His Orchestra	Majestic 1061

DATE CHARTED	PEAK POS	WKS CHRT'D	ARTIST — Record Title	Label & Number

ALFRED DRAKE
Real name Alfred Capurro; one of Broadway's great musical comedy stars of the 40s and 50s; "Oklahoma!", "Kiss Me, Kate" and "Kismet" provided his most memorable roles. (also see "Oklahoma!" Album)

DATE CHARTED	PEAK POS	WKS CHRT'D	ARTIST — Record Title	Label & Number
1/22/44	22	1	1. The Surrey With The Fringe On Top .... from the Broadway musical "Oklahoma!" orchestra directed by Jay Blackton	Decca 23284

RUSTY DRAPER

DATE CHARTED	PEAK POS	WKS CHRT'D	ARTIST — Record Title	Label & Number
3/07/53	10	8	1. No Help Wanted	Mercury 70077
7/04/53	6	18	2. Gambler's Guitar	Mercury 70167
8/01/53	23	3	3. Lighthouse	Mercury 70188
11/28/53	23	3	4. Native Dancer .... 1, 3 & 4 with the Jack Halloran Singers orchestra on all directed by David Carroll	Mercury 70256

DORIS DREW

DATE CHARTED	PEAK POS	WKS CHRT'D	ARTIST — Record Title	Label & Number
8/11/51	22	2	1. Sweet Violets .... accompanied by the Cliff Parman Orchestra & the Jack Halloran Chorus	Mercury 5673

DRIFTERS
Great R&B group led by Clyde McPhatter, with Gerhart & Andrew Thrasher and Bill Pinckney.

DATE CHARTED	PEAK POS	WKS CHRT'D	ARTIST — Record Title	Label & Number
10/16/54	21	4	● 1. Honey Love	Atlantic 1029

EDDY DUCHIN & HIS ORCHESTRA
The famous pianist-bandleader first became known with Leo Reisman before starting his own orchestra. Five years after his death of leukemia on 2/9/51 (40), Hollywood produced "The Eddy Duchin Story". Son Peter Duchin became a successful society pianist-bandleader.

DATE CHARTED	PEAK POS	WKS CHRT'D	ARTIST — Record Title	Label & Number
3/26/32	7	3	1. Snuggled On Your Shoulder (Cuddled In Your Arms)	Columbia 2625
7/30/32	11	4	2. Now You've Got Me Worryin' For You	Columbia 2680
1/01/33	2(3)	8	3. Night And Day .... [I] from the Broadway musical "Gay Divorce" listed on above records as "Eddy Duchin & His Central Park Casino Orchestra"	Brunswick 6445
4/29/33	15	3	4. I Can't Remember/	
5/06/33	11	3	5. Hold Me	Victor 24280
7/01/33	3	6	6. I Cover The Waterfront/ written to promote the film of the same name	
6/10/33	3	6	7. Isn't It Heavenly?	Victor 24325
6/10/33	10	5	8. An Orchid To You	Victor 24326
7/22/33	14	3	9. Don't Do Anything I Wouldn't Do	Victor 24327
8/26/33	18	1	10. Trouble In Paradise	Victor 24377
12/16/33	1(3)	6	11. **Did You Ever See A Dream Walking?** .... from the film "Sitting Pretty"	Victor 24477
2/10/34	1(5)	11	12. **Let's Fall In Love** .... movie title song	Victor 24510
3/10/34	5	6	13. This Little Piggie Went To Market	Victor 24512
3/10/34	8	5	14. I Was In The Mood .... vocals on 1-2, 4-14: Lew Sherwood	Victor 24518
4/07/34	3	6	15. Ill Wind (You're Blowing Me No Good) .... vocal: Harold Arlen (the song's composer); from the Cotton Club revue "Parade in Harlem"	Victor 24579
4/07/34	8	4	16. Why Do I Dream These Dreams?	Victor 24576
4/14/34	7	4	17. She Reminds Me Of You/	
4/21/34	16	2	18. May I? .... above two from the film "We're Not Dressing"	Victor 24591
5/12/34	3	7	19. Riptide/ vocal: Lew Sherwood & DeMarco Sisters	
5/12/34	4	10	20. I've Had My Moments .... from the film "Hollywood Party" vocals on 16-18 & 20: Lew Sherwood	Victor 24613

DATE CHARTED	PEAK POS	WKS CHRT'D	ARTIST — Record Title	Label & Number
5/19/34	**4**	7	21. Easy Come, Easy Go.................................... Victor 24611 vocal: DeMarco Sisters	
7/14/34	**3**	11	22. I Never Had A Chance/	
7/21/34	**4**	9	23. Dust On The Moon .... Victor 24664	
7/21/34	**12**	6	24. Dames .... Victor 24666	
8/11/34	**4**	12	25. I Only Have Eyes For You........................... Victor 24665 above two from the film "Dames"	
10/06/34	**13**	2	26. Night And Day................................... [I-R] Brunswick 6977	
2/23/35	**14**	6	27. Haunting Me .... Victor 24841	
3/09/35	**1(3)**	14	28. **I Won't Dance/** above two from the film "Roberta"	
3/09/35	**1(4)**	14	29. **Lovely To Look At** .... Victor 24871	
4/13/35+	**11**	3	30. It's An Old Southern Custom .... Victor 24875 from the film "George White's Scandals of 1935"	
7/20/35	**2(2)**	12	31. You're All I Need .... Victor 25029	
8/24/35	**2(1)**	11	32. Cheek To Cheek .... Victor 25093 from the film "Top Hat"	
10/19/35	**1(3)**	9	33. **You Are My Lucky Star/**	
11/02/35	**9**	4	34. I've Got A Feelin' You're Foolin'............... Victor 25125 above two from the film "Broadway Melody of 1936"	
1/11/36	**1(3)**	11	35. **Moon Over Miami/**	
1/18/36	**1(1)**	15	36. **Lights Out**.. Victor 25212 vocals on 22-36: Lew Sherwood	
4/04/36	**6**	5	37. A Melody From The Sky............................. Victor 25254 vocal: Pete Woolery	
4/11/36	**15**	2	38. It's Great To Be In Love Again .... Victor 25259 vocals on 38 & 40: Lew Sherwood	
7/11/36	**1(2)**	10	39. **Take My Heart** .... Victor 25343 vocals on 39 & 41: Jerry Cooper	
10/24/36	**15**	4	40. Dream Awhile .... Victor 25361	
11/14/36+	**1(2)**	13	41. **It's De-Lovely** .... Victor 25432 from the Broadway musical "Red, Hot and Blue"	
11/28/36	**1(1)**	8	42. **I'll Sing You A Thousand Love Songs** .... Victor 25393 vocal: Jimmy Newell	
12/05/36+	**2(1)**	9	43. Pennies From Heaven .... Victor 25431 movie title song	
2/27/37	**9**	3	44. Love And Learn... Victor 25472 from the film "That Girl from Paris"	
2/27/37	**5**	5	45. Moonlight And Shadows............................ Victor 25514 from the film "Jungle Princess"	
5/15/37	**20**	1	46. Let's Call The Whole Thing Off.................... Victor 25569 from the film "Shall We Dance?" vocals on 44 & 46: Jerry Cooper	
6/05/37	**2(1)**	9	47. The Merry-Go-Round Broke Down .... Victor 25585 vocals on 43, 45 & 47: Lew Sherwood	
6/18/38	**2(2)**	17	48. Ol' Man Mose .... Brunswick 8155 vocal: Patricia Norman	
9/24/38	**15**	3	49. How Can We Be Wrong?/	
10/29/38	**13**	3	50. My Reverie .... Brunswick 8224 based on Debussy's "Reverie"	
11/26/38	**12**	4	51. Heart And Soul... Brunswick 8238 above three vocals: Stanley Worth	
1/07/39	**7**	8	52. Get Out Of Town/ [I]	
12/10/38	**8**	4	53. From Now On.................................... [I] Brunswick 8252 above two & 55 from the Broadway musical "Leave It To Me"	
12/10/38	**9**	1	54. (Don't Wait Till) The Night Before Christmas.. .... [X] Brunswick 8264	
1/07/39	**9**	2	55. My Heart Belongs To Daddy........................ Brunswick 8282 MARY MARTIN WITH EDDY DUCHIN'S ORCHESTRA	
1/07/39	**15**	5	56. I Go For That .... Brunswick 8278 from the film "St. Louis Blues"	
8/26/39	**14**	4	57. Comes Love .... Brunswick 8434 vocal: Durelle Alexander; from the Broadway musical "Yokel Boy"	

DATE CHARTED	PEAK POS	WKS CHRT'D	ARTIST — Record Title	Label & Number
12/23/39	16	1	58. Honestly .... vocals on 54, 56 & 58: Stanley Worth	Columbia 35246
12/30/39	17	1	59. Smarty Pants........................ vocal: Carolyn Horton	Columbia 35255
12/30/39+	18	5	60. It's A Hap, Hap, Happy Day .... vocal: Three Earbenders; from the animated film "Gulliver's Travels"	Columbia 35259
2/10/40	15	3	61. In An Old Dutch Garden........................	Columbia 35329
4/06/40	17	2	62. The Gaucho Serenade........................	Columbia 35351
9/28/40	25	1	63. I Concentrate On You .... from the film "Broadway Melody of 1940" vocals on 61 & 63: Stanley Worth	Columbia 35369
11/02/40	15	1	64. Only Forever .... from the film "Rhythm On the River" vocals on 62 & 64: June Robbins	Columbia 35624
11/02/40	27	1	65. The Same Old Story	Columbia 35724
11/23/40	15	3	66. Down Argentina Way/ vocal: Three Earbenders	
11/30/40	22	1	67. Two Dreams Met....................... above two from the film "Down Argentine Way" vocals on 65, 67, & 70-71: Johnny Drake	Columbia 35774
12/21/40+	2(1)	7	68. I Give You My Word/	
12/21/40+	6	5	69. So You're The One	Columbia 35812
12/28/40	17	1	70. Dream Valley..........................	Columbia 35780
1/25/41	6	10	71. You Walk By..........................	Columbia 35903
2/15/41	14	1	72. It All Comes Back To Me Now	Columbia 35867
3/08/41	21	1	73. Number Ten Lullaby Lane	Columbia 35917
4/19/41	26	1	74. I Could Write a Book .... vocal by Tony Leonard; from the Broadway musical "Pal Joey"	Columbia 35941
3/14/42	23	1	75. Sometimes.......................... vocals on 68-69, 72-73 & 75: June Robbins	Columbia 36501

LAWRENCE DUCHOW'S RED RAVEN ORCHESTRA
Polka band

11/15/47	23	1	1. Swiss Boy..........................	RCA Victor 1079

S.H. DUDLEY
Real name Samuel Holland Rous; sang opera from 1886-98, then became second tenor in Edison Male Quartet and Haydn Quartet. After becoming an executive with Victor, achieved his greatest renown under his real name as editor of the Victor record catalogs and Book of the Opera; died on 6/6/47 (81). (also see Sousa's Band and aforementioned groups)

7/02/98	3	2	1. Jack's The Boy	Chicago
1/14/99	4	2	2. My Old New Hampshire Home	Berliner 1958
11/11/99	3	2	3. My Sunday Girl .... also recorded for Edison 7227 from the Broadway musical "The Man In The Moon"	Berliner 0431
11/18/99	2(3)	4	4. 'Mid The Green Fields Of Virginia .... HARRY MACDONOUGH & S.H. DUDLEY	Edison 7262
3/09/01	1(3)	7	5. **When Reuben Comes To Town**................... also issued on Victor 3001; from Broadway musical "Rogers Brothers in Central Park"	Gram-o-Phone 519
3/23/01	3	4	6. Ma Blushin' Rosie	Gram-o-Phone 517
6/22/01	2(2)	4	7. Whistling .... from the Broadway musical "Florodora"	Gram-o-Phone 706
8/24/01	3	3	8. Sweet Annie Moore	Victor 775
2/15/02	4	2	9. While The Leaves Came Drifting Down	Victor 1075
6/28/02	4	2	10. Bye And Bye You Will Forget Me .... above three: HARRY MACDONOUGH & S.H. DUDLEY	Victor 1329
8/06/04	2(2)	5	11. Meet Me In St. Louis, Louis .... commemorated the 1904 Louisiana Purchase Exposition in St. Louis	Victor 2807
6/03/05	4	1	12. Tammany...............................	Victor 4297
9/09/05	4	1	13. Give My Regards To Broadway .... from the Broadway musical "Little Johnny Jones" above two under pseudonym "Frank Kernell"	Victor 4385

DATE CHARTED	PEAK POS	WKS CHRT'D	ARTIST — Record Title	Label & Number
			DUFFY AND IMGRUND'S 5th REGIMENT BAND One of the earliest commercially-recorded bands, with 1889's "The Night Alarm" on North American, their best-known offering.	
			HOWARD DuLANY Singer with Gene Krupa 1940-41 ('High On a Windy Hill', 'It All Comes Back To Me Now").	
			DUNCAN SISTERS Rosetta and Vivian Duncan, popular on both Broadway and London stages	
2/23/24	**4**	5	1. Rememb'ring .... with Phil Ohman, piano; featured in the Broadway musical "Topsy and Eva"	Victor 19206
			MARGUERITE DUNLAP South Carolina-born contralto, died on 1/7/60 (71).	
8/05/11	**6**	2	1. Mighty Lak' A Rose.................................	Victor 5837
3/01/13	**8**	2	2. A Little Girl At Home .... from the Broadway musical "Lady of the Slipper"	Victor 17220
1/24/14	**2(2)**	5	3. You've Got Your Mother's Big Blue Eyes .... under pseudonym "Lillian Davis"	Victor 17482
1/31/14	**8**	1	4. When It's Apple Blossom Time In Normandy.. 2 & 4: HARRY MACDONOUGH & MARGUERITE DUNLAP from the Broadway musical "Roly Boly"; based on Beethoven's "Minuet in G"	Victor 17445
3/04/16	**3**	5	5. Go To Sleep, My Dusky Baby .... OLIVE KLINE, ELSIE BAKER & MARGUERITE DUNLAP based on Dvorak's "Humoresque"	Victor 17918
4/12/19	**5**	5	6. Beautiful Ohio... OLIVE KLINE & MARGUERITE DUNLAP	Victor 45161
			IRENE DUNNE Leading movie actress between 1930 and 1950, an Oscar winner in 1936 for "Theodora Goes Wild"; former opera singer.	
6/08/35	**20**	1	1. Lovely To Look At .... from the film "Roberta" accompanied by Nat Shilkret's Orchestra	Brunswick 7420
			EDDIE DUNSTEDTER Renowned organist and orchestra conductor. (see Bing Crosby)	
			FRED DUPREZ Popular vaudeville comedian, died on 10/29/38 (54).	
9/05/14	**9**	1	1. Happy Tho' Married .... [C] flip side of #1 million-seller "Cohen On the Telephone" by Joe Hayman	Columbia 1516
			JIMMY DURANTE Much-beloved comedian who started on vaudeville and became star of many Broadway shows and movies as well as his own TV show (1954-56); the great "Schnozzola" died on 1/29/80 (86).	
2/24/34	**6**	4	1. Inka Dinka Doo .... [N] jimmy's longtime theme song; from the film "Palooka"	Brunswick 6774
10/21/44	**24**	1	2. Umbriago .... [N] from the film "Music for the Millions"	Decca 23351
9/22/51	**29**	1	3. Blackstrap Molasses............................ [N] DANNY KAYE, JIMMY DURANTE, GROUCHO MARX, & JANE WYMAN	Decca 27748

DATE CHARTED	PEAK POS	WKS CHRT'D	ARTIST — Record Title	Label & Number
			DEANNA DURBIN Popular Canadian-born soprano featured in many films from 1937 (at age 15) to 1948	
2/04/39	**15**	3	1. My Own... from the film "That Certain Age"	Decca 2274

E

RAY EBERLE
Glenn Miller's featured vocalist on 'Over the Rainbow', 'Moonlight Cocktail", and many other hits; younger brother of Bob Eberly. In 1940 & 1942 Ray ranked as the #1 male band singer in Billboard's college surveys (edging out Frank Sinatra).

BOB EBERLY
Real name Robert Eberle; with Jimmy Dorsey, became one of the most popular of all band singers from 1936-43, with hits like "Blue Champagne", "The Breeze and I", and duets with Helen O'Connell. Previously sang with Dorsey Brothers band. Bob ranked #3 three straight years (1940-42) in the Billboard college polls; he died on 12/17/81 (65).

DATE CHARTED	PEAK POS	WKS CHRT'D	ARTIST — Record Title	Label & Number
10/30/48	**25**	3	1. Hair Of Gold (Eyes Of Blue)........................ with the Sunshine Serenaders; from the film "Singin' Spurs"	Decca 24491
12/20/52	**30**	1	2. When I Dream	Capitol 2239
8/08/53	**30**	1	3. You Are Too Beautiful .... from the 1933 film "Hallelujah, I'm A Bum" above two accompanied by Les Baxter's Orchestra	Capitol 2525

BILLY ECKSTINE
Possessor of of one of the most distinctive baritones in popular music, Billy Eckstine sang with Earl Hines from 1939-43 before forming a historic jazz band featuring such greats as Charlie Parker, Dizzy Gillespie, Art Blakey, Fats Navarro, and Miles Davis, with Billy and Sarah Vaughan as vocalists. As a solo star he became universally known as "Mr. B".

DATE CHARTED	PEAK POS	WKS CHRT'D	ARTIST — Record Title	Label & Number
10/06/45	**8**	2	● 1. A Cottage For Sale.................................	National 9014
1/26/46	**12**	3	2. I'm In The Mood For Love........................... from the film "Every Night at Eight"	National 9016
4/06/46	**10**	10	● 3. Prisoner Of Love....................................	National 9017
7/27/46	**13**	2	4. You Call It Madness (But I Call It Love).........	National 9019
11/08/47	**22**	1	5. The Wildest Gal In Town	MGM 10069
1/24/48	**22**	1	6. True	MGM 10123
3/20/48	**27**	1	7. Intrigue... movie title song	MGM 10154
7/31/48	**24**	1	8. Sophisticated Lady .... 1946 recording; band includes Miles Davis	National 9049
10/16/48	**30**	1	9. Everything I Have Is Yours .... accompanied by Sonny Burke & His Orchestra from the film "Dancing Lady"	MGM 10259
3/05/49	**21**	3	10. Blue Moon	MGM 10311
3/05/49	**27**	1	11. Bewildered	MGM 10340
4/23/49	**27**	1	12. Caravan .... 5-7 & 10-12 with Hugo Winterhalter's Orchestra	MGM 10368
8/06/49	**27**	3	13. Crying	MGM 10458
9/03/49	**25**	2	14. Somehow	MGM 10383
9/24/49	**27**	1	15. Body And Soul .... from the Broadway musical "Three's a Crowd"	MGM 10501
12/03/49	**24**	1	16. Fool's Paradise.................................... accompanied on 13, 15, & 16 by Buddy Baker's Orchestra	MGM 10562
2/04/50	**23**	3	17. Sitting By The Window .... with the Quartones	MGM 10602
3/11/50	**6**	19	● 18. My Foolish Heart	MGM 10623
6/17/50	**7**	15	19. I Wanna Be Loved.................................. song published in 1933 accompanied on above three & 22 by Russ Case Orchestra	MGM 10716
2/17/51	**10**	8	20. If	MGM 10896

DATE CHARTED	PEAK POS	WKS CHRT'D	ARTIST — Record Title	Label & Number
3/03/51	**6**	20	● 21. I Apologize .... above two accompanied by Pete Rugolo's Orchestra	MGM 10903
3/10/51	**26**	2	22. Be My Love.. from the film "The Toast of New Orleans"	MGM 10799
4/26/52	**16**	13	23. Kiss Of Fire .... adapted from the Argentine tango "El Choclo"	MGM 11225
4/11/53	**26**	1	24. Coquette .... with the Lee Gordon Singers	MGM 11439
7/11/53	**25**	1	25. Send My Baby Back To Me/ above four accompanied by Nelson Riddle & His Orchestra above two with the Textor Singers	
7/11/53	**29**	1	26. I Laugh To Keep From Crying	MGM 11511
9/19/53	**24**	1	27. St. Louis Blues..................................... accompanied by the Metronome All-Stars, including Roy Eldridge (trumpet), Kai Winding (trombone), Lester Young (tenor sax), Teddy Wilson (piano) & Max Roach (drums)	MGM 11573
4/10/54	**24**	3	28. Lost In Loveliness.................................. accompanied by Lou Bring's Orchestra from the film "The Girl In Pink Tights"	MGM 11694

NELSON EDDY
Baritone star of many movie musicals, but most memorably the eight he made with Jeanette MacDonald; died on 3/6/67 (65).

5/11/35	**5**	6	1. Ah! Sweet Mystery Of Life	Victor 4281
5/18/35	**4**	6	2. I'm Falling In Love With Someone............... above two from the film version of "Naughty Marietta"	Victor 4280
8/10/35	**8**	4	3. When I Grow Too Old To Dream .... from the film "The Night is Young"	Victor 4285
12/26/36+	**8**	6	● 4. Indian Love Call .... JEANETTE MACDONALD & NELSON EDDY from the film version of "Rose Marie" orchestra on all directed by Nat Shilkret	Victor 4323

EDISON MALE QUARTETTE
John Bieling, S.H. Dudley, William F. Hooley, and Harry Macdonough; famous group later known as the Haydn Quartet.

1/22/98	**1(3)**	6	1. **My Old Kentucky Home**........................	Edison 2223
4/16/98	**2(3)**	4	2. Break The News To Mother........................	Edison 2232

CLIFF EDWARDS
Universally known as "Ukelele Ike", Cliff Edwards' friendly, jazz-flavored musical style made him a popular phenomenon of the 20s, and generated a nationwide craze for the ukelele. He appeared in over fifty early movie musicals, and in 1940 served as the voice of Jiminy Cricket in the Disney animated classic "Pinocchio". Cliff died on 7/18/72 (76).

6/28/24	**14**	1	1. Where The Lazy Daisies Grow.................... also issued on Regal 9620	Banner 1328
8/16/24	**6**	3	2. It Had To Be You	Pathe 032047
10/25/24	**13**	1	3. Hard-Hearted Hannah..............................	Pathe 032054
1/31/25	**6**	3	4. All Alone .... featured in Broadway musical "Music Box Revue of 1924"	Pathe 032090
1/31/25	**11**	1	5. Somebody Loves Me .... from "George White's Scandals of 1924"	Pathe 032073
2/28/25	**15**	1	6. My Best Girl...	Pathe 032088
4/11/25	**6**	4	7. Fascinating Rhythm .... also on Perfect 11560	Pathe 025126
5/30/25	**13**	1	8. Oh Lady Be Good................................... above two from the Broadway musical "Lady, Be Good!"	Pathe 025130
6/20/25	**7**	3	9. Who Takes Care Of The Caretaker's Daughter?..................................... [C]	Pathe 025128
8/22/25	**5**	4	10. If You Knew Susie (Like I Know Susie).......... also on Perfect 11575 featured in the Broadway musical "Big Boy"	Pathe 025141
11/21/25	**3**	6	11. Paddlin' Madelin' Home	Pathe 025149
2/13/26	**10**	1	12. Remember... also on Perfect 11611	Pathe 025163

DATE CHARTED	PEAK POS	WKS CHRT'D	ARTIST — Record Title	Label & Number
3/06/26	**5**	3	13. Dinah .... also on Perfect 11598	Pathe 025164
11/27/26	**12**	1	14. When The Red, Red Robin Comes Bob-Bob- Bobbin' Along..................................	Pathe 25186

1/08/27	**3**	8	15. Sunday ....
			    also on Pathe 25199
			    from the Broadway musical "The Merry World"
				Perfect 11633

4/02/27	**7**	5	16. I'm Tellin' The Birds, I'm Tellin' The Bees
			      (How I Love You) ....
			    also on Pathe 25200
			    band on most of above records features: Cliff (ukelele), Red
			    Nichols (cornet), Miff Mole (trombone), Dick McDonough
			    (guitar); Jimmy Dorsey (clarinet/alto sax) on 15
				Perfect 11634

8/27/27	**12**	3	17. Side By Side ....
			    also on Pathe 25206; with Adrian Rollini (baritone sax), Joe
			    Ventuti (violin/piano), & Eddie Lang (guitar)
				Perfect 11640

4/07/28	**11**	3	18. After My Laughter Came Tears	Columbia 1254
4/14/28	**10**	4	19. Together/	
4/28/28	**3**	7	20. Mary Ann...................................	Columbia 1295
9/08/28	**14**	2	21. Just Like A Melody Out Of The Sky/	
9/29/28	**12**	3	22. Anything You Say!.................................	Columbia 1427
9/15/28	**1(1)**	11	23. **I Can't Give You Anything But Love**......... from the Broadway musical "Blackbirds of 1928"	Columbia 1471
3/23/29	**19**	1	24. Me And The Man In The Moon....................	Columbia 1705
7/27/29	**1(3)**	12	25. **Singin' In The Rain/**	
8/10/29	**20**	1	26. Orange Blossom Time............................ above two from the film "Hollywood Revue of 1929"	Columbia 1869
10/05/29	**13**	2	27. Just You, Just Me...................................	Columbia 1907

11/25/33	**13**	4	28. It's Only A Paper Moon ....
			    from the film "Take A Chance"; originally in the
			    nonmusical play "The Great Magoo" under the title "If
			    You Believe In Me"
				Vocalion 2587

2/17/40	**10**	6	29. When You Wish Upon A Star/	

3/02/40	**16**	1	30. Give A Little Whistle..............................
			    above two from the animated film "Pinocchio"
			    accompanied on above two by Victor Young & His Orchestra
			    with the Ken Darby Singers
				Victor 26477

TOMMY EDWARDS
Virginia-born singer who hit #1 in 1958 with a million-selling new version of "It's All in the Game". Tommy died on 10/23/69 (47).

DATE CHARTED	PEAK POS	WKS CHRT'D	ARTIST — Record Title	Label & Number
7/28/51	**24**	1	1. The Morning Side Of The Mountain .... returned to charts in new version, 1958	MGM 10989
9/15/51	**18**	9	2. It's All In The Game	MGM 11035
2/09/52	**22**	4	3. Please, Mr. Sun	MGM 11134
11/29/52	**13**	5	4. You Win Again	MGM 11326
2/21/53	**24**	1	5. A Fool Such As I....................................	MGM 11395
9/05/53	**26**	2	6. Baby, Baby, Baby .... from the film "Those Red Heads from Seattle"	MGM 11541

2/20/54	**28**	1	7. Secret Love ....
			    from the film "Calamity Jane"
			    all above records accompanied by Leroy Holmes' Orchestra
				MGM 11604

ROY ELDRIDGE
Great jazz trumpet star who played with Teddy Hill and Fletcher Henderson bands in 30s before earning national reputation with Gene Krupa (1941-43), on both trumpet and vocals. Also played with Artie Shaw (1944-45), and much later with Ella Fitzgerald.

LES ELGART
Played trumpet in 1940s with Bunny Berigan, Hal McIntyre, Charlie Spivak, Harry James, and Woody Herman; achieved greatest fame over 30 years later with his "Hooked on Swing" big-band albums.

EDDIE ELKINS & HIS ORCHESTRA
Eddie died in October, 1984 (87)

DATE CHARTED	PEAK POS	WKS CHRT'D	ARTIST — Record Title	Label & Number
4/29/22	**15**	1	1. When Buddha Smiles.............................[I]	Columbia 3528
11/25/25	**14**	1	2. Sunny...[I]	Columbia 403

DATE CHARTED	PEAK POS	WKS CHRT'D	ARTIST — Record Title	Label & Number

DUKE ELLINGTON & HIS FAMOUS ORCHESTRA

Perhaps the single most important creative talent in American popular music history, Edward Kennedy Ellington was born on 4/29/1899 in Washington, D.C. Having studied piano from age seven, Duke formed his first band about 1918. He came to New York in 1923 at Fats Waller's suggestion, and his "Washingtonians" gradually established themselves; in late 1927, they began a five-year association with the famous Cotton Club. It was in the early 30s that Duke's unparalleled genius as a jazz band composer became unmistakable, a genius that ranged from great three-minute popular songs to ambitious large-scale works like "Black, Brown, and Beige" (a 50-minute suite introduced at Carnegie Hall in 1943). From 1939 on he was aided by gifted arranger-composer Billy Strayhorn, in addition to his amazing musicians. Duke Ellington died on 5/24/74 (75).

DATE CHARTED	PEAK POS	WKS CHRT'D	ARTIST — Record Title	Label & Number
7/30/27	**10**	4	1. East St. Louis Toodle-oo .... [I]	Columbia 953
			"Duke Ellington & His Washingtonians" Duke's original theme song; previously recorded for Vocalion 1064, also for Pathe 36781 & Cameo 8182	
5/05/28	**15**	3	2. Black And Tan Fantasy/ [I]	
			previously recorded for Brunswick 3526; also for Okeh 40955 & 8521 above two featuring Bubber Miley (trumpet)	
5/05/28	**19**	1	3. Creole Love Call	Victor 21137
			vocal: Adelaide Hall	
11/24/28	**20**	1	4. Doin' The New Low Down/	
12/01/28	**17**	1	5. Diga Diga Doo	Okeh 8602
			above two vocals: Irving Mills both from the Broadway musical "Blackbirds of 1928"	
12/29/28+	**16**	2	6. The Mooche.. [I]	Okeh 8623
			also recorded for Brunswick 4122 & Cameo 9032 top sidemen in early Ellington band: Bubber Miley & Arthur Whetsol (trumpets), Joe Nanton (trombone), Johnny Hodges (alto sax), Harry Carney (baritone sax), Barney Bigard (clarinet), & Sonny Greer (drums)	
10/18/30	**1(3)**	13	7. **Three Little Words/**	
			vocal: Bing Crosby, Al Rinker, & Harry Barris (Rhythm Boys); from the film "Check and Double Check"	
11/29/30	**17**	1	8. Ring Dem Bells.....................................	Victor 22528
			vocal: Cootie Williams; Johnny Hodges (alto sax) featured	
2/07/31	**12**	2	9. Blue Again	Victor 22603
			vocal: Sid Garry	
2/14/31	**3**	10	10. Mood Indigo.. [I]	Victor 22587
			"Duke Ellington & His Cotton Club Orchestra" Ellington classic originally titled "Dreamy Blues"; selected for the NARAS Hall of Fame; featured solos by Whetsol & Bigard also recorded for Okeh 8840 (as "Harlem Footwarmers") & Brunswick 4952 (as "Jungle Band")	
3/14/31	**19**	1	11. Rockin' In Rhythm.............................. [I]	Brunswick 6038
			listed as "Jungle Band"; also recorded for Okeh 8869	
7/18/31	**18**	2	12. Creole Rhapsody, Parts 1 & 2 .... [I]	Brunswick 6093
8/22/31	**13**	3	13. Limehouse Blues .... [I]	Victor 22743
			from the London musical "A to Z"	
2/27/32	**6**	6	14. It Don't Mean A Thing (If It Ain't Got That Swing)	Brunswick 6265
			vocal: Ivie Anderson; solos by Johnny Hodges & Joe Nanton song helped give the "swing era" its name	
3/19/32	**19**	1	15. Creole Rhapsody .... [I]	Victor 36049
			different version of his 1931 hit	
3/26/32	**15**	3	16. Rose Room (In Sunny Roseland) .... [I]	Brunswick 6265
6/18/32	**14**	3	17. Moon Over Dixie	Brunswick 6317
			vocal: Sonny Greer	
7/09/32	**16**	3	18. Blue Ramble .... [I]	Brunswick 6336
5/06/33	**17**	3	19. Drop Me Off At Harlem .... [I]	Brunswick 6527
5/27/33	**3**	16	20. Sophisticated Lady/ [I]	
			solos by Toby Hardwick (alto sax), Barney Bigard (clarinet), Lawrence Brown (trombone), & Duke	
5/27/33	**4**	16	21. Stormy Weather .... [I]	Brunswick 6600
			solos by Bigard, Cootie Williams (trumpet), Ben Webster (tenor sax), & Brown	

DATE CHARTED	PEAK POS	WKS CHRT'D	ARTIST — Record Title	Label & Number
9/02/33	11	3	22. I'm Satisfied .... vocal: Ivie Anderson	Brunswick 6638
9/30/33	13	2	23. In The Shade Of The Old Apple Tree .... [I]	Brunswick 6646
2/17/34	20	1	24. Daybreak Express................................... [I]	Victor 24501
5/05/34	1(5)	15	25. **Cocktails For Two** .... [I] from the film "Murder at the Vanities"; solos by Johnny Hodges (alto sax), Bigard, & Brown	Victor 24617
10/06/34	2(2)	7	26. Moon Glow/ [I] solos by Hodges and Williams	
10/27/34+	2(1)	16	27. Solitude .... [I] featured solo by Harry Carney (baritone sax)	Brunswick 6987
11/17/34	9	3	28. Saddest Tale .... [I]	Brunswick 7310
6/08/35	6	5	29. Merry-Go-Round .... [I] 1933 version recorded for Columbia 35837	Brunswick 7440
7/13/35	14	3	30. In A Sentimental Mood .... [I] Toby Hardwick (alto sax) featured	Brunswick 7461
9/21/35	6	7	31. Accent On Youth .... [I] featured solo by Johnny Hodges	Brunswick 7514
10/12/35	4	6	32. Cotton	Brunswick 7526
3/28/36	12	3	33. Isn't Love The Strangest Thing?.................	Brunswick 7625
4/04/36	8	10	34. Love Is Like A Cigarette .... Ivie Anderson: above three vocals	Brunswick 7627
5/09/36	12	3	35. Clarinet Lament/ [I] Barney Bigard featured	
5/16/36	19	1	36. Echoes Of Harlem .... [I] Cootie Williams featured	Brunswick 7650
6/13/36	8	5	37. Oh Babe! Maybe Someday..........................	Brunswick 7667
6/20/36	20	1	38. Jazz Lips .... [I] recorded 11/14/29, issued on Victor 38129	Bluebird 6396
10/31/36	16	1	39. Yearning For Love .... [I] Lawrence Brown featured	Brunswick 7752
5/01/37	16	2	40. The New East St. Louis Toodle-Oo .... [I] new version of his 1927 hit	Master 101
5/22/37	12	2	41. There's A Lull In My Life .... vocal: Ivie Anderson; from the film "Wake Up and Live"	Master 117
6/05/37	9	5	42. Scattin' At The Kit-Kat.......................... [I]	Master 123
7/03/37	4	18	43. Caravan/ [I] featuring co-composer Juan Tizol (valve trombone); solos by Bigard, Williams, & Brown	
8/21/37	13	4	44. Azure.. [I]	Master 131
7/31/37	14	2	45. All God's Chillun Got Rhythm.................. [I] from the Marx Bros. film "A Day at the Races"; also recorded by "Ivie Anderson & Her Boys from Dixie" Ellington band on Variety 591	Master 137
2/12/38	15	2	46. Harmony In Harlem.................................	Brunswick 8044
3/19/38	10	3	47. If You Were In My Place (What Would You Do?).. vocal: Ivie Anderson	Brunswick 8093
3/26/38	1(3)	19	48. **I Let A Song Go Out Of My Heart/** [I] Johnny Hodges featured on 46 & 48; other solos on 48: Bigard, Carney, & Brown	
4/30/38	20	1	49. The Gal From Joe's............................. [I]	Brunswick 8108
9/10/38	7	7	50. Lambeth Walk/ [I]	
10/29/38	18	2	51. Prelude To A Kiss............................... [I] Johnny Hodges featured	Brunswick 8204
5/11/40	28	1	52. You, You, Darlin' .... vocal: Herb Jeffries	Victor 26537
6/01/40	25	1	53. Ko Ko.. [I] jazz classic adapted from the uncompleted score of a proposed Ellington opera; solos by Joe Nanton, Juan Tizol, Duke, & bassist Jimmy Blanton	Victor 26577
9/21/40	27	1	54. At A Dixie Roadside Diner.......................... vocal: Ivie Anderson	Victor 26719

DATE CHARTED	PEAK POS	WKS CHRT'D	ARTIST — Record Title	Label & Number
11/02/40	**24**	1	55. Sepia Panorama .... [I] Victor 26731 bassist Jimmy Blanton & Duke featured the most renowned Ellington band: Duke (piano/arranger/ director), Cootie Williams & Wallace Jones (trumpets), Rex Stewart (cornet), Joe Nanton & Lawrence Brown (trombones), Juan Tizol (valve trombone), Barney Bigard (clarinet), Johnny Hodges (alto & soprano sax), Harry Carney (baritone & alto sax), Toby Hardwick (alto sax), Ben Webster (tenor sax), Jimmy Blanton (bass), Fred Guy (guitar), Sonny Greer (drums)	
6/14/41	**11**	4	56. Flamingo... Victor 27326 vocal: Herb Jeffries	
7/26/41	**11**	7	57. Take The "A" Train............................... [I] Victor 27380 the unforgettable Ellington theme of later years written by Billy Strayhorn; selected for NARAS Hall of Fame; solos by Ray Nance (trumpet), Rex Stewart, & Duke	
10/11/41+	**13**	3	58. I Got It Bad And That Ain't Good................. Victor 27531 vocal: Ivie Anderson; from Duke's West Coast revue "Jump For Joy"; solos by Duke & Johnny Hodges	
5/01/43	**8**	14	59. Don't Get Around Much Anymore .... [I] Victor 26610 recorded 5/4/40 and issued under the title "Never No Lament"; main solos by Hodges, Williams, Brown, & Duke	
5/22/43	**21**	1	60. Perdido.. [I] Victor 27880 recorded 1/21/42; Harry Carney & Ray Nance featured	
7/03/43	**19**	1	61. Take The "A" Train .... [I-R] Victor 27380 featured in the film "Reveille With Beverly"	
8/14/43	**19**	1	62. Bojangles (A Portrait of Bill Robinson)....... [I] Victor 26644 recorded 5/28/40; Ben Webster featured	
11/06/43	**19**	1	63. A Slip Of The Lip/ vocal: Ray Nance	
11/13/43	**19**	1	64. Sentimental Lady .... [I] Victor 1528 above two recorded 7/28/42	
1/22/44	**10**	6	65. Do Nothin' Till You Hear From Me .... [I] Victor 1547 recorded 3/15/40 and issued on Victor 26598 as "Concerto for Cootie", a showcase for Cootie Williams	
3/25/44	**23**	1	66. Main Stem .... [I] Victor 1556 recorded 6/26/42; Ben Webster featured	
2/03/45	**6**	12	67. I'm Beginning To See The Light.................. Victor 1618	
2/02/46	**13**	1	68. Come To Baby, Do .... Victor 1748 above two vocals: Joya Sherrill	
6/13/53	**27**	3	69. Satin Doll... [I] Capitol 2458 main solo by Duke	
11/21/53	**30**	1	70. Boo-Dah... [I] Capitol 2598 Ellington's 1953 band features Clark Terry & Cat Anderson (trumpets), Nance & Tizol (trombones), Paul Gonsalves (tenor sax), Jimmy Hamilton (clarinet/tenor sax), Russell Procope (alto sax), & Harry Carney	

BARON ELLIOTT & HIS STARDUST MELODIES ORCHESTRA

3/20/43	**20**	1	1. Vos Zokt Eer/	
10/02/43	**18**	1	2. Stardust.. Musicraft 15010 vocals on both by Stardust Trio	

HARRY ELLIS

10/12/18	**5**	3	1. While You're Away .... Okeh 1070	

SEGER ELLIS & HIS ORCHESTRA
Singer who recorded with Louis Armstrong and the Dorsey Brothers in late 20s and early 30s; wrote many songs after 1940.

1/28/28	**17**	2	1. My Blue Heaven.................................... Okeh 40928	
9/15/28	**19**	1	2. I Can't Give You Anything But Love............ Okeh 41077 from the Broadway musical "Blackbirds of 1928"	
11/24/28	**4**	6	3. When You're Smiling............................... Columbia 1494	
1/19/29	**19**	1	4. Dream House .... Okeh 41127 band on 2 & 4 features Tommy Dorsey (trombone) & Eddie Lang (guitar)	
1/14/39	**7**	1	5. Please Come Out Of Your Dream .... Brunswick 8275	

DATE CHARTED	PEAK POS	WKS CHRT'D	ARTIST — Record Title	Label & Number
			GLEN ELLISON Born in Glasgow, Scotland	
1/29/16	**9**	1	1. Face To Face With The Girl Of My Dreams	Edison 50294
			MISCHA ELMAN Great Russian-born classical violinist, died on 4/5/67 (76). (also see Enrico Caruso)	
9/03/10	**7**	2	1. Humoresque .... [I] accompanied on piano by Percy B. Kahn	Victor 74163
2/05/16	**10**	1	2. Spanish Dance .... [I] accompanied on piano by Walter H. Golde	Victor 74455
			ZIGGY ELMAN & HIS ORCHESTRA Born Harry Finkelman, Ziggy was one of the top trumpet stars of the dance band era (a six-time Down Beat poll winner), most famous for the Benny Goodman hit "And The Angels Sing"; after five years (1936-40) with Benny, played 1940-47 with Tommy Dorsey; died on 6/26/68 (54). (also see Frank Sinatra)	
10/18/47	**25**	1	1. Body And Soul .... [I] from the Broadway musical "Three's A Crowd"	MGM 10071
			JACK EMERSON	
8/21/48	**18**	9	1. Hair Of Gold (Eyes Of Blue) .... accompanied by Chet Howard's Orchestra from the film "Singin' Spurs"	Metronome 2018
			SKINNAY ENNIS & HIS ORCHESTRA Robert (Skinnay) Ennis achieved fame singing with the Hal Kemp band from 1933-37; Claude Thornhill and Gil Evans provided some of the arrangements for his band. Died on 6/3/63 (53).	
4/15/39	**9**	1	1. Wishing (Will Make It So)...........................	Victor 26212
			ESQUIRE BOYS	
2/21/53	**27**	1	1. Caravan .... [I]	Rainbow 188
			RUTH ETTING One of Broadway's greatest torch singers, Ruth Etting was born on 11/23/07 in David City, Neb., and got her start in Chicago nightclubs. "Ziegfeld Follies of 1927" made her a star; credited as co-author of several of her hit songs, she was featured in other Broadway musicals and a few 1930s movies. Doris Day starred in Ruth's 1955 film biography, "Love Me or Leave Me"; Ruth died on 9/24/78 (70).	
6/26/26	**14**	1	1. Let's Talk About My Sweetie	Columbia 580
8/07/26	**3**	6	2. Lonesome And Sorry/	
8/14/26	**10**	1	3. But I Do, You Know I Do	Columbia 644
12/03/27	**17**	1	4. It All Belongs To Me................................. above two from the Broadway musical "Ziegfeld Follies of 1927"	Columbia 1113
2/26/27	**5**	7	5. Thinking Of You	Columbia 827
4/09/27	**2(2)**	7	6. 'Deed I Do	Columbia 865
5/21/27	**5**	6	7. Sam, The Old Accordion Man/	
5/28/27	**8**	6	8. It All Depends On You .... from the Broadway musical "Big Boy"	Columbia 908
7/02/27	**10**	4	9. Hoosier Sweetheart/	
7/16/27	**10**	4	10. Wistful And Blue	Columbia 924
7/23/27	**4**	7	11. (What Do We Do) On A Dew-Dew-Dewy Day....	Columbia 979
11/12/27	**4**	8	12. Shaking The Blues Away...........................	Columbia 1113
11/26/27	**9**	4	13. I'm Nobody's Baby	Columbia 1104
2/25/28	**7**	6	14. The Song Is Ended (But The Melody Lingers On)/	
2/25/28	**12**	3	15. Together, We Two...................................	Columbia 1196
4/07/28	**5**	7	16. Back In Your Own Back Yard/	
4/21/28	**10**	3	17. When You're With Somebody Else	Columbia 1288
4/07/28	**9**	4	18. Keep Sweeping Cobwebs Off The Moon .... Ruth Etting with Ted Lewis & His Band	Columbia 1242

DATE CHARTED	PEAK POS	WKS CHRT'D	ARTIST — Record Title	Label & Number
6/16/28	10	4	19. Ramona/ song written to promote the silent film "Ramona"	
7/14/28	11	3	20. Say "Yes" Today	Columbia 1352
8/25/28	10	3	21. Because My Baby Don't Mean Maybe Now/	
9/15/28	10	4	22. Beloved	Columbia 1420
10/06/28	9	5	23. Happy Days And Lonely Nights	Columbia 1454
12/01/28	6	4	24. Sonny Boy...............................	Columbia 1563
			from the film "The Singing Fool"	
12/22/28+	9	4	25. My Blackbirds Are Bluebirds Now	Columbia 1595
2/02/29	2(2)	11	26. Love Me Or Leave Me/	
			Ruth's trademark song	
2/23/29	15	2	27. I'm Bringing A Red, Red Rose	Columbia 1680
			above three from the Broadway musical "Whoopee"	
3/23/29	15	2	28. You're The Cream In My Coffee	Columbia 1707
			from the Broadway musical "Hold Everything"	
4/13/29	3	10	29. I'll Get By As Long As I Have You/	
6/08/29	17	2	30. Glad Rag Doll............................	Columbia 1733
5/18/29	3	9	31. Mean To Me/	
6/01/29	15	2	32. Button Up Your Overcoat	Columbia 1762
			from the Broadway musical "Follow Through"	
6/22/29	17	1	33. Deep Night...............................	Columbia 1801
10/19/29	16	1	34. Ain't Misbehavin'...........................	Columbia 1958
			from the Broadway musical "Hot Chocolates"	
11/02/29	9	3	35. What Wouldn't I Do For That Man/	
			from the films "Applause" and "Glorifying the American Girl"	
11/30/29	16	2	36. The Right Kind Of Man	Columbia 1998
12/21/29+	9	5	37. More Than You Know	Columbia 2038
			from the Broadway musical "Great Day"	
2/01/30	15	4	38. Cryin' For The Carolines......................	Columbia 2073
			from the film "Spring is Here"	
5/03/30	5	11	39. Ten Cents A Dance	Columbia 2146
			from the Broadway musical "Simple Simon"	
5/03/30	11	3	40. Exactly Like You/	
			from the Broadway musical "International Revue"	
6/14/30	19	1	41. It Happened In Monterey.....................	Columbia 2199
			from the film "The King of Jazz"	
6/21/30	10	8	42. Dancing With Tears In My Eyes..................	Columbia 2216
			Ruth also recorded this song with Ben Selvin's Orchestra on Columbia 2206	
10/04/30	6	7	43. Don't Tell Her What Happened To Me	Columbia 2280
10/18/30	10	4	44. Body And Soul	Columbia 2300
			from the Broadway musical "Three's a Crowd"	
11/08/30	10	4	45. Just A Little Closer/	
11/08/30	14	5	46. I'll Be Blue Just Thinking Of You	Columbia 2307
1/31/31	6	6	47. Reaching For The Moon/	
			movie title song	
3/07/31	18	1	48. Overnight...............................	Columbia 2377
			from the Broadway musical "Sweet and Low"	
3/28/31	5	6	49. Love Is Like That	Columbia 2398
5/30/31	11	3	50. Were You Sincere?........................	Columbia 2445
9/26/31	7	6	51. I'm Good For Nothing But Love	Columbia 2505
9/26/31	13	4	52. Now That You're Gone/	
10/03/31	4	7	53. Guilty.................................	Columbia 2529
11/28/31	17	2	54. Good Night, Sweetheart	Columbia 2557
			from the Broadway musical "Earl Carroll's Vanities of 1931"	
1/16/32	10	3	55. Cuban Love Song..........................	Columbia 2580
			movie title song	
3/26/32	8	4	56. When We're Alone	Columbia 2630
7/30/32	14	3	57. The Night When Love Was Born	Columbia 2681
9/03/32	13	2	58. It Was So Beautiful	Melotone 12450
			from the film "The Big Broadcast of 1932"	
3/18/33	16	2	59. Try A Little Tenderness........................	Melotone 12625

DATE CHARTED	PEAK POS	WKS CHRT'D	ARTIST — Record Title	Label & Number
2/24/34	**15**	3	60. Smoke Gets In Your Eyes .... from the Broadway musical "Roberta"	Brunswick 6769
4/27/35	**1(2)**	12	61. **Life Is A Song**	Columbia 3031
2/13/37	**20**	1	62. In The Chapel In The Moonlight..................	Decca 1084

GEORGE "HONEY BOY" EVANS
Famous turn-of-the-century vaudeville comedy performer who co-wrote such hits as "In the Good Old Summer Time" and "Come Take a Trip in My Air-Ship".

HENRY EVANS
Pseudonym for Evan Williams

F

SAMMY FAIN
Composer of many popular songs from 1920s to 1960s, including "I Can Dream, Can't I?", "I'll Be Seeing You", and "Love Is a Many-Splendored Thing".

11/02/29	**19**	1	1. Painting The Clouds With Sunshine .... from the film "Gold Diggers of Broadway"	Harmony 1014

PERCY FAITH & HIS ORCHESTRA
Canadian-born orchestra leader who regularly accompanied such top singers as Tony Bennett, Rosemary Clooney, and Johnny Mathis, and composed music for several films; died on 2/9/76 (67).

6/30/50	**20**	4	1. I Cross My Fingers .... vocal: Russ Emery	Columbia 38786
9/02/50	**7**	11	2. All My Love .... adapted from the French song "Bolero"	Columbia 38918
12/23/50	**28**	1	3. Christmas In Killarney .... [X] vocal: Shillelagh Singers	Columbia 39048
5/12/51	**10**	9	4. On Top Of Old Smoky .... vocal: Burl Ives; based on the traditional folk song "Little Mohee"	Columbia 39328
9/15/51	**29**	1	5. When The Saints Go Marching In/	
9/22/51	**30**	1	6. I Want To Be Near You	Columbia 39528
4/26/52	**1(1)**	22	7. **Delicado** .... [I] featuring Stan Freeman on harpsichord	Columbia 39708
3/07/53	**21**	6	8. Swedish Rhapsody (Midsummer Vigil)/ [I]	
4/04/53	**1(10)**	24	● 9. **Song From "Moulin Rouge" (Where Is Your Heart)**..................................... vocal: Felicia Sanders; movie title song	Columbia 39944
6/20/53	**19**	2	10. Return To Paradise .... [I] movie title song	Columbia 39998
12/12/53	**30**	1	11. Many Times.. [I]	Columbia 40076
5/08/54	**25**	1	12. Dream, Dream, Dream	Columbia 40185
10/23/54	**25**	1	13. The Bandit .... [I] from the Mexican film "O Cangaceiro"	Columbia 40323

CECIL FANNING

9/16/11	**2(1)**	6	1. A Perfect Day..	Columbia 5308

FARBER SISTERS

8/10/18	**3**	7	1. If He Can Fight Like He Can Love (Good Night, Germany)	Columbia 2556

DICK FARNEY

11/01/47	**13**	1	1. I Wish I Didn't Love You So .... accompanied by Paul Baron's Orchestra from the movie "The Perils of Pauline"	Majestic 7225

DATE CHARTED	PEAK POS	WKS CHRT'D	ARTIST — Record Title	Label & Number
			GERALDINE FARRAR	
			The most famous of all American-born opera singers during the early years of the century, she made her Royal Opera debut in 1901 before returning home as a star of the New York Metropolitan; died on 3/11/67 (85).	
8/31/07	**7**	1	1. Madama Butterfly: Tutti I Fior (Duet Of The Flowers).................................... [F] GERALDINE FARRAR & LOUISE HOMER	Victor 87008
7/18/08	**4**	2	2. Madama Butterfly: Finale Act I - O Quanti Acchi Fisi (O Kindly Heavens)........... [F] GERALDINE FARRAR & ENRICO CARUSO	Victor 89017
8/29/08	**4**	2	3. Boheme: Quartetto - "Addio, Dolce Svegliare" (Farewell, Sweet Love)..................... [F] CARUSO, FARRAR, ANTONIO SCOTTI, & GINA VIAFORA	Victor 96002
1/29/10	**7**	2	4. Madama Butterfly: Finale Ultimo (Butterfly's Death Scene) .... [F]	Victor 87030
4/23/10	**8**	2	5. Faust - "Mon Coeur Est Penetre Depouvante!" (My Heart Is Torn With Grief)........... [F] GERALDINE FARRAR & ENRICO CARUSO	Victor 89033
8/13/10	**9**	1	6. Contes D' Hoffman - Barcolle Belle Nuit (Oh, Night Of Love)................................. [F] GERALDINE FARRAR & ANTONIO SCOTTI	Victor 87502
10/22/10	**5**	3	7. My Old Kentucky Home	Victor 88238
3/29/13	**6**	3	8. Rigoletto: Deh! Non Parlare Al Misero (Recall Not The Past)................................. [F] GERALDINE FARRAR & ENRICO CARUSO	Victor 89058
11/15/13	**9**	2	9. Long, Long Ago	Victor 87163
2/05/16	**9**	1	10. Mighty Lak' A Rose................................ accompanied by Fritz Kreisler (violin)	Victor 88537
			BILL FARRELL	
			Baritone whose first national singing exposure was on Bob Hope's radio show; real name William Fiorelli.	
9/24/49	**26**	1	1. Circus... accompanied by Earle Hagen's Orchestra	MGM 10488
4/01/50	**20**	6	2. It Isn't Fair	MGM 10637
1/06/51	**18**	4	3. My Heart Cries For You............................ above two accompanied by Russ Case's Orchestra	MGM 10868
			MARGUERITE FARRELL	
			Popular vaudeville singer; died on 1/26/51 (62).	
9/23/16	**1(3)**	7	1. **If I Knock The 'L' Out Of Kelly (It Would Still Be Kelly To Me)/**	
11/04/16	**6**	2	2. By The Sad Luana Shore.......................... above two from the Broadway musical "Step This Way"	Victor 18105
1/06/17	**9**	1	3. You Were Just Made To Order For Me .... MARGUERITE FARRELL & M.J. O'CONNELL	Columbia 2088
			ALBERT FARRINGTON	
1/09/15	**8**	1	1. It's A Long, Long Way To Tipperary............. featured in the Broadway musicals "Chin-Chin" & "Dancing Around"	Edison Amb. 2487
			EDWARD M. FAVOR	
			Comic singer who appeared in vaudeville and on Broadway; died on 1/10/36 (80).	
3/21/95	**1(5)**	5	1. **My Best Girl's A New Yorker**	Columbia 2107
4/14/94	**1(7)**	7	2. **Say Au Revoir, But Not Goodbye**..............	North Amer. 858
1/20/00	**4**	2	3. I'd Leave My Happy Home For You..............	Berliner 0712
8/02/02	**2(2)**	4	4. On A Sunday Afternoon	Victor 1357
11/29/02	**5**	1	5. I Want To Be A Lidy................................ [C] from the Broadway musical "A Chinese Honeymoon"	Edison 8159
9/25/09	**9**	1	6. I Love My Wife, But Oh You Kid! .... [C]	Edison 10201
12/25/09	**8**	1	7. Sadie Salome, Go Home! .... [C] also recorded for Columbia 1211	Edison 10243

153

DATE CHARTED	PEAK POS	WKS CHRT'D	ARTIST — Record Title	Label & Number
			ALICE FAYE	
			Among the most beautiful and popular movie musical stars of the 1935-45 era, Alice (real name: Alice Jeanne Leppert) had first sung briefly with Rudy Vallee; married first to Tony Martin, then Phil Harris.	
5/22/37	**20**	1	1. There's A Lull In My Life .... Brunswick 7876	
			from the film "Wake Up and Live" accompanied by Cy Fever & His Orchestra	
			IRVING FAZOLA	
			Great jazz clarinetist (born Irving Prestopnik) whose most famous recordings were with Bob Crosby (1938-40) and Claude Thornhill (1941) bands; previously with Ben Pollack, and later with Teddy Powell. Died on 3/20/49 (36).	
			ELMER FELDKAMP	
			1930s band singer with Bert Lown (1931-32) and Freddy Martin (1933-38); died on 9/27/38.	
			PAUL FENNELLY & HIS ORCHESTRA	
9/04/48	**21**	2	1. A Tree In The Meadow........................... MGM 10211	
			vocal by Reggie Goff	
			CARL FENTON & HIS ORCHESTRA	
			Popular 1920s bandleader (real name: Walter Haenschen) who backed Al Jolson on a few 1920s records, and Bing Crosby on Bing's original 1931 radio show.	
9/25/20	**3**	5	1. Cuban Moon .... [I] Brunswick 2048	
3/26/21	**7**	3	2. Rosie.. [I] Brunswick 2067	
7/30/21	**3**	4	3. Cherie .... [I] Brunswick 2100	
9/24/21	**13**	1	4. Learn To Smile .... [I] Brunswick 2120	
			from the Broadway musical "The O'Brien Girl"	
3/25/22	**9**	2	5. Stealing .... [I] Brunswick 2180	
4/29/22	**5**	3	6. Three O'Clock In The Morning................. [I] Brunswick 2193	
			from the Broadway musical "Greenwich Village Follies of 1921"	
6/17/22	**6**	2	7. Georgia.. [I] Brunswick 2259	
7/29/22	**13**	1	8. Nola .... [I] Brunswick 2261	
9/02/22	**6**	3	9. Parade Of The Wooden Soldiers............... [I] Brunswick 2282	
12/30/22	**12**	1	10. I'll Build A Stairway To Paradise .... [I] Brunswick 2316	
			from the Broadway musical "George White's Scandals of 1922"	
4/21/23	**1(3)**	10	11. **Love Sends A Little Gift Of Roses** .... [I] Brunswick 2392	
			with pianists Victor Arden & Phil Ohman	
10/06/23	**8**	2	12. Tell Me A Story .... [I] Brunswick 2453	
11/03/23	**6**	3	13. Indiana Moon....................................... [I] Brunswick 2469	
3/29/24	**10**	1	14. Dream Daddy.. Brunswick 2525	
			vocal: Billy Jones & Ernest Hare	
7/19/24	**10**	1	15. Virginia (Don't Go Too Far)...................... [I] Brunswick 2585	
8/16/24	**10**	1	16. What'll I Do? .... [I] Brunswick 2604	
			from the Broadway musical "Music Box Revue of 1923"	
8/30/24	**14**	1	17. Limehouse Blues .... [I] Brunswick 2603	
			from the London musical "A to Z"	
9/27/24	**11**	1	18. Adoration Waltz .... [I] Brunswick 2617	
11/29/24	**5**	3	19. I Want To Be Happy .... Brunswick 2640	
			vocal: Billy Jones, Ernest Hare, Wilfred Glenn, & Elliott Shaw; from the Broadway musical "No, No, Nanette"	
5/02/25	**9**	1	20. Oh! Lady Be Good.................................. [I] Brunswick 2790	
			Broadway musical title song	
6/27/25	**13**	1	21. Oh Katharina! .... [I] Brunswick 2835	
7/04/25	**4**	4	22. Midnight Waltz...................................... Brunswick 2853	
			vocal: Frank Munn	
10/31/25	**15**	1	23. Collegiate... Brunswick 2913	
			vocal: Billy Jones, Ernest Hare, & Irving Kaufman	
11/07/25	**3**	5	24. Alone At Last .... Brunswick 2925	
12/26/25+	**5**	4	25. Brown Eyes, Why Are You Blue? .... Brunswick 2950	
8/20/27	**15**	2	26. The Same Old Moon .... Brunswick 3508	
			from the Broadway musical "Lucky" above two vocals: Frank Munn	

DATE CHARTED	PEAK POS	WKS CHRT'D	ARTIST — Record Title	Label & Number
			FRANK FERERA Frank Ferera and wife Helen Louise, masters of the Hawaiian guitar, played on many of the records constituting the "Hawaiian craze" of 1916-21 (also see Henry Burr & Albert Campbell, Hoarce Wright, Hawaiian Trio)	
11/24/17	6	2	1. Along The Way To Wakiki .... [I] HELEN LOUISE & FRANK FERERA	Columbia 2362
12/25/20	13	1	2. Beautiful Hawaii	Victor 18689
10/29/21	15	1	3. Hawaiian Medley .... [I] above two: FRANK FERERA & ANTHONY FRANCHINI	Columbia 3422
2/09/24	10	1	4. Aloha Oe (Farewell To Thee) .... [I] Ferera's Hawaiian Instrumental Quintet song published in 1878	Columbia 21
			MAYNARD FERGUSON One of the top modern jazz trumpeters, played with Stan Kenton in early 1950s and reached new peak of popularity in 1970s.	
			FERKO STRING BAND From Philadelphia	
3/13/48	21	3	1. Heartbreaker	Palda 109
			JOSE FERRER Academy Award-winning actor ("Cyrano de Bergerac"), formerly married to Rosemary Clooney.	
1/16/54	30	1	1. The Heat's On .... RITA HAYWORTH & JOSE FERRER from the film "Miss Sadie Thompson"	MGM 25181
1/30/54	16	7	2. Woman (Uh-Huh) .... orchestra & chorus directed by Norman Leyden	Columbia 40144
			MEL FERRER Actor, producer and director. (see Leslie Caron)	
			ARTHUR FIELDS A professional child singer at eleven, Fields co-wrote many popular songs ("Aba Daba Honeymoon" the biggest) in addition to performing on vaudeville, radio, and records. He died on 3/29/53 (64). (also see Ben Bernie)	
12/26/14+	9	2	1. Along Came Ruth .... also recorded for Columbia 1612	Victor 17637
1/30/15	9	1	2. Poor Pauline .... first written to accompany the silent film serial "The Perils of Pauline"	Columbia 1626
7/03/15	9	1	3. He Comes Up Smiling	Columbia 1696
9/18/15	9	1	4. When Sunday Comes To Town	Columbia 1769
12/09/16	2(3)	6	5. He's Got A Bungalow.............................	Columbia 2086
8/18/17	10	1	6. What Kind Of American Are You?	Columbia 2272
3/16/18	8	2	7. When Yankee Doodle Learns To Parlez Vous Francais .... also on Edison Amberol 3447	Columbia 2451
4/20/18	5	3	8. Liberty Bell (It's Time To Ring Again)..........	Columbia 2473
6/15/18	10	1	9. Any Place The Old Gang Goes (I'll Be There).. ARTHUR FIELDS & PEERLESS QUARTET	Columbia 2514
8/03/18	9	2	10. Rock-A-Bye Your Baby With A Dixie Melody ..	Pathe 20360
10/12/18	1(4)	12	11. **Oh, How I Hate To Get Up In The Morning** . from the Broadway musical "Yip, Yip, Yaphank" also recorded for Columbia 2617, Edison Amberol 3639, Pathe 20431, & Empire 6259	Victor 18489
10/12/18	8	2	12. The Last Long Mile	Columbia 2601
10/19/18	8	1	13. Oh! Frenchy.................................... also recorded for Brunswick 2569, Edison Amberol 3601, & Pathe 20411	Victor 18489
12/07/18	2(1)	6	14. Oui, Oui, Marie .... [C] also recorded for Pathe 20424 & Empire 6225	Victor 18505
12/07/18	9	1	15. The Yanks Are At It Again .... 12 & 15: ARTHUR FIELDS & PEERLESS QUARTET 15: Fields solo, Pathe 29220	Columbia 2620

DATE CHARTED	PEAK POS	WKS CHRT'D	ARTIST — Record Title	Label & Number
3/01/19	6	3	16. Would You Rather Be A Colonel With An Eagle On Your Shoulder Or A Private With A Chicken On Your Knee? .... under pseudonym "Eugene Buckley"; also recorded under real name for Okeh 1109 & Pathe 22018; from the Broadway musical "Ziegfeld Follies of 1919"	Columbia 2669
3/08/19	4	5	17. Ja-Da (Ja Da, Ja Da, Jing Jing Jing)............. also recorded for Columbia 2672, Edison Amberol 3649, Emerson 9160, Pathe 22017, & Empire 6272 flip side: "The Alcoholic Blues" (POS 5) by Billy Murray	Victor 18522
4/26/19	7	2	18. How Ya Gonna Keep 'Em Down On The Farm (After They've Seen Paree)	Victor 18537
7/12/19	4	5	19. Bring Back Those Wonderful Days...............	Victor 18555
3/25/22	12	1	20. April Showers .... featured in the Broadway musical "Bombo"	Emerson 10490

GRACIE FIELDS
Long-popular British singer and comedienne, in many 1930s and 40s movies

DATE CHARTED	PEAK POS	WKS CHRT'D	ARTIST — Record Title	Label & Number
1/31/48	3	21	1. Now Is The Hour...................................... accompanied by Phil Green's Orchestra	London 110
4/02/49	23	3	2. Forever And Ever .... accompanied by Bob Faron's Orchestra & the Wardour Singers	London 362

HERBIE FIELDS & HIS ORCHESTRA
Versatile saxophonist who played from 1944-46 with Lionel Hampton; died on 9/17/58 (39, suicide).

DATE CHARTED	PEAK POS	WKS CHRT'D	ARTIST — Record Title	Label & Number
1/18/47	14	1	1. A-Huggin' And A-Kissin'	RCA Victor 2036
3/22/47	26	1	2. Connecticut .... vocal refrain by the Romanticists band includes Al Klink (tenor sax)	RCA Victor 2104
9/12/53	24	1	3. Harlem Nocturne .... [I]	Parrot 775

IRVING FIELDS
Pianist-combo leader who specialized in Latin music

DATE CHARTED	PEAK POS	WKS CHRT'D	ARTIST — Record Title	Label & Number
6/12/48	24	1	1. The Wedding Song .... vocal by Betty Harris, the Campos Trio, & The Three-o-Niners; adapted from the Yiddish song "Raisins and Almonds"	RCA Victor 9035

SHEP FIELDS & HIS RIPPLING RHYTHM ORCHESTRA
Sweet band best remembered for its "rippling rhythm" sound introduced by blowing through a straw into a glass of water.

DATE CHARTED	PEAK POS	WKS CHRT'D	ARTIST — Record Title	Label & Number
7/11/36	17	1	1. On The Beach At Bali Bali	Bluebird 6417
8/22/36	1(4)	12	2. Did I Remember?.................................... from the film "Suzy" above two vocals: Charles Chester	Bluebird 6476
10/17/36	19	1	3. You Came To My Rescue/	
10/31/36	16	3	4. I'm Talking Through My Heart .... above two from film "Big Broadcast of 1937"	Bluebird 6547
10/31/36	13	2	5. Easy To Love .... from the film "Born to Dance" above three vocals: Dick Robertson	Bluebird 6592
11/07/36	12	2	6. One, Two, Button Your Shoe...................... vocal: Charles Chester; from the film "Pennies from Heaven"	Bluebird 6604
11/21/36	1(2)	15	7. In The Chapel In The Moonlight................	Bluebird 6640
11/21/36+	9	9	8. It's De-Lovely... from the Broadway musical "Red, Hot, and Blue"	Bluebird 6639
12/26/36+	5	11	9. There's Something In The Air .... from the film "Banjo On My Knee"	Bluebird 6683
2/06/37	9	4	10. Goodnight, My Love .... from the film "We're Not Dressing"	Bluebird 6685
2/06/37	10	8	11. On A Little Bamboo Bridge......................	Bluebird 6781
2/13/37	5	6	12. This Year's Kisses .... from the film "On the Avenue"	Bluebird 6757
3/06/37	3	9	13. Moonlight And Shadows............................ from the film "Jungle Princess"	Bluebird 6803
3/13/37	10	4	14. When My Dream Boat Comes Home..............	Bluebird 6661

DATE CHARTED	PEAK POS	WKS CHRT'D	ARTIST — Record Title	Label & Number
5/01/37	**16**	1	15. Let's Call The Whole Thing Off.................... from the film "Shall We Dance?"	Bluebird 6878
5/08/37	**12**	2	16. You're Here, You're There (You're Everywhere)/	
6/12/37	**13**	4	17. When Two Love Each Other (Just As You And I)...	Bluebird 6931
5/15/37	**8**	4	18. Little Old Lady .... from the Broadway musical "The Show Is On"	Bluebird 6747
5/29/37	**6**	8	19. It Looks Like Rain In Cherry Blossom Lane...	Bluebird 6953
6/26/37	**1(2)**	8	20. **The Merry-Go-Round Broke Down**	Bluebird 7015
8/07/37	**1(4)**	14	21. **That Old Feeling** .... from the film "Vogues of 1938"	Bluebird 7066
8/21/37	**11**	4	22. The Moon Got In My Eyes.......................... from the film "Double or Nothing"	Bluebird 7099
10/02/37	**6**	4	23. I Still Love To Kiss You Goodnight.............. from the film "Fifty-Second Street"	Bluebird 7139
10/23/37	**8**	7	24. Nice Work If You Can Get It....................... from the film "A Damsel in Distress"	Bluebird 7195
12/18/37	**15**	1	25. You Took The Words Right Out Of My Heart ..	Bluebird 7304
12/25/37+	**1(4)**	14	26. **Thanks For The Memory/** became Bob Hope's theme song	
1/08/38	**10**	7	27. Mama, That Moon Is Here Again .... above three from film "The Big Broadcast of 1938"	Bluebird 7318
1/22/38	**5**	6	28. Whistle While You Work .... from the film "Snow White and the Seven Dwarfs" all vocals from 9-28: Bob Goday	Bluebird 7343
5/14/38	**1(3)**	10	29. **Cathedral In The Pines** .... vocal: Jerry Stewart	Bluebird 7553
1/07/39	**20**	1	30. An Old Curiosity Shop	Bluebird 10056
10/07/39	**1(5)**	18	31. **South Of The Border (Down Mexico Way)**.... above two vocals: Hal Derwin	Bluebird 10376
2/17/40	**19**	1	32. Mene Mene Tekel.....................................	Bluebird 10546
11/16/40	**18**	6	33. Down Argentina Way/ vocal: Sonny Washburn; movie title song	
12/28/40	**26**	1	34. Moon Over Burma................................... vocal: Dorothy Allen	Bluebird 10886
11/15/41	**24**	1	35. City Called Heaven................................. vocal: Pat Fry	Bluebird 11255
6/06/42	**13**	1	36. Breathless .... vocal: Ken Curtis (actor, later featured on TV's "Gunsmoke" and "Ripcord")	Bluebird 11497
7/11/42	**15**	1	37. Jersey Bounce .... [I]	Bluebird 11490
3/27/43	**15**	3	38. Please Think Of Me .... vocal: Ralph Young listed on above four as "Shep Fields & His New Music"	Bluebird 0807

JACK FINA
Pianist/arranger on the huge Freddy Martin hit 'Piano Concerto in B Flat", with Martin from 1936-42; died on 5/14/70 (56).

BILL FINEGAN
Former arranger for Glenn Miller ('A Nightingale Sang in Berkeley Square", "Song of the Volga Boatmen"), co-leader of Sauter-Finegan band.

TED FIO RITO & HIS ORCHESTRA
Composer of many 1920s and 30s hits ("Toot Toot Tootsie", "Laugh Clown Laugh"), former co-leader of Russo-Fio Rito Orchestra; Betty Grable sang briefly with his band in 1933. Ted died on 7/22/71 (70).

DATE CHARTED	PEAK POS	WKS CHRT'D	ARTIST — Record Title	Label & Number
12/03/32	**17**	2	1. Willow Weep For Me	Brunswick 6422
2/04/33	**12**	3	2. (When It's) Darkness On The Delta..............	Brunswick 6478
3/11/33	**7**	7	3. I'll Take An Option On You/	
4/08/33	**12**	3	4. (I Don't Stand) A Ghost Of A Chance With You.. vocals on 1, 2, & 4: Muzzy Marcellino	Brunswick 6505
6/03/33	**12**	3	5. Hold Me	Brunswick 6555

DATE CHARTED	PEAK POS	WKS CHRT'D	ARTIST — Record Title	Label & Number
1/27/34	1(1)	14	6. **My Little Grass Shack In Kealakekua, Hawaii**	Brunswick 6736
2/03/34	15	3	7. Temptation.................................... from the film "Going Hollywood"	Brunswick 6705
5/12/34	1(5)	14	8. **I'll String Along With You**..................... vocal: Muzzy Marcellino from the film "Twenty Million Sweethearts"	Brunswick 6859
7/21/34	12	3	9. Soft Green Seas/ [I]	
9/01/34	10	5	10. King Kamahamena (Conquerer Of The Islands)................................... [I]	Brunswick 6902
12/15/34	10	4	11. June In January....................... from the film "Here Is My Heart"	Brunswick 7327
2/02/35	16	2	12. On The Good Ship Lollipop .... from the film "Bright Eyes"	Brunswick 7364
3/14/36	9	4	13. Let's Face The Music And Dance .... from the film "Follow the Fleet"	Decca 697
6/20/36	15	2	14. All My Life .... from the film "Laughing Irish Eyes" above two vocals: Stanley Hickman	Decca 784
7/17/37	10	4	15. Tomorrow Is Another Day	Decca 1257
11/06/37	17	2	16. Vieni, Vieni..................... adaptation of a Corsican popular song above two vocals: Muzzy Macellino	Decca 1450
5/20/39	16	1	17. How Strange .... vocal: Twin Fours	Decca 2381

CARL FISCHER

Pianist/conductor/arranger with Frankie Laine from 1947 until Carl's death on 3/28/54 (41); also played with Pee Wee Hunt's Dixieland band, and composed the hits "It Started All Over Again" and "Who Wouldn't Love You?".

EDDIE FISHER

One of the 1950s' most popular singers, Eddie Fisher was born on 8/10/28 in Philadelphia. At age 18 he was singing with Buddy Morrow's band, and in 1949 got his first nationwide exposure on Eddie Cantor's radio show. A year later he was a popular sensation. Married to Debbie Reynolds, then Elizabeth Taylor, Eddie appeared in several 50s movies and his own TV series. Accompanied on all solo records by Hugo Winterhalter's Orchestra. (also see Marlin Sisters, Hugo Winterhalter)

DATE CHARTED	PEAK POS	WKS CHRT'D	ARTIST — Record Title	Label & Number
10/14/50	5	18	1. Thinking Of You .... featured in the film "Three Little Words"	RCA Victor 3901
2/03/51	14	14	2. Bring Back The Thrill	RCA Victor 4016
5/05/51	17	11	3. Unless	RCA Victor 4120
7/21/51	18	9	4. I'll Hold You In My Heart	RCA Victor 4191
9/29/51	8	14	5. Turn Back The Hands Of Time	RCA Victor 4257
12/08/51+	2(2)	30	● 6. Any Time .... song published in 1921	RCA Victor 4359
1/05/52	4	19	● 7. Tell Me Why/	
2/02/52	25	2	8. Trust In Me	RCA Victor 4444
3/22/52	7	17	9. Forgive Me/	
4/05/52	10	9	10. That's The Chance You Take....................	RCA Victor 4574
5/03/52	3	19	11. I'm Yours/	
6/14/52	20	4	12. Just A Little Lovin'............................	RCA Victor 4680
6/14/52	3	18	13. Maybe/	
6/14/52	19	6	14. Watermelon Weather................... above two: PERRY COMO & EDDIE FISCHER accompanied by Mitchell Ayres' Orchestra	RCA Victor 4744
6/14/52	29	1	15. I Remember When........................	RCA Victor 4618
7/19/52	1(1)	21	● 16. **Wish You Were Here/** title song of Broadway musical	RCA Victor 4830
7/26/52	24	1	17. The Hand Of Fate	
9/27/52	6	17	● 18. Lady Of Spain/	
10/04/52	8	13	19. Outside Of Heaven	RCA Victor 4953

DATE CHARTED	PEAK POS	WKS CHRT'D	ARTIST — Record Title	Label & Number
11/22/52	23	1	20. Everything I Have Is Yours .... from the film "Dancing Lady"	RCA Victor 4841
12/27/52	22	1	21. Christmas Day .... [X]	RCA Victor 5038
1/03/53	22	1	22. You're All I Want For Christmas............. [X]	RCA Victor 5065
1/17/53	7	8	23. Even Now	RCA Victor 5106
2/07/53	5	12	24. Downhearted/	
2/07/53	14	5	25. How Do You Speak To An Angel? .... from the Broadway musical "Hazel Flagg"	RCA Victor 5137
5/09/53	1(7)	25	● 26. **I'm Walking Behind You/**	
5/30/53	24	4	27. Just Another Polka..............................	RCA Victor 5293
7/11/53	7	14	28. With These Hands...............................	RCA Victor 5365
10/10/53	4	16	29. Many Times/	
10/24/53	18	1	30. Just To Be With You	RCA Victor 5453
12/12/53+	1(8)	19	● 31. **Oh! My Pa-Pa** .... English version of song from the Swiss musical "Fireworks"	RCA Victor 5552
3/27/54	6	14	32. A Girl, A Girl (Zoom-Ba Di Alli Nella)/	
4/10/54	14	4	33. Anema E Core (With All My Heart And Soul) from the Broadway musical "John Murray Anderson's Almanac" song uses the same melody as the 1948 hit "Until"	RCA Victor 5675
6/12/54	8	8	34. Green Years/	
6/12/54	15	8	35. My Friend..	RCA Victor 5748
8/28/54	21	4	36. Heaven Was Never Like This/	
9/04/54	1(3)	24	● 37. **I Need You Now**	RCA Victor 5830
10/30/54+	5	15	38. Count Your Blessings/ from the film "White Christmas"	
11/20/54	29	1	39. Fanny.. Broadway musical title song	RCA Victor 5871

FREDDIE FISHER & HIS ORCHESTRA
Midwestern novelty band; George Rock, featured vocalist

DATE CHARTED	PEAK POS	WKS CHRT'D	ARTIST — Record Title	Label & Number
10/02/37	13	3	1. I'm A Ding Dong Daddy........................ [N]	Decca 1400
5/14/38	18	2	2. The Wild, Wild Women (Are Making A Wild Man Of Me)................................. [N]	Decca 1771
12/24/38	12	1	3. Old-Time Dance Album .... includes Tinker Polka, Cuckoo Waltz, Old Memories, Dancing Hour, & Oh Susannah	Decca 2095-2099

MARK FISHER & HIS ORCHESTRA

DATE CHARTED	PEAK POS	WKS CHRT'D	ARTIST — Record Title	Label & Number
3/04/33	16	2	1. Black-Eyed Susan Brown	Columbia 2749

FISK UNIVERSITY JUBILEE QUARTET
J.A. Myers was the leader of this world-famous gospel group.

DATE CHARTED	PEAK POS	WKS CHRT'D	ARTIST — Record Title	Label & Number
5/14/10	7	3	1. Swing Low, Sweet Chariot	Victor 16453

ELLA FITZGERALD
The most honored jazz singer of all time, Ella Fitzgerald was born on 4/25/18 in Newport News, Va. Discovered after winning the Harlem Amateur Hour in 1934, she was hired by Chick Webb and in 1938 created a popular sensation with "A-Tisket, A-Tasket". Following Chick's death in 1939 Ella took over the band for three years. Winner of the Down Beat poll as top female vocalist more than 20 times, she remains among the undisputed royalty of 20th century popular music. (Also see Benny Goodman)

DATE CHARTED	PEAK POS	WKS CHRT'D	ARTIST — Record Title	Label & Number
7/25/36	18	1	1. Sing Me A Swing Song (And Let Me Dance)	Decca 830
12/19/36	20	1	2. (If You Can't Sing It) You'll Have To Swing It .	Decca 1032
4/10/37	19	1	3. Dedicated To You/	
4/24/37	20	1	4. Big Boy Blue.................................... above two: ELLA FITZGERALD & MILLS BROTHERS	Decca 1148
7/10/37	12	4	5. If You Ever Should Leave	Decca 1302
8/14/37	20	1	6. All Over Nothing At All............................ band on above two features Louis Jordan (alto sax) & Chick Webb	Decca 1339
2/19/38	19	1	7. Rock It For Me	Decca 1586
6/11/38	18	2	8. I Got A Guy	Decca 1681

DATE CHARTED	PEAK POS	WKS CHRT'D	ARTIST — Record Title	Label & Number
6/18/38	**1(10)**	19	● 9. **A-Tisket, A-Tasket**................................. *selected for the NARAS Hall of Fame*	Decca 1840
11/12/38	**3**	6	10. I Found My Yellow Basket	Decca 2148
11/12/38	**13**	4	11. Wacky Dust	Decca 2021
11/12/38	**14**	1	12. MacPherson Is Rehearsin' To Swing	Decca 2080
11/26/38+	**8**	6	13. F.D.R. Jones .... *from the Broadway musical "Sing Out The News"*	Decca 2105
3/18/39	**8**	4	14. Undecided	Decca 2323
3/25/39	**19**	1	15. T'ain't What You Do (It's The Way That Cha Do It)..	Decca 2310
5/06/39	**14**	1	16. Chew, Chew, Chew (Your Bubble Gum).......... *1, 2 & 7-16: CHICK WEBB & HIS ORCHESTRA*	Decca 2389
9/02/39	**9**	3	17. I Want The Waiter (With The Water)............	Decca 2628
10/28/39	**16**	1	18. My Wubba Dolly	Decca 2816
4/20/40	**17**	3	19. The Starlit Hour .... *from the Broadway musical "Earl Carroll's Vanities"*	Decca 2988
4/27/40	**23**	2	20. Sing Song Swing	Decca 3126
5/18/40	**15**	3	21. Imagination/	
6/01/40	**27**	1	22. Sugar Blues....................................	Decca 3078
7/06/40	**18**	2	23. Shake Down The Stars...........................	Decca 3199
11/30/40+	**9**	5	24. Five O'Clock Whistle	Decca 3420
2/01/41	**23**	1	25. Louisville, K-Y	Decca 3441
3/15/41	**26**	1	26. Hello, Ma! I Done It Again......................	Decca 3612
8/02/41	**23**	1	27. The Muffin Man	Decca 3666
3/11/44	**10**	8	28. Cow-Cow Boogie/ *ELLA FITZGERALD & INK SPOTS*	
3/11/44	**27**	1	29. When My Sugar Walks Down The Street	Decca 18587
7/08/44	**24**	2	30. Once Too Often .... *from the film "Pin-Up Girl"*	Decca 18605
11/04/44	**1(2)**	17	● 31. **I'm Making Believe/** *from the film "Sweet and Low-Down"*	
11/11/44	**1(2)**	17	32. **Into Each Life Some Rain Must Fall** .... *above two: ELLA FITZGERALD & INK SPOTS*	Decca 23356
1/06/45	**10**	5	33. And Her Tears Flowed Like Wine............ *with Johnny Long's Orchestra & the Song Spinners*	Decca 18633
4/28/45	**5**	6	34. I'm Beginning To See The Light................... *ELLA FITZGERALD & INK SPOTS*	Decca 23399
8/25/45	**9**	3	35. It's Only A Paper Moon .... *from the film "Take a Chance"*	Decca 23425
4/06/46	**10**	2	36. You Won't Be Satisfied (Until You Break My Heart).. *ELLA FITZGERALD & LOUIS ARMSTRONG with Bob Haggart's Orchestra*	Decca 23496
7/06/46	**7**	6	37. Stone Cold Dead In The Market (He Had It Coming).. *ELLA FITZGERALD & LOUIS JORDAN*	Decca 23546
12/07/46+	**8**	14	38. (I Love You) For Sentimental Reasons .... *35 & 38 with the Delta Rhythm Boys*	Decca 23670
4/12/47	**11**	4	39. Guilty .... *with Eddie Heywood's Orchestra*	Decca 23844
6/19/48	**6**	21	40. My Happiness/ *with Song Spinners*	
6/19/48	**24**	2	41. Tea Leaves..	Decca 24446
6/11/49	**9**	13	42. Baby, It's Cold Outside .... *ELLA FITZGERALD & LOUIS JORDAN from the film "Neptune's Daughter"*	Decca 24644
11/18/50	**30**	1	43. Can Anyone Explain? (No, No, No)............... *ELLA FITZGERALD & LOUIS ARMSTRONG with Sy Oliver's Orchestra*	Decca 27209
9/08/51	**23**	6	44. Smooth Sailing .... *one of Ella's most popular scat-singing performances*	Decca 27693
9/27/52	**21**	4	45. Trying	Decca 28375

DATE CHARTED	PEAK POS	WKS CHRT'D	ARTIST — Record Title	Label & Number
11/29/52	**29**	1	46. Walkin' By The River .... Decca 28433 *above two accompanied by Leroy Kirkland's Orchestra*	
9/05/53	**15**	4	47. Crying In The Chapel................................ Decca 28762 *44 & 47 with Bill Doggett's Orchestra & the Ray Charles Singers*	
3/06/54	**25**	1	48. Melancholy Me .... Decca 29008 *with Sy Oliver's Orchestra; Taft Jordan (trumpet) on above two*	
5/29/54	**30**	1	49. I Need.. Decca 29108 *with Gordon Jenkins' Orchestra*	

FIVE RED CAPS
Mills Brothers-styled vocal group. (also see Steve Gibson)

4/15/44	**14**	2	1. I Learned A Lesson I'll Never Forget .... Beacon 7120	

NANETTE FLACK

2/03/17	**5**	3	1. Give Me All Of You................................... Columbia 2128 CHARLES HARRISON & NANETTE FLACK	

RALPH FLANAGAN & HIS ORCHESTRA
Former pianist/arranger for Sammy Kaye who also arranged for various other bands and singers; his band was credited with stimulating a 1950s revival of the Glenn Miller sound.

9/24/49	**14**	9	1. You're Breaking My Heart .... Bluebird 0001	
11/12/49	**9**	8	2. Don't Cry, Joe (Let Her Go, Let Her Go, Let Her Go).. Bluebird 0007	
11/26/49	**27**	2	3. My Hero.. Bluebird 0006 *from the Broadway musical "The Chocolate Soldier"*	
1/14/50	**24**	3	4. Dear Hearts And Gentle People .... Bluebird 0016	
2/11/50	**3**	10	5. Rag Mop... RCA Vic. 78-3688 *above five vocals: Harry Prime*	
4/29/50	**17**	3	6. Joshua .... [I] RCA Victor 3724	
6/03/50	**28**	1	7. The Stars And Stripes Forever .... [I] RCA Victor 3762	
8/05/50	**16**	5	8. Tzena Tzena Tzena .... RCA Victor 3847 *adaptation of Israeli popular song*	
9/02/50	**16**	3	9. Mona Lisa .... RCA Victor 3888 *from the film "Captain Carey, "U.S.A."*	
9/09/50	**13**	3	10. The Red We Want Is The Red We've Got (In The Old Red, White, & Blue)/	
9/23/50	**10**	14	11. Nevertheless (I'm In Love With You)........... RCA Victor 3904 *featured in the film "Three Little Words"* *above vocals: Harry Prime*	
9/23/50	**27**	1	12. La Vie En Rose....................................... [I] RCA Victor 3889 *adaptation of a popular French song*	
10/07/50	**5**	17	13. Harbor Lights .... [I] RCA Victor 3911	
11/25/50	**27**	2	14. Oh, Babe! .... RCA Victor 3954 *vocal: Steve Benoric*	
9/22/51	**15**	5	15. Blues.. [I] RCA Victor 4247 *from George Gershwin's "An American in Paris"*	
12/08/51+	**6**	14	16. Slow Poke .... RCA Victor 4373 *16, 18, & 20 with The Singing Winds*	
7/19/52	**26**	2	17. Delicado.. [I] RCA Victor 4706	
9/06/52	**4**	12	18. I Should Care .... RCA Victor 4885 *vocal: Harry Prime*	
1/17/53	**7**	16	19. Hot Toddy .... [I] RCA Victor 5095	
5/02/53	**18**	3	20. A-L-B-U-Q-U-E-R-Q-U-E .... RCA Victor 5237	
7/11/53	**18**	1	21. Rub-A-Dub-Dub .... RCA Victor 5361	
4/27/54	**27**	1	22. Angela Mia .... RCA Victor 5676	

"DUSTY" FLETCHER

2/08/47	**3**	7	1. Open The Door, Richard........................ [C] National 4012 *with Jimmy Jones' Orchestra; Fletcher had performed this comedy routine in vaudeville since the early 30s*	

DATE CHARTED	PEAK POS	WKS CHRT'D	ARTIST — Record Title	Label & Number
			FLORODORA GIRLS	
			These unidentified girls were the first cast members of a Broadway musical to record a song from their show.	
6/22/01	1(3)	6	1. **Tell Me, Pretty Maiden**	Columbia 31604
			BYRON HARLAN, FRANK STANLEY, JOE BELMONT, & FLORODORA GIRLS	
			from the Broadway musical "Florodora"	
			JOE FOLEY	
7/24/54	28	1	1. All Or Nothing At All.................................	Jubilee 5146
			with the Ray Charles Singers & Frank Hunter's Orchestra	
			RED FOLEY	
			Clyde Julian Foley - Kentucky-born Grand Ole Opry star also known as a gospel singer and composer; Pat Boone became his son-in-law. Red died on 9/18/68 (58).	
9/30/44	7	11	1. Smoke On The Water...............................	Decca 6102
9/29/45	13	1	2. Shame On You	Decca 18698
			LAWRENCE WELK & HIS ORCHESTRA WITH RED FOLEY	
1/21/50	1(8)	16	● 3. **Chattanoogie Shoe Shine Boy/**	
2/04/50	24	1	4. Sugarfoot Rag	Decca 46205
			with guitar solo by Hank "Sugarfoot" Garland	
5/13/50	14	4	5. Birmingham Bounce...............................	Decca 46234
6/10/50	22	3	6. M-I-S-S-I-S-S-I-P-P-I	Decca 46241
			with the Dixie Dons	
8/12/50	10	10	7. Goodnight, Irene.....................................	Decca 46255
			RED FOLEY & ERNEST TUBB WITH SUNSHINE TRIO	
9/02/50	7	9	8. Cincinatti Dancing Pig	Decca 46261
9/02/50	16	9	9. Our Lady Of Fatima.................................	Decca 14526
			with the Anita Kerr Singers	
2/10/51	28	6	10. My Heart Cries For You...........................	Decca 27378
			RED FOLEY & EVELYN KNIGHT	
12/15/51	28	1	11. Alabama Jubilee	Decca 27810
			with the Nashville Dixielanders, including Francis Craig on bones	
11/29/52	25	1	12. Don't Let The Stars Get In Your Eyes	Decca 28460
12/19/53+	23	2	13. Put Christ Back Into Christmas............... [X]	Decca 28940
			FONTANE SISTERS	
			Bea, Geri, & Marge Fontane from New Jersey provided supporting vocals on many Perry Como records from 1949-52.	
1/06/51	20	4	1. Tennessee Waltz	RCA Victor 3979
3/31/51	24	1	2. Let Me In..	RCA Victor 4077
			with Texas Jim Robertson	
9/08/51	27	1	3. Castle Rock	RCA Victor 4213
			with Norman Leyden's Orchestra	
11/03/51	16	3	4. Cold, Cold Heart	RCA Victor 4274
			with Mitchell Ayres' Orchestra	
1/02/54	22	1	5. Kissing Bridge..	RCA Victor 5524
			with Hugo Winterhalter's Orchestra	
7/24/54	18	4	6. Happy Days And Lonely Nights	Dot 15171
			TONY FONTANE	
11/10/51	28	2	1. Cold, Cold Heart	Mercury 5693
			accompanied by Lew Douglas' Orchestra	
			FORD & GLENN	
			"Glenn" was a singer/pianist/songwriter Glenn Rowell, who later teamed with Gene Carroll for the popular 1930s radio team of "Gene & Glenn". Glenn died on 10/9/65 (65).	
6/06/25	9	1	1. I'll See You In My Dreams	Columbia 303
6/19/26	5	4	2. Sleepy Head..	Columbia 583
10/22/27	11	3	3. Baby Your Mother....................................	Columbia 1080
5/18/29	16	2	4. I Get The Blues When It Rains	Columbia 1720
8/03/29	9	4	5. The Utah Trail/	
3/29/30	14	4	6. When It's Springtime In The Rockies..........	Columbia 1828

DATE CHARTED	PEAK POS	WKS CHRT'D	ARTIST — Record Title	Label & Number

TENNESSEE ERNIE FORD

One of the 1950s' most popular singers on television with his own 1955-65 variety series, Ernie was first known for his comedy but later concentrated on gospel singing.

DATE CHARTED	PEAK POS	WKS CHRT'D	ARTIST — Record Title	Label & Number
11/26/49	9	9	1. Mule Train	Capitol 40258
2/18/50	15	6	2. The Cry Of The Wild Goose	Capitol 40280
1/27/51	14	13	3. Shot Gun Boogie	Capitol 1295
6/16/51	18	7	4. Mister And Mississippi	Capitol 1521
6/19/54	16	2	5. The Honeymoon's Over	Capitol 2809

TENNESSEE ERNIE FORD & BETTY HUTTON
with Billy May's Orchestra
listed on all as "Tennessee Ernie"

REGINALD FORESYTHE & HIS ORCHESTRA

London-born composer-arranger-pianist

DATE CHARTED	PEAK POS	WKS CHRT'D	ARTIST — Record Title	Label & Number
11/17/34	14	2	1. Serenade For A Wealthy Widow [I]	Columbia 2916
2/09/35	18	2	2. Garden Of Weed [I]	Columbia 3000
3/02/35	11	4	3. Lullaby Of Broadway	Columbia 3012
			from the film "Gold Diggers of 1935"	
7/13/35	8	4	4. The Greener The Grass	Columbia 3060
9/14/35	18	2	5. Dodgin' A Divorcee	Columbia 3012

listed on all as "The New Music of Reginald Foresythe"
listed on all as "The New Music of Reginald Foresythe"

HELEN FORREST

Between 1938 and 1943 Helen was featured vocalist with Artie Shaw ("They Say"), Benny Goodman ("Taking a Chance on Love"), and Harry James ("I've Heard That Song Before"), placing her in the forefront of all female band singers.

DATE CHARTED	PEAK POS	WKS CHRT'D	ARTIST — Record Title	Label & Number
7/08/44	2(1)	18	1. Time Waits For No One	Decca 18600
			from the film "Shine On, Harvest Moon"; based on a theme from Strauss' "Tales Of The Vienna Woods" accompanied by Camarata's Orchestra	

HELEN FORREST & DICK HAYMES

DATE CHARTED	PEAK POS	WKS CHRT'D	ARTIST — Record Title	Label & Number
4/22/44	2(1)	18	1. Long Ago (And Far Away)	Decca 23317
			from the film "Cover Girl" accompanied by Camarata's Orchestra	
9/09/44	4	9	2. It Had To Be You/	
10/07/44	3	10	3. Together	Decca 23349
			from the film "Since You Went Away"	
9/08/45	2(1)	13	4. I'll Buy That Dream/	
			from the film "Sing Your Way Home" above three accompanied by the Victor Young Orchestra	
9/08/45	9	4	5. Some Sunday Morning	Decca 23434
			with Gordon Jenkins' Orchestra	
1/19/46+	7	5	6. I'm Alway Chasing Rainbows	Decca 23472
			from the Broadway musical "Oh Look!" featured in the film "The Dolly Sisters"	
3/02/46	4	11	7. Oh! What It Seemed To Be	Decca 23481
7/06/46	23	4	8. Come Rain or Come Shine	Decca 23548
			from the Broadway musical "St. Louis Woman"	
8/10/46	12	2	9. In Love In Vain	Decca 23528
			from the film "Centennial Summer"	
10/05/46	22	1	10. Why Does It Get So Late So Early	Decca 23611
			orchestra on above five directed by Earle Hagen	

STUART FOSTER

Vocalist with Guy Lombardo (1944, "Always"), Tommy Dorsey (1945-47, "How Are Things in Glocca Mora?"), & Hugo Winterhalter.

FOUR ACES

Al Alberts, lead singer, with Dave Mahoney, Lou Silvestri, and Sol Vocarro, from Chester, Pennsylvania.

DATE CHARTED	PEAK POS	WKS CHRT'D	ARTIST — Record Title	Label & Number
9/15/51	4	22	● 1. Sin	Victoria 101
12/08/51+	2(6)	24	● 2. Tell Me Why/	
1/05/52	14	11	3. A Garden In The Rain	Decca 27860
2/23/52	7	16	4. Perfidia	Decca 27987

DATE CHARTED	PEAK POS	WKS CHRT'D	ARTIST — Record Title	Label & Number
3/08/52	29	1	5. Two Little Kisses..	Flash 103
5/31/52	21	3	6. I'm Yours	Decca 28162
8/09/52	9	10	7. Should I..	Decca 28323
10/25/52	11	10	8. Heart And Soul/	
11/01/52	20	2	9.　Just Squeeze Me.............................	Decca 28390
1/02/53	24	2	10. La Rosita.................................	Decca 28393
2/14/53	21	2	11. I'll Never Smile Again...........................	Decca 28391
2/28/53	22	3	12. You Fooled Me	Decca 28560
5/23/53	17	5	13. Organ Grinder's Swing/	
6/06/53	24	1	14.　Honey In The Horn .... accompanied on above two and some others by Owen Bradley's Orchestra	Decca 28691
8/22/53	24	2	15. False Love................................	Decca 28744
10/17/53	22	4	16. Laughing On The Outside (Crying On The Inside)................................	Decca 28843
12/05/53+	3	16	17. Stranger In Paradise/ from the Broadway musical "Kismet"; based on Polovetsian Dances theme from the opera "Prince Igor"	
12/05/53+	7	18	18.　The Gang That Sang "Heart Of My Heart".... song published in 1926	Decca 28927
3/20/54	21	5	19. Amor/	
3/27/54	26	2	20.　So Long	Decca 29036
5/22/54	1(1)	18	● 21. **Three Coins In The Fountain/** movie title song	
5/22/54	22	5	22.　Wedding Bells (Are Breaking Up That Old Gang Of Mine)................................	Decca 29123
8/14/54	17	4	23. Dream	Decca 29217
10/23/54	11	7	24. It's A Woman's World........................... from the film "Woman's World"	Decca 29269
11/17/54+	5	14	25. Mister Sandman .... accompanied on 17-25 by Jack Pleis & His Orchestra	Decca 29344

FOUR COINS
Vocal group from Canonsburg, Pennsylvania

10/16/54	30	1	1. We'll Be Married In The Church In The Wildwood..	Epic 9074

FOUR FRESHMEN
Widely-admired close-harmony group: Ross & Don Barbour, Bob Flanagan, and Ken Errair.

8/23/52	30	1	1. It's A Blue World....................................	Capitol 2152
9/26/53	29	1	2. It Happened Once Before...........................	Capitol 2564
11/27/54	24	2	3. Mood Indigo	Capitol 2961

FOUR KNIGHTS
Bass singer Oscar Broadway, lead vocalist of North Carolina group

7/28/51	23	1	1. I Love The Sunshine Of Your Smile	Capitol 1587
10/27/51	14	10	2. (It's No) Sin.......................................	Capitol 1806
12/15/51+	21	4	3. Cry	Capitol 1875
1/24/53	8	6	4. Oh, Happy Day	Capitol 2315
1/23/54	2(1)	24	● 5. I Get So Lonely (When I Dream About You).... partly based on the 19th century melody "Gently Down the Stream"; song also known as "Oh Baby Mine"	Capitol 2654
7/31/54	22	2	6. Period...	Capitol 2847
9/25/54	30	1	7. In The Chapel In The Moonlight.................	Capitol 2840

FOUR LADS
Frank Busseri, Bernard Toorish, James Arnold, and Connie Coderini from Toronto, Canada; they backed up Johnny Ray on his #1 smash "Cry".

7/26/52	23	4	1. The Mocking Bird .... a new version of this song charted in 1956	Okeh 6885

DATE CHARTED	PEAK POS	WKS CHRT'D	ARTIST — Record Title	Label & Number
10/18/52	22	1	2. Somebody Loves Me .... from the Broadway musical "George White's Scandals of 1924"; with Mitch Miller's Orchestra	Columbia 39865
4/25/53	16	1	3. He Who Has Love......................................	Columbia 39958
7/04/53	17	5	4. Down By The Riverside.............................	Columbia 40005
10/10/53	26	1	5. I Should Have Told You Long Ago/	
10/24/53	10	13	6. Instanbul (Not Constantinople).................. accompanied on above four & 8 by Norman Leyden's Orchestra	Columbia 40082
5/01/54	30	1	7. Oh, That'll Be Joyful............................... accompanied by Jimmy Carroll's Orchestra	Columbia 40220
7/03/54	18	4	8. Gilly, Gilly, Ossenfeffer, Katzenellen Bogen By The Sea..	Columbia 40236
9/04/54	7	12	9. Skokiaan... South African song; accompanied by Neal Hefti & His Orchestra	Columbia 40306
9/18/54	21	4	10. Rain, Rain, Rain .... FRANKIE LAINE & FOUR LADS with the Buddy Cole Quartet	Columbia 40295

FOUR TUNES
Rhythm & blues group: William Best, James Nabbie, James Gordon, and Danny Owens.

DATE CHARTED	PEAK POS	WKS CHRT'D	ARTIST — Record Title	Label & Number
11/21/53	13	6	1. Marie..	Jubilee 5128
5/29/54	6	15	● 2. I Understand Just How You Feel/	
6/05/54	25	2	3. Sugar Lump.. accompanied on all by Sid Bass Orchestra	Jubilee 5132

FOUR VAGABONDS
Male quartet with guitar accompaniment

DATE CHARTED	PEAK POS	WKS CHRT'D	ARTIST — Record Title	Label & Number
4/10/43	20	1	1. Rose Ann Of Charing Cross/	
7/10/43	20	1	2. Ten Little Soldiers	Bluebird 0811
7/24/43	24	1	3. Comin' In On A Wing And A Prayer............	Bluebird 0815

FOURSOME

DATE CHARTED	PEAK POS	WKS CHRT'D	ARTIST — Record Title	Label & Number
11/17/31	9	6	1. Bidin' My Time....................................... from the Broadway musical "Girl Crazy"	Brunswick 4996

HARRY FOX
Cabaret singer, appeared in one silent film; died on 7/20/59 (77).

DATE CHARTED	PEAK POS	WKS CHRT'D	ARTIST — Record Title	Label & Number
8/17/18	5	5	1. I'm Always Chasing Rainbows.................... accompanied by Charles Prince's Orchestra; song from the Broadway musical "Oh, Look!"; melody based on Chopin's "Fantasie Impromptu in C-Sharp Minor"	Columbia 2557

ROY FOX & HIS ORCHESTRA
American bandleader who became most popular in England.

DATE CHARTED	PEAK POS	WKS CHRT'D	ARTIST — Record Title	Label & Number
12/07/29	18	1	1. Tip Toe Through The Tulips .... from the film "Gold Diggers Of Broadway"	Brunswick 4419
10/29/38	16	2	2. I Won't Tell A Soul.................................	Bluebird 7840

ARNOLD FRANK & HIS ROGER'S CAFE ORCHESTRA

DATE CHARTED	PEAK POS	WKS CHRT'D	ARTIST — Record Title	Label & Number
12/31/27	20	1	1. Rain	Okeh 40896

STAN FREBERG
Creative satirist who began career doing cartoon voices, later produced many popular radio & TV commercials.

DATE CHARTED	PEAK POS	WKS CHRT'D	ARTIST — Record Title	Label & Number
2/10/51	21	3	1. John And Marsha .... parody on soap operas	[C] Capitol 1356
8/04/51	11	5	2. I've Got You Under My Skin/ from the film "Born To Dance"	[N]
8/11/51	30	1	3. That's My Boy....................................... above two with Les Baxter & His Orchestra	[C] Capitol 1711
4/05/52	15	3	4. Try	[N] Capitol 2029
12/13/52	24	1	5. The World Is Waiting For The Sunrise ...... featuring Dick Roberts & Red Rountree on banjos	[N] Capitol 2279
10/03/53	1(4)	10	● 6. **St. George And The Dragonet/**	[C]
10/10/53	9	4	7. Little Blue Riding Hood .... above two with Daws Butler & June Foray (talking)	[C] Capitol 2596

DATE CHARTED	PEAK POS	WKS CHRT'D	ARTIST — Record Title	Label & Number
12/19/53+	13	4	8. C'est Si Bon.. [N]	Capitol 2677
			with George Burns Quintet	
12/19/53	13	3	9. Christmas Dragnet.......................... [N-X]	Capitol 2671
			featuring Daws Butler	
1/02/54	23	1	10. Dear John and Marsha Letter .... [C]	Capitol 2677
6/26/54	15	3	11. Point Of Order.................................... [C]	Capitol 2838
			takeoff on the Senate's Army-McCarthy hearings, with Butler and Burns	
10/23/54	14	1	12. Sh-Boom .... [N]	Capitol 2929
			with The Toads & Billy May's Orchestra	

BUD FREEMAN
Star tenor saxophonist with Red Nichols, Paul Whiteman, Ray Noble, Tommy Dorsey (1936-38), & Benny Goodman (1938).

STAN FREEMAN
Gifted jazz/classical harpsichordist and pianist featured on some of Rosemary Clooney's biggest hits, and on Percy Faith's #1 record "Delicado". (also see Eddie Cantor, Mitch Miller)

MARCIA FREER

DATE CHARTED	PEAK POS	WKS CHRT'D	ARTIST — Record Title	Label & Number
5/17/24	8	3	1. It's A Man, Every Time, It's A Man..............	Victor 19248
5/31/24	11	1	2. Linger Awhile	Victor 19259
			LEWIS JAMES & MARCIA FREER	
7/12/24	4	5	3. What'll I Do?....................................	Victor 19301
			HENRY BURR & MARCIA FREER	
			from the Broadway musical "Music Box Revue of 1923"	
10/25/24	12	1	4. June Brought The Roses	Victor 19347

FRENCH ARMY BAND
Under the direction of Captain Gabriel Pares.

DATE CHARTED	PEAK POS	WKS CHRT'D	ARTIST — Record Title	Label & Number
2/15/19	6	2	1. Marche Lorraine................................. [I]	Columbia 6083

FRAN FREY
Male vocalist with George Olsen's band from 1925-33

DATE CHARTED	PEAK POS	WKS CHRT'D	ARTIST — Record Title	Label & Number
7/08/33	15	3	1. Learn To Croon	Columbia 2789
			from the film "College Humor"	

LEFTY FRIZZELL
Longtime country star renowned as "honky tonk singer"; died on 7/19/75 (47).

DATE CHARTED	PEAK POS	WKS CHRT'D	ARTIST — Record Title	Label & Number
8/25/51	29	1	1. I Want To Be With You Always	Columbia 20799

FRANK FROEBA & HIS SWING BAND
Pianist-bandleader who worked with Benny Goodman, later with Riley Farley's Orchestra; co-writer of Cab Calloway's smash "The Jumpin' Jive"

DATE CHARTED	PEAK POS	WKS CHRT'D	ARTIST — Record Title	Label & Number
1/18/36	7	4	1. The Music Goes Round And Round	Columbia 3110
			vocal: Jack Purvis	
9/19/36	12	6	2. Organ Grinder's Swing/	
10/31/36	20	1	3. It All Begins And Ends With You	Columbia 3151
			above two vocals: Midge Williams band includes Bunny Berigan (trumpet) & Cozy Cole (drums)	

JANE FROMAN
Featured in many Broadway musicals and radio programs during the 1930s and 40s, Jane recovered from serious injuries in a 1943 plane crash and was honored by Hollywood in the 1952 film "With a Song in My Heart".

DATE CHARTED	PEAK POS	WKS CHRT'D	ARTIST — Record Title	Label & Number
11/10/34	20	1	1. I Only Have Eyes For You.........................	Decca 181
			from the film "Dames"	
5/03/52	14	13	2. I'll Walk Alone	Capitol 2044
			from the film "Follow the Boys" revived in the film "With A Song in My Heart"	
9/27/52	25	2	3. Wish You Were Here	Capitol 2154
			Broadway musical title song	
4/04/53	11	10	4. I Believe..	Capitol 2332
			introduced on Jane's TV show "U.S.A. Canteen" above three with Sid Feller Orchestra	
12/12/53	28	1	5. Robe Of Calvary	Capitol 2639
			accompanied by Henry Sylvern Orchestra	

DATE CHARTED	PEAK POS	WKS CHRT'D	ARTIST — Record Title	Label & Number
			EARL FULLER'S NOVELTY ORCHESTRA	
			Director Earl Fuller played trumpet and trombone, and featured Bill Scotti on clarinet and alto sax.	
9/22/17	**8**	2	1. Slippery Hank .... [I]	Victor 18321
11/03/17	**7**	3	2. 12th Street Rag .... [I]	Columbia 2298
12/15/17	**8**	2	3. Beale Street Blues .... [I]	Victor 18369
			above three: Earl Fuller's Jazz Band; with Ted Lewis (clarinet)	
9/21/18	**10**	1	4. Missouri Waltz .... [I]	Columbia 2578
12/21/18	**5**	3	5. Oriental .... [I]	Columbia 6075
5/17/19	**4**	4	6. Sand Dunes .... [I]	Columbia 2697
8/16/19	**10**	1	7. Egyptland... [I]	Columbia 2722
			JACK FULTON	
			Sang and played trombone for Paul Whiteman from 1926-34; co-wrote the 1948 hit "Until".	
3/12/49	**12**	6	1. Sunflower...	Tower 1454
			accompanied by Eddie Ballantyne & His Orchestra became the state song of Kansas; 1964 hit "Hello, Dolly!" later legally found to be based upon it	
			FURMAN & NASH	
8/26/22	**10**	1	1. Mr. Gallagher And Mr. Shean .... [C]	Columbia 3609
			from Broadway musical "Ziegfeld Follies of 1922"	

G

			SLIM GAILLARD TRIO	
			Pianist, formerly half of the popular Slim & Slam team	
5/25/46	**21**	1	1. Cement Mixer (Put-Ti, Put-Ti) .... [N]	Cadet 201
			SUNNY GALE	
2/09/52	**13**	6	1. Wheel Of Fortune...................................	Derby 787
			EDDIE WILCOX ORCHESTRA with SUNNY GALE	
9/13/52	**14**	8	2. I Laughed At Love	RCA Victor 4789
1/17/53	**12**	4	3. Teardrops On My Pillow/	
1/31/53	**18**	2	4. A Stolen Waltz......................................	RCA Victor 5103
			above three with Ralph Burns' Orchestra	
9/12/53	**22**	4	5. Love Me Again/	
10/10/53	**27**	2	6. Before It's Too Late	RCA Victor 5424
			above two & 8 with Hugo Winterhalter's Orchestra	
7/17/54	**26**	4	7. Goodnight, Sweetheart, Goodnight	RCA Victor 5746
			accompanied by Joe Reisman's Orchestra	
9/18/54	**19**	5	8. Smile..	RCA Victor 5836
			theme from the film "Modern Times"	
			GALLAGHER & SHEAN	
			Ed Gallagher and Al Shean constituted one of vaudeville's most popular comedy teams from 1910-25. German-born Shean was the uncle of the Marx Brothers.	
10/28/22	**1(6)**	12	● 1. **Mr. Gallagher And Mr. Shean** .... [C]	Victor 18941
			from the Broadway musical "Ziegfeld Follies of 1922"; one of the biggest selling comedy records of all time	
			FRANK GALLAGHER	
12/25/48	**25**	1	1. You're All I Want For Christmas............. [X]	Dana 2026
			with the Dana Serenaders	
			AMELITA GALLI-CURCI	
			World-famous Italian soprano with the New York Metropolitan Opera from 1921-31; died on 11/26/63 (81).	
2/23/24	**13**	1	1. A Kiss In The Dark	Victor 959
			from the Broadway musical "Orange Blossoms"	

DATE CHARTED	PEAK POS	WKS CHRT'D	ARTIST — Record Title	Label & Number
			CECIL GANT Nashville-born blues singer/pianist, billed as "The G.I. Sing-sation"; died on 2/4/51 (37).	
3/17/45	**20**	1	1. I Wonder .... listed as "Private Cecil Gant"	Gilt-Edge 500
			JAN GARBER & HIS ORCHESTRA Long-popular dance band leader in mellow "sweet" style.	
4/04/23	**10**	1	1. Haunting Blues .... [I]	Columbia 3781
5/03/24	**10**	1	2. You're In Kentucky Sure As You're Born ...... above two: GARBER-DAVIS ORCHESTRA (with Milton Davis)	Victor 19216
12/27/24+	**5**	5	3. I Want To Be Happy .... [I] from the Broadway musical "No, No, Nanette"	Victor 19404
9/25/26	**1(6)**	12	4. **Baby Face** .... vocal: Benny Davis	Victor 20105
7/28/28	**10**	3	5. Was It A Dream? .... vocal: Sonny Faircloth	Columbia 1372
12/22/28	**14**	2	6. Sonny Boy... from the film "The Singing Fool"	Columbia 1550
11/04/33	**6**	5	7. I'll Be Faithful..................................... vocal: Lew Palmer	Victor 24412
11/18/33	**10**	3	8. You've Got Everything/	
12/09/33	**10**	3	9. You're Gonna Lose Your Gal.....................	Victor 24444
1/27/34	**15**	2	10. On The Wrong Side Of The Fence.................	Victor 24507
2/17/34	**6**	11	11. The Boulevard Of Broken Dreams............... from the film "Moulin Rouge" vocals on 8, 10, 11, & 13: Lee Bennett	Victor 24498
6/02/34	**1(2)**	14	12. **All I Do Is Dream Of You** .... from the film "Sadie McKee" vocals on 9 & 12: Fritz Heilbron	Victor 24629
6/09/34	**11**	5	13. Why Don't You Practice What You Preach? ...	Victor 24634
6/16/34	**11**	6	14. My Dear (I Love You Truly)....................... the band's theme song	Victor 24636
9/29/34	**17**	2	15. I'm Lonesome For You, Caroline.................. vocals on above two & 17: Lew Palmer	Victor 24726
10/13/34	**8**	10	16. Rain/	
10/27/34	**19**	1	17. Blue Sky Avenue .... from the film "Gift of Gab"	Victor 24730
10/13/34	**15**	3	18. Isn't It A Shame?/	
10/13/34	**18**	2	19. Blue In Love	Victor 24727
12/15/34	**7**	5	20. The Object Of My Affection/	
1/26/35	**17**	2	21. Blame It On My Youth .... vocals on 16-18 & 20-21: Lee Bennett	Victor 24809
4/27/35	**11**	10	22. Love And A Dime .... vocal: Fritz Heilbron	Victor 24885
5/18/35	**2(2)**	8	23. In A Little Gypsy Tea-Room......................	Victor 25013
1/11/36	**3**	9	24. I Feel Like A Feather In The Breeze/ from the film "Collegiate"	
1/25/36	**3**	11	25. I'm Shooting High .... from the film "King of Burlesque" above five vocals: Lee Bennett	Decca 647
1/25/36	**1(2)**	13	26. **A Beautiful Lady In Blue/**	
2/01/36	**5**	6	27. Moon Over Miami...............................	Decca 651
3/14/36	**10**	3	28. Misty Islands Of The Highlands .... vocals on 25 & 28: Lew Palmer	Decca 717
3/28/36	**14**	2	29. I'm Putting All My Eggs In One Basket.......... vocal: Fritz Heilbron; from the film "Follow the Fleet"	Decca 699
4/11/36	**10**	3	30. Will I Ever Know? .... from the film "Palm Springs"	Decca 732
4/18/36	**16**	2	31. If You Love Me	Decca 733
4/25/36	**1(3)**	12	32. **A Melody From The Sky**	Decca 761
4/25/36	**6**	6	33. Lost	Decca 739
7/04/36	**13**	2	34. Small Town Girl .... vocal: Lew Palmer	Decca 802

DATE CHARTED	PEAK POS	WKS CHRT'D	ARTIST — Record Title	Label & Number
7/11/36	**20**	1	35. Summer Holiday .... vocals on 27, 30-33, & 35: Lee Bennett	Decca 821
8/22/36	**18**	1	36. I'm Grateful To You	Decca 860
9/05/36	**7**	6	37. A Rendezvous With A Dream	Decca 867
9/26/36	**10**	4	38. Until The Real Thing Comes Along.............. above three vocals: Russell Brown	Decca 891
1/23/37	**5**	7	39. The Night Is Young And You're So Beautiful..	Brunswick 7800
1/30/37	**12**	2	40. Serenade In The Night .... based on "Violino Tzigano"	Brunswick 7804
2/06/37	**19**	2	41. There's A Ranch In The Sky	Brunswick 7807
4/03/37	**19**	1	42. My Wild Irish Rose.................................. vocal: Tony Allen from the Broadway musical "A Romance of Athlone"	Brunswick 7843
9/25/37	**19**	1	43. I'm Feeling Like A Million .... vocal: Russell Brown from the film "Broadway Melody of 1938"	Brunswick 7906
10/02/37	**10**	3	44. That Old Feeling..................................... from the film "Vogues of 1938"	Brunswick 7935
1/01/38	**14**	3	45. I've Hitched My Wagon To A Star .... from the film "Hollywood Hotel"	Brunswick 8018
1/29/38	**16**	3	46. Outside Of Paradise................................ movie title song	Brunswick 8033
2/19/38	**18**	1	47. Ten Pretty Girls/	
2/26/38	**7**	8	48.　Love Walked In .... from the film "Goldwyn Follies"	Brunswick 8060
7/30/38	**19**	1	49. In A Little Dutch Kintergarden...................	Brunswick 8111
8/06/38	**8**	7	50. Bambina	Brunswick 8206
10/22/38	**8**	4	51. All Ashore..	Brunswick 8235
4/08/39	**9**	2	52. It's Never Too Late .... vocals on 50-52: Lee Bennett	Vocalion 4687
6/24/39	**6**	1	53. Concert In The Park................................ vocals on 49 & 53: Fritz Heilbron	Vocalion 4889
4/22/41	**22**	1	54. I Can't Remember To Forget	Okeh 6039
2/12/44	**14**	3	55. My Heart Tells Me/ vocal: Bon Davis; from the film "Sweet Rosie O'Grady"	
5/13/44	**28**	1	56.　No Love, No Nothin' .... from the film "The Gang's All Here"	Hit 7070
2/26/44	**12**	2	57. Shoo Shoo Baby .... from the film "Follow the Boys" vocals on 56 & 57: Liz Tilton	Hit 7069
6/22/46	**14**	1	58. The Gypsy	Black & White 774
5/22/48	**22**	1	59. Bedelia	Columbia 38205
1/08/49	**28**	1	60. Bella Bella Marie .... adapted from an Italian folk song	Capitol 15181
9/24/49	**19**	10	61. You're Breaking My Heart .... based on "La Mattinata"	Capitol 719
11/05/49	**22**	1	62. Jealous Heart .... above two vocals: Don Grabeau	Capitol 759
7/15/50	**30**	1	63. The Old Piano Roll Blues........................... vocal: Ernie Mathias & Bill Kleeb	Capitol 970
8/05/50	**28**	1	64. I Wanna Be Loved.................................... vocal: Dottie O'Brien	Capitol 1044
3/17/51	**26**	2	65. If .... vocal: Roy Cordell	Capitol 1351
10/06/51	**29**	2	66. The Morning Side Of The Mountain	Capitol 1594

KING GARCIA & HIS SWING BAND
Louis "King" Garcia (trumpet); band includes Herbie Haymer (tenor sax) & Adrian Rollini (piano)

DATE CHARTED	PEAK POS	WKS CHRT'D	ARTIST — Record Title	Label & Number
4/04/36	**16**	2	1. Christopher Columbus .... vocal: Dan Darcy	Bluebird 6303

DATE CHARTED	PEAK POS	WKS CHRT'D	ARTIST — Record Title	Label & Number
			JUDY GARLAND As electrifying a performer as ever sang on an American concert stage, Judy Garland was born Frances Gumm on 6/10/22 in Grand Rapids, Michigan. She made her first feature film at age 14, shot to stardom in "The Wizard of Oz", and starred in a series of hit movie musicals during the ensuing decade. "A Star Is Born" in 1954 marked her spectacular comeback from a period of personal difficulties, and in the years until her death on 1/22/69 she remained a revered concert attraction, as well as hosting a TV variety series in 1963-64. Daughter Liza Minnelli carries on the classic Garland tradition.	
9/09/39	**5**	12	1. Over The Rainbow .... Judy's trademark classic from "The Wizard of Oz"; accompanied by Victor Young's Orchestra; record selected for the NARAS Hall of Fame	Decca 2672
7/20/40	**3**	12	2. I'm Nobody's Baby .... accompanied by Bobby Sherwood's Orchestra; featured in the film "Andy Hardy Meets Debutante"	Decca 3174
1/24/42	**3**	21	3. For Me And My Gal/	
4/10/42	**19**	1	4. When You Wore A Tulip (And I Wore A Big Red Rose).. above two: JUDY GARLAND & GENE KELLY accompanied by David Rose's Orchestra both featured in the film "For Me and My Gal"	Decca 18480
7/17/43	**22**	1	5. Zing! Went The Strings Of My Heart .... recorded on 7/29/39; accompanied by Victor Young & His Orchestra; from the Broadway revue "Thumbs Up"	Decca 18543
3/18/44	**25**	1	6. A Journey To A Star .... from the film "The Girls He Left Behind"	Decca 18584
11/18/44	**4**	8	7. The Trolley Song	Decca 23361
12/23/44	**22**	1	8. Meet Me In St. Louis, Louis........................	Decca 23360
12/30/44	**27**	1	9. Have Yourself A Merry Little Christmas.... [X] flip side: Judy's famous ballad "The Boy Next Door" above three from the film "Meet Me In St. Louis" above four accompanied by Georgie Stoll's Orchestra	Decca 23362
5/12/45	**5**	7	10. Yah-Ta-Ta Yah-Ta-Ta (Talk, Talk, Talk) .... JUDY GARLAND & BING CROSBY with Joseph Lilley's Orchestra	Decca 23410
5/19/45	**22**	1	11. This Heart Of Mine..................................	Decca 18660
9/29/45	**10**	1	12. On The Atchison, Topeka, And The Santa Fe. with Merry Macs & Lyn Murray's Orchestra	Decca 23436
3/09/46+	**24**	1	13. Wait And See...................................... above two from the film "The Harvey Girls"	Decca 23459
6/08/46	**21**	1	14. You'll Never Walk Alone .... accompanied by Lyn Murray's Orchestra; from the Broadway musical "Carousel"	Decca 23539
1/18/47	**19**	1	15. For You, For Me, Forevermore.................... JUDY GARLAND & DICK HAYMES with Gordon Jenkins' Orchestra from the film "The Shocking Miss Pilgrim"	Decca 23687
7/04/53	**29**	1	16. Without A Memory.................................. accompanied by Percy Faith Orchestra	Columbia 40010
8/21/54	**22**	4	17. The Man That Got Away .... Judy's second most famous song; from the film "A Star Is Born"; accompanied by Ray Heindorf & the Warner Brothers Studio Orchestra	Columbia 40270
			ERROLL GARNER TRIO Jazz pianist whose 1954 classic composition became an enduring record standard five years later through Johnny Mathis.	
10/23/54	**30**	1	1. Misty.. [I]	Mercury 70442
			BETTY GARRETT Star of "Call me Mister" and various other Broadway musicals. Betty also appeared in many films from 1945-57 on TV's "All in the Family" (1973-76); married to actor Larry Parks ("The Jolson Story").	
11/06/48	**8**	11	1. Buttons And Bows .... with Harold Mooney's Orchestra from the film "Paleface"	MGM 10244

DATE CHARTED	PEAK POS	WKS CHRT'D	ARTIST — Record Title	Label & Number
			MABEL GARRISON Soprano with the Metropolitan Opera (1913-20); died on 8/15/63 (77).	
1/17/20	**5**	5	1. Hymn To The Sun (Coq D' Or)......................	Victor 64790
			GEORGE J. GASKIN "The Silver-Voiced Irish Tenor", born in Belfast, one of the leading pioneer recording artists of the 1890s; died around 1920.	
12/05/91	**1(5)**	5	1. **Drill, Ye Terriers, Drill**........................... also recorded for New Jersey; song from Broadway musical "A Brass Monkey"	North American
12/05/91	**2(3)**	3	2. The Picture Turned To The Wall.................	North American
1/09/92	**1(3)**	3	3. **Slide, Kelly, Slide**............................... song about 1880s baseball star Michael "King" Kelly	North American
3/04/93	**1(8)**	8	4. **O Promise Me**.................................... from the operetta "Robin Hood"	New Jersey
4/29/93	**1(10)**	10	5. **After The Ball**................................... featured in the Broadway musical "A Trip to Chinatown"	New Jersey
11/18/93	**1(8)**	8	6. **The Fatal Wedding** .... also recorded for Ohio 2231 & Ohio	New Jersey
2/03/94	**1(5)**	5	7. **Sweeet Marie** .... also recorded for Columbia & Chicago 223	New Jersey
5/05/94	**2(2)**	2	8. Say Au Revoir, But Not Goodbye	Chicago 2234
7/28/94	**1(3)**	3	9. **We Were Sweethearts, Nell And I**	Columbia
3/02/95	**2(3)**	3	10. The Sidewalks Of New York .... later recorded for Berliner 959	Chicago
1/04/96	**1(6)**	6	11. **The Sunshine Of Paradise Alley**............... also recorded for New Jersey & Chicago 2269	Columbia
2/15/96	**1(5)**	5	12. **She May Have Seen Better Days**..............	Columbia 2024
8/15/96	**2(3)**	3	13. Just Tell Them That You Saw Me .... also recorded for Edison 1565 & Berliner 189	Columbia 4020
9/12/96	**1(4)**	4	14. **Down In Poverty Row**............................ also recorded for Columbia 4047 & Edison 1509	Berliner 161
10/10/96	**1(4)**	4	15. **On The Benches In The Park** .... also recorded for Edison 1535	Columbia 4053
1/02/97	**2(3)**	4	16. A Hot Time In The Old Town......................	Chicago
4/10/97	**1(8)**	15	17. **Sweet Rosie O'Grady** .... also recorded for Columbia 4094	Edison 1551
9/25/97	**2(2)**	2	18. The Old-Fashioned Mother........................	Columbia 4112
11/06/97	**1(10)**	12	19. **On The Banks Of The Wabash** .... also recorded for Edison 1570 became the state song of Indiana	Columbia 4130
4/02/98	**1(7)**	9	20. **Break The News To Mother** .... also recorded for Edison 1583	Columbia 4156
7/09/98	**1(6)**	8	21. **She Was Bred In Old Kentucky**	Columbia 4166
12/03/98	**1(10)**	13	22. **My Old New Hampshire Home** .... also recorded for Berliner 068	Columbia 4182
12/24/98	**2(2)**	3	23. Little Old New York Is Good Enough For Me .. from the Broadway musical "Hurly Burly"	Columbia 4181
3/18/99	**3**	3	24. I Guess I'll Have To Telegraph My Baby	Columbia 4184
5/06/99	**1(3)**	14	25. **My Wild Irish Rose** .... from the Broadway musical "A Romance of Athlone"	Columbia 4188
5/13/99	**4**	2	26. 'Mid The Green Fields Of Virginia	Columbia 4185
8/26/99	**3**	4	27. A Picture No Artist Can Paint	Columbia 4198
3/10/00	**1(3)**	7	28. **When Cloe Sings A Song**	Columbia 4248
11/10/00	**1(8)**	10	29. **When You Were Sweet Sixteen**	Columbia 4281
5/25/01	**2(3)**	6	30. Absence Makes The Heart Grow Fonder........	Columbia 31549
1/23/04	**3**	3	31. Bedelia .... also on Columbia cylinder 32320	Columbia 1609
			LUCY GATES Utah-born soprano who also sang opera throughout Europe.	
4/21/17	**7**	3	1. The Nightingale Song .... with bird voices by Sybil Fagan	Columbia 5937

DATE CHARTED	PEAK POS	WKS CHRT'D	ARTIST — Record Title	Label & Number
10/26/18	**9**	2	2. My Old Kentucky Home .... Columbia 6059 LUCY GATES & COLUMBIA STELLAR QUARTET	

RUTH GAYLOR
Sang with the Hudson-DeLange, Mitchell Ayres, Bunny Berigan, Teddy Powell, and Hal McIntyre bands between 1935-45; died on 3/21/72 (53).

RONNIE GAYLORD
Lead singer of The Gaylords

DATE CHARTED	PEAK POS	WKS CHRT'D	ARTIST — Record Title	Label & Number
2/20/54	**13**	15	1. Cuddle Me .... Mercury 70285 accompanied by David Carroll's Orchestra	

GAYLORDS
Ronnie Gaylord led this Detroit trio which later became a duo with Burt Bonaldi.

DATE CHARTED	PEAK POS	WKS CHRT'D	ARTIST — Record Title	Label & Number
12/20/52	**2(1)**	22	● 1. Tell Me You're Mine .... Mercury 70030 1939 Italian song ("Per un Bacio d'amour")	
3/28/53	**16**	1	2. Spinning A Web/	
4/11/53	**12**	8	3. Ramona .... Mercury 70112 above three with Ronnie Vincent's Orchestra	
12/19/53+	**21**	4	4. The Strings Of My Heart........................... Mercury 70258 sung partly in Italian	
2/13/54	**7**	12	5. From The Vine Came The Grape .... Mercury 70296	
5/15/54	**14**	10	6. Isle Of Capri/ 1935 British popular song	
5/15/54	**23**	4	7. Love I You (You I Love)........................... Mercury 70350	
7/03/54	**2(1)**	19	8. The Little Shoemaker/ with Hugo Perelli one chorus sung in Italian above four accompanied by the George Annis Orchestra	
8/14/54	**28**	1	9. Mecque, Mecque...................................... Mercury 70403	
10/02/54	**30**	1	10. Veni-Vidi-Vici (I Came, I Saw, I Conquered) .... Mercury 70427	

PAUL GAYTEN & HIS TRIO
Jazz pianist

DATE CHARTED	PEAK POS	WKS CHRT'D	ARTIST — Record Title	Label & Number
11/22/47	**20**	1	1. Since I Fell For You................................. Dixie 1082 vocal: Annie Laurie; Lenny Welch's 1963 recording of this song was a #4 smash	

GEORGIA MINSTREL CO.
Harry Macdonough, S.H. Dudley, William F. Hooley, & Frank Banta

DATE CHARTED	PEAK POS	WKS CHRT'D	ARTIST — Record Title	Label & Number
3/30/01	**3**	4	1. Minstrel Record No. 3 .... Victor 508 featuring "Old Folks at Home"	
5/04/01	**4**	2	2. Minstrels: First Part, No. 5 .... Victor 3039 featuring "In the Evening By the Moonlight"	

GEORGIANS
Charlie Spivak (trumpet) was a member in the late 20s.

DATE CHARTED	PEAK POS	WKS CHRT'D	ARTIST — Record Title	Label & Number
3/31/23	**11**	1	1. I Wish I Could Shimmy Like My Sister Kate... Columbia 3775	
8/28/26	**13**	1	2. Horses .... Columbia 634 vocal: Johnny Morris; song based on Tchaikovsky's "Troika"	

GEORGE GERSHWIN
Perhaps America's greatest popular composer, George Gershwin was born in New York on 9/26/1898. His first major hit song was Al Jolson's "Swanee", and his remaining years were filled with enduring Broadway and movie musical scores (most with brother Ira's lyrics); "Rhapsody in Blue" and the 1935 folk opera "Porgy and Bess" stand as his greatest masterpieces. George Gershwin died of a brain tumor on 7/11/37.

DATE CHARTED	PEAK POS	WKS CHRT'D	ARTIST — Record Title	Label & Number
10/18/24	**3**	8	1. Rhapsody In Blue .... [I] Victor 55225 PAUL WHITEMAN'S CONCERT ORCHESTRA George Gershwin piano soloist; classical/jazz suite premiered at New York's Aeolian Hall on 2/12/24	
3/19/27	**17**	1	2. Someone To Watch Over Me .... [I] Columbia 812 from the Broadway musical "Oh, Kay"	
9/03/27	**7**	5	3. Rhapsody In Blue .... [I] Victor 35822 new electrically-recorded version with Paul Whiteman's Concert Orchestra, directed by Nat Shilkret	
6/22/29	**7**	6	4. An American In Paris........................... [I] Victor 35963 Victor Symphony Orchestra, George Gershwin piano soloist	

DATE CHARTED	PEAK POS	WKS CHRT'D	ARTIST — Record Title	Label & Number
			### TOM GERUN & HIS ORCHESTRA	
			West Coast-based bandleader (born Thomas Gerunovitch)	
9/21/29	18	1	1. Am I Blue?	Brunswick 4429
			vocal: Jimmy Davis; from the film "On With the Show"	
6/28/30	12	3	2. Around The Corner	Brunswick 4829
9/27/30	5	4	3. If I Could Be With You	Brunswick 4895
12/20/30	7	5	4. Cheerful Little Earful	Brunswick 4971
			from the Broadway musical "Sweet and Low"	
1/30/32	17	1	5. When We're Alone (Penthouse Serenade)	Brunswick 6236
			vocal: Scrappy Lambert	
9/10/32	11	4	6. Three's A Crowd..................................	Brunswick 6365
			vocal: Smith Ballew; with Woody Herman (clarinet) & future singer Tony Martin (tenor sax); from the film "The Crooner"	
			### STAN GETZ	
			17-time winner of Down Beat polls as top tenor saxophonist; played with Stan Kenton (1944-45), Jimmy Dorsey (1945-46), Benny Goodman (1946), and most importantly Woody Herman (1947-49).	
			### CARROLL GIBBONS & HIS ORCHESTRA	
			American pianist who became a popular British radio personality	
6/27/36	8	5	1. These Foolish Things	Columbia 3136
			### ARTHUR GIBBS & HIS GANG	
			Pianist-bandleader	
8/11/23	7	3	1. Louisville Lou...................................... [I]	Victor 19070
1/05/24	1(1)	7	2. **Charleston** .... [I]	Victor 19165
			the song which triggered the 1920s' biggest dance craze; from the Broadway musical "Runnin' Wild"	
			### GEORGIA GIBBS	
			Massachusetts-born singer formerly with Hudson-DeLange, Frankie Trumbauer, & Artie Shaw bands, first became known on late-40s Garry Moore-Jimmy Durante radio show; real name Fredda Gibbons.	
3/25/50	5	11	1. If I Knew You Were Comin' I'd've Baked A Cake	Coral 60169
			with Max Kaminsky's Dixielanders	
8/26/50	25	1	2. Play A Simple Melody	Coral 60227
			with Bob Crosby's Orchestra; from the Broadway musical "Watch Your Step"	
1/13/51	18	8	3. I Still Feel The Same About You	Coral 60353
			with the Owen Bradley Sextet	
6/16/51	21	2	4. Tom's Tune	Mercury 5644
			nearly all Mercury records with Glenn Osser's Orchestra	
7/21/51	21	2	5. Good Morning Mr. Echo...........................	Mercury 5662
8/18/51	6	9	6. While You Danced, Danced, Danced (I Walked In With A Smile)...............................	Mercury 5681
12/08/51	24	3	7. Cry	Mercury 5749
4/19/52	1(7)	20	● 8. Kiss Of Fire......................................	Mercury 5823
			adapted from the Argentine tango "El Choclo"	
7/26/52	21	3	9. So Madly In Love	Mercury 5874
10/25/52	22	5	10. My Favorite Song.................................	Mercury 5912
3/14/53	5	24	11. Seven Lonely Days................................	Mercury 70095
			with the Yale Brothers	
8/22/53	23	1	12. For Me, For Me	Mercury 70172
10/31/53	30	1	13. The Bridge Of Sighs/	
			British song	
11/14/53	30	1	14. A Home Lovin' Man................................	Mercury 70238
3/20/54	18	4	15. Somebody Bad Stole De Wedding Bell..........	Mercury 70298
			from the stage production "The Copacabana Show of 1954"	
5/01/54	21	4	16. My Sin	Mercury 70339
6/26/54	24	4	17. Wait For Me, Darling	Mercury 70386
			### PARKER GIBBS	
			Ted Weems' featured singer from 1925-39	

DATE CHARTED	PEAK POS	WKS CHRT'D	ARTIST — Record Title	Label & Number

TERRY GIBBS
Top jazz vibraphonist with Tommy Dorsey, Woody Herman (1948-49), Benny Goodman.

GINNY GIBSON

1/10/53	**25**	1	1. You Blew Me A Kiss	MGM 11383

STEVE GIBSON & THE RED CAPS

5/01/48	**21**	2	1. Wedding Bells Are Breaking Up That Old Gang Of Mine....................................	Mercury 8069
10/11/52	**20**	1	2. I Went To Your Wedding .... featuring Damita Jo	RCA Victor 4835

IRVING GILLETTE
Real name of Henry Burr

DIZZY GILLESPIE
All-time great jazz trumpet star: played with Teddy Hill (1937), Cab Calloway (1939-40), Ella Fitzgerald (1941), Lucky Millinder (1942), Earl Hines (1943), & Billy Eckstine (1944) before his historic 1945 recordings with Charlie Parker that helped give birth to "bebop".

11/24/45	**22**	1	1. Salt Peanuts .... [N]	Guild 1003

DIZZY GILLESPIE & HIS ALL-STAR QUINTET, including Charlie Parker (alto sax); vocal by Dizzy & band

ART GILLHAM
Billed as "the Whispering Pianist"; died on 6/6/61 (66).

10/31/25	**6**	2	1. Angry	Columbia 411
8/28/26	**11**	1	2. I'd Climb The Highest Mountain	Columbia 626
4/14/28	**18**	1	3. So Tired...	Columbia 1282

GILMORE'S BAND
Patrick S. Gilmore first won national acclaim in 1863 when, as bandleader of the Union Army, he co-wrote "When Johnny Comes Marching Home".

2/06/92	**2(3)**	3	1. Volunteers' March .... [I]	New York
7/02/92	**2(2)**	2	2. The Star-Spangled Banner...................... [I]	New Jersey
5/11/01	**4**	2	3. Selections From "Florodora" .... [I]	Columbia 31536

GILBERT GIRARD
Contributed to many Edison comedy records of the early 1900s, most notably through his animal impressions. (also see Len Spencer)

WILL GLAHE
European accordionist-bandleader

5/06/39	**1(4)**	21	● 1. **Beer Barrel Polka/** popular Czechoslovakian song ("Skoda Lasky"-'Lost Love')	
5/06/39	**11**	2	2. Hot Pretzels.............................	Victor V-710
5/20/39	**11**	1	3. W.P.A. Polka................................ [I]	Victor V-722
1/06/40	**12**	10	4. Woodpecker................................	Victor V-743
8/17/40	**22**	2	5. Bartender Polka .... [I]	Victor V613
			above five listed as: "Glahe Musette Orchestra"	
6/12/48	**17**	5	6. You Can't Be True Dear	RCA Victor 1117

NATHAN GLANTZ & HIS ORCHESTRA
Alto and tenor saxophonist who recorded prolifically throughout the 1920s.

9/30/22	**11**	1	1. Romany Love........................... [I]	Gennett 4888
3/10/28	**19**	1	2. Diane (I'm In Heaven When I See You Smile).. vocal: Charles Harrison	Banner 6101

JACKIE GLEASON & HIS ORCHESTRA
"The Great One", longtime star of Broadway, TV, and movies, as well as a composer and orchestra leader; his orchestra featured cornet star Bobby Hackett.

3/14/53	**22**	4	1. Melancholy Serenade .... [I]	Capitol 2361
			Jackie's famous theme for TV's "The Honeymooners"	
7/25/53	**30**	1	2. Terry's Theme From "Limelight".............. [I]	Capitol 2507

DATE CHARTED	PEAK POS	WKS CHRT'D	ARTIST — Record Title	Label & Number
			DARRELL GLENN	
			Country singer	
7/18/53	**6**	13	1. Crying In The Chapel..............................	Valley 105
			WILFRED GLENN	
			Bass singer with the Shannon Four and the Revelers.	
			(also see Haydn Quartet)	
			ALMA GLUCK	
			Born in Bucharest, Romania but raised in the U.S., Alma rose to fame with the New York Metropolitan Opera. She was frequently accompanied on record by her husband, concert violinist Efrem Zimbalist. Their son, Efrem Zimbalist Jr., starred in TV's "The F.B.I.", and granddaughter Stephanie is featured in "Remington Steele". Alma died on 10/27/38 (54).	
9/09/11	**10**	1	1. My Laddie	Victor 64183
11/18/11	**10**	1	2. From The Land Of The Sky-Blue Water........	Victor 64190
3/09/12	**6**	2	3. Home, Sweet Home	Victor 74251
6/15/12	**5**	4	4. Elegie (Song Of Mourning)......................	Victor 87101
			accompanied by Efrem Zimbalist	
7/20/12	**5**	4	5. Whispering Hope	Victrola 87107
6/14/13	**10**	1	6. Abide With Me	Victor 87132
10/10/14	**10**	1	7. Rock Of Ages	Victor 87198
2/20/15	**1(5)**	14	● 8. **Carry Me Back To Old Virginny**	Victor 88481
			only the fourth reported million-seller in history	
2/27/15	**6**	3	9. Jesus, Lover Of My Soul................	Victor 87200
			5-7 & 9: ALMA GLUCK & LOUISE HOMER	
6/19/15	**3**	5	10. The Old Folks At Home (Swanee River)	Victor 87196
11/20/15	**4**	3	11. The Fiddle And I......................	Victor 88539
			above two accompanied by Efrem Zimbalist	
5/27/16+	**3**	5	12. Listen To The Mocking Bird......................	Victor 74465
			12 & 14 with bird voices by Charles Kellogg	
6/17/16	**3**	5	13. My Old Kentucky Home	Victor 74468
8/05/16	**4**	4	14. The Nightingale Song	Victor 64566
11/25/16	**6**	4	15. Sing Me To Sleep	Victor 88573
5/26/17	**6**	2	16. I'se Gwine Back To Dixie......................	Victor 64564
			8, 13, & 16 with male chorus	
11/02/18	**10**	1	17. The Lost Chord	Victor 88593
1/25/19	**10**	1	18. Hatikva (Our Hope)............................. [F]	Victor 87296
			adopted as the Zionist anthem of Israel	
			15, 17, & 18 accompanied by Efrem Zimbalist	
3/15/19	**10**	1	19. Bring Back My Bonnie To Me	Victor 64793
			ALMA GLUCK & ORPHEUS QUARTET	
			LUD GLUSKIN & HIS ORCHESTRA	
			1930s band most popular on network radio (particularly Burns & Allen show), and for singer Buddy Clark.	
10/13/34	**6**	10	1. The Continental (You Kiss While You're Dancing)/	
			vocal: Joe Host; from the film "The Gay Divorce"	
10/27/34	**18**	3	2. La Cucharacha......................	Columbia 2952
			vocal: "Chiquita"	
3/23/35	**14**	2	3. The Rhythm Of The Rhumba......................	Columbia 3013
			vocal: Buddy Clark & Joe Host	
5/23/36	**3**	9	4. She Shall Have Music	Brunswick 7658
			movie title song	
1/23/37	**9**	7	5. May I Have The Next Romance?	Brunswick 7788
			from the British film "Head Over Heels in Love"	
			above two vocals: Buddy Clark	
			HERBERT GODDARD	
			Pseudonym for Emilo deGogorza	

DATE CHARTED	PEAK POS	WKS CHRT'D	ARTIST — Record Title	Label & Number
			ARTHUR GODFREY	
			One of the best-known stars in TV and radio history, "the Old Redhead" was a television fixture from 1949-59; he died on 3/16/83 (79).	
11/01/47	2(8)	18	1. Too Fat Polka (I Don't Want Her-You Can Have Her-She's Too Fat For Me) .... [N]	Columbia 37921
2/21/48	7	9	2. Slap 'Er Down Again, Paw	Columbia 38066
2/28/48	21	1	3. The Thousand Islands Song/ from the Broadway musical "Angel In The Wings" above two with the Too Fat Trio	
3/13/48	14	3	4. I'm Looking Over A Four-Leaf Clover	Columbia 38081
3/18/50	16	5	5. Candy And Cake.. above two with the Mariners	Columbia 38721
3/25/50	8	7	6. Go To Sleep, Go To Sleep, Go To Sleep .... MARY MARTIN & ARTHUR GODFREY	Columbia 38744
12/09/50	24	5	7. The Thing .... [N]	Columbia 919
5/19/51	13	6	8. I Like The Wide Open Spaces...................... ARTHUR GODFREY & LAURIE ANDERS	Columbia 39404
8/11/51	27	2	9. What Is A Boy .... with Mitch Miller's Orchestra	Columbia 39487
12/22/51+	6	14	10. Dance Me Loose/ with the Chordettes	
1/05/52	12	11	11. Slow Poke	Columbia 39632
8/09/52	17	2	12. I Love Girls... nearly all records with Archie Bleyer's Orchestra	Columbia 39792
			REGGIE GOFF	
			Baritone known as "the English Vaughn Monroe" (also see Paul Fennelly)	
2/05/49	13	2	1. I Love You So Much It Hurts .... with Cyril Stapleton's Orchestra	London 312
			LOU GOLD & HIS ORCHESTRA	
			Prolific New York-based bandleader	
7/09/27	20	1	1. If You See Sally	Okeh 40779
10/20/28	19	1	2. I Must Be Dreaming................................. vocal: Scrappy Lambert	Banner 7138
			BILLY GOLDEN	
			Tremendously popular comedy performer in vaudeville and in early cylinder recordings; died on 1/30/26 (67).	
10/17/91	1(7)	7	1. **Turkey In The Straw** .... [C] song first popular in 1834	Columbia
11/07/91	2(3)	3	2. Uncle Jefferson .... [C]	Columbia
6/11/98	3	1	3. Bye Bye, My Honey .... [C]	Edison 4001
4/20/01	4	2	4. Roll On The Ground .... [C] originally recorded for Columbia in 1891	Gram-o-Phone 616
12/30/05+	4	3	5. Turkey In The Straw .... [C] new version of his 1891 hit	Victor 4515
12/09/11	10	1	6. Whistling Pete.................................... [C] BILLY GOLDEN & JOE HUGHES also recorded for Edison Amberol 842	Victor 35202
			ERNIE GOLDEN & HIS ORCHESTRA	
			Pianist-bandleader	
3/27/26	15	1	1. Five Foot Two, Eyes Of Blue	Brunswick 2999
9/24/27	14	2	2. Russian Lullaby .... vocal: Vaughn DeLeath	Brunswick 3530
			JEAN GOLDKETTE & HIS ORCHESTRA	
			French-born pianist who led star-studded Detroit orchestra; died on 3/24/62 (63).	
8/30/24	12	1	1. Where The Lazy Daisies Grow................. [I]	Victor 19308
5/25/25	6	3	2. Remember .... vocal: Seymour Simons Tommy Dorsey (trombone) on above two	Victor 19548
7/03/26	9	1	3. Sorry And Blue .... vocal: Frank Bessinger	Victor 19962

DATE CHARTED	PEAK POS	WKS CHRT'D	ARTIST — Record Title	Label & Number
9/25/26	14	1	4. Lonesome And Sorry .... vocal: Carl Mathieu & James Stanley Jimmy Dorsey (alto sax/clarinet) on 1 & 3-4	Victor 20031
1/22/27	11	3	5. Sunday .... vocal: Keller Sister & Lynch from the Broadway musical "The Merry World"	Victor 20273
1/22/27	16	2	6. Don't Be Angry With Me .... [I]	Victor 20256
5/14/27	10	3	7. I'm Looking Over A Four-Leaf Clover .... vocal: Billy Murray	Victor 20466
6/18/27	13	2	8. A Lane In Spain .... vocal: The Revelers Eddie Lang (guitar) on 5 & 8	Victor 20491
6/18/27	18	1	9. Look At The World And Smile .... [I] from the Broadway musical "Yours Truly" Joe Ventuti (violin) on 1-4 & 9	Victor 20472
9/03/27	20	1	10. I'm Gonna Meet My Sweetie Now .... [I] Bix Beiderbecke (cornet) on 5 & 7-10 Frankie Trumbauer (sax) on above three	Victor 20675
9/22/28	12	3	11. Rosetta .... vocal: Frank Wilson; Pee Wee Hunt on trombone	Victor 21527
10/12/29	6	5	12. Painting The Clouds With Sunshine/	
11/02/29	5	7	13. Tip Toe Through The Tulips .... above two vocals: Frank Munn; both from the film "Gold Diggers of Broadway"; both directed by Victor Young	Victor 22027

PAUL GONSLAVES
Leading tenor saxophonist with Count Basie (1946-49) & Duke Ellington (1950-73); died on 5/15/74 (53).

AL GOODMAN & HIS ORCHESTRA
Pianist-bandleader, born in Russia (raised in U.S.); orchestra conductor for many Broadway musicals, and for first sound film "The Jazz Singer", then on radio for years; died on 1/11/72 (81).

4/12/30	17	1	1. Thank Your Father .... vocal: Scrappy Lambert; from the Broadway musical "Flying High"	Brunswick 4726

BENNY GOODMAN & HIS ORCHESTRA
Born on 5/30/09 in Chicago, Benny Goodman was playing clarinet professionally at 16 with Art Kassel, made his reputation with Ben Pollack from 1925-29, and after several years of busy studio work formed his own permanent band in 1934. The band's hard-driving sound, fueled by Fletcher Henderson's arrangements, met some early resistance but when it hit, it hit big: by the start of 1936 the Swing Era had been launched, and Benny Goodman was its king. The band's Jan. 16, 1938 Carnegie Hall concert was a historic triumph. Hollywood's "Benny Goodman Story" in 1956 honored the man who has now provided more than 50 years of classic jazz. He died on June 13, 1986 (77). (also see Red Nichols, Johnny Walker, Ethel Waters, & Teddy Wilson)

1/03/31	20	1	1. He's Not Worth Your Tears........................ vocal: Scrappy Lambert; band includes Tommy Dorsey (trombone) & Eddie Lang (guitar)	Melotone 12023
12/09/33+	6	9	2. Ain't Cha Glad?/	
1/13/34	20	1	3. I Gotta Right To Sing The Blues .... from the Broadway musical "Earl Carroll's Vanities of 1932" above two vocals: Jack Teagarden (also trombone); first Goodman hits with Gene Krupa (drums)	Columbia 2835
1/27/34	6	5	4. Riffin' The Scotch .... vocal: Billie Holiday	Columbia 2867
2/03/34	16	2	5. Love Me Or Leave Me .... [I] from the Broadway musical "Whoopee"	Columbia 2871
2/24/34	8	5	6. Ol' Pappy .... vocal: Mildred Bailey; with Coleman Hawkins (tenor sax)	Columbia 2892
5/05/34	14	3	7. Basin Street Blues .... [I]	Columbia 2914
5/26/34	6	10	8. I Ain't Lazy, I'm Just Dreamin' .... vocal: Jack Teagarden	Columbia 2923
6/16/34	1(1)	15	9. **Moon Glow**.. [I] from the Broadway musical "Blackbirds of 1934" above two with Teddy Wilson (piano)	Columbia 2927

DATE CHARTED	PEAK POS	WKS CHRT'D	ARTIST — Record Title	Label & Number
9/15/34	**5**	6	10. Take My Word/ [I]	
9/22/34	**14**	3	11. It Happens To The Best Of Friends............. Columbia 2947 vocal: Ann Graham	
10/13/34	**5**	4	12. Bugle Call Rag .... [I] Columbia 2958 above three with Claude Thornhill (piano)	
1/05/35	**8**	5	13. I'm A Hundred Percent For You.................. Columbia 2988	
1/26/35	**2(2)**	8	14. Blue Moon/	
2/16/35	**16**	2	15. Throwin' Stones At The Sun..................... Columbia 3003 above three vocals: Helen Ward	
2/16/35	**9**	10	16. Music Hall Rag .... [I] Columbia 3011	
3/30/35	**9**	6	17. Night Wind/	
3/16/35	**16**	3	18. Clouds .... Columbia 3015 vocal: Ray Hendricks	
3/30/35	**6**	8	19. I Was Lucky/	
4/20/35	**19**	1	20. Singing A Happy Song .... Columbia 3018 above two from the film "Follies Bergere"	
4/27/35	**11**	3	21. The Dixieland Band................................ Victor 25009	
5/04/35	**10**	9	22. The Dixieland Band................................ Columbia 3033 above two: different versions of same song	
5/18/35	**12**	4	23. You're A Heavenly Thing .... Victor 25021 vocals on 17 & 19-23: Helen Ward	
6/08/35	**10**	3	24. Japanese Sandman .... [I] Victor 25024	
8/17/35	**9**	4	25. Ballad In Blue .... [I] Victor 25081	
9/07/35	**5**	8	26. Body And Soul/ [I] from the Broadway musical "Three's a Crowd"	
10/19/35	**20**	1	27. After You've Gone .... [I] Victor 25115 above two: first recordings by the famous Benny Goodman Trio: Benny, Teddy Wilson & Gene Krupa	
9/14/35	**12**	4	28. Sometimes I'm Happy/ [I] from the Broadway musical "Hit the Deck"	
9/15/35	**10**	4	29. King Porter .... [I] Victor 25090 featuring one of Bunny Berigan's most famous solos	
10/26/35	**18**	1	30. Jingle Bells .... [I-X] Victor 25145	
12/21/35	**5**	5	31. No Other One .... Victor 25193	
12/21/35+	**7**	8	32. Eenie Meenie Miney Mo............................ Victor 25195 from the film "To Beat the Band"	
2/08/36	**20**	1	33. Good-Bye .... [I] Victor 25215 Benny's closing theme song 25, 28, 29 & 33 with Bunny Berigan (trumpet)	
2/15/36	**1(2)**	13	34. It's Been So Long/	
2/29/36	**1(6)**	13	35. Goody-Goody .... Victor 25245 vocals on 31-32, 34-35 by Helen Ward	
4/25/36	**9**	4	36. Christopher Columbus .... [I] Victor 25279	
5/02/36	**14**	2	37. I Know That You Know........................... [I] Victor 25290 from the Broadway musical "Oh, Please!"	
5/23/36	**1(6)**	15	38. The Glory Of Love/	
6/06/36	**2(1)**	12	39. You Can't Pull The Wool Over My Eyes....... Victor 25316	
5/30/36	**2(2)**	10	40. Star Dust .... [I] Victor 25320 flip side: Tommy Dorsey's hit version of "Star Dust"	
6/27/36	**1(2)**	13	41. These Foolish Things Remind Me Of You ... Victor 25351 from the London musical "Spread It Around" vocals on 38, 39 & 41: Helen Ward	
6/27/36	**9**	3	42. China Boy .... [I] Victor 25333 Benny Goodman Trio	
7/11/36	**11**	7	43. Stompin' At The Savoy .... [I] Victor 25247	
8/15/36	**2(1)**	5	44. Swingtime In The Rockies .... [I] Victor 25355	
8/22/36	**13**	4	45. In A Sentimental Mood .... [I] Victor 25351	
9/26/36	**8**	3	46. Moon Glow .... [I] Victor 25398 new version of 1934 hit by the Goodman Quartet: Benny, Teddy, Gene, & Lionel Hampton (vibraphone)	

DATE CHARTED	PEAK POS	WKS CHRT'D	ARTIST — Record Title	Label & Number
10/03/36	**1(2)**	10	47. **You Turned The Tables On Me/** from the film "Sing, Baby, Sing"	
11/14/36	**9**	7	48. Here's Love In Your Eyes .... [I] Victor 25391 from the film "The Big Broadcast of 1937"	
10/10/36	**4**	7	49. Love Me Or Leave Me/ [I] new version of 1934 hit	
12/12/36	**12**	2	50. Exactly Like You .... Victor 25406 Benny Goodman Trio; vocal: Lionel Hampton from the Broadway musical "International Revue"	
10/24/36	**20**	1	51. St. Louis Blues .... [I] Victor 25411 49 & 51: Benny Goodman Quartet	
11/21/36	**9**	5	52. Organ Grinder's Swing .... [I] Victor 25442	
11/21/36	**17**	1	53. When A Lady Meets A Gentleman Down South .... Victor 25434 first hit with Ziggy Elman (trumpet) vocals on 47 & 53: Helen Ward	
12/12/36	**13**	3	54. Bugle Call Rag .... [I] Victor 25467 new version of 1934 hit	
1/16/37	**1(4)**	13	55. **Goodnight, My Love** .... Victor 25461 vocal: Ella Fitzgerald; from the film "Stowaway"; the first hit with Harry James (trumpet)	
1/23/37	**4**	5	56. Smoke Dreams/	
2/13/37	**14**	3	57. Gee! But You're Swell .... Victor 25486 above two vocals: Helen Ward	
1/30/37	**1(3)**	10	58. **This Year's Kisses/**	
2/27/37	**20**	1	59. He Ain't Got Rhythm .... Victor 25505 vocal: Jimmy Rushing; above two from the film "On the Avenue"	
2/13/37	**18**	1	60. Never Should Have Told You .... Victor 25500 vocals on 58 & 60: Margaret McCrae	
2/20/37	**17**	1	61. I Want To Be Happy .... [I] Victor 25510 from the Broadway musical "No, No, Nanette"	
3/06/37	**4**	5	62. Stompin' At The Savoy .... [I] Victor 25521 new version of 1936 hit, by the Goodman Quartet	
7/31/37	**8**	3	63. Peckin' .... [I] Victor 25621 from the film "New Faces of 1937"	
8/14/37	**6**	10	64. Afraid To Dream .... Victor 25627 vocal: Betty Van; from the film "You Can't Have Everything"	
9/11/37	**20**	1	65. The Man I Love .... [I] Victor 25644 from the Broadway musical "Lady Be Good"	
10/30/37	**15**	2	66. Bob White .... Victor 25683	
12/11/37	**14**	2	67. Can't Teach My Old Heart New Tricks ....:..... Victor 25711 from the film "Hollywood Hotel"	
12/18/37+	**12**	4	68. Loch Lomond .... Victor 25717 vocal: Martha Tilton & Benny Goodman	
1/01/38	**9**	9	69. You Took The Words Right Out Of My Heart .. Victor 25720 from the film "The Big Broadcast of 1938"	
1/29/38	**4**	4	70. Bei Mir Bist Du Schoen .... Victor 25751 Goodman Quartet; song from the 1933 Yiddish musical "I Would If I Could", with new lyrics	
3/05/38	**7**	9	71. It's Wonderful .... Victor 25727 vocals on 66, 67, & above three: Martha Tilton	
3/12/38	**1(5)**	13	72. **Don't Be That Way/** [I]	
4/23/38	**8**	5	73. One O'Clock Jump .... [I] Victor 25792 the most famous Goodman band: Benny (clarinet/director), Harry James, Ziggy Elman, & Chris Griffin (trumpets), Red Ballard & Vernon Brown (trombones), Hymie Schertzer & George Koenig (alto sax), Arthur Rollini & Babe Russin (tenor sax), Jess Stacy (piano), Allan Reuss (guitar), & Gene Krupa (drums)	
4/09/38	**7**	6	74. Sing, Sing, Sing (With A Swing) .... [I] Victor 25796 the band's most renowned performance, with featured solos by Gene, Harry & Benny; selected for the NARAS Hall of Fame includes interpolation of "Christopher Columbus" Gene Krupa's final hit before leaving the band	
4/16/38	**14**	4	75. Please Be Kind .... Victor 25814 with Lester Young (tenor sax) & Lionel Hampton (drums)	

DATE CHARTED	PEAK POS	WKS CHRT'D	ARTIST — Record Title	Label & Number
5/14/38	1(1)	9	76. **I Let A Song Go Out Of My Heart/**	
7/16/38	11	4	77. Feelin' High And Happy	Victor 25840
5/21/38	12	6	78. Why'd Ya Make Me Fall In Love?	Victor 25846
			above four vocals: Martha Tilton	
6/25/38	7	5	79. The Flat Foot Floogee.........................	Victor 25871
			vocal: band	
7/09/38	12	3	80. (I've Been) Savin' Myself For You	Victor 25867
7/30/38	3	8	81. What Goes On Here In My Heart/	
9/24/38	7	1	82. A Little Kiss At Twilight	Victor 25878
			above two from the film "Give Me a Sailor"	
8/20/38	14	4	83. Lullaby In Rhythm......................... [I]	Victor 25827
9/10/38	4	9	84. I've Got A Date With A Dream/	
10/08/38	20	1	85. Could You Pass In Love?....................	Victor 26000
			above two from the film "My Lucky Star"	
11/05/38	11	5	86. When I Go A-Dreamin'/	
			from University of Pennsylvania's "Mask & Wig Club" show	
11/19/38	10	5	87. Bumble Bee Stomp........................ [I]	Victor 26087
11/19/38	15	2	88. Is That The Way To Treat A Sweetheart?......	Victor 26082
12/03/38	6	7	89. What Have You Got That Gets Me?	Victor 26053
			from the film "Artists & Models Abroad"	
12/17/38+	2(1)	13	90. This Can't Be Love.....................	Victor 26099
			from the Broadway musical "The Boys from Syracuse"	
12/17/38	14	1	91. Topsy .... [I]	Victor 26107
12/24/38	6	5	92. I Have Eyes/	
12/31/38+	6	6	93. You're A Sweet Little Headache	Victor 26071
			above two from the film "Paris Honeymoon"	
12/31/38+	13	2	94. I Must See Annie Tonight	Victor 26110
1/07/39	14	1	95. My Honey's Lovin' Arms .... [I]	Victor 26095
			also issued on Bluebird 11056; Harry James' final hit before leaving band	
4/22/39	1(5)	14	96. **And The Angels Sing**	Victor 26170
			featuring Ziggy Elman's famous trumpet chorus; adaptation of traditional Hebraic song / all vocals from 80-96: Martha Tilton	
5/20/39	10	3	97. Rose Of Washington Square .... [I]	Victor 26230
			from the Broadway musical "Ziegfeld Midnight Frolic"	
9/30/39	7	6	98. Blue Orchids/	
11/11/39	7	6	99. What's New?.........................	Columbia 35211
10/28/39	6	13	100. I Didn't Know What Time It Was.................	Columbia 35230
			from the Broadway musical "Too Many Girls"	
11/18/39	9	8	101. Scatter-Brain	Columbia 35241
			above four vocals: Louise Tobin	
12/30/39+	17	2	102. I Thought About You.........................	Columbia 35313
1/06/40	15	3	103. Bluebirds In The Moonlight....................	Columbia 35289
			from the animated film "Gulliver's Travels"	
1/27/40	1(1)	11	104. **Darn That Dream**	Columbia 35331
			from the Broadway musical "Swingin' the Dream" / Mildred Bailey: above three vocals / Fletcher Henderson at piano on above seven	
3/02/40	19	1	105. What's The Matter With Me?....................	Columbia 35374
3/23/40	6	9	106. How High The Moon/	
			from the Broadway musical "Two for the Show"	
7/20/40	20	1	107. The Fable Of The Rose..........................	Columbia 35391
5/25/40	5	9	108. I Can't Love You Any More (Any More Than I Do).....................	Columbia 35487
			first full-band hit with Charlie Christian	
5/25/40	20	1	109. Gone With "What" Wind? .... [I]	Columbia 35404
5/25/40	30	1	110. Soft Winds......................... [I]	Columbia 35320
			Benny Goodman Sextet, with Fletcher Henderson, Lionel Hampton (vibes), Charlie Christian (guitar), Artie Bernstein (bass), & Nick Fatool (drums)	
7/06/40	13	2	111. I Can't Resist You/	
10/26/40	24	1	112. Dreaming Out Loud..........................	Columbia 35574
			all vocals from 105-112: Helen Forrest	

DATE CHARTED	PEAK POS	WKS CHRT'D	ARTIST — Record Title	Label & Number
8/17/40	**19**	1	113. The Hour Of Parting .... [I]	Columbia 35527
3/01/41	**1(4)**	11	114. **There'll Be Some Changes Made**...............	Columbia 35210
			vocal: Louise Tobin; recorded 8/10/39; 1924 song revived in the 1941 film "Playgirl"	
3/22/41	**24**	1	115. As Long As I Live .... [I]	Columbia 35901
			from the 1934 stage production "Cotton Club Parade" 109 & 115: Benny Goodman & His Sextet featuring Count Basie (piano)	
3/29/41	**11**	1	116. Perfidia (Tonight)	Columbia 35962
5/03/41	**10**	2	117. Intermezzo (A Love Story) .... [I]	Columbia 36050
5/17/41	**20**	1	118. My Sister And I	Columbia 36022
7/26/41	**25**	1	119. These Things You Left Me	Columbia 35910
8/02/41	**24**	1	120. Air Mail Special................................... [I]	Columbia 36254
			previously recorded on Columbia 36099 as "Good Enough to Keep" Teddy Wilson (piano) on 116 & 120	
8/16/41	**17**	1	121. Yours	Columbia 36067
			all vocals from 116-121 by Helen Forrest	
11/15/41	**25**	1	122. I Got It Bad And That Ain't Good...............	Columbia 36421
			Peggy Lee's first hit vocal; from the West Coast revue "Jump For Joy" Cootie Williams (trumpet) on 115-116, 118-122	
1/10/42	**24**	1	123. Winter Weather	Okeh 6516
			vocal: Peggy Lee & Art Lund	
2/14/42	**20**	1	124. Blues In The Night	Okeh 6553
			movie title song; Benny Goodman & His Sextet	
3/07/42	**1(3)**	15	125. **Somebody Else Is Taking My Place**...........	Okeh 6497
			Billy Butterfield (trumpet) on 117, 120, 122 & 125	
3/21/42	**15**	2	126. A String Of Pearls/	[I]
3/28/42	**1(4)**	21	127. **Jersey Bounce**............................... [I]	Okeh 6590
4/11/42	**14**	3	128. My Little Cousin	Okeh 6606
5/23/42	**16**	2	129. We'll Meet Again	Okeh 6644
6/13/42	**22**	1	130. Full Moon (Noche De Luna).......................	Okeh 6652
6/27/42	**21**	1	131. The Way You Look Tonight	Columbia 36594
			from the film "Swing Time" Peggy Lee: all vocals from 124-131	
8/15/42	**4**	7	132. Idaho/	
8/22/42	**10**	1	133. Take Me..	Columbia 36613
10/17/42	**17**	2	134. Serenade In Blue	Columbia 36622
			from the film "Orchestra Wives" Dick Haymes: above three vocals	
1/02/43	**4**	19	135. Why Don't You Do Right?........................	Columbia 36652
			vocal: Peggy Lee	
4/24/43	**1(3)**	14	136. **Taking A Chance On Love/**	
6/12/43	**19**	1	137. Cabin In The Sky	Columbia 35869
			above two vocals by Helen Forrest, recorded on 11/29/40 both from the Broadway musical and movie "Cabin In The Sky" Cootie Williams (trumpet) on 132-134, & 136-137	
10/09/43	**12**	1	138. Mission To Moscow .... [I]	Columbia 36680
			recorded 7/30/42	
1/08/44	**20**	1	139. Solo Flight... [I]	Columbia 36684
			recorded on 3/4/41; one of Charlie Christian's most famous guitar performances	
10/28/44	**27**	1	140. And The Angels Sing............................ [R]	Victor 26170
3/10/45	**12**	3	141. Ev'ry Time We Say Goodbye	Columbia 36767
			vocal: Peggy Mann; from the Broadway musical "Seven Lively Arts"	
5/12/45	**11**	4	142. Close As Pages In A Book..........................	Columbia 36787
			vocal: Jane Harvey; from the Broadway musical "Up In Central Park"	
6/30/45	**2(1)**	17	143. Gotta Be This Or That	Columbia 36813
			vocal: Benny Goodman	
10/13/45	**9**	1	144. I'm Gonna Love That Guy/	
			above two vocals: Dottie Reid	
9/29/45	**10**	1	145. It's Only A Paper Moon	Columbia 36843
			from the film "Take a Chance"	

DATE CHARTED	PEAK POS	WKS CHRT'D	ARTIST — Record Title	Label & Number
10/06/45	**19**	4	146. How Deep Is The Ocean? .... Columbia 36754 vocal: Peggy Lee; recorded 10/8/41	
12/08/45+	**2(1)**	14	147. Symphony/	
12/08/45	**12**	3	148. My Guy's Come Back................................ Columbia 36874	
3/16/46	**13**	1	149. Give Me The Simple Life............................ Columbia 36908 from the film "Wake Up And Dream" band includes Kai Winding (trombone) above three vocals: Liza Morrow	
5/25/46	**11**	1	150. Don't Be A Baby, Baby .... Columbia 36967 BENNY GOODMAN SEXTET	
8/03/46	**12**	1	151. I Don't Know Enough About You/ Stan Getz (tenor sax) on 149 & 151	
8/17/46	**9**	4	152. Blue Skies................................ Columbia 37053 from the Broadway musical "Betsy"; title song of 1946 movie above three vocals: Art Lund	
1/11/47	**6**	6	153. A Gal In Calico .... Columbia 37187 vocal: Eve Young; from the film "The Time, the Place, & the Girl"	
4/26/47	**21**	3	154. Moon-Faced, Starry-Eyed........................... Capitol 376 Johnny Mercer, vocal	
9/13/47	**21**	3	155. I Want To Be Loved................................. Capitol 416 vocal by Lillian Lane; band includes Zoot Sims (tenor sax)	
2/28/48	**25**	2	156. For Every Man There's A Woman/ vocal: Peggy Lee; from the film "Casbah"	
3/27/48	**26**	1	157. Beyond The Sea .... [I] Capitol 15030 adaptation of Debussy's "La Mer"	
4/10/48	**24**	1	158. Give Me The Good Old Days .... Capitol 15044 vocal by the Sportsmen	
6/19/48	**30**	1	159. Somebody Else Is Taking My Place........... [R] Columbia 37187 reissue of 1942 hit (Okeh 6497)	
11/13/48+	**7**	12	160. On A Slow Boat To China .... Capitol 15208 vocal: Al Hendrickson	
4/22/50	**13**	3	161. It Isn't Fair .... Capitol 860 vocal: Buddy Greco	
12/02/50	**25**	3	162. Oh, Babe! .... Columbia 39045 BENNY GOODMAN SEXTET includes Teddy Wilson (piano) & Terry Gibbs (vibraphone) vocal by Jimmy Ricks (of the R&B group the Ravens) & Nancy Reed	
8/04/51	**28**	1	163. Wang Wang Blues................................. [I] Columbia 39478 Goodman Sextet, recorded 10/28/41	
6/13/53	**30**	1	164. I'll Never Say "Never Again" Again .... Columbia 39976 vocal: Helen Ward; band includes Billy Butterfield & Chris Griffin (trumpets) & Bobby Byrne (trombone)	

HAL GOODMAN & HIS ORCHESTRA

9/11/43	**11**	3	1. People Will Say We're In Love...................... Hit 7059 from the Broadway musical "Oklahoma!"	

GRAY GORDON & HIS ORCHESTRA
Sweet-band leader known for his "Tic-Toc Rhythm".

11/24/38	**5**	1	1. Blue In The Black Of Night .... Bluebird 7838 vocal: Cliff Grass	
9/09/39	**13**	1	2. Mexiconga .... Victor 26365 vocal: Victoria Cordova; from the Broadway musical "George White's Scandals of 1939"	
3/02/40	**17**	1	3. I Love Me .... Bluebird 10591 vocal: Rita Ray	
7/13/40	**11**	11	4. I Am An American .... Bluebird 10783 vocal: Meredith Blake & Art Perry	
9/14/40	**7**	4	5. Ferry Boat Serenade.............................. Bluebird 10819 vocal: Meredith Blake	
11/02/40	**25**	1	6. Molly Malone .... Bluebird 10861 vocal: Art Perry	

DATE CHARTED	PEAK POS	WKS CHRT'D	ARTIST — Record Title	Label & Number

ROSS GORMAN & HIS ORCHESTRA
Best remembered as clarinet soloist at the world premiere of Gershwin's "Rhapsody in Blue" (and on its original recording), Gorman also directed the Virginians; jazz stars Red Nichols (trombone) & Miff Mole (trombone) played on some of his early records. He died on 2/28/53 (about 62).

8/28/26	**12**	1	1. Valencia/
			vocal: Elliott Shaw
9/11/26	**10**	1	2. Cherie, I Love You .... [I] Columbia 631

EYDIE GORME
Talented ballad singer who got her start on Steve Allen's "Tonight Show"; often performs with her husband Steve Lawrence.

1/23/54	**19**	1	1. Fini .... Coral 61093
			accompanied by Neal Hefti's Orchestra; from the Broadway musical "John Murray Anderson's Almanac"

CONRAD GOZZO
Trumpet soloist with Isham Jones, Bob Chester, Claude Thornhill (1941-42), Benny Goodman, & Woody Herman (1945-46); died on 10/8/64 (42).

BETTY GRABLE
Hollywood's #1 female star of the 1940s, a favorite G.I. pin-up; long married to Harry James (died on 7/2/73 (56).

12/08/45+	**5**	12	1. I Can't Begin To Tell You .... Columbia 36867
			Harry James & His Orchestra; vocal: "Ruth Haag" (Betty Grable); from the film "The Dolly Sisters"

TEDDY GRACE
Singer with Mal Hallett (1937) & Bob Crosby (1939, "Over the Rainbow").

TEX GRANDE & HIS RANGE RIDERS

4/29/44	**28**	1	1. Have I Stayed Away Too Long? .... DeLuxe 5004

RACHEL GRANT
Pseudonym for Gladys Rice

LOUIS GRAVIEURE
British-born baritone who was a popular concert singer in America, then became an opera and movie star in 1930s Germany; died in November, 1965 (77).

5/27/16	**8**	1	1. Prologue From "Pagliacci" .... [F] Columbia 5792
5/26/17	**5**	3	2. America .... Columbia 5949
6/14/19	**9**	2	3. When The Boys Come Home .... Columbia 2709

DOLORES GRAY
American singer-dancer who starred in London production of "Annie Get Your Gun", also in several 50s movies

11/24/51	**16**	7	1. Shrimp Boats .... Decca 27832
			accompanied by Camarata's Orchestra
3/14/53	**23**	1	2. Kaw-Liga .... Decca 28582
			with the Commanders
5/02/53	**21**	2	3. Big Mamou .... Decca 28676
			Louisiana Cajun song
7/17/54	**29**	1	4. Lost In Loveliness................ Decca 29109
			from the film "The Girl in Pink Tights" orchestra on above two directed by Dave Terry

GLEN GRAY & THE CASA LOMA ORCHESTRA
Named for a Toronto nightclub, the Casa Loma Orchestra was formed in 1927 as an offshoot of the Jean Goldkette band in Detroit. Trombonist Pee Wee Hunt was its leading musician, and Gene Gifford's arrangements help establish the band's reputation. Alto saxist Glen Gray eventually fronted the band, and nearly all records from 1934 on bore his name; Glen died on 8/23/63 (57).

1/17/31	**15**	2	1. Casa Loma Stomp................ [I] Okeh 41492
9/19/31	**17**	1	2. Do The New York .... Brunswick 6150
			from Broadway musical "Ziegfeld Follies of 1931"
8/27/32	**16**	2	3. Blue Jazz .... [I] Brunswick 6358
7/01/33	**6**	7	4. Under A Blanket Of Blue.......... Brunswick 6584

DATE CHARTED	PEAK POS	WKS CHRT'D	ARTIST — Record Title	Label & Number
7/22/33	16	2	5. Trouble In Paradise............................ *above two vocals: Kenny Sargent*	Brunswick 6602
7/29/33	4	9	6. Sophisticated Lady .... [I]	Victor 24338
9/02/33	6	11	7. It's The Talk Of The Town........................	Brunswick 6626
9/02/33	6	4	8. Wild Goose Chase .... [I]	Brunswick 6588
9/30/33	17	1	9. Weep No More, My Baby......................... *from the Broadway musical "Murder at the Vanities" vocals on 7 & 9: Kenny Sargent*	Brunswick 6647
10/14/33	20	1	10. White Jazz .... [I] *recorded 3/24/31*	Brunswick 6092
11/18/33	10	4	11. Heat Wave.................................... *vocal: Mildred Bailey; from Broadway musical "As Thousands Cheer"*	Brunswick 6679
1/06/34	12	4	12. You're Gonna Lose Your Gal......................	Brunswick 6708
1/13/34	19	1	13. Dixie Lee.................................... *above two vocals: Pee Wee Hunt*	Brunswick 6726
2/03/34	16	2	14. You Have Taken My Heart........................	Brunswick 6738
3/24/34	15	3	15. Infatuation/	
3/31/34	15	2	16. Love Me	Brunswick 6791
4/25/34	7	8	17. Champagne Waltz/	
4/25/34	13	2	18. The House Is Haunted (By The Echo Of Your Last Goodbye) .... *above five vocals: Kenny Sargent*	Brunswick 6858
6/16/34	20	1	19. Limehouse Blues .... [I] *from the Broadway musical "Andre Charlot Revue of 1924"*	Brunswick 6886
7/07/34	10	7	20. Spellbound	Brunswick 6910
7/28/34	6	5	21. I Never Had A Chance..........................	Brunswick 6927
8/11/34	8	4	22. Moonglow .... *above three vocals: Kenny Sargent*	Brunswick 6937
8/25/34	13	3	23. Pardon My Southern Accent .... *vocal: Pee Wee Hunt*	Brunswick 6945
9/15/34	10	5	24. Two Cigarettes In The Dark .... *from the film "Kill That Story"*	Brunswick 6954
9/22/34	4	12	25. Out In The Cold Again/	
9/22/34	12	3	26. Learning .... *above three vocals: Kenny Sargent*	Brunswick 6964
11/03/34	11	3	27. You're A Builder Upper.......................... *from the Broadway musical "Life Begins at 8:40"*	Decca 193
12/01/34+	10	8	28. The Object Of My Affection........................ *above two vocals: Pee Wee Hunt*	Decca 298
1/05/35	**1(3)**	8	29. **Blue Moon**	Decca 312
2/09/35	**1(4)**	23	30. **When I Grow Too Old To Dream/**	
6/22/35	14	2	31. The Night Is Young .... *above two from the film "The Night Is Young" above three vocals: Kenny Sargent*	Decca 349
2/09/35	**2(2)**	9	32. Fare Thee Well, Annabelle .... *from the film "Sweet Music"*	Decca 352
3/16/35	7	7	33. Lookie, Lookie, Here Comes Cookie/ *above two vocals: Pee Wee Hunt*	
3/16/35	13	5	34. My Heart Is An Open Book .... *above two from the film "Love in Bloom"*	Decca 386
2/01/36	9	4	35. With All My Heart.............................	Decca 652
3/27/37	18	1	36. I've Got My Love To Keep Me Warm .... *from the film "On the Avenue"*	Decca 1126
5/22/37	7	3	37. Never In A Million Years .... *from the film "Wake Up and Live"*	Decca 1211
11/13/37	15	2	38. Smoke Rings.................................... [I] *the Casa Loma theme song*	Decca 1473
12/25/37	17	1	39. I've Got My Heart Set On You.................... *from the film "Ali Baba Goes to Town"*	Decca 1530
2/26/38	19	1	40. Sweet As A Song .... *from the film "Sally, Irene and Mary"*	Decca 1597
3/05/38	13	4	41. I See Your Face Before Me....................... *from the Broadway musical "Between the Devil"*	Decca 1608

DATE CHARTED	PEAK POS	WKS CHRT'D	ARTIST — Record Title	Label & Number
8/13/38	9	7	42. You Go To My Head..................................	Decca 1783
10/15/38	19	1	43. You Never Know Broadway musical title song	Decca 2010
11/05/38	19	1	44. Song Of India .... [I]	Decca 2031
1/14/39	6	13	45. I Cried For You.................................... recorded 12/14/37 all vocals from 34-45: Kenny Sargent	Decca 1684
3/04/39	7	4	46. This Night (Will Be My Souvenir).................. from the film "Honolulu"	Decca 2308
3/11/39	1(2)	13	47. **Heaven Can Wait**................................. above two vocals: Clyde Burke	Decca 2321
4/01/39	16	1	48. Gotta Get Some Shuteye .... vocal: Pee Wee Hunt	Decca 2307
4/08/39	1(2)	16	49. **Sunrise Serenade** .... [I] featuring Frankie Carle (pianist and composer)	Decca 2321
4/29/39	4	6	50. Tears From My Inkwell	Decca 2388
5/13/39	20	1	51. If I Had My Way....................................	Decca 2437
12/02/39	17	2	52. Tumbling Tumbleweeds	Decca 2777
5/04/40	9	9	53. A Lover's Lullaby/ [I]	
5/25/40	11	8	54. Yours Is My Heart Alone	Decca 3053
5/11/40	9	10	55. No Name Jive................................... [I] one of the band's best-known instrumentals	Decca 3089
5/09/42	22	1	56. It's The Talk Of The Town .... new version of 1933 hit vocals from 50-56: Kenny Sargent	Decca 4292
5/30/42	8	7	57. One Dozen Roses .... vocal: Pee Wee Hunt	Decca 4299
11/21/42+	20	2	58. Don't Do It, Darling/	
1/23/43	7	16	59. Don't Get Around Much Anymore .... vocal: Kenny Sargent & LeBrun Sisters	Decca 18479
11/27/43+	1(5)	21	60. **My Heart Tells Me/** from the film "Sweet Rosie O'Grady"	
12/11/43+	4	7	61. My Shining Hour................................... from the film "The Sky's the Limit"	Decca 18567
5/13/44	12	7	62. Suddenly It's Spring .... from the film "Lady In the Dark"	Decca 18596
10/07/44	26	1	63. Don't Take Your Love From Me .... Eugenie Baird: above four vocals	Decca 18615
9/08/45	9	2	64. Gotta Be This Or That .... vocal: Fats Daniels	Decca 18691

JERRY GRAY
Arranger on some of the most famous hits of the Big Band era for Artie Shaw ("Begin the Beguine") and Glenn Miller ("Chattanooga Choo Choo") and his composition "A String of Pearls").

HELEN GRAYCO
Beautiful wife of Spike Jones

10/09/54	24	1	1. Oop Shoop/	
11/13/54	29	1	2. Teach Me Tonight .... orchestra on above two directed by Harold Mooney	"X" 0051

HAROLD GRAYSON & HIS ORCHESTRA
6/21/30	17	1	1. Fight On, U.S.C. March........................... [I]	Victor 22437

GREAT WHITE WAY ORCHESTRA
4/18/23	6	3	1. You Gave Me Your Heart (So I Gave You Mine)..................................... [I]	Victor 18964
8/18/23	3	6	2. Yes! We Have No Bananas .... [N] vocal & whistling: Billy Murray	Victor 19068

BUDDY GRECO
Began as jazz pianist, played and sang with Benny Goodman in 1948, popular singer for years afterward

12/20/47	15	3	1. Ooh! Look-A-There, Ain't She Pretty?.......... with the Three Sharps	Musicraft 515
11/10/51	30	1	2. I Ran All The Way Home	Coral 60573

DATE CHARTED	PEAK POS	WKS CHRT'D	ARTIST — Record Title	Label & Number
3/21/53	**27**	1	3. I'll Always Love You Some .... Coral 60904 *above two with the Heathertones* *3: with Norman Leyden's Orchestra*	
6/20/53	**26**	1	4. You're Driving Me Crazy (What Did I Do)....... Coral 60979 *above three with the Heathertones; above two accompanied* *by Norman Leyden Orchestra*	
10/17/53	**29**	1	5. Don't Say Goodbye.................................. Coral 61038 *based on an Italian folk melody*	
5/22/54	**28**	1	6. East Side, West Side................................ Coral 61176 JOHNNY DESMOND, ALAN DALE & BUDDY GRECO, with orchestra *directed by Dick Jacobs* *remake of "The Sidewalks of New York"*	

GREEN BROTHERS NOVELTY BAND
George Hamilton Green and Joe Green, who played xylophone,
marimba, vibraphone, and drums

DATE CHARTED	PEAK POS	WKS CHRT'D	ARTIST — Record Title	Label & Number
7/03/20	**7**	2	1. La Veeda... [I] Victor 18667 *also recorded for Pathe 22365*	
9/25/20	**15**	1	2. Kismet.. [I] Okeh 4119 *also recorded for Edison Amberol 4091, Gennett 9059, &* *Pathe 22380*	
6/25/21	**14**	1	3. Mazie.. [I] Gennett 4671 *also recorded for Pathe 20498*	
7/16/21	**7**	2	4. Learning .... [I] Brunswick 2090	
11/21/25	**3**	5	5. Sometime... [I] Columbia 430	

ALICE GREEN
Pseudonym for Olive Kline

BARRY GREEN

DATE CHARTED	PEAK POS	WKS CHRT'D	ARTIST — Record Title	Label & Number
11/06/48	**16**	2	1. Brush Those Tears From Your Eyes .... Rainbow 10090	

JANE GREEN
American vaudeville singer

DATE CHARTED	PEAK POS	WKS CHRT'D	ARTIST — Record Title	Label & Number
2/21/25	**5**	4	1. Me And The Boy Friend .... Victor 19502	
10/31/25	**13**	1	2. Ida - I Do .... Victor 19707	
5/05/28	**14**	2	3. My One And Only.................................... Victor 21145 *from the Broadway musical "Funny Face"* *accompanied on all by Nat Shilkret & His Orchestra*	

JOE GREEN'S NOVELTY ORCHESTRA
Vibraphonist-bandleader

DATE CHARTED	PEAK POS	WKS CHRT'D	ARTIST — Record Title	Label & Number
4/11/31	**13**	3	1. For You .... Columbia 2429 *listed as Joe Green's Marimba Band*	
4/29/33	**4**	12	2. In The Valley Of The Moon/	
5/06/33	**12**	3	3. Remember Me .... Columbia 2768	

JOHNNY GREEN & HIS ORCHESTRA
Pianist-composer best known for co-writing the all-time classic
"Body and Soul", and as conductor/arranger on many movies from
1930s to 60s; frequent TV conductor for Academy Awards. (also see
Fred Astaire, & Ethel Merman)

DATE CHARTED	PEAK POS	WKS CHRT'D	ARTIST — Record Title	Label & Number
6/09/34	**13**	2	1. Cocktails For Two.................................... Brunswick 6797 *vocal: Howard Phillips; Benny Goodman on clarinet; from the* *film "Murder at the Vanities"*	
8/18/34	**9**	7	2. A New Moon Is Over My Shoulder .... Columbia 2940 *vocal: Bernie Park; from the film "Student Tour"*	
9/08/34	**2(3)**	8	3. Two Cigarettes In The Dark .... Columbia 2943 *vocal: George Bouler; from the film "Kill That Story"* *(Brunswick 6995: Ethel Merman with Johnny Green's Orchestra)*	
4/06/35	**6**	7	4. I Won't Dance .... Columbia 3022 *vocal: Marjorie Logan & Jimmy Farrell* *from the film "Roberta"*	
6/15/35	**20**	1	5. Go Into Your Dance/ *above two vocals: Marjorie Logan*	
4/27/35	**2(2)**	9	6. The Little Things You Used To Do .... Columbia 3028	

DATE CHARTED	PEAK POS	WKS CHRT'D	ARTIST — Record Title	Label & Number
4/27/35	**4**	8	7. She's A Latin From Manhattan/	
4/27/35	**5**	11	8. About A Quarter To Nine	Columbia 3029
			above two vocals: Jimmy Farrell	
			above four from the film "Go Into Your Dance"	
			band includes Jimmy Lytell (clarinet/alto sax) & Perry Botkin (guitar)	
			(Brunswick 7487-88, 7608-10, 7716-18, 7855-57: Fred Astaire with Johnny Green's Orchestra)	
11/16/35	**18**	1	9. Me And Marie..............................	Brunswick 7521
11/23/35	**12**	7	10. Why Shouldn't I?.........................	Brunswick 7522
			above two from Broadway musical "Jubilee"	
5/30/36	**5**	10	11. Rendezvous With A Dream	Brunswick 7662
10/03/36	**16**	2	12. The Waltz In Swing Time .... [I]	Brunswick 7716
			from the film "Swing Time"	
			flip side of Fred Astaire's #1 hit "A Fine Romance"	

LARRY GREEN & HIS ORCHESTRA
Boston society pianist-bandleader

DATE CHARTED	PEAK POS	WKS CHRT'D	ARTIST — Record Title	Label & Number
10/11/47	**3**	13	1. Near You....................................	RCA Victor 2421
12/27/47+	**23**	2	2. Gonna Get A Girl/	
			vocal trio on above two	
12/27/47+	**23**	2	3. Song Of New Orleans	RCA Victor 2560
3/06/48	**8**	7	4. Beg Your Pardon	RCA Victor 2647
			vocal: Don Grady	
11/13/48	**21**	2	5. Bella Bella Marie	RCA Victor 3072
6/03/50	**13**	9	6. Bewitched	RCA Victor 3726
			from the Broadway musical "Pal Joey"	
10/21/50	**28**	1	7. Can Anyone Explain? (No! No! No!)..............	RCA Victor 3902
			above two vocals: Honeydreamers	

LIL GREEN
Chicago-based blues singer who recorded the original version of the Benny Goodman hit "Why Don't You Do Right"; died on 4/14/54 (34).

DATE CHARTED	PEAK POS	WKS CHRT'D	ARTIST — Record Title	Label & Number
11/23/40	**23**	1	1. Romance In The Dark............................	Bluebird 8524
			with Big Bill Broonzy	

GENE GREENE
Known in vaudeville as "the Ragtime King"; died on 4/5/30 (52).

DATE CHARTED	PEAK POS	WKS CHRT'D	ARTIST — Record Title	Label & Number
7/29/11	**6**	2	1. King Of The Bungaloos	Columbia 994
5/19/17	**7**	2	2. From Here To Shanghai	Victor 18242
			GENE GREENE & PEERLESS QUARTET	

SONNY GREER & HIS MEMPHIS MEN
Duke Ellington's drummer from 1919-51.

DATE CHARTED	PEAK POS	WKS CHRT'D	ARTIST — Record Title	Label & Number
11/25/33	**14**	2	1. Saturday Night Function...................... [I]	Columbia 2832
			Ellington band, including Duke (piano), Barney Bigard (clarinet), & Johnny Hodges (alto sax)	

JIMMIE GRIER & HIS ORCHESTRA
California-based bandleader, formerly clarinetist/arranger for Gus Arnheim; widely heard on radio throughout 1930s. Co-writer of "Object of My Affection" and "What's the Reason?"; died on 6/4/59 (57). (also see Boswell Sisters)

DATE CHARTED	PEAK POS	WKS CHRT'D	ARTIST — Record Title	Label & Number
4/23/32	**2(3)**	11	1. One Hour With You/	
			movie title song	
4/23/32	**10**	3	2. Music In The Moonlight	Victor 22971
4/23/32	**11**	3	3. Bon Voyage To My Ship Of Dreams	Victor 22970
			above three vocals: Donald Novis	
11/17/34	**1(2)**	13	4. **The Object Of My Affection**	Brunswick 7308
11/24/34	**1(3)**	8	5. **Stay As Sweet As You Are**.......................	Brunswick 7307
			from the film "College Rhythm"	
2/02/35	**11**	3	6. Don't Be Afraid To Tell Your Mother	Brunswick 7355
			vocal: Pinky Tomlin	

KEN GRIFFIN
Organist who once was movie house accompanist for silent films in the 1920s

DATE CHARTED	PEAK POS	WKS CHRT'D	ARTIST — Record Title	Label & Number
4/10/48	**1(7)**	23	● 1. **You Can't Be True, Dear**	Rondo 228
			vocal: Jerry Wayne	

DATE CHARTED	PEAK POS	WKS CHRT'D	ARTIST — Record Title	Label & Number
6/05/48	**19**	8	2. Cuckoo Waltz/ vocal: Nikola Meinkoff, with Efim Schachmeister Orchestra	
7/10/48	**2(7)**	15	3. You Can't Be True, Dear .... [I]	Rondo 128
			original instrumental version	
4/30/49	**29**	1	4. You, You, You Are The One .... [I]	Rondo 186
			German waltz	
8/20/49	**26**	1	5. Beautiful Wisconsin	Rondo 192
			vocal: Johnny Hill	
9/30/50	**11**	20	6. Harbor Lights .... [I]	Columbia 38889
			accompanied by Hawaiian guitar	

MERV GRIFFIN
The long-popular TV talk show host started as featured singer with
Freddy Martin from 1948-52 ("I've Got a Lovely Bunch of
Cocoanuts")

8/04/51	**27**	1	1. The Morning Side Of The Mountain	RCA Victor 4181
11/03/51	**30**	1	2. Twenty-Three Starlets (And Me)	RCA Victor 4270
			above two accompanied by Hugo Winterhalter's Orchestra	

ANDY GRIFFITH
These records made Andy an overnight comedy star, leading to a
long and successful career in movies ("A Face in the Crowd") and
TV (as Sherriff Andy Taylor in "The Andy Griffith Show", 1960-68)

1/09/54	**9**	6	1. What It Was, Was Football ....[T-C]	Capitol 2693
			Capitol purchased the master of this record from a regional label after it became a North Carolina sensation	
2/20/54	**27**	1	2. Romeo And Juliet...............................[T-C]	Capitol 2698
			billed on both as "Deacon Andy Griffith"	

FERDE GROFE & HIS ORCHESTRA
Pianist/arranger for Paul Whiteman from 1920-32, Ferde arranged
"Rhapsody in Blue" for George Gershwin in 1924, then achieved
enduring fame for his 1931 composition "The Grand Canyon Suite";
the 1942 hit song "Daybreak" was based on his "Mississippi Suite".
Ferde died on 4/3/72 (80).

12/23/33+	**19**	2	1. Temptation..	Columbia 2851
			band includes Tommy Dorsey (trombone) & Ross Gorman (clarinet/bass); song from the film "Going Hollywood"	

LOUISE GROODY
Broadway singer-dancer-actress; died on 9/16/61 (64).

8/06/27	**9**	4	1. Sometimes I'm Happy	Victor 20609
			CHARLES KING & LOUISE GROODY from the Broadway musical "Hit the Deck"	

HARRY GROVE TRIO

9/06/52	**11**	7	1. Meet Mr. Callaghan	London 1248

GUITAR SLIM
Eddie "Guitar Slim" Jones

2/20/54	**23**	2	● 1. The Things That I Used To Do.....................	Specialty 482
			#1 R&B hit; accompanied by Ray Charles (piano)	

WOODY GUTHRIE
Folk music's most legendary figure, and perhaps its greatest songwriter ("This Land Is Your Land", "So Long, It's Been Good to Know
Ya"), made familiar to most Americans by the Weavers; Woody died
on 10/4/67 (55), and son Arlo has been a folk star in the years
since.

H

BOBBY HACKETT
Renowned cornet player, with Hoarce Heidt (1940), Glenn Miller
(1941-42), the Casa Loma band (1944-46), & Jackie Gleason
(1953-55). (also see Johnny Desmond, Frank Sinatra)

BUDDY HACKETT
Popular comedian

12/26/53	**29**	1	1. The Chinese Waiter...........................[T-C]	Coral 61105

DATE CHARTED	PEAK POS	WKS CHRT'D	ARTIST — Record Title	Label & Number
			CHARLES HACKETT Renowned American tenor who sang with the Metropolitan Opera from 1919-22 & 1924-40; died on 1/01/42 (52).	
7/30/21	12	1	1. Love Sends A Little Gift Of Roses	Columbia 79518
			CASS HAGAN & HIS ORCHESTRA New York violinist-dance band leader	
8/06/27	20	1	1. Hallelujah!.............................. vocal: Franklyn Baur; from the Broadway musical "Hit the Deck"	Columbia 966
12/17/27	15	2	2. The Varsity Drag .... vocal: Franklyn Baur, Lewis James, & Elliott Shaw; with Red Nichols (trumpet); from the Broadway musical "Good News!"	Columbia 1114
			EARLE HAGEN Played trombone for late-1930s Ray Noble band; conductor/arranger for many singers (Buddy Clark, Dick Haymes, Helen Forrest, Tony Martin); composer of the jazz classic "Harlem Nocturne" and many TV themes (including "The Andy Griffith Show" & "I Spy").	
			CONNIE HAINES Born Yvonne Marie Jamais, Connie sang with Tommy Dorsey from 1940-42 ("Kiss the Boys Goodbye")	
8/28/48	29	1	1. At The Darktown Strutters' Ball................. CONNIE HAINES & ALAN DALE	Signature 15197
4/23/49	19	2	2. How It Lies, How It Lies, How It Lies! .... with Four Hits & a Miss	Coral 60044
9/24/49	20	1	3. Maybe It's Because.................................... with the Highlighters & Roy Ross' Orchestra from the Broadway musical "Along Fifth Avenue"	Coral 60070
5/08/54	27	1	4. Make A Joyful Noise Unto The Lord - Do Lord.. JANE RUSSELL, CONNIE HAINES, BERYL DAVID & DELLA RUSSELL with orchestra directed by Lyn Murray	Coral 61113
			BILL HALEY & HIS COMETS The pioneer group of rock and roll: guitarist and lead singer Bill Haley, featured saxophonist Rudy Pompelli, with John Grande, Billy Williamson, Al Rex, Francis Beecher, & Don Raymond. Bill died on 2/9/81 (55).	
5/23/53	12	10	1. Crazy, Man, Crazy..................................	Essex 321
8/15/53	24	3	2. Fractured	Essex 327
10/24/53	25	1	3. Live It Up	Essex 332
5/29/54	23	1	4. Rock Around The Clock .... when re-released a year later, this became the seminal hit of rock & roll, eventually selling more than 20 million copies	Decca 29124
8/21/54	7	27	● 5. Shake, Rattle, And Roll............................	Decca 29204
			ADELAIDE HALL Jazz singer; star of Broadway's "Blackbirds of 1928"; recorded with Duke Ellington.	
			GEORGE HALL & HIS ORCHESTRA New York-based bandleader whose most prominent musician was guitarist Tony Mottola. Singer Dolly Dawn, who later became his adoptive daughter, made many records under her own name with the Hall band.	
12/22/34	12	3	1. Santa Claus Is Comin' To Town .... [X] vocal: Sonny Schuyler	Bluebird 5711
5/18/35	20	1	2. I Won't Dance .... vocal: Loretta Lee & Sonny Schuyler; from the film "Roberta"	Bluebird 5863
4/18/36	20	2	3. Every Minute Of The Hour	Bluebird 6282
6/13/36	5	10	4. Would You?.. from the film "San Francisco"	Bluebird 6375
12/26/36+	5	6	5. The Night Is Young And You're So Beautiful.. above two vocals: Johnny McKeever	Bluebird 6702
2/27/37	15	3	6. When The Poppies Bloom Again .... vocals on 3 & 6: Dolly Dawn	Bluebird 6801
5/08/37	5	4	7. There's A Lull In My Life .... from the film "Wake Up and Live"	Variety 526

DATE CHARTED	PEAK POS	WKS CHRT'D	ARTIST — Record Title	Label & Number
9/11/37	18	1	8. My Cabin Of Dreams................................ also on Vocalion 3775	Variety 611
3/19/38	9	4	9. Ti-Pi-Pin... adaptation of a popular Spanish song	Vocalion 3991
5/21/38	13	2	10. Oh! Ma-Ma (The Butcher Boy)...................... based on the Italian song "Luna Merro Mare"	Vocalion 4085
6/25/38	10	3	11. Says My Heart.................................... from the film "The Cocoanut Grove"	Vocalion 4098
9/17/38	8	3	12. I've Got A Date With A Dream..................... from the film "My Lucky Star"	Vocalion 4283
11/05/38	17	2	13. My Own... from the film "That Certain Age" vocals on 10 & 13, & most others 1937-38: Dolly Dawn	Vocalion 4297

HENRY HALL & THE B.B.C. DANCE ORCHESTRA
The British Broadcasting Corporation's resident dance band

DATE CHARTED	PEAK POS	WKS CHRT'D	ARTIST — Record Title	Label & Number
4/21/34	9	7	1. Play To Me, Gypsy	Columbia 2910

JAMES HALL
Pseudonym for Andrea Sarto

JUANITA HALL
Most famous for portraying Bloody Mary in both the Broadway and film versions of "South Pacific"; died on 2/28/68 (60).

DATE CHARTED	PEAK POS	WKS CHRT'D	ARTIST — Record Title	Label & Number
11/05/49	22	4	1. Don't Cry, Joe (Let Her Go, Let Her Go, Let Her Go)...	RCA Victor 3557

WENDELL HALL
Ukelele-playing Wendell Hall created a popular sensation with his debut hit, and quickly became a radio and vaudeville favorite.

DATE CHARTED	PEAK POS	WKS CHRT'D	ARTIST — Record Title	Label & Number
1/26/24	1(6)	20	● 1. **It Ain't Gonna Rain No Mo'/** sold over 2 million copies; based on traditional 19th Century Kentucky folk song; also recorded for Edison 51261 & Gennett 5271	
4/05/24	4	3	2. Red-Headed Music Maker	Victor 19171
6/28/24	9	2	3. It Looks Like Rain	Victor 19270
7/19/24	8	1	4. Oh Susanna .... WENDELL HALL & SHANNON FOUR	Victor 19290
10/04/24	10	1	5. Whistling The Blues Away......................... with whistling by Carson Robinson	Victor 19338
3/26/27	13	3	6. I'm Tellin' The Birds, I'm Tellin' The Bees (How I Love You) .... with Carson Robinson	Brunswick 3387

MAL HALLET & HIS ORCHESTRA
New England bandleader and violinist whose original bands included Toots Mondello (alto sax) and Gene Krupa. Pianist Frankie Carle was featured on most of his charted hits; Mal died on 11/20/52 (59).

DATE CHARTED	PEAK POS	WKS CHRT'D	ARTIST — Record Title	Label & Number
12/19/36+	11	3	1. In The Chapel In The Moonlight..................	Decca 1033
2/20/37	20	1	2. One In A Million .... movie title song	Decca 1116
3/27/37	3	6	3. Boo Hoo .... above three vocals by Jerry Perkins	Decca 1162
6/12/37	19	2	4. Turn Off The Moon............................... movie title song	Decca 1270
6/26/37	9	3	5. (Have You Forgotten) The You And Me That Used To Be.................................... above two vocals: Teddy Grace	Decca 1281

WILLIAM J. HALLEY
Real name William J. Hanley; the only charted artist who became a state legislator (New Jersey Assembly, 1917-18) and a judge (Hoboken District Court Judge from 1923-33). He died on 11/14/61 (68).

DATE CHARTED	PEAK POS	WKS CHRT'D	ARTIST — Record Title	Label & Number
9/27/13	6	3	1. You Made Me Love You (I Didn't Want To Do It)...	Victor 17381
5/09/14	8	1	2. Do You Take This Woman For Your Lawful Wife?	Columbia 1497

DATE CHARTED	PEAK POS	WKS CHRT'D	ARTIST — Record Title	Label & Number

STUART HAMBLEN
Country and gospel singer/songwriter (composer of "This Ole House"); started in early 30s with Beverly Hill Billies group.

11/13/54	**26**	4	1. This Ole House	RCA Victor 5739

EDWARD HAMILTON
Pseudonym for Reinald Werrenrath

GEORGE HAMILTON
Hotel band leader, conducted Chicago Opera orchestra several years; died on 3/31/57 (56).

12/19/36+	**12**	4	1. With Plenty Of Money And You	Victor 25458
			vocal: Lee Norton; from the film "Gold Diggers of 1937"	

ROY HAMILTON
Popular R&B ballad singer from New Jersey; died on 7/20/69 (40).

1/30/54	**21**	7	1. You'll Never Walk Alone	Epic 9015
5/22/54	**26**	1	2. If I Loved You	Epic 9047
			above two from the Broadway musical "Carousel"	
10/02/54	**30**	1	3. Ebb Tide	Epic 9068
			orchestra on above two directed by O.B. Masingill	

JOHNNY HAMP & HIS ORCHESTRA
Band originally billed as "Johnny Hamp & His Kentucky Serenaders".

1/30/26	**13**	1	1. Cecelia	Victor 19756
11/27/26	**9**	1	2. That's Why I Love You	Victor 20105
			above two vocals: Charles Buckwalter-Frank Master-Elwood Groff	
12/04/26	**3**	6	3. Black Bottom.................................... [I]	Victor 20101
			from the Broadway musical "George White's Scandals of 1926"; one of 1920s' most popular dances	
12/10/27	**5**	6	4. I Fell Head Over Heels In Love	Victor 20923
			vocal: Hal White; from the Broadway musical "The Merry World"	
10/20/28	**4**	9	5. I Can't Give You Anything But Love............	Victor 21514
			vocal: Joe Cassidy, Hal White & Elwood Groff from the musical "Blackbirds of 1928"	
12/22/28+	**14**	3	6. Blue Shadows	Victor 21632
			vocal: Frank Munn; from the Broadway musical "Earl Carroll's Vanities of 1928"	
11/16/29	**10**	9	7. Sunny Side Up/	
11/23/29+	**5**	8	8. If I Had A Talking Picture Of You	Victor 22124
			above two from the film "Sunny Side Up"	
5/16/31	**12**	4	9. Two Hearts In Waltz Time	Victor 22638
7/18/31	**10**	3	10. On The Beach With You...........................	Victor 22730
			above vocals: Cliff Gamet	
5/07/32	**11**	6	11. By A Rippling Stream	Victor 22999
			vocal: Cliff Gamet, Charles Socci & Carl Grobb	
5/28/32	**8**	5	12. Hummin' To Myself	Victor 24000
			vocal: Carl Grobb	

LIONEL HAMPTON & HIS ORCHESTRA
Great jazz vibraphonist also adept on piano and drums, Lionel Hampton started his career in late-1920s Chicago, gained fame playing with Benny Goodman a decade later, and remains an active performer in the 1980s. His bands featured many enduring giants of jazz, including bassist-composer Charles Mingus, trumpeter-arranger Quincy Jones, and singers Dinah Washington and Joe Williams. (All vocals by Lionel except as noted)

3/27/37	**20**	1	1. The Mood That I'm In	Victor 25527
			with Gene Krupa (drums)	
6/26/37	**16**	1	2. China Stomp.. [I]	Victor 25586
			with Johnny Hodges (alto sax)	
9/25/37	**14**	2	3. Confessin' (That I Love You)	Victor 25658
11/06/37	**6**	3	4. After You've Gone	Victor 25674
5/20/39	**10**	5	5. Wizzin' The Wiz .... [I]	Victor 26233
			Lionel's most famous piano performance Cozy Cole (drums) on above four	
9/02/39	**15**	1	6. The Jumpin' Jive....................................	Victor 26304
			with Rex Stewart (cornet), Lawrence Brown (trombone), & Harry Carney (baritone sax)	

DATE CHARTED	PEAK POS	WKS CHRT'D	ARTIST — Record Title	Label & Number
5/11/40	25	1	7. Flying Home .... [I]	Victor 26595
			Ziggy Elman (trumpet) on 1, 4, & 7	
7/18/42	23	1	8. Flying Home .... [I]	Decca 18394
			the most renowned version of Hampton's jazz classic, with tenor sax solo by Illinois Jacquet; Dexter Gordon also on tenor sax	
9/30/44	23	1	9. Hamp's Boogie Woogie........................... [I]	Decca 18613
			with Earl Bostic (alto sax)	
3/02/46	9	8	10. Hey! Ba-Ba-Re-Bop	Decca 18754
			with Herbie Fields (alto sax)	
5/10/47	21	1	11. Blow Top Blues	Decca 23792
			vocal: Dinah Washington	
2/04/50	7	10	12. Rag Mop..	Decca 24855
			vocal: Hamptones; with Wes Montgomery (guitar)	

W.C. HANDY'S ORCHESTRA
Known worldwide as "The Father of the Blues", William Christopher Handy was born on 11/16/1873 in Florence, Ala. After years as a cornetist, bandleader, & music teacher, his acclaim as a songwriter began in 1913 with "The Memphis Blues"; a year later came the most-recorded American song of all time, "St. Louis Blues". Handy died on 3/29/58, the same year Nat King Cole starred in the film based on his life.

DATE CHARTED	PEAK POS	WKS CHRT'D	ARTIST — Record Title	Label & Number
2/02/18	7	2	1. Livery Stable Blues............................... [I]	Columbia 2419
11/24/23	9	1	2. St. Louis Blues...................................... [I]	Okeh 4896

PETE HANLEY

DATE CHARTED	PEAK POS	WKS CHRT'D	ARTIST — Record Title	Label & Number
4/11/53	19	6	1. Big Mamou	Okeh 6956
			Cajun song with French & English choruses	
6/27/53	28	1	2. Help Me Mend A Broken Heart	Okeh 6980
			above two with Leydon Brothers' Orchestra	

PHIL HANNA
Sang briefly with Russ Morgan

DATE CHARTED	PEAK POS	WKS CHRT'D	ARTIST — Record Title	Label & Number
9/09/44	13	4	1. A Fellow On A Furlough.............................	Decca 4448
			accompanied by Leonard Joy's Orchestra from the film "Miss Bobby Socks"	

ANNETTE HANSHAW
New York-born radio and record star, featured in mid-30s on Glen Gray's radio show; died on 3/14/85 (74).

DATE CHARTED	PEAK POS	WKS CHRT'D	ARTIST — Record Title	Label & Number
11/10/28	10	3	1. For Old Times' Sake	Harmony 666
5/18/29	19	1	2. In A Great Big Way	Harmony 832
8/03/29	10	3	3. Big City Blues	Columbia 1812
			from the film "Fox Movietone Follies of 1929"	
10/19/29	11	2	4. Am I Blue?	Harmony 940
			from the film "On With the Show"	
11/15/30	12	2	5. Body And Soul	Harmony 1224
			from the Broadway musical "Three's a Crowd"	

HAPPINESS BOYS - see ERNEST HARE & BILLY JONES

HAPPY SIX
Band featuring Phil Ohman (piano) & George Hamilton Green (xylophone)

DATE CHARTED	PEAK POS	WKS CHRT'D	ARTIST — Record Title	Label & Number
7/31/20	8	1	1. My Sahara Rose .... [I]	Columbia 2934
4/30/21	6	2	2. Do You Ever Think Of Me? .... [I]	Columbia 3372

ROGER HARDING
Original member of the Edison Male Quartet (1894) who also made some of the earliest commercial children's records; died in 1901 (making him the first charted recording artist to die).

DATE CHARTED	PEAK POS	WKS CHRT'D	ARTIST — Record Title	Label & Number
9/11/97	2(2)	3	1. Bye And Bye You Will Forget Me	Columbia 8404
			LEN SPENCER & ROGER HARDING	
2/05/98	3	3	2. On The Banks Of The Wabash....................	Edison 2042

DATE CHARTED	PEAK POS	WKS CHRT'D	ARTIST — Record Title	Label & Number
			ERNEST HARE Former understudy to Al Jolson who became half of radio's most famous comedy singing team with Billy Jones, as gifted a ballad singer as he was at novelties; died on 3/9/39 (55). (also see Carl Fenton)	
3/08/19	**10**	1	1. A Good Man Is Hard To Find	Emerson 9112
10/04/19	**4**	3	2. I Want To Hold You In My Arms .... [C] AL BERNARD & ERNEST HARE	Edison 50558
10/23/20	**10**	1	3. Old Pal, Why Don't You Answer Me?	Brunswick 2057
11/26/21	**12**	1	4. Tuck Me To Sleep (In My Old 'Tucky Home) ...	Pathe 20612
4/08/22	**9**	1	5. April Showers .... from the Broadway musical "Bombo"	Brunswick 2188
12/23/22+	**5**	3	6. My Buddy..	Brunswick 2320
5/31/24	**12**	1	7. Mindin' My Business	Okeh 40055
			ERNEST HARE & BILLY JONES Throughout the 1920s and 30s radio audiences were entertained by the famous team of baritone Ernest Hare & tenor Billy Jones, a partnership ended only by Ernie's death in 1939.	
8/06/21	**5**	3	1. Down Yonder .... also recorded for Brunswick 2101	Okeh 4347
5/13/22	**9**	2	2. Indiana Lullaby	Columbia 3564
7/01/22	**2(2)**	8	3. In The Little Red School House .... [C] also on Edison Amberol 4553	Edison 50962
8/05/22	**1(2)**	9	4. **Mr. Gallagher And Mr. Shean**.............. [C] also recorded for Brunswick 2270	Okeh 4608
2/17/23	**9**	1	5. Toot Toot Tootsie (Goo'bye)................... [N] from the Broadway musical "Bombo"	Okeh 4726
4/04/23	**8**	1	6. You Tell Her - I Stutter .... [C] also recorded for Okeh 4756, Vocalion 14459, & Gennett 5007	Edison 51079
7/21/23	**2(2)**	7	7. Barney Google .... [C] also recorded for Brunswick 2425, Okeh 4828, Edison 51155, Vocalion 14556, & Emerson 10622	Columbia 3876
10/27/23	**12**	1	8. Oh Gee, Oh Gosh, Oh Golly (I'm In Love) ... [C] they also did vocal chorus on Ben Selvin's version of song, Vocalion 14674; from the Broadway musical "Ziegfeld Follies of 1922"	Edison 51193
12/22/23+	**6**	3	9. That Old Gang Of Mine............................	Edison 51235
2/23/24	**11**	1	10. Last Night On The Back Porch .... [C]	Okeh 4948
4/26/24	**14**	1	11. Syncopated Opera................................. [C]	Okeh 40032
6/28/24	**11**	1	12. It Ain't Gonna Rain No Mo'..................... [C]	Columbia
7/12/24	**9**	1	13. Does The Spearment Lose Its Flavor On The Bedpost Overnight? .... [C] song revived as Top Ten hit for Lonnie Donegan in 1961	Cameo 504
10/13/24	**5**	2	14. Hinky Dinky Parley Voo........................ [C] also recorded for Okeh 40128 as "Whatever Became of Hinkey Dinkey Parley Voo?"	Columbia 132
12/27/24	**14**	1	15. She Loves Me	Columbia 194
4/11/25	**8**	1	16. How Do You Do?................................... [C] the duo's famous theme song also recorded for Brunswick 2791	Edison 51500
8/01/25	**5**	4	17. Don't Bring Lulu................................. [C] also recorded for Edison 51555	Okeh 40354
9/19/25	**7**	2	18. If You Knew Susie................................ [C] Billy Jones also recorded song for Domino 1558 & Regal 9857	Brunswick 2888
10/03/25	**3**	5	19. I Miss My Swiss (My Swiss Miss Misses Me) .... [C] also recorded for Columbia 410 & Harmony 9	Victor 19718
3/20/26	**9**	1	20. That Certain Party............................... [C]	Victor 19865
3/27/26	**12**	1	21. Show Me The Way To Go Home .... also recorded for Banner 1649, Domino 3622, & Regal 9954	Edison 51660
12/18/26+	**6**	4	22. Gentlemen Prefer Blondes .... from the Broadway musical "Queen High"	Edison 51802
12/25/26	**15**	1	23. How Many Times?............................... [C]	Columbia 700
6/11/27	**16**	1	24. I've Never Seen A Straight Banana .... [C] also recorded for Edison 51973	Columbia 898

DATE CHARTED	PEAK POS	WKS CHRT'D	ARTIST — Record Title	Label & Number
10/01/27	**9**	5	25. You Don't Like It - Not Much .... [C]	Victor 20756
3/31/28	**7**	5	26. Henry's Made A Lady Out Of Lizzie .... [C] song about Henry Ford's "Tin Lizzie"; also recorded for Edison 52200 & 5476	Victor 21174
11/03/28	**17**	1	27. Mr. Hoover And Mr. Smith .... also recorded for Columbia 1483 & Edison 52367	Victor 21607

BOB HARING & HIS ORCHESTRA
Bandleader and composer, also conductor on 1930s radio; also see
Colonial Club Orchestra

DATE CHARTED	PEAK POS	WKS CHRT'D	ARTIST — Record Title	Label & Number
6/22/29	**1(4)**	11	1. **Pagan Love Song** .... Copley Plaza Orchestra; from the film "The Pagan"	Brunswick 4321
7/20/29	**19**	1	2. Fioretta .... Broadway musical title song	Brunswick 4288
8/16/30	**14**	3	3. I Love You So Much/ from the film "The Cuckoos"	
8/23/30	**4**	10	4. **Betty Co-Ed**	Brunswick 4852

BYRON G. HARLAN
Kansas-born (8/29/1861) Byron G. Harlan became famous for his long
series of hit duets with Arthur Collins, but enjoyed great success
as a solo artist as well. Many of his individual hits were
sentimental ballads, in contrast to the duo's emphasis on ragtime
and minstrel humor. Long a friend and neighbor of Thomas Edison,
Harlan died on 9/11/36. (See Collins & Harlan for duet hits)

DATE CHARTED	PEAK POS	WKS CHRT'D	ARTIST — Record Title	Label & Number
9/23/99	**2(1)**	5	1. Please, Mr. Conductor, Don't Put Me Off This Train..	Edison 7219
2/03/00	**2(2)**	6	2. In The Shadow Of The Pines .... BYRON HARLAN & A.D. MADEIRA	Edison 7347
2/02/01	**3**	4	3. When The Harvest Days Are Over .... also recorded for Edison 7670	Columbia 31521
6/22/01	**1(3)**	6	4. **Tell Me, Pretty Maiden** .... BYRON HARLAN, FRANK STANLEY, JOE BELMONT, & THE FLORODORA GIRLS from the Broadway musical "Florodora"	Columbia 31604
8/03/01	**1(5)**	9	5. **Hello Central, Give Me Heaven**................. later recorded for Columbia disc 230	Edison 7852
8/23/02	**1(3)**	10	6. **The Mansion Of Aching Hearts**	Edison 8093
8/30/02	**4**	2	7. First Rehearsal For The Huskin' Bee .... [C] later recorded for Columbia 916 & 31856	Edison 8096
11/15/02	**3**	3	8. Two Rubes In A Tavern .... [C] also recorded for Edison 8121 above two & 10: BYRON HARLAN & FRANK STANLEY	Columbia 938
11/22/02	**4**	2	9. The Birds .... BYRON HARLAN & JOE BELMONT	Columbia 927
12/13/02	**5**	1	10. Closing Time At A Country Grocery .... [C] later recorded for Columbia 1141 & 32077, also by Collins & Harlan for Victor 1728	Edison 8172
3/28/03	**3**	4	11. There's No Place Like Home	Edison 8306
4/25/03	**2(1)**	5	12. Please, Mamma, Buy Me A Baby .... also recorded for Columbia 1192 & 32127 later for Victor 2155	Edison 8369
11/14/03	**2(2)**	4	13. Always In The Way .... later recorded for Columbia 1662 & 32370	Edison 8501
1/02/04	**5**	1	14. In The Village By The Sea .... also on Victor 31191 & Edison 8533	Victor 2567
5/14/04	**1(4)**	7	15. **Blue Bell** .... BYRON HARLAN & FRANK STANLEY	Edison 8655
8/27/04	**1(2)**	8	16. **All Aboard For Dreamland** .... also recorded for Columbia 1841 & 32545	Edison 8700
10/01/04	**4**	1	17. Good-Bye, Little Girl, Good-Bye .... also on Columbia cylinder 32546	Columbia 1840
2/25/05	**9**	1	18. The Battle Cry Of Freedom	Victor 4099
3/25/05	**8**	1	19. Soldier Boy.. also on Columbia cylinder 32644; from the Broadway musical "Rogers Brothers in Paris" above two: BYRON HARLAN & FRANK STANLEY	Columbia 3067
4/15/05	**4**	2	20. It Makes Me Think Of Home, Sweet Home...... also recorded for Victor 4255, Columbia 3081 & 32658	Edison 8932

DATE CHARTED	PEAK POS	WKS CHRT'D	ARTIST — Record Title	Label & Number
7/29/05	**5**	1	21. Longing For You..	Columbia 3187
9/02/05	**5**	1	22. A Picnic For Two	Columbia 3231
9/30/05	**2(2)**	4	23. Would You Care?	Victor 4425
11/11/05	**1(5)**	11	24. **Where The Morning Glories Twine Around The Door**..	Columbia 3282
11/25/05	**4**	2	25. The Message Of The Old Church Bell	Victor 4494
2/03/06	**1(9)**	17	26. **Wait Till The Sun Shines, Nellie** .... also recorded for Edison 9130	Columbia 3321
3/17/06	**2(3)**	6	27. Daddy's Little Girl .... also recorded for Edison 9202	Victor 4604
6/02/06	**2(4)**	6	28. Keep On The Sunny Side........................ also recorded for Columbia 3398 & 32942, Imperial 44758, & International 2094	Edison 9271
9/15/06	**1(4)**	7	29. **The Good Old U.S.A.**............................ also on Columbia cylinder 32997, Edison 9350, Zon-o-Phone 539, Imperial 45187, & International 3124	Columbia 3463
2/05/07	**1(10)**	13	30. **My Gal Sal**...	Victor 4918
3/30/07	**7**	1	31. Won't You Come Over To My House?...........	Victor 4939
5/11/07	**1(11)**	16	32. **School Days (When We Were A Couple Of Kids)**	Victor 5086
			also recorded for Columbia 33128 & Edison 9562	
7/20/07	**1(3)**	7	33. **Nobody's Little Girl**............................... also recorded for Edison 9539 & Columbia 85123	Victor 5147
7/27/07	**6**	1	34. In The Wildwood Where The Blue Bells Grew . BYRON HARLAN & FRANK STANLEY	Edison 9567
8/31/07	**8**	1	35. It's Great To Be A Soldier Man	Edison 9600
9/28/07	**9**	1	36. I'm Tying The Leaves So They Won't Come Down .... later recorded for Victor 16122	Edison 9606
12/28/07+	**3**	4	37. Two Blue Eyes (Two Little Baby Shoes)........ also recorded for Edison 9766	Victor 5310
4/18/08	**3**	4	38. There Never Was A Girl Like You	Edison 9795
11/21/08	**4**	2	39. Sunbonnet Sue.......................................	Edison 9958
11/28/08	**8**	1	40. Are You Sincere?....................................	Edison 9973
3/13/09	**3**	4	41. Meet Me In Rose-Time, Rosie...................... BYRON HARLAN & FRANK STANLEY also recorded for Edison 10079	Columbia 630
6/19/09	**5**	1	42. School Mates .... also recorded for Indestructable 1053 & Zon-o-Phone 5488	Edison 10159
11/27/09	**6**	1	43. Lonesome... also recorded for Indestructable 1184	Edison 10219
12/25/09	**5**	2	44. Let's Go In To A Picture Show .... also recorded for Edison 10269; one of the first hit songs about the movies	Indestructable 1202
5/21/10	**6**	2	45. Put On Your Old Gray Bonnet	Indestructable 1303
10/15/10	**1(1)**	9	46. **Tramp! Tramp! Tramp!** .... BYRON HARLAN & FRANK STANLEY from the Broadway musical "Naughty Maruetta"	Victor 16531
10/22/10	**4**	4	47. Sweet Italian Love .... from the Broadway musical "Up and Down Broadway"	Columbia 896
5/06/11	**7**	2	48. Think It Over, Mary................................. also recorded for Columbia 965	Victor 16712
9/23/11	**4**	3	49. Chicken Reel .... BYRON HARLAN & FRANK STANLEY also recorded for Columbia 1044	Victor 16897
5/29/15	**6**	3	50. By Heck.. [C] BYRON HARLAN & WILL ROBBINS	Columbia 1722
11/13/15	**9**	1	51. The Village Gossips............................. [C] CAL STEWART & BYRON HARLAN	Victor 17854

DATE CHARTED	PEAK POS	WKS CHRT'D	ARTIST — Record Title	Label & Number
6/30/17	**6**	4	52. With His Hands In His Pockets And His Pockets In His Pants/ [C] also recorded for Edison Amberol 3124	
7/14/17	**3**	4	53. I'm A Twelve O'Clock Fellow In A Nine O'Clock Town.................. [C] Columbia 2219 also recorded for Victor 18364, Emerson 7226, & Gennett 7616	
5/10/19	**9**	1	54. How Ya Gonna Keep 'Em Down On The Farm (After They've Seen Paree) .... Edison 50518 also recorded for Emerson 9140, Pathe 22078, & Empire 21105	

HARMONICATS
Turkish-born Jerry Murad led this trend-setting harmonica group.
(also see Jerry Byrd, Richard Hayman, & Roberta Quinlan)

DATE CHARTED	PEAK POS	WKS CHRT'D	ARTIST — Record Title	Label & Number
4/26/47	**1(8)**	26	● 1. **Peg O' My Heart**.................. [I] Vitacoustic 1 from the Broadway musical "Ziegfeld Follies of 1913"	
11/15/47	**21**	1	2. Peggy O'Neil .... [I] Vitacoustic 7 song published in 1921	
8/14/48	**15**	9	3. Hair Of Gold (Eyes Of Blue).................. [I] Universal 121 from the film "Singin' Spurs"	
5/20/50	**8**	12	4. Bewitched .... [I] Mercury 5399 JAN AUGUST & JERRY MURAD'S HARMONICATS from the Broadway musical "Pal Joey"	
12/29/51	**21**	2	5. Charmaine .... [I] Mercury 5747 written to promote the 1927 silent film "What Price Glory?"	
3/21/53	**26**	1	6. Till I Waltz Again With You .... [I] Mercury 70069	

TONI HARPER & EAST BEALE SEXTET
Precocious jazz-influenced singer barely 11 years old in 1948,
later sang with Harry James.

DATE CHARTED	PEAK POS	WKS CHRT'D	ARTIST — Record Title	Label & Number
6/26/48	**22**	3	1. Candy Store Blues .... Columbia 38229	

HARPTONES
R&B group led by tenor Willie Winfield

DATE CHARTED	PEAK POS	WKS CHRT'D	ARTIST — Record Title	Label & Number
9/18/54	**25**	1	1. Why Should I Love You? .... Bruce 109 with the Shytans	

BILL HARRIS
Ten-time Down Beat poll winner as top trombonist; with Bob Chester
(1943), Benny Goodman (1944), & Woody Herman (1944-46, 48-50,
56-57).

MARION HARRIS
One of the 1920s' most popular singers, Marion was also featured
in several Broadway musicals; she died on 4/23/44 (48) in a hotel
fire.

DATE CHARTED	PEAK POS	WKS CHRT'D	ARTIST — Record Title	Label & Number
12/02/16	**8**	2	1. I'm Gonna Make Hay While The Sun Shines In Virginia.................. Victor 18143	
1/13/17	**5**	4	2. I Ain't Got Nobody Much .... Victor 18133 same song later known as "I Ain't Got Nobody"	
2/10/17	**7**	2	3. Paradise Blues .... Victor 18152	
12/15/17	**2(2)**	5	4. They Go Wild, Simply Wild, Over Me .... Victor 18343	
5/04/18	**3**	5	5. Everybody's Crazy 'Bout The Doggone Blues (But I'm Happy) .... Victor 18443	
9/14/18	**4**	4	6. When Alexander Takes His Ragtime Band To France.................. Victor 18486	
9/21/18	**8**	2	7. There's A Lump Of Sugar Down In Dixie .... Victor 18482	
1/18/19	**1(3)**	9	8. **After You've Gone** .... Victor 18509	
5/03/19	**2(2)**	9	9. A Good Man Is Hard To Find .... Victor 18535	
7/12/19	**3**	7	10. Jazz Baby .... Victor 18555	
9/27/19	**5**	4	11. Take Me To The Land Of Jazz.................. Victor 18593 accompanied on most Victor records by Rosario Bourdon's Orchestra	
7/31/20	**5**	3	12. Left All Alone Again Blues .... Columbia 2939 from the Broadway musical "The Night Boat"	
8/28/20	**1(3)**	9	13. **St. Louis Blues** .... Columbia 2944	
10/30/20	**11**	1	14. Oh! Judge (He Treats Me Mean) .... Columbia 2968	
12/18/20+	**4**	6	15. Sweet Mama (Papa's Gettin' Mad).................. Columbia 3300	

DATE CHARTED	PEAK POS	WKS CHRT'D	ARTIST — Record Title	Label & Number
2/19/21	**8**	2	16. I'm A Jazz Vampire................................	Columbia 3328
3/19/21	**7**	2	17. Grieving For You	Columbia 3353
4/23/21	**1(3)**	10	18. **Look For The Silver Lining**	Columbia 3367
			from the Broadway musical "Sally"	
6/04/21	**3**	7	19. I Ain't Got Nobody	Columbia 3371
			new version of her 1917 hit	
10/24/21	**3**	8	20. I'm Nobody's Baby	Columbia 3433
12/17/21	**5**	4	21. Beale Street Blues	Columbia 3474
6/17/22	**3**	5	22. Some Sunny Day	Columbia 3593
10/07/22	**4**	5	23. Nobody Lied (When They Said That I Cried	
			Over You)...	Columbia 3646
			accompanied on most Columbia records by Charles Prince's Orchestra	
10/21/22	**4**	5	24. I'm Just Wild About Harry	Brunswick 2309
			from the Broadway musical "Shuffle Along"	
			accompanied on some Brunswicks by Carl Fenton's Orchestra	
10/28/22	**5**	3	25. Sweet Indiana Home/	
			with Isham Jones' Orchestra	
12/23/22+	**7**	3	26. Blue (And Broken Hearted)	Brunswick 2310
1/27/23	**4**	4	27. Carolina In The Morning	Brunswick 2329
3/31/23	**3**	6	28. Aggravatin' Papa	Brunswick 2345
4/11/23	**3**	6	29. Rose Of The Rio Grande...........................	Brunswick 2370
7/28/23	**7**	4	30. Beside A Babbling Brook...........................	Brunswick 2421
9/01/23	**5**	4	31. Who's Sorry Now?..................................	Brunswick 2443
10/20/23	**6**	3	32. Dirty Hands! Dirty Face!	Brunswick 2458
7/26/24	**3**	5	33. It Had To Be You/	
8/16/24	**5**	4	34. How Come You Do Me Like You Do?	Brunswick 2610
9/06/24	**3**	6	35. Jealous..	Brunswick 2622
10/01/24	**7**	3	36. There'll Be Some Changes Made	Brunswick 2651
1/10/25	**7**	2	37. Somebody Loves Me	Brunswick 2735
			from the Broadway musical "George White's Scandals of 1924"	
1/24/25	**1(3)**	11	38. **Tea For Two**	Brunswick 2747
			from the Broadway musical "No, No, Nanette"	
3/28/25	**4**	5	39. I'll See You In My Dreams	Brunswick 2784
6/27/25	**11**	1	40. When You And I Were Seventeen.................	Brunswick 2836
3/10/28	**4**	7	41. The Man I Love/	
			from the Broadway musical "Lady, Be Good"	
3/17/28	**14**	2	42. Did You Mean It?...................................	Victor 21116
1/18/30	**20**	1	43. Nobody's Using It Now	Brunswick 4663
			from the film "The Love Parade"	

PHIL HARRIS

Best known as a movie/radio/TV personality, Phil was also a popular bandleader, having previously played drums in Francis Craig's 1920s band. Phil married actress Alice Faye, and they co-hosted a 1947-54 radio program. (All vocals by Phil)

DATE CHARTED	PEAK POS	WKS CHRT'D	ARTIST — Record Title	Label & Number
3/25/33	**8**	7	1. What Have We Got To Lose? (Heigh-Ho	
			Lackaway)	Columbia 2761
5/06/33	**10**	5	2. How's About It? .... [C]	Columbia 2766
10/26/35	**15**	4	3. I'd Love To Take Orders From You	Decca 564
			from the film "Shipmates Forever"	
3/16/46	**2(2)**	10	4. One-Zy, Two-Zy (I Love You-Zy)	ARA 136
3/23/46	**10**	3	5. The Darktown Poker Club .... [C]	ARA 116
			from the Broadway musical "Ziegfeld Follies of 1914"	
3/15/47	**21**	1	6. That's What I Like About The South .... [C]	RCA Victor 2089
			Phil's trademark song	
3/29/47	**22**	3	7. The Preacher And The Bear..................... [C]	RCA Victor 2143
8/23/47	**8**	4	8. Smoke! Smoke! Smoke! (That Cigarette).... [C]	RCA Victor 2370
12/13/47	**27**	1	9. The Dark Town Poker Club...................... [C]	RCA Victor 2471
			new version of his 1946 hit	
5/08/48	**20**	2	10. Deck Of Cards .... [C]	RCA Victor 2821
12/31/49+	**10**	8	11. The Old Master Painter	RCA Vic. 78-3608

DATE CHARTED	PEAK POS	WKS CHRT'D	ARTIST — Record Title	Label & Number
3/11/50	**8**	6	12. Chattanoogie Shoe Shine Boy	RCA Vic. 78-3692
9/02/50	**30**	1	13. Play A Simple Melody..................................	RCA Victor 3781
			from the Broadway musical "Watch Your Step"	
11/25/50	**1(5)**	15	● 14. **The Thing** .... [C]	RCA Victor 3968
			with Walter Scharf's Orchestra	
			uses melody of the traditional song "The Tailor's Boy"	
9/01/51	**24**	2	15. The Musicians...	RCA Victor 4225
			DINAH SHORE, TONY MARTIN, BETTY HUTTON & PHIL HARRIS	
			with Henri Rene's Orchestra	
			novelty adaptation of a Haydn Theme	
3/15/52	**19**	6	16. Hambone...	RCA Victor 4584
			BELL SISTERS with PHIL HARRIS	

WYNONIE HARRIS
Acclaimed blues 'shouter' who made his reputation in the 40s with
Lucky Millinder; Wynonie's 1948 R&B smash "Good Rockin' Tonight"
was a historic precursor of rock & roll. He died on 6/14/69 (53).

CHARLES HARRISON
Extremely popular tenor ballad singer, a member of Columbia
Stellar Quartet and Columbia Mixed Quartet; in 1920s he sang
briefly with the Revelers, then late in decade formed the American
Singers. Charles died on 2/2/65 (74). (also see Joseph C. Smith's
Orchestra)

DATE CHARTED	PEAK POS	WKS CHRT'D	ARTIST — Record Title	Label & Number
2/17/12	**9**	1	1. I'm Falling In Love With Someone...............	Columbia 5327
			from the Broadway musical "Naughty Marietta"	
3/16/12	**9**	1	2. Wallflower Sweet	Columbia 5329
			CHARLES HARRISON & GRACE KERNS	
			from the Broadway musical "The Siren"	
10/11/13	**6**	3	3. Last Night Was The End Of The World.........	Edison Amb. 1786
11/08/13	**1(7)**	14	4. **Peg O' My Heart**..............................'.....	Victor 17412
			from Broadway musical "Ziegfeld Follies of 1913"	
3/28/14	**4**	5	5. Little Grey Home In The West	Victor 17522
9/05/14	**4**	6	6. Love Has Wings/	
9/12/14	**6**	4	7. Love's Own Sweet Song	Columbia 5574
			above two: CHARLES HARRISON & GRACE KERNS	
			both from the Broadway musical "Sari"	
11/28/14	**4**	7	8. Mary, You're A Little Bit Old-Fashioned........	Victor 17638
2/25/15+	**8**	2	9. When You're In Love With Someone Who Is	
			Not In Love With You..........................	Victor 17877
7/17/15	**2(2)**	6	10. A Little Bit Of Heaven (Shure, They Call It	
			Ireland).......................................	Victor 17780
			from the Broadway musical "The Heart of Paddy Whack"	
10/09/15	**9**	1	11. There's A Long, Long Trail........................	Columbia 1791
			"BILLY BURTON & HERBERT STUART"	
			pseudonyms for Charles Harrison and Albert Wiederhold	
5/20/16	**9**	1	12. She's The Daughter Of Mother Machree	Victor 17948
10/21/16	**1(3)**	8	13. **Ireland Must Be Heaven, For My Mother**	
			Came From There	Victor 18111
2/03/17	**5**	3	14. Give Me All Of You..................................	Columbia 2128
			CHARLES HARRISON & NANETTE FLACK	
			from the Broadway musical "Flora Bella"	
6/02/17	**5**	2	15. Poor Butterfly	Columbia 2206
			from the Broadway musical "The Big Show"	
6/16/17	**9**	1	16. The Magic Of Your Eyes	Victor 18244
8/11/17	**2(2)**	6	17. All The World Will Be Jealous Of Me	Victor 18302
11/09/18	**1(5)**	13	18. **I'm Always Chasing Rainbows**	Victor 18496
			from the Broadway musical "Oh, Look!"; melody taken from	
			Chopin's "Fantasie Impromptu in C-Sharp Minor"	
12/14/18	**6**	2	19. Dear Little Boy Of Mine	Columbia 2613
2/01/19	**3**	5	20. Dreaming Of Home, Sweet Home.................	Victor 18508
3/08/19	**9**	1	21. Rose Of No Man's Land	Columbia 2670
			under pseudonym "Hugh Donovan"	
3/15/19	**6**	4	22. In The Land Of Beginning Again.................	Victor 18523
5/31/19	**3**	6	23. When You Look In The Heart Of A Rose........	Columbia 2699
12/20/19+	**4**	5	24. Golden Gate...	Columbia 2791
			CHARLES HARRISON & LEWIS JAMES	

DATE CHARTED	PEAK POS	WKS CHRT'D	ARTIST — Record Title	Label & Number
1/03/20	6	2	25. Broken Blossoms....................................	Columbia 2793
2/21/20	10	1	26. Waiting..	Columbia 2786
7/10/20	6	3	27. That Old Irish Mother Of Mine.....................	Columbia 2937
9/04/20	3	6	28. Pretty Kitty Kelly...................................	Victor 18679
			also recorded for Columbia 2948	
11/13/20	2(1)	10	29. I'll Be With You In Apple Blossom Time........	Victor 18693
5/14/21	7	3	30. Look For The Silver Lining.........................	Victor 18731
			CHARLES HARRISON & "EDNA BROWN" (Elsie Baker) from the Broadway musical "Sally"	
9/10/21	8	2	31. Peggy O'Neil..	Vocalion 14191
10/29/21	11	1	32. You Made Me Forget How To Cry.................	Columbia 3425
11/26/21	6	3	33. Who'll Be The Next One (To Cry Over You)....	Columbia 3463
4/29/22	11	1	34. April Showers.......................................	Victor 18862
			from the Broadway musical "Bombo"	
5/27/22	4	5	35. Play That Song Of India Again	Victor 18877

JAMES F. HARRISON
Baritone ballad singer, real name Frederick Wheeler, first known for his religious duets, also a member of Knickerbocker Quartet & other Edison groups; died on 8/7/51 (73).

DATE CHARTED	PEAK POS	WKS CHRT'D	ARTIST — Record Title	Label & Number
7/02/04	2(3)	8	1. You're The Flower Of My Heart, Sweet Adeline...	Edison 8677
			ALBERT CAMPBELL & JAMES F. HARRISON	
7/29/05	10	1	2. Excelsior..	Edison 8985
11/04/05	5	2	3. When The Mists Have Rolled Away	Edison 9105
8/11/06	5	1	4. Let The Lower Lights Be Burning	Edison 9272
			later recorded for Columbia 3556 & 33034	
11/28/08	9	1	5. Beautiful Isle Of Somewhere	Edison 9959
10/15/10	10	1	6. See The Pale Moon..................................	Victor 5780
			above four: JAMES F. HARRISON & HARRY ANTHONY (Harry's real name: John Young)	
7/05/13	5	4	7. The Land Of Golden Dreams	Victor 17334
8/09/13	9	1	8. The Trail Of The Lonesome Pine...................	Victor 17338
8/16/13	4	4	9. Sunshine And Roses.................................	Victor 17359
11/29/13	5	4	10. When It's Apple Blossom Time In Normandy..	Columbia 1383
			from the Broadway musical "Roly Boly"; based on Beethoven's "Minuet in G"	
1/31/14	9	1	11. If We Were On Our Honeymoon	Columbia 1423
			from the Broadway musical "The Doll Girl" above four: JAMES F. HARRISON & "EDNA BROWN" (Edna's real name: Elsie Baker)	
8/07/15	9	1	12. The Flame Of Love.................................	Victor 17762
			JAMES F. HARRISON & ELSIE BAKER from the Broadway musical "The Peasant Girl"	
12/18/15+	1(2)	8	13. **Keep The Home Fires Burning (Till The Boys Come Home)**	Victor 17881
			British wartime classic	
5/20/16	2(2)	4	14. Wake Up, America!	Victor 17984
			above two as Frederick J. Wheeler	

JAMES F. HARRISON & JAMES REED
Real names Frederick Wheeler and Reed Miller (tenor).

DATE CHARTED	PEAK POS	WKS CHRT'D	ARTIST — Record Title	Label & Number
4/17/15	3	8	1. The Little House Upon The Hill	Columbia 1700
			also recorded for Victor 17732	
7/31/15	1(2)	10	2. **My Little Dream Girl**	Victor 17789
			also recorded for Columbia 1755	
11/20/15	2(3)	6	3. You'll Always Be The Same Sweet Girl	Victor 17878
			also recorded for Columbia 1826	
11/27/15	6	2	4. My Sweet Adair	Victor 17852
			also recorded for Columbia 1831	
12/18/15+	1(3)	12	5. **There's A Long, Long Trail**	Victor 17882
1/29/16	4	5	6. Keep The Home Fires Burning....................	Columbia 1869
			duet version of Harrison's solo hit the only hit duet listed under their real names billed as Frederick Wheeler & James Reed	
3/11/16	2(2)	5	7. We'll Build A Little Home In The U.S.A........	Columbia 1924

DATE CHARTED	PEAK POS	WKS CHRT'D	ARTIST — Record Title	Label & Number
9/16/16	4	3	8. There's Someone More Lonesome Than You .. *also recorded for Columbia 2044*	Victor 18064
3/17/17	6	2	9. Hawaii And You	Columbia 2168
4/21/17	3	5	10. There's A Long, Long Trail [R]	Victor 17882
4/28/17	2(1)	5	11. In The Sweet Long Ago	Columbia 2164

JAMES HARROD

DATE CHARTED	PEAK POS	WKS CHRT'D	ARTIST — Record Title	Label & Number
8/11/17	1(6)	10	1. **Till The Clouds Roll By** ANNA WHEATON & JAMES HARROD *from the Broadway musical "Oh, Boy!"*	Columbia 2261

HARRY'S TAVERN BAND
This band backed up Billy Murray on some of his final 1940-41 recordings.

DATE CHARTED	PEAK POS	WKS CHRT'D	ARTIST — Record Title	Label & Number
10/26/40	26	1	1. Bartender Polka *vocal: Jimmy Ray*	Bluebird 10806
1/11/41	23	1	2. Rock And Rye Polka	Bluebird 10907

CHARLES HART
First tenor of the Shannon Four from 1917-23; performed in both opera and vaudeville, and in later years appeared on stage as an actor opposite Mae West and Katharine Hepburn. (Also see Nicholas Orlando's Orchestra & Joseph C. Smith's Orchestra)

DATE CHARTED	PEAK POS	WKS CHRT'D	ARTIST — Record Title	Label & Number
1/26/18	8	2	1. Somewhere In France Is The Lily	Victor 18409
6/08/18	9	1	2. The Last Long Mile	Victor 18455
6/22/18	10	1	3. Just A Baby's Prayer At Twilight	Gennett 7646
9/07/18	8	2	4. My Belgian Rose	Victor 18479
9/28/18	4	4	5. The Garden Of My Dreams *from the Broadway musical "Ziegfeld Follies of 1918"*	Victor 18487
1/18/19	6	2	6. Rose Of No Man's Land	Victor 18508
2/22/19	1(1)	9	7. **Till We Meet Again** CHARLES HART & LEWIS JAMES	Victor 18518
6/21/19	6	4	8. Forever Is A Long, Long Time	Okeh 1185
6/21/19	7	3	9. I'm Forever Blowing Bubbles *from the Broadway musical "The Passing Show of 1918"* 4, 6, & 9: CHARLES HART & ELLIOTT SHAW	Victor 18540
12/13/19	8	1	10. Golden Gate	Victor 18612
2/28/20	14	1	11. Let The Rest Of The World Go By CHARLES HART & LEWIS JAMES *also recorded for Empire 414*	Pathe 22259
6/25/21	7	2	12. Wyoming (Lullaby) 10 & 12: CHARLES HART & ELLIOTT SHAW *also recorded for Brunswick 2091*	Victor 18740
11/19/21	7	2	13. There's Only One Pal, After All	Victor 18786
1/28/22	10	1	14. I Wonder If You Still Care For Me	Victor 18806
12/01/23	10	1	15. Midnight Rose	Columbia 3945
3/29/24	12	1	16. I Love You *from the Broadway musical "Little Jessie James"*	Victor 19214

GLORIA HART
Sang with Art Kassel in the 40s.

DATE CHARTED	PEAK POS	WKS CHRT'D	ARTIST — Record Title	Label & Number
9/15/51	28	2	1. Oh How I Love You	Sharp 36
8/02/52	18	2	2. I Would Rather Look At You	Mercury 5881

MORTON HARVEY
Discovered in a minstrel show by Billy Murray.

DATE CHARTED	PEAK POS	WKS CHRT'D	ARTIST — Record Title	Label & Number
1/16/15	8	2	1. I Want To Go Back To Michigan (Down On The Farm)	Victor 17650
4/03/15	1(3)	12	2. **I Didn't Raise My Boy To Be A Soldier**	Victor 17716
12/02/16	10	1	3. Turn Back The Universe And Give Me Yesterday	Emerson 785
3/03/17	9	1	4. They're Wearing 'Em Higher In Hawaii	Columbia 2143

DATE CHARTED	PEAK POS	WKS CHRT'D	ARTIST — Record Title	Label & Number
			HAVANA NOVELTY ORCHESTRA	
2/14/31	10	4	1. Lady, Play Your Mandolin .... Victor 22597 vocal: Paul Small	
			JOHN HAVENS - see ESTELLA MANN	
			HAWAIIAN TRIO Helen Louise, Frank Ferera, & Irene Greenus	
7/17/20	8	2	1. Alabama Moon .... [I] Victor 18669	
			COLEMAN HAWKINS & HIS ORCHESTRA One of the great tenor saxophonists in jazz history; Coleman played with Fletcher Henderson (1924-34), and after his return from Europe recorded the historic "Body and Soul". He died on 5/19/69 (64). (also see Benny Carter, Benny Goodman, & Metronome All-Star Band)	
1/27/40	13	6	1. Body And Soul .... [I] Bluebird 10523 jazz classic, selected for NARAS Hall of Fame	
			ERSKINE HAWKINS & HIS ORCHESTRA Trumpeter-bandleader, composer of his most famous hit "Tuxedo Junction"; band featured brothers Dud & Paul Bascomb on trumpet & tenor sax.	
8/29/36	20	1	1. Until The Real Thing Comes Along.............. Vocalion 3280 vocal: Billy Daniels	
10/17/36	18	1	2. Big John's Special .... [I] Vocalion 3318	
7/03/37	17	2	3. Way Down Upon The Swanee River .... [I] Vocalion 3567	
1/14/39	16	1	4. Do You Wanna Jump, Chillun?.................... Bluebird 10019	
12/16/39+	7	15	5. Tuxedo Junction .... [I] Bluebird 10409 main trumpet solo by Dud Bascomb	
5/18/40	13	2	6. Whispering Grass................................. Bluebird 10671 vocals on 4 & 6: Jimmy Mitchelle	
8/31/40	10	7	7. Dolemite .... [I] Bluebird 10812	
11/09/40	15	2	8. Five O'Clock Whistle .... [I] Bluebird 10854	
1/04/41	21	1	9. Song Of The Wanderer............................. Bluebird 10879	
3/15/41	17	2	10. Nona .... [I] Bluebird 10979	
7/11/42	23	1	11. Wrap Your Troubles In Dreams .... Bluebird 11485	
9/11/43	11	14	12. Don't Cry, Baby.................................. Bluebird 0813 recorded 5/27/42	
2/05/44	15	4	13. Cherry .... Bluebird 0819 recorded 7/18/39 vocals on 9, 11-13: Jimmy Mitchelle	
4/28/45	9	8	14. Tippin' In .... [I] Victor 1639	
5/12/45	12	3	15. Caldonia .... Victor 1659 vocal: Ace Harris	
5/15/48	28	1	16. Gabriel's Heater .... [I] RCA Victor 2836	
			HAWKSHAW HAWKINS Country singer	
1/12/52	26	1	1. Slow-Poke .... King 998	
			HAYDN QUARTET Along with the Peerless and the American, one of the three great vocal groups in the pioneer age of popular recording. Original members were tenors John Bieling and Harry Macdonough, baritone S.H. Dudley, and bass William F. Hooley; on Edison same group was known as Edison Male Quartet. Billy Murray sang lead on many of the group's biggest hits; during the later period Reinald Werrenrath often took Dudley's place. The group disbanded in 1914, three of its members then helping to form the Orpheus Quartet. (From about 1910 on, group's name was spelled "Hayden") (Also see Cal Stewart)	
9/17/98	3	1	1. She Was Bred In Old Kentucky.................. Berliner 4295	
11/04/99	4	2	2. Cornfield Medley.................................... Berliner 0416 later recorded for Victor 125	
10/06/00	1(4)	6	3. **Because**.. Gram-o-Phone 105 previously on Berliner 0414; from the Broadway musical "The French Maid"	
6/07/02	3	3	4. In The Sweet Bye And Bye .... Victor 1316	
2/28/03	1(6)	12	5. **In The Good Old Summer Time** .... Victor 1793	

DATE CHARTED	PEAK POS	WKS CHRT'D	ARTIST — Record Title	Label & Number
6/13/03	2(3)	4	6. My Old Kentucky Home	Victor 1997
1/09/04	1(7)	11	7. **Bedelia**................................... from the Broadway musical "The Jersey Lily"	Victor 2559
4/23/04	2(2)	5	8. Dear Old Girl .... Harry Macdonough also recorded song for Edison 8613	Victor 2643
6/11/04	1(2)	8	9. **Toyland**.................................... CORRINE MORGAN & HAYDN QUARTET from the Broadway musical "Babes in Toyland"	Victor 2721
6/18/04	1(3)	7	10. **Blue Bell** .... Harry Macdonough also recorded song for Columbia 1813 & 32515 7, 8, & 10 lead vocals: Harry Macdonough	Victor 2750
8/06/04	4	2	11. The Old Folks At Home........................	Victor 2816
10/15/04	1(10)	17	12. **Sweet Adeline (You're The Flower Of My Heart)**............................ lead vocals: John Bieling & S.H. Dudley song written as instrumental in 1896 ("Down Home in New England"), lyrics added in 1903; became identified with Boston Mayor John F. "Honey" Fitzgerald	Victor 2934
11/05/04	4	2	13. I Am Longing For You, Sweetheart, Day By Day............................. Macdonough also recorded song for Columbia 32582	Victor 2933
1/21/05	2(3)	6	14. My Little Canoe............................ lead vocals: Harry Macdonough & S.H. Dudley; from the Broadway musical "The School Girl"	Victor 4064
3/04/05	3	4	15. Tell Me With Your Eyes .... also recorded as Edison Male Quartet for Edison 8945	Victor 4170
5/27/05	6	1	16. Where The Southern Roses Grow.................	Victor 4277
5/27/05	10	1	17. The Holy City................................	Victor 4256
7/01/05	2(1)	8	18. In The Shade Of The Old Apple Tree............ lead vocals on 13, 17, 18, 20 & 21: Harry Macdonough	Victor 4337
8/26/05	1(2)	8	19. **Dearie**.................................... CORRINE MORGAN & HAYDN QUARTET	Victor 4396
8/26/05	8	1	20. Come Along, Little Girl, Come Along	Victor 4347
9/16/05	4	2	21. Down Where The Silv'ry Mohawk Flows	Victor 4378
10/28/05	5	1	22. Grandfather's Clock	Victor 4473
12/16/05	2(3)	3	23. Silent Night, Hallowed Night .... [X] also recorded as Edison Male Quartet for Edison 9168	Victor 4511
1/06/06	1(2)	6	24. **How'd You Like To Spoon With Me?** .... CORRINE MORGAN & HAYDN QUARTET from the Broadway musical "The Earl and the Girl"	Victor 4532
1/20/06	3	2	25. In Dear Old Georgia................................	Victor 4522
2/24/06	2(1)	6	26. Will You Love Me In December As You Do In May?.. Macdonough also recorded song for Edison 9198	Victor 4575
4/28/06	4	2	27. Just A Little Rocking Chair And You	Victor 31501
6/30/06	6	1	28. When The Roll Is Called Up Yonder.............	Victor 4689
9/08/06	5	2	29. Waltz Me Around Again, Willie.................... from the Broadway musical "His Honor the Mayor"; Billy Murray also recorded song for Edison 9340 & Zon-a-Phone 500	Victor 4738
3/30/07	5	1	30. When The Flowers Bloom In The Springtime, Molly Dear	Victor 4967
8/03/07+	2(1)	5	31. My Wild Irish Rose............................... from the Broadway musical "A Romance of Athlone" lead vocals on 26, 28 & 31: Harry Macdonough	Victor 5149
8/17/07	2(1)	5	32. In The Wildwood Where The Blue Bells Grew .	Victor 5168
8/31/07	10	1	33. Stein Song...	Victor 5136
3/28/08	8	1	34. I'm Happy When The Band Plays Dixie	Victor 5330
4/04/08	2(2)	4	35. Keep On Smiling...................................	Victor 5379
6/27/08	7	1	36. Love Me And The World Is Mine	Victor 5437
7/04/08	5	1	37. When It's Moonlight On The Prairie..............	Victor 5448
10/24/08	1(7)	16	38. **Take Me Out To The Ball Game** .... the most popular recording of the national pastime's anthem 34, 35, 38 & 40: BILLY MURRAY & HAYDN QUARTET	Victor 5570

DATE CHARTED	PEAK POS	WKS CHRT'D	ARTIST — Record Title	Label & Number
10/31/08	1(5)	14	39. **Sunbonnet Sue**.............................. Victor 5568 lead vocals on 36-37 & 39: Harry Macdonough	
10/31/08	8	1	40. Yankee Doodle's Come To Town.................. Victor 5504	
11/28/08	7	1	41. Rainbow... Victor 5571	
12/26/08	5	1	42. Here's To The Girl!............................. Victor 5611 ALAN TURNER & HAYDN QUARTET from the Broadway musical "The Girls of Gottenburg"	
2/06/09	3	3	43. Brown Eyes, Good-Bye............................. Victor 5650	
3/06/09	5	1	44. Sullivan .... Victor 5617 from the Broadway musical "The American Idea"; Murray also recorded song for Edison 10060	
5/29/09	6	1	45. Meet Me In Rose-Time, Rosie...................... Victor 5676	
8/28/09	4	3	46. Take Me Up With You, Dearie .... Victor 5718 Murray also recorded song for Edison 10213	
10/09/09	4	3	47. Take Me Out For A Joy Ride...................... Victor 5732 above four: BILLY MURRAY & HAYDN QUARTET	
10/30/09	3	3	48. Up, Up, Up In My Aeroplane...................... Victor 16340 from the Broadway musical "Ziegfeld Follies of 1909"	
12/04/09	3	5	49. Lonesome.. Victor 5743 lead vocals on 43, 49, 55 & 62: Harry Macdonough	
12/11/09	1(11)	17	50. **Put On Your Old Gray Bonnet**.................. Victor 16377	
12/18/09	3	5	51. The Hat My Father Wore On St. Patrick's Day	Victor 16365
1/08/10	6	2	52. Tell Mother I'll Be There .... Victor 16414	
3/26/10	4	4	53. Down In Sunshine Alley............................ Victor 16450 Murray also recorded song for Edison Amberol 337	
4/16/10	1(9)	17	54. **By The Light Of The Silv'ry Moon**............ Victor 16460 from the Broadway musical "Ziegfeld Follies of 1909" above four: BILLY MURRAY & HAYDN QUARTET	
6/11/10	9	1	55. The Garden Of Roses................................ Victor 16467	
7/23/10	2(2)	6	56. I'll Make A Ring Around Rosie .... Victor 16498	
9/24/10	5	3	57. Meet Me Where The Lanterns Glow .... Victor 16509 from the Broadway musical "A Trip To Japan"	
9/24/10	7	2	58. My Heart Has Learned To Love You, Now Do Not Say Good-Bye.............................. Victor 16503	
7/22/11	7	2	59. Mary .... Victor 16828 ELIZABETH WHEELER & HAYDN QUARTET	
8/26/11	5	3	60. By The Saskatchewan .... Victor 5839 lead vocal: Reinald Werrenrath from the Broadway musical "The Pink Lady"	
5/10/13	2(2)	8	61. In The Evening By The Moonlight .... Victor 17305	
4/25/14	4	4	62. 'Cross The Great Divide (I'll Wait For You) .... Victor 17545 on this final hit, the group consisted of Macdonough, Steve Porter, Wilfred Glenn, & Robert D'Armour	

BRUCE HAYES
Sang briefly in the 40s with Vincent Lopez.

7/24/48	18	10	1. You Call Everybody Darlin'........................ DeLuxe 1178	

PETER LIND HAYES
Composed Johnny Mathis' hit "Come to Me" and other songs for television.

1/01/49	20	2	1. My Darling, My Darling .... Decca 24519 from the Broadway musical "Where's Charley?" with the Stardusters	

RICHARD HAYES

12/17/49+	2(1)	12	1. The Old Master Painter .... Mercury 5342	
5/27/50	21	2	2. My Foolish Heart .... Mercury 5362 above two accompanied by Mitch Miller's Orchestra	
9/09/50	10	12	3. Our Lady Of Fatima.............................. Mercury 5466 with Jimmy Carroll's Orchestra	
3/03/51	9	10	4. The Aba Daba Honeymoon .... Mercury 5586 above two: RICHARD HAYES & KITTY KALLEN with George Sivavo's Orchestra	
7/04/51	24	1	5. Too Young... Mercury 5599	

DATE CHARTED	PEAK POS	WKS CHRT'D	ARTIST — Record Title	Label & Number
8/11/51	**14**	1	6. Come On-A My House/ from the off-Broadway play "The Son"	
8/11/51	**23**	1	7. Go! Go! Go! Go .... above two with George Bassman's Orchestra	Mercury 5671
10/27/51	**9**	10	8. Out In The Cold Again	Mercury 5724
5/03/52	**15**	11	9. Junco Partner....................................... with Eddie Sauter's Orchestra	Mercury 5833
5/03/52	**24**	1	10. I'll Walk Alone .... from the film "Follow the Boys" 8 & 10 with Joe Reichman's Orchestra	Mercury 5821
7/12/52	**23**	1	11. The Mask Is Off .... with Jimmy Carroll's Orchestra	Mercury 5872
11/01/52	**15**	2	12. Forgetting You	Mercury 5910
7/25/53	**24**	1	13. Midnight In Paris .... with Richard Hayman's Orchestra	Mercury 70169

JOE HAYMAN
American comedian specializing in Jewish sketches, especially popular in England.

8/08/14	**1(5)**	15	● 1. **Cohen On The Telephone**....................[T-C] possibly the first million-selling spoken comedy record	Columbia 1516
2/19/16	**5**	3	2. Cohen Telephones From Brighton..........[T-C]	Columbia 1885
4/25/23	**15**	1	3. Cohen Telephones About His Auto.........[T-C]	Columbia 3772

RICHARD HAYMAN & HIS ORCHESTRA
Orchestra leader and harmonica soloist, helped arrange background music for "Meet Me in St. Louis" & other films, also arranger for Vaughn Monroe.

4/11/53	**3**	19	1. Ruby .... [I]	Mercury 70115
			theme from the film "Ruby Gentry"	
4/18/53	**12**	11	2. April In Portugal .... [I] originally written for the University of Coimbra in Portugese	Mercury 70114
6/27/53	**13**	4	3. Limelight (Terry's Theme)/ [I] Charlie Chaplin's theme from the film "Limelight"	
8/08/53	**23**	1	4. Eyes Of Blue.................................... [I] theme from the film "Shane"	Mercury 70168
9/26/53	**14**	8	5. The Story Of Three Loves...................... [I] JERRY MURAD with RICHARD HAYMAN & HIS ORCHESTRA movie title theme; based on Rachmaninoff's "18th Variation: Rhapsody on a Theme of Paganini"	Mercury 70202
1/02/54	**16**	2	6. Off Shore.. [I]	Mercury 70232
1/16/54	**20**	5	7. Sadie Thompson's Song .... [I] theme from the film "Miss Sadie Thompson"	Mercury 70237

HERBIE HAYMER
Tenor sax star with Red Norvo (1935-37), Jimmy Dorsey (1937-41), Woody Herman, & Kay Kyser (1942-43); died on 4/11/49 (34) in an automobile accident.

DICK HAYMES
One of the 1940s' finest ballad singers, born in Argentina (raised in U.S.), sang with Harry James ("I'll Get By"), Benny Goodman ("Idaho"), and Tommy Dorsey in early 40s, and appeared in various movies from 1944-53. He was briefly married to Rita Hayworth. (also see Helen Forrest)

6/26/43	**1(1)**	15	1. **It Can't Be Wrong**/	
7/17/43	**3**	13	2. In My Arms	Decca 18557
7/10/43	**1(7)**	18	3. **You'll Never Know**/ from the film "Hello, Frisco, Hello"	
7/24/43	**6**	13	4. Wait For Me, Mary	Decca 18556
9/11/43	**11**	3	5. I Never Mention Your Name/	
9/11/43	**13**	3	6. I Heard You Cried Last Night	Decca 18558
10/30/43	**5**	7	7. Put Your Arms Around Me, Honey/	
11/27/43	**13**	4	8. For The First Time (I've Fallen In Love) ...... above eight with the Song Spinners	Decca 18565

DATE CHARTED	PEAK POS	WKS CHRT'D	ARTIST — Record Title	Label & Number
6/17/44	**27**	1	9. How Many Times Do I Have To Tell You?/	
6/24/44	**11**	10	10. How Blue The Night .... above two with Emil Newman's Orchestra both from the film "Four Jills in a Jeep"	Decca 18604
11/04/44	**26**	1	11. Janie... movie title song	Decca 18633
5/26/45	**9**	3	12. Laura .... movie title song	Decca 18666
6/09/45	**7**	3	13. The More I See You/	
7/14/45	**6**	6	14. I Wish I Knew .... above two from the film "Billy Rose's Diamond Horseshoe" above four accompanied by Victor Young's Orchestra	Decca 18662
9/15/45	**3**	9	15. Till The End Of Time/ based on Chopin's "Polonaise in A-Flat Major"; from the film "A Song to Remember"	
9/29/45	**11**	1	16. Love Letters	Decca 18699
10/13/45	**6**	11	17. That's For Me/	
11/17/45	**5**	12	18. It Might As Well Be Spring	Decca 18706
2/02/46	**21**	1	19. It's A Grand Night For Singing .... accompanied by Earle Hagen's Orchestra above three from the film "State Fair"	Decca 18740
2/16/46	**12**	1	20. Slowly .... from the film "Fallen Angels" 15-18 & 20 accompanied by Victor Young's Orchestra	Decca 18747
10/26/46	**21**	1	21. You Make Me Feel So Young/	
12/02/46+	**21**	4	22. On The Boardwalk (In Atlantic City).......... above two from the film "Three Little Girls in Blue"	Decca 18914
1/18/47	**19**	1	23. For You, For Me, Forevermore.................. DICK HAYMES & JUDY GARLAND with Gordon Jenkins Orchestra from the film "The Shocking Miss Pilgrim"	Decca 23687
3/29/47	**9**	5	24. How Are Things In Glocca Mora? .... from the Broadway musical "Finian's Rainbow"	Decca 23830
5/03/47	**3**	11	25. Mam'selle.................................... from the film "The Razor's Edge"	Decca 23861
7/19/47	**25**	1	26. There's No Business Like Show Business ...... BING CROSBY, ANDREWS SISTERS, & DICK HAYMES from the Broadway musical "Annie Get Your Gun"	Decca 40039
8/09/47	**19**	1	27. Ivy .... movie title song	Decca 23877
10/04/47	**21**	3	28. Naughty Angeline/	
10/25/47	**9**	8	29. I Wish I Didn't Love You So .... from the film "The Perils of Pauline" above two with mixed quartet	Decca 23977
11/08/47	**15**	3	30. And Mimi	Decca 24172
3/20/48	**21**	1	31. Teresa .... DICK HAYMES & ANDREWS SISTERS 26 & 31 accompanied by Vic Schoen Orchestra	Decca 24320
4/10/48	**2(1)**	23	● 32. Little White Lies................................ with Four Hits & a Miss 23-25, 27, 30 & 32 accompanied by Gordon Jenkins Orchestra	Decca 24280
6/05/48	**9**	13	33. You Can't Be True, Dear/	
6/05/48	**11**	5	34. Nature Boy................................. above two with the Song Spinners	Decca 24439
7/24/48	**9**	18	35. It's Magic .... from the film "Romance on the High Seas" accompanied by Gordon Jenkins' Orchestra	Decca 23826
9/25/48	**24**	2	36. Ev'ry Day I Love You .... accompanied by Vic Schoen's Orchestra; from the film "Two Guys from Texas"	Decca 24457
3/19/49	**22**	1	37. Bouquet Of Roses.......................... with the Troubadors	Decca 24506
6/25/49	**6**	20	38. Room Full Of Roses	Decca 24632
7/16/49	**5**	18	39. Maybe It's Because	Decca 24650
12/10/49+	**4**	13	40. The Old Master Painter .... accompanied by Sonny Burke's Orchestra	Decca 24801

DATE CHARTED	PEAK POS	WKS CHRT'D	ARTIST — Record Title	Label & Number
5/27/50	**29**	1	41. Roses .... 39, 41 & 44 accompanied by Gordon Jenkins' Orchestra	Decca 27008
7/22/50	**10**	11	42. Count Every Star .... with Artie Shaw & His Orchestra	Decca 27042
9/09/50	**23**	2	43. Can Anyone Explain? (No, No, No!) .... with Four Hits & A Miss	Decca 27161
4/07/51	**30**	1	44. You're Just In Love................................... DICK HAYMES & ETHEL MERMAN from the Broadway musical "Call Me Madam"	Decca 27317
10/27/51	**28**	3	45. And So To Sleep Again .... 43 & 45 accompanied by Victor Young & His Orchestra 40, 41, 43 & 45 with Four Hits & A Miss	Decca 27731

JOE HAYMES & HIS ORCHESTRA
Former arranger for Ted Weems; Tommy Dorsey formed his first orchestra by recruiting Haymes' top musicians.

DATE CHARTED	PEAK POS	WKS CHRT'D	ARTIST — Record Title	Label & Number
6/24/33	**17**	1	1. I Cover The Waterfront .... written to promote film of same name	Columbia 2781
8/12/33	**17**	2	2. Ain't Gonna Grieve No More	Bluebird 5220
7/27/35	**20**	1	3. The Lady In Red .... vocal: Cliff Weston; from the film "In Caliente"	Bluebird 5918

LENNIE HAYTON & HIS ORCHESTRA
Pianist/arranger for Paul Whiteman 1928-30, musical director for various 1930s radio shows and for MGM movies from 1940-53 (including "Singin' In the Rain"). Lennie was married to Lena Horne; he died on 4/24/71 (63). (also see Bing Crosby)

DATE CHARTED	PEAK POS	WKS CHRT'D	ARTIST — Record Title	Label & Number
9/11/37	**19**	1	1. I Know Now .... vocal: Paul Berry from the film "The Singing Marine"	Decca 1267
4/23/49	**19**	6	2. Slaughter On 10th Avenue .... [I] "Lennie Hayton & the MGM Studio Orchestra" ballet from the Broadway musical "On Your Toes" recording from the film "Words And Music"	MGM 30174

FLORENCE HAYWARD - see HARRY MACDONOUGH

RITA HAYWORTH
One of Hollywood's top leading ladies and sex symbols of the 1940s & 50s.

DATE CHARTED	PEAK POS	WKS CHRT'D	ARTIST — Record Title	Label & Number
1/16/54	**30**	1	1. The Heat's On .... RITA HAYWORTH & JOSE FERRER from the film "Miss Sadie Thompson"	MGM 70259

NEAL HEFTI
Trumpeter most famous as arranger for Woody Herman (1944-46), Harry James, & Count Basie, then as composer of TV themes for "Batman" & other shows.

HEIDELBERG QUINTET
The American Quartet (Billy Murray, John Bieling, Steve Porter, & William F. Hooley) plus counter-tenor Will Oakland

DATE CHARTED	PEAK POS	WKS CHRT'D	ARTIST — Record Title	Label & Number
1/07/11	**5**	3	1. In The Gloaming......................................	Victor 16646
8/11/12	**9**	1	2. Under The Love Tree................................	Victor 17082
9/28/12	**1(6)**	12	3. **Waiting For The Robert E. Lee**	Victor 17141
10/12/12	**5**	3	4. 'Way Down South .... also recorded for Edison Amberol 1531	Victor 17146
11/02/12	**5**	3	5. On A Beautiful Night With A Beautiful Girl....	Victor 17152
10/18/13	**8**	1	6. You're A Great Big Blue-Eyed Baby.............	Victor 17344
7/18/14	**1(6)**	11	7. **By The Beautiful Sea**	Victor 17560
1/23/15	**8**	1	8. Roll Them Cotton Bales	Victor 17633

HOARCE HEIDT & HIS ORCHESTRA
Sweet-band leader who featured tenor saxist Frank DeVol, pianist Frankie Carle, & electric guitarist Alvino Rey.

DATE CHARTED	PEAK POS	WKS CHRT'D	ARTIST — Record Title	Label & Number
7/03/37	**1(1)**	9	1. **Gone With The Wind**/ vocal: Larry Cotton	
7/31/37	**17**	2	2. The Miller's Daughter Marianne .... vocal: Bob McCoy	Brunswick 7913
7/17/37	**5**	4	3. Hot Lips..	Brunswick 7916
8/07/37	**12**	2	4. Oh Marie-Oh, Marie	Brunswick 7920

DATE CHARTED	PEAK POS	WKS CHRT'D	ARTIST — Record Title	Label & Number
8/21/37	**5**	5	5. It's The Natural Thing To Do .... from the film "Double or Nothing" above three vocals: King Sisters	Brunswick 7927
9/11/37	**12**	2	6. Lovely One .... from the film "Vogues of 1938"	Brunswick 7939
9/18/37	**3**	5	7. Little Heaven Of The Seven Seas .... vocal: King Sisters	Brunswick 7946
11/06/37	**2(1)**	7	8. Once In A While	Brunswick 7977
11/27/37	**4**	4	9. Vieni, Vieni/ vocal: Lysabeth Hughes; adaptation of a Corsican song	
12/11/37+	**17**	2	10. In The Mission By The Sea	Brunswick 8003
12/25/37+	**5**	4	11. There's A Gold Mine In The Sky	Brunswick 8021
12/25/37+	**9**	9	12. Sweet Someone .... from the film "Love and Hisses" vocals on 6, 8, & above three: Larry Cotton	Brunswick 8013
1/15/38	**6**	4	13. Rosalie .... vocal: Lysbeth Hughes; movie title song	Brunswick 8028
1/22/38	**3**	9	14. Sweet As A Song .... from the film "Sally, Irene, and Mary"	Brunswick 8043
3/05/38	**1(6)**	13	15. **Ti-Pi-Pin** .... vocal: Lysbeth Hughes & Larry Cotton adaptation of a popular Spanish song	Brunswick 8078
3/05/38	**12**	2	16. Heigh Ho .... vocal by Kings Men & Glee Club from the animated film "Snow White and the Seven Dwarfs"	Brunswick 8074
5/07/38	**15**	4	17. The Girl In The Bonnet Of Blue	Brunswick 8133
5/14/38	**3**	14	18. Lovelight In The Starlight	Brunswick 8110
5/28/38	**6**	10	19. This Time It's Real................................	Brunswick 8121
6/25/38	**8**	4	20. My Margarita .... vocal: Larry Cotton, Bob McCoy, & Charioteers	Brunswick 8129
8/06/38	**14**	2	21. When They Played The Polka..................... vocals on 17 & 21: Charles Goodwin	Brunswick 8148
9/03/38	**7**	3	22. Tu-Li Tulip Time............................ vocal: Lysbeth Hughes & Larry Cotton	Brunswick 8192
11/26/38	**6**	5	23. This Can't Be Love.............................. from the Broadway musical "The Boys from Syracuse"	Brunswick 8257
2/11/39	**7**	5	24. Little Sir Echo/ vocal: Emily Stevenson & Larry Cotton; musical version of the Boy Scout anthem	
2/18/39	**20**	1	25. Let's Stop The Clock	Brunswick 8309
2/25/39	**12**	7	26. I Long To Belong To You........................	Brunswick 8331
3/04/39	**8**	7	27. Penny Serenade/ British song vocals on 14, 18-19, 23 & 25-27: Larry Cotton	
4/22/39	**17**	2	28. Dawn Of A New Day .... vocal: Charles Goodwin; official song of New York World's Fair	Brunswick 8313
7/22/39	**9**	3	29. Shabby Old Cabby..................................	Brunswick 8409
7/29/39	**2(1)**	10	30. The Man With The Mandolin	Brunswick 8430
12/09/39	**16**	1	31. Tomorrow Night .... vocal: Height-Lights	Columbia 35203
2/24/40	**18**	2	32. Make Love With A Guitar........................	Columbia 35327
4/20/40	**12**	5	33. When You Wish Upon A Star .... from the animated film "Pinocchio" first Heidt hit with Bobby Hackett (cornet, through 1941)	Columbia 35351
8/28/40	**26**	1	34. The Stars And Stripes Forever .... vocal: Ruth Davis, Larry Cotton & Henry Russell	Columbia 35637
4/12/41	**8**	15	35. Friendly Tavern Polka	Columbia 36006
4/26/41	**2(2)**	12	36. G'bye Now .... vocal: Ronnie Kemper	Columbia 36026
5/31/41	**3**	13	37. The Hut-Hut Song (A Swedish Serenade)	Columbia 36138
6/21/41	**3**	14	38. Goodbye Dear, I'll Be Back In A Year .... vocal: Ronnie Kemper & Don Juans (Art Carney a member)	Columbia 36148

DATE CHARTED	PEAK POS	WKS CHRT'D	ARTIST — Record Title	Label & Number
8/30/41	**14**	6	39. Mama/ [I]	
9/13/41	**1(3)**	13	40. **I Don't Want To Set The World On Fire** ... vocal: Larry Cotton, Donna Wood & Don Juans	Columbia 36295
10/25/41	**10**	10	41. Bi-I-Bi .... vocals on 37 & 41: Donna Wood & Don Juans	Columbia 36337
11/22/41	**7**	8	42. Shepherd Serenade .... vocal: Larry Cotton, Gordon MacRae & Fred Lowery	Columbia 36370
2/28/42	**22**	1	43. Carle Meets Mozart (Turkish March) .... [I]	Columbia 36453
3/14/42	**7**	6	44. Deep In The Heart Of Texas	Columbia 36525
5/16/42	**19**	2	45. Little Bo Peep Has Lost Her Jeep .... [N]	Columbia 36568
6/20/42	**18**	1	46. Three Little Sisters .... from the film "Private Buckaroo"	Columbia 36576
7/25/42	**22**	1	47. Pound Your Table Polka .... vocal: Mary Martin	Columbia 36595
10/31/42	**21**	1	48. Pennsylvania Polka............................. from the film "Give Out, Sisters"	Columbia 36645
1/09/43	**20**	1	49. This Is The Army, Mr. Jones! .... from the Broadway musical "This Is the Army"	Columbia 36667
4/03/43	**11**	3	50. That Old Black Magic .... from the film "Star-Spangled Rhythm"	Columbia 36670
3/25/44	**24**	1	51. Friendly Tavern Polka .... [R]	Columbia 36006
2/03/45	**10**	2	52. Don't Fence Me In .... vocal: Gene Walsh & Sweetswingsters; from the film "Hollywood Can-teen"	Columbia 36761

JASCHA HEIFETZ
Perhaps the most acclaimed violinist of the century, Russian-born Heifetz made his Carnegie Hall debut at age 16 in 1917, and remained active into the 1970s.

DATE CHARTED	PEAK POS	WKS CHRT'D	ARTIST — Record Title	Label & Number
3/23/18	**7**	2	1. La Capricieuse .... [I]	Victor 64760
11/23/18	**7**	2	2. La Ronde Des Lutins (Dance Of The Goblins)................................ [I]	Victor 74570
6/26/20	**8**	2	3. Nocturne In E Flat .... [I]	Victor 74616
8/21/20	**7**	2	4. Introduction And Tarantelle .... [I]	Victor 74626
10/30/20	**15**	1	5. Meditation................................... [I] accompanied on above four by Andre Benoist (piano)	Victor 64769

PERCY HEMUS
Born in New Zealand; died on 12/22/43 (65).

DATE CHARTED	PEAK POS	WKS CHRT'D	ARTIST — Record Title	Label & Number
5/04/18	**5**	5	1. On The Road To Home Sweet Home............. flip side of Henry Burr's #1 million-seller "Just A Baby's Prayer at Twilight"	Victor 18439

FLETCHER HENDERSON & HIS ORCHESTRA
Pianist leader of one of the 1920s' most celebrated jazz orchestras, Fletch went on to make further music history with his classic arrangements for Benny Goodman in the 30s, as well as for many other bands. Died on 12/29/52 (54). (Also see Bessie Smith, Ethel Waters)

DATE CHARTED	PEAK POS	WKS CHRT'D	ARTIST — Record Title	Label & Number
11/24/23	**10**	1	1. Gulf Coast Blues................................ [I]	Vocalion 14636
4/05/24	**8**	2	2. Charleston Crazy .... [I]	Vocalion 14726
10/10/25	**8**	2	3. Sugar Foot Stomp .... [I]	Columbia 395
3/20/26	**10**	1	4. Carolina Stomp .... [I] Louis Armstrong (cornet) on above two	Columbia 509
4/24/26	**13**	1	5. Dinah .... [I]	Vocalion 15204
3/12/27	**14**	2	6. Henderson Stomp .... [I]	Columbia 817
7/02/27	**17**	2	7. Stockholm Stomp .... [I]	Brunswick 3460
8/20/27	**17**	2	8. Fidgety Feet .... [I]	Brunswick 3521
12/08/28	**11**	3	9. King Porter Stomp .... [I]	Columbia 1543
12/26/31	**19**	1	10. Blues In My Heart	Columbia 2559
12/31/32	**19**	1	11. Underneath The Harlem Moon/ vocal: Katharine Handy; with Rex Stewart (trumpet) & J.C. Higginbotham (trombone)	
2/04/33	**18**	2	12. Honeysuckle Rose .... [I]	Columbia 2732
10/07/33	**20**	1	13. King Porter's Stomp............................ [I] new version of his 1928 hit	Vocalion 2527

DATE CHARTED	PEAK POS	WKS CHRT'D	ARTIST — Record Title	Label & Number
12/16/33	20	1	14. It's The Talk Of The Town........................ [I]	Columbia 2825
10/20/34	19	1	15. Tidal Wave .... [I]	Bluebird 5682
			Henry (Red) Allen (trumpet) on above three	
			Coleman Hawkins (tenor sax) leading soloist from 1923-33	
4/25/36	10	4	16. Christopher Columbus (A Rhythm Cocktail) [I]	Vocalion 3211
6/27/36	20	1	17. Where There's You, There's Me	Victor 25334
			vocal: Teddy Lewis	
9/12/36	11	8	18. Until Today .... [I]	Victor 25373
			Roy Eldridge (trumpet) on above two	
4/10/37	15	2	19. Slumming On Park Avenue.........................	Vocalion 3485
			vocal: Jerry Blake; from the film "On the Avenue"	
5/29/37	18	1	20. Great Caesar's Ghost.............................. [I]	Vocalion 3534
			Chu Berry (tenor sax) on above five	

SKITCH HENDERSON & HIS ORCHESTRA
Piano accompanist for Judy Garland, Frank Sinatra, & Bing Crosby in 1940s, became famous as bandleader on Steve Allen & early Johnny Carson "Tonight Show".

DATE CHARTED	PEAK POS	WKS CHRT'D	ARTIST — Record Title	Label & Number
10/12/46	9	9	1. Five Minutes More	Capitol 257
			vocal: Ray Kellogg; from the film "Sweetheart of Sigma Chi"	
11/08/47	27	1	2. Papa Won't You Dance With Me?	Capitol 471
			vocal: Nancy Reed	
			from the Broadway musical "High Button Shoes"	

RAY HERBECK & HIS ORCHESTRA
Alto saxophonist sweet-band leader

DATE CHARTED	PEAK POS	WKS CHRT'D	ARTIST — Record Title	Label & Number
4/13/40	17	1	1. You Little Heartbreaker You.......................	Vocalion 5495
			vocal: Ray Olsen	
7/20/40	27	1	2. Seems Like A Month Of Sundays (Since I Saw You Saturday Night)..........................	Okeh 5592
			vocal: Betty Benson	

VICTOR HERBERT & HIS ORCHESTRA
All-time great composer, born on 2/1/1859 in Dublin, Ireland; after establishing himself as a cellist in Germany, Herbert began his long career as composer of Broadway operettas in 1897. He died on 5/24/24 (65).

DATE CHARTED	PEAK POS	WKS CHRT'D	ARTIST — Record Title	Label & Number
9/23/11	4	4	1. March Of The Toys........................... [I]	Victor 70048
9/30/11	5	4	2. Naughty Marietta Selection .... [I]	Edison Amb. 729
8/31/12	5	3	3. Naughty Marietta Intermezzo.................. [I]	Victor 70075
1/11/13	10	1	4. The Toymaker's Shop........................... [I]	Victor 60080
			1 & 4 from his 1903 musical "Babes in Toyland"	
4/04/14	8	1	5. Sweethearts.................................... [I]	Victor 55039
			title song of his 1913 musical	
5/09/14	10	1	6. Dance Of The Hours .... [I]	Victor 55044
8/24/18	8	2	7. American Fantasie.............................. [I]	Victor 55093
7/26/19	7	2	8. Kiss Me Again .... [I]	Victor 45165
			from his 1906 musical "Mlle. Modiste"	

WOODY HERMAN & HIS ORCHESTRA
Born on 5/16/13 in Milwaukee, Woody Herman played clarinet and saxophone for Harry Sosnik, Gus Arnheim, & Isham Jones before assembling his own "Band That Plays the Blues". With "Woodchopper's Ball" as his trademark hit and "Blue Flame" his theme, Woody built to a peak in the late 40s with his "Second Herd". Sax stars Stan Getz and Zoot Sims led this ensemble with such famous jazz hits as "Early Autumn" and "Four Brothers" (Columbia 38304). Woody Herman has carried on into the 1980s as one of the most innovative and contemporary of all big-band leaders. (All vocals by Woody unless otherwise noted)

DATE CHARTED	PEAK POS	WKS CHRT'D	ARTIST — Record Title	Label & Number
12/25/37	18	1	1. I Double Dare You	Decca 1523
5/13/39	9	6	2. At The Woodchopper's Ball .... [I]	Decca 2440
			Woody's most famous hit	
6/17/39	9	7	3. Blue Evening	Decca 2250
1/20/40	17	2	4. Blues On Parade................................ [I]	Decca 2933
7/13/40	27	1	5. Get Your Boots Laced, Papa	Decca 3187
11/09/40	15	1	6. Looking For Yesterday	Decca 3397
1/04/41	11	2	7. There I Go	Decca 3454

DATE CHARTED	PEAK POS	WKS CHRT'D	ARTIST — Record Title	Label & Number
1/25/41	16	1	8. Frenesi .... Mexican song	Decca 3427
2/08/41	23	1	9. The Golden Wedding .... [I]	Decca 3436
3/29/41	5	7	10. Blue Flame .... [I] the band's theme song	Decca 3643
5/03/41	22	1	11. Sleepy Serenade .... [I]	Decca 3693
5/17/41	25	1	12. (Hurry Back To) Sorrento	Decca 3630
6/28/41	10	1	13. G'bye Now .... (Decca 3971 & 4162: Bing Crosby with Woody Herman's Woodchoppers)	Decca 3745
11/01/41	24	1	14. Bishop's Blues .... [I]	Decca 3972
11/29/41	8	8	15. This Time The Dream's On Me/	
12/06/41+	1(4)	18	16. **Blues In The Night** .... above two from the film "Blues In the Night" top sidemen in Herman's early-40s band: tenor saxmen Vido Musso (left 1940), Herbie Haymer, & Saxie Mansfield	Decca 4030
12/06/41+	7	8	17. By-U, By-O (The Lou'siana Lullaby) .... vocal: Muriel Lane	Decca 4024
1/03/42	8	8	18. 'Tis Autumn/	
2/28/42	21	1	19. I Guess I'll Be On My Way	Decca 4095
3/07/42	17	1	20. Rose O'Day .... vocals on 18 & 20: Woody & Carolyn Grey	Decca 4113
3/21/42	23	1	21. I'll Remember April......................	Decca 4135
6/20/42	21	1	22. Don't Tell A Lie About Me, Dear .... vocal: Billie Rogers (also trumpet, one of few female jazz musicians)	Decca 18357
6/27/42	5	9	23. Amen	Decca 18346
11/28/42	23	1	24. There Will Never Be Another You/ from the film "Iceland"	
2/13/43	19	1	25. Please Be There .... [I]	Decca 18469
3/13/43	14	1	26. Four Or Five Times	Decca 18526
4/17/43	21	1	27. I Dood It...................... vocal: Charles Peterson; movie title song	Decca 18506
7/24/43	21	1	28. At The Woodchopper's Ball .... [I-R]	Decca 2440
2/19/44	7	11	29. Do Nothin' Till You Hear From Me	Decca 18578
3/25/44	10	8	30. The Music Stopped...................... from the film "Higher and Higher"	Decca 18577
4/08/44	12	7	31. By The River Of Roses	Decca 18578
6/24/44	10	5	32. Milkman, Keep Those Bottles Quiet............ from the film "Broadway Rhythm"	Decca 18603
12/16/44	18	1	33. Let Me Love You Tonight .... vocal: Billie Rogers; recorded 7/24/42	Decca 18619
2/24/45	15	1	34. Saturday Night (Is The Loneliest Night In The Week)...................... vocals on 30 & 34: Frances Wayne	Decca 18641
4/14/45	4	12	35. Laura .... movie title song	Columbia 36785
5/05/45	2(2)	14	36. Caldonia .... top 1944-45 sidemen: Bill Harris (trombone), Flip Phillips (tenor sax), Pete Candoli (trumpet), Dave Tough (drummer), pianist-arranger Ralph Burns, trumpet-arranger Neal Hefti	Columbia 36789
7/07/45	16	1	37. Apple Honey .... [I]	Columbia 36803
7/14/45	9	6	38. A Kiss Goodnight......................	Columbia 36815
9/29/45	13	1	39. Northwest Passage .... [I]	Columbia 36835
1/05/46	17	1	40. Gee, It's Good To Hold You...................... vocal: Frances Wayne	Columbia 36870
2/16/46	7	4	41. Let It Snow! Let It Snow! Let It Snow!/	
2/16/46	11	1	42. Everybody Knew But Me	Columbia 36909
4/27/46	11	1	43. Atlanta, G.A.	Columbia 36949
6/29/46	8	10	44. Surrender......................	Columbia 36985
7/27/46	12	4	45. Mabel! Mabel!...................... [N] Red Norvo (vibraphone) on above two	Columbia 36995
5/03/47	12	2	46. Across The Alley From The Alamo	Columbia 37289

DATE CHARTED	PEAK POS	WKS CHRT'D	ARTIST — Record Title	Label & Number
6/14/47	**13**	3	47. That's My Desire .... above two: Small-group recordings	Columbia 37329
7/12/47	**15**	2	48. Tallahassee .... DINAH SHORE & WOODY HERMAN accompanied by Sonny Burke's Orchestra from the film "Variety Girl"	Columbia 37387
8/16/47	**25**	1	49. Pancho Maximillian Hernandez	Columbia 37355
11/22/47+	**15**	2	50. Civilization (Bongo, Bongo, Bongo) .... from the Broadway musical "Angel in the Wings" Jimmy Rowles (piano) on 44-45 & 50	Columbia 37885
1/24/48	**23**	1	51. I Told Ya I Love Ya, Now Get Out.................	Columbia 38047
3/20/48	**3**	12	52. Sabre Dance .... [I] based on Kachaturian's "Gayne Ballet Suite" Stan Getz (tenor sax) on above three Zoot Sims (tenor sax) on above two	Columbia 38102
11/15/52	**28**	1	53. Early Autumn .... adapted from Part IV of Ralph Burns' "Summer Sequence"; the famous original version of this song was an instrumental featuring Stan Getz, released in 1949 on Capitol 57-616	Mars 300

MILT HERTH TRIO
Organist Milt Herth, jazz pianist Willie "The Lion" Smith, & drummer O'Neill Spencer; Herth died on 6/18/69. (also see Russ Morgan)

DATE CHARTED	PEAK POS	WKS CHRT'D	ARTIST — Record Title	Label & Number
4/09/38	**18**	2	1. Pop-Corn Man	Decca 1736
8/27/38	**13**	2	2. La De Doody Doo...................................... above two vocals: O'Neill Spencer	Decca 1966
10/03/42	**22**	1	3. I Wanna Go Back To West Virginia	Decca 4370

RALPH HERZ
Born in Paris, featured in many Broadway musicals from 1905-20; died on 7/12/21 (43).

DATE CHARTED	PEAK POS	WKS CHRT'D	ARTIST — Record Title	Label & Number
2/27/09	**3**	2	1. That Wasn't All! .... from the Broadway musical "The Soul Kiss"	Victor 5654

EDDIE HEYWOOD
Jazz pianist, composer of 1956 smash "Canadian Sunset", orchestra conductor for Ella Fitzgerald and others.

DATE CHARTED	PEAK POS	WKS CHRT'D	ARTIST — Record Title	Label & Number
4/28/45	**16**	1	1. Begin The Beguine.............................. [I] from the Broadway musical "Jubilee"	Decca 23398

HI-LOS
Popular vocal quartet: Clark Burroughs, Bob Morse, Gene Puerling, & Don Shelton.

DATE CHARTED	PEAK POS	WKS CHRT'D	ARTIST — Record Title	Label & Number
5/15/54	**29**	1	1. My Baby Just Cares For Me	Trend 74

AL HIBBLER
Vocalist with Duke Ellington (1943-51); born blind

ART HICKMAN & HIS ORCHESTRA
Trend-setting West Coast dance band leader, composer of "Rose Room" and other songs. Alto saxophonist Clyde Doerr was a prominent member; Earl Burtnett directed some later records. Art died on 1/16/30 (43).

DATE CHARTED	PEAK POS	WKS CHRT'D	ARTIST — Record Title	Label & Number
1/10/20	**2(2)**	7	1. Peggy .... [I]	Columbia 2812
1/17/20	**2(2)**	8	2. Sweet And Low .... [I]	Columbia 2814
2/28/20	**13**	1	3. The Hesitating Blues .... [I]	Columbia 2813
4/10/20	**10**	1	4. Wonderful Pal...................................... [I] Art Hickman Trio	Columbia 2839
5/01/20	**5**	4	5. Rose Room .... [I]	Columbia 2858
6/19/20	**1(3)**	14	6. **Hold Me**.. [I]	Columbia 2899
10/02/20	**1(2)**	6	7. **The Love Nest**..................................... [I] from the Broadway musical "Mary"	Columbia 2955
10/23/20	**2(3)**	8	8. Tell Me, Little Gypsy .... [I] 6 & 8 from the Broadway musical "Ziegfeld Follies of 1920"	Columbia 2972
10/30/20	**9**	2	9. A Young Man's Fancy............................. [I] from the Broadway musical "What's In a Name?"	Columbia 2970
11/20/20	**6**	2	10. Cuban Moon .... [I]	Columbia 2982
12/18/20	**8**	3	11. Whispering .... [I]	Columbia 3301

DATE CHARTED	PEAK POS	WKS CHRT'D	ARTIST — Record Title	Label & Number
1/29/21	**11**	1	12. Avalon.. [I]	Columbia 3322
			featured in the Broadway musical "Bombo"	
2/26/21	**12**	1	13. Any Time, Any Day, Anywhere .... [I]	Columbia 3325
3/12/21	**2(1)**	7	14. Darling .... [I]	Columbia 3334

MINA HICKMAN

DATE CHARTED	PEAK POS	WKS CHRT'D	ARTIST — Record Title	Label & Number
8/03/01	**3**	3	1. When I Think Of You...............................	Victor 751
5/24/02	**4**	2	2. Pretty Molly Shannon...............................	Columbia 659
			from the Broadway musical "The Little Duchess"	
1/17/03	**1(5)**	11	3. **Come Down, Ma Evening Star**	Columbia 955
			also on Columbia cylinder 31894, later recorded for Victor 1980 & Zon-o-Phone 5292; from the Broadway musical "Twirly Whirly"	
9/19/03	**4**	3	4. Congo Love Song	Victor 2374
			from the Broadway musical "Nancy Brown"	
10/01/04	**3**	4	5. Good-Bye, Little Girl, Good-Bye	Victor 2908

J.C. HIGGINBOTHAM
Top jazz trombonist with Fletcher Henderson (1931-33), Mills Blue Rhythm Band (1934-36), Louis Armstrong (1937-40), & Red Allen (1940-47); died on 5/26/73 (67).

HIGH HATTERS

DATE CHARTED	PEAK POS	WKS CHRT'D	ARTIST — Record Title	Label & Number
1/18/30	**13**	2	1. I'm Following You	Victor 22218
4/19/30	**10**	4	2. Sing, You Sinners	Victor 22322
			from the film "Honey"	
6/28/30	**6**	4	3. My Future Just Passed	Victor 22444
			from the film "Safety in Numbers" flip side of "Get Happy" (POS 6) by Nat Shilkret & His Orchestra	
6/28/30	**13**	3	4. You Brought A New Kind Of Love To Me	Victor 22409
			from the film "The Big Pond"	
6/27/31	**6**	4	5. There Ought To Be A Moonlight Saving Time .	Victor 22703
			above four vocals: Frank Luther	
8/01/31	**15**	3	6. Come To Me..	Victor 22756
			vocal: Chick Bullock	

HILDEGARDE
Hildegarde Loretta Sell first became popular in England, then returned home to become one of the most popular singers in 1940s U.S. radio, ranking behind only Bing Crosby in 1944 ratings.

DATE CHARTED	PEAK POS	WKS CHRT'D	ARTIST — Record Title	Label & Number
12/26/36	**16**	2	1. Pennies From Heaven	Columbia 1598
			movie title song	
12/11/43	**21**	1	2. Darling, Je Vous Aime Beaucoup.................	Decca 23218
			Hildegarde's theme song	
3/04/44	**29**	1	3. Leave Us Face It (We're In Love)/	
4/29/44	**15**	2	4. Suddenly It's Spring................................	Decca 23297
			from the film "Lady in the Dark" above three with Harry Sosnik's Orchestra	
9/01/45	**11**	1	5. June Is Bustin' Out All Over	Decca 23428
			from the Broadway musical "Carousel"	
4/13/46	**15**	2	6. One-Zy, two-Zy (I Love You-Zy)/	
5/11/46	**7**	14	7. The Gypsy...	Decca 23511
			above three with Guy Lombardo & His Royal Canadians	

MURRY K. HILL
Real name Joseph T. Pope Jr.; well-known vaudeville comedian, died on 10/23/42 (77).

DATE CHARTED	PEAK POS	WKS CHRT'D	ARTIST — Record Title	Label & Number
9/28/07	**10**	1	1. In The Good Old Steamboat Days.................	Edison 9619

TEDDY HILL & HIS ORCHESTRA
Saxophonist who led jazz band at times featuring Roy Eldridge, Dizzy Gillespie, & Chu Berry.

DATE CHARTED	PEAK POS	WKS CHRT'D	ARTIST — Record Title	Label & Number
4/17/37	**20**	1	1. The Love Bug Will Bite You	Bluebird 6897

TINY HILL & HIS ORCHESTRA
350-pound "cornball" band leader (all vocals by Hill)

DATE CHARTED	PEAK POS	WKS CHRT'D	ARTIST — Record Title	Label & Number
9/23/39	**14**	1	1. Doodle Doo Doo.................................... [N]	Vocalion 5060
10/05/39	**13**	3	2. Angry .... [N]	Vocalion 4957

DATE CHARTED	PEAK POS	WKS CHRT'D	ARTIST — Record Title	Label & Number
6/08/40	28	1	3. I Get A Kick Outa Corn .... [N]	Vocalion 5469
8/03/40	25	1	4. Five Foot Two, Eyes Of Blue	Okeh 5635
2/08/41	25	1	5. The Guy At The End Of The Bar .... [N]	Okeh 5924
10/28/44	14	4	6. How Many Hearts Have You Broken	Decca 4447
1/27/51	29	2	7. Hot Rod Race .... [N]	Mercury 5547
1/12/52	28	2	8. Slow Poke .... [N]	Mercury 5740

FRED HILLEBRAND
Comedian/songwriter; died on 9/15/63 (69).

12/15/34	17	2	1. Home, James, And Don't Spare The Horses ... with the Cavaliers	Decca 215

HARRIET HILLIARD
Born Peggy Lou Snyder; vocalist with husband Ozzie Nelson's band, then co-star in their long-running radio & TV series "Ozzie & Harriet".

HILLTOPPERS
Jimmy Sacca, lead singer, with Don McGuire, Seymour Spiegelman, and Billy Vaughn (later an orchestra leader)

8/16/52	7	19	1. Trying	Dot 15018
1/03/53	26	1	2. I Keep Telling Myself/	
1/10/53	15	2	3. Must I Cry Again	Dot 15034
3/28/53	22	1	4. If I Were King..	Dot 15055
6/06/53	8	12	5. I'd Rather Die Young/	
6/13/53	4	21	● 6. P.S. I Love You...	Dot 15085
10/24/53	8	11	7. To Be Alone/	
10/24/53	8	10	8. Love Walked In .... from the film "The Goldwyn Follies"	Dot 15105
1/23/54	27	1	9. Time Will Tell/	
2/13/54	8	11	10. From The Vine Came The Grape................ sung half in English, half in Italian	Dot 15127
1/30/54	10	11	11. Till Then	Dot 15132
4/24/54	12	5	12. Poor Butterfly .... from the Broadway musical "The Big Show"	Dot 15156
7/03/54	24	3	13. Sweetheart (Will You Remember)	Dot 15201
8/28/54	17	2	14. If I Didn't Care	Dot 15220
11/20/54	25	1	15. Time Waits For No One .... from the film "Shine On, Harvest Moon"	Dot 15249

HILO HAWAIIAN ORCHESTRA
Nat Shilkret, director

4/12/30	1(2)	19	1. **When It's Springtime In The Rockies/** vocal: Frank Luther & Carson Robison	
6/28/30	10	10	2. Down The River Of Golden Dreams .... vocal: Johnny Marvin	Victor 22339

RICHARD HIMBER & HIS ORCHESTRA
Started as violin accompanist for Sophie Tucker; composer of many songs, including famous theme "It Isn't Fair"; died on 12/11/66 (59).

10/27/34	2(2)	7	1. Stars Fell On Alabama/	
11/03/34	12	4	2. If I Had A Million Dollars......................... from the film "Transatlantic Merry-Go-Round" above two vocals: Joey Nash	Victor 24745
6/15/35	10	5	3. Footloose And Fancy Free	Victor 25037
6/29/35	18	1	4. Kiss Me Goodnight	Victor 25073
11/30/35	10	5	5. Just One Of Those Things .... from the Broadway musical "Jubilee"	Victor 25161
1/04/36	15	6	6. If I Should Lose You.................................. from the film "Rose of the Rancho"	Victor 25179
2/01/36	9	8	7. You Hit The Spot .... from the film "Collegiate"	Victor 25189
2/08/36	6	8	8. Cling To Me/	
3/07/36	20	1	9. So This Is Heaven	Victor 25235

DATE CHARTED	PEAK POS	WKS CHRT'D	ARTIST — Record Title	Label & Number
4/25/36	10	9	10. Tormented.. with Artie Shaw (clarinet)	Victor 25293
12/05/36	7	4	11. In The Chapel In The Moonlight..................	Victor 25441
12/05/36	20	1	12. Thru The Courtesy Of Love .... above five with Bunny Berigan (trumpet)	Victor 25443
2/12/38	13	2	13. The Parade Of Bands............................. [I] Adrian Rollini (vibraphone/cello) on most above records	Victor 25754
11/26/38	4	2	14. Day After Day .... all vocals 3-14: Stuart Allen	Victor 26106
6/08/40	27	1	15. Whose Theme Song? .... [I]	Royale 1795
12/06/41	24	1	16. I Know Why (And So Do You)..................... vocal: Johnny Johnston & Joseph Lilley Ensemble	Decca 3896

HARVEY HINDERMYER
A member of the Shannon Four, Harvey became a popular radio performer in the 1920s as one of the "Gold Dust Twins"; he died on 10/22/57 (75).

| 11/21/08 | 3 | 4 | 1. Take Me Out To The Ball Game .... | Columbia 586 |
| 7/31/09 | 10 | 1 | 2. Nobody Knows, Nobody Cares .... | Victor 16321 |

EARL HINES & HIS ORCHESTRA
Widely regarded as the pioneer of modern jazz piano, Earl "Fatha" Hines first gained fame for his classic 1927-28 recordings with Louis Armstrong. His amazing early-40s band featured Charlie Parker (alto sax), Dizzy Gillespie (trumpet), and vocalists Billy Eckstine & Sarah Vaughan. Earl started a remarkable comeback in 1964 which lasted until his death on 4/22/83 (77).

9/23/33	20	1	1. 57 Varieties... [I]	Columbia 2800
4/03/37	17	1	2. Rhythm Sundae................................... [I]	Vocalion 3467
5/18/40	11	4	3. Boogie Woogie On The St. Louis Blues/	
9/21/40	28	1	4. Number 19 .... [I]	Bluebird 10674
4/24/43	23	1	5. Stormy Monday Blues............................. vocal by Billy Eckstine	Bluebird 11567
8/12/44	18	1	6. It Had To Be You .... vocal: Madeline Greene & Three Varieties; recorded 8/20/41, originally issued on Bluebird 11308	Bluebird 0825

JOHNNY HODGES & HIS ORCHESTRA
Among the great alto saxophonists in jazz history, with Duke Ellington from 1928-51 & 1955-60s; Johnny died on 5/11/70 (63). (also see Teddy Wilson)

7/24/37	17	2	1. A Sailboat In The Moonlight .... vocal: Buddy Clark	Variety 586
10/22/38	13	2	2. Prelude To A Kiss.................................... vocal: Mary McHugh; Johnny also recorded song with Ellington (Brunswick 8204); above two with Duke, Cootie Williams, & other Ellington sidemen	Vocalion 4386
9/01/51	28	1	3. Castle Rock .... [I] band includes Ellington trombonist Lawrence Brown.	Mercury 8944

CARL HOFF & HIS ORCHESTRA
Born Carl Hoffmayr, former arranger for Paul Whiteman & Vincent Lopez; co-wrote 1953 classic "Vaya Con Dios".

| 2/28/42 | 23 | 1 | 1. You're A Sap, Mr. Jap.............................
vocal by the Murphy Sisters | Okeh 6556 |

BILLIE HOLIDAY
Rivaled only by Ella Fitzgerald among all female jazz singers, the great "Lady Day" was born Eleanor Gough in Baltimore on 4/7/15, the illegitimate daughter of guitarist Clarence Holiday. Following her difficult early years she was discovered in 1933 by jazz critic John Hammond; she recorded one hit with Benny Goodman, then began her classic 1935-38 association with Teddy Wilson, accompanied by the top jazz musicians in the country. Billie also sang briefly in late 30s with Count Basie and Artie Shaw. Despite many personal problems, Billie remained a unique talent to the end (7/17/59); the 1972 movie "Lady Sings the Blues" was based on her life.

| 3/10/35 | 12 | 4 | 1. What A Little Moonlight Can Do .... | Brunswick 7498 |
| 11/23/35 | 6 | 7 | 2. Twenty-Four Hours A Day ....
from the film "Sweet Surrender" | Brunswick 7550 |

DATE CHARTED	PEAK POS	WKS CHRT'D	ARTIST — Record Title	Label & Number
12/07/35	12	3	3. If You Were Mine .... from the film "To Beat the Band"	Brunswick 7554
1/18/36	18	1	4. You Let Me Down.. from the film "Stars Over Broadway"	Brunswick 7581
8/01/36	5	5	5. These Foolish Things .... from the London musical "Spread It Around"	Brunswick 7699
8/15/36	17	2	6. It's Like Reaching For The Moon .... above six, 11-15, 17, 19-22, 24-26, 28 & 32-33: TEDDY WILSON & HIS ORCHESTRA, vocals by Billie Holiday; nearly all others listed as "Billie Holiday & Her Orchestra"	Brunswick 7702
9/12/36	9	5	7. No Regrets..	Vocalion 3276
9/12/36	12	2	8. Summertime .... from the folk opera "Porgy and Bess" Artie Shaw (clarinet) on above two	Vocalion 3288
10/31/36	9	3	9. A Fine Romance .... from the film "Swing Time"	Vocalion 3333
11/07/36	18	1	10. Let's Call A Heart A Heart...................... from the film "Pennies from Heaven" Bunny Berigan (trumpet) on above four; Irving Fazola (clarinet) on above two	Vocalion 3334
11/14/36	3	5	11. The Way You Look Tonight .... from the film "Swing Time"	Brunswick 7762
11/14/36	4	6	12. Who Loves You?.. Chu Berry (tenor sax) on 2 & 8; Gene Krupa (drums) on above two; Cozy Cole drummer on most other records	Brunswick 7768
12/19/36	5	4	13. I Can't Give You Anything But Love............. from the Broadway musical "Blackbirds of 1928"	Brunswick 7781
12/26/36	20	1	14. That's Life, I Guess/	
1/02/37	3	6	15. Pennies From Heaven........................... movie title song	Brunswick 7789
2/20/37	4	10	16. I've Got My Love To Keep Me Warm	Vocalion 3431
2/27/37	8	3	17. This Year's Kisses .... above two from the film "On The Avenue" Benny Goodman (clarinet) on 1, 13-15 & 17	Brunswick 7824
2/27/37	13	3	18. Please Keep Me In Your Dreams .... Ben Webster (tenor sax) on 1, 11-16, & 18; Jonah Jones (trumpet) on 16 & 18	Vocalion 3440
3/27/37	10	3	19. (This Is) My Last Affair .... from the Broadway musical "New Faces of 1934"	Brunswick 7840
4/03/37	8	3	20. The Mood That I'm In .... Henry (Red) Allen (trumpet) on above two	Brunswick 7844
4/24/37	1(3)	12	21. **Carelessly/**	
5/01/37	12	3	22. How Could You?................................... Cootie Williams (trumpet) on above two	Brunswick 7867
5/15/37	12	4	23. They Can't Take That Away From Me.......... from the film "Shall We Dance?"	Vocalion 3520
5/22/37	11	2	24. Moanin' Low .... from the Broadway musical "The Little Show" Harry Carney (clarinet/baritone sax) on 5-6, 21-22 & 24	Brunswick 7877
6/26/37	7	4	25. Mean To Me	Brunswick 7903
7/10/37	15	2	26. Easy Living	Brunswick 7911
7/17/37	11	3	27. Me, Myself, And I.....................................	Vocalion 3593
7/24/37	16	2	28. Yours And Mine.. from the film "Broadway Melody of 1938" Johnny Hodges (alto sax) on 4-6, 21-22, 24-25 & 28	Brunswick 7917
8/07/37	10	3	29. A Sailboat In The Moonlight	Vocalion 3605
10/23/37	10	5	30. Getting Some Fun Out Of Life	Vocalion 3701
11/20/37	18	2	31. Trav'lin' All Alone .... Lester Young (tenor sax) on 17, 25-27, & above three	Vocalion 3748
12/25/37	20	1	32. Nice Work If You Can Get It....................... from the film "A Damsel in Distress"	Brunswick 8015
1/08/38	14	2	33. My Man.. French song originally in musical "Paris qui Jazz", in the Broadway musical "Ziegfeld Follies of 1921" Teddy Wilson (piano) on 1-6, 11-26, 28, 32-33; Buck Clayton (trumpet) on 17 & 25-33	Brunswick 8008
7/30/38	20	1	34. You Go To My Head...................................	Vocalion 4126

DATE CHARTED	PEAK POS	WKS CHRT'D	ARTIST — Record Title	Label & Number
8/13/38	2(1)	9	35. I'm Gonna Lock My Heart........................... Claude Thornhill (piano) on 30-31 and above two	Vocalion 4238
7/22/39	16	2	36. Strange Fruit .... historic jazz classic selected for NARAS Hall of Fame; banned by radio networks as too controversial	Commodore 526
10/18/41	25	1	37. God Bless The Child .... Billie's most famous composition; selected for the NARAS Hall of Fame; Roy Eldridge (trumpet) on 2-3 & 37; Eddie Heywood (piano) on 37	Okeh 6270
10/31/42	23	1	38. Trav'lin' Light... PAUL WHITEMAN & HIS ORCHESTRA; vocal by "Lady Day"	Capitol 116
5/05/45	16	1	39. Lover Man (Oh, Where Can You Be)............. with Camarata's Orchestra	Decca 23391

LIBBY HOLMAN
Sultry torch singer whose vocal style and tempestuous private life led her to be labeled "the dark purple menace"; featured in many Broadway musicals from 1927-38, and in 1940s performed with popular black folk singer Josh White. Libby died on 6/18/71 (65).

DATE CHARTED	PEAK POS	WKS CHRT'D	ARTIST — Record Title	Label & Number
9/07/29	4	8	1. Am I Blue?/ from the film "On With the Show"	
9/21/29	5	6	2. Moanin' Low.. from the Broadway musical "The Little Show"; Libby also recorded song with Cotton Pickers (including Tommy & Jimmy Dorsey), Brunswick 4446	Brunswick 4445
12/28/29	19	1	3. Find Me A Primitive Man........................... with the Colonial Club Orchestra from the Broadway musical "Fifty Million Frenchmen"	Brunswick 4666
1/04/30	19	1	4. Why Was I Born?.....................................	Brunswick 4570
10/18/30	3	7	5. Body And Soul/	
12/20/30+	6	6	6. Something To Remember You By............... above 3 from the Broadway musical "Sweet Adeline"	Brunswick 4910
2/21/31	5	8	7. Love For Sale/ from the Broadway musical "The New Yorkers"	
2/28/31	14	2	8. I'm One Of God's Children	Brunswick 6044
1/12/35	11	5	9. You And The Night And The Music .... with Richard Himber's Orchestra; from the Broadway musical "Revenge With Music"	Victor 24839

LEROY HOLMES & HIS ORCHESTRA
Former arranger for Vincent Lopez & Harry James, orchestra leader for Tommy Edwards, Art Lund, other singers; winner of four Academy Awards, one for his "High and the Mighty" score.

DATE CHARTED	PEAK POS	WKS CHRT'D	ARTIST — Record Title	Label & Number
7/31/54	9	14	1. The High And The Mighty .... [I] whistling by Fred Lowry; movie title song	MGM 11761
11/27/54	21	4	2. Tara's Theme.. [I] theme from "Gone With The Wind"	MGM 11854

VIVIAN HOLT & LILLIAN ROSEDALE

DATE CHARTED	PEAK POS	WKS CHRT'D	ARTIST — Record Title	Label & Number
9/06/19	5	3	1. My Swanee Home.....................................	Victor 18566
10/18/19	4	5	2. Sweet Hawaiian Moonlight.........................	Victor 18597

LEW HOLTZ & HIS ORCHESTRA

DATE CHARTED	PEAK POS	WKS CHRT'D	ARTIST — Record Title	Label & Number
4/12/24	9	1	1. When It's Night Time In Italy	Victor 19205

HOMER & JETHRO
Real names Henry Haynes & Kenneth Burns, country music's foremost comedy duo from 40s until Homer's death on 8/7/71 (54); Jethro went on to work with popular folk singer Steve Goodman.

DATE CHARTED	PEAK POS	WKS CHRT'D	ARTIST — Record Title	Label & Number
8/20/49	22	1	1. Baby, It's Cold Outside .... [C] from the film "Neptune's Daughter"	RCA Victor 0078
5/30/53	17	4	2. That Hound Dog In The Window .... [C]	RCA Victor 5280

BEN HOMER
Arranger for Tommy & Jimmy Dorsey, Les Brown, Benny Goodman & other band; composer of the classic "Sentimental Journey".

DATE CHARTED	PEAK POS	WKS CHRT'D	ARTIST — Record Title	Label & Number
			### LOUISE HOMER	
			The most acclaimed American contralto of her time, over 20 years with the Metropolitan Opera; her nephew was the famous classical composer Samuel Barber. Louise died on 5/6/47 (76).	
10/28/05	6	1	1. The Old Folks At Home (Swanee River)	Victor 81077
8/31/07	7	1	2. Madama Butterfly: Tutti I Fior (Duet Of The Flowers).................................... [F] LOUISE HOMER & GERALDINE FERRAR	Victor 87008
8/29/08	8	1	3. Il Trovatore - Ai Nostri Monti (Home To Our Mountains).................................... [F]	Victor 89018
5/20/11	5	3	4. Aida - Aida A Me Togliesti (Aida Thou Hast Taken)... [F] above two: ENRICO CARUSO & LOUISE HOMER	Victor 89051
7/20/12	5	4	5. Whispering Hope	Victor 87107
6/14/13	10	1	6. Abide With Me	Victor 87132
10/10/14	10	1	7. Rock Of Ages	Victor 87198
2/27/15	6	3	8. Jesus, Lover Of My Soul............................ above four: LOUISE HOMER & ALMA GLUCK	Victor 87200
6/07/19	9	1	9. Samson Et Dalila - Je Viens Celebrer La Victoire (I Come To Celebrate Victory) [F] ENRICO CARUSO, LOUISE HOMER, & MARCEL JOURNET	Victor 89088
7/11/25	8	1	10. America The Beautiful.............................	Victor 1074
			### JOHN LEE HOOKER	
			Detroit-based, internationally-respected blues singer/guitarist, active professionally for nearly 50 years.	
11/17/51	30	1	1. I'm In The Mood	Modern 835
			### WILLIAM F. HOOLEY	
			Bass voice of the Haydn Quartet (1898-1914) and the American Quartet (1909 until his death on 10/12/18 at 57); born in Cork, Ireland.	
7/15/99	1(5)	14	1. **Gypsy Love Song** .... from the Broadway musical "The Fortune Teller"	Edison 7163
			### HOOSIER HOT SHOTS	
			Novelty instrumental quartet; began on National Barn Dance radio show.	
9/18/37	13	2	1. Breezin' Along With The Breeze .... [N]	Vocalion 3644
11/19/38	12	1	2. Red Hot Fannie .... [N]	Vocalion 4289
12/17/38	11	2	3. The Man With The Whiskers................... [X]	Vocalion 4502
4/01/39	15	1	4. Annabelle..	Vocalion 4697
2/09/46	12	1	5. Someday (You'll Want Me To Want You)........ vocal: Sally Foster	Decca 18736
			### BOB HOPE	
			Enduring institution of American entertainment, born on 5/29/03 in London; began in 1920s vaudeville.	
1/14/39	15	2	1. Two Sleepy People .... BOB HOPE & SHIRLEY ROSS with Harry Sosnik's Orchestra; from the film "Thanks for the Memory"; B side - duet of Bob's famous theme song	Decca 2219
11/17/45	21	1	2. The Road To Morocco............................. BING CROSBY & BOB HOPE with Vic Schoen's Orchestra; movie title song	Decca 40000
6/17/50	16	4	3. Blind Date .... MARGARET WHITING & BOB HOPE with the Starlighters & Billy May's Orchestra	Capitol 1042
			### HOPE QUINTET L	
8/26/50	19	3	1. Tenderly .... from the film "Torch Song"	Premium 851
			### SOL HOPII & HIS NOVELTY QUARTET	
1/20/34	20	1	1. Little Grass Shack	Brunswick 6752

DATE CHARTED	PEAK POS	WKS CHRT'D	ARTIST — Record Title	Label & Number
			CLAUDE HOPKINS & HIS ORCHESTRA Pianist who led accompanying band for Josephine Baker on 1920s European tour; his band featured clarinetist Ed Hall & Jabbo Smith (trumpet); did arrangements for various 1940s bands.	
4/15/33	17	2	1. California, Here I Come........................ [I] from the Broadway musical "Bombo"	Columbia 2741
1/27/34	18	1	2. Washington Squabble .... [I]	Brunswick 6750
5/19/34	15	2	3. Three Little Words................................ [I] from the film "Check and Double Check"	Brunswick 6864
7/14/34	5	4	4. Margie .... vocal: Orlando Robertson	Brunswick 6916
			DeWOLF HOPPER Successful musical comedy performer over many years, but known to all for this classic monologue; died on 9/23/35 (77).	
10/27/06	3	6	1. Casey At The Bat ....[T-C] Hopper first performed this on stage in 1888, and was subsequently to repeat it some 10,000 times	Victor 31559
			LENA HORNE Beautiful Broadway and movie musical star, long married to bandleader Lennie Hayton; Lena's remarkable career reached a new peak in the 1980s with her triumphant one-woman Broadway show.	
9/04/43	21	1	1. Stormy Weather .... movie title song, and Lena's theme ever since accompanied by Lou Bring's Orchestra	Victor 27819
3/17/45	21	1	2. One For My Baby (And One More For The Road) .... from the film "The Sky's the Limit"; with Hoarce Henderson's Orchestra; featuring Illinois Jacquet (tenor sax)	Victor 1616
5/01/48	26	1	3. 'Deed I Do .... with Luther Henderson's Orchestra	MGM 10165
			VLADAMIR HOROWITZ Possibly the greatest pianist of the century, born in Russia, a phenomenon from his 1925 European debut into the 1980s.	
6/16/28	20	1	1. Mazurka In C Sharp Minor...................... [I]	Victor 1327
			VAUGHN HORTON & HIS POLKA DEBS	
5/08/48	11	4	1. Toolie Oolie Doolie (The Yodel Polka)	Continental 1223
			HOTEL BOSSERT ORCHESTRA Freddy Martin, leader	
5/13/33	8	4	1. In The Park In Paree .... vocal: Elmer Feldkamp; from the film "The Barbarian"	Columbia 2769
			HOTEL COMMODORE ORCHESTRA	
4/29/33	3	7	1. Hold Me/	
5/06/33	7	4	2. Let's Call It A Day .... from the Broadway musical "Strike Me Pink"	Columbia 2767
			BOB HOUSTON Sang with Johnny Long band	
11/15/47	26	1	1. A Tune For Humming	MGM 10091
11/19/49	27	1	2. That Lucky Old Sun .... with Russ Case's Orchestra	MGM 10509
			CISCO HOUSTON Great folk singer and songwriter, long associated with Woody Guthrie; died on 4/29/61 (42).	
6/09/51	21	4	1. Rose, Rose, I Love You .... with Gordon Jenkins' Orchestra	Decca 27594
			BOB HOWARD & HIS ORCHESTRA Singer/pianist (born Howard Joyner) with top musicians	
3/28/36	15	1	1. Wake Up And Sing.................................. band includes Bunny Berigan (trumpet) & Dave Barbour (guitar)	Decca 720
			DON HOWARD Don was 17 years old when he recorded this hit.	
12/06/52+	4	15	● 1. Oh Happy Day...................................... [N]	Essex 311

DATE CHARTED	PEAK POS	WKS CHRT'D	ARTIST — Record Title	Label & Number
			EDDY HOWARD & HIS ORCHESTRA	
			Singer with Dick Jurgens band from 1934-40; composer of "My Last Goodbye" & "Careless"; died on 5/23/63 (48).	
8/17/40	**21**	2	1. Orchids For Remembrance	Columbia 35558
1/24/42	**21**	1	2. Miss You	Columbia 36432
6/29/46	**1(8)**	24	● 3. **To Each His Own**..............................	Majestic 7188
			written for, but not used in, film of same name	
			also recorded on Majestic 1070	
8/24/46	**6**	14	4. The Rickety Rickshaw Man......................	Majestic 7192
			also recorded on Majestic 1078	
11/16/46+	**2(1)**	20	5. (I Love You) For Sentimental Reasons	Majestic 7204
11/16/46	**17**	1	6. My Best To You..................................	Majestic 1074
2/08/47	**23**	1	7. The Girl That I Marry	Majestic 1083
			from the Broadway musical "Annie Get Your Gun"	
4/05/47	**2(5)**	15	8. My Adobe Hacienda.............................	Majestic 1117
4/19/47	**11**	5	9. Heartaches	Majestic 1111
5/19/47	**2(4)**	19	10. I Wonder, I Wonder, I Wonder	Majestic 1124
7/26/47	**16**	3	11. Ragtime Cowboy Joe/	
8/09/47	**23**	4	12. On The Old Spanish Trail	Majestic 1155
9/20/47	**7**	3	13. Kate (Have I Come Too Early Too Late)........	Majestic 1160
10/18/47	**9**	4	14. An Apple Blossom Wedding	Majestic 1156
11/08/47	**21**	2	15. A Tune For Humming	Majestic 1177
12/13/47	**21**	1	16. White Christmas....................... [X]	Majestic 1175
2/14/48	**8**	16	17. Now Is The Hour................................	Majestic 1191
			based on the traditional New Zealand song "Hearere Ra"	
5/15/48	**23**	2	18. Put 'Em In A Box..............................	Majestic 1252
			from the film "Romance On the High Seas"	
5/22/48	**20**	4	19. Just Because	Majestic 1231
11/27/48	**6**	12	20. On A Slow Boat To China	Mercury 5210
12/11/48	**27**	1	21. Dainty Brenda Lee	Mercury 5208
4/23/49	**20**	2	22. Candy Kisses	Mercury 5272
4/23/49	**24**	1	23. Love Me, Love Me, Love Me	Mercury 5238
6/04/49	**29**	1	24. Red Head	Mercury 5274
7/09/49	**4**	23	25. Room Full Of Roses/	
8/20/49	**21**	3	26. There's Yes! Yes! In Your Eyes.................	Mercury 5296
8/27/49	**9**	14	27. Maybe It's Because/	
			from the Broadway musical "Along Fifth Avenue"	
10/29/49	**25**	1	28. Tell Me Why	Mercury 5314
2/04/50	**28**	1	29. Half A Heart Is All You Left Me	Mercury 5349
3/11/50	**24**	1	30. Rag Mop......................................	Mercury 5371
7/15/50	**21**	1	31. American Beauty Rose	Mercury 5433
11/04/50	**9**	11	32. To Think You've Chosen Me	Mercury 5517
2/17/51	**14**	7	33. A Penny A Kiss	Mercury 5567
6/02/51	**27**	1	34. What Will I Tell My Heart/	
6/02/51	**28**	3	35. A Strange Little Girl............................	Mercury 5630
7/21/51	**22**	2	36. Deadly Weapon	Mercury 5663
9/22/51	**1(8)**	24	● 37. **Sin (It's No Sin)**............................	Mercury 5711
2/02/52	**11**	14	38. Stolen Love	Mercury 5771
3/08/52	**17**	14	39. Wishin'	Mercury 5784
3/29/52	**7**	16	40. Be Anything (But Be Mine).....................	Mercury 5815
6/28/52	**4**	16	41. Auf Weiderseh'n, Sweetheart/	
			German song introduced in England	
9/13/52	**26**	1	42. I Don't Want To Take That Chance	Mercury 5871
9/06/52	**14**	6	43. Mademoiselle..................................	Mercury 5898
11/22/52	**11**	5	44. It's Worth Any Price You Pay....................	Mercury 70015
3/28/53	**17**	5	45. Gomen-Nasai (Forgive Me)	Mercury 70107
			song introduced in Japan	
9/05/53	**24**	3	46. Love Every Moment You Live...................	Mercury 70176
10/31/53	**21**	4	47. Skirts	Mercury 70225

DATE CHARTED	PEAK POS	WKS CHRT'D	ARTIST — Record Title	Label & Number
3/06/54	22	2	48. Till We Two Are One/	
3/13/54	16	5	49. Melancholy Me	Mercury 70293

ROSETTA HOWARD
Chicago-born blues singer who retired to perform gospel music with Thomas A. Dorsey; died in 1974 (approximately 60).

2/14/48	21	5	1. Ebony Rhapsody..	Columbia 37573

accompanied by the Big Three Trio, including great blues bassist/songwriter Willie Dixon

SONNY HOWARD

7/18/53	24	2	1. Jig-Saw Puzzle Heart................................	RCA Victor 5304

WILLIE HOWARD
German-born Willie and brother Eugene Howard (real name Lekvowitz) starred as a vaudeville comedy team, then appeared together in Broadway musicals from 1912-39.

1/16/26	7	2	1. My Yiddishe Momme .... [C]	Columbia 473

HUDSON-DELANGE ORCHESTRA
Popular dance band led by Will Hudson & Eddie DeLange; briefly featured future vocal star Georgia Gibbs.

5/16/36	9	5	1. Organ Grinder's Swing........................... [I]	Brunswick 7656
1/09/37	16	2	2. Midnight At The Onyx .... [I]	Brunswick 7795
2/06/37	16	2	3. How Was I To Know?................................	Brunswick 7809
			vocal: Eddie DeLange	
3/06/37	14	2	4. Love Song Of A Half-Wit........................ [I]	Brunswick 7828
5/29/37	18	2	5. Wake Up And Live	Master 112
			movie title song	
7/24/37	19	1	6. You're My Desire	Master 132
			above two vocals: Ruth Gaylor	
9/04/37	11	5	7. Yours And Mine......................................	Master 138
			from the film "Broadway Melody of 1938"	
9/25/37	20	2	8. The Maid's Night Off............................. [I]	Master 103
11/27/37	15	3	9. Popcorn Man...	Brunswick 8007
			vocals on 7 & 9: Nan Wynn	
1/29/38	19	1	10. College Widow.................................... [I]	Brunswick 8040
4/02/38	11	5	11. Sunday In The Park	Brunswick 8077
			vocal: Mary McHugh	

WILL HUDSON
Co-leader of Hudson-DeLange band, composer of "Moonglow", did arrangements for Cab Calloway, Benny Goodman, Jimmie Lunceford, & Ray Noble.

8/27/38	11	1	1. The Night Is Filled With Music	Brunswick 8191

vocal: Jane Dover; from the fim "Carefree"

MARJORIE HUGHES
Frankie Carle's daughter and featured vocalist

7/23/49	18	5	1. You Told A Lie..	Columbia 38500

with Hugo Winterhalter's Orchestra

HELEN HUMES
Important jazz/blues singer; sang with Count Basie (1938-41) and Harry James; professionally active until shortly before her death on 9/13/81 (68).

PEE WEE HUNT & HIS ORCHESTRA
Singer and trombonist with the Casa Loma band from 1929-43; scored two giant hits with his own Dixieland band, including Carl Fischer (piano).

6/26/48	1(8)	32	● 1. **Twelfth Street Rag**........................... [I]	Capitol 15105
7/04/53	3	25	● 2. Oh!/ [I]	
7/11/53	24	4	3. San .... [I]	Capitol 2442

DATE CHARTED	PEAK POS	WKS CHRT'D	ARTIST — Record Title	Label & Number
			ALBERTA HUNTER	
			Pioneering blues singer, co-writer of Bessie Smith classic "Down Hearted Blues", originator of the "Black Bottom" dance. Alberta reached her greatest popularity in a 1970s comeback; she died on 10/10/84 (87).	
10/08/27	**16**	2	1. Beale Street Blues .... Victor 20771	
			with Fats Waller (organ)	
			RUSSELL HUNTING	
			A pioneer of the early recording industry. Russell started as a dramatic actor in the Boston Theatre Co.; achieved national fame for his "Casey" Irish comedy records (often playing multiple parts and supplying imaginative sound effects); went to England in 1898 to become an Edison Bell executive and finally became the longtime head of recording for the Pathe company. He died on 2/20/43 (78).	
6/13/91	**1(4)**	4	1. **Michael Casey As A Physician** ....[T-C] New York	
			also recorded for New England	
7/09/92	**1(5)**	5	2. **Michael Casey At The Telephone**........[T-C] Columbia	
			also recorded for New England & New Jersey	
10/08/92	**1(6)**	6	3. **Michael Casey Taking The Census** ......[T-C] Columbia	
			also recorded for New England & New Jersey	
2/04/93	**2(3)**	3	4. Casey At The Bat ....[T-C] Columbia	
			first recording of the famous monologue	
4/01/93	**2(2)**	2	5. Michael Casey Departing From New York En Route To Boston By Steamboat.......[T-C] Columbia	
			also recorded for New Jersey	
1/13/94	**1(3)**	3	6. **Casey As Insurance Agent**.................[T-C] New Jersey	
			also recorded for Chicago 5015	
11/03/94	**1(3)**	3	7. **Casey At Denny Murphy's Wake** ....[T-C] Columbia	
4/16/98	**3**	2	8. Casey As A Fortune Teller ....[T-C] Universal	
3/04/16	**9**	1	9. Casey's Description Of His Fight...........[T-C] Columbia 1908	
			as "Michael Casey"	
			FERLIN HUSKY	
			Longtime country-music star of Grand Ole Opry	
10/17/53	**24**	1	1. Forgive Me, John .... Capitol 2586	
			JEAN SHEPHERD WITH FERLIN HUSKY	
			WALTER HUSTON	
			Great American character actor on Broadway and in films (won 1948 best supporting Oscar in "The Treasure of the Sierra Madre); father of film director John Huston; died in 1950 (66).	
1/28/39	**12**	5	1. September Song...................................... Brunswick 8272	
			record selected for NARAS Hall of Fame	
			from the Broadway musical "Knickerbocker Holiday"	
			BETTY HUTTON	
			Dynamic Hollywood musical star of 1940s & 50s (born Elizabeth June Thornburg), also featured on Broadway & TV; sang with Vincent Lopez in 1938-39.	
6/24/44	**5**	12	1. It Had To Be You/	
			featured in the film "The Roaring Twenties"	
7/15/44	**7**	15	2. His Rocking Horse Ran Away................... Capitol 155	
			from the film "And the Angels Sing"	
4/07/45	**4**	10	3. Stuff Like That There .... Capitol 188	
			from the film "On Stage Everybody"	
10/13/45	**15**	2	4. What Do You Want To Make Those Eyes At Me For... Capitol 211	
			featured in film "Incendiary Blonde"	
12/01/45+	**1(2)**	20	5. **Doctor, Lawyer, Indian Chief**................... Capitol 220	
			from the film "Stork Club"	
			above five with Paul Weston's Orchestra	
8/17/46	**21**	4	6. My Fickle Eye .... Victor 1915	
			with the Four Hits	
			accompanied by Joe Lilley & His Orchestra	
9/20/47	**5**	12	7. I Wish I Didn't Love You So .... Capitol 409	
			accompanied on above two by Joe Lilley's Orchestra	
			from the film "The Perils of Pauline"	

DATE CHARTED	PEAK POS	WKS CHRT'D	ARTIST — Record Title	Label & Number
10/21/50	**3**	18	8. A Bushel And A Peck	RCA Victor 3930
			PERRY COMO & BETTY HUTTON with Mitchell Ayres' Orchestra; from the Broadway musical "Guys and Dolls"	
12/02/50	**24**	2	9. Orange Colored Sky	RCA Victor 3908
9/01/51	**24**	2	10. The Musicians....................................	RCA Victor 4225
			DINAH SHORE, TONY MARTIN, BETTY HUTTON & PHIL HARRIS	
9/12/53	**21**	2	11. Goin' Steady	Capitol 2522
			with Nelson Riddle's Orchestra	

INA RAY HUTTON & HER ORCHESTRA
Beautiful blonde leader of various "all-girl" bands from 1930s to 50s; real name Odessa Cowan; died on 2/21/84 (67).

12/15/34	**20**	1	1. Georgia's Gorgeous Gal............................	Vocalion 2801
			vocal: Ruth Bradley	

JUNE HUTTON
Ina Ray Hutton's half-sister; with Charlie Spivak's Stardusters vocal group 1941-43, then with Pied Pipers 1944-50; married to orchestra leader Axel Stordahl. June died on 5/2/73 (about 53).

5/02/53	**21**	4	1. Say You're Mine Again	Capitol 2429
9/05/53	**24**	4	2. No Stone Unturned	Capitol 2549
1/16/54	**26**	1	3. For The First Time (In A Long Time)	Capitol 2667
			all with Axel Stordahl's Orchestra	

MARION HUTTON
Born Marion Thornburg, older sister of Betty Hutton; featured singer with Glenn Miller 1938-42.

JACK HYLTON & HIS ORCHESTRA
Popular British bandleader of 1920s & 30s (with singer Ella Logan in 1930, tenor sax great Coleman Hawkins 1934-35) who achieved his greatest success as producer of over 30 London musicals from 1941 to his death on 1/29/65 (72).

2/27/32	**10**	4	1. Dancing On The Ceiling	Victor 22912
			from the London musical "Ever Green"	
7/02/32	**2(1)**	6	2. You're Blase	Brunswick 6328
			from the London musical "Bow Bells"	

DICK HYMAN TRIO
Talented arranger/composer/pianist/organist; played with Benny Goodman & Lester Young.

7/10/54	**29**	1	1. Unforgettable..................................... [I]	MGM 11743

I

IMPERIAL QUARTET OF CHICAGO

2/05/16	**6**	2	1. Perfect Day..	Victor 17872

RED INGLE & THE NATURAL SEVEN
Tenor saxist and singer with Ted Weems (1931-40) who perfected his novelty vocals with Spike Jones.

6/14/47	**1(1)**	15	1. **Temptation (Tim-Tayshun)**.................. [N]	Capitol 412
			vocal: Jo Stafford as "Cinderella G. Stump"; from the film "Going Hollywood"	
11/01/47	**26**	1	2. Them Durn Fool Things .... [N]	Capitol 451
			based on "These Foolish Things Remind Me of You"	
12/06/47	**24**	3	3. Nowhere .... [N]	Capitol 476
			based on the song "You Came Along"	
3/27/48	**15**	4	4. Cigarettes, Whusky, And Wild, Wild Women................................. [N]	Capitol 15045
			vocal: "Main St. Choral Society"	
10/09/48	**12**	6	5. Serutan Yob (A Song For Backward Boys And Girls Under 40) .... [N]	Capitol 15210
			takeoff of "Nature Boy"; vocal by Karen Tedder & "Hawthorne"	

DATE CHARTED	PEAK POS	WKS CHRT'D	ARTIST — Record Title	Label & Number
			ROY INGRAHAM & HIS ORCHESTRA	
12/21/29+	1(3)	8	1. **Chant Of The Jungle/**	
1/18/30	9	3	2. That Wonderful Something...................... Brunswick 4586	
			above two from the film "Untamed"	
			INK SPOTS	
			One of the 1940s' most popular vocal groups: lead tenor Bill Kenny, bass Orville "Hoppy" Jones (died Nov. 1944, replaced by Bill's brother Herb Kenny), Charlie Fuqua, & Ivory "Deek" Watson (later replaced by Billy Bowen).	
4/15/39	2(1)	9	1. If I Didn't Care .... Decca 2286	
			the group's most famous record	
9/23/39	14	2	2. You Bring Me Down/	
10/07/39	1(1)	9	3. **Address Unknown** .... Decca 2707	
10/07/39	3	12	4. My Prayer .... Decca 2790	
			revived as a #1 hit by the Platters in 1956	
11/18/39	15	1	5. Bless You .... Decca 2841	
4/27/40	29	1	6. Memories Of You .... Decca 2966	
5/04/40	26	1	7. I'm Gettin' Sentimental Over You .... Decca 3077	
			Tommy Dorsey's theme song	
7/20/40	4	14	8. When The Swallows Come Back To Capistrano .... Decca 3195	
8/10/40	10	10	9. Whispering Grass (Don't Tell The Trees)/	
8/24/40	2(6)	17	10. Maybe .... Decca 3258	
9/07/40	16	2	11. Stop Pretending/	
9/21/40	17	1	12. You're Breaking My Heart All Over Again .... Decca 3288	
10/12/40+	1(3)	15	13. **We Three (My Echo, My Shadow, And Me)/**	
10/19/40	12	2	14. My Greatest Mistake .... Decca 3379	
12/07/40+	15	3	15. Java Jive .... Decca 3432	
4/05/41	25	1	16. Please Take A Letter, Miss Brown................ Decca 3626	
5/10/41	8	6	17. Do I Worry? .... Decca 3432	
7/05/41	19	2	18. I'm Still Without A Sweetheart (Cause I'm Still In Love With You)/	
7/12/41	24	1	19. So Sorry .... Decca 3806	
9/20/41	24	1	20. Until The Real Thing Comes Along.............. Decca 3958	
10/18/41	4	10	21. I Don't Want To Set The World On Fire........ Decca 3987	
12/06/41	17	1	22. Someone's Rocking My Dream Boat .... Decca 4045	
9/19/42	17	2	23. Ev'ry Night About This Time...................... Decca 18461	
1/23/43	2(3)	28	24. Don't Get Around Much Anymore .... Decca 18503	
2/13/43	20	1	25. If I Cared A Little Bit Less........................ Decca 18528	
7/17/43	19	1	26. I'll Never Make The Same Mistake Again....... Decca 18542	
2/19/44	14	9	27. Don't Believe Everything You Dream........... Decca 18583	
3/11/44	10	8	28. Cow Cow Boogie (Cuma-Ti-Yi-Yi-Ay).............. Decca 18587	
			ELLA FITZGERALD & INK SPOTS	
3/11/44	16	1	29. A Lovely Way To Spend An Evening............. Decca 18583	
			from the film "Higher and Higher"	
5/06/44	7	14	30. I'll Get By (As Long As I Have You)/	
			featured in the film "A Guy Named Joe"	
7/29/44	14	1	31. Someday I'll Meet You Again .... Decca 18579	
			from the film "Passage to Marseilles"	
11/04/44	1(2)	17	● 32. **I'm Making Believe/**	
			from the film "Sweet and Low-Down"	
11/11/44	1(2)	17	33. **Into Each Life Some Rain Must Fall** .... Decca 23356	
4/28/45	5	6	34. I'm Beginning To See The Light .... Decca 23399	
			above three: ELLA FITZGERALD & INK SPOTS	
5/04/46	1(13)	23	● 35. **The Gypsy** .... Decca 18817	
			British song	
6/01/46	9	11	36. Prisoner Of Love..................................... Decca 18864	
8/31/46	1(1)	14	● 37. **To Each His Own**.................................. Decca 23615	
			written for, but not used in, film of same name	
4/05/47	19	2	38. You Can't See The Sun When You're Crying .. Decca 23809	

DATE CHARTED	PEAK POS	WKS CHRT'D	ARTIST — Record Title	Label & Number
8/02/47	**17**	4	39. Ask Anyone Who Knows............................	Decca 23900
11/27/48	**22**	2	40. Say Something Sweet To Your Sweetheart/	
12/04/48+	**8**	8	41. You Were Only Fooling (While I Was Falling In Love).................................	Decca 24507
8/20/49	**9**	14	42. You're Breaking My Heart/ based on "La Mattinata" (1904)	
9/24/49	**21**	1	43. Who Do You Know In Heaven (That Made You The Angel You Are?)....................	Decca 24693
1/21/50	**24**	1	44. Echoes..	Decca 24741
9/02/50	**26**	2	45. Sometime...	Decca 27102
3/03/51	**23**	5	46. If	Decca 27391

INTERNATIONAL NOVELTY ORCHESTRA
Nat Shilkret, director

DATE CHARTED	PEAK POS	WKS CHRT'D	ARTIST — Record Title	Label & Number
11/22/24	**7**	3	1. Tell Me You'll Forgive Me	Victor 19416
11/29/24	**11**	1	2. Charley, My Boy .... vocal: Billy Murray	Victor 19411
7/25/25	**10**	1	3. Let It Rain, Let It Pour .... vocal: Vernon Dalhart; reportedly the first electrically-recorded disc to be released	Victor 19624

ANDY IONA & HIS ORCHESTRA
Hawaiian group. (Also see Louis Armstrong)

DATE CHARTED	PEAK POS	WKS CHRT'D	ARTIST — Record Title	Label & Number
2/09/35	**19**	1	1. Hula O Ka Aina	Columbia 3001
8/15/36	**10**	8	2. South Sea Island Magic...........................	Columbia 3138

IPANA TROUBADORS
Sam Lanin, director

DATE CHARTED	PEAK POS	WKS CHRT'D	ARTIST — Record Title	Label & Number
2/27/26	**8**	1	1. Paddlin' Madelin' Home .... vocal: Billy Jones	Columbia 503
5/29/26	**9**	1	2. Song Of The Flame/ [I]	
6/12/26	**10**	1	3. Cossack Love Song .... [I] above two from the Broadway musical "Song of the Flame"	Columbia 565
7/31/26	**14**	1	4. Everything's Gonna Be All Right .... vocal: Irving Kaufman Red Nichols (trumpet) on above four	Columbia 593
10/30/26	**12**	1	5. When The Red, Red Robin Comes Bob-Bob-Bobbin' Along................................... vocal: Franklyn Baur	Columbia 662
11/13/26	**10**	1	6. Baby Face .... vocal: Lewis James	Columbia 696
1/01/27	**7**	4	7. Mary Lou .... vocal: Charles Kaley	Columbia 738
9/24/27	**8**	4	8. Just Like A Butterfly That's Caught In The Rain.. vocal: Irving Kaufman	Columbia 1018
11/12/27	**8**	6	9. Give Me A Night In June	Columbia 1098
2/18/28	**11**	3	10. Dream Kisses..	Columbia 1188
3/24/28	**12**	3	11. 'S Wonderful.. vocal: Scrappy Lambert; from Broadway musical "Funny Face"	Columbia 1213
10/13/28	**13**	2	12. Nagasacki...	Columbia 1463
3/16/29	**12**	4	13. A Precious Little Thing Called Love	Columbia 1717
8/24/29	**20**	1	14. Building A Nest For Mary .... vocal: Smith Ballew Jimmy Dorsey (clarinet/alto sax) on above two	Columbia 1815
1/18/30	**15**	2	15. Tea For Two .... from the Broadway musical "No, No, Nanette"	Columbia 2078
4/26/30	**14**	2	16. Blue Is The Night	Columbia 2174
11/29/30	**10**	3	17. Three Little Words................................... from the film "Check and Double Check"	Columbia 2317
9/05/31	**16**	2	18. Many Happy Returns Of The Day .... vocal: Dick Robertson Tommy Dorsey (trombone) on most of above eight	Columbia 2486

DATE CHARTED	PEAK POS	WKS CHRT'D	ARTIST — Record Title	Label & Number
			MAY IRWIN Canadian-born May was the foremost vaudeville star of the 1890s, the first to sing on stage such hits as "Ta-ra-ra-Boom-Der-e", "The Bully", and "Mister Johnson, Turn Me Loose". She also scandalized early movie audiences with her famous 1895 film "The Kiss". May died on 10/2/38 (76).	
12/28/07	7	1	1. The Bully	Victor 31642
			EDWARD ISSLER & HIS ORCHESTRA Pianist who was one of the earliest commericaly-recorded musicians (with 1889 records for North American).	
10/02/97	3	1	1. Dream Of Passion Waltz........................ [I]	New Jersey
			JOSE ITURBI Spanish-born piano virtuoso featured in several films; died on 6/28/80 (84).	
9/15/45	20	1	● 1. Chopin's Polonaise In A Flat................... [I] Iturbi played this in the film "A Song To Remember"	Victor 8848
1/05/46	21	1	2. Clair De Lune....................................... [I]	Victor 8851
			BURL IVES One of America's best-known folk singers from the 1940s to 60s, Burl has won equal renown as a dramatic actor in movies, Broadway, & TV.	
7/31/48	24	1	1. Blue Tail Fly .... BURL IVES & ANDREWS SISTERS	Decca 24463
2/12/49	16	1	2. Lavender Blue (Dilly Dilly)........................ with "Captain Stubby & The Buccaneers" from the film "So Dear To My Heart"; melody based on an 18th Century air	Decca 24547
4/30/49	21	6	3. Riders In The Sky (Cowboy Legend)............. the original recording of the pop/folk classic	Columbia 38445
5/12/51+	10	9	4. On Top Of Old Smoky .... with Percy Faith's Orchestra; adaptation of generations-old folk song; featured in the film "Valley of Fire"	Columbia 39328
7/26/52	30	1	5. The Wild Side Of Life............................. with Grady Martin & His Slow Foot Five	Decca 28055
5/15/54	23	2	6. True Love Goes On And On .... with Gordon Jenkins' Orchestra	Decca 29088

J

DATE CHARTED	PEAK POS	WKS CHRT'D	ARTIST — Record Title	Label & Number
			BULL MOOSE JACKSON R&B singer Benjamin Jackson got his start with Lucky Millinder.	
11/29/47	21	3	1. I Love You, Yes I Do................................. he hit the charts again in 1961 with a new version of this song	King 4181
			JACK JACKSON & HIS ORCHESTRA British band	
4/28/34	12	3	1. Play To Me, Gypsy	Victor 24594
7/27/35	16	2	2. What A Little Moonlight Can Do.................	Victor 25069
11/23/35	13	5	3. Red Sails In The Sunset .... British song; from the Broadway musical "Provincetown Follies"	Victor 25152
			MAHALIA JACKSON The world's greatest gospel singer; died on 1/27/72 (60).	
1/24/48	21	2	● 1. Move On Up A Little Higher	Apollo 164
			SASCHA JACOBSEN Violinist	
9/20/19	8	2	1. Dear Old Pal Of Mine .... [I]	Columbia 2753
			ILLINOIS JACQUET Tenor saxophonist most famous for records with Lionel Hampton (1941-42) Cab Calloway, & Count Basie (1945-46).	

DATE CHARTED	PEAK POS	WKS CHRT'D	ARTIST — Record Title	Label & Number
			DICK JAMES British singer	
7/03/48	19	2	1. You Can't Be True, Dear .... with instrumental trio	RCA Victor 2944
			HARRY JAMES & HIS ORCHESTRA Trumpet star Harry James was born on 3/15/16 in Albany, Ga. He played with Ben Pollack in 1935-36 before achieving fame with Benny Goodman the following two years. His own band started slowly despite vocalist Frank Sinatra, but soon became one of the 1940s' most popular. Built around its singers and Harry's trumpet, the band also featured trombonist Juan Tizol (1945), drummer Buddy Rich (1950s), and arrangers Ray Conniff & Neal Hefti. Harry was married to movie star Betty Grable. He remained active until his death on 7/5/83 (67). (Also see Doris Day and Frank Sinatra)	
2/19/38	7	5	1. One O'Clock Jump/ [I]	
5/21/38	9	3	2. It's The Dreamer In Me .... vocal: Helen Humes	Brunswick 8055
7/29/39	14	1	3. I Found A New Baby........................... [I]	Brunswick 8406
1/06/40	10	6	4. Ciribiribin .... [I] became Harry's theme song	Columbia 35316
6/08/40	20	3	5. The Flight Of The Bumble Bee................. [I] one of Harry's most famous trumpet performances	Variety 8298
4/05/41	9	5	6. Music Makers................................ [I]	Columbia 35932
8/30/41	10	1	7. Lament To Love .... [I]	Columbia 36222
10/18/41	18	1	8. Trumpet Rhapsody .... [I]	Columbia 36160
11/01/41	5	18	● 9. You Made Me Love You/ [I]	
12/13/41	15	1	10. A Sinner Kissed An Angel...................... vocal: Dick Haymes	Columbia 36296
11/15/41	22	1	11. Misirlou .... [I]	Columbia 36390
2/14/42	23	1	12. The Devil Sat Down And Cried .... vocal: Dick Haymes-Harry James-Helen Forrest	Columbia 36466
2/28/42	1(2)	15	13. **I Don't Want To Walk Without You** .... from the film "Sweater Girl"	Columbia 36478
4/04/42	11	2	● 14. Easter Parade .... [I] from the Broadway musical "As Thousands Cheer"	Columbia 36545
4/18/42	1(4)	21	15. **Sleepy Lagoon**........................... [I] adapted from a symphonic composition by Eric Coates	Columbia 36549
5/02/42	11	4	16. Skylark....................................	Columbia 36533
5/16/42	24	1	17. I Remember You............................. from the film "The Fleet's In" vocals on 13, 16-17: Helen Forrest	Columbia 36518
5/23/42	4	15	18. One Dozen Roses .... vocal: Jimmy Saunders	Columbia 36566
7/18/42	5	12	19. Strictly Instrumental...................... [I]	Columbia 36579
8/08/42	12	1	20. But Not For Me............................. from the Broadway musical "Girl Crazy"	Columbia 36599
9/05/42	7	9	21. He's My Guy	Columbia 36614
9/05/42	19	2	22. I Cried For You............................	Columbia 36623
11/14/42+	1(2)	13	23. **Mister Five By Five** .... from the film "Behind the Eight Ball"	Columbia 36650
11/21/42+	1(2)	22	● 24. **I Had The Craziest Dream**..................... from the film "Springtime in the Rockies"	Columbia 36659
11/21/42	9	4	25. Manhattan Serenade/ originally a 1928 instrumental	
12/12/42	17	2	26. Daybreak .... adapted from a theme in Ferde Grofe's "Mississippi Suite" featured in the film "Thousands Cheer"	Columbia 36644
1/16/43	1(13)	25	● 27. **I've Heard That Song Before**/ from the film "Youth on Parade" vocals on 20, 22, 25 & 27 by Helen Forrest	
1/16/43	15	4	28. Moonlight Becomes You......................... from the film "The Road to Morocco" vocals on 26 & 28: Johnny McAfee	Columbia 36668
4/10/43	2(2)	16	29. Velvet Moon/ [I]	
4/17/43	13	4	30. Prince Charming .... [I]	Columbia 36672

DATE CHARTED	PEAK POS	WKS CHRT'D	ARTIST — Record Title	Label & Number
6/19/43	**1(2)**	21	● 31. **All Or Nothing At All**............................ [R] Columbia 35587 FRANK SINATRA & HARRY JAMES' ORCHESTRA recorded 9/17/39	
6/26/43	**19**	1	32. Two O'Clock Jump............................. [I-R] Columbia 36232 recorded 1/5/38; originally issued as "One O'Clock Jump"	
7/10/43	**19**	1	33. Flash... [I-R] Columbia 35587 recorded 11/8/39	
7/24/43	**2(1)**	21	34. I Heard You Cried Last Night .... Columbia 36677 vocal: Helen Forrest; recorded 7/15/42; from the film "Cinderella Swings It"	
12/18/43	**21**	2	35. Jump Town/ [I]	
1/08/44	**4**	10	36. Cherry... [I] Columbia 36683 above two recorded 7/22/42	
4/01/44	**24**	1	37. Back Beat Boogie .... [I-R] Columbia 35456 recorded 11/30/39	
4/15/44	**1(6)**	28	38. **I'll Get By (As Long As I Have You)** .... [R] Columbia 36698 vocal: Dick Haymes; recorded 4/7/41, originally released on Columbia 36285; featured in the film "Follow the Boys"	
5/13/44	**27**	1	39. On A Little Street In Singapore/ [R] recorded 10/13/39	
5/27/44	**17**	2	40. Every Day Of My Life .... [R] Columbia 36700 recorded 11/8/39 above two vocals: Frank Sinatra	
7/08/44	**15**	2	41. Memphis Blues/ [I] recorded 7/31/42	
8/05/44	**21**	1	42. Sleepy Time Gal .... [I-R] Columbia 36713 recorded 10/13/39	
9/16/44	**12**	3	43. Estrellita.. [I] Columbia 36729 recorded 3/19/42	
10/28/44	**21**	1	44. It's Funny To Everyone But Me .... [R] Columbia 36738 vocal: Frank Sinatra; recorded 8/17/39	
1/27/45	**1(2)**	19	45. **I'm Beginning To See The Light**................ Columbia 36758	
4/07/45	**8**	1	46. I Don't Care Who Knows It/	
4/14/45	**16**	1	47. Guess I'll Hang My Tears Out To Dry.......... Columbia 36778 from the Broadway musical "Glad to See You"	
5/05/45	**11**	2	48. Yah-Ta-Ta, Yah-Ta-Ta......................... Columbia 36786 above four vocals: Kitty Kallen	
5/26/45	**12**	3	49. The More I See You .... Columbia 36794 from the film "Diamond Horseshoe"	
7/28/45	**8**	3	50. If I Loved You .... Columbia 36806 from the Broadway musical "Carousel" above two vocals: Buddy DeVito	
9/08/45	**8**	4	51. 11:60 P.M. .... Columbia 36827	
9/22/45	**2(1)**	14	52. I'll Buy That Dream............................... Columbia 36833 from the film "Sing Your Way Home"	
10/13/45	**1(3)**	17	53. **It's Been A Long, Long Time/**	
11/03/45	**16**	2	54. Autumn Serenade............................... [I] Columbia 36838	
11/34/45	**6**	10	55. Waitin' For The Train To Come In/	
12/08/45+	**5**	12	56. I Can't Begin To Tell You .... Columbia 36867 vocal: Betty Grable (under pseudonym "Ruth Haag"); from the film "The Dolly Sisters"; adapted from 1906 song "When Love Is Young in Springtime"	
2/02/46	**9**	4	57. I'm Always Chasing Rainbows.................... Columbia 36899 from the Broadway musical "Oh, Look!"; revived in the film "The Dolly Sisters"; melody taken from Chopin's "Fantasie Impromptu in C-Sharp Minor"	
4/27/46	**23**	1	58. Easter Parade .... [I-R] Columbia 36545	
6/08/46	**18**	2	59. Who's Sorry Now .... Columbia 36973 vocal: Willie Smith	
6/29/46	**15**	4	60. Do You Love Me .... Columbia 36965 vocal: Ginnie Powell; movie title song	
9/21/46	**13**	2	61. And Then It's Heaven............................ Columbia 37060 from the film "Sweetheart of Sigma Chi"	
9/28/46	**10**	2	62. This Is Always .... Columbia 37052 from the film "Three Little Girls in Blue"	

DATE CHARTED	PEAK POS	WKS CHRT'D	ARTIST — Record Title	Label & Number
1/25/47	12	2	63. Oh! But I Do.................................... Columbia 37156 from the film "The Time, The Place, and The Girl"	
4/05/47	4	9	64. Heartaches .... [I] Columbia 37305	
4/05/47	17	1	65. Jalousie (Jealousy) .... [I] Columbia 37218	
5/03/47	21	1	66. I Tipped My Hat (And Slowly Rode Away) ...... Columbia 37305 vocal by Art Lund	
5/10/47	21	1	67. Stella By Starlight .... [I] Columbia 37323 from the film "The Uninvited"	
11/08/47	23	1	68. I Still Get Jealous .... Columbia 37929 from the Broadway musical "High Button Shoes" vocals on 57, 61-63 & 68: Buddy DiVito	
8/05/50	14	8	69. Mona Lisa .... Columbia 38768 vocal: Dick Williams; from the film "Captain Carey, U.S.A." Juan Tizol (trombone) & Willie Smith (alto sax) featured with band from 1945-51	
3/10/51	10	10	70. Would I Love You (Love You, Love You)........ Columbia 39159 DORIS DAY with HARRY JAMES & HIS ORCHESTRA	
9/10/51	8	8	71. Castle Rock .... Columbia 39527 FRANK SINATRA with HARRY JAMES & HIS ORCHESTRA	
1/10/53	18	2	72. You'll Never Know .... Columbia 39905 ROSEMARY CLOONEY WITH HARRY JAMES & HIS ORCHESTRA from the film "Hello, Frisco, Hello"	
7/11/53	20	2	73. Ruby .... [I] Columbia 39994 theme from the film "Ruby Gentry" band now includes Buddy Rich (drums)	

JONI JAMES
Born Joan Carmello Babbo in Chicago; started as a dancer.

DATE CHARTED	PEAK POS	WKS CHRT'D	ARTIST — Record Title	Label & Number
10/17/52	1(6)	23	● 1. **Why Don't You Believe Me/**	
11/29/52	26	2	2. Purple Shades.....................	MGM 11333
1/03/53	4	16	● 3. Have You Heard/	
1/17/53	17	4	4. Wishing Ring	MGM 11390
2/21/53	2(3)	17	● 5. Your Cheatin' Heart	MGM 11426
5/02/53	9	9	6. Almost Always/	
5/09/53	16	4	7. Is It Any Wonder	MGM 11470
8/22/53	8	12	8. My Love, My Love/ with Jack Halloran Choir	
8/22/53	11	12	9. You're Fooling Someone	MGM 11543
11/21/53	23	2	10. I'd Never Stand In Your Way	MGM 11606
12/26/53	27	1	11. Nina-Non	MGM 11637
3/20/54	22	1	12. Maybe Next Time/	
4/03/54	22	4	13. Am I In Love...................	MGM 11696
6/26/54	22	4	14. In A Garden Of Roses	MGM 11753
9/25/54	23	3	15. Mama, Don't Cry At My Wedding	MGM 11802
11/27/54+	28	2	16. When We Come Of Age	MGM 11865
			all records with Lew Douglas' Orchestra	

LEWIS JAMES
Tenor particularly well known for his group recordings with the Shannon Four, the Revelers, & Criterion Trio; in all he reportedly made close to 3,000 records from 1917 through the 30s. Lewis sometimes performed with symphony orchestras and oratorios; he died on 2/19/59 (66). (Also see Ipana Troubadors, Joseph C. Smith's Orchestra.)

DATE CHARTED	PEAK POS	WKS CHRT'D	ARTIST — Record Title	Label & Number
7/14/17	8	1	1. Would You Take Back The Love You Gave Me? .... Columbia 2226 1-4 under pseudonym "Robert Lewis"	
9/01/17	5	2	2. When The Sun Goes Down In Dixie .... Columbia 2207 GEORGE WILSON & "ROBERT LEWIS"	
6/08/18	7	2	3. Fancy You Fancying Me .... Columbia 2520 from the Broadway musical "Odds and Ends of 1917"	
9/14/18	3	5	4. The Daughter of Rosie O'Grady .... Columbia 2561	
12/14/18	4	4	5. My Baby Boy................................... Columbia 2638	
2/22/19	1(1)	9	6. **Till We Meet Again** .... Victor 18518 LEWIS JAMES & CHARLES HART	

DATE CHARTED	PEAK POS	WKS CHRT'D	ARTIST — Record Title	Label & Number
6/14/19	7	3	7. Smile And The World Smiles With You .... LEWIS JAMES & PEERLESS QUARTET	Victor 18545
12/20/19+	4	5	8. Golden Gate............................. CHARLES HARRISON & LEWIS JAMES	Columbia 2791
2/28/20	14	1	9. Let The Rest Of The World Go By .... LEWIS JAMES & CHARLES HART also recorded for Empire 414	Pathe 22259
5/29/20	12	1	10. Daddy, You've Been A Mother To Me...........	Columbia 2894
12/25/20	11	1	11. Old Pal (Why Don't You Answer Me?) .... also recorded for Pathe 22438	Edison Amb. 4184
6/25/21	12	1	12. Look For The Silver Lining....................... from the Broadway musical "Sally"	Okeh 4292
5/27/22	15	1	13. Up In The Clouds .... Broadway musical title song above two: ELIZABETH SPENCER & LEWIS JAMES	Edison 50899
10/27/23	11	1	14. Who's Sorry Now?................................	Columbia 3937
12/08/23	10	1	15. I Wish I Had Someone To Cry Over Me......... also recorded for Okeh 4942 & Gennett 5248	Victor 19135
1/26/24	12	1	16. Just A Girl That Men Forget	Okeh 4929
2/16/24	10	1	17. I Love You.................................... from the Broadway musical "Little Jessie James"	Columbia 25
5/31/24	11	1	18. Linger Awhile .... LEWIS JAMES & MARCIA FREER	Victor 19259
6/07/24	5	3	19. Mr. Radio Man (Tell My Mammy To Come Back Home).................................... also recorded for Columbia 79 & Okeh 40056	Victor 19262
8/09/24	6	2	20. What'll I Do?.................................. from the Broadway musical "Music Box Revue of 1923"	Columbia 115
1/10/25	8	2	21. The Pal That I Loved (Stole The Gal I Loved) .	Victor 19473
1/31/25	12	1	22. Put Away A Little Ray Of Sunshine.............	Columbia 214
2/28/25	12	1	23. All Alone .... also recorded for Columbia 235; from the Broadway musical "Music Box Revue of 1924"	Victor 19495
4/18/25	9	2	24. At The End Of The Road	Columbia 263
6/27/25	12	1	25. I'll See You In My Dreams	Victor 19598
8/08/25	7	2	26. Oh How I Miss You Tonight	Victor 19623
8/22/25	3	5	27. Pal Of My Cradle Days	Columbia 375
12/26/25	11	1	28. Alone At Last	Columbia 451
2/27/26	12	1	29. Sleepy Time Gal	Columbia 499
6/26/26	12	1	30. Always	Columbia 564
8/14/26	5	3	31. Am I Wasting My Time On You?	Columbia 629
9/25/26	12	1	32. At Peace With The World .... LEWIS JAMES & FRANKLYN BAUR	Victor 20057
8/13/27	11	3	33. Charmaine!...................................	Victor 20590

ELSIE JANIS
Popular female vaudeville and Broadway performer, born Elsie
Bierbower, later a songwriter and author; died on 2/26/56 (66).

2/22/13	10	1	1. Fo' De Lawd's Sake, Play A Waltz...............	Victor 60091

ART JARRETT & HIS ORCHESTRA
Singer/guitarist/trombonist formerly with Earl Burtnett and Ted
Weems; took over the late Hal Kemp's band in 1941. Married to
Olympic swimming champion Eleanor Holm.

8/23/41	11	3	1. Foolish/ vocal: Gale Robbins (future movie actress)	
11/29/41	12	1	2. Shepherd Serenade .... vocal: Smoothies	Victor 27527
12/20/41	24	1	3. You Can Depend On Me...........................	Victor 27580
2/07/42	21	1	4. Buckle Down, Winsocki .... from the Broadway musical "Best Foot Forward" above two vocals: Art Jarrett	Victor 27665

HAROLD JARVIS
Toronto-born tenor; died on 3/31/24 (58).'

2/27/09	3	3	1. Beautiful Isle Of Somewhere	Victor 16008

DATE CHARTED	PEAK POS	WKS CHRT'D	ARTIST — Record Title	Label & Number
			JAUDAS' SOCIETY ORCHESTRA	
			Violinist Eugene A. Jaudas was Edison's longtime orchestra leader.	
10/14/16	**9**	1	1. Missouri Waltz .... [I]	Edison Amb. 2950
3/13/18	**9**	1	2. The Darktown Strutters' Ball .... [I]	Edison 50469
			HERB JEFFRIES	
			Baritone who sang with Earl Hines (1934) and Duke Ellington (1940-42)	
7/12/47	**21**	5	1. When I Write My Song	Exclusive 16
			accompanied by Buddy Baker & His Orchestra	
			song adapted from Saint-Saens' "Samson et Dalilia"	
7/16/49	**18**	3	2. The Four Winds And The Seven Seas	Columbia 38511
			with Hugo Winterhalter's Orchestra	
			GORDON JENKINS & HIS ORCHESTRA	
			Composer of many popular songs ("San Fernando Valley", "Goodbye") and larger works ("Manhattan Tower Suite", the "Future" song cycle for Frank Sinatra's 1980 "Trilogy"). Gordon was also an arranger for Isham Jones, Benny Goodman, & Andre Kostelanetz, and orchestral accompanist for Sinatra, Louis Armstrong, Dick Haymes, and many other singers. Gordon died on 5/2/84 (73).	
11/14/42	**15**	2	1. White Christmas.................................. [X]	Capitol 124
			vocal: Bob Carroll; from the film "Holiday Inn"	
12/30/44	**16**	1	2. Always	Capitol 125
6/19/48	**3**	30	● 3. Maybe You'll Be There.............................	Decca 24403
			vocal: Charles Lavere; recorded in early 1947	
4/02/49	**5**	21	4. I Don't See Me In Your Eyes Anymore	Decca 24576
			vocal: Stardusters	
4/23/49	**2(3)**	23	5. Again	Decca 24602
			vocal: Joe Graydon; from the film "Roadhouse"	
9/24/49	**3**	19	6. Don't Cry, Joe (Let Her Go, Let Her Go, Let Her Go)...	Decca 24720
			vocal: Betty Brewer	
12/17/49	**26**	2	7. A Dreamer's Holiday	Decca 24738
2/18/50	**3**	23	8. My Foolish Heart	Decca 24830
			vocal: Eileen Wilson; movie title song	
4/29/50	**4**	18	9. Bewitched	Decca 24983
			vocal: Mary Lou Williams; from the Broadway musical "Pal Joey"	
7/01/50	**2(1)**	17	● 10. Tzena, Tzena, Tzena/	
			adaptation of a popular Israeli song	
7/08/50	**1(13)**	25	11. **Goodnight, Irene**	Decca 27077
			above two: WEAVERS with GORDON JENKINS' ORCHESTRA	
			sold over 2 million copies	
9/16/50	**10**	10	12. I'm Forever Blowing Bubbles......................	Decca 27186
			with Artie Shaw (clarinet) and vocal chorus; from the Broadway musical "The Passing Show of 1918"	
1/13/51	**4**	14	13. So Long (It's Been Good To Know Ya)	Decca 27376
			THE WEAVERS WITH GORDON JENKINS' ORCHESTRA	
6/09/51	**21**	4	14. Rose, Rose, I Love You/	
			vocal: Cisco Houston	
6/23/51	**30**	1	15. Unless	Decca 27594
			vocal: Bob Stephens	
10/27/51	**27**	1	16. Whispering	Decca 27585
12/01/51	**18**	9	17. Charmaine...	Decca 27859
			vocal: Bob Carroll	
			song written to promote the 1926 film "What Price Glory?"	
2/16/52	**14**	11	18. Wimoweh	Decca 27928
			adapted from the South African Zulu song "Mbube"; revised version by the Tokens hit #1 in 1961 as "The Lion Sleeps Tonight"	
4/26/52	**19**	1	19. Around The Corner (Beneath The Berry Tree)	Decca 28054
			above two: THE WEAVERS WITH GORDON JENKINS' ORCHESTRA	
9/19/53	**26**	1	20. Fury...	Decca 28806
			vocal: Stuart Foster	
			JACK JENNEY	
			Trombone star with Isham Jones, Artie Shaw (1940-41), & Benny Goodman; died on 12/16/45 (35).	

DATE CHARTED	PEAK POS	WKS CHRT'D	ARTIST — Record Title	Label & Number
			HENRY JEROME & HIS ORCHESTRA New York bandleader and composer	
9/05/53	**22**	2	1. Here's To The Ladies..............................	MGM 11526
11/14/53	**21**	4	2. Tipica Serenada.................................... vocal: Ray DeMeno	MGM 11594
			JERRY JEROME Tenor saxophonist with Red Norvo, Benny Goodman (1938-40), Artie Shaw, & Lionel Hampton.	
			GEORGE JESSEL Star of vaudeville, Broadway, and all other media from 1917 through the 50s; lyricist on such popular songs as "Roses in December", and producer of several top Hollywood musicals. George died on 5/25/81 (83).	
4/20/29	**8**	6	1. My Mother's Eyes .... from the film "Lucky Boy" accompanied by Harry Selinger's Ensemble & Leroy Shield's Orchestra	Victor 21852
			RED JESSUP & HIS MELODY MAKERS Trombonist-bandleader	
4/10/37	**16**	2	1. You're Here, You're There.........................	Vocalion 3477
			JESTERS Red Latham, Wamp Carlson, & Guy Bonham; specialized in humorous turn-of-the-century songs.	
8/10/40	**23**	1	1. McNamara's Band .... as "King's Jesters"; six years later group backed up Bing Crosby on his version of this song	Decca 3268
6/14/41	**22**	1	2. The Band Played On................................ featured in the movie "Strawberry Blonde"	Decca 3676
6/09/45	**11**	3	3. Bell Bottom Trousers .... melody based on traditional sea chantey	Decca 4482
7/28/45	**12**	7	4. Fuzzy-Wuzzy	Decca 18688
			DAMITA JO Regular on Redd Foxx TV variety series (1977) (also see Steve Gibson)	
1/24/53	**29**	1	1. I Don't Care	RCA Victor 5022
			ALBERT & MONROE JOCKERS Violinist and pianist	
7/24/15	**8**	2	1. My Tango Girl .... [I]	Columbia 5683
5/25/18	**9**	1	2. For The Two Of Us............................. [I]	Columbia 6036
			ARNOLD JOHNSON & HIS ORCHESTRA Pianist-composer-bandleader; composer Harold Arlen was a band pianist.	
9/28/29	**20**	1	1. Breakaway	Brunswick 4348
			BETTY JOHNSON	
11/27/54	**22**	1	1. I Want Eddie Fisher For Christmas .... [X-N] orchestra directed by Jimmy Leyden	New Disc 10013
			BUDDY JOHNSON & HIS ORCHESTRA Blues band leader whose vocalists included his sister Ella and Arthur Prysock; composer of the 1963 Lenny Welch classic hit "Since I Fell for You" (Buddy's original version on Decca 48016).	
4/08/44	**23**	1	1. When My Man Comes Home.......................	Decca 8655
9/01/45	**14**	1	2. That's The Stuff You Gotta Watch	Decca 8671
9/11/48	**28**	1	3. Far Cry .... [I]	Decca 48076
11/20/48	**27**	1	4. A Tree In The Meadow............................ British song	Columbia 38279
7/30/49	**17**	8	5. Did You See Jackie Robinson Hit That Ball?.. one of three chart hits about baseball players (the other subjects: Michael "King" Kelly & Joe DiMaggio) vocals on 1, 2 & 5 by Ella Johnson	Decca 24675

DATE CHARTED	PEAK POS	WKS CHRT'D	ARTIST — Record Title	Label & Number
			GEORGE WASHINGTON JOHNSON	
			One of the very first entertainers to make recordings (on tin foil in 1877), Johnson was born into slavery and became the recording industry's first widely-known star. Published accounts that he was hanged for allegedly killing his wife are now believed to be false; George died around 1910 at approximately 64.	
4/04/91	1(10)	10	1. **The Laughing Song** .... [C]	Columbia
			probably the biggest-selling cylinder of the 1890s; also recorded for New Jersey; Johnson reportedly recorded his famous infectious laugh some 40,000 times (during the industry's pre-mass production age)	
7/11/91	1(5)	5	2. **The Whistling Coon** .... [C]	Columbia
			also recorded for New Jersey	
4/13/01	2(1)	4	3. The Laughing Song .... [C]	Gram-o-Phone 583
			new version of his 1891 hit	
			JAMES P. JOHNSON	
			Renowned jazz/ragtime pianist, died on 11/17/55 (64). (Also see Bessie Smith)	
4/22/22	10	1	1. Carolina Shout .... [I]	Okeh 4495
			JERRY JOHNSON & HIS ORCHESTRA	
9/22/34	6	4	1. Two Cigarettes In The Dark	Victor 24710
			from the film "Kill That Story"	
			J.J. JOHNSON	
			Winner of nearly 20 Down Beat polls as top trombonist; played with Benny Carter, Count Basie (1945-46), Woody Herman (1949).	
			JOHNNY JOHNSON & HIS ORCHESTRA	
			Bandleader formerly pianist with Ben Bernie.	
3/28/28	19	1	1. My Stormy Weather Pal	Victor 21227
			vocal: Scrappy Lambert	
12/08/28	12	3	2. Once In A Lifetime	Victor 21677
			vocal: Franklyn Baur	
1/05/29	20	1	3. It Goes Like This (That Funny Melody)	Victor 21701
			vocal: Bob Treaster	
			LONNIE JOHNSON	
			Acclaimed blues guitarist and singer, played in the 1920s with Louis Armstrong (on classic "Hotter Than That") and Duke Ellington; died on 6/16/70 (81).	
6/26/48	19	3	● 1. Tomorrow Night	King 4201
			#1 R&B hit	
			JOHNSTON BROTHERS	
			Baritone quartet	
4/17/54	28	1	1. Crystal Ball	London 1423
10/16/54	26	3	2. The Bandit	London 1470
			from the Mexican film "O Cangaceiro"	
			JOHNNIE JOHNSTON	
			Baritone who sang in several 40s movies, also in 1951 Broadway musical "A Tree Grows in Brooklyn".	
3/24/45	7	1	1. (All Of A Sudden) My Heart Sings	Capitol 186
			from the film "Anchors Aweigh"	
6/02/45	5	5	2. Laura/	
			movie title song	
7/14/45	9	2	3. There Must Be A Way	Capitol 196
			above three with Paul Baron's Orchestra	
1/26/46	13	2	4. One More Dream (And She's Mine)	Capitol 228
			with the Satisfiers & Lloyd Schaffer's Orchestra	

DATE CHARTED	PEAK POS	WKS CHRT'D	ARTIST — Record Title	Label & Number
			AL JOLSON	
			One of the greatest popular entertainers in American history, Al Jolson was born Asa Yoelson in St. Petersburg, Russia, March 26, 1886. Al grew up in Washington, D.C., and after performing with a minstrel show troupe and in vaudeville, he first electrified Broadway in 1911 with his dramatic vocal style, extraordinary stage presence, and personal rapport with audiences. For most of the next 20 years Jolson was the king of the American musical in 1927 with "The Jazz Singer", ushering in the age of sound motion pictures, but by the 30s his career was in decline. The hit 1946 film "The Jolson Story", with Al's newly-recorded vocals, brought about an incredible comeback. Al died on 10/23/50 (66).	
3/16/12	1(2)	11	1. **That Haunting Melody** .... Victor 17037 from the Broadway musical "Vera Violetta"	
7/06/12	1(5)	12	● 2. **Ragging The Baby To Sleep** .... Victor 17081	
7/20/12	6	2	3. Snap Your Fingers .... Victor 17075	
5/24/13	1(5)	9	● 4. **The Spaniard That Blighted My Life** ..... [C] Victor 17318 from the Broadway musical "The Honeymoon Express" accompanied on above four by Walter B. Rogers' Orchestra	
9/20/13	1(7)	13	5. **You Made Me Love You, I Didn't Want To Do It** .... Columbia 1374	
9/27/13	5	4	6. That Little German Band .... Columbia 1356	
10/04/13	5	4	7. Pullman Porters' Parade .... Columbia 1374	
1/02/15	2(3)	8	8. Back To The Carolina You Love .... Columbia 1621	
3/13/15	6	2	9. Sister Susie's Sewing Shirts For Soldiers....... Columbia 1671	
6/10/16	2(5)	7	10. Yaaka Hula Hickey Dula .... [C] Columbia 1956	
7/01/16	6	2	11. Where Did Robinson Crusoe Go With Friday On Saturday Night? .... [C] Columbia 1976 above two from Broadway musical "Robinson Crusoe, Jr."	
8/19/16	3	5	12. Down Where The Swanee River Flows .... Columbia 2007	
9/02/16	1(3)	7	13. **I Sent My Wife To The Thousand Isles**... [C] Columbia 2021	
9/16/16	2(2)	6	14. You're A Dangerous Girl .... Columbia 2041	
12/02/16	3	4	15. I'm Saving Up The Means To Get To New Orleans.. Columbia 2064	
1/20/17	2(1)	4	16. Someone Else May Be There While I'm Gone.. Columbia 2124	
4/14/17	4	4	17. Pray For Sunshine .... Columbia 2169	
5/12/17	5	2	18. Ev'ry Little While .... Columbia 2181	
6/23/17	4	4	19. From Here To Shanghai .... Columbia 2224	
3/23/18	1(3)	9	20. **I'm All Bound Round With The Mason Dixon Line** .... Columbia 2478 flip side: "The Darktown Strutters' Ball" (POS 1) by Arthur Collins & Byron Harlan	
6/01/18	2(2)	5	21. 'N Everything... Columbia 2519	
6/01/18	8	1	22. Wedding Bells (Will They Ever Ring For Me?) . Columbia 2512	
7/13/18	1(3)	8	23. **Hello Central, Give Me No Man's Land** .... Columbia 2542	
8/10/18	1(8)	14	24. **Rock-A-Bye Your Baby With A Dixie Melody**... Columbia 2560 21, 23 & 24 from the Broadway musical "Sinbad"	
1/11/19	2(1)	5	25. Tell That To The Marines .... Columbia 2657	
5/31/19	5	3	26. On The Road To Calais .... Columbia 2690	
8/09/19	1(6)	9	27. **I'll Say She Does** .... Columbia 2746	
12/27/19+	1(2)	7	28. **I've Got My Captain Working For Me Now** .. Columbia 2794	
1/31/20	3	5	29. Tell Me .... Columbia 2821	
3/06/20	6	2	30. I Gave Her That .... Columbia 2835	
3/20/20	3	5	31. You Ain't Heard Nothin' Yet .... Columbia 2836	
4/24/20	5	4	32. Chloe... Columbia 2861	
5/08/20	1(9)	18	● 33. Swanee.. Columbia 2884 27, 30 & 33 from "Sinbad"	
5/29/20	5	3	34. That Wonderful Kid From Madrid .... Columbia 2898	
9/18/20	5	3	35. In Sweet September............................... Columbia 2946	
11/27/20+	2(2)	9	36. Avalon... Columbia 2995	

DATE CHARTED	PEAK POS	WKS CHRT'D	ARTIST — Record Title	Label & Number
4/09/21	1(4)	7	37. **O-H-I-O (O-My! O!)** .... [C]	Columbia 3361
7/09/21	5	3	38. Scandanavia	Columbia 3382
1/28/22	1(11)	17	39. **April Showers**	Columbia 3500
2/18/22	4	5	40. Yoo Hoo.................................... [C]	Columbia 3513
			36, 39 & 40 from the Broadway musical "Bombo"	
4/08/22	2(4)	8	41. Give Me My Mammy	Columbia 3540
5/06/22	1(5)	8	42. **Angel Child**	Columbia 3568
8/26/22	7	2	43. Coo Coo .... [C]	Columbia 3626
			all records from 5-43 accompanied by Charles Prince's Orchestra	
12/23/22+	1(4)	10	44. **Toot Toot Tootsie (Goo'bye)**	Columbia 3705
2/10/23	4	3	45. Lost (A Wonderful Girl)............................	Columbia 3744
3/10/23	4	4	46. Who Cares?	Columbia 3779
			accompanied by Paul Biese's Orchestra 44 & 46 from "Bombo"	
6/30/23	4	3	47. Coal Black Mammy	Columbia 3854
			orchestra on 45 & 47 directed by Frank Westphal	
8/11/23	5	5	48. Morning Will Come..............................	Columbia 3880
9/08/23	4	5	49. Stella	Columbia 3913
12/29/23+	7	2	50. You've Simply Got Me Cuckoo....................	Columbia 3984
3/22/24	6	2	51. Arcady	Columbia 43
5/03/24	1(6)	12	52. **California, Here I Come!**.........................	Brunswick 2569
			with Buddy DeSylva (ukelele)	
5/10/24	2(2)	7	53. The One I Love Belongs To Someone Else	Brunswick 2567
5/10/24	2(2)	7	54. I'm Goin' South	Brunswick 2569
			also recorded for Columbia 61	
5/10/24	4	6	55. Steppin' Out	Brunswick 2567
6/14/24	4	4	56. Mr. Radio Man.....................................	Brunswick 2582
			above five accompanied by Isham Jones' Orchestra	
6/21/24	4	5	57. Lazy/	
7/26/24	11	1	58. My Papa Doesn't Two-Time No Time...........	Brunswick 2595
			above two accompanied by Gene Rodemich's Orchestra	
9/27/24	3	5	59. Mandalay	Brunswick 2650
			accompanied by Abe Lyman's Orchestra	
10/18/24	1(3)	12	60. **I Wonder What's Become Of Sally?/**	
11/01/24	3	6	61. Follow The Swallow	Brunswick 2671
1/03/25	1(5)	9	62. **All Alone**	Brunswick 2743
			accompanied by Ray Miller's Orchestra; featured in the Broadway musical "Music Box Revue of 1924"	
2/21/25	5	3	63. Hello, 'Tucky	Brunswick 2763
3/13/26	1(2)	11	64. **I'm Sitting On Top Of The World**	Brunswick 3014
4/03/26	6	3	65. Miami	Brunswick 3013
			63 & 65 from the Broadway musical "Big Boy"	
7/24/26	5	3	66. I Wish I Had My Old Gal Back Again/	
8/21/26	7	2	67. I'd Climb The Highest Mountain (If I Knew I'd Find You)..................................	Brunswick 3183
8/28/26	3	5	68. At Peace With The World	Brunswick 3196
9/18/26	1(2)	8	69. **When The Red, Red Robin Comes Bob-Bob-Bobbin' Along**................................	Brunswick 3222
			accompanied on 60-61 & 63-69 by Carl Fenton's Orchestra	
1/28/28	2(3)	8	70. Mother Of Mine, I Still Have You/	
			from the film "The Jazz Singer"	
2/11/28	16	1	71. Blue River	Brunswick 3719
5/05/28	9	4	72. Golden Gate.......................................	Brunswick 3775
5/19/28	4	5	73. Ol' Man River......................................	Brunswick 3867
			from the Broadway musical "Show Boat" orchestra on above four directed by William Wirges	
6/09/28	2(2)	7	74. My Mammy/	
			originally from the Broadway musical "Sinbad"	
6/16/28	8	4	75. Dirty Hands! Dirty Face!	Brunswick 3912
			above two from "The Jazz Singer" both with Abe Lyman's California Orchestra	

DATE CHARTED	PEAK POS	WKS CHRT'D	ARTIST — Record Title	Label & Number
10/13/28	1(12)	19	● 76. **Sonny Boy/**	
10/20/28	1(2)	13	77. **There's A Rainbow Round My Shoulder** ...	Brunswick 4033
			72 & above two from the film "The Singing Fool"	
8/24/29	1(5)	10	78. **Little Pal/**	
8/24/29	2(2)	6	79. I'm In Seventh Heaven............................	Brunswick 4400
8/24/29	4	6	80. Why Can't You?/	
9/14/29	18	1	81. Used To You	Brunswick 4401
			above four from the movie "Say It With Songs"	
9/14/29	9	4	82. Liza (All The Clouds'll Roll Away)................	Brunswick 4402
			accompanied by Bob Haring's Orchestra; from the Broadway musical "Show Girl"	
3/08/30	2(2)	10	83. Let Me Sing And I'm Happy	Brunswick 4721
3/15/30	6	7	84. When The Little Red Roses Get The Blues/	
			from the film "Hold Everything"	
4/05/30	7	7	85. To My Mammy	Brunswick 4722
			83 & 85 from the movie "Mammy"	
			orchestra on 78-81 & 83-85 directed by Louis Silvers	
3/11/33	19	1	86. Hallelujah! I'm A Bum	Brunswick 6500
			accompanied by Victor Young's Orchestra; movie title song; based on the traditional hymn "Revive Us Again"	
2/15/47	2(6)	14	● 87. The Anniversary Song	Decca 23714
			based on the 1880 song "Danube Waves"	
2/15/47	18	4	● 88. My Mammy..	Decca 23614
4/24/47	15	3	● 89. April Showers	Decca 23470
			recorded 8/10/45, accompanied by Carmen Dragon's Orchestra 87 & 89 from the film "The Jolson Story"	
6/07/47	20	2	90. Alexander's Ragtime Band	Decca 40038
			AL JOLSON & BING CROSBY	
3/06/48	26	1	91. If I Only Had A Match	Decca 24296
			above two accompanied by Morris Stoloff's Orchestra	

ADA JONES

The most popular female singer of the entire pre-1920 era, Ada was born 6/1/1873 in Lancashire, England. She began recording in 1904, and her strong contralto voice, mastery of ethnic and national dialects, and infectious humor quickly made her an enduring favorite, particularly in duets with Billy Murray and Len Spencer. Ada died on 5/22/22. (Also see Len Spencer)

DATE CHARTED	PEAK POS	WKS CHRT'D	ARTIST — Record Title	Label & Number
5/20/05	3	2	1. My Carolina Lady	Edison 8948
			later recorded for Victor 4430 & Columbia 32731	
9/16/05	3	3	2. Just Plain Folks	Edison 9085
10/07/05	5	1	3. Keep A Cosey Little Corner In Your Heart	
			For Me..	Edison 9060
11/25/05	10	1	4. Please Come And Play In My Yard	Columbia 3286
1/27/06	7	1	5. I'm The Only Star That Twinkles On	
			Broadway	Edison 9135
			also recorded for Victor 4563	
4/21/06	4	1	6. Just A Little Rocking Chair And You	Edison 9222
5/12/06	2(4)	6	7. So Long, Mary.....................................	Edison 9288
			from the Broadway musical "Forty-Five Minutes from Broadway"	
6/30/06	7	1	8. My Lovin' Henry................................... [C]	Edison 9259
8/11/06	2(2)	5	9. Waiting At The Church (My Wife Won't Let	
			Me) .... [C]	Victor 4714
			also recorded for Columbia 3436 & 32972, Edison 9315, & Zon-o-Phone 499	
12/15/06	4	3	10. It's All Right In The Summertime	Columbia 3473
			also on Columbia cylinder 33004, Victor 4863, & Zon-o-Phone 541; from the Broadway musical "The Artist's Model"	
12/29/06	6	1	11. The Moon Has His Eyes On You..................	Edison 9387
3/23/07	3	3	12. If The Man In The Moon Were A Coon ...... [C]	Edison 9372
			also recorded for Columbia 3565 & 333083, Victor 5226	
4/06/07	1(2)	6	13. **I Just Can't Make My Eyes Behave**...........	Columbia 3588
			from the Broadway musical "A Parisian Model"	
5/18/07	2(4)	6	14. My Irish Rosie	Edison 9484

DATE CHARTED	PEAK POS	WKS CHRT'D	ARTIST — Record Title	Label & Number
1/25/08	**6**	1	15. Wouldn't You Like To Have Me For A Sweetheart? .... from the Broadway musical "The Yankee Tourist"; also recorded by Ada & Billy for Victor 5384	Edison 9706
8/29/08	**6**	1	16. I Want To Be A Merry, Merry Widow .... [C] also recorded for Zon-o-Phone 1073	Victor 5473
3/20/09	**2(1)**	4	17. I Remember You... also recorded for Edison 10171	Columbia 1054
7/17/09	**2(1)**	5	18. Beautiful Eyes.. also recorded for Edison 10123, Victor 16339 & U.S. Everlasting 345	Indestructable 1100
7/31/09	**1(5)**	9	19. **The Yama Yama Man** .... ADA JONES & VICTOR LIGHT OPERA CO. also recorded for Columbia 664; from the Broadway musical "Three Twins"	Victor 16326
10/09/09	**2(2)**	4	20. My Pony Boy... also recorded for Edison Amberol 221; from the Broadway musical "Miss Innocence"	Victor 16356
10/30/09	**9**	1	21. Mister Othello .... from the Broadway musical "The Candy Shop"	Victor 16352
11/06/09	**1(4)**	12	22. **I've Got Rings On My Fingers** .... also recorded for U.S. Everlasting 204 from the Broadway musical "The Yankee Girl"	Columbia 741
11/27/09	**5**	1	23. Red Head	Victor 16360
2/12/10	**6**	3	24. Oh, You Candy Kid .... from the Broadway musical "The Candy Kid"	Victor 16429
2/26/10	**4**	5	25. Has Anybody Here Seen Kelly? .... Later recorded for Victor 16510 & Columbia 810; from the Broadway musical "The Jolly Bachelors"	Indestructable 1248
6/04/10	**2(1)**	8	26. By The Light Of The Silvery Moon .... also recorded for Indestructable 1330 from Broadway's "Ziegfeld Follies of 1909"	Edison 10362
9/03/10	**1(4)**	10	27. **Call Me Up Some Rainy Afternoon** .... ADA JONES & AMERICAN QUARTET	Victor 16508
9/10/10	**7**	2	28. The Girl With A Brogue .... also recorded for Victor 16559 & Indestructable 1388 from the Broadway musical "The Arcadians"	Columbia 829
9/24/10	**4**	4	29. Call Me Up Some Rainy Afternoon .... also recorded for Edison Amberol 485 & Indestructable 1386	Columbia 855
12/03/10	**9**	1	30. Is There Anything Else I Can Do For You?.....	Columbia 909
3/13/11	**1(3)**	11	31. **Come, Josephine, In My Flying Machine.....** ADA JONES, BILLY MURRAY & AMERICAN QUARTET Ada also recorded solo for Indestructable 1468	Victor 16844
3/18/11	**9**	1	32. The Dublin Rag .... also on Indestructable 1445; from the Broadway musical "Madame Sherry" flip side of "I Love It!" (POS 3) by Arthur Collins	Columbia 940
6/03/11	**4**	4	33. All Aboard For Blanket Bay........................	Columbia 989
6/24/11	**5**	2	34. Put Your Arms Around Me, Honey	Edison Amb. 669
7/22/11	**8**	1	35. Any Little Girl, That's A Nice Girl Is The Right Little Girl For Me	Edison 10502
7/29/11	**9**	1	36. It's Got To Be Someone I Love .... ADA JONES & WALTER VAN BRUNT also recorded by Ada solo on Victor 16896, Zon-o-Phone 5730 & Edison Amberol 777; flip side of #2 hit "Honey On Our Honeymoon" by Henry Burr	Columbia 988
8/12/11	**6**	3	37. That Was Before I Met You	Columbia 998
9/09/11	**6**	2	38. All Alone .... also on Indestructable 1496; Ada & Billy Murray recorded song for Victor 5846 & 16884	Columbia 1010
12/16/11	**5**	3	39. Knock Wood .... above three: ADA JONES & WALTER VAN BRUNT song recorded by Ada & Billy for Victor 17008	Columbia 1058
12/30/11+	**7**	3	40. They Always Pick On Me........................ [C] also recorded for Columbia 1056	Victor 17008

DATE CHARTED	PEAK POS	WKS CHRT'D	ARTIST — Record Title	Label & Number
5/25/12	7	2	41. Ring Ting A Ling .... also recorded for Columbia 1138 & Zon-o-Phone 5864; from the Broadway musical "Over The River"	Victor 17051
6/08/12	5	3	42. Bring Back My Lovin' Man........................... flip side of "Don't Take Me Home (POS 4) by Eddie Morton	Victor 17052
7/13/12	3	5	43. I'm Afraid, Pretty Maid, I'm Afraid .... ADA & WALTER VAN BRUNT also recorded by Ada & Billy Murray for Edison Amberol 1067 & Zon-o-Phone 5913	Columbia 1164
7/27/12	7	2	44. Oh Mr. Dream Man (Please Let Me Dream Some More) .... also recorded for Edison 10567, Amberol 1047, Zon-o-Phone 5907 & U.S. Everlasting 1504	Victor 17076
10/12/12	6	2	45. Whistle It .... ADA JONES & PEERLESS QUARTET Ada also recorded solo for Edison Amberol 1118 above two from the Broadway musical "The Wall Street Girl"	Columbia 1185
12/14/12	6	2	46. Be My Little Baby Bumble Bee .... ADA & WALTER VAN BRUNT also recorded by Ada & Billy for Victor 17152	Columbia 1210
1/04/13	1(3)	9	47. **Row! Row! Row!/** above two from Broadway's "Ziegfeld Follies of 1912"	
2/01/13	9	1	48. I've Got The Finest Man	Victor 17205
3/15/13	8	2	49. When I Get You Alone To-Night .... ADA JONES & WALTER VAN BRUNT also recorded for U.S. Everlasting 1602	Columbia 1237
2/14/14	9	1	50. On The Old Front Porch .... ADA JONES & HENRY BURR also recorded by Ada & Billy for Victor 17425	Columbia 1443
3/21/14	3	6	51. All Aboard For Dixie Land......................... ADA JONES & PEERLESS QUARTET also recorded by Ada solo for Edison Amberol 2212 from the Broadway musical "High Jinks"	Columbia 1481
5/09/14	9	1	52. Where Can I Meet You To-Night? .... ADA JONES & HENRY BURR also recorded by Ada & Billy Murray for Edison Amberol 2311	Columbia 1495
9/05/14	1(2)	8	53. **By The Beautiful Sea** .... ADA JONES & BILLY WATKINS	Columbia 1563
1/16/15	10	1	54. If That's Your Idea Of A Wonderful Time (Take Me Home) .... [C]	Victor 17630
6/05/15	10	1	55. She Used To Be The Slowest Girl In Town . [C]	Columbia 1694
7/17/15	7	2	56. My Little Girl .... above two: ADA JONES & WILL ROBBINS	Columbia 1724
2/26/16	6	2	57. Beatrice Fairfax, Tell Me What To Do!	Victor 17926
10/14/16	9	1	58. If I Knock The "L" Out Of Kelly .... also recorded for Indestructable 1539 from the Broadway musical "Step This Way"	Edison Amb. 2940
2/17/17	9	1	59. O'Brien Is Tryin' To Learn To Talk Hawaiian . also recorded for Indestructable 3394	Edison 50402
4/07/17	10	1	60. Put On Your Slippers & Fill Up Your Pipe (You're Not Going Bye-Bye Tonight) .... also recorded for Edison 50398, Edison Amberol 3132, & Emerson 7143	Victor 18205
4/14/17	9	1	61. M-I-S-S-I-S-S-I-P-P-I .... also recorded for Emerson 7128; from the Broadway musical "Hitchy-Koo"	Pathe 20074
12/01/17	4	4	62. Some Sunday Morning .... ADA JONES & M.J. O'CONNELL Ada also recorded song with Billy Murray for Victor 18393, & with other artists for Emerson & Empire	Columbia 2330
10/11/19	5	4	63. Uncle Josh And Aunt Nancy Put Up The Kitchen Stove..............................[T-C] CAL STEWART & ADA JONES also recorded for Edison 50599 & Columbia 2991	Victor 18595
12/27/19	7	1	64. Christmas Time At Pumpkin Center ...... [X-C] CAL STEWART, ADA JONES, & PEERLESS QUARTET	Columbia 2789

DATE CHARTED	PEAK POS	WKS CHRT'D	ARTIST — Record Title	Label & Number
			ADA JONES & BILLY MURRAY	
			Ada and Billy constituted perhaps the most popular female-male vocal pairing in recording history; their patented "conversational" duets possessed enormous appeal due to their mutually breezy, light-hearted styles.	
1/19/07	**4**	3	1. I'm Sorry.. Victor 4921	
			also recorded for Zon-o-Phone 669; from the Broadway musical "About Town"	
3/30/07	**8**	1	2. Wouldn't You Like To Flirt With Me? .... Victor 4951	
			also recorded for Zon-o-Phone 674	
4/27/07	**2(1)**	4	3. Whistle It .... Columbia 3589	
			ADA JONES, BILLY MURRAY & FRANK STANLEY	
			from the Broadway musical "The Red Mill"	
			also recorded by Ada, Billy, & S.H. Dudley for Victor 4970	
5/04/07	**3**	3	4. The Game of Peek-A-Boo (I'd Like To See A Little More Of You) .... Victor 4992	
			also recorded for Columbia 3612 & 33122, Zon-o-Phone 713; from the Broadway musical "A Parisian Model"	
7/13/07	**3**	3	5. It's Nice To Have A Sweetheart .... Victor 5137	
7/20/07	**5**	1	6. Kiss, Kiss, Kiss (If You Want To Learn To Kiss) .... Victor 5165	
			also recorded for Edison 9683, Columbia 3652, & Zon-o-Phone 715	
9/28/07+	**3**	4	7. Won't You Be My Honey? .... Columbia 3682	
			also on Columbia cylinder 33164	
11/09/07	**1(6)**	12	8. **Let's Take An Old-Fashioned Walk** .... Columbia 3714	
			also recorded for Zon-o-Phone 5395	
12/21/07	**5**	1	9. Be My Little Teddy Bear .... Edison 9659	
			also recorded for Columbia 3697	
			from the Broadway musical "A Parisian Model"	
1/11/08	**3**	6	10. Make Believe .... Victor 5317	
			also recorded for Zon-o-Phone 5396	
2/29/08	**6**	1	11. I Could Learn To Love You When You Smile, Smile, Smile .... Edison 9724	
			also recorded for Columbia 3729, Victor 5397, Zon-o-Phone 964 & Indestructable 681	
4/11/08	**1(3)**	8	12. **Wouldn't You Like To Have Me For A Sweetheart?** .... Victor 5384	
			also recorded for Zon-o-Phone 5397 & Indestructable 727	
			from the Broadway musical "The Yankee Tourist"	
8/01/08	**1(4)**	9	13. **When We Are M-A-Double-R-I-E-D**............ Edison 9875	
			also recorded for Victor 5625 & Zon-o-Phone 5108; from the Broadway musical "The Talk of New York"	
8/29/08	**2(2)**	5	14. Smarty .... Victor 5455	
			Ada also recorded song solo for Edison 9872	
9/12/08	**1(5)**	10	15. **Cuddle Up A Little Closer, Lovey Mine** ...... Victor 5532	
			also recorded for Edison 9950, Zon-o-Phone 5175 & Indestructable 876; from the Broadway musical "Three Twins"	
9/12/08	**2(2)**	6	16. I've Taken Quite A Fancy To You .... Victor 5515	
			also recorded for Edison 9923, Zon-o-Phone 5106 & Indestructable 801	
9/26/08	**6**	1	17. The ABCs Of The U.S.A............................. Victor 5502	
			also recorded for Edison 9903; from the Broadway musical "The Yankee Prince"	
10/31/08	**7**	1	18. By The Old Oaken Bucket, Louise................ Victor 5499	
12/19/08	**3**	6	19. There's No Moon Like The Honeymoon .... Victor 5609	
			also recorded for Columbia 943	
3/27/09	**8**	1	20. Pet Names... Victor 5642	
			from the Broadway musical "The American Idea"	
4/24/09	**8**	1	21. Oh, You Kid! .... Columbia 1000	
			also recorded for Victor 5673 & Edison 10090	
5/15/09	**1(5)**	11	22. **Shine On, Harvest Moon**........................... Edison 10134	
			from the Broadway musicals "Ziegfeld Follies of 1908" & "Miss Innocence"	
6/05/09	**5**	2	23. I'm Looking For A Sweetheart And I Think You'll Do .... Victor 16322	
			also recorded for Indestructable 1024; Ada & Walter Van Brunt also recorded song for Columbia 668 & Edison 10114	

238

DATE CHARTED	PEAK POS	WKS CHRT'D	ARTIST — Record Title	Label & Number
7/31/09	6	1	24. Isn't Love A Grand Old Thing? .... Edison 10150 also recorded by Ada & Van Brunt for Indestructable 1072	
10/02/09	3	3	25. I'm Awfully Glad I Met You .... Victor 16346 also recorded for Edison 10202 & Zon-o-Phone 5618	
12/25/09+	6	2	26. I'm Glad I'm A Boy - I'm Glad I'm A Girl .... Victor 5745	
3/10/10	2(1)	7	27. Emmaline .... Victor 5761 also on Zon-o-Phone 5596	
4/09/10	3	6	28. What Makes The World Go Round .... Victor 16450 also recorded for Edison 10330; from the Broadway musical "A Broken Idol"	
7/09/10	8	2	29. Just A Little Ring From You .... Edison 10359	
2/25/11	7	2	30. Silver Bell .... Edison Amb. 576 later on Edison 10492	
3/04/11	5	3	31. Kiss Me, My Honey, Kiss Me .... Edison Amb. 617	
4/08/11	7	2	32. Cheer Up, My Honey .... Victor 16697	
8/26/11	2(2)	5	33. All Alone .... Victor 5846 also on Zon-o-Phone 5750; recorded by Ada solo for Edison Amberol 725	
1/27/12	9	1	34. Knock Wood .... Victor 17008	
7/06/12	8	2	35. Lingering Love .... Victor 17071 also on Zon-o-Phone 5872	
10/19/12	1(5)	13	36. **Be My Little Baby Bumble Bee** .... Victor 17152 from "Ziegfeld Follies of 1912"	
11/23/12	4	5	37. The Wedding Glide .... Victor 17170 later recorded for Edison Amberol 1577; from the Broadway musical "The Passing Show of 1912"	
4/12/13	7	3	38. All Night Long .... [C] Victor 17278 also recorded by Ada & Peerless Quartet for Columbia 1297	
12/06/13	6	4	39. On The Old Front Porch .... Victor 17425 also recorded for Edison Amberol 2129; Ada & Henry Burr recorded song for Columbia 1443	
6/06/14	4	5	40. I'm Crying Just For You .... Victor 17562 also recorded for Edison Amberol 2224	
10/24/14	10	1	41. The Whistling Coquette .... Edison Amb. 2361 whistling by Joe Belmont; also recorded by Ada & Belmont for Columbia 1597	
3/17/17	3	5	42. What Do You Want To Make Those Eyes At Me For? .... Victor 18224	
5/18/18	9	1	43. I'll Take You Back To Italy .... Victor 18436 from the Broadway musical "Jack O'Lantern"	
2/18/22	6	4	44. When Frances Dances With Me .... Victor 18830 also recorded by Ada & Billy Jones for Edison Amberol 4425 and Edison 50852	

ALLAN JONES
Featured in many Hollywood musicals and other films from 1935-45; father of singer Jack Jones.

DATE CHARTED	PEAK POS	WKS CHRT'D	ARTIST — Record Title	Label & Number
4/23/38	8	6	1. The Donkey Serenade .... Victor 4380 from the film "The Firefly"; adapted from 1923 hit "Chansonette"; orchestra conducted by Nat Shilkret	

BILLY JONES
Half of the famous "Happiness Boys" team with Ernest Hare; also performed in vaudeville; died on 11/23/40 (51). (Also see Ipana Troubadors, Bennie Krueger)

DATE CHARTED	PEAK POS	WKS CHRT'D	ARTIST — Record Title	Label & Number
3/12/21	2(2)	5	1. (Down By The) O-H-I-O .... Victor 18723 BILLY MURRAY & "VICTOR ROBERTS" (Billy Jones)	
8/13/21	5	5	2. Peggy O'Neil .... Victor 18764	
11/26/21	15	1	3. Tuck Me To Sleep (In My Old 'Tucky Home) ... Okeh 4409	
7/22/22	8	1	4. Gee, But I Hate To Go Home Alone .... Victor 18892 also recorded for Columbia 3641	
9/24/22	12	1	5. Ain't We Got Fun? .... [C] Edison Amb. 4309	
10/07/22	3	5	6. Why Should I Cry Over You? .... Victor 18922 1-2, 4 & 6 under pseudonym "Victor Roberts"	
7/21/23	1(5)	13	7. **Yes! We Have No Bananas** .... [C] Edison 51183 Billy also recorded song for Okeh 4876, Vocalion 14579 & Emerson 10622; also sang on versions by Bernie Kreuger (Brunswick 2445) & Blue Diamond Dance Orchestra (Okeh 4866)	

DATE CHARTED	PEAK POS	WKS CHRT'D	ARTIST — Record Title	Label & Number
9/15/23	**8**	2	8. Bebe..	Columbia 3913
10/31/25	**12**	1	9. Row, Row, Rosie	Okeh 40421
7/31/26	**13**	1	10. Gimme A Little Kiss, Will Ya, Huh? .... [C]	Okeh 40585
			also recorded for Domino 3692 & Regal 8028	

ISHAM JONES & HIS ORCHESTRA
Regarded by some as the best dance band of the pre-"swing" era; leader and tenor saxophonist Isham Jones was also one of the finest songwriters of his time ("It Had To Be You", "I'll See You In My Dreams", many of the band's other hits). Gordon Jenkins was his main 1930s arranger, and the band featured Johnny Carlson (lead trumpet) & Milt Yaner (alto sax/clarinet). Isham died on on 10/19/56 (62). (Also see Bing Crosby, Marion Harris, Al Jolson)

DATE CHARTED	PEAK POS	WKS CHRT'D	ARTIST — Record Title	Label & Number
9/25/20	**12**	1	1. A Young Man's Fancy...................... [I]	Brunswick 5014
			from the Broadway musical "What's In A Name?"	
10/16/20	**4**	5	2. Kismet................................... [I]	Brunswick 5021
4/16/21	**8**	1	3. Whip-Poor-Will/ [I]	
4/30/21	**11**	1	4. Look For The Silver Lining.................. [I]	Brunswick 5045
			from the Broadway musical "Sally"	
5/28/21	**11**	1	5. My Mammy.............................. [I]	Brunswick 5046
			from the Broadway musical "Bombo"	
6/11/21	**5**	5	6. Make Believe .... [I]	Brunswick 5049
12/10/21	**1(6)**	12	● 7. **Wabash Blues** .... [I]	Brunswick 5065
			Louis Panico (trumpet) featured	
5/20/22	**1(4)**	10	8. **On The Alamo** .... [I]	Brunswick 2245
10/14/22	**4**	5	9. My Honey's Lovin' Arms .... [I]	Brunswick 2301
11/11/22	**2(1)**	6	10. The World Is Waiting For The Sunrise ...... [I]	Brunswick 2313
12/09/22	**10**	1	11. Say It While Dancing........................ [I]	Brunswick 2314
3/10/23	**2(1)**	7	12. Broken-Hearted Melody .... [I]	Brunswick 2343
4/07/23	**5**	3	13. Ivy, Cling To Me .... [I]	Brunswick 5177
5/26/23	**5**	5	14. Saw Mill River Road/ [I]	
6/16/23	**8**	1	15. Farewell Blues .... [I]	Brunswick 2406
8/04/23	**1(6)**	15	16. **Swingin' Down The Lane/** [I]	
8/11/23	**3**	8	17. Who's Sorry Now? .... [I]	Brunswick 2438
			revived as a 1958 million-seller by Connie Francis	
8/18/23	**8**	2	18. Marcheta........................... [I]	Brunswick 2439
9/29/23	**4**	7	19. When You Walked Out, Someone Else Walked Right In .... [I]	Brunswick 2456
3/15/24	**8**	2	20. Mama Loves Papa .... [I]	Brunswick 2506
4/19/24	**5**	4	21. The One I Love Belongs To Somebody Else. [I]	Brunswick 2555
			ISHAM JONES WITH RAY MILLER'S ORCHESTRA	
4/26/24	**7**	3	22. You're In Kentucky Sure As You're Born ... [I]	Brunswick 2557
6/07/24	**2(1)**	6	23. Nobody's Sweetheart........................ [I]	Brunswick 2578
6/21/24	**1(2)**	12	24. **Spain**................................ [I]	Brunswick 2600
6/28/24	**5**	3	25. Never Again............................ [I]	Brunswick 2577
7/19/24	**1(5)**	15	26. **It Had To Be You** .... [I]	Brunswick 2614
12/06/24	**2(2)**	5	27. Some Other Day, Some Other Girl................	Brunswick 2678
1/10/25	**8**	2	28. Tell Me, Dreamy Eyes........................ [I]	Brunswick 2738
2/14/25	**4**	4	29. My Best Girl/ [I]	
2/21/25	**10**	1	30. Gotta Getta Girl .... [I]	Brunswick 2750
3/14/25	**1(7)**	16	31. **I'll See You In My Dreams/** [I]	
4/18/25	**8**	2	32. Why Couldn't It Be Poor Little Me?........ [I]	Brunswick 2788
			above two: Isham Jones conducting Ray Miller's Orchestra	
5/09/25	**10**	1	33. Alabamy Bound................................ [I]	Brunswick 2789
7/04/25	**5**	3	34. Riverboat Shuffle/ [I]	
8/08/25	**8**	2	35. Swanee Butterfly........................ [I]	Brunswick 2854
9/26/25	**5**	4	36. Sweet Georgia Brown .... [I]	Brunswick 2913
10/10/25	**3**	5	37. I'm Tired Of Everything But You.............. [I]	Brunswick 2933
10/10/25	**7**	2	38. Ida - I Do........................... [I]	Brunswick 2915
12/12/25	**1(1)**	8	39. **Remember** .... [I]	Brunswick 2963
2/06/26	**5**	3	40. The Original Charleston......................... [I]	Brunswick 2970

DATE CHARTED	PEAK POS	WKS CHRT'D	ARTIST — Record Title	Label & Number
4/17/26	5	3	41. My Castle In Spain .... [I] from the Broadway musical "By the Way"	Brunswick 3015
9/04/26	5	3	42. At Peace With The World .... [I]	Brunswick 3199
12/25/26+	3	8	43. It Made You Happy When You Made Me Cry... vocal: Frank Munn	Brunswick 3335
12/25/26+	3	5	44. I Lost My Heart In Monterey (When I Found You).. vocal: Alfie Evans	Brunswick 3333
1/21/28	5	5	45. Together, We Two .... vocal: Keller Sisters	Brunswick 3685
7/19/30	2(2)	7	46. What's The Use?...................................	Brunswick 4810
8/23/30	13	4	47. Trees/ [I] musical adaptation of the Joyce Kilmer poem	
9/13/30+	1(1)	20	48. **Star Dust** .... [I] not the first recording of this song, but the one which established it as a classic	Brunswick 4586
11/29/30	10	4	49. Sweet Jennie Lee!.................................	Brunswick 4909
1/31/31	8	4	50. Lonesome Lover .... vocal: Frank Sylvano	Brunswick 6015
2/27/32	16	1	51. Snuggled On Your Shoulder (Cuddled In Your Arms)..	Brunswick 6249
6/11/32	4	7	52. My Silent Love/ vocal: Billy Scott; adapted from the instrumental "Jazz Nocturne"	
8/06/32	5	4	53. I Can't Believe It's True ...,......................	Brunswick 6308
9/24/32	10	4	54. Everyone Says "I Love You"........................ above two vocals: Eddie Stone	Victor 24118
11/05/32	7	4	55. I'll Never Have To Dream Again.................. vocal: Dave Franks	Victor 24134
12/03/32	6	8	56. Just A Little Street Where Old Friends Meet.. vocal: Frank Hazzard	Victor 24161
9/02/33	8	5	57. It Isn't Fair .... vocal: Rita Smith	Victor 24367
9/09/33	13	3	58. Shadows On The Swanee...........................	Victor 24368
9/30/33	14	3	59. This Time It's Love	Victor 24392
3/24/34	14	3	60. I Knew You When	Victor 24583
3/31/34	6	6	61. Over Somebody Else's Shoulder/ vocals on 59 & 61: Joe Martin	
4/07/34	6	7	62. Neighbors..	Victor 24582
4/28/34	17	1	63. I Hate Myself (For Being So Mean To You) ..... vocals on 58, 60, 62-63: Eddie Stone	Victor 24595
6/16/34	11	3	64. With My Eyes Wide Open I'm Dreaming........ from the film "Shoot the Works"	Victor 24643
6/23/34	10	5	65. Little Man, You've Had A Busy Day.............	Victor 24633
8/18/34	12	3	66. From Now On .... from the film "Student Tour"	Victor 24682
8/18/34	16	2	67. For All We Know/	
8/25/34	15	2	68. Say It	Victor 24681
5/18/35	13	3	69. China Boy .... [I]	Decca 443
3/21/36	20	1	70. Life Begins When You're In Love/ from the film "The Music Goes 'Round"	
4/11/36	20	1	71. (There Is) No Greater Love....................... above two vocals: Woody Herman (only hits with Woody)	Decca 704
12/18/37+	13	5	72. I Wanna Be In Winchell's Column .... from the film "Love and Hisses" vocals on 65-66 & 72: Eddie Stone	Vocalion 3862
2/19/38	13	3	73. There's A Gold Mine In The Sky .... vocals on 64, 67-68 & 73: Joe Martin	Vocalion 3910

JONAH JONES

Trumpet star with Jimmie Lunceford, Stuff Smith (1932-40), Billie
Holiday, Cab Calloway (1941-50).

DATE CHARTED	PEAK POS	WKS CHRT'D	ARTIST — Record Title	Label & Number
			SPIKE JONES & HIS CITY SLICKERS Former Hollywood studio drummer who became leader of the zaniest novelty band of all, using such instruments as pistols, cowbells, & toy whistles; he died on 5/1/64 (52).	
5/02/42	23	1	1. Clink, Clink, Another Drink .... [N] with Mel Blanc	Bluebird 11466
10/03/42	3	16	● 2. Der Fuehrer's Face .... [N] vocal: Carl Grayson & Willie Spicer animated film title song	Bluebird 11586
6/19/43	19	1	3. The Sheik Of Araby/ [N]	
7/17/43	20	1	4. Oh! By Jingo! (Oh! By Gee, By Gosh, By Gum, By Juu) .... [N]	Bluebird 0812
1/27/45	4	8	● 5. Cocktails For Two/ [N] vocal: Carl Grayson; from the film "Murder at the Vanities"	
3/03/45	14	1	6. Leave The Dishes In The Sink, Ma .... [N] vocals on 1 & 6: Del Porter	Victor 1628
4/28/45	5	6	7. Chloe .... [N] vocal: Red Ingle; featured in the film "Bring On The Girls"	Victor 1654
11/15/45	10	1	8. Holiday For Strings .... [N]	Victor 1733
7/27/46	8	1	9. Hawaiian War Chant (Ta-Hu-Wa-Hu-Wai) ... [N] vocal: "Wacky Wakakians"	RCA Victor 1893
6/12/48	6	15	10. William Tell Overture .... [N]	RCA Victor 2861
11/27/48+	1(3)	8	● 11. **All I Want For Christmas (Is My Two Front Teeth)** .... [X-N]	RCA Victor 3177
4/16/49	24	2	12. Ya Wanna Buy A Bunny? .... [N] above two vocals: George Rock	RCA Victor 3359
8/27/49	13	9	13. Dance Of The Hours .... [N] vocals on 10 & 13: Doodles Weaver also recorded on RCA Victor 45-2992	RCA Vic. 78-3516
1/07/50	18	1	14. All I Want For Christmas (Is My Two Front Teeth) .... [X-N-R] also recorded on RCA Victor 45-2963	RCA Vic. 78-3177
4/29/50	16	3	15. Chinese Mule Train .... [N] with "Fleddy Morgan"; from the film "Singing Guns"	RCA Victor 3741
12/23/50	7	3	16. Rudolph, The Red-Nosed Reindeer .... [X-N] with "Rudolph & the Reindeers"	RCA Victor 3934
1/20/51	13	5	17. Tennessee Waltz .... [N] vocal: Sara Berner & "Sir Frederic Gas"	RCA Victor 4011
12/20/52+	4	3	18. I Saw Mommy Kissing Santa Claus/ [X-N] vocal: George Rock	
1/03/53	23	1	19. Winter .... [N] vocal: Mello Men	RCA Victor 5067
1/31/53	20	1	20. I Went To Your Wedding .... [N] vocal: "Sir Frederic Gas"	RCA Victor 5107
			SCOTT JOPLIN The pioneer composer of the ragtime classics ("Maple Leaf Rag", "The Entertainer", & many others) made no recordings, only piano rolls; he died on 4/11/17 (48).	
			LOUIS JORDAN & HIS TYMPANY FIVE Regarded by many as the father of modern rhythm & blues, Louis Jordan was born on 7/8/08 in Brinkley, Ark. He played alto sax with Chick Webb (1936-38), formed the Tympany Five band, and soon began pouring out his long series of dance/R&B classics, featuring his own distinctive vocals, which were to dominate the 'race' charts throughout the decade. Louis died on 2/4/75 (66).	
1/15/44	11	4	1. Ration Blues	Decca 8654
5/06/44	1(2)	25	● 2. **G.I. Jive/**	
7/29/44	2(3)	19	3. Is You Is Or Is You Ain't (Ma' Baby) .... from the film "Follow the Boys"	Decca 8659
4/21/45	11	1	4. You Can't Get That No More	Decca 8668
6/03/45	6	8	● 5. Caldonia Boogie	Decca 8670
7/21/45	14	1	6. My Baby Said Yes .... BING CROSBY & LOUIS JORDAN WITH TYMPANY FIVE	Decca 23417
1/05/46	9	2	7. Buzz Me	Decca 18734
5/18/46	20	1	8. Beware (Brother, Beware)	Decca 18818

DATE CHARTED	PEAK POS	WKS CHRT'D	ARTIST — Record Title	Label & Number
7/06/46	**7**	6	9. Stone Cold Dead In The Market (He Had It Coming) .... ELLA FITZGERALD & LOUIS JORDAN	Decca 23546
8/31/46	**7**	16	● 10. Choo Choo Ch'boogie....................	Decca 23610
11/02/46	**17**	2	11. Ain't That Just Like A Woman....................	Decca 23669
1/04/47	**6**	6	12. Ain't Nobody Here But Us Chickens	Decca 23741
3/08/47	**6**	4	13. Open The Door, Richard.................... [C]	Decca 23841
3/15/47	**20**	3	14. Texas And Pacific	Decca 23810
7/11/47	**21**	1	15. Jack, You're Dead	Decca 23901
9/13/47	**21**	1	16. Boogie Woogie Blue Plate	Decca 24108
7/03/48	**23**	3	17. Run, Joe	Decca 24448
6/11/49	**9**	13	18. Baby, It's Cold Outside .... ELLA FITZGERALD & LOUIS JORDAN from the film "Neptune's Daughter"	Decca 24644
10/22/49	**21**	5	● 19. Saturday Night Fish Fry.................... band membership changed regularly; all records featured Louis on alto; main tenor saxists: Josh Jackson & James Wright	Decca 24725

TAFT JORDAN
Featured trumpet with Chick Webb (1933-39), Willie Bryant, Ella Fitzgerald, & Duke Ellington (1943-47).

RICHARD JOSE
British-born counter-tenor famous in vaudeville from 1890s; died on 10/20/41 (72).

2/06/04	**1(4)**	11	1. **Silver Threads Among The Gold** .... later on Victor 31342	Victor 2556
4/15/05	**3**	4	2. The Day That You Grew Colder	Victor 31348
4/15/05	**4**	2	3. When I'm Away From You, Dear.................	Victor 4259
4/28/06	**7**	1	4. When You And I Were Young, Maggie	Victor 31485
8/04/06	**3**	3	5. Home, Sweet Home	Victor 31515
11/24/06	**9**	1	6. Nearer My God To Thee	Victor 4818

MARCEL JOURNET
Bass, long the #1 French operatic star, with New York Met 1900-08; died on 9/9/33 (66). (see Frances Alda, Victor Military Band)

JIMMY JOY & HIS ORCHESTRA
Clarinetist-bandleader (born James Maloney) whose 1947 Chicago radio show gave early boost to Patti Page. Jimmy died on 3/7/62 (59).

3/28/25+	**15**	1	1. Milenberg Joys..................... [I]	Okeh 40251

JUBILAIRES
Close-harmony vocal group.

5/11/46	**14**	1	1. I Know..................... with Andy Kirk & His Orchestra	Decca 18782
6/17/50	**25**	1	2. The Old Piano Roll Blues.....................	Capitol 845

DICK JURGENS & HIS ORCHESTRA
Hotel bandleader best known for singer Eddy Howard; co-wrote such hits as "Careless", "Elmer's Tune", & "One Dozen Roses".

3/04/39	**17**	2	1. Rainbow Valley	Vocalion 4678
8/05/39	**6**	3	2. My Last Good-Bye.....................	Vocalion 4874
9/30/39	**6**	7	3. It's A Hundred To One (I'm In Love)	Vocalion 5063
10/21/39	**15**	1	4. If I Knew Then (What I Know Now).............	Vocalion 5074
12/09/39+	**6**	12	5. Careless.....................	Vocalion 5235
12/16/39+	**3**	19	6. In An Old Dutch Garden (By An Old Dutch Mill)	Vocalion 5263
12/16/39+	**9**	6	7. Bluebirds In The Moonlight..................... from the animated film "Gulliver's Travels"	Vocalion 5081
3/30/40	**13**	5	8. On The Isle Of May..................... based on Tchaikovsky's "Quartet in D" Eddy Howard: above eight vocals	Vocalion 5361
4/06/40	**8**	12	9. Cecelia .... vocal: Ronnie Kemper	Vocalion 5405

DATE CHARTED	PEAK POS	WKS CHRT'D	ARTIST — Record Title	Label & Number
8/03/40	17	2	10. Make Believe Island	Vocalion 5540
8/10/40	12	6	11. A Million Dreams Ago...........................	Okeh 5628
10/19/40	10	2	12. Our Love Affair .... from the film "Strike Up the Band"	Okeh 5759
10/19/40	25	1	13. Goodnight, Mother	Okeh 5730
1/18/41	6	5	14. Along The Santa Fe Trail .... from the film "Santa Fe Trail"	Okeh 5858
6/14/41	24	1	15. Nighty Night .... Harry Cool: above six vocals	Okeh 6166
8/02/41	8	18	16. Elmer's Tune .... [I]	Okeh 6209
12/13/41	7	11	17. The Bells Of San Raquel/ vocal: Harry Cool	
1/24/42	24	1	18. Cuddle Up A Little Closer...................... from the Broadway musical "The Three Twins"; revived in the film "Birth of The Blues"	Okeh 6456
1/31/42	21	1	19. How About You?................................. from the film "Babes on Broadway"	Okeh 6535
4/18/42	3	15	20. One Dozen Roses .... vocal: Buddy Moreno	Okeh 6636
6/06/42	21	1	21. On Echo Hill/	
6/27/42	19	1	22. Happy In Love..................................	Columbia 36586
1/16/43	4	11	23. Why Don't You Fall In Love With Me? .... vocal: Harry Cool	Columbia 36643
2/15/47	14	1	24. (Oh Why, Oh Why, Did I Ever Leave) Wyoming .... vocal: Jimmy Castle & Al Galante	Columbia 37210
10/04/47	17	1	25. When You Were Sweet Sixteen.................. vocal: Jimmy Castle	Columbia 37803

K

ISH KABIBBLE
Real name Merwyn Bogue, Kay Kyser's popular comic singer also on trumpet from 1935-45.

ART KAHN & HIS ORCHESTRA
Chicago-based pianist-bandleader

4/19/24	9	1	1. Shanghai Lullaby .... [I]	Columbia 45
10/15/27	18	1	2. When Day Is Done .... [I]	Okeh 40857

ROGER WOLFE KAHN & HIS ORCHESTRA
Millionaire's son who became a popular alto saxist-bandleader; often featured Miff Mole (trombone), Joe Ventuti (violin), & Eddie Lang (guitar); died on 7/12/62 (54).

2/13/26	9	1	1. I'm Sitting On Top Of The World.............. [I]	Victor 19845
3/20/26	8	1	2. A Little Bungalow............................. [I] from the Broadway musical "The Cocoanuts"	Victor 19860
9/18/26	4	5	3. Mountain Greenery/ [I] from the Broadway musical "Garrick Gaieties"	
10/02/26	8	2	4. Cross Your Heart.............................. vocal: Henry Burr; from the Broadway musical "Queen High"	Victor 20071
2/05/27	9	6	5. Clap Yo' Hands................................. [I] from the Broadway musical "Oh, Kay!"	Victor 20327
2/19/27	11	4	6. Tonight You Belong To Me	Victor 20359
7/09/27	5	7	7. Sometimes I'm Happy .... from the Broadway musical "Hit the Deck" above two vocals: Franklyn Baur flip side of "Hallelujah" (POS 3) by Nat Shilkret & His Orchestra	Victor 20599
7/16/27	1(3)	15	8. **Russian Lullaby** .... vocal: Henry Garden	Victor 20602
7/30/27	11	3	9. I Can't Believe That You're In Love With Me...................................... [I]	Victor 20573
9/24/27	19	1	10. Where The Wild, Wild Flowers Grow.......... [I]	Victor 20717

DATE CHARTED	PEAK POS	WKS CHRT'D	ARTIST — Record Title	Label & Number
2/04/28	**17**	2	11. An Old Guitar And An Old Refrain	Victor 21078
3/17/28	**12**	2	12. Among My Souvenirs................................. vocal: Scrappy Lambert	Victor 21084
4/21/28	**6**	6	13. Let A Smile Be Your Umbrella....................	Victor 21233
6/23/28	**14**	2	14. She's A Great, Great Girl........................ [I] featuring trombone solo by Jack Teagarden	Victor 21326
8/11/28	**10**	4	15. Crazy Rhythm .... from the Broadway musical "Here's Howe"	Victor 21368
3/02/29	**18**	2	16. Dance, Little Lady .... from the Broadway musical "This Year of Grace" vocals on 11, 13, 15 & 16: Franklyn Baur	Victor 21801
6/25/32	**8**	4	17. My Silent Love .... vocal: Elmer Feldkamp; adapted from the instrumental "Jazz Nocturne"	Columbia 2653
11/26/32	**12**	4	18. A Shine On Your Shoes........................... from the Broadway musical "Flying Colors" Artie Shaw (clarinet) on above two	Columbia 2722

KITTY KALLEN
Leading big band singer with Jack Teagarden, Jimmy Dorsey ("They're Either Too Young or Too Old") & Harry James ("I'm Beginning to See the Light").

DATE CHARTED	PEAK POS	WKS CHRT'D	ARTIST — Record Title	Label & Number
4/30/49	**30**	1	1. Kiss Me Sweet .... with Mitch Miller's Orchestra	Mercury 5265
5/13/50	**17**	1	2. Juke Box Annie....................................... with Harry Geller's Orchestra	Mercury 5417
9/09/50	**10**	12	3. Our Lady Of Fatima................................. with Jimmy Carroll's Orchestra	Mercury 5466
3/03/51+	**9**	10	4. The Aba Daba Honeymoon .... with George Siravo's Orchestra; song revived in the film "Two Weeks With Love" above two: RICHARD HAYES & KITTY KALLEN	Mercury 5586
11/07/53	**27**	3	5. Are You Looking For A Sweetheart?/	
4/17/54	**1(9)**	26	● 6. **Little Things Mean A Lot**	Decca 28904
7/17/54	**4**	14	● 7. In The Chapel In The Moonlight..................	Decca 29130
11/13/54	**23**	4	8. I Want You All To Myself (Just You)............. above four accompanied by Jack Pleis' Orchestra	Decca 29268

MAX KAMINSKY
Trumpet star with Leo Reisman, Tommy Dorsey (1936), Tony Pastor, Artie Shaw (1941).

HELEN KANE
The famous baby-voiced "boop-boop-a-doop" girl, born Helen Schroder, in several Broadway and film musicals; she died on 9/26/66 (62).

DATE CHARTED	PEAK POS	WKS CHRT'D	ARTIST — Record Title	Label & Number
9/15/28	**5**	6	1. That's My Weakness Now/	
9/15/28	**7**	5	2. Get Out And Under The Moon .... above two with Nat Shilkret's Orchestra	Victor 21557
11/17/28	**2(2)**	11	3. I Wanna Be Loved By You .... Helen's trademark song; with Leonard Joy's Orchestra	Victor 21684
2/23/29	**8**	5	4. Me And The Man In The Moon/	
4/06/29	**16**	2	5. Don't Be Like That.................................. 3 & 5 from the Broadway musical "Good Boy"	Victor 21830
3/23/29	**3**	8	6. Button Up Your Overcoat/	
6/29/29	**18**	1	7. I Want To Be Bad................................... above two from the Broadway musical "Follow Through"	Victor 21863
7/20/29	**12**	3	8. Do Something...................................... from the film "Syncopation"	Victor 21917

WILLIAM KAPELL
American pianist who was a featured soloist with major American orchestras and throughout Europe. He died in a plane crash on 10/29/53 (31).

DATE CHARTED	PEAK POS	WKS CHRT'D	ARTIST — Record Title	Label & Number
11/13/53	**19**	2	1. The Eighteenth Variation (Rachmaninoff: Rhapsody On A Theme of Paganini) .... [I] featured in the film "Story of Three Loves" accompanied by Fritz Reiner & the Robin Hood Dell Orchestra of Philadelphia	RCA Victor 4210

ANTON KARAS
Austrian zither player, the most remarkable of all one-hit artists; died on 1/10/84 (78).

2/18/50	1(11)	27	● 1. **The Third Man Theme** .... [I] movie theme; sold over two million copies	London 536

GENE KARDOS & HIS ORCHESTRA
Alto saxophonist-bandleader

6/04/32	20	1	1. My Extraordinary Gal .... vocal: Dick Robertson	Victor 22986

HARRY KARI & HIS SIX SAKI SIPPERS
"Harry" is actually Yorgi Yorgesson.

4/04/53	22	1	1. Yokohama Mama .... [N]	Capitol 2392

ART KARLE & HIS BOYS

2/15/36	14	2	1. Moon Over Miami .... vocal: Chick Bullock	Vocalion 3146

THEO KARLE
Tenor, real name Theo Karle Johnston.

3/25/22	14	1	1. The World Is Waiting For The Sunrise	Brunswick 13031

ART KASSEL & HIS "KASSELS-IN-THE-AIR"
Sweet-band leader, tenor saxist and songwriter ("Hell's Bells"); died on 2/3/65 (69).

5/07/32	14	2	1. Goodnight, My Love	Columbia 2636
7/30/32	2(1)	21	2. Hell's Bells .... vocal: Ralph Morris-Ding Johnson-Floyd Townes	Columbia 2682
2/11/33	6	4	3. Moon Song (That Wasn't Meant For Me) .... from the film "Hello, Everybody"	Columbia 2742
4/22/33	14	4	4. Chant Of The Swamp.......................... [I]	Columbia 2765
10/09/37	8	6	5. The One Rose (That's Left In My Heart)........	Bluebird 7184
12/18/37+	16	3	6. Thrill Of A Lifetime................................. movie title song	Bluebird 7255
6/25/38	4	9	7. Music, Maestro, Please........................... above three vocals: Billy Leach	Bluebird 7619
5/04/40	25	2	8. A Guy Needs A Gal .... vocal: Art Kassel	Bluebird 10656
7/27/40	24	1	9. Back In The Saddle Again .... vocal: Harvey Crawford; Gene Autry's theme song	Bluebird 10772
8/03/40	21	2	10. It's All Over Now (I Won't Worry)	Bluebird 10750
2/15/41	21	1	11. Alexander The Swoose (Half Swan, Half Goose) .... [N] vocal: Marion Holmes	Bluebird 10990
1/03/42	16	2	12. Angeline .... vocals on 10 & 12: Kassel Trio	Bluebird 11356
6/10/44	27	1	13. I'm In Love With Someone.........................	Hit 7090
1/18/47	15	1	14. (I Love You) For Sentimental Reasons .... above two vocals: Jimmy Featherstone	Vogue 781

MICKEY KATZ & HIS ORCHESTRA
Formerly with Spike Jones; specialized in Yiddish humor. The father of actor Joel Grey, Mickey died on 4/30/85 (75).

3/11/50	18	2	1. Music! Music! Music!............................ [N]	Capitol 862
9/29/51	22	3	2. Come On-A My House .... [N] from the off-Broadway play "The Son"	Capitol 1788
3/01/52	28	1	3. Herring Boats .... [N] parody of "Shrimp Boats"	Capitol 1961

IRVING KAUFMAN
Dynamic New York-born singer who was a member of Avon Comedy Four; perhaps the most prolific of all band singers, by one account he recorded with some 62 different orchestras from 1923-33 (including Carl Fenton, Ipana Troubadors, Sam Lanin, & Ben Selvin). Irving died on 1/3/76 (85).

10/03/14	4	5	1. California And You	Victor 17613
2/20/15	9	1	2. Underneath The Japanese Moon................. from Broadway's "Ziegfeld Follies of 1914"	Victor 17653

DATE CHARTED	PEAK POS	WKS CHRT'D	ARTIST — Record Title	Label & Number
8/14/15	5	5	3. If We Can't Be The Same Old Sweethearts, We'll Just Be The Same Old Friends	Victor 17813
12/04/15	7	3	4. We'll Build A Little Home In The U.S.A.	Edison Amb. 2695
4/08/16	6	2	5. Are You From Dixie? ('cause I'm From Dixie Too) .... BILLY MURRAY & IRVING KAUFMAN	Victor 17942
1/20/17	7	2	6. Way Down In Iowa, I'm Going To Hide Away ..	Victor 18184
2/24/17	7	2	7. It's A Long, Long Time Since I've Been Home	Victor 18196
1/26/18	6	3	8. I'm All Bound Round With The Mason-Dixon Line .... also recorded for Columbia 2328	Victor 18353
3/02/18	1(4)	8	9. **Hail! Hail! The Gang's All Here** .... IRVING KAUFMAN & COLUMBIA QUARTET uses melody of "Pirates of Penzance" song, which in turn was based on "Anvil Chorus"	Columbia 2443
11/30/18	5	3	10. Oh! How I Hate To Get Up In The Morning ..... also recorded for Indestructable 1569 from the Broadway musical "Yip, Yip, Yaphank"	Okeh 1074
12/14/18	8	1	11. Oui, Oui, Marie .... [C]	Columbia 2637
10/11/19	10	1	12. Take Your Girlie To The Movies (If You Can't Make Love At Home)	Columbia 2756
1/03/20	4	4	13. Nobody Knows (And Nobody Seems To Care) . IRVING & JACK KAUFMAN	Columbia 2795
1/31/20	8	2	14. You'd Be Surprised .... from Broadway's "Ziegfeld Follies of 1919"	Columbia 2815
1/28/22	7	2	15. Ten Little Fingers And Ten Little Toes (Down In Tennessee)	Columbia 3477
9/30/22	12	1	16. Mr. Gallagher And Mr. Shean .... [C] from Broadway's "Ziegfeld Follies of 1922"	Gennett 4870
7/28/23	11	1	17. Who's Sorry Now?	Emerson 10594
9/15/23	6	3	18. Dirty Hands! Dirty Face! .... IRVING KAUFMAN WITH BEN SELVIN'S ORCHESTRA	Vocalion 14602
11/24/23	11	1	19. That Old Gang Of Mine .... 16 & 19: IRVING & JACK KAUFMAN	Emerson 10657
8/30/24	11	1	20. What'll I Do? .... from the Broadway musical "Music Box Revue of 1923"	Vocalion 14797
11/29/24	6	2	21. Where The Dreamy Wabash Flows	Vocalion 14836
9/26/25	11	1	22. Oh How I Miss You Tonight	Vocalion 15023
12/25/26	11	2	23. Tonight You Belong To Me .... also on Domino 3773, Harmony 301, & Regal 8115	Banner 1804
1/08/27	6	7	24. The Little White House (At The End Of Honeymoon Lane) .... also recorded for Banner 1897, Domino 3863, & Regal 8214 from the Broadway musical "Honeymoon Lane"	Columbia 762
11/10/28	16	2	25. Do I Hear You Saying "I Love You"? .... VAUGHN DELEATH & "FRANK HARRIS" (Irving Kaufman) from the Broadway musical "Present Arms"	Columbia 1470

JACK KAUFMAN
Irving Kaufman's older brother; died on 2/27/48 (65).

DATE CHARTED	PEAK POS	WKS CHRT'D	ARTIST — Record Title	Label & Number
1/03/20	4	4	1. Nobody Knows (And Nobody Seems To Care) . IRVING & JACK KAUFMAN Jack also recorded song for Gennett 9013	Columbia 2795
7/31/20	14	1	2. I'll See You In C-U-B-A .... from the "Greenwich Village Follies of 1919"	Emerson 10158
9/30/22	12	1	3. Mr. Gallagher And Mr. Shean .... [C] from Broadway's "Ziegfeld Follies of 1922"	Gennett 4870
11/24/23	11	1	4. That Old Gang Of Mine .... above two: IRVING & JACK KAUFMAN	Emerson 10657

AL KAVELIN & HIS ORCHESTRA
Band featured pianist Carmen Cavallaro in 1930s

DATE CHARTED	PEAK POS	WKS CHRT'D	ARTIST — Record Title	Label & Number
10/12/40	12	3	1. Practice Makes Perfect .... vocal; Bill Darnell	Okeh 5746

DATE CHARTED	PEAK POS	WKS CHRT'D	ARTIST — Record Title	Label & Number
			BEATRICE KAY Popular on radio and stage for vocal parodies of turn-of-the-century songs.	
2/05/49	21	2	1. I've Been Waitin' For Your Phone Call For Eighteen Years .... [N] accompanied by Mitchell Ayres & His Orchestra	Columbia 38373
			DOLLY KAY	
4/29/22	13	1	1. Wabash Blues	Columbia 3534
4/28/23	5	4	2. You've Got To See Mama Ev'ry Night (Or You Can't See Mama At All) .... accompanied by Frank Westphal & His Orchestra	Columbia 3808
12/15/23	10	1	3. My Sweetie Went Away............................... accompanied by Phil Phillips (piano)	Columbia 3955
10/04/24	3	6	4. Hard-Hearted Hannah...............................	Columbia 151
			HERBIE KAY & HIS ORCHESTRA Midwestern hotel band; Kay was married from 1935-39 to movie star Dorothy Lamour, who also sang with the band on Brunswick records. He died on 5/11/44 (40).	
2/29/36	16	2	1. Precious Little One	Columbia 3109
6/13/36	17	2	2. Swing, Mr. Charlie..................................	Columbia 3125
8/08/36	16	2	3. Za Zu Za .... [I]	Columbia 3126
			BUDDY KAYE QUINTET Lyricist on many popular songs, including "Till the End of Time" and "'A' You're Adorable"; also saxophonist	
2/21/48	22	3	1. Thoughtless.. vocal: Tune Timers	MGM 10137
5/07/49	27	1	2. "A" - You're Adorable .... vocal: Artie Malvin	MGM 10310
			DANNY KAYE Great comedy/musical entertainer (born David Kuminsky) on Broadway ("Lady In the Dark"), movies ("Hans Christian Andersen"), and TV ("The Danny Kaye Show", 1963-67) from 1941 onward. In recent years Danny has won equal renown as a tireless international spokesman for UNICEF.	
8/09/47	21	3	1. Bloop Bleep .... [N] accompanied by Billy May & His Orchestra	Decca 23950
11/22/47+	3	11	2. Civilization (Bongo, Bongo, Bongo)............... from the Broadway musical "Angel In the Wings"	Decca 23940
7/19/48	18	6	3. The Woody Woodpecker........................... [N] above two: DANNY KAYE & ANDREWS SISTERS	Decca 24462
1/14/50	26	2	4. I've Got A Lovely Bunch Of Cocoanuts ..... [N] with the Harmonaires	Decca 24784
6/03/50	21	1	5. C'est Si Bon.. with the Lee Gordon Singers above four accompanied by Vic Schoen & His Orchestra	Decca 24932
9/22/51	29	1	6. Blackstrap Molasses............................. [N] DANNY KAYE, JIMMY DURANTE, JANE WYMAN, & GROUCHO MARX accompanied by Sonny Burke's Orchestra & 4 Hits & A Miss	Decca 27748
10/11/52	28	1	7. Thumbelina .... accompanied by Gordon Jenkins & His Orchestra from the film "Hans Christian Andersen"	Decca 28380
			MARY KAYE TRIO	
12/20/52	26	1(1)	1. I Wish I Could Shimmy Like My Sister Kate...	Capitol 2278
2/27/54	24	1	2. Do You Believe In Dreams?	RCA Victor 5586
			SAMMY KAYE & HIS ORCHESTRA Durable leader of popular "sweet" dance band with the slogan "Swing and Sway with Sammy Kaye" (also listed on most of the band's early records); also clarinet/alto saxman, and composer ("Remember Pearl Harbor") (also see Eddie Cantor)	
10/02/37	15	2	1. Swing And Sway...................................... vocal: Three Barons	Vocalion 3669
10/09/37	15	2	2. Josephine .... [I]	Vocalion 3681
10/23/37+	1(2)	15	3. **Rosalie**.. movie title song	Vocalion 3700

DATE CHARTED	PEAK POS	WKS CHRT'D	ARTIST — Record Title	Label & Number
2/05/38	18	1	4. Sometimes I'm Happy .... from the Broadway musical "Hit the Deck"	Vocalion 3909
2/19/38	11	3	5. True Confession .... vocals: Charlie Wilson	Vocalion 3871
3/19/38	1(3)	16	6. **Love Walked In** .... from the film "Goldwyn Follies"	Vocalion 4017
6/25/38	4	5	7. When They Played The Polka....................	Vocalion 4152
7/02/38	17	2	8. I Married An Angel................................. Broadway musical title song	Vocalion 4140
10/08/38	3	13	9. All Ashore..	Victor 26059
11/05/38	6	5	10. Two Sleepy People .... from the film "Thanks for the Memory"	Victor 26067
11/12/38	15	1	11. Carolina Moon....................................	Victor 26072
11/26/38	11	5	12. They Say.. vocals on 3, 4, 6, 9, 11-12: Tommy Ryan	Victor 26075
12/17/38+	4	10	13. Hurry Home...................................... vocals on 5, 10 & 13: Charlie Wilson	Victor 26084
1/28/39	16	1	14. Star Dust .... [I]	Vocalion 4433
1/28/39	17	1	15. My Blue Heaven.................................	Vocalion 4199
2/18/39	2(1)	9	16. Penny Serenade................................. British song vocals on 8, 15 & 16: Jimmy Brown	Victor 26150
2/18/39	10	5	17. There's A Hole In The Ole Oaken Bucket	Victor 26157
3/18/39	8	4	18. We've Come A Long Way Together..............	Victor 26178
7/15/39	4	8	19. White Sails (Beneath A Yellow Moon)	Victor 26267
7/22/39	14	5	20. My Heart Has Wings	Victor 26238
8/05/39	7	3	21. Shabby Old Cabby................................	Victor 26298
12/16/39	16	1	22. In Our Little Part Of Town........................	Victor 26436
3/16/40	17	2	23. Last Night's Gardenias	Victor 26472
4/06/40	4	8	24. Let There Be Love	Victor 26564
7/27/40	19	1	25. Make Believe Island/	
8/03/40	11	1	26. Where Was I?................................... vocals on 19-20, 22 & 26: Clyde Burke	Victor 26594
12/07/40+	1(1)	13	27. **Dream Valley/**	
12/21/40+	21	2	28. A Nightingale Sang In Berkeley Square....... from the London musical "New Faces" vocals on 18, 23-25, 27-28: Tommy Ryan	Victor 26795
12/21/40+	9	4	29. Along The Santa Fe Trail .... vocal: Jimmy Brown; from the film "Santa Fe Trail"	Victor 27220
2/22/41	24	1	30. The Mem'ry Of A Rose .... vocal: Arthur Wright	Victor 27287
4/05/41	10	9	31. Until Tomorrow (Goodnight, My Love)..........	Victor 27262
5/24/41	1(8)	18	32. **Daddy** .... this and all other unidenified vocals by Kaye Choir or Three Kaydets	Victor 27391
7/26/41	12	4	33. The Reluctant Dragon .... vocal: George Gingell & Maury Cross animated movie title song	Victor 27449
9/06/41	22	1	34. Harbor Of Dreams	Victor 27498
12/13/41	14	2	35. Minka .... above two vocals: Tommy Ryan	Victor 27567
1/03/42	7	3	36. The Shrine Of St. Cecelia	Victor 27691
1/10/42	11	6	37. (There'll Be Bluebirds Over) The White Cliffs Of Dover/ vocal: Arthur Wright	
1/17/42	9	7	38. Madelaine	Victor 27704
1/24/42	3	8	39. Remember Pearl Harbor/	
4/04/42	21	1	40. Dear Mom .... vocals on 36, 38 & 40: Allan Foster	Victor 27738
3/07/42	21	1	41. On The Street Of Regret	Victor 27750

DATE CHARTED	PEAK POS	WKS CHRT'D	ARTIST — Record Title	Label & Number
5/30/42	**25**	1	42. Here You Are/ vocal: Elaine Beatty	
7/11/42	**13**	2	43. Johnny Doughboy Found A Rose In Ireland .	Victor 27870
8/08/42	**19**	1	44. Wonder When My Baby's Coming Home	Victor 27922
8/29/42	**3**	14	45. I Left My Heart At The Stage Door Canteen ... from the Broadway musical "This Is the Army"	Victor 27932
8/29/42	**20**	1	46. Where The Mountains Meet The Sky	Victor 27944
9/26/42	**8**	10	47. I Came Here To Talk For Joe .... vocals on 45 & 47: Don Cornell	Victor 27994
11/14/42	**23**	1	48. My Buddy.. vocals on 41, 43 & 48: Tommy Ryan	Victor 27811
1/23/43	**20**	1	49. There Will Never Be Another You .... from the film "Iceland"	Victor 27949
4/24/43	**13**	2	50. Taking A Chance On Love .... from the Broadway musical "Cabin In the Sky"; recorded in Nov. 1940	Victor 27239
12/30/44+	**8**	8	51. There Goes That Song Again/ from the film "Carolina Blues" vocals on 44, 49 & 51: Nancy Norman	
1/13/45	**10**	3	52. You Always Hurt The One You Love	Victor 1606
1/13/45	**10**	5	53. Always/ vocal: Tony Alamo	
1/20/45	**4**	7	54. Don't Fence Me In.................................. from the film "Hollywood Canteen"	Victor 1610
2/17/45	**6**	7	55. Saturday Night (Is The Loneliest Night Of The Week)..	Victor 1635
4/14/45	**10**	5	56. Just A Prayer Away/	
4/14/45	**10**	1	57. All Of My Life .... vocals on 46, 52, 54 & 56-57: Billy Williams	Victor 1642
8/11/45	**6**	7	58. Gotta Be This Or That/	
8/11/45	**10**	1	59. Good, Good, Good (That's You-That's You) ..	Victor 1684
10/20/45	**1(4)**	16	60. **Chickery Chick**	Victor 1726
10/27/45	**10**	5	61. Walkin' With My Honey (Soon, Soon, Soon)/ above three vocals: Nancy Norman & Billy Williams	
11/10/45	**17**	1	62. Promises...	Victor 1713
12/08/45+	**9**	7	63. I Can't Begin To Tell You .... from the film "The Dolly Sisters"; based on 1906 song "When Love Is Young In Springtime" vocals on 55, 58 & 63: Nancy Norman	Victor 1720
12/15/45+	**4**	10	64. It Might As Well Be Spring......................... from the film "State Fair"	Victor 1738
3/02/46	**6**	8	65. Atlanta, G.A.	Victor 1795
3/30/46	**1(1)**	15	66. **I'm A Big Girl Now** .... vocals on 66 & 70: Betty Barclay	Victor 1812
5/11/46	**3**	17	67. The Gypsy... vocals on 67 & 72: Mary Marlow	RCA Victor 1844
5/18/46	**3**	11	68. Laughing On The Outside, Crying On The Inside..	RCA Victor 1856
11/02/46	**1(7)**	17	69. **The Old Lamp-Lighter** .... vocals on 62, 64-65, & 68-69: Billy Williams	RCA Victor 1963
11/16/46	**8**	8	70. Sooner Or Later (You're Gonna Be Comin' Around)/	
12/21/46+	**11**	5	71. Zip-A-Dee-Doo-Dah................................. above two from the animated film "Song of the South"	RCA Victor 1976
5/10/47	**16**	1	72. The Egg And I/ movie title song	
7/09/47	**22**	3	73. After Graduation Day .... vocal by Johnnie Ryan & Glee Club	RCA Victor 2209
5/24/47	**2(1)**	22	74. That's My Desire/	
5/24/47	**8**	8	75. The Red Silk Stockings And Green Perfume	RCA Victor 2251
9/20/47	**17**	1	76. The Echo Says "No'/	
10/04/47	**5**	5	77. An Apple Blossom Wedding......................	RCA Victor 2330
11/08/47	**24**	2	78. The Little Old Mill (Went Round And Round) .	RCA Victor 2434

DATE CHARTED	PEAK POS	WKS CHRT'D	ARTIST — Record Title	Label & Number
11/15/47+	**3**	16	79. Serenade Of The Bells.............................. vocals on 74-75, 77 & 79: Don Cornell	RCA Victor 2372
11/15/47	**21**	4	80. Hand In Hand..	RCA Victor 2482
11/29/47+	**21**	4	81. Dream Again/	
12/06/47	**20**	3	82. I'll Hate Myself In The Morning .... vocals on 80 & 82: Don Cornell & Laura Leslie	RCA Victor 2524
3/20/48	**10**	4	83. I Love You, Yes I Do.................................	RCA Victor 2674
5/15/48	**8**	10	84. Tell Me A Story	RCA Victor 2761
5/29/48	**11**	7	85. Baby Face	RCA Victor 2879
11/13/48+	**14**	6	86. Down Among The Sheltering Palms/ vocals on 83-84 & 86: Don Cornell	
12/11/48+	**4**	16	87. Lavender Blue (Dilly Dilly)....................... from the animated film "So Dear to My Heart"; based on a traditional English folk song	RCA Victor 3100
2/05/49	**3**	22	88. Careless Hands/	
2/05/49	**13**	10	89. Powder Your Face With Sunshine	RCA Vic. 78-3321
5/28/49	**29**	1	90. Kiss Me Sweet	RCA Victor 3420
6/11/49	**2(1)**	24	91. Room Full Of Roses................................	RCA Vic. 78-3441
6/18/49	**3**	11	92. The Four Winds And The Seven Seas	RCA Vic. 78-3459
6/18/49	**12**	10	93. Baby, It's Cold Outside .... from the film "Neptune's Daughter" vocals on 90 & 93: Don Cornell & Laura Leslie	RCA Vic. 78-3448
10/01/49	**24**	6	94. Dime A Dozen	RCA Vic. 78-3532
2/04/50	**2(6)**	24	● 95. It Isn't Fair .... vocals on 88, 91 & 95: Don Cornell	RCA Vic. 78-3609
3/25/50	**11**	10	96. Wanderin'	RCA Vic. 78-3680
5/06/50	**5**	12	97. Roses .... vocals on 71, 78, 81, 85, 87, 89, 94, 97 & 100: Three Kaydets (also backing vocals on many other records)	RCA Victor 3754
9/09/50	**1(4)**	27	98. **Harbor Lights**	Columbia 78- 38963
8/18/51	**16**	8	99. Longing For You..................................... vocals on 92, 96 & 98-99: Tony Alamo	Columbia 39499
11/17/51	**25**	2	100. Sin	Columbia 39567
6/07/52	**28**	1	101. You	Columbia 39724
8/02/52	**11**	13	102. Walkin' To Missouri .... vocal: Tony Russo	Columbia 39769
10/17/53	**15**	7	103. In The Mission Of St. Augustine.................. vocal: Jeffrey Clay	Columbia 40061

RUBY KEELER
Singer/dancer who co-starred in classic 1930s film musicals '42nd Street" & "Gold Diggers of 1933", among others; married to Al Jolson 1928-39. She made a smash Broadway comeback in the 1970 revival of "No, No, Nanette".

GRETA KELLER
Vienna-born international singing star; died on 11/4/77 (75).

5/20/33	**15**	2	1. Lover.. from the film "Love Me Tonight"	Brunswick 6544

CHARLES KELLOGG
"The Nature Singer", a nationally-known master of bird voices; died on 9/4/49 (80). (also see Alma Gluck)

7/10/15	**4**	4	1. Songs Of Our Native Birds .... featuring the songs of the Loon, California Mountain Quail, Cardinal Redbird, & Red Wing Blackbird	Victor 55049

DAN KELLY
Next to Russell Hunting, the best-known comic recording artist of the 1890s; during the previous two decades he performed with Christy's & other minstrel companies.

5/02/91	**2(2)**	2	1. Pat Kelly's Plea In His Own Defense.......[T-C]	Ohio
9/19/91	**1(4)**	4	2. **Pat Kelly As A Police Justice** ....[T-C]	Ohio
12/28/91	**2(3)**	3	3. Pat Kelly On A Spree..........................[T-C]	Ohio

DATE CHARTED	PEAK POS	WKS CHRT'D	ARTIST — Record Title	Label & Number
			GENE KELLY	
			Along with Fred Astaire the greatest dancer-singer in movie history, Gene started on Broadway and went on to star in and choreograph such classic Hollywood musicals as "An American in Paris" and "Singin' In the Rain".	
1/24/42	**3**	21	1. For Me And My Gal/	
4/10/42	**19**	1	2. When You Wore A Tulip (And I Wore A Big Red Rose)...	Decca 18480
			above two: JUDY GARLAND & GENE KELLY with David Rose's Orchestra from the film "For Me and My Gal"	
			MONTY KELLY & HIS ORCHESTRA	
			Played trumpet for Paul Whiteman in the early 40s. (also see Bob Manning, Al Martino)	
7/18/53	**19**	5	1. Tropicana.. [I]	Essex 325
10/03/53	**21**	3	2. Three O'Clock In The Morning.................. [I]	Essex 328
			from Broadway's "Greenwich Village Follies of 1921"	
			PAULA KELLY	
			Sang with Al Donohue band 1938-40, then achieved her greatest fame as a featured member of the Modernaires, first with Glenn Miller ("Chattanooga Choo Choo") and then on their own.	
			WILLIE KELLY & HIS ORCHESTRA	
5/29/43	**2(2)**	10	1. Comin' In On A Wing And A Prayer/	
6/12/43	**6**	5	2. You'll Never Know	Hit 7046
			from the film "Hello, Frisco, Hello"	
11/13/43	**17**	2	3. I Dug A Ditch	Hit 7062
			from the film "As Thousands Cheer"	
			MAY KELSO	
			Following her brief recording career, May was a successful stage and movie actress into the 1920s; she died on 6/5/46 (79).	
11/18/99	**4**	1	1. Kentucky Babe.....................................	Edison 7177
			HAL KEMP & HIS ORCHESTRA	
			Popular sweet band leader and saxophonist featuring John Scott Trotter's arrangements (through 1935) and singer Skinnay Ennis; died on 12/21/40 (35) following an auto accident.	
1/11/30	**17**	1	1. H'lo, Baby	Brunswick 4580
6/21/30	**14**	2	2. If I Had A Girl Like You	Brunswick 4807
5/16/31	**2(2)**	7	3. (There Ought To Be A) Moonlight Saving Time	Brunswick 6108
3/04/33	**2(1)**	12	4. Shuffle Off To Buffalo/	
3/18/33	**7**	7	5. Forty-Second Street	Brunswick 6471
			above two from the film "Forty-Second Street"	
3/25/33	**13**	3	6. You've Got Me Crying Again	Brunswick 6528
6/17/33	**16**	2	7. The Gold Digger's Song............................	Brunswick 6582
6/24/33	**13**	2	8. I've Got To Sing A Torch Song	Brunswick 6583
			above two from the film "Gold Diggers of 1933"	
9/16/33	**14**	2	9. Love Is The Sweetest Thing	Brunswick 6636
			nearly all above vocals: Skinnay Ennis	
3/31/34	**9**	4	10. Good Night, Lovely Little Lady....................	Brunswick 6790
			vocal: Bob Allen; from the film "We're Not Dressing"	
8/18/34	**3**	8	11. For All We Know	Brunswick 6947
8/18/34	**12**	4	12. Love In Bloom....................................	Brunswick 6943
			from the film "She Loves Me Not"	
10/20/34	**10**	2	13. Irresistable	Brunswick 6985
11/24/34	**9**	3	14. Hands Across The Table	Brunswick 7315
			from the Broadway musical "Continental Follies"	
12/29/34	**16**	1	15. Got A Date With An Angel........................	Brunswick 7319
			Hal's theme song vocals on 11-12, 14-15: Skinnay Ennis	
12/29/34	**18**	1	16. Will Love Find A Way?	Brunswick 7334
			vocal: Deane Janis	
2/23/35	**10**	6	17. A Little White Gardenia	Brunswick 7340
			from the Broadway musical "All the King's Horses"	

DATE CHARTED	PEAK POS	WKS CHRT'D	ARTIST — Record Title	Label & Number
3/02/35	**17**	2	18. So Red The Rose.....................................	Brunswick 7360
3/30/35	**14**	3	19. Lullaby Of Broadway................................ from the film "Gold Diggers of 1935"	Brunswick 7369
4/20/35	**16**	3	20. Restless/ vocal: Maxine Gray	
4/27/35	**15**	3	21. Once Upon A Midnight...........................	Brunswick 7413
5/25/35	**2(2)**	14	22. In The Middle Of A Kiss/	
6/15/35	**6**	9	23. Thrilled	Brunswick 7437
8/03/35	**15**	4	24. You're So Darn Charming/ vocals on 18-19, 21 & 24: Bob Allen	
8/10/35	**6**	8	25. Page Miss Glory................................ vocals on 17, 22 & 25: Skinnay Ennis	Brunswick 7493
12/28/35+	**9**	4	26. Alone/ from the film "A Night at the Opera"	
12/07/35	**17**	3	27. It's Dangerous To Love Like This	Brunswick 7552
12/21/35+	**3**	8	28. With All My Heart/	
12/28/35+	**12**	3	29. Where Am I? (Am I In Heaven?)................. from the film "Stars Over Broadway"	Brunswick 7565
1/11/36	**4**	6	30. The Music Goes Round And Round/	
2/01/36	**13**	4	31. Dinner For One, Please, James.................	Brunswick 7587
2/22/36	**14**	2	32. I Can't Get Started..................................... from the Broadway musical "Ziegfeld Follies of 1936"	Brunswick 7600
3/28/36	**7**	4	33. Lost/	
4/04/36	**3**	6	34. The Touch Of Your Lips...........................	Brunswick 7626
4/04/36	**4**	4	35. Gloomy Sunday .... famous Hungarian "suicide song" subsequently banned from network radio	Brunswick 7630
4/18/36	**1(2)**	15	36. **There's A Small Hotel**........................... from the Broadway musical "On Your Toes"	Brunswick 7634
4/18/36	**12**	4	37. I Don't Want To Make History (I Just Want To Make Love) .... from the film "Palm Springs"	Brunswick 7636
7/25/36	**1(2)**	13	38. **When I'm With You**................................ from the film "Poor Little Rich Girl"	Brunswick 7681
8/15/36	**3**	12	39. A Star Fell Out Of Heaven/	
8/22/36	**8**	9	40. Me And The Moon....................................	Brunswick 7707
10/24/36	**8**	7	41. I've Got You Under My Skin....................... from the film "Born to Dance" vocals on 32, 34, 38 & 41: Skinnay Ennis	Brunswick 7745
10/31/36	**8**	5	42. Pennies From Heaven .... movie title song vocals on 37 & 42: Maxine Gray	Brunswick 7749
12/26/36+	**10**	3	43. Goodnight, My Love .... from the film "Stowaway" vocals on 33, 35 & 43: Bob Allen	Brunswick 7783
2/13/37	**1(4)**	8	44. **This Year's Kisses**................................ from the film "On the Avenue"	Brunswick 7812
2/20/37	**8**	5	45. With Plenty Of Money And You .... from the film "Gold Diggers of 1937"	Brunswick 7769
3/13/37	**9**	4	46. What Will I Tell My Heart?	Brunswick 7830
5/15/37	**1(1)**	16	47. **Where Or When**/	
6/12/37	**15**	3	48. Johnny One-Note..................................... above two from the Broadway musical "Babes in Arms" vocals on 44-45 & 48: Skinnay Ennis	Brunswick 7856
7/03/37	**11**	3	49. Whispers In The Dark............................... from the film "Artists and Models"	Victor 25598
7/23/38	**7**	6	50. Where In The World .... from the film "Josette"	Victor 25855
9/17/38	**18**	4	51. If I Loved You More................................	Victor 26040
11/12/38	**13**	1	52. The Night Is Filled With Music .... from the film "Carefree"	Victor 26009
3/11/39	**10**	1	53. You've Got Me Crying Again	Victor 26165

DATE CHARTED	PEAK POS	WKS CHRT'D	ARTIST — Record Title	Label & Number
4/01/39	5	15	54. Don't Worry 'Bout Me .... from the "World's Fair" edition of the Cotton Club show vocals on 46-47, 49-54 & 60: Bob Allen	Victor 26188
4/22/39	5	8	55. Three Little Fishies/ [N]	
4/22/39	12	3	56. The Chestnut Tree .... vocal: Saxie Dowell; British song	Victor 26204
7/08/39	14	3	57. Love For Sale.................................... from the Broadway musical "The New Yorkers"	Victor 26278
10/28/39	11	5	58. What's New?... vocal: Nan Wynn	Victor 26336
1/20/40+	14	4	59. The Little Red Fox .... from the film "That's Right - You're Wrong" vocals on 55, 57 & 59: Smoothies	Victor 26416
2/01/41	5	6	60. It All Comes Back To Me Now	Victor 27255
2/08/41	8	4	61. So You're The One/	
5/24/41	19	1	62. Walkin' By The River .... above two vocals: Janet Blair (later movie star)	Victor 27222

RONNIE KEMPER
Singer and pianist with Dick Jurgens 1934-40 ("Cecelia"), also with Hoarce Heidt ("G'bye Now").

BILL KENNY
Lead tenor voice of the Ink Spots from the 1930s to the 50s.

DATE CHARTED	PEAK POS	WKS CHRT'D	ARTIST — Record Title	Label & Number
2/10/51	18	11	1. It Is No Secret .... with the Song Spinners	Decca 27326
12/27/52	23	1	2. (That's Just My Way Of) Forgetting You........ orchestra directed by Leroy Kirkland	Decca 28462

STAN KENTON & HIS ORCHESTRA
One of the most consistently successful bandleaders of the postwar era, Stan Kenton started as pianist for Gus Arnheim and lesser bands before bringing his talents as composer ("Artistry in Rhythm") and arranger to his own big band. A leader of the "progressive jazz" movement, Kenton's orchestras always featured top musicians and vocalist (particularly June Christy). Stan died on 8/25/79 (67).

DATE CHARTED	PEAK POS	WKS CHRT'D	ARTIST — Record Title	Label & Number
2/26/44	10	8	1. Do Nothin' Till You Hear From Me .... vocal: Red Dorris	Capitol 145
9/16/44	4	18	2. And Her Tears Flowed Like Wine/ vocal: Anita O'Day	
11/04/44	9	4	3. How Many Hearts Have You Broken? .... vocal: Gene Howard Stan Getz (alto sax) on above two	Capitol 166
11/04/44	16	1	● 4. Artistry In Rhythm ....[I] Stan's famous theme	Capitol 159
7/28/45	3	15	● 5. Tampico..	Capitol 202
11/03/45	6	9	6. It's Been A Long, Long Time......................	Capitol 219
1/26/46	13	3	7. Artistry Jumps/ [I] "Jump" version of "Artistry in Rhythm"	
3/02/46	16	1	8. Just A-Sittin' And A-Rockin'	Capitol 229
3/09/46	6	11	● 9. Shoo-Fly Pie And Apple Pan Dowdy	Capitol 235
2/29/47	12	1	10. His Feet Too Big For De Bed	Capitol 361
5/03/47	11	5	11. Across The Alley From The Alamo .... Kai Winding (trombone) on above two; Vido Musso (tenor sax) on above four	Capitol 387
11/22/47	23	1	12. Curiosity	Capitol 15005
1/10/48	26	1	13. I Told Ya I Love Ya, Now Get Out................	Capitol 15018
6/05/48	23	1	14. Lonely Woman .... June Christy: all vocals from 5-14	Capitol 10125
7/10/48	20	1	15. How High The Moon ....[I]	Capitol 15117
9/30/50	5	14	16. Orange Colored Sky .... NAT "KING" COLE with STAN KENTON & HIS ORCHESTRA	Capitol 1184
4/28/51	17	11	17. September Song......................................	Capitol 1480

DATE CHARTED	PEAK POS	WKS CHRT'D	ARTIST — Record Title	Label & Number
8/04/51	**12**	5	18. Laura .... Capitol 1704 movie title song Art Pepper (alto sax) on 1, 14-18; Shelly Manne (drums) on most 1947-51 records; Bud Shank (alto sax), Maynard Ferguson & Shorty Rogers (trumpets) on above three	Capitol 1704
6/07/52	**25**	2	19. Delicado.. [I] Capitol 2040	[I] Capitol 2040
3/21/53	**30**	1	20. And The Bull Walked Around, Olay............. Capitol 2388 vocal by Chris Connor	Capitol 2388
4/04/53	**27**	1	21. Hush-A-Bye .... Capitol 2373 from the new film version of "The Jazz Singer" 17, 18 & 21: ensemble vocals	Capitol 2373
2/13/54	**28**	1	22. The Creep .... [I] Capitol 2685 Lee Konitz (alto sax) on 20 & 22	[I] Capitol 2685

KENTUCKY SERENADERS

DATE CHARTED	PEAK POS	WKS CHRT'D	ARTIST — Record Title	Label & Number
6/19/20	**3**	9	1. Rose Of Washington Square.................... [I] Columbia 2908 from the Broadway musical "Ziegfeld Midnight Frolic"	[I] Columbia 2908

JANE KENYON
Pseudonym for Elizabeth Wheeler

FRANK KERNELL
Pseudonym for S.H. Dudley

GRACE KERNS
Popular concert soprano, a college music professor after her retirement; died on 9/10/36 (50) in a car accident

DATE CHARTED	PEAK POS	WKS CHRT'D	ARTIST — Record Title	Label & Number
11/04/11	**9**	2	1. My Beautiful Lady .... Columbia 2613 from the Broadway musical "The Pink Lady"	Columbia 2613
3/16/12	**9**	1	2. Wallflower Sweet .... Columbia 5329 GRACE KERNS & CHARLES HARRISON from the Broadway musical "The Siren"	Columbia 5329
10/04/13	**6**	2	3. Sweethearts.. Columbia 1359 Broadway musical title song	Columbia 1359
2/28/14	**10**	1	4. The One I Love....................................... Columbia 1442 GRACE KERNS & REED MILLER from the Broadway musical "The Marriage Market"	Columbia 1442
9/05/14	**4**	6	5. Love Has Wings/	
9/12/14	**6**	4	6. Love's Own Sweet Song .... Columbia 5574 above two: GRACE KERNS & CHARLES HARRISON both from the Broadway musical "Sari"	Columbia 5574
1/30/15	**3**	8	7. Chinatown, My Chinatown......................... Columbia 1624 GRACE KERNS & JOHN BARNES WELLS from the Broadway musical "Up and Down Broadway"	Columbia 1624
4/30/15	**8**	2	8. The Song Of Songs .... Columbia 5625	Columbia 5625
7/22/16	**8**	1	9. They Didn't Believe Me .... Columbia 1442 GRACE KERNS & REED MILLER from the Broadway musical "The Girl from Utah"	Columbia 1442
3/31/17	**7**	2	10. Poor Butterfly .... Columbia 2167 under pseudonym "Katharine Clark"; from the Broadway musical "The Big Show"	Columbia 2167

BARNEY KESSEL
Five-time Down Beat poll winner as top guitarist; played in 40s with Charlie Parker, Charlie Barnet, Artie Shaw, & Benny Goodman.

MARGARET KEYES

DATE CHARTED	PEAK POS	WKS CHRT'D	ARTIST — Record Title	Label & Number
4/15/16	**9**	1	1. Some Day I'll Wander Back Again................ Columbia 5785 with the Columbia Stellar Quartet	Columbia 5785

KEYNOTES - see PRIMO SCALA

JACK KILTY
Sang briefly with Leo Reisman

DATE CHARTED	PEAK POS	WKS CHRT'D	ARTIST — Record Title	Label & Number
4/30/49	**28**	1	1. Sunflower... MGM 10339 became the official state song of Kansas	MGM 10339

KING COLE TRIO - see NAT KING COLE

DATE CHARTED	PEAK POS	WKS CHRT'D	ARTIST — Record Title	Label & Number
			KING SISTERS	
			Alyce, Donna, Louise, & Yvonne (real last name: Driggs); sang with Hoarce Heidt (1936-38) and, most prominently, with Alvino Rey (Louise's husband) from 1939-43. Billed on most records as the Four King Sisters, they reached an even wider audience with the 1960s TV series "The King Family".	
6/07/41	7	8	1. The Hut-Hut Song (A Swedish Serenade)	Bluebird 11154
6/14/41	25	1	2. Bless 'Em All	Victor 27407
			BARRY WOOD & KING SISTERS	
1/17/42	18	1	3. Rose O'Day (The Filla-Da-Gusha Song)	Bluebird 11349
5/02/42	21	1	4. Arthur Murray Taught Me Dancing In A Hurry	Bluebird 11431
			from the film "The Fleet's In"	
9/05/42	11	4	5. My Devotion	Bluebird 11555
4/03/43	20	1	6. Gobs Of Love	Bluebird 11576
4/08/44	12	4	7. I'll Get By...........................	Bluebird 0821
			featured in the film "Follow The Boys"	
4/15/44	4	11	8. It's Love-Love-Love/	
			from the film "Stars Over Broadway"	
4/15/44	21	1	9. Mairzy Doats .... [N]	Bluebird 0822
6/10/44	13	5	10. Milkman, Keep Those Bottles Quiet.............	Bluebird 0824
			from the film "Broadway Rhythm"	
11/25/44	13	7	11. The Trolley Song	Bluebird 0829
			from the film "Meet Me In St. Louis"	
3/31/45	15	2	12. Candy/	
			7 & 12 with Buddy Cole Orchestra	
3/31/45	15	1	13. Saturday Night (Is The Loneliest Night In The Week)........................	Victor 1633
			CHARLES KING	
			Star of many Broadway musicals from 1911-30, and in some of the first Hollywood musicals; he died on 1/11/44 (49).	
7/29/11	5	3	1. Let Me Live And Stay In Dixieland	Victor 5843
			from the Broadway musical "The Slim Princess"	
7/08/16	10	1	2. That Hula Hula.............................	Columbia 1944
			from the Broadway musical "Stop! Look! Listen!"	
10/28/16	3	5	3. My Own Iona.........................	Columbia 2059
7/07/17	6	2	4. Hawaiian Butterfly......................	Columbia 2226
12/01/17	8	1	5. In Lilac Time (When You Stole This Heart Of Mine).......................	Columbia 2339
			above five: CHARLES KING & ELIZABETH BRICE	
8/06/27	9	4	6. Sometimes I'm Happy	Victor 20609
			CHARLES KING & LOUISE GROODY accompanied by Frank Banta (piano); from the Broadway "Hit the Deck"	
7/20/29	10	4	7. Broadway Melody/	
8/03/29	8	4	8. The Wedding Of The Painted Doll	Victor 21964
			above two from the film "Broadway Melody"	
			DENNIS KING	
			British-born star of New York and London musical theater; born Dennis Pratt; he died on 5/21/71 (73).	
4/17/26	5	4	1. Song Of The Vagabonds	Victor 19897
			with the Victor Light Opera Co. from the Broadway musical "The Vagabond King" accompanied by Rosario Bourdon's Orchestra	
			HENRY KING & HIS ORCHESTRA	
			Pianist and leader of hotel band	
11/25/33	7	6	1. Good Night, Little Girl Of My Dreams/	
12/23/33+	16	3	2. Don't You Remember Me?	Victor 24457
12/30/33+	14	2	3. April In Paris.............................	Victor 24478
			from the Broadway musical "Walk a Little Faster"	
9/15/34	7	6	4. You're A Builder Upper...........................	Columbia 2945
			from the Broadway musical "Life Begins at 8:40"	
9/15/34	17	1	5. Fun To Be Fooled	Columbia 2941
1/12/35	9	7	6. Dancing With My Shadow..........................	Columbia 2992

DATE CHARTED	PEAK POS	WKS CHRT'D	ARTIST — Record Title	Label & Number
2/16/35	14	2	7. So Close To The Forest	Columbia 3010
7/06/35	7	5	8. Chasing Shadows...............................	Columbia 3048
5/09/36	4	11	9. Would You?/ from the film "San Francisco" all above vocals: Joe Sudy	
5/09/36	19	1	10. I've Got A Heavy Date .... Decca 760 vocal: Sidney Sudy	Decca 760
10/17/36	13	2	11. A Fine Romance .... vocal: Joe Sudy; from the film "Swing Time"	Decca 890
5/21/38	14	3	12. A Garden In Grenada............................... vocal: Sunny Schuyler	Decca 1767
5/11/40	24	2	13. Palms Of Paradise................................... vocal: Bob Carroll	Decca 3072
5/15/48	14	4	14. Baby Face .... vocal: Siggy Lane	Decca 25356

PEE WEE KING & HIS GOLDEN WEST COWBOYS
Composer of the classics "Tennessee Waltz" and "You Belong to Me",
in addition to "Slow Poke"; featured for years earlier on Grand
Ole Opry. (Vocals by Redd Stewart)

DATE CHARTED	PEAK POS	WKS CHRT'D	ARTIST — Record Title	Label & Number
4/10/48	30	1	1. Tennessee Waltz	RCA Victor 2680
11/03/51+	1(3)	24	● 2. **Slow Poke**...................................	RCA Victor 0489
3/08/52	18	4	3. Silver And Gold	RCA Victor 4458
6/14/52	27	1	4. Busybody	RCA Victor 4655

TEMPO KING & HIS KINGS OF TEMPO
Swing band featuring pianist Queenie Ada Rubin and guitarist Eddie
Condon; King (featured on all vocals) died on 6/25/39 (24).

DATE CHARTED	PEAK POS	WKS CHRT'D	ARTIST — Record Title	Label & Number
9/12/36	10	5	1. Organ Grinder's Swing...........................	Bluebird 6533
9/26/36	2(1)	8	2. I'll Sing You A Thousand Love Songs	Bluebird 6535
11/07/36	12	6	3. To Mary With Love	Bluebird 6637

WAYNE KING & HIS ORCHESTRA
Midwestern dance band favorite, known as "the Waltz King", alto
saxphonist, and composer of theme "The Waltz You Saved for Me",
"Goofus", and some of his other hits. Wayne died on 7/16/85 (84).

DATE CHARTED	PEAK POS	WKS CHRT'D	ARTIST — Record Title	Label & Number
3/22/30	12	4	1. Song Of The Islands .... [I]	Victor 22301
5/24/30	17	1	2. On A Blue And Moonless Night....................	Victor 22399
12/20/30+	4	15	3. The Waltz You Saved For Me .... [I] Wayne's familiar theme	Victor 22575
12/20/30	14	2	4. (I Am Only The Words) You Are The Melody .. from the film "Just Imagine"	Victor 22573
1/31/31	10	3	5. Goofus... [I]	Victor 22600
3/14/31	16	1	6. Hello, Beautiful .... vocal: Ernie Burchill & Bill Enger	Victor 22642
3/28/31	4	11	7. Wabash Moon/	
4/04/31	1(4)	12	8. **Dream A Little Dream Of Me** .... vocals on 2, 4, 8 & 12: Ernie Burchill	Victor 22643
6/06/31	17	2	9. Star Dust .... [I]	Victor 22656
10/17/31	1(7)	15	10. **Good Night, Sweetheart** .... [I] from the Broadway musical "Earl Carroll's Vanities of 1931"	Victor 22825
10/17/31	2(2)	6	11. I Don't Know Why (I Just Do)/ vocals on 7 & 11: Ernie Burchill, Andy Hansen & Bill Enger	
10/24/31	11	3	12. Guilty..	Victor 22817
8/06/32	16	2	13. Goofus .... [I-R]	Victor 22600
9/17/32	3	7	14. Sweethearts Forever .... vocal: Gordon Graham; from the film "The Crooner"	Victor 24117
2/11/33	3	5	15. The Moon Song....................................... from the film "Hello, Everybody"	Brunswick 6474
2/18/33	14	3	16. Blue Danube .... [I]	Brunswick 6475
6/03/33	14	3	17. When It's Lamp-Lightin' Time In The Valley ..	Brunswick 6563
6/17/33	11	3	18. Adorable .... vocal: Wayne King	Brunswick 6581
1/06/34	18	2	19. The Waltz You Saved For Me .... [I-R]	Victor 24472

DATE CHARTED	PEAK POS	WKS CHRT'D	ARTIST — Record Title	Label & Number
2/10/34	**16**	2	20. Song Of Surrender .... from the film "Moulin Rouge"	Brunswick 6735
10/24/36	**17**	1	21. Lost In My Dreams................................. [I]	Victor 25416
10/31/36	**19**	1	22. Mickey Mouse's Birthday Party	Victor 25419
1/16/37	**5**	10	23. Trust In Me/ [I]	
2/06/37	**15**	3	24. The Night Is Young And You're So 　　Beautiful .... [I]	Victor 25495
1/30/37	**15**	2	25. You're Laughing At Me .... [I] from the film "On the Avenue"	Victor 25506
3/06/37	**3**	10	26. Josephine .... [I]	Victor 25518
11/26/37	**14**	1	27. Emaline .... [I]	Victor 26070
5/13/39	**9**	5	28. My Man.. [I] French song ("Mon Homme") from Broadway's "Ziegfeld Follies of 1921"	Victor 26231
8/12/39	**6**	4	29. The Man With The Mandolin	Victor 26314
5/24/41	**2(1)**	8	30. Maria Elena/ [I] Mexican song	
11/09/40+	**20**	2	31. You Are My Sunshine............................	Victor 26767
			vocal: Wayne King	
3/01/41	**12**	1	32. You Walk By... [I]	Victor 27206
4/12/41	**5**	18	33. Intermezzo (Souvenir De Vienne) .... [I]	Victor 26659
8/23/41	**19**	1	34. 'Til Reveille	Victor 27511
10/11/41	**26**	1	35. Darling, How You Lied/	
11/01/41	**22**	1	36. Jumpin' Jupiter .... [I]	Victor 27575

JOHN KIRBY & HIS ONYX CLUB BOYS
Bassist and leader of respected jazz sextet; previously played with Fletcher Henderson (1930-33, 35-36), Chick Webb (1933-35), & Mills Blue Rhythm Band. Married to singer Maxine Sullivan; John died on 6/14/52 (43).

DATE CHARTED	PEAK POS	WKS CHRT'D	ARTIST — Record Title	Label & Number
3/18/39	**19**	1	1. Undecided .... [I] sextet includes Charlie Shavers (trumpet) & Buster Bailey (clarinet)	Decca 2216

ANDY KIRK & HIS TWELVE CLOUDS OF JOY
Andy played tuba & bass sax for various bands in the 1920s before his swing band became one of Kansas City's most popular; featuring his wife, pianist-arranger-composer Mary Lou Williams, tenor saxist Dick Wilson, and (in the 40s) Howard McGee (trumpet).

DATE CHARTED	PEAK POS	WKS CHRT'D	ARTIST — Record Title	Label & Number
4/04/36	**2(1)**	14	1. Christopher Columbus........................... [I]	Decca 729
7/04/36	**1(2)**	13	2. **Until The Real Thing Comes Along**........... Andy's theme song	Decca 809
1/16/37	**2(2)**	9	3. What Will I Tell My Heart?	Decca 1035
4/10/37	**11**	2	4. Dedicated To You	Decca 1146
8/21/37	**20**	1	5. Skies Are Blue	Decca 1349
10/22/38	**1(2)**	12	6. **I Won't Tell A Soul (I Love You)**	Decca 2127
11/16/40	**19**	1	7. Now I Lay Me Down To Dream.................... all above vocals: Pha Terrell	Decca 3306
5/11/46	**14**	1	8. I Know...................................... JUBILAIRES with ANDY KIRK & HIS ORCHESTRA	Decca 18782

LISA KIRK
Appeared in "Kiss Me, Kate" and many other Broadway musicals from the late 40s to the 70s.

DATE CHARTED	PEAK POS	WKS CHRT'D	ARTIST — Record Title	Label & Number
3/18/50	**22**	5	1. Dearie .... LISA KIRK & FRAN WARREN with Henri Rene's Orchestra	RCA Vic. 78-3696
6/24/50	**27**	1	2. The Old Piano Roll Blues........................... EDDIE CANTOR & LISA KIRK with Sammy Kaye's Orchestra, featuring Stan Freeman on piano	RCA Victor 3751
12/13/52+	**25**	2	3. Boomerang	RCA Victor 5016
4/18/53	**27**	1	4. Ohio .... from the Broadway musical "Wonderful Town"	RCA Victor 5187

DATE CHARTED	PEAK POS	WKS CHRT'D	ARTIST — Record Title	Label & Number
			EARTHA KITT Seductive American singer/actress who performed in Paris before becoming a sensation in Broadway's "New Faces of 1952".	
5/16/53	**23**	3	1. Uska Dara - A Turkish Tale .... [F] sung mostly in Turkish	RCA Victor 5284
7/18/53	**8**	14	2. C'est Si Bon.. [F]	RCA Victor 5358
9/26/53	**22**	4	3. I Want To Be Evil....................................	RCA Victor 5442
12/05/53	**4**	5	4. Santa Baby.................................... [X]	RCA Victor 5502
2/13/54	**16**	4	5. Somebody Bad Stole De Wedding Bell (Who's Got De Ding Dong)/ [N] from Copacabana show of 1954	
2/13/54	**20**	3	6. Lovin' Spree .... accompanied on all by Henri Rene & His Orchestra	RCA Victor 5610
			MANNIE KLEIN Trumpet star who played with Boswell Sisters, Dorsey Brothers, Ben Selvin, Claude Thornhill (1937), & Artie Shaw (1940), among many others. (also see Frankie Laine)	
			OLIVE KLINE American concert soprano popular for years, regularly featured in Victor Light Opera Co. recordings, and also a member of the Lyric Quartet.	
1/11/13	**4**	6	1. Say Not Love Is A Dream .... from the Broadway musical "The Count of Luxembourg"	Victor 35266
5/17/13	**5**	5	2. When A Maid Comes Knocking At Your Door . from the Broadway musical "The Firefly"	Victor 35278
2/28/14	**7**	3	3. Isle D'amour .... from the "Ziegfeld Follies of 1915"	Victor 17509
6/27/14	**10**	1	4. You're Here And I'm Here .... OLIVE KLINE & HARRY MACDONOUGH from the Broadway musical "The Laughing Husband"	Victor 17555
3/20/15	**6**	3	5. When You're Away .... from the Broadway musical "The Only Girl"	Victor 17690
9/18/15	**1(6)**	10	6. **Hello, Frisco!** .... "ALICE GREEN & EDWARD HAMILTON" (Olive & Reginald Werrenrath) from Broadway's "Ziegfeld Follies of 1915"	Victor 17837
11/06/15	**2(1)**	7	7. Auf Wiedersehen .... from the Broadway musical "The Blue Paradise"	Victor 17858
11/13/15	**1(7)**	12	8. **They Didn't Believe Me** .... from the Broadway musical "The Girl from Utah" above two: "ALICE GREEN" (Olive) & HARRY MACDONOUGH	Victor 35491
11/27/15	**10**	1	9. Teach Me To Smile................................. "ALICE GREEN & EDWARD HAMILTON" from the Broadway musical "The Girl Who Smiles"	Victor 17858
3/04/16	**3**	5	10. Go To Sleep, My Dusky Baby .... OLIVE KLINE, ELSIE BAKER, & MARGARET DUNLAP song based on Dvorak's "Humoresque"	Victor 17918
4/22/16	**6**	3	11. So Long, Letty .... "ALICE GREEN & RAYMOND DIXON" (Olive & Lambert Murphy) Broadway musical title song	Victor 17974
5/13/16	**5**	5	12. Kiss Me Again .... from the Broadway musical "Mlle. Modiste"	Victor 17954
10/07/16	**3**	6	13. Have A Heart .... from Broadway's "Ziegfeld Follies of 1916"	Victor 18104
1/19/18	**3**	7	14. Will You Remember?................................ from the Broadway musical "Maytime" above two: "ALICE GREEN & RAYMOND DIXON"	Victor 18399
2/16/18	**9**	1	15. Wait Till The Cows Come Home.................. "ALICE GREEN" & HARRY MACDONOUGH from the Broadway musical "Jack O'Lantern"	Victor 18408
8/03/18	**8**	2	16. Bring Back My Soldier Boy To Me	Victor 45152
4/12/19	**5**	5	17. Beautiful Ohio...................................... OLIVE KLINE & MARGUERITE DUNLAP became the official state song of Ohio	Victor 45161
3/27/20	**5**	4	18. I Might Be Your Once-In-A-While................. from the Broadway musical "Angel Face"	Victor 45173
11/12/21	**6**	2	19. Where The Lazy Mississippi Flows	Victor 45252

DATE CHARTED	PEAK POS	WKS CHRT'D	ARTIST — Record Title	Label & Number
7/01/22	**5**	3	20. Marcheta.. *above two:* OLIVE KLINE & ELSIE BAKER	Victor 45309

ORVILLE KNAPP & HIS ORCHESTRA
Hotel band leader, former saxophonist with Coon-Sanders & Paul Specht bands; died on 7/16/36 (28) in a plane crash.

6/13/36	**11**	2	1. Robins And Roses.....................................	Brunswick 7649

KNICKERBOCKER QUARTET
Led by Lewis James

4/14/17	**1(5)**	10	1. **Pack Up Your Troubles In Your Old Kit Bag (And Smile, Smile, Smile)**............ JAMES F. HARRISON & KNICKERBOCKER QUARTET	Columbia 2181

KNICKERBOCKERS - see BEN SELVIN

EVELYN KNIGHT
Born in Washington, D.C.

8/26/44	**6**	17	1. Dance With A Dolly (With A Hole In Her Stocking) .... *with Camarata's Orchestra; melody adapted from the 1844 song "Lubly Fan (Buffalo Gals, Won't You Come Out Tonight)"*	Decca 18614
12/15/45+	**10**	5	2. Chickery Chick... *with Three Jesters & Bob Haggart's Orchestra*	Decca 18725
11/17/48+	**9**	15	3. Brush Those Tears From Your Eyes/	
11/20/48+	**1(7)**	21	● 4. **A Little Bird Told Me**	Decca 24514
11/20/48	**14**	8	5. Buttons And Bows .... *with Mannie Klein's Orchestra; from the film "Paleface"*	Decca 24489
12/25/48+	**1(1)**	20	6. **Powder Your Face With Sunshine** .... *above four with Stardusters*	Decca 24530
6/18/49	**22**	2	7. It's Too Late Now/ *accompanied by Sonny Burke's Orchestra*	
8/06/49	**21**	3	8. You're So Understanding .... *above two with Four Hits & a Miss*	Decca 24636
4/15/50	**20**	1	9. Candy And Cake.................................... *with Lee Gordon Singers*	Decca 24943
8/19/50	**25**	1	10. All Dressed Up To Smile .... *with the Ray Charles Singers*	Decca 27103
2/10/51	**28**	6	11. My Heart Cries For You............................. RED FOLEY & EVELYN KNIGHT	Decca 27378

ANDRE KOSTELANETZ
Russian-born conductor whose radio program was one of America's most popular from the 1930s to the 50s. He died on 1/14/80 (78). (see Perry Como)

FRITZ KREISLER
All-time great violin virtuoso born in Austria, also a successful composer ("The Old Refrain", Broadway score "Apple Blossoms"). Kreisler served as accompanist on many John McCormack recordings. He died on 1/29/62 (86). (also see Geraldine Farrar)

12/17/10	**10**	1	1. Gavotte In E Major .... [I]	Victor 64132
1/21/11	**4**	5	2. Liebesfreud (Old Vienna Waltz) .... [I]	Victor 74196
1/21/11	**6**	2	3. Meditation From "Thais" .... [I]	Victor 74182
6/29/12	**7**	3	4. Humoresque .... [I]	Victor 64241
4/26/13	**5**	5	5. Liebesleid (Love's Sorrow) .... [I]	Victor 74333
9/29/16	**6**	2	6. The Old Refrain.................................... [I]	Victor 64529
6/02/17	**9**	2	7. Poor Butterfly .... [I] *from the Broadway musical "The Big Show"*	Victor 64655
9/13/19	**7**	2	8. Beautiful Ohio...................................... [I]	Victor 64817
6/26/20	**15**	1	9. Gypsy Serenade.................................... [I]	Victor 64857
11/29/24	**13**	1	10. A Kiss In The Dark .... [I] *from the Broadway musical "Orange Blossoms"* *6 & 10 accompanied by Carl Lamson (piano)*	Victor 1029

BENNY KRUEGER & HIS ORCHESTRA
Sweet-band leader, former saxophonist with Original Dixieland Jazz Band (1920-21) & Carl Fenton; he died on 4/29/67 (68).

5/14/21	**4**	5	1. Spread Yo' Stuff .... [I]	Brunswick 2083

DATE CHARTED	PEAK POS	WKS CHRT'D	ARTIST — Record Title	Label & Number
10/22/21	6	3	2. All By Myself .... [I]	Brunswick 2130
8/25/23	8	1	3. Yes! We Have No Bananas .... [N] vocal by Billy Jones	Brunswick 2445
9/29/23	2(1)	10	4. I Cried For You...................................... [I]	Brunswick 2453
12/08/23	3	5	5. That Old Gang Of Mine............................	Brunswick 2485
7/12/24	10	1	6. I Wonder Who's Dancing With You Tonight?.. [I]	Brunswick 2576
7/26/24	5	4	7. Deep In My Heart................................. [I] from the Broadway musical "The Student Prince"	Brunswick 2605
11/21/25	5	5	8. If I Had A Girl Like You .... [I]	Brunswick 2936
9/04/26	7	2	9. Bye Bye Blackbird	Brunswick 3186
10/23/26	3	6	10. How Many Times?................................	Brunswick 3237
10/24/31	8	3	11. I Don't Know Why................................ vocal: Smith Ballew	Brunswick 6185
2/20/32	18	1	12. Was That The Human Thing To Do?............ vocal: Frank Sylvano	Brunswick 6246
5/26/34	7	4	13. Goodnight, Lovely Little Lady................... from the film "We're Not Dressing"	Columbia 2918

GENE KRUPA & HIS ORCHESTRA
Rivaled only by Buddy Rich as the most acclaimed drummer of the Big Band Era, Gene Krupa achieved national fame with Benny Goodman (1934-38), climaxed by the band's historic Carnegie Hall concert. Gene's orchestra achieved renown of its own due mostly to Roy Eldridge and Anita O'Day. He died on 10/16/73 (64).

DATE CHARTED	PEAK POS	WKS CHRT'D	ARTIST — Record Title	Label & Number
5/28/38	15	3	1. Grandfather's Clock .... [I]	Brunswick 8124
6/25/38	18	1	2. Fare Thee Well, Annie Laurie .... vocal: Jerry Kruger	Brunswick 8139
2/18/39	15	1	3. Ta-Ra-Ra-Boom-Der-E .... [I]	Brunswick 8296
8/05/39	17	1	4. You Taught Me To Love Again	Brunswick 8400
5/25/40	13	4	5. Boog It...	Columbia 35415
9/21/40	26	1	6. Blue Rhythm Fantasy........................... [I]	Okeh 5627
11/20/40	24	1	7. Drummer Boy	Okeh 5747
11/30/40+	23	1	8. Moon Over Burma	Okeh 5814
12/14/40	15	2	9. Down Argentina Way............................. movie title song	Okeh 5826
2/01/41	2(3)	11	10. It All Comes Back To Me Now/	
2/01/41	2(1)	9	11. High On A Windy Hill	Okeh 5883
2/01/41	15	1	12. Tonight (Perfidia)	Okeh 5715
3/29/41	12	1	13. There'll Be Some Changes Made	Okeh 6021
4/05/41	26	1	14. Drum Boogie..................................... Irene Daye: vocals on 4-5, 7-9, 13-14	Okeh 6046
6/14/41	4	9	15. Just A Little Bit South Of North Carolina......	Okeh 6130
6/21/41	16	1	16. The Things I Love	Okeh 6143
6/28/41	17	1	17. Georgia On My Mind .... vocals on 15 & 17: Anita O'Day	Okeh 6118
7/26/41	10	12	18. Let Me Off Uptown .... vocal: Anita O'Day & Roy Eldridge; trumpet solo by Roy	Okeh 6210
10/04/41	19	2	19. Have You Changed? .... vocals on 10-12, 16, & 19: Howard Dulany	Okeh 6306
1/10/42	21	1	20. Keep 'Em Flying .... vocal: Johnny Desmond; movie title song	Okeh 6506
6/20/42	24	1	21. Knock Me A Kiss .... vocal: Roy Eldridge (also trumpet on above four)	Columbia 36591
10/13/45	7	2	22. Along The Navajo Trail	Columbia 36846
12/08/45	10	5	23. Chickery Chick/	
12/22/45+	20	4	24. Just A Little Fond Affection .... vocals on 22 & 24: Buddy-Stewart	Columbia 36877
7/06/46	9	6	25. Boogie Blues .... Anita O'Day: vocals on 23 & 25 Charlie Ventura (tenor sax) on above four	Columbia 36986

DATE CHARTED	PEAK POS	WKS CHRT'D	ARTIST — Record Title	Label & Number
5/10/47	21	1	26. Old Devil Moon... vocal: Carolyn Grey from the Broadway musical "Finian's Rainbow"	Columbia 37270
6/10/50	9	15	27. Bonaparte's Retreat .... vocal: Bobby Scots	RCA Victor 3766

DICK KUHN & HIS ORCHESTRA

DATE CHARTED	PEAK POS	WKS CHRT'D	ARTIST — Record Title	Label & Number
10/18/41	23	1	1. The Window Washer Man .... vocal: Lennie Herman	Decca 3826
9/12/42	19	2	2. Put Your Arms Around Me, Honey	Decca 4337
9/25/43	4	10	3. Put Your Arms Around Me, Honey/ [R]	
12/18/43	20	1	4. I've Got Rings On My Fingers .... from the Broadway musical "The Midnight Sons"	Decca 4337

KAY KYSER & HIS ORCHESTRA
Among the most popular of "sweet" dance bands, best known for his radio "Kollege of Musical Knowledge", singers Harry Babbitt & Ginny Simms, and trumpet personality Ish Kabibble. Kay died on 7/23/85 (79).

DATE CHARTED	PEAK POS	WKS CHRT'D	ARTIST — Record Title	Label & Number
6/29/35	20	1	1. (I've Grown So Lonesome) Thinking Of You ... the band's longtime theme song	Brunswick 7449
7/20/35	14	5	2. Star Gazing .... [I]	Brunswick 7465
11/07/36	6	6	3. Did You Mean It?	Brunswick 7759
7/17/37	12	3	4. 'Cause My Baby Says It's So .... from the film "The Singing Marine"	Brunswick 7891
4/30/38	3	9	5. Cry, Baby, Cry..	Brunswick 8114
7/02/38	5	6	6. Music, Maestro, Please!............................	Brunswick 8149
8/20/38	6	7	7. Stop Beatin' Round The Mulberry Bush	Brunswick 8197
8/20/38	14	4	8. Don't Cross Your Fingers, Cross Your Heart ..	Brunswick 8193
10/15/38	9	5	9. Ya Got Me .... from the University of Pennsylvania's "Mask & Wig Club" show	Brunswick 8220
10/22/38	11	3	10. Monday Morning...................................... vocals on 6 & 10: Ginny Simms	Brunswick 8234
11/19/38	7	4	11. Two Sleepy People .... from the film "Thanks for the Memory"	Brunswick 8244
12/03/38+	1(1)	11	12. **The Umbrella Man** .... above two vocals: Ginny Simms & Harry Babbitt	Brunswick 8225
12/10/38	16	1	13. Hark The Sound Of Tar Heel Voices .... [R] recorded 11/26/29, originally issued on Victor 40258 University of North Carolina school song	Bluebird 7892
2/18/39	7	5	14. I Promise You/	
3/18/39	14	2	15. Heaven Can Wait ....••••	**Brunswick 8317**
2/25/39	5	3	16. Cuckoo In The Clock/	
3/04/39	6	7	17. (Gotta Get Some) Shut-Eye	Brunswick 8312
3/25/39	20	2	18. Chopsticks .... vocals on 5, 8-9, 16 & 18: Sully Mason	Brunswick 8308
5/06/39	1(2)	9	19. **Three Little Fishies**............................. [N] vocal: Ginny Simms Ish Kabibble-Harry Babbitt	Brunswick 8368
6/03/39	5	2	20. The Tinkle Song .... [I]	Brunswick 8377
6/17/39	4	7	21. Stairway To The Stars	Brunswick 8381
7/08/39	10	2	22. Concert In The Park.................................	Brunswick 8385
10/14/39	11	5	23. Day In - Day Out...................................... vocals on 14-15, 17, 21 & 23: Harry Babbitt	Columbia 35202
12/09/39+	4	9	24. The Little Red Fox .... vocal: Kay Kyser-Harry Babbitt-'Little Audrey"-Pokey Carriere	Columbia 35295
12/23/39+	6	9	25. Chatter Box .... above two from the film "That's Right-You're Wrong" vocals on 22 & 25: Ginny Simms & Harry Babbitt	Columbia 35307
12/23/39	13	1	26. Hello, Mr. Kringle .... [X] vocals: Ginny Simms, Ish Kabibble, Sully Mason & Harry Babbitt	Columbia 35248
3/02/40	17	2	27. Confucius Say	Columbia 35343
4/20/40	10	6	28. You, You, Darlin'	Columbia 35395
4/27/40	2(2)	14	29. Playmates .... [N]	Columbia 35375

DATE CHARTED	PEAK POS	WKS CHRT'D	ARTIST — Record Title	Label & Number
5/04/40	**4**	9	30. With The Wind And The Rain In Your Hair	Columbia 35350
5/25/40	**15**	4	31. Let There Be Love	Columbia 35439
6/01/40	**11**	4	32. Friendship .... vocal: Ginny Simms-Harry Babbitt-Jack Martin-Ish Kabibble from the Broadway musical "DuBarry Was A Lady"	Columbia 35368
6/08/40	**7**	6	33. Blue Love Bird .... from the film "Lillian Russell" vocals on 28, 30 & 33: Ginny Simms	Columbia 35488
7/13/40	**9**	4	34. Tennessee Fish Fry .... from the New York World's Fair production "Jubilee"	Columbia 35574
8/24/40	**12**	2	35. Who's Yehoodi?/ [N] vocal: Kay Kyser-Sully Mason-Harry Babbitt	
9/21/40	**11**	2	36. Blueberry Hill	Columbia 35554
10/19/40+	**6**	12	37. Ferry Boat Serenade	Columbia 35627
12/07/40	**24**	1	38. The Bad Humor Man .... [N]	Columbia 35767
			vocal: Ish Kabibble-Sully Mason-Harry Babbitt	
12/21/40	**12**	7	39. You've Got Me This Way .... above two from film "You'll Find Out"	Columbia 35762
3/22/41	**22**	1	40. You Stepped Out Of A Dream .... vocals on 31, 36-37, 39-40: Harry Babbitt	Columbia 35946
4/12/41	**24**	1	41. We'll Meet Again	Columbia 35870
4/19/41	**3**	4	42. Alexander The Swoose (Half Swan, Half Goose)..	Columbia 36040
5/10/41	**22**	2	43. The Wise Old Owl	Columbia 36051
7/26/41	**1(2)**	15	44. **(Lights Out) 'Til Reveille**..................... vocal: Harry Babbitt-Ginny Simms-Max Williams-Jack Martin	Columbia 36137
8/30/41	**13**	9	45. The Cowboy Serenade	Columbia 36244
9/13/41	**8**	17	46. Why Don't We Do This More Often? .... vocals on 41 & 46: Ginny Simms & Harry Babbitt	Columbia 36253
12/20/41+	**1(1)**	13	47. **(There'll Be Bluebirds Over) The White Cliffs Of Dover**..................................	Columbia 36445
3/14/42	**7**	10	48. A Zoot Suit (For My Sunday Girl) .... vocals: Sully Mason, "Trudy", Jack Martin & Max Williams	Columbia 36517
4/18/42	**1(2)**	23	● 49. **Who Wouldn't Love You** .... vocal: Trudy & Harry Babbitt	Columbia 36526
5/09/42	**2(1)**	17	50. Johnny Doughboy Found A Rose In Ireland ...	Columbia 36558
5/30/42	**17**	2	51. Got The Moon In My Pocket....................... from the film "My Favorite Spy"	Columbia 36575
7/04/42	**1(8)**	13	● 52. **Jingle, Jangle, Jingle**/ vocal: Julie Conway & Harry Babbitt from the film "The Forest Rangers"	
7/18/42	**1(4)**	14	53. **He Wears A Pair Of Silver Wings** .... British song vocals on 45 & 53: Harry Babbitt	Columbia 36604
10/03/42	**1(2)**	11	● 54. **Strip Polka**/ vocal: Jack Martin	
10/31/42+	**18**	2	55. Ev'ry Night About This Time	Columbia 36635
10/17/42+	**1(3)**	14	● 56. **Praise The Lord And Pass The Ammunition!** .... vocals on 50 & 56: Glee Club	Columbia 36640
11/28/42+	**4**	11	57. Can't Get Out Of This Mood/ vocal: Harry Babbitt-Julie Conway-Trudy-Jack Martin-Max Williams; from the film "Seven Days Leave"	
2/20/43	**13**	3	58. Moonlight Mood...............................	Columbia 36657
5/15/43	**4**	11	59. Let's Get Lost/ vocal: Julie Conway-Max Williams-Harry Babbitt-Jack Martin	
6/05/43	**11**	1	60. The Fuddy Duddy Watchmaker .... vocal: Julie Conway; from the film "Happy-Go-Lucky"	Columbia 36673
7/10/43	**18**	1	61. Pushin' Sand..	Columbia 36676
1/20/45	**7**	4	62. There Goes That Song Again...................... vocal: Georgia Carroll	Columbia 36757
2/24/45	**12**	2	63. Ac-Cent-Tchu-Ate The Positive................... vocal: Dolly Mitchell; from the film "Here Come the Waves"	Columbia 36771

DATE CHARTED	PEAK POS	WKS CHRT'D	ARTIST — Record Title	Label & Number
6/09/45	**3**	10	64. Bell-Bottom Trousers/ vocal: Ferdy & Slim; based on traditional sea chantey	
7/07/45	**10**	1	65. Can't You Read Between The Lines?	Columbia 36801
8/18/45	**10**	4	66. Rosemary/	
8/25/45	**11**	2	67. Horses Don't Bet On People .... vocal: Clyde Rogers	Columbia 36824
11/03/45	**12**	2	68. That's For Me... from the film "State Fair"	Columbia 36844
2/09/46	**11**	1	69. Slowly .... Mike Douglas & Campus Kids: vocals on 66, 68 & 69	Columbia 36900
4/20/46	**5**	2	70. One-Zy, Two-Zy (I Love You-Zy) .... vocal: Moonbeams	Columbia 36960
9/21/46	**1(2)**	19	71. **Ole Buttermilk Sky** .... from the film "Canyon Passage" Mike Douglas & Campus Kids: vocals on 71 & 73	Columbia 37073
11/30/46+	**3**	13	72. The Old Lamp-Lighter/ above two vocals: Mike Douglas & Campus Kids	
11/16/46	**8**	9	73. Huggin' And Chalkin' .... [N] vocal: Jack Martin & Campus Kids	Columbia 37095
2/01/47	**6**	12	74. Managua, Nicaragua	Columbia 37214
1/03/48	**13**	1	75. Serenade Of The Bells .... vocal: Harry Babbitt	Columbia 37956
2/07/48	**21**	3	76. Saturday Date.......................................	Columbia 38049
6/05/48	**1(6)**	15	● 77. **Woody Woodpecker**.............................. [N] vocals on 74 & 77: Gloria Wood & Campus Kids	Columbia 38197
10/23/48	**2(7)**	20	● 78. On A Slow Boat To China .... vocals on 76 & 78: Harry Babbitt & Gloria Wood	Columbia 38301

L

FRANKIE LAINE

Born Frank Paul Lovecchio on 3/30/13 in Chicago, Frankie's swirling musical melodramas made him one of the top singing stars of the decade after World War II.

DATE CHARTED	PEAK POS	WKS CHRT'D	ARTIST — Record Title	Label & Number
3/22/47	**4**	26	● 1. That's My Desire .... with Mannie Klein's All-Stars	Mercury 5007
5/19/47	**14**	2	2. Mam'selle .... with Harry Geller's Orchestra from the film "The Razor's Edge".	Mercury 5048
11/22/47	**21**	3	3. Two Loves Have I	Mercury 5064
11/22/47	**27**	1	4. Black And Blue .... with Carl Fischer's Swingtet	Mercury 1026
1/24/48	**9**	9	5. Shine...	Mercury 5091
4/03/48	**24**	1	6. Monday Again	Mercury 5105
4/10/48	**20**	3	7. Baby, That Ain't Right.............................	Mercury 5114
8/21/48	**21**	1	8. Ah, But It Happens	Mercury 5158
12/18/48+	**11**	3	9. You're All I Want For Christmas.............. [X] above five accompanied by Carl Fischer's Orchestra	Mercury 5177
8/27/49	**1(8)**	22	● 10. **That Lucky Old Sun** .... with Judd Conlon's Rhythmaires, Harry Geller & His Orchestra, & Carl Fischer (piano)	Mercury 5316
9/24/49	**20**	5	11. Now That I Need You .... from the film "Red, Hot, and Blue"	Mercury 5311
11/12/49	**1(6)**	13	● 12. **Mule Train** .... with the Muleskinners	Mercury 5345
1/07/50	**29**	1	13. You're All I Want For Christmas........... [X-R]	Mercury 5177
2/11/50	**1(2)**	11	● 14. **The Cry Of The Wild Goose**......................	Mercury 5363
3/25/50	**28**	1	15. Satan Wears A Satin Gown........................ with Judd Conlon's Rhythmaires	Mercury 5358
4/01/50	**12**	4	16. Swamp Girl...	Mercury 5390
5/20/50	**20**	4	17. The Stars And Stripes Forever	Mercury 5421

DATE CHARTED	PEAK POS	WKS CHRT'D	ARTIST — Record Title	Label & Number
8/26/50	**13**	9	18. Music, Maestro, Please!/	
9/09/50	**18**	5	19. Dream A Little Dream Of Me....................	Mercury 5488
			14, 16-19 accompanied by Harry Geller's Orchestra	
11/11/50	**11**	10	20. Nevertheless (I'm In Love With You)............	Mercury 5495
			featured in the film "Three Little Words"	
11/18/50	**30**	1	21. If I Were A Bell...	Mercury 5500
			from the Broadway musical "Guys and Dolls"	
4/14/51	**19**	6	22. Metro Polka	Mercury 5581
5/05/51	**2(2)**	21	● 23. Jezebel/	
5/12/51	**3**	19	24. Rose, Rose, I Love You	Columbia 39367
			above two with Mitch Miller's Orchestra	
5/19/51	**13**	10	25. Pretty Eyed Baby.....................................	Columbia 39388
8/11/51	**17**	4	26. In The Cool, Cool, Cool Of The Evening........	Columbia 39466
			from the film "Here Comes the Groom"	
			above two: FRANKIE LAINE & JO STAFFORD	
8/11/51	**23**	2	27. The Girl In The Wood/	
9/01/51	**17**	3	28. Wonderful, Wasn't It?...........................	Columbia 39489
10/20/51	**9**	8	29. Hey, Good Lookin'/	
10/27/51	**19**	4	30. Gambella (The Gamblin' Lady)	Columbia 39570
			above two: FRANKIE LAINE & JO STAFFORD	
11/10/51	**3**	14	● 31. Jealousy (Jalousie)	Columbia 39585
3/08/52	**6**	10	32. Hambone...	Columbia 39672
3/15/52	**21**	7	33. The Gaudy Dancers' Ball/	
5/17/52	**30**	1	34. When You're In Love	Columbia 39685
6/21/52	**7**	14	● 35. Sugarbush..	Columbia 39693
			FRANKIE LAINE & DORIS DAY	
7/12/52	**5**	19	● 36. High Noon (Do Not Forsake Me)/	
			theme from the film "High Noon"	
7/19/52	**20**	5	37. The Rock Of Gibraltar	Columbia 39770
			above two & 40 accompanied by Jimmy Carroll's Orchestra	
10/18/52	**21**	3	38. Tonight We're Setting The Woods On Fire	Columbia 39867
1/03/53	**25**	1	39. Chow, Willy	Columbia 39893
			32, 38-39: FRANKIE LAINE & JO STAFFORD	
1/17/53	**14**	7	40. I'm Just A Poor Bachelor/	
2/28/53	**26**	2	41. Tonight You Belong To Me	Columbia 39903
2/21/53	**2(3)**	23	● 42. I Believe/	
3/14/53	**18**	6	43. Your Cheatin' Heart	Columbia 39938
			29, 38 & 43 written by Hank Williams	
3/14/53	**4**	12	44. Tell Me A Story/	
3/28/53	**24**	1	45. The Little Boy And The Old Man	Columbia 39570
			above two: FRANKIE LAINE & JIMMY BOYD	
5/23/53	**27**	1	46. I Let Her Go...	Columbia 39979
			orchestra directed by Carl Fischer on 23, 35 & 46	
8/22/53	**6**	16	47. Hey Joe!...	Columbia 40036
10/24/53	**21**	4	48. Blowing Wild (The Ballad Of Black Gold)/	
			from the film "Blowing Wild"	
			orchestra & chorus directed by Mitch Miller, with Carl Fischer	
10/31/53	**24**	2	49. Answer Me, Lord Above	Columbia 40079
11/28/53	**26**	1	50. Way Down Yonder In New Orleans	Columbia 40116
			FRANKIE LAINE & JO STAFFORD	
			all Laine-Stafford records accompanied by Paul Weston & His Orchestra, with Carl Fischer (piano)	
1/23/54	**17**	4	51. Grenada...	Columbia 40136
3/20/54	**20**	4	52. The Kid's Last Fight................................	Columbia 40170
7/03/54	**14**	7	53. Some Day	Columbia 40235
9/18/54	**21**	4	54. Rain, Rain, Rain/	
			with Four Lads & the Buddy Cole Quartet	
10/16/54	**28**	1	55. Your Heart, My Heart	Columbia 40295
			nearly all Columbias not directed by Carl Fischer are accompanied by Paul Weston's Orchestra, most with the Norman Luboff Choir	

DATE CHARTED	PEAK POS	WKS CHRT'D	ARTIST — Record Title	Label & Number
			ARTHUR LALLY & HIS ORCHESTRA	
7/30/32	**12**	3	1. Hold My Hand	Brunswick 6328
			vocal: The Million-Airs	
			SCRAPPY LAMBERT	
			Sang with many bands during 1920s & early 30s, including Arden-Ohman, Ben Bernie, Ipana Troubadors, Roger Wolfe Kahn, Nat Shilkret, & Victor Young.	
6/23/28	**18**	1	1. Ramona	Brunswick 3870
			written to promote the silent film "Ramona"	
8/11/28	**16**	2	2. My Angel..	Brunswick 3926
			from the film "Street Angel"	
			DOROTHY LAMOUR	
			Glamourous star of many 30s & 40s movies, including the "Road" films with Bing Crosby & Bob Hope; real name Dorothy Stanton.	
2/27/37	**10**	4	1. Moonlight And Shadows..........................	Brunswick 7829
			from the film "The Jungle Princess"	
6/12/37	**16**	2	2. Swing High, Swing Low	Brunswick 7838
			movie title song	
			orchestra on above two directed by Cy Feuer	
5/28/38	**14**	3	3. Lovelight In The Starlight	Brunswick 8132
			accompanied by Herbie Kay's Orchestra (her then-husband)	
2/04/39	**15**	2	4. I Go For That	Brunswick 8291
			from the film "St. Louis Blues"; orchestra directed by Jerry Joyce	
5/27/39	**5**	6	5. Strange Enchantment..............................	Bluebird 10265
			from the film "Man About Town"; orchestra directed by Lou Bring	
			LANCERS	
			Group provided background vocals on some Kay Starr records.	
10/17/53	**13**	5	1. Sweet Mama Tree Top Tall	Trend 63
3/27/54	**26**	1	2. Stop Chasin' Me, Baby	Trend 70
12/11/54	**28**	1	3. Mister Sandman	Coral 61288
			above three accompanied by the Van Alexander Orchestra	
			ART LANDRY & HIS ORCHESTRA	
			Violinist-bandleader	
5/26/23	**1(3)**	10	● 1. Dreamy Melody .... [I]	Gennett 5052
3/13/26	**10**	1	2. Sleepy Time Gal	Victor 19843
			vocal: Henry Burr	
4/10/26	**10**	1	3. Five Foot Two, Eyes Of Blue	Victor 19850
			vocal: Denny Curtis	
2/05/27	**17**	2	4. Song Of The Wanderer (Where Shall I Go?)	Victor 20300
			vocal: Al Marineau	
			EDDIE LANG	
			Renowned jazz guitarist (born Salvatore Massaro), played with Bing Crosby, Seger Ellis, Jean Goldkette, Red Nichols, Joe Venuti, & Paul Whiteman, among others; he died on 3/26/33 (30).	
			FRANCES LANGFORD	
			Born Frances Newbern, featured in many Hollywood musicals from 1935-54; Frances also won fame entertaining troops in World War II & Korea with Bob Hope.	
9/21/35	**15**	2	1. I Feel A Song Comin' On	Brunswick 7512
10/12/35	**15**	2	2. I'm In The Mood For Love..........................	Brunswick 7513
			above two from the film "Every Night at Eight"	
			above two accompanied by Mahlon Merrick & His Music	
11/14/36	**20**	1	3. Easy To Love	Decca 940
			from the film "Born to Dance"	
5/22/37	**11**	6	4. Was It Rain?	Decca 1202
			from the film "Hit Parade"	
10/23/37	**6**	6	5. Harbor Lights.......................................	Decca 1441
11/06/37	**17**	3	6. So Many Memories	Decca 1440
			above four accompanied by Victor Young & His Orchestra	
3/18/39	**18**	1	7. Falling In Love With Love	Decca 2247
			accompanied by Harry Sosnik & His Orchestra	
			from the Broadway musical "The Boys from Syracuse"	

DATE CHARTED	PEAK POS	WKS CHRT'D	ARTIST — Record Title	Label & Number
			HOWARD LANIN & HIS ORCHESTRA	
			Hotel bandleader, brother of Sam Lanin.	
1/23/26	**10**	1	1. Don't Wake Me Up, Let Me Dream............ [I]	Victor 19797
			SAM LANIN & HIS ORCHESTRA	
			One of the most heavily-recorded bandleaders of the 20s & early 30s, also musical director of the popular Ipana Troubadors.	
9/29/23	**15**	1	1. Yes! We Have No Bananas...................... [I]	Columbia 3924
3/29/24	**13**	1	2. Mama Goes Where Papa Goes .... [I]	Okeh 40014
9/06/24	**10**	1	3. It Had To Be You .... [I]	Okeh 40084
4/25/25	**13**	1	4. Fascinating Rhythm.............................. [I]	Columbia 276
			from the Broadway musical "Lady Be Good"	
8/14/26	**9**	1	5. The Blue Room .... [I]	Okeh 40603
			listed as "Melody Sheiks" from the Broadway musical "The Girl Friend"	
3/12/27	**12**	2	6. In A Little Spanish Town	Okeh 40740
5/28/27	**14**	2	7. Yankee Rose.....................................	Okeh 40754
			vocal: Vaughn DeLeath Tommy Dorsey (trombone) & Jimmy Dorsey (clarinet/alto sax) on above two	
3/17/28	**16**	2	8. Rain..	Banner 6148
3/31/28	**12**	3	9. Let A Smile Be Your Umbrella	Okeh 40977
			Irving Kaufman: vocals on 6, 8 & 9 Red Nichols (cornet) on nearly all of above eight	
5/31/30	**19**	1	10. Exactly Like You	Perfect 15313
			vocal: Smith Ballew; with Tommy Dorsey (trombone) from the Broadway musical "International Revue"	
			SNOOKY LANSON	
			Roy "Snooky" Lanson, former Ray Noble vocalist, became best known as star of TV's "Hit Parade" show from 1950-57.	
11/27/48	**24**	4	1. On A Slow Boat To China	Mercury 5191
12/10/49+	**12**	8	2. The Old Master Painter	London 555
			accompanied by Beasley Smith & His Orchestra	
			MARIO LANZA	
			Born Alfredo Cocozza in Philadelphia, Mario Lanza became the most spectacularly popular operatic tenor since Caruso, his voice featured in seven movies (though no theatrical operas) before his death on 10/7/59 (38).	
12/16/50+	**1(1)**	34	● 1. **Be My Love**	RCA Vic. 78-1561
			sold two million copies; with Ray Sinatra's Orchestra & the Jeff Alexander Choir; from the film "Toast of New Orleans"	
3/17/51	**21**	3	2. Vesti La Giubba................................. [F]	RCA Victor 3228
			from the opera "I Pagliacci"	
4/14/51	**3**	34	● 3. The Loveliest Night Of The Year.................	RCA Victor 3300
			melody adapted from the 1888 waltz "Sobre las Olas" (Over the Waves) above two from the film "The Great Caruso"	
6/23/51	**16**	14	4. Because	RCA Victor 3207
9/13/52	**7**	19	● 5. Because You're Mine	RCA Victor 3914
			movie title song; with the Jeff Alexander Choir	
8/22/53	**20**	1	6. Song Of India	RCA Victor 4209
			"Chanson Indoue" from the opera "Sadko"	
10/16/54	**21**	4	7. Drink, Drink, Drink	RCA Victor 4220
			from the film "The Student Prince" most above records accompanied by Constantine Callinicos' Victor Orchestra	
			JULIUS LAROSA	
			Became famous on TV's Arthur Godfrey show (1951 until his celebrated on-air firing in late 1953)	
1/31/53	**21**	3	1. This Is Heaven/	
2/07/53	**4**	9	2. Anywhere I Wander	Cadence 1230
			from the film "Hans Christian Andersen"	
5/16/53	**21**	4	3. My Lady Loves To Dance	Cadence 1231
9/12/53	**2(1)**	20	● 4. Eh Cumpari .... [F]	Cadence 1232
			adaptation of a traditional Italian song	

DATE CHARTED	PEAK POS	WKS CHRT'D	ARTIST — Record Title	Label & Number
5/22/54	**21**	3	5. Three Coins In The Fountain .... movie title song	Cadence 1240
11/27/54	**21**	4	6. Mobile .... accompanied on nearly all records by Archie Bleyer's Orchestra	Cadence 1251

JACK LATHROP & THE DRUGSTORE COWBOYS
Singer/guitarist formerly with Glenn Miller and Hal McIntyre

9/25/48	**27**	2	1. You Call Everybody Darling/	
10/23/48	**19**	3	2. Hair Of Gold, Eyes Of Blue...................... from the film "Silver Spurs"	RCA Victor 3109
1/29/49	**26**	1	3. My Darling, My Darling .... EVE YOUNG & JACK LATHROP from the Broadway musical "Where's Charley"	RCA Victor 3187

HARRY LAUDER
Scottish comedian and folk singer famed in every English-speaking country. wrote many of his songs; ultimately knighted, possibly the only artist in American chart history to receive the honor. Sir Harry died on 2/25/50 (79).

11/09/07	**2(1)**	5	1. I Love A Lassie (My Scotch Bluebell) .... later on Victor 60001 & Edison Amberol 1821	Victor 52002
11/18/08	**10**	1	2. The Wedding Of Sandy McNab................. [C]	Victor 58001
2/27/09	**7**	1	3. When I Get Back Again To Bonnie Scotland...	Victor 58002
9/11/09	**2(2)**	5	4. She Is My Daisy.................................... later on Victor 70006	Victor 58007
9/25/09	**7**	1	5. He Was Very Kind To Me.........................	Victor 58008
4/02/10	**4**	3	6. Stop Your Ticklin', Jock .... [C] previously on Victor 52003	Victor 60002
6/25/10	**10**	1	7. The Bounding Bounder, Or "On The Bounding Sea".. [C]	Victor 70010
8/20/10	**7**	2	8. We Parted On The Shore	Victor 70013
10/15/10	**7**	2	9. The Blarney Stone .... [C]	Victor 70018
2/17/12	**5**	5	10. Roamin' In The Gloamin'........................... later on Victor 60105	Victor 70061
3/16/12	**8**	1	11. The Picnic (Every Laddie Loves A Lassie)......	Victor 70060
7/05/13	**10**	1	12. She's The Lass For Me...........................	Victor 70096
7/01/16	**9**	1	13. My Bonny Bonny Jean.............................	Victor 70115

JOHN LAURENZ
Baritone ballad singer

8/07/48	**26**	2	1. My Happiness....................................	Mercury 5144
8/21/48	**18**	7	2. A Tree In The Meadow	Mercury 5148
9/04/48	**22**	5	3. Hair Of Gold (Eyes Of Blue) .... accompanied by Dick Maltby Orchestra from the film "Silver Spurs"	Mercury 5172
12/04/48	**29**	1	4. The Mountaineer And The Jabberwock........ inspired by Lewis Carroll's "Alice in Wonderland"	Mercury 5202
4/09/49	**21**	5	5. Red Roses For A Blue Lady	Mercury 5201
7/16/49	**28**	1	6. Some Enchanted Evening .... from the Broadway musical "South Pacific" accompanied by Mitch Miller's Orchestra	Mercury 5276

PAUL LAVALLE & HIS ORCHESTRA
Radio conductor, often a guest symphony orchestra conductor

11/11/44	**29**	1	1. Always	Musicraft 297

BILL LAWRENCE
Sang in the late 40s with Jimmy Dorsey.

10/01/49	**14**	8	1. Jealous Heart .... orchestra directed by Henri Rene	RCA Vic. 78-3539

ELLIOT LAWRENCE & HIS ORCHESTRA
Pianist-bandleader (born Elliot Lawrence Broza) who briefly featured saxophone star Gerry Mulligan; he hosted a daily CBS radio show in the 1950s, and served as musical director for some of the 1960s' top Broadway musicals. (Also see Red Buttons)

7/20/46	**9**	2	1. Who Do You Love I Hope...........................	Columbia 37047

DATE CHARTED	PEAK POS	WKS CHRT'D	ARTIST — Record Title	Label & Number
11/02/46	**16**	1	2. You Broke The Only Heart That Ever Loved You.................. vocal: Rosalind Patton & Jack Hunter Mitch Miller (oboe) on above two	Columbia 37084
10/04/47	**4**	14	3. Near You..	Columbia 37838
6/26/48	**21**	1	4. At The Flying "W"..................................... vocals on 1, 3 & 4: Rosalind Patton	Columbia 38215

GERTRUDE LAWRENCE
London-born all-time great of Broadway and London musical theater; she climaxed her long career starring with Yul Brynner in "The King and I" (1951), and died on 9/6/52 (54).

DATE CHARTED	PEAK POS	WKS CHRT'D	ARTIST — Record Title	Label & Number
3/27/26	**5**	4	1. A Cup Of Coffee, A Sandwich, And You........ GERTRUDE LAWRENCE & JACK BUCHANAN	Columbia 512
4/24/26	**11**	1	2. Poor Little Rich Girl................................ above two from the Broadway musical "Andre Charlot Revue of 1925"	Columbia 513
2/05/27	**2(1)**	11	3. Someone To Watch Over Me/	
2/05/27	**8**	5	4. Do-Do-Do.. above two from the Broadway musical "Oh, Kay!" both accompanied by Tom Waring (piano)	Victor 20331

STEVE LAWRENCE
Popular singer-actor, long married to Eydie Gorme, got his start on TV's "Steve Allen Show".

DATE CHARTED	PEAK POS	WKS CHRT'D	ARTIST — Record Title	Label & Number
6/14/52	**21**	3	1. Poinciana... barely age 17 when recorded	King 15185
1/17/53	**26**	4	2. How Many Stars Have To Shine.................... both with Dewey Bergman's Orchestra	King 15208

YANK LAWSON
Trumpet star formerly with Ben Pollack, became famous with Bob Crosby (1935-38, 41-42) & Tommy Dorsey (1938-39); also briefly with Benny Goodman, and played in TV "Tonight Show" band in 60s.

HIPOLITO LAZARO
Barcelona-born operatic tenor

DATE CHARTED	PEAK POS	WKS CHRT'D	ARTIST — Record Title	Label & Number
11/11/16	**9**	1	1. Aida: Celeste Aida (Heavenly Aida) .... [F]	Columbia 48762

SILAS LEACHMAN
Popular early minstrel-style recording artist; died on 4/28/36 (76).

DATE CHARTED	PEAK POS	WKS CHRT'D	ARTIST — Record Title	Label & Number
6/30/94	**1(4)**	4	1. **Dem Golden Slippers**	Columbia
4/01/99	**4**	2	2. I Guess I'll Have To Telegraph My Baby	Chicago 0140
9/14/01	**5**	1	3. I'm Living Easy	Victor 793
10/11/02	**4**	2	4. Bill Bailey, Won't You Please Come Home? ...	Victor 1458

HUDDIE LEDBETTER
Great folk/blues singer-songwriter best known as "Leadbelly", composed the all-time hit "Goodnight, Irene" (his version was on Capitol 40130). Huddie died on 12/6/49 (60).

JACKIE LEE & HIS ORCHESTRA
Pianist-bandleader

DATE CHARTED	PEAK POS	WKS CHRT'D	ARTIST — Record Title	Label & Number
5/08/54	**17**	11	1. Isle Of Capri..	Coral 61149

JULIA LEE & HER BOY FRIENDS
Jazz/R&B singer from Kansas City who first recorded in the 1920s; died on 12/8/58 (56).

DATE CHARTED	PEAK POS	WKS CHRT'D	ARTIST — Record Title	Label & Number
8/16/47	**25**	1	1. My Sin .... with Red Nichols (cornet) & Red Norvo (xylophone)	Capitol Am. 40056
11/01/47	**24**	1	2. Snatch And Grab It	Capitol Am. 40028
3/27/48	**15**	3	3. King Size Papa .... above two were #1 on R&B charts for a total of 17 weeks Dave Cavanaugh (tenor sax) on above three Benny Carter (alto sax) on 3	Capitol Am. 40082
4/16/49	**29**	1	4. I Didn't Like It The First Time....................	Capitol 15367

DATE CHARTED	PEAK POS	WKS CHRT'D	ARTIST — Record Title	Label & Number
			PEGGY LEE A leading jazz singer for four decades, Peggy Lee was born Norma Jean Egstrom in Jamestown, N.D. on 5/26/20. She sang briefly with Will Osborne before becoming famous with with Benny Goodman (1941-43). Peggy and then-husband Dave Barbour co-wrote many of her early hits ("It's A Good Day", "Manana").	
11/10/45	4	14	1. Waitin' For The Train To Come In/	
3/30/46	24	2	2. I'm Glad I Waited For You .... from the film "Tars and Spars"	Capitol 218
5/25/46	7	6	3. I Don't Know Enough About You	Capitol 236
9/28/46	16	2	4. Linger In My Arms A Little Longer, Baby	Capitol 263
11/23/46	10	6	5. It's All Over Now	Capitol 292
1/18/47	16	2	6. It's A Good Day	Capitol 322
2/08/47	21	3	7. Everything's Movin' Too Fast	Capitol 343
6/28/47+	10	4	8. Chi-Baba, Chi-Baba (My Bambino Go To Sleep)	Capitol 419
11/15/47+	2(1)	18	9. Golden Earrings/ movie title song	
12/20/47+	11	4	10. I'll Dance At Your Wedding	Capitol 15009
1/24/48	1(9)	21	● 11. **Manana (Is Soon Enough For Me)/**	
1/31/48	21	1	12. All Dressed Up With A Broken Heart..........	Capitol 15022
2/28/48	25	2	13. For Every Man There's A Woman................. with Benny Goodman & His Orchestra from the film "Casbah"	Capitol 15030
4/03/48	13	4	14. Laroo, Laroo, Lili Bolero/	
4/17/48	23	1	15. Talking To Myself About You...................	Capitol 15048
5/15/48	22	2	16. Don't Smoke In Bed	Capitol 10120
6/05/48	13	5	17. Caramba! It's The Samba/ 11, 14 & 17 with Dave Barbour & the Brazilians	
6/05/48	21	3	18. Baby Don't Be Mad At Me........................ Benny Carter (alto sax), Herbie Haymer (tenor sax), Red Norvo (vibraphone) & Buddy Cole (piano) on 9-10 & 18	Capitol 15090
7/03/48	23	4	19. Bubble Loo, Bubble Loo	Capitol 15118
3/12/49	27	1	20. Blum Blum, I Wonder Who I Am .... Peggy Lee & Her Dixieland Band, with some members of Woody Herman's band	Capitol 15371
4/23/49	17	1	21. Similau (See-Me-Lo)	Capitol 15416
5/14/49	13	16	22. Bali Ha'i... from the Broadway musical "South Pacific"	Capitol 543
5/28/49	2(1)	9	23. Riders In The Sky (A Cowboy Legend) .... with the Jud Conlon Singers	Capitol 608
1/07/50	9	7	24. The Old Master Painter............................. PEGGY LEE & MEL TORME with the Mellomen	Capitol 791
8/26/50	28	1	25. Show Me The Way To Get Out Of This World . nearly all above solo records accompanied by Dave Barbour's Orchestra	Capitol 1105
9/08/51	14	8	26. I Get Ideas....................................... with Billy May's Orchestra adaptation of Argentine tango ("Adios Muchachos")	Capitol 1573
5/24/52	21	3	27. Be Anything (But Be Mine)........................	Decca 28142
6/07/52	3	13	● 28. Lover .... from the film "Love Me Tonight"	Decca 28215
7/26/52	28	2	29. Watermelon Weather.............................. PEGGY LEE & BING CROSBY	Decca 28238
8/02/52	14	4	30. Just One Of Those Things .... from the Broadway musical "Jubilee"	Decca 28313
11/22/52	23	2	31. River, River .... 27-28, 30-31 accompanied by Gordon Jenkins' Orchestra	Decca 28395
5/23/53	22	2	32. Who's Gonna Pay The Check?.................... accompanied by Dave Barbour's Orchestra	Decca 28631
12/05/53	30	1	33. Baubles, Bangles, And Beads .... from the Broadway musical "Kismet"	Decca 28890
3/13/54	28	2	34. Where Can I Go Without You?....................	Decca 29003

DATE CHARTED	PEAK POS	WKS CHRT'D	ARTIST — Record Title	Label & Number
12/18/54	**26**	2	35. Let Me Go, Lover .... Decca 29373 accompanied by Victor Young's Orchestra	

ROBERTA LEE
R&B singer

12/08/51	**13**	10	1. Slow Poke .... Decca 27792
			    accompanied by Neal Hefti & His Orchestra, featuring
			    Kai Winding (trombone)	

JACK LEONARD
Tommy Dorsey's star vocalist from 1935-39 ("Marie", "All the Things You Are").

8/03/40	**24**	1	1. All This And Heaven Too .... Okeh 5631 movie title song	
1/18/41	**16**	1	2. I Give You My Word .... Okeh 5886	
2/22/41	**21**	1	3. I'm Gettin' Sentimental Over You .... Okeh 5951 Tommy Dorsey's theme song	
9/04/43	**8**	13	4. I Never Mention Your Name .... Okeh 6715 accompanied on all by Ray Bloch's Orchestra	

TOMMY LEONETTI
Died on 9/15/79 (50)

6/26/54	**29**	1	1. The Happy Wanderer .... Capitol 2788 orchestra & chorus directed by Nelson Riddle	
8/07/54	**30**	1	2. I Cried .... Capitol 2861	

LES COMPAGNONS DE LA CHANSON
French group which sometimes accompanied Edith Piaf.

1/19/52	**14**	9	1. The Three Bells (The Jimmy Brown Song) ..... Columbia 39657 also released on Columbia 4105	

JERRY LESTER
Comedian, featured on TV's "Candid Camera" (1948-53) and other shows

12/02/50	**30**	1	1. Orange Colored Sky .... Coral 60325	

JULES LEVY
Acclaimed as "the world's greatest cornet player" during the late 19th century, also the first nationally-known musician to be extensively recorded; born in London, he died on 11/28/03 (45).

7/08/93	**1(3)**	3	1. **My Country 'Tis Of Thee** .... [I] North Amer. 470	
3/20/97	**3**	2	2. Alice, Where Art Thou........................... [I] Columbia	
2/08/02	**3**	3	3. Absence Makes The Heart Grow Fonder..... [I] Victor 1052	
3/01/02	**4**	2	4. The Palms.. [I] Victor 1054 later recorded for Columbia 917 & 31857	

LOUIS LEVY & HIS ORCHESTRA
British leader of large concert orchestra

5/16/36	**14**	3	1. She Shall Have Music .... Columbia 3130	

JERRY LEWIS
Comic star of over thiry movies, also director/producer; born Joseph Levitch.

12/04/48	**22**	1	1. That Certain Party................................. [C] Capitol 15249 DEAN MARTIN & JERRY LEWIS	

MONICA LEWIS
Daughter of an opera singer & an orchestra conductor; became a successful TV and movie actress.

4/26/47	**16**	1	1. Midnight Masquerade................................ Signature 15078 accompanied by Ray Bloch & His Orchestra	
8/21/48	**21**	3	2. A Tree In The Meadow .... Decca 24411 with the Ames Brothers & the Mary Osborne Trio	

ROBERT LEWIS
Pseudonym for Lewis James

ROBERT Q. LEWIS
Former disc jockey, host of many early TV game shows and his own daytime variety series (1954-56).

11/03/51	**22**	3	1. Where's A Your House........................... [N] MGM 11056 accompanied by Leroy Holmes' Orchestra	

DATE CHARTED	PEAK POS	WKS CHRT'D	ARTIST — Record Title	Label & Number
			TED LEWIS & HIS BAND Colorful, long-popular bandleader (born Theodore Friedman) whose showmanship was honed during early years in vaudeville. Clarinetist, singer, & sometimes songwriter (his theme "When My Baby Smiles at Me"), Ted's famous slogan was "Is everybody happy?" He died on 8/25/71 (79). (All vocals by Ted, unless otherwise noted) (Also see Ruth Etting & Sophie Tucker)	
1/10/20	**5**	3	1. Blues (My Naughty Sweetie Gives To Me).... [I]	Columbia 2798
3/27/20	**13**	1	2. O (Oh!)	Columbia 2844
5/29/20	**1(7)**	18	3. **When My Baby Smiles At Me**.................. from the Broadway musical "Greenwich Village Follies of 1919"	Columbia 2908
6/26/20	**4**	5	4. I'll See You In C-U-B-A....................... [I] from the Broadway musical "Ziegfeld Midnight Frolic"	Columbia 2927
6/26/20	**14**	1	5. Bo-La-Bo .... [I]	Columbia 2895
1/08/21	**9**	1	6. Fair One............................ [I]	Columbia 2998
2/05/21	**10**	1	7. I Love You, Sunday .... [I]	Columbia 3306
2/26/21	**15**	1	8. Tired Of Me .... [I]	Columbia 3329
3/19/21	**4**	5	9. Margie .... [I]	Columbia 3351
9/24/21	**1(4)**	12	10. **All By Myself** .... [I]	Columbia 3434
9/24/21	**11**	1	11. Love Me .... [I]	Columbia 3411
11/12/21	**2(2)**	7	12. Second Hand Rose/ [I] from the "Ziegfeld Follies of 1921"	
12/03/21	**9**	1	13. Sally, Won't You Come Back? .... [I]	Columbia 3453
1/21/22	**7**	2	14. Ma! .... [I]	Columbia 3473
2/04/22	**3**	6	15. Everybody Step .... [I] from the Broadway musical "Music Box Revue"	Columbia 3499
4/22/22	**5**	3	16. Marie............................ [I]	Columbia 3538
6/17/22	**7**	2	17. Every Day .... [I]	Columbia 3590
9/23/22	**8**	2	18. Sunshine Alley .... [I]	Columbia 3647
11/18/22	**8**	3	19. Georgette .... [I]	Columbia 3662
12/30/22	**11**	1	20. Hot Lips.......................... [I]	Columbia 3676
2/17/23	**5**	3	21. Bees' Knees .... [I]	Columbia 3730
4/18/23	**9**	1	22. Runnin' Wild .... [I]	Columbia 3790
5/12/23	**8**	1	23. Tiger Rag .... [I]	Columbia 3813
9/01/23	**7**	2	24. Aunt Hagar's Blues .... [I]	Columbia 3879
9/29/23	**11**	1	25. Louisville Lou .... [I]	Columbia 3892
10/27/23	**5**	3	26. Cut Yourself A Piece Of Cake................... [I]	Columbia 3944
12/29/23	**14**	1	27. 12th Street Rag .... [I]	Columbia 3972
4/19/24	**6**	3	28. Twelve O'Clock At Night .... [I]	Columbia 52
4/26/24	**11**	1	29. Steppin' Out .... [I]	Columbia 48
8/23/24	**4**	4	30. San/ [I]	
9/13/24	**7**	2	31. She's Everybody's Sweetheart..................	Columbia 122
9/20/24	**2(2)**	6	32. June Night/ [I]	
11/15/24	**7**	2	33. I Wonder What's Become Of Sally? .... [I]	Columbia 157
10/25/24	**5**	4	34. There'll Be Some Changes Made .... [I]	Columbia 170
2/21/25	**9**	1	35. Show Me The Way................................ [I]	Columbia 241
4/25/25	**1(1)**	9	36. **O! Katharina** .... [I]	Columbia 295
11/28/25	**15**	1	37. Angry .... [I]	Columbia 416
12/26/25	**14**	1	38. Tin Roof Blues .... [I]	Columbia 439
2/06/26	**9**	1	39. Bam, Bam, Bamy Shore .... [I]	Columbia 478
4/10/26	**8**	1	40. That Certain Party....................	Columbia 551
7/03/26	**2(1)**	6	41. I've Found A New Baby .... [I]	Columbia 600
9/18/26	**3**	6	42. Where'd You Get Those Eyes?....................	Columbia 667
1/15/27	**10**	4	43. Tiger Rag .... [I] new version of 1923 hit (Columbia 826: Sophie Tucker with Ted Lewis & His Band)	Columbia 770
4/09/27	**7**	5	44. If You See Sally	Columbia 844
7/30/27	**8**	4	45. One Sweet Letter From You......................	Columbia 988

DATE CHARTED	PEAK POS	WKS CHRT'D	ARTIST — Record Title	Label & Number
9/03/27	9	5	46. Frankie And Johnny .... folk song dating back to 1840s	Columbia 1017
9/24/27	9	4	47. The Memphis Blues .... [I]	Columbia 1050
11/12/27	12	3	48. The Darktown Strutters' Ball	Columbia 1084
3/10/28	10	3	49. Is Everybody Happy Now? .... (Columbia 1242: Ruth Etting with Ted Lewis & His Band)	Columbia 1207
5/05/28	10	4	50. Mary Ann	Columbia 1313
6/23/28	5	6	51. Laugh, Clown, Laugh!/ based on a theme from the opera "I Pagliacci"	
7/07/28	16	2	52. Hello, Montreal!	Columbia 1346
8/18/28	19	1	53. Oh Baby!	Columbia 1391
8/25/28	8	4	54. A Good Man Is Hard To Find	Columbia 1428
10/13/28	5	6	55. King For A Day/	
11/24/28	17	1	56. Moonlight Madness (Then You Were Gone) ..	Columbia 1485
2/02/29	15	2	57. She's Funny That Way	Columbia 1656
2/23/29	10	4	58. Glad Rag Doll	Columbia 1709
8/10/29	13	2	59. I'm Walking Around In A Dream	Columbia 1854
8/31/29	3	6	60. I Love You (My Love Song)	Columbia 1916
8/31/29	10	3	61. I'm The Medicine Man For The Blues .... from the film "Is Everybody Happy?"	Columbia 1882
10/12/29	4	6	62. Lonely Troubador	Columbia 1957
11/02/29	3	7	63. Lady Luck .... from the film "Show of Shows"	Columbia 1999
11/02/29	10	3	64. Through! (How Can You Say We're Through?)	Columbia 1957
12/07/29	2(1)	7	65. Farewell Blues/ [I]	
1/04/30	16	2	66. Wabash Blues .... [I]	Columbia 2029
1/18/30	4	5	67. You've Got That Thing .... from the Broadway musical "Fifty Million Frenchmen"	Columbia 2088
3/08/30	6	5	68. Aunt Hagar's Blues/	
3/29/30	18	1	69. San .... [I] new version of 1924 hit	Columbia 2113
4/05/30	2(2)	7	70. On The Sunny Side Of The Street .... from the Broadway musical "International Revue"	Columbia 2144
5/10/30	3	7	71. The Lonesome Road/ from the film version of "Show Boat"	
5/10/30	8	7	72. Dinah .... above two vocals: Ted Lewis & Four Dusty Travelers (black group)	Columbia 2181
7/19/30	4	5	73. Yellow Dog Blues .... [I]	Columbia 2217
8/02/30	2(2)	8	74. Three O'Clock In The Morning .... from the Broadway musical "Greenwich Village Follies of 1921" Jimmy Dorsey (alto sax/clarinet) on above eight	Columbia 2246
11/15/30	14	2	75. Homemade Sunshine .... with Jack Teagarden (trombone)	Columbia 2311
12/20/30+	14	4	76. Somebody Stole My Gal/	
1/03/31	16	2	77. Some Day, Sweetheart	Columbia 2336
1/31/31	1(2)	8	78. **Just A Gigolo** .... adaptation of Viennese song ("Schoner Gigolo")	Columbia 2378
3/28/31	12	3	79. At Last I'm Happy	Columbia 2408
4/09/31+	2(2)	9	80. Somebody Loves You/	
4/16/32	9	4	81. My Woman!	Columbia 2635
4/25/31	9	4	82. Egyptian Ella	Columbia 2428
5/23/31	6	6	83. Ho Hum!	Columbia 2452
8/08/31	7	6	84. I'm All Dressed Up With A Broken Heart	Columbia 2492
10/03/31	7	7	85. Dallas Blues .... Fats Waller, vocal (also piano on 82 & 85)	Columbia 2527
12/05/31	2(1)	7	86. An Ev'ning In Caroline	Columbia 2560
6/04/32	1(10)	22	87. **In A Shanty In Old Shanty Town** .... from the film "The Crooner"	Columbia 2652

DATE CHARTED	PEAK POS	WKS CHRT'D	ARTIST — Record Title	Label & Number
6/25/32	14	2	88. Ted Lewis Presents A Miniature Dance Program.............................. *reissue of songs on Columbia 2181, together on one side*	Columbia 56000
11/19/32	6	7	89. Headin' For Better Times/ [R] *recorded 1/12/31, originally on Columbia 2378* Benny Goodman (clarinet) on 78-86 & 89	
12/10/32	16	2	90. New Farewell Blues........................... [I-R] *reissue of Columbia 2029*	Columbia 2721
12/24/32+	4	6	91. Play, Fiddle, Play.....................................	Columbia 2728
2/25/33	6	10	92. Try A Little Tenderness.............................	Columbia 2748
3/18/33	12	2	93. There's A New Day Comin'/	
3/25/33	8	8	94. Have You Ever Been Lonely?.....................	Columbia 2753
4/08/33	11	3	95. All Aboard For Dreamland, Baby.................	Columbia 2758
5/20/33	5	7	96. The Gold Diggers' Song (We're In The Money). *from the film "Gold Diggers of 1933"*	Columbia 2775
5/27/33	6	7	97. Stormy Weather .... *vocal: Shirley Jay*	Columbia 2774
6/03/33	9	4	98. An Old, Old Man With An Old, Old Pipe (And An Old, Old Lady Beside Him)...............	Columbia 2777
7/15/33	1(4)	11	99. **Lazybones**	Columbia 2786
8/26/33	13	3	100. Here You Come With Love..........................	Columbia 2799
11/10/34	9	6	101. Pop! Goes Your Heart .... *from the film "Happiness Ahead"* *Muggsy Spanier (cornet) on vast majority of records from 59-101*	Decca 239
11/11/38	18	1	102. When My Baby Smiles At Me....................... *new version of Ted's theme song*	Decca 2054

J. ALDRICH LIBBEY
Top vaudeville entertainer famous for introducing the classic "After the Ball" in 1892.

7/12/02	3	3	1. On A Sunday Afternoon	Edison 8018
2/28/03	2(2)	3	2. In The Sweet Bye And Bye	Edison 8300

LIBERACE
The pianist born Wladziu Valentino Liberace in Milwaukee became a nationwide sensation in the 50s with his flamboyant style, and nearly 30 years later his loyal legion of fans enabled him to shatter Radio City Music Hall attendance records.

5/03/52	27	1	1. September Song...................................... [I] *from the Broadway musical "Knickerbocker Holiday"*	Columbia 39709
10/24/53	21	6	2. The Story Of Three Loves (18th Variation - Rachmaninoff: Rhapsody On A Theme Of Paganini) .... [I] *movie title theme*	Columbia 40099
12/26/53	21	2	3. Christmas Medley .... [I-X] *"White Christmas", "Jingle Bells", "O Come All Ye Faithful", "Silent Night"*	Columbia 48001
3/27/54	30	1	4. Indiscretion .... JO STAFFORD with LIBERACE & THE PAUL WESTON ORCHESTRA *Italian song*	Columbia 40170
4/24/54	26	1	5. Easter Parade .... [I] *orchestra directed by George Liberace; from the Broadway musical "As Thousands Cheer"*	Columbia 48007
5/08/54	23	1	6. Twelfth Street Rag................................ [I]	Columbia 40217

JOE LIGGINS
Popular R & B singer and pianist

10/20/45	13	3	● 1. The Honeydripper .... *17 weeks at #1 on R&B chart*	Exclusive 207
2/16/46	12	1	2. Got A Right To Cry	Exclusive 210
6/10/50	30	1	3. Pink Champagne...................................... *eleven weeks at #1 on R&B chart*	Specialty 355

DATE CHARTED	PEAK POS	WKS CHRT'D	ARTIST — Record Title	Label & Number
			ENOCH LIGHT & HIS LIGHT BRIGADE Bandleader who achieved enormous popularity in the early 1960s with his elaborately-arranged stereo albums.	
2/06/37	**19**	1	1. Summer Night .... vocal: Johnny Muldowney	Vocalion 3421
			LITTLE JACK LITTLE & HIS ORCHESTRA Popular pianist-singer on 1920s radio before forming his band; co-wrote various popular songs, including "Hold Me" and the blockbuster "In a Shanty in Old Shanty Town". Born in London; died on 4/9/56 (55, suicide). (All vocals by Little)	
3/10/34	**2(2)**	9	1. You Oughta Be In Pictures .... from the film "New York Town"	Columbia 2895
3/17/34	**12**	3	2. Old Roses	Columbia 2900
12/01/34	**16**	2	3. Stay As Sweet As You Are......................... from the film "College Rhythm"	Columbia 2969
12/08/34	**7**	6	4. June In January...................................... from the film "Here Is My Heart"	Columbia 2978
1/12/35	**13**	2	5. Little Boy Blue	Columbia 2984
2/23/35	**5**	8	6. Lullaby Of Broadway/	
3/02/35	**16**	2	7. I'm Goin' Shopping With You .... above two from the film "Gold Diggers of 1935"	Columbia 3009
8/17/35	**1(3)**	14	8. **I'm In The Mood For Love** .... from the film "Every Night at Eight"	Columbia 3069
8/24/35	**13**	2	9. I Wished On The Moon............................. from the film "The Big Broadcast of 1936"	Columbia 3068
11/23/35	**4**	6	10. On Treasure Island/	
11/23/35	**7**	4	11. No Other One	Columbia 3095
11/30/35	**7**	6	12. Where Am I? (Am I In Heaven?)................... from the film "Stars Over Broadway"	Columbia 3096
2/15/36	**15**	2	13. I'm Shooting High .... from the film "King of Burlesque"	Columbia 3108
5/01/37	**17**	1	14. It's Swell Of You..................................... from the film "Wake Up And Live"	Vocalion 3498
			ELLA LOGAN Born Ella Allan in Glasgow, Scotland, Ella was featured in a number of movie and Broadway musicals, and achieved her greatest fame as star of the 1947 Broadway classic "Finian's Rainbow"; she died on 5/1/69 (56).	
2/12/38	**4**	6	1. Oh Dear! What Can The Matter Be?............. accompanied by Bill Harty & His Orchestra	Brunswick 8057
8/13/38	**8**	5	2. My Bonnie Lies Over The Ocean	Brunswick 8196
10/22/38	**12**	2	3. Come To The Fair	Brunswick 8232
11/12/38	**13**	3	4. Two Sleepy People .... ELLA LOGAN & HOAGY CARMICHAEL from the film "Thanks for the Memory" accompanied on above three by Perry Botkin & His Orchestra featuring Mannie Klein (trumpet)	Brunswick 8250
			LAURIE LOMAN	
10/09/54	**21**	4	1. Whither Thou Goest .... accompanied by Hank Russell's Orchestra	Century 106
			CARMEN LOMBARDO Lead saxophonist and featured vocalist for brother Guy Lombardo from 1925-70; born in Ontario, Canada. Also a prolific composer ("Sweethearts on Parade", "A Sailboat In the Moonlight", "Seems Like Old Times"), and arranger for the band. He died on 4/17/71 (67).	

DATE CHARTED	PEAK POS	WKS CHRT'D	ARTIST — Record Title	Label & Number
			GUY LOMBARDO & HIS ROYAL CANADIANS	
			The man who became leader of the only dance band ever to sell more than 100 million records was born on 6/19/02 in London, Ontario, Canada. The Lombardo brothers formed their band in 1925, with Guy as leader and Carmen as lead saxophonist and singer, and by decade's end "The Sweetest Music This Side of Heaven" had settled in for a long stay as one of America's favorites. It was of course Guy's annual New Year's Eve broadcasts, always climaxed by his theme "Auld Lang Syne", that made him most familiar to modern audiences. He died on 11/5/77. (Nearly all 1927-40 vocals by Carmen Lombardo.) (Also see Bing Crosby, Hildegarde, & Kate Smith)	
9/10/27	1(7)	15	1. **Charmaine!**..	Columbia 1048
6/16/28	6	5	2. Coquette/	
7/14/28	9	4	3. Beloved	Columbia 1345
8/04/28	16	2	4. Japansy...	Columbia 1364
12/29/28+	1(3)	12	5. **Sweethearts On Parade**.........................	Columbia 1628
1/26/29	20	1	6. High Up On A Hill Top	Columbia 1653
2/09/29	4	6	7. Where The Shy Little Violets Grow	Columbia 1679
8/17/29	8	4	8. I Get The Blues When It Rains	Columbia 1888
10/26/29	18	1	9. (You Made Me Love You) Why Did You?	Columbia 1927
11/02/29	6	5	10. College Medley Fox Trot (The Big Ten)....... [I] themes from Chicago, Northwestern, Wisconsin, etc.	Columbia 1996
11/23/29+	11	4	11. A Little Kiss Each Morning (A Little Kiss Each Night) .... from the film "The Vagabond Lover"	Columbia 2017
12/21/29	10	3	12. Singin' In The Bathtub............................. from the film "Show of Shows"	Columbia 2045
1/04/30	3	4	13. Have A Little Faith In Me/	
2/08/30	6	4	14. Crying For The Carolines .... above two from the film "Spring Is Here"	Columbia 2062
3/01/30	5	10	15. Under A Texas Moon .... movie title song	Columbia 2089
3/22/30	10	5	16. Lazy Lou'siana Moon	Columbia 2135
4/05/30	4	10	17. A Cottage For Sale................................	Columbia 2156
5/03/30	17	2	18. With You.. from the film "Puttin' On the Ritz"	Columbia 2107
5/24/30	7	5	19. You're The Sweetest Girl This Side Of Heaven/	
7/12/30	9	5	20. Rollin' Down The River...........................	Columbia 2188
6/14/30	4	7	21. Singing A Song To The Stars.......................	Columbia 2206
8/02/30	3	7	22. Swingin' In A Hammock............................	Columbia 2237
9/06/30	2(1)	6	23. Confessin' (That I Love You)	Columbia 2259
10/04/30	8	5	24. Go Home And Tell Your Mother.................. from the film "Love in the Rough"	Columbia 2276
10/25/30	5	4	25. I Still Get A Thrill (Thinking Of You)	Columbia 2286
11/22/30	7	8	26. Baby's Birthday Party	Columbia 2319
11/29/30	1(4)	12	27. **You're Driving Me Crazy! (What Did I Do?).** from the Broadway musical "Smiles"	Columbia 2335
2/28/31	12	5	28. Heartaches	Columbia 2390
3/14/31	1(3)	11	29. **By The River St. Marie/**	
3/21/31	17	1	30. Running Between The Rain-Drops..............	Columbia 2401
4/25/31	3	9	31. Whistling In The Dark	Columbia 2444
5/30/31	1(3)	8	32. **(There Ought To Be A) Moonlight Saving Time**...	Columbia 2457
7/04/31	3	5	33. Without That Gal!..................................	Columbia 2475
8/15/31	2(5)	9	34. Sweet And Lovely/	
8/22/31	4	6	35. Begging For Love................................. from the Broadway musical "Shoot the Works"	Columbia 2500
9/26/31	2(3)	8	36. Now That You're Gone.............................	Columbia 2528
11/07/31	1(2)	11	37. **Goodnight, Sweetheart** .... from the Broadway musical "Earl Carroll's Vanities of 1931"	Columbia 2547

DATE CHARTED	PEAK POS	WKS CHRT'D	ARTIST — Record Title	Label & Number
12/12/31	**8**	4	38. You Try Somebody Else (We'll Be Back Together Again) .... (Columbia 2578: Kate Smith with Guy Lombardo & Royal Canadians)	Columbia 2567
3/05/32	**1(2)**	9	39. **Too Many Tears**	Brunswick 6261
4/23/32	**1(3)**	10	40. **Paradise/**	
5/21/32	**8**	5	41. My Extraordinary Gal	Brunswick 6290
5/07/32	**4**	5	42. Lawd, You Made The Night Too Long	Brunswick 6300
6/18/32	**11**	2	43. Sharing (My Love For You)	Brunswick 6315
8/20/32	**1(5)**	8	44. **We Just Couldn't Say Goodbye/**	
9/03/32	**8**	4	45. I'll Never Be The Same	Brunswick 6350
9/03/32	**11**	4	46. I Guess I'll Have To Change My Plan (The Blue Pajamas Song).......................... from the Broadway musical "The Little Show"	Brunswick 6363
10/01/32	**5**	5	47. Puh-Leeze, Mr. Hemingway	Brunswick 6390
10/29/32	**4**	6	48. How Deep Is The Ocean? (How High Is The Sky?)/	
11/05/32	**10**	4	49. Pink Elephants............................	Brunswick 6399
12/03/32	**9**	5	50. I'm Sure Of Everything But You..................	Brunswick 6426
12/24/32	**5**	4	51. Just A Little Home For The Old Folks (A Token From Me)	Brunswick 6440
12/24/32	**9**	3	52. Waltzing In A Dream	Brunswick 6441
1/14/33	**5**	5	53. Street Of Dreams .... (Brunswick 6472 & 6477: Bing Crosby with Guy Lombardo & Royal Canadians)	Brunswick 6455
2/18/33	**7**	6	54. Going, Going, Gone!................................	Brunswick 6499
4/22/33	**11**	4	55. Maybe It's Because I Love You Too Much/	
4/29/33	**8**	5	56. Lover .... from the film "Love Me Tonight"	Brunswick 6535
4/22/33	**11**	2	57. You'll Never Get Up To Heaven That Way......	Brunswick 6536
4/29/33	**2(4)**	10	58. Stormy Weather (Keeps Rainin' All The Time)	Brunswick 6550
6/24/33	**11**	4	59. Shadow Waltz .... from the film "Gold Diggers of 1933"	Brunswick 6590
7/22/33	**9**	4	60. Don't Blame Me.................................... from the film "Dinner at Eight"	Brunswick 6608
8/26/33	**12**	3	61. Time To Go....................................	Brunswick 6634
9/23/33	**6**	4	62. This Time It's Love	Brunswick 6641
10/14/33	**6**	6	63. By A Waterfall .... from the film "Footlight Parade"	Brunswick 6653
10/21/33	**1(3)**	8	64. **The Last Round-Up/** featured in Broadway's "Ziegfeld Follies of 1934"	
11/11/34+	**2(2)**	8	65. Annie Doesn't Live Here Anymore	Brunswick 6662
12/16/33	**2(2)**	7	66. Did You Ever See A Dream Walking?/ from the film "Sitting Pretty"	
1/20/34	**17**	2	67. I Raised My Hat.................................	Brunswick 6713
2/10/34	**7**	7	68. Night On The Water/	
1/13/34	**11**	4	69. Inka Dinka Doo .... Jimmy Durante's theme song; from the film "Palooka"	Brunswick 6714
3/24/34	**13**	2	70. Little Dutch Mill	Brunswick 6781
5/05/34	**2(2)**	6	71. Riptide/	
5/12/34	**14**	4	72. How Do I Know It's Sunday?.................... from the film "Harold Teen"	Brunswick 6866
5/26/34	**20**	1	73. The Sweetest Music This Side Of Heaven/	
6/02/34	**8**	5	74. Fare Thee Well, Annabelle .... vocal: Lebert Lombardo	Brunswick 6874
6/23/34	**7**	5	75. My Old Flame.................................... from the film "Belle of the Nineties"	Brunswick 6909
10/27/34	**1(4)**	9	76. **Stars Fell On Alabama**..........................	Decca 104
10/27/34	**11**	2	77. Love In Bloom .... from the film "She Loves Me Not"	Decca 102

DATE CHARTED	PEAK POS	WKS CHRT'D	ARTIST — Record Title	Label & Number
11/24/34	**15**	2	78. Stay As Sweet As You Are................................ *from the film "College Rhythm"*	Decca 274
12/01/34	**2(1)**	9	79. Winter Wonderland ....[X]	Decca 294
1/19/35	**14**	2	80. June In January....................................... *from the film "Here Is My Heart"*	Decca 307
3/23/35	**1(2)**	15	81. **What's The Reason (I'm Not Pleasin' You)/**	
6/08/35	**14**	2	82. Down By The River .... *from the film "Mississippi"*	Decca 393
5/04/35	**17**	2	83. Would There Be Love?...............................	Decca 425
5/11/35	**13**	4	84. Everything's Been Done Before .... *from the film "Reckless"*	Decca 424
6/08/35	**10**	4	85. Seein' Is Believin'	Decca 454
9/28/35	**2(3)**	10	86. Cheek To Cheek/ *from the film "Top Hat"*	
10/05/35	**9**	6	87. Broadway Rhythm .... *from the film "Broadway Melody of 1936"*	Decca 549
10/26/35	**1(4)**	16	88. **Red Sails In The Sunset** .... *British song* *from the Broadway musical "Provincetown Follies"*	Decca 554
11/16/35	**6**	9	89. I'm Sittin' High On A Hill Top.....................	Decca 589
1/11/36	**3**	7	90. The Broken Record/	
1/25/36	**13**	7	91. Alone At A Table For Two	Victor 25210
4/04/36	**14**	2	92. I'm Putting All My Eggs In One Basket......... *from the film "Follow the Fleet"*	Victor 25242
4/18/36	**1(2)**	13	93. **Lost**	Victor 25271
8/15/36	**1(2)**	15	94. **When Did You Leave Heaven?** .... *from the film "Sing, Baby, Sing"*	Victor 25357
9/12/36	**3**	10	95. The Way You Look Tonight/	
11/07/36	**13**	2	96. A Fine Romance .... *above two from the film "Swing Time"*	Victor 25372
11/07/36	**11**	7	97. You Do The Darndest Things, Baby .... *from the film "Pigskin Parade"*	Victor 25421
11/14/36+	**19**	2	98. Sweetheart, Let's Grow Old Together............	Victor 25417
12/12/36+	**3**	18	99. When My Dream Boat Comes Home/ *vocal: Lebert Lombardo*	
2/06/37	**15**	2	100. Rainbow On The River .... *movie title song*	Victor 25435
12/26/36+	**13**	5	101. Gone	Victor 25475
3/13/37	**1(5)**	12	102. **Boo Hoo/**	
4/03/37	**11**	3	103. I Can't Lose That Longing For You	Victor 25522
4/10/37	**1(4)**	16	104. **September In The Rain** .... *from the films "Stars Over Broadway" and "Melody for Two"*	Victor 25526
5/15/37	**1(5)**	16	105. **It Looks Like Rain In Cherry Blossom Lane/**	
7/03/37	**14**	3	106. Toodle-oo	Victor 25572
5/15/37	**10**	4	107. The Love Bug Will Bite You	Victor 25548
6/19/37	**1(3)**	14	108. **A Sailboat In The Moonlight/**	
8/21/37	**16**	1	109. Gone With The Wind	Victor 25594
7/10/37	**2(2)**	12	110. I Know Now .... *from the film "The Singing Marine"*	Victor 25566
7/31/37	**17**	1	111. The Folks Who Live On The Hill/	
8/28/37	**13**	4	112. Can I Forget You?.................................. *above two from the film "High, Wide, and Handsome"*	Victor 25615
8/07/37	**1(1)**	8	113. **So Rare**	Victor 25626
9/18/37	**17**	1	114. You Can't Stop Me From Dreaming..............	Victor 25656
11/20/37	**14**	4	115. When The Mighty Organ Played "Oh Promise Me"...	Victor 25702
12/25/37+	**12**	7	116. I See Your Face Before Me......................... *from the Broadway musical "Between the Devil"*	Victor 25684

DATE CHARTED	PEAK POS	WKS CHRT'D	ARTIST — Record Title	Label & Number
1/01/38	**2(1)**	7	117. Bei Mir Bist Du Schoen/ adapted from song featured in the 1933 Yiddish musical "I Would If I Could"	
3/12/38	**11**	1	118. It's Easier Said Than Done	Victor 25739
3/05/38	**3**	10	119. Ti-Pi-Pin/ adaptation of Spanish popular song	
3/19/38	**10**	5	120. Let's Sail To Dreamland..........................	Victor 25786
3/19/38	**14**	5	121. In My Little Red Book..............................	Victor 25798
4/09/38	**13**	3	122. Two Bouquets	Victor 25787
5/07/38	**7**	5	123. So Little Time/	
5/28/38	**9**	10	124. Little Lady Make Believe..........................	Victor 25823
12/10/38	**20**	1	125. Girl Friend Of The Whirling Dervish/ from the film "Garden of the Moon"	
12/17/38	**2(1)**	6	126. I Must See Annie Tonight	Decca 2195
12/17/38	**7**	3	127. It's A Lonely Trail (When You're Travelin' All Alone)/	
1/07/39	**6**	4	128. I Ups To Her And She Ups To Me (And The Next Thing I Knows I'm In Love) .... [N]	Decca 2196
1/28/39	**9**	1	129. Deep Purple	Decca 2215
3/04/39	**1(1)**	11	130. **Penny Serenade**	Decca 2291
			British song	
3/11/39	**2(1)**	12	131. Little Sir Echo....................................	Decca 2306
			musical adaptation of the Boy Scouts anthem	
4/01/39	**11**	1	132. Easter Parade	Decca 2345
			from the Broadway musical "As Thousands Cheer"	
6/17/39	**11**	1	133. St. Louis Blues....................................	Decca 2478
			B side: Guy's famous theme "Auld Lang Syne"	
7/15/39	**3**	9	134. Cinderella, Stay In My Arms	Decca 2520
			British song	
7/22/39	**5**	2	135. South American Way..............................	Decca 2566
			from the Broadway musical "The Streets of Paris"	
8/05/39	**7**	1	136. I'm Sorry For Myself...............................	Decca 2550
			from the film "Second Fiddle"	
10/07/39	**8**	3	137. In An 18th Century Drawing Room	Decca 2701
			based on Mozart's "Piano Sonata No. 3 in C"	
11/04/39	**8**	8	138. South Of The Border (Down Mexico Way).......	Decca 2768
1/13/40	**9**	12	139. Confucius Say	Decca 2917
			vocals on 126, 136 & 139: Carmen Lombardo, Larry Owen & Fred Henry	
4/13/40	**5**	7	140. When You Wish Upon A Star......................	Decca 2969
			from the animated film "Pinocchio"	
10/19/40	**13**	3	141. Now I Lay Me Down To Dream....................	Decca 3330
11/02/40	**28**	1	142. Notre Dame Medley .... [I]	Decca 3368
1/04/41	**3**	6	143. A Nightingale Sang In Berkeley Square	Decca 3453
			from the London musical "New Faces"	
2/01/41	**24**	1	144. We'll Meet Again....................................	Decca 3575
2/15/41	**22**	1	145. The Moon Fell In The River.......................	Decca 3487
			from the Broadway musical "It Happens On Ice" Carmen Lombardo: nearly all above vocals	
4/12/41	**1(2)**	14	146. **The Band Played On**	Decca 3675
			vocal: Kenny Gardner & the Leonardo Trio featured in the movie "Strawberry Blonde"	
5/10/41	**1(1)**	13	147. **Intermezzo (Souvenir De Vienne)**............ [I]	Decca 3674
8/23/41	**11**	5	148. Ma! I Miss Your Apple Pie........................	Decca 3822
			vocal: Carmen Lombardo-Mert Curtis-Fred Henry	
12/20/41	**21**	1	149. Sail Boat In The Sky................................	Decca 4066
3/14/42	**21**	1	150. Frankie And Johnny.................................	Decca 4177
5/09/42	**9**	4	151. Johnny Doughboy Found A Rose In Ireland ...	Decca 4278
10/24/42	**20**	1	152. Beale Street Blues/	
1/23/43	**17**	1	153. For Me And My Gal	Decca 4371
			movie title song vocals on 149, 151 & 153: Kenny Gardner	

DATE CHARTED	PEAK POS	WKS CHRT'D	ARTIST — Record Title	Label & Number
7/24/43	19	1	154. Where Or When .... from the Broadway musical "Babes in Arms"	Decca 18548
1/08/44	5	9	155. Speak Low (When You Speak, Love)/ vocal: Billy Leach from the Broadway musical "One Touch of Venus"	
1/29/44	11	10	156. Take It Easy	Decca 18573
3/18/44	1(2)	19	157. **It's Love-Love-Love** .... vocal: Skip Nelson; from the film "Stars on Parade"	Decca 18589
6/24/44	11	4	158. Long Ago (And Far Away)/ from the film "Cover Girl"	
7/15/44	20	1	159. Humoresque .... [I]	Decca 18602
			featuring Fred Kreitzer & Francis Vigneau (pianos)	
9/30/44	7	11	160. Together .... from the film "Since You Went Away" vocals on 158 & 160: Tony Craig	Decca 18617
12/09/44	13	3	161. Meet Me In St. Louis, Louis.......................	Decca 18626
1/06/45	19	2	162. The Trolley Song/ above 2 from the film "Meet Me In St. Louis"	
1/20/45	10	5	163. Always	Decca 18634
2/24/45	5	13	164. A Little On The Lonely Side/	
4/07/45	21	1	165. My Heart Sings........................... vocal by Stuart Foster	Decca 18642
3/31/45	18	1	166. Oh! Moytle/ [N]	
4/21/45	11	8	167. Poor Little Rhode Island .... from the film "Carolina Blues" vocals on 162-163 & 167: Stuart Foster	Decca 18651
6/23/45	2(1)	13	168. Bell Bottom Trousers .... adaptation of traditional sea chantey vocals on 164, 166 & 168: Jimmy Brown	Decca 18683
9/08/45	17	1	169. Stars In Your Eyes	Decca 18696
11/10/45	8	6	170. No Can Do .... vocal: Don Rodney & Rose Marie Lombardo (Guy's sister)	Decca 18712
1/12/46	10	8	171. Symphony/	
3/02/46	7	7	172. Seems Like Old Times	Decca 18737
4/06/46	6	7	173. Shoo-Fly Pie And Apple Pan Dowdy/	
5/04/46	12	8	174. Give Me The Moon Over Brooklyn .... (Decca 23428 & 23511: Hildegarde with Guy Lombardo & His Royal Canadians)	Decca 18809
6/29/46	23	4	175. Love On A Greyhound Bus .... from the film "No Leave, No Love"	Decca 18873
8/24/46	14	5	176. I'd Be Lost Without You...........................	Decca 18901
1/25/47	1(1)	15	177. **Managua, Nicaragua**...........................	Decca 23782
2/22/47	2(2)	13	178. Anniversary Song .... vocal: Kenny Gardner melody based on the 1880 song "Danube Wayes"	Decca 23799
4/12/47	21	1	●179. Easter Parade .... new version of the band's 1939 hit	Decca 23817
5/03/47	9	4	180. April Showers .... featured in the film "The Jolson Story"	Decca 23845
5/24/47	3	17	181. I Wonder, I Wonder, I Wonder	Decca 23865
10/11/47	16	1	182. The Echo Said "No" .... (Decca 24156: Mary Martin with Guy Lombardo & His Royal Canadians)	Decca 24115
3/13/48	22	1	183. Thoughtless...........................	Decca 24318
31/24/48	10	6	184. I'm My Own Grandpaw...........................[N]	Decca 24288
2/12/49	8	19	185. Red Roses For A Blue Lady/	
4/09/49	19	9	186. Everywhere You Go........................... most vocals from 172-186: Don Rodney	Decca 24549
2/26/49	20	5	187. Down By The Station...........................	Decca 24555
5/28/49	18	8	188. Merry-Go-Round Waltz........................... adaptation of "Over the Waves"	Decca 24624
6/11/49	30	1	189. Need You...........................	Decca 24614
8/06/49	19	4	190. The Four Winds And The Seven Seas .... vocal: Don Rodney	Decca 24648

DATE CHARTED	PEAK POS	WKS CHRT'D	ARTIST — Record Title	Label & Number
10/01/49	16	5	191. Hop-Scotch Polka (Scotch Hot)	Decca 24704
10/22/49	30	1	192. The Blue Skirt Waltz	Decca 24714
1/21/50	10	19	193. Enjoy Yourself (It's Later Than You Think)/ vocals on 188-89, 191 & 193: Kenny Gardner	
3/11/50	1(11)	27	●194. **The Third Man Theme** .... [I] from the film "The Third Man" featuring Don Rodney on guitar	Decca 24839
3/18/50	28	1	195. The Wedding Samba	Decca 24838
3/25/50	5	14	196. Dearie... from the stage production "The Copacabana Show of 1950"	Decca 24899
6/10/50	24	1	197. Tiddley Winkie Woo	Decca 27005
8/26/50	19	3	198. Our Little Ranch House...........................	Decca 27092
9/16/50	25	1	199. Nola .... [I]	Decca 27178
10/07/50	10	15	200. All My Love .... melody based on Ravel's "Bolero"	Decca 27118
10/07/50	22	3	201. The Petite Waltz (La Petite Valse)/ [I] "twin pianos" of Fred Kreitzer & Buddy Brennan featured on 199 & 201	
10/14/50	2(1)	20	202. Harbor Lights.......................................	Decca 27208
12/16/50+	6	16	203. Tennessee Waltz...................................	Decca 27336
1/06/51	28	1	204. Frosty The Snowman........................... [X]	Decca 27257
2/03/51	29	1	205. Get Out Those Old Records....................... vocal: Kenny Gardner & Carmen Lombardo	Decca 27336
2/17/51	21	1	206. Velvet Lips/	
2/17/51	22	5	207. The Chicken Song (I Ain't Gonna Take It Settin' Down) .... vocal: Cliff Grass	Decca 27393
3/17/51	20	5	208. If .... vocals on 200 & 208: Bill Flanagan	Decca 27449
9/08/51	11	12	209. Because Of You .... Gloria DeHaven (movie star), vocal	Decca 27666
12/22/51	28	1	210. Undecided	Decca 27835
1/19/52	20	5	211. Crazy Heart	Decca 27888
3/29/52	9	19	212. Blue Tango .... [I]	Decca 28031
7/26/52	30	1	213. Kiss Of Fire	Decca 28179
8/02/52	13	9	214. Auf Wiederseh'n Sweetheart/	
8/16/52	20	6	215. Half As Much	Decca 28271
9/27/52	26	2	216. Wish You Were Here................................ Broadway musical title song (Decca 29054: Bing Crosby with Guy Lombardo & Royal Canadians)	Decca 28308
2/07/53	26	1	217. John, John, John (Every Tom, Dick and Harry's Called John) .... [N]	Decca 28546
7/07/54	14	4	218. Hernando's Hideaway .... from the Broadway musical "The Pajama Game" unless otherwise noted, nearly all vocals from 195-218 are by Kenny Gardner	Decca 29173

LONDON MAYFAIR ORCHESTRA - see RAY NOBLE

JIMMY LONG - see GENE AUTRY

JOHNNY LONG & HIS ORCHESTRA
Violinist-bandleader who featured singer Dick Robertson; died
on 10/31/72 (56).

DATE CHARTED	PEAK POS	WKS CHRT'D	ARTIST — Record Title	Label & Number
8/16/41	22	1	1. Blue Skies .... vocal: Bob Houston; from the Broadway musical "Betsy"	Decca 3823
3/21/42	21	1	2. Russian Rose	Decca 4126
11/07/42	20	1	3. Can't Get Out Of This Mood .... vocal: Four Teens; from the film "Seven Day Leave"	Decca 4369
1/23/43	10	1	4. Why Don't You Fall In Love With Me?	Decca 4375
2/12/44	5	9	5. No Love, No Nothin' .... from the film "The Gang's All Here"	Decca 4427
2/26/44	23	2	6. I've Had This Feeling Before .... vocals on 4 & 6: Bob Houston & Helen Young	Decca 4429

DATE CHARTED	PEAK POS	WKS CHRT'D	ARTIST — Record Title	Label & Number
7/29/44	**8**	8	7. Time Waits For No One .... from the film "Shine On, Harvest Moon" based on a theme from Strauss' "Tales of the Vienna Woods" vocals on 5 & 7: Patti Dugan	Decca 4439
4/14/45	**3**	12	8. My Dreams Are Getting Better All The Time/ from the film "In Society"	
5/05/45	**8**	8	9. Candy..	Decca 18661
11/24/45	**7**	10	10. Waitin' For The Train To Come In................ Dick Robertson: above three vocals	Decca 18718
10/12/46	**13**	7	11. In A Shanty In Old Shanty Town .... from the film "The Crooner"	Decca 23622
1/08/49	**19**	3	12. Sweet Sue, Just You...............................	Signature 15243
1/21/50	**22**	3	13. We'll Build A Bungalow .... above three vocals by ensemble	King 15018

VINCENT LOPEZ & HIS ORCHESTRA
Long-popular pianist and bandleader who broadcast the first live band performance on radio in 1921; he remained active through the 1960s, and died on 9/20/75 (80).

DATE CHARTED	PEAK POS	WKS CHRT'D	ARTIST — Record Title	Label & Number
7/01/22	**3**	8	1. Nola .... [I] his theme song and most famous piano performance also recorded for Edison Disc 50961 & Edison Amberol 4556	Okeh 4579
7/22/22	**6**	3	2. Teasin' .... [I] also recorded for Edison 50964	Okeh 4591
8/26/22	**3**	7	3. Parade Of The Wooden Soldiers................ [I] also recorded for Okeh 4638	Edison 50987
11/25/22	**11**	1	4. I'm Just Wild About Harry .... [I] from the Broadway musical "Shuffle Along" also recorded for Edison Amberol 4604	Okeh 4647
2/24/23	**11**	1	5. Toot Toot Tootsie (Goo'bye).................... [I] from the Broadway musical "Bombo"	Okeh 4706
4/25/23	**13**	1	6. Away Down East In Maine .... vocal: Aileen Stanley	Okeh 4736
1/19/24	**4**	5	7. Sun-Kist Rose .... [I]	Okeh 4944
2/02/24	**5**	3	8. Covered Wagon Days............................... [I]	Okeh 4946
4/26/24	**9**	2	9. Learn To Do The Strut.............................. [I]	Okeh 4987
5/31/24	**9**	1	10. Steppin' Out .... [I]	Okeh 40024
8/09/24	**8**	2	11. What'll I Do? .... [I] 9 & 11 from the Broadway musical "Music Box Revue of 1923"	Okeh 40097
12/13/24+	**2(2)**	7	12. I Want To Be Happy .... [I] from the Broadway musical "No, No, Nanette"	Okeh 40175
2/07/25	**8**	2	13. You're Just A Flower From An Old Bouquet .. vocal: Bruce Wallace	Okeh 40218
5/09/25	**5**	5	14. O Katharina!.. [I] from the French musical "Chauve Souris"	Okeh 40307
12/12/25	**9**	2	15. Don't Wake Me Up (Let Me Dream)........... [I]	Okeh 40535
2/20/26	**3**	6	16. Show Me The Way To Go Home .... [I]	Okeh 40516
4/03/26	**9**	1	17. Song Of The Vagabonds .... [I] from the Broadway musical "The Vagabond King"	Okeh 40540
5/08/26	**1(2)**	9	18. **Always**... [I]	Okeh 40567
6/12/26	**5**	3	19. Song Of The Flame.................................. [I] Broadway musical title song	Okeh 40586
2/12/27	**3**	7	20. Hello, Bluebird .... vocal: Keller Sisters & Lynch	Brunswick 3368
4/23/27	**9**	5	21. Blue Skies .... from the Broadway musical "Betsy"	Brunswick 3425
7/16/27+	**13**	2	22. So Blue...	Brunswick 3473
10/01/27	**16**	2	23. Just Like A Butterfly (That's Caught In The Rain) .... vocal: Franklyn Baur	Brunswick 3573
12/03/27	**11**	3	24. Just A Memory.. vocals on 21-22 & 24: Frank Munn	Brunswick 3633
7/21/28	**2(2)**	7	25. My Angel (Angela Mia) .... vocal: Lewis James; from the film "Street Angel" Jimmy Dorsey (alto sax/clarinet) on above four	Brunswick 3927
6/30/34	**20**	1	26. Spellbound	Bluebird 5523

DATE CHARTED	PEAK POS	WKS CHRT'D	ARTIST — Record Title	Label & Number
6/25/38	8	10	27. There's Honey On The Moon Tonight........... above two vocals: Johnny Morris	Vocalion 4141
6/10/39	14	1	28. Dark Eyes .... [I]	Bluebird 10283
7/22/39	15	1	29. Igloo.. Betty Hutton, vocal	Bluebird 10300

DENISE LOR

9/01/54	8	12	1. If I Give My Heart To You .... accompanied by Joe Candulo's Orchestra	Major 27

CARL LORCH & HIS ORCHESTRA
Saxophonist/bandleader

2/10/40	18	1	1. Does Your Heart Beat For Me? .... vocal: Shirley Dean	Bluebird 10418

JOE LOSS & HIS ORCHESTRA

9/18/48	17	1	1. A Tree In The Meadow............................ vocal by Howard Jones	RCA Victor 2965

HELEN LOUISE & FRANK FERERA
Husband and wife, masters of the Hawaiian guitar, they played on many of the records constituting this period's "Hawaiian craze". (see Henry Burr & Albert Campbell, Hoarce Wright)

11/24/17	6	2	1. Along The Way To Wakiki...................... [I]	Columbia 2362

JIM LOWE
Songwriter and former disc jockey; hit #1 in 1956 with "The Green Door".

7/18/53	26	1	1. Gambler's Guitar	Mercury 70163

FRED LOWERY
Blind whistler best known for the Leroy Holmes hit "The High and the Mighty"; previously with Hoarce Heidt & Vince Lopez.

BERT LOWN & HIS ORCHESTRA
Pianist-bandleader who featured Ed Farley (trumpet) & Adrian Rollini (baritone sax); co-wrote "Bye Bye Blues".

8/23/30	5	7	1. Bye Bye Blues.. the band's theme song	Columbia 2258
11/01/30	3	7	2. I'm Yours/	
11/01/30	14	3	3. Here Comes The Sun	Victor 22541
1/17/31	11	5	4. You're The One I Care For	Victor 22583
4/18/31	10	5	5. Please Don't Talk About Me When I'm Gone ..	Victor 22652
5/30/31	3	7	6. Now You're In My Arms/	
6/13/31	3	6	7. I Wanna Sing About You .... vocals on 1-3 & 7: Biltmore Rhythm Boys	Victor 22689
2/13/32	6	4	8. Was That The Human Thing To Do?............ Elmer Feldkamp: vocals on 4-6 & 8	Victor 22908

CLYDE LUCAS & HIS CALIFORNIA DONS
Trombonist-bandleader

9/18/37	8	5	1. The Big Apple .... [I]	Variety 631
6/21/41	21	1	2. Intermezzo (A Love Story)...................... [I]	Columbia 36017

NICK LUCAS
Former banjoist for the Russo-Fio Rito band, Nick's easygoing vocal and guitar style made him a national favorite in the late 20s, particularly with the blockbuster hit "Tip Toe Through the Tulips". Long billed as "The Singing Troubador", he reappeared in 1974 singing on the film soundtrack of "The Great Gatsby". Nick died on 7/28/82 (84). (Accompanied on most records only by his own guitar and a pianist.)

2/28/25	4	5	1. My Best Girl...	Brunswick 2768
12/19/25	2(3)	6	2. Brown Eyes, Why Are You Blue?	Brunswick 2961
2/27/26	3	6	3. Sleepy Time Gal	Brunswick 2990
5/22/26	4	4	4. Always	Brunswick 3088
8/14/26	4	4	5. Bye Bye, Blackbird	Brunswick 3184
2/12/27	9	4	6. Hello, Bluebird	Brunswick 3370
4/30/27	2(2)	10	7. I'm Looking Over A Four-Leaf Clover	Brunswick 3439

DATE CHARTED	PEAK POS	WKS CHRT'D	ARTIST — Record Title	Label & Number
7/30/27	**3**	9	8. Side By Side	Brunswick 3512
7/30/27	**13**	2	9. So Blue	Brunswick 3492
10/29/27	**10**	3	10. Broken Hearted	Brunswick 3602
1/28/28	**7**	5	11. My Blue Heaven	Brunswick 3684
3/17/28	**12**	3	12. Together	Brunswick 3749
3/31/28	**4**	8	13. My Ohio Home/	
5/05/28	**12**	2	14. Without You, Sweetheart	Brunswick 3773
5/26/28	**12**	2	15. Sunshine...	Brunswick 3850
9/08/28	**9**	4	16. You're A Real Sweetheart	Brunswick 3966
11/10/28	**5**	5	17. Someday - Somewhere	Brunswick 4026
3/23/29	**11**	3	18. My Tonia	Brunswick 4141
5/11/29	**12**	3	19. I'll Get By	Brunswick 4156
9/28/29	**1(10)**	19	20. **Tip Toe Through The Tulips/**	
10/05/29	**2(5)**	15	21. Painting The Clouds With Sunshine .... above two from the film "Gold Diggers of Broadway"	Brunswick 4418
6/21/30	**15**	2	22. Telling It To The Daisies	Brunswick 4834
12/20/30+	**7**	5	23. You're Driving Me Crazy .... with his Crooning Troubadors from the Broadway musical "Smiles"	Brunswick 4987
1/24/31	**5**	5	24. Lady, Play Your Mandolin	Brunswick 6013
3/07/31	**8**	5	25. Walkin' My Baby Back Home	Brunswick 6048
8/01/31	**7**	6	26. When The Moon Comes Over The Mountain ...	Brunswick 6147

JIMMIE LUNCEFORD & HIS ORCHESTRA

Among the most exciting of all the swing bands of the 30s & 40s;
saxophonist Jimmie Lunceford featured arrangements by trumpeter Sy
Oliver and top musicians Willie Smith (alto sax), Tommy Stevenson
(trumpet), & drummer Jimmy Crawford. Jimmie died on 7/13/47 (45).

DATE CHARTED	PEAK POS	WKS CHRT'D	ARTIST — Record Title	Label & Number
11/10/34	**19**	1	1. Mood Indigo.............................. [I]	Decca 131
5/11/35	**1(1)**	16	2. **Rhythm Is Our Business/** vocal: Willie Smith	
6/29/35	**10**	5	3. Star Dust .... vocal: Henry Wells	Decca 369
5/25/35	**19**	1	4. Black And Tan Fantasy .... [I]	Decca 453
2/15/36	**19**	1	5. Swanee River............................ [I]	Decca 668
10/24/36	**2(3)**	8	6. Organ Grinder's Swing................ [I]	Decca 908
11/28/36	**19**	1	7. T'ain't Good (Like A Nickel Made Of Wood)....	Decca 960
1/09/37	**7**	5	8. (This Is) My Last Affair .... from the Broadway musical "New Faces of 1934"	Decca 1035
3/20/37	**18**	1	9. Slumming On Park Avenue........................ from the film "On the Avenue"	Decca 1128
7/24/37	**7**	4	10. The Merry-Go-Round Broke Down .... vocal: Sy Oliver	Decca 1318
8/07/37	**7**	3	11. For Dancers Only.......................... [I]	Decca 1340
8/28/37	**9**	2	12. 'Posin'	Decca 1355
9/04/37	**8**	6	13. The First Time I Saw You...................... vocals on 8 & 13: Dan Grissom	Decca 1364
12/04/37	**11**	2	14. Put On Your Old Grey Bonnet .... vocal: Eddie Tompkins	Decca 1506
2/04/39	**11**	8	15. T'ain't What You Do (It's The Way That You Do It).. Sy Oliver's most famous Lunceford arrangement	Vocalion 4582
2/07/42	**4**	8	16. Blues In The Night .... vocal: Willie Smith	Decca 4125
5/09/42	**21**	1	17. Life Is Fine .... vocals on 15 & 17: Trummy Young	Decca 4289
5/30/42	**12**	2	18. I'm Gonna Move To The Outskirts Of Town....	Decca 18324
4/15/44	**28**	1	19. Back Door Stuff............................... [I]	Decca 18594
10/21/44	**23**	1	20. I Dream A Lot About You...................... recorded 7/14/42 vocals on 18 & 20: Dan Grissom	Decca 18618

DATE CHARTED	PEAK POS	WKS CHRT'D	ARTIST — Record Title	Label & Number
11/24/45	**10**	3	21. The Honeydripper .... Decca 23451 vocal: Delta Rhythm Boys	Decca 23451
6/15/46	**13**	2	22. Cement Mixer (Put-Ti, Put-Ti) .... [N] Majestic 1045 vocal: Joe Thomas	Majestic 1045

ART LUND
Baritone first known as Art London with Benny Goodman ("Blue Skies"). He had a starring role in the classic 1956 Broadway musical "The Most Happy Fella".

DATE CHARTED	PEAK POS	WKS CHRT'D	ARTIST — Record Title	Label & Number
4/19/47	**1(2)**	13	● 1. **Mam'selle** .... MGM 10011 from the film "The Razor's Edge"	MGM 10011
6/28/47	**4**	13	2. Peg O' My Heart........................... MGM 10037 from Broadway's "Ziegfeld Follies of 1913"	MGM 10037
11/01/47	**14**	2	3. And Mimi .... MGM 10082	MGM 10082
1/24/48	**25**	1	4. But Beautiful/ from the film "The Road to Rio"	
1/31/48	**24**	2	5. Love Is So Terrific .... MGM 10126	MGM 10126
9/25/48	**20**	4	6. Hair Of Gold/ with the Crew Chiefs; from the film "Silver Spurs"	
9/25/48	**22**	1	7. You Call Everybody Darlin' .... MGM 10258	MGM 10258
11/06/48	**12**	12	8. On A Slow Boat To China .... MGM 10269	MGM 10269
2/26/49	**22**	2	9. I've Got My Love To Keep Me Warm .... MGM 10348 from the film "On the Avenue" accompanied on above nine by Johnny Thompson's Orchestra	MGM 10348
7/08/50	**14**	7	10. Mona Lisa .... MGM 10689 from the film "Captain Carey, U.S.A."	MGM 10689
10/11/52	**27**	1	11. Cincinatti Ding Dong .... Coral 60834	Coral 60834
9/26/53	**23**	2	12. Crying In The Chapel...................... Coral 61018 with Ray Charles Singers above three accompanied by Leroy Holmes' Orchestra	Coral 61018

NELLIE LUTCHER & HER RHYTHM
Energetic West Coast singer-pianist

DATE CHARTED	PEAK POS	WKS CHRT'D	ARTIST — Record Title	Label & Number
9/06/47	**20**	5	1. Hurry On Down .... Capitol 40002	Capitol 40002
11/01/47	**15**	1	2. He's A Real Gone Guy .... Capitol Am. 40017	Capitol Am. 40017
1/03/48	**23**	1	3. The Song Is Ended (But The Melody Lingers On) .... Capitol Am. 40063	Capitol Am. 40063
3/20/48	**21**	2	4. Fine Brown Frame .... Capitol 15032	Capitol 15032

FRANK LUTHER
Born Frank Crow, prolific band vocalist (with Arden-Ohman, Johnny Hamp, High Hatters & Hilo Hawaiian) and hillbilly singer. During the 1940s and 50s he achieved his greatest fame with a long series of records and original songs for children, and a network radio show. Frank died on 11/19/80 (75).

DATE CHARTED	PEAK POS	WKS CHRT'D	ARTIST — Record Title	Label & Number
8/17/29	**19**	1	1. The Utah Trail .... Brunswick 4296 FRANK LUTHER & CARSON ROBISON	Brunswick 4296
10/12/29	**13**	2	2. Barnacle Bill The Sailor .... Brunswick 4371	Brunswick 4371
1/31/31	**4**	12	3. When Your Hair Has Turned To Silver/ "BUD & JOE BILLINGS" (Frank Luther & Carson Robison)	
2/14/31	**9**	5	4. I'm Alone Because I Love You................. Victor 22588 as "Bud Billings"	Victor 22588

ABE LYMAN & HIS CALIFORNIA ORCHESTRA
Drummer-bandleader (born Abraham Simon) who co-wrote the hit songs I Cried for You", "Mary Lou", and others. He died on 10/23/57 (60). (Also see Al Jolson)

DATE CHARTED	PEAK POS	WKS CHRT'D	ARTIST — Record Title	Label & Number
11/24/23	**5**	5	1. Midnight Rose .... Brunswick 2478	Brunswick 2478
1/24/25	**10**	1	2. All Alone .... [I] Brunswick 2742 from the Broadway musical "Music Box Revue of 1924"	Brunswick 2742
5/22/26+	**6**	3	3. After I Say I'm Sorry .... Brunswick 3069	Brunswick 3069
7/10/26	**3**	5	4. Mary Lou .... Brunswick 3135 all above vocals: Charles Kaley	Brunswick 3135
7/10/26	**9**	2	5. There's A Blue Ridge In My Heart, Virginia. [I] Brunswick 3139	Brunswick 3139
10/30/26	**11**	1	6. Breezin' Along With The Breeze .... Brunswick 3240	Brunswick 3240
1/01/27	**7**	5	7. Just A Bird's Eye View Of My Old Kentucky Home .... Brunswick 3322	Brunswick 3322

DATE CHARTED	PEAK POS	WKS CHRT'D	ARTIST — Record Title	Label & Number
1/08/27	**13**	3	8. Beside A Garden Wall.................................	Brunswick 3317
1/12/29	**8**	5	9. Sweethearts On Parade...........................	Brunswick 4117
2/23/29	**14**	3	10. Dream Train...	Brunswick 4137
4/25/31	**13**	3	11. In A Cafe On The Road To Calais................	Brunswick 6094
6/27/31	**12**	3	12. It Looks Like Love..................................	Brunswick 6119
7/04/31	**6**	4	13. Just One More Chance............................	Brunswick 6125
8/22/31	**10**	3	14. Give Me Your Affection, Honey................... Brunswick 6154 above five vocals: Phil Neely	Brunswick 6154
1/30/32	**10**	3	15. Of Thee I Sing (Dance Medley) .... Brunswick 20103 vocal: Dick Robertson, Phil Neely & Frank Sylvano medley from the Broadway musical "Of Thee I Sing": Who Cares/Love Is Sweeping The Country	Brunswick 20103
3/19/32	**13**	2	16. Auf Wiedersehen, My Dear	Brunswick 6255
11/18/33	**16**	2	17. Heaven Only Knows .... above two vocals: Phil Neely	Brunswick 6672
2/17/34	**19**	1	18. Keep Young And Beautiful .... from the film "Roman Scandals"	Brunswick 6698
9/22/34	**10**	4	19. I'm In Love .... vocal: Louis Rapp	Brunswick 6968
3/06/37	**2(3)**	8	20. Little Old Lady...................................... vocal: Sonny Schuyler; with Carmen Cavallaro (piano) from the Broadway musical "The Show Is On"	Decca 1120
10/21/39	**10**	7	21. Good Morning .... from the film version of "Babes In Arms"	Bluebird 10424
2/17/40	**13**	5	22. At The Balalaika .... vocal: Ed Holly; from the film "Balalaika"	Bluebird 10533
3/23/40	**19**	1	23. Love Song Of Renaldo............................... vocal: Irving Kahal	Bluebird 10572
6/22/40	**14**	1	24. How Can I Ever Be Alone? .... vocal: Frank Parrish	Bluebird 10731
12/14/40	**11**	7	25. He's My Uncle	Bluebird 10924
3/22/41	**11**	2	26. Help Me (Cuatro Vidas) .... vocal: Dale Evans (Roy Rogers' wife) & Lucia Garcia	Bluebird 10887
8/22/42	**4**	8	27. Amen	Bluebird 11542
2/19/44	**21**	2	28. Besame Mucho .... Hit 7072 with Si Zentner (trombone); song based on "nightingale" aria from "Goyescas"	Hit 7072
3/10/45	**8**	5	29. Rum And Coca-Cola .... Columbia 36775 uses calypso melody from Trinidad ("L'Anee Passee", 1906) Rose Blane: vocals on 21, 25, 27-29	Columbia 36775

VERA LYNN
England's most popular female singer during World War II, formerly
with Ambrose orchestra; on British TV for many years.

DATE CHARTED	PEAK POS	WKS CHRT'D	ARTIST — Record Title	Label & Number
5/22/48	**9**	7	1. You Can't Be True, Dear .... with Bob Farndon's Orchestra	London 202
1/29/49	**23**	3	2. Again .... with Bruce Campbell's Orchestra; from the film "Roadhouse"	London 310
6/21/52	**1(9)**	21	● 3. **Auf Wiederseh'n Sweetheart**....................	London 1227
10/25/52	**7**	10	4. Yours (Quierme Mucho)............................ Spanish song; from the film "Orchestra Wives"	London 1261
1/02/54	**29**	1	5. We'll Meet Again .... this recording was heard at the climax of the 1964 film "Dr. Strangelove"; above two with Soldiers, Sailors, & Airmen of Her Majesty's Forces accompanied on above three by Roland Shaw's Orchestra	London 1348
4/03/54	**21**	5	6. If You Love Me (Really Love Me)	London 1412
11/20/54	**28**	1	7. My Son, My Son...................................... with Frank Weir's Orchestra	London 1501

LYRIC QUARTET
Originally composed of Harry Macdonough, Frank Stanley (died in
1910), Elise Stevenson, & Corrine Morgan, its membership from 1913
on was Macdonough, Reinald Werrenrath, Olive Kline, & Elsie Baker.

DATE CHARTED	PEAK POS	WKS CHRT'D	ARTIST — Record Title	Label & Number
2/18/11	**5**	4	1. Winter	Victor 5814
4/15/11	**10**	1	2. Merry Wedding Bells .... from the Broadway musical "He Came from Miwaukee"	Victor 5815

DATE CHARTED	PEAK POS	WKS CHRT'D	ARTIST — Record Title	Label & Number
9/30/11	**6**	2	3. For Every Boy Who's Lonely, There's A Girl Who's Lonely.................................... *from the Broadway musical "Dr. DeLuxe"*	Victor 5849
1/06/12	**6**	2	4. There's A Girl In Havana.......................... *from the Broadway musical "The Never Homes"*	Victor 16985
3/02/12	**7**	2	5. Day Dreams, Visions Of Bliss .... CHRISTIE MACDONALD & LYRIC QUARTET *from the Broadway musical "The Spring Maid"*	Victor 60061
8/03/12	**7**	2	6. A Girl Like Me.............................. ELIZABETH WHEELER & LYRIC QUARTET *from the Broadway musical "A Winsome Widow"*	Victor 17095
1/04/13	**6**	3	7. Where The Edelweiss Is Blooming................ *from the Broadway musical "Hanky Panky"*	Victor 17194
8/01/14	**8**	2	8. When The Angelus Is Ringing	Victor 17587
7/31/15	**3**	7	9. Down Among The Sheltering Palms..............	Victor 17778
8/26/16	**9**	1	10. My Dreamy China Lady............................	Victor 18034
7/14/17	**7**	2	11. You're In Love .... *Broadway musical title song*	Victor 18260

JIMMY LYTELL & HIS ALL-STAR SEVEN
Jazz clarinetist (born James Sarrapede), with Original Dixieland Jazz Band & Cotton Pickers in 1920s, Broadway show bandleader in 30s, later an orchestra conductor & radio musical director; died on 11/26/72 (67). (Also see Teresa Brewer, & Morton Downey)

1/02/43	**11**	3	1. Fat Meat Is Good Meat .... *Savannah Churchill, vocal*	Beacon 104

LYTTLE SISTERS - see TONY MARTIN

M

CHRISTIE MacDONALD
Canadian-born star of many Broadway musicals from 1898-1920; Victor Herbert wrote "Sweethearts" especially for her. Christie died on 7/25/62 (87).

2/03/12	**5**	3	1. Two Little Love Bees................................ CHRISTIE MacDONALD & REINALD WERRENRATH	Victor 60060
3/02/12	**7**	2	2. Day Dreams, Visions Of Bliss .... CHRISTIE MacDONALD & LYRIC QUARTET *above two from the Broadway musical "The Spring Maid"*	Victor 60061
7/26/13	**3**	9	3. The Angelus .... CHRISTIE MacDONALD, REINALD WERRENRATH & VICTOR MALE CHORUS	Victor 70099
8/09/13	**2(2)**	9	4. Sweethearts... *above two from the Broadway musical "Sweethearts"*	Victor 60101

JEANETTE MacDONALD
Beautiful soprano star of over two dozen movie musicals, including eight with Nelson Eddy. She died on 1/14/65 (63).

9/27/30	**9**	4	1. Beyond The Blue Horizon........................ *from the film "Monte Carlo" accompanied by Leroy Shield's Orchestra*	Victor 22514
12/26/36+	**8**	6	● 2. Indian Love Call .... JEANETTE MacDONALD & NELSON EDDY *accompanied by Nat Shilkret's Orchestra from the film "Rose Marie"*	Victor 4323

HARRY MacDONOUGH
Born John S. MacDonald in Ontario, Canada on 3/30/1871, tenor Harry Macdonough became second only to Henry Burr among the great ballad singers of recordings' pioneer pre-1920 era. A member of the Edison, Haydn, Lyric, and Orpheus Quartets, and also of the Victor Light Opera Co., Harry was a top record company executive after World War I; he died on 9/26/31. (also see Nicholas Orlando, Joseph C. Smith, & Sousa's Band, and aforementioned groups)

11/18/99	**2(3)**	4	1. 'Mid The Green Fields Of Virginia .... HARRY MACDONOUGH & S.H. DUDLEY	Edison 7262
12/02/99	**4**	2	2. Just As The Sun Went Down .... HARRY MACDONOUGH & JOHN BIELING	Berliner 0552

DATE CHARTED	PEAK POS	WKS CHRT'D	ARTIST — Record Title	Label & Number
3/10/00	**3**	3	3. Mandy Lee..	Berliner 0801
6/16/00	**2(2)**	3	4. My Sunny Southern Home	Berliner 0940
9/08/00	**2(2)**	4	5. When We Are Married................................	Edison 7558
			HARRY MACDONOUGH & GRACE SPENCER from the Broadway musical "The Belle of New York" later recorded for Victor 904	
10/06/00	**3**	4	6. My Wild Irish Rose	Gram-o-Phone 99
			from the Broadway musical "A Romance of Athlone"	
10/20/00	**2(3)**	4	7. A Bird In A Gilded Cage	Edison 7587
11/10/00	**2(2)**	7	8. I Can't Tell Why I Love You, But I Do	Edison 7595
			later recorded for Gram-o-Phone 533	
11/24/00	**2(1)**	5	9. The Holy City...	Gram-o-Phone 94
			also on Victor 3012	
12/01/00	**4**	2	10. I Love You Just The Same	Edison 7610
4/27/01	**1(7)**	11	11. **Tell Me, Pretty Maiden**	Edison 7758
			HARRY MACDONOUGH & GRACE SPENCER from the Broadway musical "Florodora" later recorded for Victor 1362 & 3501	
5/11/01	**2(1)**	4	12. When The Harvest Days Are Over	Gram-o-Phone 652
			also recorded on Gram-o-Phone 3079	
5/18/01	**2(2)**	5	13. Good-Bye, Dolly Gray	Gram-o-Phone 655
			also on Victor 3083	
6/08/01	**4**	2	14. Hearts And Flowers..................................	Edison 7789
8/17/01	**3**	2	15. When You Were Sweet Sixteen	Victor 769
			also recorded for Zon-o-Phone 9473	
8/24/01	**3**	3	16. Sweet Annie Moore	Victor 775
			HARRY MACDONOUGH & S.H. DUDLEY also on Victor 3318	
9/21/01	**3**	3	17. In The Shade Of The Palm	Gram-o-Phone 55
			from the Broadway musical "Florodora"; this recording was substituted in 1901 for a previous Gram-o-Phone 55	
10/05/01	**1(4)**	7	18. The Tale Of The Bumble Bee.....................	Victor 908
			from the Broadway musical "King Dodo"; also on Victor 3508	
10/12/01	**1(3)**	8	19. **Absence Makes The Heart Grow Fonder**	Victor 907
			also recorded for Edison 7870	
10/12/01	**3**	4	20. I've A Longing In My Heart For You, Louise...	Victor 909
12/21/01	**3**	4	21. I'll Be With You When The Roses Bloom Again	Edison 7942
12/21/01	**4**	2	22. The Wedding Of Reuben And The Maid	Victor 951
			from the Broadway musical "Rogers Brothers in Washington"	
2/15/02	**4**	2	23. Bye And Bye You Will Forget Me	Victor 1329
			HARRY MACDONOUGH & S.H. DUDLEY	
4/26/02	**3**	4	24. Home, Sweet Home	Victor 1214
			with Charles D'Almaine (violin)	
6/07/02	**4**	2	25. My Carolina Lady	Victor 1269
8/16/02	**5**	2	26. On A Sunday Afternoon............................	Victor 1391
8/30/02	**3**	3	27. Jennie Lee	Victor 1395
8/30/02	**4**	2	28. Josephine, My Jo....................................	Victor 1393
9/13/02	**1(4)**	11	29. **The Mansion Of Aching Hearts**	Victor 1415
12/06/02	**3**	2	30. My Beautiful Irish Maid...........................	Victor 1617
1/24/03	**2(2)**	7	31. In The Good Old Summer Time...................	Victor 1655
			from the Broadway musical "The Defender" Harry also recorded this classic with Sousa's Band (Victor 1833)	
4/25/03	**1(4)**	11	32. **In The Sweet Bye And Bye**......................	Victor 1855
			HARRY MACDONOUGH & JOHN BIELING	
5/02/03	**5**	2	33. Two Eyes Of Blue...................................	Edison 8353
			also recorded for Victor 1921	
5/16/03	**3**	4	34. Heidelberg..	Victor 1920
			from the Broadway musical "The Prince of Pilsen"	
5/23/03	**4**	3	35. Since I First Met You..............................	Victor 1922
7/04/03	**1(4)**	9	36. **Hiawatha**	Edison 8425
			also recorded for Victor 2351	

DATE CHARTED	PEAK POS	WKS CHRT'D	ARTIST — Record Title	Label & Number
7/11/03	4	2	37. Tessie.. HARRY MACDONOUGH & S.H. DUDLEY from the Broadway musical "The Silver Slipper"	Victor 2056
9/05/03	2(1)	6	38. Beautiful Bird, Sing On .... with bird singing by Joe Belmont	Victor 2332
12/12/03	4	1	39. When Kate And I Were Comin' Thro' The Rye	Victor 2458
12/26/03+	3	4	40. By The Sycamore Tree............................ from the Broadway musical "Rogers Brothers in London"	Edison 8526
1/16/04	3	3	41. I Love Only One Girl In The Wide, Wide World... from the Broadway musical "The Wizard of Oz"	Victor 2515
2/13/04	5	2	42. The Girl You Love.................................. from the Broadway musical "The Silver Slipper"	Victor 2565
2/27/04	5	1	43. Peggy Brady .... from the Broadway musical "The Isle of Spice"	Victor 2574
4/30/04	3	4	44. Navajo .... also recorded for Edison 8640 from the Broadway musical "Nancy Brown"	Victor 2656
6/25/04	5	1	45. My San Domingo Maid .... from the Broadway musical "The Yankee Consul"	Victor 2697
9/03/04	5	1	46. Good-Bye, My Lady Love........................ also recorded for Edison 8684	Victor 2851
1/28/05	3	4	47. Sweet Thoughts Of Home	Victor 4132
1/28/05	7	1	48. My Cozy Corner Girl............................... from the Broadway musical "The School Girl"	Victor 4062
3/18/05	3	4	49. Marguerite... HARRY MACDONOUGH & JOHN BIELING	Edison 8938
4/29/05	9	1	50. You And I... HARRY MACDONOUGH & FLORENCE HAYWARD from the Broadway musical "The Isle of Spice"	Victor 4272
6/24/05	6	1	51. Tale Of The Turtle Dove........................... from the Broadway musical "Woodland"	Columbia 32687
9/30/05	6	1	52. Dearie	Edison 9054
12/09/05	3	3	53. In The Valley Of Yesterday	Victor 4504
4/28/06	4	2	54. If A Girl Like You Loved A Boy Like Me........ also recorded for Edison 9175	Victor 4601
4/28/06	6	1	55. When The Mocking Birds Are Singing In The Wildwood...	Victor 4665
6/23/06	3	4	56. My Old Kentucky Home	Victor 4672
9/22/06	2(2)	5	57. Where The River Shannon Flows	Edison 9344
11/10/06	3	3	58. Ain't You Coming Back To Old New Hampshire, Molly?............................	Victor 4828
1/05/07	3	3	59. In The Evening By The Moonlight, Dear Louise...	Victor 4871
1/26/07	8	1	60. A Flower From Home, Sweet Home .... HARRY MACDONOUGH & JOHN BIELING	Victor 4877
2/23/07	8	1	61. Almost Persuaded................................... HARRY MACDONOUGH & FRANK STANLEY	Victor 4917
4/20/07	1(2)	7	62. **Because You're You** .... HARRY MACDONOUGH & ELISE STEVENSON also recorded for Columbia 3590; from the Broadway musical "The Red Mill"; Macdonough & Florence Hinkle recorded song for Edison 9478	Victor 5020
6/15/07	3	3	63. The Tale The Church Bell Tolled .... also recorded for Edison 9522	Victor 5121
9/07/07	5	1	64. Sweet Julienne......................................	Victor 5176
10/26/07	6	1	65. Dreaming	Victor 5189
12/14/07+	1(5)	12	66. **My Dear**	Victor 5293
12/28/07	9	1	67. Messiah: Every Valley Shall Be Exalted .... [X]	Victor 31672
2/22/08	3	6	68. I Love You So.. HARRY MACDONOUGH & ELISE STEVENSON	Victor 5340
3/28/08	4	1	69. Some Day You'll Come Back To Me .... HARRY MACDONOUGH & FRANK STANLEY	Victor 5366

DATE CHARTED	PEAK POS	WKS CHRT'D	ARTIST — Record Title	Label & Number
4/25/08	8	1	70. One Sweet Little Girl .... Victor 5352	
			from the Broadway musical "O'Neill of Derry"	
5/30/08	4	2	71. Maxim's .... Victor 5394	
			68 & 71 from the Broadway musical "The Merry Widow"	
6/06/08	4	2	72. Sweetheart Days .... Victor 5407	
6/27/08	3	5	73. Kiss Duet (Sweetest Maid Of All)................. Victor 5446	
			HARRY MACDONOUGH & ELISE STEVENSON	
			from the Broadway musical "A Waltz Dream"	
9/19/08	2(1)	5	74. Over The Hills And Far Away...................... Victor 5506	
10/31/08	6	1	75. When Sweet Marie Was Sweet Sixteen .... Victor 5505	
			above two: HARRY MACDONOUGH & JOHN BIELING	
2/27/09	8	1	76. There Never Was A Girl Like You .... Victor 5630	
4/10/09	1(9)	14	77. Shine On, Harvest Moon............................ Victor 16259	
			from Broadway's "Ziegfeld Follies of 1908"	
4/24/09	9	1	78. The Message Of The Red Rose.................... Victor 5667	
			from the Broadway musical "Marcelle"	
			above two duets with unidentified "Miss Walton" -	
			believed to be Elise Stevenson	
2/05/10	4	3	79. When I Marry You................................... Victor 16433	
			HARRY MACDONOUGH & ELIZABETH WHEELER	
2/12/10	1(6)	13	80. Where The River Shannon Flows.............. Victor 16440	
			new version of his 1906 hit	
8/06/10	8	2	81. Ring O' Roses............................... Victor 31783	
			from the Broadway musical "The Dollar Princess"	
9/03/10	1(4)	13	82. Every Little Movement........................... Victor 5784	
			from the Broadway musical "Madame Sherry"	
			above two: HARRY MACDONOUGH & LUCY ISABELLE MARSH	
10/08/10	1(2)	11	83. In The Valley Of Yesterday .... Victor 16535	
12/11/11+	1(7)	18	84. Down By The Old Mill Stream.................. Victor 17000	
6/01/12	3	7	85. When I Was Twenty-One And You Were	
			Sweet Sixteen .... Victor 17057	
			HARRY MACDONOUGH & AMERICAN QUARTET	
3/01/13	8	2	86. A Little Girl At Home .... Victor 17220	
			HARRY MACDONOUGH & MARGUERITE DUNLAP	
			from the Broadway musical "Lady of the Slipper"	
7/26/13	3	7	87. When Irish Eyes Are Smiling.................... Victor 17317	
			from the Broadway musical "The Isle O' Dreams"	
10/18/13	2(4)	12	88. There's A Girl In The Heart Of Maryland	
			(With A Heart That Belongs To Me)........ Victor 17401	
10/18/13	5	5	89. On The Banks Of The Wabash.................... Victor 17397	
			HARRY MACDONOUGH & AMERICAN QUARTET	
1/31/14	8	1	90. When It's Apple Blossom Time In Normandy.. Victor 17445	
			HARRY MACDONOUGH & MARGUERITE DUNLAP	
			from the Broadway musical "Roly Poly"	
			song based on Beethoven's "Minuet in G"	
6/27/14	10	1	91. You're Here And I'm Here .... Victor 17555	
			HARRY MACDONOUGH & OLIVE KLINE	
			from the Broadway musical "The Laughing Husband"	
5/22/15	5	3	92. Sweet Kentucky Lady (Dry Your Eyes)........ Victor 17723	
11/06/15	2(1)	7	93. Auf Wiedersehen .... Victor 17858	
			from the Broadway musical "The Blue Paradise"	
11/13/15	1(7)	12	94. They Didn't Believe Me .... Victor 35491	
			from the Broadway musical "The Girl from Utah"	
			above two: HARRY MACDONOUGH & "ALICE GREEN" (Olive Kline)	
2/12/16	3	5	95. Araby .... Victor 17889	
4/15/16	1(3)	9	96. The Girl On The Magazine .... Victor 17945	
			from the Broadway musical "Stop! Look! Listen!"	
			flip side of Billy Murray's #1 hit "I Love a Piano"	
			the first double-sided #1 hit record	
1/06/17	2(1)	6	97. Babes In The Wood .... Victor 18172	
			HARRY MACDONOUGH & "ANNA HOWARD" (Lucy Isabelle Marsh)	
			from the Broadway musical "Very Good, Eddie"	
2/16/18	9	1	98. Wait Till The Cows Come Home................. Victor 18408	
			HARRY MACDONOUGH & "ALICE GREEN" (Olive Kline)	
			from the Broadway musical "Jack O' Lantern"	
10/12/18	9	1	99. Good-Bye, Mother Machree .... Victor 18488	
			HARRY MACDONOUGH & SHANNON FOUR	

DATE CHARTED	PEAK POS	WKS CHRT'D	ARTIST — Record Title	Label & Number
			GEORGE MacFARLANE Canadian-born baritone who starred on Broadway and in Gilbert & Sullivan operettas; he died on 2/22/32 (54).	
8/15/14	**6**	3	1. When It's Night Time Down In Burghandy	Victor 60121
10/24/14	**4**	5	2. Can't You Hear Me Calling, Caroline?	Victor 60123
5/01/15	**1(5)**	15	3. **A Little Bit Of Heaven ("Shure, They Call It Ireland")** .... from the Broadway musical "The Heart of Paddy Whack"	Victor 60132
2/05/16	**8**	1	4. My Own Home Town In Ireland	Victor 45074
			GISELE MacKENZIE Born Gisele Lefleche in Winnipeg, Canada, she became popular singing on TV's "Your Hit Parade" (1953-57); also a pianist & violinist.	
2/02/52	**20**	1	1. La Fiacre	Capitol 1907
8/09/52	**14**	4	2. Adios	Capitol 2156
11/29/52	**21**	3	3. Water Can't Quench The Fire Of Love	Capitol 2266
12/06/52+	**11**	3	4. Don't Let The Stars Get In Your Eyes	Capitol 2256
			all solo records with Buddy Cole's Orchestra	
4/25/53	**25**	1	5. Lipstick-a-Powder-'n Paint .... 3 & 5: GISELE MacKENZIE & HELEN O'CONNELL both accompanied by "Dave Cavanaugh's Music"	Captiol 2404
			FRED MacMURRAY Longtime movie and TV star ("My Three Sons", 1960-72) who played tenor sax for Gus Arnheim & George Olsen bands in early 1930s.	
			GORDON MacRAE Baritone star of the classic movie musicals "Oklahoma!" and "Carousel", Gordon sang with Hoarce Heidt (1942-43), and recorded numerous duet hits with Jo Stafford. In 1967 he was featured in the Broadway hit "I Do, I Do!". Gordon died on 1/24/86 (64). (also see Jo Stafford)	
11/15/47	**25**	2	1. I Still Get Jealous	Capitol 15002
12/20/47+	**20**	4	2. At The Candlelight Cafe .... from the film "Tisa"	Capitol 15014
2/21/48	**28**	1	3. Thoughtless/	
3/06/48	**22**	2	4. You Were Meant For Me	Capitol 15027
4/03/48	**27**	1	5. That Feathery Feelin'	Capitol 15041
7/03/48	**9**	17	6. It's Magic .... accompanied by Carlyle Hall's Orchestra from the film "Romance On the High Seas"	Capitol 15072
7/24/48	**23**	1	7. Hankerin'	Capitol 15128
8/28/48	**7**	14	8. Hair Of Gold, Eyes Of Blue/ from the film "Silver Spurs"	
10/23/48	**27**	1	9. Rambling Rose .... above two with the Starlighters	Capitol 15178
3/05/49	**20**	9	10. So In Love .... from the Broadway musical "Kiss Me, Kate"	Capitol 15357
7/16/49	**30**	1	11. Younger Than Springtime .... from the Broadway musical "South Pacific" unless otherwise noted, most above records accompanied by Paul Weston's Orchestra	Capitol 598
11/26/49	**14**	4	12. Mule Train/	
12/24/49	**19**	2	13. Dear Hearts And Gentle People .... above two with Andy Parker's Orchestra & the Plainsmen	Capitol 777
2/28/53	**30**	1	14. How Do You Speak To An Angel?/ from the Broadway musical "Hazel Flagg"	
3/28/53	**28**	2	15. Congratulations To Someone	Capitol 2352
6/06/53	**29**	1	16. C'est Magnifique .... with Axel Stordahl's Orchestra from the Broadway musical "Can-Can"	Capitol 2465
12/05/53	**29**	1	17. Stranger In Paradise .... with Van Alexander's Orchestra from the Broadway musical "Kismet"	Capitol 2652
6/12/54	**30**	1	18. Face To Face	Capitol 2760

DATE CHARTED	PEAK POS	WKS CHRT'D	ARTIST — Record Title	Label & Number
			JOHNNY MADDOX & THE RHYTHMASTERS Honky tonk pianist-bandleader	
9/20/52	26	1	1. The Little Grass Shack .... [I]	Dot 15020
1/31/53	16	5	2. In The Mood .... [I]	Dot 15045
5/02/53	21	1	3. Twilight Time....................................... [I]	Dot 15062
8/08/53	21	1	4. Eight Beat Boogie .... [I]	Dot 15090
11/07/53	15	2	5. Dipsy Doodle .... [I]	Dot 15182
			A.D. MADEIRA Baritone Addison Dashiell Madeira was an opera singer before his recording career; also a member of the Big Four Quartet. He died on 10/8/30 (71).	
2/03/00	2(2)	6	1. In The Shadow Of The Pines .... BYRON HARLAN & A.D. MADEIRA	Edison 7347
			BETTY MADIGAN	
5/29/54	12	8	1. Joey...	MGM 11716
10/09/54	21	4	2. Always You .... with The Ray Charles Singers orchestra on above two directed by Joe Lipman	MGM 11812
			ENRIC MADRIGUERA & HIS ORCHESTRA Violinist-bandleader born in Barcelona, helped popularize Latin-American music. He died on 9/7/73 (69).	
8/13/32	7	4	1. It Was So Beautiful .... from the film "The Big Broadcast of 1932"	Columbia 18006
1/28/33	12	2	2. May I Have This Waltz, Madame	Columbia 2740
1/28/33	19	1	3. At The Baby Parade	Columbia 2735
2/17/34	6	9	4. Orchids In The Moonlight/	
2/24/34	1(2)	10	5. **The Carioca**...................................... [I] vocal: Patricia Gilmore; above two from the film "Flying Down To Rio"	Columbia 2885
3/03/34	13	3	6. There Goes My Heart..............................	Columbia 2888
3/17/34	3	11	7. True..	Columbia 2896
1/19/35	13	3	8. Blow, Gabriel, Blow .... from the Broadway musical "Anything Goes"	Victor 24818
2/02/35	17	2	9. If There Is Someone Lovelier Than You .... from the Broadway musical "Revenge With Music"	Victor 24768
6/22/35	11	2	10. Chasing Shadows...................................	Victor 25047
9/28/35	20	1	11. Nothing Lives Longer Than Love	Victor 25114
11/02/35	3	8	12. I Found A Dream .... from the film "Redheads on Parade"	Victor 25162
11/02/35	5	5	13. Here's To Romance .... [I] movie title song	Victor 25154
11/09/35	19	1	14. When The Leaves Bid The Trees Goodbye/ vocals on 10 & 14: Bob Bunch	
12/07/35	14	2	15. It Never Dawned On Me............................ vocals on 8-9, 11, 13, & 15: Tony Sacco	Victor 25163
4/26/41	21	1	16. Intermezzo .... [I]	Victor 27355
4/08/44	7	3	17. I Love You/ from the Broadway musical "Mexican Hayride"	
5/06/44	24	2	18. Someday I'll Meet You Again .... above two vocals: Bob Lido	Hit 7077
			JERE MAHONEY Member of the Edison Male Quartet (1896-1900).	
3/03/00	1(5)	11	1. **When You Were Sweet Sixteen**.................	Edison 7410
4/14/00	1(5)	10	2. **A Bird In A Gilded Cage**...........................	Edison 7440
2/02/02	3	4	3. For Old Times' Sake	Edison 7680
			MATTY MALNECK Played violin with Paul Whiteman (1927-38), composed many popular songs ("Pardon My Southern Accent", "Goody Goody"); orchestra conductor for Bing Crosby.	

DATE CHARTED	PEAK POS	WKS CHRT'D	ARTIST — Record Title	Label & Number
			### RICHARD MALTBY & HIS ORCHESTRA Bandleader who previously played trumpet for Little Jack Little & Henry Busse.	
10/02/54	21	5	1. St. Louis Blues Mambo .... [I]	"X" 0042
12/25/54	27	1	2. Stardust Mambo .... [I]	"X" 0075
			### SILVANA MANGANO Sultry Italian movie star	
4/11/53	5	17	● 1. Anna .... [F] movie title song	MGM 11457
			### MANHANSETT QUARTETTE The first vocal group to make commercial records in its own name: George J. Gaskin, Gilbert Girard, Joe Riley, & "Evans"; John Bieling became a member in 1894.	
3/26/92	1(6)	6	1. **The Picture Turned Toward The Wall**....... also recorded for New Jersey	North American
5/07/92	1(3)	3	2. **Sally In Our Alley** .... also recorded for New Jersey	North American
1/06/94	2(2)	2	3. The Old Oaken Bucket...........................	New Jersey
			### ESTELLA MANN & JOHN HAVENS Concert soprano Estella Mann was one of the first women to make commercial records, as a member of the Lyric Trio in the late 1890s; she died in August, 1947.	
11/26/98	3	2	1. When We Are Married........................ from the Broadway musical "The Belle of New York"	New Jersey
			### SHELLY MANNE Leading modern jazz drummer with Bobby Byrne, Raymond Scott, Stan Kenton (1946-47, 50-51) & Woody Herman (1949), later bandleader.	
			### BOB MANNING	
4/11/53	16	6	1. The Nearness Of You............................. from the film "Romance in the Dark"	Capitol 2383
8/15/53	27	1	2. All I Desire .... with Sid Feller's Orchestra; movie title song	Capitol 2493
2/27/54	29	1	3. Venus De Milo.................................... 1 & 3 accompanied by Monty Kelly & His Orchestra	Capitol 2694
			### WINGY MANONE & HIS ORCHESTRA Trumpet star who lost his right arm in a childhood accident; he composed "Tar Paper Stomp", which Glenn Miller later made famous in revised form as "In the Mood". (All vocals by Wingy)	
8/10/35	20	1	1. Rhythm Is Our Business...........................	Vocalion 2990
2/15/36	5	8	2. Please Believe Me	Vocalion 3159
3/21/36	14	2	3. Nickel In The Slot .... vocal: Wingy Manone & Nappy Lamare; recorded 1/15/35, originally released on Okeh 41573	Vocalion 3171
5/16/36	14	4	4. You Started Me Dreaming/	
6/06/36	16	2	5. Tormented .... Eddie Miller (tenor sax) on above three	Bluebird 6359
11/27/37	18	2	6. Everything You Said Came True	Bluebird 7197
7/23/38	18	1	7. The Flat Foot Floogee.............................	Bluebird 7621
			### MANTOVANI & HIS ORCHESTRA Annunzio Paulo Mantovani was born in Venice, and played classical violin in England before forming his own orchestra in the early 30s, but only achieved international fame twenty years later with his 40-piece orchestra and distinctive "cascading strings" sound.	
11/30/35	2(1)	7	1. Red Sails In The Sunset .... [I] British song from the Broadway musical "Provincetown Follies"	Columbia 3097
12/26/36+	7	6	2. Serenade In The Night .... [I] based on "Violino Tzigano"	Columbia 3159
11/17/51	10	19	● 3. Charmaine .... [I] written to promote the 1927 silent film "What Price Glory?"	London 1020
3/15/52	25	1	4. Greensleeves .... [I]	London 1171
4/19/52	26	1	5. Dancing With Tears In My Eyes................ [I]	London 1175

DATE CHARTED	PEAK POS	WKS CHRT'D	ARTIST — Record Title	Label & Number
12/27/52	**23**	1	6. White Christmas................................... [I-X] from the film "Holiday Inn"	London 1280
5/16/53	**8**	10	● 7. The "Moulin Rouge" Theme (Where Is Your Heart)... [I]	London 1328
8/14/54	**10**	18	● 8. Cara Mia .... DAVID WHITFIELD WITH MANTOVANI	London 1486

TOMMY MARA

6/13/53	**28**	1	1. I'll Try... accompanied by Monty Kelly & His Orchestra	Jubilee 6040

MUZZY MARCELLINO
Featured vocalist & guitarist with Ted Fio Rito in 30s ("Willow Weep for Me", "I'll String Along With You"); his whistling was featured on 1954 sountrack of "The High and the Mighty".

MARINERS
Vocal group featured on Arthur Godfrey's TV show.

7/29/50	**16**	10	1. Sometime	Columbia 38781
12/29/51	**30**	1	2. They Call The Wind Maria .... from the Broadway musical "Paint Your Wagon" above two accompanied by Archie Bleyer & His Orchestra	Columbia 39568
9/19/53	**14**	14	3. I See The Moon.. accompanied by David Rhodes & His Orchestra	Columbia 40047

MIKE MARKEL'S ORCHESTRA
Pianist-bandleader

5/18/18	**8**	1	1. Sweet Emmaline, My Gal......................... [I] "Sargeant Markel's Orchestra"	Victor 18450
9/30/22	**15**	1	2. Suez... [I]	Okeh 4614

MARLIN SISTERS

6/12/48	**19**	4	1. You Can't Be True, Dear/ MARLIN SISTERS WITH EDDIE FISHER	
6/26/48	**30**	1	2. Toolie Oolie Doolie (The Yodel Polka)	Columbia 38211
7/24/48	**24**	4	3. My Happiness.. above three with the Columbians	Columbia 38217

MARIAN MARLOWE
Ballad singer featured with Frank Parker on Arthur Godfrey's TV show.

10/30/54	**27**	1	1. Whither Thou Goest .... orchestra directed by Will Roland	Columbia 40315

CHARLES MARSH

6/18/92	**1(3)**	3	1. **Throw Him Down, McCloskey**....................	Columbia

LUCY ISABELLE MARSH
Popular concert soprano, also a member of The Victor Light Opera Co.; she died on 1/20/56 (77).

6/20/08	**1(5)**	10	1. **The Glow-Worm**...................................... from the 1902 German operetta "Lysistrata"; featured in the Broadway musical "The Girl Behind the Counter"	Columbia 3791
6/18/10	**2(2)**	7	2. My Hero .... from the Broadway musical "The Chocolate Soldier"	Victor 60012
8/06/10	**8**	2	3. Ring O' Roses.. from the Broadway musical "The Dollar Princess"	Victor 31783
9/03/10	**1(4)**	13	4. **Every Little Movement**............................ from the Broadway musical "Madame Sherry" above two: HARRY MACDONOUGH & LUCY ISABELLE MARSH	Victor 5784
3/04/11	**2(2)**	9	5. Italian Street Song .... LUCY ISABELLE MARSH & THE VICTOR LIGHT OPERA CO. from the Broadway musical "Naughty Marietta"	Victor 60031
7/08/11	**3**	8	6. My Beautiful Lady .... from the Broadway musical "The Pink Lady"	Victor 60040
3/02/12	**10**	1	7. Melody Of Love .... from the Broadway musical "Gypsy Love"	Victor 60059
3/30/12	**5**	4	8. The Maids Of Cadiz (Les Filles De Cadiz)	Victor 60069

DATE CHARTED	PEAK POS	WKS CHRT'D	ARTIST — Record Title	Label & Number
4/13/12	5	3	9. To The Land Of My Own Romance (I Have A Dream, By Night, By Day).................... *from the Broadway musical "The Enchantress"*	Victor 60066
1/25/13	6	3	10. Homeland............................ *from the Broadway musical "The Merry Countess"*	Victor 70086
2/13/15	9	1	11. Aida - O Terra Addio ("Farewell, Oh Earth") [F] JOHN McCORMACK & LUCY ISABELLE MARSH	Victor 74398
8/05/16	10	1	12. Just A-Wearyin' For You...........................	Victor 45090
1/06/17	2(1)	6	13. Babes In The Wood .... HARRY MACDONOUGH & "ANNA HOWARD" (Lucy) *from the Broadway musical "Very Good, Eddie"*	Victor 18172
4/30/21	15	1	14. Deep In Your Eyes .... *from the Broadway musical "The Half Moon"*	Victor 45214
4/15/22	2(1)	8	15. The Song Of Love .... LUCY ISABELLE MARSH & ROYAL DADMUN *from the Broadway musical "Blossom Time" · melody adapted from a theme in Schubert's "Unfinished" Symphony*	Victor 45304

RALPH MARTERIE & HIS ORCHESTRA
Very popular early-50s bandleader, born in Naples, Italy (grew up in Chicago); played trumpet in the 40s for Enric Madriguera, and other bands.

DATE CHARTED	PEAK POS	WKS CHRT'D	ARTIST — Record Title	Label & Number
3/03/51	26	1	1. So Long (It's Been Good To Know Yuh)	Mercury 5570
1/10/53	6	10	2. Pretend.. [I]	Mercury 70045
3/21/53	6	11	● 3. Caravan .... [I]	Mercury 70097
6/20/53	13	4	4. Crazy, Man, Crazy................................... *vocal: Larry Rogen & Smarty-Airs*	Mercury 70153
11/14/53	27	1	5. Warsaw Concerto............................... [I] *from the film "Suicide Squadron"*	Mercury 70221
1/09/54	25	1	6. The Creep .... [I] *from the Mexican film "O Cangaceiro"*	Mercury 70281
8/28/54	3	15	7. Skokiaan.. [I] *South African song, named for a Zulu tribal drink*	Mercury 70432

CHRIS MARTIN

DATE CHARTED	PEAK POS	WKS CHRT'D	ARTIST — Record Title	Label & Number
11/21/53	28	1	1. Six Buzzard Feathers And A Mocking Bird's Tail.. *accompanied by Buddy DuFault & His Orchestra*	Smart 355

DEAN MARTIN
Born Dino Crocetti, he began as half of the famed team with Jerry Lewis, then established himself as a successful romantic singer and personality in movies and TV ("Dean Martin Show", 1965-74).

DATE CHARTED	PEAK POS	WKS CHRT'D	ARTIST — Record Title	Label & Number
12/04/48	22	1	1. That Certain Party............................. [C] DEAN MARTIN & JERRY LEWIS	Capitol 15249
2/19/49	10	4	2. Powder Your Face With Sunshine (Smile, Smile, Smile)	Capitol 15351
9/02/50	11	16	3. I'll Always Love You .... *above two with Paul Weston's Orchestra* *from the film "My Friend Irma Goes West"*	Capitol 1028
2/10/51	14	6	4. If .... *with Lou Busch's Orchestra*	Capitol 1342
9/06/52	12	10	5. You Belong To Me	Capitol 2165
7/04/53	25	2	6. Love Me, Love Me .... *with the Herman McCoy Singers*	Capitol 2485
11/14/53	2(5)	22	● 7. That's Amore.. *from the film "The Caddy"*	Capitol 2589
4/24/54	21	4	8. I'd Cry Like A Baby.................................	Capitol 2749
7/24/54	15	10	9. Sway/ *Mexican song ("Quien Sera")*	
7/24/54	23	4	10. Money Burns A Hole In My Pocket .... *from the film "Living It Up"* *orchestra on above five directed by Dick Stabile*	Capitol 2818

DATE CHARTED	PEAK POS	WKS CHRT'D	ARTIST — Record Title	Label & Number
			FREDDY MARTIN & HIS ORCHESTRA Leader of one of the most popular "sweet" bands, his tenor saxophone style led to the nickname "Mr. Silvertone". Pianist Jack Fina was a featured sideman, Merv Griffin his late-40s singing star. Freddy died on 10/1/83 (76). (Also see Hotel Bossert Orchestra)	
9/16/33	**14**	3	1. Bless Your Heart .... vocal: Terry Shand	Brunswick 6631
12/23/33+	**5**	7	2. April In Paris	Brunswick 6717
1/20/34	**13**	3	3. In The Valley Of Yesterday .... vocal: Russ Morgan	Banner 32926
2/17/34	**12**	3	4. When Tomorrow Comes	Brunswick 6760
3/17/34	**15**	3	5. Neighbors.. [I]	Brunswick 6777
6/30/34	**11**	4	6. All I Do Is Dream Of You .... from the film "Sadie McKee"	Brunswick 6888
7/28/34	**14**	2	7. Born To Be Kissed	Brunswick 6930
8/25/34	**1(4)**	11	8. **I Saw Stars/**	
9/01/34	**12**	4	9. Then I'll Be Tired Of You	Brunswick 6948
10/27/34	**5**	8	10. Be Still, My Heart!.................................	Brunswick 6998
11/17/34	**18**	2	11. Must We Say Goodnight (So Soon?)	Brunswick 7309
2/02/35	**2(2)**	9	12. Isle Of Capri/	
2/16/35	**20**	1	13. Where There's Smoke-There's Fire	Brunswick 7344
4/13/35	**8**	7	14. Everything's Been Done Before .... from the film "Reckless" Elmer Feldkamp: all above vocals except 1 & 3	Brunswick 7395
4/20/35	**11**	2	15. (There's A) Little Picture Playhouse In My Heart	Brunswick 7418
5/04/35	**10**	5	16. Life Is A Song .... vocal: Elmer Feldkamp	Brunswick 7422
5/18/35	**7**	11	17. Tell Me That You Love Me	Brunswick 7438
5/25/35	**16**	2	18. Reckless .... movie title song	Brunswick 7439
7/13/35	**6**	12	19. I Couldn't Believe My Eyes	Brunswick 7462
7/13/35	**17**	1	20. Get Rhythm In Your Feet	Brunswick 7447
8/03/35	**9**	5	21. Paris In The Spring	Brunswick 7459
11/30/35	**3**	8	22. A Little Bit Independent (But Easy On The Eyes)/	
12/21/35+	**15**	6	23. One Night In Monte Carlo	Brunswick 7559
1/25/36	**4**	6	24. The Broken Record	Brunswick 7591
3/21/36	**5**	5	25. Goody Goody	Brunswick 7621
4/11/36	**8**	4	26. It's Been So Long/ vocals on 15 & 26: Terry Shand	
4/11/36	**11**	3	27. You... from the film "The Great Ziegfeld"	Brunswick 7631
8/13/38	**14**	2	28. Beside A Moonlit Stream..........................	Bluebird 7636
11/04/39	**4**	10	29. Scatter-Brain .... vocal: Glen Hughes	Bluebird 10436
3/02/40	**18**	1	30. One Cigarette For Two	Bluebird 10554
3/08/41	**23**	1	31. It's A Great Day For The Irish....................	Bluebird 10947
5/10/41	**7**	9	32. Intermezzo	Bluebird 11123
5/31/41	**2(1)**	13	33. The Hut-Hut Song (A Swedish Serenade) .... vocals on 30-31 & 33: Eddie Stone	Bluebird 11147
6/28/41	**19**	1	34. 'Til Reveille .... vocals on 32 & 34: Clyde Rogers	Bluebird 11167
8/09/41	**1(8)**	25	● 35. **Piano Concerto In B Flat/** [I] adaptation of the Tchaikovsky classic pianist Jack Fina featured	
8/16/41	**14**	1	36. Why Don't We Do This More Often?	Bluebird 11211
10/18/41	**24**	1	37. Be Honest With Me................................ vocal: Clyde Rogers & Eddie Stone	Bluebird 11256
12/06/41	**14**	1	38. Symphonie Moderne............................... [I]	Bluebird 11328

DATE CHARTED	PEAK POS	WKS CHRT'D	ARTIST — Record Title	Label & Number
12/27/41+	**8**	3	39. Tonight We Love .... vocal version of "Piano Concerto in B Flat"	Bluebird 11320
1/10/42	**1(2)**	11	40. **Rose O'Day (The Filla-Da-Gusha Song)/** vocals on 36 & 40: Eddie Stone	
3/14/42	**22**	1	41. Miss You..	Bluebird 11286
2/21/42	**21**	1	42. Grieg Piano Concerto .... [I]	Bluebird 11430
3/28/42	**22**	1	43. When There's A Breeze On Lake Louise....... from the film "The Mayor of 44th Street"	Bluebird 11437
6/06/42	**24**	1	44. Just Plain Lonesome .... from the film "My Favorite Spy"	Bluebird 11524
6/27/42	**11**	3	45. Johnny Doughboy Found A Rose In Ireland ...	Bluebird 11503
8/15/42	**15**	1	46. Jingle, Jangle, Jingle/ vocal: Clyde Rogers & Stuart Wade from the film "The Forest Rangers"	
10/03/42	**8**	12	47. I Met Her On Monday.............................	Victor 27909
10/17/42	**24**	1	48. White Christmas/ [X] vocals on 39, 41, 43-45 & 48: Clyde Rogers	
11/07/42	**22**	1	49. Abraham... above two from the film "Holiday Inn"	Victor 27946
12/19/42+	**12**	4	50. A Touch Of Texas .... vocal: Eddie Stone & Glen Hughes	Victor 1504
1/09/43	**15**	2	51. I Get The Neck Of The Chicken .... above two from the film "Seven Days' Leave" vocals on 47 & 51: Eddie Stone	Victor 1515
8/21/43	**11**	1	52. Warsaw Concerto/ [I] from the film "Suicide Squadron"	
9/04/43	**21**	1	53. From Twilight 'Til Dawn .... vocal: Bob Haymes	Victor 1535
4/14/45	**9**	7	54. Dream/ vocal: Artie Wayne originally Johnny Mercer's closing radio theme	
4/28/45	**15**	2	55. Everytime .... vocals on 49 & 55: Glen Hughes	Victor 1645
4/28/45	**6**	7	56. Laura .... movie title song	Victor 1655
9/29/45	**7**	2	57. Lily Belle .... vocal by Gene Conklin & Martin Men	Victor 1712
12/01/45+	**1(2)**	17	58. **Symphony/** vocals on 58 & 70: Clyde Rogers	
12/01/45	**13**	4	59. In The Middle Of May	Victor 1747
12/22/45	**16**	1	60. White Christmas............................ [X-R]	Victor 27946
3/23/46	**4**	9	61. One-Zy, Two-Zy (I Love You-Zy)	RCA Victor 1826
5/04/46	**7**	6	62. Bumble Boogie .... [I] featuring Jack Fina (piano) based on Rimsky-Korsakov's "Flight of the Bumble Bee"	RCA Victor 1829
6/22/46	**2(1)**	13	63. Doin' What Comes Natur'lly..................... from the Broadway musical "Annie Get Your Gun"	RCA Victor 1878
8/10/46	**1(2)**	17	64. **To Each His Own**................................... written for, but not included in, the film of the same name	RCA Victor 1921
1/18/47	**1(3)**	13	65. **Managua, Nicaragua**............................. vocals on 64-65, 69 & 72: Stuart Wade	RCA Victor 2026
3/19/47	**20**	5	66. Santa Catalina (Island Of Romance) .... vocal by Stuart Wade & the Martin Men	RCA Victor 2136
5/03/47	**14**	1	67. Moon-Faced, Starry-Eyed......................... vocal: Murray Arnold from the Broadway musical "Street Scene"	RCA Victor 2176
8/16/47	**5**	9	68. The Lady From 29 Palms	RCA Victor 2347
9/13/47	**16**	1	69. Come To The Mardi Gras.........................	RCA Victor 2288
11/08/47	**23**	3	70. Don't You Love Me Anymore?....................	RCA Victor 2473
1/24/48	**23**	1	71. Treasure Of The Sierra Madre/ movie title theme	
3/13/48	**23**	1	72. Don't Call It Love .... from the film "I'll Walk Alone"	RCA Victor 2590

DATE CHARTED	PEAK POS	WKS CHRT'D	ARTIST — Record Title	Label & Number
4/03/48	**6**	11	73. Sabre Dance Boogie .... RCA Victor 2721 vocal: Barclay Allen; based on Khachaturian's "Gayne Ballet Suite"	RCA Victor 2721
4/17/48	**21**	3	74. The New Look	RCA Victor 2769
5/01/48	**5**	11	75. The Dickey-Bird Song .... from the film "Three Daring Daughters"	RCA Victor 2617
11/06/48	**4**	17	76. On A Slow Boat To China .... vocals on 63, 75-76: Glen Hughes	RCA Victor 3123
10/29/49	**8**	17	● 77. I've Got A Lovely Bunch Of Coconuts .... [N]	RCA Vic. 78-3554
3/11/50	**5**	10	78. Music! Music! Music!	RCA Vic. 78-3693
6/10/50	**17**	6	79. The Third Man Theme .... from the film "The Third Man"	RCA Victor 3797
3/31/51	**12**	7	80. The Aba Daba Honeymoon .... featured in the film "Two Weeks With Love"	RCA Victor 4065
4/14/51	**19**	6	81. Never Been Kissed	RCA Victor 4099
7/14/51	**18**	3	82. My Truly, Truly Fair................................ Merv Griffin: vocals on 77-79 & 81-82	RCA Victor 4159
10/13/51	**15**	7	83. Down Yonder .... vocal: Murray Arnold	RCA Victor 4267
4/04/53	**15**	6	84. April In Portugal (The Whisp'ring Serenade) .. written for the University of Coimbra in Portugese East Africa	RCA Victor 5052
9/18/54	**27**	1	85. Lonesome Polecat.................................... from the film "Seven Brides for Seven Brothers"	RCA Victor 5833

MARY MARTIN

One of the all-time greats of the American musical stage from her 1938 Broadway debut, Mary is most famous for her starring roles in "South Pacific" and "The Sound of Music". She is the mother of TV star Larry Hagman.

DATE CHARTED	PEAK POS	WKS CHRT'D	ARTIST — Record Title	Label & Number
1/07/39	**9**	2	1. My Heart Belongs To Daddy...................... with Eddy Duchin's Orchestra the song that made her famous in the Broadway musical "Leave It to Me"	Decca 8282
11/08/41	**23**	1	2. The Waiter And The Porter And The Upstairs Maid .... BING CROSBY, MARY MARTIN, & JACK TEAGARDEN with Jack Teagarden's Orchestra from the film "Birth of the Blues"	Decca 3970
7/25/42	**22**	1	3. Pound Your Table Polka .... with Hoarce Heidt & His Musical Knights	Columbia 36595
8/26/44	**6**	13	4. I'll Walk Alone .... from the film "Follow the Boys" accompanied by Camarata & His Orchestra	Decca 23340
10/25/47	**21**	1	5. Almost Like Being In Love .... with Guy Lombardo & His Royal Canadians from the Broadway musical "Brigadoon"	Decca 24156
3/25/50	**8**	7	6. Go To Sleep, Go To Sleep, Go To Sleep .... MARY MARTIN & ARTHUR GODFREY	Columbia 38744

TONY MARTIN

Born Alvin Morris, Tony played saxophone in Tom Gerun's band before launching his long and successful singing career. He was featured in many films from 1936-57, and frequently performed on stage with his wife, movie star Cyd Charisse. (also see Ray Noble)

DATE CHARTED	PEAK POS	WKS CHRT'D	ARTIST — Record Title	Label & Number
7/30/38	**13**	3	1. Now It Can Be Told .... with Ray Noble's Orchestra	Brunswick 8153
12/23/39	**16**	2	2. South Of The Border .... with Abe Lyman's Orchestra	Decca 2788
2/03/40	**2(2)**	13	3. It's A Blue World .... from the film "Music In My Heart"	Decca 2932
8/03/40	**14**	1	4. Fools Rush In (Where Angels Fear To Tread).. above two with Ray Sinatra's Orchestra	Decca 3119
11/01/41	**5**	11	5. Tonight We Love .... vocal version of Tchaikovsky's "Piano Concerto in B Flat" accompanied by David Rose's Orchestra	Decca 3988
1/31/42	**22**	1	6. Cancel The Flowers................................... with Harry Sosnik's Orchestra	Decca 4101

DATE CHARTED	PEAK POS	WKS CHRT'D	ARTIST — Record Title	Label & Number
7/27/46	**4**	16	● 7. To Each His Own .... with the Starlighters; written for but not used in film of same name	Mercury 3022
10/12/46	**9**	7	8. Rumors Are Flying................................ above two with Al Sack's Orchestra	Mercury 3032
11/29/47	**23**	3	9. I'll Dance At Your Wedding	RCA Victor 2512
3/13/48	**21**	1	10. Hooray For Love....................................	RCA Victor 2690
5/15/48	**25**	1	11. Confess..	RCA Victor 2812
6/12/48	**30**	1	12. For Every Man There's A Woman................ 10 & 12 from the film "Casbah"	RCA Victor 2689
8/07/48	**11**	14	13. It's Magic .... from the film "Romance On the High Seas"	RCA Victor 2862
5/21/49	**17**	3	14. If You Stub Your Toe On The Moon .... from the film "A Connecticut Yankee in King Arthur's Court" 8, 11, & 14 with the Lyttle Sisters above six with Earle Hagen's Orchestra	RCA Victor 3383
8/27/49	**24**	3	15. Circus.. with Skip Martin's Orchestra also on RCA Victor 45-2947	RCA Vic. 78-3488
11/12/49	**2(1)**	27	16. There's No Tomorrow .... melody derived from "O Sole Mio" from the film "Two Tickets to Broadway" also on RCA Victor 45-3078	RCA Vic. 78-3582
12/24/49+	**15**	6	17. Marta (Rambling Rose Of The Wildwood) .... also recorded on RCA Victor 45-3104	RCA Vic. 78-3598
1/21/50	**3**	13	18. I Said My Pajamas (And Put On My Pray'rs) ... TONY MARTIN & FRAN WARREN also on RCA Victor 45-3119	RCA Vic. 78-3613
5/13/50	**18**	6	19. Valencia..	RCA Victor 3755
7/15/50	**9**	17	20. La Vie En Rose...................................... adaptation of a popular French song	RCA Victor 3819
3/03/51	**19**	6	21. Would I Love You (Love You, Love You)........	RCA Victor 4056
6/02/51+	**3**	30	● 22. I Get Ideas.. adapted from the Argentine tango "Adios Muchachos"	RCA Victor 4141
6/09/51	**20**	1	23. I Apologize	RCA Victor 4056
9/01/51	**24**	2	24. The Musicians.................................... DINAH SHORE, TONY MARTIN, BETTY HUTTON & PHIL HARRIS	RCA Victor 4225
9/15/51	**18**	1	25. Vanity	RCA Victor 4246
9/22/51	**17**	4	26. Over A Bottle Of Wine	RCA Victor 4220
11/03/51	**9**	12	27. Domino..	RCA Victor 4343
5/03/52	**6**	15	28. Kiss Of Fire	RCA Victor 4671
8/16/52	**24**	1	29. Some Day/ from the film "The Vagabond King"	
8/30/52	**27**	1	30. Luna Rossa (Blushing Moon).....................	RCA Victor 4836
11/08/52	**27**	1	31. Dance Of Destiny	RCA Victor 5008
5/30/53	**17**	2	32. April In Portugal (The Whisp'ring Serenade) .. written for the University of Coimbra in Portugese East Africa; accompanied by Lennie Hayton's Orchestra	RCA Victor 5279
7/11/53	**26**	1	33. Sorta On The Border	RCA Victor 5352
1/02/54	**10**	11	34. Stranger In Paradise............................... with Hugo Winterhalter's Orchestra from the Broadway musical "Kismet" based on a theme from "Polovetsian Dances" in the opera "Prince Igor"	RCA Victor 5535
3/27/54	**5**	16	35. Here.. adapted from the classical "Caro Nome" accompanied on 16-31, 33 & 35 by Henri Rene's Orchestra	RCA Victor 5665

AL MARTINO

Internationally-popular singer born in Philadelphia, continued to hit the charts for 25 years

DATE CHARTED	PEAK POS	WKS CHRT'D	ARTIST — Record Title	Label & Number
5/17/52	**1(3)**	19	● 1. **Here In My Heart**	B.B.S. 101
6/28/52	**12**	8	2. Take My Heart	Capitol 2122
2/28/53	**30**	1	3. Rachel.. above three with Monty Kelly's Orchestra	Capitol 2353

DATE CHARTED	PEAK POS	WKS CHRT'D	ARTIST — Record Title	Label & Number
7/11/53	**27**	1	4. When You're Mine..................................... with Les Baxter's Orchestra	Capitol 2480

JOHNNY MARVIN
One of the 1920s' most popular band singers, he later wrote songs for Gene Autry movies. Johnny died on 12/20/44 (47). (Also see Arden-Ohman, Columbians, Hilo Hawaiian Orchestra, Vincent Lopez, Nat Shilkret)

DATE CHARTED	PEAK POS	WKS CHRT'D	ARTIST — Record Title	Label & Number
5/08/26	**8**	2	1. Clap Hands! Here Comes Charley.................	Okeh 40558
10/09/26	**1(2)**	10	2. **Breezin' Along With The Breeze**............... also recorded for Edison 51793	Columbia 699
1/22/27	**12**	2	3. Half A Moon... also recorded with Nat Shilkret for Victor 20231, & with the Knickerbockers for Columbia 832	Columbia 750
1/29/27	**3**	7	4. The Little White House (At The End Of Honeymoon Lane)............................... above two from the Broadway musical "Honeymoon Lane"	Okeh 40704
3/12/27	**4**	6	5. 'Deed I Do .... also recorded for Edison 51928	Victor 20397
4/30/27	**9**	5	6. Blue Skies .... JOHNNY MARVIN & ED SMALLE from the Broadway musical "Betsy"	Victor 20457
6/04/27	**14**	2	7. Ain't She Sweet?	Okeh 40769
8/27/27	**7**	4	8. Side By Side .... JOHNNY MARVIN & AILEEN STANLEY	Victor 20714
9/24/27	**10**	4	9. Ain't That A Grand And Glorious Feeling?	Victor 20731
9/24/27	**15**	1	10. Me And My Shadow..................................	Columbia 1020
1/21/28	**18**	1	11. Give Me A Night In June	Victor 20984
9/08/28	**18**	1	12. I Still Love You	Victor 21435
12/15/28	**19**	1	13. If You Don't Love Me	Victor 21609
6/01/29	**16**	2	14. Precious Little Thing Called Love/	
6/29/29	**20**	1	15. Caressing You...................................... above two: JOHNNY MARVIN & ED SMALLE	Victor 21892
11/09/29	**11**	3	16. Tip Toe Through The Tulips .... from the film "Gold Diggers of Broadway"	Victor 22113

GROUCHO MARX
All-time comedy great, star of thirteen Marx Brothers films with Harpo & Chico, and TV series "You Bet Your Life" (1950-61); died on 8/19/77 (86). (see Danny Kaye)

LOUISE MASSEY & THE WESTERNERS
Country group including Louise's brothers Curt & Allen

DATE CHARTED	PEAK POS	WKS CHRT'D	ARTIST — Record Title	Label & Number
8/10/40	**20**	4	1. Rock And Rye Polka	Vocalion 5511
1/25/41	**25**	1	2. Beer And Skittles	Okeh 5916
9/13/41	**23**	1	3. My Adobe Hacienda..............................	Okeh 6077
10/09/43	**19**	1	4. Honey, I'm In Love With You	Okeh 6687
6/14/47	**16**	1	5. My Adobe Hacienda.............................. new version of 1941 hit	Columbia 37332

FRANKIE MASTERS & HIS ORCHESTRA
Sweet band leader and songwriter; in 1942 David Rose served as arranger.

DATE CHARTED	PEAK POS	WKS CHRT'D	ARTIST — Record Title	Label & Number
10/21/39	**1(8)**	16	1. **Scatter-Brain**	Vocalion 4915
2/10/40	**14**	3	2. All The Things You Are .... vocal: Harlan Rogers from the Broadway musical "Very Warm for May"	Vocalion 5265
4/06/40	**7**	13	3. Alice Blue Gown .... from the Broadway musical & film "Irene"	Vocalion 5455
5/11/40	**12**	6	4. Charming Little Faker	Vocalion 5394
5/25/40	**25**	1	5. A Lover's Lullaby	Vocalion 5443
11/02/40	**12**	9	6. Ferry-Boat Serenade/ vocals on 3 & 6: Marion Francis	
11/16/40	**16**	1	7. The Same Old Story .... Frankie Master: vocals on 1, 4 & 7	Okeh 5716
3/15/41	**21**	1	8. Let's Dream This One Out	Okeh 5998

DATE CHARTED	PEAK POS	WKS CHRT'D	ARTIST — Record Title	Label & Number
7/05/41	21	1	9. Daddy.. Okeh 6232	
			above two vocals: Swingmasters	
1/17/42	23	1	10. How Long Did I Dream? .... Okeh 6507	
			vocal: Lou Hurst	

MATTY MATLOCK
Jazz clarinetist with Bob Crosby's band; he accompanied Bing Crosby on some early 50s hits.

MATYS BROTHERS

9/18/54	25	2	1. Muskrat Ramble .... 20th Century 5024

BOBBY MAXWELL & HIS SWINGING HARPS

2/09/52	24	2	1. Chinatown, My Chinatown........................ Mercury 5773
			from the Broadway musical "Up and Down Broadway"

JOE MAXWELL

8/20/10	6	3	1. You Taught Me How To Love You, Now Teach Me To Forget .... Edison Amb. 456

BILLY MAY & HIS ORCHESTRA
Played trumpet with Charlie Barnet (1938-39) & Glenn Miller (1940-42), and did arrangements for Miller, Woody Herman, & Alvino Rey. After leading his own band in the early 50s, Billy went on to arrange and conduct for Frank Sinatra and compose movie & TV scores. (also see Nat King Cole)

2/02/52	17	2	1. Charmaine .... [I] Capitol 1919
			written to promote the silent film "What Price Glory?" band includes Mannie Klein, & Conrad Gozzo (trumpets), Si Zentner (trombone), and Skeets Herfurt (alto sax)

PERCY MAYFIELD
Los Angeles-based R&B singer/songwriter ("Hit the Road, Jack").

11/18/50	26	1	● 1. Please Send Me Someone To Love............... Specialty 375
			long-running R&B hit

MARGARET MAYHEW
Probable pseudonym for Elise Stevenson

REGINALD McALL
pipe organist

11/18/16	10	1	1. Hallelujah Chorus............................. [I-X] Victor 35547
			from Handel's "Messiah"

MARY ANN McCALL
Singer with Charlie Barnet (1939-40) & Woody Herman (1946-49)

HARRY McCLASKEY
Real name of, and pseudonym for, Henry Burr.

JAMES McCOOL
Tenor; died in 1936 (61).

10/13/06	3	3	1. There Never Was A Girl Like You .... Victor 4797

JOHN McCORMACK
The most famous Irish tenor of all time, John McCormack was born in Athlone, Ireland on 6/14/1884. Shortly after making his first recordings for Edison Bell in 1904 and singing at the St. Louis international exposition, McCormack made his operatic debut in Italy. It was in 1910 that he became an American sensation, and by 1915 was so monumentally popular he largely abandoned opera to concentrate on solo concert performances. During these years no one else save Caruso did more to establish the importance and value of commercial recordings (and probably not even Caruso sold so many Victor Red Seals). John McCormack died on 8/16/45 (61).

5/07/10	5	5	1. Killarney... Victor 74157
7/23/10	9	1	2. Come Back To Erin .... Victor 74158
8/13/10	10	1	3. Carmen - Il Flor Che Aveci A Me (Flower Song) .... [F] Victor 88216
8/20/10	4	5	4. When Shadows Gather............................ Victor 64127
11/12/10	8	2	5. Annie Laurie... Victor 64138
4/22/11	6	3	6. Drink To Me Only With Thine Eyes .... Victor 74204

DATE CHARTED	PEAK POS	WKS CHRT'D	ARTIST — Record Title	Label & Number
6/03/11	**1(7)**	13	7. **I'm Falling In Love With Someone**............ from the Broadway operetta "Naughty Marietta"	Victor 64174
7/01/11	**1(5)**	13	8. **Mother Machree**..................................... from the Broadway musical "Barry of Ballymore"	Victor 64181
9/02/11	**3**	6	9. Kathleen Mavourneen...............................	Victor 74236
9/02/11	**10**	1	10. Believe Me If All Those Endearing Young Charms..	Victor 64180
8/31/12	**6**	3	11. Silver Threads Among The Gold	Victor 64260
10/26/12	**4**	6	12. The Rosary.......................................	Victor 64257
1/18/13	**4**	6	13. Take, Oh Take Those Lips Away	Victor 64252
3/29/13	**3**	6	14. Where The River Shannon Flows	Victor 64311
6/28/13	**5**	4	15. Say "Au Revoir" But Not Goodbye..............	Victor 64328
1/10/14	**6**	4	16. I'll Sing Thee Songs Of Araby....................	Victor 64375
5/02/14	**8**	2	17. Nearer My God To Thee	Victor 64345
8/08/14	**7**	4	18. Ave Maria... by Mascagni & Weatherly; in English	Victor 87192
9/20/14+	**4**	6	19. A Little Love, A Little Kiss	Victor 64343
10/24/14	**7**	2	20. Good-Bye	Victor 74346
12/12/14	**5**	4	21. Lullaby From Jocelyn ("Angels Guard Thee") . accompanied on 18 & 21 by Fritz Kreisler (violin)	Victor 88483

1/16/15	**1(8)**	13	22. **It's A Long, Long Way To Tipperary** ....
			    featured in the Broadway musicals "Chin-Chin" &
			    "Dancing Around"
				Victor 64476

2/06/15	**7**	2	23. My Wild Irish Rose............................. from the Broadway musical "A Romance of Athlone"	Victor 64426
2/13/15	**9**	1	24. Aida - O Terra Addio ("Farewell, Oh Earth")[F] JOHN McCORMACK & LUCY ISABELLE MARSH	Victor 74398
3/27/15	**4**	5	25. Ave Maria .... [F] by Bach & Gounod; in Latin	Victor 88481
9/18/15	**8**	1	26. Evening Song	Victor 64496
10/23/15	**5**	4	27. Serenata .... [F] accompanied by Fritz Kreisler (violin) on 25 & 27	Victor 87230
12/11/15	**2(1)**	4	28. Adeste Fidelis (Oh, Come All Ye Faithful)[F-X] with chorus & chimes	Victor 74436
1/22/16	**1(2)**	9	29. **Somewhere A Voice Is Calling**..................	Victor 64405
4/29/16	**4**	4	30. Beautiful Isle Of Somewhere	Victor 64428
5/20/16	**2(1)**	6	31. The Old Refrain...................................	Victor 64559
5/27/16+	**9**	1	32. A Little Bit Of Heaven (Shure, They Call It Ireland)...	Victor 64543

9/30/16	**3**	5	33. Tales Of Hoffman: Barcolle ("Belle Nuit" - Oh
			    Night Of Love)....................................
			    accompanied by Fritz Kreisler
				Victor 87245

11/18/16	**3**	5	34. Cradle Song 1915................................. adapted from "Caprice Viennois"	Victor 64606
12/23/16	**1(4)**	7	35. **The Sunshine Of Your Smile**....................	Victor 64622
2/03/17	**6**	3	36. Love, Here Is My Heart!...........................	Victor 64623
5/12/17	**4**	3	37. When Irish Eyes Are Smiling...................... from the Broadway musical "The Isle o' Dreams"	Victor 64631
5/26/17	**1(3)**	8	38. **The Star-Spangled Banner**	Victor 64664
9/01/17	**3**	5	39. There's A Long, Long Trail A-Winding..........	Victor 64694
9/29/17	**4**	4	40. Keep The Home Fires Burning....................	Victor 64696
12/22/17+	**1(4)**	10	41. **Send Me Away With A Smile**....................	Victor 64741
12/22/17	**6**	2	42. The Crucifix...................................... JOHN McCORMACK & REINALD WERRENRATH	Victor 64712
3/16/18	**5**	3	43. The Rainbow Of Love	Victor 64732
6/15/18	**3**	5	44. God Be With Our Boys Tonight..................	Victor 64773
6/29/18	**3**	7	45. Little Mother Of Mine	Victor 64778
11/02/18	**3**	6	46. Love's Garden Of Roses	Victor 64787
2/08/19	**4**	4	47. When You Come Back	Victor 64791
5/24/19	**4**	4	48. Calling Me Home To You	Victor 64803

DATE CHARTED	PEAK POS	WKS CHRT'D	ARTIST — Record Title	Label & Number
7/26/19	2(3)	7	49. When You Look In The Heart Of A Rose........	Victor 64817
12/20/19	9	1	50. Roses Of Picardy	Victor 64825
4/24/20	5	5	51. That Tumble-Down Shack In Athlone	Victor 64837
5/22/20	6	4	52. Your Eyes Have Told Me So	Victor 64860
7/31/20	6	3	53. The Barefoot Trail	Victor 64878
10/04/20	5	3	54. When Night Descends...............................	Victor 87571
12/04/20	8	2	55. Thank God For A Garden	Victor 64900
10/15/21	4	5	56. Learn To Smile.......................................	Victor 64982
1/28/22	13	1	57. The Last Hour	Victor 87576
			54 & 57 accompanied by Fritz Kreisler	
2/04/22	10	1	58. Rose Of My Heart.....................................	Victor 66012
5/27/22	11	1	59. Sweet Peggy O'Neil..................................	Victor 66028
8/12/22	8	2	60. Somewhere...	Victor 64976
6/16/23	10	1	61. The Lost Chord	Victor 74791
1/05/24	5	3	62. Love Sends A Little Gift Of Roses	Victor 961
2/23/24	5	5	63. Somewhere In The World	Victor 968
8/30/24	9	1	64. Indiana Moon/	
9/27/24	12	1	65. Marcheta..	Victor 1011
2/28/25	1(2)	8	66. **All Alone**/	
			from the Broadway musical "Music Box Revue of 1924"	
3/14/25	5	4	67. Rose Marie	Victor 1067
			Broadway musical title song	
8/15/25	5	3	68. When You and I Were Seventeen	Victor 1086
8/29/25	3	5	69. Moonlight And Roses...............................	Victor 1092
			based on Lamare's "Andante"	
2/27/26	11	1	70. You Forgot To Remember..........................	Victor 1121
3/27/26	4	5	71. Just A Cottage Small...............................	Victor 1113
4/09/27	6	6	72. The Far Away Bells..................................	Victor 1215
2/16/29	15	2	73. Jeannine, I Dream Of Lilac Time	Victor 1360
			theme from the silent film "Lilac Time"	

OWEN McCORMACK

7/04/14	4	4	1. In The Town Where I Was Born	Edison Amb. 2304

CLYDE McCOY & HIS ORCHESTRA
Trumpeter known for his "wah-wah" sound.

2/21/31	2(1)	20	1. Sugar Blues... [I]	Columbia 2389
			Clyde's famous theme	
8/19/33	8	4	2. Smoke Rings.. [I]	Columbia 2794
9/09/33	12	3	3. In The Cool Of The Night....................... [I]	Columbia 2801
10/07/33	12	3	4. Wah Wah Lament .... [I]	Columbia 2824
4/18/34	18	1	5. Tear It Down... [I]	Columbia 2909
4/27/35	6	9	6. Sugar Blues... [I]	Decca 381
			new version of his 1931 hit	
2/13/37	5	4	7. The Goona Goo .... [I]	Decca 1109
3/08/41	22	1	8. Love Can Do The Darndest Things	Decca 3581
			vocal: Bennett Sisters	

DICK McDONOUGH
Top guitarist who played on chart hits by Dorsey Brothers, Benny Goodman, Billie Holiday, Red Nichols, & Ethel Waters. Dick died on 5/28/38 (34).

McFARLAND TWINS

3/28/42	23	1	1. Hey, Zeke! .... [N]	Bluebird 11449

"STICK" McGHEE & HIS BUDDIES
Granville "Stick" McGhee, the brother of folk/blues singer "Brownie" McGhee; died on 8/15/61 (43).

8/27/49	26	1	1. Drinking Wine, Spo-Dee-O-Dee, Drinking Wine	Atlantic 873
			the first of Atlantic Records' many R&B hits	

DATE CHARTED	PEAK POS	WKS CHRT'D	ARTIST — Record Title	Label & Number

McGUIRE SISTERS

Christine, Dorothy, & Phyllis McGuire got their first break on Kate Smith's radio show before winning an Arthur Godfrey "Talent Scouts" contest; they hit #1 in 1955 with "Sincerely".

4/03/54	26	1	1. Pine Tree, Pine Over Me .... Coral 61126 JOHNNY DESMOND, EILEEN BARTON, & McGUIRE SISTERS	
6/26/54	7	15	2. Goodnight, Sweetheart, Goodnight .... Coral 61187	
10/16/54	10	10	3. Muskrat Ramble/	
11/06/54	28	1	4. Lonesome Polecat.................................... Coral 61278 from the film "Seven Brides for Seven Brothers" 2 & 4 accompanied by Neal Hefti & His Orchestra	
12/25/54	25	2	5. Christmas Alphabet .... [X] Coral 61303 orchestra on 1, 3 & 5 directed by Dick Jacobs	

HAL McINTYRE & HIS ORCHESTRA

Glenn Miller's lead alto saxophonist (1937-41), Hal had Miller's assistance in starting his own band. He died on 5/5/59 (44) in an apartment fire.

9/26/42	18	1	1. This Is The Army, Mr. Jones..................... Victor 27952 vocal: Jack Lathrop from the Broadway musical "This Is the Army"	
9/11/43	19	1	2. This Is The Army, Mr. Jones................. [R] Victor 27952	
2/17/45	14	1	3. I'm Making Believe................................... Bluebird 0831	
2/24/45	16	1	4. My Funny Valentine .... Bluebird 0837 from the Broadway musical "Babes in Arms" above two vocals: Ruth Gaylor	
4/28/45	3	19	5. Sentimental Journey .... Victor 1643	
10/30/45	8	5	6. I'll Buy That Dream.................................. Victor 1679 from the film "Sing Your Way Home"	
6/01/46	8	4	7. The Gypsy/	
6/01/46	18	3	8. Cement Mixer (Put-Ti, Put-Ti)................ [N] Cosmo 475	
7/06/46	17	1	9. There's No One But You........................... Cosmo 479 above four vocals: Frankie Lester	

McKEE'S ORCHESTRA

8/28/15	9	1	1. Estrellita... [I] Victor 35475	
12/04/15	4	3	2. A Perfect Day .... [I] Victor 17835 listed as McKee Trio	

RAY McKINLEY & HIS ORCHESTRA

Drummer for the Dorsey Brothers, Jimmy Dorsey (1935-39), then co-leader of the Will Bradley band. Ray played from 1943-45 with Glenn Miller's Army Air Force band before his own postwar band caught on, with Eddie Sauter arrangements. He led the Glenn Miller Orchestra in the late 50s & eary 60s.

5/08/43	14	4	1. Big Boy .... Capitol 131 vocal: Imogene Lynn	
3/29/47	15	1	2. Hoodle-Addle .... Majestic 7207 vocal: Louis Stein, Mundell Lowe & Ward Erwin	
5/03/47	10	3	3. Red Silk Stockings And Green Perfume........ Majestic 7216	
11/22/47	8	5	4. Civilization (Bongo, Bongo, Bongo).............. Majestic 7274 from the Broadway musical "Angel in the Wings"	
12/27/47+	22	2	5. Your Red Wagon..................................... Majestic 7275 movie title song	
3/27/48	21	3	6. Airizay .... RCA Victor 2736	
5/01/48	24	2	7. A Man Could Be A Wonderful Thing .... RCA Victor 2768 vocal: Marcy Lutes	
8/07/48	13	16	8. You Came A Long Way (From St. Louis)........ RCA Victor 2913 ensemble vocal	
3/12/49	19	3	9. Sunflower.. RCA Victor 3334 vocal: Jean Friley; became the state song of Kansas later found in court to be direct inspiration for "Hello, Dolly!"	

McKINNEY'S COTTON PICKERS

Jazz band founded by Bill McKinney, directed by alto saxophonist Don Redman; Coleman Hawkins & Fats Waller played with the band in 1929.

12/22/28	17	2	1. Milenberg Joys...................................... [I] Victor 21611	

DATE CHARTED	PEAK POS	WKS CHRT'D	ARTIST — Record Title	Label & Number
8/16/30	1(2)	12	2. **If I Could Be With You One Hour Tonight** .. vocal: George Thomas; with Benny Carter (alto sax)	Victor 38118

BETTE McLAURIN
Jazz-influenced singer

5/10/52+	23	3	1. I May Hate Myself In The Morning .... accompanied by Rex Kearney & His Orchestra	Derby 790
9/19/53	25	1	2. Only A Rose .... accompanied by Sy Oliver & His Orchestra	Coral 61026

JIMMY McPARTLAND
Jazz cornet star in Dixieland style, played with Ben Pollack (1927-29), Russ Columbo, Smith Ballew, Hoarce Heidt, Jack Teagarden.

JAY McSHANN & HIS ORCHESTRA
Pianist-bandleader who featured (on both hits) all-time jazz great Charlie Parker (alto sax)

7/26/41	24	1	1. Confessin' The Blues .... vocal: Walter Brown	Decca 8559
7/03/43	18	1	2. Get Me On Your Mind .... vocal: Al Hibbler	Decca 4418

JACK McVEA & HIS ALL-STARS
Tenor and baritone saxophonist with Lionel Hampton in the early 40s.

1/25/47	3	9	1. Open The Door, Richard! .... [C]	Black & White 792
			vocal by McVea & John "Red" Kelly	

GEORGE MEADER

3/13/20	10	1	1. Wonderful Pal	Columbia 2821

EDWARD MEEKER
Staff announcer and comic sound effects specialist on many Edison records into the 1920s; died on 4/19/37 (63).

9/28/07	8	1	1. Harrigan .... from the Broadway musical "Fifty Miles from Boston"	Edison 9616
10/17/08	5	1	2. Take Me Out To The Ball Game	Edison 9926

NELLIE MELBA
World-famous operatic soprano born Helen Mitchell, took her stage name from birthplace Melbourne, Australia. Renowned with the New York Metropolitan and throughout Europe from 1890; Nellie died on 2/23/31 (69).

1/28/05	10	1	1. Good-Bye	Victor 95012
7/27/07	8	1	2. La Boheme - O Soave Faniculla (Thou Sweetest Maiden) .... [F] ENRICO CARUSO & NELLIE MELBA	Victor 95200
2/04/11	10	1	3. La Boheme - Mi Chiamano Mimi (My Name Is Mimi) .... [F]	Victor 88074
3/14/14	10	1	4. Comin' Thro' The Rye	Victor 88449

JOSE MELLIS & HIS ORCHESTRA
Pianist and rhumba band leader.

11/29/47	26	1	1. Don't You Love Me Anymore? .... vocal by Jeannie Williams	Mercury 5070

MELODY SHEIKS
Sam Lanin, director

8/14/26	9	1	1. The Blue Room .... [I] from the Broadway musical "The Girl Friend"	Okeh 40603

MELODY THREE

8/17/29	7	4	1. My Song Of The Nile .... from the film "The Drag"	Victor 22028

JAMES MELTON
Acclaimed tenor who sang with the popular Revelers in the late 1920s and was featured in 1930s movie musicals. James sang with the Chicago Opera (1940-42) and the New York Metropolitan Opera (1942-50), and hosted a popular network radio program and a 1951 TV series. He died on 4/21/61 (57).

7/27/29	11	4	1. Sleepy Valley	Columbia 1797

DATE CHARTED	PEAK POS	WKS CHRT'D	ARTIST — Record Title	Label & Number
8/24/29	**18**	1	2. **With A Song In My Heart**................................	Columbia 1853
			from the Broadway musical "Spring Is Here"	
11/26/32	**20**	1	3. **You Are Love**...	Brunswick 20115
			accompanied by Victor Young & His Orchestra	
			from the Broadway musical "Show Boat"	
6/05/37	**16**	2	4. **September In The Rain**	Decca 1247
			accompanied by Bobby Dolan's Orchestra	
			from the film "Melody for Two"	
4/28/45	**21**	1	5. **Strange Music**	Victor 8746
			accompanied by Al Goodman & His Orchestra	
			from the Broadway musical "Song of Norway"	

HAMISH MENZIES
Scottish male singer-songwriter

DATE CHARTED	PEAK POS	WKS CHRT'D	ARTIST — Record Title	Label & Number
3/28/53	**22**	4	1. **Less Than Tomorrow**................................	Decca 28601
			with the Jack Halloran Chorus & Lew Douglas' Orchestra	
9/05/53	**25**	1	2. **Dare I?**	Decca 28811

JOHNNY MERCER
The lyricist for more popular songs than any other songwriter in history, Johnny Mercer was born on 11/18/09 in Savannah, Ga. Among his 1,000-plus songs were "Blues In the Night", "That Old Black Magic", "Dream", & "Moon River"; his genial vocal style proved popular in its own right. In 1942 Johnny founded Capitol Records. He died on 6/25/76 (66).

DATE CHARTED	PEAK POS	WKS CHRT'D	ARTIST — Record Title	Label & Number
8/13/38	**7**	5	1. **Mr. Gallagher And Mr. Shean**/ [C]	
8/27/38	**3**	13	2. **Small Fry**	Decca 1960
			from the film "Sing, You Sinners"	
7/20/40	**18**	1	3. **Mister Meadowlark**....................................	Decca 3182
			above three: BING CROSBY & JOHNNY MERCER	
8/08/42	**7**	13	4. **Strip Polka**	Capitol 103
1/09/43	**18**	1	5. **I Lost My Sugar In Salt Lake City**	Capitol 122
			with Freddie Slack's Orchestra	
			featured in the film "Stormy Weather"	
1/15/44	**11**	9	6. **G.I. Jive**	Capitol 141
4/29/44	**21**	1	7. **San Fernando Valley**	Capitol 150
			with the Berries	
9/16/44	**24**	1	8. **Sam's Got Him**	Capitol 164
1/06/45	**1(2)**	16	9. **Ac-Cent-Tchu-Ate The Positive**................	Capitol 180
			from the film "Here Come the Waves"	
2/24/45	**1(1)**	18	10. **Candy**/	
			JOHNNY MERCER, JO STAFFORD, & PIED PIPERS	
3/10/45	**12**	2	11. **I'm Gonna See My Baby**	Capitol 183
7/14/45	**1(8)**	19	12. **On The Atchison, Topeka, And The Santa**	
			Fe	Capitol 195
			from the film "The Harvey Girls"	
11/17/45	**16**	1	13. **Surprise Party**.......................................	Capitol 217
1/26/46	**1(2)**	15	14. **Personality**..	Capitol 230
			from the film "The Road to Utopia"	
8/10/46	**11**	9	15. **My Sugar Is So Refined**/	
9/28/46	**22**	1	16. **Ugly Chile (You're Some Pretty Doll)**	Capitol 268
12/07/46+	**8**	8	17. **Zip-A-Dee-Doo-Dah**....................................	Capitol 323
			from the animated film "Song of the South"	
12/14/46	**5**	10	18. **A Gal In Calico**/	
			from the film "The Time, the Place, & the Girl"	
1/04/47	**4**	1	19. **Winter Wonderland**............................[X]	Capitol 316
			from Broadway's "Ziegfeld Follies of 1935"	
			Pied Pipers: backing vocals on nearly all of above	
			eleven & also on 26	
1/11/47	**8**	7	20. **Huggin' And A-Chalkin'**	Capitol 334
4/12/47	**13**	2	21. **I Do Do Do Like You**.................................	Capitol 367
4/26/47	**21**	3	22. **Moon Faced, Starry-Eyed**	Capitol 1376
			with Benny Goodman & His Orchestra	
9/20/47	**4**	8	23. **Sugar Blues** ....[N]	Capitol 448
			6·21 & 23 accompanied by Paul Weston's Orchestra	

DATE CHARTED	PEAK POS	WKS CHRT'D	ARTIST — Record Title	Label & Number
10/25/47	**12**	1	24. Save The Bones For Henry Jones (Cause Henry Don't Eat Meat)/	
11/01/47	**12**	3	25. Harmony.. Capitol 15000 from the film "Variety Girl" above two: JOHNNY MERCER & KING COLE TRIO	
2/28/48	**28**	1	26. The Thousand Islands Song/ from the Broadway musical "Angel In the Wings"	
3/06/48	**25**	1	27. Hooray For Love.................................... Capitol 15028 from the film "Casbah"	
5/14/49	**3**	19	28. Baby, It's Cold Outside .... Capitol 567 MARGARET WHITING & JOHNNY MERCER from the film "Neptune's Daughter"	
10/25/52	**30**	1	29. The Glow-Worm.................................[R] Capitol 2248 accompanied by Alvino Rey's Orchestra; originally released in 1949 on Capitol 15412 Johnny's new lyrics to the 1902 German operetta hit featured in the Broadway musical "The Girl Behind the Counter"	

TOMMY MERCER
Best known as singer with Ray Anthony in nearly 50s, also sang with Charlie Spivak & Buddy Morrow bands.

ETHEL MERMAN
All-time Broadway musical great, born Ethel Zimmerman. She raised the rafters with her unmistakably brassy style in thirteen Broadway shows, including "Anything Goes", "Annie Get Your Gun" (which provided her trademark song, "There's No Business Like Show Business"), and "Gypsy". Ethel died on 2/15/84 (75).

DATE CHARTED	PEAK POS	WKS CHRT'D	ARTIST — Record Title	Label & Number
11/05/32	**14**	3	1. How Deep Is The Ocean? .... Victor 24146 accompanied by Nat Shilkret's Orchestra	
1/21/33	**8**	4	2. Eadie Was A Lady................................. Brunswick 6456 accompanied by Victor Young's Orchestra from the Broadway musical "Take a Chance"	
11/10/34+	**11**	9	3. An Earful Of Music................................. Brunswick 6995 from the film "Kid Millions"	
12/22/34+	**4**	9	4. You're The Top/	
1/05/35	**12**	5	5. I Get A Kick Out Of You.......................... Brunswick 7342 above two from the Broadway musical "Anything Goes" above three accompanied by Johnny Green's Orchestra	
2/20/43	**14**	1	6. Move It Over .... Victor 1521	
9/14/46	**20**	1	7. They Say It's Wonderful........................... Decca 23586 ETHEL MERMAN & RAY MIDDLETON with Jay Blackton's Orchestra from the Broadway musical "Annie Get Your Gun"	
3/04/50	**12**	11	8. Dearie/ from the "Copacabana Show of 1950"	
3/11/50	**20**	2	9. I Said My Pajamas (And Put On My Prayers) Decca 24873	
4/29/50	**15**	3	10. If I Knew You Were Comin' I'd've Baked A Cake .... Decca 24944 above three: ETHEL MERMAN & RAY BOLGER	
4/07/51	**30**	1	11. You're Just In Love................................ Decca 27317 ETHEL MERMAN & DICK HAYMES accompanied by Gordon Jenkins' Orchestra from the Broadway musical "Call Me Madam"	
5/05/51	**29**	1	12. Once Upon A Nickel .... Decca 27506 ETHEL MERMAN & RAY BOLGER 8-10 & 12 accompanied by Sy Oliver & His Orchestra	

BENNY MEROFF & HIS ORCHESTRA
Bandleader who for a time featured jazz cornet star Wild Bill Davison. He died in 1973 (72).

DATE CHARTED	PEAK POS	WKS CHRT'D	ARTIST — Record Title	Label & Number
2/01/30	**1(3)**	6	1. Happy Days Are Here Again .... Brunswick 4709 vocal: Dusty Rhodes; from the film "Chasing Rainbows"; became President Franklin D. Roosevelt's theme song	

JOAN MERRILL

DATE CHARTED	PEAK POS	WKS CHRT'D	ARTIST — Record Title	Label & Number
8/23/41	**13**	2	1. Daddy.. Bluebird 11171	

DATE CHARTED	PEAK POS	WKS CHRT'D	ARTIST — Record Title	Label & Number
			ROBERT MERRILL One of the modern era's best-known opera stars. Robert made his New York Metropolitan debut in 1945, the same year he sang before both houses of Congress at the FDR memorial services.	
6/07/47	**14**	1	1. The Whiffenpoof Song .... accompanied by Russ Case's Orchestra written in 1909 for a branch of the Yale Glee Club	RCA Victor 1313
			MERRY MACS Original members brothers Joe, Ted, & Judd McMichael, & Cherry MacKay; popular four-part harmony vocal group. Joe was replaced during war by Lynn Allen, female spot underwent many changes. (also see Bing Crosby)	
3/25/39	**14**	1	1. Ta Hu Wa Nu Wa (Hawaiian War Chant)	Decca 2333
6/14/41+	**13**	3	2. The Hut-Hut Song	Decca 3810
3/07/42	**11**	3	3. Deep In The Heart Of Texas	Decca 4136
6/20/42+	**4**	10	4. Jingle, Jangle, Jingle .... from the film "The Forest Rangers"	Decca 18361
6/20/42	**23**	1	5. Breathless	Decca 4265
8/15/42	**21**	1	6. Cheatin' On The Sandman	Decca 18361
11/14/42	**8**	5	7. Praise The Lord And Pass The Ammunition ..	Decca 18498
2/19/44	**1(5)**	15	8. **Mairzy Doats** .... [N]	Decca 18588
7/29/44	**7**	14	9. Pretty Kitty Blue Eyes	Decca 18610
6/30/45	**4**	12	10. Sentimental Journey	Decca 18684
4/20/46	**9**	6	11. Laughing On The Outside (Crying On The Inside)/	
6/01/46	**21**	4	12. Ashby de la Zooch	Decca 18811
			JOHNNY MESSNER & HIS ORCHESTRA Saxophonist-bandleader, started with Five Messner Brothers band	
1/07/39	**12**	3	1. The Umbrella Man .... vocal: Three Jacks	Bluebird 10048
2/04/39	**3**	12	2. Could Be	Bluebird 10107
3/18/39	**19**	1	3. Among Those Sailing................................ above two vocals: Jeanne d'Arcy	Bluebird 10058
			METRONOME ALL-STAR BAND	
4/12/41	**13**	1	1. One O'Clock Jump .... [I] Count Basie (piano); Harry James, Cootie Williams, Ziggy Elman (trumpets); Tommy Dorsey & J.C. Higginbotham (trombones); Benny Goodman (clarinet); Benny Carter & Toots Mondello (alto sax); Coleman Hawkins & Tex Beneke (tenor sax); Charlie Christian (electric guitar); Artie Bernstein (bass); Buddy Rich (drums)	Victor 27314
			METROPOLITAN ORCHESTRA The first regular studio recording orchestra	
1/25/02	**4**	1	1. Creole Belles.................................... [I]	Victor 1023
			JOHN MEYER Sang bass with both the Peerless Quartet (1911-25) and the American Quartet (1921-25). He died on 5/3/49 (71).	
1/31/20	**13**	1	1. Carolina Sunshine	Okeh 4006
2/28/20	**12**	1	2. I Never Knew .... above two: HENRY BURR & JOHN MEYER	Okeh 4043
			MIDNIGHTERS Top rhythm & blues group led by Hank Ballard	
6/05/54	**22**	3	1. Work With Me, Annie	Federal 12169
10/02/54	**23**	1	2. Annie Had A Baby .... both #1 R & B hits	Federal 12195
			ALLEN MILLER & HIS ORCHESTRA	
5/08/43	**3**	8	1. It Can't Be Wrong	Hit 7045
			EDDIE MILLER Tenor saxophone soloist with Ben Pollack (1930-34), Bob Crosby (1935-42), Wingy Manone, & Paul Weston (mid-40s to early 50s).	

EDDIE "PIANO" MILLER
Honky-tonk pianist

DATE CHARTED	PEAK POS	WKS CHRT'D	ARTIST — Record Title	Label & Number
12/10/49	14	3	1. She Wore A Yellow Ribbon	Rainbow 80033

GLENN MILLER & HIS ORCHESTRA
Leader of the most universally beloved of all big bands, Glenn Miller was born on 3/1/04 in Clarinda, Iowa. He played trombone for Ben Pollack, Red Nichols, Benny Goodman, & the Dorsey Brothers, became de facto leader of Ray Noble's 1935 American band, and did arrangements for Glen Gray and others before starting his own band in 1937. It failed, as did a 1938 successor, but in 1939 Glenn developed his trademark reed sound (four saxophones and clarinet) and soared to the top. Vital ingredients in the band's staggering success were arrangers Jerry Gray & Bill Finegan, and featured soloists Bobby Hackett, Tex Beneke, Billy May & Hal McIntyre. At the band's peak after four years of extraordinary popularity, Glenn left to enlist in the Army Air Force in Sept. 1942, and formed the war's most famous service band. His plane was lost over the English Channel on a 12/15/44 flight. Tex Beneke carried on the legacy with a new Miller orchestra, and Hollywood's 1954 "Glenn Miller Story" further immortalized the music and the man.

DATE CHARTED	PEAK POS	WKS CHRT'D	ARTIST — Record Title	Label & Number
7/13/35	7	5	1. Solo Hop .... [I]	Columbia 3058
			with members of Ray Noble's Orchestra, including Bunny Berigan & Charlie Spivak (trumpets), Eddie Miller (tenor sax), & Claude Thornhill (piano)	
2/05/38	17	1	2. Every Day's A Holiday	Brunswick 8041
			vocal: Kathleen Lane; band includes Irving Fazola (clarinet); movie title song	
11/05/38	11	3	3. My Reverie	Bluebird 7853
			based on Debussy's "Reverie"	
7/29/39	3	15	● 4. Moonlight Serenade/ [I]	
			Glenn's immortal theme song (his composition), originally titled "Now I Lay Me Down to Weep"; Wilbur Schwartz (clarinet) featured	
4/29/39	7	11	5. Sunrise Serenade .... [I]	Bluebird 10214
			featuring Tex Beneke (tenor sax)	
5/13/39	1(4)	14	6. Wishing (Will Make It So)	Bluebird 10219
			from the film "Love Affair"	
5/13/39	2(1)	12	7. The Lady's In Love With You/	
			vocal: Tex Beneke; from the film "Some Like It Hot"	
6/10/39	13	2	8. My Last Good-Bye...............................	Bluebird 10229
6/11/39	12	1	9. Runnin' Wild .... [I]	Bluebird 10269
6/17/39	1(4)	13	10. Stairway To The Stars...........................	Bluebird 10276
			based on a theme from "Park Avenue Fantasy"	
6/17/39	10	7	11. Little Brown Jug .... [I]	Bluebird 10286
7/01/39	1(4)	16	12. Moon Love/	
			adapted from the 2nd movement of Tschaikovsky's Fifth Symphony	
8/12/39	16	2	13. Cinderella (Stay In My Arms)	Bluebird 10303
			vocals on 3, 6, 8, 10, 12 & 13: Ray Eberle	
7/02/39	8	5	14. Back To Back	Bluebird 10299
7/22/39	8	2	15. Ain'tcha Comin' Out Tonight?....................	Bluebird 10329
			above two vocals: Marion Hutton & Tex Beneke	
8/19/39	1(7)	15	16. Over The Rainbow/	
11/11/39	17	2	17. Ding-Dong! The Witch Is Dead..................	Bluebird 10366
			above two from the film "The Wizard of Oz"	
8/26/39	7	11	18. The Little Man Who Wasn't There/	
			vocal: Tex Beneke	
9/02/39	1(3)	10	19. The Man With The Mandolin	Bluebird 10358
			vocals on 17 & 19: Marion Hutton	
9/09/39	1(1)	12	20. Blue Orchids..	Bluebird 10372
			Tex featured on tenor sax	
9/30/39	15	1	21. My Isle Of Golden Dreams .... [I]	Bluebird 10399
10/07/39+	1(12)	30	● 22. In The Mood .... [I]	Bluebird 10416
			Glenn's most gargantuan hit, based on a riff theme first heard in Wingy Manone's "Tar Paper Stomp"; solos by Tex & Al Klink (ts) & Clyde Hurley (trumpet); record selected for the NARAS Hall of Fame	

DATE CHARTED	PEAK POS	WKS CHRT'D	ARTIST — Record Title	Label & Number
10/21/39	**2(2)**	15	23. My Prayer .... with trombone solo by Glenn; song revived as a #1 hit for The Platters in 1956	Bluebird 10404
10/28/39	**5**	10	24. (Why Couldn't It Last) Last Night/	
11/18/39	**15**	3	25. Melancholy Lullaby...................... vocals on 16, 20, 23-25: Ray Eberle	Bluebird 10423
12/16/39+	**4**	11	26. Faithful Forever/ above two from the animated film "Gulliver's Travels"	
11/25/39	**9**	5	27. Bluebirds In The Moonlight .... vocal: Marion Hutton	Bluebird 10465
12/02/39	**8**	7	28. Speaking Of Heaven	Bluebird 10455
1/06/40	**1(5)**	13	29. **Careless/**	
2/03/40	**16**	1	30. Vagabond Dreams................................	Bluebird 10520
1/06/40	**8**	6	31. This Changing World	Bluebird 10526
3/02/40	**1(5)**	16	32. **When You Wish Upon A Star/** with tenor sax solo by Tex; from the animated film "Pinocchio"	
1/27/40	**8**	11	33. The Gaucho Serenade............................	Bluebird 10570
2/03/40	**8**	10	34. Indian Summer.. song published in 1919	Bluebird 10495
2/10/40	**8**	8	35. In An Old Dutch Garden (By An Old Dutch Mill)/	
4/13/40	**10**	8	36. Starlit Hour.. from the Broadway musical "Earl Carroll's Vanities" vocals on 26, 28-36: Ray Eberle	Bluebird 10553
2/24/40	**1(9)**	19	● 37. **Tuxedo Junction/** [I] solos by Dale McMickle (muted trumpet), Clyde Hurley (trumpet),& Chummy MacGregor (piano)	
3/09/40	**17**	2	38. Danny Boy (Londonderry Air) .... [I]	Bluebird 10612
3/02/40	**13**	6	39. Ooh! What You Said .... from the musical comedy "Three After Three"	Bluebird 10561
3/30/40	**14**	4	40. It's A Blue World .... from the film "Music In My Heart"	Bluebird 10536
4/06/40	**1(7)**	16	41. **The Woodpecker Song**............................ based on "Reginella Campagnola"	Bluebird 10598
5/11/40	**1(3)**	11	42. **Imagination/**	
4/20/40	**15**	2	43. Say "Si Si" (Para Vigo Me Voy)..................	Bluebird 10622
4/27/40	**4**	10	44. Shake Down The Stars/	
5/04/40	**7**	12	45. Boog It.. vocals on 39, 41 & 45: Marion Hutton	Bluebird 10689
5/04/40	**2(2)**	11	46. Say It .... from the film "Buck Benny Rides Again"	Bluebird 10631
5/04/40	**16**	2	47. The Sky Fell Down................................ [I]	Bluebird 10580
6/01/40	**18**	2	48. Alice Blue Gown...................................... [I] from the Broadway musical "Irene"	Bluebird 10701
6/08/40	**7**	7	49. Devil May Care/	
6/29/40	**7**	6	50. I'm Stepping Out With A Memory Tonight ...	Bluebird 10717
6/08/40	**9**	10	51. Slow Freight .... [I]	Bluebird 10740
6/15/40	**1(1)**	13	52. **Fools Rush In (Where Angels Fear To Tread)**................ revived by Rick Nelson in 1963	Bluebird 10728
6/29/40	**5**	11	53. The Nearness Of You..............................	Bluebird 10745
7/06/40	**5**	12	● 54. Pennsylvania 6-5000 .... [I] Unison vocal; solos by Tex (tenor sax) & Johnny Best (trumpet); this was the telephone number of the Cafe Rouge at New York's Hotel Pennsylvania	Bluebird 10754
7/06/40	**9**	8	55. Hear My Song, Violetta	Bluebird 10684
8/03/40	**2(2)**	12	56. When The Swallows Come Back To Capistrano	Bluebird 10776
8/03/40	**17**	2	57. Sierra Sue	Bluebird 10638
8/10/40	**1(1)**	20	58. **Blueberry Hill/** revived by Fats Domino in 1956	
11/09/40	**24**	1	59. A Million Dreams Ago............................	Bluebird 10768

DATE CHARTED	PEAK POS	WKS CHRT'D	ARTIST — Record Title	Label & Number
8/10/40	**16**	1	60. I'll Never Smile Again	Bluebird 10673
10/26/40	**8**	7	61. Our Love Affair/ from the film "Strike Up the Band"	
9/28/40	**10**	10	62. The Call Of The Canyon	Bluebird 10845
			Ray Eberle: except as noted, all vocals from 40-62	
10/05/40	**9**	9	63. Crosstown	Bluebird 10832
10/19/40	**23**	1	64. I Wouldn't Take A Million	Bluebird 10860
			from the film "Young People"	
10/26/40+	**20**	1	65. Star Dust .... [I]	Bluebird 10665
11/09/40	**5**	10	66. Five O'Clock Whistle	Bluebird 10900
11/09/40	**9**	10	67. Falling Leaves/ [I]	
11/23/40	**15**	2	68. Beat Me, Daddy (Eight To The Bar)...........	Bluebird 10876
			vocals on 63 & 68: Jack Lathrop	
11/23/40	**10**	7	69. A Handful Of Stars/ from the film "Hullabaloo"	
11/30/40	**14**	1	70. Yesterthoughts	Bluebird 10893
12/28/40	**12**	1	71. You've Got Me This Way/ above two from the film "You'll Find Out"	
12/14/40	**24**	1	72. I'd Know You Anywhere	Bluebird 10906
12/21/40	**2(2)**	6	73. A Nightingale Sang In Berkeley Square	Bluebird 10931
			from the London musical "New Faces"	
1/11/41	**3**	17	74. Anvil Chorus .... [I]	Bluebird 10982
			solos by Tex (tenor sax) & Billy May (trumpet) from the opera "Il Trovatore"	
1/11/41	**7**	5	75. Along The Santa Fe Trail/ movie title song vocals on 64, 69-70, 72-73, & 75: Ray Eberle	
2/08/41	**9**	8	76. Yes, My Darling Daughter......................	Bluebird 10970
			vocals on 66, 71 & 76: Marion Hutton	
2/15/41	**16**	3	77. Frenesi .... [I]	Bluebird 10994
			Mexican song	
2/22/41	**1(1)**	10	78. **Song Of The Volga Boatmen** .... [I]	Bluebird 11029
			adaptation of Russian folk song; solos by Billy May & Ernie Caceres (alto sax)	
3/22/41	**3**	5	79. I Dreamt I Dwelt In Harlem.................... [I]	Bluebird 11063
4/19/41	**11**	4	80. Perfidia (Tonight)...........................	Bluebird 11095
			vocal; Dorothy Claire & Modernaires	
4/26/41	**23**	1	81. When That Man Is Dead And Gone..............	Bluebird 11069
5/17/41	**29**	1	82. Ida (Sweet As Apple Cider)...................	Bluebird 11079
			vocal: Tex Beneke	
6/28/41	**18**	2	83. Boulder Bluff/ [I]	
7/19/41	**7**	13	84. The Booglie Wooglie Piggy.....................	Bluebird 11163
			vocals on 81 & 84: Tex Beneke & Modernaires	
8/23/41	**4**	15	85. I Guess I'll Have To Dream The Rest	Bluebird 11187
8/30/41	**1(5)**	11	86. **You And I**	Bluebird 11215
			with muted trombone solo by Glenn	
8/30/41	**13**	5	87. Adios .... [I]	Bluebird 11219
9/06/41	**15**	2	88. The Cowboy Serenade	Bluebird 11235
9/13/41	**1(9)**	25	● 89. **Chattanooga Choo Choo/** the first record formally certified as a million seller Glenn Miller, Jimmy Priddy, Paul Tanner, & Frank D'Annolfo (trombones); Billy May, Ray Anthony, Dale McMickle, & Johnny Best (trumpets); Hal McIntyre & Ernie Caceres (alto saxes), Wilbur Schwartz (clarinet & alto sax), Tex Beneke & Al Klink (tenor sax); Chummy MacGregor (piano), Jack Lathrop (guitar), Herman Alpert (bass), & Maurice Purtill (drums)	
11/08/41	**18**	1	90. I Know Why..	Bluebird 11230
			above two & 94 from the film "It Happened in Sun Valley"	
9/27/41	**23**	1	91. Delilah/ vocals on 89 & 91: Tex Beneke & Modernaires with Paula Kelly	
10/04/41	**1(1)**	20	92. **Elmer's Tune**	Bluebird 11274
			solos by Tex & Glenn vocals on 85 & 92: Ray Eberle & Modernaires	
11/08/41	**11**	3	93. This Time The Dream's On Me	Bluebird 11315
			from the film "Blues In the Night"	

DATE CHARTED	PEAK POS	WKS CHRT'D	ARTIST — Record Title	Label & Number
11/15/41	18	1	94. It Happened In Sun Valley .... vocal: Paula Kelly-Ray Eberle-Tex Beneke-Modernaires	Bluebird 11263
11/29/41	16	2	95. I'm Thrilled	Bluebird 11287
12/20/41	23	1	96. Orange Blossom Lane	Bluebird 11326
12/27/41	5	2	97. Jingle Bells .... [X] vocal: Tex Beneke, Ernie Caceres, & Modernaires	Bluebird 11353
1/03/42+	1(2)	21	● 98. **A String Of Pearls**.............................. [I] Jerry Gray's most famous song & arrangement; featured cornet solo by Bobby Hackett; other solos by Beneke & Caceres (as) & Al Klink (ts)	Bluebird 11382
1/03/42	6	9	99. (There'll Be Bluebirds Over) The White Cliffs Of Dover/	
3/14/42	24	1	100. We're The Couple In The Castle................. from the animated film "Mr. Bug Goes to Town"	Bluebird 11397
1/17/42	7	10	101. Ev'rything I Love .... from the Broadway musical "Let's Face It" vocals on 86, 88, 93, 95-96, 99-101: Ray Eberle	Bluebird 11365
1/31/42	17	2	102. This Is No Laughing Matter/	
2/07/42	23	1	103. Humpty Dumpty Heart...........................	Bluebird 11369
2/07/42	1(10)	19	●104. **Moonlight Cocktail** .... with solos by MacGregor (piano) & Tex (tenor sax)	Bluebird 11401
3/07/42	10	5	105. Always In My Heart................................ movie title song	Bluebird 11438
4/04/42	7	12	106. Skylark/	
4/18/42	15	1	107. The Story Of A Starry Night.................... based on 1st movement of Tchaikovsky's Sixth Symphony	Bluebird 11462
4/11/42	1(2)	17	108. **Don't Sit Under The Apple Tree (With Anyone Else But Me)**......................... vocal: Marion Hutton-Tex Beneke-Modernaires; from the Broadway musical "Yokel Boy"; featured in the film "Private Buckaroo"	Bluebird 11474
7/04/42	7	14	109. Sweet Eloise	Victor 27879
7/04/42	15	2	110. American Patrol .... [I] featured trumpet solo by Billy May; song published in 1885	Victor 27873
7/11/42	22	1	111. Knit One, Purl Two	Victor 27894
8/01/42	1(8)	20	●112. **(I've Got A Gal In) Kalamazoo/** with solos by Billy & Tex vocals on 111-112: Marion Hutton & the Modernaires	
10/17/42	9	9	113. At Last .... vocals on 102-103, 105-107, & 113: Ray Eberle	Victor 27934
9/12/42	2(1)	18	114. Serenade In Blue .... 109 & 114: featured cornet solos by Bobby Hackett above three from the film "Orchestra Wives"	Victor 27935
9/26/42	19	1	115. Yesterday's Gardenias .... vocals on 104, 109, 114-115: Ray Eberle & the Modernaires	Victor 27933
10/31/42+	4	10	116. Dearly Beloved.................................... vocal: Skip Nelson; from the film "You Were Never Lovelier"	Victor 27953
11/28/42	7	11	117. Juke Box Saturday Night .... vocal: Marion Hutton, Tex Beneke, & Modernaires; with famous takeoffs on Harry James & Ink Spots	Victor 1509
12/19/42+	5	12	118. Moonlight Becomes You/ from the film "The Road to Morocco"	
1/16/43	11	3	119. Moonlight Mood......................................	Victor 1520
2/20/43	1(1)	19	120. **That Old Black Magic** .... from the film "Star-Spangled Rhythm" above three vocals: Skip Nelson & Modernaires	Victor 1523
5/01/43	20	1	121. In The Mood...................................... [I-R]	Bluebird 10416
9/11/43	8	14	122. Blue Rain .... vocal: Ray Eberle; recorded 10/3/39, originally released on Bluebird 10486	Victor 1536
10/09/43	13	7	123. Rhapsody In Blue .... [I] featured solos by Bobby & Tex	Victor 1529

DATE CHARTED	PEAK POS	WKS CHRT'D	ARTIST — Record Title	Label & Number
1/01/44	**20**	1	124. Rainbow Rhapsody/ [I]	
1/08/44	**12**	8	125. It Must Be Jelly ('cause Jam Don't Shake Like That) .... Victor 1546 vocal: The Modernaires above three recorded July 15-16, 1942	
1/08/44	**23**	1	126. Sunrise Serenade................................ [I-R]	Bluebird 10214
3/04/44	**27**	1	127. A String Of Pearls............................. [I-R] reissue of Bluebird 11382	Victor 1552
4/01/44	**25**	1	128. Here We Go Again.................................. [I] recorded 7/14/42	Victor 1563
7/10/48	**28**	1	129. Adios... [I-R] reissue of Bluebird 11219	Victor 2942

MITCH MILLER & HIS ORCHESTRA
Mitch began as a classical oboist, playing with Andre Kostelanetz & other large orchestras, & also with the Elliot Lawrence band. He became a top record producer and executive with Columbia, conductor-producer for Guy Mitchell, Tony Bennett, & other singers, and finally achieved his greatest fame with the "Sing Along with Mitch" best-selling albums & TV series.
(also see Frank Sinatra, Frankie Laine)

DATE CHARTED	PEAK POS	WKS CHRT'D	ARTIST — Record Title	Label & Number
7/15/50	**3**	12	1. Tzena, Tzena, Tzena .... Columbia 38885 adaptation of an Israeli song	
9/27/52	**23**	1	2. Meet Mister Callaghan	Columbia 39851
3/14/53	**25**	1	3. Without My Lover .... [I] featuring Stan Freeman on harpsichord	Columbia 39901
12/05/53	**26**	1	4. Under Paris Skies .... title song of the French film	Columbia 40100
7/24/54	**25**	1	5. Napoleon .... vocal adaptation of Tchaikovsky's "1812 Overture"	Columbia 40261

RAY MILLER & HIS ORCHESTRA
Popular 1920s bandleader who briefly featured jazz stars Frankie Trumbauer & Muggsy Spanier. (Also see Al Jolson)

DATE CHARTED	PEAK POS	WKS CHRT'D	ARTIST — Record Title	Label & Number
4/29/22	**8**	2	1. On The Gin-Gin-Ginny Shore .... [I]	Columbia 3550
5/13/22	**3**	5	2. The Sheik (Of Araby) .... [I]	Okeh 4498
8/05/22	**7**	2	3. Stumbling... [I]	Columbia 3611
9/09/22	**4**	5	4. I'm Just Wild About Harry .... [I] from the Broadway musical "Shuffle Along"	Columbia 3640
6/30/23	**9**	2	5. Bambalina .... [I] from the Broadway musical "Wildflower"	Columbia 3860
4/19/24	**5**	4	6. The One I Love Belongs To Somebody Else . [I] ISHAM JONES with RAY MILLER'S ORCHESTRA	Brunswick 2555
12/13/24	**4**	4	7. Somebody Loves Me .... [I] from "George White's Scandals of 1924"	Brunswick 2669
3/14/25	**1(7)**	16	8. **I'll See You In My Dreams/** [I]	
4/18/25	**8**	2	9. Why Couldn't It Be Poor Little Me.......... [I] above two: Isham Jones conducting Ray Miller's Orchestra	Brunswick 2788
5/23/25	**9**	2	10. Tessie (Stop Teasing Me) .... [I]	Brunswick 2830
9/05/25	**9**	1	11. Moonlight And Roses.............................. vocal: Frank Wright & Frank Bessinger; based on Lamare's "Andante" Frankie Trumbauer (cornet) on above five	Brunswick 2866
12/26/25	**12**	1	12. Save Your Sorrow (For Tomorrow) .... [I]	Brunswick 2935
4/27/29	**20**	1	13. Who Wouldn't Be Jealous Of You?.............. vocal: Dick Teela; with Muggsy Spanier (cornet)	Brunswick 4131
1/18/30	**14**	2	14. Funny, Dear, What Love Can Do................. vocal: Al Cameron	Brunswick 4675
4/26/30	**15**	2	15. Kiss Me With Your Eyes/	
5/10/30	**5**	7	16. When It's Springtime In The Rockies..........	Brunswick 4735

DATE CHARTED	PEAK POS	WKS CHRT'D	ARTIST — Record Title	Label & Number
			REED MILLER	
			Prolific concert tenor who also sang in opera, particularly popular for his duets with Frederick Wheeler under the names "James Reed & James F. Harrison"; also a member of the Columbia Stellar Quartet. Reed died on 12/29/23 (43). (also see James F. Harrison)	
3/05/10	7	3	1. Roses In June .... Victor 5753	
			later released on Victor 16675	
1/07/11	2(3)	7	2. It's Always June When You're In Love .... Columbia 924	
			under pseudonym "James Reed"	
7/01/11	9	2	3. Tell Her I Love Her So .... Victor 5829	
8/10/12	3	5	4. A Stein Song.. Columbia 5386	
			REED MILLER & FRANK CROXTON	
9/13/13	9	1	5. Every Lover Must Meet His Fate .... Victor 17333	
			also recorded for Columbia 1359	
9/13/13	10	1	6. Santa Lucia .... [F] Columbia 1340	
2/28/14	10	1	7. The One I Love.. Columbia 1442	
			REED MILLER & GRACE KERNS	
			from the Broadway musical "The Marriage Market"	
2/19/16	10	1	8. Love, Here Is My Heart!............................. Victor 17916	
7/01/16	5	3	9. Fair Hawaii .... Victor 18032	
			"EDNA BROWN & JAMES REED" (Elsie Baker & Reed Miller)	
7/22/16	8	1	10. They Didn't Believe Me .... Columbia 1982	
			GRACE KERNS & REED MILLER	
			from the Broadway musical "The Girl from Utah"	
6/16/17	10	1	11. Love Will Find A Way.............................. Victor 18234	
			from the Broadway musical "The Maid of the Mountains"	
9/25/20	11	1	12. I'll Be With You In Apple Blossom Time........ Emerson 10213	
5/28/21	14	1	13. Love Will Find The Way .... Edison 80590	
			from the Broadway musical "Shuffle Along"	
			LUCKY MILLINDER & HIS ORCHESTRA	
			Vocalist and front man for Mills Blue Rhythm Band in 1930s before leading this swing band featuring blues singers Sister Rosetta Tharpe & Wynonie Harris, and all-time jazz trumpet great Dizzy Gillespie; pianist Bill Doggett was a regular member. Lucky died on 9/28/66 (66).	
1/31/42	23	1	1. Big Fat Mama .... Decca 4041	
7/18/42	21	1	2. Shout, Sister, Shout!/	
8/22/42	13	1	3. I Want A Tall, Skinny Papa .... Decca 18386	
			above two vocals: Sister Rosetta Tharpe	
12/19/42+	12	4	4. When The Lights Go On Again (All Over The World) .... Decca 18496	
4/24/43	20	1	5. Are You Ready? .... Decca 18529	
			Dizzy Gillespie (trumpet) on above two	
12/25/43	20	1	6. When The Lights Go On Again (All Over The World) .... [R] Decca 18496	
1/15/44	12	2	7. Sweet Slumber .... Decca 18569	
			vocals on 1, 4-7: Trevor Bacon	
8/12/44	24	1	8. Hurry, Hurry! .... Decca 18609	
6/30/45	7	10	9. Who Threw The Whiskey In The Well? .... Decca 18674	
			above two vocals: Wynonie Harris	
7/28/51	19	8	10. I'm Waiting Just For You .... King 4453	
			vocal: Annisteen Allen	
			MILLS BLUE RHYTHM BAND	
			Swing band led by Lucky Millinder, featuring Henry "Red" Allen (trumpet) & J.C. Higginbotham (trombone), with arrangements by Will Hudson.	
3/30/35	8	5	1. Solitude .... Columbia 2994	
6/01/35	15	3	2. Dancing Dogs.................................... [I] Columbia 3044	
10/12/35	11	4	3. Truckin'.. Columbia 3078	
			vocal: Henry "Red" Allen	
10/12/35	17	2	4. Dinah Lou .... Columbia 3083	
			from the stage production of "Cotton Club Parade"	
			vocals on 1 & 4: Chuck Richards	

DATE CHARTED	PEAK POS	WKS CHRT'D	ARTIST — Record Title	Label & Number
10/19/35	**9**	17	5. Ride, Red, Ride.. vocal: Lucky Millinder	Columbia 3087
11/23/35	**19**	1	6. Harlem Heat .... [I]	Columbia 3071
10/17/36	**15**	2	7. Merry-Go-Round .... [I]	Columbia 3147
10/31/36	**19**	1	8. In A Sentimental Mood .... [I]	Columbia 3148
11/21/36	**11**	2	9. Barrelhouse... [I]	Columbia 3156
12/26/36+	**15**	3	10. Mr. Ghost Goes To Town .... [I]	Columbia 3158
8/07/37	**18**	1	11. The Image Of You .... [I]	Variety 3531

MILLS BROTHERS

No other vocal group in history turned out hit records over a longer span of time than the Mills Brothers. Herbert, Harry, & Donald Mills, all born 1912-15 in Piqua, Ohio, began perfecting their distinctively smooth, relaxed sound on Cincinatti radio in the late 1920s. Accompanied by older brother John with bass-note vocals and guitar, they scored with the first of many hits in late 1931. John died in late 1935, replaced by father John Sr. (until his retirement in 1956). Surviving two generations of changing musical styles with their same patented sound, the Mills continued to hit the charts through the end of the 60s. Harry Mills died on 6/28/82 (68).

DATE CHARTED	PEAK POS	WKS CHRT'D	ARTIST — Record Title	Label & Number
11/21/31	**1(4)**	13	1. **Tiger Rag/**	
11/28/31+	**4**	9	2. Nobody's Sweetheart............................. on nearly all their records through 1950, the brothers had no instrumental accompaniment other than guitar	Brunswick 6197
11/21/31	**3**	11	3. Gems From "George White's Scandals" .... BING CROSBY, MILLS BROTHERS, & BOSWELL SISTERS with Victor Young's Orchestra medley from the Broadway musical: "The Thrill Is Gone"/ "Life Is Just a Bowl of Cherries"	Brunswick 20102
1/09/32	**1(2)**	9	4. **Dinah/**	
2/20/32	**10**	4	5. Can't We Talk It Over? .... above two: BING CROSBY & MILLS BROTHERS	Brunswick 6240
1/16/32	**3**	8	6. You Rascal, You/	
2/20/32	**20**	1	7. Baby, Won't You Please Come Home	Brunswick 6225
3/05/32	**3**	9	8. I Heard	Brunswick 6269
4/16/32	**4**	7	9. Good-Bye, Blues/	
5/14/32	**4**	6	10. Rockin' Chair......................................	Brunswick 6278
4/16/32	**7**	5	11. Shine... BING CROSBY & MILLS BROTHERS	Brunswick 6276
5/21/32	**10**	6	12. Chinatown, My Chinatown........................ from the Broadway musical "Up and Down Broadway"	Brunswick 6305
7/02/32	**2(2)**	8	13. St. Louis Blues/	
7/09/32	**8**	6	14. Sweet Sue	Brunswick 6330
8/20/32	**2(1)**	5	15. Bugle Call Rag	Brunswick 6357
9/17/32	**7**	5	16. It Don't Mean A Thing (If It Ain't Got That Swing)	Brunswick 6377
4/04/34	**19**	1	17. I Found A New Baby.................................	Brunswick 6785
6/02/34	**2(1)**	6	18. Swing It, Sister/	
6/23/34	**12**	3	19. Money In My Pockets .... from the Broadway musical "Strictly Dynamite"	Brunswick 6894
6/30/34	**2(1)**	9	20. Sleepy Head... also recorded for Melotone 13177	Brunswick 6913
4/10/37	**19**	1	21. Dedicated To You/	
4/24/37	**20**	1	22. Big Boy Blue.. above two: ELLA FITZGERALD & MILLS BROTHERS	Decca 1148
6/12/37	**19**	1	23. Darling Nelly Gray	Decca 1245
7/16/38	**20**	1	24. Flat Foot Floogee................................ [N] above two: LOUIS ARMSTRONG & MILLS BROTHERS	Decca 1876
11/05/38	**8**	8	25. Sixty Seconds Got Together......................	Decca 1964
3/18/39	**10**	2	26. Sweet Adeline/	
8/12/39	**14**	2	27. You Tell Me Your Dream, I'll Tell You Mine .	Decca 2285
5/25/40	**30**	1	28. Old Black Joe	Decca 3132

DATE CHARTED	PEAK POS	WKS CHRT'D	ARTIST — Record Title	Label & Number
7/13/40	26	1	29. W.P.A. .... LOUIS ARMSTRONG & MILLS BROTHERS	Decca 3151
10/24/42	20	1	30. Paper Doll	Decca 18318
7/17/43	1(12)	36	● 31. **Paper Doll/** [R] biggest non-holiday hit of the decade, with sales over six million	
11/06/43	17	2	32. I'll Be Around	Decca 18318
6/03/44	1(5)	33	● 33. **You Always Hurt The One You Love/**	
6/24/44	8	16	34. Till Then	Decca 18599
5/19/45	6	11	35. I Wish/	
5/19/45	14	5	36. Put Another Chair At The Table	Decca 18663
4/20/46	12	4	37. Don't Be A Baby, Baby	Decca 18753
5/18/46	7	15	38. I Don't Know Enough About You/	
7/13/46	22	4	39. There's No One But You	Decca 18834
9/28/46	12	7	40. I Guess I'll Get The Papers (And Go Home)	Decca 23638
5/10/47	2(2)	15	41. Across The Alley From The Alamo	Decca 23863
9/20/47	21	2	42. Oh! My Achin' Heart	Decca 23979
10/25/47	15	1	43. When You Were Sweet Sixteen	Decca 23627
11/20/48	17	11	44. Gloria	Decca 24509
2/12/49	8	9	45. I Love You So Much It Hurts/	
2/19/49	9	11	46. I've Got My Love To Keep Me Warm	Decca 24550
			from the film "On the Avenue"	
8/20/49	5	15	47. Someday (You'll Want Me To Want You)	Decca 24694
11/31/49	24	1	48. Who'll Be The Next One (To Cry Over You)	Decca 24749
2/25/50	5	14	49. Daddy's Little Girl	Decca 24872
11/11/50+	4	17	50. Nevertheless (I'm In Love With You)	Decca 27253
			featured in the film "Three Little Words"	
2/02/52	7	12	51. Be My Life's Companion	Decca 27889
			above two with Sy Oliver's Orchestra	
9/27/52	1(3)	21	● 52. **The Glow-Worm** .... with Hal McIntyre's Orchestra; adaptation of the 1908 hit (from the German operetta "Lysistrata", & the Broadway musical "The Girl Behind The Counter") with new lyrics	Decca 28384
12/13/52	22	2	53. Lazy River .... previously recorded for Decca 25046	Decca 28458
3/14/53	14	4	54. Twice As Much	Decca 28586
5/23/53	12	6	55. Say "Si Si" .... above two with Sonny Burke's Orchestra	Decca 28670
7/18/53	21	3	56. Pretty Butterfly	Decca 28736
10/17/53	23	2	57. Who Put The Devil In Evelyn's Eyes .... above two with Owen Bradley's Orchestra	Decca 28818
12/19/53+	15	5	58. The Jones Boy/	
1/16/54	27	1	59. She Was Five And He Was Ten	Decca 28945
3/13/54	22	2	60. You Didn't Want Me When You Had Me (So Why Do You Want Me Now)	Decca 29019
5/22/54	26	1	61. A Carnival In Venice .... based on Ludovic Gobbaerts' "Carnival de Venise"	Decca 29115
9/04/54	25	1	62. How Blue? .... 58-60 & 62 with Sy Oliver's Orchestra	Decca 29185

IRVING MILLS & HIS HOTSY TOTSY BAND

Lyricist on many popular hits ("It Don't Mean a Thing",
"Solitude", "Straighten Up and Fly Right"), early manager for Duke
Ellington, publisher; also assembled all-star jazz record
sessions, sometimes including Benny Goodman & the Dorsey brothers.
Irving died in April, 1985 (91).

DATE CHARTED	PEAK POS	WKS CHRT'D	ARTIST — Record Title	Label & Number
10/26/29	8	3	1. Ain't Misbehavin' .... Bill "Bojangles" Robinson, accompanied by Mills' band from the Broadway musical "Hot Chocolates"	Brunswick 4535
1/04/30	20	1	2. Star Dust .... [I] the first charted version of this classic, with composer Hoagy Carmichael (piano) & Jimmy Dorsey (clarinet/alto sax)	Brunswick 4587

DATE CHARTED	PEAK POS	WKS CHRT'D	ARTIST — Record Title	Label & Number
			ROY MILTON & HIS SOLID SENDERS Influential West Coat R&B singer/drummer	
8/17/46	**20**	1	● 1. R.M. Blues .... Juke Box 504 long-running R&B hit	
			JOHNNY MINCE Jazz clarinetist (born John Henry Muenzenberger) with Buddy Rogers, Ray Noble (1935-37), Red Norvo, & Tommy Dorsey (1937-41).	
			CARMEN MIRANDA Flamboyant Portugese-born entertainer (born Maria Do Carmo Miranda Da Cunha) billed as "the Brazilian Bombshell", and featured in 1940s movies and Broadway shows. Carmen died on 8/5/55 (46).	
5/03/41	**25**	1	1. Mama Euquero (I Want My Mama) .... [F] Decca 23132 accompanied by Bando da Lua	
10/09/48	**12**	14	2. Cuanto La Gusta .... Decca 24479 from the film "A Date With Judy"	
1/28/50	**23**	3	3. The Wedding Samba................................ Decca 24841 above two: CARMEN MIRANDA & ANDREWS SISTERS accompanied by Vic Shoen & His Orchestra	
			MR. GOON BONES & MR. FORD Used same bones-and-organ instrumentation as Brother Bones; featuring Barney Lantz.	
7/23/49	**14**	7	1. Ain't She Sweet .... Crystalette 1803	
			GUY MITCHELL Popular baritone who started as a child performer, and sang briefly with Carmen Cavallaro in the late 40s; his biggest hit was the 1956 million-seller "Singing the Blues". (Accompanied on all records by Mitch Miller & His Orchestra)	
12/09/50+	**2(7)**	21	● 1. My Heart Cries For You/ adapted from the 18th century French melody "Chanson de Marie Antoinette"	
12/16/50+	**4**	17	2. The Roving Kind............................. Col. 78-39067 adapted from the English folk song "The Pirate Ship"	
2/24/51	**24**	2	3. You're Just In Love.................................. Columbia 39052 ROSEMARY CLOONEY & GUY MITCHELL from the Broadway musical "Me Madam"	
3/03/51	**8**	15	4. Sparrow In The Tree Top/	
3/17/51	**27**	2	5. Christopher Columbus........................... Columbia 39190	
5/05/51	**17**	11	6. Unless .... Columbia 39331	
6/02/51	**2(1)**	19	● 7. My Truly, Truly Fair................................. Columbia 39415	
8/18/51	**9**	9	8. Belle, Belle, My Liberty Belle/	
8/18/51	**23**	1	9. Sweetheart Of Yesterday........................ Columbia 39512	
11/17/51	**20**	1	10. There's Always Room At Our House/	
11/17/51	**28**	2	11. I Can't Help It .... Columbia 39595 Hank Williams' country classic	
3/15/52	**4**	21	● 12. Pittsburgh, Pennsylvania/	
6/21/52	**26**	1	13. Day Of Jubilo.................................... Columbia 39753	
8/23/52	**14**	6	14. Feet Up (Pat Him On The Po-Po)................... Columbia 39822	
11/01/52	**24**	2	15. 'Cause I Love You, That's A-Why................. Columbia 39879	
1/31/53	**19**	4	16. She Wears Red Feathers .... Columbia 39909	
7/18/53	**23**	1	17. Tell Us Where The Good Times Are............. Columbia 39992 15 & 17: GUY MITCHELL & MINDY CARSON	
			MODERNAIRES WITH PAULA KELLY Paula, Hal Dickinson, Ralph Brewster, Chuck Goldstein, & Bill Conway first achieved great popularity singing with Glenn Miller ("Chattanooga Choo Choo", "Moonlight Cocktail", "Kalamazoo"). There were various male personnel changes, with Dickinson (Paula's husband) & Brewster remaining into the 50s. (Also see Les Brown & Frank Sinatra)	
7/21/45	**11**	1	1. There! I've Said It Again .... Columbia 36800	
7/27/46	**18**	1	2. Salute To Glenn Miller .... Columbia 36992 medley featuring "Elmer's Tune" & "Chattanooga Choo Choo"	
8/17/46	**3**	14	3. To Each His Own .... Columbia 37063 written for, but not included in, the film of the same name	

DATE CHARTED	PEAK POS	WKS CHRT'D	ARTIST — Record Title	Label & Number
1/11/47	**11**	3	4. Zip-A-Dee-Doo-Dah .... from the animated film "Song of the South" above four accompanied by Mitchell Ayres' Orchestra	Columbia 37147
3/07/53	**23**	2	5. New Juke Box Saturday Night .... new version of their famous hit with Glenn Miller accompanied by George Cates' Orchestra	Coral 60899
2/27/54	**29**	2	6. Salute To Glenn Miller .... new medley	Coral 61110

MIFF MOLE
Renowned jazz trombonist, played with Roger Wolfe Kahn (1926-27), Red Nichols, Paul Whiteman (1938-40), & Benny Goodman (1943); died on 4/29/61 (63).

CARLOS MOLINA & HIS ORCHESTRA
Latin-American band.

3/28/36	**19**	1	1. Thinking Of You	Columbia 3122

TOOTS MONDELLO
Six-time Metronome poll winner as top alto saxophonist; played with Roger Wolfe Kahn, Benny Goodman (1934, 39-40), Ray Noble (1935), & Andre Kostelanetz.

MARILYN MONROE
The most legendary of all postwar movie stars and the definitive American sex symbol, born Norma Jean Baker; died on 8/5/62 (36).

7/10/54	**30**	1	1. River Of No Return .... movie title song	RCA Victor 5745

VAUGHN MONROE & HIS ORCHESTRA
Big-voiced baritone, trumpeter, & bandleader; very popular on radio, and featured in several movies. He died on 5/21/73 (61). (Except as noted, all vocals by Vaughn)

10/19/40	**1(3)**	12	1. **There I Go**	Bluebird 10848
11/16/40	**26**	1	2. Is It Love Or Is It Conscription?/	
2/08/41	**16**	4	3. So You're The One	Bluebird 10901
2/15/41	**13**	3	4. High On A Windy Hill	Bluebird 10976
3/01/41	**24**	1	5. There'll Be Some Changes Made	Bluebird 11025
4/12/41	**25**	2	6. Racing With The Moon........................ Vaughn's famous theme song	Bluebird 11070
6/14/41	**12**	2	7. G'bye Now .... from the Broadway musical "Hellzapoppin"	Bluebird 11114
8/02/41	**22**	1	8. The Worm Who Loved The Little Tater Bug .... [N]	Bluebird 11207
8/09/41	**16**	2	9. Yours .... vocals on 7 & 9: Marilyn Duke	Vocals on 7
9/06/41	**23**	1	10. If It's You	Bluebird 11245
1/17/42	**21**	3	11. The Shrine Of St. Cecelia	Bluebird 11344
5/23/42	**11**	1	12. Tangerine............................	Bluebird 11433
5/23/42+	**13**	2	13. Three Little Sisters .... from the film "Private Buckaroos"	Bluebird 11508
8/15/42	**1(1)**	14	14. **My Devotion**............................	Victor 27925
10/03/42	**20**	1	15. Hip, Hip, Hooray/ vocals on 15 & 17: Four V's	
10/31/42+	**1(3)**	15	16. **When The Lights Go On Again (All Over The World)**	Victor 27945
5/08/43	**1(3)**	14	17. **Let's Get Lost** .... vocal: Vaughn Monroe & Four Lee Sisters from the film "Happy-Go-Lucky"	Victor 1524
12/09/44+	**4**	7	18. The Trolley Song/ vocal: Vaughn & Marilyn Duke from the film "Meet Me in St. Louis"	
12/16/44	**19**	1	19. The Very Thought Of You........................	Victor 1605
3/03/45	**8**	1	20. Rum And Coca-Cola/ uses a calypso melody from Trinidad ("L'Anee' Passee'")	
3/17/45	**1(6)**	29	● 21. **There! I've Said It Again**........................ hit #1 again in 1964 for Bobby Vinton	Victor 1637
11/10/45	**12**	2	22. Something Sentimental............................	Victor 1714

DATE CHARTED	PEAK POS	WKS CHRT'D	ARTIST — Record Title	Label & Number
11/10/45	**17**	1	23. Just A Blue Serge Suit.............................	Victor 1725
11/24/45	**17**	1	24. Fishin' For The Moon/	
1/26/46	**12**	1	25. Are These Really Mine?	Victor 1736
12/22/45+	**1(5)**	14	26. **Let It Snow! Let It Snow! Let It Snow!**.......	Victor 1759
3/30/46	**7**	5	27. Seems Like Old Times	Victor 1811
			backing vocals on above eight: Norton Sisters	
7/13/46	**15**	3	28. Who Told You That Lie?/	
7/20/46	**16**	2	29. It's My Lazy Day	Victor 1892
11/16/46	**13**	4	30. The Things We Did Last Summer................	Victor 1972
2/01/47	**21**	5	31. You Can't See the Sun When You're Cryin'....	RCA Victor 2053
6/21/47	**22**	4	32. Dreams Are A Dime A Dozen	Victor 2226
9/20/47	**2(5)**	15	33. I Wish I Didn't Love You So	RCA Victor 2294
			from the film "The Perils of Pauline"	
10/25/47	**10**	1	34. Kokomo, Indiana/	
11/01/47	**5**	8	35. You Do	RCA Victor 2361
			above two from the film "Mother Wore Tights"	
11/08/47	**1(10)**	22	● 36. **Ballerina**	RCA Victor 2433
11/22/47+	**3**	13	37. How Soon (Will I Be Seeing You)	RCA Victor 2523
12/27/47+	**21**	4	38. In A Little Book Shop/	
2/07/48	**24**	2	39. Passing Fancy....................................	RCA Victor 2573
1/31/48	**20**	4	40. Matinee..	RCA Victor 2671
3/13/48	**22**	1	41. Completely Yours	RCA Victor 2712
5/01/48	**21**	1	42. It's The Sentimental Thing To Do	RCA Victor 2748
5/01/48	**22**	2	43. Melody Time/	
5/15/48	**26**	1	44. Blue Shadows On The Trail	RCA Victor 2785
			above two from the animated film "Melody Time"	
5/15/48	**23**	1	45. What Do I Have To Do (To Make You Love Me)	RCA Victor 2811
			from the Broadway musical "Are You With It?"	
6/26/48	**19**	9	46. The Maharajah Of Magador..................... [N]	RCA Victor 2851
			featuring Ziggy Talent	
7/24/48	**9**	14	47. Cool Water	RCA Victor 2923
			with the Sons of the Pioneers	
10/30/48	**22**	1	48. Ev'rday I Love You (Just A Little Bit More)....	RCA Victor 2957
			from the film "Two Guys from Texas"	
11/27/48	**20**	2	49. In My Dreams......................................	RCA Victor 3133
			most records from 28-50 with the Moon Maids	
1/15/49	**3**	22	50. Red Roses For A Blue Lady	RCA Victor 3319
4/23/49	**1(12)**	22	● 51. **Riders In The Sky (A Cowboy Legend)**........	RCA Victor 3411
8/06/49	**1(2)**	18	52. **Someday**...	RCA Vic. 78-3510
9/24/49	**6**	17	53. That Lucky Old Sun (Just Rolls Around Heaven All Day)	RCA Vic. 78-3531
			51, 53 & 54 with the Moon Men	
11/05/49	**29**	1	54. Vieni Su (Say You Love Me Too)	RCA Vic. 78-3549
11/19/49	**10**	9	55. Mule Train...	RCA Vic. 78-3600
1/28/50	**4**	7	56. Bamboo	RCA Vic. 78-3627
6/17/50	**20**	1	57. Thanks, Mister Florist	RCA Victor 3773
4/21/51	**3**	17	58. Sound Off..	RCA Victor 4113
4/21/51	**8**	16	59. On Top Of Old Smoky	RCA Victor 4114
			based on the traditional folk song "Little Mohee" with the Moon Maids & the Moon Men	
5/12/51	**7**	8	60. Old Soldiers Never Die	RCA Victor 4146
			inspired by Douglas MacArthur's "farewell" speech to Congress	
10/20/51	**28**	2	61. Meanderin'	RCA Victor 4271
1/19/52	**27**	1	62. Charmaine...	RCA Victor 4375
			originally written to promote the silent film "What Price Glory?"	
3/08/52	**22**	1	63. Mountain Laurel.....................................	RCA Victor 4479

DATE CHARTED	PEAK POS	WKS CHRT'D	ARTIST — Record Title	Label & Number
4/12/52	18	5	64. Lady Love/	
5/03/52	20	6	65. Idaho State Fair	RCA Victor 4611
5/30/53	27	1	66. Ruby .... theme from the film "Ruby Gentry"	RCA Victor 5286
8/07/54	7	16	67. They Were Doin' The Mambo	RCA Victor 5767

PATSY MONTANA & THE PRAIRIE RAMBLERS
Born Rubye Blevins, one of the first widely popular solo female country singers

1/25/36	10	4	1. I Wanna Be A Cowboy's Sweetheart	Vocalion 3010

LOU MONTE
New Jersey-born singer

2/13/54	7	11	1. At The Darktown Strutters' Ball..................	RCA Victor 5611
4/17/54	21	4	2. Somewhere There Is Someone.................... accompanied by Henri Rene & His Orchestra	RCA Victor 5691
8/28/54	30	1	3. Italian Hucklebuck .... [N] 1 & 3 accompanied by Hugo Winterhalter & His Orchestra	RCA Victor 5832

MONTGOMERY & STONE
Dave Montgomery & Fred Stone, popular musical comedy duo in many Broadway shows, also in minstrel shows and vaudeville; Montgomery died on 4/20/17 (46), Stone on 3/6/59 (85).

11/18/11	9	1	1. Moriah - Scotch Medley......................... [C]	Victor 70044

ART MOONEY & HIS ORCHESTRA
Detroit-based band featuring some arrangements by Neal Hefti, most successful with singalong remakes of 1920s standards.

1/24/48	1(5)	18	● 1. **I'm Looking Over A Four-Leaf Clover** .... featuring Mike Pingatore (banjo)	MGM 10119
4/03/48	3	15	● 2. Baby Face	MGM 10156
7/03/48	5	22	● 3. Bluebird Of Happiness .... vocal: Bud Brees & Galli Sister, with poem recitation by Art; British song	MGM 10207
2/26/49	18	8	4. Beautiful Eyes/	
3/12/49	21	2	5. Doo De Doo On An Old Kazoo	MGM 10357
5/07/49	7	17	6. Again .... vocal: Johnny Martin & Madely Russell from the film "Road House"	MGM 10398
6/04/49	29	1	7. Merry-Go-Round Waltz............................	MGM 10405
7/16/49	13	6	8. Twenty-Four Hours Of Sunshine.................	MGM 10446
9/17/49	16	11	9. Hop-Scotch Polka (Scotch Hot)	MGM 10500
10/29/49	19	4	10. Toot Toot Tootsie (Good-Bye)/ featured in the film "The Jolson Story"	
11/19/49	21	1	11. I Never See Maggie Alone .... lead vocal by Tex Fletcher	MGM 10548
4/22/50	28	2	12. If I Knew You Were Comin' I'd've Baked A Cake .... lead vocal by Betty Harris	MGM 10660
7/01/50	23	1	13. M-I-S-S-I-S-S-I-P-P-I .... vocal by Allan Brooks & The Four Clovers	MGM 10721
12/20/52	29	1	14. Lazy River....................................... vocals by Cathy Ryan & the Clover Leafs	MGM 11347
12/27/52	24	1	15. Heartbreaker	MGM 11386

GRACE MOORE
The most popular opera star of the 1930s, Grace started in Broadway musicals before becoming a featured soprano with the New York Metropolitan Opera in 1928; the 1934 film "One Night of Love" and subsequent movie musicals spread her fame further. Grace remained with the Met until her death on 1/26/47 in a plane crash; the 1953 film "So This Is Love" was based on her life.

6/27/25	5	4	1. Listening/	
7/11/25	8	2	2. Tell Her In The Springtime .... above two from the Broadway musical "Music Box Revue of 1924"; both accompanied by Rosario Bourdon's Orchestra	Victor 19613

DATE CHARTED	PEAK POS	WKS CHRT'D	ARTIST — Record Title	Label & Number
10/20/34	1(4)	10	**3. One Night Of Love/**	
11/03/34	15	2	4. Ciribiribin .... above two from the film "One Night of Love" both accompanied by Wilifred Pelletier's Orchestra, and the Metropolitan Opera Chorus	Brunswick 6994
			PHIL MOORE FOUR Pianist-singer, wrote arrangements for Jack Teagarden & Mildred Bailey, composed the hit "Shoo Shoo Baby".	
3/17/45	3	10	1. My Dreams Are Getting Better All The Time/ from the film "In Society"	
5/05/45	22	1	2. A Little On The Lonely Side .... both vocals: Phil Moore & Billy Daniels	Victor 1641
			ESY MORALES & HIS LATIN-AMERICAN ORCHESTRA Flute virtuoso with rumba band	
3/27/48	27	1	1. Jungle Fantasy	Rainbow 10050
			MORAN & MACK George Moran (1881-1949) and Charles Mack (1888-1934, real name Charles Sellers), vaudeville comedy team whose record debut was one of the 1920s' fastest sellers.	
6/25/27	1(5)	12	● **1. Two Black Crows-Parts 1 & 2 (The Early Bird Catches The Worm)**..............[T-C]	Columbia 935
10/29/27	4	5	2. Two Black Crows-Parts 3 & 4 (All About Lions).....................................[T-C]	Columbia 1094
2/18/28	6	4	3. Two Black Crows-Part 5 (Curiosities On The Farm) ....[T-C]	Columbia 1198
6/23/28	13	2	4. Two Black Crows-Part 7 (No Matter How Hungry A Horse Is, He Cannot Eat A Bit) ....[T-C]	Columbia 1350
10/05/29	14	1	5. Foolishments ....[T-C]	Columbia 1929
			AL MORGAN Chicago-based singer-pianist	
7/30/49	4	26	1. Jealous Heart .... also issued on Universal 148	London 500
1/28/50	26	1	2. Half A Heart Is All You Left Me (When You Broke My Heart In Two)......................	London 571
12/02/50	29	1	3. The Place Where I Worship (Is The Wide Open Spaces) .... with recitation by John McCormick	London 784
1/13/51	24	2	4. My Heart Cries For You.......................... with the Key Tones & Jack Pleis' Orchestra	London 877
			CORRINE MORGAN Real name Corrine Morgan Welsh, popular contralto best known for her duets with Frank Stanley. Corrine died in 1945 (about 70).	
8/08/03	4	3	1. It's A Lovely Day For A Walk..................... also recorded for Columbia 1461 CORRINE MORGAN & FRANK STANLEY	Edison 8469
6/11/04	1(2)	8	**2. Toyland**.. CORRINE MORGAN & HAYDN QUARTET from the Broadway musical "Babes in Toyland"	Victor 2721
7/16/04	5	1	3. Then You'll Remember Me...................... also on Victor 31213	Victor 2756
8/27/04	3	5	4. Listen To The Mocking Bird...................... later recorded for Columbia 1833 & 32531, Victor 4080 & 31316	Edison 8715
1/28/05	6	1	5. Love's Old Sweet Song............................	Victor 4095
6/10/05	5	1	6. Just My Style... also recorded for Edison 8997	Victor 4332
8/26/05	1(2)	8	**7. Dearie**..	Victor 4396
9/20/05	4	2	8. When You And I Were Young, Maggie .... 4, 6 & 8: FRANK STANLEY & CORRINE MORGAN	Victor 4428

DATE CHARTED	PEAK POS	WKS CHRT'D	ARTIST — Record Title	Label & Number
1/06/06	1(2)	6	9. **How'd You Like To Spoon With Me?** .... from the Broadway musical "The Earl and the Girl" 7 & 9: CORRINE MORGAN & HAYDN QUARTET	Victor 4532
4/14/06	1(3)	6	10. **So Long, Mary**.. from the Broadway musical "Forty-Five Minutes from Broadway" also recorded for Columbia 3359	Victor 4590
6/23/06	4	2	11. The Moon Has His Eyes On You.................. also recorded for Columbia 3412 & 32955	Victor 4696
8/25/06	8	1	12. By The Light Of The Honeymoon .... above two: FRANK STANLEY & CORRINE MORGAN	Victor 31532
2/23/07	3	3	13. Oh Promise Me .... from the Broadway operetta "Robin Hood"	Victor 4964

GEORGE MORGAN
Major country star often featured on Grand Ole Opry.

DATE CHARTED	PEAK POS	WKS CHRT'D	ARTIST — Record Title	Label & Number
10/29/49	25	1	1. Room Full Of Roses..................................	Columbia 20594

HELEN MORGAN
The 1920s' definitive "torch singer"; Helen started in Chicago and became a top Broadway musical star, famed above all for the classic "Show Boat" and for her trademark piano-top singing. She died on 10/8/41 (41).

DATE CHARTED	PEAK POS	WKS CHRT'D	ARTIST — Record Title	Label & Number
9/10/27	9	1	1. A Tree In The Park .... from the Broadway musical "Peggy Ann"	Brunswick 111
4/21/28	4	7	2. Bill/	
5/26/28	7	4	3. Can't Help Lovin' Dat Man...................... above two from "Show Boat" both accompanied by Victor Bavaralli's Orchestra	Victor 21238
6/29/29	11	3	4. Mean To Me	Victor 21930
1/04/30	8	5	5. Why Was I Born?...................................... from the Broadway musical "Sweet Adeline"	Victor 22199
11/08/30	16	2	6. Body And Soul .... from the Broadway musical "Three's A Crowd" above three accompanied by Leonard Joy's Orchestra	Victor 22532

JAYE P. MORGAN
Featured on many TV variety and game shows from the 1950s to the 70s.

DATE CHARTED	PEAK POS	WKS CHRT'D	ARTIST — Record Title	Label & Number
9/19/53	22	1	1. Just A Gigolo...	Derby 828
12/19/53+	26	2	2. Life Is Just A Bowl Of Cherries .... orchestra directed by Frank DeVol from the Broadway musical "George White's Scandals of 1931"	Derby 837

RUSS MORGAN & HIS ORCHESTRA
Trombonist and popular sweet-band leader, former pianist, arranger for Jean Goldkette, Fletcher Henderson, Dorsey Brothers, others. Russ was also an extremely successful composer ("Somebody Else Is Taking My Place", "You're Nobody Till Somebody Loves You", "So Tired"). He died on 8/8/69 (65). (also see Andrews Sisters)

DATE CHARTED	PEAK POS	WKS CHRT'D	ARTIST — Record Title	Label & Number
6/22/35	10	3	1. Tidal Wave .... [I]	Columbia 3050
7/20/35	7	9	2. Love Me Forever...................................... movie title song	Columbia 3063
7/27/35	10	4	3. In A Little Gypsy Tea Room..................... Claude Thornhill (piano), Will Bradley (trombone), & Joe Ventuti (violin) on above three	Columbia 3064
8/24/35	9	8	4. The Rose In Her Hair................................ from the film "The Broadway Gondolier"	Columbia 3063
10/17/36	12	5	5. Midnight Blue .... from Broadway's "Ziegfeld Follies of 1936"	Brunswick 7737
10/24/36	20	1	6. Fancy Meeting You (The Evolution Song)....... from the film "Stage Struck"	Brunswick 7742
12/12/36+	5	5	7. I'm In A Dancing Mood/	
1/02/37	16	2	8. Someone To Care For Me .... from the film "Three Smart Girls"	Brunswick 7777
1/16/37	17	1	9. Gee, But You're Swell...............................	Brunswick 7799
2/27/37	20	1	10. The Girl On The Police Gazette .... vocal: Russ Morgan; from the film "On the Avenue"	Brunswick 7822
3/20/37	13	5	11. Swing High, Swing Low............................ vocal: Judy Richards; movie title song	Brunswick 7833
4/03/37	8	4	12. When The Poppies Bloom Again	Brunswick 7845

DATE CHARTED	PEAK POS	WKS CHRT'D	ARTIST — Record Title	Label & Number
5/08/37	**13**	5	13. On A Little Dream Ranch	Brunswick 7866
6/05/37	**1(2)**	10	14. **The Merry-Go-Round Broke Down** .... vocal: Jimmy Lewis	Brunswick 7888

7/21/37	**10**	7	15. Stop! You're Breaking My Heart ....
			     vocal: Russ Morgan & Dave Franklin
			     from the film "Artists and Models"
				Brunswick 7910

9/04/37	**17**	2	16. The Loveliness Of You .... from the film "Love in Bloom"	Brunswick 7931
9/25/37	**8**	6	17. So Many Memories	Brunswick 7959
10/30/37	**14**	2	18. Goodbye, Jonah .... from the Broadway musical "Virginia"	Brunswick 7955
11/20/37	**7**	6	19. Farewell, My Love/ vocals on 12-13, 16-17, & 19: Mert Curtis	
12/18/37	**13**	2	20. True Confession .... vocals on 18 & 20: Lewis Julian	Brunswick 8009
12/04/37	**2(2)**	6	21. The Dipsy Doodle .... [I]	Brunswick 8005
1/01/38	**2(3)**	14	22. I Double Dare You/ vocal: Bernice Parks	

1/15/38	**3**	6	23. Bei Mir Bist Du Schoen (Means That You're
			     Grand)..
			     adaptation of a song from the Yiddish musical "I Would
			     If I Could"; vocal by Bernice Parks
				Brunswick 8037

7/23/38	**7**	5	24. Will You Remember Tonight Tomorrow?	Brunswick 8119

8/20/38	**1(2)**	13	25. **I've Got A Pocketful Of Dreams** ....
			     from the film "Sing, You Sinners"
			     above three vocals: Russ Morgan
				Decca 1936

10/01/38	**4**	12	26. Lambeth Walk.. vocal: Jimmy Lewis; from the London musical "Me and My Girl"	Decca 2009
1/21/39	**17**	2	27. Wabash Blues .... [I]	Decca 2251
7/08/39	**4**	6	28. Wishing (Will Make It So)......................... vocal: Mert Curtis; from the film "Love Affair"	Decca 2436
9/21/40.	**14**	5	29. Blueberry Hill .... vocal: Carol Kay	Decca 3290
3/21/42	**5**	13	30. Somebody Else Is Taking My Place.............. vocal: Morganaires; from the film "Strictly In the Groove"	Decca 4098
5/23/42	**21**	1	31. All Those Wonderful Years...................... [I]	Decca 4300
10/17/42	**21**	1	32. Don't Cry, Sweetheart .... [I]	Decca 18348
5/27/44	**6**	16	33. Good Night, Wherever You Are....................	Decca 18598

11/04/44	**3**	12	34. Dance With A Dolly (With A Hole In Her
			     Stocking)/
			     vocal: Al Jennings; adaptation of the 1844 song "Lubly
			     Fan (Buffalo Gals, Won't You Come Out Tonight?)"	

11/18/44+	**4**	12	35. There Goes That Song Again .... from the film "Carolina Blues"	Decca 18625
1/12/46	**17**	1	36. (Did You Ever Get) That Feeling In The Moonlight/	
1/26/46	**14**	1	37. You're Nobody 'Til Somebody Loves You	Decca 18724
2/21/48	**6**	13	38. I'm Looking Over A Four-Leaf Clover/ vocal: Ames Brothers	
2/28/48	**20**	2	39. Bye Bye Blackbird .... above two with the Milt Herth Trio	Decca 24319
11/27/48+	**3**	25	40. So Tired.. vocal by Russ Morgan	Decca 24521
2/26/49	**1(7)**	22	● 41. **Cruising Down The River**/	

2/26/49	**5**	15	42. Sunflower..
			     became the state song of Kansas; a court ruling found the
			     1964 hit "Hello, Dolly" to be directly based on this song
				Decca 24568

3/19/49	**1(3)**	26	43. **Forever And Ever**/	

3/26/49	**17**	6	44. You, You, You Are The One ....
			     adaptation of a German waltz
			     above four vocals: Skylarks
				Decca 24569

5/07/49	**20**	5	45. Barroom Polka	Decca 24608
9/03/49	**17**	6	46. That's My Weakness Now	Decca 24692
12/24/49	**13**	3	47. Blue Christmas .... [X]	Decca 24766

DATE CHARTED	PEAK POS	WKS CHRT'D	ARTIST — Record Title	Label & Number
12/31/49+	7	10	48. Johnson Rag.................................	Decca 25442
1/14/50	24	1	49. Careless Kisses	Decca 24814
4/22/50	7	17	50. Sentimental Me............................	Decca 24904
5/27/50	15	4	51. Hoop-De-Doo..............................	Decca 24986
6/10/50	28	1	52. You Dreamer, You/	
10/07/50	28	1	53. Beloved, Be Faithful.....................	Decca 27006
			above seven vocals: Morganaires	
3/31/51	16	10	54. Mockin' Bird Hill	Decca 27444
2/02/52	30	1	55. Dance Me Loose	Decca 27906
1/17/53	23	1	56. Till I Waltz Again With You	Decca 28539
			vocal: Russ Morgan & Morganaires	
3/28/53	21	4	57. I'll Be Hangin' Around	Decca 28590
			vocal: Al Jennings	

ELIDA MORRIS
Dynamic Philadelphia-born singer who started in minstrel shows,
and later appeared in opera; she founded the Women's Aeronautical
Association, of which Amelia Earhart was a member.

DATE CHARTED	PEAK POS	WKS CHRT'D	ARTIST — Record Title	Label & Number
10/15/10	5	2	1. Angel Eyes	Victor 5782
			BILLY MURRAY & ELIDA MORRIS	
11/26/10	4	5	2. Kiss Me, My Honey, Kiss Me	Columbia 906
			also on Indestructable 1439	
2/11/11	4	5	3. Stop, Stop, Stop (Come Over And Love Me Some More)	Victor 16687
			also recorded for Columbia 953 & Indestructable 1457	
2/25/11	2(1)	6	4. I've Got Your Number......................	Columbia 3191
			ELIDA MORRIS & WALTER VAN BRUNT	
6/06/14	2(3)	8	5. If I Had Someone At Home Like You........	Columbia 1523
11/07/14	3	7	6. I Want To Go Back To Michigan (Down On The Farm)/	
12/19/14	8	2	7. The High Cost Of Loving	Columbia 1592
10/09/15	3	5	8. Hello, Frisco!	Columbia 1801
			ELIDA MORRIS & SAM ASH	
			from Broadway's "Ziegfeld Follies of 1915"	
			all Columbias accompanied by Charles Prince's Orchestra	

JOE MORRISON
Tenor ballad singer best known for vocal on George Olsen's #1
smash "The Last Round-Up"; also appeared in several films.

DATE CHARTED	PEAK POS	WKS CHRT'D	ARTIST — Record Title	Label & Number
1/12/35	18	1	1. Me Without You..........................	Brunswick 7347
			from the film "One Hour Late"	

BUDDY MORROW & HIS ORCHESTRA
Born Muni Zudekoff, trombone star with Paul Whiteman (1934-36),
Artie Shaw, Tommy Dorsey (1938), Bob Crosby, & Jimmy Dorsey (1945)
Buddy's early 50s swing band was a hit; he later played with
Johnny Carson's "Tonight Show" band. (also see Sarah Vaughan)

DATE CHARTED	PEAK POS	WKS CHRT'D	ARTIST — Record Title	Label & Number
5/19/51	8	10	1. Rose, Rose, I Love You	RCA Victor 4135
8/30/52	27	2	2. Night Train............................ [I]	RCA Victor 4693
			famous instrumental based on the climactic riff of Duke Ellington's "Happy Go Lucky Local"	
11/29/52	30	1	3. One-Mint Julep........................ [I]	RCA Victor 4868
12/06/52	19	2	4. Greyhound	RCA Victor 5041
1/31/53	16	5	5. I Don't Know...........................	RCA Victor 5117
3/14/53	28	1	6. Train, Train, Train......................	RCA Victor 5212
11/21/53	27	1	7. Re-enlistment Blues	RCA Victor 5466
			from the film "From Here to Eternity"	
			above four vocals: Frankie Lester	
12/04/54	20	1	8. Mr. Sandman	Mercury 70477

DATE CHARTED	PEAK POS	WKS CHRT'D	ARTIST — Record Title	Label & Number
			ELLA MAE MORSE Ella's jazz-flavored vocal style first reached a wide audience with Freddie Slack's band ("Cow Cow Boogie", "The House of Blue Lights") after a brief 1939 stay with Jimmy Dorsey.	
12/18/43+	4	18	1. Shoo Shoo Baby/ from the film "Three Cheers for the Boys"	
1/22/44	4	12	2. No Love, No Nothin' .... from the film "The Gang's All Here"	Capitol 143
4/29/44	11	5	3. Tess' Torch Song (I Had A Man)/ from the film "Up in Arms"	
5/06/44	7	16	4. Milkman, Keep Those Bottles Quiet .... from the film "Broadway Rhythm" above four with Dick Walters' Orchestra	Capitol 151
9/09/44	10	5	5. The Patty Cake Man.....................................	Capitol 163
5/26/45	17	1	6. Captain Kidd...	Capitol 193
1/19/46	15	1	7. Buzz Me .... above two with Billy May's Orchestra	Capitol 226
2/16/52	3	22	● 8. The Blacksmith Blues................................	Capitol 1922
6/07/52	23	2	9. Oakie Boogie.. above two with Nelson Riddle's Orchestra	Capitol 2072
8/22/53	26	1	10. 40 Cups of Coffee..................................... with "Dave Cavanaugh's Music"	Capitol 2539
			LEE MORSE Female vocalist with top jazz support. She died in 1954 (at about 54).	
9/13/30	20	1	1. I Still Get A Thrill..................................	Columbia 2270
4/04/31	18	1	2. Walkin' My Baby Back Home .... with Tommy Dorsey (trombone), Benny Goodman (clarinet), Eddie Lang (guitar)	Columbia 2417
9/24/32	16	2	3. Something In The Night	Columbia 2705
			EDDIE MORTON Popular vaudeville comedy performer, died on 4/11/38 (67).	
10/03/08	4	1	1. The Right Church, But The Wrong Pew..... [C]	Victor 5501
10/10/08	4	2	2. Don't Take Me Home .... also on Zon-o-Phone 1176	Victor 5545
3/12/10	2(2)	6	3. You Ain't Talking To Me	Columbia 777
11/04/11	5	4	4. Oceana Roll .... flip side of "Alexander's Ragtime Band" (POS 1) by Arthur Collins & Byron Harlan	Victor 16908
7/20/12	9	1	5. The Last Shot Got Him (The Great Bloo-ie Song) .... [C]	Victor 17071
3/07/14	7	2	6. I'm Crying Just For You...........................	Columbia 1456
6/13/14	8	2	7. He's A Devil In His Own Home Town .... accompanied on all Columbias by Charles Prince's Orchestra	Columbia 1525
			JELLY ROLL MORTON'S RED HOT PEPPERS Pioneering jazz pianist and composer ("King Porter Stomp"), born Ferdinand Joseph La Menthe Morton near New Orleans. Died on 7/10/41 (55).	
1/01/27	13	3	1. Black Bottom Stomp .... [I]	Victor 20221
4/16/27	17	2	2. Original Jelly Roll Blues .... [I]	Victor 20405
5/28/27	17	2	3. Grandpa's Spells...................................... [I] Kid Ory (trombone) on above three	Victor 20431
3/17/28	19	1	4. Wolverine Blues .... [I] with Johnny Dodds (clarinet)	Victor 21064
			JOE MOSS & HIS SOCIETY DANCE ORCHESTRA	
7/23/32	13	2	1. Banking On The Weather	Columbia 18003
11/16/35	8	5	2. On Treasure Island .... vocal: Dick Robertson	Brunswick 7545
			BENNIE MOTEN'S KANSAS CITY ORCHESTRA Top Midwestern jazz pianist-bandleader, Count Basie was a member of his early-30s band; died on 4/2/35 (40).	
4/25/25	12	1	1. South .... [I]	Okeh 8194
7/02/27	18	1	2. Kansas City Shuffle .... [I]	Victor 20485

DATE CHARTED	PEAK POS	WKS CHRT'D	ARTIST — Record Title	Label & Number
1/07/28	**16**	2	3. Moten Stomp .... [I] Victor 20955	
1/26/29	**10**	4	4. South .... [I] Victor 38021	
			new version of his 1925 hit	
12/02/44	**22**	1	5. South .... [I-R] Victor 24893	
			reissue of Victor 38021	

TONY MOTTOLA
Guitarist with George Hall (1939-41), often accompanied Frank Sinatra in the 40s; featured on TV by Perry Como, and later in Johnny Carson's "Tonight Show" band. (also see Hugo Winterhalter)

MULCAYS
Harmonica group

11/14/53	**26**	2	1. My Happiness.. [I] Cardinal 1011	
4/03/54	**24**	1	2. Alabamy Bound...................................... [I] Cardinal 1014	

MOON MULLICAN
Country singer billed as "King of Hillbilly Piano Playing"; died on 1/1/67 (57).

1/11/47	**21**	1	1. New Pretty Blonde .... King 578	
			MOON MULLICAN & THE SHOWBOYS	
			Cajun song also known as "Jole Blon"	
6/17/50	**17**	3	● 2. I'll Sail My Ship Alone .... King 830	
			long-running #1 country hit	

GERRY MULLIGAN
Twenty-time Down Beat poll winner as top baritone saxophonist; played and arranged for Gene Krupa (1947), Elliot Lawrence, Miles Davis, Claude Thornhill (1951).

JAMES MUNDY
Star arranger for Earl Hines, Benny Goodman ("These Foolish Things", "Sing, Sing, Sing"), Count Basie, Harry James, and many other bands.

FRANK MUNN
Prolific tenor band singer; had hits with Ben Bernie, Carl Fenton, Jean Goldkette, Vincent Lopez, Ben Selvin, & Nat Shilkret, among others. Frank died on 10/1/53 (58).

1/16/26	**9**	2	1. Lullaby Lane .... Brunswick 2969	

PATRICE MUNSEL
American opera star whose 1943 New York Met debut made her the youngest (age 18) singer who had ever appeared there; she starred in the 1953 film biography of Nellie Melba.

10/13/51	**27**	2	1. Bela Bimba.. RCA Victor 4255	
			accompanied by Norman Leyden's Orchestra	

JERRY MURAD - see HARMONICATS, RICHARD HAYMAN

LAMBERT MURPHY
Leading concert tenor who sang with the Metropolitan Opera, also a member of the Orpheus Quartet; died on 7/24/54 (69).

3/21/14	**9**	1	1. La Forza Del Destino - Solenne In Quest Ora (Swear In This Hour) .... [F] Victor 70103	
			LAMBERT MURPHY & REINALD WERRENRATH	
4/10/15	**3**	5	2. Goodbye, Girls, I'm Through .... Victor 17715	
			from the Broadway musical "Chin-Chin"	
4/22/16	**6**	3	3. So Long, Letty .... Victor 17974	
			Broadway musical title song	
4/22/16	**8**	2	4. Underneath The Stars .... Victor 17946	
			2 & 4 under pseudonym "Raymond Dixon"	
10/07/16	**3**	6	5. Have A Heart .... Victor 18104	
			from Broadway's "Ziegfeld Follies of 1916"	
1/19/18	**3**	7	6. Will You Remember? .... Victor 18399	
			from the Broadway musical "Maytime"	
			3, 5 & 6: "ALICE GREEN & RAYMOND DIXON" (Olive Kline & Lambert Murphy)	
5/25/18	**3**	4	7. Roses Of Picardy .... Victor 45130	
12/07/18	**5**	3	8. Smiles .... Victor 45155	
			from Broadway's "The Passing Show of 1918"	

DATE CHARTED	PEAK POS	WKS CHRT'D	ARTIST — Record Title	Label & Number
1/22/21	**8**	2	9. Waiting For The Sun To Come Out	Victor 45199
11/25/22	**12**	1	10. I Dream Of Jeannie With The Light Brown Hair	Victor 45324
12/28/24	**14**	1	11. Rose Marie .... Broadway musical title song	Victor 45458

ROSE MURPHY
Pianist-singer known as "the Chee-Chee Girl"

DATE CHARTED	PEAK POS	WKS CHRT'D	ARTIST — Record Title	Label & Number
12/27/47+	**13**	4	1. I Can't Give You Anything But Love .... from Broadway musical "Blackbirds of 1928"	Majestic 1204

BILLY MURRAY
The most sensational record seller of the entire pre-1920 pioneer era, Billy Murray was born on 5/25/1877 in Philadelphia to Irish parents. Raised in Denver (his early nickname: "the Denver Nightingale"), Billy sang in vaudeville and honkytonks before making his first commercial recordings in 1903. Almost immediately, his clear tenor, rapid-fire style, and amiable humor sent him skyrocketing to the top of the music world. His many hit duets with Ada Jones made them the king and queen of the era's popular recordings; Billy also established himself as the official interpreter of George M. Cohan, since he recorded the definitive hit version of nearly every Cohan song from 1905 on. No other performer sang lead on so many group hits - with the Haydn and American Quartets and the Heidelberg Quintet. Billy died on 8/17/54. (In addition to Ada and groups, also see Columbia Comedy Trio, Jean Goldkette, Great White Way Orchestra, International Novelty Orchestra, Jack Shilkret, & Joseph C. Smith's Orchestra)

DATE CHARTED	PEAK POS	WKS CHRT'D	ARTIST — Record Title	Label & Number
4/25/03	**3**	2	1. Tessie (You Are the Only, Only) .... from the Broadway musical "The Silver Slipper"; this became the "official" song of Boston Red Sox fans in the first World Series (1903)	Columbia 1163
11/14/03	**3**	5	2. Up In A Cocoanut Tree .... [C]	Victor 2453
1/23/04	**1(3)**	10	3. **Bedelia**.. from the Broadway musical "The Jersey Lily"	Edison 8550
2/20/04	**2(1)**	9	4. Under The Anhauser Bush .... [C] also recorded for Columbia 1676 & 32384	Edison 8575
3/12/04	**1(5)**	11	5. **Navajo**.. from the Broadway musical "Nancy Brown"	Columbia 1655
4/23/04	**4**	1	6. I Can't Do The Sum .... from the Broadway musical "The Wizard of Oz"	Columbia 1687
6/25/04	**4**	3	7. Ain't It Funny What A Difference A Few Hours Can Make............................... also recorded for Columbia 1790 & 32489 from the Broadway musical "The Yankee Consul"	Victor 2731
7/23/04	**1(9)**	14	8. **Meet Me In St. Louis, Louis** .... also recorded for Victor 2850, Columbia 1792 & 32488; inspired by the Louisiana Purchase Exposition in St. Louis	Edison 8722
8/06/04	**5**	1	9. In The Days Of Old................................... also recorded for Edison 8704	Victor 2803
9/10/04	**1(3)**	9	10. **Alexander** .... [C]	Edison 8765
11/05/04	**2(1)**	4	11. Teasing (I Was Only Teasing You) .... [C]	Columbia 1857
1/14/05	**1(4)**	9	12. **Come Take A Trip In My Air-Ship**............. also recorded for Edison 8874; inspired by the Wright Brothers' historic flight at Kitty Hawk	Victor 2986
1/28/05	**9**	1	13. Runaway Motor Car .... [C] also on Columbia cylinder 32427	Columbia 1886
2/11/05	**4**	3	14. Can't You See My Heart Beats All For You .... BILLY MURRAY & LEN SPENCER also recorded by Billy & Bob Roberts for Edison 8942	Victor 4152
2/25/05	**1(8)**	14	15. **Yankee Doodle Boy** .... also recorded for Victor 4229 & Zon-o-Phone 75	Columbia 3051
5/27/05	**9**	1	16. Oh! Oh! Sallie .... [C] BILLY MURRAY & ROB ROBERTS	Victor 4276
6/17/05	**1(5)**	11	17. **Give My Regards To Broadway**................. also recorded for Edison 9095 & Zon-o-Phone 140 15 & 17 from the Broadway musical "Little Johnny Jones"	Columbia 3165
9/09/05	**3**	2	18. My Irish Molly-O .... also recorded for Columbia 32778 from the Broadway musical "Sargeant Brue"	Edison 9063

DATE CHARTED	PEAK POS	WKS CHRT'D	ARTIST — Record Title	Label & Number
9/30/05	7	1	19. Tammany .... [C] from the Broadway musical "Fantana"	Columbia 32775
10/14/05	1(7)	10	20. **In My Merry Oldsmobile** .... later recorded for Columbia 3564 & 33063; inspired by the first transcontinental auto race, won by an Oldsmobile	Victor 4467
12/23/05+	1(3)	8	21. **Everybody Works But Father** .... [C]	Victor 4519
12/30/05	6	1	22. The Irish Girl I Love	Columbia 32821
1/27/06	6	1	23. Just A Little Rocking Chair And You .... also recorded for Zon-o-Phone 346	Columbia 32860
2/10/06	3	4	24. Forty-Five Minutes From Broadway............. also recorded for Edison 9231; Broadway musical title song	Columbia 32877
4/28/06	4	2	25. Just A Little Rocking Chair And You	Victor 31501
5/05/06	1(10)	15	26. **The Grand Old Rag**................................ the biggest-selling record of Victor's first decade; also recorded for Edison 9226, Columbia 3388 & 32920, Zon-o-Phone 425, & International 2098; from the Broadway musical "George Washington, Jr."; song better known as "You're a Grand Old Flag"	Victor 4634
6/16/06+	5	2	27. Keep On The Sunny Side...........................	Victor 31507
7/21/06	2(3)	7	28. Cheyenne (Shy Ann) .... also recorded for Columbia 3389 & 32944 from the Broadway musical "The Earl and The Girl"	Victor 4719
7/28/06	9	1	29. You Look Awful Good To Father .... [C] from the Broadway musical "The Umpire"	Victor 4684
9/08/06	2(1)	3	30. College Life .... [C]	Victor 4742
9/08/06	5	2	31. Waltz Me Around Again, Willie................... from the Broadway musical "His Honor the Mayor"; Billy Murray also recorded song for Edison 9340 & Zon-o-Phone 500 25 & 31: BILLY MURRAY & HAYDN QUARTET	Victor 4738
10/27/06	8	1	32. Is Your Mother In, Molly Malone? .... also recorded for Columbia 3464	Victor 4803
11/24/06	4	3	33. Not Because Your Hair Is Curly .... [C] also recorded for Columbia 3489 & 33015, Zon-o-Phone 546	Victor 4861
11/24/06	8	1	34. Pat And Mike McGee .... [C] BILLY MURRAY & LEN SPENCER	Victor 31567
1/26/07	3	2	35. The Streets Of New York .... also on Columbia cylinder 33062	Columbia 3544
1/26/07	9	1	36. An Evening At Mrs. Clancy's Boarding House... [C] BILLY MURRAY & STEVE PORTER	Columbia 3526
2/09/07	2(4)	7	37. On San Francisco Bay .... from the Broadway musical "A Parisian Model"	Columbia 3548
2/09/07	4	2	38. Rose Bud (Call And I'll Come To You) .... also recorded for Zon-o-Phone 548	Columbia 3543
5/25/07	3	4	39. San Antonio (Cowboy Song) .... also recorded for Edison 9547, and on Columbia 3608 with the Rambler Minstrel Co.	Victor 5099
5/25/07	6	1	40. You Can Have Broadway .... also recorded for Columbia 3600 & 33094, Zon-o-Phone 675	Victor 5084
6/15/07	2(3)	5	41. No Wedding Bells For Me .... [C] also recorded for Zon-o-Phone 742	Victor 5123
7/06/07	2(1)	5	42. He Goes To Church On Sunday .... [C] also recorded for Victor 5124, Columbia 3671, & Zon-o-Phone 786 above two from the Broadway musical "The Orchid"	Edison 9612
8/03/07	4	2	43. Because I'm Married Now .... also recorded for Columbia 3670 & Edison 9586	Victor 5115
9/14/07	1(9)	14	44. **Harrigan** .... later recorded for Zon-o-Phone 5376 from the Broadway musical "Fifty Miles from Boston"	Victor 5197
9/28/07	6	1	45. It's Great To Be A Soldier Man	Victor 5161
11/30/07	5	1	46. Honey Boy... with whistling chorus by Edward Ables	Victor 5207
11/30/07	9	1	47. Always Leave Them Laughing When You Say Good-Bye .... later recorded for Victor 5296	Columbia 33179
12/07/07	2(1)	5	48. Take Me Around Again	Columbia 33171

DATE CHARTED	PEAK POS	WKS CHRT'D	ARTIST — Record Title	Label & Number
12/28/07	6	1	49. Take Me Back To New York Town .... also on Columbia cylinder 33196	Columbia 3717
1/25/08	7	1	50. Two Blue Eyes	Columbia 33205
2/01/08	1(6)	11	51. **Under Any Old Flag At All** .... also recorded for Columbia 3768 & 33226, Edison 9796, Zon-o-Phone 5089, & Indestructable 732 47 & 51 from the Broadway musical "The Talk of New York"	Victor 5339
2/29/08	7	1	52. Dixie Dan .... [C] from the Broadway musical "The Gay White Way"	Edison 9742
3/07/08	3	3	53. I'm Afraid To Come Home In The Dark ..... [C] later recorded for Edison 9780 & Columbia 3767	Victor 5355
3/28/08	8	1	54. I'm Happy When The Band Plays Dixie	Victor 5330
4/04/08	2(2)	4	55. Keep On Smiling	Victor 5379
4/25/08	7	1	56. I'm Looking For The Man That Wrote The Merry Widow Waltz .... [C] also recorded for Zon-o-Phone 5086	Victor 5358
6/27/08	8	1	57. Bon-Bon Buddy .... from the Broadway musical "Bandana Land"	Victor 5433
10/24/08	1(7)	16	58. **Take Me Out To The Ball Game** .... the most popular recording of the national pastime's anthem 54-55, 58-59 & 61: BILLY MURRAY & HAYDN QUARTET	Victor 5570
10/31/08	8	1	59. Yankee Doodle's Come To Town	Victor 5504
11/07/08	3	3	60. It Looks Like A Big Night To-Night .... also recorded for Columbia 864, Zon-o-Phone 5174, & Indestructable 864	Victor 5550
11/28/08	7	1	61. Rainbow	Victor 5571
12/26/08	4	2	62. I'm Glad I'm Married .... [C] also recorded for Edison 10018 & Zon-o-Phone 5174	Victor 5591
2/20/09	4	1	63. Good Evening, Caroline .... also recorded for Zon-o-Phone 5372 & Indestructable 957	Edison 10038
3/06/09	5	1	64. Sullivan .... 64 & 68 from the Broadway musical "The American Idea" Murray also recorded song for Edison 10060	Victor 5617
3/27/09	6	1	65. When A Fellow's On The Level With A Girl Who's On The Square .... from the Broadway musical "The Talk of New York"	Victor 5626
5/08/09	2(1)	6	66. I Wish I Had A Girl	Victor 16291
5/29/09	6	1	67. Meet Me In Rose-Time, Rosie	Victor 5676
5/29/09	7	1	68. American Ragtime	Victor 16144
8/14/09	5	2	69. My Cousin Caruso .... [C] from Broadway's "Ziegfeld Follies of 1909"	Victor 16327
8/28/09	4	3	70. Take Me Up With You, Dearie .... Murray also recorded song for Edison 10213	Victor 5718
10/09/09	4	3	71. Take Me Out For A Joy Ride .... 64, 67, 70 & 71: BILLY MURRAY & HAYDN QUARTET	Victor 5732
12/04/09	3	3	72. Dixie Land, I Love You	Victor 16366
12/18/09	3	5	73. The Hat My Father Wore On St. Patrick's Day	Victor 16365
1/08/10	6	2	74. Tell Mother I'll Be There	Victor 16414
1/15/10	1(2)	11	75. **Carrie (Carrie Marry Harry)** .... [C]	Victor 5758
1/22/10	4	5	76. I Wonder Who's Kissing Her Now .... from the Broadway musical "The Prince of Pilsen"	Victor 16426
2/26/10	10	1	77. She Sells Sea Shells .... [C] from the Broadway musical "The Beauty Spot"	Victor 16429
3/26/10	4	4	78. Down In Sunshine Alley .... Murray also recorded song for Edison Amberol 337	Victor 16450
4/16/10	1(9)	17	79. **By The Light Of The Silvery Moon** .... from the Broadway musical "Ziegfeld Follies of 1909" 73-74, 78-79: BILLY MURRAY & HAYDN QUARTET	Victor 16460
4/23/10	9	1	80. It's Moonlight All The Time On Broadway ..... also recorded for Zon-o-Phone 5593	Edison 10503
6/04/10	6	3	81. The Cubanola Glide	Victor 5769
7/02/10	3	5	82. Casey Jones .... also on Edison 10499; million-selling version of song by Billy & the American Quartet on Victor 16483	Edison Amb. 450

DATE CHARTED	PEAK POS	WKS CHRT'D	ARTIST — Record Title	Label & Number
7/30/10	2(3)	8	83. What's The Matter With Father?.............. [C] also recorded for Edison 10369	Victor 16499
8/27/10	10	1	84. Two Gentlemen From Ireland.................. [C] BILLY MURRAY & LEN SPENCER	Edison Amb. 442
10/15/10	5	2	85. Angel Eyes .... BILLY MURRAY & ELIDA MORRIS	Victor 5782
10/22/10	9	1	86. I've Got Rings On My Fingers .... from the Broadway musical "The Midnight Sons"	Victor 16510
10/29/10	8	1	87. Sweet Italian Love .... from "Up and Down Broadway"	Edison 10427
11/26/10	5	3	88. That Italian Rag	Victor 16608
4/22/11	5	4	89. Gee, But It's Great To Meet A Friend From Your Home Town..................... also recorded for Zon-o-Phone 5717; later for Victor 16897	Edison Amb. 631
5/27/11	5	3	90. To The Strains Of That Wedding March (It's A Long, Long Walk) .... [C]	Victor 16833
6/10/11	3	5	91. Piano Man	Edison Amb. 673
7/15/11	9	1	92. That's Why I Never Married .... also recorded for Edison Amberol 692 from the Broadway musical "The Slim Princess"	Victor 16851
11/11/11	2(1)	7	93. Alexander's Ragtime Band .... also on Edison Amberol 817	Edison 10522
11/11/11	9	1	94. The Camptown Races (Gwine To Run All Night)	Victor 16888
2/17/12	3	7	95. Any Place The Old Flag Flies .... also recorded for Edison Amberol 875 & Zon-o-Phone 5820 from the Broadway musical "The Little Millionaire"	Victor 17031
3/02/12	9	1	96. Who Are You With To-Night? .... from the Broadway musical "Girlies"	Victor 16992
3/30/12	6	2	97. If You Talk In Your Sleep, Don't Mention My Name	Victor 17025
3/30/12	9	1	98. Just As My Father Used To Do	Edison Amb. 905
6/15/12	3	5	99. The Gaby Glide.. also recorded for Edison Amberol 1049 from the Broadway musical "Vera Violetta"	Victor 17077
1/04/13	5	4	100. Oh! Oh! Delphine .... Broadway musical title song	Victor 17196
2/01/13	2(3)	9	101. Bagdad .... from the Broadway musical "Lady of the Slipper"	Victor 17220
4/19/13	5	4	102. Good-Night, Nurse................................. [C]	Victor 17286
5/03/13	9	1	103. On The Mississippi	Edison Amb. 1637
5/31/13	4	4	104. Snookey Ookums.................................. [C]	Victor 17313
12/20/13	10	1	105. Come On Over Here................................. BILLY MURRAY & HELEN CLARK also recorded by Billy & Elizabeth Spencer for Edison Amberol 2066; from the Broadway musical "The Doll Girl"	Victor 17441
1/10/14	6	3	106. On The Old Fall River Line	Victor 17427
2/07/14	2(3)	8	107. He'd Have To Get Under - Get Out And Get Under (To Fix Up His Automobile)...... [C] also recorded for Edison Amberol 2194 from the Broadway musical "The Pleasure Seekers"	Victor 17491
3/07/14	3	6	108. When You're All Dressed Up And No Place To Go .... also recorded for Edison Amberol 2256 from the Broadway musical "The Beauty Shop"	Victor 17527
3/07/14	6	3	109. Sit Down (You're Rocking The Boat)............ also recorded for Edison Amberol 2216	Victor 17516
7/04/14	2(2)	6	110. He's A Devil In His Own Home Town .... [C]	Victor 17576
7/11/14	6	2	111. This Is The Life .... also recorded for Edison Amberol 2375	Victor 17584
9/19/14	3	5	112. The 20th Century Rag	Victor 17605
10/10/14	4	6	113. Just For To-Night.............................. BILLY MURRAY & WILL OAKLAND	Victor 17622
11/14/14	10	1	114. I'll Do It All Over Again.............................	Victor 17637

DATE CHARTED	PEAK POS	WKS CHRT'D	ARTIST — Record Title	Label & Number
12/05/14	6	3	115. They Start The Victrola (And Go Dancing Around The Floor)	Victor 17631
2/06/15	7	2	116. Sister Susie's Sewing Shirts For Soldiers....... also recorded for Edison 50202 & Edison Amberol 2530	Victor 17659
2/20/15	8	1	117. When The Grown-Up Ladies Act Like Babies (I've Got To Love 'Em, That's All) ...... [C] flip side of "Tip-Top Tippearary Mary" (POS 2) by the Peerless Quartet	Victor 17678
2/27/15	10	1	118. When You're Wearing The Ball And Chain..... from the Broadway musical "The Only Girl"	Victor 17679
7/31/15	3	7	119. The Little Ford Rambled Right Along .... also recorded for Edison 50227	Victor 17755
8/21/15	9	1	120. The Magic Melody .... from the Broadway musical "Nobody Home"	Victor 17790
3/18/16	9	1	121. When I Get Back To The U.S.A. .... also recorded for Edison 50337 & Edison Amberol 2845	Victor 17930
4/01/16	2(2)	6	122. Hello, Hawaii, How Are You?......................	Victor 17944
4/08/16	1(1)	8	123. **I Love A Piano** .... flip side of Harry Macdonough's #1 hit "The Girl On the Magazine" - the first double-sided #1 record 121 & 123 from the Broadway musical "Stop! Look! Listen!"	Victor 17945
4/08/16	6	2	124. Are You From Dixie? ('cause I'm From Dixie Too) .... BILLY MURRAY & IRVING KAUFMAN also recorded by Billy solo for Edison 50357 & Edison Amberol 2942	Victor 17942
6/17/16	10	1	125. Some Sort Of Somebody .... from the Broadway musical "Very Good, Eddie"	Victor 17992
8/19/16	4	6	126. Simple Melody.. from the Broadway musical "Watch Your Step" song better known as "Play a Simple Melody" above two: BILLY MURRAY & "EDNA BROWN" (Elsie Baker)	Victor 18051
10/07/16	1(1)	6	127. **Pretty Baby/** from Broadway's "The Passing Show of 1916" also recorded for Indestructable 3374	
10/14/16	10	1	128. When You Drop Off At Cairo, Illinois .... from the Broadway musical "Step This Way"	Victor 18102
11/18/16	4	5	129. There's A Little Bit Of Bad In Every Good Little Girl.. orchestra on most Victor records from 1908-16 directed by Walter B. Rogers	Victor 18143
8/18/17	9	1	130. For Me And My Gal	Edison 50407
12/01/17	5	2	131. Over There .... also on Edison Amberol 3275; Billy's biggest version of song recorded with American Quartet (Victor 18333)	Edison 50443
6/01/18	3	4	132. K-K-K-Katy (Stammering Song)................. [C]	Victor 18455
7/27/18	3	5	133. They Were All Out Of Step But Jim.......... [C]	Victor 18465
3/08/19	5	4	134. The Alcoholic Blues .... [C] later recorded for Columbia 2707 & Paramount 30097 one of the first hit songs about the newly-ratified Prohibition flip side of "Ja Da" (POS 4) by Arthur Fields	Victor 18522
3/22/19	9	1	135. After You've Gone.................................. BILLY MURRAY & "RACHEL GRANT" (Gladys Rice)	Edison Amb. 3666
8/16/19	2(1)	6	136. Just As We Used To Do............................ also recorded for Okeh 1253	Columbia 2746
9/27/19	5	6	137. Take Your Girlie To The Movies (If You Can't Make Love At Home)......................... also recorded for Gennett 4542	Victor 18592
10/25/19	6	3	138. And He'd Say Oo-La-La! Wee Wee! .... [C] also recorded for Gennett 4541, Emerson 9207, Pathe 22156, Empire 404 & Victor 18610	Columbia 2765
11/22/19	6	3	139. I've Got My Captain Working For Me Now...... also recorded for Emerson 1042, Vocalion 12208, & Paramount 33020	Victor 18604

DATE CHARTED	PEAK POS	WKS CHRT'D	ARTIST — Record Title	Label & Number
1/10/20	**7**	3	140. Wait Till You Get Them Up In The Air, Boys .. also recorded for Victor 18628, Pathe 22262, & Empire 21135 flip side of "I've Got My Captain Working for Me Now" (POS 1) by Al Jolson	Columbia 2794
1/31/20	**13**	1	141. Poor Little Butterfly (Is A Fly Gal Now)	Okeh 4027
3/27/20	**11**	1	142. That Wonderful Kid From Madrid .... also recorded for Emerson 10138, Vocalion 14019, & Lyric 5214	Okeh 4050
5/29/20	**3**	5	143. I'll See You In C-U-B-A .... also recorded for Okeh 4079, Gennett 9029, Vocalion 14035, Pathe 22322 & Empire 421	Victor 18652
6/19/20	**10**	1	144. He Went In Like A Lion And Came Out Like A Lamb .... [C]	Victor 18657
6/26/20	**12**	1	145. Oh By Jingo! Oh By Gee! You're The Only Girl For Me.. also recorded for Empire 6005	Emerson 10177
7/31/20	**12**	1	146. Marion (You'll Soon Be Marryin' Me)............ also recorded for Okeh 4112 & Edison Amberol 4065	Victor 18671
8/14/20	**8**	1	147. When My Baby Smiles At Me...................... 143 & 147 from Broadway's "Greenwich Village Follies of 1919"	Edison 50651
8/28/20	**14**	1	148. Oh! How I Laugh When I Think That I Cried Over You... above three: BILLY MURRAY & "RACHEL GRANT" (Gladys Rice)	Edison Amb. 4048
11/13/20	**9**	1	149. Dardanella Blues	Victor 18688
3/12/21	**2(2)**	5	150. (Down By The) O-H-I-O (I've Got The Sweetest Little O, My! O!)................................. BILLY MURRAY & "VICTOR ROBERTS" (Billy Jones)	Victor 18723
2/25/22	**12**	1	151. Ten Little Fingers And Ten Little Toes (Down In Tennessee) .... 149 & 151: BILLY MURRAY & ED SMALLE	Victor 18830
8/19/22	**4**	4	152. Stumbling..	Victor 18906
12/23/22	**9**	1	153. All Over Nothing At All............................	Victor 18943
2/10/23	**10**	1	154. Yankee Doodle Blues.............................. from the Broadway musical "Spice of 1922"	Victor 18959
3/03/23	**8**	1	155. You Tell Her - I Stutter .... [C]	Victor 18975
5/26/23	**12**	1	156. I Gave You Up Just Before You Threw Me Down .... BILLY MURRAY & "RACHEL GRANT" (Gladys Rice)	Victor 19023
6/30/23	**11**	1	157. You've Got To See Mama Ev'ry Night (Or You Can't See Mama At All)....................... 153 & 157: BILLY MURRAY & AILEEN STANLEY	Victor 19431
9/29/23	**1(6)**	14	158. **That Old Gang Of Mine** .... 154 & 158: BILLY MURRAY & ED SMALLE	Victor 19095
11/24/23	**12**	1	159. Cut Yourself A Piece Of Cake	Victor 19114
12/22/23	**8**	2	160. My Sweetie Went Away	Victor 19144
6/28/24	**15**	1	161. Home In Pasadena	Victor 19293
10/25/24	**8**	1	162. It Had To Be You .... BILLY MURRAY & AILEEN STANLEY	Victor 19373
10/25/24	**11**	1	163. Hinky Dinky Parley Voo......................... [C] 159-160 & 163: BILLY MURRAY & ED SMALLE	Victor 19388
8/01/25	**5**	4	164. Don't Bring Lulu................................. [C]	Victor 19628
9/26/25	**15**	1	165. Titina .... BILLY MURRAY & ED SMALLE from the Broadway musical "Puzzles of 1925"	Victor 19640
1/30/26	**10**	1	166. Keep Your Skirts Down, Mary Ann..............	Victor 19795
3/06/26	**7**	2	167. I Wonder Where My Baby Is To-Night? .... BILLY MURRAY & HENRY BURR the superstars' only duet together accompanied by Frank Banta (piano) & Carl Mathew	Victor 19864
12/11/26	**6**	2	168. I Can't Get Over A Girl Like You (Loving A Boy Like Me)	Victor 20148

DATE CHARTED	PEAK POS	WKS CHRT'D	ARTIST — Record Title	Label & Number
1/08/27	**14**	2	169. Bridget O'Flynn (Where've Ya Been?) .... [C] known for its whispering introduction 166, 168 & 169: BILLY MURRAY & AILEEN STANLEY	Victor 20240

KEN MURRAY & THE OSWALD COMEDIANS
Real name Don Court; comedy actor in vaudeville, radio, and his own 1950-53 TV series.

10/17/36	**7**	6	1. Mama, That Man's Here Again................ [C]	Victor 25418

VIDO MUSSO
Tenor sax star with Benny Goodman (1936-37, 41-42), Teddy Wilson, Gene Krupa (1938), Harry James, Woody Herman, & Stan Kenton (1946-47). Vido died on 1/9/82 (68).

J.W. MYERS
John W. Meyers, born in Wales, the foremost baritone ballad singer of his era: a former theatrical manager, he was immediately recognizable for his distinctive handlebar mustache, and died shortly before 1920 (in his early 50s).

DATE CHARTED	PEAK POS	WKS CHRT'D	ARTIST — Record Title	Label & Number
3/05/92	**2(2)**	2	1. Sing Those Pretty Songs Again....................	New York
8/19/93	**1(4)**	4	2. **Two Little Girls In Blue**	New Jersey
2/03/94	**2(2)**	2	3. The Heart Bowed Down............................ also recorded for New Jersey	Columbia
4/13/95	**1(4)**	4	4. **The Sidewalks Of New York**.................... also recorded for Chicago 2609 & Ohio	Columbia
8/01/95	**1(6)**	6	5. **Just Tell Them That You Saw Me**............	Columbia 6009
6/05/97	**2(4)**	5	6. Sweet Rosie O'Grady	Columbia 6036
5/21/00	**2(1)**	4	7. Good-Bye, Dolly Gray	Columbia 7502
6/08/01	**3**	3	8. When You Were Sweet Sixteen	Victor 3135
8/24/01	**1(1)**	7	9. **In The Shade Of The Palm**...................... from the Broadway musical "Florodora"	Columbia 31620
4/19/02	**1(6)**	10	10. **On A Sunday Afternoon** .... also on Columbia cylinder 31755	Columbia 106
5/17/02	**1(5)**	12	11. **Way Down In Old Indiana**.......................	Victor 1228
5/17/02	**3**	4	12. Pretty Molly Shannon .... from the Broadway musical "The Little Duchess"	Victor 1240
6/28/02	**2(2)**	6	13. The Mansion Of Aching Hearts .... also on Columbia cylinder 31776	Columbia 861
7/19/02	**3**	4	14. Nancy Brown	Columbia 856
10/25/02	**1(7)**	12	15. **In The Good Old Summer Time** .... from the Broadway musical "The Defender"	Columbia 940
12/06/02	**4**	2	16. My Little Gipsy Maid .... 14 & 16 from the Broadway musical "The Wild Rose"	Columbia 947
2/14/03	**3**	4	17. Heidelberg	Columbia 1054
2/14/03	**4**	2	18. In The City Of Sighs And Tears .... also recorded for Columbia 1014	Victor 1696
3/14/03	**5**	2	19. My Own United States............................ also recorded for Victor 1795 from the Broadway musical "When Johnny Comes Marching Home"	Columbia 1055
4/04/03	**5**	1	20. The Message Of The Violets .... also recorded for Columbia 1055 17 & 20 from the Broadway musical "The Prince of Pilsen"	Victor 1796
5/30/03	**3**	3	21. If I But Knew	Columbia 1252
11/14/03	**2(3)**	6	22. Dear Old Girl......................................	Columbia 1573
12/19/03	**4**	2	23. You're As Welcome As The Flowers In May ...	Columbia 1600
3/05/04	**5**	1	24. I'm Wearing My Heart Away For You...........	Columbia 1650
4/16/04	**3**	3	25. Navajo .... from the Broadway musical "Nancy Brown"	Columbia 1721
9/10/04	**3**	3	26. Meet Me In St. Louis, Louis......................	Columbia 1848
10/08/04	**5**	1	27. On A Good Old Trolley Ride	Columbia 1836
12/31/04+	**2(1)**	5	28. Come Take A Trip In My Air-Ship	Columbia 1878
3/25/05	**6**	1	29. While The Brass Band Played	Columbia 32614
6/24/05	**7**	1	30. He's Me Pal.......................................	Columbia 3104
9/26/06	**7**	1	31. The Good Old U.S.A..............................	Victor 4761

DATE CHARTED	PEAK POS	WKS CHRT'D	ARTIST — Record Title	Label & Number
6/29/07	5	1	32. My Irish Rosie	Columbia 3615

N

JOEY NASH
Vocalist with Richard Himber in mid-30s

JOE NATUS
Member of the Big Four Quartet; died on 4/26/17 (57).

5/28/92	1(3)	3	1. **The Song That Reached My Heart**	North Amer.
7/13/01	3	3	2. I Never Trouble Trouble Until Trouble	
			Troubles Me .... [C]	Edison 7816
2/08/02	2(2)	5	3. Tell Me, Dusky Maiden............................	Edison 8000

from the Broadway musical "Sleeping Beauty and the Beast"
above two: ARTHUR COLLINS & JOE NATUS

NEAPOLITAN TRIO

12/29/17	7	1	1. Silent Night, Holy Night .... [X]	Victor 18389

GRACE NELSON

2/25/05	7	1	1. My Little Canoe......................................	Edison 8858

OZZIE NELSON & HIS ORCHESTRA
Familiar to a generation of TV viewers for the long-running show "Ozzie and Harriet" (1952-66, previously on radio from 1944), Ozzie Nelson was first a popular sweet-band leader. Wife Harriet Hilliard was his featured singer, Abe Lincoln (trombone) and Harry Johnson (trumpet) his top sidemen. Son Rick became a top star of the 50s & 60s. Ozzie died on 6/3/75 (68).

9/27/30	8	3	1. I Still Get A Thrill (Thinking Of You)	Brunswick 4897
12/20/30	18	1	2. Body And Soul	Brunswick 4922
			from the Broadway musical "Three's a Crowd"	
1/24/31	9	3	3. Truly (I Love You)....................................	Brunswick 6018
7/11/31	18	1	4. On The Beach With You............................	Brunswick 6131
			Charlie Spivak (trumpet) on above records	
8/20/32	16	2	5. It Was So Beautiful	Brunswick 6347
			from the film "The Big Broadcast"	
9/17/32	8	3	6. Say It Isn't So	Brunswick 6372
10/20/34	17	2	7. If I Had A Million Dollars........................	Brunswick 6991
			from the film "Transatlantic Merry Go-Round" most above vocals: Ozzie Nelson	
3/16/35	20	1 •	8. Oh Susanna, Dust Off The Old Pianna...........	Brunswick 7375
			vocal: Ozzie Nelson & Harriet Hilliard	
5/11/35	3	12	9. About A Quarter To Nine/	
5/25/35	15	2	10. She's A Latin From Manhattan	Brunswick 7425
			above two from the film "Go Into Your Dance"	
6/08/35	4	12	11. I'll Never Say "Never Again" Again..............	Brunswick 7426
7/06/35	1(1)	12	12. **And Then Some**....................................	Brunswick 7464
12/28/35+	16	2	13. Quicker Than You Can Say Jack Robinson/	
12/28/35	19	1	14. I Picked A Flower The Color Of Your Eyes...	Brunswick 7576
2/22/36	14	2	15. Cling To Me	Brunswick 7597
			most vocals 9-15 by Ozzie	
3/28/36	18	1	16. But Where Are You?	Brunswick 7607
			vocal: Harriet Hilliard; from the film "Follow the Fleet"	
5/16/36	4	7	17. Is It True What They Say About Dixie?........	Brunswick 7651
5/30/36	12	2	18. Stompin' At The Savoy .... [I]	Brunswick 7659
12/05/36	13	2	19. T'ain't Good (Like A Nickel Made Of Wood)....	Brunswick 7770
4/03/37	6	4	20. They Can't Take That Away From Me...........	Bluebird 6873
			from the film "Shall We Dance?"	
6/12/37	6	4	21. Our Penthouse On Third Avenue/	
7/24/37	14	2	22. Love Is Never Out Of Season....................	Bluebird 6987
			above two from the film "New Faces of 1937"	
7/31/37	3	11	23. Roses In December...............................	Bluebird 7034
			from the film "Life of the Party"	

DATE CHARTED	PEAK POS	WKS CHRT'D	ARTIST — Record Title	Label & Number
12/04/37	5	6	24. You Can't Stop Me From Dreaming	Bluebird 7159
4/30/38	11	2	25. The Old Apple Tree	Bluebird 7430
			vocals on 17, 19-20, 22, 24-25 by Ozzie Nelson	
6/04/38	5	9	26. Says My Heart/	
			vocals on 21, 23, & 26: Harriet Hilliard	
6/18/38	11	6	27. You Leave Me Breathless	Bluebird 7528
			above two from the film "Cocoanut Grove"	
8/27/38	6	5	28. Change Partners...................................	Bluebird 7734
			from the film "Carefree"	
9/17/38	3	10	29. At Long Last Love	Bluebird 7825
			from the Broadway musical "You Never Know"	
10/22/38	16	1	30. Who Blew Out The Flame?	Bluebird 7814
12/17/38	13	1	31. What Do You Know About Love?................	Bluebird 7681
			from the film "Love Finds Andy Hardy"	
4/29/39	3	3	32. Little Skipper...................................	Bluebird 10187
7/01/39	2(2)	10	33. White Sails (Beneath A Yellow Moon)	Bluebird 10311
			above seven vocals by Ozzie Nelson	
7/08/39	8	3	34. Strange Enchantment............................	Bluebird 10196
			from the film "Man About Town"	
12/23/39	15	1	35. Who Told You I Cared?	Bluebird 10469
			vocal: Harriet Hilliard	
2/24/40	16	4	36. Leanin' On The Ole Top Rail	Bluebird 10499
5/11/40	16	3	37. Alice Blue Gown	Bluebird 10659
			from the Broadway musical & film "Irene"	
8/24/40	14	1	38. I'm Nobody's Baby	Bluebird 10722
			featured in the film "Andy Hardy Meets Debutante" vocals on 33 & above three: Rose Ann Stevens	

NEW YORK MILITARY BAND

1/07/11	8	2	1. Blaze Of Glory.................................... [I]	Edison 10455

RUBY NEWMAN & HIS ORCHESTRA
Violinist-bandleader from Boston

6/25/32	3	6	1. My Silent Love	Victor 24042
			adapted from the instrumental "Jazz Nocturne"	
8/13/32	12	5	2. So Ashamed	Victor 24073
			above two vocals: Gordon Graham	
7/18/36	18	1	3. On Your Toes....................................	Brunswick 7633
			Broadway musical title song	
9/26/36	4	6	4. Sing, Baby, Sing	Victor 25401
			vocal: Barry McKinley; movie title song	
12/17/38	8	2	5. Please Come Out Of Your Dream	Decca 2191
			vocal; Ruby Newman	

JOY NICHOLS & BENNY LEE

2/12/49	21	1	1. The Pussy Cat Song	London 365
			with the Keynotes, & Stanley Black & The Blacksmiths	

RED NICHOLS & HIS FIVE PENNIES
Cornetist and leader of famous all-star jazz band which often featured Benny Goodman, Glenn Miller, & the Dorsey brothers. Red also led the Charleston Chasers, and played with Paul Whiteman & other bands; the 1959 film "The Five Pennies" was based on his life; he died on 6/28/65 (60). (also see Frank Sinatra)

4/16/27	13	3	1. Washboard Blues................................ [I]	Brunswick 3407
			also recorded for Vocalion 15498	
10/15/27	14	2	2. Bugle Call Rag .... [I]	Brunswick 3490
			Eddie Lang (guitar) on above two	
11/12/27	1(3)	15	● 3. Ida, Sweet As Apple Cider.................... [I]	Brunswick 3626
			also recorded for Vocalion 15622; 1903 song featured in the 1919 Broadway musical "Roly Boly Eyes"	
1/07/28	14	2	4. Riverboat Shuffle............................... [I]	Brunswick 3627
7/28/28	13	3	5. Nobody's Sweetheart	Brunswick 3854
			Miff Mole (trombone) on above four	
10/26/29	19	1	6. Indiana .... [I]	Brunswick 4373
2/01/30	7	7	7. Strike Up The Band..............................	Brunswick 4695
			Broadway musical title song	

DATE CHARTED	PEAK POS	WKS CHRT'D	ARTIST — Record Title	Label & Number
5/24/30	**19**	1	8. I Want To Be Happy .... [I] from the Broadway musical "No, No, Nanette" Adrian Rollini (baritone sax) on 3, 4 & 8	Brunswick 4724
10/11/30	**18**	1	9. China Boy .... [I]	Brunswick 4877
11/22/30+	**2(1)**	9	10. Embraceable You/	
12/06/30+	**5**	8	11. I Got Rhythm .... above two from the Broadway musical "Girl Crazy"	Brunswick 4957
11/22/30	**19**	1	12. It Had To Be You .... [I] vocal: Scrappy Lambert; recorded on 6/7/29 Manny Klein (trumpet) on 4, 6, 8 & 12	Brunswick 20092
2/07/31	**5**	4	13. The Peanut Vendor .... vocal: Paul Small Jack Teagarden (trombone) on 6, 8, 12 & 13	Brunswick 6035
2/07/31	**10**	6	14. Blue Again .... vocals on 10-11 & 14: Dick Robertson	Brunswick 6014
3/28/31	**18**	1	15. Corrine Corrina .... vocal: Wingy Manone (also trumpet) Benny Goodman (clarinet) on 6, 9, 10, & 12-15	Brunswick 6058
7/18/31	**17**	1	16. You Rascal, You	Brunswick 6133
9/19/31	**20**	1	17. Fan It .... above two vocals: Ray McKinley Glenn Miller (trombone) & Gene Krupa (drums) on nearly all of above twelve	Brunswick 6160
6/18/32	**15**	2	18. Goofus.. vocal: Dick Robertson	Brunswick 6312
7/09/32	**20**	1	19. California Medley............................... vocal: Boswell Sisters, Sid Garry & Art Jarrett Jimmy Dorsey (alto sax/clarinet) on 1-2, 7-8, 12 & 16-19	Brunswick 20107
5/29/37	**17**	1	20. Wake Up And Live .... vocal: Russell Cromwell; movie title song	Variety 524
5/13/39	**13**	3	21. Tears From My Inkwell .... vocal: Bill Darnell	Bluebird 10200

ALICE NIELSEN
American soprano who sang with the Metropolitan Opera from 1909-13. Died on 3/8/43 (66).

10/26/07	**7**	1	1. Rigoletto - E Il Sol Dell Prima (Love Is The Sun) .... [F] ALICE NIELSEN & FLORENCIO CONSTANTINO	Columbia 3681
2/08/13	**10**	1	2. In The Gloaming.....................................	Columbia 5425
6/26/15	**6**	2	3. By The Waters Of Minnetonka/	
9/04/15	**10**	1	4.　From The Land Of Sky-Blue Water.............	Columbia 1732
7/03/15	**1(2)**	8	5. **Home, Sweet Home** .... written in 1823	Columbia 5283

GERTRUDE NIESEN
Popular ballad singer who started in vaudeville, and was featured in several Broadway musicals and films.

4/01/33	**19**	2	1. Tony's Wife .... accompanied by Ben Selvin's Orchestra	Columbia 2759
8/05/33	**14**	3	2. Hold Your Man	Columbia 2787
6/05/37	**14**	2	3. Where Are You? .... accompanied by Cy Fever's Orchestra from the film "Top of the Town"	Brunswick 7837
3/03/45	**10**	1	4. I Wanna Get Married .... accompanied by Harry Sosnik's Orchestra from the film "Follow the Girls"	Decca 23382

RAY NOBLE & HIS ORCHESTRA
The most popular and acclaimed of all 1930s British bands; pianist/arranger Ray Noble composed some of the decade's top hits ("Love Is the Sweetest Thing", "The Very Thought of You", "The Touch of Your Lips"). Vocalist Al Bowlly was the band's star, but Glenn Miller also assembled for Ray in late 1934 a topflight new U.S. orchestra filled with great musicians. Ray also accompanied Fred Astaire on several late-30s hits. He died on 4/3/79 (75).

9/26/31	**5**	15	1. Lady Of Spain	Victor 22774
6/04/32	**5**	7	2. Lights Of Paris	Victor 24004
7/02/32	**5**	8	3. Hold My Hand	Victor 24034

DATE CHARTED	PEAK POS	WKS CHRT'D	ARTIST — Record Title	Label & Number
10/22/32	**5**	9	4. Sailing On The Robert E. Lee	Victor 24128
1/21/33	**7**	9	5. We've Got The Moon And Sixpence	Victor 24212
			above records listed as "London Mayfair Orchestra"	
5/20/33	**13**	4	6. Lying In The Hay	Victor 24297
7/15/33	**1(5)**	16	7. **Love Is The Sweetest Thing**......................	Victor 24333
10/21/33+	**1(3)**	22	8. **The Old Spinning Wheel**...........................	Victor 24357
2/03/34	**18**	2	9. Love Locked Out	Victor 24485
4/18/34	**15**	2	10. Who Walks In When I Walk Out?	Victor 24594
5/05/34	**6**	5	11. Tiger Rag	Victor 24577
6/30/34	**12**	6	12. My Hat's On The Side Of My Head	Victor 24624
			from the British film "Jack Ahoy"	
7/07/34	**1(5)**	14	13. **The Very Thought Of You**	Victor 24657
10/06/34	**12**	2	14. It's All Forgotten Now................................	Victor 24724
11/24/34	**8**	8	15. I'll Follow My Secret Heart	Victor 24749
			from the Broadway musical "Conversation Piece"	
12/22/34+	**3**	18	16. Blue Danube	Victor 24806
12/29/34+	**1(7)**	16	17. **Isle Of Capri**.....................................	Victor 24777
2/02/35	**5**	6	18. Blue Moon	Victor 24849
2/23/35	**5**	9	19. Clouds	Victor 24865
3/16/35	**15**	2	20. It's Bad For Me......................................	Victor 24872
			Al Bowlly: all above vocals	
3/30/35	**11**	9	21. Flowers For Madame	Victor 24865
6/29/35	**1(1)**	11	22. **Paris In The Spring**..............................	Victor 25040
			vocal: Freshmen	
7/06/35	**1(2)**	7	23. **Let's Swing It/**	
8/10/35	**14**	2	24. Chinatown, My Chinatown................... [I]	Victor 25070
			from the Broadway musical "Up and Down Broadway"	
8/17/35	**4**	6	25. Top Hat	Victor 25094
8/17/35	**12**	10	26. Double Trouble	Victor 25105
			vocal: the Freshmen & Ray Noble	
8/17/35	**19**	1	27. Mad About The Boy................................	Victor 25020
8/31/35	**14**	2	28. The Piccolino	Victor 25094
			25 & 28 from the film "Top Hat"	
12/21/35+	**16**	4	29. Where Am I? (Am I In Heaven?)/	
			from the film "Stars Over Broadway"	
1/04/36	**7**	10	30. Dinner For One, Please, James.................	Victor 25187
1/04/36	**19**	1	31. I Built A Dream One Day.........................	Victor 25200
			from the Broadway musical "May Wine"	
1/25/36	**13**	3	32. A Beautiful Lady In Blue..........................	Victor 25209
2/29/36	**20**	1	33. It's Great To Be In Love	Victor 25232
4/18/36	**12**	4	34. The Touch Of Your Lips	Victor 25277
			Will Bradley (trombone), Bud Freeman (tenor sax), & Claude Thornhill (piano) on 19-34	
8/08/36	**15**	4	35. When I'm With You/	
8/22/36	**20**	1	36. But Definately.......................................	Victor 25336
			above two from the film "Poor Little Rich Girl"	
12/05/36	**3**	13	37. I've Got You Under My Skin/	
12/19/36+	**7**	9	38. Easy To Love	Victor 25422
			above two from the film "Born to Dance" Al Bowlly: nearly all above vocals	
2/06/37	**3**	9	39. I've Got My Love To Keep Me Warm	Victor 25507
			vocal: Howard Phillips; from the film "On the Avenue" Glenn Miller (trombone) & Charlie Spivak (trumpet) on 19-39 (Brunswick 7982-83, 8189-90: Fred Astaire, accompanied by Ray Noble & His Orchestra)	
3/12/38	**15**	2	40. The Moon Of Manakoora/	
			from the film "The Hurricane"	
4/30/38	**4**	12	41. I Hadn't Anyone Till You	Brunswick 8079
5/14/38	**16**	1	42. You Couldn't Be Cuter.............................	Brunswick 8076
			from the film "Joy of Living"	
7/30/38	**17**	2	43. My Walking Stick...................................	Brunswick 8153
			Tony Martin: above four vocals	

DATE CHARTED	PEAK POS	WKS CHRT'D	ARTIST — Record Title	Label & Number
9/10/38	**6**	4	44. Alexander's Ragtime Band ....[I] above two from the film "Alexander's Ragtime Band"	Brunswick 8180
8/05/39	**20**	1	45. Is It Possible? .... from the Broadway musical "Streets of Paris"	Brunswick 8399
8/03/40	**26**	1	46. Louisiana Purchase...................................... vocal: Don Bonnee; Broadway musical title song	Columbia 35507
12/07/40	**10**	3	47. A Nightingale Sang In Berkeley Square .... from the London musical "New Faces"	Columbia 35733
3/28/42	**12**	7	48. By The Light Of The Silv'ry Moon .... record moved in & out of regional best sellers for nearly a year; from Broadway's "Ziegfeld Follies of 1909"	Columbia 36479
7/01/44	**23**	1	49. By The Light Of The Silv'ry Moon ....[R]	Columbia 36479
3/31/45	**14**	2	50. Sweet Dreams, Sweetheart .... vocals on 45, 47 & 50: Larry Stewart	Columbia 36765
2/23/46	**18**	1	51. Full Moon And Empty Arms........................ based on Rachmaninoff's Piano Concerto No. 2 in C-Minor vocals on 48 & 51: Snooky Lanson	Columbia 36893
2/15/47	**1(2)**	23	52. **Linda**	Columbia 37215
9/20/47	**11**	4	53. I Wonder Who's Kissing Her Now................ vocal: Snooky Lanson & the Sportsmen; movie title song	Columbia 37544
12/06/47+	**3**	15	54. I'll Dance At Your Wedding .... Buddy Clark: vocals on 52 & 54	Columbia 37967
5/01/48	**25**	1	55. Suspicion	Columbia 38146
6/19/48	**21**	3	56. It's A Most Unusual Day .... vocal: Anita Gordon; from the film "A Date With Judy"	Columbia 38206
2/09/49	**19**	7	57. Lady Of Spain ....[R] reissue of 1931 recording, with Al Bowlly's original vocal replaced by dubbed-in vocal trio	RCA Victor 3302

HELENE NOLDI

2/29/08	**9**	1	1. Vilia Song..	Victor 31688

JIMMIE NOONE'S APEX CLUB ORCHESTRA
Jazz clarinetist-bandleader whose professional career began in 1913 in New Orleans; Earl Hines played in his 1928 band; died on 4/19/44 (48).

3/07/31	**20**	1	1. Trav'lin' All Alone .... Mildred Bailey, vocal	Vocalion 1580

PATRICIA NORMAN
Singer with Paul Pendarvis & Eddy Duchin ("Ol' Man Mose")

12/31/38	**11**	4	1. Pluckin' On A Golden Harp........................ "with music by Meakin"	Vocalion 4547

RED NORVO & HIS ORCHESTRA
Born Kenneth Norville, great jazzman with long career on xylophone & vibraphone. Red played in the early 30s with Paul Whiteman; his own band featured his wife, superb jazz singer Mildred Bailey, with arrangements by Eddie Sauter, and top regular sideman Herbie Haymer (tenor sax). In the 40s he played with Benny Goodman & Woody Herman, and remained active through the 70s. (also see Mildred Bailey)

1/26/35	**20**	1	1. I Surrender, Dear....................................[I] with Artie Shaw (clarinet) & Charlie Barnet (tenor sax)	Columbia 2977
7/27/35	**9**	4	2. Honeysuckle Rose................................[I]	Columbia 3059
8/01/36	**19**	1	3. Bughouse ....[I] Bunny Berigan (trumpet), Chu Berry (tenor sax), & Gene Krupa (drums) on 2 & 3; Teddy Wilson (piano) on above three	Columbia 3079
11/14/36	**17**	1	4. It Can Happen To You	Brunswick 7761
2/13/37	**11**	4	5. I've Got My Love To Keep Me Warm/	
2/27/37	**8**	4	6. Slummin' On Park Avenue .... above two from the film "On the Avenue"	Brunswick 7813
10/30/37	**10**	2	7. Worried Over You	Brunswick 7970
2/26/38	**16**	2	8. Love Is Here To Stay .... from the film "Goldwyn Follies"	Brunswick 8068
3/12/38	**1(2)**	16	9. **Please Be Kind/**	
5/07/38	**10**	7	10. Weekend Of A Private Secretary................	Brunswick 8088
6/04/38	**1(4)**	12	11. **Says My Heart**	Brunswick 8135

DATE CHARTED	PEAK POS	WKS CHRT'D	ARTIST — Record Title	Label & Number
9/03/38	6	4	12. Garden Of The Moon .... movie title song	Brunswick 8202
11/12/38	5	8	13. Have You Forgotten So Soon? .... Mildred Bailey: all above vocals	Vocalion 4432
2/25/39	3	10	14. I Get Along Without You Very Well .... vocal: Terry Allen	Vocalion 4648
3/18/39	20	1	15. I Go For That .... vocal: Mildred Bailey; from the film "St. Louis Blues"	Vocalion 4548

JACK NORWORTH

Famous vaudeville entertainer and songwriter ("Shine On, Harvest Moon", lyrics for "Take Me Out to the Ball Game"), co-starred in five Broadway musicals with his wife Nora Bayes. Film "Shine On Harvest Moon" about Nora & Jack. He died on 9/1/59 (80).

6/25/10	3	6	1. Come Along, My Mandy............................ NORA BAYES & JACK NORWORTH from the Broadway musical "The Jolly Bachelors"	Victor 70016
10/01/10	9	2	2. Back To My Old Home Town	Victor 60020
10/22/10	8	1	3. Rosa Rosetta	Victor 70019
10/14/11	7	2	4. Turn Off Your Light, Mr. Moon Man............. from the Broadway musical "Little Miss Fix-It" above two: NORA BAYES & JACK NORWORTH	Victor 70038

FRANK NOVAK & HIS ORCHESTRA

Clarinetist/bandleader

2/05/38	15	1	1. Dear Old Girl (Medley)..............................	Vocalion 3913
10/05/40	26	1	2. You're On The Right Side Of The Ocean .... FRANK NOVAK & HIS ROOTIN' TOOTIN' BOYS	Okeh 04171

DONALD NOVIS

Tenor ballad singer featured on 1930s radio and in 1935 hit Broadway musical "Jumbo", also sang on hits by Jimmie Grier; died on 7/23/66 (60).

8/27/32	17	2	1. As You Desire Me .... accompanied by Leonard Joy's Orchestra	Victor 24071
3/25/33	18	2	2. The Whisper Waltz.................................	Brunswick 6489
5/06/33	12	3	3. Trees.. musical version of the famous Joyce Kilmer poem above two accompanied by Victor Young's Orchestra	Brunswick 6538

O

WILL OAKLAND

Known for his exceptionally high counter-tenor voice, Will's professional career stretched from early-century vaudeville to television before his death on 5/15/56 (76). His real name was Herman Hinricks. (Also see Heidelberg Quintet).

12/26/08	7	1	1. When You And I Were Young, Maggie .... later recorded for Victor 5682	Edison 9980
6/26/09	4	3	2. Silver Threads Among The Gold .... previously recorded for Edison Amberol 47	Victor 5691
7/31/09	2(1)	5	3. Nobody Knows, Nobody Cares	Edison 10163
3/05/10	6	3	4. I'm Tired Of Living Without You	Victor 16439
12/17/10	5	3	5. Wait Till The Clouds Roll By .... later recorded for Edison Amberol 710	Victor 16608
1/07/11	5	3	6. In The Gloaming .... WILL OAKLAND & AMERICAN QUARTET	Victor 16646
2/11/11	1(2)	10	7. **Mother Machree** .... later recorded for Columbia 1204	Edison Amb. 583
4/08/11	1(2)	9	8. **I Love The Name Of Mary** .... above two from the Broadway musical "Barry of Ballymore"	Columbia 969
6/29/12	5	4	9. Say "Au Revoir" But Not Goodbye .... later recorded for U.S. Everlasting 1493	Edison Amb. 1022
11/09/12	6	3	10. I'll Take You Home Again, Kathleen.............	Edison Ambersol 1102

DATE CHARTED	PEAK POS	WKS CHRT'D	ARTIST — Record Title	Label & Number
8/23/13	6	3	11. With All Her Faults, I Love Her Still .... accompanied by Charles Prince's Orchestra previously recorded for Edison Amberol 1124	Columbia 1306
9/06/13	2(2)	10	12. The Curse Of An Aching Heart .... also recorded for Edison Amberol 2022	Victor 17372
2/14/14	1(6)	12	13. **I'm On My Way To Mandalay** .... 13 & 15: HENRY BURR, ALBERT CAMPBELL, & WILL OAKLAND (Lyric Trio)	Victor 17503
10/10/14	4	6	14. Just For To-Night .... BILLY MURRAY & WILL OAKLAND	Victor 17622
10/31/14	10	1	15. Dear Love Days .... later recorded by trio for Victor 17789	Columbia 1577
8/30/19	7	2	16. Dear Little Boy Of Mine	Edison 50526

OBREGON'S ORCHESTRA

1/15/38	16	1	1. Cachita	Decca 1574

DOTTIE O'BRIEN

8/12/50	23	2	1. I Wanna Be Loved .... with Jan Garber's Orchestra	Capitol 1044

HELEN O'CONNELL
Famous as featured vocalist for Jimmy Dorsey from 1939-43, usually in duets with Bob Eberly ("Amapola", "Green Eyes", "Tangerine"). She & Bob starred in 1953 TV show with Ray Anthony; in recent years Helen has often been seen on TV.

3/17/51	16	10	1. Would I Love You (Love You, Love You)........ with Dave Cavanaugh's Orchestra	Capitol 1368
12/08/51+	8	13	2. Slow Poke .... with Cliffie Stone's Orchestra	Capitol 1837
5/10/52	27	1	3. Be Anything (But Be Mine)........................ with Harold Mooney's Orchestra	Capitol 2011
11/29/52	21	3	4. Water Can't Quench The Fire Of Love.......... HELEN O'CONNELL & GISELLE MacKENZIE	Capitol 2266
4/25/53	25	1	5. Lipstick-a-Powder-'n Paint........................ above two: HELEN O'CONNELL & GISELE MacKENZIE accompanied by "Dave Cavanaugh's Music"	Capitol 2404

M.J. O'CONNELL

9/02/16	9	1	1. It's A Hundred To One You're In Love	Columbia 2021
1/06/17	9	1	2. You Were Just Made To Order For Me .... MARGUERITE FARRELL & M.J. O'CONNELL	Columbia 2088
5/12/17	8	1	3. Keep Your Eye On The Girlie You Love	Columbia 2188
12/01/17	4	4	4. Some Sunday Morning .... ADA JONES & M.J. O'CONNELL	Columbia 2330
12/29/17+	5	3	5. Send Me Away With A Smile	Columbia 2355

DONALD O'CONNOR
Co-star of the classic movie musical "Singin' In the Rain" as well as many other popular film musicals and comedies from 1938-69, equally talented as a dancer, singer, & comic actor.

10/25/52	25	2	1. No Two People .... DORIS DAY & DONALD O'CONNOR accompanied by Paul Weston & His Orchestra from the film "Hans Christian Andersen"	Columbia 39863

GEORGE O'CONNOR
Minstrel-show comedian who entertained several times at the White House; died on 9/28/46 (72).

5/15/15	8	2	1. Everybody Rag With Me	Columbia 1706
2/24/17	9	1	2. Pray For The Lights To Go Out...................	Columbia 2143

KITTY O'CONNOR

10/10/28	18	1	1. Forgetting You	Columbia 1421

DATE CHARTED	PEAK POS	WKS CHRT'D	ARTIST — Record Title	Label & Number

ANITA O'DAY
Trend-setting, husky-voiced jazz singer who made her reputation with Gene Krupa ("Let Me Off Uptown") and Stan Kenton ("And Her Tears Flowed Like Wine") in the 1940s; she overcame personal difficulties to continue singing into the 80s.

12/27/47	**24**	1	1. Hi Ho Trailus Boot Whip	Signature 15162

with Toots Mondello (alto sax) & Stan Freeman (piano)

2/24/51	**24**	1	2. Tennessee Waltz	London 867

with Doc Severinsen & Charlie Shavers (trumpet), Al Klink (alto sax), & Teddy Wilson (piano)
both records with Will Bradley's Orchestra (Will on trombone)

PAT O'DAY & THE FOUR HORSEMEN

8/22/53	**17**	4	1. A Dear John Letter	MGM 11566

GEOFFREY O'HARA
Canadian-born singer-songwriter known as a leading authority on American Indian music; died in 1955 (73).

7/08/16	**2(1)**	4	1. All I Want Is A Cottage, Some Roses, And You...	Victor 18022
8/12/16	**5**	2	2. They Made It Twice As Nice As Paradise (And They Called It Dixieland)	Victor 18051

flip side of "Simple Melody" (POS 4) by Billy Murray & Elsie Baker

PHIL OHMAN & HIS ORCHESTRA
Pianist, composer of 1936 hit "Lost", co-leader with Victor Arden of the popular Arden-Ohman Orchestra. Died on 8/8/54 (57).

8/31/35	**5**	7	1. Cheek To Cheek	Columbia 3077
9/28/35	**16**	2	2. Isn't This A Lovely Day?...........................	Columbia 3076

both from the film "Top Hat"

WALTER O'KEEFE
Vaudeville and concert entertainer

1/06/34	**6**	7	1. The Man On The Flying Trapeze	Victor 24172

with Jack Shilkret's Orchestra
featured in the film "George White's Scandals"

OKEH LAUGHING RECORD

5/05/23	**8**	1	1. The Okeh Laughing Record .... [N]	Okeh 4678

recorded anonymously in Germany; not to be confused with George Washington Johnson's equally famous "Laughing Song"

OKEH SYNCOPATORS
Harry Reser, leader

"OKLAHOMA!" ALBUM
The Rodgers & Hammerstein musical often called Broadway's greatest ever also made history as the first album (before 1949 meaning a package of 78s) to become a major chart hit, and the first significant original-cast album.

12/18/43	**9**	4	● 1. Oklahoma! Cast Album	Decca 359

featuring Alfred Drake, Joan Roberts, Celeste Holm, Howard da Silva, & Lee Dixon, with orchestra & chorus directed by Jay Blackton
songs include "Oh What a Beautiful Mornin'", "People Will Say We're in Love", "The Surrey With the Fringe on Top", "Kansas City", "I Cain't Say No", & "Oklahoma!"

CHAUNCEY OLCOTT
World-famous tenor and composer of Irish ballads, most notably his first three chart hits. American-born, he started in 1890s minstrel shows before hitting it big on Broadway; died on 3/18/32 (74).

6/21/13	**1(7)**	16	1. **When Irish Eyes Are Smiling**	Columbia 1310

from the Broadway musical "The Ise o' Dreams"

7/26/13	**5**	5	2. My Wild Irish Rose...............................	Columbia 1308

from his 1899 musical "A Romance of Athlone"

8/30/13	**7**	4	3. Mother Machree....................................	Columbia 1337

from the Broadway musical "Barry of Ballymore"

12/20/13+	**1(4)**	13	4. **Too-Ra-Loo-Ra-Loo-Ral (That's An Irish Lullaby)**	Columbia 1410

DATE CHARTED	PEAK POS	WKS CHRT'D	ARTIST — Record Title	Label & Number

KING OLIVER & HIS JAZZ BAND

Joseph Oliver was the "king" of New Orleans jazz cornet just after World War I, and when he took his band to Chicago and invited young protege Louis Armstrong to join, the results were jazz history. Oliver's was the first black jazz band to make commercial records. He also wrote such standards as Armstrong's classic "West End Blues"; died on 4/8/38 (52).

DATE CHARTED	PEAK POS	WKS CHRT'D	ARTIST — Record Title	Label & Number
1/19/24	9	1	1. Dipper Mouth Blues..................... vocal: Bill Johnson; also recorded for Gennett 5132	Okeh 4918
1/26/24	15	1	2. High Society Rag .... [I] Louis Armstrong (cornet) & Johnny Dodds (clarinet) on above two	Okeh 4933
4/09/27	15	2	3. Someday, Sweetheart .... [I]	Vocalion 15493
12/05/27	20	1	4. Willie The Weeper..................... [I] Kid Ory (trombone) & Barney Bigard (clarinet/alto sax) on above two	Vocalion 1112
12/08/28	17	2	5. Four Or Five Times .... vocal: Andy Pendleton & Willie Jackson	Brunswick 4028
2/22/30	9	3	6. St. James' Infirmary..................... vocal: Frank Marvin; with Bubber Miley (trumpet)	Victor 22298

SY OLIVER

One of the great arrangers of the Big Band Era, also on vocals and trumpet; crucial to success of Jimmie Lunceford band (1933-39), then with Tommy Dorsey (1939-43, 45-46), and composer of such Dorsey classics as "Opus No. 1" and "Yes Indeed". Sy later served as arranger/orchestra leader for Louis Armstrong, Bing Crosby, Ella Fitzgerald, Peggy Lee, the Mills Brothers, & Frank Sinatra, among many others.

GEORGE OLSEN & HIS ORCHESTRA

Popular sweet-band leader with featured vocalists Fran Frey (male) & Ethel Shutta (George's wife); the band played in several hit Broadway musicals, including "Sunny". He died on 3/18/71 (78th birthday).

DATE CHARTED	PEAK POS	WKS CHRT'D	ARTIST — Record Title	Label & Number
12/26/25+	7	3	1. I'm Knee Deep In Daisies (And Head Over Heels In Love)..................... vocal: Fran Frey & Bob Rice	Victor 19761
1/30/26	1(6)	12	● 2. Who?/	
2/06/26	2(2)	8	3. Sunny .... [I] above two from the Broadway musical "Sunny"	Victor 19840
4/24/26	1(3)	10	4. Always .... vocal: Edward Joyce, Fran Frey & Bob Rice	Victor 19955
5/22/26	3	6	5. Drifting And Dreaming (Sweet Paradise)........	Victor 19969
6/12/26	2(1)	6	6. Horses .... vocal: Fran Frey, with George Olsen (speaking) based on Tchaikovsky's "Troika"	Victor 19977
8/21/26	3	6	7. The Girl Friend..................... vocal: Larry Murphy, Bob Borger & Fran Frey Broadway musical title song	Victor 20029
10/30/26	5	4	8. Katinka	Victor 20100
11/13/26	5	4	9. Lucky Day..................... from the Broadway musical "George White's Scandals of 1926"	Victor 20101
2/05/27	5	7	10. Do-Do-Do.....................	Victor 20327
3/12/27	3	7	11. Someone To Watch Over Me .... [I] above two from the Broadway musical "Oh, Kay!"	Victor 20392
4/16/27	2(2)	10	12. Blue Skies/ from the Broadway musical "Betsy"	
5/14/27	12	3	13. Where's That Rainbow? .... from the Broadway musical "Peggy Ann"	Victor 20455
4/16/27	10	4	14. Ev'ry Little While	Victor 20409
5/14/27	1(3)	12	15. At Sundown (When Love Is Calling Me Home) .... all vocals from 8-15: Fran Frey, Bob Borger & Bob Rice	Victor 20476
10/29/27	3	9	16. The Best Things In Life Are Free/ vocal: Bob Borger	
11/05/27	9	4	17. Lucky In Love.....................	Victor 20872

DATE CHARTED	PEAK POS	WKS CHRT'D	ARTIST — Record Title	Label & Number
11/05/27	**4**	7	18. The Varsity Drag/	
11/19/27	**6**	6	19.　Good News .... Victor 20875 above four from the Broadway musical "Good News"	
1/21/28	**5**	7	20. My Heart Stood Still .... Victor 21034 from the Broadway musical "A Connecticut Yankee" vocals on 17, 19 & 20: Fran Frey, Bob Borger & Bob Rice	
9/29/28	**7**	6	21. Old Man Sunshine, Little Boy Bluebird .... Victor 21566 vocals on 18 & 21: Fran Frey	
10/27/28	**15**	2	22. I'm On The Crest Of A Wave .... Victor 21500 from the Broadway musical "George White's Scandals of 1928"	
12/01/28	**5**	5	23. Doin' The Raccoon.............................. Victor 21701 vocal: Fran Frey-Bob Borger-Bob Rice-Jack Gifford	
2/16/29	**1(2)**	11	24. **A Precious Little Thing Called Love** .... Victor 21832	
2/08/30	**14**	2	25. South Sea Rose .... Victor 22213 vocals on 24 & 25: Ethel Shutta	
5/17/30	**7**	5	26. The Moon Is Low .... Victor 22392 vocal by Fran Frey; from the film "Montana Moon"	
5/17/30	**9**	5	27. I'm In The Market For You .... Victor 22391 from the film "High Society Blues"	
5/17/30	**10**	5	28. It Happened In Monterey......................... Victor 22370 from the film "The King of Jazz"	
9/06/30	**6**	6	29. The Kiss Waltz................................. Victor 22462	
11/01/30	**5**	6	30. Beyond The Blue Horizon........................ Victor 22530 from the film "Monte Carlo" vocals on 22, & 27-30: Bob Borger	
4/02/32	**10**	4	31. By The Fireside .... Victor 22947 vocal: Bob Borger & Ethel Shutta; British song	
4/30/32	**18**	1	32. There's Nothing The Matter With Me .... Victor 22968 from the Broadway musical "Hot-cha"	
5/14/32	**1(2)**	10	33. **Lullaby Of The Leaves** .... Victor 22998 group vocal	
8/20/32	**14**	2	34. It Was So Beautiful .... Victor 24070	
9/17/32	**1(2)**	9	35. **Say It Isn't So**/	
10/08/32	**14**	3	36.　Love Me Tonight..................... Victor 24124 movie title song above three vocals: Paul Small	
9/24/32	**6**	6	37. All-American Girl .... Victor 24125	
10/22/32	**5**	6	38. Please....................................... Victor 24139 vocal: Bob Borger 34 & 38 from the film "The Big Broadcast of 1932"	
10/22/32	**8**	5	39. Pink Elephants.......................... [I] Victor 24138	
11/12/32+	**15**	3	40. Rock-A-Bye Moon/	
11/19/32	**16**	2	41.　Play, Fiddle, Play.................................. Victor 24165 vocal: Dave Marshall	
2/18/33	**13**	2	42. The Girl In The Little Green Hat................. Victor 24220 vocals on 37 & 42: Fran Frey	
3/11/33	**11**	3	43. Underneath The Arches........................... Victor 24229	
7/22/33	**6**	4	44. Louisiana Lullaby............................... Columbia 2790	
7/29/33	**1(9)**	24	45. **The Last Round-Up** .... Columbia 2791 vocal: Joe Morrison featured in Broadway's "Ziegfeld Follies of 1934"	
10/07/33	**14**	3	46. Night Owl .... Columbia 2820 vocals on 32, 40, 43 & 46: Ethel Shutta	
12/23/33	**17**	1	47. Everything I Have Is Yours .... Columbia 2842 from the film "Dancing Lady"	
1/13/34	**12**	5	48. Throw Another Log On The Fire .... Columbia 2857	
12/22/45	**12**	2	49. Chickery Chick............................... Majestic 7155 vocal: Judith Blair & Ray Adams	

DANNY O'NEIL
Tenor ballad singer

12/14/46	**12**	1	1. Ole Buttermilk Sky .... Majestic 7199 with Virgil Davis' Orchestra; from the film "Canyon Passage"	

DATE CHARTED	PEAK POS	WKS CHRT'D	ARTIST — Record Title	Label & Number

ORIGINAL DIXIELAND JAZZ BAND
Historic band led by Nick LaRocca (cornet) which was the first jazz group to be commercially recorded, and the first to make jazz nationally popular. Larry Shields (clarinet), Eddie Edwards (trombone), Harry Ragas (piano), & Tony Sbarbaro (drums) were the other original members. LaRocca was credited as composer of the enduring jazz standards "Tiger Rag" & "Livery Stable Blues"; he died on 2/22/61 at age 71.

DATE CHARTED	PEAK POS	WKS CHRT'D	ARTIST — Record Title	Label & Number
6/02/17	4	4	1. Livery Stable Blues...................... [I]	Victor 18255
10/13/17	2(1)	7	2. Darktown Strutters' Ball/ [I]	
10/20/17	8	2	3. Indiana........................ [I]	Columbia 2297
7/13/18	8	1	4. At The Jazz Band Ball............. [I]	Victor 18457
8/17/18	1(2)	11	5. **Tiger Rag**..................... [I]	Victor 18472
3/05/21	3	5	6. Palesteena/ [I]	
3/26/21	9	1	7. Margie .... [I]	Victor 18717
3/26/21	12	1	8. Sweet Mama (Papa's Gettin' Mad)........	Victor 18722
			group vocal	
4/02/21	2(1)	6	9. Home Again Blues .... [I]	Victor 18729
8/27/21	3	6	10. St. Louis Blues/	
9/17/21	9	1	11. Jazz Me Blues................... [I]	Victor 18772
11/19/21	3	5	12. Royal Garden Blues	Victor 18798
			vocals on 10 & 12 by Al Bernard	
2/25/22	9	1	13. Bow Bow Blues (My Mama Treats Me Like A Dog)..................	Victor 18850
			Benny Krueger (alto sax) on above seven	
4/25/23	5	3	14. Some Of These Days.............. [I]	Okeh 4738

ORIGINAL MEMPHIS FIVE
Jazz band featuring Phil Napoleon (trumpet) & Jimmy Lytell (clarinet).

DATE CHARTED	PEAK POS	WKS CHRT'D	ARTIST — Record Title	Label & Number
7/21/23	8	1	1. Who's Sorry Now? .... [I]	Victor 19052

ORIOLES
Tenor Sonny Til (died on 12/9/81 at age 56) led this trend-setting R&B group, originally from Baltimore.

DATE CHARTED	PEAK POS	WKS CHRT'D	ARTIST — Record Title	Label & Number
11/06/48	13	7	1. It's Too Soon To Know............	Natural 5000
8/22/53	11	10	● 2. Crying In The Chapel............	Jubilee 5122

NICHOLAS ORLANDO'S ORCHESTRA

DATE CHARTED	PEAK POS	WKS CHRT'D	ARTIST — Record Title	Label & Number
3/22/19	1(2)	10	1. **Till We Meet Again**	Victor 18526
			vocal: Harry Macdonough & Charles Hart	
			flip side of #1 hit "Beautiful Ohio" by the Waldorf-Astoria Dance Orchestra	

ORPHEUS QUARTET
Tenors Harry Macdonough & Lambert Murphy. baritone Reinald Werrenrath. & bass William F. Hooley.

DATE CHARTED	PEAK POS	WKS CHRT'D	ARTIST — Record Title	Label & Number
2/14/14	10	1	1. The Girl In The Gingham Gown	Victor 17468
			from the Broadway musical "America"	
11/11/16	1(3)	10	2. **Turn Back The Universe And Give Me Yester Day**	Victor 18112
2/17/17	5	3	3. Mammy's Little Coal Black Rose	Victor 18183
10/13/17	10	1	4. For The Freedom Of The World	Victor 18337
6/22/18	5	3	5. Some Day They're Coming Home Again	Victor 18468
			2, 4-5: "HARRY MACDONOUGH & ORPHEUS QUARTET"	
1/04/19	9	1	6. When You Come Back, And You Will Come Back	Victor 18494
3/15/19	9	2	7. Bring Back My Bonnie To Me	Victor 64793
			ALMA GLUCK & ORPHEUS QUARTET	

KID ORY
The career of jazz trombonist Edward "Kid" Ory extended from 1912-19, when he led New Orleans' hottest jazz band (at times including King Oliver, Louis Armstrong, & Sidney Bechet) to the 70s. The composer of long-popular "Muskrat Ramble", he recorded in the 20s with Oliver, Armstrong, & Jelly Roll Morton; died on 1/23/73 (86).

DATE CHARTED	PEAK POS	WKS CHRT'D	ARTIST — Record Title	Label & Number
			WILL OSBORNE & HIS ORCHESTRA Vocalist and sweet-band leader, born William Oliphant in Canada; co-wrote several popular songs ("Pompton Turnpike"). (All vocals by Osborne)	
6/02/34	**15**	2	1. Cocktails For Two.. from the film "Murder at the Vanities"	Melotone 12996
4/20/35	**20**	1	2. Soon.. from the film "Mississippi"	Melotone 13330
8/24/35	**13**	4	3. That's What You Think.............................. from the film "King Solomon of Broadway"	Columbia 3080
1/16/37	**14**	3	4. It's De-Lovely.. from the Broadway musical "Red, Hot, and Blue"	Decca 1058
7/09/38	**17**	1	5. So Lovely	Decca 1905
10/29/38	**20**	1	6. Silver On The Sage....................................	Decca 1951
			VESS OSSMAN Sylvester Louis Ossman, "The King of the Banjo" from the 1890s to World War I, was born on 8/21/1868 in Hudson, N.Y. The foremost recorded ragtime musician of the original ragtime era died on 12/8/23 (55). (also see Arthur Collins)	
6/02/94	**1(4)**	4	1. **Yankee Doodle** .... [I] also recorded for New Jersey	North Amer. 905
5/30/95	**1(3)**	3	2. **Cocoanut Dance** .... [I]	Columbia 1069
6/20/96	**1(3)**	3	3. **A Hot Time On The Levee**........................ [I] LEN SPENCER & VESS OSSMAN	Columbia 7200
6/12/97	**3**	3	4. Hot Stuff Patrol .... [I] also recorded for Edison 2616 & Chicago 721	Columbia 3811
7/10/97	**3**	2	5. Yankee Doodle .... [I] new version of 1894 hit also recorded for Edison 2635 & New Jersey	Columbia 3814
12/11/97	**2(3)**	3	6. Ragtime Medley .... [I]	Berliner 467
12/10/98	**3**	2	7. At A Georgia Camp Meeting.................... [I] also recorded for Chicago 702	Columbia 3837
2/04/99	**2(1)**	5	8. A Bunch Of Rags .... [I] his most famous original; later recorded for Edison 7305	Columbia 3861
1/27/00	**2(1)**	5	9. The Old Folks At Home........................... [I] also recorded for Edison 7340, later for Victor 3371	Berliner 084
9/22/00	**2(2)**	4	10. A Coon Band Contest .... [I] also recorded for Columbia 31412, later for Gram-o-Phone 154 & 3042; later issued on Columbia disc 461	Edison 7561
4/27/01	**5**	1	11. Florodora: Selections .... [I]	Gram-o-Phone 624
4/02/04	**3**	1	12. Razzle Dazzle .... [I]	Edison 8618
2/04/05	**3**	3	13. St. Louis Rag .... [I] also recorded for Edison 8726	Columbia 32576
9/30/05	**8**	1	14. Little Johnny Jones Medley..................... [I]	Victor 4382
10/28/05	**8**	1	15. Turkey In The Straw Medley.................... [I]	Victor 4424
2/24/06	**9**	1	16. My Irish Molly O .... [I] from the Broadway musical "Sargeant Brue"	Victor 4533
5/12/06	**3**	4	17. St. Louis Tickle...................................... [I]	Victor 4624
6/16/06	**4**	1	18. The Buffalo Rag .... [I] also recorded for Columbia 3360	Victor 4628
9/29/06	**6**	1	19. On The Rocky Road To Dublin .... [I]	Columbia 3447
12/15/06	**5**	2	20. Sunflower Dance .... [I] also on Columbia cylinder 33016	Columbia 3507
2/23/07	**6**	1	21. Popularity .... [I] later recorded for Edison 9521	Columbia 3529
4/27/07	**7**	1	22. The Motor March .... [I] also on Columbia cylinder 33084 later recorded for Victor 5073	Columbia 3569
6/29/07+	**9**	1	23. Panama Rag Two-Step .... [I] 17 & 23 by the Ossman-Dudley Trio, with brothers George & Audley Dudley on harp-guitar & mandolin	Columbia 85109
7/07/07	**3**	3	24. Maple Leaf Rag .... [I] also on Columbia cylinder 33133	Columbia 3626
3/20/09	**7**	1	25. A Gay Gossoon....................................... [I]	Victor 16092

DATE CHARTED	PEAK POS	WKS CHRT'D	ARTIST — Record Title	Label & Number
4/02/10	9	1	26. Moose March.. [I] also on Indestructable 1249, later recorded for Edison 10383	Columbia 787
7/08/11	10	1	27. The Smiler .... [I] previously recorded for Edison 9765	Columbia 972

JACK OWENS
Singer featured on Don McNeill's "Breakfast Club" network radio show

DATE CHARTED	PEAK POS	WKS CHRT'D	ARTIST — Record Title	Label & Number
9/20/47	2(1)	20	1. How Soon (Will I Be Seeing You) .... with Eddie Bellantyne's Orchestra	Tower 1258
10/01/49	11	12	2. Jealous Heart	Decca 24711
1/07/50	22	2	3. You're The Only One I Care For.................. above two with Danny Mendelsohn's Orchestra	Decca 24712
4/08/50	29	1	4. You're A Sweetheart .... with Sy Oliver's Orchestra, & Three Beaus & A Peep	Decca 24935
9/09/50	14	11	5. Dream A Little Dream Of Me......................	Decca 27096

P

IGNACE JAN PADEREWSKI
Great Polish-born pianist and composer who first achieved international acclaim in 1888; died on 6/29/41 (80).

DATE CHARTED	PEAK POS	WKS CHRT'D	ARTIST — Record Title	Label & Number
11/24/17	8	1	1. Chopin Etude In G Flat Major.................. [I]	Victor 64706

HOT LIPS PAGE & HIS BAND
Jazz trumpet player and singer, born Oran Thaddeus Page; played with Bennie Moten (1931-35) & Artie Shaw (1941-42); died on 11/5/54 (46).

DATE CHARTED	PEAK POS	WKS CHRT'D	ARTIST — Record Title	Label & Number
5/28/38	9	4	1. I Let A Song Go Out Of My Heart .... [I]	Bluebird 7567

PATTI PAGE
Born Clara Ann Fowler in Oklahoma, Patti Page sold more records than any other female vocalist of the 1950s. After singing briefly with Benny Goodman in early 1948, her first major hits created a great stir since they were among the first widely-heard multi-track vocal recordings, in which she seemed to be singing duets with herself. Patti hosted a late-50s TV series, and continued to hit the charts through the 60s.

DATE CHARTED	PEAK POS	WKS CHRT'D	ARTIST — Record Title	Label & Number
6/26/48	12	8	1. Confess.. accompanied by George Barnes Trio	Mercury 5129
10/30/48	23	4	2. Say Something Sweet To Your Sweetheart..... VIC DAMONE & PATTI PAGE with Eric Robinson's Orchestra	Mercury 5192
2/12/49	13	1	3. So In Love .... from the Broadway musical "Kiss Me, Kate"	Mercury 5230
4/23/49	27	1	4. Money, Marbles And Chalk .... accompanied by Zeb Masher's Orchestra	Mercury 5251
9/03/49	26	1	5. I'll Keep The Lovelight Burning..................	Mercury 5310
1/07/50	11	11	● 6. With My Eyes Wide Open I'm Dreaming........ listed as "Patti Page Quartet" from the film "Shoot the Works"	Mercury 5344
5/20/50	8	9	7. I Don't Care If The Sun Don't Shine .... accompanied by D'Artega's Orchestra	Mercury 5396
8/26/50	1(5)	23	● 8. All My Love .... melody based on Ravel's "Bolero"	Mercury 5455
10/07/50	23	1	9. Back In Your Own Back Yard......................	Mercury 5463
11/18/50	1(13)	26	● 10. The Tennessee Waltz .... one of the biggest hits of all time, with sales over six million	Mercury 5534
2/10/51	4	19	● 11. Would I Love You (Love You, Love You)........	Mercury 5571
2/24/51	2(1)	22	● 12. Mockin' Bird Hill .... accompanied by Jimmy Carroll's Orchestra	Mercury 5595
5/05/51	17	7	13. Down The Trail Of Achin' Hearts/ accompanied by the Jack Rael Quartet	
5/05/51	24	2	14. Ever True Ever More .... 8-9, 11, & 14 accompanied by Harry Geller's Orchestra	Mercury 5579

DATE CHARTED	PEAK POS	WKS CHRT'D	ARTIST — Record Title	Label & Number
5/19/51	**8**	14	● 15. Mister And Mississippi/ 10 & 15 accompanied by Jack Rael's Orchestra	

6/30/51	**26**	2	16. These Things I Offer You........................ Mercury 5645
			    accompanied by Joe Reisman's Orchestra
			    (Joe arranged many of Patti's other hits)	

8/04/51	**5**	16	● 17. Detour .... Mercury 5682	
9/22/51	**4**	13	18. And So to Sleep Again .... Mercury 5706 on 6 & 18 Patti is a one-woman quartet through overdubbing	
1/26/52	**22**	4	19. Retreat (Cries My Heart)/	
2/09/52	**9**	11	20. Come What May .... Mercury 5772	
3/29/52	**16**	11	21. Whispering Winds.................................... Mercury 5816	
6/28/52	**9**	11	22. Once In Awhile.. Mercury 5867	
8/30/52	**1(10)**	22	● 23. **I Went To Your Wedding/**	
8/30/52	**4**	17	24. You Belong To Me................................... Mercury 5899	
11/29/52+	**4**	13	25. Why Don't You Believe Me/	
12/06/52	**18**	4	26. Conquest... Mercury 70025	
1/31/53	**1(8)**	20	● 27. **The Doggie In The Window/**	
2/07/53	**17**	5	28. My Jealous Eyes..................................... Mercury 70070	
5/16/53	**18**	2	29. Now That I'm In Love/	
5/30/53	**16**	1	30. Oo! What You Do To Me .... Mercury 70127	
7/18/53	**10**	11	31. Butterflies/	
8/08/53	**20**	2	32. This Is My Song...................................... Mercury 70183 Patti's theme for her 1952-53 NBC TV series	

10/10/53	**21**	1	33. Father, Father... Mercury 70222
			    based on the Hebraic song "Eli, Eli"
			    all records from 17-33 accompanied by Jack Rael's Orchestra	

11/07/53	**23**	2	34. Milwaukee Polka .... Mercury 70230 accompanied by Joe Reisman & His Polka Dots	
11/28/53	**3**	19	● 35. Changing Partners .... Mercury 70260	
2/27/54	**2(4)**	21	● 36. Cross Over The Bridge/	
2/27/54	**21**	4	37. My Restless Lover................................... Mercury 70302	
6/05/54	**8**	8	38. Steam Heat... Mercury 70380 from the Broadway musical "The Pajama Game"	
8/14/54	**13**	8	39. I Cried/	
8/28/54	**10**	8	40. What A Dream .... Mercury 70416	
10/16/54	**30**	1	41. I Can't Tell A Waltz From A Tango/	
10/30/54	**24**	3	42. The Mama Doll Song .... Mercury 70458 35-42 accompanied by Jack Rael's Orchestra	

RAYMOND PAIGE & HIS ORCHESTRA
Violinist-bandleader, frequently on radio, later directed the orchestra at Radio City Music Hall; died on 8/7/65.

DATE CHARTED	PEAK POS	WKS CHRT'D	ARTIST — Record Title	Label & Number

5/19/34	**19**	1	1. Love Thy Neighbor.................................. Victor 24604
			    vocal: Three Rhythm Kings
			    from the film "We're Not Dressing"	

CHARLIE PARKER
Alto saxophonist regarded by many as the single greatest jazz musician of the postwar era; the man known as "Bird" won five Down Beat poll awards, and played with Billy Eckstine, Earl Hines, Andy Kirk, Lucky Millinder, & Cootie Williams in the early 40s. His own original band, featuring trumpet great Dizzy Gillespie, made jazz history by setting into motion the "bebop" movement. Charlie Parker died on 3/12/55 (34).

FRANK PARKER
Tenor balladeer who briefly sang with the Revelers, and was the first singer on Jack Benny's radio show (1933-35); in several movies, many other radio programs, 1944 Broadway hit "Follow the Girls", and on TV in early 50s with Arthur Godfrey.

DATE CHARTED	PEAK POS	WKS CHRT'D	ARTIST — Record Title	Label & Number
10/06/34	**6**	4	1. Two Cigarettes In The Dark .... Columbia 2944 from the film "Kill That Story"	

KATHLEEN PARLOW
Canadian-born violinist with an international concert career; died on 8/19/63 (72).

DATE CHARTED	PEAK POS	WKS CHRT'D	ARTIST — Record Title	Label & Number
10/28/16	**9**	1	1. Thais: Meditation.................................. [I] Columbia 5843	

DATE CHARTED	PEAK POS	WKS CHRT'D	ARTIST — Record Title	Label & Number
			TONY PASTOR & HIS ORCHESTRA	
			Born Antonio Pestritto, former tenor saxophonist-singer with Irving Aaronson (1928-30), Vincent Lopez, and most importantly Artie Shaw (1936-39). Johnny McAfee (alto sax) his featured sideman, with late-40s arrangements by Ralph Flanagan; during later period Rosemary & Betty Clooney were band's vocalists. Tony died on 10/31/69 (62).	
6/28/41	9	3	1. Maria Elena	Bluebird 11127
7/26/41	21	1	2. Green Eyes	Bluebird 11168
			above two vocals: Dorsey Anderson	
9/13/41	25	1	3. Twenty-One Dollars A Day-Once A Month	Bluebird 11231
6/13/42	21	1	4. That Ain't The Way I Dreamed It	Bluebird 11502
			vocal: Johnny McAfee	
1/30/43	20	1	5. Hey, Mabel! .... [N]	Bluebird 0802
10/21/44	9	10	6. Dance With A Dolly (With A Hole In Her Stocking)	Bluebird 0827
			adapted from the 1844 song "Lubly Fan (Buffalo Gals, Won't You Come Out Tonight)"	
5/19/45	2(2)	15	7. Bell-Bottom Trousers/	
			vocal Ruth McCullough	
			based on a traditional sea chantey	
7/14/45	11	3	8. Five Salted Peanuts	Victor 1661
8/18/45	13	1	9. Please No Squeeza Da Banana .... [N]	Victor 1693
			vocal: Charles Trotta	
3/02/46	10	2	10. Sioux City Sue	Cosmo 471
5/31/47	8	2	11. Red Silk Stockings And Green Perfume .... [N]	Columbia 37330
6/14/47	11	9	12. I Wonder, I Wonder, I Wonder	Columbia 37353
8/16/47	10	7	13. The Lady From Twenty-Nine Palms	Columbia 37562
			Tony Pastor: vocals on 3-4, 6, & most of above eight	
11/27/48	16	3	14. You Started Something	Columbia 38297
2/05/49	21	1	15. It's Like Taking Candy From A Baby	Columbia 38355
2/19/49	11	5	16. Grieving For You	Columbia 38383
			Rosemary Clooney: above three vocals	
5/07/49	12	8	17. "A" You're Adorable (The Alphabet Song)	Columbia 38449
			vocal: Clooney Sisters	
			BUNNY PAUL	
			female vocalist	
10/17/53	23	4	1. Magic Guitar	Dot 15107
3/27/54	23	4	2. Such A Night	Essex 352
6/05/54	24	2	3. Lovey Dovey	Essex 359
			orchestra on above two directed by Sy Oliver	
			LES PAUL	
			One of the greatest creative talents in modern popular music, Les Paul (born Lester Pollfuss) played guitar for Fred Waring (1938-40) and accompanied Bing Crosby on his 1945 #1 hit "It's Been a Long, Long Time". During this period he put his electronic wizardry to work in designing the first solid-body amplified electric guitar, and developing the sound-on-sound and multi-track recording techniques that marked his many hits with wife Mary Ford, and which later became standard in the record industry. In 1976 Les won a best-instrumental Grammy Award for an album with Chet Atkins.	
10/19/46	4	13	1. Rumors Are Flying	Decca 23656
			ANDREWS SISTERS & LES PAUL	
2/21/48	21	4	2. Lover/ [I]	
			from the film "Love Me Tonight"	
2/21/48	22	2	3. Brazil .... [I]	Capitol 15037
			breakthrough record with Les playing six guitars, overdubbed	
5/15/48	11	1	4. What Is This Thing Called Love? .... [I]	Capitol 15070
			from the Broadway musical "Wake Up and Dream"	
6/24/50	9	17	5. Nola .... [I]	Capitol 1014
			Les on Spanish guitar and steel guitar	
10/07/50	21	2	6. Goofus .... [I]	Capitol 1192
12/16/50+	18	7	7. Little Rock Getaway .... [I]	Capitol 1316
1/10/51	23	2	8. Jazz Me Blues .... [I]	Capitol 1825

DATE CHARTED	PEAK POS	WKS CHRT'D	ARTIST — Record Title	Label & Number
7/07/51	**12**	12	9. Josephine .... [I]	Capitol 1592
8/18/51	**7**	16	10. Whispering .... [I]	Capitol 1748
12/15/51+	**10**	4	11. Jingle Bells .... [I-X]	Capitol 1881
5/17/52	**14**	9	12. Carioca .... [I]	Capitol 2080
			from the film "Flying Down to Rio"	
8/30/52	**5**	14	13. Meet Mister Callaghan .... [I]	Capitol 2193
11/08/52	**8**	8	14. Lady Of Spain .... [I]	Capitol 2265
4/04/53	**21**	1	15. Sleep .... [I]	Capitol 2400
			Fred Waring's theme song	
10/31/53	**25**	2	16. The Kangaroo .... [I]	Capitol 2614

LES PAUL & MARY FORD

Mary's real name was Colleen Summers; she and Les were married until 1962 (she died on 10/1/77). Their records used Les' multi-track recording process superimposing his several guitar parts behind her voice.

DATE CHARTED	PEAK POS	WKS CHRT'D	ARTIST — Record Title	Label & Number
12/30/50+	**6**	14	1. Tennessee Waltz	Capitol 1316
2/17/51	**2(6)**	24	● 2. Mockin' Bird Hill	Capitol 1373
3/31/51	**1(9)**	25	● 3. **How High The Moon**.................	Capitol 1451
			record selected for NARAS Hall of Fame	
			from the Broadway musical "Two for the Show"	
7/28/51	**18**	6	4. I Wish I Had Never Seen Sunshine	Capitol 1592
8/18/51	**2(2)**	16	● 5. The World Is Waiting For The Sunrise	Capitol 1748
10/27/51	**5**	13	6. Just One More Chance...........................	Capitol 1825
1/05/52	**2(1)**	12	7. Tiger Rag	Capitol 1920
5/17/52	**13**	11	8. I'm Confessin' (That I Love You)	Capitol 2080
6/21/52	**15**	7	9. In The Good Old Summertime/	
6/28/52	**14**	7	10. Smoke Rings...........................	Capitol 2123
9/06/52	**15**	8	11. Take Me In Your Arms And Hold Me	Capitol 2193
11/22/52	**7**	10	12. My Baby's Coming Home/	
1/03/53	**5**	7	13. Bye Bye Blues...........................	Capitol 2316
3/28/53	**10**	6	14. I'm Sitting On Top Of The World.................	Capitol 2400
			featured in the film "The Jolson Story"	
6/20/53	**1(11)**	31	● 15. **Vaya Con Dios (May God Be With You)**/	
6/27/53	**15**	5	16. Johnny (Is The Boy For Me).....................	Capitol 2486
11/07/53	**13**	4	17. Don'cha Hear Them Bells	Capitol 2614
4/03/54	**11**	10	18. I Really Don't Want To Know.....................	Capitol 2735
7/10/54	**6**	14	19. I'm A Fool To Care.................................	Capitol 2839
10/16/54	**10**	9	20. Whither Thou Goest/	
11/27/54	**19**	1	21. Mandolino	Capitol 2928

JAN PEERCE

Tenor who was featured on broadcasts of Radio City Music Hall 1933-38 before debuting with the Metropolitan Opera. Chosen by Toscanini to star in his radio opera productions from 1944-54, in 1955 he became the first American singer to appear on the stage of Moscow's Bolshoi Theater. Jan died on 12/15/84 (80).

DATE CHARTED	PEAK POS	WKS CHRT'D	ARTIST — Record Title	Label & Number
10/02/48	**23**	2	1. Bluebird Of Happiness	RCA Victor 9007
6/16/51	**22**	4	2. What Is A Boy?/	
7/14/51	**12**	8	3. Because Of You.......................	RCA Victor 3425
			above two accompanied by Hugo Winterhalter's Orchestra	

DATE CHARTED	PEAK POS	WKS CHRT'D	ARTIST — Record Title	Label & Number
			PEERLESS QUARTET	
			All-time great vocal group which began as the Columbia Male Quartet, composed on most 1904-05 hits of tenors Henry Burr & Albert Campbell, baritone Steve Porter, and bass Tom Daniels. By 1906 Frank Stanley had replaced Daniels, and he became both lead singer and manager as the group became known as the Peerless. Arthur Collins took Porter's place in 1909; upon Stanley's death in 1910 John Meyer became the new bass, and Burr took over as leader. Collins departed in late 1918, succeeded by Frank Croxton, and the Burr-Campbell-Meyer-Croxton combination remained intact through 1925, when Burr formed a new Peerless Quartet with three lesser-known partners, until a final 1928 dissolution.	
11/19/04	**1(3)**	10	1. **You're The Flower Of My Heart, Sweet Adeline** .... written as an instrumental in 1896 ("Down Home in New England")	Columbia 32584
3/04/05	**5**	2	2. Kentucky Babe...	Columbia 3055
5/13/05	**3**	2	3. Tell Me With Your Eyes	Columbia 32706
7/29/05	**7**	1	4. In The Sweet Bye And Bye	Columbia 32722
12/30/05	**7**	1	5. O Come, All Ye Faithful .... [X]	Columbia 32823
10/27/06	**9**	1	6. While The Old Mill Wheel Is Turning	Columbia 3453
8/31/07	**2(2)**	5	7. Honey Boy... also recorded as Peerless Quartet for Zon-o-Phone 5423 all above records: Columbia Male Quartet	Columbia 3669
3/28/08	**7**	1	8. As Long As The World Rolls On	Zon-o-Phone 957
5/30/08	**7**	1	9. Women .... from the Broadway musical "The Merry Widow"	Victor 5392
8/15/08	**4**	2	10. Come Where My Love Lies Dreaming........... also recorded for U.S. Everlasting 343	Victor 5481
10/31/08	**10**	1	11. Rah, Rah, Rah... from the Broadway musical "The Soul Kiss"	Victor 5460
12/26/08	**10**	1	12. Old Black Joe	Victor 5562
4/29/09	**6**	1	13. Roses Bring Dreams Of You .... also on Columbia cylinder 85185 flip side of "In the Garden of My Heart" (POS 2) by Frank Stanley & Henry Burr	Columbia 641
8/21/09	**3**	3	14. My Pony Boy.. from the Broadway musical "Miss Innocence"	Columbia 713
11/27/09	**8**	1	15. Sweetheart's A Pretty Name When It's Y-O-U .	Victor 16352
4/09/10	**6**	4	16. Medley Of Foster Songs............................. including "My Old Kentucky Home" & "The Old Folks at Home"	Victor 35095
4/30/10	**2(2)**	7	17. By The Light Of The Silvery Moon .... also recorded for Zon-o-Phone 5648 & U.S. Everlasting 1078 from Broadway's "Ziegfeld Follies of 1909"	Columbia 799
10/15/10	**8**	1	18. Big Bass Viol .... listed as Frank Stanley & Peerless Quartet; also released under Stanley's name on Zon-o-Phone 5634 & Indestructable 1123	Victor 16507
12/10/10	**2(3)**	9	19. Silver Bell .... also recorded for U.S. Everlasting 1105 flip side of Will Oakland & American Quartet's #5 hit "In The Gloaming" Frank Stanley: lead vocals on nearly all 1906-10 records	Victor 16646
3/18/11	**9**	1	20. The Old Oaken Bucket..............................	Columbia 3195
6/17/11	**9**	1	21. Way Down East .... also recorded for Columbia 970, U.S. Everlasting 1121 & Zon-o-Phone 5843	Edison 10489
9/23/11	**2(5)**	8	22. I Want A Girl Just Like The Girl That Married Dear Old Dad.........................	Columbia 1034
11/04/11	**1(7)**	17	23. **Let Me Call You Sweetheart**	Columbia 1057
11/04/11	**3**	5	24. Jimmy Valentine .... also recorded for Victor 17036, & Edison Amberol 1042	Columbia 1043
4/06/12	**6**	2	25. Everybody's Doing It Now..........................	Columbia 112
4/27/12	**6**	3	26. It's A Long Lane That Has No Turning.......... also recorded for Columbia 1141 group listed on nearly all above Columbias as Columbia Male Quartet	Victor 17030
9/21/12	**4**	5	27. Bring Back My Golden Dreams	Victor 17124

DATE CHARTED	PEAK POS	WKS CHRT'D	ARTIST — Record Title	Label & Number
9/21/12	7	2	28. That Aeroplane Glide .... also recorded for Columbia 1197 & Edison Amberol 1143 flip side of Dolly Connolly's #4 hit "Waiting For The Robert E. Lee"	Victor 17113
10/12/12	6	2	29. Whistle It .... ADA JONES & PEERLESS QUARTET from the Broadway musical "The Wall Street Girl"	Columbia 1185
10/26/12	6	3	30. The Ragtime Jockey Man .... MAURICE BURKHART & PEERLESS QUARTET	Columbia 1188
11/30/12	3	6	31. Kentucky Days..	Columbia 1223
1/25/13	2(4)	8	32. The Ghost Of The Violin.............................	Columbia 1244
2/22/13	7	3	33. My Little Persian Rose...............................	Columbia 1247
5/17/13	6	4	34. At The Devil's Ball.................................... also recorded with Maurice Burkhart for Columbia 1282	Victor 17315
6/07/13	6	4	35. Goodbye, Boys	Columbia 1301
7/05/13	4	3	36. You're A Great Big Blue-Eyed Baby.............	Columbia 1300
10/25/13	10	1	37. San Francisco Bound................................. also recorded for Columbia 1333	Victor 17367
11/22/13	5	3	38. Good-By, Summer! So Long Fall! Hello, Winter Time! .... also recorded for Columbia 1403	Victor 17430
2/07/14	4	5	39. Oh You Million Dollar Doll........................ flip side of "On the Old Front Porch" (POS 9) by Henry Burr & Ada Jones	Columbia 1443
3/21/14	3	6	40. All Aboard For Dixie Land......................... ADA JONES & PEERLESS QUARTET from the Broadway musical "High Jinks"	Columbia 1481
4/11/14	2(3)	7	41. Don't Blame It All On Broadway .... also recorded for Columbia 1497	Victor 17539
5/23/14	3	8	42. This Is The Life	Columbia 1509
5/23/14	3	6	43. If I Had My Way......................................	Victor 17534
6/06/14	8	2	44. While They Were Dancing Around	Victor 17571
7/25/14	3	6	45. When The Angelus Is Ringing	Columbia 1533
8/01/14	4	5	46. When It's Moonlight On The Alamo	Victor 17591
1/30/15	3	5	47. He's A Rag Picker .... also recorded for Columbia 1628 & Edison Amberol 2513	Victor 17655
2/13/15	2(3)	8	48. Tip Top Tipperary Mary	Victor 17678
3/27/15	6	2	49. I'm Coming Back To Dixie And You............. previously recorded for Columbia 1547	Victor 17685
4/17/15	1(4)	13	50. **I Didn't Raise My Boy To Be A Soldier**.......	Columbia 1697
4/24/15	4	5	51. Virginia Lee...	Victor 17723
5/22/15	3	7	52. I'm On My Way To Dublin Bay/	
6/12/15	2(2)	6	53. Don't Take My Darling Boy Away	Victor 17736
7/24/15	1(4)	11	54. **My Bird Of Paradise** .... also recorded for Columbia 1760	Victor 17770
8/07/15	8	2	55. Cows May Come, Cows May Go, But The Bull Goes On Forever	Columbia 1696
8/28/15	4	4	56. Jane..	Victor 17813
1/08/16	3	4	57. I Think We've Got Another Washington (Wilson Is His Name) .... one of only two chart songs about a President ("F.D.R. Jones" the other)	Columbia 1864
2/12/16	7	2	58. When Old Bill Bailey Plays The Ukelele .... also recorded for Victor 17904	Columbia 1865
3/25/16	1(2)	7	59. **The Lights Of My Home Town**	Victor 17943
7/22/16	7	2	60. Arrah Go On, I'm Going Back To Oregon	Victor 18046
7/29/16	5	4	61. There's A Quaker Down In Quaker Town ...... #1 hit version of song by Campbell & Burr (Victor 18034)	Columbia 2005
9/09/16	9	1	62. The Honolulu Blues..................................	Victor 18068
9/30/16	10	1	63. Welcome, Honey, To Your Old Plantation Home .... with Fred Van Eps (banjo); also recorded for Columbia 2039	Victor 18120

DATE CHARTED	PEAK POS	WKS CHRT'D	ARTIST — Record Title	Label & Number
10/21/16	7	2	64. Dear Old Dreamy Honolulu Town................	Victor 18101
3/03/17	8	2	65. Keep Your Eye On The Girlie You Love........	Victor 18204
5/19/17	3	5	66. America, Here's My Boy............................	Victor 18256
5/19/17	7	2	67. From Here To Shanghai .... GENE GREENE & PEERLESS QUARTET	Victor 18242
6/23/17	6	2	68. When The Sun Goes Down In Dixie (And The Moon Begins To Rise)	Victor 18272
8/04/17	5	4	69. Hong Kong..	Victor 18295
9/08/17	5	4	70. For Your Country And My Country	Columbia 2273
10/13/17	1(2)	10	71. **Over There/** George M. Cohan's World War I classic	
10/20/17	4	4	72. I May Be Gone For A Long, Long Time........ from the Broadway musical "Hitchy-Koo"	Columbia 2306
10/27/17	7	2	73. Musical Sam From Alabam'	Victor 18350
11/03/17	5	3	74. Good-Bye Broadway, Hello France .... from "The Passing Show of 1917"	Columbia 2333
11/10/17	9	1	75. Somewhere In France Is Daddy...................	Columbia 2336
12/29/17+	3	4	76. We're Going Over...................................... also recorded for Victor 18383	Columbia 2399
1/05/18	1(2)	10	77. **I Don't Know Where I'm Going But I'm On My Way**... also recorded for Columbia 2329	Victor 18383
1/19/18	6	3	78. Say A Prayer For The Boys Out There	Victor 18411
2/23/18	10	1	79. Long Boy.. BYRON HARLAN & PEERLESS QUARTET also recorded for Victor 18413	Columbia 2409
4/06/18	8	1	80. Liberty Bell (It's Time To Ring Again).......... also recorded for Pathe 20313	Victor 18434
4/27/18	8	2	81. Au Revoir But Not Good-Bye, Soldier Boy......	Victor 18438
6/15/18	10	1	82. Any Place The Old Gang Goes (I'll Be There)..	Columbia 2514
6/22/18	4	5	83. Just Like Washington Crossed the Delaware, General Pershing Will Cross the Rhine/ also recorded with Arthur Fields for Columbia 2545	
6/22/18	5	2	84. I May Stay Away A Little Longer	Victor 18469
9/21/18	4	4	85. I'm Gonna Pin My Medal On The Girl I Left Behind.. from the "Ziegfeld Follies of 1918"	Victor 18486
10/12/18	8	2	86. The Last Long Mile	Columbia 2601
10/26/18	4	4	87. For Your Boy And My Boy .... also recorded for Columbia 2635 & Emerson 981	Victor 18494
12/07/18	9	1	88. The Yanks Are At It Again .... 82, 86 & 88: ARTHUR FIELDS & PEERLESS QUARTET	Columbia 2620
12/21/18+	2(2)	5	89. While You're Away (Pack Up Your Cares In A Bundle Of Joy)	Columbia 2642
3/01/19	9	1	90. Goodbye, France.......................................	Victor 18514
6/14/19	7	3	91. Smile And The World Smiles With You .... LEWIS JAMES & PEERLESS QUARTET	Victor 18545
12/27/19	7	1	92. Christmas Time At Pumpkin Center ...... [C-X] CAL STEWART, ADA JONES, & PEERLESS QUARTET	Columbia 2789
1/17/20	9	1	93. When I'm Gone You'll Soon Forget..............	Victor 18609
6/26/20	11	1	94. Who'll Take The Place Of Mary?.................	Columbia 2913
11/20/20	5	4	95. I'd Love To Fall Asleep And Wake Up In My Mammy's Arms .... also recorded for Okeh 4127	Victor 18692
11/27/20	11	1	96. Swanee	Victor 18688
2/12/21	7	3	97. Broadway Rose... also recorded for Columbia 3333	Victor 18710
4/02/21	8	2	98. I Used To Love You, But It's All Over Now.....	Victor 18725
4/16/21	4	5	99. My Mammy .... 96 & 99 from the Broadway musical "Sinbad"	Victor 18730
10/08/21	9	1	100. Down Yonder	Victor 18775

DATE CHARTED	PEAK POS	WKS CHRT'D	ARTIST — Record Title	Label & Number
12/10/21	5	3	101. Auld Lang Syne.................[X]	Victor 18792
1/14/22	3	5	102. My Sunny Tennessee.................	Victor 18812
			from the Broadway musical "Midnight Rounders of 1921"	
3/25/22	11	1	103. Weep No More, My Mammy................	Victor 18847
5/27/22	9	2	104. Georgia.................	Victor 18876
7/29/22	14	1	105. Pick Me Up And Lay Me Down In Dear Old Dixieland.................	Victor 18884
12/16/22	9	2	106. Way Down Yonder In New Orleans.............	Victor 18942
6/28/24	13	1	107. A Smile Will Go A Long, Long Way.............	Victor 19281
2/27/26	14	1	108. Let Me Linger Longer In Your Arms.............	Victor 19827
			Henry Burr: lead vocals on nearly all records after 1910	

PAUL PENDARVIS & HIS ORCHESTRA
Violinist and sweet-band leader

DATE CHARTED	PEAK POS	WKS CHRT'D	ARTIST — Record Title	Label & Number
12/15/34+	8	6	1. I've Got An Invitation To A Dance.............	Columbia 2974
9/21/35	15	2	2. Accent On Youth.................	Columbia 3082
10/26/35	5	9	3. Thanks A Million.................	Columbia 3091
			movie title song	

ART PEPPER
Alto saxophone star who first achieved prominence with Stan Kenton (1943-44, 47-52); died on 6/15/82 (56).

FRANK PETTY TRIO
Featuring pianist Mike DiNapoli

DATE CHARTED	PEAK POS	WKS CHRT'D	ARTIST — Record Title	Label & Number
5/06/50	17	5	1. Rain....................	MGM 10669
11/17/51	26	1	2. Down Yonder.................[I]	MGM 11057

NORMAN PETTY TRIO

DATE CHARTED	PEAK POS	WKS CHRT'D	ARTIST — Record Title	Label & Number
9/18/54	14	9	1. Mood Indigo.................[I]	"X" 0040
12/11/54	29	1	2. On The Alamo.................[I]	"X" 0071

PHILADELPHIA ORCHESTRA (LEOPOLD STOKOWSKI, Conductor)
London-born Leopold Stokowski was the dynamic, flamboyant director of the Philadelphia Orchestra from 1912-38, making the "Philadelphia sound" known worldwide. He remained an active and popular conductor until shortly before his death on 9/13/77 (95), but probably his greatest fame came through his collaboration on the classic 1940 film "Fantasia"

DATE CHARTED	PEAK POS	WKS CHRT'D	ARTIST — Record Title	Label & Number
3/02/18	9	1	1. A Midsummer Night's Dream - Scherzo......[I]	Victor 74560
1/04/19	9	2	2. Peer Gynt Suite No. 1 (Anitra's Dance).......[I]	Victor 64768
1/31/20	9	2	3. Invitation To The Waltz.................[I]	Victor 74598
4/16/21	8	2	4. Hungarian Rhapsody No. 2.................[I]	Victor 74647
9/17/21	9	2	5. The Young Prince And The Young Princess [I]	Victor 74691
			from "Scheherazade"	
9/30/22	13	1	6. Tannhauser Overture - Part 1.................[I]	Victor 74758
8/02/24	10	1	7. Concerto No. 2 In C Minor, Parts 1 & 2......[I]	Victor 8064
			Sergei Rachmaninoff, piano soloist	
5/02/25	9	2	8. The Fire Bird, Parts 1 & 2.................[I]	Victor 6492
12/31/27	19	1	9. Afternoon Of A Faun, Parts 1 & 2.............[I]	Victor 6696

PHILHARMONIC ORCHESTRA OF NEW YORK
Directed by Joseph Stransky

DATE CHARTED	PEAK POS	WKS CHRT'D	ARTIST — Record Title	Label & Number
12/21/18	9	2	1. Waltz Of The Flowers.................[I-X]	Victor 6070
			from "The Nutcracker Suite"	

FLIP PHILLIPS
Two-time Down Beat poll winner as top tenor saxophonist; with Woody Herman, 1944-46.

HOWARD PHILLIPS
1930s band vocalist with Johnny Green, Ray Noble, Leo Reisman, & Ben Selvin ("I Only Have Eyes for You"), among others.

DATE CHARTED	PEAK POS	WKS CHRT'D	ARTIST — Record Title	Label & Number
			JOSEPH PHILLIPS New York-born baritone	
7/10/15	9	1	1. Don't Take My Darling Boy Away .... HELEN CLARK & JOSEPH PHILLIPS	Edison Amb. 2622
			TEDDY PHILLIPS & HIS ORCHESTRA	
3/08/52	29	1	1. Wishin'	King 15156
			EDITH PIAF Legendary French chanteuse, born Edith Giovanna Gassion, as teenager sang for pennies in streets of Paris, eventually became idolized international music-hall and cabaret star. She died on 10/11/63 (47).	
10/21/50	23	3	● 1. La Vie En Rose... sung in English; accompanied by the Robert Chavigny Orchestra	Columbia 38938
			PICKENS SISTERS Jane, Patti, & Helen Pickens	
1/27/34	20	1	1. Did You Ever See A Dream Walking?........... from the film "Sitting Pretty"	Victor 24468
			PIED PIPERS Popular seven-member male vocal group with female leads Jo Stafford (1942-44), then June Hutton; became famous with Tommy Dorsey in early 40s, often accompanying Frank Sinatra ("I'll Never Smile Again", "There Are Such Things"); appeared in several movies. (Also see Johnny Mercer)	
4/08/44	8	1	1. Mairzy Doats .... [N]	Capitol 148
10/14/44	2(2)	14	2. The Trolley Song .... from the film "Meet Me in St. Louis"	Capitol 168
3/10/45	1(1)	18	● 3. **Dream**... originally heard as closing theme for composer Johnny Mercer's radio show	Capitol 185
9/22/45	16	1	4. Lily Belle	Capitol 207
12/29/45	18	1	5. Aren't You Glad You're You?/ from the film "The Bells of St. Mary's"	
1/12/46	14	2	6. In The Middle Of May ....,..........	Capitol 225
4/27/46	8	4	7. In The Moon Mist....................................	Capitol 243
3/01/47	8	3	8. Open The Door, Richard........................ [N]	Capitol 369
5/03/47	3	11	9. Mam'selle.. from the film "The Razor's Edge"	Capitol 396
12/27/47	28	1	10. Penny..	Capitol 478
3/13/48	25	1	11. Ok'l Baby Dok'l	Capitol 495
6/05/48	3	27	● 12. My Happiness.. nearly all above records accompanied by Paul Weston & His Orchestra	Capitol 15094
			WEBB PIERCE One of country music's leading stars of the 1950s, often featured on the Grand Ole Opry.	
11/20/54	22	1	● 1. More And More.. long-running #1 country hit	Decca 29252
			PINETOPPERS	
3/03/51	10	17	1. Mockin' Bird Hill .... with the Beaver Valley Sweethearts	Coral 64061
7/14/51	14	9	2. Lonely Little Robin .... with the Marlin Sisters & Ray Smith	Coral 60508
			EZIO PINZA Renowned Italian bass vocalist with New York Metropolitan Opera from 1926-48; his greatest fame came in 1949 starring in the all-time Broadway classic "South Pacific", also featured in several movies and the 1954 Broadway hit "Fanny"; died on 5/9/57 (64).	
9/10/49	7	9	● 1. Some Enchanted Evening .... accompanied by Salvadore Dell Isola's Orchestra from the Broadway musical "South Pacific"	Columbia 4559

DATE CHARTED	PEAK POS	WKS CHRT'D	ARTIST — Record Title	Label & Number
			PETER PIPER & HIS ORCHESTRA	
2/06/43	**16**	2	1. Rose Ann Of Charing Cross .... Hit 7033	
			British song	
			BEN POLLACK & HIS ORCHESTRA	
			Drummer and leader of one of the top bands of the pre-swing era, featuring such future stars as Benny Goodman, Glenn Miller, & Harry James. Ben appeared in the 1956 movie "The Benny Goodman Story". He died on 6/7/71 (67, suicide)	
7/28/28	**3**	7	1. Sweet Sue - Just You............................. Victor 21437	
			vocal: Franklyn Baur	
8/17/29	**20**	1	2. Yellow Dog Blues................................... Victor 21971	
			Glenn Miller (trombone) on above two	
8/02/30	**18**	1	3. Rollin' Down The River .... Perfect 15328	
5/09/31	**19**	1	4. I've Got Five Dollars.............................. Perfect 15431	
			from the Broadway musical "America's Sweetheart" Benny Goodman (clarinet) on above four vocals on above three: Ben Pollack	
1/27/34	**9**	4	5. Got The Jitters.................................... Columbia 2870	
			vocal: Nappy Lamare Jack Teagarden (trombone) on above two	
2/17/34	**10**	7	6. My Little Grass Shack In Kealakekua, Hawaii Columbia 2886	
			vocal: Doris Robbins-Nappy Lamare-Joe Harris	
3/24/34	**2(2)**	14	7. The Beat O' My Heart .... Columbia 2905	
6/23/34	**8**	4	8. Freckle Face, You're Beautiful ....∴. Columbia 2931	
6/23/34	**13**	2	9. Sleepy Head...................................... Columbia 2929	
			above two vocals: Joe Harris	
7/28/34	**20**	1	10. I've Got A Warm Spot In My Heart For You.... Columbia 2931	
			vocals on 7 & 10: Doris Robbins	
10/24/36	**19**	1	11. Thru' The Courtesy Of Love....................... Brunswick 7747	
			vocal: Ben Pollack; with Harry James (trumpet), Glenn Miller (trombone), Irving Fazola (clarinet), & Freddy Slack (piano)	
			COLE PORTER	
			Among the greatest of all popular composers, with a long string of hit Broadway musicals and a longer list of classic songs ("Night and Day", "Begin the Beguine", "I've Got You Under My Skin", "What Is This Thing Called Love?"); died on 10/15/64 (72).	
1/12/35	**10**	4	1. You're The Top .... Victor 24766	
			self-accompanied on piano from his Broadway musical "Anything Goes"	
			STEVE PORTER	
			Began as a vaudeville comedian in 1890s; sang baritone in Columbia Male Quartet and American Quartet (1909-19); died on 1/13/46 (81).	
1/08/98	**1(4)**	7	1. **On The Banks Of The Wabash** .... Berliner 1784	
			also recorded for Columbia 4548	
8/06/98	**2(3)**	4	2. She Was Bred In Old Kentucky................... Columbia 4570	
8/20/98	**1(4)**	6	3. **She's More To Be Pitied Than Censured** .... Columbia 4576	
9/03/98	**3**	2	4. Break The News To Mother....................... Columbia 4586	
9/02/99	**1(2)**	10	5. **A Picture No Artist Can Paint** .... Columbia 4599	
9/30/99	**4**	2	6. My Creole Sue .... Columbia 4597	
10/28/99	**3**	3	7. Those Cruel Words, Good-Bye .... Columbia 4605	
5/26/00	**1(6)**	11	8. **A Bird In A Gilded Cage**........................... Columbia 4608	
7/28/00	**3**	3	9. The Little Brown Jug .... Columbia 4617	
5/26/06	**6**	1	10. Flanagan's Night Off............................. [C] Edison 9244	
			LEN SPENCER & STEVE PORTER	
1/26/07	**9**	1	11. An Evening At Mrs. Clancy's Boarding House .... [C] Columbia 3526	
			BILLY MURRAY & STEVE PORTER also on Columbia cylinder 33043	
4/27/07	**8**	1	12. Flanagan's Troubles In A Restaraunt .... [C] Edison 9495	
			also recorded for Columbia 3567	
2/02/10	**9**	2	13. Flanagan And His Motor Car................... [C] Victor 16436	
			also recorded for Edison 10295	

DATE CHARTED	PEAK POS	WKS CHRT'D	ARTIST — Record Title	Label & Number
			BUD POWELL	
			Great jazz pianist of the postwar "bop" era, played in the 1940s with Cootie Williams and Dizzy Gillespie; died on 8/1/66 (41). (also see Sarah Vaughan)	
			DICK POWELL	
			Star of many 1930s Hollywood musicals (most importantly "42nd Street"), he went on to featured roles in crime and detective movies the next two decades, and also hosted a TV series; died on 1/3/63 (58).	
6/24/33	18	1	1. The Gold Digger's Song (We're In The Money). from the film "Gold Diggers of 1933"	Perfect 12919
5/19/34	19	1	2. Fair And Warmer................................... flip side of Ted Fio Rito's #1 hit "I'll String Along With You"	Brunswick 6859
11/10/34	14	2	3. Happiness Ahead .... above two from the film "Happiness Ahead"	Brunswick 6979
2/16/35	19	1	4. Mr. And Mrs. Is The Name .... from the film "Flirtation Walk"	Brunswick 7328
4/27/35	20	1	5. I'm Goin' Shoppin' With You...................... with Jimmie Grier's Orchestra from the film "Gold Diggers of 1935"	Brunswick 7407
10/24/36	18	1	6. My Kingdom For A Kiss .... with Victor Young's Orchestra from the film "Hearts Divided"	Decca 900
8/21/37	14	3	7. I Know Now .... with Lou Forbes' Orchestra from the film "The Singing Marine"	Decca 1310
			ELEANOR POWELL	
			Ranks alongside Ann Miller as the best tap-dancer in movie musical history, also singer, in such film classics as "Born to Dance" and "Broadway Melody of 1940"; she died on 2/11/82 (69).	
11/09/35	10	6	1. You Are My Lucky Star .... Eleanor Powell (vocal) with Tommy Dorsey & His Orchestra from the film "Broadway Melody of 1936"	Victor 25158
			JANE POWELL	
			Star of many 1950s movie musicals and romances. (see Fred Astaire)	
			MEL POWELL	
			Five-time Down Beat poll winner as top pianist; with Benny Goodman (1941, 47-48), Raymond Scott (1942), Glenn Miller AAF band (1943-45).	
			TEDDY POWELL & HIS ORCHESTRA	
			Born Alfred Paolella, sweet-band leader who formerly played guitar & banjo for Abe Lyman (1926-34), also a successful songwriter ("Boots and Saddle").	
4/19/41	18	1	1. The Wise Old Owl	Bluebird 11089
6/21/41	11	1	2. The Things I Love.................................	Bluebird 11113
11/08/41	23	1	3. I Went Out Of My Way .... above three vocals: Ruth Gaylor	Bluebird 11152
2/14/42	21	1	4. Goodbye, Mama (I'm Off To Yokohama)........ vocal: Dick Judge & Peggy Mann	Bluebird 11412
7/18/42	22	1	5. Somebody's Thinking Of You Tonight........... vocal: Peggy Mann; with Irving Fazola (clarinet)	Bluebird 11520
			PEREZ PRADO & HIS ORCHESTRA	
			Cuban-born pianist/organist and mambo band leader; he scored a gigantic #1 hit in 1955 with "Cherry Pink and Apple Blossom White".	
8/08/53	29	1	1. Anna.. [I] movie title theme	RCA Victor 5367
9/25/54	26	1	2. Skokiaan... [I] South African song	RCA Victor 5839
			PREMIER QUARTET - see AMERICAN QUARTET	
			GEORGIE PRICE	
			Popular vaudeville singer-comedian who founded the American Guild of Variety Artists; died on 5/10/64 (64).	
7/21/23	9	1	1. Morning Will Come.................................	Victor 19047

DATE CHARTED	PEAK POS	WKS CHRT'D	ARTIST — Record Title	Label & Number
8/25/23	12	1	2. Barney Google .... [C]	Victor 19066
6/07/24	7	2	3. California, Here I Come.............................	Victor 19261
			from the Broadway musical "Big Boy"	
9/05/25	10	1	4. Isn't She The Sweetest Thing?	Victor 19654

LOUIS PRIMA & HIS ORCHESTRA
Durable jazz trumpeter-singer-bandleader; co-writer of the classic songs "Sing, Sing, Sing" and "A Sunday Kind of Love", continued hitting the charts through 1960, including duets with wife Keely Smith; died on 8/24/78 (67).

DATE CHARTED	PEAK POS	WKS CHRT'D	ARTIST — Record Title	Label & Number
6/01/35	13	8	1. I'm Living In A Great Big Way....................	Brunswick 7419
7/06/35	14	2	2. Chasing Shadows/	
7/13/35	8	5	3. The Lady In Red.................................	Brunswick 7448
			from the film "In Caliente"	
7/20/35	4	6	4. In A Little Gypsy Tea Room......................	Brunswick 7479
			above four vocals: Louis Prima	
1/30/37	20	1	5. The Goose Hangs High........................... [I]	Vocalion 3388
11/11/44	14	6	6. Angelina	Hit 7106
			vocal by Louis Prima	
5/26/45	6	6	7. Bell-Bottom Trousers	Majestic 7134
			based on a traditional sea chantey	
			vocal: Lily Ann Carol	
10/11/47	8	8	8. Civilization (Bongo, Bongo, Bongo).......... [N]	RCA Victor 2400
			group vocal; from the Broadway musical "Angel In the Wings"	
11/11/50	12	7	9. Oh, Babe!	Robin Hood 101
			vocal: Keely Smith	

HARRY PRIME
Postwar band singer with Tommy Dorsey ("Until") and Ralph flanagan ("Rag Mop").

PRINCE'S ORCHESTRA
Pianist & celesta player Charles Adams Prince, said to be a distant relative of President John Adams, was musical director of Columbia Records from the turn of the century to the early 20s. During that period his band accompanied virtually every singer recording for Columbia. He died on 10/10/37 (68). (Also see Columbia Orchestra, Marion Harris, Al Jolson)

DATE CHARTED	PEAK POS	WKS CHRT'D	ARTIST — Record Title	Label & Number
4/01/05	3	2	1. "Coax Me" Medley .... [I]	Columbia 3095
			also on Columbia cylinder 32650	
3/31/06	5	1	2. Wait Till The Sun Shines, Nellie .... [I]	Columbia 32883
3/09/07	4	2	3. Selections From "The Red Mill" .... [I]	Columbia 3552
4/27/07	9	1	4. Manhattan Beach March .... [I]	Columbia 85102
3/28/08	6	1	5. Merry Widow Waltz............................. [I]	Columbia 30106
			from the Broadway musical "The Merry Widow"	
7/25/08	9	1	6. Summertime Medley............................. [I]	Columbia 3790
3/20/09	5	2	7. Washington Post March .... [I]	Indestructable 997
			most early records listed as "Prince's Military Band"	
7/02/10	10	1	8. Cubanola Glide................................. [I]	Columbia 811
8/27/10	7	2	9. Overture "1812" .... [I]	Columbia 5174
12/31/10+	5	4	10. The Birth Of Passion .... [I]	Columbia 925
			from the Broadway musical "Madame Sherry"	
1/07/11	3	5	11. Ciribiribin Waltz............................. [I]	Columbia 5235
1/21/11	9	1	12. Peer Gynt Suite No. 1........................ [I]	Columbia 5227
8/26/11	3	4	13. Selections From "The Pink Lady"............. [I]	Columbia 5307
4/13/12	3	5	14. Alexander's Ragtime Band .... [I]	Columbia 1126
2/15/13	7	2	15. Fireflies .... [I]	Columbia 1239
7/19/13	7	3	16. The Angelus .... [I]	Columbia 5422
			from the Broadway musical "Sweethearts"	
9/20/13	10	1	17. Turkey-Trot Dance Medley, Part II .... [I]	Columbia 5459
3/28/14	8	1	18. That International Rag .... [I]	Columbia 5532
7/11/14	6	3	19. Fascination .... [I]	Columbia 5555
8/01/14	6	2	20. Kitty McKay .... [I]	Columbia 5560
8/08/14	5	5	21. Puppchen .... [I]	Columbia 5531
8/22/14	3	5	22. Love's Melody .... [I]	Columbia 5566

DATE CHARTED	PEAK POS	WKS CHRT'D	ARTIST — Record Title	Label & Number
9/26/14	6	4	23. By The Beautiful Sea/ [I]	
10/03/14	8	2	24. That's A-Plenty .... [I]	Columbia 5582
10/17/14	1(3)	12	25. **Ballin' The Jack** .... [I]	Columbia 5595
10/31/14	7	2	26. The Old Homestead .... [I]	Columbia 5600
11/07/14	4	8	27. Memphis Blues .... [I]	Columbia 5591
			the first hit recording of a "blues" song	
1/02/15	2(3)	10	28. It's A Long, Long Way To Tipperary	Columbia 1620
			with men's chorus; featured in the Broadway musicals "Chin-Chin" & "Dancing Around"	
2/27/15	8	1	29. Underneath The Japanese Moon............... [I]	Columbia 5623
			from Broadway's "Ziegfeld Follies of 1914"	
3/06/15	9	1	30. Syncopated Walk................................. [I]	Columbia 5632
			from the Broadway musical "Watch Your Step"	
3/20/15	8	2	31. Chin-Chin... [I]	Columbia 5634
			Broadway musical title song	
5/15/15	9	1	32. I Want To Go To Tokio .... [I]	Columbia 5659
5/22/15	6	2	33. I Want To Linger .... [I]	Columbia 5662
6/05/15	8	2	34. Chinatown, My Chinatown...................... [I]	Columbia 5674
			from the Broadway musical "Up and Down Broadway"	
7/17/15	5	2	35. Shadowland Fox-Trot .... [I]	Columbia 5680
8/28/15	5	4	36. On, Wisconsin! .... [I]	Columbia 1762
1/01/16	5	3	37. Back Home In Tennessee .... [I]	Columbia 5729
4/08/16	1(5)	12	38. **Hello, Hawaii, How Are You?** .... [I]	Columbia 5780
5/13/16	4	4	39. St. Louis Blues .... [I]	Columbia 5772
6/03/16	6	3	40. Underneath The Stars .... [I]	Columbia 5780
6/03/16	10	1	41. The Hesitating Blues .... [I]	Columbia 5772
6/24/16	5	2	42. So Long, Letty .... [I]	Columbia 5796
			Broadway musical title song	
7/22/16	1(2)	8	43. **The Star-Spangled Banner**.................... [I]	Columbia 1991
9/02/16	5	3	44. Babes In The Wood .... [I]	Columbia 5816
			from the Broadway musical "Very Good, Eddie"	
9/23/16	4	5	45. Missouri Waltz .... [I]	Columbia 5838
11/04/16	4	4	46. Joe Turner Blues................................. [I]	Columbia 5854
3/24/17	3	6	47. Poor Butterfly .... [I]	Columbia 5930
			from the Broadway musical "The Big Show"	
4/28/17	6	2	48. Marche Slave, Parts 1 & 2 .... [I]	Columbia 5933
6/02/17	5	3	49. For Me And My Gal .... [I]	Columbia 5957
6/30/17	5	2	50. American Republic March .... [I]	Columbia 2223
7/21/17	9	1	51. American Patrol .... [I]	Columbia 2237
7/28/17	3	5	52. The Man Behind The Hammer And The Plow .... [I]	Columbia 5973
8/25/17	2(1)	8	53. Till The Clouds Roll By.......................... [I]	Columbia 2266
			from the Broadway musical "Oh, Boy!"	
9/15/17	4	4	54. The Old Grey Mare............................... [I]	Columbia 2285
			derived from the 1858 song "Down in Alabam'", which under new title "Old Abe Lincoln" was used in the 1860 presidential campaign	
9/15/17	7	2	55. You're A Grand Old Flag .... [I]	Columbia 5978
			from the Broadway musical "George Washington, Jr."	
11/17/17	5	4	56. Beale Street Blues .... [I]	Columbia 2327
11/24/17	9	1	57. For The Freedom Of The World .... [I]	Columbia 2347
1/05/18	6	2	58. Over There .... [I]	Columbia 2387
3/09/18	5	3	59. For You A Rose .... [I]	Columbia 2424
3/23/18	4	4	60. Wait Till The Cows Come Home............... [I]	Columbia 2448
			from the Broadway musical "Jack O' Lantern"	
4/06/18	5	3	61. Long Boy .... [I]	Columbia 2424
4/13/18	4	5	62. Indianola .... [I]	Columbia 6018
4/13/18	8	1	63. Hello, My Dearie .... [I]	Columbia 5986
6/01/18	6	2	64. Just A Baby's Prayer At Twilight .... [I]	Columbia 6029

DATE CHARTED	PEAK POS	WKS CHRT'D	ARTIST — Record Title	Label & Number
7/20/18	7	2	65. Just Like Washington Crossed The Delaware, General Pershing Will Cross The Rhine [I]	Columbia 6049
10/26/18	6	3	66. I'm Always Chasing Rainbows.................. [I] from the Broadway musical "Oh, Look!"	Columbia 6064
11/23/18	4	4	67. Everything Is Peaches Down In Georgia ..... [I]	Columbia 6073
12/21/18	6	2	68. Cathedral Chimes .... [I-X]	Columbia 2644
1/11/19	2(1)	7	69. Beautiful Ohio.................................. [I]	Columbia 6081
5/03/19	10	1	70. Till We Meet Again.............................. [I]	Columbia 6098
11/08/19	3	6	71. Yearning .... [I]	Columbia 2773
3/27/20	5	4	72. Dardanella (An Echo Of The Past)............ [I]	Columbia 2851
5/29/20	10	1	73. Afghanistan .... [I]	Columbia 2883
10/09/20	7	2	74. Manyana .... [I]	Columbia 2963
1/29/21	7	2	75. Beautiful Annabelle Lee....................... [I]	Columbia 6175
10/15/21	8	2	76. Deep In Your Eyes .... [I] from the Broadway musical "The Half Moon"	Columbia 6187
12/31/21+	8	2	77. Mississippi Cradle................................ [I]	Columbia 6191
3/11/22	8	2	78. The Song Of Love .... [I] from the Broadway musical "Blossom Time"	Columbia 3504
4/29/22	12	1	79. When Shall We Meet Again? .... [I]	Columbia 6208
5/06/22	5	3	80. Selections From "Blossom Time" .... [I]	Columbia 6209
6/24/22	9	1	81. Swanee River Moon............................. [I]	Columbia 6213
1/20/23	9	1	82. Nellie Kelly, I Love You .... [I] from the Broadway musical "Little Nellie Kelly"	Columbia 3698

TOMMY PRISCO

DATE CHARTED	PEAK POS	WKS CHRT'D	ARTIST — Record Title	Label & Number
7/17/54	30	1	1. Friends And Neighbors	Mercury 70396

ARTHUR PRYOR'S BAND

First trombonist of John Philip Sousa's famous band, he actually served as conductor on the vast majority of Sousa recordings. Pryor's own band became a major concert attraction in its own right. He died on 6/18/42 (71).

DATE CHARTED	PEAK POS	WKS CHRT'D	ARTIST — Record Title	Label & Number
1/30/04	3	3	1. Bedelia .... [I] from the Broadway musical "The Jersey Lily"	Victor 2558
7/30/04	4	1	2. The St. Louis Rag .... [I]	Victor 2783
12/03/04	3	4	3. Meet Me In St. Louis Medley .... [I]	Victor 2960
1/14/05	5	1	4. A Coon Band Contest .... [I]	Victor 4069
5/06/05	3	2	5. Hearts And Flowers .... [I]	Victor 31371
7/15/05	5	1	6. Tammany... [I] from the Broadway musical "Fantana"	Victor 31397
8/26/05	7	1	7. The Chirpers.................................... [I] with Joe Belmont (bird whistling)	Victor 4370
8/26/05	9	1	8. In The Shade Of The Old Apple Tree .... [I]	Victor 4381
11/25/05	9	1	9. Dance Of The Hours .... [I]	Victor 31443
2/24/06	6	1	10. Silver Heels .... [I]	Victor 4552
6/30/06	9	1	11. American Fantasie.............................. [I]	Victor 31504
8/25/06	3	4	12. You're A Grand Old Flag .... [I] from the Broadway musical "George Washington, Jr."	Victor 31539
12/01/06	2(3)	5	13. On The Rocky Road To Dublin .... [I]	Victor 4842
2/15/08	4	5	14. International March .... [I]	Victor 5324
3/28/08	9	1	15. King Of Rags.................................... [I]	Victor 5301
6/27/08	9	1	16. Happy Days March .... [I]	Victor 5411
8/29/08	4	2	17. Red Wing Medley .... [I]	Victor 5490
1/30/09	9	1	18. National Emblem March .... [I]	Victor 5576
7/24/09	4	2	19. 1812 Overture................................... [I]	Victor 31739
6/25/10	5	5	20. Shine On, Harvest Moon .... [I] from Broadway's "Ziegfeld Follies of 1908"	Victor 16475
7/16/10	8	2	21. Popular Medley No. 2............................ [I] including "I've Got Rings On My Fingers" & "Good Evening Caroline"	Victor 16480
7/30/10	10	1	22. Dill Pickles Rag .... [I]	Victor 16482

DATE CHARTED	PEAK POS	WKS CHRT'D	ARTIST — Record Title	Label & Number
9/10/10	6	2	23. Popular Medley No. 4.............................. [I] including "Put On Your Old Gray Bonnet" & "By the Light of the Silv'ry Moon"	Victor 16494
12/30/11	9	1	24. Nut Cracker Ballet-Characteristic Dance.... [I]	Victor 16974
6/15/12	6	3	25. The Gaby Glide .... [I] from the Broadway musical "Vera Violetta"	Victor 17063
8/31/12	6	2	26. Everybody's Doin' It Two-Step Medley .... [I]	Victor 17091
7/15/16	9	1	27. National Emblem March.......................... [I] new version of 1909 hit	Victor 17957

RILEY PUCKETT
Blind country guitarist and singer, key member of Gid Tanner & His Skillet Lickers. Died on 7/13/46.

1/01/27	16	1	1. My Carolina Home	Columbia 15095

ROBERTA QUINLAN
Hosted her own NBC TV musical series from 1949-51.

6/03/50	22	2	1. Buffalo Billy .... with Jan August & Jerry Murad's Harmonicats	Mercury 5420
11/18/50	30	1	2. Molasses, Molasses .... with Jan August (pianola), and orchestra & chorus directed by Marty Manning variation on melody of "A-Tisket, A-Tasket"	Mercury 5504

DAN QUINN
One of the three top vocal recording stars of the 1890s (along with George J. Gaskin & Len Spencer). Dan recorded some 2,500 titles in his 20-year career. He died on 11/7/38 (79).

12/31/92	1(4)	4	1. **Daddy Wouldn't Buy Me A Bow-Wow** ..... [N]	New Jersey
1/28/93	1(5)	5	2. **The Bowery** .... from Broadway musical "A Trip to Chinatown"	New Jersey
9/16/93	1(9)	9	3. **Daisy Bell**.. also recorded for Chicago 2429; song better known as "A Bicycle Built for Two"	New Jersey
8/18/94	1(3)	3	4. **Lindley, Does You Love Me?**	Columbia
10/06/94	1(4)	4	5. **My Pearl Is A Bowery Girl** .... also recorded for Ohio	Columbia
11/24/94	1(6)	6	6. **And Her Golden Hair Was Hanging Down Her Back**... also recorded for New Jersey & Chicago; later issued on Columbia 5128	Columbia
2/09/95	1(9)	9	7. **The Sidewalks Of New York**...................... also recorded for New Jersey; later issued on Columbia 5079	Columbia
8/24/95	1(10)	10	8. **The Band Played On** .... also recorded for New Jersey & Ohio 2400 later for Berliner 961	Columbia 2045
11/02/95	1(5)	5	9. **The Little Lost Child** .... also recorded for New Jersey & Chicago 2437; later on Columbia 5006	Columbia 2048
11/07/96	1(5)	5	10. **In The Baggage Coach Ahead**	US Phono. Co.
12/12/96	1(7)	9	11. **A Hot Time In The Old Town**	Edison 1038
3/27/97	1(5)	9	12. **My Mother Was A Lady**	Columbia 5093
5/08/97	2(2)	4	13. You're Not The Only Pebble On The Beach .... also recorded for Chicago	Columbia 5122
9/04/97	1(4)	5	14. **There's A Little Star Shining For You**.......	Edison 1098
10/08/98	1(4)	6	15. **She Was Happy Till She Met You**	Columbia 5354
10/29/98	2(2)	4	16. Soldiers In The Park................................. later recorded for Edison 6942 from the Broadway musical "A Runaway Girl"	Columbia 5347
11/05/98	1(4)	7	17. **At A Georgia Camp Meeting** .... later recorded for Edison 6903	Columbia 5353
11/19/98	2(2)	2	18. Poor O'Hoolihan .... from the Broadway musical "Yankee Doodle Dandy"	Columbia 5350

DATE CHARTED	PEAK POS	WKS CHRT'D	ARTIST — Record Title	Label & Number
10/21/99	**1(7)**	10	19. **Curse Of The Dreamer**	Columbia 5822
2/17/00	**4**	2	20. Nothing's Too Good For The Irish	Edison 7359
9/01/00	**3**	3	21. San Francisco Sadie	Gram-o-Phone 11
12/15/00	**2(3)**	5	22. When Reuben Comes To Town	Columbia 31481
			later recorded for Edison 7708; from the Broadway musical "Rogers Brothers in Central Park"	
7/20/01	**2(2)**	6	23. You Can't Keep A Good Man Down	Victor 746
10/26/01	**3**	3	24. Ain't Dat A Shame? .... [C]	Victor 923
			also on Victor 3525	
10/26/01	**4**	2	25. When Mister Shakespeare Comes To Town [C]	Edison 7906
			also recorded for Victor 922 & 3524	
11/09/01	**1(3)**	8	26. **Good Evening, Carrie**.............................	Victor 920
			also recorded for Edison 7893	
11/09/01	**4**	2	27. Tell Us, Pretty Ladies	Edison 7905
			from the Broadway musical "Fiddle Dee Dee"	
6/21/02	**3**	4	28. Oh! Didn't He Ramble! .... [C]	Victor 1327
9/13/02	**2(2)**	8	29. Bill Bailey, Won't You Please Come Home . [C]	Victor 1411
11/08/02	**2(2)**	5	30. Mister Dooley.............................	Victor 1466
			from the Broadway musical "A Chinese Honeymoon"	
6/20/03	**3**	4	31. There's A Lot Of Things You Never Learn At School.............................	Columbia 1360
			later recorded for Victor 2409 from the Broadway musical "The Wizard of Oz"	
7/18/03	**3**	3	32. Hiawatha..............................	Columbia 1406
10/24/03	**3**	3	33. The Beer That Made Milwaukee Famous ... [C]	Victor 2410
			from the Broadway musical "Blue Beard"	
2/23/07	**10**	1	34. Is Marriage A Failure? .... [C]	Victor 4914
			HELEN TRIX & DAN QUINN	

QUINTET OF THE HOT CLUB OF FRANCE
Internationally-renowned combo featuring two enduring jazz greats: Belgian gypsy guitarist Django Reinhardt (died on 5/16/53 at age 43) and French violinist Stephane Grappelli (still an active jazzman in the 1980s).

DATE CHARTED	PEAK POS	WKS CHRT'D	ARTIST — Record Title	Label & Number
3/27/37	**20**	1	1. After You've Gone .... [I]	Victor 25511

R

SERGEI RACHMANINOFF
Great Russian-born composer, pianist and conductor whose concertos remain among the most-performed musical creations in the world; died on 3/28/43 (69).

DATE CHARTED	PEAK POS	WKS CHRT'D	ARTIST — Record Title	Label & Number
8/28/20	**10**	1	1. Prelude In G Minor............................. [I]	Victor 74628
8/02/24	**10**	1	2. Concert No. 2 In C Minor, Parts 1 & 2 .... [I]	Victor 8064
			with the Philadelphia Orchestra conducted by Leopold Stokowski	

HARRY RADERMAN'S JAZZ ORCHESTRA
Trombonist-bandleader who also played with Ted Lewis.

2/28/20	**9**	1	1. Dardanella .... [I]	Edison 50637
7/30/21	**15**	1	2. Cherie .... [I]	Edison 50783

RADIOLITES
Some records directed by Ben Selvin

12/24/27	**18**	1	1. Dancing Tambourine .... [I]	Columbia 1114
8/08/31	**15**	2	2. When The Moon Comes Over The Mountain ...	Columbia 2485
			Kate Smith's theme song	

LORRY RAINE
Previously sang with Mark Warnow's Orchestra.

9/23/50	**24**	4	1. Strangers	London 30178
			with Cliff Parman's Orchestra	
6/13/53	**22**	4	2. A-Wooin' We Will Go/	
7/11/53	**21**	4	3. There's Nothin' Left To Do (But Cry)	Kem 2723
			above two with Nelson Riddle's Orchestra	

DATE CHARTED	PEAK POS	WKS CHRT'D	ARTIST — Record Title	Label & Number
12/26/53	**24**	3	4. I'm In Love With A Guy	Kem 2729
11/06/54	**22**	4	5. What Would I Do .... with Russ Garcia's Orchestra	Dot 15224

MA RAINEY
Gertrude Malissa Pridgett (married to vaudevillian William "Pa" Rainey), pioneer blues singer who was a model for Bessie Smith, and whose life inspired the 1985 Broadway musical "Ma Rainey's Black Bottom"; died on 12/22/39 (53).

1/31/25	**14**	1	1. See See Rider Blues .... with Louis Armstrong (cornet), Fletcher Henderson (piano)	Paramount 12252

GRAY RAINS & HIS ORCHESTRA

7/22/44	**28**	1	1. Swinging On A Star .... from the film "Going My Way"	Hit 7086

RAMONA
Ramona Myers, singer-pianist with Paul Whiteman (1932-37)

4/15/33	**13**	2	1. What Have We Got To Lose? .... ROY BARGY & RAMONA	Victor 24268
9/28/35	**11**	4	2. Every Now And Then..............................	Victor 25138

SLATZ RANDALL & HIS ORCHESTRA
Midwestern pianist-singer

5/31/30	**16**	1	1. Skirts	Brunswick 4779

WAYNE RANEY
Country singer and harmonica player.

10/01/49	**22**	4	1. Why Don't You Haul Off And Love Me?	King 791

RAVENS
Rhythm & Blues quartet featuring bass Jimmy Ricks. (also see Benny Goodman)

12/13/47	**24**	1	1. Write Me A Letter	National 9038

JOHNNIE RAY
Partially deaf from age twelve, Johnnie's passionate, soulful vocal style made him a 1950s sensation; 20 years later he made a popular comeback in England.

11/24/51	**1(11)**	27	● 1. **Cry/** sold over two million copies; Johnnie's trademark song	
11/24/51+	**2(2)**	22	2. The Little White Cloud That Cried	Okeh 6840
1/26/52	**6**	18	● 3. Please, Mr. Sun/	
1/26/52	**8**	15	4. Here Am I - Broken Hearted......................	Columbia 39636
4/12/52	**13**	8	5. What's The Use?................................... above five with Four Lads above three with Jimmy Carroll's Orchestra	Columbia 39698
5/24/52	**4**	20	6. Walkin' My Baby Back Home	Columbia 39750
7/26/52	**12**	8	7. All Of Me/	
8/09/52	**20**	2	8. A Sinner Am I...................................... with Four Lads & Jimmy Carroll's Orchestra	Columbia 39788
9/27/52	**25**	1	9. Love Me (Baby Can't You Love Me)..............	Columbia 39837
12/13/52	**20**	2	10. A Full-Time Job/	
12/27/52	**23**	1	11. Ma Says, Pa Says.................................. South African song	Columbia 39898
1/17/53	**24**	1	12. I'm Gonna Walk and Talk With My Lord	Columbia 39908
4/11/53	**8**	6	13. Somebody Stole My Gal	Columbia 39961
6/13/53	**17**	2	14. Candy Lips .... 10, 11 & 14: DORIS DAY & JOHNNIE RAY	Columbia 40001
8/15/53	**29**	1	15. With These Hands................................ 12 & 15 with the Four Lads & the Buddy Cole Quartet	Columbia 40026
8/29/53	**27**	1	16. All I Do Is Dream Of You	Columbia 40046
10/31/53	**29**	1	17. Please Don't Talk About Me When I'm Gone .. 6-7, 13, 16 & 17 with the Buddy Cole Quartet	Columbia 40090
2/20/54	**25**	1	18. You'd Be Surprised	Columbia 40154
4/17/54	**19**	1	19. Such A Night	Columbia 40200

DATE CHARTED	PEAK POS	WKS CHRT'D	ARTIST — Record Title	Label & Number
5/29/54	27	3	20. Hey There/	
6/12/54	14	7	21. Hernando's Hideaway	Columbia 40224
			above two from the Broadway musical "The Pajama Game" *both accompanied by Joe Reisman's Orchestra*	
9/04/54	26	3	22. To Ev'ry Girl - To Ev'ry Boy (The Meaning Of Love)..	Columbia 40252

MARTHA RAYE
Longtime movie & TV comedienne (real name Martha Reed), also a talented singer.

9/09/39	18	2	1. Melancholy Mood......................................	Brunswick 8394
			with Dave Rose (Martha's then-husband) & His Orchestra	

DON REDMAN & HIS ORCHESTRA
Arranger and saxophonist for Fletcher Henderson & McKinney's Cotton Pickers; in the 40s he also did arrangements for Count Basie, Harry James, & others. Don died on 11/30/64 (64).

12/12/31	15	2	1. Chant Of The Weed .... [I]	Brunswick 6211
			Don's theme song	
1/30/32	7	7	2. I Heard	Brunswick 6233
			vocal: Don Redman *Henry (Red) Allen (trumpet) on above two*	
11/19/32	17	2	3. Underneath The Harlem Moon....................	Brunswick 6401
6/03/33	19	1	4. Sophisticated Lady .... [I]	Brunswick 6560
8/19/33	4	5	5. Lazy Bones......................................	Brunswick 6622
			vocals on 3 & 5: Harlan Lattimore	
7/17/37	14	2	6. Exactly Like You	Variety 580
			from the Broadway musical "International Revue"	
1/14/39	15	1	7. Margie	Bluebird 10061
			above two: group vocals	

WILLIAM REDMOND

10/11/02	3	5	1. In The Good Old Summer Time....................	Edison 8118
			from the Broadway musical "The Defender"	

JAMES REED
Pseudonym for Reed Miller

JIM REEVES
Important country-western star who was reaching his peak of popularity when a private plane crash took his life on 7/31/64 (39).

4/25/53	23	2	● 1. Mexican Joe	Abbott 116
			JIM REEVES & HIS CIRCLE O RANCH BOYS *one of the year's biggest country hits*	
1/02/54	26	1	2. Bimbo..	Abbott 148

GAYLA REEVEY
Eleven years old

12/12/53	24	2	1. I Want A Hippopotamus For Christmas.. [N-X]	Columbia 40106
			orchestra directed by Norman Leyden	

JOAN REGAN

8/29/53	23	1	1. Till They've All Gone Home	London 1353
			orchestra directed by Roland Shaw	

REGENT CLUB ORCHESTRA
Bob Haring directed many of this band's records.

5/03/30	5	5	1. It Happened In Monterey	Brunswick 4756
			from the film "The King of Jazz"	
6/07/30	2(1)	6	2. Dancing With Tears In My Eyes	Brunswick 4795

REGIMENTAL BAND OF H.M. GRENADIER GUARDS

12/30/16	8	1	1. 1812 Overture, Parts 1 & 2 .... [I]	Columbia 5874

JOE REICHMAN & HIS ORCHESTRA
Pianist-bandleader; died on 4/14/70 (72).

6/28/41	24	1	1. Afraid To Say Hello (Since You Said Goodbye)	Victor 27357
			vocal: Marion Shaw	

DATE CHARTED	PEAK POS	WKS CHRT'D	ARTIST — Record Title	Label & Number
			DOTTIE REID Sang with Benny Goodman ("It's Only A Paper Moon")	
3/26/49	**24**	5	1. Hurry! Hurry! Hurry!	Peak 800
5/07/49	**23**	3	2. Don't Be Afraid To Dream	Peak 809
			LEO REISMAN & HIS ORCHESTRA Durable violinist-bandleader who featured at piano future leaders Eddy Duchin & Johnny Green; he accompanied Fred Astaire on the blockbuster hits "Night and Day" and "Cheek to Cheek". Leo died on 12/18/61 (64). (Also see Fred Astaire)	
4/30/21	**4**	4	1. Bright Eyes .... [I]	Columbia 3366
3/07/25	**6**	3	2. Indian Love Call .... [I] from the Broadway musical "Rose Marie"	Columbia 242
5/22/26	**7**	3	3. Here In My Arms .... [I] from the Broadway musical "Dearest Enemy"	Columbia 573
9/25/26	**11**	1	4. Bye Bye Blackbird .... [I]	Columbia 653
8/27/27	**14**	2	5. Collette..	Columbia 973
8/04/28	**7**	5	6. Ah! Sweet Mystery Of Life .... from the Broadway musical "Naughty Marietta"	Columbia 1377
3/23/29	**13**	3	7. A Love Tale Of Alsace-Lorraine...................	Columbia 1682
5/25/29	**1(4)**	12	8. **The Wedding Of The Painted Doll** .... from the film "Broadway Melody"	Columbia 1780
5/25/29	**3**	9	9. With A Song In My Heart......................... from the Broadway musical "Spring Is Here"	Victor 21923
7/20/29	**13**	3	10. I Kiss Your Hand, Madame .... above two vocals: Ran Weeks	Victor 21920
8/31/29	**2(1)**	7	11. Ain't Misbehavin'..................................... vocal: Lew Conrad from the Broadway musical "Hot Chocolates"	Victor 22047
11/09/29	**15**	2	12. Look What You've Done To Me...................	Victor 22115
12/14/29	**5**	5	13. My Sweeter Than Sweet .... from the film "Sweetie"	Victor 22194
1/18/30	**10**	3	14. I'll See You Again .... from the Broadway musical "Bitter Sweet"	Victor 22246
1/25/30	**11**	3	15. You've Got That Thing..............................	Victor 22244
2/01/30	**3**	9	16. Happy Days Are Here Again....................... from the film "Chasing Rainbows" became President Franklin D. Roosevelt's theme song vocals on 12-14 & 16: L. Levin	Victor 22221
2/01/30	**13**	2	17. You Do Something To Me .... above two from the Broadway musical "Fifty Million Frenchmen"	Victor 22244
2/15/30	**5**	9	18. What Is This Thing Called Love? .... from the Broadway musical "Wake Up and Dream"	Victor 22282
4/05/30	**20**	1	19. Puttin' On The Ritz .... movie title song vocals on 11 & 18-19: Lew Conrad	Victor 22306
7/19/30	**17**	2	20. Around The Corner/ vocal: Don Howard	
8/30/30	**17**	1	21. Bye Bye Blues................................... vocal: Philip Steele	Victor 22459
12/25/30+	**15**	2	22. Body And Soul .... from the Broadway musical "Three's a Crowd" vocals on 15, 17 & 22: Frank Luther Eddy Duchin (piano) on nearly all of above twelve	Victor 22537
2/21/31	**15**	2	23. Just A Gigolo....................................	Victor 22606
5/16/31	**6**	4	24. Out Of Nowhere .... vocal: Frank Munn	Victor 22668
7/25/31	**12**	5	25. When The Moon Comes Over The Mountain ... vocals on 23 & 25: Ben Gordon	Victor 22746
8/01/31	**4**	7	26. I Love Louisa/	
8/01/31	**10**	4	27. New Sun In The Sky............................ Fred Astaire, above two vocals both from the Broadway musical "The Band Wagon"	Victor 22755
8/08/31	**8**	4	28. Without That Gal!	Victor 22746

DATE CHARTED	PEAK POS	WKS CHRT'D	ARTIST — Record Title	Label & Number
12/12/31	6	4	29. Time On My Hands.. vocal: Lee Wiley; from the Broadway musical "Smiles"	Victor 22839
1/02/32	10	4	30. The Night Was Made For Love/	
1/02/32	13	4	31. She Didn't Say "Yes" .... above two from the Broadway musical "The Cat and the Fiddle"	Victor 22839
1/23/32	1(6)	17	32. **Paradise**.. vocal: Frances Maddux	Victor 22904
3/12/32	7	4	33. Jalousie (Jealousy) .... [I] recorded 2/25/31	Victor 22928
3/12/32	16	2	34. Drums In My Heart.................................. from the Broadway musical "Through the Years"	Victor 22915
5/07/32	10	4	35. Lovable.. vocal: Dick Robertson	Victor 22954
10/01/32	15	4	36. She Didn't Say "Yes" .... [R]	Victor 22870
11/05/32	9	5	37. Alone Together .... from the Broadway musical "Flying Colors" vocals on 30-31, 34 & 37: Frank Luther	Victor 24131
12/03/32	10	4	38. Louisiana Hayride.................................. vocal: Arthur Schwartz (composer) & Eva Jessye Choir above two from the Broadway musical "Flying Colors"	Victor 24157
12/17/32	1(10)	18	39. **Night And Day/**	
2/11/33	17	2	40. I've Got You On My Mind......................... Fred Astaire, above two vocals both from the Broadway musical "Gay Divorce"	Victor 24193
3/25/33	1(8)	19	41. **Stormy Weather/** Harold Arlen (composer), vocal	
4/22/33	17	1	42. Maybe It's Because I Love You Too Much.... Fred Astaire, vocal	Victor 24262
5/27/33	7	5	43. Love Songs Of The Nile............................ vocal: Howard Phillips; from the film "The Barbarian"	Victor 24312
10/28/33	5	12	44. Easter Parade .... vocal: Clifton Webb from the Broadway musical "As Thousands Cheer"	Victor 24418
11/11/33	6	6	45. By A Waterfall/	
12/09/33	13	3	46. Honeymoon Hotel .... above two from the film "Footlight Parade"	Victor 24399
11/25/33	3	8	47. Yesterdays	Brunswick 6701
1/06/34	3	6	48. (When Your Heart's On Fire) Smoke Gets In Your Eyes/ vocal: Tamara	
1/13/34	10	5	49. The Touch Of Your Hand .... above three from the Broadway musical "Roberta" vocals on 45 & 49: Arthur Wright	Brunswick 6715
1/20/34	17	3	50. Our Big Love Scene................................. from the film "Going Hollywood" vocals on 46-47 & 50: Frank Luther	Victor 24448
3/31/34	17	1	51. Ill Wind (You're Blowing Me No Good).......... vocal: Thelma Nevins	Brunswick 6789
6/09/34	10	4	52. Night On The Desert/	
7/21/34	19	1	53. Tonight Is Mine .... from the film "Stingaree"	Brunswick 6903
6/30/34	3	11	54. With My Eyes Wide Open I'm Dreaming........ from the film "Shoot the Works" above three vocals: George Bueler	Brunswick 6896
8/25/34	6	6	55. You're A Builder Upper............................ Harold Arlen (composer), vocal from the Broadway musical "Life Begins at 8:40"	Brunswick 6941
9/22/34	11	3	56. Don't Let It Bother You	Brunswick 6963
10/06/34	1(2)	7	57. **The Continental (You Kiss While You're** **Dancing)/** [I]	
11/03/34	16	2	58. A Needle In A Haystack .... vocal: Lew Conrad above three from the film "The Gay Divorcee"	Brunswick 6973
1/19/35	20	1	59. I Get A Kick Out Of You........................... from the Broadway musical "Anything Goes" vocals on 56 & 59: Sally Singer	Brunswick 7332

DATE CHARTED	PEAK POS	WKS CHRT'D	ARTIST — Record Title	Label & Number
2/02/35	18	1	60. **You And The Night And The Music** .... from the Broadway musical "Revenge With Music"	Brunswick 7331
3/23/35	10	4	61. **Lovely To Look At/**	
5/04/35	9	4	62. **I Won't Dance** .... above two from the film "Roberta" above three vocals: Phil Dewey	Brunswick 7393
9/07/35	18	1	63. **I'm In The Mood For Love**...................... vocal: Frank Luther; from the film "Every Night at Eight" (Brunswick 7486: "Cheek to Cheek", Fred Astaire with Leo Reisman's Orchestra)	Brunswick 7482
11/30/35	5	7	64. **I Got Plenty O' Nuttin'/**	
12/14/35	16	2	65. **It Ain't Necessarily So** .... above two from the folk opera "Porgy and Bess"	Brunswick 7562
12/28/35+	18	2	66. **I Dream Too Much** .... movie title song	Brunswick 7561
1/18/36	19	1	67. **I Wanna Woo** .... vocal: Honey Dean	Brunswick 7584
4/04/36	14	6	68. **Yours Truly Is Truly Yours**...................... vocal: Benny Davis	Brunswick 7614
7/18/36	14	5	69. **Afterglow/**	
7/25/36	6	5	70. **On The Beach At Bali Bali**....................... 	Brunswick 7696
11/07/36	7	6	71. **It's De-Lovely**................................... from the Broadway musical "Red, Hot, and Blue!"	Brunswick 7753
3/27/37	16	1	72. **Too Marvelous For Words** .... from the film "Ready, Willing, and Able"	Brunswick 7831
12/25/37+	9	7	73. **In The Still Of The Night** .... from the film "Rosalie"	Brunswick 7985
5/28/38	14	3	74. **Spring Is Here** .... vocal: Felix Knight from the Broadway musical "I Married an Angel"	Victor 25842
2/03/40	7	8	75. **Do I Love You?**.................................. from the Broadway musical "DuBarry Was A Lady" vocals on 73 & 75: Lee Sullivan	Victor 26421
10/26/40	23	1	76. **I Want To Live (As Long As You Love Me)** ..... vocal: Joan Whitney from the Broadway musical "Boys and Girls Together"	Victor 26758
11/16/40	7	9	77. **Down Argentina Way**............................ vocal: Sara Horn; movie title song	Victor 26765
12/28/40	22	1	78. **Ferry Boat Serenade**	Victor 26718
6/07/41	25	1	79. **Bewitched** .... from the Broadway musical "Pal Joey" above two vocals: Anita Boyer	Victor 27344
			KEN REMO	
3/14/53	29	1	1. **Mexico**.................................... orchestra directed by Joe Lipman	MGM 11419
			JACQUES RENARD & HIS ORCHESTRA Sweet-band leader featured on several 30s radio shows	
10/25/30	6	6	1. **Sing Something Simple** .... from the Broadway musical "The Second Little Show"	Brunswick 4918
11/08/30	3	6	2. **Three Little Words**.................................. from the film "Check and Double Check"	Brunswick 4939
7/04/31	16	2	3. **Come To Me**.................................... from the film "Indiscreet"	Brunswck 6106
7/25/31	20	1	4. **Dancing In The Dark** .... vocal: Frank Munn from the Broadway musical "The Band Wagon"	Brunswick 6136
10/24/31	19	1	5. **Who Am I?** .... vocals on 3 & 5: Paul Small	Brunswick 6183
11/14/31	7	4	6. **Cuban Love Song**................................ movie title song	Brunswick 6206
11/21/31	13	4	7. **As Time Goes By** .... from the Broadway musical "Everybody's Welcome"	Brunswick 6205
11/09/35	14	4	8. **I'd Rather Listen To Your Eyes** .... vocal: Smith Ballew; from the film "Shipmates Forever"	Columbia 3086
3/27/43	3	16	9. **As Time Goes By** .... [R] featured in the film "Casablanca"	Brunswick 6205

DATE CHARTED	PEAK POS	WKS CHRT'D	ARTIST — Record Title	Label & Number

HENRI RENE & HIS ORCHESTRA
German-raised bandleader who became an arranger-conductor for Perry Como, Dinah Shore, Eartha Kitt, Mindy Carson, & other singers. (Also see Hugo Winterhalter)

DATE CHARTED	PEAK POS	WKS CHRT'D	ARTIST — Record Title	Label & Number
12/14/40+	20	3	1. Lo-Lo-Lita	Victor V-771
6/14/41	26	1	2. Pound Your Table Polka	Victor V-783
			above two: Rene's Musette Orchestra	
6/19/48	30	1	3. Toolie Oolie Doolie (The Yodel Polka)	RCA Victor 1114
			vocal: Three-o-Niners	
4/25/53	24	1	4. The Song From "Moulin Rouge" (Where Is Your Heart?).....................................	RCA Victor 5264
			vocal: Alvy West	
5/08/54	8	15	5. The Happy Wanderer...............................	RCA Victor 5715
			Swiss song	

HARRY RESER'S ORCHESTRA
The 1920s' foremost banjo player, also musical director of Clevelanders and Clicquot Club Eskimos. He died on 9/27/65.

DATE CHARTED	PEAK POS	WKS CHRT'D	ARTIST — Record Title	Label & Number
2/24/23	15	1	1. I Wish I Could Shimmy Like My Sister Kate [I]	Okeh 4694
			Okeh Syncopators	
8/01/25	9	1	2. Yearning (Just For You)......................... [I]	Columbia 319
12/25/26	10	1	3. Someone Is Losin' Susan........................ [I]	Columbia 708
7/28/28	15	2	4. Imagination	Columbia 1378
11/02/29+	15	2	5. Piccolo Pete.................................... [N]	Brunswick 4457
			Six Jumping Jacks	
			above two vocals: Tom Stacks	
1/06/34	13	2	6. You're Gonna Lose Your Gal.......................	Columbia 2840

REVELERS
The 1920s' most famous vocal group, it evolved out of the Shannon Four, which had been recording since 1917. Tenor Lewis James, baritone Elliott Shaw, & bass Wilfred Glenn carried over from the Shannon, joined by first tenor Franklyn Baur and pianist-arranger Ed Smalle. Baur was replaced in 1928 by James Melton, later a renowned opera and movie star. The group recorded for different companies under various names, including the Singing Sophomores. (also see Shannon Four, Arden-Ohman Orchestra, & Nat Shilkret)

DATE CHARTED	PEAK POS	WKS CHRT'D	ARTIST — Record Title	Label & Number
1/16/26	4	6	1. Dinah	Victor 19796
7/31/26	11	1	2. Just Around The Corner	Victor 19968
9/18/26	5	4	3. Valencia (A Song Of Spain)/	
10/09/26	3	5	4. The Blue Room	Victor 20082
			from the Broadway musical "The Girl Friend"	
11/21/26	11	1	5. Birth Of The Blues/	
12/04/26	10	1	6. Lucky Day..	Victor 20111
			above two from "George White's Scandals of 1926"	
1/01/27	17	1	7. Breezin' Along With The Breeze	Victor 20140
			also recorded as Singing Sophomores for Columbia 4235	
7/09/27	18	1	8. Yankee Rose...................................	Victor 20564
			with Charles Harrison as first tenor	
8/06/27	11	3	9. Hallelujah!....................................	Victor 20609
			also recorded as Singing Sophomores for Columbia 4620	
			from the Broadway musical "Hit the Deck"	
9/10/27	17	1	10. Russian Lullaby	Columbia 985
			as Singing Sophomores	
3/03/28	10	4	11. Among My Souvenirs...............................	Victor 21100
6/02/28	10	3	12. Ol' Man River	Victor 21241
			from the Broadway musical "Show Boat"	
5/17/30	18	1	13. A Cottage For Sale................................	Victor 22382

ALVINO REY & HIS ORCHESTRA
Real name Alvin McBurney, one of the first important electric guitarists; played with Hoarce Heidt 1934-39. His band featured alto saxist Skeets Herfurt, pianist Buddy Cole, and the King Sisters on vocals, with arranger Frank DeVol.

DATE CHARTED	PEAK POS	WKS CHRT'D	ARTIST — Record Title	Label & Number
2/22/41	23	1	1. Tiger Rag	Bluebird 11002
5/03/41	13	2	2. Nighty Night	Bluebird 11041

DATE CHARTED	PEAK POS	WKS CHRT'D	ARTIST — Record Title	Label & Number
1/17/42	**2(1)**	10	3. I Said No!/ from the film "Sweater Girl"	
2/14/42	**1(1)**	10	4. **Deep In The Heart Of Texas** .... Bluebird 11391 vocal: Bill Schallen & Skeets Herfurt	
7/25/42	**3**	11	5. Idaho.. Bluebird 11331 vocals on 2-3 & 5: Yvonne King	
9/05/42	**22**	1	6. When It's Moonlight On The Blue Pacific....... Victor 27948	
9/19/42	**6**	6	7. Strip Polka .... Bluebird 11573 vocals on 1 & 7: Four King Sisters	
12/12/42	**21**	1	8. Dearly Beloved........................... Bluebird 11579 vocal: Bill Schallen; from film "You Were Never Lovelier" Kai Winding (trombone) on above three	
6/05/43	**19**	1	9. The Army Air Corps...................... Bluebird 11476 vocals on 6 & 9: Bill Schallen & Four King Sisters	
4/20/46	**5**	9	10. Cement Mixer (Put-Ti, Put-Ti) .... [N] Capitol 248	
7/19/47	**13**	3	11. Bloop-Bleep .... [N] Capitol 428 above two vocals: Rocky Coluccio	
9/20/47	**3**	14	12. Near You.............................. Capitol 452 vocal: Jimmy Joyce	
2/21/48	**6**	8	13. I'm Looking Over A Four-Leaf Clover .... Capitol 491 featured in film "Jolson Sings Again"	

CHUY REYES & HIS HOLLYWOOD MOCAMBO ORCHESTRA
Well-known Latin-American rumba band.

DATE CHARTED	PEAK POS	WKS CHRT'D	ARTIST — Record Title	Label & Number
5/15/48	**27**	1	1. Rhumba Boogie .... [I] Capitol 15067	

DEBBIE REYNOLDS
Long-popular movie ("Singin' In the Rain") and Broadway ("Irene" revival) star, successful in both musicals and comedies; married to Eddie Fisher from 1955-59; their daughter is actress Carrie Fisher.

DATE CHARTED	PEAK POS	WKS CHRT'D	ARTIST — Record Title	Label & Number
2/03/51	**3**	17	● 1. Aba Daba Honeymoon .... MGM 30282 DEBBIE REYNOLDS & CARLETON CARPENTER featured in the film "Two Weeks With Love" accompanied by George Stoll & His MGM Studio Orchestra	

TOMMY REYNOLDS & HIS ORCHESTRA
Clarinetist and swing band leader

DATE CHARTED	PEAK POS	WKS CHRT'D	ARTIST — Record Title	Label & Number
9/07/40	**25**	1	1. On A Simmery Summery Day..................... Vocalion 5569 vocal: Sally Richards	

BETTY JANE RHODES
Singer featured on radio and in many 40s movies.

DATE CHARTED	PEAK POS	WKS CHRT'D	ARTIST — Record Title	Label & Number
9/28/46	**5**	11	1. Rumors Are Flying................................. RCA Victor 1944	
11/29/47	**21**	1	2. Tonight Be Tender To Me .... RCA Victor 2227 accompanied by Charles Dant Orchestra	
11/13/48	**9**	9	3. Buttons And Bows .... RCA Victor 3078 accompanied by Harry Zimmerman's Orchestra from the film "The Paleface"	

RHYTHM WRECKERS

DATE CHARTED	PEAK POS	WKS CHRT'D	ARTIST — Record Title	Label & Number
9/25/37	**19**	1	1. September In The Rain .... Vocalion 3608 vocal: Pauline Byrne; with Muggsy Spanier (cornet) from the film "Melody For Two"	

LIEUTENANT GITZ RICE OF THE FIRST CANADIANS
Died on 10/16/47 (56).

DATE CHARTED	PEAK POS	WKS CHRT'D	ARTIST — Record Title	Label & Number
1/26/18	**10**	1	1. Life In A Trench In Belgium...................... Columbia 2410 LT. GITZ RICE & HENRY BURR	

GLADYS RICE
Philadelphia-born singer, real name Gladys Hilberg; her father starred with May Irwin in the famous 1896 silent movie "The Kiss". Gladys died on 9/7/83 (92).

DATE CHARTED	PEAK POS	WKS CHRT'D	ARTIST — Record Title	Label & Number
1/08/16	**9**	1	1. They Didn't Believe Me .... Edison Amb. 2759 later on Edison Diamond Disc 80279 from the Broadway musical "The Girl from Utah"	

DATE CHARTED	PEAK POS	WKS CHRT'D	ARTIST — Record Title	Label & Number
8/05/16	8	2	2. Babes In The Wood .... also on Edison Amberol 2900 from the Broadway musical "Very Good, Eddie" above two: WALTER VAN BRUNT & GLADYS RICE	Edison 50344
5/04/18	8	2	3. The Siren's Song .... HELEN CLARK & GLADYS RICE from the Broadway musical "Leave It to Jane"	Edison 80382
3/22/19	9	1	4. After You've Gone .... BILLY MURRAY & "RACHEL GRANT" (Gladys Rice)	Edison Amb. 3666
3/29/19	9	2	5. Till We Meet Again................................... VERNON DALHART & GLADYS RICE	Edison Amb. 3670
7/31/20	12	1	6. Marion (You'll Soon Be Marryin' Me)............ also recorded for Okeh 4112 & Edison Amberol 4065	Victor 18671
8/14/20	8	1	7. When My Baby Smiles At Me....................... from the "Greenwich Village Follies of 1919"	Edison 50651
8/28/20	14	1	8. Oh! How I Laugh When I Think That I Cried Over You	Edison Amb. 4048
5/26/23	12	1	9. I Gave You Up Just Before You Threw Me Down .... above four: BILLY MURRAY & "RACHEL GRANT"	Victor 19023

BUDDY RICH
Acclaimed by his many fans as "the world's greatest drummer" from his early days with Bunny Berigan (1938), Artie Shaw (1939), Tommy Dorsey (1939-42, 44-46, 54-55), & Harry James (1953-54) into the 1980s. (see Metronome All-Star Band)

FRED RICH & HIS ORCHESTRA
Polish-born pianist-bandleader, featured many top jazz stars, later served as composer & musical director for 1940s movies; died on 9/8/56 (58).

DATE CHARTED	PEAK POS	WKS CHRT'D	ARTIST — Record Title	Label & Number
1/01/27	10	3	1. Play Gypsies - Dance Gypsies/ [I] from the Broadway musical "Countess Maritza"	
1/08/27	17	2	2. Moonlight On The Ganges .... [I]	Columbia 734
2/19/27	18	1	3. Just A Little Longer................................ vocal: Crooners	Columbia 773
11/19/27	15	2	4. Good News .... vocal: Franklyn Baur-Frank Luther-Elliott Shaw Broadway musical title song	Columbia 1108
3/21/28	19	1	5. The Man I Love .... vocal: Vaughn DeLeath from the Broadway musical "Lady Be Good"	Columbia 1241
3/08/30	19	1	6. What Is This Thing Called Love? .... Tommy Dorsey (trombone) & Bunny Berigan (trumpet) featured from the Broadway musical "Wake Up and Dream"	Columbia 2099
2/20/34	8	4	7. Let's Fall In Love................................... vocal: Phil Regan; movie title song	Columbia 2868

CAROL RICHARDS - see BING CROSBY

JACK RICHARDS & THE MARKSMEN

DATE CHARTED	PEAK POS	WKS CHRT'D	ARTIST — Record Title	Label & Number
5/15/54	27	1	1. Hers And His .... orchestra directed by Dick Jacobs	Coral 61164

TRUDY RICHARDS
Husky-voiced singer formerly with Charlie Barnet.

DATE CHARTED	PEAK POS	WKS CHRT'D	ARTIST — Record Title	Label & Number
5/09/53	19	3	1. The Breeze (That's Bringin' My Honey Back To Me)... orchestra directed by Eddie Wilcox	Derby 823

HARRY RICHMAN
Born Harry Reichman, colorful night club, Broadway, and movie musical star; formerly vaudeville pianist for top performers like Nora Bayes & Mae West. As a pilot in 1935, he set a world altitude record, and the following year made the first-ever trans-ocean round-trip flight. Harry died on 11/3/72 (77).

DATE CHARTED	PEAK POS	WKS CHRT'D	ARTIST — Record Title	Label & Number
10/23/26	4	5	1. The Birth Of The Blues .... from "George White's Scandals of 1926"	Vocalion 15412
4/30/27	10	4	2. Muddy Water	Brunswick 3435
5/14/27	13	2	3. Blue Skies .... from the Broadway musical "Betsy"	Vocalion 15511

DATE CHARTED	PEAK POS	WKS CHRT'D	ARTIST — Record Title	Label & Number
9/03/27	**11**	3	4. C'est Vous (It's You)	Brunswick 3538
10/27/28	**19**	1	5. I'm On The Crest Of A Wave .... from "George White's Scandals of 1927"	Brunswick 4008
2/15/30	**1(1)**	8	6. **Puttin' On The Ritz**................................	Brunswick 4677
3/01/30	**4**	8	7. There's Danger In Your Eyes, Cherie/	
3/08/30	**7**	7	8. Singing A Vagabond Song .... above three accompanied by Earl Burtnett & His Los Angeles Biltmore Hotel Orchestra; all from the film "Puttin' On The Ritz"	Brunswick 4678
4/19/30	**13**	2	9. On The Sunny Side Of The Street/	
5/10/30	**12**	3	10. Exactly Like You.................................... above two from the Broadway musical "International Revue"	Brunswick 4747
8/27/32	**7**	6	11. It Was So Beautiful .... from the film "The Big Broadcast of 1932"	Columbia 2701

NELSON RIDDLE & HIS ORCHESTRA
Trombonist-arranger with Charlie Spivak & Tommy Dorsey in the 40s; became one of the most in-demand of all arranger-conductors: for Frank Sinatra (several classic 50s albums), Nat King Cole, Ella Mae Morse, and (in the 1980s) Linda Ronstadt; also arranger & musical director on many films. His 1956 record "Lisbon Antigua" was a million-seller. Nelson died on 10/6/85 (64).

4/10/54	**23**	3	1. Brother John .... [I] adaptation of the French song "Frere Jacques"	Capitol 2744

RILEY-FARLEY ORCHESTRA
Joe Riley (tuba & trumpet), formerly with Rudy Vallee, Vincent Lopez, Will Osborne, & other bands; and Eddie Farley (trumpet), previously with Bert Lown & Osborne; they introduced this huge novelty hit.

12/07/35+	**1(3)**	11	1. **The Music Goes Round And Round** .... [N] vocal: Riley & Farley	Decca 578
12/31/38	**15**	1	2. The Music Goes Round And Round .... [N-R]	Decca 578

JOE RINES & HIS ORCHESTRA
Violinist-bandleader

12/03/32	**6**	6	1. Underneath The Harlem Moon..................... vocal: Joe Rines	Victor 24151
10/23/37	**19**	1	2. The Lady Is A Tramp................................. vocal: Bebe Best; from the Broadway musical "Babes in Arms"	Brunswick 7967

BLANCHE RING
Star of many Broadway musicals from 1902-1938; in her first musical she introduced classic hit "In the Good Old Summer Time"; died on 1/13/61 (83).

7/17/09	**4**	1	1. Yip-I-Addy-I-Aye .... later on Victor 60017	Victor 5692
10/23/09	**1(2)**	5	2. **I've Got Rings On My Fingers** .... later on Victor 60016 from the Broadway musical "The Midnight Song"	Victor 5737
10/30/09	**8**	1	3. The Billiken Man	Victor 5731
1/28/11	**9**	1	4. Nora Malone	Victor 60024
4/15/11	**1(2)**	10	5. **Come, Josephine, In My Flying Machine**.....	Victor 60032

TEX RITTER
Star of some 85 Hollywood Westerns from 1935-45, Tex (Maurice Woodeward Ritter) sang the famous title song in the movie "High Noon". He died on 1/2/74 (67); his son is TV comedian John Ritter.

11/25/44	**11**	4	1. I'm Wasting My Tears On You/	
12/09/44	**26**	1	2. There's A New Moon Over My Shoulder	Capitol 174
9/20/52	**12**	8	3. High Noon (Do Not Forsake Me)	Capitol 2120
11/06/54	**30**	1	4. The Bandit .... from the Mexican film "O Cangaceiro"	Capitol 2916

RKO STUDIO ORCHESTRA
Directed by the famous composer Max Steiner.

3/17/34	**13**	3	1. Carioca... [I] movie soundtrack recording from "Flying Down to Rio"	Victor 24515

DATE CHARTED	PEAK POS	WKS CHRT'D	ARTIST — Record Title	Label & Number
			MAX ROACH Important jazz "bop" drummer, played with Dizzy Gillespie, Charlie Parker, Benny Carter, and Miles Davis. (see Billy Eckstine)	
			WILL ROBBINS	
5/29/15	6	3	1. By Heck .... BYRON HARLAN & WILL ROBBINS	Columbia 1722
6/05/15	10	1	2. She Used To Be The Slowest Girl In Town	Columbia 1694
7/17/15	7	2	3. My Little Girl .... above two: ADA JONES & WILL ROBBINS	Columbia 1724
			BOB ROBERTS Popular baritone novelty singer; died on 1/21/30 (51).	
7/25/03	2(1)	5	1. Hurrah For Baffin's Bay .... from the Broadway musical "The Wizard of Oz"	Columbia 1404
7/25/03	5	1	2. I'm A Jonah Man .... [C]	Columbia 1388
8/01/03+	5	1	3. Marriage Is Sublime .... [C] also on Columbia cylinder 32185	Columbia 1420
8/08/03	3	4	4. I'm Thinkin' Of You All De While	Columbia 1441
12/19/03	2(2)	4	5. By The Sycamore Tree .... [C] also on Columbia cylinder 32328 & Zone-o-Phone 5795 from the Broadway musical "Rogers Brothers in London"	Columbia 1617
3/26/04	3	3	6. The Woodchuck Song .... [C] Bob's most famous comedy hit; also recorded for Columbia 1658 & 32366, Victor 22624, & Zon-o-Phone 5795; from the Broadway musical "The Runaways"	Edison 8617
6/18/04	5	1	7. The Ghost That Never Walked .... [C] from the Broadway musical "Piff! Paff! Pouf!"	Columbia 32428
10/22/04	3	3	8. Teasing	Edison 8804
12/17/04	3	4	9. I May Be Crazy, But I Ain't No Fool .... [C] also recorded for Victor 4108 & Zon-o-Phone 43; from the Broadway musical "In Dahomey"	Columbia 1889
5/27/05	9	1	10. Oh! Oh! Sallie .... [C] BILLY MURRAY & BOB ROBERTS	Victor 4276
12/16/05	4	1	11. Everybody Works But Father .... [C] also recorded for Columbia 32830 & Zon-o-Phone 258	Edison 9100
1/26/07	7	1	12. He's A Cousin Of Mine .... [C] from the Broadway musical "Marrying Mary"	Edison 9412
6/29/07	6	1	13. No Wedding Bells For Me .... [C] also recorded for Columbia 3659 & 33139 from the Broadway musical "The Orchid"	Edison 9538
8/31/07	6	1	14. You'll Have To Wait Till My Ship Comes In....	Columbia 3660
4/25/08	6	1	15. I've Got A Tickling Sensation 'Round My Heart For You	Columbia 3743
12/26/08	8	1	16. Don't Take Me Home .... [C]	Indestructable 889
6/26/09	6	1	17. Shine On, Harvest Moon .... from Broadway's "Ziegfeld Follies of 1908"	Columbia 668
8/21/09	5	1	18. I Love My Wife, But Oh You Kid! .... [C]	Indestructable 1129
10/30/09	7	1	19. My Wife's Gone To The Country, Hurrah! Hurrah! .... [C]	Indestructable 1145
4/02/10	5	4	20. Sadie Salome (Go Home) .... [C]	Columbia 789
10/21/11	2(1)	5	21. Woodman, Woodman, Spare That Tree .... [C] also recorded for Edison Amberol 837 from the "Ziegfeld Follies of 1911"	Victor 16909
7/13/12	1(6)	14	22. **Ragtime Cowboy Joe** .... later recorded for U.S. Everlasting 509 among artists with more than one charted record, this was the biggest final hit by any recording artist	Victor 17090
			KENNEY ROBERTS Country singer and well-known yodeller	
9/10/49	9	13	● 1. I Never See Maggie Alone .... 1926 British song; Kenney originally recorded this with Nancy Lee for Vitacoustic 506	Coral 64012

DATE CHARTED	PEAK POS	WKS CHRT'D	ARTIST — Record Title	Label & Number
			VICTOR ROBERTS	
			Pseudonym for Billy Jones	
			DICK ROBERTSON & HIS ORCHESTRA	
			Soft-voiced band singer whose own band featured top musicians; also credited as co-writer of several hit songs ("Goodnight, Wherever You Are"). (also see Ipana Troubadors, Johnny Long, Ben Selvin, Peter Van Steeden, Victor Young)	
6/05/37	16	2	1. Toodle-Oo..	Decca 1260
7/10/37	14	2	2. On A Little Dream Ranch	Decca 1283
7/31/37	12	2	3. The Merry-Go-Round Broke Down/	
8/14/37	20	1	4. Good Mornin'..	Decca 1334
			from the film "Mountain Music" Bobby Hackett (cornet) on above four	
9/04/37	10	2	5. Sailboat In The Moonlight	Decca 1367
10/02/37	5	11	6. Blossoms On Broadway/	
10/16/37	11	2	7. You Can't Stop Me From Dreaming	Decca 1415
12/18/37	16	1	8. Rollin' Plains	Decca 1498
			Buddy Morrow (trombone) on 5 & 8	
12/25/37+	14	2	9. That Old Gang Of Mine.............................	Decca 1536
3/26/38	9	3	10. Cry, Baby, Cry/	
4/30/38	7	7	11. Oh, Ma, Ma (The Butcher Boy)............... [N]	Decca 1726
			based on the Italian song "Luna Merro Mare" Frank Froeba (piano) on most of above records	
9/10/38	5	5	12. Rancho Grande	Decca 1979
4/22/39	10	2	13. I'm Building A Sailboat Of Dreams	Decca 2364
6/24/39	12	2	14. Pippinella...	Decca 2497
2/24/40	12	6	15. Ma (He's Making Eyes At Me) .... [N]	Decca 2920
9/07/40	22	1	16. Goodbye, Little Darlin', Goodbye	Decca 3304
2/14/42	22	1	17. We Did It Before (And We Can Do It Again)....	Decca 4117
			vocal: Dick Robertson & American Four	
			TEXAS JIM ROBERTSON	
			Country bass singer	
4/19/41	21	1	1. I'll Be Back In A Year, Little Darlin'............	Bluebird 8606
3/31/53+	24	1	2. Let Me In...	RCA Victor 4077
			FONTANE SISTERS & TEXAS JIM ROBERTSON	
			PAUL ROBESON	
			Great bass singer, son of a minister who escaped from slavery, he was one of the best-ever college football offensive tackles, and also a law school graduate. Paul was internationally renowned for both his singing and his Shakespearian acting and was featured in several films. His 1940 recording "Ballad for Americans" (Victor 26516 & 26517) was later selected for the NARAS Hall of Fame. Paul died on 1/23/76 (77).	
12/26/25	13	1	1. Steal Away	Victor 19742
10/22/27	19	1	2. Deep River..	Victor 20793
6/02/28	7	4	3. Ol' Man River	Victor 35912
			Paul Whiteman & His Orchestra, Paul Robeson vocal, his most famous song; from the Broadway musical "Show Boat"	
			BILL ROBINSON	
			Known to all as "Bojangles", all-time great tap dancer in Broadway musicals and Shirley Temple movies. Bill died in Nov. 1949 (71).	
10/26/29	8	3	1. Ain't Misbehavin'.....................................	Brunswick 4535
			vocal with tap dancing accompanied by Irving Mills & His Hotsy-Totsy Gang from the Broadway musical "Hot Chocolates"	
			CARSON ROBISON	
			Important country-western singer-songwriter, composed standards "Carry Me Back to the Lone Prairie" & "My Blue Ridge Mountain Home"; died on 3/24/57 (66).	
10/04/24	10	1	1. Whistling The Blues Away.........................	Victor 19338
			WENDELL HALL & CARSON ROBISON	
7/25/25	9	1	2. Way Down Home	Victor 19637
			GENE AUSTIN & CARSON ROBISON	

DATE CHARTED	PEAK POS	WKS CHRT'D	ARTIST — Record Title	Label & Number
10/08/27	7	4	3. My Carolina Home .... *previously recorded for Okeh 45085*	Victor 20795
3/31/28	19	1	4. A Memory That Time Cannot Erase............. *recorded for several companies (see Vernon Dalhart)* *above three: VERNON DALHART & CARSON ROBISON*	Victor 21094
8/17/29	19	1	5. The Utah Trail .... FRANK LUTHER & CARSON ROBISON	Brunswick 4296
1/31/31	4	12	6. When Your Hair Has Turned To Silver .... LUTHER & ROBISON as "Bud & Joe Billings"	Victor 22588
3/28/42	21	1	7. Mussolini's Letter to Hitler .... [N]	Bluebird 11459
4/04/42	22	1	8. 1942 Turkey In The Straw..................... [N]	Bluebird 11460
4/10/43	21	1	9. That Old Grey Mare Is Back Where She Used To Be .... [N]	Bluebird 0808
10/02/48	14	9	10. Life Gets Tee-Jus, Don't It?	MGM 10224

WILLIAM ROBYN

DATE CHARTED	PEAK POS	WKS CHRT'D	ARTIST — Record Title	Label & Number
10/30/20	7	2	1. I'm In Heaven When I'm In My Mother's Arms	Victor 18686

"ROCHESTER"
Real name Eddie Anderson, famous for years on radio & TV as Jack Benny's gravel-voiced, wisecracking servant.

DATE CHARTED	PEAK POS	WKS CHRT'D	ARTIST — Record Title	Label & Number
4/20/40	13	6	1. My! My!.. [N] *from the film "Buck Benny Rides Again"*	Columbia 35442

HOMER RODEHEAVER
Most famous for singing hymns at Billy Sunday's revival meetings; died on 12/18/55 (75).

DATE CHARTED	PEAK POS	WKS CHRT'D	ARTIST — Record Title	Label & Number
6/19/15	6	4	1. Brighten The Corner Where You Are .... *later recorded for Columbia 1990*	Victor 17763
2/28/20	10	1	2. When I Look In His Face	Columbia 2833
3/05/21	5	3	3. The Old Rugged Cross............................... *above two: HOMER RODEHEAVER & VIRGINIA ASHER*	Victor 18706

GENE RODEMICH & HIS ORCHESTRA
Pianist-bandleader

DATE CHARTED	PEAK POS	WKS CHRT'D	ARTIST — Record Title	Label & Number
10/16/20	7	3	1. Margie .... [I]	Brunswick 2060
11/10/23	7	2	2. Wolverine Blues .... [I]	Brunswick 2455

JIMMIE RODGERS
"The Father of Country Music", Jimmie Rodgers was born on 9/8/1897 in Meridian, Miss. He contracted tuberculosis while working as a railroad brakeman, and while recuperating began singing and writing songs; by merging hillbilly and Negro blues sounds, he developed a new style that made him a legend following his death on 5/26/33 (35).

DATE CHARTED	PEAK POS	WKS CHRT'D	ARTIST — Record Title	Label & Number
12/31/27+	9	5	1. The Soldier's Sweetheart...........................	Victor 20864
3/31/28	2(1)	11	● 2. Blue Yodel... *country classic also known as "T for Texas"*	Victor 21142
7/07/28	14	3	3. In The Jail House Now	Victor 21245
8/04/28	7	7	4. The Brakeman's Blues...............................	Victor 21291
11/17/28	10	4	5. Blue Yodel No. 3	Victor 21531
4/06/29	14	3	6. Waiting For A Train	Victor 40014
10/11/30	19	1	7. Anniversary Yodel (Blue Yodel No. 7)	Victor 22488
3/19/32	18	1	8. Roll Along, Kentucky Moon	Victor 23651

BUDDY ROGERS & HIS ORCHESTRA
Star of many films from 1926-48, including the silent classic "Wings"; married movie star Mary Pickford; singer, played various instruments. (All vocals by Buddy)

DATE CHARTED	PEAK POS	WKS CHRT'D	ARTIST — Record Title	Label & Number
4/26/30	18	1	1. Anytime's The Time To Fall In Love............. *from the film "Paramount on Parade"*	Columbia 2143
7/09/32	14	3	2. In My Hideaway	Victor 24015
6/04/38	10	4	3. Lovelight In The Starlight	Vocalion 4058
10/08/38	2(1)	9	4. While A Cigarette Was Burning	Vocalion 4408

DATE CHARTED	PEAK POS	WKS CHRT'D	ARTIST — Record Title	Label & Number
			ROY ROGERS "The King of the Cowboys", born Leonard Slye; original member of the famous country group the Sons of the Pioneers. Roy starred in close to 100 movie Westerns, then a popular radio & TV series with his wife Dale Evans. Like his counterpart Gene Autry, Roy has become a multi-millionaire businessman.	
7/23/38	13	2	1. Hi-Yo, Silver	Vocalion 4190
12/04/43	18	1	2. Think Of Me..	Decca 6092
			WALTER B. ROGERS Featured cornet player for John Philip Sousa's famous band, also conducted some Sousa records; director of the Victor Light Opera Co. & Victor Military Band, and orchestral conductor for nearly all Victor artists from about 1908-16, including Enrico Caruso, Al Jolson, & Billy Murray. Walter died on 12/24/39 (74).	
			WILL ROGERS Oklahoma's nationally-beloved humorist, killed in an August 1935 plane crash at the peak of his film and stage stardom at 55.	
11/24/23	13	1	1. Will Rogers Tells Traffic Chiefs How To Direct Traffic.............................[T-C]	Victor 45369
3/15/24	10	1	2. Will Rogers' First Political Speech ....[T-C]	Victor 45374
			ADRIAN ROLLINI & THE GANG Jazz baritone & bass saxophonist also adept on other instruments; played with Bix Beiderbecke, Red Nichols, Frankie Trumbauer, Joe Venuti, & other bands; died on 5/15/56 (51).	
4/25/34	20	1	1. A Thousand Goodnights............................. vocal: Joey Nash; with Benny Goodman (clarinet) & Bunny Berigan (trumpet)	Vocalion 2672
7/20/35	11	3	2. Weather Man .... vocal: Wingy Manone (also trumpet) & Putney Dandridge (also piano)	Victor 25072
			MANUEL ROMAIN Top early tenor ballad singer (American-born, of Spanish ancestry), in minstrel shows & vaudeville for years; died on 12/22/26 (56).	
3/27/09	7	1	1. I Wish I Had A Girl...................................	Edison 10068
5/08/09	4	2	2. To The End Of The World With You	Edison Amb. 118
10/30/09	5	1	3. I Wish I Had My Old Gal Back Again............	Edison Amb. 216
1/29/10	6	3	4. I Wonder Who's Kissing Her Now................. from the Broadway musical "The Prince of Tonight"	Edison 10287
5/03/13	2(1)	5	5. When I Lost You......................................	Columbia 1288
11/29/13	9	1	6. The Curse Of An Aching Heart	Columbia 1380
2/21/14	2(2)	6	7. I Miss You Most Of All .... also recorded for Edison Amberol 2258	Columbia 1454
6/20/14	5	4	8. That's A Real Moving Picture From Life........	Columbia 1524
10/31/14	3	6	9. You're More Than The World To Me .... also recorded for Edison Amberol 2425	Columbia 1577
5/20/16	10	1	10. She's The Daughter Of Mother Machree	Columbia 1951
			SIGMUND ROMBERG Hungarian-born composer of many operetta-styled Broadway musicals from World War I to the 40s; died on 11/9/51 (64). (see Perry Como)	
			RONDOLIERS & PIANO PALS	
7/23/32	10	2	1. Love's Old Sweet Song.............................	Columbia 18004
			EDMUNDO ROS & HIS ORCHESTRA Venezuela-born bandleader enormously popular in England & Japan	
1/21/50	16	7	1. The Wedding Samba.................................	London 499
			ROSE MARIE Major child star of the 1930s who became still better known in 1960s as Sally on TV's "Dick Van Dyke Show"	
5/02/32	19	1	1. Say That You Were Teasing Me .... billed as "Baby Rose Marie" (no more than age seven at recording), accompanied by Fletcher Henderson's Orchestra	Victor 22960

DATE CHARTED	PEAK POS	WKS CHRT'D	ARTIST — Record Title	Label & Number

DAVID ROSE & HIS ORCHESTRA

British-born composer and orchestra leader, former pianist-arranger with Ted Fio Rito, also arranged Benny Goodman's #1 hit "It's Been So Long". He wrote scores for several 50s movies, and had the 1962 #1 million-seller "The Stripper". David was married briefly to Martha Raye and Judy Garland.

6/19/43+	**2(3)**	21	● 1. Holiday For Strings .... [I]	Victor 27853
2/19/44	**11**	6	2. Poinciana (Song Of The Tree) .... [I]	Victor 1554

FREDERIC ROSE

12/05/08	**5**	1	1. If You Cared For Me	Edison 9965

JULIAN ROSE

Popular Jewish sketch comedian

6/08/18	**5**	2	1. Levinsky At The Wedding, Parts 3 & 4 ...[T-C]	Columbia 2366

LILLIAN ROSEDALE - see VIVIAN HOLT

HARRY ROSENTHAL & HIS ORCHESTRA

1/26/35	**18**	1	1. All Through The Night	Columbia 2986

vocal: Helen Ward
with Benny Goodman (clarinet), & Toots Mondello (alto sax)
from the Broadway musical "Anything Goes"

LANNY ROSS

Tenor star of 30s & 40s radio shows, also in several movies

12/22/34	**20**	1	1. Stay As Sweet As You Are........................	Brunswick 7318

from the film "College Rhythm"
accompanied by Nat Finston & His Paramount Recording Orchestra

ROY ROSS & HIS ORCHESTRA

Pianist and accordionist, frequently accompanied the Ames Brothers.

6/10/50	**28**	1	1. Bewitched .... [I]	Coral 60182

from the Broadway musical "Pal Joey"

SHIRLEY ROSS

Singer-actress in many 1930s movies; born Bernice Gaunt

1/14/39	**15**	2	1. Two Sleepy People	Decca 2219

SHIRLEY ROSS & BOB HOPE
accompanied by Harry Sosnik's Orchestra
from the film "Thanks for the Memory"
B side: duet on the famous title song

PETE RUGOLO

Chief arranger for Stan Kenton 1945-49, orchestra conductor on records by Billy Eckstine & Mel Torme, musical director of Capitol, then of Mercury Records.

JIMMY RUSHING

Acclaimed jazz and blues singer, with Count Basie from 1936-48; died on 6/8/72 (68). (see Benny Goodman)

ANDY RUSSELL

Popular romantic singer, born Andy Rabajos to Mexican-Spanish parents.

4/15/44	**10**	5	1. Besame Mucho	Capitol 149

based on "nightingale" aria from the opera "Goyescas"

6/01/44	**5**	10	2. Amor..	Capitol 156

Spanish song, featured in the film "Broadway Rhythm"
above two accompanied by Al Sack's Orchestra

10/21/44	**14**	8	3. What A Diff'rence A Day Made/	
12/30/44	**5**	5	4. I Dream Of You	Capitol 167
12/15/45+	**7**	9	5. I Can't Begin To Tell You	Capitol 221

from the film "The Dolly Sisters"

5/11/46	**4**	12	6. Laughing On The Outside (Crying On The Inside)/	
6/01/46	**10**	5	7. They Say It's Wonderful...........................	Capitol 252

from the Broadway musical "Annie Get Your Gun"

8/17/46	**10**	8	8. Pretending...	Capitol 271

DATE CHARTED	PEAK POS	WKS CHRT'D	ARTIST — Record Title	Label & Number
3/08/47	**4**	10	9. Anniversary Song .... Capitol 368	
			based on the 1880 song "Danube Waves" from the film "The Jolson Story" above eight accompanied by Paul Weston's Orchestra	
3/08/47	**15**	1	10. I'll Close My Eyes .... Capitol 342	
8/02/47	**22**	2	11. Je Vous Aime .... Capitol 417	
			from the film "Copacabana" nearly all from 3-11 accompanied by Paul Weston's Orchestra	
9/25/48	**13**	9	12. Underneath The Arches .... Capitol 15183	
			with Pied Pipers	

CONNIE RUSSELL

1/30/54	**30**	1	1. You've Changed............................ Capitol 2666	
			orchestra directed by Harold Mooney	

JANE RUSSELL
One of Hollywood's most glamorous stars of the 1940s & 50s.

5/08/54	**27**	1	1. Make A Joyful Noise Unto The Lord - Do Lord................................... Coral 61113	
			JANE RUSSELL, CONNIE HAINES, BERYL DAVIS & DELLA RUSSELL, with the Lyn Murray Orchestra	

LUIS RUSSELL & HIS ORCHESTRA
Pianist-jazz band leader born in Panama, played in late 20s with King Oliver; Louis Armstrong took over his band in 1935; died on 12/11/63 (61).

9/15/34	**19**	1	1. Ol' Man River .... Perfect 15995	
			vocal: Sonny Woods; featuring Rex Stewart (cornet) from the Broadway musical "Show Boat"	

BABE RUSSIN
Tenor saxophonist with Red Nichols (1927-32), Roger Wolfe Kahn, Benny Goodman (1937-38), Tommy Dorsey (1938-40), Jimmy Dorsey (1942-43).

RUSSO & FIORITO'S ORIOLE ORCHESTRA
Led by Dan Russo (violin) & Ted Fio Rito (piano)

10/18/24	**10**	1	1. The Little Old Clock On The Mantel .... [I] Brunswick 2637	

DAN RUSSO & HIS ORIOLE ORCHESTRA

5/21/32	**5**	4	1. Goofus.................................... Columbia 2641	
5/28/32	**20**	1	2. Old MacDonald Had A Farm...................... Columbia 2647	

TOMMY RYAN
Sammy Kaye's featured singer from 1938-43 ("Love Walked In", "Dream Valley").

S

AL SACK & HIS ORCHESTRA
Bandleader who accompanied Dinah Shore on some mid-40s hits

9/30/44	**20**	1	1. A Fellow On A Furlough........................... AS 101	

EDGAR SAMPSON
Saxophonist-arranger with Fletcher Henderson (1931-33) & Chick Webb (1933-37), composed & arranged Benny Goodman hits "Stompin' At the Savoy" & "Don't Be That Way"; died on 1/16/73 (65).

FELICIA SANDERS
Vocalist on Percy Faith's #1 hit "Song from Moulin Rouge"

JOE SANDERS & HIS ORCHESTRA
Co-leader of Coon-Sanders Orchestra in 1920s, pianist, singer, & songwriter; died on 5/15/65 (68).

8/01/36	**17**	1	1. These Foolish Things .... Decca 843	

KENNY SARGENT
Popular singer and tenor saxist with Casa Loma Orchestra from 1931-42 ("Under a Blanket of Blue", "You Go to My Head", "Tears from My Inkwell"); died on 12/20/69 (63).

DATE CHARTED	PEAK POS	WKS CHRT'D	ARTIST — Record Title	Label & Number

ANDREA SARTO
Male vocalist who usually recorded under pseudonyms; original member of Columbia Stellar Quartet.

DATE CHARTED	PEAK POS	WKS CHRT'D	ARTIST — Record Title	Label & Number
11/25/11	9	1	1. Spanish Love	Columbia 1031
10/25/13	4	6	2. There's A Girl In The Heart Of Maryland	Columbia 1360
			HENRY BURR & "EDGAR STODDARD" (Sarto)	
8/18/17	6	2	3. The Man Behind The Hammer And The Plow .	Columbia 2271
			as "James Hall"	

RED SAUNDERS & HIS ORCHESTRA
Theodore "Red" Saunders, Chicago-based drummer/vibraphonist who worked with Duke Ellington and Louis Armstrong; in the early 50s the great Joe Williams sang with Saunders before joining Count Basie.

DATE CHARTED	PEAK POS	WKS CHRT'D	ARTIST — Record Title	Label & Number
3/15/52	20	1	1. Hambone..	Okeh 6862
			vocal: Dolores Hawkins & the Hambone Kids	

SAUTER-FINEGAN ORCHESTRA
One of the 1950s' most innovative bands, led by two of the swing era's foremost arrangers: Eddie Sauter, arranger for Red Norvo & Mildred Bailey (1936-39), Benny Goodman (1939-42), Tommy Dorsey, & others; and Bill Finegan, one of Glenn Miller's top arrangers. Their band featured such instruments as piccolo, oboe, & English horn. Sauter arranged in the 1960s for Andre Kostelanetz and Broadway musicals. Eddie died on 4/21/81 (66).

DATE CHARTED	PEAK POS	WKS CHRT'D	ARTIST — Record Title	Label & Number
8/23/52	12	10	1. Doodletown Fifers................................. [I]	RCA Victor 4866
			adaptation of a Civil War song	
12/20/52	13	4	2. Nina Never Knew	RCA Victor 5065
			vocal: Joe Mooney; featuring Kai Winding (trombone)	
1/03/53	29	1	3. Midnight Sleighride .... [I]	RCA Victor 4995
			based on a Prokofiev classical suite	
			Al Klink (tenor sax) & Ralph Burns (piano/celeste) on above three	
8/29/53	20	3	4. The Moon Is Blue....................................	RCA Victor 5359
			vocal: Sally Sweetland; movie title song	
			Doc Severinsen (trumpet) on 2 & 4	

JAN SAVITT & HIS ORCHESTRA
Russian-born, American-raised dance band leader, child prodigy on violin, featured vocalist "Bon Bon" and arranger-pianist Jack Pleis; died on 10/4/48 (35).

DATE CHARTED	PEAK POS	WKS CHRT'D	ARTIST — Record Title	Label & Number
7/23/38	14	2	1. Hi-Yo, Silver	Bluebird 7666
			vocal: Bon Bon	
8/27/38	19	1	2. That's A-Plenty .... [I]	Bluebird 7733
12/10/38	19	2	3. Sugarfoot Stomp................................ [I]	Bluebird 10005
12/16/39	17	2	4. 720 In The Books .... [I]	Decca 2771
			the band's best-known instrumental	
5/11/40	15	3	5. Tuxedo Junction .... [I]	Decca 2989
6/29/40	14	4	6. Where Was I?..	Decca 3153
8/03/40	8	2	7. Make Believe Island	Decca 3188
			vocal: Bon Bon	
7/05/41	20	1	8. The Things I Love....................................	Victor 27403
			vocals on 5 & 7: Alan DeWitt	

PRIMO SCALA & HIS BANJO & ACCORDION ORCHESTRA WITH THE KEYNOTES
British band (all vocals by the Keynotes).

DATE CHARTED	PEAK POS	WKS CHRT'D	ARTIST — Record Title	Label & Number
8/14/48	6	16	1. Underneath The Arches............................	London 238
1/01/49	24	1	2. Jingle Bells/ [X]	
1/08/49	27	1	3. The Mistletoe Kiss .... [X]	London 302
3/12/49	27	1	4. Cruising Down The River..........................	London 356

WALTER SCANLAN
Pseudonym for Walter Van Brunt

HYMIE SCHERTZER
Alto saxophonist with Benny Goodman (1935-39, 1942-44) and Tommy Dorsey (1939-40), later in Johnny Carson's "Tonight Show" band.

DATE CHARTED	PEAK POS	WKS CHRT'D	ARTIST — Record Title	Label & Number

VIC SCHOEN
Arranger-conductor on nearly all Andrews Sisters records, also for Patti Page & the Weavers.

ADRIAN SCHUBERT & HIS SALON ORCHESTRA
Musical director of minor 1920s labels (Banner, Domino, Crown), made hundreds of band records

5/12/28	**20**	1	1. Mississippi Sweetheart............................ Banner 7012 vocal: Frank Luther	

ERNESTINE SCHUMANN-HEINK
Famous German-born contralto, with the Hamburg opera (1883-98), then long stay with the New York Metropolitan Opera (1899-1932); died on 11/17/36 (75).

5/30/08	**8**	1	1. The Rosary.. Victor 88108	
12/26/08	**6**	1	2. Stille Nacht, Helige Nacht (Silent Night, Holy Night).........................[F-X] Victor 88138	
1/19/18	**5**	4	3. Danny Boy .... Victor 88592 adaptation of the traditional Irish folk song "Londonberry Air"	

VOICES OF WALTER SCHUMANN
Choral group

11/14/53	**26**	3	1. I See The Moon...................................... RCA Victor 5478	

SONNY SCHUYLER
Sang with George Hall (1934-36), Abe Lyman (1936-37), Vincent Lopez (1939-43); became an important composer under the name Sunny Skylar: "Besame Mucho", "Amor", "You're Breaking My Heart".

ARTHUR SCHWARTZ
Great popular composer who collaborated with lyricist Howard Dietz on such enduring standards as "Dancing In the Dark", "Alone Together", and "That's Entertainment".

12/03/32	**10**	4	1. Louisiana Hayride.............................. Victor 24157 LEO REISMAN & HIS ORCHESTRA vocals by Arthur Schwartz & the Eva Jessye Choir from the Broadway musical "Flying Colors"	

GEORGE SCHWEINFEST
Flutist, violinist and band pianist, one of the first musicians to make commercial records (from 1889 on North American), played in Columbia orchestras until 1915. He died on 6/8/49 (87).

8/14/97	**2(1)**	3	1. Departure From The Mountains............... [I] New Jersey	

RAYMOND SCOTT & HIS ORCHESTRA
Pianist-arranger-composer, born Harry Warnow, later musical director for CBS Radio, replaced his late brother Mark Warnow as conductor of "Hit Parade" on 1950s TV.

4/24/37	**11**	9	1. Twilight In Turkey .... [I] Master 108	
5/08/37	**17**	3	2. The Toy Trumpet.............................. [I] Master 111	
8/07/37	**7**	12	3. Dinner Music For A Pack Of Hungry Cannibals .... [I] Master 136	
4/30/38	**15**	2	4. The Toy Trumpet.............................. [I-R] Brunswick 7993 reissue of Master 111 above four: RAYMOND SCOTT QUINTETTE	
9/21/40	**12**	3	5. Huckleberry Duck................................. [I] Columbia 35363	
8/01/42	**21**	1	6. Secret Agent.. [I] Decca 18377 above two: RAYMOND SCOTT & HIS NEW ORCHESTRA	

ANTONIO SCOTTI
Italian baritone who sang with the New York Metropolitan longer than anybody else, 34 years (1889-1933); died on 2/26/36 (70).

6/30/06	**2(1)**	6	1. La Forza Del Destino - Solenne In Quest' Ora (Swear In This Hour) .... [F] Victor 89001 ENRICO CARUSO & ANTONIO SCOTTI	
8/29/08	**4**	2	2. La Boheme: Quartetto .... [F] Victor 96002 ENRICO CARUSO, GERALDINE FARRAR, ANTONIO SCOTTI, & GINA VIAFORA	
8/13/10	**9**	1	3. Contes D' Hoffman - Barcolle, "Belle Nuit" (Oh, Night Of Love") .... [F] Victor 87502 GERALDINE FARRAR & ANTONIO SCOTTI	

DATE CHARTED	PEAK POS	WKS CHRT'D	ARTIST — Record Title	Label & Number
9/24/10	6	3	4. Madama Butterfly - Duet, Act I: "Amore Ogrillo" (Love Or Fancy?)...............[F] ENRICO CARUSO & ANTONIO SCOTTI	Victor 89043

OSCAR SEAGLE
American concert baritone; died on 12/19/45 (68).

DATE CHARTED	PEAK POS	WKS CHRT'D	ARTIST — Record Title	Label & Number
2/23/18	4	3	1. There's A Long, Long Trail........................	Columbia 245
3/02/18	4	3	2. Calling Me Home To You	Columbia 2452
5/11/18	4	3	3. Pack Up Your Troubles In Your Old Kit Bag...	Columbia 6028
2/08/19	8	2	4. The Old Folks At Home............................	Columbia 6082
			1, 3-4: OSCAR SEAGLE & COLUMBIA STELLAR QUARTETTE	

BLOSSOM SEELEY
Energetic singer-dancer in vaudeville and on Broadway, married first to Hall of Fame pitcher Rube Marquard, then to entertainer Lew Fields (the 1952 movie "Somebody Loves Me" was based on their lives); died on 4/17/74 (82).

DATE CHARTED	PEAK POS	WKS CHRT'D	ARTIST — Record Title	Label & Number
2/24/23	5	3	1. Way Down Yonder In New Orleans	Columbia 3731
7/26/24	9	1	2. Lazy/	
8/23/24	8	1	3. Don't Mind The Rain	Columbia 114
			above two accompanied by the Georgians	
10/04/24	10	1	4. Bringin' Home The Bacon..........................	Columbia 136
5/16/25	2(1)	7	5. Alabamy Bound.....................................	Columbia 304
9/12/25	2(2)	6	6. Yes Sir, That's My Baby	Columbia 386
8/07/26	10	1	7. Spanish Shawl......................................	Columbia 613

TOSCHA SEIDEL
Russian-born violinist, made his American debut in 1918; died on 11/15/62 (62).

DATE CHARTED	PEAK POS	WKS CHRT'D	ARTIST — Record Title	Label & Number
5/17/41	12	2	1. Intermezzo (Hungarian Dance No. 1).........[I]	Victor 4458

BEN SELVIN & HIS ORCHESTRA
No other bandleader made more recordings than Ben Selvin, the violinist whose 2,000-plus records included many with jazz stars such as Benny Goodman and Tommy & Jimmy Dorsey. Ben died on 7/15/80 (82). (also see Irving Kaufman, Kate Smith, Ethel Waters).

DATE CHARTED	PEAK POS	WKS CHRT'D	ARTIST — Record Title	Label & Number
10/18/19	1(4)	11	1. **I'm Forever Blowing Bubbles**................[I] most 1919-21 records listed as "Selvin's Novelty Orchestra"	Victor 18603
12/20/19+	5	3	2. Mandy ....[I] introduced by "A Pretty Girl Is Like a Melody"; "Mandy" from the Broadway musicals "Yip, Yip, Yaphank" & "Ziegfeld Follies of 1919"	Victor 18614
1/24/20	1(13)	24	● 3. **Dardanella**/ [I] the first record to sell more than five million copies also recorded for Paramount 20001	
2/14/20	4	6	4. My Isle Of Golden Dreams ....[I] also recorded for Paramount 20002	Victor 18633
4/24/20	13	1	5. In Your Arms...	Victor 18650
6/05/20	4	4	6. Afghanistan.......................................[I] also recorded for Paramount 20007	Okeh 4087
7/24/20	9	1	7. Venetian Moon ....[I]	Paramount 20007
9/25/20	5	3	8. Wond'ring ....[I]	Victor 18682
12/25/20	14	1	9. Dance-O-Mania ....[I]	Victor 18699
1/29/21	15	1	10. The Japanese Sandman ....[I]	Lyric 4229
4/02/21	9	1	11. Now And Then ....[I] also recorded for Vocalion 14128	Emerson 10315
6/25/21	11	1	12. Make Believe	Vocalion 14169
7/23/21	5	2	13. Cherie ....[I] introduced by "I'm Nobody's Baby"	Vocalion 14182
9/24/21	14	1	14. All By Myself .... vocal: Ernest Hare	Arto 9067
12/17/21	6	3	15. Say It With Music ....[I] from the Broadway musical "Music Box Revue"	Vocalion 14239
2/11/22	7	3	16. Love Will Find A Way ....[I] from the Broadway musical "Shuffle Along"	Brunswick 2144
5/27/22	7	3	17. Angel Child ....[I] from the Broadway musical "Spice of 1922"	Brunswick 2249

DATE CHARTED	PEAK POS	WKS CHRT'D	ARTIST — Record Title	Label & Number
8/12/22	**6**	3	18. Romany Love.. [I]	Brunswick 2273
11/11/22	**5**	5	19. Chicago .... [I]	Banner 1104
1/27/23	**8**	1	20. I'll Build A Stairway To Paradise .... [I] from "George White's Scandals of 1922"	Vocalion 14434
3/24/23	**8**	1	21. Three O'Clock In The Morning..................... from Broadway's "Greenwich Village Follies of 1921"	Vocalion 14488
6/30/23	**12**	1	22. Wonderful One .... [I]	Vocalion 14508
9/01/23	**1(2)**	12	23. **Yes! We Have No Bananas** .... [N] vocal: Irving Kaufman	Vocalion 14590
9/29/23	**2(2)**	9	24. Indiana Moon .... [I]	Vocalion 14621
12/29/23	**12**	1	25. Dirty Hands! Dirty Face! .... [I]	Vocalion 14660
1/26/24	**9**	1	26. Sleep... [I]	Vocalion 14695
1/26/24	**11**	1	27. So This Is Love .... [I] from the Broadway musical "Little Miss Bluebeard"	Vocalion 14690
3/29/24	**5**	3	28. Take, Oh Take, Those Lips Away.............. [I]	Vocalion 14723
9/27/24	**13**	1	29. Jealous .... [I]	Vocalion 14798
2/28/25+	**9**	2	30. Honest And Truly .... [I] also recorded for Vocalion 14932	Columbia 224
2/28/25	**11**	1	31. All Alone .... [I] from Broadway's "Music Box Revue of 1923"	Columbia 235
6/13/25	**7**	2	32. Will You Remember Me? .... [I]	Vocalion 14981
8/29/25	**11**	1	33. The Original Charleston........................ [I]	Columbia 355
8/29/25	**13**	1	34. Let It Rain, Let It Pour .... vocal: Irving Kaufman	Vocalion 15003
9/19/25	**1(3)**	12	35. **Oh, How I Miss You Tonight** .... [I] 30-31 & 35 listed as "Cavaliers"	Columbia 359
10/24/25	**1(4)**	10	36. **Manhattan/** [I]	
11/14/25	**2(2)**	6	37. Sentimental Me .... [I] above two from the Broadway musical "The Garrick Gaieties" 33, 36 & 37 listed as "Knickerbockers"	Columbia 422
10/31/25	**11**	1	38. I'm Tired Of Everything But You.............. [I] also recorded for Harmony 7-H	Vocalion 15049
12/26/25	**12**	1	39. Brown Eyes, Why Are You Blue? .... [I]	Vocalion 15110
3/27/26	**11**	1	40. Sleepy-Time Gal	Vocalion 15154
6/19/26	**4**	5	41. A Night Of Love................................... [I]	Columbia 597
7/24/26	**3**	6	42. Valencia.. also recorded for Banner 1749	Brunswick 3172
7/24/26	**10**	1	43. Tamiani Trail....................................	Vocalion 15277
9/18/26	**10**	1	44. Only You And Lonely Me...................... vocal: Keller Sisters & Lynch	Vocalion 15365
10/23/26	**6**	3	45. Baby Face	Brunswick 3253
10/30/26	**5**	4	46. Am I Wasting My Time On You? .... vocal: Franklyn Baur	Columbia 703
11/13/26	**3**	5	47. Barcelona....................................... vocals on 42 & 47: Irving Kaufman	Brunswick 3284
1/15/27	**17**	2	48. That's A Good Girl .... vocals on 40, 44 & 48: Ben Selvin	Brunswick 3340
1/29/27	**4**	6	49. In A Little Spanish Town .... 41, 45 & 49 listed as "Cavaliers"	Columbia 805
4/09/27	**1(2)**	9	50. **Blue Skies** .... from the Broadway musical "Betsy"	Columbia 860
5/21/27	**4**	6	51. Rio Rita .... vocal: Charles Kaley; Broadway musical title song	Columbia 893
6/25/27	**17**	1	52. I Found A Million-Dollar Baby (In A Five-And- Ten-Cent Store)	Columbia 870
10/22/27	**8**	5	53. Miss Annabelle Lee .... vocal by Irving Kaufman above four listed as "Knickerbockers"	Columbia 1088
12/10/27	**17**	1	54. Ooh! Maybe It's You .... vocal: Franklyn Baur; from the "Ziegfeld Follies of 1927"	Brunswick 3639
1/14/28	**16**	2	55. Wherever You Are .... from the Broadway musical "Sidewalks of New York"	Columbia 1133

DATE CHARTED	PEAK POS	WKS CHRT'D	ARTIST — Record Title	Label & Number
1/21/28	**8**	7	56. My Heart Stood Still/	
2/18/28	**10**	4	57. Thou Swell .... Columbia 1187	
			above two from the Broadway musical "A Connecticut Yankee"	
1/28/28	**3**	10	58. Among My Souvenirs........................ Columbia 1188	
2/11/28	**17**	2	59. Thinking Of You .... Columbia 1164	
			from the Broadway musical "The Five O'Clock Girl"	
			56-57 & 59 listed as "Broadway Nitelites"	
6/30/28	**13**	3	60. My Stormy Weather Pal .... Columbia 1331	
			as "Cavaliers"	
8/04/28	**19**	1	61. Indian Cradle Song........................ Columbia 1399	
			vocal: Lewis James	
9/01/28	**2(1)**	14	62. I Can't Give You Anything But Love/	
10/27/28	**10**	4	63. I Must Have That Man!........................ Columbia 1424	
			above two from the Broadway musical "Blackbirds of 1928"	
11/10/28	**6**	5	64. Jeannine, I Dream Of Lilac Time .... Columbia 1512	
			from the silent film "Lilac Time"	
12/01/28	**12**	3	65. Masquerade .... Columbia 1557	
12/15/28+	**2(1)**	9	66. You're The Cream In My Coffee .... Columbia 1604	
			vocal: Jack Palmer	
			from the Broadway musical "Hold Everything"	
12/29/28+	**13**	2	67. Happy Days And Lonely Nights .... Columbia 1596	
			62-63, 65 & 67 listed as "Knickerbockers"	
1/05/29	**8**	4	68. I Wanna Be Loved By You .... Columbia 1604	
			from the Broadway musical "Good Boy"	
			Vaughn DeLeath: vocals on 62-63 & 68	
1/12/29	**9**	5	69. Pompanola .... Columbia 1622	
			vocal: Larry Murphy	
			from the Broadway musical "Three Cheers"	
2/16/29	**10**	5	70. A Room With A View........................ Columbia 1693	
			from the Broadway musical "This Year of Grace"	
3/09/29	**5**	7	71. Carolina Moon........................ Columbia 1719	
4/20/29	**3**	10	72. Broadway Melody/	
5/04/29	**13**	3	73. You Were Meant For Me........................ Columbia 1738	
			above two from the film "Broadway Melody"	
6/01/29	**2(1)**	10	74. My Sin/	
6/01/29	**10**	4	75. Honey........................ Columbia 1800	
9/07/29	**8**	4	76. My Song Of The Nile/	
			from the film "The Drag"	
10/05/29	**17**	1	77. Am I Blue? .... Columbia 1900	
			from the film "On With the Show"	
11/23/29	**10**	4	78. Love, Your Spell Is Everywhere .... Columbia 1994	
			above three vocals: Smith Ballew	
2/15/30	**10**	2	79. Funny, Dear, What Love Can Do........ Columbia 2096	
3/01/30	**1(2)**	7	80. **Happy Days Are Here Again** .... Columbia 2116	
			from the film "Chasing Rainbows"	
			became President Franklin D. Roosevelt's theme song	
6/07/30	**1(3)**	11	81. **When It's Springtime In The Rockies/**	
6/14/30	**5**	10	82. Dancing With Tears In My Eyes........ Columbia 2206	
			Ruth Etting, vocal	
7/19/30	**18**	2	83. Around The Corner .... Columbia 2221	
8/30/30	**10**	6	84. Somewhere In Old Wyoming/	
9/06/30	**7**	10	85. Moonlight On The Colorado .... Columbia 2266	
10/04/30	**8**	8	86. When The Organ Played At Twilight........ Columbia 2279	
1/17/31	**14**	2	87. Yours And Mine........................ Columbia 2366	
			vocals on 83 & 87: Smith Ballew	
4/11/31	**14**	2	88. Smile, Darn Ya, Smile........................ Columbia 2421	
			vocal: Joe & Don Mooney	
7/11/31	**10**	4	89. Dancing In The Dark .... Columbia 2473	
			from the Broadway musical "The Band Wagon"	
			also recorded for Harmony 1334	
7/18/31	**20**	1	90. Just One More Chance........................ Columbia 2487	
			with Bunny Berigan (trumpet)	
9/05/31	**8**	3	91. Slow But Sure .... Columbia 2502	

DATE CHARTED	PEAK POS	WKS CHRT'D	ARTIST — Record Title	Label & Number
11/14/31	9	5	92. Call Me Darling (Call Me Sweetheart, Call Me Dear)............. listed as "Cavaliers"	Columbia 2555
1/09/32	17	2	93. Now's The Time To Fall In Love .... from the film "Palmy Days" Benny Goodman (clarinet) on above six	Columbia 2575
1/23/32	12	3	94. Goodnight, Moon .... also recorded for Okeh 41545 Dick Robertson: vocals on 90-91 & 93-94	Columbia 2592
2/06/32	19	1	95. All Of Me..................................... Tommy Dorsey (trombone) & Manny Klein (trumpet) on vast majority of sides recorded from 1929-31	Columbia 2585
2/13/32	8	4	96. Of Thee I Sing .... Broadway musical title song 91 & 96 listed as "Knickerbockers"	Columbia 2598
2/20/32	12	2	97. You're My Everything......................... from the Broadway musical "The Laugh Parade"	Columbia 2596
3/12/32	15	2	98. Auf Wiedersehen, My Dear .... listed as "Mickey Alpert"; also recorded for Okeh 41545	Columbia 2614
4/02/32	14	2	99. Just Friends	Columbia 2618
6/25/32	10	3	100. Is I In Love? I Is......................	Columbia 2661
7/09/32	12	3	101. (I've Got The Words-I've Got The Tune) Hummin' To Myself......................	Columbia 2669
1/21/33	5	5	102. Street Of Dreams	Columbia 2734
6/17/33	8	6	103. Sweetheart Darlin'	Columbia 2778
10/21/33	14	4	104. Dinner At Eight .... movie title song	Columbia 2813
7/21/34	9	6	105. The Prize Waltz.......................	Columbia 2965
7/28/34	2(1)	8	106. I Only Have Eyes For You/ from the film "Dames"	
8/04/34	16	2	107. Born To Be Kissed .... above two vocals: Howard Phillips	Columbia 2966

SEVEN DWARFS

2/12/38	2(1)	13	1. Whistle While You Work	Victor 25736
2/12/38	3	12	2. Heigh Ho .... above two from the soundtrack of the animated film "Snow White and The Seven Dwarfs"	Victor 25735

DOC SEVERINSEN
Before his long reign as leader of Johnny Carson's "Tonight Show" band, Doc played trumpet for Charlie Barnet (1947-49), Tommy Dorsey (1949-50), & Sauter-Finegan (1952-53) bands. (also see Anita O'Day)

TERRY SHAND & HIS ORCHESTRA
Pianist-singer with Freddy Martin (1933-38), co-wrote several hit songs ("I Double Dare You", "Cry, Baby, Cry")

8/03/40	16	1	1. I Can't Love You Any More (Any More Than I Do)................. vocal: Terry Shand	Decca 3127

SHANNON FOUR
Original members Charles Hart & Harvey Hindermyer (tenors), baritone Elliott Shaw, & bass Wilfred Glenn. In 1918 Lewis James replaced Hindermyer; by 1926, the group was transformed into the Revelers.

10/20/17	9	1	1. I May Be Gone For A Long, Long Time......... also recorded for Edison Amberol 3319 from the Broadway musical "Hitchy-Koo" flip side of #1 classic "Over There" by the American Quartet	Victor 18333
12/15/17	6	2	2. Break The News To Mother........................	Victor 18358
1/12/18	6	2	3. Melody Land	Victor 18400
3/16/18	5	3	4. Hail! Hail! The Gang's All Here .... uses melody of a song from "Pirates of Penzance", in turn based on "Anvil Chorus"	Victor 18414
3/30/18	4	4	5. Sweet Little Buttercup............................. ELIZABETH SPENCER & SHANNON FOUR	Victor 18427

DATE CHARTED	PEAK POS	WKS CHRT'D	ARTIST — Record Title	Label & Number
5/25/18	**6**	2	6. A Little Bit Of Sunshine	Victor 18453
8/03/18	**8**	1	7. What Are You Going To Do To Help The Boys?	Victor 18467
10/12/18	**9**	1	8. Good-Bye, Mother Machree HARRY MACDONOUGH & SHANNON FOUR	Victor 18488
11/01/19	**4**	6	9. Mandy from the Broadway musicals "Yip, Yip, Yaphank" & "Ziegfeld Follies of 1919"	Victor 18605
9/11/20	**8**	2	10. Wond'ring	Brunswick 2039
5/26/23	**14**	1	11. Kentucky Babe	Victor 19013
7/19/24	**8**	1	12. Oh Susanna WENDELL HALL & SHANNON FOUR	Victor 19290
2/28/25	**13**	1	13. I Want To Be Happy from the Broadway musical "No, No, Nanette"	Columbia 222
11/07/25	**7**	2	14. Save Your Sorrow (For Tomorrow)	Columbia 404

CHARLIE SHAVERS

Down Beat poll-winning trumpet star with John Kirby (1937-44), Tommy Dorsey (1945-49), remained active until his death on 7/8/71 (53).

ARTIE SHAW & HIS ORCHESTRA

Rivaled only by Benny Goodman as the greatest clarinetist of the swing era, Artie was born Arthur Arshawsky on 5/23/10 in New York City. He played with Irving Aaronson, Red Nichols, Vincent Lopez, & Roger Wolfe Kahn before forming his own band in 1936. Fueled by Jerry Gray's arrangements, singer Helen Forrest, and featured soloists (in addition to Artie) Tony Pastor & George Auld (tenor saxes), the band was one of the nation's hottest by late 1938. A year later Artie abruptly left music, but his 1940 return from Mexico led to even greater success with imaginative full-band arrangements with strings, and jazz combo recordings with his "Gramercy Five". He married eight times, including movie stars Lana Turner & Ava Gardner; later became a theatrical producer, and in the 80s began fronting a new band. (also see Gordon Jenkins).

DATE CHARTED	PEAK POS	WKS CHRT'D	ARTIST — Record Title	Label & Number
12/12/36	**10**	4	1. There's Frost On The Moon	Brunswick 7771
1/02/37	**11**	6	2. Love And Learn from the film "That Girl from Paris"	Brunswick 7787
3/27/37	**20**	1	3. Love Is Good For Anything That Ails You from the film "The Hit Parade" above three vocals: Peg LaCentra Buddy Morrow (trombone) on above two	Brunswick 7841
6/26/37	**15**	3	4. All God's Chillun Got Rhythm from the film "A Day at the Races"	Brunswick 7895
11/20/37	**13**	3	5. Free Wheeling vocal: Leo Watson	Brunswick 7976
2/19/38	**15**	3	6. One Song from the animated film "Snow White and the Seven Dwarfs"	Brunswick 8050
2/26/38	**2(1)**	13	7. Goodnight, Angel from the film "Radio City Revels" above two vocals: Nita Bradley	Brunswick 8054
8/20/38	**6**	8	8. Indian Love Call/ from the Broadway musical "Rose Marie" vocals on 4 & 8: Tony Pastor	
9/03/38	**1(6)**	18	● 9. **Begin The Beguine** [I] Billboard Disc jockey poll voted this the #3 all-time record and #5 all-time song, featuring Artie's most famous solo; from the Broadway musical "Jubilee"	Bluebird 7746
9/24/38	**8**	6	10. Back Bay Shuffle [I]	Bluebird 7759
11/12/38	**7**	7	11. Nightmare [I] Artie's famous theme (original composition)	Bluebird 7875
11/19/38	**10**	1	12. I Have Eyes from the film "Paris Honeymoon"	Bluebird 7889
11/26/38	**14**	2	13. The Blues [I] recorded on 8/4/37; from William Grant Still's "Lenox Avenue Suite"	Vocalion 4401
12/03/38	**12**	1	14. Let 'Er Go [I] recorded 10/18/37	Brunswick 7986
12/10/38	**3**	13	15. Deep In A Dream	Bluebird 10046
12/31/38+	**1(2)**	8	16. **They Say**	Bluebird 10075

DATE CHARTED	PEAK POS	WKS CHRT'D	ARTIST — Record Title	Label & Number
1/07/39	1(1)	8	17. **Thanks For Ev'rything/** movie title song	
1/28/39	13	3	18. Between A Kiss And A Sigh........................ Bluebird 10055 Helen Forrest: vocals on 12 & 15-18	
2/04/39	15	1	19. Jungle Drums .... [I] Bluebird 10091	
2/11/39	15	1	20. What Is This Thing Called Love? .... [I] Bluebird 10001 from the Broadway musical "Wake Up and Dream"	
2/25/39	12	2	21. Artie Shaw Album .... Bluebird 10124 (Bill / Carioca); 10125 (My Heart Stood Still / Donkey Serenade); 10126 (Lover Come Back to Me / Rosalie); 10127 (Zigeuner / Supper Time); 10128 (The Man I Love / Vilia)	
3/04/39	15	1	22. Delightful Delirium .... Bluebird 10134	
4/08/39	12	1	23. Pastel Blue/ [I]	
4/15/39	17	1	24. Deep Purple.. Bluebird 10178	
5/27/39	15	3	25. You Grow Sweeter As The Years Go By........ Bluebird 10195	
7/01/39	4	12	26. I Poured My Heart Into A Song/	
7/01/39	6	1	27. When Winter Comes............................... Bluebird 10307 above two from the film "Second Fiddle" vocals on 22 & 27: Tony Pastor	
8/05/39	4	10	28. Comes Love .... Bluebird 10324 from the Broadway musical "Yokel Boy" Helen Forrest: vocals on 24-26 & 28	
9/09/39	9	6	29. Traffic Jam .... [I] Bluebird 10385 one of the band's most renowned jazz instrumentals	
9/30/39	8	4	30. Melancholy Mood.................................... Bluebird 10334	
9/30/39	11	7	31. Day In-Day Out.................................... Bluebird 10406	
11/11/39	11	5	32. Many Dreams Ago.................................. Bluebird 10446	
1/13/40	8	8	33. All The Things You Are .... Bluebird 10492 from the Broadway musical "Very Warm for May" Helen Forest: above four vocals Tony Pastor (tenor sax) on all above records Buddy Rich (drums) on 21-33	
7/27/40	1(13)	30	● 34. **Frensei/** [I]	
9/14/40	18	1	35. Adios, Marquita Linda .... [I] Victor 26542 vocal: Anita Boyer; above two both Mexican songs	
11/30/40	25	1	36. An Old, Old Castle In Scotland .... Victor 26760	
1/11/41	10	7	● 37. Summit Ridge Drive .... [I] Victor 26763 voted the #8 all-time record in Billboard disc jockey poll	
1/18/41	2(1)	11	38. Star Dust .... [I] Victor 27230 voted the greatest record and the greatest song of all time in Billboard disc jockey polls; solos by Billy Butterfield (trumpet), Artie, & Jack Jenney (trombone)	
2/08/41	10	6	39. Concerto For Clarinet........................... [I] Victor 36383 featured solo by Artie; from the film "Second Chorus"	
3/08/41	9	3	● 40. Dancing In The Dark/ [I] from the Broadway musical "The Band Wagon"	
3/15/41	24	1	41. Smoke Gets In Your Eyes..................... [I] Victor 27335 from the Broadway musical "Roberta" 37 & 41: ARTIE SHAW & GRAMERCY FIVE	
10/25/41	22	1	42. It Had To Be You .... [I] Victor 27536 Billy Butterfield (trumpet) on above six	
11/29/41	10	2	43. Blues In The Night .... Victor 27609 movie title song	
2/21/42	20	2	44. Begin The Beguine.............................. [I-R] Bluebird 7746	
8/08/42	18	1	45. St. James' Infirmary.............................. Victor 27895 vocals on 43 & 45: Hot Lips Page (also trumpet) Ray Conniff (trombone) on 39-43 & 45	
1/01/44	21	1	46. Temptation.. [I] Victor 27230 recorded 9/7/40; from the film "Going Hollywood"	
3/25/44	25	1	47. Dancing In The Dark .... [I-R] Victor 1544 reissue of Victor 27335	
4/15/44	29	1	48. Summit Ridge Drive .... [I-R] Victor 26763	
9/09/44	10	4	49. It Had To Be You .... [I-R] Victor 1593 reissue of Victor 27536	

DATE CHARTED	PEAK POS	WKS CHRT'D	ARTIST — Record Title	Label & Number
1/20/45	**5**	7	50. Ac-cent-tchu-ate The Positive .... Victor 1612 vocal: Imogene Lynn from the film "Here Come the Waves" with Roy Eldridge (trumpet) & Barney Kessel (guitar)	
7/20/46	**17**	1	51. I Got The Sun In The Morning .... Musicraft 365 Mel Torme, vocal from the Broadway musical "Annie Get Your Gun"	
10/12/46	**22**	3	52. My Heart Belongs To Daddy .... Musicraft 392 vocal by Kitty Kallen from the Broadway musical "Leave It To Me!"	
7/22/50	**10**	11	53. Count Every Star .... Decca 27042 DICK HAYMES with ARTIE SHAW & HIS ORCHESTRA	
11/22/52	**25**	2	54. My Little Nest Of Heavenly Blue .... Decca 28377 CONNEE BOSWELL with ARTIE SHAW & HIS GRAMERCY FIVE from the Broadway operetta "Frasquito" featured in the film "Rich, Young, and Pretty"	

ELLIOTT SHAW
Baritone who sang with Shannon Four and the Revelers.
(also see Nat Shilkret, Paul Whiteman)

4/01/22	**3**	6	1. Ka-Lu-A .... Victor 18854 from the Broadway musical "Good Morning, Dearie" "EDNA BROWN" (Elsie Baker) & ELLIOTT SHAW	
6/07/24	**10**	1	2. Days Of Yesterday .... Victor 19268	

GEORGIE SHAW

1/23/54	**7**	14	1. Till We Two Are One .... Decca 28937	
8/28/54	**29**	1	2. Someone Else's Love Song......................... Decca 29160 above two with Jimmy Leyden's Orchestra & Chorus	

DOROTHY SHAY
Known as "The Park Avenue Hillbilly"

7/12/47	**4**	11	1. Feudin' And Fightin' .... Columbia 37189 accompanied by Mischa Russell's Orchestra from the Broadway musical "Laffing Room Only"	

GEORGE SHEARING QUINTET
Blind British pianist who earned wide jazz reputation by 1950, and
in the 1970s & 80s collaborated with Mel Torme on a series of
award-winning albums.

5/28/49	**25**	1	1. September In The Rain .... [I] MGM 30250 international million-seller; from the film "Melody for Two"	

ANNE SHELTON
Popular British singer

1/01/49	**25**	3	1. Be Mine .... London 239	
2/05/49	**27**	2	2. Galway Bay .... London 287 with the Wardour Singers both accompanied by Roy Robertson's Orchestra	

BURT SHEPARD
English comedian who had reported international million-seller in
1910 with new Zon-o-Phone recording of George Washington Johnson's
famous "Laughing Song".

JEAN SHEPARD

9/05/53	**4**	10	1. A Dear John Letter .... Capitol 2502	
10/17/53	**24**	1	2. Forgive Me, John .... Capitol 2586 with narration by Ferlin Husky	

SHORTY SHERLOCK
Featured on trumpet with Ben Pollack, Jimmy Dorsey (1937-39), Bob
Crosby, Gene Krupa (1940-41), Tommy Dorsey (1941).

BOBBY SHERWOOD & HIS ORCHESTRA
Versatile musician who played guitar for Bing Crosby & Artie Shaw
(1940), and trumpet & trombone in his own band. Bobby died on
1/23/80 (66). (also see Judy Garland)

10/12/46	**11**	1	1. Sherwood's Forest .... [I] Capitol 286 band includes Sherwood & Manny Klein (trumpet), Herbie Haymer & Dave Cavanaugh (tenor sax)	

DATE CHARTED	PEAK POS	WKS CHRT'D	ARTIST — Record Title	Label & Number
			LEW SHERWOOD Eddy Duchin's featured singer ("Let's Fall in Love", "Cheek to Cheek", "Pennies from Heaven") from 1933-41, also on trumpet.	
			JACK SHILKRET & HIS ORCHESTRA Pianist-bandleader, brother of Nat Shilkret; died on 6/16/64 (67).	
9/05/25	8	1	1. If You Knew Susie (Like I Know Susie)......... Billy Murray, vocal; from the Broadway musical "Big Boy"	Victor 19675
4/24/26	10	1	2. Here In My Arms .... [I] from the Broadway musical "Dearest Enemy"	Victor 19868
			NAT SHILKRET & THE VICTOR ORCHESTRA Former classical clarinetist with New York Philharmonic, played in John Philip Sousa's and other concert bands; served as Victor's Director of Light Music from 1915-45, and led orchestral accompaniment for many Victor artists during these years.	
11/22/24	7	3	1. Tell Me You'll Forgive Me/	
11/29/24	11	1	2. Charley, My Boy .... Billy Murray, vocal	Victor 19416
1/24/25	7	2	3. June Brought The Roses........................ [I] listed as "Troubadors"	Victor 19458
7/25/25	10	1	4. Let It Rain, Let It Pour .... Vernon Dalhart, vocal 1-2 & 4: INTERNATIONAL NOVELTY ORCHESTRA	Victor 19624
5/21/26+	8	5	5. Rio Rita .... vocal: Lewis James; Broadway musical title song	Victor 20474
11/27/26	6	3	6. On The Riviera .... vocal: Carl Mathieu	Victor 20113
1/08/27	2(2)	7	7. All Alone Monday .... Johnny Marvin, vocal from the Broadway musical "The Ramblers"	Victor 20259
2/26/27	4	7	8. One Alone/ [I]	
3/05/27	9	5	9. The Riff Song................................... the Revelers, vocal above two from the Broadway musical "The Desert Song"	Victor 20373
3/19/27	12	3	10. Maybe... from the Broadway musical "Oh, Kay!"	Victor 20392
4/23/27	5	7	11. I Know That You Know.................... from the Broadway musical "Oh, Please!"	Victor 20437
4/23/27	6	5	12. Flapperette... [I]	Victor 20429
5/07/27	8	6	13. When Day Is Done .... [I]	Victor 20456
5/28/27	10	4	14. What Does It Matter Now?....................... vocal: Elliott Shaw	Victor 20471
6/11/27	6	6	15. The Doll Dance .... [I]	Victor 20503
7/02/27	3	7	16. Hallelujah!....................................... from the Broadway musical "Hit the Deck" flip side: "Sometimes I'm Happy" (POS 5) by Roger Wolfe Kahn & His Orchestra	Victor 20599
7/02/27	19	1	17. The Desert Song .... accompanied by Mischa Russell & His Orchestra from the film "The Affairs of Bel Ami"	Columbia 37213
8/13/27	5	7	18. Me And My Shadow..............................	Victor 20675
10/15/27	7	4	19. It's A Million To One You're In Love............	Victor 20837
12/10/27	9	5	20. Paree! (Ca C'est Paris).............................. INTERNATIONAL NOVELTY ORCHESTRA vocals on 11, 16 & 19-20: Franklyn Baur	Victor 20884
12/24/27	13	2	21. Baby's Blue .... Johnny Marvin, vocals on 18 & 21	Victor 20882
12/31/27+	2(3)	8	22. Diane (I'm In Heaven When I See You Smile) .. listed as "Troubadors" vocal: Franklyn Baur, Lewis James & Elliott Shaw	Victor
1/07/28	5	6	23. Thinking Of You/	
1/14/28	13	2	24. Up In The Clouds.................................... above two from the Broadway musical "The Five O'Clock Girl"	Victor 20996
2/25/28	5	6	25. Did You Mean It?......................................	Victor 21105
3/24/28	16	2	26. Dawn... above four vocals: Lewis James	Victor 21097

DATE CHARTED	PEAK POS	WKS CHRT'D	ARTIST — Record Title	Label & Number
6/02/28	**9**	4	27. Why Do I Love You?.. Victor 21215 from the Broadway musical "Show Boat"	
7/28/28	**20**	1	28. Without You, Sweetheart .... Victor 21259 vocal: Johnny Marvin	
8/18/28	**2(1)**	7	29. The Sidewalks Of New York .... Victor 21493 vocal: Lewis James; revived as the theme song of New York Governor Al Smith's presidential campaign	
8/25/28	**14**	2	30. Dream House .... Victor 21392 vocal: Scrappy Lambert	
9/15/28	**2(3)**	8	31. Jeannine (I Dream Of Lilac Time)................. Victor 21572 from the silent film "Lilac Time"	
9/22/28	**10**	3	32. Dusky Stevedore .... Victor 21515 vocal: Elliott Shaw & Wilfred Glenn	
10/20/28	**8**	5	33. Out Of The Dawn .... Victor 21572	
11/10/28	**11**	3	34. Neapolitan Nights (Oh, Night Of Splendor)...... Victor 21633	
12/29/28+	**12**	3	35. I Can't Give You Anything But Love............. Victor 21688 from the Broadway musical "Blackbirds of 1928"	
1/19/29	**5**	6	36. Softly, As In A Morning Sunrise/ vocals on 27, 31, 33 & 36: Franklyn Baur	
1/19/29	**6**	5	37. One Kiss .... Victor 21775 above two from the Broadway musical "The New Moon"	
1/19/29	**9**	6	38. Marie.. Victor 21746	
3/30/29	**15**	2	39. Carolina Moon/	
4/20/29	**19**	1	40. When Summer Is Gone .... Victor 21847	
5/04/29	**2(2)**	12	41. You Were Meant For Me/	
6/08/29	**13**	2	42. Broadway Melody .... Victor 21886 vocal: Four Rajahs above two from the film "Broadway Melody"	
7/06/29	**3**	7	43. Pagan Love Song .... Victor 21931 from the film "The Pagan" 34, 39, 43 & 47 listed as Troubadors Orchestra	
7/20/29	**15**	2	44. Some Sweet Day .... Victor 21896 vocal: Franklyn Baur	
8/10/29	**10**	3	45. The Lonesome Road................................. Victor 21996 Willard Robinson, vocal featured in the film version of "Show Boat"	
9/07/29	**12**	3	46. Am I Blue? .... Victor 22004 vocal: Don Howard; from the film "On With the Show"	
10/19/29	**17**	1	47. My Song Of The Nile............................... Victor 22073 from the film "The Drag" vocals on 39, 41 & 47: Scrappy Lambert	
11/09/29	**4**	7	48. Love Me .... Victor 22152	
1/04/30	**3**	6	49. Chant Of The Jungle .... Victor 22203 from the film "Untamed" vocals on 37, 40, 43, & 48-49: Frank Munn	
6/21/30	**1(7)**	11	50. **Dancing With Tears In My Eyes** .... Victor 22425 vocals on 38 & 50: Lewis James	
7/05/30	**6**	7	51. Get Happy .... Victor 22444 vocal: Phil Dewey-Frank Luther-Leo O'Rourke from the Broadway musical "9:15 Revue" flip side: "My Future Just Passed" (POS 6) by the High Hatters	
10/10/31	**12**	3	52. I Apologize .... Victor 22781 with Jimmy Dorsey (clarinet/alto sax)	
1/23/32	**8**	3	53. Delishious .... Victor 22902 movie title song above two vocals: Paul Small	
3/19/32	**17**	2	54. The Wooden Soldier And The China Doll....... Victor 22925 vocal: Scrappy Lambert	

MERVIN SHINER
country singer

DATE CHARTED	PEAK POS	WKS CHRT'D	ARTIST — Record Title	Label & Number
3/25/50	**8**	6	● 1. Peter Cottontail.................................... Decca 46221	

DATE CHARTED	PEAK POS	WKS CHRT'D	ARTIST — Record Title	Label & Number
			DINAH SHORE	
			Born Frances Rose Shore on 3/1/17 in Winchester, Tenn., Dinah was one of the most popular female vocalists of the 1940-55 era. She became a solo star almost immediately after her brief stay with Xavier Cugat band, but her greatest fame came with her 1951-62 TV variety series, which was followed in the 70s by a popular talk show.	
9/14/40	24	1	1. You Can't Brush Me Off .... DINAH SHORE & DICK TODD from the Broadway musical "Louisiana Purchase"	Bluebird 10720
12/28/40+	10	9	2. Yes, My Darling Daughter...........................	Bluebird 10920
1/25/41	23	1	3. My Man.. from Broadway's "Ziegfeld Follies of 1921"	Bluebird 10978
3/08/41	9	2	4. I Hear A Rhapsody/	
3/15/41	22	2	5. I Do, Do You?..	Bluebird 11003
7/26/41	21	2	6. Do You Care?...	Bluebird 11191
9/13/41	5	12	7. Jim	Bluebird 11204
2/14/42	4	11	● 8. Blues In The Night .... movie title song	Bluebird 11436
3/21/42	8	11	9. Miss You .... featured in the film "Strictly In the Groove"	Bluebird 11322
3/21/42	12	3	10. I Don't Want To Walk Without You .... from the film "Sweater Girl"	Bluebird 11423
4/18/42	23	1	11. Goodnight, Captain Curly-Head/	
5/16/42	5	5	12. Skylark... above two accompanied by Rosario Bourdon's Orchestra	Bluebird 11473
6/20/42	8	7	13. One Dozen Roses	Victor 27881
6/20/42	12	1	14. Sleepy Lagoon... 1-10 & 13-14 accompanied by Leonard Joy's Orchestra	Victor 27875
8/01/42	16	3	15. He Wears A Pair Of Silver Wings.................. British song	Victor 27931
8/22/42	18	1	16. Mad About Him, Sad Without Him, How Can I Be Glad Without Him Blues..................	Victor 27940
12/05/42	20	1	17. He's My Guy	Victor 27963
12/26/42	10	3	18. Dearly Beloved/ from the film "You Were Never Lovelier"	
1/02/43	3	12	19. (As Long As You're Not In Love With Anyone Else) Why Don't You Fall In Love With Me?	Victor 27970
1/23/43	3	18	20. You'd Be So Nice To Come Home To............ from the film "Something to Shout About" above four accompanied by Paul Weston's Orchestra	Victor 1519
4/10/43	5	11	21. Murder, He Says/ from the film "Happy-Go-Lucky"	
5/01/43	18	1	22. Something To Remember You By.............. from the Broadway musical "Three's A Crowd" 15-16, 21-22 accompanied by Gordon Jenkins' Orchestra	Victor 1525
7/08/44	1(4)	25	23. **I'll Walk Alone**.................................... with a mixed chorus; from the film "Follow the Boys"	Victor 1586
11/11/44	19	1	24. Together .... from the film "Since You Went Away"	Victor 1594
2/24/45	8	1	25. Sleigh Ride In July................................... from the film "Belle of the Yukon"	Victor 1617
3/10/45	5	11	26. Candy/	
4/07/45	11	1	27. He's Home For A Little While....................	Victor 1632
9/15/45	7	2	28. Along The Navajo Trail .... above four accompanied by Al Sack's Orchestra	Victor 1666
11/10/45	16	1	29. But I Did	Victor 1732
11/24/45	14	3	30. My Guy's Come Back................................	Victor 1731
3/02/46	10	4	31. Personality .... from the film "The Road to Utopia" above three accompanied by Russ Case's Orchestra	Victor 1781
3/09/46	6	9	32. Shoo-Fly Pie And Apple Pan Dowdy	Columbia 36943

DATE CHARTED	PEAK POS	WKS CHRT'D	ARTIST — Record Title	Label & Number
4/20/46	**3**	12	33. Laughing On The Outside (Crying On The Inside)/	
4/27/46	**1(8)**	21	34. **The Gypsy**	Columbia 36964
5/11/46	**9**	4	35. All That Glitters Is Not Gold	Columbia 36971
			above four accompanied by Sonny Burke's Orchestra	
6/01/46	**3**	14	36. Doin' What Comes Natur'lly................	Columbia 36976
			from the Broadway musical "Annie Get Your Gun" accompanied by Spade Cooley's Orchestra	
11/09/46	**5**	3	37. You Keep Coming Back Like A Song	Columbia 37072
			from the film "Blue Skies"	
1/04/47	**2(2)**	16	38. (I Love You) For Sentimental Reasons	Columbia 37188
3/01/47	**1(2)**	12	39. **Anniversary Song**..................	Columbia 37234
			accompanied by Morris Stoloff's Orchestra from the film "The Jolson Story" based on the 1880 song "Danube Waves"	
4/19/47	**16**	2	40. The Egg And I	Columbia 37278
5/03/47	**23**	2	41. When Am I Gonna Kiss You Good Morning? ..	Columbia 37291
7/12/47	**15**	2	42. Tallahassee	Columbia 37387
			DINAH SHORE & WOODY HERMAN from the film "Variety Girl"	
10/11/47	**2(3)**	12	43. I Wish I Didn't Love You So	Columbia 37506
			from the film "The Perils of Pauline"	
10/25/47	**4**	11	44. You Do	Columbia 37587
			from the film "Mother Wore Tights"	
11/01/47	**23**	1	45. It Takes A Long, Long Train With A Red Caboose (To Carry My Blues Away)........	Columbia 37840
11/08/47	**25**	3	46. Golden Earrings	Columbia 37932
12/20/47+	**8**	9	47. How Soon (Will I Be Seeing You)	Columbia 37952
12/27/47	**24**	1	48. At The Candlelight Cafe/	
2/28/48	**18**	2	49. The Best Things In Life Are Free	Columbia 37984
			with Four Hits & a Miss from the Broadway musical "Good News" above nine accompanied by Sonny Burke's Orchestra	
6/19/48	**11**	7	50. Little White Lies....................	Columbia 38114
9/18/48	**1(10)**	25	● 51. **Buttons And Bows**................	Columbia 38284
			with the Happy Valley Boys; from the film "Paleface"	
12/18/48+	**9**	12	52. Lavender Blue (Dilly Dilly)............	Columbia 38299
			from the film "So Dear To My Heart" based on an English folk song	
1/22/49	**14**	8	53. Far Away Places....................	Columbia 38356
			accompanied by piano duo	
3/19/49	**20**	4	54. So In Love	Columbia 38399
			from the Broadway musical "Kiss Me, Kate"	
4/23/49	**12**	15	55. Forever And Ever	Columbia 38410
5/07/49	**4**	19	56. Baby, It's Cold Outside	Columbia 38463
			DINAH SHORE & BUDDY CLARK accompanied by Ted Dale's Orchestra from the film "Neptune's Daughter"	
6/11/49	**22**	2	57. A Wonderful Guy	Columbia 38460
			from the Broadway musical "South Pacific"	
11/19/49+	**2(1)**	17	58. Dear Hearts And Gentle People	Columbia 38605
2/11/50	**25**	1	59. Bibbidi-Bobbidi-Boo.................	Columbia 38659
			from the animated film "Cinderella"	
2/18/50	**20**	3	60. It's So Nice To Have A Man Around The House............................	Columbia 38689
9/16/50	**29**	1	61. Can Anyone Explain? (No! No! No!)........	Columbia 38927
			52, 54-55, & 57-61 accompanied by Harry Zimmerman's Orchestra	
12/09/50+	**3**	19	62. My Heart Cries For You/	
			adapted from the French folk song "Chanson de Marie Antoinette"	
12/23/50	**18**	3	63. Nobody's Chasing Me.................	RCA Victor 3978
			from the Broadway musical "Out of This World"	

DATE CHARTED	PEAK POS	WKS CHRT'D	ARTIST — Record Title	Label & Number
2/03/51	**8**	12	64. A Penny A Kiss/	
3/03/51	**24**	2	65. In Your Arms.. RCA Victor 4019 above two: DINAH SHORE & TONY MARTIN	
7/07/51	**3**	17	66. Sweet Violets .... RCA Victor 4174	
9/01/51	**24**	2	67. The Musicians................................... RCA Victor 4225 DINAH SHORE, TONY MARTIN, BETTY HUTTON, & PHIL HARRIS	
6/07/52	**28**	1	68. Delicado.................................... RCA Victor 4729	
10/11/52	**20**	5	69. Blues In Advance.............................. RCA Victor 4926 above six accompanied by Henri Rene's Orchestra	
3/21/53	**22**	1	70. Salomee (With Her Seven Veils) .... RCA Victor 5176 from the Broadway musical "Hazel Flagg"	
5/16/53	**27**	1	71. Sweet Thing... RCA Victor 5247 above two accompanied by Harry Zimmerman's Orchestra	
8/01/53	**11**	4	72. Blue Canary..................................... RCA Victor 5390	
1/09/54	**12**	5	73. Changing Partners .... RCA Victor 5515 accompanied by Hugo Winterhalter's Orchestra	
3/06/54	**28**	1	74. Pass The Jam, Sam................................... RCA Victor 5622 accompanied by Henri Rene's Orchestra	
10/02/54	**28**	1	75. If I Give My Heart To You.......................... RCA Victor 5838	

ETHEL SHUTTA
Featured singer for and wife of George Olsen ("A Precious Little Thing Called Love"); appeared in many Broadway musicals.

MONROE SILVER
Yiddish-dialect comedian, discovered by Billy Murray; died in 1947 (approximately age 67).

2/15/19	**9**	1	1. Cohen On His Honeymoon ....[T-C] Victor 18501	

GINNY SIMMS
Extremely popular singer with Kay Kyser from 1934-41; voted the #1 female band vocalist in 1941 Billboard college poll after ranking second the previous year. Appeared in several movies, and hosted own radio & TV shows in early 50s.

4/19/41	**16**	1	1. Walkin' By The River .... Okeh 6025 accompanied by Nat Brandwynne's Orchestra	
4/15/44	**27**	1	2. Irresistable You...................................... Columbia 36693 from the film "Broadway Rhythm"	

LU ANN SIMMS

2/28/53	**30**	1	1. Moving Away .... Columbia 39928 accompanied by Percy Faith & His Orchestra	

LEE SIMS
Piano soloist and composer; died on 5/7/66 (68).

8/08/31	**20**	1	1. Star Dust .... [I] Brunswick 6132	

ZOOT SIMS
One of the modern era's leading jazz tenor saxophonists; greatest fame as one of Woody Herman's "Four Brothers" sax section (1947-49), also played with Benny Goodman (1944 & 1946), & Stan Kenton (1953).

DATE CHARTED	PEAK POS	WKS CHRT'D	ARTIST — Record Title	Label & Number
			FRANK SINATRA Francis Albert Sinatra, perhaps the greatest popular singer in recording history, was born on 12/12/15 in Hoboken, N.J. He and his group the Hoboken Four won a 1935 Major Bowes Amateur Hour contest, and on his own did local engagements for three years until Harry James heard him on a New York radio station in 1939 and hired him as vocalist. Sinatra remained largely unknown, however, until joining Tommy Dorsey in early 1940. Influenced by Dorsey's breath control on trombone and his singing idols Billie Holiday and Bing Crosby, Sinatra found the distinctive style that would captivate two generations. By late 1942, with a long list of unforgettable hits ("I'll Never Smile Again", "There Are Such Things") with Dorsey, Sinatra decided to strike out on his own, and solo appearances at New York's Paramount Theater generated such unprecedented frenzy that the legend of "The Voice" was born. After many solo hits and movie appearances, his career almost ran aground in the early 50s until an Academy Award-winning performance in "From Here to Eternity". A series of classic albums with Nelson Riddle and other top arrangers, and the song-styling mastery that continued into the 1980s, ensured his place in music history. (Unless otherwise noted, all Columbia records are accompanied by Axel Stordahl's Orchestra).	
3/28/42	**16**	2	1. Night And Day .... accompanied by Alex Stordahl & His Orchestra from the Broadway musical "Gay Divorce"	Bluebird 11463
6/19/43	**1(2)**	21	● 2. **All Or Nothing At All**........................... [R] FRANK SINATRA with HARRY JAMES & HIS ORCHESTRA recorded on 9/17/39	Columbia 35587
7/24/43	**2(2)**	16	3. You'll Never Know/ from the film "Hello, Frisco, Hello"	
8/28/43	**10**	9	4. Close To You	Columbia 36678
8/07/43	**9**	11	5. Sunday, Monday, Or Always	Columbia 36679
10/02/43	**3**	18	6. People Will Say We're In Love/	
11/27/43	**12**	4	7. Oh, What A Beautiful Mornin' .... above two from the Broadway musical "Oklahoma!"	Columbia 36682
2/12/44	**4**	14	8. I Couldn't Sleep A Wink Last Night/	
3/18/44	**11**	4	9. A Lovely Way To Spend An Evening .... above two from film "Higher and Higher" above seven with the Bobby Tucker Singers (no orchestra)	Columbia 36687
5/13/44	**27**	1	10. On A Little Street In Singapore/ recorded 10/13/39	
5/27/44	**17**	2	11. Every Day Of My Life............................. recorded 11/8/39	Columbia 36700
9/02/44	**15**	3	12. Night And Day .... [R] reissue of Bluebird 11463	Victor 1589
10/28/44	**21**	1	13. It's Funny To Everyone But Me .... recorded 8/17/39 10-11 & 13: FRANK SINATRA with HARRY JAMES & HIS ORCHESTRA	Columbia 36738
12/30/44	**7**	2	● 14. White Christmas................................. [X] from the film "Holiday Inn"	Columbia 36756
2/03/45	**2(1)**	12	15. Saturday Night (Is The Loneliest Night Of The Week)/	
1/27/45	**7**	5	16. I Dream Of You	Columbia 36762
1/27/45	**19**	1	17. If You Are But A Dream...........................	Columbia 36786
5/05/45	**13**	1	18. What Makes The Sun Set .... from the film "Anchors Aweigh"	Columbia 36774
6/02/45	**5**	7	19. Dream .... originally Johnny Mercer's closing radio theme	Columbia 36797
6/23/45	**8**	2	20. I Should Care..................................... from the film "Thrill of a Romance"	Columbia 36791
9/08/45	**7**	2	21. If I Loved You/	
9/15/45	**9**	1	22. You'll Never Walk Alone .... above two from the Broadway musical "Carousel"	Columbia 36825
10/27/45	**23**	1	23. Homesick - That's All .... above two with Ken Lane Singers	Columbia 36820
11/10/45	**9**	4	24. Don't Forget Tonight Tomorrow .... with The Charioteers, and small band featuring Red Nichols (trumpet)	Columbia 36854

DATE CHARTED	PEAK POS	WKS CHRT'D	ARTIST — Record Title	Label & Number
12/08/45	10	2	25. Nancy (With The Laughing Face) .... written for Frank's two-year-old daughter	Columbia 36868
12/15/45+	5	4	26. White Christmas.............................. [X-R]	Columbia 36860
1/19/46	22	1	27. The House I Live In	Columbia 36886
2/16/46	1(8)	17	28. **Oh! What It Seemed To Be/**	
2/16/46	5	10	29. Day By Day	Columbia 36905
4/13/46	17	2	30. Full Moon And Empty Arms..................... based on Rachmaninoff's Piano Concerto No. 2 in C-Minor	Columbia 36947
5/18/46	2(1)	14	31. They Say It's Wonderful/	
6/01/46	11	2	32. The Girl That I Marry .... above two from the Broadway musical "Annie Get Your Gun"	Columbia 36975
5/18/46	7	3	33. All Through The Day................................. from the film "Centennial Summer"	Columbia 36962
7/13/46	18	1	34. From This Day Forward	Columbia 36898
8/03/46	1(4)	22	35. **Five Minutes More**................................. featured in the film "Sweetheart of Sigma Chi"	Columbia 37048
9/28/46	6	12	36. The Coffee Song	Columbia 37089
10/05/46	21	1	37. Something Old, Something New	Columbia 36987
10/19/46	23	3	38. Begin The Beguine................................. from the Broadway musical "Jubilee"	Columbia 37064
10/26/46	8	6	39. The Things We Said Last Summer	Columbia 37089
12/21/46	8	2	40. September Song.................................... from the Broadway musical "Knickerbocker Holiday" Dave Barbour (guitar) on most records from 19-40	Columbia 37161
12/28/46	6	4	41. White Christmas.............................. [X-R]	Columbia 37132
2/01/47	11	1	42. This Is The Night .... nearly all records from 14-42 accompanied by Axel Stordahl's Orchestra	Columbia 37193
3/08/47	10	5	43. That's How Much I Love You .... with the Page Cavanaugh Trio	Columbia 37231
5/03/47	5	6	44. I Believe/	
5/17/47	16	5	45. Time After Time .... above two from the film "It Happened in Brooklyn"	Columbia 37300
5/10/47	1(1)	10	46. **Mam'selle** .... from the film "The Razor's Edge"	Columbia 37343
7/12/47	20	5	47. Almost Like Being In Love .... from the Broadway musical "Brigadoon"	Columbia 37382
7/12/47	21	4	48. Stella By Starlight	Columbia 37343
9/20/47	13	2	49. I Have But One Heart/	
9/20/47	21	4	50. Ain'tcha Ever Comin' Back......................	Columbia 37554
11/08/47	8	2	51. So Far/	
11/08/47	24	1	52. A Fellow Needs A Girl .... above two from the Broadway musical "Allegro" Ray Linn (trumpet) on most from 31-52	Columbia 37883
12/06/47	21	4	53. The Dum-Dot Song/ [N]	
1/03/48	23	3	54. You're My Girl .... with the Pied Pipers from the Broadway musical "High Button Shoes"	Columbia 37966
12/13/47	26	1	55. Christmas Dreaming........................... [X]	Columbia 37809
1/31/48	23	2	56. What'll I Do?/ with trio including Tony Mottola (guitar) from the Broadway musical "Music Box Revue of 1923"	
1/24/48	24	2	57. My Cousin Louella .... with trio: Johnny Guanieri (piano), Herman Alpert (bass), & Tony Mottola (guitar)	Columbia 38045
1/31/48	14	4	58. But Beautiful	Columbia 38053
4/10/48	21	2	59. I've Got A Crush On You .... featuring Bobby Hackett (trumpet); from the Broadway musical "Treasure Girl"	Columbia 38151
5/01/48	21	3	60. All Of Me	Columbia 38163
5/29/48	7	4	61. Nature Boy .... with the Jeff Alexander Choir (no orchestra)	Columbia 38210

DATE CHARTED	PEAK POS	WKS CHRT'D	ARTIST — Record Title	Label & Number
7/03/48	**21**	3	62. Just For Now/	
7/03/48	**25**	1	63. Everybody Loves Somebody	Columbia 38225
			revived as a #1 record by Dean Martin in 1964	
8/07/48	**19**	1	64. It Only Happens When I Dance With You.......	Columbia 38192
			from the film "Easter Parade"	
1/29/49	**27**	1	65. Autumn In New York...............................	Columbia 38316
3/19/49	**14**	5	66. Sunflower..	Columbia 38391
			with "hillbilly" band	
			became the official state song of Kansas	
6/11/49	**6**	13	67. Some Enchanted Evening/	
7/02/49	**18**	5	68. Bali Ha'i..	Columbia 38446
			above two from the Broadway musical "South Pacific"	
6/11/49	**10**	14	69. The Hucklebuck	Columbia 38486
			based on Charlie Parker's jazz instrumental "Now's the Time"	
			Si Zenter (trombone) on 35, 44 & 69	
			Herbie Haymer (tenor sax) on a great majority of records	
			from 20-69	
8/06/49	**17**	6	70. Let's Take An Old-Fashioned Walk	Columbia 38513
			FRANK SINATRA & DORIS DAY	
			from the Broadway musical "Miss Liberty"	
10/08/49	**9**	12	71. Don't Cry, Joe (Let Her Go, Let Her Go, Let	
			Her Go)..	Columbia 38555
			band includes Buddy Morrow (trombone)	
10/29/49	**16**	4	72. That Lucky Old Sun	Columbia 38608
12/24/49+	**13**	7	73. The Old Master Painter	Columbia 38650
1/21/50	**28**	1	74. Sorry..	Columbia 38662
			above two with Paula Kelly & the Modernaires	
2/25/50	**10**	7	75. Chattanoogie Shoe Shine Boy/	
2/25/50	**25**	1	76. God's Country....................................	Columbia 38708
			72 & above two with the Jeff Alexander Choir	
			Ziggy Elman (trumpet) on 69, 72, & 74-76	
5/27/50	**26**	2	77. American Beauty Rose	Columbia 38809
			with Dixieland band directed by Mitch Miller, and featuring	
			Will Bradley (trombone)	
8/05/50	**5**	12	78. Goodnight Irene................................	Columbia 38892
			with Mitch Miller & trio	
11/04/50	**9**	16	79. One Finger Melody	Columbia 39014
12/02/50	**14**	5	80. Nevertheless	Columbia 39044
			with trumpet solo by Billy Butterfield; song featured in	
			the film "Three Little Words" (Butterfield also on 71)	
5/05/51	**17**	1	81. You're The One	Columbia 39213
			Lou McGarity (trombone) on 72, 74-76 & 81	
6/02/51	**22**	2	82. We Kiss In A Shadow	Columbia 39294
			from the Broadway musical "The King and I"	
6/23/51	**14**	7	83. I'm A Fool To Want You/	
6/23/51	**21**	5	84. Mama Will Bark .... [N]	Columbia 39425
			FRANK SINATRA & DAGMAR	
			Chris Griffin (trumpet) on 28, 30, 60, 63-65, 80 & 83-84	
9/01/51	**8**	8	85. Castle Rock	Columbia 39527
			with Harry James & His Orchestra	
3/22/52	**24**	3	86. I Hear A Rhapsody	Columbia 39652
			with the Jeff Alexander Choir	
9/13/52	**20**	4	87. Bim Bam Baby/	
9/27/52	**30**	1	88. Azure-Te (Paris Blues)	Columbia 39819
11/15/52	**19**	5	89. The Birth Of The Blues	Columbia 39882
			from the Broadway musical "George White's Scandals of 1926"	
			Babe Russin (tenor sax) on 44, 53, many from 70-89, & some	
			Capitols	
5/16/53	**7**	10	90. I'm Walking Behind You/	
			British song	
5/16/53	**25**	3	91. Lean Baby..	Capitol 2450
			except as noted, all records from 14-91 accompanied by Axel	
			Stordahl's Orchestra	
7/04/53	**14**	4	92. I've Got The World On A String/	
8/01/53	**28**	1	93. My One And Only Love	Capitol 2505

DATE CHARTED	PEAK POS	WKS CHRT'D	ARTIST — Record Title	Label & Number
9/26/53	**15**	6	94. From Here To Eternity	Capitol 2560
			inspired by, but not written for, the film above three with Nelson Riddle's Orchestra	
11/28/53	**18**	4	95. South Of The Border..................................	Capitol 2638
			listed as accompanied by Billy May's Orchestra, but may be Riddle	
2/13/54	**2(1)**	22	● 96. Young-At-Heart	Capitol 2703
			became movie title song	
5/08/54	**17**	6	97. Don't Worry 'Bout Me/	
5/08/54	**21**	4	98. I Could Have Told You............................	Capitol 2787
5/29/54	**4**	13	99. Three Coins In The Fountain	Capitol 2816
			movie title song	
7/31/54	**21**	4	100. The Gal That Got Away/	
			from the film "A Star Is Born"	
8/07/54	**23**	4	101. Half As Lovely (Twice As True)	Capitol 2864
10/30/54	**30**	1	102. It Worries Me	Capitol 2922
			96-102 accompanied by Nelson Riddle's Orchestra	

GEORGE SIRAVO
Alto saxophonist with Glenn Miller (1937) & Gene Krupa (1938),
arranger for various bands and for Frank Sinatra,
conductor/arranger for Connee Boswell, Vic Damone & Doris Day.

NOBLE SISSLE
Best known for his association with Eubie Blake as lyricist
(Broadway hit "Shuffle Along") and singer, also a bandleader who
featured great jazzman Sidney Bechet in 1930s; died on 12/17/75
(86).

1/14/22	**10**	1	1. Arkansas Blues	Emerson 10443
9/29/23	**13**	1	2. Down-Hearted Blues.................................	Victor 19086
			above two: NOBLE SISSLE (vocals) & EUBIE BLAKE (piano)	
3/21/31	**14**	2	3. Got The Bench, Got The Park.....................	Brunswick 6073
			"Noble Sissle & His Orchestra" featuring Sidney Bechet (clarinet/soprano sax)	

SIX BROWN BROTHERS - see "BROWN"

SIX HITS & A MISS
vocal group

3/06/43	**11**	2	1. You'd Be So Nice To Come Home To............	Capitol 127
			from the film "Something to Shout About"	

SIX JUMPING JACKS
Directed by Harry Reser (banjo)

11/02/29	**15**	2	1. Piccolo Pete.. [N]	Brunswick 4457
			vocal: Tom Stacks	

SKYLARKS
Vocal group which worked in late 40s with Russ Morgan.

4/18/53	**28**	1	1. I Had The Craziest Dream..........................	RCA Victor 5257
			from the film "Springtime In the Rockies"	

BOB SKYLES & HIS SKYROCKETS
country-western band

4/24/37	**19**	1	1. The Arkansas Bazooka Swing	Bluebird 6876

FREDDIE SLACK & HIS ORCHESTRA
Boogie-woogie pianist who played with Ben Pollack (1935-36), Jimmy
Dorsey (1936-39), & Will Bradley (1940 smash "Beat Me, Daddy
(Eight to a Bar)". His band featured vocalists Ella Mae Morse &
Margaret Whiting. Slack wrote several of his hits, including
"House of Blue Lights"; he died on 8/10/65 (55). (Also see Johnny
Mercer.)

7/25/42	**9**	10	1. Cow Cow Boogie	Capitol 102
			from the film "Ride 'Em, Cowboy"	
9/26/42	**10**	20	2. Mr. Five By Five	Capitol 115
			from the film "Behind the Eight Ball" Ella Mae Morse: above two vocals	
2/13/43	**10**	8	3. That Old Black Magic/	
6/12/43	**16**	2	4. Hit The Road To Dreamland	Capitol 126
			vocal: Mellowaires 3 & 5 from the film "Star-Spangled Rhythm"	

DATE CHARTED	PEAK POS	WKS CHRT'D	ARTIST — Record Title	Label & Number
5/01/43	**19**	2	5. Riffette .... [I]	Capitol 129
7/24/43	**17**	2	6. Get On Board, Little Chillun'	Capitol 133
3/04/44	**19**	2	7. Silver Wings In The Moonlight.....................	Capitol 146
			Margaret Whiting: vocals on 3 & 7	
11/11/44	**13**	5	8. Cuban Sugar Mill.. [I]	Capitol 172
7/28/45	**12**	1	9. A Kiss Goodnight......................................	Capitol 203
			vocal: Liza Morrow	
5/18/46	**8**	13	10. The House Of Blue Lights..........................	Capitol 251
			Ella Mae Morse: vocals on 6 & 10	

SLIM & SLAM

Pianist/guitarist Bulee "Slim" Gaillard and bassist Leroy "Slam" Stewart, novelty & jazz combo leaders; nearly all hits written by Gaillard (both on vocals).

DATE CHARTED	PEAK POS	WKS CHRT'D	ARTIST — Record Title	Label & Number
4/09/38	**2(2)**	17	1. Flat Foot Floogee................................ [N]	Vocalion 4021
7/23/38	**3**	11	2. Tutti Fruti....................................... [N]	Vocalion 4225
10/15/38	**7**	5	3. Jump Session...................................	Vocalion 4346
12/03/38	**15**	2	4. Laughing In Rhythm .... [N]	Vocalion 4461
1/21/39	**12**	2	5. Buck Dance Rhythm	Vocalion 4521

PAUL SMALL

Depression-era band vocalist with Jack Denny, George Olsen, Nat Shilkret, and many others.

ED SMALLE

Singer often paired with superstar Billy Murray; also served as piano accompanist for the Revelers; died on 11/23/68 (81).

DATE CHARTED	PEAK POS	WKS CHRT'D	ARTIST — Record Title	Label & Number
11/13/20	**9**	1	1. Dardanella Blues	Victor 18688
2/25/22	**12**	1	2. Ten Little Fingers And Ten Little Toes (Down	
			In Tennessee)	Victor 18830
2/10/23	**10**	1	3. Yankee Doodle Blues............................	Victor 18959
			from the Broadway musical "Spice of 1922"	
9/29/23	**1(6)**	14	4. **That Old Gang Of Mine**	Victor 19095
12/22/23	**8**	2	5. My Sweetie Went Away............................	Victor 19144
6/28/24	**15**	1	6. Home In Pasadena	Victor 19293
10/25/24	**12**	1	7. Hinky Dinky Parley Voo........................ [N]	Victor 19388
			above seven: BILLY MURRAY & ED SMALLE	
12/25/26	**12**	1	8. Cross Your Heart	Columbia 711
			from the Broadway musical "Queen High"	
4/30/27	**9**	5	9. Blue Skies	Victor 20457
			from the Broadway musical "Betsy"	
2/04/28	**13**	3	10. Together, We Two..................................	Victor 21042
			8-10: VAUGHN DELEATH & ED SMALLE	
6/01/29	**16**	2	11. Precious Little Thing Called Love/	
6/29/29	**20**	1	12. Caressing You......................................	Victor 21892
			9, 11-12: JOHNNY MARVIN & ED SMALLE	

SMITH BROTHERS

DATE CHARTED	PEAK POS	WKS CHRT'D	ARTIST — Record Title	Label & Number
3/06/54	**21**	1	1. Melancholy Me	"X" 0003
6/12/54	**23**	2	2. (These Are) The Things I Love....................	"X" 0009
			orchestra directed by Danny Mendelsohn	

ARTHUR SMITH & HIS CRACKER-JACKS

Guitarist, also played mandolin and banjo.

DATE CHARTED	PEAK POS	WKS CHRT'D	ARTIST — Record Title	Label & Number
7/10/48	**25**	1	1. Guitar Boogie...................................... [I]	MGM 10293
			originally released on Super Disc 1004	

DATE CHARTED	PEAK POS	WKS CHRT'D	ARTIST — Record Title	Label & Number
			BESSIE SMITH	
			The greatest of all blues singers, Bessie Smith was born on 4/15/1895 in Chattanooga, Tenn. Her first major professional experience was touring with blues singer Ma Rainey, and it was after performing regularly in Philadelphia that her legendary recording career began with the million-selling "Down-Hearted Blues", an astounding achievement for a "race" record. Her records proved so popular that they were largely responsible for saving Columbia from bankruptcy. The depth and power of Bessie's voice were without equal, and she was often accompanied by Louis Armstrong and other top jazzmen. The Depression all but ended her career, and Bessie Smith died following an auto accident on 9/26/37 (42).	
6/09/23	1(4)	12	● 1. **Down Hearted Blues/**	
7/07/23	5	4	2. Gulf Coast Blues.................... above two accompanied by only Clarence Williams (piano)	Columbia 3844
8/25/23	12	1	3. Aggravatin' Papa	Columbia 3877
9/01/23	6	4	4. Baby Won't You Please Come Home Blues.....	Columbia 3888
10/20/23	9	1	5. T'ain't Nobody's Biz-Ness If I Do................ above three accompanied by Down-Home Boys, including Clarence Williams	Columbia 3989
6/13/25	3	6	6. The St. Louis Blues...................	Columbia 14064
10/31/25	5	3	7. Careless Love Blues	Columbia 14083
11/28/25	8	3	8. I Ain't Gonna Play No Second Fiddle .... Louis Armstrong (cornet) featured on above three	Columbia 14090
2/20/26	8	1	9. I Ain't Got Nobody	Columbia 14095
9/25/26	5	4	10. Lost Your Head Blues...................	Columbia 14158
8/06/27	7	4	11. After You've Gone .... with Buster Bailey (clarinet) Fletcher Henderson (piano) on above five	Columbia 14197
10/15/27	17	1	12. Alexander's Ragtime Band .... with Coleman Hawkins (clarinet)	Columbia 14219
3/10/28	13	2	13. A Good Man Is Hard To Find......................	Columbia 14250
6/30/28	20	1	14. Empty Bed Blues .... record selected for the NARAS Hall of Fame	Columbia 14312
8/31/29	15	2	15. Nobody Knows You When You're Down And Out .... with Clarence Williams (piano)	Columbia 14451
			CLARA SMITH	
			Early blues singer, sometimes accompanied by jazz greats Louis Armstrong & Coleman Hawkins; died in 1935 (41).	
7/26/24	15	1	1. Chicago Blues .... band includes Fletcher Henderson (piano) & Don Redman (clarinet)	Columbia 14009
			ETHEL SMITH	
			Popular organist who sometimes played with symphony orchestras; appeared in several movies.	
11/25/44+	14	6	1. Tico Tico................................... [I] Ethel Smith with the Bando Carioca Brazilian song featured in the film "Saludos Amigos"	Decca 23353
10/20/51	16	4	2. Down Yonder .... [I]	King 986
			JACK SMITH	
			Tenor who sang on radio from late 30s, later TV actor	
5/31/47	18	1	1. Jack! Jack! Jack!	Capitol 403
10/18/47	9	7	2. Civilization (Bongo, Bongo, Bongo).............. accompanied by Frank DeVol's Orchestra	Capitol 465
2/28/48	26	1	3. Big Brass Band From Braziil .... above 2 from the Broadway musical "Angel In the Wings"	Capitol 15029
3/13/48	26	1	4. Shaunty O'Shea........................ from the Broadway musical "Look Ma, I'm Dancing"	Capitol 484
5/22/48	13	3	5. Baby Face	Capitol 15078
5/22/48	26	1	6. Takin' Miss Mary To The Ball .... from the film "On An Island With You"	Capitol 15073
6/19/48	17	2	7. Tea Leaves.....................................	Capitol 15102

DATE CHARTED	PEAK POS	WKS CHRT'D	ARTIST — Record Title	Label & Number
8/21/48	**13**	9	8. You Call Everybody Darling/	
12/04/48	**14**	4	9. Cuanto Le Gusta (La Parranda) .... Capitol 15280 from the film "A Date With Judy"	
1/22/49	**17**	4	10. Lavender Blue (Dilly Dilly)........................ Capitol 15225 from the film "So Dear to My Heart"; based on an 18th century English folk song 4 & 10 accompanied by Earl Sheldon's Orchestra	
2/26/49	**3**	14	11. Cruising Down The River........................ Capitol 15372 Clark Sisters: accompanying vocals on nearly all above records	
4/09/49	**13**	4	12. Sunflower... Capitol 15394 with the Crew Chiefs above two accompanied by Frank DeVol's Orchestra	

JOSEPH C. SMITH'S ORCHESTRA
Important early dance band

DATE CHARTED	PEAK POS	WKS CHRT'D	ARTIST — Record Title	Label & Number
8/21/17	**4**	3	1. Havanola Fox-Trot .... [I] Victor 35615	
11/10/17	**10**	1	2. Gems From "Ziegfeld Follies Of 1917" .... [I] Victor 18334	
2/23/18	**9**	1	3. Some Sunday Morning .... [I] Victor 18407	
8/10/18	**1(1)**	10	4. **Smiles** .... Victor 18473 Harry Macdonough, vocal; from "The Passing Show of 1918"	
11/30/18	**8**	1	5. Oriental .... [I] Victor 35676	
12/28/18+	**3**	5	6. Hindustan .... [I] Victor 18507	
2/08/19	**6**	2	7. Mary .... Victor 18500 vocal: Charles Harrison, Lewis James & Harry Macdonough	
5/10/19	**6**	2	8. Sometime... [I] Victor 35684 Broadway musical title song	
8/23/19	**6**	2	9. Oh My Dear!.. [I] Victor 35690	
9/27/19	**3**	8	10. The Vamp.. Victor 18594 Billy Murray & Harry Macdonough, vocal	
12/06/19	**3**	4	11. Yearning .... [I] Victor 18603	
2/07/20	**4**	4	12. Yellow Dog Blues .... [I] Victor 18618	
2/28/20	**15**	1	13. Taxi .... [I] Victor 18640	
4/10/20	**3**	6	14. That Naughty Waltz .... [I] Victor 18650	
6/12/20	**10**	1	15. Whose Baby Are You? .... [I] Victor 18661 from the Broadway musical "The Night Booat"	
6/19/20	**6**	2	16. Irene .... [I] Victor 35695 Broadway musical title song	
7/31/20	**6**	2	17. Alexandria .... [I] Victor 18673	
9/25/20	**6**	4	18. The Love Nest....................................... [I] Victor 18678 from the Broadway musical "Mary"	
10/30/20	**12**	1	19. Cuban Moon .... [I] Victor 35698	
2/11/22	**3**	6	20. Sally - Medley .... [I] Victor 35706 from the Broadway musical: Look for the Silver Lining / Whippoor-Will / Wild Rose	
5/13/22	**5**	3	21. Three O'Clock In The Morning................. [I] Victor 18866 from Broadway's "Greenwich Village Follies of 1921"	

KATE SMITH
Large, tremendously popular soprano who was for years one of the most-listened-to of all radio singers, and later hosted a TV series. Kate introduced the classic "God Bless America". She died on 6/17/86 (79).

DATE CHARTED	PEAK POS	WKS CHRT'D	ARTIST — Record Title	Label & Number
7/02/27	**14**	2	1. One Sweet Letter From You...................... Columbia 911 with Red Nichols' Charleston Chasers	
9/12/31	**1(2)**	8	2. **When The Moon Comes Over The Mountain** Columbia 2516 Kate's familiar radio theme	
11/07/31	**15**	2	3. I Don't Know Why.................................. Columbia 2539	
12/12/31	**12**	3	4. That's Why Darkies Were Born .... Columbia 2563 from the Broadway musical "George White's Scandals of 1931"	
1/02/32	**1(2)**	8	5. **River, Stay 'Way From My Door/**	
1/16/32	**9**	4	6. Too Late .... Columbia 2578 above two: KATE SMITH WITH GUY LOMBARDO & HIS ROYAL CANADIANS	
3/26/32	**10**	3	7. Snuggled On Your Shoulder .... Columbia 2624	

DATE CHARTED	PEAK POS	WKS CHRT'D	ARTIST — Record Title	Label & Number
4/16/32	8	4	8. Medley From "Face The Music"................... with the Three Nitecaps	Columbia 18000
4/23/32	10	4	9. My Mom .... Ben Selvin's Orchestra accompanies Kate on 2-4 & above three	Columbia 2637
6/25/32	17	1	10. Kate Smith Presents A Memory Program.......	Columbia 56000
4/24/33+	19	1	11. Shine On, Harvest Moon........................... revived in the film "Hello, Frisco, Hello"	Columbia 36674
2/05/38	15	2	12. Bei Mir Bist Du Schoen (Means That You're Grand).. from the Yiddish musical "I Would If I Could"	Victor 25752
4/08/39	10	4	13. God Bless America................................. Irving Berlin originally wrote this for the 1918 show "Yip, Yip, Haphank", but deleted & shelved it until giving the song to Kate	Victor 26198
1/11/40+	8	11	14. The Last Time I Saw Paris........................ written in response to the Nazi takeover of Paris featured in the film "Lady Be Good"	Columbia 35802
3/30/40	14	5	15. The Woodpecker Song/ based on "Reginella Campagnola"	
7/27/40	25	1	16. I'm Stepping Out With A Memory Tonight ...	Columbia 35398
7/27/40	5	11	17. God Bless America.............................. [R]	Victor 26198
1/03/42	23	1	18. God Bless America.............................. [R]	Victor 26198
1/10/42	8	11	19. Rose O'Day (The Filla-Da-Gusha Song)/	
1/10/42	9	8	20. (There'll Be Bluebirds Over) The White Cliffs Of Dover	Columbia 36448
4/11/42	21	1	21. How Do I Know It's Real?........................	Columbia 36534
6/20/42	10	7	22. I Threw A Kiss In The Ocean	Columbia 36552
1/20/45	8	2	23. Don't Fence Me In/ with Four Chicks & Chuck; from the film "Hollywood Canteen"	
1/20/45	12	3	24. There Goes That Song Again .... from the film "Carolina Blues"	Columbia 36759
10/13/45	21	1	25. And There You Are	Columbia 36821
4/27/46	12	1	26. Seems Like Old Times	Columbia 36950
3/20/48	12	2	27. Now Is The Hour................................ based on the traditional New Zealand song "Hearera Ra" except as noted, all records from 1938-1948 accompanied by Jack Miller's Orchestra	MGM 10125

MAMIE SMITH & HER JAZZ HOUNDS
The first blues singer to be commercially recorded, Mamie created a popular sensation with "Crazy Blues" and paved the way for (unrelated) Bessie Smith. Mamie died on 10/30/46 (56).

DATE CHARTED	PEAK POS	WKS CHRT'D	ARTIST — Record Title	Label & Number
12/11/20+	3	11	1. Crazy Blues	Okeh 4169
2/26/21	9	2	2. Fare Thee Honey Blues	Okeh 4194
5/28/21	13	1	3. Royal Garden Blues	Okeh 4254
7/09/21	4	5	4. You Can't Keep A Good Man Down .... Mamie previously recorded this for Okeh 4113	Okeh 4305
9/24/21	6	3	5. Dangerous Blues........................... Buster Bailey (clarinet) on above two	Okeh 4351
9/30/22	6	4	6. Lonesome Mama Blues	Okeh 4630
2/24/23	13	1	7. You Can Have Him, I Don't Want Him Blues .. with Bubber Miley (cornet)	Okeh 4670
6/30/23	13	1	8. You've Got To See Mama Ev'ry Night (Or You Can't See Mama At All) .... Coleman Hawkins (tenor sax) on above three	Okeh 4781

PINE TOP SMITH
Acclaimed boogie woogie pianist; died on 3/15/29 (24, night club shooting)

DATE CHARTED	PEAK POS	WKS CHRT'D	ARTIST — Record Title	Label & Number
2/09/29	20	1	1. Pine Top's Boogie Woogie....................... [I] selected for NARAS Hall of Fame; most famous as recorded by Tommy Dorsey ("Boogie Woogie")	Vocalion 1245

DATE CHARTED	PEAK POS	WKS CHRT'D	ARTIST — Record Title	Label & Number
			STUFF SMITH & HIS ONYX CLUB BOYS Great jazz violinist, born Hezekiah Smith, composed 1938 hit "It's Wonderful", featured future piano star Erroll Garner in 40s; died on 9/25/65 (56).	
3/28/36	**19**	1	1. I'se A-Muggin' .... vocal: Stuff Smith; featuring Jonah Jones (trumpet)	Vocalion 3169
			TAB SMITH & HIS ORCHESTRA Jazz alto saxophonist with Mills Blue Rhythm Band (1936-38), Count Basie (1940-42), & Lucky Millinder (1942-44); died on 8/19/71 (62)	
11/03/51	**20**	6	1. Because Of You .... [I] listed as "Tab Smith, His Fabulous Alto, & Orchestra"	United 104
			"WHISPERING" JACK SMITH Singer who was just as popular in England as he was in U.S., he was forced to develop his famous intimate half-singing, half-talking style by an exploding gas shell in World War I; died in May 1951 (52).	
1/30/26	**7**	2	1. Cecelia	Victor 19787
3/06/26	**9**	1	2. Then I'll Be Happy	Victor 19856
5/29/26	**11**	1	3. Some Other Bird Whistled A Tune	Victor 19914
6/05/26	**1(2)**	8	4. **Gimme A Lil' Kiss, Will Ya, Huh?**.............	Victor 19978
7/31/26	**10**	1	5. Poor Papa..	Victor 19998
10/02/26	**9**	1	6. When The Red, Red Robin Comes Bob, Bob, Bobbin' Along/	
10/30/26	**13**	1	7. Tonight's My Night With Baby..................	Victor 20069
12/18/26	**6**	3	8. Baby Face/	
1/01/27	**13**	2	9. I'm On My Way Home	Victor 20229
1/29/27	**3**	6	10. There Ain't No Maybe In My Baby's Eyes	Victor 20312
3/19/27	**15**	2	11. Clap Yo' Hands.. from the Broadway musical "Oh, Kay!"	Victor 20372
7/16/27	**1(4)**	14	12. **Me And My Shadow**	Victor 20626
2/04/28	**14**	2	13. The Song Is Ended (But The Melody Lingers On)	Victor 21028
			WILLIE SMITH Alto sax star with Jimmie Lunceford (1930-41), Charlie Spivak (194243), Harry James (1944-51), & Duke Ellington (1951-52); died on 3/7/67 (56).	
			SMOOTHIES Vocal group which recorded with Hal Kemp (1939-40) & Art Jarrett	
7/06/40	**29**	1	1. Down By The O-Hi-O	Bluebird 10710
			HANK SNOW & THE RAINBOW RANCH BOYS "The Singing Ranger", great 1950s ountry music star, born in Canada, frequently featured on The Grand Ole Opry.	
7/15/50	**27**	1	1. I'm Movin' On.. #1 for 18 weeks on country chart	RCA Victor 4593
7/10/54	**22**	3	● 2. I Don't Hurt Anymore.............................. #1 for 20 weeks on country chart	RCA Victor 5698
			BILL SNYDER ORCHESTRA Pianist/composer/bandleader from Chicago.	
4/22/50	**3**	19	● 1. Bewitched .... [I] from the Broadway musical "Pal Joey"	Tower 1473
			SANDY SOLO	
12/13/52	**23**	2	1. Close Your Dreamy Eyes (And Dream Of Me).. with Bobby Byrne's Orchestra	Barry 712
			DEBROY SOMERS BAND British	
7/09/32	**13**	3	1. Got A Date With An Angel........................	Columbia 2663

DATE CHARTED	PEAK POS	WKS CHRT'D	ARTIST — Record Title	Label & Number
			SONG SPINNERS Vocal group which enjoyed burst of popularity during musicians' record ban; accompanied Dick Haymes on "You'll Never Know" & several other hits.	
6/19/43	1(3)	12	1. **Comin' In On A Wing And A Prayer/**	
6/19/43	4	9	2. Johnny Zero	Decca 18553
			SONS OF THE PIONEERS Famous country-western group founded in 1934 by Roy Rogers and Bob Nolan (composer of the country classics "Tumbling Tumbleweeds" & "Cool Water"). Rogers left for Hollywood in 1937; the group appeared in several movies. (Also see Vaughn Monroe)	
12/15/34	13	2	1. Tumbling Tumbleweeds	Decca 5047
8/02/41	25	1	2. Cool Water .... record selected for the NARAS Hall of Fame a 1948 version recorded with Vaughn Monroe also hit the charts	Decca 5939
8/30/49	26	2	3. Room Full Of Roses..................................	RCA Victor 0065
			HARRY SOSNIK & HIS EDGEWATER BEACH HOTEL ORCHESTRA Chicago-based pianist/bandleader, arranged for Paul Whiteman & other bands, also songwriter, later record company executive.	
1/20/34	2(3)	8	1. Carioca .... [I] Victor 24488 from the film "Flying Down to Rio"	
			SOUSA'S BAND John Philip Sousa, America's "March King", was born 11/6/1854 in Washington, D.C. The son of a U.S. Marine Band trombonist, he played violin in various orchestras before himself becoming director of the Marine Band from 1880-91; his epic march compositions soon made Sousa the nation's most famous bandmaster. Arthur Pryor was featured trombone soloist from the late 1890s, and actually directed the great majority of the band's recordings due to Sousa's disdain for "canned music". Cornetists Walter B. Rogers and Herbert L. Clarke also served as Sousa conductors on records. Over the years Sousa's band gave more than ten thousand concerts around the world; he died on 3/5/32 (77). (also see U.S. Marine Band)	
6/15/95	1(7)	7	1. **El Capitan March**................................ [I] Columbia later recorded for Berliner 42; title theme of Sousa's comic opera	
7/06/95	2(3)	3	2. King Cotton March................................ [I] Columbia later recorded for Berliner 143	
8/03/95	1(3)	3	3. **Washington Post March** .... [I] Columbia later recorded for Berliner 140	
7/03/97	1(8)	11	4. **The Stars And Stripes Forever** .... [I] Columbia 532 the most famous of all marches; also recorded for Berliner 61, & later on Berliner 0228	
7/24/97	2(2)	3	5. Dancing In The Dark .... [I] Columbia 529	
6/24/99	2(2)	8	6. Hands Across The Sea .... [I] Berliner 075 also recorded for Chicago 304, later for Gram-o-Phone 300	
2/02/01	1(3)	8	7. **The Stars And Stripes Forever** .... [I] Gram-o-Phone 306 new version of 1897 hit	
2/02/01	4	2	8. The Bride Elect: March .... [I] Gram-o-Phone 303	
2/16/01	3	3	9. William Tell Overture: Finale .... [I] Gram-o-Phone 321	
3/02/01	3	3	10. American Patrol .... [I] Gram-o-Phone 382	
10/12/01	4	2	11. The Invincible Eagle March .... [I] Victor 844	
4/19/02	3	1	12. Semper Fidelis .... [I] Victor 1175 new version of his 1890 U.S. Marine Band hit, written at the request of President Chester A. Arthur	
3/28/03	1(4)	13	13. **In The Good Old Summer Time** .... Victor 1833 vocal refrain: Harry Macdonough & S.H. Dudley from the Broadway musical "The Defender"	
10/17/03	4	3	14. Jack Tar March.................................. [I] Victor 2419	
11/14/03	3	2	15. Hiawatha Two-Step .... [I] Victor 2443	
10/14/05	3	5	16. America.. [I] Victor 4452	
12/02/05	4	2	17. Blue Danube Waltz .... [I] Victor 31450	
1/06/06	3	3	18. Moonlight...................................... [I] Victor 4528	

DATE CHARTED	PEAK POS	WKS CHRT'D	ARTIST — Record Title	Label & Number
2/13/09	3	3	19. Under The Double Eagle.......................... [I]	Victor 5639
2/27/09	9	1	20. Fairest Of The Fair March .... [I]	Victor 5621
4/17/09	3	4	21. El Capitan March.................................. [I]	Victor 35052
			new version of band's 1895 hit	
12/21/12	10	1	22. Sardinia March.................................... [I]	Victor 17162
1/04/13	9	1	23. Venus On Earth Waltz .... [I]	Victor 35164
4/12/13	10	1	24. On The Mississippi (Medley) .... [I]	Victor 17249
7/21/17	4	3	25. The Stars And Stripes Forever March..... [I-R]	Victor 16777
			recorded 12/13/12	
3/16/18	3	4	26. Liberty Loan March .... [I]	Victor 18430
			one of the very few recordings conducted by Sousa	

PAUL SOUTHE
Vaudeville entertainer; died on 8/5/46 (58).

DATE CHARTED	PEAK POS	WKS CHRT'D	ARTIST — Record Title	Label & Number
4/16/10	4	4	1. He's A College Boy...............................	Columbia 790

JERI SOUTHERN
Nebraska-born singer/pianist who became a Chicago favorite in the early 50s.

DATE CHARTED	PEAK POS	WKS CHRT'D	ARTIST — Record Title	Label & Number
12/29/51+	30	1	1. You Better Go Now..............................	Decca 27840
			orchestra directed by Camarata	
8/07/54	25	1	2. Joey...	Decca 29184
			orchestra directed by Sonny Burke	

SPANIELS
Rhythm & Blues group led by "Pookie" Hudson

DATE CHARTED	PEAK POS	WKS CHRT'D	ARTIST — Record Title	Label & Number
6/19/54	24	4	1. Goodnite, Sweetheart, Goodnite	Vee Jay 107

MUGGSY SPANIER & HIS ORCHESTRA
Jazz cornetist with Ray Miller, Ted Lewis (1929-36), Ben Pollack, & Bob Crosby (1940-41); his 1941 band featured clarinet star Irving Fazola; died on 2/12/67 (60).

DATE CHARTED	PEAK POS	WKS CHRT'D	ARTIST — Record Title	Label & Number
2/27/43	21	1	1. Two O'Clock Jump............................. [I]	Decca 4336

PAUL SPECHT & HIS ORCHESTRA
Bandleader who at various times featured future leaders Russ Morgan, Charlie Spivak, & Artie Shaw; died in 1954 (about 59).

DATE CHARTED	PEAK POS	WKS CHRT'D	ARTIST — Record Title	Label & Number
1/20/23	10	1	1. Goodbye.. [I]	Columbia 3708
2/24/23	11	1	2. When The Leaves Come Tumbling Down.... [I]	Columbia 3726
3/24/23	7	2	3. When Hearts Are Young......................... [I]	Columbia 3760
			from the Broadway musical "Lady in Ermine"	
4/25/23	14	1	4. Porcelain Maid................................... [I]	Columbia 3778
7/28/23	6	2	5. Roses Of Picardy .... [I]	Columbia 3870
			with Russ Morgan (trombone)	
2/23/24	6	3	6. Waltz Of Long Ago .... [I]	Columbia 13
			from "Music Box Revue of 1923"	
7/26/24	8	1	7. Morvanna... [I]	Columbia 103
9/13/24	8	2	8. Memory Lane...................................... [I]	Columbia 121
12/20/24	7	2	9. Bagdad .... [I]	Columbia 188
3/21/25	8	2	10. You And I.. [I]	Columbia 261
			from the Broadway musical "My Girl"	
2/19/27	15	2	11. I've Grown So Lonesome, Thinking Of You . [I]	Columbia 819
			Charlie Spivak (trumpet) on above two	
12/14/29	13	4	12. Chant Of The Jungle	Columbia 2002
			from the film "Untamed"	
2/08/30	12	2	13. I'm Following You.................................	Columbia 2056
			from the film "It's a Great Life"	

ELIZABETH SPENCER
Died in April 1930 (about 54).

DATE CHARTED	PEAK POS	WKS CHRT'D	ARTIST — Record Title	Label & Number
9/09/11	9	1	1. My Beautiful Lady	Edison Amb. 762
			from the Broadway musical "The Pink Lady"	
7/25/14	7	2	2. In The Valley Of The Moon	Edison Amb. 2300
11/28/14	10	1	3. Somewhere A Voice Is Calling...................	Edison Amb. 2453
			above two: ELIZABETH SPENCER & VERNON ARCHIBALD	
2/09/18	3	4	4. Where The Morning Glories Grow	Victor 18403
			ELIZABETH SPENCER & STERLING TRIO	

DATE CHARTED	PEAK POS	WKS CHRT'D	ARTIST — Record Title	Label & Number
3/30/18	**4**	4	5. Sweet Little Buttercup.......................... Victor 18427 ELIZABETH SPENCER & SHANNON FOUR	
4/06/18	**10**	1	6. I'm Going To Follow The Boys..................... Victor 18433 HENRY BURR & ELIZABETH SPENCER	
1/18/19	**10**	1	7. The Bluebird.. Victor 18452	
2/28/20	**2(3)**	7	8. Let The Rest Of The World Go By .... Victor 18638 8 & 11: ELIZABETH SPENCER & CHARLES HART	
6/25/21	**12**	1	9. Look For The Silver Lining........................ Okeh 4292 from the Broadway musical "Sally"	
5/27/22	**15**	1	10. Up In The Clouds.................................... Edison 50899 Broadway musical title song above two: ELIZABETH SPENCER & LEWIS JAMES	
3/31/23	**14**	1	11. In Rose Time... Edison 51097	

GRACE SPENCER
Soprano who was the first woman to record for Victor.

DATE CHARTED	PEAK POS	WKS CHRT'D	ARTIST — Record Title	Label & Number
9/08/00+	**2(2)**	4	1. When We Are Married............................... Edison 7558 from the Broadway musical "Belle of New York" later recorded for Victor 904	
4/27/01	**1(7)**	11	2. Tell Me, Pretty Maiden .... Edison 7758 from the Broadway musical "Florodora" later recorded for Victor 1362 & 3501 both: HARRY MACDONOUGH & GRACE SPENCER	

LEN SPENCER
Leonard Garfield Spencer, one of the giants of the pioneer recording era, was born 2/12/1867 in Washington, D.C.; his mother was a renowned suffragist & political activist, his father a famous educator who developed the "Spencerian" method of penmanship long taught in schools. Spencer became America's first nationally-known recording star in the 1890s. In the early 1900s he recorded many dramatic recitations, and had a series of hit comic duets with Ada Jones, in which he played a wide variety of ethnic roles. Len died on 12/15/14 (47).

DATE CHARTED	PEAK POS	WKS CHRT'D	ARTIST — Record Title	Label & Number
3/07/91	**1(4)**	4	1. Little 'Liza Loves You............................. Columbia	
1/30/92	**1(8)**	8	2. Ta-Ra-Ra-Boom Der E............................. Columbia above two also recorded for New Jersey	
8/13/92	**1(6)**	6	3. The Old Folks At Home............................ New Jersey	
11/19/92	**1(2)**	2	4. Near It .... New Jersey from the Broadway musical "The Pearl of Pekin"	
7/29/93	**1(3)**	3	5. Mamie, Come And Kiss Your Honey Boy ..... New Jersey also recorded for Chicago 2055 & Ohio	
10/07/93	**2(3)**	3	6. Carry Me Back To Old Virginny .... New Jersey also recorded for Ohio	
11/03/94	**2(2)**	3	7. Maggie Murphy's Home .... Chicago 2091 from the Broadway musical "Reilly and the Four Hundred"	
1/05/95	**1(5)**	5	8. Little Alabama Coon................................. Columbia 7256 also recorded for Chicago 2093 & New Jersey	
2/02/95	**2(2)**	2	9. I Love My Love In The Spring Time .... Chicago 2095	
4/25/95	**1(5)**	5	10. Dat New Bully.. Columbia 2107	
6/20/96	**1(3)**	3	11. A Hot Time On The Levee........................ Columbia 7200 LEN SPENCER & VESS OSSMAN (banjo)	
9/05/96	**2(3)**	3	12. You've Been A Good Ole Wagon But You've Done Broke Down.............................. Columbia 7209 later recorded for Berliner 0145	
11/07/96	**2(3)**	3	13. All Coons Look Alike To Me .... Columbia 7236 also recorded for Chicago 4000	
1/23/97	**1(3)**	8	14. A Hot Time In The Old Town .... Columbia 7266 later recorded for Berliner 0163	
1/30/97	**1(4)**	8	15. Oh, Mr. Johnson, Turn Me Loose............... Columbia 7239	
2/20/97	**1(4)**	9	16. My Gal Is A Highborn Lady .... Columbia 7252 also recorded for Chicago 4045	
5/29/97	**2(2)**	2	17. You're Not The Only Pebble On The Beach .... Columbia 7263	
8/07/97	**2(3)**	3	18. Crappy Dan .... Columbia 7281 also recorded for Chicago 4007	
9/11/97	**2(2)**	3	19. Bye And Bye You Will Forget Me .... Columbia 8404 LEN SPENCER & ROGER HARDING	
6/04/98	**1(3)**	7	20. I Don't Like No Cheap Man...................... Columbia 7440	

DATE CHARTED	PEAK POS	WKS CHRT'D	ARTIST — Record Title	Label & Number
7/16/98	**2(2)**	3	21. All I Wants Is My Chickens..................... [C]	Columbia 7446
3/04/99	**3**	2	22. Kiss Me, Honey, Do .... also recorded for Berliner 07	Columbia 7456
4/01/99	**2(4)**	6	23. I Guess I'll Have To Telegraph My Baby	Columbia 7466
4/29/99	**1(6)**	12	24. **Hello! Ma Baby**....................................... also recorded for Columbia 7470	Berliner 05
5/13/99	**5**	1	25. When You Ain't Got No More Money, Well, You Needn't Come 'Round.............. [C]	Berliner 017
9/30/99	**4**	4	26. Everything Is Rag-Time Now	Columbia 7479
10/21/99	**2(2)**	4	27. Smoky Mokes...	Columbia 7480
7/14/00	**1(5)**	10	28. **Ma Tiger Lily**.......................................	Columbia 7502
11/03/00	**2(3)**	7	29. Arkansaw Traveler .... [C] original version of song published in 1851	Columbia 11098
6/29/01	**2(3)**	6	30. Reuben Haskins From Skowhegan, Maine . [C] later recorded for Victor 1972 & Edison 8441	Columbia 31582
9/21/01	**3**	3	31. Con Clancy's Christening .... [C] later recorded for Victor 1104 & Edison 8279	Columbia 31634
11/02/01	**3**	2	32. Scene At A Dog Fight ....[T-N] with animal impressions by Gilbert Girard	Victor 860

3/01/02	**1(11)**	14	33. **Arkansaw Traveler** .... [C]
			     the biggest-selling record of the pre-1905 era; new version
			     of 1900 hit; also on Columbia disc 21, later recorded for
			     Edison 8202
			     Charles D'Almaine (violin) accompanies 29, 31-33
				Victor 1101

8/09/02	**3**	3	34. Daybreak At Calamity Farm .... [C]
			     with Gilbert Girard; also recorded for Victor 1381, later
			     for Columbia 916 & 31856
				Edison 8034

10/17/03	**2(3)**	4	35. Reuben Haskins' Ride On A Cyclone Auto. [C] later recorded for Edison 8619	Columbia 1528

8/27/04+	**5**	1	36. Reuben Haskins' Ride 'Round The World In
			       His Air-Ship................................... [C]
			     with Parke Hunter (banjo)
			     also recorded for Victor 2803 & 31215
				Edison 8704

1/28/05	**8**	1	37. The Transformation Scene From "Dr. Jekyll
			       and Mr. Hyde"................................. [T]
			     also recorded for Edison 8879, later for Victor 4233
				Columbia 1908

2/11/05	**4**	3	38. Can't You See My Heart Beats All For You .... BILLY MURRAY & LEN SPENCER	Victor 4152
4/29/05	**6**	1	39. Reuben Haskins' Ride In The "Red Devil" .. [C]	Victor 4216
10/28/05	**10**	1	40. Barn Dance In Dixie .... [C]	Victor 4436
1/27/06	**10**	1	41. The Musical Yankee .... [C]	Victor 31444

5/26/06	**6**	1	42. Flanagan's Night Off............................ [C]
			     LEN SPENCER & STEVE PORTER
			     also recorded for Zon-o-Phone 515
				Edison 9244

11/24/06	**8**	1	43. Pat And Mike McGee .... [C]	Victor 31567
7/31/09	**8**	1	44. Uncle Josh's Trip To Coney Island.........[T-C] CAL STEWART & LEN SPENCER	Edison 10149
8/27/10	**10**	1	45. Two Gentlemen From Ireland.................. [C] 43 & 45: BILLY MURRAY & LEN SPENCER	Edison Amb. 442

LEN SPENCER & ADA JONES

Billy Murray was originally to play the female role in these
comedy records, but when he discovered Ada Jones, she became Len's
protege and half of two of the era's most popular record teams.

5/27/05	**8**	1	1. Mr. And Mrs. Murphy........................... [C]	Columbia 3108
6/03/05	**5**	1	2. Heinie... [C]	Edison 8982
6/17/05	**4**	3	3. Ev'ry Little Bit Helps........................... [C] also recorded for Columbia 3148 & 32730	Edison 9016
6/24/05	**8**	1	4. Reuben And Cynthia .... [C]	Victor 4302

7/08/05	**5**	1	5. Pals .... [C]
			     introducing the song "He's Me Pal"
			     also recorded for Victor 4363 & Zon-o-Phone 321
				Columbia 3148

10/21/05	**4**	1	6. Jimmie And Maggie At The Hippodrome .[T-C] later recorded for Victor 31483 & Imperial 44777	Edison 9079

DATE CHARTED	PEAK POS	WKS CHRT'D	ARTIST — Record Title	Label & Number
12/30/05	9	1	7. Courtship Of Barney And Eileen ....[T-C] also recorded for Victor 31441	Edison 9143
1/27/06	4	2	8. The Golden Wedding .... [C] also recorded for Edison 9148, Columbia 3314, Zon-o-Phone 342, Indestructable 3093, & Imperial 44778	Victor 4549
2/24/06	7	1	9. Fritz And Louisa ....[T-C] also recorded for Victor 4550, Columbia 3325 & 32868	Edison 9172
3/31/06	6	1	10. The Original Cohens...........................[T-C] also on Columbia cylinder 32901, Victor 4605, & Edison 9215	Columbia 3340
8/25/06	4	1	11. Bashful Henry And His Lovin' Lucy .... [C] also recorded for Edison 9335 & Zon-o-Phone 513	Victor 31531
10/06/06	3	3	12. Peaches And Cream .... [C] also recorded for Edison 9359, Columbia 3468 & 32999, & Zon-o-Phone 497	Victor 4720
11/24/06	6	1	13. Let Me See You Smile .... [C] also recorded for Columbia 85081	Edison 9383
12/29/06	8	1	14. Jimmie And Maggie At The Ball Game....[T-C]	Victor 4864
2/23/07	7	1	15. Down On The Farm .... [C] also recorded for Victor 31597 & Zon-o-Phone 617	Edison 9431
7/27/07	7	1	16. Meet Me Down At The Corner .... [C] also recorded for Edison 9552, later for Victor 5252	Columbia 3665
11/30/07	7	1	17. Herman And Minnie ....[T-C] also recorded for Edison 9643, Columbia 3690 & 33169	Victor 5186
12/28/07	8	1	18. You've Got To Love Me A Lot .... [C] later recorded for Victor 5334	Columbia 3719
5/16/08	5	2	19. Jimmie And Maggie At "The Merry Widow".......................................[T-C] also recorded for Edison 9820, Zon-o-Phone 5109 & Indestructable 718	Victor 5386
10/29/10	9	1	20. Return Of The Arkansas Traveler .... [C]	Columbia 3108

PHIL SPITALNY & HIS ORCHESTRA
Russian-born bandleader, clarinet prodigy who came to U.S. in 1917. In 1934 formed the "all-girl" orchestra for which he became most famous; his "Hour of Charm" radio show a long-running hit through 1940s; died on 10/11/70 (79).

DATE CHARTED	PEAK POS	WKS CHRT'D	ARTIST — Record Title	Label & Number
1/01/27	14	1	1. Someone Is Losin' Susan........................ [I]	Victor 20196
1/22/27	14	3	2. Just A Little Longer.............................. vocal: Charles Hart	Victor 20272
10/25/30	18	1	3. Beyond The Blue Horizon......................... from the film "Monte Carlo"	Brunswick 4917
4/18/42	21	1	4. We Must Be Vigilant .... Phil Spitalny & His All-Girl Orchestra song based on "American Patrol"	Columbia 36550
10/28/50	23	5	5. Our Lady Of Fatima................................ vocal: Hour of Charm Choir	RCA Victor 3920

CHARLIE SPIVAK & HIS ORCHESTRA
Played trumpet with Paul Specht (1925-31), Ben Pollack (1931-34), Dorsey Brothers, Ray Noble, Tommy Dorsey (1938), & Jack Teagarden; Glenn Miller helped him form band in 1940. Sonny Burke & Nelson Riddle wrote arrangements, vocals by Garry Stevens and Stardusters (including June Hutton); 1942 band featured Willie Smith (alto sax) & Dave Tough (drums). Charlie later married singer Irene Daye. He died of cancer on 3/1/82 (75).

DATE CHARTED	PEAK POS	WKS CHRT'D	ARTIST — Record Title	Label & Number
6/07/41	10	6	1. Intermezzo (A Love Story)...................... [I]	Okeh 6120
12/20/41+	8	9	2. This Is No Laughing Matter.......................	Okeh 6458
12/27/41	15	1	3. Let's Go Home .... [I]	Okeh 6366
8/01/42	20	1	4. Brother Bill .... vocal: Stardusters	Columbia 36596
9/05/42	8	6	5. I Left My Heart At The Stage Door Canteen/ from the Broadway musical "This Is the Army"	
9/12/42	2(2)	12	6. My Devotion	Columbia 36620
11/07/42	12	5	7. White Christmas................................. [X] from the film "Holiday Inn" vocals on 2, 5-7: Garry Stevens	Columbia 36649
4/28/45	16	1	8. Sweetheart Of All My Dreams .... from the film "Thirty Seconds Over Tokyo"	Victor 1646

DATE CHARTED	PEAK POS	WKS CHRT'D	ARTIST — Record Title	Label & Number
5/26/45	**6**.	6	9. You Belong To My Heart/ from the animated film "The Three Caballeros"	
5/26/45	**9**	6	10. There Must Be A Way............................	Victor 1663
10/13/45	**4**	12	11. It's Been A Long, Long Time......................	Victor 1721
			vocals on 8 & 11: Irene Daye	
3/16/46	**5**	7	12. Oh! What It Seemed To Be.........................	RCA Victor 1806
12/14/46	**5**	14	13. (I Love You) For Sentimental Reasons	RCA Victor 1981
			vocals on 9-10 & 12-13: Jimmy Saunders	
3/29/47	**5**	11	14. Linda	RCA Victor 2047
7/26/47	**25**	1	15. Tomorrow	Victor 2287
			vocal by Rusty Nichols	
3/20/48	**14**	2	16. Now Is The Hour (Maori Farewell Song)........	RCA Victor 2704
			based on the traditional New Zealand song "Hearare Ra" vocals on 14 & 16: Tommy Mercer	
6/12/48	**23**	1	17. Inner Spectrum	RCA Victor 2864
7/29/50	**16**	7	18. Mona Lisa	London 619
			from the film "Captain Carey, U.S.A."	

SPORTSMEN
Group accompanied Mel Blanc on 1948 smash "Woody Woodpecker"
(also see Benny Goodman)

DATE CHARTED	PEAK POS	WKS CHRT'D	ARTIST — Record Title	Label & Number
10/23/43	**22**	1	1. What Did You Do In The Infantry?	Decca 18562
3/13/48	**24**	1	2. Tutti Tutti Pizzicato............................. [N]	Capitol 496
5/28/48	**6**	14	3. You Can't Be True, Dear/	
6/12/48	**11**	6	4. Toolie Oolie Doolie................................	Capitol 15077
7/17/48	**2(5)**	9	5. Woody Woodpecker................................ [N]	Capitol 15145
			SPORTSMEN & MEL BLANC	

DICK STABILE
Featured alto saxophonist with Ben Bernie 1928-36, then bandleader
who for a time featured singer Paula Kelly; in 50s accompanied
Dean Martin on radio & records.

JESS STACY
Four-time Down Beat poll winner as top pianist: with Benny Goodman
(1935-39, 42-44, 46-47), Bob Crosby (1940-42), Tommy Dorsey
(1944).

JO STAFFORD
Sang with Tommy Dorsey 1940-42 both as member of Pied Pipers and
individually ("Yes Indeed", "Manhattan Serenade"). Jo left Pied
Pipers in 1944, had smash hits with Red Ingle & Johnny Mercer
("Candy"), and ran up a string of solo and duet successes.
(Except as noted, all records are accompanied by Paul Weston & His
Orchestra)

DATE CHARTED	PEAK POS	WKS CHRT'D	ARTIST — Record Title	Label & Number
1/08/44	**15**	2	1. Old Acquaintance/ movie title song	
2/15/44	**14**	1	2. How Sweet You Are................................	Capitol 142
			from the film "Thank Your Lucky Stars"	
4/29/44	**8**	6	3. I Love You/ from the Broadway musical "Mexican Hayride"	
5/06/44	**6**	14	4. Long Ago (And Far Away)	Capitol 153
			from the film "Cover Girl"	
7/29/44	**10**	10	5. It Could Happen To You...........................	Capitol 158
			from the film "And the Angels Sing"	
2/17/45	**14**	3	6. Let's Take The Long Way Home	Capitol 181
			from film "Here Come the Waves"	
2/24/45	**1(1)**	18	7. **Candy**	Capitol 183
			JOHNNY MERCER, JO STAFFORD & PIED PIPERS	
5/12/45	**7**	7	8. There's No You/	
7/28/45	**9**	1	9. Out Of This World................................	Capitol 191
			movie title song	
7/07/45	**17**	1	10. On The Sunny Side Of The Street.................	Capitol 199
			with the Pied Pipers from the Broadway musical "International Revue"	
11/03/45	**4**	4	11. That's For Me.....................................	Capitol 213
			from the film "State Fair"	
12/29/45+	**4**	12	12. Symphony/	
3/09/46	**8**	2	13. Day By Day	Capitol 227

405

DATE CHARTED	PEAK POS	WKS CHRT'D	ARTIST — Record Title	Label & Number
9/28/46	11	1	14. This Is Always .... from the film "Three Little Girls in Blue"	Capitol 277
11/09/46	11	5	15. You Keep Coming Back Like A Song/ from the film "Blue Skies"	
11/16/46	10	2	16. The Things We Did Last Summer..............	Capitol 297
12/28/46	9	1	17. White Christmas................................[X] from the film "Holiday Inn"	Capitol 319
1/18/47	10	5	18. Sonata.. accompanied by Carlyle Hall's Orchestra	Capitol 337
5/03/47	13	4	19. Ivy/ movie title song	
6/07/47	15	1	20. A Sunday Kind Of Love	Capitol 388
8/16/47	21	4	21. I'm So Right Tonight	Capitol 423
8/30/47	7	11	22. Feudin' And Fightin' .... with the Starlighters from the Broadway musical "Laffing Room Only"	Capitol 443
10/11/47	11	2	23. The Stanley Steamer .... featured in the film "Summer Holiday"	Capitol 454
10/18/47	25	1	24. Love And The Weather	Capitol 443
11/29/47	20	3	25. The Gentleman Is A Dope/ from the Broadway musical "Allegro"	
12/20/47	6	11	26. Serenade Of The Bells	Capitol 15007
1/03/48	21	3	27. The Best Things In Life Are Free/ from the Broadway musical "Good News"	
1/10/48	23	1	28. I Never Loved Anyone	Capitol 15017
1/24/48	21	2	29. I'm My Own Grandmaw/ [N] with the Starlighters & Paul Weston's Mountain Boys	
2/07/48	23	4	30. Haunted Heart .... from the Broadway musical "Inside U.S.A."	Capitol 15023
5/01/48	23	1	31. Suspicion	Capitol 15068
5/29/48	26	2	32. Better Luck Next Time	Capitol 15084
9/25/48	25	1	33. Ev'ry Day I Love You (Just A Little Bit More). from the film "Two Guys from Texas"	Capitol 15139
1/15/49	13	11	34. Congratulations/	
1/29/49	28	1	35. Here I'll Stay	Capitol 15319
4/23/49	16	6	36. Once And For Always...............................	Capitol 15424
5/14/49	4	17	37. Some Enchanted Evening .... from the Broadway musical "South Pacific"	Capitol 544
8/13/49	11	8	38. Homework/	
8/20/49	12	6	39. Just One Way To Say I Love You..............	Capitol 665
9/17/49	10	7	40. Ragtime Cowboy Joe/	
10/15/49	16	5	41. The Last Mile Home	Capitol 710
11/19/49	20	2	42. If I Ever Love Again	Capitol 742
1/07/50	14	4	43. Scarlet Ribbons (For Her Hair).....................	Capitol 785
3/04/50	30	1	44. Diamonds Are A Girl's Best Friend .... with the Starlighters from the Broadway musical "Gentlemen Prefer Blondes"	Capitol 824
7/01/50	18	3	45. Play A Simple Melody.............................. with "Paul Weston's Dixie Eight" from the Broadway musical "Watch Your Step" 32, 40 & 45 with the Starlighters	Capitol 1039
8/19/50	8	11	46. No Other Love/ from the Broadway musical "Me and Juliet"	
9/02/50	27	3	47. Sometime..	Capitol 1053
8/26/50	9	7	48. Goodnight, Irene...................................... accompanied by Harold Mooney's Orchestra	Capitol 1142
12/02/50+	7	13	49. Tennessee Waltz/	
12/16/50	14	4	50. If You've Got The Money, I've Got The Time	Col. 78-39065
1/13/51	8	18	51. If/	
3/10/51	15	3	52. It Is No Secret	Col. 78-39082
5/19/51	13	10	53. Pretty Eyed Baby......................................	Columbia 39388
6/02/51	12	5	54. Somebody	Columbia 39389

DATE CHARTED	PEAK POS	WKS CHRT'D	ARTIST — Record Title	Label & Number
8/11/51	**17**	4	55. In The Cool, Cool, Cool Of The Evening......... from the film "Here Comes the Groom"	Columbia 39466
9/15/51	**20**	2	56. Kissing Bug Boogie	Columbia 39529
10/20/51	**9**	8	57. Hey, Good Lookin'/	
10/27/51	**19**	4	58. Gambella (The Gamblin' Lady) .... 53, 55 & 57-58: JO STAFFORD & FRANKIE LAINE	Columbia 39570
11/10/51	**2(2)**	17	● 59. Shrimp Boats............................... 54, 58-59 with the Norman Luboff Choir	Columbia 39581
3/08/52	**6**	10	60. Hambone...................................	Columbia 39672
3/08/52	**9**	12	61. A-Round The Corner	Columbia 39653
8/09/52	**1(12)**	25	● 62. **You Belong To Me** .... Jo's biggest-selling hit (close to 2 million copies)	Columbia 39811
8/30/52	**3**	20	● 63. Jambalaya	Columbia 39838
10/18/52	**21**	3	64. Tonight We're Setting The Woods On Fire	Columbia 39867
10/25/52	**23**	3	65. Early Autumn	Columbia 39838
11/15/52+	**4**	18	66. Keep It A Secret	Columbia 39891
1/03/53	**25**	1	67. Chow, Willy .... 60, 64 & 67: JO STAFFORD & FRANKIE LAINE	Columbia 39893
2/21/53	**16**	4	68. (Now And Then There's) A Fool Such As I	Columbia 39930
3/21/53	**27**	2	69. Without My Lover	Columbia 39951
6/20/53	**22**	1	70. Just Another Polka.......................... 65, 67 & 70 with the Norman Luboff Choir	Columbia 40000
11/28/53	**26**	1	71. Way Down Yonder In New Orleans .... JO STAFFORD & FRANKIE LAINE Carl Fischer (piano) on all Stafford-Laine records	Columbia 40116
1/23/54	**1(7)**	24	● 72. **Make Love To Me!**....................... based on 1923 jazz instrumental "Tin Roof Blues"	Columbia 40143
3/27/54	**30**	1	73. Indiscretion .... with Liberace (piano) from the Italian film "Indiscretion of an American Wife"	Columbia 40170
7/03/54	**12**	5	74. Thank You For Calling......................	Columbia 40250
12/04/54	**15**	6	75. Teach Me Tonight	Columbia 40351

JO STAFFORD & GORDON MacRAE

DATE CHARTED	PEAK POS	WKS CHRT'D	ARTIST — Record Title	Label & Number
10/16/48	**10**	6	1. Say Something Sweet To Your Sweetheart/	
10/16/48	**16**	4	2. Bluebird Of Happiness .... with male choir	Capitol 15207
11/13/48+	**1(1)**	17	3. **My Darling, My Darling** .... from the Broadway musical "Where's Charley?" 1 & 3 with the Starlighters	Capitol 15270
2/12/49	**26**	2	4. The Pussy Cat Song	Capitol 15342
3/19/49	**4**	15	5. "A"-You're Adorable (The Alphabet Song)/	
4/02/49	**7**	12	6. Need You	Capitol 15393
8/20/49	**4**	23	● 7. Whispering Hope .... song written in 1868	Capitol 690
12/24/49+	**13**	7	8. Bibbidi-Bobbidi-Boo/ from the animated film "Cinderella"	
12/24/49+	**18**	5	9. Echoes....................................	Capitol 782
3/11/50	**10**	11	10. Dearie .... from the stage production "The Copacabana Show of 1950"	Capitol 858

JOHNNY STANDLEY

DATE CHARTED	PEAK POS	WKS CHRT'D	ARTIST — Record Title	Label & Number
10/04/52	**1(2)**	19	● 1. **It's In The Book** .... [C] with Hoarce Heidt & His Musical Knights a parody of fundamentalist preachers	Capitol 2249

AILEEN STANLEY

Chicago-born singer particularly popular in duets with Billy Murray; appeared in three Broadway musicals. Aileen died on 3/24/82 (89).

DATE CHARTED	PEAK POS	WKS CHRT'D	ARTIST — Record Title	Label & Number
1/29/21	**12**	1	1. Singin' The Blues................................	Victor 18703
6/11/21	**8**	2	2. My Mammy .... from the Broadway musical "Sinbad"	Okeh 4275
7/30/21	**11**	1	3. I'm Nobody's Baby .... later recorded for Edison 50791	Vocalion 14172

DATE CHARTED	PEAK POS	WKS CHRT'D	ARTIST — Record Title	Label & Number
8/13/21	7	2	4. My Man (Mon Homme)......................... Okeh 4326 French song; from the "Ziegfeld Follies of 1921"	
8/27/21	6	2	5. Home Again Blues .... Victor 18760	
10/01/21	5	3	6. All By Myself .... Victor 18774 most above records accompanied by Rosario Bordon's Orchestra	
9/30/22	2(2)	5	7. Sweet Indiana Home.............................. Victor 18922	
12/16/22	7	2	8. The Dixie Highway .... Victor 18935	
12/23/22	9	1	9. All Over Nothing At All............................ Victor 18943	
6/30/23	11	1	10. You've Got To See Mama Ev'ry Night........... Victor 19027	
10/25/24	8	1	11. It Had To Be You .... Victor 19373 accompanied by Prince's Orchestra above three: BILLY MURRAY & AILEEN STANLEY	
2/07/25	5	3	12. Everybody Loves My Baby......................... Victor 19486	
5/02/25	3	6	13. When My Sugar Walks Down The Street....... Victor 19585 GENE AUSTIN & AILEEN STANLEY accompanied by Nat Shilkret's Orchestra	
1/30/26	10	1	14. Keep Your Skirts Down, Mary Ann.............. Victor 19795	
5/15/26	10	1	15. I Love My Baby (My Baby Loves Me)............ Victor 19950	
12/11/26	6	2	16. I Can't Get Over A Girl Like You (Loving A Boy Like Me) .... Victor 200148 accompanied by Frank Banta (piano)	
1/08/27	14	2	17. Bridget O'Flynn (Where've Ya Been?) .... Victor 20240 record known for its whispering introduction 14, 16 & 17: BILLY MURRAY & AILEEN STANLEY	
8/27/27	7	4	18. Side By Side .... Victor 20714 AILEEN STANLEY & JOHNNY MARVIN	
9/10/27	18	1	19. I'm Back In Love Again............................ Victor 20643	
10/22/27	17	2	20. Broken Hearted .... Victor 20825 accompanied by Leroy Shield's Orchestra	
6/08/29	16	2	21. I'll Never Ask For More .... Victor 21874	
6/15/29	18	1	22. I'll Get By, As Long As I Have You............... Victor 21839 accompanied by Leonard Joy's Orchestra	

FRANK STANLEY

The dominant popular bass voice of his era, Frank Stanley (born William Stanley Grinsted) started as a banjo player, and accompanied Arthur Collins on some late-1890s cylinders. He became most famous as leader (and manager) of the Peerless Quartet, and for his many duets with Henry Burr, Corrine Morgan, & others. Frank also found time to be elected alderman and public school commissioner of Orange, N.J. He died of pneumonia on 12/12/10 (41). (also see Peerless Quartet)

DATE CHARTED	PEAK POS	WKS CHRT'D	ARTIST — Record Title	Label & Number
1/14/99	2(2)	4	1. My Old New Hampshire Home .... Columbia 5636	
2/25/99	4	2	2. 'Mid The Green Fields Of Virginia .... Columbia 5634	
8/30/02	4	2	3. First Rehearsal For The Huskin' Bee........ [C] Edison 8096 later recorded for Columbia 916 & 31856	
11/15/02	3	3	4. Two Rubes In A Tavern .... [C] Columbia 938 also recorded for Edison 8121	
12/13/02	5	1	5. Closing Time At A Country Grocery .... [C] Edison 8172 later recorded for Columbia 1141 & 32077 above three: FRANK STANLEY & BYRON HARLAN	
8/08/03	4	3	6. It's A Lovely Day For A Walk..................... Edison 8469 also recorded for Columbia 1461	
5/14/04	1(4)	7	7. **Blue Bell** .... Edison 8655	
8/27/04	3	5	8. Listen To The Mocking Bird...................... Edison 8715 later recorded for Columbia 1833 & 32531, & Victor 4080 & 31316 6 & 8: FRANK STANLEY & CORRINE MORGAN	
2/25/05	9	1	9. The Battle Cry Of Freedom .... Victor 4099	
3/25/05	2(2)	4	10. In The Shadow Of The Pyramid .... Victor 4210	
3/25/05	8	1	11. Soldier Boy..................................... Columbia 3067 from the Broadway musical "Rogers Brothers in Paris" 7, 9 & 11: FRANK STANLEY & BYRON HARLAN	
3/25/05	9	1	12. Juanita... Edison 8916	
4/29/05	5	1	13. Listen To The Big Brass Band .... Victor 4259	

DATE CHARTED	PEAK POS	WKS CHRT'D	ARTIST — Record Title	Label & Number
6/10/05	**5**	1	14. Just My Style..	Victor 4332
			also recorded for Edison 8997	
9/23/05	**4**	2	15. When You And I Were Young, Maggie	Victor 4428
			12, 14-15: FRANK STANLEY & CORRINE MORGAN	
11/18/05	**3**	4	16. In Dear Old Georgia.....................................	Victor 4503
			also recorded for Columbia 3256 & 32805	
11/25/05	**7**	1	17. Little Girl, You'll Do.....................................	Columbia 3257
			also on Columbia cylinder 32790	
			from the Broadway musical "That Rollicking Girl"	
3/31/06	**7**	1	18. When The Mocking Birds Are Singing In The	
			Wildwood..	Columbia 3336
5/19/06	**3**	4	19. Good-Bye, Sweetheart, Good-Bye	Edison 9283
			first recorded for Zon-o-Phone 216	
6/23/06	**4**	2	20. The Moon Has His Eyes On You....................	Victor 4696
			also recorded for Columbia 3412 & 32955	
7/07/06	**3**	3	21. I Want What I Want When I Want It	Edison 9307
			from the Broadway musical "Mile, Modiste"	
			also recorded for Zon-o-Phone 414	
8/25/06	**8**	1	22. By The Light Of The Honeymoon	Victor 31532
			20 & 22: FRANK STANLEY & CORRINE MORGAN	
9/29/06	**10**	1	23. The Belle Of The Ball	Columbia 3421
			also on Columbia cylinder 32962	
1/12/07	**3**	3	24. The Linger Longer Girl	Victor 4876
			later recorded for Columbia 3573 & Zon-o-Phone 716	
			FRANK STANLEY & ELISE STEVENSON	
1/26/07	**6**	1	25. In The Evening By The Moonlight, Dear	
			Louise...	Columbia 3521
2/23/07	**8**	1	26. Almost Persuaded.......................................	Victor 4917
4/27/07	**2(1)**	4	27. Whistle It	Columbia 3589
			ADA JONES, BILLY MURRAY, & FRANK STANLEY	
			from the Broadway musical "The Red Mill"	
4/27/07	**6**	1	28. Somebody's Waiting For You	Columbia 3577
5/25/07	**7**	1	29. The Tale The Church Bell Tolled	Columbia 33111
			also recorded for Zon-o-Phone 7022	
7/27/07	**6**	1	30. In The Wildwood Where The Blue Bells Grew .	Edison 9567
			FRANK STANLEY & BYRON HARLAN	
			also recorded for Zon-o-Phone 793	
12/14/07	**2(1)**	3	31. Auld Lang Syne.............................. [X]	Columbia 3731
1/25/08	**8**	1	32. You...	Columbia 3732
3/28/08	**4**	1	33. Some Day You'll Come Back To Me	Victor 5366
			26 & 33: FRANK STANLEY & HARRY MACDONOUGH	
5/09/08	**4**	2	34. The Cavalier	Victor 5389
			also recorded for Zon-o-Phone 5145	
5/30/08	**6**	1	35. From Your Dear Heart To Mine	Columbia 3757
10/10/08	**2(1)**	4	36. Any Old Port In A Storm	Victor 5547
			also recorded for Indestructable 799 & Zon-o-Phone 5097	
1/02/09	**1(5)**	11	37. **Good Evening, Caroline**...........................	Victor 5627
			also recorded for Columbia 5080	
			34 & 37: FRANK STANLEY & ELISE STEVENSON	
3/13/09	**3**	4	38. Meet Me In Rose-Time, Rosie......................	Columbia 630
			FRANK STANLEY & BYRON HARLAN	
			also recorded for Edison 10079	
10/30/09	**6**	1	39. Cupid's Telephone	Columbia 729
			from the Broadway musical "Havana"	
12/25/09+	**5**	3	40. It's Hard To Kiss Your Sweetheart (When The	
			Last Kiss Means Good-Bye)	Columbia 734
1/08/10	**4**	4	41. What Makes The World Go Round................	Columbia 756
			from the Broadway musical "A Broken Idol"	
3/26/10	**5**	3	42. That Would Be Lovely	Columbia 781
			from the Broadway musical "The Chocolate Soldier"	
			above three: FRANK STANLEY & ELISE STEVENSON	
10/15/10	**1(1)**	9	43. **Tramp! Tramp! Tramp!**	Victor 16531
			from the Broadway musical "Naughty Marietta"	
9/23/11	**4**	3	44. Chicken Reel	Victor 16897
			also recorded for Columbia 1044	
			above two: FRANK STANLEY & BYRON HARLAN	

DATE CHARTED	PEAK POS	WKS CHRT'D	ARTIST — Record Title	Label & Number
			FRANK STANLEY & HENRY BURR	
			The leaders of the Peerless Quartet	
9/07/07	**2(4)**	9	1. Red Wing (An Indian Fable)	Columbia 3681
11/30/07	**8**	1	2. When Summer Tells Autumn Good-Bye.........	Columbia 3696
			also on Columbia cylinder 33175	
6/13/08	**2(3)**	8	3. She's The Fairest Little Flower Old Dixie Ever Grew	Columbia 3785
			also on Indestructable 678	
8/29/08	**10**	1	4. Bye Bye Dearie...............................	Columbia 3803
			also on Columbia cylinder 33241	
12/12/08	**4**	2	5. Rainbow..	Columbia 600
4/10/09	**2(4)**	7	6. In The Garden Of My Heart	Columbia 641
			also on Indestructable 1107	
5/29/09	**10**	1	7. Softly And Tenderly	Columbia 5089
6/19/09	**2(1)**	6	8. Shine On, Harvest Moon..........................	Indestructable 1075
			also recorded for Zon-o-Phone 5509 from the Broadway musicals "Ziegfeld Follies of 1908" and "Miss Innocence"	
8/06/10	**10**	1	9. We Shall Meet Bye And Bye.......................	Edison 10370
12/03/10	**5**	3	10. Silver Bell	Columbia 917
			also on Indestructable 1413	
12/17/10	**9**	1	11. My Prairie Song Bird	Victor 16560
			also recorded for Indestructable 1220	
4/22/11+	**8**	2	12. The Moonlight, The Rose, And You	Victor 16702
			above two also on Zon-o-Phone 5647	
			STARLIGHTERS	
			Sang background on some Jo Stafford records	
6/26/48	**23**	1	1. Maria From Bahia	Capitol 15114
2/19/49	**26**	1	2. I've Got My Love To Keep Me Warm	Capitol 15330
			from the film "On the Avenue"	
8/20/49	**21**	3	3. Room Full Of Roses...............................	Capitol 617
2/18/50	**12**	7	4. Rag Mop..	Capitol 844
			accompanied on all by Paul Weston's Orchestra	
			KAY STARR	
			Born Katherine Starks on an Oklahoma Indian reservation, Kay sang briefly with Glenn Miller, Charlie Barnet, & other bands before launching her successful solo career.	
12/04/48	**16**	8	1. You Were Only Foolin' (While I Was Falling In Love)	Capitol 15226
1/15/49	**7**	16	2. So Tired.....................................	Capitol 15314
5/28/49	**28**	1	3. How It Lies, How It Lies, How It Lies	Capitol 15419
5/06/50	**2(1)**	15	4. Hoop-Dee-Doo	Capitol 980
5/27/50	**4**	27	5. Bonaparte's Retreat	Capitol 936
			accompanied by Lou Busch's Orchestra	
7/15/50	**18**	1	6. M-I-S-S-I-S-S-I-P-P-I	Capitol 1072
8/19/50	**3**	20	7. I'll Never Be Free/	
8/19/50	**22**	2	8. Ain't Nobody's Business But My Own	Capitol 1124
			above two: KAY STARR & TENNESSEE ERNIE FORD	
11/18/50	**7**	8	9. Oh, Babe!	Capitol 1278
			3-4, 6, & 9 accompanied by Frank DeVol's Orchestra	
6/30/51	**15**	6	10. Oceans Of Tears/	
6/30/51	**22**	1	11. You're My Sugar..............................	Capitol 1567
			above two: KAY STARR & TENNESSEE ERNIE FORD	
8/04/51	**8**	9	12. Come On-A My House	Capitol 1710
			from the off-Broadway play "The Son"	
10/27/51	**26**	1	13. Angry	Capitol 1796
			above two accompanied by Dave Cavanaugh's Orchestra	
2/16/52	**1(10)**	25	● 14. **Wheel Of Fortune**	Capitol 1964
5/31/52	**20**	6	15. I Waited A Little Too Long	Capitol 2062

DATE CHARTED	PEAK POS	WKS CHRT'D	ARTIST — Record Title	Label & Number
7/26/52	**18**	3	16. Kay's Lament/	
8/09/52	**13**	8	17. Fool, Fool, Fool	Capitol 2151
			above two with the Lancers	
9/27/52	**9**	9	18. Comes A-Long A-Love/	
10/11/52	**22**	4	19. Three Letters....................................	Capitol 2213
1/31/53	**3**	13	20. Side By Side	Capitol 2334
6/06/53	**7**	15	21. Half A Photograph/	
6/20/53	**11**	9	22. Allez-Vous-En	Capitol 2464
			from the Broadway musical "Can-Can"	
			14, 18-22 accompanied by Harold Mooney's Orchestra	
10/17/53	**18**	4	23. When My Dreamboat Comes Home/	
10/31/53	**30**	1	24. Swamp Fire	Capitol 2595
			above two accompanied by Dave Cavanaugh's Orchestra	
12/05/53+	**7**	13	25. Changing Partners	Capitol 2657
4/17/54	**7**	17	26. The Man Upstairs/	
4/24/54	**4**	18	27. If You Love Me (Really Love Me)	Capitol 2769
			above three accompanied by Harold Mooney's Orchestra	
9/11/54	**22**	3	28. Am I A Toy Or A Treasure?/	
10/06/54	**17**	4	29. Fortune In Dreams..............................	Capitol 2887

JOHN STEEL
Tenor star of several Broadway musicals; died on 6/24/71 (71).

DATE CHARTED	PEAK POS	WKS CHRT'D	ARTIST — Record Title	Label & Number
8/02/19	**2(1)**	7	1. A Rose, A Kiss, And You...........................	Victor 18551
9/20/19	**1(5)**	15	2. **A Pretty Girl Is Like A Melody**..................	Victor 18588
			from Broadway's "Ziegfeld Follies of 1919"	
11/08/19	**6**	3	3. Dear Heart	Victor 18606
1/03/20	**7**	2	4. The Hand That Rocked The Cradle Rules My Heart	Victor 18611
8/21/20	**1(4)**	10	5. **The Love Nest**	Victor 18676
			from the Broadway musical "Mary"	
10/16/20	**3**	5	6. Tell Me, Little Gypsy/	
11/13/20	**5**	4	7. The Girls Of My Dreams..........................	Victor 18687
			above two from Broadway's "Ziegfeld Follies of 1920"	
12/25/20+	**8**	2	8. Whispering	Victor 18695
1/28/22	**11**	1	9. Say It With Music	Victor 18828
			from the Broadway musical "Music Box Revue"	
3/25/22	**4**	5	10. The World Is Waiting For The Sunrise	Victor 18844
4/25/23	**4**	5	11. Lady Of The Evening	Victor 18990
			from the "Music Box Revue of 1922"	
3/22/24	**4**	4	12. Little Butterfly/	
3/29/24	**11**	1	13. An Orange Grove In California	Victor 19219
			above two from the "Music Box Revue of 1923"	

JON & SANDRA STEELE

DATE CHARTED	PEAK POS	WKS CHRT'D	ARTIST — Record Title	Label & Number
5/15/48	**2(2)**	30	● 1. My Happiness......................................	Damon 11133

GEORGE STEHL, MARSHALL LUFSKY, & PAUL SURTH
Violin, flute, & harp.

DATE CHARTED	PEAK POS	WKS CHRT'D	ARTIST — Record Title	Label & Number
12/19/08	**5**	1	1. The Herd Girl's Dream........................... [I]	Columbia 587

MAX STEINER
One of the great Hollywood film score composers ("Gone With The Wind", "A Summer Place"); Austrian-born, died on 12/28/71 (83).
(see RKO Studio Orchestra)

STERLING TRIO
Three-quarters of the Peerless Quartet: Henry Burr, Albert Campbell, & John Meyer

DATE CHARTED	PEAK POS	WKS CHRT'D	ARTIST — Record Title	Label & Number
11/11/16	**7**	2	1. On The South Sea Isle	Victor 18113
			with Louise & Ferera (Hawaiian guitars)	
			also recorded for Columbia 2045 & Pathe 20027	
12/16/16	**7**	2	2. In Florida Among The Palms.....................	Victor 18138
			from Broadway's "Ziegfeld Follies of 1916"	
6/16/17	**4**	6	3. Hawaiian Butterfly.................................	Victor 18272

DATE CHARTED	PEAK POS	WKS CHRT'D	ARTIST — Record Title	Label & Number
2/09/18	3	4	4. Where The Morning Glories Grow/ ELIZABETH SPENCER & STERLING TRIO	
3/16/18	8	1	5. My Sunshine Jane	Victor 18403
9/28/18	9	1	6. When We Meet In The Sweet Bye And Bye..... also recorded for Columbia 2582, Okeh 1088, & Pathe 20426	Victor 18484
11/09/18	5	3	7. When You Sang "Hush-A-Bye" To Me	Victor 18493
2/22/19	9	1	8. Dreaming Of Home, Sweet Home.................	Columbia 2668
6/14/19	3	6	9. That Tumble-Down Shack In Athlone .... also recorded for Victor 18545; later for Okeh 1173 & gennett 4550	Columbia 2698
8/16/19	5	4	10. Friends	Columbia 2744
11/29/19	6	3	11. Carolina Sunshine	Columbia 2770
7/23/21	5	3	12. I Found A Rose In The Devil's Garden	Victor 18746
3/25/22	13	1	13. Georgia Rose.................................	Victor 18837

HAROLD STERN & HIS ORCHESTRA
hotel band

DATE CHARTED	PEAK POS	WKS CHRT'D	ARTIST — Record Title	Label & Number
10/08/32	13	3	1. Isn't It Romantic? .... from the film "Love Me Tonight"	Columbia 2718

APRIL STEVENS
Known for her sensuous, intimate whispering vocal style; in 1963 she and brother Nino Tempo hit #1 with their remake of "Deep Purple."

DATE CHARTED	PEAK POS	WKS CHRT'D	ARTIST — Record Title	Label & Number
6/09/51	6	15	1. I'm In Love Again	RCA Victor 4148
8/11/51	10	5	2. Gimme A Little Kiss, Will Ya, Huh?.............	RCA Victor 4208
10/13/51	27	1	3. And So To Sleep Again .... all with Henri Rene's Orchestra	RCA Victor 4283

GARRY STEVENS
Vocalist with Charlie Spivak ("My Devotion") and Tex Beneke ("The Anniversary Song") in 1940s.

ELISE STEVENSON
Soprano born in Liverpool, England, member of Lyric Quartet and Trinity Choir, also on early Victor Light Opera Co. records; frequent duet partner Frank Stanley was also her manager.

DATE CHARTED	PEAK POS	WKS CHRT'D	ARTIST — Record Title	Label & Number
1/12/07	3	3	1. The Linger Longer Girl .... later recorded for Columbia 3573 & Zon-o-Phone 716	Victor 4876
4/20/07	1(2)	7	2. Because You're You .... also recorded for Columbia 3590 from the Broadway musical "The Red Mill"	Victor 5020
2/22/08	3	6	3. I Love You So................................ above two: HARRY MACDONOUGH & ELISE STEVENSON	Victor 5340
5/09/08+	4	2	4. The Cavalier .... also recorded for Zon-o-Phone 5145 1 & 4: FRANK STANLEY & ELISE STEVENSON	Victor 5389
5/30/08	3	3	5. The Vilia Song................................ 3 & 5 from the Broadway musical "The Merry Widow"	Victor 5391
6/27/08	3	5	6. Kiss Duet (Sweetest Maid Of All) .... from the Broadway musical "A Waltz Dream"	Victor 5446
7/11/08	1(4)	10	7. Are You Sincere?	Victor 5467
1/02/09	1(5)	11	8. Good Evening, Caroline......................... also recorded for Columbia 5080 6 & 8: FRANK STANLEY & ELISE STEVENSON	Victor 5627
4/10/09	1(9)	14	9. Shine On, Harvest Moon......................... from Broadway's "Ziegfeld Follies of 1908"	Victor 16259
4/24/09	9	1	10. The Message Of The Red Rose.................... from the Broadway musical "Marcelle" above two: HARRY MACDONOUGH & "MISS WALTON" (believed to be Elise Stevenson)	Victor 5667
12/25/09+	5	3	11. It's Hard To Kiss Your Sweetheart (When The Last Kiss Means Good-Bye)	Columbia 734
1/08/10	4	4	12. What Makes The World Go Round............... from the Broadway musical "A Broken Idol"	Columbia 756
1/22/10	8	3	13. Dear Heart	Indestructable 1219

DATE CHARTED	PEAK POS	WKS CHRT'D	ARTIST — Record Title	Label & Number
3/26/10	**5**	3	14. That Would Be Lovely .... *from the Broadway musical "A Chocolate Soldier"* *11-12 & 14: FRANK STANLEY & ELISE STEVENSON*	Columbia 781
12/24/10	**6**	2	15. Every Little Movement.............................. HENRY BURR & "MARGARET MAYHEW" (believed to be Elise Stevenson) *from the Broadway musical "Madama Sherry"*	Columbia 894
6/24/11	**7**	2	16. Day Dreams, Visions Of Bliss .... *from the Broadway musical "The Spring Maid"; also released on Zon-o-Phone 5707*	Victor 5830
8/05/11	**7**	2	17. Love Is Like A Red, Red Rose .... *from the Broadway musical "He Came from Milwaukee"*	Victor 16854
10/14/11	**5**	3	18. Save Up Your Kisses For A Rainy Day .... *also on Zon-o-Phone 5768*	Victor 16907
10/14/11	**6**	2	19. When You're In Town .... *also recorded for Columbia 1021 & Zon-o-Phone 5747* *above four: HENRY BURR & ELISE STEVENSON*	Victor 16898

CLIFF STEWARD & THE SAN FRANCISCO BOYS

DATE CHARTED	PEAK POS	WKS CHRT'D	ARTIST — Record Title	Label & Number
5/13/50	**18**	5	1. The Old Piano Roll Blues........................... *vocal by Ray Staunton*	Coral 60177
4/07/51	**19**	3	2. The Aba Daba Honeymoon .... *revived in the film "Two Weeks With Love"*	Coral 60374

BUDDY STEWART
Sang with group Snowflakes for Claude Thornhill, then featured with Gene Krupa (1944-46); died on 2/2/50 (28, auto accident).

CAL STEWART
Virginia-born Cal Stewart made his rural New England character of "Uncle Josh Weathersby" and the mythical town of "Pumpkin Center" beloved symbols of Americana during the early years of the century. Cal worked on trains and in circuses, medicine shows, & vaudeville before his remarkable recording career. A friend of Mark Twain and later Will Rogers, his droll, philosophic humor was often linked with theirs. Cal died on 12/7/19 (63).

DATE CHARTED	PEAK POS	WKS CHRT'D	ARTIST — Record Title	Label & Number
5/07/98	**1(5)**	8	1. **Uncle Josh's Arrival In New York** ....[T-C] *also recorded for Edison 3875 & Chicago 7600; later for Berliner 047*	Columbia 14000
5/14/98	**2(2)**	4	2. Uncle Josh At The Opera ....[T-C] *also recorded for Columbia 14002*	Edison 3877
6/18/98	**2(1)**	3	3. Uncle Josh In A Department Store.........[T-C] *later recorded for Berliner 6007 & Chicago 7611*	Columbia 14004
7/23/98	**3**	2	4. Uncle Josh On A Street Car.................[T-C] *later recorded for Berliner 038*	Columbia 14003
8/06/98	**3**	2	5. Uncle Josh On A Bicycle.....................[T-C] *later recorded for Gram-o-Phone 652*	Columbia 14011
9/17/98	**1(3)**	6	6. **I'm Old But I'm Awfully Tough (Laughing Song)**... [C] *also recorded for Columbia 14032 & Berliner 1910*	Edison 3903
9/24/98	**2(1)**	2	7. Uncle Josh On A Fifth Avenue Bus ....[T-C]	Columbia 14008
1/07/99	**2(2)**	3	8. Uncle Josh At A Camp Meeting ....[T-C] *also recorded for Chicago 7601*	Columbia 14016
1/07/99	**4**	2	9. Uncle Josh At A Baptizing At Hickory Corners Square ....[T-C] *also recorded for Chicago 7615*	Columbia 14014
8/26/99	**3**	3	10. Uncle Josh In Society.......................[T-C]	Columbia 14027
9/16/99	**3**	2	11. Uncle Josh And The Lightning Rod Agent..................................[T-C]	Columbia 14029
5/25/01	**4**	2	12. Uncle Josh Weathersby On A Trip To Boston ....[T-C]	Gram-o-Phone 663
7/13/01	**1(3)**	5	13. **Jim Lawson's Horse Trade With Deacon Witherspoon**...............................[T-C] *also recorded for Columbia 31574, Gram-o-Phone 3102 & Zon-o-Phone 9897*	Edison 7847
8/31/01	**1(3)**	8	14. **Uncle Josh's Huskin' Bee Dance** .... [C] *later recorded for Victor 16109*	Edison 7861
6/14/02	**2(1)**	4	15. Last Day Of School At Pumpkin Center ..[T-C]	Columbia 784

DATE CHARTED	PEAK POS	WKS CHRT'D	ARTIST — Record Title	Label & Number
2/07/03	5	1	16. Uncle Josh's Troubles In A Hotel...........[T-C] previously recorded for Berliner 041 & Zon-o-Phone 9196	Victor 1636
3/14/03	4	2	17. Uncle Josh And Aunt Nancy Smith On A Visit To New York ....[T-C] later recorded for Victor 2347 & Zon-o-Phone 5747	Columbia 1140
8/22/03	1(4)	8	18. **Uncle Josh On An Automobile**.............[T-C] later recorded for Victor 2541 & 31146	Columbia 1518
6/04/04	3	2	19. Evening Time At Pumpkin Center..........[T-C]	Columbia 1757
11/26/04	3	3	20. Uncle Josh And The Insurance Company [T-C]	Columbia 1868
3/25/05	7	1	21. The Wedding Of Uncle Josh And Aunt Nancy Smith.....................................[T-C] MR. & MRS. CAL STEWART & CO.	Columbia 3058
6/10/05	4	1	22. Uncle Josh At The White House ....[T-C]	Columbia 3112
6/24/05	9	1	23. Uncle Josh And Aunt Nancy In The Subway ....[T-C]	Columbia 3151
6/30/06	10	1	24. Sunday School Picnic At Pumpkin Center ..... later recorded for Zon-o-Phone 722 with Peerless Quartet	Columbia 3435
3/09/07	4	1	25. Uncle Josh's Second Visit To The Metropolis..................................[T-C]	Victor 4980
5/18/07	3	2	26. The Wedding Of Uncle Josh And Aunt Nancy Smith.. [C] new version of 1905 hit	Victor 5071
6/29/07	7	1	27. Uncle Josh And Aunt Nancy Go To Housekeeping .... [C] above two: MR. & MRS. CAL STEWART WITH HAYDN QUARTET	Victor 5082
7/27/07	9	1	28. And Then I Laughed........................... [C] also recorded for Columbia 3611 & 33120, & Zon-o-Phone 775	Victor 5101
8/31/07	9	1	29. Uncle Josh At The Dentist's ....[T-C] also recorded for Victor 5282	Columbia 3640
8/01/08	4	2	30. Uncle Josh's Letter From Home ....[T-C] previously recorded for Columbia 3737 & 85157	Victor 5377
4/24/09	7	1	31. Uncle Josh On A Fifth Avenue Bus ....[T-C] new version of his 1898 hit; also recorded for Victor 16228	Edison 10085
7/31/09	8	1	32. Uncle Josh's Trip To Coney Island.........[T-C] CAL STEWART & LEN SPENCER Cal previously recorded for Zon-o-Phone 5849	Edison 10149
8/28/09	7	1	33. Uncle Josh At A Baseball Game ....[T-C] also recorded for Indestructable 923	Edison 10169
12/28/12	10	1	34. Town Topics Of Pumpkin Center ....[T-C]	Edison Amb. 1507
8/22/14	10	1	35. Fourth Of July At Pumpkin Center ....[T-C]	Edison Amb. 2326
9/25/15	9	1	36. Uncle Josh In A Barber Shop/ [T-C] also recorded for Edison 50264	
10/02/15	5	3	37. War Talk At Pun'kin Center ....[T-C] also recorded for Columbia 1797 & Edison Amberol 2657	Victor 17820
11/13/15	9	1	38. The Village Gossips..........................[T-C] CAL STEWART & BYRON HARLAN Cal previously recorded this with Steve Porter for Edison Amberol 1594	Victor 17854
10/11/19	5	4	39. Uncle Josh And Aunt Nancy Put Up The Kitchen Stove.............................[T-C] CAL STEWART & ADA JONES	Victor 18595
12/27/19	7	1	40. Christmas Time At Pumpkin Center ...... [C-X] CAL STEWART, ADA JONES, & PEERLESS QUARTET	Columbia 2789
10/30/20	14	1	41. Uncle Josh Takes The Census..............[T-C]	Columbia 2962
11/05/21	9	1	42. Uncle Josh Buys A Victrola.................[T-C]	Victor 18793

LARRY STEWART
Sang with Leo Reisman (1936-37), Ray Noble (1938-41), & Phil Harris (1941-42).

MARTHA STEWART
Wife of band singer Buddy Stewart, she sang with Claude Thornhill's group the Snowflakes, and appeared in several movies.

DATE CHARTED	PEAK POS	WKS CHRT'D	ARTIST — Record Title	Label & Number
2/17/45	12	2	1. (All Of A Sudden) My Heart Sings................ from the film "Anchors Aweigh"	Bluebird 0832

DATE CHARTED	PEAK POS	WKS CHRT'D	ARTIST — Record Title	Label & Number
			REX STEWART Cornet star with Duke Ellington (1934-45), also played with Fletcher Henderson & Lionel Hampton, later a lecturer & jazz writer; died 9/7/67 (60).	
			SANDY STEWART Singer who made some recordings with Louis Armstrong.	
2/14/53	27	1	1. Since You Went Away From Me .... accompanied by the Joe Reisman Orchestra	Okeh 6941
			LEOPOLD STOKOWSKI - see PHILADELPHIA ORCHESTRA	
			GEORGIE STOLL Orchestra conductor on hits by Bing Crosby in mid-30s and Judy Garland in 40s, also musical director on many MGM movies from 30s to 60s, including classic "Meet Me in St. Louis".	
			CLIFFIE STONE Leader of square dance band which achieved great popularity on network radio. (see Helen O'Connell)	
			EDDIE STONE Vocalist and violinist with Isham Jones (1929-38) and Freddy Martin (1939-42).	
			LEW STONE & HIS ORCHESTRA Popular British bandleader who featured England's #1 vocalist, Al Bowlly; died 2/13/69 (69).	
2/02/35	3	10	1. Isle Of Capri .... vocal: Al Bowlly	Decca 247
			ERNEST VAN (POP) STONEMAN Important early country music star who performed with wife, uncle, and children; the family appeared regularly on the Grand Ole Opry in the 1960s until his death on 6/14/68 (75).	
5/16/25	3	10	● 1. The Titanic	Okeh 40288
			AXEL STORDAHL Arranger for Tommy Dorsey from 1936-43, best known as conductor/arranger on nearly all Frank Sinatra records from 1943-53, also on some records by Eddie Fisher, Dinah Shore, and Axel's wife June Hutton; he died on 8/30/63 (50).	
			RICCARDO STRACCIARI Italian baritone with New York Met 1906-08 & Chicago Opera 1917-19; died on 10/10/55 (80).	
2/22/19	10	1	1. There's A Long, Long Trail .... with Columbia Stellar Quartet	Columbia 49517
			TED STRAETER & HIS ORCHESTRA Pianist-singer and leader of society band, also the orchestra leader on Kate Smith's radio show from 1938-43.	
6/29/40	29	1	1. Imagination .... vocal by Dorothy Rochelle	Columbia 35406
9/20/52	27	1	2. The Most Beautiful Girl In The World .... vocal by Ted on his theme song; from the Broadway musical "Jumbo"; previously recorded for Hit 3017, Sonora 1207 & Varsity 112	MGM 11275
			BENNY STRONG & HIS ORCHESTRA Singer and hotel bandleader from Chicago.	
9/11/48	9	14	1. That Certain Party	Tower 1271
5/07/49	30	1	2. Five Foot Two, Eyes Of Blue	Tower 1456
1/14/50	19	3	3. Dear Hearts And Gentle People	Capitol 757
4/01/50	11	6	4. If I Knew You Were Comin' I'd've Baked A Cake	Capitol 915
			JOSEPH SUDY Featured vocalist with Henry King band in 1930s, also violinist	

DATE CHARTED	PEAK POS	WKS CHRT'D	ARTIST — Record Title	Label & Number
			JOE SULLIVAN Jazz pianist who played with Russ Columbo, Bing Crosby, Benny Goodman, & Red Nichols, also composer; died on 10/13/71 (64).	
6/02/34	**9**	8	1. Onyx Bringdown .... [I] Columbia 2925 piano solo	
10/12/40	**24**	1	2. I've Got A Crush On You .... Okeh 5647 Joe Sullivan's Cafe Society Orchestra; vocal: Helen Ward from the Broadway musicals "Treasure Girl" & "Strike Up the Band"	
			MAXINE SULLIVAN Born Marietta Williams, popular singer who started with Claude Thornhill, married to jazz bandleader John Kirby; she made a comeback in the late 60s jazz festivals and remains active in the 80s.	
12/04/37+	**10**	4	1. Nice Work If You Can Get It .... Vocalion 3848 from the film "Damsel in Distress"	
12/28/37	**9**	3	2. Loch Lomond .... Vocalion 3654 Maxine's trademark song above two with Claude Thornhill's Orchestra	
9/25/43+	**11**	1	3. My Ideal .... Decca 18555 from the film "Playboy of Paris" recorded 1/28/42	
			SUPER-SONICS	
6/13/53	**22**	3	1. Sheik Of Araby .... Rainbow 214	
			ELLEN SUTTON	
2/09/52	**21**	2	1. I Wanna Say Hello .... Kem 2710 with "Sir H. Pimm"	
			WILBUR SWEATMAN'S ORIGINAL JAZZ BAND Began as clarinetist in turn-of-the-century circus bands; died on 3/9/61 (79).	
7/20/18	**5**	3	1. Everybody's Crazy 'Bout The Doggone Blues (But I'm Happy) .... [I] Columbia 2548	
11/16/18	**5**	3	2. Indianola .... [I] Columbia 2611	
6/18/19	**5**	4	3. A Good Man Is Hard To Find .... [I] Columbia 2721	
9/06/19	**4**	3	4. I'll Say She Does .... [I] Columbia 2752 from the Broadway musical "Sinbad"	
12/13/19	**4**	4	5. Slide, Kelly, Slide .... [I] Columbia 2775	
			SWEET VIOLET BOYS	
6/27/36	**12**	3	1. Sweet Violets .... Vocalion 3110	
8/01/36	**16**	2	2. Sweet Violets No. 2 .... Vocalion 3256	
1/23/37	**15**	2	3. I Haven't Got A Pot To Cook In .... Vocalion 3402	

T

DATE CHARTED	PEAK POS	WKS CHRT'D	ARTIST — Record Title	Label & Number
			ZIGGY TALENT Novelty singer and saxophonist with Vaughn Monroe from 1944-early 50s	
11/04/50	**25**	2	1. Please Say Goodnight To The Guy, Irene .... RCA Victor 3925	
			HARRY TALLY Tenor associated with vaudeville's famous Empire City Quartet from about 1900-1915; died on 8/16/39 (73).	
11/12/04	**3**	4	1. Seminole .... Columbia 1852 later recorded for Victor 2937	
11/19/04	**5**	1	2. Egypt (My Cleopatra) .... Columbia 1853 from the Broadway musical "The Girl from Kay's"	
9/30/05	**9**	1	3. My Irish Molly O .... Columbia 3238 from the Broadway musical "Sergeant Brue"	
2/10/06	**1(1)**	8	4. **Wait Till The Sun Shines, Nellie** .... Victor 4551	
2/24/06	**8**	1	5. Silver Heels .... Victor 4579	
4/28/06	**10**	1	6. On An Automobile Afternoon .... Victor 4592 also recorded for Zon-o-Phone 320	

DATE CHARTED	PEAK POS	WKS CHRT'D	ARTIST — Record Title	Label & Number
10/19/07	**2(2)**	5	7. Take Me Back To New York Town	Victor 5230
4/17/09	**4**	2	8. I Wish I Had A Girl	Columbia 642
5/01/09	**5**	1	9. In Those Good Old Country Days	Victor 16259
			flip side of "Shine On, Harvest Moon" (POS 1) by Harry Macdonough	
11/27/09	**10**	1	10. When I Dream In The Gloaming Of You	Columbia 733
5/27/11	**7**	2	11. Come, Josephine, In My Flying Machine	Columbia 966

TAMPA RED & HIS CHICAGO FIVE
Great blues guitarist and singer, born Hudson Whittaker; frequently recorded with Thomas A. Dorsey ("Georgia Tom") before Dorsey became gospel's foremost songwriter.

7/25/36	**14**	4	1. Let's Get Drunk And Truck	Bluebird 6353

ELMO TANNER
Famous whistler and singer with Ted Weems for years, featured in huge Weems hit "Heartaches".

GID TANNER & HIS SKILLET LICKERS
Important early country group led by fiddler James Gideon Tanner and blind guitarist/singer Riley Puckett; Tanner died on 5/13/60 (74).

12/25/26	**14**	1	1. Turkey In The Straw	Columbia 15084
9/17/27	**20**	1	2. John Henry (Steel-Drivin' Man)	Columbia 15142
8/04/34	**10**	6	3. Down Yonder	Bluebird 5562
			country classic with claimed (unverified) sales over a million	

ART TATUM
The greatest pianist in jazz history, admired even by classical virtuosos, mostly blind all of his life; died on 11/5/56 (46).

5/15/37	**19**	1	1. Body And Soul .... [I]	Decca 1197
			"Art Tatum & His Swingsters" from the Broadway musical "Three's A Crowd"	
8/12/39	**18**	1	2. Tea For Two .... [I]	Decca 2456
			piano solo; from the Broadway musical "No, No, Nanette" record selected for the NARAS Hall of Fame	

TAYLOR TRIO
Led by cellist Albert Taylor

10/16/15	**5**	4	1. Mother Machree .... [I]	Columbia 1735
			TAYLOR, HACKEL, & BERGE from the Broadway musical "Barry of Ballymore"	
1/22/16	**8**	1	2. The Rosary .... [I]	Columbia 1815
			STELL, TAYLOR, & BERGE	
3/11/16	**4**	4	3. The Old Folks At Home .... [I]	Columbia 1915

JACK TEAGARDEN & HIS ORCHESTRA
One of the great jazz trombonists, also singer; played with Roger Wolfe Kahn, Ben Pollack (1928-33), Red Nichols, Benny Goodman, & Paul Whiteman (1934-38), then bandleader; later with Louis Armstrong All-Stars. Brother of jazz trumpeter Charlie Teagarden, Jack died on 1/15/64 (58). (also see Bing Crosby, Ethel Waters)

9/09/33	**7**	4	1. Someone Stole Gabriel's Horn	Columbia 2802
5/19/34	**16**	2	2. I've Got "It" .... [I]	Columbia 2913
6/03/39	**14**	1	3. The Sheik Of Araby	Brunswick 8370
			vocal: Jack Teagarden & Meredith Blake	
6/10/39	**19**	1	4. Cinderella, Stay In My Arms	Brunswick 8378
			Jack Teagarden: vocals on 1 & 4 Charlie Spivak (trumpet) on above two	
11/08/41	**23**	1	5. The Waiter And The Porter And The Upstairs Maid	Decca 3970
			BING CROSBY, MARY MARTIN & JACK TEAGARDEN with Jack's Orchestra	

PHA TERRELL
Male vocalist with the Andy Kirk band from 1933-41 ("Until the Real Thing Comes Along", "I Won't Tell A Soul"); died on 10/14/45 (35).

DATE CHARTED	PEAK POS	WKS CHRT'D	ARTIST — Record Title	Label & Number

CLARK TERRY
Trumpet star with Count Basie (1948-51) and Duke Ellington (1951-59), featured from 1960s to 1972 in Johnny Carson's "Tonight Show" band.

PAT TERRY
Male vocalist

10/10/53	**23**	1	1. Love Me Again	Jubilee 6044

JACK TETER TRIO
Piano, guitar & organ

10/08/49	**6**	23	1. Johnson Rag...	London 501

MAGGIE TEYTE
British soprano with the Chicago Opera from 1911-14 & the Boston Opera from 1914-17, long popular in concerts; made a Dame of the British Empire by Queen Elizabeth II.

4/11/14	**5**	4	1. Little Grey Home In The West	Columbia 1472
5/27/16	**5**	3	2. A Little Love, A Little Kiss.........................	Columbia 1957

SISTER ROSETTA THARPE
Gospel and folk singer, born Rosetta Nubin, who first achieved acclaim with Lucky Millinder in the early 1940s; died on 10/9/73 (58).

"THAT GIRL" QUARTET
One of the first female vocal groups to make commercial records: Harriet Keys, Allie Thomas, Precis Thompson & Helen Summers.

2/25/11	**9**	1	1. Silver Bell	Victor 16695
4/22/11	**6**	2	2. Put Your Arms Around Me, Honey	Victor 5827
6/10/11	**4**	4	3. Honey Love	Victor 16848
12/30/11+	**5**	4	4. Make Me Love You Like I Never Loved Before	Victor 16990
4/19/13	**10**	1	5. My Little Persian Rose.............................	Victor 17270
			flip side of #1 hit "Sympathy" by Helen Clark & Walter Van Brunt	

CONRAD THIBAULT
Baritone who sang with Philadelphia Grand Opera Co. (1928-31), later frequently heard on radio.

10/21/33	**18**	1	1. The Last Round-Up	Victor 22404
			accompanied by Ferde Grofe & His Orchestra	

DICK THOMAS

12/15/45	**16**	1	1. Sioux City Sue	National 5007

CAROLYN THOMPSON
Featured in original American production of "The Vagabond King"

5/01/26	**7**	2	1. Only A Rose..	Victor 19897
			accompanied by Leroy Shields' Orchestra & Victor Light Opera Co.; from the Broadway musical "The Vagabond King"	

HANK THOMPSON & HIS BRAZOS VALLEY BOYS
Texas-born country music star

6/14/52	**27**	1	● 1. The Wild Side Of Life.................................	Capitol 1942
			#1 on country chart for 15 weeks	
1/17/53	**21**	2	2. You're Walking On My Heart.......................	Capitol 2269

SONNY THOMPSON WITH HIS THREE SHARPS & FLATS
Chicago-born rhythm & blues pianist

7/10/48	**29**	1	1. Gone	Miracle 126
			long-running R&B hit	

WILLIAM H. THOMPSON
Baritone; died on 7/24/45 (72).

12/27/02+	**2(1)**	6	1. The Rosary...	Edison 8214
1/27/12	**3**	5	2. The Harbor Of Love.................................	Columbia 1087
			FRANK COOMBS & WILLIAM H. THOMPSON	

DATE CHARTED	PEAK POS	WKS CHRT'D	ARTIST — Record Title	Label & Number
			CLAUDE THORNHILL & HIS ORCHESTRA	
			Pianist/arranger who led one of the 1940s' most admired bands, known for its classically-styled instrumentals, its ballads sung by Fran Warren, and its late 40s progressive jazz. Claude previously played with Freddy Martin, Leo Reisman, Paul Whiteman, & other bands. Claude and Gil Evans did most of the band's arrangements. In the mid-50s Claude was musical director for Tony Bennett; he died on 7/1/65 (55).	
8/21/37	**19**	1	1. Gone With The Wind/	
8/28/37	**7**	8	2. Harbor Lights	Vocalion 3595
			vocal: Jimmy Farrell	
12/18/37	**9**	3	3. Loch Lomond..	Vocalion 3654
			vocals on 1 & 3: Maxine Sullivan	
12/18/37	**15**	2	4. Ebb Tide	Brunswick 7957
			vocal: Barry McKinley	
			Charlie Spivak & Manny Klein (trumpets), Toots Mondello (alto sax) on above four	
6/28/41	**27**	1	5. Sleepy Serenade .... [I]	Okeh 6178
10/18/41	**15**	3	6. Snowfall.. [I]	Columbia 36268
			Claude's haunting theme song (original composition)	
12/27/41	**16**	1	7. Autumn Nocturne................................... [I]	Columbia 36435
12/27/41	**25**	1	8. Concerto For Two (A Love Song).................	Columbia 36371
			based on a theme from the 1st movement of Tchaikovsky's Piano Concerto No. 1	
1/10/42	**22**	1	9. I Found You In The Rain	Columbia 36431
			above two vocals: Dick Harding	
			Conrad Gozzo (trumpet) & Irving Fazola (clarinet) on above five	
5/03/47	**16**	6	10. A Sunday Kind Of Love............................	Columbia 37219
			Fran Warren's most famous vocal	
10/04/47	**25**	1	11. You're Not So Easy To Forget	Columbia 37558
1/17/48	**26**	1	12. Warsaw Concerto/ [I]	
11/29/47	**28**	1	13. Love For Love..	Columbia 37940
			with Lee Konitz (alto sax)	
12/06/47	**22**	1	14. Early Autumn	Columbia 37593
			Fran Warren: vocals on 10-11, 13-14	
2/04/50	**24**	4	15. Johnson Rag...	RCA Vic. 78-3604
			vocal: Joe Derisi & Snowflakes	
9/26/53	**29**	2	16. Summer Is Gone	Trend 60
			vocal: Tony Becker	
			THREE CHUCKLES	
11/13/54	**20**	8	1. Runaround	"X" 0066
			THREE FLAMES	
			New York R&B trio which hosted its own NBC TV summer series in 1949 and was later featured in the 1956-57 series "Washington Square".	
2/08/47	**1(1)**	8	1. **Open The Door, Richard**....................... [C]	Columbia 37268
			THREE KEYS	
1/14/33	**16**	2	1. Fit As A Fiddle......................................	Brunswick 6411
			THREE PEPPERS	
8/26/39	**14**	1	1. Love Grows On The White Oak Tree............	Decca 2557
			THREE SUNS	
			Popular instrumental trio: original members Al Nevins (guitar), brother Morty Nevins (accordion), & Artie Dunn (organ)	
7/01/44	**16**	1	1. Long Ago (And Far Away) .... [I]	Hit 7085
			from the film "Cover Girl"	
8/12/44	**7**	18	2. How Many Hearts Have You Broken/	
11/11/44	**14**	6	3. Twilight Time .... [I]	Hit 7092
			the group's theme song, later recorded for Victor 2137	
4/28/45	**10**	1	4. All Of My Life..	Hit 7126
9/07/46	**7**	13	5. Five Minutes More	Majestic 7197
			featured in the film "Sweetheart of Sigma Chi"	
11/09/46	**7**	6	6. Rumors Are Flying...................................	Majestic 7205

DATE CHARTED	PEAK POS	WKS CHRT'D	ARTIST — Record Title	Label & Number
6/21/47	1(4)	19	7. **Peg O' My Heart**.. [I] from the Broadway musical "Ziegfeld Follies of 1913"	RCA Victor 2272
11/15/47	21	3	8. I Still Get Jealous .... from the Broadway musical "High Button Shoes"	RCA Victor 2469
2/28/48	10	8	9. I'm Looking Over A Four-Leaf Clover .... vocals on 2, 5, 8 & 9 by Artie Dunn	RCA Victor 2688
7/24/48	24	1	10. Just For Now	RCA Victor 2946
4/02/49	21	1	11. You, You, You Are The One .... above two vocals by Artie Dunn & The Sun Maids	RCA Victor 3322
4/02/49	24	5	12. Cruising Down The River........................... vocal duet	RCA Victor 3349
8/01/50+	21	3	13. Don't Take Your Love From Me	RCA Victor 5347
2/06/54	22	1	14. The Creep .... [I] British song	RCA Victor 5553
7/24/54	24	4	15. Moonlight And Roses (Bring Memories of You)... [I]	RCA Victor 5768

LAWRENCE TIBBETT
Baritone star with the Metropolitan Opera from 1923-49, featured in several movie musicals; died on 7/15/60 (63) in a traffic accident.

DATE CHARTED	PEAK POS	WKS CHRT'D	ARTIST — Record Title	Label & Number
2/15/30	10	10	1. The White Dove/	
3/01/30	12	5	2. When I'm Looking At You	Victor 1447
2/22/30	18	1	3. The Rogue Song .... above three from the film "The Rogue Song" all accompanied by Nat Shilkret's Orchestra	Victor 1446

MERLE TILLOTSON
Real name Merle Alcock

DATE CHARTED	PEAK POS	WKS CHRT'D	ARTIST — Record Title	Label & Number
4/22/11	7	2	1. 'Neath The Southern Moon .... from the Broadway musical "Naughty Marietta"	Columbia 5255

MARTHA TILTON
First achieved prominence singing with Benny Goodman from 1937-39 ("I Let a Song Go Out of My Heart", "And the Angels Sing")

DATE CHARTED	PEAK POS	WKS CHRT'D	ARTIST — Record Title	Label & Number
6/24/44	30	1	1. Texas Polka/	
7/15/44	4	24	2. I'll Walk Alone .... from the film "Follow the Boys"	Capitol 157
3/24/45	10	3	3. I Should Care/ from the film "Thrill of a Romance"	
7/28/45	10	1	4. Stranger In Town.............................. above two accompanied by Eddie Miller's Orchestra	Capitol 184
3/08/47	8	5	5. How Are Things In Glocca Mora? .... from the Broadway musical "Finian's Rainbow"	Capitol 345
6/07/47	10	9	6. That's My Desire/	
7/12/47	9	2	7. I Wonder, I Wonder, I Wonder .... above three accompanied by Dean Elliott's Orchestra	Capitol 395
3/20/48	22	3	8. That's Gratitide..................................	Capitol 15042
10/28/50	23	1	9. I'll Always Love You .... accompanied by Lee Gordon's Orchestra from the film "My Friend Irma Goes West"	Coral 60258

FRANK TINNEY
Comedian-singer in many Broadway musicals from 1911-26; died on 11/28/49 (62).

DATE CHARTED	PEAK POS	WKS CHRT'D	ARTIST — Record Title	Label & Number
12/25/15+	7	2	1. Frank Tinney's First Record .... [C]	Columbia 1854

DIMITRI TIOMKIN & HIS ORCHESTRA
Russian-born, one of Hollywood's leading composers from the 1930s through the 60s (including the scores for "Lost Horizon", "High Noon" and "The High and the Mighty").

DATE CHARTED	PEAK POS	WKS CHRT'D	ARTIST — Record Title	Label & Number
8/14/54	29	1	1. The High And The Mighty .... [I]	Coral 61211

JUAN TIZOL
Valve trombonist born in Puerto Rico, featured with Duke Ellington (1929-44, 51-53) & Harry James (1944-50 & later); composer or co-writer of jazz classics "Caravan" and "Perdido"; died on 4/25/84 (84).

DATE CHARTED	PEAK POS	WKS CHRT'D	ARTIST — Record Title	Label & Number
			DICK TODD Canadian-born baritone briefly with Larry Clinton (1938)	
5/07/38+	**9**	5	1. The Girl In The Bonnet Of Blue	Victor 25839
10/15/38	**20**	1	2. Love Doesn't Grow On Trees.....................	Victor 26058
12/17/38	**9**	2	3. When Paw Was Courtin' Maw.....................	Bluebird 10034
4/01/39	**10**	4	4. Little Sir Echo................................. adaptation of the Boy Scouts anthem	Bluebird 10169
10/07/39	**12**	4	5. It's A Hundred To One (I'm In Love)	Bluebird 10398
2/03/40	**10**	3	6. To You, Sweetheart, Aloha	Bluebird 10445
3/02/40	**4**	7	7. The Gaucho Serenade.............................	Bluebird 10559
4/27/40	**13**	3	8. Angel In Disguise................................ from the film "It All Came True"	Bluebird 10636
5/04/40	**16**	2	9. The Singing Hills	Bluebird 10596
6/22/40	**14**	4	10. Make Believe Island	Bluebird 10729
8/31/40	**20**	1	11. All This And Heaven Too .... movie title song	Bluebird 10789
9/14/40	**24**	1	12. You Can't Brush Me Off .... DINAH SHORE & DICK TODD accompanied by Leonard Joy's Orchestra from the Broadway musical "Louisiana Purchase"	Bluebird 10720
12/21/40	**24**	1	13. Goodnight, Mother .... one of the few anti-war songs of World War II	Bluebird 10912
1/21/50	**11**	16	14. Daddy's Little Girl .... with Phil Ellis Choristers & Eddie Miller's Orchestra	Rainbow 80080
3/14/53	**17**	1	15. Till I Waltz Again With You .... accompanied by Jerry Jerome's Orchestra	Decca 28506
			JO ANN TOLLEY	
5/30/53	**29**	1	1. I'd Never Forgive Myself...........................	MGM 11471
			PINKY TOMLIN Singer with Jimmie Grier (Pinky's composition "The Object of My Affection"), writer of such other hits as "What's the Reason?" & "The Love Bug Will Bite You"; appeared in several movies.	
4/10/37	**9**	3	1. The Love Bug Will Bite You (If You Don't Watch Out)............................... with Joe Haymes' Orchestra	Brunswick 7849
5/13/39	**14**	2	2. Ragtime Cowboy Joe	Decca 2014
			TOP HATTERS	
4/04/36	**15**	2	1. Wah-Hoo! .... vocal trio, accompanied by band including Eddie Farley (trumpet) & Mike Riley (trombone)	Decca 711
			MEL TORME A man of many talents: singer, songwriter ("Lament to Love", the all-time holiday classic "The Christmas Song"), arranger, pianist, drummer, dramatic actor, & author. In his first wave of popularity as leader of vocal group the Mel-Tones, he was known as "The Velvet Fog"; Mel has reached the pinnacle of his career in the 70s & 80s as one of the world's most honored jazz singers, usually working with pianist George Shearing. (Also see Artie Shaw)	
10/27/45	**20**	1	1. I Fall In Love Too Easily .... EUGENE BAIRD with MEL TORME'S MEL-TONES from the film "Anchors Aweigh"	Decca 18707
3/23/46	**15**	1	2. Day By Day .... BING CROSBY WITH MEL TORME & HIS MEL-TONES	Decca 18746
5/03/47	**24**	1	3. It's Dreamtime .... with the Mel-Tones, accompanied by Sonny Burke & His Orchestra	Musicraft 15102
3/05/49	**1(1)**	18	4. **Careless Hands** .... accompanied by Sonny Burke's Orchestra	Capitol 15379
4/02/49	**3**	18	5. Again/ from the film "Roadhouse"	
4/16/49	**20**	5	6. Blue Moon .... featured in the film "Words and Music"	Capitol 15428
7/02/49	**10**	8	7. The Four Winds And The Seven Seas .... accompanied by Frank DeVol's Orchestra	Capitol 671

DATE CHARTED	PEAK POS	WKS CHRT'D	ARTIST — Record Title	Label & Number
1/07/50	9	7	8. The Old Master Painter .... Capitol 791 PEGGY LEE & MEL TORME with the Mellowmen	Capitol 791
5/13/50	8	12	9. Bewitched .... from the Broadway musical "Pal Joey" 5-6 & 9 accompanied by Pete Rugolo & His Orchestra	Capitol 1000
11/15/52	30	1	10. Anywhere I Wander................................ accompanied by Al Pelligrini's Orchestra from the film "Hans Christian Andersen"	Capitol 2263

MITCHELL TOROK & LOUISIANA HAYRIDE BAND

8/29/53	26	2	1. Caribbean.. Abbott 140	Abbott 140

ARTURO TOSCANINI & LA SCALA ORCHESTRA
World-famous Italian-born conductor who led the New York
Metropolitan Opera Orchestra (1908-15), the New York Symphony
Orchestra (1928-36), & finally the NBC Symphony Orchestra on the
radio from 1937-54; died on 1/16/57 (89).

4/30/21	12	1	1. Symphony In E Flat Major (Finale) .... [I] Victor 74669	Victor 74669

DAVE TOUGH
Two-time poll-winning jazz drummer with Red Nichols, Tommy Dorsey
(1936-37,38-39), Bunny Berigan, Benny Goodman (1938, 1941), Artie
Shaw, & Woody Herman (1944-45); died on 12/6/48 (40).

AL TRACE & HIS ORCHESTRA
Bandleader and composer of his smash hits "Mairzy Doats" & "You
Call Everybody Darlin'" as well as "If I Knew You Were Comin'
I'd've Baked a Cake".

2/05/44	7	9	1. Mairzy Doats .... [N] Hit 8079 "AL TRACE & HIS SILLY SYMPHONISTS" vocal by Red Maddock & group	Hit 8079
6/19/48	1(6)	24	2. **You Call Everybody Darlin'** .... Regent 117	Regent 117
9/11/48	21	3	3. You Call Everybody Darlin'........................ vocal by Bob Vincent	Sterling 3023
5/26/51	26	10	4. Pretty Eyed Baby................................. vocal by Lola Ameche	Mercury 5609
7/28/51	24	3	5. Hitsity Hotsity .... [N] Mercury 5675 LOLA AMECHE & AL TRACE	Mercury 5675

ARTHUR TRACY
Philadelphia-born ballad singer & accordionist known as "The
Street Singer", popular on 1930s radio.

2/20/32	19	1	1. Marta (Rambling Rose Of The Wildwood) .... Brunswick 6216	Brunswick 6216
5/14/32+	14	3	2. Kiss Me Goodnight .... Brunswick 6279	Brunswick 6279
4/11/34	19	1	3. Play To Me, Gypsy .... Vocalion 2659	Vocalion 2659

MERLE TRAVIS
Enormously popular country singer/guitarist/songwriter who
composed Tennessee Ernie Ford's all-time classic "Sixteen Tons";
died on 10/20/83 (65).

11/02/46	25	1	1. Divorce Me C.O.D................................... #1 on country chart for 14 weeks	Capitol 290
2/22/47	21	1	2. So Round, So Firm, So Fully Packed............ #1 on country chart for 14 weeks	Capitol 349

JUDY TREMAINE

5/01/54	28	1	1. Chain Lightning..................................... accompanied by Dick Jacobs & His Orchestra	Coral 61150

PAUL TREMAINE & HIS ORCHESTRA
Tenor saxophonist, singer, bandleader

3/08/30	18	1	1. Hand Me Down My Walking Cane................ Columbia 2130	Columbia 2130
5/31/30	18	1	2. Anchors Aweigh .... theme song of the U.S. Navy, written for the 1906 Army-Navy football game	Columbia 2200

TRINITY CHOIR
Elise Stevenson was a member

12/16/11	5	3	1. Joy To The World............................... [X] Victor 16996	Victor 16996
12/14/12	4	3	2. Hark! The Herald Angels Sing .... [X] Victor 17164	Victor 17164

DATE CHARTED	PEAK POS	WKS CHRT'D	ARTIST — Record Title	Label & Number

HELEN TRIX
Very popular vaudeville entertainer who became even bigger in England in the 1920s performing with her sister Josephine; died on 11/18/51 (early 60s).

2/23/07	**10**	1	1. Is Marriage A Failure? .... [C]	Victor 4914
			HELEN TRIX & DAN QUINN from the Broadway musical "The Mayor of Tokio"	
3/02/07	**3**	3	2. The Bird On Nellie's Hat .... [C]	Victor 4904
			also recorded for Edison 9450	

JOHN SCOTT TROTTER
Musical director on the vast majority of Bing Crosby records from 1937 to the early 50s, previously pianist/arranger for Hal Kemp; also arranged for Judy Garland, Al Jolson & Mary Martin.

TROUBADORS ORCHESTRA -   see NAT SHILKRET

FRANKIE TRUMBAUER & HIS ORCHESTRA
Jazz star on C-melody saxophone whose band featured all-time cornet great Bix Beiderbecke. Frankie also played with Ray Miller, Jean Goldkette, & Paul Whiteman (1927-32, 33-36) and was a World War II test pilot; he died on 6/11/56 (56).

6/18/27	**9**	6	1. Singin' The Blues .... [I]	Okeh 40772
			selected for NARAS Hall of Fame	
9/10/27	**5**	7	2. I'm Coming, Virginia .... [I]	Okeh 40843
9/10/27	**16**	2	3. Riverboat Shuffle................................ [I]	Okeh 40822
12/03/27	**10**	4	4. There's A Cradle In Caroline......................	Okeh 40879
			vocal: Seger Ellis	
4/28/28	**18**	1	5. Mississippi Mud	Okeh 40979
			Bing Crosby & Frankie Trumbauer, vocal	
10/13/28	**17**	1	6. Dusky Stevedore	Okeh 41100
			vocal: Frankie Trumbauer & Dee Orr Bix Beiderbecke (cornet) on above six	
6/28/30	**15**	3	7. Get Happy	Okeh 41431
			vocal: Frankie Trumbauer from the Broadway musical "9:15 Revue" Eddie Lang (guitar) on 1-4 & 7	
8/22/31	**10**	4	8. Georgia On My Mind	Brunswick 6159
			vocal: Art Jarrett	
5/21/32	**6**	6	9. Medley Of Isham Jones Dance Hits	Columbia 18002
			On the Alamo/Swinging Down the Lane (vocal: Helen Rowland)/ I'll See You In My Dreams	

ERNEST TUBB
"The Texas Troubador", one of country music's most durable stars, long featured on radio's Grand Ole Opry; died on 9/6/84 (70).

8/23/41	**23**	1	● 1. Walking The Floor Over You	Decca 5958
			long-running country classic	
1/22/44	**18**	3	2. Try Me One More Time............................	Decca 6093
6/24/44	**29**	1	3. Yesterday's Tears/	
8/19/44	**16**	2	4. Soldier's Last Letter	Decca 6098
9/18/48	**30**	1	5. Forever Is Ending Today	Decca 46134
5/07/49	**30**	1	6. I'm Bitin' My Fingernails And Thinking Of You..	Decca 24592
			ERNEST TUBB & ANDREWS SISTERS	
11/26/49	**17**	3	7. Slippin' Around	Decca 46173
12/24/49+	**21**	2	8. Blue Christmas .... [X]	Decca 46186
			revived in the 1960s by Elvis Presley	
8/12/50	**10**	10	9. Goodnight, Irene	Decca 46255
			RED FOLEY & ERNEST TUBB with the Sunshine Trio	
2/28/53	**22**	1	10. I'll Miss You When You Go	Decca 28550
11/14/53	**25**	1	11. Counterfeit Kisses	Decca 28869

ORRIN TUCKER & HIS ORCHESTRA
Dance band best known for singer "Wee" Bonnie Baker; saxophonist-leader Tucker wrote several of his hits.

6/03/39	**12**	4	1. Wishing (Will Make It So)........................	Vocalion 4762
			vocal: Orrin Tucker	

DATE CHARTED	PEAK POS	WKS CHRT'D	ARTIST — Record Title	Label & Number
11/04/39	2(4)	14	2. Oh, Johnny, Oh, Johnny, Oh! .... from the 1916 Broadway musical "Follow Me"	Columbia 35228
12/09/39+	5	7	3. Stop! It's Wonderful	Columbia 35249
12/30/39	10	2	4. Billy .... above three vocals: Bonnie Baker	Vocalion 4914
1/06/40	3	13	5. At The Balalaika/ vocal: Gil Mershon; from the film "Balalaika"	
1/13/40	15	3	6. Would'ja Mind?	Columbia 35332
2/03/40	5	10	7. You'd Be Surprised .... from Broadway's "Ziegfeld Follies of 1919"	Columbia 35344
2/10/40	10	2	8. Pinch Me .... above five vocals: Bonnie Baker	Columbia 35328
3/30/40	20	3	9. If I Could Be The Dummy On Your Knee ... [N]	Columbia 35390
4/20/40	8	5	10. Apple Blossoms And Chapel Bells	Columbia 35405
5/18/40	13	5	11. Where Do I Go From You?	Columbia 35452
5/25/40	14	4	12. My Resistance Is Low .... vocals on 6-9 & 11-12: Bonnie Baker	Columbia 35468
1/11/41	21	2	13. You're The One (For Me)............................	Columbia 35848
12/20/41	22	1	14. Hi, Neighbor!....................................... from the film "San Antonio Rose"	Columbia 36362
4/04/42	22	1	15. Dear Mom.. vocals on 10 & 15: Orrin Tucker	Columbia 36515
5/16/42	21	1	16. She Don't Wanna .... [N]	Columbia 36490

SOPHIE TUCKER

Born Sonia Kalish in Russia, Sophie Tucker used her brassy, flamboyant vocal style to become one of vaudeville's greatest stars. She helped introduce many hit songs she did not record ("Carrie", "The Cubanola Glide", "The Darktown Strutters' Ball"), but her lifelong theme song was also her biggest hit, "Some Of These Days". Billed as "The Last of the Red-Hot Mamas", Sophie died on 2/9/66 (81).

DATE CHARTED	PEAK POS	WKS CHRT'D	ARTIST — Record Title	Label & Number
7/30/10	3	5	1. That Lovin' Rag..	Edison 10360
11/12/10	9	1	2. That Lovin' Two-Step Man...........................	Edison 10411
6/17/11	8	1	3. That Loving Soul Kiss	Edison 10493
7/08/11	2(3)	9	4. Some Of These Days.................................. Sophie's most famous song	Edison Amb. 691
1/06/12	9	1	5. Knock Wood...	Edison Amb. 852
6/24/22	6	3	6. High Brown Blues	Okeh 4565
7/28/23	6	3	7. You've Gotta See Mama Ev'ry Night (Or You Can't See Mama At All)/	
8/04/23	10	1	8. Aggravatin' Papa	Okeh 4817
5/31/24	10	1	9. The One I Love Belongs To Somebody Else....	Okeh 40054
9/27/24	7	2	10. Red-Hot Mama.......................................	Okeh 40129
2/26/27	1(5)	12	● 11. **Some Of These Days/** new version of her trademark song	
3/19/27	10	3	12. Bugle Call Rag .... above two: SOPHIE TUCKER WITH TED LEWIS & HIS BAND	Columbia 826
8/13/27	13	3	13. Fifty Million Frenchmen Can't Be Wrong.......	Okeh 40813
9/03/27	10	3	14. After You've Gone/	
9/03/27+	12	3	15. I Ain't Got Nobody .... above two with Miff Mole's Molers, including Red Nichols (trumpet), Miff Mole (trombone), Jimmy Dorsey (clarinet/ alto sax), Eddie Lang (guitar) & Ted Shapiro (piano)	Okeh 40837
12/17/27	10	3	16. Blue River	Okeh 40895
1/28/28	10	4	17. There'll Be Some Changes Made .... accompanied on 10 & 16-17 by Ted Shapiro (piano)	Okeh 40921
6/02/28	11	3	18. The Man I Love .... from the Broadway musical "Lady Be Good"	Okeh 41010
10/06/28	5	8	19. My Yiddishe Momme .... above two accompanied by Ted Shapiro's Orchestra	Columbia 4962
9/14/29+	15	2	20. I'm The Last Of The Red-Hot Mamas	Victor 21994

DATE CHARTED	PEAK POS	WKS CHRT'D	ARTIST — Record Title	Label & Number
11/13/37	**19**	1	21. The Lady Is A Tramp................................. Decca 1472 *accompanied by Harry Sosnik & His Orchestra* *from the Broadway musical "Babes In Arms"*	Decca 1472

TOMMY TUCKER & HIS ORCHESTRA
Pianist and sweet-band leader; listed on records 1-8 as "Tommy Tucker Time"

DATE CHARTED	PEAK POS	WKS CHRT'D	ARTIST — Record Title	Label & Number
12/30/39+	**9**	11	1. The Man Who Comes Around................. [N] *vocal: Kelly Rand*	Vocalion 5199
9/21/40	**29**	1	2. Buds Won't Bud .... *vocal: Al Knapp*	Okeh 5634
11/09/40	**10**	4	3. There I Go..	Okeh 5789
12/07/40	**23**	1	4. Seven Beers With The Wrong Woman....... [N] *vocal: Kerwin Somerville*	Okeh 5815
2/08/41	**7**	6	5. You Walk By.. *vocal: Amy Arnell & Don Brown*	Okeh 5973
9/06/41	**4**	13	6. I Don't Want To Set The World On Fire........ *vocals on 3 & 6: Amy Arnell*	Okeh 6320
5/30/42	**13**	3	7. Johnny Doughboy Found A Rose In Ireland... *vocal: Don Brown*	Okeh 6620
6/26/43	**21**	1	8. I Love You................................... [R] *the band's theme song* *reissue of Okeh 6145; recorded 3/27/41*	Okeh 6633
8/25/45	**10**	3	9. On The Atchison, Topeka, And The Santa Fe. *vocal: Don Brown & Three Two-Timers* *from the film "The Harvey Girls"*	Columbia 36829

ALAN TURNER
British operatic baritone

DATE CHARTED	PEAK POS	WKS CHRT'D	ARTIST — Record Title	Label & Number
7/28/06	**8**	1	1. The Rosary...	Victor 4676
2/08/08	**1(6)**	14	2. **As Long As The World Rolls On**	Victor 31693
4/04/08	**5**	1	3. Good-Bye, Sweetheart, Good-Bye	Victor 5351
5/02/08	**4**	2	4. Carmen - Toreador Song .... [F]	Victor 5376
12/26/08+	**5**	1	5. Here's To The Girl!................................... ALAN TURNER & HAYDN QUARTET *from the Broadway musical "The Girls of Gottenburg"*	Victor 5611
12/14/12+	**1(3)**	10	6. **Till The Sands Of The Desert Grow Cold**....	Victor 35259
1/25/13	**9**	1	7. Oh Promise Me .... *from the operetta "Robin Hood"*	Victor 17189
5/16/14	**9**	1	8. O Sole Mio (My Sunshine)	Victor 17536

JOE TURNER
Known as "Big Joe", one of the top blues singers for some 15 years before he reached a new audience by introducing the rock classic "Shake, Rattle and Roll"; died on 11/24/85 (74).

DATE CHARTED	PEAK POS	WKS CHRT'D	ARTIST — Record Title	Label & Number
9/15/51	**30**	1	● 1. Chains Of Love...................................... *long-running R&B hit; with Van "Piano Man" Walls*	Atlantic 939
12/19/53	**23**	2	● 2. Honey Hush...	Atlantic 1001
8/14/54	**22**	2	3. Shake, Rattle, And Roll	Atlantic 1026

JANE TURZY
Singer from Chicago

DATE CHARTED	PEAK POS	WKS CHRT'D	ARTIST — Record Title	Label & Number
6/30/51	**12**	5	1. Good Morning, Mister Echo........................ *"Jane Turzy Trio" (Jane with vocal overdubbing)*	Decca 27622
7/28/51	**11**	10	2. Sweet Violets .... *adapted from a traditional folk song*	Decca 27668
11/24/51	**20**	4	3. I Like It .... *all accompanied by Remo Biondi's Orchestra*	Decca 27851

DATE CHARTED	PEAK POS	WKS CHRT'D	ARTIST — Record Title	Label & Number
			T. TEXAS TYLER Country singer known for his "growl", with the group "Oklahoma Melody Boys".	
4/24/48	**21**	2	1. Deck Of Cards .... 4 Star 1228	

U

DATE CHARTED	PEAK POS	WKS CHRT'D	ARTIST — Record Title	Label & Number
			U.S. MARINE BAND Under the leadership of John Philip Sousa, "the President's band" was the first to make commercially successful recordings.	
8/02/90	**1(6)**	6	1. **Semper Fidelis** .... [I] Columbia America's first #1 record; written at the request of President Chester A. Arthur	
9/13/90	**1(6)**	6	2. **Washington Post** .... [I] Columbia written on commission for this newspaper's awards ceremonies	
10/25/90	**1(4)**	4	3. **The Thunderer** .... [I] Columbia	
4/02/92	**2(3)**	3	4. Ta-Ra-Ra-Boom (Medley) .... [I] Columbia above four with John Philip Sousa, director	
8/05/93	**2(2)**	2	5. A Trip To Chinatown - Selection .... [I] Columbia	
3/10/94	**1(5)**	5	6. **The Liberty Bell** .... [I] Columbia	
12/01/94	**2(3)**	3	7. Manhattan Beach .... [I] Columbia	
3/16/07	**2(1)**	5	8. Maple Leaf Rag .... [I] Victor 4911 conducted by Lt. William H. Santelmann	
			U.S. NAVAL ACADEMY BAND	
2/26/21	**13**	1	1. Anchors Aweigh .... [I] Columbia 3331 written for the 1906 Army-Navy football game	
			UNNATURAL SEVEN - see RED INGLE	
			UPTOWN STRING BAND	
1/31/48	**11**	2	1. I'm Looking Over A Four-Leaf Clover .... Mercury 5100 vocal by Joseph Giardino	
			ANTHONY URATO	
11/26/21	**13**	1	1. They Needed A Song Bird In Heaven (So God Took Caruso Away) .... Cardinal 2040	

V

DATE CHARTED	PEAK POS	WKS CHRT'D	ARTIST — Record Title	Label & Number
			JERRY VALE Popular ballad singer born Genero Louis Vitaliano in the Bronx	
3/07/53	**29**	1	1. You Can Never Give Me Back My Heart .... Columbia 39929 accompanied by Percy Faith & His Orchestra	
1/30/54	**20**	4	2. Two Purple Shadows .... Columbia 40131	
5/22/54	**29**	1	3. I Live Each Day .... Columbia 40201 orchestra on above two directed by Jimmy Carroll	
			JUDY VALENTINE Baby-voiced singer in tradition of Helen Kane and Bonnie Baker.	
11/21/53	**21**	4	1. She Was Five And He Was Ten .... Epic 9004 orchestra directed by Bill Leaviff	
			RUDY VALLEE & HIS CONNECTICUT YANKEES Sensationally popular Depression-era singer and bandleader, born Herbert Pryor Vallee 7/28/01 in Island Pond, Vt. A Yale graduate known for singing into a megaphone and his regular greeting "High-ho, everybody!" Rudy played alto sax & clarinet in the early period with his band, starred in several movie musicals & Broadway's "George White's Scandals of 1931". Later he was in the 1961 Broadway hit "How to Succeed in Business Without Really Trying".	
2/16/29	**5**	6	1. Sweetheart Of All My Dreams .... Harmony 811	
3/02/29	**7**	5	2. If I Had You .... Harmony 825	

DATE CHARTED	PEAK POS	WKS CHRT'D	ARTIST — Record Title	Label & Number
3/16/29	**2(1)**	8	3. Marie...	Harmony 834
3/30/29	**1(8)**	15	4. **Honey**	Victor 21869
4/06/29	**2(4)**	10	5. Weary River/	
4/13/29	**2(2)**	10	6. Deep Night	Victor 21868
4/27/29	**9**	5	7. Lover, Come Back To Me/ from the Broadway musical "The New Moon"	
5/04/29	**10**	3	8. Coquette	Victor 21880
6/01/29	**8**	5	9. My Time Is Your Time	Victor 21924
			Rudy's familiar radio theme	
7/13/29	**5**	8	10. I'm Just A Vagabond Lover	Victor 21967
			from the film "The Vagabond Lover"	
7/27/29	**7**	4	11. S'posin'...	Victor 21998
9/21/29	**10**	3	12. Pretending...	Victor 22062
9/28/29	**11**	3	13. Heigh-Ho, Everybody, Heigh-Ho!	Victor 22029
10/26/29	**16**	1	14. Baby Oh Where Can You Be......................	Victor 22034
11/09/29	**2(1)**	8	15. Lonely Troubador	Victor 22136
1/04/30	**3**	7	16. A Little Kiss Each Morning (A Little Kiss Each Night)	Victor 22193
			from "The Vagabond Lover"	
3/15/30	**1(10)**	21	17. **Stein Song (University Of Maine)/** originated in 1901 as an instrumental march (based on one of Brahms' "Hungarian Dances"); rewritten with lyrics in 1910; became the theme song for the University of Maine	
5/10/30	**15**	4	18. St. Louis Blues......................................	Victor 22321
5/17/30	**16**	2	19. I Still Remember...................................	Victor 22361
6/07/30	**3**	10	20. If I Had A Girl Like You	Victor 22419
8/09/30	**4**	7	21. Betty Co-Ed	Victor 22473
9/08/30	**8**	4	22. Just A Little Longer................................	Victor 22489
9/27/30	**4**	5	23. Confessin' (That I Love You)	Victor 22506
11/22/30	**9**	4	24. Sweetheart Of My Student Days	Victor 22560
12/13/30+	**3**	9	25. You're Driving Me Crazy! (What Did I Do?).....	Victor 22572
			from the Broadway musical "Smiles"	
1/24/31	**12**	4	26. Tears..	Victor 22585
3/07/31	**4**	7	27. Would You Like To Take A Walk?	Victor 22611
			from the Broadway musical "Sweet and Low"	
7/18/31	**2(1)**	7	28. When Yuba Plays The Rhumba On The Tuba .	Victor 22742
			from the Broadway musical "The Third Little Show"	
9/12/31	**3**	5	29. Life Is Just A Bowl Of Cherries	Victor 22783
9/12/31	**10**	3	30. The Thrill Is Gone/	
9/19/31	**10**	4	31. My Song...	Victor 22784
			above three from the Broadway musical "George White's Scandals of 1931"	
9/19/31	**15**	2	32. As Time Goes By	Victor 22773
			from the Broadway musical "Everybody's Welcome"	
8/27/32	**2(3)**	10	33. I Guess I'll Have To Change My Plan (The Blue Pajama Song)...........................	Columbia 2700
			from the Broadway musical "The Little Show"	
9/10/32	**6**	4	34. Strange Interlude...................................	Columbia 2702
9/17/32	**15**	2	35. Maori..	Columbia 2700
10/01/32	**2(3)**	8	36. Let's Put Out The Lights..........................	Columbia 2715
			from the Broadway musical "George White's Music Hall Varieties"	
10/08/32	**12**	6	37. Say It Isn't So	Columbia 2714
11/26/32	**1(2)**	8	38. **Brother, Can You Spare A Dime?**	Columbia 2725
			from the Broadway musical "New Americana"	
11/26/32	**7**	4	39. How Deep Is The Ocean? (How-High-Is-The- Sky?)	Columbia 2724
12/31/32+	**10**	3	40. Here It Is Monday	Columbia 2730
1/14/33	**3**	6	41. Just An Echo In The Valley	Columbia 2733
1/28/33	**11**	3	42. Linger A Little Longer In The Twilight.........	Columbia 2738
2/18/33	**6**	4	43. Whisper Waltz.......................................	Columbia 2746

DATE CHARTED	PEAK POS	WKS CHRT'D	ARTIST — Record Title	Label & Number
2/25/33	10	3	44. The Girl In The Little Green Hat..................	Columbia 2744
2/25/33	11	4	45. Pretending You Care	Columbia 2746
3/18/33	6	4	46. Maybe It's Because I Love You Too Much	Columbia 2756
4/22/33	16	2	47. Here Is My Heart....................................	Columbia 2764
5/27/33	6	7	48. The Shadow Waltz/	
6/10/33	18	1	49. I've Got To Sing A Torch Song .... above two from the film "Gold Diggers of 1933"	Columbia 2773
11/04/33	15	2	50. By A Waterfall	Bluebird 5171
1/06/34	3	7	51. Everything I Have Is Yours .... from the film "Dancing Lady"	Victor 24458
1/06/34	4	11	52. Orchids In The Moonlight/	
1/13/34	6	7	53. Flying Down To Rio............................... above two from the film "Flying Down to Rio"	Victor 24459
1/06/34	13	2	54. Puddin' Head Jones	Victor 24475
3/17/34	12	5	55. Dancing In The Moonlight	Victor 24558
3/24/34	5	6	56. You Oughta Be In Pictures .... from the film "New York Town"	Victor 24580
4/14/34	10	5	57. Nasty Man/	
4/14/34	11	4	58. Hold My Hand .... above two from the film "George White's Scandals"	Victor 24581
9/29/34	4	9	59. Lost In A Fog/	
10/13/34	6	7	60. The Drunkard Song (There Is A Tavern In The Town)..................................... [N] written in 1883, since associated with Ivy League colleges	Victor 24721
11/10/34	12	6	61. P.S. I Love You......................................	Victor 24723
1/19/35	4	10	62. On The Good Ship Lollipop........................ from the Shirley Temple film "Bright Eyes"	Victor 24838
4/18/36	13	3	63. There's Always A Happy Ending.................	Victor 25260
9/04/37	6	4	64. The Old Sow Song..................................	Bluebird 7079
10/23/37	1(1)	13	65. **Vieni, Vieni** .... adaptation of a popular Corsican song	Bluebird 7069
11/06/37	11	2	66. In The Mission By The Sea	Bluebird 7226
3/12/38	19	1	67. I'll Take Romance.................................... with the Gentlemen Songsters	Bluebird 7331
5/07/38	5	10	68. Oh, Ma, Ma (The Butcher Boy) .... based on the Italian song "Luna Merro Mare"	Bluebird 7543
6/18/38	8	4	69. Day Dreaming	Victor 25836
8/13/38	19	1	70. Naturally...	Bluebird 7645
9/23/39	15	1	71. Lydia, The Tattooed Lady .... [N] from the film "The Marx Brothers at the Circus"	Decca 2708
3/27/43	1(4)	16	72. **As Time Goes By** .... [R] reissue of Victor 22773 (recorded 7/25/31); originally from the Broadway musical "Everybody's Welcome", featured in the film "Casablanca"	Victor 1526
9/14/46	20	1	73. The Whiffenpoof Song.............................. with the Sportsmen; theme song for a branch of the Yale Glee Club; Rudy first recorded this in 1937 (Bluebird 7135)	Enterprise 181
			JUNE VALLI Got her start by winning on Arthur Godfrey's "Talent Scouts" program.	
7/19/52	23	4	1. Strange Sensation....................................	RCA Victor 4759
12/06/52	24	2	2. A Shoulder To Weep On .... with a male quartet	RCA Victor 5017
8/01/53	4	17	3. Crying In The Chapel............................... accompanied by Joe Riesman's Orchestra	RCA Victor 5368
11/14/53	24	1	4. Don't Forget To Write...............................	RCA Victor 5488
6/12/54	8	12	5. I Understand... accompanied by Hugo Winterhalter's Orchestra	RCA Victor 5740
10/23/54	16	4	6. Tell Me, Tell Me..................................... 4 & 6 accompanied by Henri Rene's Orchestra	RCA Victor 5837

DATE CHARTED	PEAK POS	WKS CHRT'D	ARTIST — Record Title	Label & Number
			VAN & SCHENCK	
			Gus Van & Joe Schenck, comedy-musical team featured in several Broadway musicals, in vaudeville, & on radio. Joe Schenck died on 6/28/30 (39), and Gus Kahn on 3/12/68 (80).	
3/17/17	6	3	1. Yaddie Kaddie Kiddie Kaddie Koo .... [C]	Victor 18220
5/26/17	1(3)	10	2. **For Me And My Gal**................................	Victor 18258
			accompanied by Rosario Bourdon & His Orchestra	
9/15/17	9	1	3. Huckleberry Finn.....................................	Victor 18318
3/09/18	8	1	4. I Don't Want To Get Well	Victor 18413
5/11/18	2(3)	5	5. In The Land O' Yamo Yamo .... [C]	Victor 18443
			1 & 3-5 accompanied by Eddie King & His Orchestra	
11/15/19	6	3	6. Oh! How She Can Sing .... [C]	Columbia 2757
			accompanied on most Columbias through 1923 by Charles Prince's Orchestra	
12/06/19	2(2)	7	7. Mandy	Columbia 2780
			from Broadway's "Ziegfeld Follies of 1919"	
8/21/20	6	3	8. All The Boys Love Mary...........................	Columbia 2942
10/09/20	2(2)	6	9. After You Get What You Want, You Don't Want It...................................... [C]	Columbia 2966
1/22/21	5	4	10. All She'd Say Was "Umh-Hum" .... [C]	Columbia 3319
8/13/21	1(2)	9	11. **Ain't We Got Fun?**..............................	Columbia 3412
5/27/22	4	4	12. Virginia Blues	Columbia 3577
8/05/22	5	3	13. California	Columbia 3614
12/30/22+	5	3	14. When You And I Were Young, Maggie, Blues..	Columbia 3694
1/13/23	1(3)	14	15. **Carolina In The Morning**	Columbia 3712
			from "The Passing Show of 1922"	
2/03/23	5	4	16. You Can Have Him, I Don't Want Him....... [C]	Columbia 3735
4/11/23	5	3	17. You Tell Her - I Stutter .... [C]	Columbia 3770
7/24/24	14	1	18. Down Where The South Begins..................	Columbia 101
10/11/24	6	2	19. I Wonder What's Become Of Sally	Columbia 148
3/17/28	10	4	20. Is She My Girl Friend?	Columbia 1221
			WALTER VAN BRUNT	
			Thomas Edison's favorite tenor, Walter Van Brunt is said to have sold more Edison Diamond Discs than anyone except Billy Murray; he recorded his first hit at age 17. In 1917, at Edison's suggestion, he changed his last name to Scanlan, and starred in the Broadway musical "Eileen". He was featured on the radio with Murray from 1929-33.	
11/20/09	3	4	1. When I Dream In The Gloaming Of You........	Victor 16363
1/01/10	2(1)	6	2. It's Hard To Kiss Your Sweetheart (When The Last Kiss Means Good-Bye)	Victor 16414
2/25/11	2(1)	6	3. I've Got Your Number	Columbia 3191
			ELIDA MORRIS & WALTER VAN BRUNT	
7/29/11	9	1	4. It's Got To Be Someone I Love	Columbia 988
8/12/11	6	3	5. That Was Before I Met You.......................	Columbia 998
			also recorded solo for Zon-o-Phone 5733 above two: ADA JONES & WALTER VAN BRUNT	
8/19/11	3	5	6. Don't Wake Me Up, I'm Dreaming................	Victor 16880
8/19/11	4	3	7. That Railroad Rag..................................	Victor 16876
9/09/11	6	2	8. All Alone	Columbia 1010
			also on Indestructable 1496	
9/23/11	6	2	9. June	Victor 16871
			from the Broadway musical "The Hen-Pecks"	
10/07/11	3	4	10. That Was Before I Met You	Victor 16904
			solo version of 5	
11/11/11	2(2)	10	11. I Want A Girl Just Like The Girl That Married Dear Old Dad...........................	Victor 16962
			WALTER VAN BRUNT & AMERICAN QUARTET solo version released on Zon-o-Phone 5810	
11/18/11	6	2	12. I'm Just Pining For You	Victor 16906
12/16/11	5	3	13. Knock Wood	Columbia 1058
			8 & 13: ADA JONES & WALTER VAN BRUNT	

DATE CHARTED	PEAK POS	WKS CHRT'D	ARTIST — Record Title	Label & Number
1/13/12	9	1	14. Her Bright Smile Haunts Me Still .... WALTER VAN BRUNT & JOHN BIELING	Victor 16970
1/20/12	7	2	15. After The Honeymoon	Columbia 1073
3/02/12	7	2	16. One O'Clock In The Morning	Columbia 1098
4/13/12	5	3	17. The Harbor Of Love..............................	Victor 17034
6/29/12	6	2	18. Take Me Back To The Garden Of Love	Victor 17076
7/13/12	3	5	19. I'm Afraid, Pretty Maid, I'm Afraid	Columbia 1164
8/17/12	5	3	20. I'd Love To Live In Loveland With A Girl Like You............................... also recorded for Edison 10572	Victor 17089
9/28/12	7	2	21. I Love The Name Of Mary .... from the Broadway musical "Barry of Ballymore"	Victor 17107
10/26/12	10	1	22. Goodbye, Everybody............................. from the Broadway musical "A Modern Eve"	Victor 17136
12/07/12	7	2	23. That Mellow Melody	Victor 17170
12/14/12	6	2	24. Be My Little Baby Bumble Bee .... from Broadway's "Ziegfeld Follies of 1912"	Columbia 1210
12/28/12	9	1	25. Rose Of Pyramid Land	Victor 17173
1/04/13	3	6	26. Ghost Of The Violin.............................. WALTER VAN BRUNT & MAURICE BURKHARDT	Victor 17195
3/15/13	8	2	27. When I Get You Alone To-Night .... 19, 24 & 27: ADA JONES & WALTER VAN BRUNT	Columbia 1237
3/22/13	1(2)	8	28. **Sympathy**.................................. from the Broadway musical "The Firefly" 25 & 28: WALTER VAN BRUNT & HELEN CLARK	Victor 17270
4/19/13	4	4	29. And The Green Grass Grew All Around.........	Columbia 1277
6/14/13	6	3	30. In My Harem	Columbia 1302
11/12/13	10	1	31. There's A Girl In The Heart Of Maryland	Edison Amb. 1943
11/29/13	6	3	32. Where Did You Get That Girl?.................... also recorded for Columbia 1407	Victor 17414
1/31/14	7	2	33. Peg O' My Heart.............................. from Broadway's "Ziegfeld Follies of 1913"	Edison Amb. 2036
9/19/14	5	5	34. Something Seems Tingle-Ingling .... from the Broadway musical "High Jinks"	Edison Amb. 2404
10/17/14	7	2	35. Mary, You're A Little Bit Old-Fashioned........	Edison Amb. 2386
4/17/15	9	1	36. My Melancholy Baby .... later issued on Edison Disc 50923	Edison Amb. 2542
7/24/15	8	2	37. Simple Melody.............................. WALTER VAN BRUNT & MARY CARSON from the Broadway musical "Watch Your Step"	Edison Amb. 2607
1/08/16	9	1	38. They Didn't Believe Me .... from the Broadway musical "The Girl from Utah" later on Edison Diamond Disc 80279	Edison Amb. 2759
8/05/16	8	2	39. Babes In The Wood .... from the Broadway musical "Very Good, Eddie" also on Edison Amberol 2900 above two: WALTER VAN BRUNT & GLADYS RICE	Edison 50344
12/09/16	3	4	40. I'll Take You Home Again, Kathleen............. also on Edison Amberol 2987	Edison 80160

ART VAN DAMME
Jazz accordionist who led group backing Dinning Sisters on 1948 smash "Buttons and Bows".

FRED VAN EPS
Successor to Vess Ossman as "king of the banjo"; his trio included pianist Felix Arndt, and later saxophonist Nathan Glantz. Fred died on 11/22/60 (81); his son George was a guitarist with Ray Noble, and three other sons were also successful musicians. (also see Peerless Quartet)

DATE CHARTED	PEAK POS	WKS CHRT'D	ARTIST — Record Title	Label & Number
8/09/02	5	2	1. Blaze Away .... [I]	Edison 8025
8/19/11+	9	1	2. Infanta March .... [I] also recorded for Edison Amberol 747 & Zon-o-Phone 5783	Victor 16847
5/04/12	5	3	3. Red Pepper - A Spicy Rag .... [I]	Victor 17033
6/21/13	10	1	4. Florida Rag.......................... [I]	Victor 17308

DATE CHARTED	PEAK POS	WKS CHRT'D	ARTIST — Record Title	Label & Number
4/17/14	10	1	5. Old Folks Rag .... [I] Van Eps' Banjo Orchestra	Columbia 5618
6/12/14	8	2	6. The Original Fox Trot .... [I]	Victor 17677
9/23/16	7	2	7. Hill And Dale .... [I]	Columbia 2034
8/02/19	7	2	8. Oh, Susy, Behave................................. [I]	Victor 18556
3/20/20	10	1	9. Where The Lanterns Glow .... [I] 4, 6-9: VAN EPS TRIO	Victor 18640

PETER VAN STEEDEN & HIS ORCHESTRA
Orchestra conductor on many radio shows, also composer; born in Holland.

DATE CHARTED	PEAK POS	WKS CHRT'D	ARTIST — Record Title	Label & Number
12/26/31+	2(3)	9	1. Home/	
1/30/32	13	3	2. I Promise You .... above two vocals: Dick Robertson	Victor 22868
4/09/32	12	2	3. Somebody Loves You .... vocal: Chick Bullock	Victor 22948

CAROLINE VAUGHAN - see HENRY BURR

SARAH VAUGHAN
"The Divine One", among the greatest jazz singers of the postwar era; she sang in the 40s with Earl Hines, Billy Eckstine, & Dizzy Gillespie (with whom she recorded the classic "Lover Man"); she remains one of the world's most respected singers in the 1980s.

DATE CHARTED	PEAK POS	WKS CHRT'D	ARTIST — Record Title	Label & Number
11/15/47	27	1	1. Tenderly .... accompanied by George Treadwell's Orchestra	Musicraft 504
7/03/48	9	1	2. Nature Boy	Musicraft 567
8/14/48	11	11	3. It's Magic .... accompanied by Richard Maltby's Orchestra from the film "Romance On the High Seas"	Musicraft 557
6/04/49	13	4	4. Black Coffee	Columbia 38462
9/17/49	14	4	5. That Lucky Old Sun (Just Rolls Around Heaven All Day)/	
10/01/49	20	5	6. Make Believe (You Are Glad When You're Sorry)... above three accompanied by Joe Lipman's Orchestra	Columbia 38559
6/03/50	26	3	7. I'm Crazy To Love You .... with Billy Butterfield & Taft Jordan (trumpets)	Columbia 38701
8/05/50	15	6	8. Our Very Own .... movie title song	Columbia 38860
9/16/50	10	7	9. I Love The Guy/	
11/11/50	16	7	10. Thinking Of You.................................... above three accompanied by Norman Leyden's Orchestra Bud Powell (piano) & Al Klink (tenor sax) on above two Buddy Morrow (trombone) on 4-6, 9-10	Columbia 38925
6/02/51	11	13	11. These Things I Offer You (For A Lifetime)......	Columbia 39370
8/11/51	19	2	12. Vanity .... accompanied by Paul Weston's Orchestra with Ziggy Elman (trumpet) & Babe Russin (tenor sax)	Columbia 39446
11/10/51	18	2	13. I Ran All The Way Home......................... Stan Freeman (piano) on 11 & 13 Toots Mondello (alto sax) on 13	Columbia 39576
11/08/52	22	2	14. Sinner Or Saint	Columbia 39873
11/22/52	27	1	15. My Tormented Heart .... Chris Griffin (trumpet) on 4, 9-10, 14-15	Columbia 39839
2/14/53	28	1	16. A Lover's Quarrel .... band includes Lou Stein (piano)	Columbia 39932
10/17/53	30	1	17. Time .... Will Bradley (trombone) on 7, 9-10, & 16-17 11, 13-15 & 17 accompanied by Percy Faith & His Orchestra	Columbia 40041

EMIL VELASCO

DATE CHARTED	PEAK POS	WKS CHRT'D	ARTIST — Record Title	Label & Number
1/20/34	9	3	1. The Old Spinning Wheel...........................	Columbia 2864

VENETIAN TRIO
Violin, cello, & harp

DATE CHARTED	PEAK POS	WKS CHRT'D	ARTIST — Record Title	Label & Number
5/01/15	6	2	1. Love's Dream After The Ball................... [I]	Victor 17720

DATE CHARTED	PEAK POS	WKS CHRT'D	ARTIST — Record Title	Label & Number
			CHARLIE VENTURA Top jazzman on tenor sax & other reed instruments, featured with Gene Krupa (1942-43, 44-46), then successful bandleader.	
			JOE VENTUTI & HIS ORCHESTRA Great jazz violinist born at sea to Italian immigrant parents; played with Jean Goldkette, Roger Wolfe Kahn, & Paul Whiteman, among other bands, active into 1970s.	
7/18/31	**4**	6	1. Little Girl .... Harold Arlen, vocal, with Joe Ventuti's Blue Four	Columbia 2488
1/23/32	**20**	1	2. Beale Street Blues .... [I] VENTUTI-LANG ALL-STAR ORCHESTRA vocal: Jack Teagarden (also trombone) Benny Goodman (clarinet)	Melotone 12294
6/17/33	**19**	1	3. Jig Saw Puzzle Blues........................... [I] VENTUTI-LANG BLUE FIVE Eddie Lang (guitar) on above three; Jimmy Dorsey (alto sax/clarinet) on above two; Adrian Rollini (baritone sax) on 3	Columbia 2782
12/21/35+	**5**	6	4. Stop, Look, And Listen .... vocal: Ruth Lee	Columbia 3104
12/28/35+	**7**	5	5. Twenty-Four Hours A Day .... vocal: Tony Pasteur; from the film "Sweet Surrender" Toots Camarata (trumpet) on above two	Columbia 3103
			VERNON COUNTRY CLUB BAND	
7/09/21	**9**	1	1. Whip-Poor-Will/Look For The Silver Lining (medley).................................. [I] both songs from the Broadway musical "Sally"	Columbia 3378
			VICTOR CONCERT ORCHESTRA Conducted by Walter B. Rogers.	
10/28/11	**10**	1	1. Pink Lady Selection .... [I]	Victor 35193
			VICTOR LIGHT OPERA CO. Virtually every singing star recording for Victor took part in these records, including Harry Macdonough, Lucy Isabelle Marsh, Olive Kline, Reinald Werrenrath, Billy Murray, Ada Jones, Elsie Baker, John Bieling, Elise Stevenson, & members of the Revelers. Walter B. Rogers was conductor on all records through 1916, and Nat Shilkret on the later hits. (also see Dennis King)	
7/31/09	**1(5)**	9	1. **The Yama Yama Man** .... ADA JONES & VICTOR LIGHT OPERA CO. from the Broadway musical "The Three Twins"	Victor 1632
11/27/09	**7**	1	2. Gems From "The Prince Of To-Night"	Victor 31748
7/09/10	**7**	2	3. Gems From "The Chocolate Soldier" .... including "My Hero" & "That Would Be Lovely"	Victor 31780
10/29/10	**7**	2	4. Gems From "Mlle. Modiste"	Victor 31790
11/19/10	**7**	2	5. Gems From "The Red Mill"........................ including "Because You're You" & "Good-a-Bye John"	Victor 31794
2/25/11	**6**	3	6. Gems From "The Merry Widow"	Victor 31805
3/04/11	**2(2)**	9	7. Italian Street Song .... LUCY ISABELLE MARSH & VICTOR LIGHT OPERA CO. from the Broadway musical "Naughty Marietta"	Victor 60031
5/06/11	**10**	1	8. Gems From "The Pirates Of Penzance"..........	Victor 31808
5/20/11	**10**	1	9. Gems From "Babes In Toyland"	Victor 31814
9/16/11	**9**	1	10. Gems From "Florodora"............................	Victor 31817
10/21/11	**6**	3	11. Gems From "Madame Sherry"...................... including "Every Little Movement" & "Come to the Ball"	Victor 31824
11/04/11	**10**	1	12. Gems From "The Fortune Teller"	Victor 31830
2/03/12	**7**	2	13. Gems From "The Quaker Girl".....................	Victor 31847
2/24/12	**2(2)**	8	14. Gems From "Naughty Marietta" .... including "I'm Falling In Love With Someone" & "Tramp Tramp Tramp"	Victor 31852
4/05/13	**9**	2	15. Gems From "Lady Of The Slipper"................	Victor 31877
11/01/13	**7**	3	16. Gems From "Sweethearts".........................	Victor 31885
8/01/14	**9**	1	17. Gems From "High Jinks"	Victor 35382
12/05/14	**7**	3	18. Gems From "The Girl From Utah" .... including "Same Sort of Girl" & "They Didn't Believe Me"	Victor 35404
6/12/15	**7**	2	19. Gems From "Maid In America"	Victor 35440

DATE CHARTED	PEAK POS	WKS CHRT'D	ARTIST — Record Title	Label & Number
9/25/15	**10**	1	20. Gems From "Nobody Home"	Victor 35471
4/22/16	**6**	2	21. Gems From "Very Good, Eddie" .... including "Babes In the Wood" & "Some Sort of Somebody"	Victor 35529
2/03/17	**9**	1	22. Gems From "Miss Springtime"	Victor 35592
3/09/18	**3**	4	23. Gems From "Leave It To Jane" .... including title song & "The Siren's Song"	Victor 35666
8/28/20	**12**	1	24. Gems From "Irene"	Victor 35697
5/26/23	**13**	1	25. Gems From "Blossom Time"	Victor 35722
9/26/25	**12**	1	26. Gems From "The Student Prince" .... including "The Drinking Song" & "Deep In My Heart"	Victor 35757
6/26/26	**13**	1	27. Song Of The Flame .... Broadway musical title song	Victor 19954
			VICTOR MILITARY BAND Walter B. Rogers, director	
1/13/12	**4**	4	1. Alexander's Ragtime Band .... [I]	Victor 17006
5/10/13	**9**	1	2. When The Midnight Choo-Choo Leaves For Alabam'... [I]	Victor 35277
1/24/14	**6**	3	3. That International Rag .... [I]	Victor 17487
3/28/14	**6**	2	4. La Golondria (The Swallow) .... [I]	Victor 17515
11/21/14	**9**	1	5. The Memphis Blues .... [I]	Victor 17619
2/27/15	**7**	2	6. My Tango Girl .... [I]	Victor 35422
3/11/16	**10**	1	7. Stop, Look, And Listen (Medley) .... [I]	Victor 35521
7/22/16	**3**	6	8. Missouri Waltz .... [I]	Victor 18026
2/17/17	**1(6)**	10	9. **Poor Butterfly/** [I] from the Broadway musical "The Big Show"	
3/03/17	**2(2)**	5	10. Katinka (Medley) .... [I]	Victor 35605
3/10/17	**4**	5	11. Pack Up Your Troubles In Your Old Kit Bag And Smile, Smile, Smile......................	Victor 18218
6/23/17	**8**	1	12. Boy Scouts Of America March .... [I]	Victor 18209
1/05/18	**9**	1	13. Sailin' Away On The Henry Clay............. [I]	Victor 35654
7/06/18	**6**	3	14. Liberty Forever! .... [I]	Victor 18471
4/26/19	**3**	5	15. Madelon/ vocal refrain by opera star Marcel Journet	
5/10/19	**10**	1	16. Marche Francaise .... [I]	Victor 18534
			VICTOR MIXED CHORUS Walter B. Rogers, director	
9/25/15	**4**	4	1. Songs Of The Past, Parts 1 & 2 .... medley: Good-bye Dolly Gray / After the Ball / Sweet Marie / Where Did You Get That Hat? / Say "Au Revoir" But Not Goodbye / Daisy Bell / A Hot Time In the Old Town	Victor 35477
			VICTOR ORCHESTRA Walter B. Rogers, conductor	
10/05/07	**2(1)**	6	1. Merry Widow Waltz.............................. [I] from the Broadway musical "The Merry Widow"	Victor 5208
5/02/08	**5**	1	2. The Dream Waltz................................. [I] from the Broadway musical "The Waltz Dream"	Victor 5369
5/16/08	**1(5)**	9	3. **The Glow-Worm**.................................. [I] from the German operetta "Lysistrata"; featured in the Broadway musical "The Girl Behind the Counter"	Victor 5408
			VICTOR SYMPHONY ORCHESTRA	
6/22/29	**7**	6	1. An American In Paris .... [I] George Gershwin, piano soloist	Victor 35963
10/19/29	**12**	2	2. Patriotic March Medley .... [I]	Victor 22013
			VESTA VICTORIA Famous British entertainer featured in several Broadway musicals.	
9/14/07	**4**	1	1. Waiting At The Church (My Wife Won't Let Me)	Victor 5182
			ANNE VINCENT	
7/31/48	**6**	16	1. You Call Everybody Darlin'........................	Mercury 5155

DATE CHARTED	PEAK POS	WKS CHRT'D	ARTIST — Record Title	Label & Number
			LARRY VINCENT & THE FEILDEN FOURSOME	
3/29/47	20	6	1. If I Had My Life To Live Over	20th Century 13
			EDDIE (CLEANHEAD) VINSON Durable blues singer who had the 1944 hit with Cootie Williams, "Cherry Red Blues".	
			VIRGINIANS Directed by Ross Gorman (clarinet), featuring Paul Whiteman stars Henry Busse (cornet) & Ferde Grofe (piano)	
11/25/22	15	1	1. Why Should I Cry Over You? .... [I]	Victor 18933
2/03/23	3	7	2. I Wish I Could Shimmy Like My Sister Kate [I]	Victor 18965
			DON VOORHEES & HIS ORCHESTRA Pianist-bandleader who went on to become a top radio conductor from the 1930s to 50s.	
4/09/27	19	1	1. One Alone .... from the Broadway musical "The Desert Song"	Columbia 835
7/09/27	18	2	2. Dancing The Devil Away .... vocal: Charles Kaley; from the Broadway musical "Lucky" above two: DON VOORHEES & HIS EARL CARROLL VANITIES ORCH.	Columbia 954
12/31/27+	9	4	3. My Blue Heaven....................................... vocal: Lewis James	Columbia 1129
1/07/28+	15	2	4. When The Morning Glories Wake Up In The Morning (Then I'll Kiss Your Two Lips Goodnight)................................... vocal: Irving Kaufman; with Red Nichols (trumpet) Miff Mole (trombone) on above four	Columbia 1124

W

DATE CHARTED	PEAK POS	WKS CHRT'D	ARTIST — Record Title	Label & Number
			STUART WADE Vocalist with Freddy Martin in 1940s ("Jingle, Jangle, Jingle", "To Each His Own", "Managua, Nicaragua").	
			BEA WAIN Voted the #1 female band vocalist in the 1939 Billboard college poll thanks to her smash hits with Larry Clinton ("My Reverie", "Heart and Soul", "Deep Purple"); she later hosted her own radio show.	
8/24/40	11	2	1. I'm Nobody's Baby .... accompanied by Walter Grass & His Orchestra song featured in the film "Andy Hardy Meets DeButante"	Victor 26603
4/12/41	23	1	2. Do I Worry?	Victor 27353
5/17/41	15	2	3. My Sister And I	Victor 27363
7/12/41	8	11	4. Kiss The Boys Goodbye .... movie title song	Victor 27445
			JIMMY WAKELY Popular country performer who appeared in over 50 movie Westerns during 1940s, and scored his biggest hits in duets with Margaret Whiting. Jimmy died on 9/23/82 (68).	
3/20/43	14	2	1. There's A Star-Spangled Banner Waving Somewhere	Decca 6059
10/23/48	10	8	2. One Has My Name (The Other Has My Heart)..	Capitol 15162
12/18/48	21	8	3. I Love You So Much It Hurts	Capitol 15243
9/10/49	1(3)	23	● 4. **Slippin' Around**/	
10/22/49	30	1	5. Wedding Bells Will Soon Be Ringing..........	Capitol 40224
11/05/49	8	10	6. I'll Never Slip Around Again	Capitol 40246
2/11/50	12	7	7. Broken Down Merry-Go-Round/	
2/25/50	17	7	8. The Gods Were Angry With Me................. above five: MARGARET WHITING & JIMMY WAKELY	Capitol 800
4/15/50	13	6	9. Let's Go To Church (Next Sunday Morning)....	Capitol 960
4/15/50	26	1	10. Peter Cottontail...................................	Capitol 929
10/28/50	6	15	11. A Bushel And A Peck .... from the Broadway musical "Guys and Dolls"	Capitol 1234

DATE CHARTED	PEAK POS	WKS CHRT'D	ARTIST — Record Title	Label & Number
1/06/51	**12**	13	12. My Heart Cries For You.............................. Capitol 1328	Capitol 1328
			adapted from the French folk song "Chanson de Marie Antoinette"	
3/17/51	**12**	14	13. Beautiful Brown Eyes	Capitol 1393
			accompanied by Les Baxter's Orchestra	
5/12/51	**20**	2	14. When You And I Were Young, Maggie	Capitol 1500
			9, 11 & 14: MARGARET WHITING & JIMMY WAKELY	

JERRY WALD & HIS ORCHESTRA
Clarinetist-bandleader who featured alto saxophonist Larry Elgart and arrangements by Ray Conniff & Jerry Gray; died in 1973 (55).

DATE CHARTED	PEAK POS	WKS CHRT'D	ARTIST — Record Title	Label & Number
9/30/44	**24**	1	1. Since You Went Away	Decca 4446
			vocal: Ginnie Powell	
4/14/45	**8**	3	2. Laura/	
			vocal: Dick Merrick; movie title song	
5/19/45	**18**	1	3. Candy...	Majestic 7129

WALDORF-ASTORIA DANCE ORCHESTRA
Joseph Knecht, director

DATE CHARTED	PEAK POS	WKS CHRT'D	ARTIST — Record Title	Label & Number
4/06/18	**9**	1	1. Maytime Waltz (Will You Remember?) .... [I]	Victor 18432
4/05/19	**1(1)**	9	2. Beautiful Ohio .... [I]	Victor 18526
			flip side of #1 hit "Till We Meet Again" by Nicholas Orlando & His Orchestra	
5/17/19	**6**	3	3. Arabian Nights .... [I]	Victor 18536
9/27/19	**7**	2	4. The Vamp...	Columbia 2758
			vocal: Irving & Jack Kaufman	

GEORGE WALKER - see BERT WILLIAMS

JOHNNY WALKER & HIS ORCHESTRA - see CHARLESTON CHASERS

JERRY WALLACE

DATE CHARTED	PEAK POS	WKS CHRT'D	ARTIST — Record Title	Label & Number
2/06/54	**30**	1	1. Little Miss One	Allied 5015
			with Eddie Oliver & The Oliver Twisters	

TED WALLACE & HIS CAMPUS BOYS
Real name Wallace T. "Ed" Kirkeby, manager of the California Ramblers

DATE CHARTED	PEAK POS	WKS CHRT'D	ARTIST — Record Title	Label & Number
3/01/30	**17**	2	1. When You're Smiling (The Whole World Smiles With You)...............................	Columbia 2104
4/19/30	**8**	4	2. Stein Song..	Columbia 2151
			University of Maine theme song	
			above two vocals: Smith Ballew	
8/23/30	**3**	6	3. Little White Lies.................................	Columbia 2254
			vocal: Elmer Feldkamp	
11/29/30	**14**	3	4. Sweetheart Of My Student Days/	
12/06/30	**11**	3	5. The Little Things In Life	Columbia 2334
			above two vocals: Dick Dixon (may be pseudonym for Dick Robertson)	
8/15/31	**8**	4	6. I'm An Unemployed Sweetheart (Looking For Somebody To Love)............................	Columbia 2493
3/12/32	**14**	2	7. Starlight (Help Me Find The One I Love)	Columbia 2601

FATS WALLER
Thomas "Fats" Waller was born on 5/21/04 in New York City. He worked as a piano and organ accompanist during the 20s until his first big break, collaborating on Broadway musical scores "Keep Shufflin'" & "Hot Chocolates" (including his classic "Ain't Misbehavin'"). But it was in 1934 that Fats burst through as one of the country's most popular entertainers, with his playful, high-spirited vocals, distinctive stride piano style, and jazz accompaniment. Bill Coleman (trumpet), Gene Sedric (clarinet/tenor sax), & Rudy Powell (clarinet) were his top sidemen. Shortly after his hit movie appearance in "Stormy Weather", Fats Waller died on 12/15/43. The late-70s hit Broadway musical "Ain't Misbehavin'" celebrated his great songs and spirit.

DATE CHARTED	PEAK POS	WKS CHRT'D	ARTIST — Record Title	Label & Number
11/09/29	**17**	1	1. Ain't Misbehavin'................................ [I]	Victor 22108
			selected for the NARAS Hall of Fame	
			from the Broadway musical "Hot Chocolates"	
6/16/34	**8**	8	2. I Wish I Were Twins	Victor 24641

DATE CHARTED	PEAK POS	WKS CHRT'D	ARTIST — Record Title	Label & Number
9/29/34	9	4	3. Then I'll Be Tired Of You............................	Victor 24708
10/13/34	10	5	4. Don't Let It Bother You .... from the film "Gay Divorcee"	Victor 24714
10/20/34	7	7	5. Sweetie Pie/	
10/27/34	16	2	6. How Can You Face Me?...........................	Victor 24737
11/24/34	20	1	7. A Porter's Love Song To A Chambermaid......	Victor 24648
12/22/34+	5	11	8. Believe It, Beloved	Victor 24808
2/09/35	16	2	9. Because Of Once Upon A Time	Victor 24846
2/09/35	17	1	10. Honeysuckle Rose...................................	Victor 24826
2/16/35	10	4	11. I Believe In Miracles	Victor 24853
3/30/35	13	3	12. Whose Honey Are You?	Victor 24892
5/11/35	20	1	13. Pardon My Love	Victor 24889
6/22/35	8	10	14. Lulu's Back In Town .... from the film "Broadway Gondolier"	Victor 25063
6/29/35	5	9	15. I'm Gonna Sit Right Down And Write Myself A Letter..	Victor 25044
8/24/35	13	4	16. Sweet And Slow....................................	Victor 25063
8/31/35	1(3)	13	17. **Truckin'**	Victor 25116
8/31/35	19	1	18. 12th Street Rag	Victor 25087
9/28/35	8	6	19. Rhythm And Romance.............................	Victor 25131
12/21/35	1(2)	7	20. **A Little Bit Independent**	Victor 25196
2/22/36	11	3	21. I've Got My Fingers Crossed....................... from the film "King of Burlesque"	Victor 25211
2/22/36	13	5	22. Sing An Old-Fashioned Song/	
2/29/36	11	5	23. West Wind....................................	Victor 25253
5/02/36	1(1)	11	24. **All My Life** .... from the film "Laughing Irish Eyes"	Victor 25296
5/09/36	6	5	25. Us On A Bus	Victor 25295
5/23/36	7	9	26. Cross Patch	Victor 25315
6/27/36	1(4)	12	27. **It's A Sin To Tell A Lie**	Victor 25342
7/18/36	4	6	28. Let's Sing Again .... movie title song	Victor 25348
8/01/36	7	9	29. You're Not The Kind	Victor 25353
8/22/36	7	3	30. Black Raspberry Jam ....[I]	Victor 25359
8/29/36	4	11	31. Bye Bye Baby..	Victor 25388
9/05/36	3	7	32. Until The Real Thing Comes Along..............	Victor 25374
9/26/36	4	5	33. The Curse Of An Aching Heart	Victor 25394
10/24/36	5	5	34. S'posin'...	Victor 25415
12/12/36	7	4	35. Dinah .... from the Broadway musical "Kid Boots"	Victor 25471
12/26/36+	9	3	36. T'ain't Good (Like A Nickel Made Of Wood)....	Victor 25478
1/02/37	8	4	37. A Thousand Dreams Of You........................ from the film "Rainbow On the River"	Victor 25483
1/30/37	6	5	38. Please Keep Me In Your Dreams	Victor 25498
2/13/37	8	3	39. Who's Afraid Of Love .... from the film "One in a Million"	Victor 25499
2/20/37	3	6	40. I'm Sorry I Made You Cry	Victor 25515
3/06/37	4	4	41. You're Laughing At Me	Victor 25530
4/10/37	20	1	42. Where Is The Sun?.................................	Victor 25550
4/17/37	3	6	43. Spring Cleaning....................................	Victor 25554
4/24/37	4	4	44. Honeysuckle Rose.................................... "A Jam Session at Victor": Fats Waller, Tommy Dorsey (trombone), Bunny Berigan (trumpet), & Dick McDonough (guitar)	Victor 25559
4/24/37	17	1	45. When Love Is Young.................................	Victor 25537
5/01/37	17	1	46. To A Sweet And Pretty Thing......................	Victor 25551
5/15/37	19	1	47. You Showed Me The Way	Victor 25565
7/10/37	1(2)	8	48. **Smarty**...	Victor 25608
10/09/37	19	1	49. You're My Dish....................................	Victor 25679

DATE CHARTED	PEAK POS	WKS CHRT'D	ARTIST — Record Title	Label & Number
10/23/37	7	4	50. Our Love Was Meant To Be......................	Victor 25681
11/13/37	17	1	51. The Joint Is Jumpin'.................................	Victor 25689
12/25/37+	13	2	52. What Will I Do In The Morning?................	Victor 25712
4/09/38+	5	6	53. I Love To Whistle...................................	Victor 25806
4/30/38	11	7	54. Something Tells Me................................	Victor 25817
8/06/38	17	2	55. There's Honey On The Moon Tonight...........	Victor 25891
11/12/38	1(2)	11	56. **Two Sleepy People**............................. from the film "Thanks for the Memory"	Bluebird 10000
1/14/39	15	1	57. You Look Good To Me	Bluebird 10028
2/18/39	7	6	58. Good For Nothin' But Love	Bluebird 10129
3/04/39	11	4	59. Hold Tight	Bluebird 10116
12/30/39	15	2	60. Your Feet's Too Big.......................... [N]	Bluebird 10500
4/27/40	6	11	61. Little Curly Hair In A High Chair .... [N] from the film "Forty Little Mothers"	Bluebird 10698
12/06/41	22	1	62. Come And Get It....................................	Bluebird 11262
9/11/43	21	1	63. Your Socks Don't Match...........................	Bluebird 0814

RUTH WALLIS
First became known for her risque recordings.

11/21/53	25	1	1. Dear Mr. Godfrey .... inspired by Arthur Godfrey's on-air TV firing of singer Julius La Rosa	Monarch 3005

TEDDY WALTERS
Sang briefly with Jimmy Dorsey

4/06/46	4	12	1. Laughing On The Outside (Crying On The Inside)... accompanied by Lou Bring & His Orchestra	ARA 135

HELEN WARD
Benny Goodman's featured vocalist from 1934-36 ("Blue Moon", "Goody Goody", "These Foolish Things"), Helen also sang with Teddy Wilson, Joe Sullivan, & Harry James.

11/14/53	30	1	1. You Brought A New Kind Of Love To Me .... accompanied by Percy Faith & His Orchestra	Columbia 49709

FRED WARING'S PENNSYLVANIANS
Extremely popular dance band leader best known for his "glee club" featured on radio shows from 1933 through 40s, and as inventor of the famous Waring Blender. Younger brother Tom Waring was one of band's singers; Johnny "Scat" Davis (trumpet) its most prominent musician. While at his peak of radio popularity, Fred ceased recording for nearly a decade after 1932; he hosted TV show in the early 50s. Fred died on 7/29/84 (84). (Also see Bing Crosby)

12/29/23+	1(5)	11	1. **Sleep**.. Fred's theme song; vocal: Fred & Tom Waring	Victor 19172
2/23/24	14	1	2. Stack O' Lee Blues................................. [I]	Victor 19189
8/02/24	1(5)	17	3. **Memory Lane/** vocal: Tom Waring	
9/27/24	10	1	4. Down Home Blues............................... [I]	Victor 19303
10/25/24	7	2	5. June Night .... [I]	Victor 19380
11/01/24	7	2	6. Maytime................................... [I]	Victor 19367
6/13/25	6	2	7. At The End Of The Road .... [I]	Victor 19603
7/25/25	3	6	8. Collegiate...	Victor 19648
1/02/26	8	2	9. Freshie	Victor 19784
4/24/26+	5	4	10. Thanks For The Buggy Ride.......................	Victor 19913
5/01/26	6	3	11. I Love My Baby	Victor 19905
10/16/26	4	5	12. Looking At The World Thro' Rose-Colored Glasses... vocal: Fred & Tom Waring	Victor 20076
10/30/26	14	1	13. Cherie, I Love You	Victor 20074
1/29/27	2(4)	8	14. It Made You Happy When You Made Me Cry...	Victor 20315
1/29/27	11	4	15. The Little White House (At The End Of Honeymoon Lane)............................... from the Broadway musical "Honeymoon Lane"	Victor 20289

DATE CHARTED	PEAK POS	WKS CHRT'D	ARTIST — Record Title	Label & Number
3/05/27	**6**	5	16. Where Do You Work-A, John?/	
3/12/27	**11**	3	17. I Love The College Girls...........................	Victor 20378
			8-11, 16-17 ensemble vocals	
5/14/27	**12**	2	18. Hello, Swanee, Hello!................................	Victor 20467
8/27/27	**3**	7	19. Just Another Day Wasted Away (Waiting For	
			You)..	Victor 20724
			vocals on 13-15, 18-19: Tom Waring	
10/08/27	**3**	7	20. Sweetheart Of Sigma Chi...........................	Victor 20820
2/18/28	**3**	6	21. I Scream-You Scream-We All Scream- For Ice	
			Cream	Victor 21099
			vocal: Fred Waring, Poley McClintock, & group	
5/26/28	**1(1)**	12	22. **Laugh, Clown, Laugh!**...........................	Victor 21308
			vocal: Fred Waring	
			based on a theme from the opera "I Pagliacci"	
6/02/28	**5**	5	23. I Can't Do Without You............................	Victor 21327
6/16/28	**16**	1	24. That Melody Of Love/	
			vocal: Fred & Tom Waring	
7/21/28	**11**	3	25. Was It A Dream?	Victor 21297
7/21/28	**2(1)**	9	26. Ah! Sweet Mystery Of Life	Victor 35921
			from the Broadway musical "Naughty Marietta"	
			vocals on 20, 23, 25-26: Tom Waring & ensemble	
11/24/28	**7**	5	27. Roses Of Yesterday .... [I]	Victor 21676
12/08/28+	**6**	7	28. I'm Sorry, Sally	Victor 21755
2/02/29	**14**	2	29. How About Me?......................................	Victor 21792
2/16/29	**9**	5	30. The Song I Love	Victor 21810
4/13/29	**11**	3	31. Button Up Your Overcoat	Victor 21861
4/27/29	**12**	3	32. Jericho/	
			vocals on 30 & 32: Fred Waring	
5/25/29	**3**	8	33. I'll Always Be In Love With You	Victor 21870
			above two from the film "Syncopation"	
5/18/29	**11**	3	34. My Lucky Star	Victor 21861
			vocal: Roy Cropper	
			above two from the Broadway musical "Follow Through"	
6/22/29	**18**	1	35. I Used To Love Her In The Moonlight...........	Victor 21900
7/20/29	**7**	4	36. My Sin	Victor 21977
			vocals on 28-29, 34-36: Clare Hanlon	
2/08/30	**3**	6	37. Cryin' For The Carolines........................	Victor 22272
			vocal: Will Morgan; from the film "Spring Is Here"	
3/22/30	**13**	2	38. There's Danger In Your Eyes, Cherie	Victor 22293
			from the film "Puttin' On the Ritz"	
8/16/30	**1(6)**	12	39. **Little White Lies**	Victor 22494
			above two vocals: Clare Hanlon	
8/16/30	**3**	6	40. So Beats My Heart For You......................	Victor 22486
			vocal: Stuart Churchill & Three Girl Friends	
3/14/31	**14**	2	41. Love For Sale..	Victor 22598
			from the Broadway musical "The New Yorkers"	
6/27/31	**19**	1	42. Elizabeth..	Victor 22655
			from the Broadway musical "The Wonder Bar"	
7/04/31	**1(3)**	6	43. **I Found A Million-Dollar Baby (In A Five-**	
			And-Ten-Cent Store)	Victor 22707
			vocal: Clare Hanlon & Three Waring Girls	
			from the Broadway musical "Billy Rose's Crazy Quilt"	
7/11/31	**3**	11	44. Dancing In The Dark/	
8/08/31	**12**	3	45. High And Low	Victor 22708
			above two from the Broadway musical "The Band Wagon"	
3/19/32	**5**	7	46. Let's Have Another Cup O' Coffee/	
			vocal: Chick Bullock & the Three Waring Girls	
4/02/32	**8**	5	47. Soft Lights And Sweet Music	Victor 22936
			above two from the Broadway musical "Face the Music"	
			vocals on 41-42, 44-45 & 47: Three Waring Girls	
6/25/32	**18**	2	48. With Summer Coming On	Victor 24016
			vocal: Fred Waring-Nelson Keller-Clare Hanlon-Tom Waring	
11/26/32	**4**	6	49. Fit As A Fiddle.......................................	Victor 24168
			vocal: Frank Zullo	

DATE CHARTED	PEAK POS	WKS CHRT'D	ARTIST — Record Title	Label & Number
3/11/33	**15**	2	50. You're Getting To Be A Habit With Me.......... *from the film "Forty-Second Street"*	Victor 24214
2/13/43	**21**	1	51. Yankee Doodle Boy .... *featured in the film "Yankee Doodle Dandy"*	Decca 18454
4/15/44	**14**	1	52. Holiday For Strings .... [I]	Decca 23311
12/04/54	**29**	1	53. Fanny... *Broadway musical title song*	Decca 29304

TOM WARING
Featured vocalist for brother Fred Waring's band; died on 12/29/60 (58).

WARNER'S SEVEN ACES
Byron Warner, director

5/30/25	**14**	1	1. When My Sugar Walks Down The Street .... [I]	Columbia 305

MARK WARNOW & HIS ORCHESTRA
Orchestra conductor on radio's "Your Hit Parade" from 1937-47, older brother of bandleader Raymond Scott; died in Oct. 1949 (47).

4/10/48	**26**	1	1. Who Put That Dream In Your Eye? .... *vocal by Lorry Raine*	Coast 8026

FRAN WARREN
Popular singer best remembered for her late-40s work with Claude Thornhill ("A Sunday Kind of Love").

7/16/49	**17**	5	1. A Wonderful Guy .... *from the Broadway musical "South Pacific"*	RCA Victor 3403
10/22/49	**12**	9	2. Envy	RCA Vic. 78-3551
1/21/50	**3**	13	3. I Said My Pajamas (And Put On My Prayers)... *TONY MARTIN & FRAN WARREN*	RCA Vic. 78-3613
3/18/50	**22**	5	4. Dearie .... *FRAN WARREN & LISA KIRK* *from the stage production "Copacabana Show of 1950"*	RCA Vic. 78-3696
9/02/50	**22**	1	5. I Love The Guy.. *above five accompanied by Henri Rene's Orchestra*	RCA Victor 3848
12/26/53	**26**	1	6. It's Anybody's Heart .... *accompanied by Lew Douglas & His Orchestra*	MGM 11616

DINAH WASHINGTON
Acclaimed jazz/rhythm & blues singer (born Ruth Jones) featured with Lionel Hampton from 1943-45, and known during the early 50s as "Queen of the Juke Boxes" for her many R&B hits. Dinah scored a classic 1959 hit with "What a Diff'rence a Day Makes"; she died on 12/14/63 (39).

6/17/50	**22**	4	1. I Wanna Be Loved.................................... *accompanied by Teddy Stewart's Orchestra*	Mercury 8181
12/18/54	**23**	1	2. Teach Me Tonight	Mercury 70497

ETHEL WATERS
Extremely popular blues singer who started in vaudeville, then became a star through recordings and Broadway musicals. The all-time classic "Stormy Weather", which she introduced at the Cotton Club, became her trademark song. Ethel appeared in a number of movies and subsequent Broadway shows as a dramatic actress through the 50s.

9/17/21	**5**	4	1. Down Home Blues....................................	Black Swan 2010
12/24/21+	**5**	5	2. There'll Be Some Changes Made	Black Swan 2021
9/16/22	**7**	2	3. Spread Yo' Stuff	Black Swan 10070
10/28/22	**14**	1	4. Tiger Rag	Black Swan 10073
11/17/23	**10**	1	5. Georgia Blues...	Black Swan 14120
9/19/25	**6**	2	6. Sweet Georgia Brown	Columbia 379
1/23/26	**2(2)**	8	7. Dinah .... *from the Broadway musical "Kid Boots"*	Columbia 487
6/26/26	**11**	1	8. I've Found A New Baby.............................. *Fletcher Henderson (piano) on 1-6 & 8*	Columbia 561
7/10/26	**9**	1	9. Sugar	Columbia 14146
2/12/27	**10**	4	10. I'm Coming, Virginia................................	Columbia 14170
7/20/29	**1(2)**	15	11. **Am I Blue?**/	
9/07/29	**20**	1	12. Birmingham Bertha.................................. *above two from the film "On With the Show"*	Columbia 1837

DATE CHARTED	PEAK POS	WKS CHRT'D	ARTIST — Record Title	Label & Number
9/07/29	15	2	13. True Blue Lou.. from the film "Dance of Life"	Columbia 1871
1/10/31	8	4	14. Three Little Words/ from the film "Check and Double Check"	
1/17/31	17	1	15. I Got Rhythm.. from the Broadway musical "Girl Crazy" Ben Selvin (violin) on above three	Columbia 2346
7/18/31	13	3	16. You Can't Stop Me From Loving You .... from the Broadway musical "Rhapsody in Black"	Columbia 2481
9/12/31	9	4	17. Shine On, Harvest Moon/ revived in the Broadway musical "Ziegfeld Follies of 1931"	
10/03/31	18	1	18. River, Stay 'Way From My Door.................	Columbia 2511
1/02/32	17	2	19. You Can't Stop Me From Loving You .... [R] Manny Klein (trumpet) on 11-12, 14-19	Columbia 2481
5/20/33	1(3)	11	20. **Stormy Weather** .... Ethel's definitive classic	Brunswick 6564
8/19/33	6	8	21. Don't Blame Me ....,.................................	Brunswick 6617
10/28/33	7	6	22. Heat Wave... from the Broadway musical "As Thousands Cheer"	Columbia 2826
12/23/33	7	4	23. A Hundred Years From Today .... accompanied by Benny Goodman & His Orchestra, with Jack Teagarden (trombone) & Gene Krupa (drums) from the Broadway musical "Blackbirds of 1933" Benny Goodman (clarinet) on 16-19 & 22-23	Columbia 2853
5/19/34	9	4	24. Come Up And See Me Sometime .... from the Mae West film "Take a Chance" Bunny Berigan (trumpet) on 20-22 & 24	Brunswick 6885
12/08/34	19	1	25. Miss Otis Regrets (She's Unable To Lunch Today).. from the London musical "Hi Diddle Diddle" Tommy Dorsey (trombone) on 11-22, 24-25; Jimmy Dorsey (alto sax/clarinet) on 11-15, 20-22, 24-25	Decca 140
2/19/38	16	2	26. You're A Sweetheart .... movie title song	Decca 1613
			BILLY WATKINS Died on 9/3/45 (57).	
9/05/14	1(2)	8	1. **By The Beautiful Sea** .... ADA JONES & BILLY WATKINS	Columbia 1563
11/28/14	9	1	2. I Can't Believe You Really Love Me (It's Like A Wonderful Dream)	Victor 17630
			PAULA WATSON R&B singer/pianist	
11/27/48+	6	16	1. A Little Bird Told Me................................	Supreme 1507
			ARTIE WAYNE Sang briefly in the mid-40s with Freddy Martin ("Dream")	
1/31/53	21	4	1. Rachel	Kem 2718
11/21/53	21	4	2. My Hymn (To Her)/ accompanied by Harold Mooney's Orchestra	
3/13/54	23	4	3. Watermelon In December .... accompanied by Tony Iavello's Orchestra	Mercury 70241
			BERNIE WAYNE Pianist-singer best known as composer of the famous Miss America theme "There She Is".	
11/28/53	29	1	1. Zsa-Zsa	Coral 61085
			BOBBY WAYNE	
3/24/51	26	1	1. Let Me In.. accompanied by Richard Hayman & His Orchestra	London 973
8/18/51	23	2	2. Belle, Belle, My Liberty Belle .... accompanied by George Bassman's Orchestra	Mercury 5690
12/29/51+	17	6	3. Mother At Your Feet Is Kneeling/ with the Choir of the Shrine Church of St. Bernadette	
2/23/52	6	13	4. Wheel Of Fortune	London 968
3/15/52	29	1	5. If I Had The Heart Of A Clown..................... above two accompanied by Joe Reisman's Orchestra	Mercury 5779

DATE CHARTED	PEAK POS	WKS CHRT'D	ARTIST — Record Title	Label & Number
3/14/53	30	1	6. Gone	Mercury 70074
7/18/53	18	1	7. Love Me, Love Me .... accompanied by Jimmy Carroll's Orchestra	Mercury 70148
10/03/53	21	2	8. Oh Mis'rable Love .... accompanied by Richard Hayman & His Orchestra	Mercury 70211

FRANCES WAYNE
Sang in the 40s with Charlie Barnet ("That Old Black Magic") & Woody Herman ("The Music Stopped"); married top jazz arranger Neal Hefti.

JERRY WAYNE
Vocalist on Ken Griffin's 1948 million-seller "You Can't Be True, Dear", he later starred in the London production of "Guys and Dolls".

DATE CHARTED	PEAK POS	WKS CHRT'D	ARTIST — Record Title	Label & Number
9/04/48	14	6	1. You Call Everybody Darling .... with organ accompaniment	Columbia 38286
1/29/49	15	5	2. A Little Bird Told Me............................... JERRY WAYNE WITH JANETTE DAVIS	Columbia 38386
8/27/49	6	7	3. Room Full Of Roses................................. accompanied by Hugo Winterhalter & His Orchestra	Columbia 38525

VINCE WAYNE

DATE CHARTED	PEAK POS	WKS CHRT'D	ARTIST — Record Title	Label & Number
4/18/53	29	1	1. Blue Piano...	Triple A 2506

WEAVERS
The historic group which made folk music a popular phenomenon had its roots in the Almanac Singers, which during the early 40s included Pete Seeger, Lee Hays, & the legendary Woody Guthrie. Pete & Lee went on to form the Weavers with female lead Ronnie Gilbert & Fred Hellerman. Political blacklisting cut short the group's recording career, but the group's 1955 Carnegie Hall concert helped trigger a new folk boom, and such Seeger-Hays songs as "If I Had a Hammer" kept it alive. The 1981 documentary "Wasn't That a Time?" chronicled the Weavers just before Lee Hays' death (8/26/81 at age 68). Pete remains a tireless performer and activist, and Ronnie has performed in the 80s with folk singer/songwriter Holly Near.

DATE CHARTED	PEAK POS	WKS CHRT'D	ARTIST — Record Title	Label & Number
7/01/50	2(1)	17	● 1. Tzena, Tzena, Tzena/ adaptation of an Israeli song; the Weavers also issued a Hebrew version of the song on Decca 27053	
7/08/50	1(13)	25	2. **Goodnight, Irene** .... sold over two million copies	Decca 27077
12/23/50+	11	13	3. The Roving Kind...................................... accompanied by Leroy Holmes' Orchestra based on the English folk song "The Pirate Ship" flip side: "Wreck of the John B", later adapted by the Beach Boys as "Sloop John B"	Decca 27332
1/13/51	4	14	4. So Long (It's Been Good To Know Ya).......... one of Woody Guthrie's most famous songs, written about the Oklahoma "Dust Bowl" experience 1-2 & 4 with Gordon Jenkins' Orchestra	Decca 27376
3/30/51	2(8)	23	● 5. On Top Of Old Smoky .... with the Terry Gilkyson chorus & Vic Schoen's Orchestra adaptation of a traditional Southern Highlands folk song	Decca 27515
8/18/51	19	6	6. Kisses Sweeter Than Wine/	
8/25/51	27	2	7. When The Saints Go Marching In.............. above two accompanied by Leo Diamond & His Orchestra	Decca 27670
2/16/52	14	11	8. Wimoweh .... adapted from the South African Zulu song "Mbube"; in 1961 The Tokens took a revised version to #1 as "The Lion Sleeps Tonight"	Decca 27928
4/26/52	19	1	9. Around The Corner (Beneath the Berry Tree).	Decca 28054
9/06/52	30	1	10. Midnight Special...................................... above three accompanied by Gordon Jenkins & His Orchestra	Decca 28272
1/23/54	27	2	11. Sylvie .... accompanied by Larry Clinton & His Orchestra 2, 10 & 11 written by Huddie Ledbetter (Leadbelly)	Decca 28919

CHICK WEBB & HIS ORCHESTRA

One of the 1930s' hottest jazz bands, led by hunchbacked drummer William "Chick" Webb. The great Ella Fitzgerald was the band's focal point; alto saxist/arranger Edgar Sampson & trumpet star Taft Jordan were key members. Chick died on 6/16/39 (30), after which Ella fronted band until 1942.

DATE CHARTED	PEAK POS	WKS CHRT'D	ARTIST — Record Title	Label & Number
6/02/34	20	1	1. I Can't Dance (I Got Ants In My Pants).......... vocal: Taft Jordan	Columbia 2920
6/30/34	10	7	2. Stompin' At The Savoy ....[I] Chick's most famous original	Columbia 2926
8/24/35	20	1	3. Don't Be That Way...............................[I] Benny Goodman classic composed by Sampson	Decca 483
7/25/36	18	1	4. Sing Me A Swing Song (And Let Me Dance)	Decca 830
8/01/36	18	2	5. Stompin' At The Savoy ....[I-R] reissue of 1934 hit	Vocalion 3246
12/19/36	20	1	6. (If You Can't Sing It) You'll Have To Swing It . Ella Fitzgerald: vocals on 4 & 6	Decca 1032
6/26/37	17	1	7. Rusty Hinge... Louis Jordan, vocal	Decca 1273
8/28/37	19	1	8. That Naughty Waltz ....[I]	Decca 1356
2/19/38	19	1	9. Rock It For Me	Decca 1586
6/11/38	18	2	10. I Got A Guy	Decca 1681
6/18/38	1(10)	19	● 11. **A-Tisket, A-Tasket**............................ Ella's breakthrough record, the 1930s' biggest seller record selected for the NARAS Hall of Fame Louis Jordan (alto sax) on above six	Decca 1840
11/12/38	3	6	12. I Found My Yellow Basket	Decca 2148
11/12/38	13	4	13. Wacky Dust..	Decca 2021
11/12/38	14	1	14. MacPherson Is Rehearsin' To Swing	Decca 2080
11/26/38+	8	6	15. F.D.R. Jones .... from the Broadway musical "Sing Out the News"	Decca 2105
3/18/39	8	4	16. Undecided	Decca 2323
3/25/39	19	1	17. T'ain't What You Do (It's The Way That 'Cha Do It)...	Decca 2310
5/06/39	14	1	18. Chew, Chew, Chew (Your Bubble Gum).......... Ella Fitzgerald: all vocals from 9-18	Decca 2389

CLIFTON WEBB

Born Webb Hollenbeck, best known as a character actor in some 20 movies; started as a singer/dancer in many Broadway musicals; died in 1966 (74).

DATE CHARTED	PEAK POS	WKS CHRT'D	ARTIST — Record Title	Label & Number
10/28/33	5	12	1. Easter Parade .... LEO REISMAN'S ORCHESTRA, vocal by Clifton Webb from the Broadway musical "As Thousands Cheer"	Victor 24418

WEBER & FIELDS

Joe Weber & Lew Fields (born Moses Schanfield), famous vaudeville comedy team from the 1880s through World War I, which also starred in several Broadway productions. They originated the deathless "That was no lady, that was my wife" joke. Fields, the father of all-time great popular lyricist Dorothy Fields, died on 7/20/41 (75); Weber on 5/10/42 (74).

DATE CHARTED	PEAK POS	WKS CHRT'D	ARTIST — Record Title	Label & Number
8/24/12	10	1	1. Hypnotic Scene - Mike And Meyer..........[T-C]	Columbia 1159
12/18/15	9	1	2. Restaurant Scene ....[T-C]	Columbia 1855
1/13/17	4	3	3. The Baseball Game ....[T-C]	Columbia 2092

MAREK WEBER & HIS ORCHESTRA

Austrian-born leader of large orchestra

DATE CHARTED	PEAK POS	WKS CHRT'D	ARTIST — Record Title	Label & Number
2/22/41	25	1	1. Blue Danube Waltz ....[I]	Victor 25199

BEN WEBSTER

Great tenor saxophonist featured with Duke Ellington (1935-36, 40-43), Cab Calloway, Fletcher Henderson (1937-38), & Teddy Wilson; died on 9/20/73 (64).

ANSON WEEKS & HIS ORCHESTRA

West Coast hotel dance band leader; died on 2/7/69 (72).

DATE CHARTED	PEAK POS	WKS CHRT'D	ARTIST — Record Title	Label & Number
6/10/33	15	2	1. It Was A Night In June .... vocal: Harriet Lee	Brunswick 6569

DATE CHARTED	PEAK POS	WKS CHRT'D	ARTIST — Record Title	Label & Number
9/01/34	**7**	4	2. The Breeze/ vocal: Kay St. Germaine	
9/08/34	**20**	1	3. And I Still Do... vocal: Pete Fylling	Brunswick 6946
3/20/37	**7**	4	4. How Could You?....................................... vocal: Maggie Dee	Decca 1134

TED WEEMS & HIS ORCHESTRA
Born Wilfred Theodore Weymes, leader of popular Chicago-based dance band whose blockbuster 1947 hit "Heartaches" was a 14-year-old reissue. Perry Como got his first major exposure with the band in the late 30s. Ted died on 2/7/69 (72).

DATE CHARTED	PEAK POS	WKS CHRT'D	ARTIST — Record Title	Label & Number
7/29/22	**11**	1	1. Every Day .... [I]	Columbia 3590
2/16/24	**1(5)**	14	● 2. **Somebody Stole My Gal/** [I]	
2/23/24	**10**	1	3. Covered Wagon Days.......................... [I] from the Broadway musical "The Newcomers"	Victor 19212
4/19/24	**4**	4	4. A Smile Will Go A Long, Long Way .... [I]	Victor 19258
3/28/25	**3**	4	5. Blue Eyed Sally .... [I]	Victor 19547
9/04/26	**6**	2	6. Love Bound .... [I]	Victor 20033
11/05/27	**11**	3	7. Barbara	Victor 20846
11/26/27	**6**	6	8. Highways Are Happy Ways/ vocal: Parker Gibbs & Dusty Rhodes	
12/03/27	**13**	3	9. It Was Only A Sun Shower .... vocals on 7 & 9: Dusty Rhodes	Victor 20910
4/07/28	**18**	1	10. Cobble-Stones	Victor 21105
10/06/28	**20**	1	11. Who Wouldn't Be Blue? .... above two vocals: Parker Gibbs-Art Jarrett-Sam Olver	Victor 21511
12/29/28+	**7**	4	12. You're The Cream In My Coffee .... from the Broadway musical "Hold Everything"	Victor 21767
3/16/29	**12**	2	13. Me And The Man In The Moon...................	Victor 21809
9/14/29	**2(4)**	15	14. Piccolo Pete.................................... [N]	Victor 22037
1/11/30	**1(1)**	7	15. **The Man From The South**........................ vocal: Art Jarrett & Parker Gibbs	Victor 22238
10/04/30	**4**	7	16. My Baby Just Cares For Me .... from the film "Whoopee"	Victor 22499
11/01/30	**18**	1	17. I Still Get A Thrill (Thinking Of You) .... Art Jarrett: vocals on 13, 16-17	Victor 22515
4/04/31	**8**	5	18. Walkin' My Baby Back Home	Victor 22637
10/31/31	**14**	3	19. I Love To Hear A Military Band	Victor 22822
10/20/34	**7**	4	20. Talkin' To Myself.................................... Red Ingle, vocal	Columbia 2957
11/24/34	**14**	3	21. I'm Growing Fonder Of You........................ vocal: Fred Waldmar	Columbia 2975
12/08/34+	**13**	5	22. Winter Wonderland .... [X] Parker Gibbs: vocals on 12, 14, 18-19, & 22	Columbia 2976
9/05/36	**10**	4	23. Knock! Knock! Who's There? .... vocal chorus	Decca 895
7/16/38	**9**	4	24. Three Shif'less Skonks .... [N]	Decca 1884
1/20/40	**15**	1	25. Goody Goodbye	Decca 2794
2/22/41	**11**	2	26. There'll Be Some Changes Made .... vocal: Mary Lee; recorded 10/4/30	Decca 3044
3/15/41	**22**	1	27. It All Comes Back To Me Now	Decca 3627
3/21/42	**23**	1	28. Deep In The Heart Of Texas....................... Perry Como: vocals on 25, 27-28	Decca 4138
3/01/47	**1(13)**	20	● 29. **Heartaches** .... whistling by Elmo Tanner; reissue of Bluebird 5131, recorded on 8/4/33; sold over 2 million copies	Victor 2175
6/14/47	**14**	1	30. Violets/	
6/28/47	**5**	6	31. Peg O' My Heart .... from Broadway's "Ziegfeld Follies of 1913"	Mercury 5052
8/02/47	**2(5)**	17	32. I Wonder Who's Kissing Her Now .... Perry Como, vocal; reissue of Decca 2919, recorded 10/5/39; revived as 1947 movie title song	Decca 25078
10/25/47	**3**	11	● 33. Mickey... [R] vocal: Bob Edwards & Elmo Tanner	Mercury 5062

DATE CHARTED	PEAK POS	WKS CHRT'D	ARTIST — Record Title	Label & Number
11/08/47	**28**	1	34. There'll Be Some Changes Made .... reissue of Decca 3044	Decca 25288
12/20/47	**20**	3	35. The Secretary Song .... vocal:Shirley Richards	Mercury 5081
9/11/48	**24**	4	36. Hindustan .... whistling chorus by Elmo Tanner	Mercury 5139

BRUCIE WEIL
5 1/2 years old in 1953.

8/22/53	**18**	3	1. God Bless Us All .... accompanied by Don Costa & His Orchestra	Barbour 451

FRANK WEIR & HIS ORCHESTRA
Soprano saxophonist-bandleader. (also see Vera Lynn)

5/01/54	**4**	19	1. The Happy Wanderer .... German song, best known for its singalong "Val-de-Ri, Val-de-Ra" chorus	London 1448

LAWRENCE WELK & HIS ORCHESTRA
Perennially popular accordionist-sweet band leader who started in 1920s. The band's "champagne music" style reached its greatest national audience through Welk's TV show, which began regionally in 1951 and continued on ABC and then in syndication through the 70s.

9/10/38	**17**	1	1. Colorado Sunset	Vocalion 4284
10/15/38	**13**	3	2. Change Partners .... vocal: Lois Best; from the film "Carefree"	Vocalion 4270
11/26/38	**8**	1	3. I Won't Tell A Soul (I Love You)/	
11/26/38	**13**	4	4. Two Sleepy People .... from the film "Thanks for the Memory"	Vocalion 4435
2/18/39	**10**	2	5. Annabelle .... [I]	Vocalion 4610
3/25/39	**7**	8	6. The Moon Is A Silver Dollar .... vocals on 1, 3-4, & 6: Walter Bloom	Vocalion 4681
5/27/39	**13**	1	7. Bubbles In The Wine .... [I] the band's theme song	Vocalion 4368
6/10/39	**18**	1	8. I'm Happy About The Whole Thing .... vocal: Lois Best & Jules Herman from the film "Naughty But Nice"	Vocalion 4680
1/11/41	**21**	1	9. Daddy's Lullaby/ vocal: Jayne Walton & Parnell Grina	
2/08/41	**22**	2	10. Maria Elena	Okeh 5939
3/29/41	**21**	1	11. Little Sleepy Head	Okeh 5976
7/04/42	**21**	1	12. Dear Home In Holland .... [I]	Decca 3940
2/05/44	**23**	1	13. Cleanin' My Rifle (And Dreamin' Of You)/	
2/12/44	**20**	1	14. I Wish That I Could Hide Inside This Letter.	Decca 4428
3/25/44	**2(1)**	20	15. Don't Sweetheart Me/ vocal: Wayne Marsh	
4/01/44	**16**	2	16. Mairzy Doats .... [N] vocals on 13 & 16: Bobby Beers	Decca 4434
4/22/44	**13**	5	17. Is My Baby Blue Tonight? .... vocals on 10-11, 14 & 17: Jayne Walton	Decca 4438
9/29/45	**13**	1	18. Shame On You .... LAWRENCE WELK & HIS ORCHESTRA with RED FOLEY	Decca 18698
1/24/53	**5**	9	19. Oh Happy Day .... vocal: Larry Hooper	Coral 60893

JOHN BARNES WELLS
Tenor concert singer, died on 8/8/35 (54).

5/27/11	**10**	1	1. The Story Of The Rose .... song later revised as "The Gang That Sang 'Heart of My Heart'"	Victor 16705
1/10/14	**7**	3	2. My Wonderful Dream Girl .... from the Broadway musical "The Tik-Tok Man of Oz"	Victor 17441
1/09/15	**9**	1	3. Same Sort Of Girl .... INEZ BARBOUR & JOHN BARNES WELLS from the Broadway musical "The Girl from Utah"	Columbia 1609
1/30/15	**3**	8	4. Chinatown, My Chinatown .... GRACE KERNS & JOHN BARNES WELLS from the Broadway musical "Up and Down Broadway"	Columbia 1624

DATE CHARTED	PEAK POS	WKS CHRT'D	ARTIST — Record Title	Label & Number
3/06/15	8	2	5. A Little Bit Of Heaven (Shure, They Call It Ireland).. *from the Broadway musical "Heart of Paddy Whack"*	Columbia 1662
4/29/16	4	3	6. Memories	Victor 17968

KITTY WELLS
Top country-music star who broke through with her 1952 classic "It Wasn't God Who Made Honky Tonk Angels"

DATE CHARTED	PEAK POS	WKS CHRT'D	ARTIST — Record Title	Label & Number
8/23/52	27	1	1. It Wasn't God Who Made Honky Tonk Angels	Decca 28232
2/14/53	22	1	2. The Things I Might Have Been......................	Decca 28525

REINALD WERRENRATH
American baritone, son of a Danish opera tenor, Reinald sang with the New York Metropolitan (1919-21), and is said to have made over 3,000 concert appearances. Long the featured baritone on Victor Light Opera Co. records, he also sang with the Orpheus Quartet; died on 9/12/53 (70).

DATE CHARTED	PEAK POS	WKS CHRT'D	ARTIST — Record Title	Label & Number
9/21/07	5	1	1. My Dear	Edison 9604
1/04/08	2(1)	5	2. As Long As The World Rolls On	Edison 9662
7/08/11	5	4	3. Two Little Love Bees................................. REINALD WERRENRATH & ELIZABETH WHEELER *from the Broadway musical "The Spring Maid"*	Victor 5836
8/26/11	5	3	4. By The Saskatchewan .... REINALD WERRENRATH & HAYDEN QUARTET *from the Broadway musical "The Pink Lady"*	Victor 5839
9/23/11	7	2	5. Dear, Delightful Women .... *from the Broadway musical "The Balkan Princess"*	Victor 16872
2/03/12	5	3	6. Two Little Love Bees................................. CHRISTIE MACDONALD & REINALD WERRENRATH new version of #5	Victor 60060
6/22/12	9	1	7. Let Us Have Peace	Victor 5861
7/26/13	3	9	8. The Angelus .... CHRISTIE MACDONALD, REINALD WERRENRATH, & VICTOR MALE CHORUS *from the Broadway musical "Sweethearts"*	Victor 70099
3/02/14	9	1	9. La Forza Del Destino - Solenne In Quest' Ora (Swear In This Hour) .... [F] REINALD WERRENRATH & LAMBERT MURPHY	Victor 70103
9/18/15	1(6)	10	10. **Hello, Frisco!** .... *from Broadway's "Ziegfeld Follies of 1915"*	Victor 17837
11/27/15	10	1	11. Teach Me To Smile................................... *from the Broadway musical "The Girl Who Smiles"* above two: "EDWARD HAMILTON & ALICE GREEN" (Reinald Werrenrath & Olive Kline)	Victor 17858
3/18/16	4	4	12. Neapolitan Love Song .... *from the Broadway musical "Princess Pat"*	Victor 17879
4/07/17	4	3	13. Pack Up Your Troubles In Your Old Kit Bag And Smile, Smile, Smile!...................... "EDWARD HAMILTON" & MIXED CHORUS *from the Broadway musical "Her Soldier Boy"*	Victor 18222
7/21/17	4	3	14. The Battle Hymn Of The Republic...............	Victor 45121
12/22/17	6	2	15. The Crucifix.. JOHN McCORMACK & REINALD WERRENRATH	Victor 64712
7/06/18	10	1	16. Lafayette (We Hear You Calling)	Victor 45151
5/31/19	8	2	17. After All	Victor 45162
9/20/19	4	5	18. Smilin' Through	Victor 45166
11/27/20	14	1	19. Gypsy Love Song .... *from the Broadway musical "The Fortune Teller"*	Victor 64897
7/30/21	4	6	20. Love Sends A Little Gift Of Roses	Victor 64964

WESSON BROTHERS
Dick & Gene Wesson, vaudeville comedy team.

DATE CHARTED	PEAK POS	WKS CHRT'D	ARTIST — Record Title	Label & Number
4/16/49	11	3	1. All Right Louie, Drop The Gun .... [N]	National 9070

DATE CHARTED	PEAK POS	WKS CHRT'D	ARTIST — Record Title	Label & Number

MAE WEST
One of the greatest stars of Hollywood's "Golden Era", Mae's sexy, suggestive style first found an audience in Broadway comedies from 1918-31 before her movie debut; she died on 11/22/80 (88).

4/01/33	**5**	5	1. I Like A Guy What Takes His Time .... from the film "She Done Him Wrong"	Brunswick 6495

PAUL WESTON & HIS ORCHESTRA
Born Paul Wetstein, he arranged for Tommy Dorsey & Bob Crosby before becoming Capitol Record's foremost conductor/arranger (later with Columbia), backing many singers (his wife Jo Stafford, Doris Day, Frankie Laine, Pied Pipers) and recording "mood music" albums. Composer of the hits "I Should Care" & "Shrimp Boats"; Paul later served as conductor for several TV shows.

10/27/45	**6**	11	1. It Might As Well Be Spring......................... Margaret Whiting, vocal; from the film "State Fair"	Capitol 214
11/02/46	**6**	13	2. Ole Buttermilk Sky/ from the film "Canyon Passage"	
12/28/46+	**21**	4	3. Just Squeeze Me (But Don't Tease Me)........	Capitol 285
4/19/47	**8**	8	4. Linda .... above three vocals: Matt Dennis	Capitol 362
9/04/48	**15**	14	5. Clair De Lune................................... [I] from the "Suite Bergamasque" by Debussy	Capitol 15153
1/15/49	**20**	5	6. Deep Purple... [I]	Capitol 15294
3/05/49	**12**	17	7. The Hot Canary.................................. [I] featuring Paul Nero (violin)	Capitol 15373
6/18/49	**10**	3	8. Bali Ha'i/ [I]	
7/16/49	**9**	11	9. Some Enchanted Evening...................... [I] above two from the Broadway musical "South Pacific"	Capitol 629
9/03/49	**23**	2	10. Reckon I'm In Love	Capitol 697
10/08/49	**16**	3	11. Lingering Down The Lane/	
11/12/49	**25**	2	12. I Know, I Know, I Know .... from the film "That Midnight Kiss" above two vocals: Jud Conlon Singers	Capitol 57725
3/04/50	**30**	1	13. Fairy Tales .... [I]	Capitol 826
6/24/50	**12**	16	14. La Vie En Rose.................................... [I]	Capitol 890
10/07/50	**2(1)**	18	15. Nevertheless (I'm In Love With You)............ featured in the film "Three Little Words"	Columbia 38982
2/17/51	**19**	4	16. Across The Wide Missouri/ adaptation of a traditional folk song	
2/24/51	**21**	5	17. So Long (It's Been Good To Know Yuh).......	Columbia 39160
7/07/51	**16**	7	18. The Morningside Of The Mountain	Columbia 39424
12/01/51	**30**	1	19. And So To Sleep Again	Columbia 39569
12/29/51+	**8**	6	20. Charmaine....................................... written to accompany the silent film "What Price Glory?" above six vocals: Norman Luboff Choir	Columbia 39616
7/11/53	**29**	1	21. Shane (The Call Of The Far-Away Hills) ..... [I] from the film "Shane"	Columbia 40014
5/22/54	**30**	1	22. I Went Out Of My Way	Columbia 40237

FRAN WESTPHAL & HIS ORCHESTRA
Pianist/bandleader

8/25/23	**15**	1	1. Bugle Call Rag .... [I]	Columbia 3872

ANNA WHEATON

6/30/17	**2(1)**	7	1. M-I-S-S-I-S-S-I-P-P-I .... from the Broadway musical "Hitchy-Koo"	Columbia 2224
8/11/17	**1(6)**	10	2. **Till The Clouds Roll By**......................... ANNA WHEATON & JAMES HARROD from the Broadway musical "Oh, Boy!"	Columbia 2261

ELIZABETH WHEELER
Soprano most famous for her duets with husband William Wheeler

11/27/09	**9**	1	1. The Last Rose Of Summer	Victor 5739
2/05/10	**4**	3	2. When I Marry You.................................... HARRY MACDONOUGH & ELIZABETH WHEELER	Victor 16433
2/12/10	**4**	5	3. Meet Me To-Night In Dreamland................. ELIZABETH WHEELER & HARRY ANTHONY	Edison 10290

DATE CHARTED	PEAK POS	WKS CHRT'D	ARTIST — Record Title	Label & Number
10/29/10	**6**	3	4. Abide With Me	Victor 16506
5/13/11	**10**	1	5. Oh, That We Two Were Maying....................	Victor 16705
			above two: ELIZABETH & WILLIAM WHEELER	
7/08/11	**5**	4	6. Two Little Love Bees..............................	Victor 5836
			REINALD WERRENRATH & ELIZABETH WHEELER from the Broadway musical "The Spring Maid"	
7/22/11	**7**	2	7. Mary	Victor 16828
			ELIZABETH WHEELER & HAYDEN QUARTET	
8/03/12	**7**	2	8. A Girl Like Me..	Victor 17095
			ELIZABETH WHEELER & LYRIC QUARTET from the Broadway musical "Winsome Widow"	
9/02/16	**2(2)**	5	9. At The End Of A Beautiful Day..................	Victor 18065
			under the pseudonym "Jane Kenyon"	

FREDERICK J. WHEELER
Pseudonym James F. Harrison

WILLIAM WHEELER - see ELIZABETH WHEELER

EDNA WHITE'S TRUMPET QUARTET
One of the first successful female musicians, leading on all-female group; Edna remained a popular performer into the 1950s.

DATE CHARTED	PEAK POS	WKS CHRT'D	ARTIST — Record Title	Label & Number
7/13/18	**7**	2	1. Just A Baby's Prayer At Twilight (For Her Daddy Over There)...........................[I]	Columbia 2538

FRANCES WHITE
Featured in Broadway cast of "Hitchy-Koo"

DATE CHARTED	PEAK POS	WKS CHRT'D	ARTIST — Record Title	Label & Number
4/20/18	**5**	2	1. I'd Like To Be A Monkey In The Zoo	Victor 45149

PAUL WHITEMAN & HIS ORCHESTRA
The most popular bandleader of the pre-swing era was born on 3/28/1890 in Denver. Paul played violin & viola in the Denver & San Francisco Symphony Orchestras before forming his band in 1919 featuring Henry Busse (trumpet) and Ferde Grofe (piano/arranger). Almost immediately after the blockbuster debut hit "Whispering", the Whiteman band became the dominant force in American popular recording, with a staggering profusion of hits. Whiteman's historic premiere of George Gershwin's classic "Rhapsody in Blue", his late-20s addition of Bix Beiderbecke and other jazz greats, and his introduction to America of Bing Crosby, solidified his stature in popular music history. Paul died on 12/29/67 (77).

DATE CHARTED	PEAK POS	WKS CHRT'D	ARTIST — Record Title	Label & Number
10/30/20	**1(11)**	20	● 1. **Whispering/**	[I]
			sold over two million copies	
11/13/20	**1(2)**	12	2. **The Japanese Sandman** .... [I]	Victor 18690
12/04/20+	**1(6)**	17	● 3. **Wang Wang Blues/**	[I]
			featuring trumpet solo by Henry Busse	
1/01/21	**5**	4	4. Anytime, Anyday, Anywhere .... [I]	Victor 18694
2/05/21	**3**	6	5. Grieving For You - Feather Your Nest .... [I]	Victor 35703
3/19/21	**5**	5	6. Caresses .... [I]	Victor 35704
4/23/21	**2(4)**	7	7. Bright Eyes .... [I]	Victor 18735
5/07/21	**1(5)**	12	8. **My Mammy/**	[I]
			from the Broadway musical "Sinbad"	
7/02/21	**5**	3	9. Humming .... [I]	Victor 18737
5/14/21	**4**	4	10. Do You Ever Think Of Me?/	[I]
6/11/21	**7**	3	11. I Never Knew .... [I]	Victor 18734
5/21/21	**2(2)**	9	12. Make Believe .... [I]	Victor 18742
7/16/21	**1(6)**	12	13. **Cherie/**	[I]
7/23/21	**2(3)**	7	14. My Man (Mon Homme) .... [I]	Victor 18758
			French song featured in the "Ziegfeld Follies of 1921"	
8/27/21	**1(5)**	14	15. **Song Of India** .... [I]	Victor 18777
			"Chanson Indoue" from the Rimsky-Korsakov 1897 opera "Sadko"	
9/17/21	**3**	5	16. Learn To Smile .... [I]	Victor 18778
			from the Broadway musical "The O'Brien Girl"	
10/15/21	**3**	6	17. Sweetheart .... [I]	Victor 18789
11/12/21	**1(5)**	14	18. **Say It With Music** .... [I]	Victor 18803
			18, 21 & 24 from the Broadway musical "Music Box Revue"	
12/31/21+	**4**	5	19. Canadian Capers .... [I]	Victor 18824

DATE CHARTED	PEAK POS	WKS CHRT'D	ARTIST — Record Title	Label & Number
2/04/22	2(1)	6	20. April Showers .... [I] from the Broadway musical "Bombo"	Victor 18825
2/25/22	11	1	21. Everybody Step .... [I]	Victor 18826
3/18/22	2(2)	7	22. When Buddha Smiles/	[I]
3/25/22	4	4	23. Gypsy Blues .... [I]	Victor 18839
4/08/22	5	5	24. They Call It Dancing/	[I]
4/22/22	7	2	25. Dear Old Southland............................. [I]	Victor 18856
6/03/22	1(2)	9	26. **Do It Again**................................... [I] from the Broadway musical "The French Doll"	Victor 18882
6/03/22	7	3	27. Old-Fashioned Girl .... [I]	Victor 18879
7/01/22	1(6)	12	28. **Stumbling/**	[I]
7/01/22	5	4	29. Georgia .... [I]	Victor 18899
7/01/22	5	3	30. Some Sunny Day .... [I]	Victor 18891
9/02/22	7	3	31. 'Neath The South Sea Moon.................... [I]	Victor 18911
9/09/22	1(6)	11	32. **Hot Lips**....................................... [I] featuring Henry Busse trumpet solo	Victor 18920
10/21/22	7	3	33. My Rambler Rose.................................. [I] 31 & 33 from Broadway's "Ziegfeld Follies of 1922"	Victor 18923
10/28/22	4	4	34. I'm Just Wild About Harry .... [I] from the Broadway musical "Shuffle Along"	Victor 18938
11/18/22	1(8)	20	● 35. **Three O'Clock In The Morning/** [I] Whiteman classic, with famous bell-tolling from the Broadway musical "Greenwich Village Follies of 1921"	
12/30/22+	8	2	36. Oriental .... [I]	Victor 18940
11/25/22	6	4	37. Coal Black Mammy .... [I]	Victor 18939
12/09/22+	1(1)	9	38. **I'll Build A Stairway To Paradise** .... [I] from "George White's Scandals of 1922"	Victor 18949
2/03/23	5	4	39. Carolina In The Morning .... [I] from "The Passing Show of 1922"	Victor 18962
2/03/23	9	2	40. Romany Love...................................... [I]	Victor 18966
3/03/23	2(2)	6	41. Journey's End/	[I]
3/31/23	12	1	42. When Hearts Are Young .... [I] from the Broadway musical "Lady in Ermine"	Victor 18985
3/17/23	2(3)	9	43. Crinoline Days .... [I] 43 & 47 from the Broadway musical "Music Box Revue of 1922"	Victor 18983
4/07/23	1(7)	13	44. **Parade Of The Wooden Soldiers** .... [I]	Victor 19007
5/19/23	3	5	45. Wonderful One/	[I]
5/26/23	5	3	46. Underneath The Mellow Moon............... [I]	Victor 19019
5/26/23	11	1	47. Lady Of The Evening .... [I]	Victor 19016
6/02/23	1(1)	8	48. **Bambalina**... [I] from the Broadway musical "Wildflower"	Victor 19035
6/16/23	4	5	49. Dearest (You're The Nearest To My Heart)/ [I]	
6/23/23	5	3	50. Way Down Yonder In New Orleans.......... [I]	Victor 19030
12/01/23+	3	8	51. Last Night On The Back Porch .... Victor 19139 vocal: American Quartet (Billy Murray, Albert Campbell, John Meyer, & Frank Croxton)	
12/15/23+	4	6	52. Chansonette .... [I] from Broadway's "Ziegfeld Follies of 1923"	Victor 19145
1/12/24	3	5	53. I Love You.. [I] from the Broadway musical "Little Jessie James"	Victor 19151
1/26/24	5	3	54. An Orange Grove In California .... [I] from the "Music Box Revue of 1923"	Victor 19169
2/16/24	1(4)	10	● 55. **Linger Awhile** .... [I]	Victor 19211
2/23/24	12	1	56. Raggedy Ann .... [I] from the Broadway musical "Stepping Stones"	Victor 19187
4/19/24	7	2	57. Someone Loves You After All .... [I] from the Broadway musical "Kid Boots"	Victor 19244
4/26/24	8	1	58. I'm Goin' South .... [I] from the Broadway musical "Bombo"	Victor 19229
5/17/24	4	5	59. Limehouse Blues .... [I] from the Broadway musical "Andre Charlot Revue of 1924"	Victor 19264

DATE CHARTED	PEAK POS	WKS CHRT'D	ARTIST — Record Title	Label & Number
6/28/24	6	3	60. Why Did I Kiss That Girl? .... Victor 19267 vocal: American Quartet	
7/05/24	1(5)	15	61. **What'll I Do?/** [I] from the "Music Box Revue of 1923"	
8/02/24	9	1	62. Lazy .... [I] Victor 19299	
8/30/24	5	3	63. There's Yes! Yes! In Your Eyes .... Victor 19309	
8/30/24	7	2	64. Spain.. [I] Victor 19330	
10/18/24	5	3	65. Driftwood/ [I]	
9/20/24	6	2	66. Mandalay .... [I] Victor 35744	
10/11/24	6	2	67. Pale Moon .... [I] Victor 19345	
10/18/24	3	8	68. Rhapsody In Blue, Parts 1 & 2 .... [I] Victor 55225 Paul Whiteman's Concert Orchestra, George Gershwin piano soloist; they introduced this classic at New York's Aeolian Hall on 2/12/24; arrangement by Ferde Grofe; selected for the NARAS Hall of Fame	
10/27/24	8	1	69. It Had To Be You .... [I] Victor 19339	
11/01/24	1(5)	12	70. **Somebody Loves Me/** [I] from the Broadway musical "George White's Scandals of 1924"	
11/22/24	7	2	71. Lonely Little Melody .... [I] Victor 19414	
12/06/24	7	2	72. Song Of Songs .... [I] Victor 19402	
12/13/24	6	3	73. Adoring You .... [I] Victor 19429 71 & 73 from Broadway's "Ziegfeld Follies of 1924"	
12/27/24	11	1	74. Where The Dreamy Wabash Flows .... [I] Victor 19428	
1/10/25	3	6	75. Rose-Marie .... [I] Victor 19461	
1/17/25	1(3)	9	76. **All Alone** .... [I] Victor 19487	
1/31/25	4	4	77. Mandy, Make Up Your Mind................... [I] Victor 19492 from the Broadway musical "Dixie to Broadway"	
2/28/25	3	7	78. Indian Love Call/ [I] 75 & 78 from the Broadway musical "Rose-Marie"	
3/14/25	8	2	79. Tell Her In The Springtime .... [I] Victor 19517 76 & 79 from the "Music Box Revue of 1924"	
4/04/25	2(2)	7	80. Oh! Lady Be Good................................. [I] Victor 19551 from the Broadway musical "Lady Be Good"	
4/11/25	5	5	81. I'll See You In My Dreams/ [I]	
4/25/25	7	3	82. When The One You Love Loves You........ [I] Victor 19553	
9/19/25	4	4	83. Honey, I'm In Love With You/ [I]	
10/24/25	5	4	84. Charleston .... [I] Victor 19671 from the Broadway musical "Running Wild"	
9/26/25	10	1	85. Pal Of My Cradle Days .... Victor 19690 vocal: Lewis James	
11/21/25	6	2	86. I Miss My Swiss (My Swiss Miss Misses Me) .... Victor 19753 vocal: John Sperzel; yodeling by Fritz Zimmerman	
12/05/25	3	6	87. Manhattan.. [I] Victor 19769 from the Broadway musical "Garrick Gaieties"	
5/01/26	5	3	88. That Certain Feeling .... [I] Victor 19920	
6/26/26	1(11)	17	89. **Valencia** .... Victor 20007 vocal chorus by Franklyn Baur; French song featured in the Broadway musical "Great Temptations"; famous for its distinctive 6/8 rhythm	
11/20/26	1(4)	12	90. **The Birth Of The Blues**............................ Victor 20138 from the Broadway musical "George White's Scandals of 1926"	
11/27/26	2(4)	10	91. Moonlight On The Ganges......................... Victor 20139 vocal: Austin Young	
12/11/26	7	2	92. When The Red, Red Robin Comes Bob, Bob, Bobbin' Along................................... Victor 20177	
12/18/26	9	1	93. Why Do Ya Roll Those Eyes? .... Victor 20197 vocals on 90, 92-93: Jack Fulton-Charles Gaylord-Austin Young	
1/01/27	1(8)	15	94. **In A Little Spanish Town** .... Victor 20266 vocal: Jack Fulton	
6/04/27	2(1)	8	95. It All Depends On You .... [I] Victor 20513	

DATE CHARTED	PEAK POS	WKS CHRT'D	ARTIST — Record Title	Label & Number
6/11/27	**6**	5	96. **Your Land And My Land/** vocal: Charles Harrison-Lewis James-Elliott Shaw-Wilfred Glenn	
6/25/27	**12**	2	97. Silver Moon .... [I] above two from the Broadway musical "My Maryland"	Victor 20505
6/11/27	**11**	2	98. Muddy Water .... Bing Crosby's first hit vocal	Victor 20508
7/02/27	**5**	6	99. So Blue	Victor 20570
7/30/27	**3**	8	100. Side By Side..	Victor 20627
9/03/27	**7**	5	101. Rhapsody In Blue, Parts 1 & 2 .... [I] new electrically-recorded version of 1924 classic, again with George Gershwin as piano soloist; directed by Nat Shilkret	Victor 35822
9/10/27	**2(4)**	12	102. When Day Is Done .... [I] featuring Henry Busse trumpet solo; adaptation of a Viennese popular song ("Madonna") above two: PAUL WHITEMAN'S CONCERT ORCHESTRA	Victor 35828
9/17/27	**3**	8	103. Broken Hearted	Victor 20757
9/24/27	**6**	4	104. I'm Coming, Virginia/ vocals on 100 & 104: Rhythm Boys (Bing Crosby-Al Rinker-Harry Barris)	
9/24/27	**15**	2	105. Just Once Again..................................... vocals on 99 & 105: Austin Young	Victor 20751
10/15/27	**1(1)**	16	106. **My Blue Heaven**................................... vocal: Jack Fulton-Charles Gaylord-Austin Young-Bing Crosby-Al Rinker Red Nichols (trumpet) on 100, 103-106	Victor 20828
11/12/27	**7**	5	107. The Calinda (Boo-Joom, Boo-Joom, Boo!) ...... vocal: Bing Crosby-Jack Fulton-Charles Gaylord-Austin Young from the Broadway musical "A La Carte"	Victor 20882
11/19/27	**3**	8	108. Just A Memory....................................... [I]	Victor 20881
11/26/27	**14**	2	109. Shaking The Blues Away........................ [I] from Broadway's "Ziegfeld Follies of 1927"	Victor 20885
12/24/27	**4**	7	110. A Shady Tree/ vocal: Mildred Hunt	
12/24/27+	**6**	5	111. Dancing Tambourine .... [I]	Victor 20972
2/04/28	**1(4)**	13	112. **Among My Souvenirs/** vocals on 103 & 112: Jack Fulton-Charles Gaylord-Austin Young	
3/24/28	**17**	1	113. Washboard Blues................................... Hoagy Carmichael, vocal & piano	Victor 35877
2/25/28	**4**	8	114. Changes .... vocal: Crosby-Rinker-Barris-Fulton-Gaylord-Young; featuring one of Bix Beiderbecke's most famous cornet solos with Whiteman Tommy Dorsey (trombone) on 106-109, 112-114	Victor 21103
3/10/28	**1(2)**	12	115. **Together/** vocal: Jack Fulton	
3/17/28	**11**	2	116. My Heart Stood Still .... vocal: Rinker-Fulton-Gaylord-Young from the Broadway musical "A Connecticut Yankee"	Victor 35883
3/31/28	**1(3)**	12	117. **Ramona**.. vocal: Austin Young written to promote the silent film "Ramona"	Victor 21214
3/31/28	**1(1)**	11	118. **Ol' Man River/**	
4/21/28	**7**	5	119. Make Believe .... Bing Crosby: above two vocals both from the Broadway musical "Show Boat"	Victor 21218
5/12/28	**6**	4	120. Sunshine...	Victor 21240
5/26/28	**6**	5	121. Mississippi Mud/ vocal: Irene Taylor-Bing Crosby-Al Rinker-Harry Barris-Jack Fulton-Charles Gaylord-Austin Young	
6/09/28	**14**	2	122. From Monday On .... vocals on 120 & 122: Crosby-Rinker-Fulton-Gaylord-Young	Victor 21274
6/02/28	**7**	4	123. Ol' Man River .... Paul Robeson, vocal on different version of "Show Boat" classic; with chorus including Olive Kline, Elsie Baker, Helen Clark, Lambert Murphy, Charles Harrison, Lewis James, Elliott Shaw, Frank Croxton, & Wilfred Glenn	Victor 35912

DATE CHARTED	PEAK POS	WKS CHRT'D	ARTIST — Record Title	Label & Number
6/23/28	7	5	124. Chloe (Song Of The Swamp) .... vocal: Austin Young	Victor 35921
6/23/28	17	1	125. Parade Of The Wooden Soldiers................ [I] new version of 1923 hit jimmy Dorsey (alto sax/clarinet) on many Whiteman records from 103-125	Victor 21304
6/30/28	1(6)	16	126. **My Angel** .... vocal: Jack Fulton-Charles Gaylord-Al Rinker theme from the silent film "Street Angel"	Victor 21388
6/30/28	11	4	127. Little Log Cabin Of Dreams........................	Victor 21325
7/21/28	4	6	128. C-O-N-S-T-A-N-T-I-N-O-P-L-E/ vocal: Rinker-Barris-Fulton-Gaylord-Young	
8/04/28	4	6	129. Get Out And Under The Moon	Columbia 1402
7/28/28	7	4	130. Last Night I Dreamed You Kissed Me/	
8/25/28	15	2	131. Evening Star	Columbia 1401
8/11/28	9	5	132. You Took Adavantage Of Me .... from the Broadway musical "Present Arms"	Victor 21398
8/25/28	4	6	133. Chiquita .... vocals on 127, 130, & 133: Jack Fulton	Columbia 1448
8/25/28	19	1	134. Sugar .... [I]	Victor 21464
9/08/28	12	2	135. Louisiana	Victor 21438
9/08/28	15	1	136. The Man I Love .... Vaughn DeLeath, vocal from the Broadway musical "Lady Be Good"	Columbia 50058
9/15/28	19	1	137. It Was The Dawn Of Love .... vocal: Crosby-Rinker-Gaylord-Young	Victor 21453
9/22/28	6	6	138. I'm On The Crest Of A Wave .... from the Broadway musical "George White's Scandals of 1928"	Columbia 1465
9/29/28	15	2	139. Just Like A Melody Out Of The Sky	Columbia 1441
12/22/28	6	3	140. Silent Night, Holy Night .... [X] Bing Crosby, vocal; Bing's 1934 solo recording of this song became an all-time Christmas standard	Columbia 50098
12/22/28	16	2	141. Out Of Town Gal.. vocal: Crosby-Rinker-Barris	Columbia 1505
1/12/29	10	5	142. Concerto In F, Parts 1 & 2 .... [I] Paul Whiteman's Concert Orchestra Roy Bargy, featured piano soloist on the George Gershwin classic	Columbia 50139
2/16/29	5	7	143. Let's Do It (Let's Fall In Love) .... from the Broadway musical "Paris" vocals on 139 & 143: Fulton, Gaylord & Young	Columbia 1701
2/16/29	8	5	144. Makin' Whoopee .... from the Broadway musical "Whoopee" vocals on 132, 135, 138 & 144: Bing Crosby, Jack Fulton, Charles Gaylord & Austin Young	Columbia 1683
3/30/29	5	6	145. Button Up Your Overcoat/ Vaugn DeLeath, vocal	
4/06/29	4	8	146. My Lucky Star .... vocal: Norman Clark above two from the Broadway musical "Follow Through"	Columbia 1736
4/13/29	3	8	147. Lover, Come Back To Me.......................... from the Broadway musical "The New Moon"	Columbia 1731
6/22/29	6	5	148. Louise/ from the film "Innocents of Paris"	
7/06/29	12	3	149. Blue Hawaii .... vocal: Jack Fulton & Charles Gaylord	Columbia 1771
9/07/29	9	4	150. Little Pal.. from the film "Say It With Songs"	Columbia 1877
9/14/29	10	6	151. When My Dreams Come True .... from the film version of "The Cocoanuts"	Columbia 1822
9/28/29	16	2	152. Your Mother And Mine............................ from the film "Show of Shows"	Columbia 1844
10/19/29	5	4	153. Love Me/ vocals on 147, 151 & 153: Jack Fulton	
11/02/29	12	3	154. Waiting At The End Of The Road .... Columbia 1974 from the film "Hallelujah" Bix Beiderbecke (cornet) on many records from 112-154	Columbia 1974

DATE CHARTED	PEAK POS	WKS CHRT'D	ARTIST — Record Title	Label & Number
11/16/29	**6**	11	155. (I'm A Dreamer) Aren't We All?/ vocal: Crosby-Fulton-Rinker-Barris	
11/16/29	**7**	7	156. If I Had A Talking Picture Of You............. above two from the film "Sunny Side Up" Bing Crosby: vocals on 148, 150, 154 & 156	Columbia 2010
12/09/29	**13**	2	157. China Boy .... [I]	Columbia 1945
12/14/29	**1(2)**	9	158. **Great Day/**	
12/21/29+	**6**	7	159. Without A Song.............................. above two from the Broadway musical "Great Day!"	Columbia 2098
1/11/30	**10**	3	160. A Bundle Of Old Love Letters................... from the film "Lord Byron of Broadway"	Columbia 2047
2/01/30	**2(2)**	8	161. Nobody's Sweetheart/ [I]	
2/22/30	**14**	2	162. After You've Gone	Columbia 2098
4/19/30	**2(1)**	9	163. It Happened In Monterey/	
4/26/30	**19**	1	164. I Like To Do Things For You.................. above two from the Whiteman film "King of Jazz" vocals on 152 & 164: Bing Crosby, Al Rinker & Harry Barris	Columbia 2170
5/03/30	**3**	8	165. You Brought A New Kind Of Love To Me/	
6/07/30	**16**	2	166. Living In The Sunlight, Loving In The Moonlight..................................... above two from the film "The Big Pond" Bing Crosby: vocals on 158-160, 162, 165-66	Columbia 2171
7/12/30	**2(1)**	8	167. Old New England Moon	Columbia 2224
9/27/30	**10**	4	168. The New Tiger Rag............................. [I]	Columbia 2277
10/11/30	**1(6)**	15	169. **Body And Soul** .... from the Broadway musical "Three's a Crowd" voted the #3 all-time song in Billboard disc jockey poll vocals on 163, 167 & 169: Jack Fulton	Columbia 2297
8/01/31	**16**	3	170. Choo Choo.................................. [I]	Columbia 2491
11/07/31	**4**	5	171. A Faded Summer Love...........................	Victor 22827
11/14/31	**6**	10	172. When It's Sleepy Time Down South .... Mildred Bailey & Romancers, vocal	Victor 22828
11/21/31	**13**	2	173. Cuban Love Song .... movie title song vocals on 171 & 173: Jack Fulton & Romancers	Victor 22834
1/09/32	**1(3)**	10	174. **All Of Me/** Mildred Bailey, vocal	
1/23/32	**12**	4	175. By The Sycamore Tree..........................	Victor 22879
6/04/32	**10**	5	176. The Voice In The Old Village Choir.............	Victor 22998
6/11/32	**15**	3	177. Chinese Lullaby .... [I] recorded 1/10/29, with Bix Beiderbecke	Columbia 2656
7/02/32	**13**	3	178. Grand Canyon Suite (On The Trail, Part 1)..... vocal chorus by Fulton on the classic by longtime Whiteman arranger Ferde Grofe	Victor 36053
8/27/32	**3**	5	179. Three On A Match................................	Victor 24089
9/03/32	**3**	6	180. We Just Couldn't Say Goodbye/	
9/10/32	**14**	3	181. I'll Never Be The Same........................... above two vocals by Mildred Bailey	Victor 24088
10/15/32	**2(1)**	6	182. Let's Put Out The Lights (And Go To Sleep) ... from the Broadway musical "George White's Music Hall Varieties"	Victor 24140
10/22/32	**5**	5	183. How Deep Is The Ocean? (How-High-Is-The- Sky?)/ vocals on 175-76 & 183: Jack Fulton	
11/05/32	**19**	1	184. I'll Follow You................................. vocals on 179, 182 & 184: Red McKenzie	Victor 24141
12/17/32+	**2(2)**	7	185. Willow Weep For Me .... vocal: Irene Taylor	Victor 24187
1/28/33	**11**	4	186. You're An Old Smoothie/	
2/04/33	**17**	2	187. Eadie Was A Lady................................ vocal: Ramona Davies & Rhythm Boys (not the Crosby group) above three from the Broadway musical "Take A Chance"	Victor 24202
1/28/33	**16**	2	188. Rise 'N Shine/	Victor 24197
2/25/33	**4**	8	189. Farewell To Arms	Victor 24236

DATE CHARTED	PEAK POS	WKS CHRT'D	ARTIST — Record Title	Label & Number
4/22/33	3	7	190. Lover... from the film "Love Me Tonight"	Victor 24283
8/19/33	11	3	191. My Moonlight Madonna .... above three vocals: Jack Fulton	Victor 24364
9/16/33+	13	3	192. Are You Makin' Any Money?...................... from the film "Moonlight and Pretzels" vocals on 186, 188 & 192: Ramona Davies	Victor 24365
10/07/33	9	8	193. It's Only A Paper Moon .... originally in the Broadway nonmusical play "The Great Magoo" under the title "If You Believe in Me"; featured in the film "Take a Chance"	Victor 24400
12/09/33+	1(6)	15	194. **Smoke Gets In Your Eyes** .... from the Broadway musical "Roberta" Bunny Berigan (trumpet) on above two	Victor 24455
2/17/34	1(1)	12	195. **Wagon Wheels**/	
2/24/34	16	3	196. If I Love Again .... from the Broadway musical "Hold Your Horses" above three vocals: Bob Lawrence	Victor 24517
5/12/34	15	3	197. The House Is Haunted............................... 195 & 197 from the Broadway musical "Ziegfeld Follies of 1934"	Victor 24597
6/02/34	15	3	198. Christmas Night In Harlem .... Jack Teagarden, vocal from the Broadway musical "Blackbirds of 1934"	Victor 24615
8/11/34	4	10	199. Love In Bloom...................................... vocal: Jack Fulton; from the film "She Loves Me Not"	Victor 24672
9/15/34	4	6	200. I Saw Stars .... vocal: Peggy Healy	Victor 24705
11/24/34	2(3)	10	201. You're The Top/ vocal: Peggy Hely & John Hauser	
12/15/34+	3	11	202. I Get A Kick Out Of You..........................	Victor 24769
12/22/34	5	8	203. Anything Goes/	
12/29/34+	8	6	204. All Through The Night............................ above four from the Broadway musical "Anything Goes" vocal: Bob Lawrence	Victor 24770
3/02/35	8	8	205. If The Moon Turns Green .... vocals on 202-03 & 205: Ramona Davies	Victor 24860
12/07/35	11	5	206. Thanks A Million .... movie title song	Victor 25151
1/04/36	20	1	207. I'm The Echo... vocal: King's Men	Victor 25198
2/29/36	9	8	208. Wah-Hoo!/	
3/14/36	7	8	209. What's The Name Of That Song? .... vocals on 206 & 209: John Hauser	Victor 25252
3/14/36	19	1	210. Saddle Your Blues To A Wild Mustang.......... vocal: Bob Lawrence & King's Men	Victor 25251
4/18/36	19	1	211. I'se A-Muggin' .... Paul Whiteman's "Three T's": Jack Teagarden (trombone), Charlie Teagarden (trumpet), & Frankie Trumbauer (saxophone)	Victor 25273
6/20/36	18	1	212. My Romance .... vocal by Donald Novis & Gloria Grafton from the Broadway musical "Jumbo"	Victor 25269
7/11/36	19	1	213. There's A Small Hotel .... from the Broadway musical "On Your Toes" vocals on 208 & 213: Durelle Alexander Frankie Trumbauer (C-melody saxophone) on vast majority of hits from 115-213	Victor 25270
10/08/38	17	1	214. While A Cigarette Was Burning .... vocal: Joan Edwards	Decca 2083
12/10/38	12	1	215. I'm Comin', Virginia .... new version of 1927 hit Jack Teagarden (trombone) on most hits from 197-217	Decca 2145
5/13/39	11	4	216. Three Little Fishies............................. [N]	Decca 2417
8/12/39	8	7	217. Moon Love... based on the second movement of Tchaikovsky's Symphony No. 5 in E	Decca 2578

DATE CHARTED	PEAK POS	WKS CHRT'D	ARTIST — Record Title	Label & Number
10/31/42	**23**	1	218. Trav'lin' Light .... Billie Holiday (listed only as "Lady Day"), vocal	Capitol 116
11/27/43	**19**	1	219. The Old Music Master .... Johnny Mercer & Jack Teagarden, vocal	Capitol 137
9/04/54	**29**	1	220. Whispering .... "Paul Whiteman & His New Ambassador Hotel Orchestra" new version of Whiteman's 1920 classic, with vocal by Dick Ridgely	Coral 61228

DAVID WHITFIELD

8/14/54	**10**	18	● 1. Cara Mia .... with Mantovani's Orchestra	London 1486
9/11/54	**25**	1	2. Smile... music written by Charlie Chaplin for the 1936 film "Modern Times" orchestra directed by Eric Rogers	London 1494
12/11/54	**19**	4	3. Santo Natale.....................................[X]	London 1508
			accompanied by Stanley Black & His Orchestra	

MARGARET WHITING

The daughter of great popular composer Richard Whiting ("Till We Meet Again"), Margaret scored major hits in the early 40s with Freddie Slack ("That Old Black Music"), Billy Butterfield ("Moonlight in Vermont"), & Paul Weston ("It Might As Well Be Spring") before her string of solo and duet hits.

4/13/46	**11**	4	1. All Through The Day/	
5/11/46	**12**	3	2. In Love In Vain .... above two from the film "Centennial Summer" both accompanied by Carl Kress' Orchestra	Capitol 240
6/15/46	**17**	1	3. Come Rain Or Come Shine................. from the Broadway musical "St. Louis Woman" accompanied by Paul Weston's Orchestra	Capitol 247
8/31/46	**13**	1	4. Along With Me .... from the Broadway musical "Call Me Mister"	Capitol 269
10/26/46	**12**	4	5. Passe...	Capitol 294
12/07/46+	**4**	17	6. Guilty/	
12/14/46+	**7**	7	7. Oh, But I Do... from the film "The Time, the Place, and the Girl" above four accompanied by Jerry Gray's Orchestra	Capitol 324
4/19/47	**21**	1	8. Beware My Heart	Capitol 360
6/07/47	**11**	6	9. Old Devil Moon/ from the Broadway musical "Finian's Rainbow"	
8/02/47	**21**	5	10. Ask Anyone Who Knows.........................	Capitol 410
6/21/47	**25**	1	11. Little Girl Blue .... from the Broadway musical "Jumbo"	Capitol 20116
11/01/47	**5**	10	12. You Do... from the film "Mother Wore Tights"	Capitol 438
11/08/47	**21**	1	13. Lazy Countryside.................................... from the film "Fun And Fancy Free"	Capitol 461
12/06/47+	**8**	4	14. Pass That Peace Pipe/ from the film "Good News"	
1/03/48	**22**	1	15. Let's Be Sweethearts Again	Capitol 15010
1/24/48	**21**	2	16. But Beautiful/ from the film "The Road to Rio"	
2/14/48	**2(1)**	16	17. Now Is The Hour (Maori Farewell Song)....... based on the traditional New Zealand song "Hearere Ra"	Capitol 15024
3/20/48	**29**	1	18. What's Good About Goodbye? .... from the film "Casbah"	Capitol 15042
5/01/48	**23**	1	19. Please Don't Kiss Me .... from the film "The Lady from Shangha"	Capitol 15058
7/17/48	**1(5)**	23	● 20. **A Tree In The Meadow** .... British song	Capitol 15122
12/04/48+	**2(6)**	23	21. Far Away Places...................................... with Crew Chiefs	Capitol 15278
4/16/49	**5**	17	22. Forever And Ever.................................... adaptation of a Swiss popular song	Capitol 15386

DATE CHARTED	PEAK POS	WKS CHRT'D	ARTIST — Record Title	Label & Number
5/07/49	**12**	12	23. A Wonderful Guy .... Capitol 542 from the Broadway musical "South Pacific" nearly all from 9-23 accompanied by Frank DeVol's Orchestra	
5/14/49	**3**	19	24. Baby, It's Cold Outside .... Capitol 567 MARGARET WHITING & JOHNNY MERCER accompanied by Paul Weston's Orchestra from the film "Neptune's Daughter"	
9/10/49	**1(3)**	23	● 25. **Slippin' Around/**	
10/22/49	**30**	1	26. Wedding Bells Will Soon Be Ringing .... Capitol 40224 above two, 28-30: MARGARET WHITING & JIMMY WAKELY	
9/24/49	**19**	2	27. Dime A Dozen .... Capitol 709	
11/05/49	**8**	10	28. I'll Never Slip Around Again .... Capitol 40246	
2/11/50	**12**	7	29. Broken Down Merry-Go-Round/	
2/25/50	**17**	7	30. The Gods Were Angry With Me................. Capitol 800	
3/04/50	**21**	3	31. I Said My Pajamas (And Put On My Pray'rs) ... Capitol 841	
4/15/50	**13**	6	32. Let's Go To Church (Next Sunday Morning).... Capitol 960	
5/06/50	**17**	8	33. My Foolish Heart .... Capitol 934 nearly all above solo hits accompanied by Frank DeVol's Orchestra	
6/17/50	**16**	4	34. Blind Date .... Capitol 1042 MARGARET WHITING & BOB HOPE accompanied by Billy May's Orchestra	
10/28/50	**6**	15	35. A Bushel And A Peck .... Capitol 1234 from the Broadway musical "Guys and Dolls"	
5/12/51	**20**	2	36. When You And I Were Young, Maggie, Blues.. Capitol 1500 32, 35-36: MARGARET WHITING & JIMMY WAKELY	
7/21/51	**14**	5	37. Good Morning, Mr. Echo............................ Capitol 1702	
3/22/52	**29**	1	38. I'll Walk Alone .... Capitol 2000 featured in the film "With a Song In My Heart"	
11/05/52	**22**	2	39. Outside Of Heaven .... Capitol 2217	
2/14/53	**29**	1	40. Why Don't You Believe Me? .... Capitol 2292	
2/13/54	**29**	1	41. Moonlight In Vermont................................. Capitol 2681 new version of her 1945 classic with Billy Butterfield above four accompanied by Lou Busch's Orchestra	

SLIM WHITMAN
More than a quarter-century after his biggest chart hits, the country balladeer and yodeller reached his greatest fame with best-selling compilation albums sold solely over TV.

7/26/52	**9**	14	● 1. Indian Love Call .... Imperial 8156	
5/01/54	**22**	4	2. Rose-Marie .... Imperial 8236 both from the Broadway musical "Rose-Marie"	

HENRY WHITTIER
Early country-western singer

5/31/24	**12**	1	1. The Wreck Of The Southern Old 97 .... Okeh 40015	

RUDY WIEDOEFT
The first important saxophone virtuoso, featured on some 1920s Henry Burr hits; Rudy Vallee named himself after him. Died on 2/18/40 (47).

EDDIE WILCOX & HIS ORCHESTRA
Acclaimed pianist/arranger for Jimmie Lunceford band throughout its career (1929-47), then bandleader; died on 9/29/68 (about 59).

2/09/52	**13**	6	1. Wheel Of Fortune.................................... Derby 787 vocal by Sunny Gale	

LEE WILEY
1930s band singer with Johnny Green, Leo Reisman ("Time On My Hands"), & Victor Young.

BERT WILLIAMS
Born on 11/12/1874 in Nassau, West Indies, Bert Williams was the first black entertainer to become a headlined Broadway star. He and partner George Walker debuted on Broadway in 1896, and by 1910 Williams was one of the country's most popular comedians and singers. Co-writer of many of his hits, including the classic "Nobody"; Bert died on 3/4/22 (47).

1/04/02	**1(5)**	10	1. **Good Morning, Carrie** .... [C] Victor 997	

DATE CHARTED	PEAK POS	WKS CHRT'D	ARTIST — Record Title	Label & Number
1/04/02	**3**	3	2. I Don't Like That Face You Wear............ [C] above two: BERT WILLIAMS & GEORGE WALKER	Victor 987
1/18/02	**2(4)**	5	3. When It's All Going Out And Nothing Coming In .... [C]	Victor 994
2/22/02	**4**	2	4. The Fortune Telling Man........................ [C]	Victor 1083
7/14/06	**1(9)**	14	5. **Nobody**... selected for the NARAS Hall of Fame; Bert's trademark song	Columbia 3423
8/25/06	**7**	1	6. Pretty Desdamone .... [C] WILLIAMS & WALKER	Columbia 3410
9/15/06	**3**	4	7. Here It Comes Again .... [C]	Columbia 3454
12/15/06	**1(2)**	5	8. **Let It Alone**.. [C]	Columbia 3504
1/19/07	**1(2)**	7	9. **He's A Cousin Of Mine** .... [C] from the Broadway musical "Marrying Mary"	Columbia 3536
3/30/07	**6**	1	10. The Mississippi Stoker........................... [C]	Columbia 3557
4/06/07	**3**	3	11. I've Such A Funny Feeling When I Look At You..	Columbia 3574
5/07/10	**4**	4	12. The Mississippi Stoker........................... [C] new version of 1907 hit flip side of "That Mesmerizing Mendelssohn Tune" (POS 2) by Arthur Collins & Byron Harlan	Columbia 801
11/19/10	**2(2)**	6	13. Constantly/ [C]	
12/17/10	**8**	1	14. I'll Lend You Everything I've Got Except My Wife... [C]	Columbia 915
12/24/10	**1(6)**	10	15. **Play That Barber-Shop Chord**	Columbia 929
6/21/13	**4**	4	16. Nobody .... new version of 1906 classic	Columbia 1289
7/19/13	**2(2)**	7	17. Woodman, Woodman, Spare That Tree .... from Broadway's "Ziegfeld Follies of 1911"	Columbia 1321
5/02/14	**3**	6	18. The Darktown Poker Club .... [C]	Columbia 1504
10/30/15+	**4**	5	19. I'm Neutral .... [C]	Columbia 1817
12/25/15+	**3**	5	20. Never Mo'... [C]	Columbia 1853
3/11/16	**5**	2	21. Everybody	Columbia 1909
2/23/18	**5**	3	22. No Place Like Home	Columbia 2438
1/04/19	**1(2)**	6	23. **O Death, Where Is Thy Sting?** .... [C]	Columbia 2652
6/28/19	**4**	5	24. Bring Back Those Wonderful Days..............	Columbia 2710
9/13/19	**1(2)**	6	25. **It's Nobody's Business But My Own/** from the "Ziegfeld's Midnight Frolics"	Columbia 2750
9/13/19	**2(2)**	7	26. Everybody Wants A Key To My Cellar .... [C] one of Bert's several Prohibition laments	
3/27/20	**2(2)**	5	27. When The Moon Shines On The Moonshine [C] from Broadway's "Ziegfeld Follies of 1919"	Columbia 2849
4/24/20	**5**	3	28. Elder Eatmore's Sermon On Generosity .... [C]	Columbia 6141
5/22/20	**6**	2	29. Sorry, I Ain't Got It .... [C]	Columbia 2877
8/07/20	**3**	6	30. Ten Little Bottles .... [C]	Columbia 2941
11/20/20	**9**	1	31. Save A Little Dram For Me .... [C]	Columbia 2979
5/28/21	**8**	2	32. Just Snap Your Fingers At Care	Columbia 3360
6/10/22+	**4**	4	33. Not Lately	Columbia 3589

BILLY WILLIAMS QUARTET
Black group featured for several years on TV's "Your Show of Shows"; Billy was previously a member of the Charioteers.

DATE CHARTED	PEAK POS	WKS CHRT'D	ARTIST — Record Title	Label & Number
4/26/47	**13**	4	1. My Adobe Hacienda.................................	RCA Victor 2150
8/18/51	**20**	6	2. Shanghai...	MGM 10998
10/13/51	**28**	2	3. Sin...	MGM 11066
3/07/53	**30**	1	4. Pour Me A Glass Of Teardrops...................	Mercury 70094
8/21/54	**21**	3	5. Sh-Boom (Life Could Be A Dream)................	Coral 61212

DATE CHARTED	PEAK POS	WKS CHRT'D	ARTIST — Record Title	Label & Number
			CLARENCE WILLIAMS' BLUE FIVE	
			Important jazz composer ("West End Blues", "Royal Garden Blues"), pianist and combo leader, also musical director of Okeh Records. Clarence frequently accompanied blues greats Bessie Smith and Ethel Waters; he died on 11/6/65 (67).	
3/22/24	**9**	1	1. 'Tain't Nobody's Bus'ness If I Do .... [I]	Okeh 4966
4/04/25	**10**	1	2. Everybody Loves My Baby (But My Baby Don't Love Nobody But Me)	Okeh 8181
7/25/25	**13**	1	3. Cake Ealking Babies From Home	Okeh 40321
			above two vocals: Eva Taylor (Clarence's wife) Louis Armstrong (cornet) on above two Sidney Bechet (clarinet) on 1 & 3	
12/31/27+	**13**	2	4. Baby, Won't You Please Come Home?........ [I]	Okeh 8510
			Clarence Williams' Blue Seven	
			COOTIE WILLIAMS & HIS ORCHESTRA	
			Great jazz trumpet star who became famous with Duke Ellington (1929-40), then with Benny Goodman for a year; his band included jazz greats Charlie Parker & Bud Powell. Cootie & Thelonious Monk co-wrote the classic "Round About Midnight"; died on 9/15/85 (77).	
4/29/44	**19**	1	1. Tess' Torch Song	Hit 7075
			Pearl Bailey, vocal	
8/26/44	**23**	1	2. Cherry Red Blues.....................................	Hit 7084
			Eddie (Cleanhead) Vinson, vocal record stayed on R&B chart for nearly 40 weeks Bud Powell (piano), Vinson (alto sax), & Eddie (Lockjaw) Davis (tenor sax) on both	
			EVAN WILLIAMS	
			Famous American tenor, born Ffrangeon Davies to Welsh parents, gave over 1,000 concert recitals in U.S. and many more in England; died on 5/24/18 (50).	
3/27/09	**9**	1	1. The Song That Reached My Heart	Victor 5643
			under pseudonym "Harry Evans"	
11/05/10	**10**	1	2. Because	Victor 64133
3/30/12	**10**	1	3. Loch Lomond...	Victor 64210
			HANK WILLIAMS & HIS DRIFTING COWBOYS	
			Country music's greatest legend, he created a vast new audience for postwar country through his urgent vocals and his many great compositions ("Cold, Cold Heart", "Your Cheatin' Heart", "Jambalaya"). Hank died on 1/1/53 at 29; his son Hank Williams, Jr. has been a major country star in his own right.	
5/14/49	**24**	1	● 1. Lovesick Blues...............................	MGM 10352
			the #1 country hit of 1949	
4/14/51	**27**	1	2. Cold, Cold Heart	MGM 10904
			44 weeks on country chart; #1 smash for Tony Bennett	
9/15/51	**29**	1	● 3. Hey, Good Lookin'	MGM 11000
9/06/52	**20**	6	● 4. Jambalaya (On The Bayou).........................	MGM 11283
			14 weeks at #1 on country chart	
2/21/53	**23**	1	● 5. Kaw-Liga/	
			13 weeks at #1 on country chart	
3/28/53	**25**	2	6. Your Cheatin' Heart	MGM 11416
			HOD WILLIAMS & HIS ORCHESTRA	
8/28/37	**17**	2	1. The Big Apple .... [I]	Bluebird 7104
			MARY LOU WILLIAMS	
			Great jazz pianist/composer/arranger (born Mary Elfreida Winn) with Andy Kirk from 1929-42; she also did arrangements for Duke Ellington.	
			TEX WILLIAMS & THE WESTERN CARAVAN	
			Popular country music singer/guitarist	
7/05/47	**1(6)**	17	● 1. **Smoke! Smoke! Smoke! (That Cigarette)**.....	Capitol Am. 40001
			sold over two million copies	
1/31/48	**27**	1	2. Don't Telephone, Don't Telegraph, Tell A Woman..	Capitol Am. 40081
5/08/48	**24**	1	3. Suspicion	Capitol Am. 40108
12/04/48	**27**	2	4. Life Gets Tee-Jus, Don't It?	Capitol 15271

DATE CHARTED	PEAK POS	WKS CHRT'D	ARTIST — Record Title	Label & Number
			BOB WILLS & HIS TEXAS PLAYBOYS The "King of Western Swing", great country bandleader who introduced jazz band influence to create new sound. Bob played violin and composed (classic "San Antonio Rose"). Tommy Duncan was the band's featured singer, and Leon McAuliffe (steel guitar) its star soloist. Bob died on 5/13/75 (70).	
6/03/39	15	2	1. San Antonio Rose	Vocalion 4755
11/30/40+	11	5	● 2. New San Antonio Rose.............................. new version of Bob's classic	Okeh 5694
5/17/41	27	1	3. Worried Mind .... above three vocals: Tommy Duncan	Okeh 6101
11/07/42	21	1	4. Ten Years..............................	Okeh 6692
3/27/43	19	1	5. New San Antonio Rose.......................... [R]	Okeh 5694
9/25/43	21	1	6. Home In San Antone .... vocal: Danny Alguire	Okeh 6710
9/23/44	11	2	7. We Might As Well Forget It/ vocals on 4 & 7 by Leon Huff	
10/14/44	14	3	8. You're From Texas .... vocal by Leon McAuliffe; from the film "A Tornado In the Saddle"	Okeh 6722
7/13/46	20	1	9. New Spanish Two-Step............................. vocal: Tommy Duncan; 15 weeks at #1 on country chart	Columbia 36966
			JOHNNIE LEE WILLS brother of famed western swing bandleader, Bob Wills	
2/04/50	9	11	1. Rag Mop....................................	Bullet 696
			NAT WILLS Popular vaudeville comedian who also appeared on Broadway; died on 12/9/17 (44).	
1/30/09	4	1	1. No News, Or What Killed The Dog............ [C]	Victor 5612
10/30/09	10	1	2. The Traveling Man................................ [C]	Victor 5725
			EDITH WILSON Blues and jazz singer; died on 3/30/81 (84).	
6/10/22	10	1	1. Birmingham Blues .... featuring Johnny Dunn (cornet)	Columbia 3558
			EILEEN WILSON Former band singer with Les Brown, best known as one of the featured performers on "Your Hit Parade" radio & TV shows.	
10/13/51	19	1	1. Cold, Cold Heart	Decca 27761
			GEORGE WILSON	
3/24/17	10	1	1. There's Egypt In Your Dreamy Eyes.............	Columbia 2168
9/01/17	5	2	2. When The Sun Goes Down In Dixie (And The Moon Begins To Rise) .... GEORGE WILSON & "ROBERT LEWIS" (Lewis James)	Columbia 2207
			MARGARET WOODROW WILSON Daughter of President Woodrow Wilson	
5/08/15	7	2	1. The Star-Spangled Banner.........................	Columbia 1685
			TEDDY WILSON & HIS ORCHESTRA Great jazz pianist, member of Benny Goodman Trio & Quartet, also played with Red Norvo. Billie Holiday shot to stardom as the band's vocalist, and Teddy's band was filled with top jazz stars; he remained active through the 70s. (also see Billy Eckstine)	
8/10/35	12	4	1. What A Little Moonlight Can Do.................	Brunswick 7498
10/19/35	17	1	2. Sweet Lorraine..................................... [I]	Brunswick 7520
11/23/35	6	7	3. Twenty-Four Hours A Day .... from the film "Sweet Surrender"	Brunswick 7550
12/07/35	12	3	4. If You Were Mine .... from the film "To Beat the Band" Roy Eldridge (trumpet) on above four	Brunswick 7554
12/28/35	16	2	5. On Treasure Island .... [I] piano solo	Brunswick 7572
1/18/36	18	1	6. You Let Me Down.................................... from the film "Stars Over Broadway" Billie Holiday: all above vocals	Brunswick 7581

DATE CHARTED	PEAK POS	WKS CHRT'D	ARTIST — Record Title	Label & Number
4/25/36	12	4	7. Christopher Columbus/ [I]	
4/25/36	13	2	8. All My Life .... from the film "Laughing Irish Eyes"	Brunswick 7640
8/01/36	5	5	9. Theses Foolish Things	Brunswick 7699
8/15/36	17	2	10. It's Like Reaching For The Moon	Brunswick 7702
9/19/36	6	9	11. My Melancholy Baby .... Ella Fitzgerald: vocals on 8 & 11	Brunswick 7729
10/03/36	12	5	12. Sing, Baby, Sing .... vocal: Red Harper, with Lionel Hampton (vibraphone) movie title song	Brunswick 7736
11/14/36	3	5	13. The Way You Look Tonight .... from the film "Swing Time"	Brunswick 7762
11/14/36	4	6	14. Who Loves You?........................... Chu Berry (tenor sax) on 3 & 14	Brunswick 7768
12/19/36	5	4	15. I Can't Give You Anything But Love............ from the Broadway musical "Blackbirds of 1928"	Brunswick 7781
12/26/36	20	1	16. That's Life, I Guess/	
1/02/37	3	6	17. Pennies From Heaven........................... movie title song Billie Holiday: vocals on 9-10, 13-17	Brunswick 7789
1/16/37	7	4	18. Where The Lazy River Goes By .... vocal: Midge Williams	Brunswick 7797
2/13/37	18	2	19. Tea For Two .... [I] from the Broadway musical "No, No, Nanette" Ben Webster (tenor sax) on 1-2, 13-19	Brunswick 7816
2/27/37	8	3	20. This Year's Kisses .... from the film "On the Avenue"	Brunswick 7824
3/27/37	10	3	21. (This Is) My Last Affair .... from the Broadway musical "New Faces of 1934"	Brunswick 7840
4/03/37	8	3	22. The Mood That I'm In .... Henry (Red) Allen (trumpet) on above two	Brunswick 7844
4/24/37	1(3)	12	23. Carelessly/	
5/01/37	12	3	24. How Could You?...........................	Brunswick 7867
5/22/37	2(2)	10	25. There's A Lull In My Life	Brunswick 7884
5/22/37	11	2	26. Moanin' Low .... from the Broadway musical "The Little Show" Cootie Williams (trumpet) on above three; Harry Carney (clarinet/baritone sax) on 9-10, 23-24 & 26	Brunswick 7877
6/12/37	10	3	27. I'm Coming, Virginia .... [I]	Brunswick 7893
6/12/37	18	1	28. It's Swell Of You........................... above two vocals: Helen Ward both from the film "Wake Up and Live"	Brunswick 7884
6/26/37	7	4	29. Mean To Me...........................	Brunswick 7903
7/10/37	15	2	30. Easy Living .... Lester Young (tenor sax) on 20, 29-30	Brunswick 7911
7/24/37	16	2	31. Yours And Mine........................... from the film "Broadway Melody of 1937" Billie Holiday: vocals on 20-25, 29-31	Brunswick 7917
9/11/37	2(3)	10	32. Remember Me?/ from film "Mr. Dodds Takes the Air"	
9/11/37	16	1	33. You're My Desire........................... above two vocals: Boots Castle Benny Goodman (clarinet) on 1, 15-17, 20, 32-33; Gene Krupa (drums) on 12-14 & 33 (Cozy Cole drummer on most other records)	Brunswick 7940
10/02/37	1(2)	7	34. You Can't Stop Me From Dreaming .... [I]	Brunswick 7954
10/23/37	6	3	35. Ain't Misbehavin'........................... [I] Teddy Wilson Quartet, including Red Norvo (xylophone) song from the Broadway musical "Hot Chocolates" Harry James (trumpet) on 25, 27-28 & 35 Vido Musso (tenor sax/clarinet) on 18-19, 32-35	Brunswick 7964
12/25/37	20	1	36. Nice Work If You Can Get It........................... from the film "A Damsel in Distress"	Brunswick 8015
1/08/38	14	2	37. My Man........................... from Broadway's "Ziegfeld Follies of 1921" Billie Holiday: above two vocals Buck Clayton (trumpet) on 20, 30-31, 36-37	Brunswick 8008

DATE CHARTED	PEAK POS	WKS CHRT'D	ARTIST — Record Title	Label & Number
6/18/38	20	1	38. You Go To My Head...................................... vocal: Nan Wynn; with Bobby Hackett (cornet) Johnny Hodges (alto sax) on 6, 9-10, 23-29, 31 & 38	Brunswick 8141

DANNY WINCHELL

| 11/29/52 | 30 | 2 | 1. Carolina In The Morning .... accompanied by Leroy Holmes & His Orchestra | MGM 11335 |

KAI WINDING

Danish-born star jazz trombonist, with Benny Goodman & Stan Kenton in mid-40s; had 1963 smash hit "More". Kai died on 5/6/83 (60). (also see Billy Eckstine)

HUGO WINTERHALTER & HIS ORCHESTRA

Arranger in 40s for Count Basie, Tommy & Jimmy Dorsey, Claude Thornhill, & others, musical director for Victor, conductor/arranger for Eddie Fisher, Perry Como, Billy Eckstine, & other top singers; died on 9/17/73 (64).

DATE CHARTED	PEAK POS	WKS CHRT'D	ARTIST — Record Title	Label & Number
10/15/49	10	6	1. Jealous Heart .... vocal: Johnny Thompson	Columbia 38593
12/24/49+	9	3	2. Blue Christmas .... [X]	Columbia 38635
3/25/50	17	5	3. Music! Music! Music!............................. vocal: Five Gems	Columbia 38704
4/15/50	10	20	4. Count Every Star	RCA Vic. 78-3697
4/22/50	21	4	5. The Third Man Theme .... [I] Tony Mottola featured on guitar	Columbia 38706
5/20/50	29	1	6. My Foolish Heart .... above two both movie title themes	Columbia 38697
6/03/50	11	9	7. I Wanna Be Loved................................. vocal: Fontane Sisters	RCA Victor 3772
9/30/50	25	1	8. I Need You So .... vocal: Don Cornell	RCA Victor 3884
10/07/50	9	7	9. Mr. Touchdown, U.S.A.	RCA Victor 3913
12/16/50	20	2	10. Blue Christmas .... [X-R]	Columbia 38635
2/10/51	21	4	11. Across The Wide Missouri .... vocal: Stuart Foster	RCA Victor 4017
8/25/51	25	1	12. Belle, Belle, My Liberty Belle .... vocal: Merv Griffin	RCA Victor 4217
11/03/51	23	3	13. Beyond The Blue Horizon......................... from the film "Monte Carlo"	RCA Victor 4288
1/05/52	18	1	14. Blue December	RCA Victor 4412
1/26/52	10	9	15. A Kiss To Build A Dream On...................... vocal: Johnny Parker; from the film "The Strip"	RCA Victor 4455
3/08/52	6	17	16. Blue Tango... [I]	RCA Victor 4518
6/14/52	9	14	17. Vanessa .... [I]	RCA Victor 4691
11/01/52	19	3	18. Blue Violins/	[I]
11/22/52	30	1	19. Fandango .... [I]	RCA Victor 4997
4/04/53	24	2	20. The Magic Touch	RCA Victor 5209
9/12/53	8	5	21. The Velvet Glove .... [I] featuring Henri Rene (musette accordion)	RCA Victor 5405
3/13/54	22	4	22. Latin Lady .... [I]	RCA Victor 5655
7/03/54	9	11	23. The Little Shoemaker/	
7/10/54	22	4	24. The Magic Tango .... Eddie Fisher leads chorus on above two, which are billed "Hugo Winterhalter's Orchestra & Chorus and a Friend"	RCA Victor 5769
11/13/54	28	1	25. Land Of Dreams/ Eddie Heywood (piano) featured	[I]
12/18/54	25	5	26. Song Of The Barefoot Contessa .... movie title theme all unidentified vocals by chorus	RCA Victor 5888

CHARLES WOLCOTT & HIS ORCHESTRA

DATE CHARTED	PEAK POS	WKS CHRT'D	ARTIST — Record Title	Label & Number
8/26/44	18	3	1. Tico Tico.. Brazilian song featured in the film "Saludos Amigos"	Decca 23318

DATE CHARTED	PEAK POS	WKS CHRT'D	ARTIST — Record Title	Label & Number
			BARRY WOOD	
			Baritone who sang briefly with Abe Lyman, later a TV producer; died on 7/19/70 (61).	
5/17/41	**13**	1	1. The Things I Love	Victor 27369
8/16/41	**21**	1	2. Any Bonds Today?...................................	Victor 27478
1/24/42	**23**	1	3. One For All - All For One...........................	Victor 27708
			above two with the Lynn Murray Singers and Leonard Joy's Orchestra	
7/04/42	**16**	2	4. Put-Put-Put (Put Your Arms Around Me) ... [N]	Bluebird 11523
			with The Wood-Nymphs	
			DEL WOOD	
			Female country pianist, also singer, longtime "Grand Ole Opry" performer	
9/01/51	**4**	25	● 1. Down Yonder .... [I]	Tennessee 775
5/30/53	**24**	1	2. Elmer's Tune	Republic 7043
			ILENE WOODS	
			The voice of Cinderella in the Walt Disney animated classic	
1/14/50	**22**	2	1. Bibbidi-Bobbidi-Boo..............................	Bluebird 0019
			from the animated film "Cinderella" accompanied by Harold Mooney & His Orchestra	
			WRIGHT BROTHERS	
9/25/54	**25**	2	1. If I Give My Heart To You	MGM 11776
			EDYTHE WRIGHT	
			Sang with Tommy Dorsey from 1935-39 ("On Treasure Island", "The Music Goes Round and Round"); died on 10/28/65.	
			HOARCE WRIGHT	
1/06/17	**1(4)**	9	1. **My Own Iona**.....................	Victor 18171
			HOARCE WRIGHT & RENE DIETRICH	
1/27/17	**2(3)**	7	2. O'Brien Is Tryin' To Learn To Talk Hawaiian .	Victor 18167
			both accompanied by Helen Louise & Frank Ferera (Hawaiian guitars)	
			JANE WYMAN	
			Movie star who won the Academy Award in 1948 for "Johnny Belinda"; formerly married to Ronald Reagan.	
8/04/51	**11**	6	1. In The Cool, Cool, Cool Of The Evening........	Decca 27678
			from the film "Here Comes the Groom"	
9/22/51	**29**	1	2. Blackstrap Molasses............................. [C]	Decca 27748
			DANNY KAYE, JIMMY DURANTE, JANE WYMAN, & GROUCHO MARX accompanied by Sonny Burke's Orchestra and Four Hits & a Miss	
8/09/52	**18**	6	3. Zing A Little Zong...................................	Decca 28255
			from the film "Just for You" 1 & 3: BING CROSBY & JANE WYMAN	
			NAN WYNN	
			Sang with Hudson-DeLange, Hal Kemp, & Raymond Scott bands in late 30s, dubbed Rita Hayworth's vocals in several 40s movies.	

Y

DATE CHARTED	PEAK POS	WKS CHRT'D	ARTIST — Record Title	Label & Number
			FRANKIE YANKOVIC & HIS YANKS	
			Cleveland-based accordionist and polka band leader; in 1986 Frank won the first-ever Grammy Award for best polka recording.	
5/08/48	**9**	14	1. Just Because	Columbia 12359
3/05/49	**12**	26	● 2. Blue Skirt Waltz	Columbia 12394
			vocal: Marlin Sisters	
			YERKES JAZARIMBA ORCHESTRA	
			Harry A. Yerkes, director	
4/12/19	**3**	6	1. Kentucky Dreams................................. [I]	Columbia 6092
			YERKES MARIMBAPHONE BAND	
8/23/19	**8**	2	2. Mammy O' Mine................................... [I]	Columbia 6108

DATE CHARTED	PEAK POS	WKS CHRT'D	ARTIST — Record Title	Label & Number
4/30/21	**8**	2	3. My Mammy.........................[I] from the Broadway musical "Sinbad"	Columbia 3372
7/02/21	**3**	5	4. Mazie ....[I] Ted Fiorito (piano) on above two; Joe Green & George Hamilton Green (xylophone/drums) on 1, 3, & 4	Columbia 3393
			YOGI YORGESSON with The Johnny Duffy Trio Real name Harry Stewart (also see Harry Kari & His Six Saki Sippers)	
12/10/49	**5**	5	● 1. I Yust Go Nuts At Christmas/ [X-N]	
12/17/49	**7**	4	2. Yingle Bells ....[X-N]	Capitol 781
			EVE YOUNG	
12/11/48	**29**	1	1. Cuanto La Gusta .... EVE YOUNG & THE DRUGSTORE COWBOYS from the film "A Date With Judy"	RCA Victor 3077
1/29/49	**26**	1	2. My Darling, My Darling .... EVE YOUNG & JACK LATHROP from the Broadway musical "Where's Charley?"	RCA Victor 3187
			JOHN YOUNG Pseudonym Harry Anthony	
			LESTER YOUNG All-time great tenor saxophonist who made his reputation with Count Basie (1936-40); also played with Benny Goodman, Billie Holiday and Teddy Wilson. Lester died on 3/15/59 (49). (also see Billy Eckstine)	
			RALPH YOUNG Baritone who sang in early 40s with Les Brown & Shep Fields bands	
			TRUMMY YOUNG Trombone star with Earl Hines (1933-37), Jimmie Lunceford (1937-43) & Benny Goodman (1945).	
			VICKI YOUNG	
6/27/53	**26**	1	1. I Love You So Much	Capitol 2478
10/02/54	**25**	2	2. Honey Love	Capitol 2865
			VICTOR YOUNG & HIS ORCHESTRA Composer of many enduring songs ("A Ghost of a Chance", "Stella by Starlight", "My Foolish Heart"); began as concert violinist; bandleader, radio conductor for Al Jolson & others, wrote film background music. Shortly after composing the music for "Around the World in 80 Days"; he died on 11/11/56 (56). (Also see Boswell Sisters, & Bing Crosby)	
10/17/31	**20**	1	1. Gems From "The Band Wagon".............[I] Dancing in the Dark / High and Low / Sweet Music / I Love Louisa	Brunswick 6172
9/30/33	**3**	12	2. The Last Round-Up/ above two vocals: Songsmiths	
9/30/33	**3**	8	3. Who's Afraid Of The Big Bad Wolf?........... from the animated film "The Three Little Pigs"	Brunswick 6651
1/20/34	**10**	5	4. The Old Spinning Wheel.................... vocal: Scrappy Lambert	Brunswick 6725
2/10/34	**6**	6	5. This Little Piggie Went To Market.............. vocal: Peg LaCentra Jimmy Dorsey (clarinet/alto sax), Bunny Berigan (trumpet) & Joe Venuti (violin) on most of above five	Brunswick 6747
12/15/34	**10**	5	6. Flirtation Walk/	
12/22/34	**17**	2	7. Mr. And Mrs. Is The Name .... above two vocals: Paul Small both from the film "Flirtation Walk"	Decca 279
3/02/35	**7**	11	8. Ev'ry Day/	
3/09/35	**19**	1	9. Sweet Music .... above two from the film "Sweet Music"	Decca 350
5/11/35	**3**	6	10. About A Quarter To Nine .... vocal: Hal Burke	Decca 418
5/25/35	**6**	5	11. Way Back Home .... vocal: Milton Watson	Decca 452

DATE CHARTED	PEAK POS	WKS CHRT'D	ARTIST — Record Title	Label & Number
6/01/35	1(4)	10	12. **She's A Latin From Manhattan**................ Decca 418 vocal: Hal Burke & Tune Twisters above two from the film "Go Into Your Dance"	
11/16/35	18	2	13. It Never Dawned On Me........................... Decca 582	
12/07/35	20	1	14. Take Me Back To My Boots And Saddle .... Decca 581 above two vocals: Frank Luther	
3/07/36	13	2	15. Lights Out .... Decca 703	
5/02/36	5	9	16. It's A Sin To Tell A Lie .... Decca 751 above two vocals: Dick Robertson	
4/24/37	14	3	17. Will You Remember?................................ Decca 1199 vocal: Tommy Haris	
6/19/37	17	1	18. Johnny One-Note .... Decca 1280 from the Broadway musical "Babes in Arms"	
6/10/50	27	1	19. La Vie En Rose...................................... Decca 24816	
7/01/50	7	15	20. Mona Lisa/ from the film "Captain Carey, U.S.A."	
7/08/50	22	2	21. The Third Man Theme .... Decca 27048 vocals on above two by Don Cherry	
2/24/51	29	1	22. My Heart Cries For You........................... Decca 27333 vocal: Joe Graydon & unbilled female	
5/30/53	20	2	23. Ruby .... Decca 28675 with George Fields & Singing Strings; movie title theme	
7/25/53	26	2	24. Limelight Theme .... Decca 28735	
8/07/54	6	14	25. The High And The Mighty .... [I] Decca 29203 movie title theme	

Z

FLORIAN ZABACH
Classically-trained violinist from Chicago

3/31/51	13	10	● 1. The Hot Canary.................................. [I] Decca 27509 orchestra directed by Al Rickey adapted from the Belgian song "Le Canari"	
4/11/53	22	2	2. Red Canary .... [I] Decca 28646	

SI ZENTNER
Jazz trombone star, played in 40s with Les Brown, Harry James, & Jimmy Dorsey.

EFREM ZIMBALIST
Famous concert violinist, married to opera star Alma Gluck (whom he often accompanied), father of TV star Efrem Zimbalist, Jr., grandfather of actress Stephanie Zimbalist. Efrem died in February, 1985 (94).

4/30/21	9	2	1. Serenade.. [I] Victor 64936	

BOB ZURKE & HIS DELTA RHYTHM BAND
Down Beat poll-winning pianist with Bob Crosby (1936-39); died on 2/16/44 (33).

6/29/40	30	1	1. I Love You Much Too Much .... Victor 26561 vocal: Evelyn Poe	

THE SONGS

This section cross references, alphabetically, all titles listed in the artist section. The artist's name is listed next to each title along with the peak position and the year of peak popularity (position/year).

A song with more than one charted version is listed once, with the artist's names listed below in chronoligical order. It was very common during this era to have many artists record the same song, and now you can tell at a glance who had the biggest hit versions. Songs that have the same title, but are actually different songs, are listed separately in chronological order.

In most cases the titles are listed in perfect alphabetical order, which means if an apostrophe is used in a word it will come before a title using the complete spelling (ex.: Walkin' comes before Walking), etc. Cross reference have been used throughout to help in finding titles.

A

A-Huggin' ... *see: Huggin'*

A-Tisket, A-Tasket
1/38 Ella Fitzgerald with Chick Webb
12/38 Tommy Dorsey

22/53 **A-Wooin' We Will Go** ... Lorry Raine

"A"-You're Adorable (The Alphabet Song)
1/49 Perry Como
4/49 Jo Stafford & Gordon MacRae
12/49 Tony Pastor
27/49 Buddy Kaye Quintet

6/08 **ABCs Of The U.S.A.** ...
Ada Jones & Billy Murray

Aba Daba Honeymoon
1/14 Arthur Collins & Byron Harlan
9/50 Kitty Kallen
3/51 Carleton Carpenter & Debbie Reynolds
9/51 Richard Hayes
12/51 Freddy Martin
19/51 Cliff Stewart
23/51 Hoagy Carmichael & Cass Daley

17/38 **Abba Dabba (One Of The Arabian Knights)** ... Larry Clinton

Abide With Me
6/10 Elizabeth Wheeler
10/13 Alma Gluck & Louise Homer

About A Quarter To Nine
3/35 Ozzie Nelson
3/35 Victor Young
5/35 Johnny Green

22/42 **Abraham** ... Freddy Martin

Absence Makes The Heart Grow Fonder
1/01 Harry Macdonough
2/01 George J. Gaskin
3/02 Jules Levy

7/30 **Absence Makes The Heart Grow Fonder (For Somebody Else)** ...
Bernie Cummins

Ac-cent-tchu-ate The Positive
1/45 Johnny Mercer
2/45 Bing Crosby & Andrews Sisters
5/45 Artie Shaw
12/45 Kay Kyser

Accent On Youth
6/35 Duke Ellington
15/35 Paul Pendarvis

Across The Alley From The Alamo
2/47 Mills Brothers
11/47 Stan Kenton
12/47 Woody Herman

Across The Great Divide ...
see: 'Cross

Across The Wide Missouri
19/51 Paul Weston
21/51 Hugo Winterhalter

Addio ... *see: Goodbye*

1/39 **Address Unknown** ... Ink Spots

Adeste Fideles ...
see: O Come, All Ye Faithful

Adios
13/41 Glenn Miller
28/48 Glenn Miller
14/52 Gisele MacKenzie

18/40 **Adios, Marquita Linda** ...
Artie Shaw

11/33 **Adorable** ... Wayne King

11/24 **Adoration Waltz** ... Carl Fenton

6/24 **Adoring You** ... Paul Whiteman

22/51 **Aeluna Mezzumare (Butcher Boy)** ...
Emil Dewan Quartones

Afghanistan
4/20 Ben Selvin
10/20 Prince's Orchestra

6/37 **Afraid To Dream** ... Benny Goodman

Afraid To Say Hello (Since You Said Goodbye)
23/41 Charlie Barnet
24/41 Joe Reichman

8/19 **After All** ... Reinald Werrenrath

15/39 **After All** ... Tommy Dorsey

22/47 **After Graduation Day** ...
Sammy Kaye

6/24 **After I Say I'm Sorry** ... Abe Lyman

After I Say I'm Sorry ...
see: (What Can I Say)

11/28 **After My Laughter Came Tears** ...
Cliff Edwards

After The Ball
1/93 George J. Gaskin
2/93 John Yorke Atlee

7/12 **After The Honeymoon** ...
Walter Van Brunt

2/20 **After You Get What You Want, You Don't Want It** ... Van & Schenck

After You've Gone
2/18 Henry Burr & Albert Campbell
1/19 Marion Harris
9/19 Billy Murray & Gladys Rice
7/27 Bessie Smith
10/27 Sophie Tucker
14/30 Paul Whiteman
15/32 Louis Armstrong
20/35 Benny Goodman
6/37 Lionel Hampton
20/37 Quintet Of The Hot Club Of France

14/36 **Afterglow** ... Leo Reisman

19/27 **Afternoon Of A Faun, Parts 1 & 2** ...
Philadelphia Orchestra

Again
2/49	Doris Day
2/49	Gordon Jenkins
3/49	Mel Torme
6/49	Vic Damone
6/49	Tommy Dorsey
7/49	Art Mooney
23/49	Vera Lynn

Aggravatin' Papa
3/23	Marion Harris
10/23	Sophie Tucker
12/23	Bessie Smith

21/48 **Ah, But It Happens** ...
Frankie Laine

Ah! Sweet Mystery Of Life
2/28	Fred Waring's Pennsylvanians
7/28	Leo Reisman
5/35	Nelson Eddy
12/39	Bing Crosby

5/11 **Aida - Aida A Me Togliesti (Aida Thou Hast Taken)** ... Enrico Caruso & Louise Homer

Aida - Celeste Aida (Heavenly Aida)
3/04	Enrico Caruso
5/12	Enrico Caruso
9/16	Hipolito Lazaro

9/15 **Aida - O Terra Addio ("Farewell, Oh Earth")** ... John McCormack & Lucy Isabelle Marsh

6/34 **Ain't Cha Glad?** ... Benny Goodman

3/01 **Ain't Dat A Shame?** ... Dan Quinn

17/33 **Ain't Gonna Grieve No More** ...
Joe Haymes

4/04 **Ain't It Funny What A Difference A Few Hours Can Make** ... Billy Murray

Ain't Misbehavin'
2/29	Leo Reisman
7/29	Louis Armstrong
8/29	Bill Robinson with Irving Mills
9/29	Gene Austin
16/29	Ruth Etting
17/29	Fats Waller
6/37	Teddy Wilson

6/47 **Ain't Nobody Here But Us Chickens** ...
Louis Jordan

22/50 **Ain't Nobody's Business But My Own** ... Kay Starr

Ain't She Sweet?
1/27	Ben Bernie
4/27	Gene Austin
14/27	Johnny Marvin
14/49	Mr. Goon Bones & Mr. Ford

10/27 **Ain't That A Grand And Glorious Feeling?** ... Johnny Marvin

17/46 **Ain't That Just Like A Woman** ...
Louis Jordan

Ain't We Got Fun?
1/21	Van & Schenck
9/21	Benson Orchestra Of Chicago
12/22	Billy Jones

3/06 **Ain't You Coming Back To Old New Hampshire, Molly?** ... Harry Macdonough

8/39 **Ain'tcha Comin' Out Tonight?** ...
Glenn Miller

21/47 **Ain'tcha Ever Comin' Back** ...
Frank Sinatra

24/41 **Air Mail Special** ... Benny Goodman

21/48 **Airizay** ... Ray McKinley

4/09 **Alabam'** ...
Arthur Collins & Byron Harlan

Alabama Jubilee
2/15	Arthur Collins & Byron Harlan
28/51	Red Foley

8/20 **Alabama Moon** ... Hawaiian Trio

Alabamy Bound
2/25	Blossom Seeley
10/25	Isham Jones
24/54	Mulcays

18/53 **A-L-B-U-Q-U-E-R-Q-U-E** ...
Ralph Flanagan

5/19 **Alcoholic Blues** ... Billy Murray

1/04 **Alexander** ... Billy Murray

Alexander The Swoose (Half Swan, Half Goose)
3/41	Kay Kyser
21/41	Art Kassel

Alexander's Ragtime Band
1/11	Arthur Collins & Byron Harlan
2/11	Billy Murray
3/12	Prince's Orchestra
4/12	Victor Military Band
17/27	Bessie Smith
9/35	Boswell Sisters
12/37	Louis Armstrong
1/38	Bing Crosby & Connee Boswell
4/38	Boswell Sisters
6/38	Ray Noble
20/47	Bing Crosby & Al Jolson

6/20 **Alexandria** ...
Joseph C. Smith's Orchestra

4/37 **Alibi Baby** ... Tommy Dorsey

Alice Blue Gown
1/20	Edith Day
7/40	Frankie Masters
16/40	Ozzie Nelson
18/40	Glenn Miller

3/97 **Alice, Where Art Thou** ...
Jules Levy

4/11 **All Aboard For Blanket Bay** ...
Ada Jones

All Aboard For Dixieland
3/14	Ada Jones & Peerless Quartet
5/14	American Quartet

1/04 **All Aboard For Dreamland** ...
Byron G. Harlan

11/33 **All Aboard For Dreamland, Baby** ...
Ted Lewis

All Alone
2/11   Ada Jones & Billy Murray
6/11   Ada Jones & Walter Van Brunt

All Alone (by Irving Berlin)
1/25   Al Jolson
1/25   John McCormack
1/25   Paul Whiteman
6/25   Cliff Edwards
10/25   Abe Lyman
11/25   Ben Selvin
12/25   Lewis James

22/41   **All Alone And Lonely ...**
     Jimmy Dorsey

2/27   **All Alone Monday ...** Nat Shilkret

6/32   **All-American Girl ...** George Olsen

All Ashore
3/38   Sammy Kaye
8/38   Jan Garber

All By Myself
1/21   Ted Lewis
5/21   Frank Crumit
5/21   Aileen Stanley
6/21   Benny Krueger
13/21   Vaughn Deleath
14/21   Ben Selvin

19/29   **All By Yourself In The Moonlight ...**
     Irving Aaronson

2/96   **All Coons Look Alike To Me ...**
     Len Spencer

25/50   **All Dressed Up To Smile ...**
     Evelyn Knight

21/48   **All Dressed Up With A Broken Heart ...** Peggy Lee

18/43   **All For You ...** Nat "King" Cole

All God's Chillun Got Rhythm
14/37   Duke Ellington
15/37   Artie Shaw

27/53   **All I Desire ...** Bob Manning

All I Do Is Dream Of You
1/34   Jan Garber
9/34   Henry Busse
11/34   Freddy Martin
27/53   Johnnie Ray

11/39   **All I Remember Is You ...**
     Tommy Dorsey

All I Want For Christmas (Is My Two Front Teeth)
1/49   Spike Jones
18/50   Spike Jones

2/16   **All I Want Is A Cottage, Some Roses, And You ...** Geoffrey O'Hara

2/98   **All I Wants Is My Chickens ...**
     Len Spencer

All My Life
1/36   Fats Waller
13/36   Teddy Wilson
15/36   Ted Fio Rito

All My Love
1/50   Patti Page
7/50   Percy Faith
10/50   Guy Lombardo
11/50   Bing Crosby
22/50   Dennis Day

7/13   **All Night Long ...**
     Ada Jones & Billy Murray

25/54   **All Night Long ...** Rusty Bryant

(All Of A Sudden) My Heart Sings
7/45   Johnnie Johnston
12/45   Martha Stewart

All Of Me
1/32   Louis Armstrong
1/32   Paul Whiteman
19/32   Ben Selvin
14/43   Count Basie
21/48   Frank Sinatra
12/52   Johnnie Ray

All Of My Life
10/45   Sammy Kaye
10/45   Three Suns
12/45   Bing Crosby

All Or Nothing At All
1/43   Frank Sinatra with Harry James
28/54   Joe Foley

All Over Nothing At All
3/22   Nora Bayes
9/22   Billy Murray & Aileen Stanley

20/37   **All Over Nothing At All ...**
     Ella Fitzgerald

11/49   **All Right Louie, Drop The Gun ...**
     Wesson Brothers

5/21   **All She'd Say Was "Umh-Hum" ...**
     Van & Schenck

9/46   **All That Glitters Is Not Gold ...**
     Dinah Shore

2/10   **All That I Ask Of You Is Love ...**
     Henry Burr

All The Boys Love Mary
6/20   Van & Schenck
9/20   Eddie Cantor

All The Things You Are
1/40   Tommy Dorsey
8/40   Artie Shaw
14/40   Frankie Masters

All The World Will Be Jealous Of Me
2/17   Charles Harrison
4/17   Henry Burr

All This And Heaven Too
9/40   Jimmy Dorsey
12/40   Tommy Dorsey
14/40   Charlie Barnet
20/40   Dick Todd
24/40   Jack Leonard

21/42   **All Those Wonderful Years ...**
     Russ Morgan

All Through The Day
7/46   Frank Sinatra
8/46   Perry Como
11/46   Margaret Whiting

3/12 **Any Place The Old Flag Flies** ...
Billy Murray

10/18 **Any Place The Old Gang Goes (I'll Be There)** ... Arthur Fields & Peerless Quartet

1/03 **Any Rags?** ... Arthur Collins

2/52 **Any Time** ... Eddie Fisher

27/54 **Anyone Can Fall In Love** ...
Doris Day

5/34 **Anything Goes** ... Paul Whiteman

9/19 **Anything Is Nice If It Comes From Dixie** ... American Quartet

12/28 **Anything You Say!** ... Cliff Edwards

17/48 **Anytime** ... Eddy Arnold

Anytime, Anyday, Anywhere
5/21 Paul Whiteman
12/21 Art Hickman

18/30 **Anytime's The Time To Fall In Love** ... Buddy Rogers

Anywhere I Wander
30/52 Mel Torme
4/53 Julius LaRosa

Apple Blossom Wedding
5/47 Sammy Kaye
9/47 Eddy Howard
14/47 Buddy Clark

8/40 **Apple Blossoms And Chapel Bells** ...
Orrin Tucker

2/39 **Apple For The Teacher** ...
Bing Crosby & Connee Boswell

16/45 **Apple Honey** ... Woody Herman

April In Paris
5/34 Freddy Martin
14/34 Henry King

April In Portugal
2/53 Les Baxter
10/53 Vic Damone
12/53 Richard Hayman
15/53 Freddy Martin
17/53 Tony Martin

10/40 **April Played The Fiddle** ...
Bing Crosby

April Showers
1/22 Al Jolson
2/22 Paul Whiteman
9/22 Ernest Hare
11/22 Charles Harrison
12/22 Arthur Fields
9/47 Guy Lombardo
15/47 Al Jolson

6/19 **Arabian Nights** ...
Waldorf-Astoria Dance Orchestra

3/16 **Araby** ... Harry Macdonough

6/24 **Arcady** ... Al Jolson

12/46 **Are These Really Mine?** ...
Vaughn Monroe

6/16 **Are You From Dixie? ('cause I'm From Dixie Too)** ... Billy Murray & Irving Kaufman

3/18 **Are You From Heaven?** ...
Henry Burr

6/39 **Are You Having Any Fun?** ...
Tommy Dorsey

Are You Lonesome Tonight?
4/27 Vaughn Deleath
10/27 Henry Burr
19/50 Blue Barron

27/53 **Are You Looking For A Sweetheart?** ... Kitty Kallen

13/30 **Are You Makin' Any Money?** ...
Paul Whiteman

20/43 **Are You Ready?** ... Lucky Millinder

Are You Sincere?
1/08 Elise Stevenson
8/08 Byron G. Harlan

9/25 **Are You Sorry?** ... Ben Bernie

Aren't You Glad You're You?
18/45 Pied Pipers
8/46 Bing Crosby
11/46 Les Brown
14/46 Tommy Dorsey

Argentines, The Portugese, And The Greeks
9/20 Nora Bayes
11/20 Eddie Cantor
15/20 Arthur Collins

19/37 **Arkansas Bazooka Swing** ...
Bob Skyles

10/22 **Arkansas Blues** ...
Noble Sissle & Eubie Blake

Arkansaw Traveler
2/00 Len Spencer
1/02 Len Spencer
14/24 Fiddlin' John Carson

19/43 **Army Air Corps** ... Alvino Rey

Around The Corner
12/30 Tom Gerun
17/30 Leo Reisman
18/30 Ben Selvin

Around The Corner (Beneath The Berry Tree)
9/52 Jo Stafford
19/52 Weavers with Gordon Jenkins

7/16 **Arrah Go On, I'm Going Back To Oregon** ... Peerless Quartet

Arthur Murray Taught Me Dancing In A Hurry
18/42 Jimmy Dorsey
21/42 King Sisters

12/39 **Artie Shaw Album** ... Artie Shaw

16/44 **Artistry In Rhythm** ... Stan Kenton

13/46 **Artistry Jumps** ... Stan Kenton

24/41 **As Long As I Live** ...
Benny Goodman

21/47 **As Long As I'm Dreaming** ...
Tex Beneke

Bambalina
1/23 Paul Whiteman
9/23 Ray Miller

Bambina
8/38 Jan Garber
16/38 Henry Busse

4/50 **Bamboo** ... Vaughn Monroe

Band Played On
1/95 Dan Quinn
1/41 Guy Lombardo
22/41 Jesters

8/21 **Bandana Days** ... Eubie Blake

Bandit, The
25/54 Percy Faith
26/54 Johnston Brothers
30/54 Tex Ritter

Banking On The Weather
12/32 Ted Black
13/32 Joe Moss

11/27 **Barbara** ... Ted Weems

3/26 **Barcelona** ... Ben Selvin

6/20 **Barefoot Trail** ... John McCormack

10/05 **Barn Dance In Dixie** ... Len Spencer

13/29 **Barnacle Bill The Sailor** ...
Frank Luther

Barney Google
2/23 Ernest Hare & Billy Jones
12/23 Georgie Price

11/36 **Barrelhouse** ...
Mills Blue Rhythm Band

23/42 **Barrelhouse Bessie From Basin
Street** ... Bob Crosby

20/49 **Barroom Polka** ... Russ Morgan

Bartender Polka
22/40 Will Glahe
26/40 Harry's Tavern Band

4/17 **Baseball Game** ... Weber & Fields

4/06 **Bashful Henry And His Lovin' Lucy** ...
Len Spencer & Ada Jones

Basin Street Blues
14/31 Charleston Chasers
14/34 Benny Goodman
12/37 Bing Crosby & Connee Boswell
20/38 Louis Armstrong

9/05 **Battle Cry Of Freedom** ...
Frank Stanley & Byron Harlan

Battle Hymn Of The Republic
6/12 Columbia Mixed Quartet
5/16 Columbia Mixed Double Quartet
4/17 Reinald Werrenrath
1/18 Columbia Stellar Quartet
10/18 Thomas Chalmers

30/53 **Baubles, Bangles, And Beads** ...
Peggy Lee

15/54 **(Bazoom) I Need Your Lovin'** ...
Cheers

Be Anything (But Be Mine)
7/52 Eddy Howard
21/52 Peggy Lee
26/52 Champ Butler
27/52 Helen O'Connell

Be Careful, It's My Heart
2/42 Bing Crosby
13/42 Tommy Dorsey

Be Honest With Me
19/41 Bing Crosby
23/41 Gene Autry
24/41 Freddy Martin

25/49 **Be Mine** ... Anne Shelton

Be My Life's Companion
7/52 Mills Brothers
18/52 Rosemary Clooney

Be My Little Baby Bumble Bee
1/12 Ada Jones & Billy Murray
6/12 Ada Jones & Walter Van Brunt

5/07 **Be My Little Teddy Bear** ...
Ada Jones & Billy Murray

Be My Love
1/51 Mario Lanza
13/51 Ray Anthony
26/51 Billy Eckstine

5/34 **Be Still, My Heart!** ... Freddy Martin

Beale Street Blues
5/17 Prince's Orchestra
8/17 Earl Fuller
5/21 Marion Harris
16/27 Alberta Hunter
20/32 Joe Venuti
20/42 Guy Lombardo

Beat Me, Daddy, Eight To The Bar
1/40 Will Bradley
15/40 Glenn Miller
2/41 Andrews Sisters

2/34 **Beat O' My Heart** ... Ben Pollack

6/16 **Beatrice Fairfax, Tell Me What To
Do!** ... Ada Jones

7/21 **Beautiful Annabelle Lee** ...
Prince's Orchestra

2/03 **Beautiful Bird, Sing On** ...
Harry Macdonough & Joe Belmont

Beautiful Brown Eyes
11/51 Rosemary Clooney
12/51 Jimmy Wakely

7/13 **Beautiful Doll, Good-Bye** ...
American Quartet

2/09 **Beautiful Eyes** ... Ada Jones

18/49 **Beautiful Eyes** ... Art Mooney

11/33 **Beautiful Girl** ... Bing Crosby

13/20 **Beautiful Hawaii** ... Frank Ferera

Beautiful Isle Of Somewhere
9/08 Harry Anthony & James Harrison
3/09 Harold Jarvis
4/16 John McCormack

Beautiful Lady In Blue
1/36 Jan Garber
13/36 Ray Noble

Beautiful Ohio
1/19 Henry Burr
1/19 Waldorf-Astoria Dance Orchestra
2/19 Prince's Orchestra
5/19 Olive Kline & Marguerite Dunlap
7/19 Fritz Kreisler
8/19 Sam Ash

26/49 **Beautiful Wisconsin** ... Ken Griffin

8/23 **Bebe** ... Billy Jones

Because
2/99 Albert Campbell
1/00 Haydn Quartet

Because
10/10 Evan Williams
4/13 Enrico Caruso
4/48 Perry Como
16/51 Mario Lanza

Because ... *also see: 'Cause*

12/27 **Because I Love You** ... Henry Burr

4/07 **Because I'm Married Now** ...
Billy Murray

10/28 **Because My Baby Don't Mean Maybe Now** ... Ruth Etting

16/35 **Because Of Once Upon A Time** ...
Fats Waller

17/51 **Because Of Rain** ... Nat "King" Cole

Because Of You
23/41 Larry Clinton
1/51 Tony Bennett
4/51 Les Baxter
11/51 Gloria DeHaven with Guy Lombardo
12/51 Jan Peerce
17/51 Johnny Desmond
20/51 Tab Smith
23/51 Ray Barber

Because You're Mine
7/52 Mario Lanza
16/52 Nat "King" Cole

1/07 **Because You're You** ...
Harry Macdonough & Elise Stevenson

Bedelia
1/04 Haydn Quartet
1/04 Billy Murray
3/04 George J. Gaskin
3/04 Arthur Pryor's Band
22/48 Jan Garber

25/41 **Beer And Skittles** ... Louise Massey

Beer Barrel Polka
1/39 Will Glahe
4/39 Andrews Sisters
13/39 Eddie DeLange

3/03 **Beer That Made Milwaukee Famous** ...
Dan Quinn

5/23 **Bees' Knees** ... Ted Lewis

27/53 **Before It's Too Late** ... Sunny Gale

Beg Your Pardon
3/48 Francis Craig
5/48 Frankie Carle
8/48 Larry Green
12/48 Dinning Sisters

4/31 **Begging For Love** ... Guy Lombardo

Begin The Beguine
13/35 Xavier Cugat
1/38 Artie Shaw
20/42 Artie Shaw
16/45 Eddie Heywood
23/46 Frank Sinatra

Beginner's Luck ... *see: (I've Got)*

Bei Mir Bist Du Schoen
1/38 Andrews Sisters
2/38 Guy Lombardo
3/38 Russ Morgan
4/38 Benny Goodman
7/38 Jerry Blaine
15/38 Kate Smith

27/51 **Bela Bimba** ... Patrice Munsel

3/18 **Belgian Rose** ...
Henry Burr & Albert Campbell

22/54 **Believe In Me** ... Don Cornell

5/35 **Believe It, Beloved** ... Fats Waller

10/11 **Believe Me If All Those Endearing Young Charms** ... John McCormack

12/40 **Believing** ... Bob Crosby

17/54 **Bell Bottom Blues** ... Teresa Brewer

Bell-Bottom Trousers
2/45 Guy Lombardo
2/45 Tony Pastor
3/45 Kay Kyser
6/45 Louis Prima
9/45 Jerry Colonna
11/45 Jesters

Bella Bella Marie
21/48 Larry Green
23/48 Andrews Sisters
28/49 Jan Garber

Belle, Belle, My Liberty Belle
9/51 Guy Mitchell
23/51 Bobby Wayne
25/51 Don Cherry
25/51 Hugo Winterhalter

10/06 **Belle Of The Ball** ... Frank Stanley

7/41 **Bells Of San Raquel** ... Dick Jurgens

Bells Of St. Mary's
7/20 Frances Alda
21/46 Bing Crosby

Beloved
9/28 Guy Lombardo
10/28 Ruth Etting
16/33 Don Bestor

28/50 **Beloved, Be Faithful** ... Russ Morgan

Beneath ... *see: 'Neath*

Bermuda
7/52 Bell Sisters
24/52 Ray Anthony

Besame Mucho
1/44 Jimmy Dorsey
10/44 Andy Russell
21/44 Abe Lyman

7/23 **Beside A Babbling Brook** ...
Marion Harris

3/26	**Black Bottom** ... Johnny Hamp
13/27	**Black Bottom Stomp** ... Jelly Roll Morton
13/49	**Black Coffee** ... Sarah Vaughan
16/33	**Black-Eyed Susan Brown** ... Mark Fisher
7/36	**Black Raspberry Jam** ... Fats Waller
3/52	**Blacksmith Blues** ... Ella Mae Morse
29/51	**Blackstrap Molasses** ... Danny Kaye, Jimmy Durante, Groucho Marx & Jane Wyman
13/39	**Blame It On My Last Affair** ... Mildred Bailey
17/35	**Blame It On My Youth** ... Jan Garber
7/10	**Blarney Stone** ... Harry Lauder
5/02	**Blaze Away** ... Fred Van Eps
8/11	**Blaze Of Glory** ... New York Military Band
25/41	**Bless 'Em All** ... King Sisters
15/39	**Bless You** ... Ink Spots
14/33	**Bless Your Heart** ... Freddy Martin
16/50	**Blind Date** ... Margaret Whiting & Bob Hope
8/45	**Blond Sailor** ... Andrews Sisters

Bloop-Bleep

13/47	Alvino Rey
21/47	Danny Kaye

Blossoms On Broadway

4/37	Dolly Dawn
5/37	Dick Robertson

13/35	**Blow, Gabriel, Blow** ... Enric Madriguera
21/47	**Blow Top Blues** ... Lionel Hampton
21/53	**Blowing Wild (The Ballad Of Black Gold)** ... Frankie Laine

Blue Again

10/31	Red Nichols
12/31	Duke Ellington

7/23	**Blue (And Broken Hearted)** ... Marion Harris
21/48	**Blue And Sentimental** ... Count Basie

Blue Bell

1/04	Haydn Quartet
1/04	Frank Stanley & Byron G. Harlan
4/04	Henry Burr

20/42	**Blue Blazes** ... Tommy Dorsey
11/53	**Blue Canary** ... Dinah Shore
1/41	**Blue Champagne** ... Jimmy Dorsey

Blue Christmas

13/49	Russ Morgan
9/50	Hugo Winterhalter
20/50	Hugo Winterhalter
21/50	Ernest Tubb

Blue Danube Waltz

4/05	Sousa's Band
14/33	Wayne King
3/35	Ray Noble
25/41	Marek Weber

18/52	**Blue December** ... Hugo Winterhalter
9/39	**Blue Evening** ... Woody Herman
3/25	**Blue Eyed Sally** ... Ted Weems
5/41	**Blue Flame** ... Woody Herman
12/29	**Blue Hawaii** ... Paul Whiteman
5/37	**Blue Hawaii** ... Bing Crosby
18/34	**Blue In Love** ... Jan Garber
5/38	**Blue In The Black Of Night** ... Gray Gordon
14/30	**Blue Is The Night** ... Ipana Troubadors
16/32	**Blue Jazz** ... Glen Gray

Blue Love Bird

7/40	Kay Kyser
14/40	Mitchell Ayres

Blue Moon

1/35	Glen Gray
2/35	Benny Goodman
5/35	Al Bowlly with Ray Noble
20/49	Mel Torme
21/49	Billy Eckstine

Blue Orchids

1/39	Glenn Miller
7/39	Benny Goodman
8/39	Bob Crosby

29/53	**Blue Piano** ... Vince Wayne
10/33	**Blue Prelude** ... Bing Crosby
8/43	**Blue Rain** ... Glenn Miller
16/32	**Blue Ramble** ... Duke Ellington
26/40	**Blue Rhythm Fantasy** ... Gene Krupa

Blue River

10/27	Sophie Tucker
16/28	Al Jolson

Blue Room

3/26	Revelers
9/26	Sam Lanin
9/26	Melody Sheiks
18/49	Perry Como

14/29	**Blue Shadows** ... Johnny Hamp

Blue Shadows On The Trail

23/48	Bing Crosby
26/48	Vaughn Monroe

Blue Skies

1/27	Ben Selvin
2/27	George Olsen
9/27	Vincent Lopez
9/27	Johnny Marvin & Ed Smalle
13/27	Harry Richman
15/27	Vaughn Deleath
22/41	Johnny Long
8/46	Count Basie
9/46	Benny Goodman

Blue Skirt Waltz
12/49 Frankie Yankovic
30/49 Guy Lombardo

19/34 **Blue Sky Avenue** ... Jan Garber

20/43 **Blue Surreal** ... Bob Crosby

24/48 **Blue Tail Fly** ...
Andrews Sisters & Burl Ives

Blue Tango
1/52 Leroy Anderson
6/52 Hugo Winterhalter
9/52 Guy Lombardo
10/52 Les Baxter

16/51 **Blue Velvet** ... Tony Bennett

19/52 **Blue Violins** ... Hugo Winterhalter

2/28 **Blue Yodel** ... Jimmie Rodgers

10/28 **Blue Yodel No. 3** ... Jimmie Rodgers

Blueberry Hill
1/40 Glenn Miller
11/40 Kay Kyser
14/40 Russ Morgan

10/19 **Bluebird** ... Elizabeth Spencer

Bluebird Of Happiness
5/48 Art Mooney
16/48 Jo Stafford & Gordon MacRae
23/48 Jan Peerce

19/49 **Bluebird On Your Windowsill** ...
Doris Day

Bluebirds In The Moonlight
9/39 Glenn Miller
9/40 Dick Jurgens
15/40 Benny Goodman

14/38 **Blues, The** ... Artie Shaw

15/51 **Blues (from "An American In
Paris")** ... Ralph Flanagan

20/52 **Blues In Advance** ... Dinah Shore

19/31 **Blues In My Heart** ...
Fletcher Henderson

Blues In The Night
10/41 Artie Shaw
1/42 Woody Herman
4/42 Jimmie Lunceford
4/42 Dinah Shore
8/42 Cab Calloway
20/42 Benny Goodman
17/52 Rosemary Clooney

5/20 **Blues (My Naughty Sweetie Gives To
Me)** ... Ted Lewis

17/40 **Blues On Parade** ... Woody Herman

11/49 **Blues Stay Away From Me** ...
Owen Bradley

27/49 **Blum Blum, I Wonder Who I Am** ...
Peggy Lee

14/20 **Bo-La-Bo** ... Ted Lewis

15/37 **Bob White** ... Benny Goodman

**Bob White (Whatcha Gonna Swing
Tonight?)**
1/37 Bing Crosby & Connee Boswell
14/37 Mildred Bailey

Body And Soul
1/30 Paul Whiteman
3/30 Libby Holman
10/30 Ruth Etting
12/30 Annette Hanshaw
16/30 Helen Morgan
18/30 Ozzie Nelson
15/31 Leo Reisman
7/32 Louis Armstrong
5/35 Benny Goodman
17/35 Henry Allen
19/37 Art Tatum
13/40 Coleman Hawkins
25/47 Ziggy Elman
27/49 Billy Eckstine

4/08 **Boheme: Quartetto - "Addio, Dolce
Svegliare" (Farewell, Sweet Love)** ..
Geraldine Farrar

19/43 **Bojangles (A Portrait Of Bill
Robinson)** ... Duke Ellington

17/36 **Bojangles Of Harlem** ... Fred Astaire

19/42 **Bombadier Song** ... Bing Crosby

8/08 **Bon-Bon Buddy** ... Billy Murray

11/32 **Bon Voyage To My Ship Of Dreams** ...
Jimmie Grier

Bonaparte's Retreat
4/50 Kay Starr
9/50 Gene Krupa

30/53 **Boo-Dah** ... Duke Ellington

Boo Hoo
1/37 Guy Lombardo
3/37 Mal Hallet

Boog It
7/40 Glenn Miller
13/40 Gene Krupa

9/46 **Boogie Blues** ... Gene Krupa

Boogie Woogie
3/38 Tommy Dorsey
5/44 Tommy Dorsey
21/44 Tommy Dorsey
4/45 Tommy Dorsey
*(also see: Pine Top's Boogie
Woogie)*

21/47 **Boogie Woogie Blue Plate** ...
Louis Jordan

6/41 **Boogie Woogie Bugle Boy** ...
Andrews Sisters

11/40 **Boogie Woogie On The St. Louis
Blues** ... Earl Hines
(also see: St. Louis Blues)

7/41 **Booglie Wooglie Piggy** ...
Glenn Miller

25/53 **Boomerang** ... Lisa Kirk

Born To Be Kissed
14/34 Freddy Martin
16/34 Ben Selvin

19/43 **Born To Lose** ... Ted Daffan

2/52 **Botch-A-Me (Ba-Ba-Baciami
Piccina)** ... Rosemary Clooney

18/41 **Boulder Bluff** ... Glenn Miller

Bye Bye Blackbird
1/26	Gene Austin
4/26	Nick Lucas
7/26	Benny Krueger
11/26	Leo Reisman
20/48	Russ Morgan

Bye Bye Blues
5/30	Bert Lown
17/30	Leo Reisman
24/41	Cab Calloway
5/53	Les Paul & Mary Ford

10/08 **Bye Bye Dearie** ...
Frank Stanley & Henry Burr

3/98 **Bye Bye, My Honey** ... Billy Golden

C

29/53 **C'est Magnifique** ... Gordon MacRae

C'est Si Bon
21/50	Danny Kaye
25/50	Johnny Desmond
8/53	Eartha Kitt
13/54	Stan Freberg

11/27 **C'est Vous (It's You)** ...
Harry Richman

28/54 **Cabbages And Kings** ...
Charlie Applewhite

Cabin In The Cotton
11/32	Bing Crosby
17/32	Cab Calloway

19/43 **Cabin In The Sky** ...
Benny Goodman

16/38 **Cachita** ... Obregon's Orchestra

13/25 **Cake Ealking Babies From Home** ...
Clarence Williams' Blue Five

Caldonia
2/45	Woody Herman
6/45	Louis Jordan
12/45	Erskine Hawkins

5/22 **California** ... Van & Schenck

California And You
4/14	Irving Kaufman
8/14	Henry Burr & Albert Campbell

California, Here I Come
1/24	Al Jolson
7/24	Georgie Price
10/24	California Ramblers
17/33	Claude Hopkins

20/32 **California Medley** ... Red Nichols

7/27 **Calinda (Boo-Joom, Boo-Joom, Boo!)** ...
Paul Whiteman

9/31 **Call Me Darling (Call Me Sweetheart, Call Me Dear)** ... Ben Selvin

Call Me Up Some Rainy Afternoon
1/10	Ada Jones & American Quartet
4/10	Ada Jones

Call Of The Canyon
10/40	Glenn Miller
14/40	Tommy Dorsey

13/51 **Calla Calla** ... Vic Damone

Calling Me Home To You
4/18	Oscar Seagle
4/19	John McCormack

1/07 **Camp Meetin' Time** ...
Arthur Collins & Byron Harlan

9/14 **Camp Meeting Band** ...
Arthur Collins & Byron Harlan

9/11 **Camptown Races (Gwine To Run All Night)** ... Billy Murray

Can Anyone Explain? (No! No! No!)
5/50	Ames Brothers
5/50	Ray Anthony
23/50	Dick Haymes
25/50	Vic Damone
28/50	Larry Green
29/50	Dinah Shore
30/50	Louis Armstrong
30/50	Ella Fitzgerald

Can I Forget You?
8/37	Bing Crosby
13/37	Henry Allen
13/37	Guy Lombardo

8/39 **Can I Help It?** ... Bob Crosby

17/35 **Can The Circle Be Unbroken (Bye and Bye)** ... Carter Family

11/30 **Can This Be Love?** ...
Arden-Ohman Orchestra

8/40 **Can't Get Indiana Off My Mind** ...
Bing Crosby

Can't Get Out Of This Mood
20/42	Johnny Long
4/43	Kay Kyser

Can't Help Lovin' Dat Man
7/28	Helen Morgan
19/28	Ben Bernie

Can't I?
16/53	Nat "King" Cole
23/53	Ames Brothers

14/37 **Can't Teach My Old Heart New Tricks** ... Benny Goodman

Can't We Talk It Over?
10/32	Bing Crosby & Mills Brothers
22/50	Andrews Sisters

4/14 **Can't You Hear Me Calling, Caroline?** ... George MacFarlane

Can't You Read Between The Lines?
8/45	Jimmy Dorsey
10/45	Kay Kyser

4/05 **Can't You See My Heart Beats All For You** ... Billy Murray & Len Spencer

Canadian Capers
4/22	Paul Whiteman
15/49	Doris Day

22/42 **Cancel The Flowers** ... Tony Martin

Candy
1/45   Johnny Mercer & Jo Stafford
5/45   Dinah Shore
8/45   Johnny Long
15/45   King Sisters
18/45   Jerry Wald

Candy And Cake
12/50   Mindy Carson
16/50   Arthur Godfrey
20/50   Evelyn Knight

20/49 **Candy Kisses** ... Eddy Howard

17/53 **Candy Lips** ...
       Doris Day & Johnny Ray

22/48 **Candy Store Blues** ...
       Toni Harper & East Beale Sextet

4/12 **Canta Pe' Me (Neapolitan Song)** ...
       Enrico Caruso

17/45 **Captain Kidd** ... Ella Mae Morse

10/54 **Cara Mia** ...
       David Whitfield with Mantovani

13/48 **Caramba! It's The Samba** ...
       Peggy Lee

Caravan
4/37   Duke Ellington
20/37   Barney Bigard
27/49   Billy Eckstine
6/53   Ralph Marterie
27/53   Esquire Boys

Careless
1/40   Glenn Miller
6/40   Dick Jurgens

Careless Hands
1/49   Mel Torme
3/49   Sammy Kaye
12/49   Bing Crosby
21/49   Bob & Jeanne

24/50 **Careless Kisses** ... Russ Morgan

5/25 **Careless Love Blues** ... Bessie Smith

1/37 **Carelessly** ...
       Teddy Wilson featuring Billie Holiday

5/21 **Caresses** ... Paul Whiteman

20/29 **Caressing You** ...
       Johnny Marvin & Ed Smalle

26/53 **Caribbean** ... Mitchell Torok

Carioca
1/34   Enric Madriguera
2/34   Harry Sosnik
4/34   Castillian Troubadors
13/34   RKO Studio Orchestra
14/52   Les Paul

22/42 **Carle Meets Mozart (Turkish March)** ... Hoarce Heidt

5/10 **Carmen - Air De La Fleur (Flower Song)** ... Enrico Caruso

10/10 **Carmen - Il Flor Che Aveci A Me (Flower Song)** ... John McCormack

Carmen - Toreador Song
6/05   Emilio DeGogorza
4/08   Alan Turner

26/54 **Carnival In Venice** ... Mills Brothers

Carolina In The Morning
1/23   Van & Schenck
4/23   Marion Harris
5/23   Paul Whiteman
8/23   American Quartet
30/52   Danny Winchell

11/21 **Carolina Lullaby** ...
       Henry Burr & Albert Campbell

Carolina Moon
1/29   Gene Austin
5/29   Ben Selvin
15/29   Nat Shilkret
15/38   Sammy Kaye

10/22 **Carolina Shout** ... James P. Johnson

10/26 **Carolina Stomp** ...
       Fletcher Henderson

Carolina Sunshine
6/19   Sterling Trio
13/20   Henry Burr & John Meyer

1/10 **Carrie (Carrie Marry Harry)** ...
       Billy Murray

10/23 **Carry Me Back To My Carolina Home** ... Henry Burr & Albert Campbell

Carry Me Back To Old Virginny
2/93   Len Spencer
1/15   Alma Gluck

15/31 **Casa Loma Stomp** ... Glen Gray

3/98 **Casey As A Fortune Teller** ...
       Russell Hunting
       (also see: Michael Casey)

1/94 **Casey As Insurance Agent** ...
       Russell Hunting

1/94 **Casey At Denny Murphy's Wake** ...
       Russell Hunting

Casey At The Bat
2/93   Russell Hunting
3/06   DeWolf Hopper

Casey Jones
1/10   American Quartet
3/10   Billy Murray
5/10   Arthur Collins & Byron Harlan

9/16 **Casey's Description Of His Fight** ...
       Russell Hunting

Castle Rock
8/51   Frank Sinatra with Harry James
27/51   Fontane Sisters
28/51   Johnny Hodges

6/18 **Cathedral Chimes** ...
       Prince's Orchestra

1/38 **Cathedral In The Pines** ...
       Shep Fields

24/52 **'Cause I Love You, That's A-Why** ...
       Guy Mitchell & Mindy Carson

12/37 **'Cause My Baby Says It's So** ...
       Kay Kyser

4/08 **Cavalier, The** ...
Frank Stanley & Elise Stevenson

6/05 **Cavalleria Rusticana - Brindisi (Drinking Song)** ... Enrico Caruso

Cecelia
7/26 "Whispering" Jack Smith
13/26 Johnny Hamp
8/40 Dick Jurgens

3/14 **Celebratin' Day In Tennessee** ...
Arthur Collins & Byron Harlan

19/40 **Celery Stalks At Midnight** ...
Will Bradley

Cement Mixer (Put-Ti, Put-Ti)
5/46 Alvino Rey
13/46 Charlie Barnet
13/46 Jimmie Lunceford
18/46 Hal McIntyre
21/46 Slim Gaillard Trio

28/54 **Chain Lightning** ... Judy Tremaine

30/51 **Chains Of Love** ... Joe Turner

7/34 **Champagne Waltz** ... Glen Gray

Change Partners
1/38 Fred Astaire
1/38 Jimmy Dorsey
6/38 Ozzie Nelson
13/38 Lawrence Welk

4/28 **Changes** ... Paul Whiteman

Changing Partners
3/53 Patti Page
7/54 Kay Starr
12/54 Dinah Shore
13/54 Bing Crosby

9/17 **Chanson De Juin (Song Of June)** ...
Enrico Caruso

4/24 **Chansonette** ... Paul Whiteman

Chant Of The Jungle
13/29 Paul Specht
1/30 Roy Ingraham
3/30 Nat Shilkret

14/33 **Chant Of The Swamp** ... Art Kassel

15/31 **Chant Of The Weed** ... Don Redman

6/16 **Chantique De Noel (Holy Night)** ...
Enrico Caruso

Charleston
1/24 Arthur Gibbs
5/25 Paul Whiteman
(also see: Original Charleston)

24/41 **Charleston Alley** ... Charlie Barnet

8/24 **Charleston Crazy** ...
Fletcher Henderson

15/50 **Charley My Boy** ... Andrews Sisters

Charley, My Boy
3/24 Eddie Cantor
11/24 International Novelty Orchestra

Charmaine
1/27 Guy Lombardo
11/27 Lewis James
25/44 Frankie Carle
10/51 Mantovani
18/51 Gordon Jenkins
21/51 Harmonicats
8/52 Paul Weston
17/52 Billy May
27/52 Vaughn Monroe

12/40 **Charming Little Faker** ...
Frankie Masters

Chasing Shadows
1/35 Dorsey Brothers Orchestra
7/35 Henry King
11/35 Enric Madriguera
14/35 Louis Prima

1/41 **Chattanooga Choo Choo** ...
Glenn Miller

Chattanoogie Shoe Shine Boy
1/50 Red Foley
4/50 Bing Crosby
8/50 Phil Harris
10/50 Frank Sinatra
17/50 Bradford & Romano
18/50 Bill Darnel

6/40 **Chatter Box** ... Kay Kyser

8/25 **Cheatin' On Me** ... Ben Bernie

21/42 **Cheatin' On The Sandman** ...
Merry Macs

Cheek To Cheek
1/35 Fred Astaire
2/35 Eddy Duchin
2/35 Guy Lombardo
5/35 Phil Ohman
10/35 Boswell Sisters

7/11 **Cheer Up, My Honey** ...
Ada Jones & Billy Murray

7/30 **Cheerful Little Earful** ... Tom Gerun

Cherie
1/21 Paul Whiteman
3/21 Carl Fenton
5/21 Nora Bayes
5/21 Ben Selvin
15/21 Harry Raderman's Jazz Orchestra

Cherie, I Love You
4/26 Ben Bernie
10/26 Ross Gorman
14/26 Fred Waring's Pennsylvanians

15/39 **Cherokee** ... Charlie Barnet

Cherry
4/44 Harry James
15/44 Erskine Hawkins

23/44 **Cherry Red Blues** ... Cootie Williams

12/39 **Chestnut Tree** ... Hal Kemp

14/39 **Chew, Chew, Chew (Your Bubble Gum)** ... Ella Fitzgerald with Chick Webb

2/06 **Cheyenne (Shy Ann)** ... Billy Murray

Chi-Baba, Chi-Baba
1/47 Perry Como
14/47 Blue Barron
16/47 Charioteers
10/48 Peggy Lee

26/41 **Chica, Chica, Boom, Chic** ...
Xavier Cugat

Chicago
5/22 Ben Selvin
13/22 Bar Harbor Society Orchestra

15/24 **Chicago Blues** ... Clara Smith

Chicken Reel
4/11 Frank Stanley & Byron G. Harlan
6/11 Arthur Collins

22/51 **Chicken Song (I Ain't Gonna Take It Settin' Down)** ... Guy Lombardo

Chickery Chick
1/45 Sammy Kaye
10/45 Gene Krupa
12/45 George Olsen
10/46 Evelyn Knight

11/39 **Chico's Love Song** ...
Andrews Sisters

4/20 **Chili Bean** ...
Paul Biese Trio & Frank Crumit

8/15 **Chin-Chin** ... Prince's Orchestra

China Boy
13/29 Paul Whiteman
18/30 Red Nichols
13/35 Isham Jones
9/36 Benny Goodman

16/37 **China Stomp** ... Lionel Hampton

Chinatown, My Chinatown
1/15 American Quartet
3/15 Grace Kerns & John Barnes Wells
8/15 Prince's Orchestra
5/32 Louis Armstrong
10/32 Mills Brothers
14/35 Ray Noble
24/52 Bobby Maxwell

15/32 **Chinese Lullaby** ... Paul Whiteman

16/50 **Chinese Mule Train** ... Spike Jones

6/34 **Chinese Rhythm** ... Cab Calloway

29/53 **Chinese Waiter** ... Buddy Hackett

4/28 **Chiquita** ... Paul Whiteman

7/05 **Chirpers** ...
Joe Belmont & Arthur Pryor's Band

Chloe ... Al Jolson

Chloe (Song Of The Swamp)
7/28 Paul Whiteman
5/45 Spike Jones
26/53 Louis Armstrong

2/19 **Chong** ...
Columbia Saxophone Sextette

16/31 **Choo Choo** ... Paul Whiteman

7/46 **Choo Choo Ch'boogie** ...
Louis Jordan

20/53 **Choo Choo Train (Ch-Ch-Foo)** ...
Doris Day

17/50 **Choo'n Gum** ... Teresa Brewer

8/17 **Chopin Etude In G Flat Major** ...
Ignace Jan Paderewski

3/45 **Chopin's Polonaise** ...
Carmen Cavallaro

20/45 **Chopin's Polonaise In A Flat** ...
Jose Iturbi

20/39 **Chopsticks** ... Kay Kyser

25/53 **Chow, Willy** ...
Jo Stafford & Frankie Laine

25/54 **Christmas Alphabet** ...
McGuire Sisters

22/52 **Christmas Day** ... Eddie Fisher

13/53 **Christmas Dragnet** ... Stan Freberg

26/47 **Christmas Dreaming** ...
Frank Sinatra

22/53 **Christmas Festival** ...
Leroy Anderson

28/50 **Christmas In Killarney** ...
Percy Faith

Christmas Island
7/47 Andrews Sisters with Guy Lombardo
20/47 Andrews Sisters with Guy Lombardo
26/49 Andrews Sisters with Guy Lombardo

21/53 **Christmas Medley** ... Liberace

15/34 **Christmas Night In Harlem** ...
Paul Whiteman

Christmas Song
3/46 Nat "King" Cole
12/47 Les Brown
23/47 Nat "King" Cole
24/49 Nat "King" Cole
30/53 Nat "King" Cole
29/54 Nat "King" Cole

7/19 **Christmas Time At Pumpkin Center** ... Cal Stewart, Ada Jones & Peerless Quartet

Christopher Columbus
2/36 Andy Kirk
9/36 Benny Goodman
10/36 Fletcher Henderson
12/36 Teddy Wilson
16/36 King Garcia

27/51 **Christopher Columbus** ...
Guy Mitchell

15/48 **Cigarettes, Whusky, And Wild, Wild Women** ... Red Ingle

7/50 **Cincinatti Dancing Pig** ... Red Foley

27/52 **Cincinatti Ding Dong** ... Art Lund

11/50 **Cincinnati Dancing Pig** ...
Vic Damone

Cinderella, Stay In My Arms
3/39 Guy Lombardo
16/39 Glenn Miller
19/39 Jack Teagarden

2/01 **Cindy, I Dreams About You** ...
Arthur Collins

8/54 **Cinnamon Sinner** ... Tony Bennett

5/08 **Come On And Kiss Yo' Baby** ...
Arthur Collins & Byron Harlan

10/13 **Come On Over Here** ...
Billy Murray & Helen Clark

7/19 **Come On, Papa** ...
Avon Comedy Four

Come Rain Or Come Shine
17/46 Margaret Whiting
23/46 Helen Forrest & Dick Haymes

Come Take A Trip In My Air-Ship
1/05 Billy Murray
2/05 J.W. Myers

Come To Baby, Do
13/46 Les Brown
13/46 Duke Ellington

Come To Me
15/31 High Hatters
16/31 Jacques Renard

5/12 **Come To The Ball** ... Henry Burr

12/38 **Come To The Fair** ... Ella Logan

16/47 **Come To The Mardi Gras** ...
Freddy Martin

9/34 **Come Up And See Me Sometime** ...
Ethel Waters

9/52 **Come What May** ... Patti Page

4/08 **Come Where My Love Lies
Dreaming** ... Peerless Quartet

9/52 **Comes A-Long A-Love** ... Kay Starr

Comes Love
4/39 Artie Shaw
7/39 Larry Clinton
14/39 Eddy Duchin

Comin' In On A Wing And A Prayer
1/43 Song Spinners
2/43 Willie Kelly
24/43 Four Vagabonds

10/14 **Comin' Thro' The Rye** ...
Nellie Melba

22/48 **Completely Yours** ... Vaughn Monroe

3/01 **Con Clancy's Christening** ...
Len Spencer

Concert In The Park
6/39 Jan Garber
10/39 Kay Kyser

10/41 **Concerto For Clarinet** ... Artie Shaw

25/41 **Concerto For Two (A Love Song)** ...
Claude Thornhill

10/29 **Concerto In F, Parts 1 & 2** ...
Paul Whiteman

10/24 **Concerto No. 2 In C Minor, Parts 1 &
2** ... Sergei Rachmaninoff with
Philadelphia Orchestra

Confess
12/48 Patti Page
16/48 Doris Day & Buddy Clark
25/48 Tony Martin

Confessin' (That I Love You)
2/30 Guy Lombardo
4/30 Rudy Vallee
14/37 Lionel Hampton
12/45 Perry Como
13/52 Les Paul & Mary Ford

24/41 **Confessin' The Blues** ...
Jay McShann

Confucius Say
9/40 Guy Lombardo
17/40 Kay Kyser

17/37 **Congo** ... Cab Calloway

4/03 **Congo Love Song** ... Mina Hickman

12/29 **Congratulations** ... Jack Denny

13/49 **Congratulations** ... Jo Stafford

Congratulations To Someone
20/53 Tony Bennett
28/53 Gordon MacRae

26/47 **Connecticut** ... Herbie Fields

18/52 **Conquest** ... Patti Page

4/28 **C-O-N-S-T-A-N-T-I-N-O-P-L-E** ...
Paul Whiteman

2/10 **Constantly** ... Bert Williams

13/43 **Constantly** ... Bing Crosby

9/10 **Contes D' Hoffman - Barcolle Belle
Nuit (Oh, Night Of Love)** ...
Geraldine Farrar & Antonio Scotti

**Continental (You Kiss While You're
Dancing)**
1/34 Leo Reisman
2/34 Jolly Coburn
6/34 Lud Gluskin

9/26 **Convict And The Rose** ...
Vernon Dalhart

7/22 **Coo Coo** ... Al Jolson

Cool Water
25/41 Sons Of The Pioneers
9/48 Vaughn Monroe with Sons Of The
Pioneers

Coon Band Contest
2/00 Vess Ossman
5/05 Arthur Pryor's Band

5/25 **Copenhagen** ...
Benson Orchestra Of Chicago

13/36 **Copper Colored Gal** ... Cab Calloway

Coquette
6/28 Guy Lombardo
20/28 Dorsey Brothers Orchestra
10/29 Rudy Vallee
26/53 Billy Eckstine

Corabelle ...
see: (I'm A-Comin', I'm A-Courtin')

4/99 **Cornfield Medley** ... Haydn Quartet

21/45 **Corns For My Country** ...
Andrews Sisters

18/31 **Corrine Corrina** ... Red Nichols

10/26 **Cossack Love Song** ...
Ipana Troubadors

	Cottage For Sale	
4/30	Guy Lombardo	
18/30	Revelers	
8/45	Billy Eckstine	

4/35 **Cotton** ... Duke Ellington

3/39 **Could Be** ... Johnny Messner

20/38 **Could You Pass In Love?** ...
Benny Goodman

	Count Every Star	
4/50	Ray Anthony	
10/50	Dick Haymes with Artie Shaw	
10/50	Hugo Winterhalter	

	Count Your Blessings (Instead Of Sheep)	
27/54	Rosemary Clooney	
27/54	Bing Crosby	
5/55	Eddie Fisher	

25/53 **Counterfeit Kisses** ... Ernest Tubb

17/45 **Counting The Days** ... Frankie Carle

9/05 **Courtship Of Barney And Eileen** ...
Len Spencer & Ada Jones

	Covered Wagon Days	
5/24	Vincent Lopez	
10/24	Ted Weems	

23/41 **Cow Cow Blues** ... Bob Crosby

	Cow Cow Boogie	
9/42	Freddie Slack	

10/44 **Cow-Cow Boogie** ...
Ella Fitzgerald & Ink Spots

	Cowboy Serenade	
13/41	Kay Kyser	
15/41	Glenn Miller	

8/15 **Cows May Come, Cows May Go, But The Bull Goes On Forever** ...
Peerless Quartet

3/16 **Cradle Song 1915** ...
John McCormack

2/97 **Crappy Dan** ... Len Spencer

8/54 **Crazy 'Bout Ya Baby** ... Crew-Cuts

3/21 **Crazy Blues** ... Mamie Smith

20/52 **Crazy Heart** ... Guy Lombardo

	Crazy, Man, Crazy	
12/53	Bill Haley	
13/53	Ralph Marterie	

10/28 **Crazy Rhythm** ... Roger Wolfe Kahn

9/27 **Crazy Words-Crazy Tune** ...
Frank Crumit

	Creep, The	
22/54	Three Suns	
25/54	Ralph Marterie	
28/54	Stan Kenton	

4/02 **Creole Belles** ...
Metropolitan Orchestra

19/28 **Creole Love Call** ... Duke Ellington

	Creole Rhapsody	
18/31	Duke Ellington	
19/32	Duke Ellington	

2/23 **Crinoline Days** ... Paul Whiteman

7/21 **Crooning** ...
Benson Orchestra Of Chicago

22/50 **Crosby Christmas** ... Bing Crosby

2/54 **Cross Over The Bridge** ... Patti Page

7/36 **Cross Patch** ... Fats Waller

4/14 **'Cross The Great Divide (I'll Wait For You)** ... Haydn Quartet

	Cross Your Heart	
8/26	Roger Wolfe Kahn	
12/26	Vaughn Deleath & Ed Smalle	

9/40 **Crosstown** ... Glenn Miller

	Crucifix, The	
9/12	Enrico Caruso	
6/17	John McCormack & Reinald Werrenrath	

	Cruising Down The River	
1/49	Blue Barron	
1/49	Russ Morgan	
3/49	Jack Smith	
8/49	Frankie Carle	
24/49	Three Suns	
27/49	Primo Scala	
29/49	Ames Brothers	
29/49	Helen Carroll	

	Cry	
1/51	Johnnie Ray	
24/51	Georgia Gibbs	
10/52	Eileen Barton	
21/52	Four Knights	

	Cry, Baby, Cry	
1/38	Larry Clinton	
3/38	Kay Kyser	
9/38	Dick Robertson	

	Cry Of The Wild Goose	
1/50	Frankie Laine	
15/50	Tennessee Ernie Ford	

	Cryin' For The Carolines	
3/30	Fred Waring's Pennsylvanians	
6/30	Guy Lombardo	
13/30	Ben Bernie	
15/30	Ruth Etting	

23/44 **Cryin' The Boogie Blues** ...
Will Bradley

27/49 **Crying** ... Billy Eckstine

	Crying In The Chapel	
4/53	June Valli	
6/53	Darrell Glenn	
8/53	Rex Allen	
11/53	Orioles	
15/53	Ella Fitzgerald	
23/53	Art Lund	

28/54 **Crystal Ball** ... Johnston Brothers

	Cuanto La Gusta	
12/48	Andrews Sisters & Carmen Miranda	
14/48	Jack Smith	
29/48	Eve Young	
27/49	Xavier Cugat	

	Cuban Love Song	
7/31	Jacques Renard	
13/31	Paul Whiteman	
10/32	Ruth Etting	

Cuban Moon
3/20 Carl Fenton
6/20 Art Hickman
12/20 Joseph C. Smith's Orchestra

13/44 **Cuban Sugar Mill** ... Freddie Slack

Cubanola Glide
3/10 Arthur Collins & Byron Harlan
6/10 Billy Murray
10/10 Prince's Orchestra

5/39 **Cuckoo In The Clock** ... Kay Kyser

19/48 **Cuckoo Waltz** ... Ken Griffin

13/54 **Cuddle Me** ... Ronnie Gaylord

Cuddle Up A Little Closer, Lovey Mine
1/08 Ada Jones & Billy Murray
24/42 Dick Jurgens
19/43 Kay Armen

5/26 **Cup Of Coffee, A Sandwich, And You** ... Gertrude Lawrence & Jack Buchanan

6/09 **Cupid's Telephone** ... Frank Stanley

23/47 **Curiosity** ... Stan Kenton

Curse Of An Aching Heart
2/13 Will Oakland
9/13 Manuel Romain
4/36 Fats Waller

1/99 **Curse Of The Dreamer** ... Dan Quinn

Cut Yourself A Piece Of Cake
5/23 Ted Lewis
12/23 Billy Murray

15/46 **Cynthia's In Love** ... Tex Beneke

D

Daddy
1/41 Sammy Kaye
13/41 Joan Merrill
21/41 Frankie Masters

2/13 **Daddy Has A Sweetheart And Mother Is Her Name** ... Elsie Baker

1/92 **Daddy Wouldn't Buy Me A Bow-Wow** ... Dan Quinn

Daddy, You've Been A Mother To Me
9/20 Henry Burr
12/20 Lewis James

2/06 **Daddy's Little Girl** ... Byron G. Harlan

Daddy's Little Girl
5/50 Mills Brothers
11/50 Dick Todd

21/41 **Daddy's Lullaby** ... Lawrence Welk

27/48 **Dainty Brenda Lee** ... Eddy Howard

5/10 **Daisies Won't Tell** ... Arthur Clough

1/93 **Daisy Bell** ... Dan Quinn

7/31 **Dallas Blues** ... Ted Lewis

12/34 **Dames** ... Eddy Duchin

18/29 **Dance, Little Lady** ... Roger Wolfe Kahn

Dance Me Loose
6/52 Arthur Godfrey
30/52 Russ Morgan

14/20 **Dance-O-Mania** ... Ben Selvin

25/40 **Dance Of An Ear Of Corn** ... Fabian Andre

27/52 **Dance Of Destiny** ... Tony Martin

9/11 **Dance Of The Grizzly Bear** ... American Quartet

Dance Of The Hours
9/05 Arthur Pryor's Band
10/14 Victor Herbert
13/49 Spike Jones

Dance With A Dolly (With A Hole In Her Stocking)
3/44 Russ Morgan
6/44 Evelyn Knight
9/44 Tony Pastor

17/53 **Dancin' With Someone (Longin' For You)** ... Teresa Brewer

15/35 **Dancing Dogs** ... Mills Blue Rhythm Band

8/22 **Dancing Fool** ... Club Royal Orchestra

2/97 **Dancing In The Dark** ... Sousa's Band

Dancing In The Dark
3/31 Bing Crosby
3/31 Fred Waring's Pennsylvanians
10/31 Ben Selvin
20/31 Jacques Renard
9/41 Artie Shaw
25/44 Artie Shaw

12/34 **Dancing In The Moonlight** ... Rudy Vallee

10/32 **Dancing On The Ceiling** ... Jack Hylton

Dancing Tambourine
18/27 Radiolites
6/28 Paul Whiteman

18/27 **Dancing The Devil Away** ... Don Voorhees

9/35 **Dancing With My Shadow** ... Henry King

Dancing With Tears In My Eyes
1/30 Nat Shilkret
2/30 Regent Club Orchestra
5/30 Ben Selvin
10/30 Ruth Etting
26/52 Mantovani

6/21 **Dangerous Blues** ... Mamie Smith

Danny Boy
5/18 Ernestine Schumann-Heink
17/40 Glenn Miller

5/22 **Dapper Dan** ... Frank Crumit

Dardanella

1/20	Ben Selvin
5/20	Prince's Orchestra
9/20	Harry Raderman's Jazz Orchestra
12/20	Henry Burr & Albert Campbell

Dardanella Blues

9/20	Billy Murray
9/20	Ed Smalle

25/53 **Dare I?** ... Hamish Menzies

Dark Eyes

11/37	Tommy Dorsey
14/39	Vincent Lopez

Darkness On The Delta ...
see: (When It's)

Darktown Poker Club

3/14	Bert Williams
10/46	Phil Harris
27/47	Phil Harris

Darktown Strutters' Ball

2/17	Original Dixieland Jazz Band
10/17	(Six) Brown Brothers
1/18	Arthur Collins & Byron Harlan
9/18	Jaudas' Society Orchestra
12/27	Ted Lewis
29/48	Alan Dale & Connie Haines
7/54	Lou Monte

2/21 **Darling** ... Art Hickman

26/41 **Darling, How You Lied** ...
Wayne King

21/43 **Darling, Je Vous Aime Beaucoup** ...
Hildegarde

19/37 **Darling Nelly Gray** ...
Louis Armstrong & Mills Brothers

Darn That Dream

1/40	Benny Goodman
14/40	Blue Barron
16/40	Tommy Dorsey

Dat New Bully ... see: Bully

3/18 **Daughter of Rosie O'Grady** ...
Lewis James

16/28 **Dawn** ... Nat Shilkret

17/39 **Dawn Of A New Day** ... Hoarce Heidt

13/39 **Dawn On The Desert** ...
Tommy Dorsey

4/38 **Day After Day** ... Richard Himber

15/44 **Day After Forever** ... Bing Crosby

Day By Day

5/46	Frank Sinatra
8/46	Jo Stafford
15/46	Les Brown
15/46	Bing Crosby & Mel Torme

8/38 **Day Dreaming** ... Rudy Vallee

Day Dreams, Visions Of Bliss

7/11	Henry Burr & Elise Stevenson
7/12	Christie MacDonald & Lyric Quartet

Day In-Day Out

1/39	Bob Crosby
11/39	Kay Kyser
11/39	Artie Shaw

26/52 **Day Of Jubilo** ... Guy Mitchell

3/05 **Day That You Grew Colder** ...
Richard Jose

3/33 **Day You Came Along** ... Bing Crosby

Daybreak

10/42	Tommy Dorsey
17/42	Harry James
18/42	Jimmy Dorsey

3/02 **Daybreak At Calamity Farm** ...
Len Spencer

20/34 **Daybreak Express** ... Duke Ellington

10/24 **Days Of Yesterday** ... Elliott Shaw

22/51 **Deadly Weapon** ... Eddy Howard

7/11 **Dear, Delightful Women** ...
Reinald Werrenrath

Dear Heart

8/10	Elise Stevenson
6/19	John Steel

Dear Hearts And Gentle People

19/49	Gordon MacRae
2/50	Bing Crosby
2/50	Dinah Shore
14/50	Dennis Day
19/50	Benny Strong
24/50	Ralph Flanagan

21/42 **Dear Home In Holland** ...
Lawrence Welk

Dear John Letter

4/53	Jean Shepard
17/53	Pat O'Day & The Four Horsemen

23/54 **Dear John and Marsha Letter** ...
Stan Freberg

Dear Little Boy Of Mine

6/18	Charles Harrison
7/19	Will Oakland

10/14 **Dear Love Days** ...
Henry Burr, Albert Campbell & Will
Oakland

Dear Mom

21/42	Sammy Kaye
22/42	Orrin Tucker

25/53 **Dear Mr. Godfrey** ... Ruth Wallis

7/16 **Dear Old Dreamy Honolulu Town** ...
Peerless Quartet

Dear Old Girl

2/03	J.W. Myers
2/04	Haydn Quartet

15/38 **Dear Old Girl (Medley)** ...
Frank Novak

8/19 **Dear Old Pal Of Mine** ...
Sascha Jacobsen

Dear Old Southland

7/22	Paul Whiteman
12/22	Vernon Dalhart

**Dearest (You're The Nearest To My
Heart)**

4/23	Paul Whiteman
7/23	Nora Bayes

Don't Be A Baby, Baby
11/46   Benny Goodman
12/46   Mills Brothers

23/49   **Don't Be Afraid To Dream ...**
Dottie Reid

11/35   **Don't Be Afraid To Tell Your Mother ...** Jimmie Grier

16/27   **Don't Be Angry With Me ...**
Jean Goldkette

16/29   **Don't Be Like That ...** Helen Kane

Don't Be That Way
20/35   Chick Webb
1/38   Benny Goodman
9/38   Mildred Bailey

14/44   **Don't Believe Everything You Dream ...** Ink Spots

2/14   **Don't Blame It All On Broadway ...**
Peerless Quartet

Don't Blame Me
6/33   Ethel Waters
9/33   Guy Lombardo
13/33   Charles Agnew
21/48   Nat "King" Cole

Don't Bring Lulu
5/25   Ernest Hare & Billy Jones
5/25   Billy Murray

23/48   **Don't Call It Love ...** Freddy Martin

27/53   **Don't Call My Name ...** Helene Dixon

14/38   **Don't Cross Your Fingers, Cross Your Heart ...** Kay Kyser

11/43   **Don't Cry, Baby ...** Erskine Hawkins

Don't Cry, Joe (Let Her Go, Let Her Go, Let Her Go)
3/49   Gordon Jenkins
9/49   Ralph Flanagan
9/49   Frank Sinatra
22/49   Johnny Desmond
22/49   Juanita Hall

8/19   **Don't Cry, Little Girl, Don't Cry ...**
Henry Burr

21/42   **Don't Cry, Sweetheart ...**
Russ Morgan

14/33   **Don't Do Anything I Wouldn't Do ...**
Eddy Duchin

20/43   **Don't Do It, Darling ...** Glen Gray

Don't Fence Me In
1/44   Bing Crosby & Andrews Sisters
4/45   Sammy Kaye
8/45   Kate Smith
10/45   Hoarce Heidt

24/53   **Don't Forget To Write ...** June Valli

9/45   **Don't Forget Tonight Tomorrow ...**
Frank Sinatra

Don't Get Around Much Anymore
2/43   Ink Spots
7/43   Glen Gray
8/43   Duke Ellington

9/35   **Don't Give Up The Ship ...**
Tommy Dorsey

15/52   **Don't Leave My Poor Heart Breaking ...** Cowboy Copas

Don't Let It Bother You
10/34   Fats Waller
11/34   Leo Reisman

19/38   **Don't Let That Moon Get Away ...**
Bing Crosby

Don't Let The Stars Get In Your Eyes
25/52   Red Foley
1/53   Perry Como
11/53   Gisele MacKenzie
24/53   Eileen Barton

23/53   **Don't Let Your Eyes Go Shopping (For Your Heart) ...** Nat "King" Cole

8/24   **Don't Mind The Rain ...**
Blossom Seeley

23/49   **Don't Rob Another Man's Castle ...**
Eddy Arnold

29/53   **Don't Say Goodbye ...** Buddy Greco

Don't Sit Under The Apple Tree (With Anyone Else But Me)
1/42   Glenn Miller
16/42   Andrews Sisters

22/48   **Don't Smoke In Bed ...** Peggy Lee

2/44   **Don't Sweetheart Me ...**
Lawrence Welk

Don't Take Me Home
4/08   Eddie Morton
8/08   Bob Roberts

Don't Take My Darling Boy Away
2/15   Peerless Quartet
9/15   Helen Clark & Joseph Phillips

Don't Take Your Love From Me
26/44   Glen Gray
21/53   Three Suns

27/48   **Don't Telephone, Don't Telegraph, Tell A Woman ...** Tex Williams

21/42   **Don't Tell A Lie About Me, Dear ...**
Woody Herman

6/30   **Don't Tell Her What Happened To Me ...** Ruth Etting

9/38   **(Don't Wait Till) The Night Before Christmas ...** Eddy Duchin

3/11   **Don't Wake Me Up, I'm Dreaming ...**
Walter Van Brunt

Don't Wake Me Up (Let Me Dream)
9/25   Vincent Lopez
10/26   Howard Lanin

Don't Worry 'Bout Me
5/39   Hal Kemp
17/54   Frank Sinatra

Don't You Love Me Anymore?
22/47   Buddy Clark
23/47   Freddy Martin
26/47   Jose Mellis

15/38   **Don't You Make Me High ...**
Blu Lu Barker

Don't You Remember Me?
16/34	Henry King
21/46	Johnny Desmond

8/38 **Donkey Serenade** ... Allan Jones

21/49 **Doo De Doo On An Old Kazoo** ...
Art Mooney

Doodle-Doo-Doo
5/25	Eddie Cantor
14/39	Tiny Hill

12/52 **Doodletown Fifers** ...
Sauter-Finegan Orchestra

15/45 **Door Will Open** ... Tommy Dorsey

4/08 **Dorn Sebastian - In Terra Solo (On Earth Alone)** ... Enrico Caruso

12/35 **Double Trouble** ... Ray Noble

Down Among The Sheltering Palms
3/15	Lyric Quartet
14/49	Sammy Kaye

2/09 **Down Among The Sugar Cane** ...
Arthur Collins & Byron Harlan

Down Argentina Way
7/40	Leo Reisman
15/40	Eddy Duchin
15/40	Gene Krupa
18/40	Shep Fields
2/41	Bob Crosby

7/09 **Down At The Huskin' Bee** ...
Arthur Collins & Byron Harlan

Down By The O-HI-O
2/21	Billy Murray & Billy Jones
21/40	Andrews Sisters
29/40	Smoothies

Down By The Old Mill Stream
1/11	Arthur Clough
1/12	Harry Macdonough

Down By The River
14/35	Guy Lombardo
17/35	Bing Crosby

17/53 **Down By The Riverside** ...
Four Lads

28/54 Bing Crosby & Gary Crosby

Down By The Station
11/49	Tommy Dorsey
20/49	Guy Lombardo

Down-Hearted Blues
1/23	Bessie Smith
13/23	Noble Sissle & Eubie Blake

5/21 **Down Home Blues** ... Ethel Waters

10/24 **Down Home Blues** ...
Fred Waring's Pennsylvanians

4/14 **Down In Chattanooga** ...
Arthur Collins & Byron Harlan

5/08 **Down In Dear Old New Orleans** ...
Arthur Collins & Byron Harlan

4/08 **Down In Jungle Town** ...
Arthur Collins & Byron Harlan

1/96 **Down In Poverty Row** ...
George J. Gaskin

Down In Sunshine Valley
4/10	Billy Murray & Haydn Quartet
8/12	Henry Burr & Albert Campbell

20/44 **Down In The Valley** ...
Andrews Sisters

7/07 **Down On The Farm** ...
Len Spencer & Ada Jones

8/33 **Down The Old Ox Road** ...
Bing Crosby

10/30 **Down The River Of Golden Dreams** ...
Hilo Hawaiian Orchestra

10/40 **Down The Road A Piece** ...
Will Bradley

17/51 **Down The Trail Of Achin' Hearts** ...
Patti Page

6/10 **Down Where The Big Bananas Grow** ...
Arthur Collins & Byron Harlan

Down Where The Silv'ry Mohawk Flows
4/05	Haydn Quartet
7/05	Harry Anthony

14/24 **Down Where The South Begins** ...
Van & Schenck

16/28 **Down Where The Sun Goes Down** ...
Coon-Sanders Orchestra

3/16 **Down Where The Swanee River Flows** ... Al Jolson

Down Where The Wurzburger Flows
1/03	Arthur Collins & Byron Harlan
4/03	Arthur Collins

Down Yonder
5/21	Ernest Hare & Billy Jones
9/21	Peerless Quartet
10/34	Gid Tanner
4/51	Del Wood
14/51	Joe "Fingers" Carr
15/51	Freddy Martin
16/51	Ethel Smith
17/51	Champ Butler
22/51	Lawrence (Piano Roll) Cook
26/51	Frank Petty Trio

5/53 **Downhearted** ... Eddie Fisher

Dr. Jekyll And Mr. Hyde ...
see: Transformation Scene From

2/53 **Dragnet** ... Ray Anthony

Dream
1/45	Pied Pipers
5/45	Frank Sinatra
9/45	Freddy Martin
15/45	Jimmy Dorsey
17/54	Four Aces

13/21 **Dream, A** ... Enrico Caruso

Dream A Little Dream Of Me
1/31	Wayne King
14/50	Jack Owens
18/50	Frankie Laine

21/48 **Dream Again** ... Sammy Kaye

Dream Awhile
15/36	Eddy Duchin
28/50	Frank DeVol

10/24 **Dream Daddy** ... Carl Fenton

25/54	**Dream, Dream, Dream** ... Percy Faith
	Dream House
14/28	Nat Shilkret
19/29	Seger Ellis
11/28	**Dream Kisses** ... Ipana Troubadors
12/29	**Dream Mother** ... Gene Austin
3/97	**Dream Of Passion Waltz** ... Edward Issler
14/29	**Dream Train** ... Abe Lyman
	Dream Valley
17/40	Eddy Duchin
1/41	Sammy Kaye
5/08	**Dream Waltz** ... Victor Orchestra
7/44	**Dreamer, The** ... Kay Armen
	Dreamer's Holiday
12/49	Buddy Clark
26/49	Gordon Jenkins
3/50	Perry Como
11/50	Ray Anthony
	Dreaming
4/07	Albert Campbell
6/07	Harry Macdonough
	Dreaming Of Home, Sweet Home
3/19	Charles Harrison
9/19	Sterling Trio
24/40	**Dreaming Out Loud** ... Benny Goodman
22/47	**Dreams Are A Dime A Dozen** ... Vaughn Monroe
9/23	**Dreams Of India** ... Benson Orchestra Of Chicago
	Dreams Of Long Ago
2/12	Enrico Caruso
5/21	Enrico Caruso
25/48	**Dreamy Lullaby** ... Frankie Carle
1/23	**Dreamy Melody** ... Art Landry
3/26	**Drifting And Dreaming (Sweet Paradise)** ... George Olsen
5/24	**Driftwood** ... Paul Whiteman
1/91	**Drill, Ye Terriers, Drill** ... George J. Gaskin
21/54	**Drink, Drink, Drink** ... Mario Lanza
	Drink To Me Only With Thine Eyes
6/07	Emilio DeGogorza
6/11	John McCormack
26/49	**Drinking Wine, Spo-Dee-O-Dee, Drinking Wine** ... "Stick" McGhee
17/33	**Drop Me Off At Harlem** ... Duke Ellington
26/41	**Drum Boogie** ... Gene Krupa
24/40	**Drummer Boy** ... Gene Krupa
16/32	**Drums In My Heart** ... Leo Reisman
6/34	**Drunkard Song (There Is A Tavern In The Town)** ... Rudy Vallee
9/11	**Dublin Rag** ... Ada Jones
21/47	**Dum-Dot Song** ... Frank Sinatra

30/53	**Dummy Song** ... Louis Armstrong
	Dusky Stevedore
10/28	Nat Shilkret
17/28	Frankie Trumbauer
4/34	**Dust On The Moon** ... Eddy Duchin

E

	Eadie Was A Lady
8/33	Ethel Merman
17/33	Paul Whiteman
9/14	**Eagle Rock** ... Arthur Collins & Byron Harlan
11/35	**Earful Of Music** ... Ethel Merman
	Early Autumn
22/47	Claude Thornhill
23/52	Jo Stafford
28/52	Woody Herman
18/43	**East Of The Rockies** ... Andrews Sisters
1/35	**East Of The Sun (And West Of The Moon)** ... Tom Coakley
6/39	**East Side Of Heaven** ... Bing Crosby
	East Side, West Side
28/54	Alan Dale
28/54	Johnny Desmond
28/54	Buddy Greco
10/27	**East St. Louis Toodle-oo** ... Duke Ellington *(also see: New East St. Louis)*
	Easter Parade
5/33	Leo Reisman & Clifton Webb
11/39	Guy Lombardo
11/42	Harry James
23/46	Harry James
21/47	Guy Lombardo
22/47	Bing Crosby
22/48	Bing Crosby
26/54	Liberace
4/34	**Easy Come, Easy Go** ... Eddy Duchin
	Easy Does It
27/40	Bobby Byrne
28/40	Count Basie
15/37	**Easy Living** ... Teddy Wilson featuring Billie Holiday
	Easy To Love
13/36	Shep Fields
20/36	Frances Langford
7/37	Ray Noble
	Ebb Tide
5/37	Bunny Berigan
15/37	Claude Thornhill
	Ebb Tide
2/53	Frank Chacksfield
10/53	Vic Damone
30/54	Roy Hamilton

17/35 **Every Single Little Tingle Of My Heart** ... Dorsey Brothers Orchestra

5/16 **Everybody** ... Bert Williams

7/20 **Everybody Calls Me Honey** ...
Nora Bayes

11/46 **Everybody Knew But Me** ...
Woody Herman

Everybody Loves My Baby
5/25 Aileen Stanley
10/25 Clarence Williams' Blue Five

25/48 **Everybody Loves Somebody** ...
Frank Sinatra

8/15 **Everybody Rag With Me** ...
George O'Connor

Everybody Step
3/22 Ted Lewis
11/22 Paul Whiteman

1/12 **Everybody Two-Step** ...
American Quartet

2/19 **Everybody Wants A Key To My Cellar** ... Bert Williams

Everybody Works But Father
4/05 Lew Dockstader
4/05 Bob Roberts
1/06 Billy Murray

Everybody's Crazy 'Bout The Doggone Blues (But I'm Happy)
3/18 Marion Harris
5/18 Wilbur Sweatman's Original Jazz Band

6/12 **Everybody's Doin' It Two-Step Medley** ... Arthur Pryor's Band

Everybody's Doing It Now
2/12 Arthur Collins & Byron Harlan
6/12 Peerless Quartet

10/32 **Everyone Says "I Love You"** ...
Isham Jones

9/41 **Everything Happens To Me** ...
Tommy Dorsey

Everything I Have Is Yours
17/33 George Olsen
3/34 Rudy Vallee
30/48 Billy Eckstine
23/52 Eddie Fisher

9/25 **Everything Is Hotsy Totsy Now** ...
Gene Austin

Everything Is Peaches Down In Georgia
4/18 Prince's Orchestra
5/18 American Quartet

4/99 **Everything Is Rag-Time Now** ...
Len Spencer

18/37 **Everything You Said Came True** ...
Wingy Manone

Everything's Been Done Before
8/35 Freddy Martin
13/35 Guy Lombardo

14/26 **Everything's Gonna Be All Right** ...
Ipana Troubadors

21/47 **Everything's Movin' Too Fast** ...
Peggy Lee

15/45 **Everytime** ... Freddy Martin

Everywhere You Go
19/49 Guy Lombardo
22/49 Doris Day

Exactly Like You
11/30 Ruth Etting
12/30 Harry Richman
19/30 Sam Lanin
12/36 Benny Goodman
14/37 Don Redman

10/05 **Excelsior** ...
Harry Anthony & James Harrison

23/53 **Eyes Of Blue** ... Richard Hayman

F

F'r ... *see: For*

F.D.R. Jones
8/39 Ella Fitzgerald with Chick Webb
14/39 Cab Calloway

20/40 **Fable Of The Rose** ...
Benny Goodman

Face The Music ... *see: Medley From*

30/54 **Face To Face** ... Gordon MacRae

9/16 **Face To Face With The Girl Of My Dreams** ... Glen Ellison

3/23 **Faded Love Letters** ... Henry Burr

Faded Summer Love
4/31 Paul Whiteman
8/31 Bing Crosby

19/34 **Fair And Warmer** ... Dick Powell

5/16 **Fair Hawaii** ...
Elsie Baker & Reed Miller

9/21 **Fair One** ... Ted Lewis

9/09 **Fairest Of The Fair March** ...
Sousa's Band

30/50 **Fairy Tales** ... Paul Weston

24/52 **Faith Can Move Mountains** ...
Nat "King" Cole

4/40 **Faithful Forever** ... Glenn Miller

18/39 **Falling In Love With Love** ...
Frances Langford

9/40 **Falling Leaves** ... Glenn Miller

24/53 **False Love** ... Four Aces

20/31 **Fan It** ... Red Nichols

20/36 **Fancy Meeting You (The Evolution Song)** ... Russ Morgan

28/54 **Fancy Pants** ... Floyd Cramer

7/18 **Fancy You Fancying Me** ...
Lewis James

4/11	**For You Alone** ... Enrico Caruso	
19/47	**For You, For Me, Forevermore** ...	
	Judy Garland & Dick Haymes	
4/18	**For Your Boy And My Boy** ...	
	Peerless Quartet	
	For Your Country And My Country	
5/17	Peerless Quartet	
9/17	Frances Alda	
	Forever And Ever	
1/49	Russ Morgan	
2/49	Perry Como	
5/49	Margaret Whiting	
12/49	Dinah Shore	
23/49	Gracie Fields	
6/19	**Forever Is A Long, Long Time** ...	
	Charles Hart	
30/48	**Forever Is Ending Today** ...	
	Ernest Tubb	
10/24	**Forget-Me-Not (Means Remember Me)** ... Benson Orchestra Of Chicago	
18/28	**Forgetting You** ... Kitty O'Connor	
	Forgetting You	
15/52	Richard Hayes	
23/52	Bill Kenny	
	Forgive Me	
1/27	Gene Austin	
7/52	Eddie Fisher	
24/53	**Forgive Me, John** ...	
	Jean Shepard with Ferlin Husky	
17/54	**Fortune In Dreams** ... Kay Starr	
4/02	**Fortune Telling Man** ...	
	Bert Williams	
26/53	**40 Cups Of Coffee** ... Ella Mae Morse	
3/06	**Forty-Five Minutes From Broadway** ...	
	Billy Murray	
	Forty-Second Street	
1/33	Don Bestor	
7/33	Hal Kemp	
	Forza Del Destino ... *see: La Forza*	
	Four Or Five Times	
17/28	King Oliver	
14/43	Woody Herman	
	Four Winds And The Seven Seas	
3/49	Sammy Kaye	
10/49	Mel Torme	
16/49	Vic Damone	
18/49	Herb Jeffries	
19/49	Guy Lombardo	
10/14	**Fourth Of July At Pumpkin Center** ...	
	Cal Stewart	
24/53	**Fractured** ... Bill Haley	
7/16	**Frank Tinney's First Record** ...	
	Frank Tinney	
	Frankie And Johnny	
9/27	Ted Lewis	
18/27	Frank Crumit	
21/42	Guy Lombardo	
8/34	**Freckle Face, You're Beautiful** ...	
	Ben Pollack	

7/47	**Free Eats** ... Count Basie
13/37	**Free Wheeling** ... Artie Shaw
21/47	**Freedom Train** ...
	Bing Crosby & Andrews Sisters
	Frenesi
1/40	Artie Shaw
16/41	Woody Herman
16/41	Glenn Miller
8/26	**Freshie** ...
	Fred Waring's Pennsylvanians
9/45	**Friend Of Yours** ... Tommy Dorsey
	Friendly Tavern Polka
8/41	Hoarce Heidt
24/44	Hoarce Heidt
5/19	**Friends** ... Sterling Trio
30/54	**Friends And Neighbors** ...
	Tommy Prisco
11/40	**Friendship** ... Kay Kyser
19/46	**Frim Fram Sauce** ... Nat "King" Cole
7/06	**Fritz And Louisa** ...
	Len Spencer & Ada Jones
14/40	**From Another World** ...
	Charlie Barnet
15/53	**From Here To Eternity** ...
	Frank Sinatra
	From Here To Shanghai
4/17	Al Jolson
7/17	Gene Greene & Peerless Quartet
14/28	**From Monday On** ... Paul Whiteman
	From Now On
12/34	Isham Jones
8/38	Eddy Duchin
	From The Land Of The Sky-Blue Water
10/11	Alma Gluck
10/15	Alice Nielsen
10/35	**From The Top Of Your Head** ...
	Bing Crosby
	From The Vine Came The Grape
7/54	Gaylords
8/54	Hilltoppers
18/46	**From This Day Forward** ...
	Frank Sinatra
21/43	**From Twilight 'Til Dawn** ...
	Freddy Martin
6/08	**From Your Dear Heart To Mine** ...
	Frank Stanley
	Frosty The Snowman
7/51	Gene Autry
9/51	Nat "King" Cole
28/51	Guy Lombardo
23/52	Gene Autry
11/43	**Fuddy Duddy Watchmaker** ...
	Kay Kyser
	Full Moon
19/42	Jimmy Dorsey
22/42	Benny Goodman

500

20/37	**Girl On The Police Gazette** ... Russ Morgan	3/16	**Go To Sleep, My Dusky Baby** ... Olive Kline, Elsie Baker & Marguerite Dunlap
	Girl That I Marry	20/43	**Gobs Of Love** ... King Sisters
11/46	Frank Sinatra		
23/47	Eddy Howard	3/18	**God Be With Our Boys Tonight** ... John McCormack
7/10	**Girl With A Brogue** ... Ada Jones		**God Bless America**
5/04	**Girl You Love** ... Harry Macdonough	10/39	Kate Smith
5/20	**Girls Of My Dreams** ... John Steel	17/39	Bing Crosby
16/40	**Give A Little Whistle** ... Cliff Edwards	5/40	Kate Smith
		23/42	Kate Smith
12/34	**Give Me A Heart To Sing To** ... Bing Crosby	25/41	**God Bless The Child** ... Billie Holiday
	Give Me A Night In June	18/53	**God Bless Us All** ... Brucie Weil
8/27	Ipana Troubadors		**God's Country**
18/28	Johnny Marvin	25/50	Frank Sinatra
	Give Me All Of You	27/50	Vic Damone
5/17	Nanette Flack	17/50	**Gods Were Angry With Me** ... Margaret Whiting & Jimmy Wakely
5/17	Charles Harrison		
	Give Me Five Minutes More ... see: Five Minutes More	30/52	**Goin' Home** ... Fats Domino
		21/53	**Goin' Steady** ... Betty Hutton
2/22	**Give Me My Mammy** ... Al Jolson	25/41	**Goin' To Chicago Blues** ... Count Basie
24/48	**Give Me The Good Old Days** ... Benny Goodman	24/53	**Goin' To The River** ... Fats Domino
12/46	**Give Me The Moon Over Brooklyn** ... Guy Lombardo	7/33	**Going, Going, Gone!** ... Guy Lombardo
10/18	**Give Me The Moonlight, Give Me The Girl (And Leave The Rest To Me)** ... Sam Ash	15/44	**Going My Way** ... Bing Crosby
		16/38	**Going To Shout All Over God's Heaven** ... Louis Armstrong
	Give Me The Simple Life		**Gold Digger's Song (We're In The Money)**
13/46	Benny Goodman		
16/46	Bing Crosby with Jimmy Dorsey	5/33	Ted Lewis
10/31	**Give Me Your Affection, Honey** ... Abe Lyman	16/33	Hal Kemp
		18/33	Dick Powell
23/49	**Give Me Your Hand** ... Perry Como		**Golden Earrings**
	Give My Regards To Broadway	25/47	Dinah Shore
1/05	Billy Murray	2/48	Peggy Lee
4/05	S.H. Dudley		**Golden Gate**
	Glad Rag Doll	8/19	Charles Hart
10/29	Ted Lewis	4/20	Charles Harrison & Lewis James
17/29	Ruth Etting	9/28	**Golden Gate** ... Al Jolson
4/36	**Gloomy Sunday** ... Hal Kemp	4/06	**Golden Wedding** ... Len Spencer & Ada Jones
17/48	**Gloria** ... Mills Brothers		
1/36	**Glory Of Love** ... Benny Goodman	23/41	**Golden Wedding** ... Woody Herman
	Glow-Worm		**Gomen Nasai (Forgive Me)**
1/08	Lucy Isabelle Marsh	15/53	Richard Bowers
1/08	Victor Orchestra	17/53	Eddy Howard
1/52	Mills Brothers	19/53	Harry Belafonte
30/52	Johnny Mercer	13/37	**Gone** ... Guy Lombardo
10/39	**Go Fly A Kite** ... Bing Crosby	29/48	**Gone** ... Sonny Thompson
23/51	**Go! Go! Go! Go** ... Richard Hayes	30/53	**Gone** ... Bobby Wayne
	Go Home And Tell Your Mother	19/51	**Gone Fishin'** ... Bing Crosby & Louis Armstrong
3/30	Gus Arnheim		
8/30	Guy Lombardo		**Gone With The Wind**
20/35	**Go Into Your Dance** ... Johnny Green	1/37	Hoarce Heidt
		16/37	Guy Lombardo
8/50	**Go To Sleep, Go To Sleep, Go To Sleep** ... Mary Martin & Arthur Godfrey	19/37	Claude Thornhill

18/43 **Goodbye, Sue** ... Perry Como	17/42 **Got The Moon In My Pocket** ...
5/13 **Good-By Summer! So Long Fall! Hello,**	Kay Kyser
Winter Time! ... Peerless Quartet	**Gotta Be This Or That**
Goodbye, Sweetheart, Goodbye	2/45 Benny Goodman
3/06 Frank Stanley	6/45 Sammy Kaye
5/08 Alan Turner	9/45 Glen Gray
2/38 **Goodnight, Angel** ... Artie Shaw	**(Gotta Get Some) Shut-Eye**
23/42 **Goodnight, Captain Curly-Head** ...	6/39 Kay Kyser
Dinah Shore	16/39 Glen Gray
Goodnight Irene	10/25 **Gotta Getta Girl** ... Isham Jones
5/50 Frank Sinatra	8/26 **Governor's Pardon** ...
17/50 Dennis Day	Vernon Dalhart
26/50 Alexander Brothers	**Grand Canyon Suite** ...
Goodnight, Irene	see: *On The Trail*
1/50 Weavers with Gordon Jenkins	**Grand Old Rag** ...
9/50 Jo Stafford	see: *You're A Grand Old Flag*
10/50 Red Foley	**Grandfather's Clock**
10/50 Ernest Tubb	5/05 Haydn Quartet
7/34 **Goodnight, Lovely Little Lady** ...	15/38 Gene Krupa
Benny Krueger	17/27 **Grandpa's Spells** ...
12/32 **Goodnight, Moon** ... Ben Selvin	Jelly Roll Morton
Goodnight, Mother	18/37 **Great Caesar's Ghost** ...
24/40 Dick Todd	Fletcher Henderson
25/40 Dick Jurgens	1/29 **Great Day** ... Paul Whiteman
18/39 **Goodnight, My Beautiful** ...	13/38 **Great Speckle Bird** ... Roy Acuff
Tommy Dorsey	23/41 **Greechee Joe** ... Cab Calloway
Goodnight, My Love	**Green Eyes**
14/32 Art Kassel	1/41 Jimmy Dorsey
1/37 Benny Goodman	16/41 Xavier Cugat
9/37 Shep Fields	21/41 Tony Pastor
10/37 Hal Kemp	8/54 **Green Years** ... Eddie Fisher
1/31 **Goodnight, Sweetheart** ...	8/35 **Greener The Grass** ...
Guy Lombardo	Reginald Foresythe
Goodnight, Sweetheart, Goodnight	25/52 **Greensleeves** ... Mantovani
7/54 McGuire Sisters	**Grenada**
24/54 Spaniels	17/54 Frankie Laine
26/54 Sunny Gale	24/54 Clark Dennis
Goody Goodbye	19/52 **Greyhound** ... Buddy Morrow
9/39 Dolly Dawn	21/42 **Grieg Piano Concerto** ...
15/40 Ted Weems	Freddy Martin
Goody-Goody	**Grieving For You**
1/36 Benny Goodman	7/21 Marion Harris
5/36 Freddy Martin	11/49 Tony Pastor
7/36 Bob Crosby	3/21 **Grieving For You - Feather Your**
Goofus	**Nest** ... Paul Whiteman
10/31 Wayne King	**Grizzly Bear**
5/32 Dan Russo	4/11 American Quartet
15/32 Red Nichols	6/11 Arthur Collins
16/32 Wayne King	16/45 **Guess I'll Hang My Tears Out To**
21/50 Les Paul	**Dry** ... Harry James
5/37 **Goona Goo** ... Clyde McCoy	**Guilty**
20/37 **Goose Hangs High** ... Louis Prima	4/31 Ruth Etting
Got A Date With An Angel	11/31 Wayne King
13/32 Debroy Somers Band	13/31 Russ Columbo
16/34 Hal Kemp	4/47 Margaret Whiting
12/46 **Got A Right To Cry** ... Joe Liggins	11/47 Ella Fitzgerald
14/31 **Got The Bench, Got The Park** ...	12/47 Johnny Desmond
Noble Sissle	25/48 **Guitar Boogie** ... Arthur Smith
9/34 **Got The Jitters** ... Ben Pollack	

H

Hard-Hearted Hannah
3/24 Dolly Kay
13/24 Belle Baker
13/24 Cliff Edwards

Hark! The Herald Angels Sing
4/12 Trinity Choir
5/16 Columbia Mixed Quartet

16/38 **Hark The Sound Of Tar Heel Voices** ...
Kay Kyser

19/35 **Harlem Heat** ...
Mills Blue Rhythm Band

24/53 **Harlem Nocturne** ... Herbie Fields

12/47 **Harmony** ...
Johnny Mercer & King Cole Trio

15/38 **Harmony In Harlem** ...
Duke Ellington

1/03 **Harrah For Baffin's Bay** ...
Arthur Collins & Byron Harlan

Harrigan
1/07 Billy Murray
8/07 Edward Meeker

Has Anybody Here Seen Kelly?
2/10 Nora Bayes
4/10 Ada Jones

3/09 **Hat My Father Wore On St. Patrick's Day** ... Billy Murray & Haydn Quartet

10/19 **Hatikva (Our Hope)** ... Alma Gluck

Haunted Heart
20/48 Perry Como
23/48 Jo Stafford

10/23 **Haunting Blues** ... Jan Garber

14/35 **Haunting Me** ... Eddy Duchin

4/17 **Havanola Fox-Trot** ...
Joseph C. Smith's Orchestra

16/52 **Have A Good Time** ... Tony Bennett

3/16 **Have A Heart** ...
Olive Kline & Lambert Murphy

9/16 **Have A Heart - "Ziegfeld Follies Of 1915" Medley** ... Conway's Band

3/30 **Have A Little Faith In Me** ...
Guy Lombardo

Have I Stayed Away Too Long?
19/44 Perry Como
28/44 Tex Grande

24/50 **Have I Told You Lately That I Love You?** ... Bing Crosby & Andrews Sisters

19/41 **Have You Changed?** ... Gene Krupa

8/33 **Have You Ever Been Lonely?** ...
Ted Lewis

(Have You Forgotten) ...
see: You And Me That Used To Be

5/38 **Have You Forgotten So Soon?** ...
Red Norvo

Have You Got Any Castles, Baby?
2/37 Tommy Dorsey
8/37 Dolly Dawn
11/37 Gus Arnheim

4/53 **Have You Heard** ... Joni James

27/44 **Have Yourself A Merry Little Christmas** ... Judy Garland

6/17 **Hawaii And You** ...
James F. Harrison & James Reed

Hawaiian Butterfly
4/17 Sterling Trio
6/17 Charles King & Elizabeth Brice

15/21 **Hawaiian Medley** ... Frank Ferera

Hawaiian War Chant (Ta-Hu-Wa-Hu-Wai)
8/46 Spike Jones
21/51 Ames Brothers

20/37 **He Ain't Got Rhythm** ...
Benny Goodman

9/15 **He Comes Up Smiling** ...
Arthur Fields

2/07 **He Goes To Church On Sunday** ...
Billy Murray

9/23 **He Loves It** ... Eddie Cantor

21/53 **He Loves Me** ... Jenny Barrett

He Treats Your Daughter Mean ...
see: (Mama)

7/09 **He Was Very Kind To Me** ...
Harry Lauder

He Wears A Pair Of Silver Wings
1/42 Kay Kyser
16/42 Dinah Shore

10/20 **He Went In Like A Lion And Came Out Like A Lamb** ... Billy Murray

16/53 **He Who Has Love** ... Four Lads

2/14 **He'd Have To Get Under - Get Out And Get Under (To Fix Up His Automobile)** ... Billy Murray

He's A College Boy
4/10 American Quartet
4/10 Paul Southe

He's A Cousin Of Mine
1/07 Bert Williams
7/07 Bob Roberts

He's A Devil In His Own Home Town
2/14 Billy Murray
8/14 Eddie Morton

3/15 **He's A Rag Picker** ...
Peerless Quartet

15/47 **He's A Real Gone Guy** ...
Nellie Lutcher & Her Rhythm

He's Funny That Way ...
see: She's Funny That Way

2/16 **He's Got A Bungalow** ...
Arthur Fields

11/45 **He's Home For A Little While** ...
Dinah Shore

7/05 **He's Me Pal** ... J.W. Myers

He's My Guy
7/42 Harry James
20/42 Dinah Shore

11/40 **He's My Uncle** ... Abe Lyman

20/28	**Here Comes The Showboat** ...	30/53	**Hi-Lili, Hi-Lo** ...

20/28 **Here Comes The Showboat** ...
    Vaughn Deleath

14/30 **Here Comes The Sun** ... Bert Lown

28/49 **Here I'll Stay** ... Jo Stafford

Here In My Arms
7/26   Leo Reisman
10/26   Jack Shilkret

Here In My Heart
8/51   Vic Damone
1/52   Al Martino
15/52   Tony Bennett

16/33 **Here Is My Heart** ... Rudy Vallee

Here It Comes Again
3/06   Bert Williams
5/06   Arthur Collins

10/33 **Here It Is Monday** ... Rudy Vallee

11/32 **Here Lies Love** ... Bing Crosby

25/44 **Here We Go Again** ... Glenn Miller

25/42 **Here You Are** ... Sammy Kaye

13/33 **Here You Come With Love** ...
    Ted Lewis

Here's Love In Your Eyes
9/36   Benny Goodman
17/37   Henry Allen

5/35 **Here's To Romance** ...
    Enric Madriguera

5/05 **Here's To The Girl!** ...
    Alan Turner & Haydn Quartet

22/53 **Here's To The Ladies** ...
    Henry Jerome

7/07 **Herman And Minnie** ...
    Len Spencer & Ada Jones

Hernando's Hideaway
2/54   Archie Bleyer
14/54   Guy Lombardo
14/54   Johnnie Ray

28/52 **Herring Boats** ... Mickey Katz
    (also see: Shrimp Boats)

27/54 **Hers And His** ...
    Jack Richards & The Marksmen

Hesitating Blues
10/16   Prince's Orchestra
13/20   Art Hickman

Hey! Ba-Ba-Re-Bop
4/46   Tex Beneke
9/46   Lionel Hampton

Hey, Good Lookin'
9/51   Frankie Laine & Jo Stafford
29/51   Hank Williams

6/53 **Hey Joe!** ... Frankie Laine

20/43 **Hey, Mabel!** ... Tony Pastor

Hey There
1/54   Rosemary Clooney
16/54   Sammy Davis, Jr.
27/54   Johnnie Ray

23/42 **Hey, Zeke!** ... McFarland Twins

24/47 **Hi Ho Trailus Boot Whip** ...
    Anita O'Day

30/53 **Hi-Lili, Hi-Lo** ...
    Leslie Caron & Mel Ferrer

22/41 **Hi, Neighbor!** ... Orrin Tucker

Hi-Yo, Silver
13/38   Roy Rogers
14/38   Jan Savitt

Hiawatha
1/03   Harry Macdonough
3/03   Columbia Orchestra
3/03   Dan Quinn
    (also see: Parody On Hiawatha)

3/03 **Hiawatha Two-Step** ... Sousa's Band

12/31 **High And Low** ...
    Fred Waring's Pennsylvanians

High And The Mighty
4/54   Les Baxter
6/54   Victor Young
9/54   Leroy Holmes
17/54   Johnny Desmond
29/54   Dimitri Tiomkin

6/22 **High Brown Blues** ... Sophie Tucker

8/14 **High Cost Of Loving** ... Elida Morris

High Noon (Do Not Forsake Me)
5/52   Frankie Laine
12/52   Tex Ritter

High On A Windy Hill
1/41   Jimmy Dorsey
2/41   Gene Krupa
9/41   Will Bradley
13/41   Vaughn Monroe

15/24 **High Society Rag** ... King Oliver

20/29 **High Up On A Hill Top** ...
    Guy Lombardo

6/27 **Highways Are Happy Ways** ...
    Ted Weems

7/16 **Hill And Dale** ... Fred Van Eps

Hindustan
3/19   Joseph C. Smith's Orchestra
6/19   Henry Burr & Albert Campbell
24/48   Ted Weems

Hinky Dinky Parley Voo
5/24   Ernest Hare & Billy Jones
11/24   Billy Murray & Ed Smalle

20/42 **Hip, Hip, Hooray** ... Vaughn Monroe

12/47 **His Feet Too Big For De Bed** ...
    Stan Kenton

7/44 **His Rocking Horse Ran Away** ...
    Betty Hutton

15/54 **Hit And Run Affair** ... Perry Como

27/40 **Hit The Road** ... Andrews Sisters

16/43 **Hit The Road To Dreamland** ...
    Freddie Slack

5/13 **Hitchy-Koo** ... American Quartet

24/51 **Hitsity Hotsity** ...
    Lola Ameche & Al Trace

8/30 **Hittin' The Bottle** ...
    Colonial Club Orchestra

I

I Get A Kick Out Of You
3/35 Paul Whiteman
12/35 Ethel Merman
20/35 Leo Reisman

28/40 **I Get A Kick Outa Corn** ... Tiny Hill

I Get Along Without You Very Well
3/39 Red Norvo
9/39 Jimmy Dorsey

I Get Ideas
3/50 Tony Martin
10/51 Louis Armstrong
14/51 Peggy Lee

2/54 **I Get So Lonely (When I Dream About You)** ... Four Knights

I Get The Blues When It Rains
8/29 Guy Lombardo
16/29 Ford & Glenn

15/43 **I Get The Neck Of The Chicken** ... Freddy Martin

I Give You My Word
7/40 Mitchell Ayres
2/41 Eddy Duchin
16/41 Jack Leonard

I Go For That
15/39 Eddy Duchin
15/39 Dorothy Lamour
20/39 Red Norvo

18/38 **I Got A Guy** ... Chick Webb featuring Ella Fizgerald

I Got It Bad And That Ain't Good
25/41 Benny Goodman
13/42 Duke Ellington

5/35 **I Got Plenty O' Nuttin'** ... Leo Reisman

I Got Rhythm
5/31 Red Nichols
17/31 Ethel Waters
17/32 Louis Armstrong

I Got The Sun In The Morning
10/46 Les Brown
17/46 Artie Shaw

13/29 **I Gotta Great Big Date With A Little Bitta Girl** ... Coon-Sanders Orchestra

I Gotta Right To Sing The Blues
17/33 Cab Calloway
18/33 Louis Armstrong
20/34 Benny Goodman

21/42 **I Guess I'll Be On My Way** ... Woody Herman

I Guess I'll Get The Papers (And Go Home)
11/46 Les Brown
12/46 Mills Brothers

I Guess I'll Have To Change My Plan (The Blue Pajama Song)
2/32 Rudy Vallee
11/32 Guy Lombardo

I Guess I'll Have To Dream The Rest
4/41 Glenn Miller
12/41 Tommy Dorsey

I Guess I'll Have To Telegraph My Baby
1/99 Arthur Collins
2/99 Len Spencer
3/99 George J. Gaskin
4/99 Silas Leachman

I Had The Craziest Dream
1/43 Harry James
28/53 Skylarks

I Hadn't Anyone Till You
4/38 Ray Noble
10/38 Tommy Dorsey

17/34 **I Hate Myself (For Being So Mean To You)** ... Isham Jones

14/48 **I Hate To Lose You** ... Andrews Sisters

I Have But One Heart
7/47 Vic Damone
13/47 Frank Sinatra

I Have Eyes
6/38 Benny Goodman
10/38 Artie Shaw
4/39 Bing Crosby

12/38 **I Haven't Changed A Thing** ... Jimmy Dorsey

15/37 **I Haven't Got A Pot To Cook In** ... Sweet Violet Boys

13/40 **I Haven't Time To Be A Millionare** ... Bing Crosby

I Hear A Rhapsody
1/41 Jimmy Dorsey
2/41 Charlie Barnet
9/41 Dinah Shore
22/41 Al Donohue
24/52 Frank Sinatra

I Heard
3/32 Mills Brothers
7/32 Don Redman

I Heard You Cried Last Night
2/43 Harry James
13/43 Dick Haymes

13/36 **I Hope Gabriel Likes My Music** ... Louis Armstrong

I Just ... *also see: I Yust*

1/07 **I Just Can't Make My Eyes Behave** ... Ada Jones

27/40 **I Just Wanna Play With You** ... Mitchell Ayres

26/53 **I Keep Telling Myself** ... Hilltoppers

I Kiss Your Hand, Madame
12/29 Smith Ballew
13/29 Leo Reisman

14/34 **I Knew You When** ... Isham Jones

I Know
9/46 Tex Beneke
14/46 Jubilaires
14/46 Andy Kirk

25/49 **I Know, I Know, I Know** ... Paul Weston

I Know Now
2/37	Guy Lombardo
14/37	Dick Powell
19/37	Lennie Hayton

I Know That You Know
5/27	Nat Shilkret
14/36	Benny Goodman

I Know Why
18/41	Glenn Miller
24/41	Richard Himber

29/53 **I Laugh To Keep From Crying** ...
Billy Eckstine

14/52 **I Laughed At Love** ... Sunny Gale

14/44 **I Learned A Lesson I'll Never Forget** ... Five Red Caps

I Left My Heart At The Stage Door Canteen
3/42	Sammy Kaye
8/42	Charlie Spivak

I Let A Song Go Out Of My Heart
1/38	Duke Ellington
1/38	Benny Goodman
5/38	Connee Boswell
8/38	Mildred Bailey
9/38	Hot Lips Page

27/53 **I Let Her Go** ... Frankie Laine

5/33 **I Like A Guy What Takes His Time** ...
Mae West

20/51 **I Like It** ... Jane Turzy

13/51 **I Like The Wide Open Spaces** ...
Arthur Godfrey & Laurie Anders

19/30 **I Like To Do Things For You** ...
Paul Whiteman

29/54 **I Live Each Day** ... Jerry Vale

12/39 **I Long To Belong To You** ...
Hoarce Heidt

3/27 **I Lost My Heart In Monterey (When I Found You)** ... Isham Jones

18/43 **I Lost My Sugar In Salt Lake City** ...
Johnny Mercer

2/07 **I Love A Lassie (My Scotch Bluebell)** ... Harry Lauder

13/32 **I Love A Parade** ...
Arden-Ohman Orchestra

1/16 **I Love A Piano** ... Billy Murray

3/08 **I Love, And The World Is Mine** ...
Henry Burr

17/52 **I Love Girls** ... Arthur Godfrey

3/22 **I Love Her-She Loves Me (I'm Her He-She's My She)** ... Eddie Cantor

I Love It
3/11	Arthur Collins
8/11	American Quartet

4/31 **I Love Louisa** ...
Leo Reisman with Fred Astaire

6/12 **I Love Love (I Love You, Dear)** ...
Henry Burr & Carolyn Vaughan

17/40 **I Love Me** ... Gray Gordon

I Love My Baby (My Baby Loves Me)
6/26	Fred Waring's Pennsylvanians
10/26	Aileen Stanley

2/95 **I Love My Love In The Spring Time** ...
Len Spencer

I Love My Wife, But Oh You Kid!
2/09	Arthur Collins
5/09	Bob Roberts
9/09	Edward M. Favor

3/04 **I Love Only One Girl In The Wide, Wide World** ... Harry Macdonough

13/53 **I Love Paris** ... Les Baxter

11/27 **I Love The College Girls** ...
Fred Waring's Pennsylvanians

I Love The Guy
10/50	Sarah Vaughan
22/50	Fran Warren

1/14 **I Love The Ladies** ...
Arthur Collins & Byron Harlan

I Love The Name Of Mary
1/11	Will Oakland
7/12	Walter Van Brunt

23/51 **I Love The Sunshine Of Your Smile** ...
Four Knights

14/31 **I Love To Hear A Military Band** ...
Ted Weems

5/37 **I Love To Whistle** ... Fats Waller

I Love You
3/24	Paul Whiteman
10/24	Lewis James
12/24	Charles Hart

I Love You
21/43	Tommy Tucker
1/44	Bing Crosby
7/44	Enric Madriguera
8/44	Jo Stafford
12/44	Perry Como

(I Love You) For Sentimental Reasons
1/46	Nat "King" Cole
5/46	Charlie Spivak
2/47	Eddy Howard
2/47	Dinah Shore
8/47	Ella Fitzgerald
15/47	Art Kassel

4/00 **I Love You Just The Same** ...
Harry Macdonough

30/40 **I Love You Much Too Much** ...
Bob Zurke

3/29 **I Love You (My Love Song)** ...
Ted Lewis

3/08 **I Love You So** ...
Harry Macdonough & Elise Stevenson

I Love You So Much
14/30	Bob Haring
26/53	Vicki Young

I Love You So Much It Hurts
21/48	Jimmy Wakely
8/49	Mills Brothers
13/49	Reggie Goff
24/49	Buddy Clark

5/02	**I Want To Be A Lidy** ... Edward M. Favor	
6/08	**I Want To Be A Merry, Merry Widow** ... Ada Jones	
18/29	**I Want To Be Bad** ... Helen Kane	
22/53	**I Want To Be Evil** ... Eartha Kitt	

I Want To Be Happy
5/24	Carl Fenton
2/25	Vincent Lopez
5/25	Jan Garber
13/25	Shannon Four
19/30	Red Nichols
17/37	Benny Goodman

I Want To Be Loved
21/47	Savannah Churchill
21/47	Benny Goodman

I Want To Be Near You
30/51	Johnny Desmond
30/51	Percy Faith

29/51 **I Want To Be With You Always** ...
Lefty Frizzell

I Want To Go Back To Michigan (Down On The Farm)
3/14	Elida Morris
8/15	Morton Harvey

9/15 **I Want To Go To Tokio** ...
Prince's Orchestra

4/19 **I Want To Hold You In My Arms** ...
Al Bernard & Ernest Hare

6/15 **I Want To Linger** ...
Prince's Orchestra

23/40 **I Want To Live (As Long As You Love Me)** ... Leo Reisman

21/47 **I Want To Thank Your Folks** ...
Perry Como

3/06 **I Want What I Want When I Want It** ...
Frank Stanley

7/08 **I Want You** ... Henry Burr

23/54 **I Want You All To Myself (Just You)** ...
Kitty Kallen

8/34 **I Was In The Mood** ... Eddy Duchin

6/35 **I Was Lucky** ... Benny Goodman

I Went Out Of My Way
23/41	Teddy Powell
30/54	Paul Weston

I Went To Your Wedding
1/52	Patti Page
20/52	Steve Gibson
20/53	Spike Jones

6/45 **I Wish** ... Mills Brothers

I Wish I Could Shimmy Like My Sister Kate
3/23	Virginians
11/23	Georgians
15/23	Harry Reser's Orchestra
1/52	Mary Kaye Trio

I Wish I Didn't Love You So
2/47	Vaughn Monroe
2/47	Dinah Shore
5/47	Betty Hutton
9/47	Dick Haymes
13/47	Dick Farney

20/41 **I Wish I Had A Dime (For Ev'ry Time I Missed You)** ... Andrews Sisters

I Wish I Had A Girl
2/09	Billy Murray
4/09	Harry Tally
7/09	Manuel Romain

I Wish I Had My Old Gal Back Again
5/09	Manuel Romain
5/26	Al Jolson
13/26	Henry Burr

18/51 **I Wish I Had Never Seen Sunshine** ...
Les Paul & Mary Ford

10/23 **I Wish I Had Someone To Cry Over Me** ... Lewis James

6/45 **I Wish I Knew** ... Dick Haymes

7/35 **I Wish I Were Aladdin** ...
Bing Crosby

I Wish I Were Twins
8/34	Emil Coleman
8/34	Fats Waller
20/34	Henry Allen

27/51 **I Wish I Wuz** ... Rosemary Clooney

20/44 **I Wish That I Could Hide Inside This Letter** ... Lawrence Welk

I Wished On The Moon
2/35	Bing Crosby
13/35	Little Jack Little

12/51 **I Won't Cry Anymore** ...
Tony Bennett

I Won't Dance
1/35	Eddy Duchin
6/35	Johnny Green
9/35	Leo Reisman
20/35	George Hall

I Won't Tell A Soul
1/38	Andy Kirk
8/38	Lawrence Welk
16/38	Roy Fox

20/45 **I Wonder** ... Cecil Gant

I Wonder, I Wonder, I Wonder
2/47	Eddy Howard
3/47	Guy Lombardo
9/47	Martha Tilton
11/47	Tony Pastor

10/22 **I Wonder If You Still Care For Me** ...
Charles Hart

I Wonder What's Become Of Sally?
1/24	Al Jolson
6/24	Van & Schenck
7/24	Ted Lewis

7/26 **I Wonder Where My Baby Is To-Night?** ... Henry Burr & Billy Murray

10/24 **I Wonder Who's Dancing With You Tonight?** ... Benny Krueger

I Wonder Who's Kissing Her Now
1/09 Henry Burr
4/10 Billy Murray
6/10 Manuel Romain
2/47 Perry Como with Ted Weems
11/47 Ray Noble
12/47 Dinning Sisters

18/52 **I Would Rather Look At You** ...
Gloria Hart

23/40 **I Wouldn't Take A Million** ...
Glenn Miller

11/41 **I, Yi, Yi, Yi, Yi (I Like You Very
Much)** ... Andrews Sisters

5/49 **I Yust Go Nuts At Christmas** ...
Yogi Yorgesson

I'd Be Lost Without You
14/46 Frankie Carle
14/46 Guy Lombardo

**I'd Climb The Highest Mountain (If I
Knew I'd Find You)**
7/26 Al Jolson
11/26 Art Gillham

21/54 **I'd Cry Like A Baby** ... Dean Martin

24/40 **I'd Know You Anywhere** ...
Glenn Miller

I'd Leave My Happy Home For You
1/99 Arthur Collins
4/00 Edward M. Favor

5/18 **I'd Like To Be A Monkey In The
Zoo** ... Frances White

**I'd Like To See A Little More Of
You** ... see: Game Of Peek-A-Boo

5/20 **I'd Love To Fall Asleep And Wake Up
In My Mammy's Arms** ... Peerless
Quartet

**I'd Love To Live In Loveland With A
Girl Like You**
5/12 Walter Van Brunt
7/12 Henry Burr & Albert Campbell

15/35 **I'd Love To Take Orders From You** ...
Phil Harris

29/53 **I'd Never Forgive Myself** ...
Jo Ann Tolley

23/53 **I'd Never Stand In Your Way** ...
Joni James

16/29 **I'd Rather Be Blue Over You (Than Be
Happy With Somebody Else)** ...
Fanny Brice

8/53 **I'd Rather Die Young** ... Hilltoppers

12/36 **I'd Rather Lead A Band** ...
Fred Astaire

14/35 **I'd Rather Listen To Your Eyes** ...
Jacques Renard

I'll Always Be In Love With You
3/29 Fred Waring's Pennsylvanians
9/29 Morton Downey

I'll Always Love You
11/50 Dean Martin
23/50 Martha Tilton

27/53 **I'll Always Love You Some** ...
Buddy Greco

17/43 **I'll Be Around** ... Mills Brothers

21/41 **I'll Be Back In A Year, Little
Darlin'** ... Texas Jim Robertson

14/30 **I'll Be Blue Just Thinking Of You** ...
Ruth Etting

I'll Be Faithful
6/33 Jan Garber
18/33 Bernie Cummins

I'll Be Glad When You're Dead ...
see: You Rascal, You

I'll Be Hangin' Around
21/53 Russ Morgan
26/53 Les Brown

I'll Be Home For Christmas
3/43 Bing Crosby
16/44 Bing Crosby

I'll Be Seeing You
1/44 Bing Crosby
4/44 Tommy Dorsey

I'll Be With You In Apple Blossom Time
2/20 Charles Harrison
5/20 Henry Burr & Albert Campbell
11/20 Reed Miller
5/41 Andrews Sisters

3/01 **I'll Be With You When The Roses
Bloom Again** ... Harry Macdonough

I'll Build A Stairway To Paradise
12/22 Carl Fenton
1/23 Paul Whiteman
8/23 Ben Selvin

I'll Buy That Dream
2/45 Helen Forrest & Dick Haymes
2/45 Harry James
8/45 Hal McIntyre

15/47 **I'll Close My Eyes** ... Andy Russell

5/34 **I'll Close My Eyes To Everyone Else** ...
Don Bestor

I'll Dance At Your Wedding
23/47 Tony Martin
3/48 Buddy Clark
3/48 Ray Noble
11/48 Peggy Lee

10/14 **I'll Do It All Over Again** ...
Billy Murray

14/38 **I'll Dream Tonight** ...
Tommy Dorsey

20/43 **I'll Find You** ... Jimmy Dorsey

8/34 **I'll Follow My Secret Heart** ...
Ray Noble

19/32 **I'll Follow You** ... Paul Whiteman

26/44 **I'll Forgive You, But I Can't Forget** ...
Roy Acuff

26/48 **I'll Get Along Somehow** ...
Sam Donohue

I'm A Jonah Man
3/03   Arthur Collins
5/03   Bob Roberts

21/47 **I'm A Lonely Little Petunia (In An Onion Patch)** ... Two-Ton Baker

4/21 **I'm A Lonesome Little Raindrop** ... Frank Crumit

3/17 **I'm A Twelve O'Clock Fellow In A Nine O'Clock Town** ... Byron G. Harlan

3/12 **I'm Afraid, Pretty Maid, I'm Afraid** ... Ada Jones & Walter Van Brunt

5/39 **(I'm Afraid) The Masquerade Is Over** ... Larry Clinton

3/08 **I'm Afraid To Come Home In The Dark** ... Billy Murray

I'm All Bound Round With The Mason Dixon Line
1/18   Al Jolson
6/18   Irving Kaufman

7/31 **I'm All Dressed Up With A Broken Heart** ... Ted Lewis

9/31 **I'm Alone Because I Love You** ... Frank Luther

I'm Always Chasing Rainbows
1/18   Charles Harrison
5/18   Harry Fox
6/18   Prince's Orchestra
9/18   Sam Ash
5/45   Perry Como
7/45   Helen Forrest & Dick Haymes
9/46   Harry James

9/22 **I'm An Indian** ... Fanny Brice

2/36 **I'm An Old Cowhand** ... Bing Crosby with Jimmy Dorsey

8/31 **I'm An Unemployed Sweetheart (Looking For Somebody To Love)** ... Ted Wallace

3/09 **I'm Awfully Glad I Met You** ... Ada Jones & Billy Murray

18/27 **I'm Back In Love Again** ... Aileen Stanley

I'm Beginning To See The Light
1/45   Harry James
5/45   Ella Fitzgerald & Ink Spots
6/45   Duke Ellington

30/49 **I'm Bitin' My Fingernails And Thinking Of You** ... Andrews Sisters & Ernest Tubb

15/29 **I'm Bringing A Red, Red Rose** ... Ruth Etting

10/39 **I'm Building A Sailboat Of Dreams** ... Dick Robertson

4/36 **I'm Building Up To An Awful Letdown** ... Fred Astaire

6/15 **I'm Coming Back To Dixie And You** ... Peerless Quartet

I'm Coming, Virginia
5/27   Frankie Trumbauer
6/27   Paul Whiteman
10/27 Ethel Waters
10/37 Teddy Wilson
12/38 Paul Whiteman

I'm Confessin' ... *see: Confessin'*

4/06 **I'm Crazy 'Bout It!** ... Arthur Collins & Byron Harlan

8/18 **I'm Crazy Over Every Girl In France** ... Avon Comedy Four

26/50 **I'm Crazy To Love You** ... Sarah Vaughan

I'm Crying Just For You
4/14   Ada Jones & Billy Murray
7/14   Eddie Morton

I'm Falling In Love With Someone
1/11   John McCormack
9/12   Charles Harrison
4/35   Nelson Eddy

19/37 **I'm Feeling Like A Million** ... Jan Garber

I'm Following You
12/30 Paul Specht
13/30 High Hatters

I'm Forever Blowing Bubbles
1/19   Henry Burr & Albert Campbell
1/19   Ben Selvin
7/19   Charles Hart
10/19 Helen Clark & George Wilton Ballard
10/50 Gordon Jenkins with Artie Shaw

I'm Gettin' Sentimental Over You
20/34 Dorsey Brothers Orchestra
8/36   Tommy Dorsey
26/40 Ink Spots
21/41 Jack Leonard

19/43 **I'm Getting Tired So I Can Sleep** ... Jimmy Dorsey

24/46 **I'm Glad I Waited For You** ... Peggy Lee

6/10 **I'm Glad I'm A Boy - I'm Glad I'm A Girl** ... Ada Jones & Billy Murray

4/08 **I'm Glad I'm Married** ... Billy Murray

I'm Goin' Shopping With You
16/35 Little Jack Little
20/35 Dick Powell

I'm Goin' South
2/24   Al Jolson
8/24   Paul Whiteman

8/12 **I'm Going Back To Dixie** ... Arthur Collins & Byron Harlan

10/18 **I'm Going To Follow The Boys** ... Henry Burr & Elizabeth Spencer

I'm Gonna Lock My Heart
2/38   Billie Holiday
7/38   Henry Busse

4/45 **I'm Gonna Love That Gal** ... Perry Como

9/45	**I'm Gonna Love That Guy** ... Benny Goodman
8/16	**I'm Gonna Make Hay While The Sun Shines In Virginia** ... Marion Harris
20/27	**I'm Gonna Meet My Sweetie Now** ... Jean Goldkette
12/42	**I'm Gonna Move To The Outskirts Of Town** ... Jimmie Lunceford
4/18	**I'm Gonna Pin My Medal On The Girl I Left Behind** ... Peerless Quartet
12/45	**I'm Gonna See My Baby** ... Johnny Mercer
	I'm Gonna Sit Right Down And Write Myself A Letter
5/35	Fats Waller
3/36	Boswell Sisters
29/53	Connee Boswell
24/53	**I'm Gonna Walk and Talk With My Lord** ... Johnnie Ray
7/31	**I'm Good For Nothing But Love** ... Ruth Etting
18/36	**I'm Grateful To You** ... Jan Garber
14/34	**I'm Growing Fonder Of You** ... Ted Weems
18/39	**I'm Happy About The Whole Thing** ... Lawrence Welk
8/08	**I'm Happy When The Band Plays Dixie** ... Billy Murray & Haydn Quartet
	I'm In A Dancing Mood
16/36	Ambrose
5/37	Tommy Dorsey
5/37	Russ Morgan
	I'm In Heaven When I'm In My Mother's Arms
7/20	William Robyn
12/20	Henry Burr
10/34	**I'm In Love** ... Abe Lyman
6/51	**I'm In Love Again** ... April Stevens
24/53	**I'm In Love With A Guy** ... Lorry Raine
27/44	**I'm In Love With Someone** ... Art Kassel
2/29	**I'm In Seventh Heaven** ... Al Jolson
9/30	**I'm In The Market For You** ... George Olsen
30/51	**I'm In The Mood** ... John Lee Hooker
	I'm In The Mood For Love
1/35	Little Jack Little
3/35	Louis Armstrong
15/35	Frances Langford
18/35	Leo Reisman
12/46	Billy Eckstine
14/53	**I'm Just A Poor Bachelor** ... Frankie Laine
5/29	**I'm Just A Vagabond Lover** ... Rudy Vallee
6/11	**I'm Just Pining For You** ... Walter Van Brunt

	I'm Just Wild About Harry
4/22	Marion Harris
4/22	Ray Miller
4/22	Paul Whiteman
10/22	Vaughn Deleath
11/22	Vincent Lopez
7/26	**I'm Knee Deep In Daisies (And Head Over Heels In Love)** ... George Olsen
5/01	**I'm Living Easy** ... Silas Leachman
13/35	**I'm Living In A Great Big Way** ... Louis Prima
17/34	**I'm Lonesome For You, Caroline** ... Jan Garber
5/11	**I'm Looking For A Nice Young Fellow Who Is Looking For A Nice Young Girl** ... American Quartet
5/09	**I'm Looking For A Sweetheart And I Think You'll Do** ... Ada Jones & Billy Murray
7/08	**I'm Looking For The Man That Wrote The Merry Widow Waltz** ... Billy Murray
	I'm Looking Over A Four-Leaf Clover
2/27	Nick Lucas
3/27	Ben Bernie
10/27	Jean Goldkette
1/48	Art Mooney
6/48	Russ Morgan
6/48	Alvino Rey
10/48	Three Suns
11/48	Uptown String Band
14/48	Arthur Godfrey
	I'm Making Believe
1/44	Ella Fitzgerald & Ink Spots
14/45	Hal McIntyre
27/50	**I'm Movin' On** ... Hank Snow
	I'm My Own Grandpaw
10/48	Guy Lombardo
21/48	Jo Stafford (Grandmaw)
4/14	**I'm Neutral** ... Bert Williams
22/52	**I'm Never Satisfied** ... Nat "King" Cole
15/33	**I'm No Angel** ... Gus Arnheim
	I'm Nobody's Baby
3/21	Marion Harris
11/21	Aileen Stanley
9/27	Ruth Etting
3/40	Judy Garland
11/40	Bea Wain
14/40	Ozzie Nelson
1/98	**I'm Old But I'm Awfully Tough (Laughing Song)** ... Cal Stewart
23/43	**I'm Old-Fashioned** ... Fred Astaire
3/35	**I'm On A See-Saw** ... Ambrose
13/27	**I'm On My Way Home** ... "Whispering" Jack Smith
3/15	**I'm On My Way To Dublin Bay** ... Peerless Quartet

In An Old Dutch Garden
3/40 Dick Jurgens
8/40 Glenn Miller
15/40 Eddy Duchin

In Dear Old Georgia
3/05 Frank Stanley
6/05 Henry Burr
3/06 Haydn Quartet

7/16 **In Florida Among The Palms** ...
Sterling Trio

8/17 **In Lilac Time (When You Stole This Heart Of Mine)** ... Charles King & Elizabeth Brice

In Love In Vain
12/46 Helen Forrest & Dick Haymes
12/46 Margaret Whiting

2/22 **In May Time (I Learned To Love)** ...
Edwin Dale

3/43 **In My Arms** ... Dick Haymes

14/28 **In My Bouquet Of Memories** ...
Gene Austin

20/48 **In My Dreams** ... Vaughn Monroe

6/13 **In My Harem** ... Walter Van Brunt

14/32 **In My Hideaway** ... Buddy Rogers

14/38 **In My Little Red Book** ...
Guy Lombardo

In My Merry Oldsmobile
1/05 Billy Murray
7/05 Arthur Collins & Byron Harlan

16/39 **In Our Little Part Of Town** ...
Sammy Kaye

6/12 **In Ragtime Land** ... Arthur Collins

14/23 **In Rose Time** ... Elizabeth Spencer

5/20 **In Sweet September** ... Al Jolson

In The Baggage Coach Ahead
1/96 Dan Quinn
14/25 Vernon Dalhart

1/43 **In The Blue Of The Evening** ...
Tommy Dorsey

In The Chapel In The Moonlight
1/36 Shep Fields
7/36 Richard Himber
11/37 Mal Hallet
20/37 Ruth Etting
4/54 Kitty Kallen
30/54 Four Knights

4/03 **In The City Of Sighs And Tears** ...
J.W. Myers

In The Cool, Cool, Cool Of The Evening
11/51 Bing Crosby & Jane Wyman
17/51 Frankie Laine & Jo Stafford

12/33 **In The Cool Of The Night** ...
Clyde McCoy

5/04 **In The Days Of Old** ... Billy Murray

In The Evening By The Moonlight, Dear Louise
3/07 Harry Macdonough
6/07 Frank Stanley
2/13 Haydn Quartet

2/09 **In The Garden Of My Heart** ...
Frank Stanley & Henry Burr

In The Gloaming
5/11 Will Oakland & American Quartet
10/13 Alice Nielsen

10/07 **In The Good Old Steamboat Days** ...
Murry K. Hill

In The Good Old Summer Time
1/02 J.W. Myers
3/02 William Redmond
1/03 Haydn Quartet
1/03 Sousa's Band
2/03 Harry Macdonough
15/52 Les Paul & Mary Ford

3/14 **In The Heart Of The City That Has No Heart** ... Henry Burr

14/28 **In The Jail House Now** ...
Jimmie Rodgers

2/18 **In The Land O' Yamo Yamo** ...
Van & Schenck

In The Land Of Beginning Again
6/19 Charles Harrison
18/46 Bing Crosby

In The Land Of Harmony
5/11 Arthur Collins
9/11 American Quartet

9/15 **In The Land Of Love With The Songbirds** ... Henry Burr & Albert Campbell

In The Little Red School House
2/22 Ernest Hare & Billy Jones
5/22 American Quartet

7/39 **In The Middle Of A Dream** ...
Tommy Dorsey

2/35 **In The Middle Of A Kiss** ...
Hal Kemp

In The Middle Of May
13/45 Freddy Martin
14/46 Pied Pipers

In The Mission By The Sea
11/37 Rudy Vallee
17/38 Hoarce Heidt

15/53 **In The Mission Of St. Augustine** ...
Sammy Kaye

In The Mood
1/40 Glenn Miller
20/43 Glenn Miller
16/53 Johnny Maddox

8/46 **In The Moon Mist** ... Pied Pipers

8/33 **In The Park In Paree** ...
Hotel Bossert Orchestra

In The Shade Of The Old Apple Tree
1/05 Henry Burr
2/05 Albert Campbell
2/05 Haydn Quartet
9/05 Arthur Pryor's Band
13/33 Duke Ellington

12/31	**It Looks Like Love** ... Abe Lyman
9/24	**It Looks Like Rain** ... Wendell Hall
	It Looks Like Rain In Cherry Blossom Lane
1/37	Guy Lombardo
6/37	Shep Fields
	It Made You Happy When You Made Me Cry
2/27	Fred Waring's Pennsylvanians
3/27	Isham Jones
4/05	**It Makes Me Think Of Home, Sweet Home** ... Byron G. Harlan
	It Makes No Difference Now
16/38	Cliff Bruner's Texas Wanderers
23/41	Bing Crosby
	It Might As Well Be Spring
5/45	Dick Haymes
6/45	Paul Weston
4/46	Sammy Kaye
12/44	**It Must Be Jelly ('cause Jam Don't Shake Like That)** ... Glenn Miller
	It Must Be True
4/30	Gus Arnheim
13/30	Earl Burtnett
	It Never Dawned On Me
14/35	Enric Madriguera
18/35	Victor Young
19/48	**It Only Happens When I Dance With You** ... Frank Sinatra
4/43	**It Started All Over Again** ... Tommy Dorsey
23/47	**It Takes A Long, Long Train With A Red Caboose (To Carry My Blues Away)** ... Dinah Shore
15/33	**It Was A Night In June** ... Anson Weeks
13/27	**It Was Only A Sun Shower** ... Ted Weems
	It Was So Beautiful
7/32	Enric Madriguera
7/32	Harry Richman
13/32	Ruth Etting
14/32	George Olsen
16/32	Ozzie Nelson
19/28	**It Was The Dawn Of Love** ... Paul Whiteman
27/52	**It Wasn't God Who Made Honky Tonk Angels** ... Kitty Wells
30/54	**It Worries Me** ... Frank Sinatra
25/49	**It's A Big, Wide, Wonderful World** ... Buddy Clark
	It's A Blue World
2/40	Tony Martin
14/40	Glenn Miller
30/52	Four Freshmen
16/47	**It's A Good Day** ... Peggy Lee
21/46	**It's A Grand Night For Singing** ... Dick Haymes

23/41	**It's A Great Day For The Irish** ... Freddy Martin
18/40	**It's A Hap, Hap, Happy Day** ... Eddy Duchin
9/16	**It's A Hundred To One (I'm In Love)** ... M.J. O'Connell
	It's A Hundred To One (I'm In Love)
6/39	Dick Jurgens
12/39	Dick Todd
	It's A Lonely Trail (When You're Travelin' All Alone)
7/38	Guy Lombardo
17/39	Bing Crosby
16/30	**It's A Lonesome Old Town (When You're Not Around)** ... Ben Bernie
6/12	**It's A Long Lane That Has No Turning** ... Peerless Quartet
7/17	**It's A Long, Long Time Since I've Been Home** ... Irving Kaufman
	It's A Long, Long Way To Tipperary
1/14	American Quartet
1/15	John McCormack
2/15	Prince's Orchestra
8/15	Albert Farrington
4/03	**It's A Lovely Day For A Walk** ... Frank Stanley & Corrine Morgan
30/51	**It's A Lovely Day Today** ... Doris Day
8/24	**It's A Man, Every Time, It's A Man** ... Marcia Freer
7/27	**It's A Million To One You're In Love** ... Nat Shilkret
21/48	**It's A Most Unusual Day** ... Ray Noble
	It's A Sin To Tell A Lie
1/36	Fats Waller
5/36	Victor Young
11/54	**It's A Woman's World** ... Four Aces
8/40	**It's A Wonderful World** ... Charlie Barnet
12/34	**It's All Forgotten Now** ... Ray Noble
18/51	**It's All In The Game** ... Tommy Edwards
	It's All Over Now
6/46	Frankie Carle
10/46	Peggy Lee
21/40	**It's All Over Now (I Won't Worry)** ... Art Kassel
4/06	**It's All Right In The Summertime** ... Ada Jones
19/49	**It's All So New To Me** ... Joan Crawford
2/11	**It's Always June When You're In Love** ... Reed Miller
3/43	**It's Always You** ... Tommy Dorsey
11/34	**It's An Old Southern Custom** ... Eddy Duchin

J

4/19 **Ja-Da (Ja Da, Ja Da, Jing Jing Jing)** ... Arthur Fields

18/47 **Jack! Jack! Jack!** ... Jack Smith

4/03 **Jack Tar March** ... Sousa's Band

21/47 **Jack, You're Dead** ... Louis Jordan

3/98 **Jack's The Boy** ... S.H. Dudley

Jalousie (Jealousy)
7/32   Leo Reisman
13/38 Boston Pops Orchestra
17/47 Harry James
3/51   Frankie Laine

Jambalaya
3/52   Jo Stafford
20/52 Hank Williams

4/15 **Jane** ... Peerless Quartet

26/44 **Janie** ... Dick Haymes

Japanese Sandman
1/20   Paul Whiteman
7/21   Nora Bayes
15/21 Ben Selvin
10/35 Benny Goodman

16/28 **Japansy** ... Guy Lombardo

15/41 **Java Jive** ... Ink Spots

3/19 **Jazz Baby** ... Marion Harris

20/36 **Jazz Lips** ... Duke Ellington

Jazz Me Blues
9/21   Original Dixieland Jazz Band
23/51 Les Paul

22/47 **Je Vous Aime** ... Andy Russell

Jealous
3/24   Marion Harris
13/24 Ben Selvin
12/41 Andrews Sisters

Jealous Heart
4/49   Al Morgan
10/49 Hugo Winterhalter
11/49 Jack Owens
14/49 Bill Lawrence
22/49 Jan Garber

Jealousy ... see: Jalousie

Jeannine (I Dream Of Lilac Time)
1/28   Gene Austin
2/28   Nat Shilkret
6/28   Ben Selvin
15/29 John McCormack

Jeepers Creepers
1/39   Al Donohue
12/39 Louis Armstrong
12/39 Larry Clinton

3/02 **Jennie Lee** ... Harry Macdonough

12/29 **Jericho** ...
       Fred Waring's Pennsylvanians

Jersey Bounce
1/42   Benny Goodman
9/42   Jimmy Dorsey
15/42 Shep Fields

6/15 **Jesus, Lover Of My Soul** ...
       Alma Gluck & Louise Homer

20/51 **Jet** ... Nat "King" Cole

2/51 **Jezebel** ... Frankie Laine

19/33 **Jig Saw Puzzle Blues** ... Joe Venuti

24/53 **Jig-Saw Puzzle Heart** ...
       Sonny Howard

6/54 **Jilted** ... Teresa Brewer

Jim
2/41   Jimmy Dorsey
5/41   Dinah Shore

1/01 **Jim Lawson's Horse Trade With Deacon Witherspoon** ... Cal Stewart

8/06 **Jimmie And Maggie At The Ball Game** ... Len Spencer & Ada Jones

4/05 **Jimmie And Maggie At The Hippodrome** ... Len Spencer & Ada Jones

5/08 **Jimmie And Maggie At The Merry Widow** ... Len Spencer & Ada Jones

3/11 **Jimmy Valentine** ... Peerless Quartet

10/45 **Jimmy's Blues** ... Count Basie

Jingle Bells
18/35 Benny Goodman
5/41   Glenn Miller
19/43 Bing Crosby & Andrews Sisters
21/47 Bing Crosby & Andrews Sisters
24/49 Primo Scala
10/52 Les Paul
       (also see: Yingle Bells)

Jingle, Jangle, Jingle
1/42   Kay Kyser
14/42 Gene Autry
15/42 Freddy Martin
4/44   Merry Macs

20/34 **Jitter Bug** ... Cab Calloway

12/46 **Jivin' Joe Jackson** ... Count Basie

2/17 **Joan Of Arc** ... Henry Burr

4/16 **Joe Turner Blues** ...
       Prince's Orchestra

Joey
12/54 Betty Madigan
25/54 Jeri Southern

21/51 **John And Marsha** ... Stan Freberg

10/24 **John Henry Blues** ...
       Fiddlin' John Carson

20/27 **John Henry (Steel-Drivin' Man)** ...
       Gid Tanner

26/53 **John, John, John (Every Tom, Dick and Harry's Called John)** ... Guy Lombardo

9/25 **John Peel** ...
       Associated Glee Clubs Of America

13/38 **John Silver** ... Jimmy Dorsey

Johnny Doughboy Found A Rose In Ireland

2/42	Kay Kyser
9/42	Guy Lombardo
11/42	Kenny Baker
11/42	Freddy Martin
13/42	Sammy Kaye
13/42	Tommy Tucker

15/53 **Johnny (Is The Boy For Me)** ...
Les Paul & Mary Ford

Johnny One-Note

15/37	Hal Kemp
17/37	Victor Young

4/43 **Johnny Zero** ... Song Spinners

Johnson Rag

16/40	Larry Clinton
6/49	Jack Teter Trio
7/50	Russ Morgan
13/50	Jimmy Dorsey
24/50	Claude Thornhill

17/37 **Joint Is Jumpin'** ... Fats Waller

12/41 **Joltin' Joe DiMaggio** ... Les Brown

15/54 **Jones Boy** ... Mills Brothers

18/38 **Joseph, Joseph** ... Andrews Sisters

Josephine

3/37	Tommy Dorsey
3/37	Wayne King
15/37	Sammy Kaye
12/51	Les Paul

4/02 **Josephine, My Jo** ...
Harry Macdonough

17/50 **Joshua** ... Ralph Flanagan

25/44 **Journey To A Star** ... Judy Garland

2/23 **Journey's End** ... Paul Whiteman

5/11 **Joy To The World** ... Trinity Choir

Juanita

9/05	Frank Stanley
6/19	Emilio DeGogorza

17/50 **Juke Box Annie** ... Kitty Kallen

7/42 **Juke Box Saturday Night** ...
Glenn Miller
(also see: New Juke Box Saturday Night)

7/38 **Jump Session** ... Slim & Slam

22/52 **Jump Through The Ring** ...
Vic Damone

21/43 **Jump Town** ... Harry James

11/39 **Jumpin' At The Woodside** ...
Count Basie

Jumpin' Jive

2/39	Cab Calloway
15/39	Lionel Hampton

22/41 **Jumpin' Jupiter** ... Wayne King

15/52 **Junco Partner** ... Richard Hayes

6/11 **June** ... Walter Van Brunt

June Brought The Roses

12/24	Marcia Freer
7/25	Nat Shilkret

June In January

1/34	Bing Crosby
7/34	Little Jack Little
10/34	Ted Fio Rito
14/35	Guy Lombardo

11/45 **June Is Bustin' Out All Over** ...
Hildegarde with Guy Lombardo

June Night

2/24	Ted Lewis
7/24	Fred Waring's Pennsylvanians

15/39 **Jungle Drums** ... Artie Shaw

27/48 **Jungle Fantasy** ... Esy Morales

Just A Baby's Prayer At Twilight (For Her Daddy Over There)

1/18	Henry Burr
6/18	Prince's Orchestra
7/18	Edna White's Trumpet Quartet
10/18	Charles Hart

7/27 **Just A Bird's Eye View Of My Old Kentucky Home** ... Abe Lyman

17/45 **Just A Blue Serge Suit** ...
Vaughn Monroe

Just A Cottage Small

4/26	John McCormack
9/26	Franklyn Baur

Just A Gigolo

1/31	Ted Lewis
3/31	Ben Bernie
12/31	Bing Crosby
15/31	Leo Reisman
22/53	Jaye P. Morgan

Just A Girl That Men Forget

3/23	Henry Burr
12/24	Lewis James

Just A Little Bit South Of North Carolina

4/41	Gene Krupa
11/41	Mitchell Ayres

10/30 **Just A Little Closer** ... Ruth Etting

20/46 **Just A Little Fond Affection** ...
Gene Krupa

5/32 **Just A Little Home For The Old Folks (A Token From Me)** ... Guy Lombardo

Just A Little Longer

14/27	Phil Spitalny
18/27	Fred Rich
8/30	Rudy Vallee

Just A Little Lovin'

13/48	Eddy Arnold
20/52	Eddie Fisher

8/10 **Just A Little Ring From You** ...
Ada Jones & Billy Murray

Just A Little Rocking Chair And You

4/06	Ada Jones
4/06	Billy Murray & Haydn Quartet
6/06	Billy Murray

Just A Little Street Where Old Friends Meet

6/32	Isham Jones
15/32	Gene Austin

K

Kiss To Build A Dream On
10/52   Hugo Winterhalter
16/52   Louis Armstrong

Kiss Waltz
6/30   George Olsen
18/30   Ben Bernie

19/51   **Kisses Sweeter Than Wine** ...
Weavers

22/54   **Kissing Bridge** ... Fontane Sisters

20/51   **Kissing Bug Boogie** ... Jo Stafford

Kitten On The Keys
5/21   Zez Confrey
5/22   Zez Confrey

6/14   **Kitty McKay** ... Prince's Orchestra

22/42   **Knit One, Purl Two** ... Glenn Miller

10/36   **Knock! Knock! Who's There?** ...
Ted Weems

24/42   **Knock Me A Kiss** ... Gene Krupa

Knock Wood
5/11   Ada Jones & Walter Van Brunt
9/12   Ada Jones & Billy Murray
9/12   Sophie Tucker

15/39   **Knockin' At The Famous Door** ...
Charlie Barnet

25/40   **Ko Ko** ... Duke Ellington

10/47   **Kokomo, Indiana** ... Vaughn Monroe

L

10/11   **La Boheme - Mi Chiamano Mimi (My Name Is Mimi)** ... Nellie Melba

8/07   **La Boheme - O Soave Fanciulla (Thou Sweetest Maiden)** ... Enrico Caruso & Nellie Melba

4/08   **La Boheme - Quartetto: "Addio, Dolce Svegliare" (Farewell, Sweet Love)** ...
Enrico Caruso, Geraldine Farrar, Antonio Scotti & Gina Viafora

6/06   **La Boheme - Raccantodi Radolfo (Rudolph's Recital, Act I)** ... Enrico Caruso

7/18   **La Capricieuse** ... Jascha Heifetz

18/34   **La Cucharacha** ... Lud Gluskin

13/38   **La De Doody Doo** ... Milt Herth Trio

20/52   **La Fiacre** ... Gisele MacKenzie

La Forza Del Destino - Solenne In Quest Ora (Swear In This Hour)
2/06   Enrico Caruso & Antonio Scotti
9/14   Reinald Werrenrath & Lambert Murphy

6/14   **La Golondria (The Swallow)** ...
Victor Military Band

8/17   **La Marseillaise** ... Frances Alda

8/15   **La Mia Canzone (My Song To Thee)** ...
Enrico Caruso

7/18   **La Ronde Des Lutins (Dance Of The Goblins)** ... Jascha Heifetz

24/53   **La Rosita** ... Four Aces

7/20   **La Veeda** ...
Green Brothers Novelty Band

La Vie En Rose
9/50   Tony Martin
12/50   Paul Weston
13/50   Bing Crosby
23/50   Edith Piaf
27/50   Ralph Flanagan
27/50   Victor Young
28/50   Louis Armstrong

Laddie Boy ...
see: (Goodbye, And Luck Be With You)

Lady From 29 Palms
5/47   Freddy Martin
7/47   Andrews Sisters
10/47   Tony Pastor

Lady In Red
3/35   Xavier Cugat
8/35   Louis Prima
20/35   Joe Haymes

Lady Is A Tramp
15/37   Tommy Dorsey
16/37   Bernie Cummins
19/37   Joe Rines
19/37   Sophie Tucker

18/52   **Lady Love** ... Vaughn Monroe

3/29   **Lady Luck** ... Ted Lewis

Lady Of Spain
5/31   Ray Noble
19/49   Ray Noble
6/52   Eddie Fisher
8/52   Les Paul

Lady Of The Evening
4/23   John Steel
11/23   Paul Whiteman

Lady, Play Your Mandolin
5/31   Nick Lucas
10/31   Havana Novelty Orchestra

Lady's In Love With You
2/39   Glenn Miller
13/39   Bob Crosby

10/18   **Lafayette (We Hear You Calling)** ...
Reinald Werrenrath

Lambeth Walk
4/38   Russ Morgan
7/38   Al Donohue
7/38   Duke Ellington

Lament To Love
10/41   Harry James
25/41   Les Brown

3/39   **Lamp Is Low** ... Tommy Dorsey

23/42   **Lamplighter's Serenade** ...
Bing Crosby

14/45 **Leave The Dishes In The Sink, Ma ...**
Spike Jones

29/44 **Leave Us Face It (We're In Love) ...**
Hildegarde

5/20 **Left All Alone Again Blues ...**
Marion Harris

22/53 **Less Than Tomorrow ...**
Hamish Menzies

Let A Smile Be Your Umbrella
6/28 Roger Wolfe Kahn
12/28 Sam Lanin

12/38 **Let 'Er Go ...** Artie Shaw

1/06 **Let It Alone ...** Bert Williams

Let It Rain, Let It Pour
6/25 Gene Austin
10/25 Nat Shilkret
13/25 Ben Selvin

Let It Snow! Let It Snow! Let It Snow!
1/46 Vaughn Monroe
7/46 Woody Herman
9/46 Connee Boswell
14/46 Bob Crosby

Let Me Call You Sweetheart
1/11 Peerless Quartet
2/11 Arthur Clough

26/54 **Let Me Go, Lover ...** Peggy Lee

Let Me In
24/51 Fontane Sisters & Texas Jim
Robertson
26/51 Blue Barron
26/51 Bobby Wayne

14/26 **Let Me Linger Longer In Your Arms ...**
Peerless Quartet

5/11 **Let Me Live And Stay In Dixieland ...**
Charles King & Elizabeth Brice

18/44 **Let Me Love You Tonight ...**
Woody Herman

10/41 **Let Me Off Uptown ...** Gene Krupa

6/06 **Let Me See You Smile ...**
Len Spencer & Ada Jones

2/30 **Let Me Sing And I'm Happy ...**
Al Jolson

7/38 **Let Me Whisper I Love You ...**
Bing Crosby

5/06 **Let The Lower Lights Be Burning ...**
Harry Anthony & James F. Harrison

Let The Rest Of The World Go By
2/20 Elizabeth Spencer
14/20 Lewis James & Charles Hart

Let There Be Love
4/40 Sammy Kaye
15/40 Kay Kyser

9/12 **Let Us Have Peace ...**
Reinald Werrenrath

2/36 **Let Yourself Go ...** Fred Astaire

6/17 **Let's All Be Americans Now ...**
American Quartet

18/33 **Let's All Sing Like The Birdies**
Sing ... Ben Bernie

25/40 **Let's Be Buddies ...** Connee Boswell

22/48 **Let's Be Sweethearts Again ...**
Margaret Whiting

Let's Call A Heart A Heart
18/36 Billie Holiday
10/37 Bing Crosby

7/33 **Let's Call It A Day ...**
Hotel Commodore Orchestra

Let's Call The Whole Thing Off
5/37 Fred Astaire
16/37 Shep Fields
20/37 Eddy Duchin

Let's Do It (Let's Fall In Love)
5/29 Irving Aaronson
5/29 Paul Whiteman
9/29 Dorsey Brothers Orchestra

21/41 **Let's Dream This One Out ...**
Frankie Masters

Let's Face The Music And Dance
5/36 Fred Astaire
9/36 Ted Fio Rito

Let's Fall In Love
1/34 Eddy Duchin
8/34 Fred Rich
19/34 Harold Arlen

7/41 **Let's Get Away From It All ...**
Tommy Dorsey

14/36 **Let's Get Drunk And Truck ...**
Tampa Red

Let's Get Lost
1/43 Vaughn Monroe
4/43 Kay Kyser
11/43 Jimmy Dorsey

15/41 **Let's Go Home ...** Charlie Spivak

5/09 **Let's Go In To A Picture Show ...**
Byron G. Harlan

13/50 **Let's Go To Church (Next Sunday**
Morning) ... Margaret Whiting &
Jimmy Wakely

5/32 **Let's Have Another Cup O' Coffee ...**
Fred Waring's Pennsylvanians

18/28 **Let's Misbehave ...** Ben Bernie

Let's Put Out The Lights (And Go To
Sleep)
2/32 Rudy Vallee
2/32 Paul Whiteman
11/32 Ben Bernie

10/38 **Let's Sail To Dreamland ...**
Guy Lombardo

Let's Sing Again
4/36 Fats Waller
14/36 Bobby Breen

18/43 **Let's Start The New Year Right ...**
Bing Crosby

20/39 **Let's Stop The Clock ...**
Hoarce Heidt

1/35 **Let's Swing It ...** Ray Noble

1/07 **Let's Take An Old-Fashioned Walk ...**
Ada Jones & Billy Murray

Little Bird Told Me
1/49 Evelyn Knight
4/49 Blu Lu Barker
6/49 Paula Watson
15/49 Jerry Wayne

Little Bit Independent
1/35 Fats Waller
3/35 Freddy Martin
8/36 Bob Crosby

Little Bit Of Heaven (Shure, They Call It Ireland)
1/15 George MacFarlane
2/15 Charles Harrison
8/15 John Barnes Wells
9/15 John McCormack

6/18 **Little Bit Of Sunshine** ...
Shannon Four

9/53 **Little Blue Riding Hood** ...
Stan Freberg

19/42 **Little Bo Peep Has Lost Her Jeep** ...
Hoarce Heidt

24/53 **Little Boy And The Old Man** ...
Frankie Laine & Jimmy Boyd

13/35 **Little Boy Blue** ... Little Jack Little

Little Brown Jug
3/00 Steve Porter
10/39 Glenn Miller

8/26 **Little Bungalow** ...
Roger Wolfe Kahn

4/24 **Little Butterfly** ... John Steel

Little Curly Hair In A High Chair
6/40 Fats Waller
16/40 Jimmy Dorsey

14/29 **Little Darling, Pal Of Mine** ...
Carter Family

Little Dutch Mill
1/34 Bing Crosby
13/34 Don Bestor
13/34 Guy Lombardo

3/15 **Little Ford Rambled Right Along** ...
Billy Murray

Little Girl
4/31 Joe Venuti featuring Harold Arlen
20/40 Mitchell Ayres
25/48 Nat "King" Cole

8/13 **Little Girl At Home** ...
Harry Macdonough & Marguerite Dunlap

25/47 **Little Girl Blue** ... Margaret Whiting

7/05 **Little Girl, You'll Do** ...
Frank Stanley

Little Grass Shack
20/34 Sol Hopii
26/52 Johnny Maddox

Little Grey Home In The West
4/14 Charles Harrison
5/14 Maggie Teyte

3/37 **Little Heaven Of The Seven Seas** ...
Hoarce Heidt

3/15 **Little House Upon The Hill** ...
James F. Harrison & James Reed

8/05 **Little Johnny Jones Medley** ...
Vess Ossman

7/38 **Little Kiss At Twilight** ...
Benny Goodman

Little Kiss Each Morning (A Little Kiss Each Night)
3/30 Rudy Vallee
11/30 Guy Lombardo

9/38 **Little Lady Make Believe** ...
Guy Lombardo

11/28 **Little Log Cabin Of Dreams** ...
Paul Whiteman

1/95 **Little Lost Child** ... Dan Quinn

28/53 **Little Love** ... Bob Carroll

Little Love, A Little Kiss
4/13 John McCormack
5/16 Maggie Teyte

Little Man Who Wasn't There
7/39 Glenn Miller
11/39 Larry Clinton

Little Man, You've Had A Busy Day
2/34 Emil Coleman
10/34 Isham Jones

30/54 **Little Miss One** ... Jerry Wallace

11/28 **Little Mother** ... Vaughn Deleath

3/18 **Little Mother Of Mine** ...
John McCormack

10/24 **Little Old Clock On The Mantel** ...
Russo & Fiorito's Oriole Orchestra

Little Old Lady
2/37 Abe Lyman
8/37 Shep Fields

9/23 **Little Old Log Cabin In The Lane** ...
Fiddlin' John Carson

24/47 **Little Old Mill (Went Round And Round)** ... Sammy Kaye

2/98 **Little Old New York Is Good Enough For Me** ... George J. Gaskin

Little On The Lonely Side
4/45 Frankie Carle
5/45 Guy Lombardo
22/45 Phil Moore Four

16/29 **Little Orphan Annie** ...
Coon-Sanders Orchestra

Little Pal
1/29 Al Jolson
7/29 Gene Austin
9/29 Paul Whiteman

Little Picture Playhouse In My Heart ... see: (There's A)

Little Red Fox (N'ya, N'ya, Ya Can't Catch Me)
4/40 Kay Kyser
14/41 Hal Kemp

22/53 **Little Red Riding Hood** ...
Al (Jazzbo) Collins

13/36 **Little Rendezvous In Hawaii** ...
    Tommy Dorsey

18/51 **Little Rock Getaway** ... Les Paul

Little Shoemaker
2/54   Gaylords
9/54   Hugo Winterhalter

Little Sir Echo
2/39   Guy Lombardo
3/39   Bing Crosby
7/39   Hoarce Heidt
10/39 Dick Todd

Little Skipper
3/39   Ozzie Nelson
4/39   Tommy Dorsey

21/41 **Little Sleepy Head** ...
    Lawrence Welk

Little Things In Life
11/30 Ted Wallace
4/31   Gus Arnheim

1/54 **Little Things Mean A Lot** ...
    Kitty Kallen

2/35 **Little Things You Used To Do** ...
    Johnny Green

2/52 **Little White Cloud That Cried** ...
    Johnnie Ray

10/35 **Little White Gardenia** ... Hal Kemp

Little White House (At The End Of Honeymoon Lane)
3/27   Johnny Marvin
6/27   Irving Kaufman
11/27 Fred Waring's Pennsylvanians

Little White Lies
1/30   Fred Waring's Pennsylvanians
3/30   Ted Wallace
4/30   Earl Burtnett
2/48   Dick Haymes
11/48 Dinah Shore

19/38 **Little White Lighthouse** ...
    Tommy Dorsey

25/53 **Live It Up** ... Bill Haley

Livery Stable Blues
4/17   Original Dixieland Jazz Band
7/18   W.C. Handy's Orchestra

Living In The Sunlight, Loving In The Moonlight
16/30 Paul Whiteman
20/30 Bernie Cummins

9/29 **Liza (All The Clouds'll Roll Away)** ...
    Al Jolson

20/41 **Lo-Lo-Lita** ... Henri Rene

Loch Lomond
10/12 Evan Williams
9/37   Maxine Sullivan & Claude Thornhill
12/38 Benny Goodman

8/17 **Lohengrin, Act III Prelude** ...
    Boston Symphony Orchestra

20/35 **London On A Rainy Night** ...
    Ambrose

23/41 **Lone Star Trail** ... Bing Crosby

7/24 **Lonely Little Melody** ...
    Paul Whiteman

Lonely Little Robin
14/51 Pinetoppers
25/51 Mindy Carson

Lonely Troubador
2/29   Rudy Vallee
4/29   Ted Lewis

26/52 **Lonely Wine** ... Les Baxter

23/48 **Lonely Woman** ... Stan Kenton

Lonesome
3/09   Haydn Quartet
6/09   Byron G. Harlan

Lonesome And Sorry
3/26   Ruth Etting
14/26 Jean Goldkette

8/31 **Lonesome Lover** ... Isham Jones

6/22 **Lonesome Mama Blues** ...
    Mamie Smith

Lonesome Polecat
27/54 Freddy Martin
28/54 McGuire Sisters

Lonesome Road
10/28 Gene Austin
10/29 Nat Shilkret
3/30   Ted Lewis
12/39 Bing Crosby

15/31 **Lonesome Valley** ... Carter Family

12/26 **Lonesomest Girl In Town** ...
    Morton Downey

20/36 **Long Ago And Far Away** ...
    Ben Bernie

Long Ago (And Far Away)
2/44   Helen Forrest & Dick Haymes
5/44   Bing Crosby
6/44   Jo Stafford
8/44   Perry Como
11/44 Guy Lombardo
16/44 Three Suns

Long Boy
5/18   Prince's Orchestra
10/18 Peerless Quartet

9/13 **Long, Long Ago** ... Geraldine Farrar

5/05 **Longing For You** ... Byron G. Harlan

Longing For You
12/51 Vic Damone
16/51 Sammy Kaye
23/51 Teresa Brewer

18/27 **Look At The World And Smile** ...
    Jean Goldkette

Look For The Silver Lining
1/21   Marion Harris
7/21   Elsie Baker
7/21   Charles Harrison
11/21 Isham Jones
12/21 Lewis James
12/21 Elizabeth Spencer

9/21 **Look For The Silver Lining (Medley)** ... Vernon Country Club Band

Love Locked Out
10/34 Ambrose
18/34 Ray Noble

11/21 **Love Me** ... Ted Lewis

Love Me
4/29 Nat Shilkret
5/29 Paul Whiteman

15/34 **Love Me** ... Glen Gray

Love Me Again
22/53 Sunny Gale
23/53 Pat Terry

Love Me And The World Is Mine
1/06 Henry Burr
1/06 Albert Campbell
6/06 Harry Anthony
7/08 Haydn Quartet

25/52 **Love Me (Baby Can't You Love Me)** ...
Johnnie Ray

7/35 **Love Me Forever** ... Russ Morgan

Love Me, Love Me
18/53 Bobby Wayne
25/53 Dean Martin

24/49 **Love Me, Love Me, Love Me** ...
Eddy Howard

Love Me Or Leave Me
2/29 Ruth Etting
16/34 Benny Goodman
4/36 Benny Goodman

9/20 **Love Me Or Not** ... Enrico Caruso

Love Me Tonight
4/32 Bing Crosby
14/32 George Olsen

Love Nest
1/20 Art Hickman
1/20 John Steel
6/20 Joseph C. Smith's Orchestra

Love Never Dies
5/12 Harry Anthony
5/12 Inez Barbour

23/46 **Love On A Greyhound Bus** ...
Guy Lombardo

Love Sends A Little Gift Of Roses
4/21 Reinald Werrenrath
12/21 Charles Hackett
1/23 Carl Fenton
7/23 Bar Harbor Society Orchestra
10/23 Sam Ash
10/23 Columbia Orchestra
5/24 John McCormack

1/48 **Love Somebody** ...
Doris Day & Buddy Clark

14/37 **Love Song Of A Half-Wit** ...
Hudson-DeLange Orchestra

19/40 **Love Song Of Renaldo** ...
Abe Lyman

7/33 **Love Songs Of The Nile** ...
Leo Reisman

13/29 **Love Tale Of Alsace-Lorraine** ...
Leo Reisman

7/23 **Love Tales** ... Ben Bernie

Love Thy Neighbor
2/34 Bing Crosby
19/34 Raymond Paige

Love Walked In
1/38 Sammy Kaye
7/38 Jimmy Dorsey
7/38 Jan Garber
14/38 Kenny Baker
19/38 Louis Armstrong
8/53 Hilltoppers

10/17 **Love Will Find A Way** ... Reed Miller

Love Will Find A Way
7/22 Ben Selvin
14/22 Edwin Dale

14/21 **Love Will Find The Way** ...
Reed Miller

4/32 **Love, You Funny Thing** ...
Louis Armstrong

10/29 **Love, Your Spell Is Everywhere** ...
Ben Selvin

6/15 **Love's Dream After The Ball** ...
Venetian Trio

3/18 **Love's Garden Of Roses** ...
John McCormack

3/14 **Love's Melody** ... Prince's Orchestra

Love's Old Sweet Song
1/92 Thomas Bott
6/05 Corrine Morgan
10/32 Rondoliers & Piano Pals

6/14 **Love's Own Sweet Song** ...
Charles Harrison & Grace Kerns

3/51 **Loveliest Night Of The Year** ...
Mario Lanza

Lovelight In The Starlight
3/38 Hoarce Heidt
10/38 Buddy Rogers
14/38 Dorothy Lamour

17/37 **Loveliness Of You** ... Russ Morgan

12/36 **Lovely Lady** ... Tommy Dorsey

12/37 **Lovely One** ... Hoarce Heidt

Lovely To Look At
1/35 Eddy Duchin
10/35 Leo Reisman
20/35 Irene Dunne

Lovely Way To Spend An Evening
11/44 Frank Sinatra
16/44 Ink Spots

Lover
3/33 Paul Whiteman
8/33 Guy Lombardo
15/33 Greta Keller
21/48 Les Paul
3/52 Peggy Lee

Lover, Come Back To Me
3/29 Paul Whiteman
6/29 Arden-Ohman Orchestra
9/29 Rudy Vallee
20/30 Perry Askam
16/53 Nat "King" Cole

Make Believe
1/21 Nora Bayes
2/21 Paul Whiteman
5/21 Isham Jones
11/21 Ben Selvin

7/28 **Make Believe** ... Paul Whiteman

Make Believe Island
1/40 Mitchell Ayres
8/40 Jan Savitt
14/40 Dick Todd
17/40 Dick Jurgens
19/40 Sammy Kaye

20/49 **Make Believe (You Are Glad When You're Sorry)** ... Sarah Vaughan

19/54 **Make Her Mine** ... Nat "King" Cole

18/39 **Make It With The Kisses** ...
Les Brown

1/54 **Make Love To Me!** ... Jo Stafford

18/40 **Make Love With A Guitar** ...
Hoarce Heidt

5/12 **Make Me Love You Like I Never Loved Before** ... "That Girl" Quartet

Makin' Whoopee
2/29 Eddie Cantor
8/29 Paul Whiteman
16/29 Ben Bernie

Mam'selle
1/47 Art Lund
1/47 Frank Sinatra
3/47 Dick Haymes
3/47 Pied Pipers
7/47 Ray Dorey
8/47 Dennis Day
14/47 Frankie Laine

14/41 **Mama** ... Hoarce Heidt

24/54 **Mama Doll Song** ... Patti Page

23/54 **Mama, Don't Cry At My Wedding** ...
Joni James

17/38 **Mama Don't Want No Peas An' Rice An' Coconut Oil** ... Count Basie

25/41 **Mama Euquero (I Want My Mama)** ...
Carmen Miranda

13/24 **Mama Goes Where Papa Goes** ...
Sam Lanin

23/53 **(Mama) He Treats Your Daughter Mean** ... Ruth Brown

20/37 **Mama, I Wanna Make Rhythm** ...
Cab Calloway

18/31 **Mama Inez** ... Maurice Chevalier

8/24 **Mama Loves Papa** ... Isham Jones

7/36 **Mama, That Man's Here Again** ...
Ken Murray & The Oswald Comedians

10/38 **Mama, That Moon Is Here Again** ...
Shep Fields

21/51 **Mama Will Bark** ...
Frank Sinatra & Dagmar

10/54 **Mambo Italiano** ...
Rosemary Clooney

27/50 **Mambo (Que Rico El Mambo)** ...
Dave Barbour

1/93 **Mamie, Come And Kiss Your Honey Boy** ... Len Spencer

8/19 **Mammy O' Mine** ...
Yerkes Jazarimba Orchestra

5/17 **Mammy's Little Coal Black Rose** ...
Orpheus Quartet

4/39 **Man And His Dream** ... Bing Crosby

Man Behind The Hammer And The Plow
3/17 Prince's Orchestra
6/17 Andrea Sarto

24/48 **Man Could Be A Wonderful Thing** ...
Ray McKinley

1/30 **Man From The South** ... Ted Weems

Man I Love
4/28 Marion Harris
11/28 Sophie Tucker
15/28 Paul Whiteman
19/28 Fred Rich
20/37 Benny Goodman

30/54 **Man, Man, Is For The Woman Made** ...
Ames Brothers

6/34 **Man On The Flying Trapeze** ...
Walter O'Keefe

Man That Got Away ... *see: Gal*

7/54 **Man Upstairs** ... Kay Starr

9/40 **Man Who Comes Around** ...
Tommy Tucker

7/18 **Man Who Put The Germ In Germany** ... Nora Bayes

6/54 **Man With The Banjo** ...
Ames Brothers

Man With The Mandolin
1/39 Glenn Miller
2/39 Hoarce Heidt
6/39 Wayne King

11/38 **Man With The Whiskers** ...
Hoosier Hot Shots

Managua, Nicaragua
1/47 Guy Lombardo
1/47 Freddy Martin
6/47 Kay Kyser

1/48 **Manana (Is Soon Enough For Me)** ...
Peggy Lee

11/21 **Mandalay** ...
Henry Burr & Albert Campbell

Mandalay
3/24 Al Jolson
6/24 Paul Whiteman

19/54 **Mandolino** ... Les Paul & Mary Ford

Mandy
2/19 Van & Schenck
4/19 Shannon Four
5/20 Ben Selvin

Mandy Lee
1/00	Arthur Collins
2/00	Albert Campbell
3/00	Harry Macdonough

Mandy, Make Up Your Mind
4/25	Paul Whiteman
16/43	Tommy Dorsey

12/22 **Mandy'n Me** ... American Quartet

Manhattan
1/25	Ben Selvin
3/25	Paul Whiteman

2/94 **Manhattan Beach** ...
U.S. Marine Band

9/07 **Manhattan Beach March** ...
Prince's Orchestra

Manhattan Serenade
9/42	Harry James
19/42	Jimmy Dorsey
4/43	Tommy Dorsey

Mansion Of Aching Hearts
1/02	Byron G. Harlan
1/02	Harry Macdonough
2/02	J.W. Myers

11/39 **Many Dreams Ago** ... Artie Shaw

Many Happy Returns Of The Day
3/31	Bing Crosby
16/31	Ipana Troubadors

Many Times
4/53	Eddie Fisher
30/53	Percy Faith

7/20 **Manyana** ... Prince's Orchestra

15/32 **Maori** ... Rudy Vallee

Maple Leaf Rag
2/07	U.S. Marine Band
3/07	Vess Ossman

March Of The Toys
4/11	Victor Herbert
14/39	Tommy Dorsey

10/19 **Marche Francaise** ...
Victor Military Band

6/19 **Marche Lorraine** ...
French Army Band

6/17 **Marche Slave, Parts 1 & 2** ...
Prince's Orchestra

Marcheta
5/22	Olive Kline & Elsie Baker
8/23	Isham Jones
12/24	John McCormack

10/33 **Marching Along Together** ...
Ben Bernie

Margie
7/20	Gene Rodemich
1/21	Eddie Cantor
4/21	Ted Lewis
7/21	Frank Crumit
9/21	Original Dixieland Jazz Band
5/34	Claude Hopkins
15/39	Don Redman

3/05 **Marguerite** ...
Harry Macdonough & John Bieling

Maria Elena
1/41	Jimmy Dorsey
2/41	Wayne King
9/41	Tony Pastor
22/41	Lawrence Welk

23/48 **Maria From Bahia** ... Starlighters

15/29 **Marianne** ... Arden-Ohman Orchestra

5/22 **Marie** ... Ted Lewis

Marie
2/29	Rudy Vallee
9/29	Nat Shilkret
15/29	Franklyn Baur
1/37	Tommy Dorsey
16/38	Tommy Dorsey
13/53	Four Tunes

20/52 **Marilyn** ... Ray Anthony

6/16 **Marimba March** ...
Blue & White Marimba Band

12/20 **Marion (You'll Soon Be Marryin' Me)** ... Billy Murray & Gladys Rice

5/05 **Marriage Is Sublime** ... Bob Roberts

24/51 **Marshmellow World** ... Bing Crosby

Marta (Rambling Rose Of The Wildwood)
19/32	Arthur Tracy
15/50	Tony Martin

2/38 **Martha** ... Larry Clinton

10/12 **Martha - Quartetto Nocturno (Good Night Quartet)** ... Enrico Caruso,
Frances Alda & Marcel Journet

Mary
7/11	Elizabeth Wheeler & Haydn Quartet
6/19	Joseph C. Smith's Orchestra

Mary Ann
3/28	Cliff Edwards
10/28	Ted Lewis

10/23 **Mary, Dear** ... Henry Burr

Mary Lou
3/26	Abe Lyman
7/27	Ipana Troubadors

10/12 **Mary Was My Mother's Name** ...
American Quartet

Mary, You're A Little Bit Old-Fashioned
4/14	Charles Harrison
7/14	Walter Van Brunt

20/43 **Mary's A Grand Old Name** ...
Bing Crosby

23/52 **Mask Is Off** ... Richard Hayes

Masquerade
12/28	Ben Selvin
3/32	Ted Black

4/39 **Masquerade Is Over** ...
Jimmy Dorsey

Masquerade Is Over ...
see: (I'm Afraid)

Matinee
20/48	Vaughn Monroe
22/48	Buddy Clark

4/08 **Maxim's** ... Harry Macdonough

May I Have The Next Romance?
9/37   Lud Gluskin
11/37   Tommy Dorsey

12/33 **May I Have This Waltz, Madame** ...
  Enric Madriguera

15/41 **May I Never Love Again** ...
  Bob Chester

25/50 **May I Take Two Giant Steps** ...
  Eileen Barton

May I?
4/34   Bing Crosby
16/34   Eddy Duchin

12/27 **Maybe** ... Nat Shilkret

Maybe
2/40   Ink Spots
18/40   Bobby Byrne
3/52   Perry Como & Eddie Fisher

4/15 **Maybe A Day, Maybe A Year** ...
  Henry Burr

14/35 **Maybe I'm Wrong Again** ...
  Bing Crosby

Maybe It's Because
5/49   Dick Haymes
9/49   Eddy Howard
20/49   Connie Haines
22/49   Bob Crosby

Maybe It's Because I Love You Too Much
6/33   Rudy Vallee
11/33   Guy Lombardo
17/33   Leo Reisman

22/54 **Maybe Next Time** ... Joni James

3/48 **Maybe You'll Be There** ...
  Gordon Jenkins

7/24 **Maytime** ...
  Fred Waring's Pennsylvanians

9/18 **Maytime Waltz (Will You Remember?)** ... Waldorf-Astoria Dance Orchestra

Mazie
3/21   Yerkes Jazarimba Orchestra
14/21   Green Brothers Novelty Band

20/28 **Mazurka In C Sharp Minor** ...
  Vladamir Horowitz

McNamara's Band
23/40   Jesters
10/46   Bing Crosby

11/31 **Me!** ... Ben Bernie

18/35 **Me And Marie** ... Johnny Green

Me And My Shadow
1/27   "Whispering" Jack Smith
5/27   Nat Shilkret
15/27   Johnny Marvin

13/35 **Me And My Wonderful One** ...
  Cleo Brown

5/25 **Me And The Boy Friend** ...
  Jane Green

Me And The Man In The Moon
8/29   Helen Kane
12/29   Ted Weems
19/29   Cliff Edwards

Me And The Moon
8/36   Hal Kemp
9/36   Bing Crosby

11/37 **Me, Myself, And I** ... Billie Holiday

18/35 **Me Without You** ... Joe Morrison

21/48 **Meadowlands** ... Tex Beneke

Mean To Me
3/29   Ruth Etting
11/29   Helen Morgan
7/37   Teddy Wilson with Billie Holiday

28/51 **Meanderin'** ... Vaughn Monroe

28/54 **Mecque, Mecque** ... Gaylords

15/20 **Meditation** ... Jascha Heifetz

6/11 **Meditation From "Thais"** ...
  Fritz Kreisler

8/32 **Medley From "Face The Music"** ...
  Kate Smith

6/10 **Medley Of Foster Songs** ...
  Peerless Quartet

6/32 **Medley Of Isham Jones Dance Hits** ..
  Frankie Trumbauer

9/06 **Medley Of Old-Time Reels** ...
  Charles D'almaine

7/07 **Meet Me Down At The Corner** ...
  Len Spencer & Ada Jones

Meet Me In Rose-Time, Rosie
3/09   Frank Stanley & Byron Harlan
6/09   Billy Murray & Haydn Quartet

Meet Me In St. Louis, Louis
1/04   Billy Murray
2/04   S.H. Dudley
3/04   J.W. Myers
13/44   Guy Lombardo
22/44   Judy Garland

3/04 **Meet Me In St. Louis Medley** ...
  Arthur Pryor's Band

16/37 **Meet Me In The Moonlight** ...
  Henry Allen

Meet Me Tonight In Dreamland
1/10   Henry Burr
4/10   Harry Anthony
4/10   Elizabeth Wheeler
13/38   Jimmie Davis

5/10 **Meet Me Where The Lanterns Glow** ..
  Haydn Quartet

Meet Mister Callaghan
5/52   Les Paul
11/52   Harry Grove Trio
23/52   Mitch Miller
28/52   Carmen Cavallaro

15/40 **Meet The Sun Half-Way** ...
  Bing Crosby

Melancholy Baby ...
  see: My Melancholy Baby

15/39 **Melancholy Lullaby** ... Glenn Miller

Melancholy Me
16/54 Eddy Howard
21/54 Smith Brothers
25/54 Ella Fitzgerald

Melancholy Mood
8/39 Artie Shaw
18/39 Martha Raye

22/53 **Melancholy Serenade ...**
Jackie Gleason

2/13 **Melinda's Wedding Day ...**
Arthur Collins & Byron Harlan

Melody From The Sky
1/36 Jan Garber
6/36 Eddy Duchin
17/36 Bunny Berigan

6/18 **Melody Land ...** Shannon Four

10/12 **Melody Of Love ...**
Lucy Isabelle Marsh

22/48 **Melody Time ...** Vaughn Monroe

Memories
4/16 John Barnes Wells
9/16 Henry Burr

Memories Of France
6/28 Gene Austin
19/28 Henry Burr

Memories Of You
18/30 Louis Armstrong
29/40 Ink Spots

Memory Lane
1/24 Fred Waring's Pennsylvanians
8/24 Paul Specht

24/41 **Mem'ry Of A Rose ...** Sammy Kaye

19/28 **Memory That Time Cannot Erase ...**
Vernon Dalhart & Carson Robison

Memphis Blues
4/14 Prince's Orchestra
9/14 Victor Military Band
8/15 Arthur Collins & Byron Harlan
9/27 Ted Lewis
15/44 Harry James

19/40 **Mene Mene Tekel ...** Shep Fields

18/50 **Merry Christmas Polka ...**
Andrews Sisters

Merry-Go-Round
6/35 Duke Ellington
15/36 Mills Blue Rhythm Band

Merry-Go-Round Broke Down
1/37 Shep Fields
1/37 Russ Morgan
2/37 Eddy Duchin
7/37 Jimmie Lunceford
12/37 Dick Robertson

Merry-Go-Round Waltz
18/49 Guy Lombardo
29/49 Art Mooney

10/11 **Merry Wedding Bells ...**
Lyric Quartet

Merry Widow Waltz
2/07 Victor Orchestra
6/08 Prince's Orchestra

4/05 **Message Of The Old Church Bell ...**
Byron G. Harlan

Message Of The Red Rose
9/09 Harry Macdonough & Elise Stevenson

9/09 **Message Of The Red Rose ...**
Elise Stevenson

5/03 **Message Of The Violets ...**
J.W. Myers

9/07 **Messiah: Every Valley Shall Be
Exalted ...** Harry Macdonough

19/51 **Metro Polka ...** Frankie Laine

3/38 **Mexicali Rose ...** Bing Crosby

23/53 **Mexican Joe ...** Jim Reeves

29/53 **Mexico ...** Ken Remo

16/44 **Mexico Joe ...** Ivie Anderson

13/39 **Mexiconga ...** Gray Gordon

6/26 **Miami ...** Al Jolson

14/27 **Miami Storm ...** Vernon Dalhart

1/91 **Michael Casey As A Physician ...**
Russell Hunting

1/92 **Michael Casey At The Telephone ...**
Russell Hunting

2/93 **Michael Casey Departing From New
York En Route To Boston By
Steamboat ...** Russell Hunting

1/92 **Michael Casey Taking The Census ...**
Russell Hunting

3/47 **Mickey ...** Ted Weems

19/36 **Mickey Mouse's Birthday Party ...**
Wayne King

'Mid The Green Fields Of Virginia
2/99 Harry Macdonough & S.H. Dudley
4/99 George J. Gaskin
4/99 Frank Stanley

16/37 **Midnight At The Onyx ...**
Hudson-DeLange Orchestra

Midnight Blue
12/36 Russ Morgan
15/36 Henry Allen

24/53 **Midnight In Paris ...** Richard Hayes

16/47 **Midnight Masquerade ...**
Monica Lewis

Midnight Rose
5/23 Abe Lyman
10/23 Charles Hart

29/53 **Midnight Sleighride ...**
Sauter-Finegan Orchestra

30/52 **Midnight Special ...** Weavers

4/25 **Midnight Waltz ...** Carl Fenton

9/18 **Midsummer Night's Dream -
Scherzo ...** Philadelphia Orchestra

Mighty Like A Rose
3/03 George Alexander
6/11 Marguerite Dunlap
9/16 Geraldine Farrar

Milenberg Joys
15/15   Jimmy Joy
17/28   McKinney's Cotton Pickers

Milkman, Keep Those Bottles Quiet
7/44   Ella Mae Morse
10/44   Woody Herman
13/44   King Sisters

17/37   **Miller's Daughter Marianne ...**
     Hoarce Heidt

Million Dreams Ago
12/40   Dick Jurgens
24/40   Glenn Miller

23/53   **Milwaukee Polka ... Patti Page**

Mimi
10/21   Paul Biese Trio & Frank Crumit
9/32   Maurice Chevalier

Mindin' My Business
8/24   Frank Crumit
12/24   Ernest Hare

12/33   **Mine ... Emil Coleman**

14/41   **Minka ... Sammy Kaye**

1/31   **Minnie The Moocher ...**
     Cab Calloway

8/32   **Minnie The Moocher's Wedding Day ...**
     Cab Calloway

9/15   **Minstrel Parade ...**
     Arthur Collins & Byron Harlan

3/01   **Minstrel Record No. 3 ...**
     Georgia Minstrel Co.

4/01   **Minstrels: First Part, No. 5 ...**
     Georgia Minstrel Co.

Misirlou
22/41   Harry James
7/46   Jan August
26/53   Leon Berry

8/27   **Miss Annabelle Lee ... Ben Selvin**

19/34   **Miss Otis Regrets (She's Unable To Lunch Today) ... Ethel Waters**

Miss You
8/42   Dinah Shore
9/42   Bing Crosby
21/42   Eddy Howard
22/42   Freddy Martin

12/43   **Mission To Moscow ...**
     Benny Goodman

M-I-S-S-I-S-S-I-P-P-I
2/17   Anna Wheaton
9/17   Ada Jones

M-I-S-S-I-S-S-I-P-P-I
18/50   Kay Starr
22/50   Red Foley
23/50   Art Mooney
26/50   Bill Darnel

8/22   **Mississippi Cradle ...**
     Prince's Orchestra

10/11   **Mississippi Dippy Dip ...**
     Arthur Collins & Byron Harlan

17/27   **Mississippi Flood ... Vernon Dalhart**

Mississippi Mud
6/28   Paul Whiteman
18/28   Frankie Trumbauer

Mississippi Stoker
6/07   Bert Williams
4/10   Bert Williams

20/28   **Mississippi Sweetheart ...**
     Adrian Schubert

Missouri Waltz
3/16   Victor Military Band
4/16   Prince's Orchestra
9/16   Jaudas' Society Orchestra
1/17   Elsie Baker
3/17   Henry Burr & Albert Campbell
10/18   Earl Fuller

Mister And Mississippi
8/51   Patti Page
13/51   Dennis Day
18/51   Tennessee Ernie Ford

Mr. And Mrs. Is The Name
17/34   Victor Young
19/35   Dick Powell

8/05   **Mr. And Mrs. Murphy ...**
     Len Spencer & Ada Jones

2/02   **Mister Dooley ... Dan Quinn**

Mister Five By Five
10/42   Freddie Slack
14/42   Andrews Sisters
1/43   Harry James

Mr. Gallagher And Mr. Shean
1/22   Gallagher & Shean
1/22   Ernest Hare & Billy Jones
10/22   Furman & Nash
12/22   Irving Kaufman & Jack Kaufman
7/38   Bing Crosby
7/38   Johnny Mercer

15/37   **Mr. Ghost Goes To Town ...**
     Mills Blue Rhythm Band

17/28   **Mr. Hoover And Mr. Smith ...**
     Ernest Hare & Billy Jones

18/40   **Mister Meadowlark ...**
     Bing Crosby & Johnny Mercer

9/09   **Mister Othello ... Ada Jones**

Mr. Radio Man
4/24   Al Jolson
5/24   Lewis James

Mister Sandman
1/54   Chordettes
20/54   Buddy Morrow
28/54   Lancers
5/55   Four Aces

10/53   **Mister Tap Toe ... Doris Day**

19/38   **Mister Toscanini, Swing For Minnie ...**
     Cab Calloway

9/50   **Mr. Touchdown, U.S.A. ...**
     Hugo Winterhalter

27/49   **Mistletoe Kiss ... Primo Scala**

30/54   **Misty ... Erroll Garner Trio**

10/36   **Misty Islands Of The Highlands ...**
     Jan Garber

22/51	**Mixed Emotions** ... Rosemary Clooney		**Moon Glow**	
		1/34	Benny Goodman	
	Moanin' Low	2/34	Duke Ellington	
5/29	Libby Holman	7/34	Cab Calloway	
19/29	Charleston Chasers	8/34	Glen Gray	
11/37	Teddy Wilson with Billie Holiday	8/36	Benny Goodman	
			Moon Got In My Eyes	
21/54	**Mobile** ... Julius LaRosa	1/37	Bing Crosby	
	Mockin' Bird Hill	11/37	Shep Fields	
2/51	Patti Page		**Moon Has His Eyes On You**	
2/51	Les Paul & Mary Ford	4/06	Frank Stanley & Corrine Morgan	
10/51	Pinetoppers	6/06	Ada Jones	
16/51	Russ Morgan	7/39	**Moon Is A Silver Dollar** ... Lawrence Welk	
23/52	**Mocking Bird** ... Four Lads *(also see: Listen To The Mockingbird)*	20/53	**Moon Is Blue** ... Sauter-Finegan Orchestra	
30/50	**Molasses, Molasses** ... Roberta Quinlan	7/30	**Moon Is Low** ... George Olsen	
			Moon Love	
25/40	**Molly Malone** ... Gray Gordon	1/39	Glenn Miller	
28/44	**Moment I Laid Eyes On You** ... Cab Calloway	7/39	Al Donohue	
		8/39	Paul Whiteman	
11/46	**Moment I Met You** ... Tommy Dorsey	14/39	Mildred Bailey	
	Mona Lisa		**Moon Of Manakoora**	
1/50	Nat "King" Cole	10/38	Bing Crosby	
7/50	Victor Young	15/38	Ray Noble	
14/50	Harry James	29/44	**Moon On My Pillow** ... Jimmy Dorsey	
14/50	Art Lund		**Moon Over Burma**	
16/50	Ralph Flanagan	26/40	Shep Fields	
16/50	Charlie Spivak	23/49	Gene Krupa	
29/50	Dennis Day	14/32	**Moon Over Dixie** ... Duke Ellington	
24/48	**Monday Again** ... Frankie Laine		**Moon Over Miami**	
19/28	**Monday Date** ... Louis Armstrong	19/35	Connee Boswell	
11/38	**Monday Morning** ... Kay Kyser	1/36	Eddy Duchin	
23/54	**Money Burns A Hole In My Pocket** ... Dean Martin	5/36	Jan Garber	
		14/36	Art Karle	
12/34	**Money In My Pockets** ... Mills Brothers		**Moon Song**	
		3/33	Wayne King	
9/46	**Money Is The Root Of All Evil** ... Andrews Sisters	5/33	Jack Denny	
		6/33	Art Kassel	
27/49	**Money, Marbles And Chalk** ... Patti Page	13/34	**Moon Was Yellow (And The Night Was Young)** ... Bing Crosby	
16/29	**Mooche, The** ... Duke Ellington	5/21	**Moonbeams** ... All-Star Trio	
	Mood Indigo	3/06	**Moonlight** ... Sousa's Band	
3/31	Duke Ellington		**Moonlight And Roses**	
19/34	Jimmie Lunceford	3/25	John McCormack	
14/54	Norman Petty Trio	9/25	Ray Miller	
24/54	Four Freshmen	24/54	Three Suns	
	Mood That I'm In		**Moonlight And Shadows**	
8/37	Teddy Wilson with Billie Holiday	3/37	Shep Fields	
20/37	Lionel Hampton	5/37	Eddy Duchin	
19/37	**Moon At Sea** ... Cab Calloway	10/37	Bing Crosby	
	Moon-Faced, Starry-Eyed	10/37	Dorothy Lamour	
14/47	Freddy Martin		**Moonlight Bay**	
21/47	Benny Goodman with Johnny Spencer	1/12	American Quartet	
22/41	**Moon Fell In The River** ... Guy Lombardo	3/12	Dolly Connolly	
		14/51	Bing Crosby & Gary Crosby	
		6/12	**Moonlight Bay Medley** ... Conway's Band	

Moonlight Becomes You
1/43	Bing Crosby
5/43	Glenn Miller
15/43	Harry James

1/42 **Moonlight Cocktail** ... Glenn Miller

7/10 **Moonlight In Jungle Land** ...
Arthur Collins & Byron Harlan

Moonlight In Vermont
15/45	Billy Butterfield
29/54	Margaret Whiting

10/24 **Moonlight Kisses** ...
California Ramblers

17/28 **Moonlight Madness (Then You Were Gone)** ... Ted Lewis

25/41 **Moonlight Masquerade** ...
Jimmy Dorsey

Moonlight Mood
22/42	Connee Boswell
11/43	Glenn Miller
13/43	Kay Kyser

7/30 **Moonlight On The Colorado** ...
Ben Selvin

Moonlight On The Ganges
2/26	Paul Whiteman
17/27	Fred Rich

Moonlight Saving Time ...
see: (There Ought To Be A)

3/39 **Moonlight Serenade** ... Glenn Miller

8/12 **Moonlight, The Rose, And You** ...
Frank Stanley & Henry Burr

26/48 **Moonlight Whispers** ... Tex Beneke

20/36 **Moonrise On The Lowlands** ...
Willie Bryant

9/10 **Moose March** ... Vess Ossman

More And More
10/45	Tommy Dorsey
14/45	Perry Como

22/54 **More And More** ... Webb Pierce

30/49 **More Beer!** ... Andrews Sisters

More I See You
7/45	Dick Haymes
12/45	Harry James

25/53 **More Luck Than Money** ...
Lily Ann Carol

6/38 **More Than Ever** ... Tommy Dorsey

More Than You Know
9/30	Ruth Etting
15/37	Mildred Bailey
19/46	Perry Como

9/11 **Moriah - Scotch Medley** ...
Montgomery & Stone

Morning Side Of The Mountain
16/51	Paul Weston
24/51	Tommy Edwards
27/51	Merv Griffin
29/51	Jan Garber

Morning Will Come
5/23	Al Jolson
9/23	Georgie Price

8/24 **Morvanna** ... Paul Specht

Most Beautiful Girl In The World
27/52	Ted Straeter
21/53	Tommy Dorsey

16/28 **Moten Stomp** ... Bennie Moten

2/98 **Moth And The Flame** ...
Albert Campbell

M-O-T-H-E-R (A Word That Means The World To Me)
1/16	Henry Burr
7/16	George Wilton Ballard

17/52 **Mother At Your Feet Is Kneeling** ...
Bobby Wayne

Mother Machree
1/11	John McCormack
1/11	Will Oakland
7/13	Chauncey Olcott
5/15	Taylor Trio

2/28 **Mother Of Mine, I Still Have You** ...
Al Jolson

7/07 **Motor March** ... Vess Ossman

Moulin Rouge Theme ...
see: Song From

4/26 **Mountain Greenery** ...
Roger Wolfe Kahn

22/52 **Mountain Laurel** ... Vaughn Monroe

29/48 **Mountaineer And The Jabberwock** ...
John Laurenz

14/43 **Move It Over** ... Ethel Merman

21/48 **Move On Up A Little Higher** ...
Mahalia Jackson

30/53 **Moving Away** ... Lu Ann Simms

Mr. ... see: Mister

Muddy Water
5/27	Ben Bernie
10/27	Harry Richman
11/27	Paul Whiteman

23/41 **Muffin Man** ... Ella Fitzgerald

Mule Train
1/49	Frankie Laine
4/49	Bing Crosby
9/49	Tennessee Ernie Ford
10/49	Vaughn Monroe
14/49	Gordon MacRae

5/43 **Murder, He Says** ... Dinah Shore

18/51 **Music By The Angels** ... Vic Damone

Music Goes Round And Round
1/36	Tommy Dorsey
1/36	Riley-Farley Orchestra
4/36	Hal Kemp
7/36	Frank Froeba
15/38	Riley-Farley Orchestra

9/35 **Music Hall Rag** ... Benny Goodman

10/32 **Music In The Moonlight** ...
Jimmie Grier

Music, Maestro, Please
1/38	Tommy Dorsey
4/38	Art Kassel
5/38	Kay Kyser
13/50	Frankie Laine

9/41 **Music Makers** ... Harry James

Music Makes Me
14/34	Fred Astaire
15/34	Emil Coleman

Music! Music! Music!
1/50	Teresa Brewer
5/50	Carmen Cavallaro
5/50	Freddy Martin
14/50	Ames Brothers
17/50	Hugo Winterhalter
18/50	Mickey Katz

10/44 **Music Stopped** ... Woody Herman

7/17 **Musical Sam From Alabam'** ...
Peerless Quartet

10/06 **Musical Yankee** ... Len Spencer

24/51 **Musicians, The** ...
Dinah Shore, Betty Hutton, Tony
Martin, & Phil Harris

Muskrat Ramble
8/26	Louis Armstrong
10/54	McGuire Sisters
25/54	Matys Brothers
28/54	Louis Armstrong

21/42 **Mussolini's Letter To Hitler** ...
Carson Robison

15/53 **Must I Cry Again** ... Hilltoppers

18/34 **Must We Say Goodnight (So Soon?)** ...
Freddy Martin

My ... *also see: Ma*

My Adobe Hacienda
23/41	Louise Massey
2/47	Eddy Howard
9/47	Dinning Sisters
13/47	Billy Williams Quartet
16/47	Kenny Baker
16/47	Louise Massey

My Angel (Angela Mia)
1/28	Paul Whiteman
2/28	Vincent Lopez
16/28	Scrappy Lambert
23/54	Don, Dick, N' Jimmy
27/54	Ralph Flanagan

4/18 **My Baby Boy** ... Lewis James

My Baby Just Cares For Me
4/30	Ted Weems
29/54	Hi-Los

14/45 **My Baby Said Yes** ...
Bing Crosby & Louise Jordan

7/52 **My Baby's Coming Home** ...
Les Paul & Mary Ford

3/02 **My Beautiful Irish Maid** ...
Harry Macdonough

My Beautiful Lady
3/11	Lucy Isabelle Marsh
9/11	Grace Kerns
9/11	Elizabeth Spencer

8/18 **My Belgian Rose** ... Charles Hart

My Best Girl
4/25	Isham Jones
4/25	Nick Lucas
15/25	Cliff Edwards

1/95 **My Best Girl's A New Yorker** ...
Edward M. Favor

17/46 **My Best To You** ... Eddy Howard

1/15 **My Bird Of Paradise** ...
Peerless Quartet

9/29 **My Blackbirds Are Bluebirds Now** ...
Ruth Etting

My Blue Heaven
1/27	Gene Austin
1/27	Paul Whiteman
7/28	Nick Lucas
9/28	Don Voorhees
17/28	Seger Ellis
17/39	Sammy Kaye

7/28 **My Blue Ridge Mountain Home** ...
Vernon Dalhart

10/49 **My Bolero** ... Vic Damone

8/38 **My Bonnie Lies Over The Ocean** ...
Ella Logan

9/16 **My Bonny Bonny Jean** ...
Harry Lauder

My Buddy
1/22	Henry Burr
5/23	Ernest Hare
11/23	Ben Bernie
23/42	Sammy Kaye

My Cabin Of Dreams
3/37	Tommy Dorsey
11/37	Gus Arnheim
18/37	George Hall

My Carolina Home
7/27	Vernon Dalhart & Carson Robison
16/27	Riley Puckett

My Carolina Lady
4/02	Harry Macdonough
3/05	Ada Jones

5/26 **My Castle In Spain** ... Isham Jones

5/04 **My Cosey Corner Girl** ... Henry Burr

1/93 **My Country 'Tis Of Thee** ...
Jules Levy
(also see: America)

5/09 **My Cousin Caruso** ... Billy Murray

24/48 **My Cousin Louella** ... Frank Sinatra

7/05 **My Cozy Corner Girl** ...
Harry Macdonough

4/99 **My Creole Sue** ... Steve Porter

9/33 **My Darling** ... Don Bestor

My Ideal
12/31	Maurice Chevalier
12/43	Billy Butterfield
5/44	Jimmy Dorsey
11/44	Maxine Sullivan

My Irish Molly O
3/05	Arthur Collins
3/05	Billy Murray
9/05	Harry Tally
9/06	Vess Ossman

My Irish Rosie
2/07	Ada Jones
5/07	J.W. Myers

My Isle Of Golden Dreams
4/20	Ben Selvin
15/39	Glenn Miller
18/39	Bing Crosby

17/53 **My Jealous Eyes** ... Patti Page

17/38 **My Kid's Singing Swing Songs** ...
Eddie DeLange

18/36 **My Kingdom For A Kiss** ...
Dick Powell

10/11 **My Laddie** ... Alma Gluck

21/53 **My Lady Loves To Dance** ...
Julius LaRosa

10/37 **My Last Affair** ... Mildred Bailey

My Last Affair ... see: (This Is)

My Last Good-Bye
6/39	Henry Busse
6/39	Dick Jurgens
13/39	Glenn Miller

6/20 **My Little Bimbo Down On The Bimbo
Isle** ... Frank Crumit

19/37 **My Little Buckaroo** ... Bing Crosby

My Little Canoe
2/05	Haydn Quartet
3/05	Henry Burr
7/05	Grace Nelson

14/42 **My Little Cousin** ... Benny Goodman

1/15 **My Little Dream Girl** ...
James F. Harrison & James Reed

4/02 **My Little Gipsy Maid** ... J.W. Myers

My Little Girl
2/15	Henry Burr & Albert Campbell
7/15	Ada Jones & Will Robbins

My Little Grass Shack In Kealakekua, Hawaii
1/34	Ted Fio Rito
10/34	Ben Pollack

25/52 **My Little Nest Of Heavenly Blue** ...
Connee Boswell with Artie Shaw

My Little Persian Rose
7/13	Peerless Quartet
10/13	"That Girl" Quartet

4/33 **My Love** ... Bing Crosby

22/52 **My Love And Devotion** ...
Perry Como

29/53 **My Love, My Life, My Happiness** ...
Ames Brothers

8/53 **My Love, My Love** ... Joni James

15/30 **My Love Parade** ...
Maurice Chevalier

7/06 **My Lovin' Henry** ... Ada Jones

My Lucky Star
4/29	Paul Whiteman
11/29	Fred Waring's Pennsylvanians

My Mammy
1/21	Paul Whiteman
4/21	Peerless Quartet
8/21	Aileen Stanley
8/21	Yerkes Jazarimba Orchestra
11/21	Isham Jones
2/28	Al Jolson
18/47	Al Jolson

My Man
2/21	Paul Whiteman
7/21	Aileen Stanley
1/22	Fanny Brice
12/28	Fanny Brice
20/29	Belle Baker
14/38	Teddy Wilson with Billie Holiday
9/39	Wayne King
23/41	Dinah Shore

8/38 **My Margarita** ... Hoarce Heidt

My Melancholy Baby
9/15	Walter Van Brunt
3/28	Gene Austin
20/35	Al Bowlly
6/36	Teddy Wilson
14/39	Bing Crosby
5/47	Sam Donohue

10/32 **My Mom** ... Kate Smith

11/33 **My Moonlight Madonna** ...
Paul Whiteman

1/97 **My Mother Was A Lady** ...
Dan Quinn

8/29 **My Mother's Eyes** ... George Jessel

4/16 **My Mother's Rosary** ... Henry Burr

My! My!
13/40	Tommy Dorsey
13/40	"Rochester"

4/28 **My Ohio Home** ... Nick Lucas

7/34 **My Old Flame** ... Guy Lombardo

My Old Kentucky Home
1/98	Edison Male Quartette
2/03	Haydn Quartet
3/06	Harry Macdonough
5/10	Geraldine Farrar
3/16	Alma Gluck
9/18	Columbia Stellar Quartet
9/18	Lucy Gates

My Old New Hampshire Home
1/98	George J. Gaskin
2/99	Frank Stanley
4/99	Albert Campbell
4/99	S.H. Dudley

My One And Only
14/28	Jane Green
18/29	Fred Astaire

11/53 **My One And Only Heart** ...
    Perry Como

28/53 **My One And Only Love** ...
    Frank Sinatra

My Own
5/38   Tommy Dorsey
17/38   George Hall
15/39   Deanna Durbin

8/16 **My Own Home Town In Ireland** ...
    George MacFarlane

My Own Iona
3/16   Charles King & Elizabeth Brice
1/17   Hoarce Wright

My Own True Love ...
    see: Tara's Theme

5/03 **My Own United States** ...
    J.W. Myers

11/24 **My Papa Doesn't Two-Time No
Time** ... Al Jolson

1/94 **My Pearl Is A Bowery Girl** ...
    Dan Quinn

18/28 **My Pet** ... Paul Ash

My Pony Boy
2/09   Ada Jones
3/09   Peerless Quartet

9/10 **My Prairie Song Bird** ...
    Frank Stanley & Henry Burr

My Prayer
2/39   Glenn Miller
3/39   Ink Spots

15/30 **My Pretty Quadroon** ...
    Beverly Hill Billies

7/22 **My Rambler Rose** ... Paul Whiteman

14/40 **My Resistance Is Low** ...
    Orrin Tucker

21/54 **My Restless Lover** ... Patti Page

My Reverie
1/38   Larry Clinton
3/38   Bing Crosby
10/38   Mildred Bailey
11/38   Glenn Miller
13/38   Eddy Duchin

18/36 **My Romance** ... Paul Whiteman

8/20 **My Sahara Rose** ... Happy Six

5/04 **My San Domingo Maid** ...
    Harry Macdonough

16/34 **My Shawl** ... Castillian Troubadors

4/44 **My Shining Hour** ... Glen Gray

My Silent Love
3/32   Ruby Newman
4/32   Isham Jones
8/32   Roger Wolfe Kahn

My Sin
2/29   Ben Selvin
7/29   Fred Waring's Pennsylvanians
19/29   Belle Baker
25/47   Julia Lee
21/54   Georgia Gibbs

My Sister And I
1/41   Jimmy Dorsey
15/41   Bea Wain
17/41   Bob Chester
20/41   Benny Goodman

28/54 **My Son, My Son** ... Vera Lynn

10/31 **My Song** ... Rudy Vallee

My Song Of The Nile
7/29   Melody Three
8/29   Ben Selvin
17/29   Nat Shilkret

5/10 **My Southern Rose** ... Henry Burr

My Stormy Weather Pal
13/28   Ben Selvin
19/28   Johnny Johnson

11/46 **My Sugar Is So Refined** ...
    Johnny Mercer

3/99 **My Sunday Girl** ... S.H. Dudley

2/00 **My Sunny Southern Home** ...
    Harry Macdonough

My Sunny Tennessee
11/21   Broadway Quartet
3/22   Peerless Quartet

8/18 **My Sunshine Jane** ... Sterling Trio

5/19 **My Swanee Home** ...
    Vivian Holt & Lillian Rosedale

6/15 **My Sweet Adair** ...
    James F. Harrison & James Reed

5/29 **My Sweeter Than Sweet** ...
    Leo Reisman

2/92 **My Sweetheart's The Man In The
Moon** ... F.F. Burnham

My Sweetie Went Away
8/23   Billy Murray & Ed Smalle
10/23   Dolly Kay

8/15 **My Tango Girl** ...
    Albert & Monroe Jockers

7/15 **My Tango Girl** ...
    Victor Military Band

8/29 **My Time Is Your Time** ...
    Rudy Vallee

11/29 **My Tonia** ... Nick Lucas

27/52 **My Tormented Heart** ...
    Sarah Vaughan

My Truly, Truly Fair
2/51   Guy Mitchell
4/51   Vic Damone
18/51   Freddy Martin
28/51   Ray Anthony

My Walking Stick
8/38   Tommy Dorsey
17/38   Ray Noble

**My Wife's Gone To The Country
(Hurrah! Hurrah!)**
4/09   Arthur Collins & Byron Harlan
7/09   Bob Roberts

My Wild Irish Rose
1/99	Albert Campbell
1/99	George J. Gaskin
3/00	Harry Macdonough
2/05	Haydn Quartet
5/13	Chauncey Olcott
7/15	John McCormack
19/37	Jan Garber

9/32 **My Woman!** ... Ted Lewis

7/14 **My Wonderful Dream Girl** ...
John Barnes Wells

16/39 **My Wubba Dolly** ... Ella Fitzgerald

My Yiddishe Momme
7/26	Willie Howard
5/28	Sophie Tucker

4/20 **Mystery** ... Paul Biese Trio

N

2/18 **'N Everything** ... Al Jolson

13/28 **Nagasacki** ... Ipana Troubadors

3/02 **Nancy Brown** ... J.W. Myers

10/45 **Nancy (With The Laughing Face)** ...
Frank Sinatra

25/54 **Napoleon** ... Mitch Miller

10/34 **Nasty Man** ... Rudy Vallee

National Emblem March
9/09	Arthur Pryor's Band
9/16	Arthur Pryor's Band

23/53 **Native Dancer** ... Rusty Draper

19/38 **Naturally** ... Rudy Vallee

Nature Boy
1/48	Nat "King" Cole
7/48	Frank Sinatra
9/48	Sarah Vaughan
11/48	Dick Haymes

21/47 **Naughty Angeline** ... Dick Haymes

5/12 **Naughty Marietta Intermezzo** ...
Victor Herbert

5/11 **Naughty Marietta Selection** ...
Victor Herbert

Navajo
1/04	Billy Murray
3/04	Harry Macdonough
3/04	J.W. Myers

4/16 **Neapolitan Love Song** ...
Reinald Werrenrath

11/28 **Neapolitan Nights (Oh, Night Of Splendor)** ... Nat Shilkret

1/92 **Near It** ... Len Spencer

Near You
1/47	Francis Craig
2/47	Andrews Sisters
3/47	Larry Green
3/47	Alvino Rey
4/47	Elliot Lawrence
12/47	Two-Ton Baker

Nearer My God To Thee
9/06	Richard Jose
8/14	John McCormack

Nearness Of You
5/40	Glenn Miller
16/53	Bob Manning

7/22 **'Neath The South Sea Moon** ...
Paul Whiteman

7/11 **'Neath The Southern Moon** ...
Merle Tillotson

Need You
7/49	Jo Stafford & Gordon MacRae
30/49	Guy Lombardo

16/34 **Needle In A Haystack** ...
Leo Reisman

Neighbors
6/34	Isham Jones
15/34	Freddy Martin

Nellie Kelly I Love You
7/23	American Quartet
9/23	Prince's Orchestra

5/24 **Never Again** ... Isham Jones

19/51 **Never Been Kissed** ... Freddy Martin

5/36 **Never Gonna Dance** ... Fred Astaire

Never In A Million Years
2/37	Bing Crosby with Jimmy Dorsey
7/37	Glen Gray
8/37	Mildred Bailey

3/16 **Never Mo'** ... Bert Williams

18/37 **Never Should Have Told You** ...
Benny Goodman

Nevertheless (I'm In Love With You)
5/31	Jack Denny
4/49	Mills Brothers
2/50	Paul Weston
9/50	Ray Anthony
10/50	Ralph Flanagan
11/50	Frankie Laine
14/50	Frank Sinatra

16/37 **New East St. Louis Toodle-oo** ...
Duke Ellington
(also see: East St. Louis Toodle-oo)

16/32 **New Farewell Blues** ... Ted Lewis

23/53 **New Juke Box Saturday Night** ...
Modernaires With Paula Kelly
(also see: Juke Box)

21/48 **New Look** ... Freddy Martin

5/39 **New Moon And An Old Serenade** ...
Tommy Dorsey

9/34 **New Moon Is Over My Shoulder** ...
Johnny Green

21/47 **New Pretty Blonde** ... Moon Mullican

New San Antonio Rose
7/41   Bing Crosby
11/41   Bob Wills
19/43   Bob Wills
         (also see: San Antonio Rose)

20/46   **New Spanish Two-Step** ... Bob Wills

10/31   **New Sun In The Sky** ...
         Leo Reisman with Fred Astaire

10/30   **New Tiger Rag** ... Paul Whiteman

Nice Work If You Can Get It
8/37   Shep Fields
20/37   Teddy Wilson with Billie Holiday
1/38   Fred Astaire
10/38   Maxine Sullivan
12/38   Andrews Sisters

14/36   **Nickel In The Slot** ... Wingy Manone

22/41   **Nickel Serenade** ... Andrews Sisters

17/32   **Night** ... Jack Denny

Night And Day
1/32   Leo Reisman with Fred Astaire
2/33   Eddy Duchin
13/34   Eddy Duchin
24/40   Charlie Barnet
16/42   Frank Sinatra
15/44   Frank Sinatra
21/46   Bing Crosby

Night Before Christmas ...
         see: (Don't Wait Till)

9/52   **Night Before Christmas Song** ...
         Rosemary Clooney & Gene Autry

10/24   **Night Hawk Blues** ...
         Coon-Sanders Orchestra

Night Is Filled With Music
11/38   Will Hudson
13/38   Hal Kemp

Night Is Young
14/35   Glen Gray
17/35   Smith Ballew

Night Is Young And You're So Beautiful
5/37   Jan Garber
5/37   George Hall
15/37   Wayne King
26/51   Ray Anthony

9/39   **Night Must Fall** ... Xavier Cugat

4/26   **Night Of Love** ... Ben Selvin

10/34   **Night On The Desert** ...
         Leo Reisman

7/34   **Night On The Water** ...
         Guy Lombardo

14/33   **Night Owl** ... George Olsen

8/17   **Night Time In Little Italy** ...
         Arthur Collins & Byron Harlan

27/52   **Night Train** ... Buddy Morrow

3/00   **Night Trip To Buffalo** ...
         American Quartet

10/32   **Night Was Made For Love** ...
         Leo Reisman

14/32   **Night When Love Was Born** ...
         Ruth Etting

Night Wind
9/35   Benny Goodman
10/35   Dorsey Brothers Orchestra

Nightingale Sang In Berkeley Square
2/40   Glenn Miller
10/40   Ray Noble
3/41   Guy Lombardo
21/41   Sammy Kaye

Nightingale Song
4/16   Alma Gluck
7/17   Lucy Gates

7/38   **Nightmare** ... Artie Shaw

Nighty Night
13/41   Alvino Rey
24/41   Dick Jurgens

Nina Never Knew
13/52   Sauter-Finegan Orchestra
19/52   Johnny Desmond

27/53   **Nina-Non** ... Joni James

22/42   **1942 Turkey In The Straw** ...
         Carson Robison

13/31   **Ninety-Nine Out Of A Hundred (Wanna Be Loved)** ... Ben Bernie

8/45   **No Can Do** ... Guy Lombardo

No Greater Love ... *see: (There Is)*

10/53   **No Help Wanted** ... Rusty Draper

9/43   **No Letter Today** ... Ted Daffan

No Love, No Nothin'
4/44   Ella Mae Morse
5/44   Johnny Long
28/44   Jan Garber

21/53   **No Moon At All** ...
         Ames Brothers with Les Brown

26/54   **No More** ... De John Sisters

9/40   **No Name Jive** ... Glen Gray

4/09   **No News, Or What Killed The Dog** ...
         Nat Wills

1/23   **No, No, Nora** ... Eddie Cantor

26/54   **No One But You** ...
         Charlie Applewhite

No Other Love
8/50   Jo Stafford
1/53   Perry Como

No Other One
5/35   Benny Goodman
7/35   Little Jack Little

5/18   **No Place Like Home** ...
         Bert Williams

No Regrets
4/36   Tommy Dorsey
9/36   Billie Holiday

24/53   **No Stone Unturned** ... June Hutton

9/35   **No Strings** ... Fred Astaire

25/52   **No Two People** ...
         Doris Day & Donald O'Connor

O

6/19	**Oh My Dear!** ...
	Joseph C. Smith's Orchestra
	Oh, My (Mein) Papa
1/54	Eddie Fisher
6/54	Eddie Calvert
15/54	Ray Anthony
5/13	**Oh! Oh! Delphine** ... Billy Murray
9/05	**Oh! Oh! Sallie** ...
	Billy Murray & Bob Roberts
	Oh Promise Me
1/93	George J. Gaskin
7/05	Henry Burr
3/07	Corrine Morgan
9/13	Alan Turner
8/24	**Oh Susanna** ...
	Wendell Hall & Shannon Four
20/35	**Oh Susanna, Dust Off The Old Pianna** ... Ozzie Nelson
7/19	**Oh, Susy, Behave** ... Fred Van Eps
3/10	**Oh That Beautiful Rag** ...
	Arthur Collins
8/11	**Oh That Moonlight Glide** ...
	Arthur Collins & Byron Harlan
9/12	**Oh That Navajo Rag** ...
	American Quartet
10/11	**Oh, That We Two Were Maying** ...
	Elizabeth Wheeler
30/54	**Oh, That'll Be Joyful** ... Four Lads
	Oh, What A Beautiful Mornin'
12/43	Frank Sinatra
4/44	Bing Crosby
	Oh! What A Pal Was Mary
1/19	Henry Burr
10/20	Edward Allen
	Oh! What It Seemed To Be
1/46	Frankie Carle
1/46	Frank Sinatra
4/46	Helen Forrest & Dick Haymes
5/46	Charlie Spivak
14/47	**(Oh Why, Oh Why, Did I Ever Leave) Wyoming** ... Dick Jurgens
1/12	**Oh, You Beautiful Doll** ...
	American Quartet
6/10	**Oh, You Candy Kid** ... Ada Jones
3/12	**Oh! You Circus Day** ...
	Arthur Collins & Byron Harlan
2/39	**Oh, You Crazy Moon** ...
	Tommy Dorsey
8/09	**Oh, You Kid!** ...
	Ada Jones & Billy Murray
4/14	**Oh You Million Dollar Doll** ...
	Peerless Quartet with James F. Harrison
27/53	**Ohio** ... Lisa Kirk
1/21	**O-H-I-O (O-My! O!)** ... Al Jolson
25/48	**Ok'l Baby Dok'l** ... Pied Pipers
19/34	**Okay, Toots** ... Eddie Cantor

8/23	**Okeh Laughing Record** ...
	Okeh Laughing Record
9/43	**Oklahoma! Cast Album** ...
	"Oklahoma!" Album
2/38	**Ol' Man Mose** ... Eddy Duchin
	Ol' Man River
1/28	Paul Whiteman
4/28	Al Jolson
7/28	Paul Robeson with Paul Whiteman
10/28	Revelers
19/34	Luis Russell
8/34	**Ol' Pappy** ... Benny Goodman
	Old ... *also see: Ol and Ole*
15/44	**Old Acquaintance** ... Jo Stafford
11/38	**Old Apple Tree** ... Ozzie Nelson
	Old Black Joe
10/08	Peerless Quartet
30/40	Mills Brothers
20/39	**Old Curiosity Shop** ... Shep Fields
10/25	**Old Dan Tucker** ...
	Fiddlin' John Carson
	Old Devil Moon
11/47	Margaret Whiting
21/47	Gene Krupa
7/22	**Old-Fashioned Girl** ...
	Paul Whiteman
4/24	**Old-Fashioned Love** ...
	Frank Crumit
2/97	**Old-Fashioned Mother** ...
	George J. Gaskin
20/37	**Old Flame Never Dies** ...
	Tommy Dorsey
4/38	**Old Folks** ... Larry Clinton
8/19	**Old Folks At Home** ...
	Columbia Stellar Quartet
	Old Folks At Home (Swanee River)
1/92	Len Spencer
2/00	Vess Ossman
4/04	Haydn Quartet
6/05	Louise Homer
3/15	Alma Gluck
4/16	Taylor Trio
8/19	Oscar Seagle & Columbia Stellar Quartet
19/36	Jimmie Lunceford
18/37	Bunny Berigan
10/14	**Old Folks Rag** ... Fred Van Eps
	Old Grey Mare
4/17	Prince's Orchestra
3/18	Arthur Collins & Byron Harlan
17/28	**Old Guitar And An Old Refrain** ...
	Roger Wolfe Kahn
7/14	**Old Homestead** ... Prince's Orchestra
	Old Lamplighter
1/46	Sammy Kaye
5/46	Hal Derwin
16/46	Morton Downey
3/47	Kay Kyser
11/47	Kenny Baker

On The Banks Of The Wabash
1/97   George J. Gaskin
1/98   Steve Porter
3/98   Roger Harding
5/13   Harry Macdonough & American Quartet

On The Beach At Bali Bali
3/36   Connee Boswell
6/36   Leo Reisman
9/36   Tommy Dorsey
17/36   Shep Fields
18/36   Henry Allen

On The Beach With You
10/31   Johnny Hamp
18/31   Ozzie Nelson

1/96   **On The Benches In The Park ...**
George J. Gaskin

On The Boardwalk In Atlantic City
12/46   Charioteers
21/47   Dick Haymes

On The 5:15
2/15   American Quartet
7/15   Arthur Collins & Byron Harlan

8/22   **On The Gin-Gin-Ginny Shore ...**
Ray Miller

On The Good Ship Lollipop
4/35   Rudy Vallee
16/35   Ted Fio Rito

6/14   **On The Honeymoon Express ...**
Arthur Collins & Byron Harlan

On The Isle Of May
3/40   Connee Boswell
13/40   Dick Jurgens

On The Mississippi
3/13   American Quartet
9/13   Billy Murray

10/13   **On The Mississippi (Medley) ...**
Sousa's Band

On The Old Fall River Line
5/14   Arthur Collins & Byron Harlan
6/14   Billy Murray

On The Old Front Porch
6/13   Ada Jones & Billy Murray
9/14   Ada Jones & Henry Burr

23/47   **On The Old Spanish Trail ...**
Eddy Howard

16/50   **On The Outgoing Tide ...**
Perry Como

6/26   **On The Riviera ...** Nat Shilkret

5/19   **On The Road To Calais ...** Al Jolson

5/18   **On The Road To Home Sweet Home ...**
Percy Hemus

3/13   **On The Road To Mandalay ...**
Frank Croxton

On The Rocky Road To Dublin
2/06   Arthur Pryor's Band
6/06   Vess Ossman

4/38   **On The Sentimental Side ...**
Bing Crosby

7/16   **On The South Sea Isle ...**
Sterling Trio

21/42   **On The Street Of Regret ...**
Sammy Kaye

On The Sunny Side Of The Street
2/30   Ted Lewis
13/30   Harry Richman
16/45   Tommy Dorsey
17/45   Jo Stafford

On The Trail ("Grand Canyon Suite")
13/32   Paul Whiteman
26/53   Ray Anthony

15/34   **On The Wrong Side Of The Fence ...**
Jan Garber

On Top Of Old Smoky
10/49   Burl Ives
2/51   Weavers
8/51   Vaughn Monroe
10/51   Percy Faith

On Treasure Island
1/35   Tommy Dorsey
4/35   Little Jack Little
8/35   Bing Crosby
8/35   Joe Moss
16/35   Teddy Wilson

5/15   **On, Wisconsin! ...** Prince's Orchestra

18/36   **On Your Toes ...** Ruby Newman

16/49   **Once And For Always ...** Jo Stafford

11/34   **Once In A Blue Moon ...** Bing Crosby

12/28   **Once In A Lifetime ...**
Johnny Johnson

Once In A While
1/37   Tommy Dorsey
2/37   Hoarce Heidt
15/38   Louis Armstrong
9/52   Patti Page

16/49   **Once In Love With Amy ...**
Ray Bolger

24/44   **Once Too Often ...** Ella Fitzgerald

15/35   **Once Upon A Midnight ...** Hal Kemp

29/51   **Once Upon A Nickel ...**
Ethel Merman & Ray Bolger

One Alone
4/27   Nat Shilkret
19/27   Don Voorhees

18/40   **One Cigarette For Two ...**
Freddy Martin

8/18   **One Day In June (It Might Have Been You) ...** Henry Burr & Albert Campbell

One Dozen Roses
3/42   Dick Jurgens
4/42   Harry James
8/42   Glen Gray
8/42   Dinah Shore

9/50   **One Finger Melody ...** Frank Sinatra

23/42   **One For All - All For One ...**
Barry Wood

P

Peggy O'Neil
5/21	Billy Jones
8/21	Charles Harrison
21/47	Frankie Carle
21/47	Harmonicats

Pennies From Heaven
1/36	Bing Crosby
8/36	Hal Kemp
16/36	Hildegarde
19/36	Jimmy Dorsey
2/37	Eddy Duchin
3/37	Teddy Wilson with Billie Holiday

5/40 **Pennsylvania 6-5000** ...
Glenn Miller

Pennsylvania Polka
17/42	Andrews Sisters
21/42	Hoarce Heidt

28/47 **Penny** ... Pied Pipers

Penny A Kiss
8/51	Dinah Shore
14/51	Eddy Howard
17/51	Andrews Sisters

Penny Serenade
1/39	Guy Lombardo
2/39	Sammy Kaye
8/39	Hoarce Heidt

Penthouse Serenade ...
see: When We're Alone

People Will Say We're In Love
2/43	Bing Crosby
3/43	Frank Sinatra
11/43	Hal Goodman

21/43 **Perdido** ... Duke Ellington

Perfect Day
2/11	Cecil Fanning
6/13	Elsie Baker
4/15	McKee's Orchestra

6/16 **Perfect Day** ...
Imperial Quartet Of Chicago

Perfidia (Tonight)
3/41	Xavier Cugat
9/41	Jimmy Dorsey
11/41	Benny Goodman
11/41	Glenn Miller
15/41	Gene Krupa
7/52	Four Aces

22/54 **Period** ... Four Knights

Personality
1/46	Johnny Mercer
9/46	Bing Crosby
10/46	Dinah Shore

8/09 **Pet Names** ...
Ada Jones & Billy Murray

Peter Cottontail
5/50	Gene Autry
8/50	Mervin Shiner
26/50	Fran Allison
26/50	Jimmy Wakely
19/51	Gene Autry

22/50 **Petite Waltz (La Petite Valse)** ...
Guy Lombardo

30/54 **Philadelphia Waltz** ...
Connee Boswell

21/48 **Pianissimo** ... Perry Como

1/41 **Piano Concerto In B Flat** ...
Freddy Martin
(also see: Tonight We Love)

3/11 **Piano Man** ... Billy Murray

Piccolino, The
10/35	Fred Astaire
14/35	Ray Noble

Piccolo Pete
15/28	Harry Reser's Orchestra
2/29	Ted Weems
15/29	Six Jumping Jacks

14/22 **Pick Me Up And Lay Me Down In Dear
Old Dixieland** ... Peerless Quartet

7/36 **Pick Yourself Up** ... Fred Astaire

8/12 **Picnic (Every Laddie Loves A
Lassie)** ... Harry Lauder

5/05 **Picnic For Two** ... Byron G. Harlan

20/50 **Picnic Song** ... Johnny Desmond

Picture No Artist Can Paint
1/99	Steve Porter
3/99	George J. Gaskin

Picture Turned Toward The Wall
2/91	George J. Gaskin
1/92	Manhansett Quartette

22/42 **Pig Foot Pete** ... Dolly Dawn

10/40 **Pinch Me** ... Orrin Tucker

20/29 **Pine Top's Boogie Woogie** ...
Pine Top Smith

26/54 **Pine Tree, Pine Over Me** ...
Johnny Desmond, Eileen Barton &
McGuire Sisters
(also see: Boogie Woogie)

30/50 **Pink Champagne** ... Joe Liggins

Pink Elephants
8/32	George Olsen
10/32	Guy Lombardo

10/11 **Pink Lady Selection** ...
Victor Concert Orchestra

19/43 **Pins And Needles (In My Heart)** ...
Bob Atcher & Bonnie Blue Eyes

12/39 **Pippinella** ... Dick Robertson

Pistol Packin' Mama
1/43	Al Dexter
2/43	Bing Crosby & Andrews Sisters

4/52 **Pittsburgh, Pennsylvania** ...
Guy Mitchell

29/50 **Place Where I Worship (Is The Wide
Open Spaces)** ... Al Morgan

Play A Simple Melody
8/15	Walter Van Brunt & Mary Carson
4/16	Billy Murray & Elsie Baker
2/50	Bing Crosby & Gary Crosby
18/50	Jo Stafford
25/50	Georgia Gibbs & Bob Crosby
30/50	Phil Harris

8/46	**Put That Kiss Back Where You Found It** ... Sam Donohue
	Put Your Arms Around Me, Honey
1/11	Arthur Collins & Byron Harlan
5/11	Ada Jones
6/11	"That Girl" Quartet
19/42	Dick Kuhn
4/43	Dick Kuhn
5/43	Dick Haymes
17/38	**Put Your Heart In A Song** ... Larry Clinton
	Puttin' On The Ritz
1/30	Harry Richman
17/30	Earl Burtnett
20/30	Leo Reisman

Q

16/36	**Quicker Than You Can Say Jack Robinson** ... Ozzie Nelson
	Quicksilver
6/50	Bing Crosby & Andrews Sisters
20/50	Doris Day
	Quierme Mucho ... *see: Yours*
17/40	**Quiero A Mi Mama (I Want My Mama)** ... Xavier Cugat

R

20/46	**R.M. Blues** ... Roy Milton
	Rachel
21/53	Artie Wayne
30/53	Al Martino
25/41	**Racing With The Moon** ... Vaughn Monroe
	Rag Mop
1/50	Ames Brothers
3/50	Ralph Flanagan
7/50	Lionel Hampton
9/50	Johnnie Lee Wills
12/50	Starlighters
15/50	Jimmy Dorsey
24/50	Eddy Howard
12/24	**Raggedy Ann** ... Paul Whiteman
1/12	**Ragging The Baby To Sleep** ... Al Jolson
5/15	**Ragging The Scale** ... Conway's Band
1/53	**Rags To Riches** ... Tony Bennett

	Ragtime Cowboy Joe
1/12	Bob Roberts
14/39	Pinky Tomlin
16/47	Eddy Howard
10/49	Jo Stafford
9/14	**Ragtime Dream** ... American Quartet
6/12	**Ragtime Jockey Man** ... Maurice Burkhardt & Peerless Quartet
2/97	**Ragtime Medley** ... Vess Ossman
7/12	**Ragtime Mocking Bird** ... Dolly Connolly
9/12	**Ragtime Soldier Man** ... Arthur Collins & Byron Harlan
3/12	**Ragtime Violin** ... American Quartet
10/08	**Rah, Rah, Rah** ... Peerless Quartet
	Rain
20/27	Arnold Frank
16/28	Sam Lanin
17/50	Frank Petty Trio
8/34	**Rain** ... Jan Garber
21/54	**Rain, Rain, Rain** ... Frankie Laine & Four Lads
	Rainbow
4/08	Frank Stanley & Henry Burr
7/08	Billy Murray & Haydn Quartet
5/18	**Rainbow Of Love** ... John McCormack
15/37	**Rainbow On The River** ... Guy Lombardo
20/44	**Rainbow Rhapsody** ... Glenn Miller
17/39	**Rainbow Valley** ... Dick Jurgens
24/50	**Rainy Day Refrain** ... Mindy Carson
7/47	**Rainy Night In Rio** ... Sam Donohue
	Rambling Rose
18/48	Perry Como
27/48	Gordon MacRae
	Ramona
1/28	Gene Austin
1/28	Paul Whiteman
10/28	Ruth Etting
18/28	Scrappy Lambert
12/53	Gaylords
5/38	**Rancho Grande** ... Dick Robertson
2/93	**Rastus And The Watermillion** ... D.C. Bangs
11/44	**Ration Blues** ... Louis Jordan
3/04	**Razzle Dazzle** ... Vess Ossman
2/26	**Reaching For The Moon** ... Ben Bernie
6/31	**Reaching For The Moon** ... Ruth Etting
20/28	**Ready For The River** ... Coon-Sanders Orchestra
	Rebecca Of Sunny-brook Farm
1/14	American Quartet
7/14	Henry Burr & Helen Clark
18/48	**Recess In Heaven** ... Deep River Boys

572

Room Full Of Roses
2/49	Sammy Kaye
4/49	Eddy Howard
6/49	Dick Haymes
6/49	Jerry Wayne
21/49	Starlighters
25/49	George Morgan
26/49	Sons Of The Pioneers

Room With A View
10/29	Ben Selvin
13/39	Tommy Dorsey

8/10	**Rosa Rosetta** ... Nora Bayes & Jack Norworth

Rosalie
1/38	Sammy Kaye
6/38	Hoarce Heidt

29/44	**Rosalita** ... Al Dexter
23/52	**Rosanne** ... Vic Damone

Rosary, The
2/03	William H. Thompson
3/03	Henry Burr
8/06	Alan Turner
8/03	Ernestine Schumann-Heink
4/12	John McCormack
8/16	Taylor Trio

5/21	**Rose** ... Paul Biese Trio
2/19	**Rose, A Kiss, And You** ... John Steel

Rose Ann Of Charing Cross
16/43	Peter Piper
20/43	Four Vagabonds

4/07	**Rose Bud (Call And I'll Come To You)** ... Billy Murray
9/35	**Rose In Her Hair** ... Russ Morgan

Rose-Marie
14/24	Lambert Murphy
3/25	Paul Whiteman
5/25	John McCormack
15/25	Jesse Crawford
22/54	Slim Whitman

Rose O'Day (The Filla-Da-Gusha Song)
1/42	Freddy Martin
8/42	Kate Smith
17/42	Woody Herman
18/42	King Sisters

10/22	**Rose Of My Heart** ... John McCormack

Rose Of No Man's Land
6/19	Charles Hart
9/19	Charles Harrison

9/12	**Rose Of Pyramid Land** ... Walter Van Brunt & Helen Clark
3/23	**Rose Of The Rio Grande** ... Marion Harris

Rose Of Washington Square
3/20	Kentucky Serenaders
5/20	Henry Burr
10/39	Benny Goodman

Rose Room (In Sunny Roseland)
5/20	Art Hickman
15/32	Duke Ellington

Rose, Rose, I Love You
3/51	Frankie Laine
8/51	Buddy Morrow
21/51	Gordon Jenkins with Cisco Houston

10/45	**Rosemary** ... Kay Kyser

Roses
5/50	Sammy Kaye
19/50	Ray Anthony
29/50	Dick Haymes

6/09	**Roses Bring Dreams Of You** ... Peerless Quartet
3/37	**Roses In December** ... Ozzie Nelson
7/10	**Roses In June** ... Reed Miller
9/47	**Roses In The Rain** ... Frankie Carle

Roses Of Picardy
3/18	Lambert Murphy
9/19	John McCormack
6/23	Paul Specht

7/28	**Roses Of Yesterday** ... Fred Waring's Pennsylvanians
12/28	**Rosetta** ... Jean Goldkette
7/21	**Rosie** ... Carl Fenton

	Route 66 ... *see: Get Your Kicks On Route 66*

Roving Kind
4/51	Guy Mitchell
11/51	Weavers
20/51	Rex Allen

Row, Row, Rosie
9/25	Eddie Cantor
12/25	Billy Jones

Row! Row! Row!
1/13	Ada Jones
7/13	Arthur Collins & Byron Harlan
8/13	American Quartet
15/40	Mitchell Ayres

Royal Garden Blues
3/21	Original Dixieland Jazz Band
13/21	Mamie Smith

18/53	**Rub-A-Dub-Dub** ... Ralph Flanagan

Ruby
3/53	Richard Hayman
7/53	Les Baxter
20/53	Harry James
20/53	Victor Young
27/53	Vaughn Monroe
29/53	Les Brown

23/52	**Ruby And The Pearl** ... Nat "King" Cole

Rudolph, The Red-Nosed Reindeer
1/50	Gene Autry
3/50	Gene Autry
7/50	Spike Jones
14/50	Bing Crosby
16/51	Gene Autry
12/52	Gene Autry
26/53	Gene Autry

	San Fernando Valley
1/44	Bing Crosby
21/44	Johnny Mercer
10/36	**San Francisco** ... Tommy Dorsey
10/13	**San Francisco Bound** ... Peerless Quartet
3/00	**San Francisco Sadie** ... Dan Quinn
4/19	**Sand Dunes** ... Earl Fuller
24/41	**Sand In My Shoes** ... Connee Boswell
24/54	**Santa And The Doodle-Li-Boop** ... Art Carney
4/53	**Santa Baby** ... Eartha Kitt
20/47	**Santa Catalina (Island Of Romance)** ... Freddy Martin
	Santa Claus Is Comin' To Town
12/34	George Hall
22/47	Bing Crosby & Andrews Sisters
	Santa Lucia (Neapolitan Folk Song)
10/13	Reed Miller
4/16	Enrico Caruso
19/54	**Santo Natale** ... David Whitfield
10/12	**Sardinia March** ... Sousa's Band
1/37	**Satan Takes A Holiday** ... Tommy Dorsey
28/50	**Satan Wears A Satin Gown** ... Frankie Laine
27/53	**Satin Doll** ... Duke Ellington
18/29	**Satisfied** ... Henry Busse
9/21	**Saturday** ... Nora Bayes
21/48	**Saturday Date** ... Kay Kyser
21/49	**Saturday Night Fish Fry** ... Louis Jordan
14/33	**Saturday Night Function** ... Sonny Greer
	Saturday Night (Is The Loneliest Night Of The Week)
2/45	Frank Sinatra
6/45	Sammy Kaye
8/45	Frankie Carle
15/45	Woody Herman
15/45	King Sisters
9/20	**Save A Little Dram For Me** ... Bert Williams
12/47	**Save The Bones For Henry Jones (Cause Henry Don't Eat Meat)** ... Johnny Mercer & King Cole Trio
5/11	**Save Up Your Kisses For A Rainy Day** ... Henry Burr & Elise Stevenson
	Save Your Sorrow (For Tomorrow)
7/25	Shannon Four
12/25	Ray Miller
13/26	Gene Austin
	Savin' Myself For You ... *see: (I've Been)*
5/23	**Saw Mill River Road** ... Isham Jones
24/48	**Saxa-Boogie** ... Sam Donohue

15/31	**Say A Little Prayer For Me** ... Smith Ballew
6/18	**Say A Prayer For The Boys Out There** ... Peerless Quartet
	Say Au Revoir, But Not Goodbye
1/94	Edward M. Favor
2/94	George J. Gaskin
5/12	Will Oakland
5/13	John McCormack
	Say It
15/34	Isham Jones
2/40	Glenn Miller
12/40	Tommy Dorsey
	Say It Isn't So
1/32	George Olsen
8/32	Ozzie Nelson
10/32	Connee Boswell
12/32	Rudy Vallee
	Say It While Dancing
4/22	Benson Orchestra Of Chicago
10/22	Isham Jones
8/24	**Say It With A Ukelele** ... Frank Crumit
	Say It With Music
1/21	Paul Whiteman
6/21	Ben Selvin
11/22	John Steel
12/22	Columbians
14/53	**Say It With Your Heart** ... Bob Carroll
4/13	**Say Not Love Is A Dream** ... Olive Kline
	Say "Si Si"
19/36	Xavier Cugat
4/40	Andrews Sisters
15/40	Glenn Miller
12/53	Mills Brothers
26/53	Eugenie Baird
	Say Something Sweet To Your Sweetheart
10/48	Jo Stafford & Gordon MacRae
22/48	Ink Spots
23/48	Vic Damone
23/48	Patti Page
19/32	**Say That You Were Teasing Me** ... Rose Marie
11/28	**Say "Yes" Today** ... Ruth Etting
	Say You're Mine Again
3/53	Perry Como
21/53	June Hutton
	Says My Heart
4/38	Red Norvo
5/38	Ozzie Nelson
7/38	Tommy Dorsey
10/38	Andrews Sisters
10/38	George Hall
5/21	**Scandanavia** ... Al Jolson
	Scarlet Ribbons (For Her Hair)
14/50	Jo Stafford
30/52	Harry Belafonte

Shadow Waltz
1/33   Bing Crosby
6/33   Rudy Vallee
11/33   Guy Lombardo

5/15   **Shadowland Fox-Trot ...**
Prince's Orchestra

Shadows On The Swanee
13/33   Isham Jones
17/33   Paul Ash

4/27   **Shady Tree ...** Paul Whiteman

Shake A Hand
22/53   Faye Adams
22/53   Savannah Churchill

Shake Down The Stars
4/40   Glenn Miller
18/40   Ella Fitzgerald

Shake, Rattle, And Roll
7/54   Bill Haley
22/54   Joe Turner

Shaking The Blues Away
4/27   Ruth Etting
14/27   Paul Whiteman

3/37   **Shall We Dance? ...** Fred Astaire

13/45   **Shame On You ...**
Red Foley with Lawrence Welk

29/53   **Shane (The Call Of The Far-Away Hills) ...** Paul Weston

Shanghai
7/51   Doris Day
20/51   Billy Williams Quartet
21/51   Bing Crosby
22/51   Bob Crosby

9/24   **Shanghai Lullaby ...** Art Kahn

11/32   **Sharing (My Love For You) ...**
Guy Lombardo

6/11   **Sharpshooters' March ...**
Guido Deiro

26/48   **Shaunty O'Shea ...** Jack Smith

She Didn't Say "Yes"
13/32   Leo Reisman
15/32   Leo Reisman

21/42   **She Don't Wanna ...** Orrin Tucker

2/09   **She Is My Daisy ...** Harry Lauder

3/17   **She Is The Sunshine Of Virginia ...**
Henry Burr & Albert Campbell

14/24   **She Loves Me ...**
Ernest Hare & Billy Jones

23/53   **She Loves Me ...** Don Cornell

1/96   **She May Have Seen Better Days ...**
George J. Gaskin

She Reminds Me Of You
7/34   Eddy Duchin
8/34   Earl Burtnett
10/34   Bing Crosby

10/10   **She Sells Sea Shells ...** Billy Murray

She Shall Have Music
3/36   Lud Gluskin
14/36   Louis Levy

10/15   **She Used To Be The Slowest Girl In Town ...** Ada Jones & Will Robbins

(She Walks Like You, She Talks Like You) ... *see: She Riminds Me Of You*

She Was Bred In Old Kentucky
1/98   George J. Gaskin
2/98   Albert Campbell
2/98   Steve Porter
3/98   Haydn Quartet

She Was Five And He Was Ten
21/53   Judy Valentine
27/54   Mills Brothers

1/98   **She Was Happy Till She Met You ...**
Dan Quinn

19/53   **She Wears Red Feathers ...**
Guy Mitchell

She Wore A Yellow Ribbon
14/49   Eddie "Piano" Miller
22/49   Andrews Sisters

14/28   **She's A Great, Great Girl ...**
Roger Wolfe Kahn

She's A Latin From Manhattan
1/35   Victor Young
4/35   Johnny Green
15/35   Ozzie Nelson

She's Everybody's Sweetheart (But Nobody's Gal)
7/24   Ted Lewis
15/24   Henry Burr

She's Funny That Way
3/29   Gene Austin
15/29   Ted Lewis

1/98   **She's More To Be Pitied Than Censured ...** Steve Porter

17/37   **She's Tall, She's Tan, She's Terrific ...** Cab Calloway

She's The Daughter Of Mother Machree
9/16   Charles Harrison
10/16   Manuel Romain

2/08   **She's The Fairest Little Flower Old Dixie Ever Grew ...** Frank Stanley & Henry Burr

10/13   **She's The Lass For Me ...**
Harry Lauder

Sheik Of Araby
3/22   Club Royal Orchestra
3/22   Ray Miller
14/39   Jack Teagarden
19/43   Spike Jones
22/53   Super-Sonics

9/17   **Shenandoah ...**
Henry Burr & Albert Campbell

Shepherd Serenade
7/41   Hoarce Heidt
12/41   Art Jarrett
4/42   Bing Crosby

3/02   **Shepherd's Dance ...**
Charles D'almaine

11/46	**Sherwood's Forest** ...	
	Bobby Sherwood	

Shine
10/24	California Ramblers
7/32	Bing Crosby & Mills Brothers
17/32	Louis Armstrong
9/48	Frankie Laine

Shine On, Harvest Moon
1/09	Harry Macdonough & Elise Stevenson
1/09	Ada Jones & Billy Murray
2/09	Frank Stanley & Henry Burr
6/09	Bob Roberts
5/10	Arthur Pryor's Band
9/31	Ethel Waters
19/43	Kate Smith

12/32	**Shine On Your Shoes** ...
	Roger Wolfe Kahn

Shoo-Fly Pie And Apple Pan Dowdy
6/46	Stan Kenton
6/46	Guy Lombardo
6/46	Dinah Shore

Shoo Shoo Baby
1/44	Andrews Sisters
4/44	Ella Mae Morse
12/44	Jan Garber

16/38	**Shortenin' Bread** ... Andrews Sisters

14/51	**Shot Gun Boogie** ...
	Tennessee Ernie Ford

3/30	**Should I** ... Arden-Ohman Orchestra

9/52	**Should I** ... Four Aces

24/52	**Shoulder To Weep On** ... June Valli

21/42	**Shout, Sister, Shout!** ...
	Lucky Millinder

9/25	**Show Me The Way** ... Ted Lewis

28/50	**Show Me The Way To Get Out Of This World** ... Peggy Lee

Show Me The Way To Go Home
3/26	Vincent Lopez
12/26	Ernest Hare & Billy Jones

Shrimp Boats
2/51	Jo Stafford
16/51	Dolores Gray
	(also see: Herring Boats)

Shrine Of St. Cecelia
3/41	Andrews Sisters
7/42	Sammy Kaye
21/42	Vaughn Monroe

Shuffle Off To Buffalo
2/33	Don Bestor
2/33	Hal Kemp

9/16	**Siam** ... American Quartet

17/31	**Siboney** ... Alfredo Brito

Side By Side
3/27	Nick Lucas
3/27	Paul Whiteman
7/27	Aileen Stanley & Johnny Marvin
12/27	Cliff Edwards
3/53	Kay Starr

Sidewalks Of New York
1/95	J.W. Myers
1/95	Dan Quinn
2/95	George J. Gaskin
2/28	Nat Shilkret

	Sierra Madre ... *see: (Treasure Of)*

Sierra Sue
1/40	Bing Crosby
17/40	Glenn Miller

Silent Night
2/05	Haydn Quartet
6/08	Ernestine Schumann-Heink
6/12	Elsie Baker
7/17	Neapolitan Trio
6/28	Paul Whiteman
7/36	Bing Crosby
10/38	Bing Crosby
11/42	Bing Crosby
22/47	Bing Crosby

18/52	**Silver And Gold** ... Pee Wee King

Silver Bell
2/10	Peerless Quartet
5/10	Frank Stanley & Henry Burr
7/11	Ada Jones & Billy Murray
9/11	"That Girl" Quartet

20/53	**Silver Bells** ...
	Bing Crosby & Carol Richards

Silver Heels
6/06	Arthur Pryor's Band
8/06	Harry Tally

12/27	**Silver Moon** ... Paul Whiteman

20/38	**Silver On The Sage** ... Will Osborne

Silver Threads Among The Gold
1/04	Richard Jose
4/09	Will Oakland
6/12	John McCormack
10/15	Charles Adams

19/44	**Silver Wings In The Moonlight** ...
	Freddie Slack

17/49	**Similau (See-Me-Lo)** ... Peggy Lee

12/38	**Simple And Sweet** ...
	Connee Boswell

	Simple Melody ...
	see: Play A Simple Melody

Sin
1/51	Eddy Howard
4/51	Four Aces
5/51	Savannah Churchill
14/51	Four Knights
25/51	Sammy Kaye
28/51	Billy Williams Quartet

20/47	**Since I Fell For You** ... Paul Gayten

4/03	**Since I First Met You** ...
	Harry Macdonough

24/44	**Since You Went Away** ... Jerry Wald

27/53	**Since You Went Away From Me** ...
	Sandy Stewart

8/39	**Sing A Song Of Sunbeams** ...
	Bing Crosby

5/26	**Sleepy Head** ... Ford & Glenn
	Sleepy Head
2/34	Mills Brothers
13/34	Ben Pollack
	Sleepy Lagoon
1/42	Harry James
12/42	Dinah Shore
	Sleepy Serenade
22/41	Andrews Sisters
22/41	Woody Herman
27/41	Claude Thornhill
	Sleepy Time Gal
1/26	Ben Bernie
3/26	Gene Austin
3/26	Nick Lucas
10/26	Art Landry
11/26	Ben Selvin
12/26	Lewis James
21/44	Harry James
	Sleepy Valley
2/29	Gus Arnheim
11/29	James Melton
24/49	**Sleigh Ride** ... Boston Pops Orchestra
	Sleigh Ride In July
8/45	Dinah Shore
14/45	Bing Crosby
15/45	Tommy Dorsey
18/45	Les Brown
1/92	**Slide, Kelly, Slide** ... George J. Gaskin
4/19	**Slide, Kelly, Slide** ... Wilbur Sweatman's Original Jazz Band
19/43	**Slip Of The Lip** ... Duke Ellington
8/17	**Slippery Hank** ... Earl Fuller
	Slippin' Around
1/49	Margaret Whiting & Jimmy Wakely
17/49	Ernest Tubb
8/31	**Slow But Sure** ... Ben Selvin
9/40	**Slow Freight** ... Glenn Miller
	Slow Poke
13/51	Roberta Lee
1/52	Pee Wee King
6/52	Ralph Flanagan
8/52	Helen O'Connell
12/52	Arthur Godfrey
	Slow-Poke
26/52	Hawkshaw Hawkins
28/52	**Slow Poke** ... Tiny Hill
	Slowly
11/46	Kay Kyser
12/46	Dick Haymes
	Slummin' On Park Avenue
8/37	Red Norvo
15/37	Fletcher Henderson
18/37	Jimmie Lunceford
	Small Fry
3/38	Bing Crosby & Johnny Mercer
9/38	Mildred Bailey

8/11	**Small-Town Gal** ... George M. Cohan
13/36	**Small Town Girl** ... Jan Garber
2/08	**Smarty** ... Ada Jones & Billy Murray
	Smarty
1/37	Fats Waller
18/37	Bing Crosby
17/39	**Smarty Pants** ... Eddy Duchin
	Smile
10/54	Nat "King" Cole
19/54	Sunny Gale
25/54	David Whitfield
10/18	**Smile And Show Your Dimple** ... Sam Ash
7/19	**Smile And The World Smiles With You** ... Lewis James & Peerless Quartet
14/31	**Smile, Darn Ya, Smile** ... Ben Selvin
	Smile Will Go A Long, Long Way
4/24	Ted Weems
13/24	Peerless Quartet
10/11	**Smiler, The** ... Vess Ossman
	Smiles
1/18	Joseph C. Smith's Orchestra
3/18	Henry Burr & Albert Campbell
5/18	Lambert Murphy
4/19	**Smilin' Through** ... Reinald Werrenrath
4/37	**Smoke Dreams** ... Benny Goodman
	Smoke Gets In Your Eyes
1/34	Paul Whiteman
3/34	Leo Reisman
4/34	Emil Coleman
15/34	Ruth Etting
24/41	Artie Shaw
7/44	**Smoke On The Water** ... Red Foley
	Smoke Rings
8/33	Clyde McCoy
15/37	Glen Gray
14/52	Les Paul & Mary Ford
	Smoke! Smoke! Smoke! (That Cigarette)
1/47	Tex Williams
8/47	Phil Harris
2/99	**Smoky Mokes** ... Len Spencer
23/51	**Smooth Sailing** ... Ella Fitzgerald
17/38	**Snake Charmer** ... Jerry Blaine
6/12	**Snap Your Fingers** ... Al Jolson
24/47	**Snatch And Grab It** ... Julia Lee
	Snookey Ookums
4/13	Arthur Collins & Byron Harlan
4/13	Billy Murray
9/20	**Snoops, The Lawyer** ... Eddie Cantor
15/41	**Snowfall** ... Claude Thornhill
	Snuggled On Your Shoulder (Cuddled In Your Arms)
7/32	Eddy Duchin
10/32	Kate Smith
11/32	Bing Crosby
16/32	Isham Jones

20/41	**Southern Fried** ... Charlie Barnet
	Spain
1/24	Isham Jones
7/24	Paul Whiteman
1/13	**Spaniard That Blighted My Life** ... Al Jolson
10/16	**Spanish Dance** ... Mischa Elman
9/11	**Spanish Love** ... Andrea Sarto
10/26	**Spanish Shawl** ... Blossom Seeley
	Sparrow In The Tree Top
8/51	Bing Crosby & Andrews Sisters
8/51	Guy Mitchell
28/51	Rex Allen
27/54	**Sparrow Sings** ... Vic Damone
5/44	**Speak Low (When You Speak, Love)** ... Guy Lombardo
5/34	**Speak To Me Of Love (Parlez-Moi D'amour)** ... Lucienne Boyer
8/39	**Speaking Of Heaven** ... Glenn Miller
	Spellbound
10/34	Glen Gray
20/34	Vincent Lopez
16/53	**Spinning A Web** ... Gaylords
4/19	**Spirit Of Independence March** ... Conway's Band
	S'posin'
7/29	Rudy Vallee
5/36	Fats Waller
28/53	Don Cornell
	Spread Yo' Stuff
4/21	Benny Krueger
7/22	Ethel Waters
3/37	**Spring Cleaning** ... Fats Waller
	Spring Is Here
14/38	Leo Reisman
19/38	Buddy Clark
25/44	**Spring Will Be A Little Late This Year** ... Morton Downey
1/53	**St. George And The Dragonet** ... Stan Freberg
	St. James' Infirmary
15/29	Louis Armstrong
9/30	King Oliver
3/31	Cab Calloway
18/42	Artie Shaw

	St. Louis Blues
4/16	Prince's Orchestra
9/19	Al Bernard
1/20	Marion Harris
3/21	Original Dixieland Jazz Band
9/23	W.C. Handy's Orchestra
3/25	Bessie Smith
11/30	Louis Armstrong
15/30	Rudy Vallee
16/30	Cab Calloway
2/32	Mills Brothers
15/35	Boswell Sisters
20/36	Benny Goodman
11/39	Guy Lombardo
18/43	Cab Calloway
24/53	Billy Eckstine
	(also see: Boogie Woogie On)
21/54	**St. Louis Blues Mambo** ... Richard Maltby
5/48	**St. Louis Blues March** ... Tex Beneke
	St. Louis Rag
4/04	Arthur Pryor's Band
3/05	**St. Louis Rag** ... Vess Ossman
3/06	**St. Louis Tickle** ... Vess Ossman
14/24	**Stack O' Lee Blues** ... Fred Waring's Pennsylvanians
	Stairway To The Stars
1/39	Glenn Miller
4/39	Kay Kyser
8/39	Jimmy Dorsey
12/39	Al Donohue
11/47	**Stanley Steamer** ... Jo Stafford
	Star Dust
20/30	Irving Mills
1/31	Isham Jones
5/31	Bing Crosby
16/31	Louis Armstrong
17/31	Wayne King
20/31	Lee Sims
10/35	Jimmie Lunceford
2/36	Benny Goodman
8/36	Tommy Dorsey
16/39	Sammy Kaye
2/41	Artie Shaw
7/41	Tommy Dorsey
20/41	Glenn Miller
18/43	Baron Elliott
23/43	Tommy Dorsey
3/44	**Star Eyes** ... Jimmy Dorsey
	Star Fell Out Of Heaven
3/36	Hal Kemp
14/36	Ben Bernie
14/35	**Star Gazing** ... Kay Kyser
	Star-Spangled Banner
2/92	Gilmore's Band
7/15	Margaret Woodrow Wilson
1/16	Prince's Orchestra
1/17	John McCormack
27/54	**Stardust Mambo** ... Richard Maltby
9/37	**Stardust On The Moon** ... Tommy Dorsey

Sunflower

5/49	Russ Morgan
12/49	Jack Fulton
13/49	Jack Smith
14/49	Frank Sinatra
19/49	Ray McKinley
28/49	Jack Kilty

5/06 **Sunflower Dance** ... Vess Ossman

Sunny

14/25	Eddie Elkins
2/26	George Olsen

Sunny Side Up

9/29	Earl Burtnett
10/29	Johnny Hamp

Sunrise Serenade

1/39	Glen Gray
7/39	Glenn Miller
23/44	Glenn Miller

Sunshine

6/28	Paul Whiteman
12/28	Nick Lucas

8/22 **Sunshine Alley** ... Ted Lewis

4/13 **Sunshine And Roses** ...
Elsie Baker & James F. Harrison

1/16 **Sunshine Of Your Smile** ...
John McCormack

16/45 **Surprise Party** ... Johnny Mercer

Surrender

1/46	Perry Como
8/46	Woody Herman

22/44 **Surrey With The Fringe On Top** ...
Alfred Drake

7/06 **Susan, Kiss Me Good And Hard** ...
Arthur Collins & Byron Harlan

Suspicion

23/48	Jo Stafford
24/48	Tex Williams
25/48	Ray Noble

30/53 **Swamp Fire** ... Kay Starr

12/50 **Swamp Girl** ... Frankie Laine

10/20 **Swan, The** ... Pablo Casals

Swanee

1/20	Al Jolson
11/20	All-Star Trio
11/20	Peerless Quartet

8/25 **Swanee Butterfly** ... Isham Jones

Swanee River ...
see: Old Folks At Home

25/53 **Swanee River Boogie** ...
Commanders

Swanee River Moon

9/22	Columbia Stellar Quartet
9/22	Prince's Orchestra

Sway

15/54	Dean Martin
21/54	Eileen Barton

21/53 **Swedish Rhapsody (Midsummer Vigil)** ... Percy Faith

1/94 **Sweeet Marie** ... George J. Gaskin

Sweet Adeline (You're The Flower Of My Heart)

1/04	Haydn Quartet
1/04	Peerless Quartet
2/04	Albert Campbell & James F. Harrison
10/39	Mills Brothers

Sweet And Lovely

1/31	Gus Arnheim
2/31	Guy Lombardo
9/31	Bing Crosby
12/31	Ben Bernie
19/31	Russ Columbo
27/44	Bing Crosby

Sweet And Low

2/20	Art Hickman
14/20	Elsie Baker

10/26 **Sweet And Low-Down** ...
Harry Archer

13/35 **Sweet And Slow** ... Fats Waller

3/01 **Sweet Annie Moore** ...
Harry Macdonough & S.H. Dudley

Sweet As A Song

3/38	Hoarce Heidt
19/38	Glen Gray

13/26 **Sweet Child (I'm Wild About You)** ...
Gene Austin

14/45 **Sweet Dreams, Sweetheart** ...
Ray Noble

7/42 **Sweet Eloise** ... Glenn Miller

8/18 **Sweet Emmaline, My Gal** ...
Mike Markel's Orchestra

Sweet Georgia Brown

1/25	Ben Bernie
5/25	Isham Jones
6/25	Ethel Waters
2/32	Bing Crosby
10/49	Brother Bones

4/19 **Sweet Hawaiian Moonlight** ...
Vivian Holt & Lillian Rosedale

Sweet Indiana Home

2/22	Aileen Stanley
5/22	Marion Harris

8/37 **Sweet Is The Word For You** ...
Bing Crosby

Sweet Italian Love

4/10	Byron G. Harlan
8/10	Billy Murray

10/30 **Sweet Jennie Lee!** ... Isham Jones

5/07 **Sweet Julienne** ...
Harry Macdonough

5/15 **Sweet Kentucky Lady (Dry Your Eyes)** ... Harry Macdonough

3/22 **Sweet Lady** ... Frank Crumit

1/37 **Sweet Leilani** ... Bing Crosby

4/18 **Sweet Little Buttercup** ...
Elizabeth Spencer & Shannon Four

17/35 **Sweet Lorraine** ... Teddy Wilson

Sweet Mama (Papa's Gettin' Mad)
4/21 Marion Harris
12/21 Original Dixieland Jazz Band

13/53 **Sweet Mama Tree Top Tall** ...
Lancers

Sweet Marie ... *see: Sweeet*

19/35 **Sweet Music** ... Victor Young

11/22 **Sweet Peggy O'Neil** ...
John McCormack

11/40 **Sweet Potato Piper** ... Bing Crosby

Sweet Rosie O'Grady
1/97 George J. Gaskin
2/97 J.W. Myers

12/44 **Sweet Slumber** ... Lucky Millinder

9/38 **Sweet Someone** ... Hoarce Heidt

Sweet Sue
3/28 Earl Burtnett
3/28 Ben Pollack
8/32 Mills Brothers
13/39 Tommy Dorsey
19/49 Johnny Long

27/53 **Sweet Thing** ... Dinah Shore

3/05 **Sweet Thoughts Of Home** ...
Harry Macdonough

12/36 **Sweet Violets** ... Sweet Violet Boys

Sweet Violets
3/51 Dinah Shore
11/51 Jane Turzy
22/51 Doris Drew

16/36 **Sweet Violets No. 2** ...
Sweet Violet Boys

4/09 **Sweetest Gal In Town** ...
Arthur Collins & Byron Harlan

20/34 **Sweetest Music This Side Of
Heaven** ... Guy Lombardo

3/21 **Sweetheart** ... Paul Whiteman

8/33 **Sweetheart Darlin'** ... Ben Selvin

4/08 **Sweetheart Days** ...
Harry Macdonough

19/37 **Sweetheart, Let's Grow Old
Together** ... Guy Lombardo

Sweetheart Of All My Dreams
5/29 Rudy Vallee
16/45 Charlie Spivak

Sweetheart Of My Student Days
9/30 Rudy Vallee
14/30 Ted Wallace

Sweetheart Of Sigma Chi
3/27 Fred Waring's Pennsylvanians
8/28 Gene Austin

23/51 **Sweetheart Of Yesterday** ...
Guy Mitchell

9/12 **Sweetheart Sue** ...
Henry Burr & Albert Campbell

24/54 **Sweetheart (Will You Remember)** ...
Hilltoppers

8/09 **Sweetheart's A Pretty Name When It's
Y-O-U** ... Peerless Quartet

Sweethearts
2/13 Christie MacDonald
6/13 Grace Kerns
8/14 Victor Herbert

3/32 **Sweethearts Forever** ... Wayne King

Sweethearts On Parade
1/29 Guy Lombardo
8/29 Abe Lyman
6/32 Louis Armstrong

7/34 **Sweetie Pie** ... Fats Waller

15/37 **Swing And Sway** ... Sammy Kaye

Swing High, Swing Low
13/37 Russ Morgan
16/37 Dorothy Lamour

2/34 **Swing It, Sister** ... Mills Brothers

7/10 **Swing Low, Sweet Chariot** ...
Fisk University Jubilee Quartet

17/36 **Swing, Mr. Charlie** ... Herbie Kay

16/39 **Swingin' At The Sugar Bowl** ...
Bob Crosby

Swingin' Down The Lane
1/23 Isham Jones
2/23 Ben Bernie
11/23 Columbians

3/30 **Swingin' In A Hammock** ...
Guy Lombardo

Swinging On A Star
1/44 Bing Crosby
28/44 Gray Rains

2/36 **Swingtime In The Rockies** ...
Benny Goodman

15/33 **Swingy Little Thingy** ... Don Bestor

23/47 **Swiss Boy** ... Lawrence Duchow

27/54 **Sylvie** ... Weavers

1/13 **Sympathy** ...
Helen Clark & Walter Van Brunt

14/41 **Symphonie Moderne** ...
Freddy Martin

Symphony
1/46 Freddy Martin
2/46 Benny Goodman
3/46 Bing Crosby
4/46 Jo Stafford
10/46 Guy Lombardo

12/21 **Symphony In E Flat Major (Finale)** ...
Arthur Toscanini

Syncopated Clock
12/51 Leroy Anderson
28/51 Boston Pops Orchestra

14/24 **Syncopated Opera** ...
Ernest Hare & Billy Jones

9/15 **Syncopated Walk** ...
Prince's Orchestra

T

22/53 **TV Rhumba** ... Bob Bachelder

14/39 **Ta Hu Wa Nu Wa (Hawaiian War Chant)** ... Merry Macs

Ta-Ra-Ra-Boom-Der-E
1/92 Len Spencer
2/92 U.S. Marine Band
15/39 Gene Krupa

21/48 **Tacos, Enchiladas, & Beans** ... Sam Donohue

'Tain't Good (Like A Nickel Made Of Wood)
13/36 Ozzie Nelson
19/36 Jimmie Lunceford
9/37 Fats Waller

10/45 **'Tain't Me** ... Les Brown

'Tain't Nobody's Bus'ness If I Do
9/23 Bessie Smith
9/24 Clarence Williams' Blue Five

'Tain't What You Do (It's The Way That You Do It)
11/39 Jimmie Lunceford
19/39 Ella Fitzgerald with Chick Webb

17/27 **Take In The Sun, Hang Out The Moon** ... Clevelanders

11/44 **Take It Easy** ... Guy Lombardo

Take Me
5/42 Tommy Dorsey
7/42 Jimmy Dorsey
10/42 Benny Goodman

2/07 **Take Me Around Again** ... Billy Murray

29/54 **Take Me Back Again** ... Tony Bennett

Take Me Back To My Boots And Saddle
4/35 Tommy Dorsey
20/35 Victor Young

Take Me Back To New York Town
2/07 Harry Tally
6/07 Billy Murray

Take Me Back To The Garden Of Love
3/12 Columbia Stellar Quartet
6/12 Walter Van Brunt

15/52 **Take Me In Your Arms And Hold Me** ... Les Paul & Mary Ford

4/09 **Take Me Out For A Joy Ride** ... Billy Murray & Haydn Quartet

Take Me Out To The Ball Game
1/08 Billy Murray & Haydn Quartet
3/08 Harvey Hindermyer
5/08 Edward Meeker

5/19 **Take Me To The Land Of Jazz** ... Marion Harris

4/09 **Take Me Up With You, Dearie** ... Billy Murray & Haydn Quartet

Take My Heart
1/36 Eddy Duchin
7/36 Nat Brandywynne

Take My Heart
12/52 Al Martino
30/52 Vic Damone

5/34 **Take My Word** ... Benny Goodman

5/24 **Take, Oh Take, Those Lips Away** ... Ben Selvin

4/13 **Take, Oh Take Those Lips Away** ... John McCormack

Take The "A" Train
11/41 Duke Ellington
19/43 Duke Ellington

Take Your Girlie To The Movies (If You Can't Make Love At Home)
5/19 Billy Murray
10/19 Irving Kaufman

Takes Two To Tango
7/52 Pearl Bailey
19/52 Louis Armstrong

26/48 **Takin' Miss Mary To The Ball** ... Jack Smith

Taking A Chance On Love
1/43 Benny Goodman
13/43 Sammy Kaye

1/01 **Tale Of The Bumble Bee** ... Harry Macdonough

6/05 **Tale Of The Turtle Dove** ... Harry Macdonough

Tale The Church Bell Tolled
3/07 Harry Macdonough
7/07 Frank Stanley

3/16 **Tales Of Hoffman: Barcolle ("Belle Nuit" - Oh Night Of Love)** ... John McCormack

7/34 **Talkin' To Myself** ... Ted Weems

23/48 **Talking To Myself About You** ... Peggy Lee

Tallahassee
10/47 Bing Crosby & Andrews Sisters
15/47 Dinah Shore & Woody Herman

10/26 **Tamiani Trail** ... Ben Selvin

Tammany
2/05 Arthur Collins & Byron Harlan
4/05 S.H. Dudley
5/05 Arthur Pryor's Band
7/05 Billy Murray

3/45 **Tampico** ... Stan Kenton

Tangerine
1/42 Jimmy Dorsey
11/42 Vaughn Monroe

13/22 **Tannhauser Overture - Part 1** ... Philadelphia Orchestra

Tara's Theme (My Own True Love)
21/54 Leroy Holmes
23/54 Johnny Desmond

15/20 **Taxi** ... Joseph C. Smith's Orchestra

Twilight In Turkey
11/37 Raymond Scott
18/37 Tommy Dorsey

Twilight Time
14/44 Three Suns
16/45 Les Brown
21/53 Johnny Maddox

6/28 **Two Black Crows-Part 5 (Curiosities On The Farm)** ... Moran & Mack

13/28 **Two Black Crows-Part 7 (No Matter How Hungry A Horse Is, He Cannot Eat A Bit)** ... Moran & Mack

1/27 **Two Black Crows-Parts 1 & 2 (The Early Bird Catches The Worm)** ... Moran & Mack

4/27 **Two Black Crows-Parts 3 & 4 (All About Lions)** ... Moran & Mack

15/38 **Two Blind Loves** ... Kenny Baker

Two Blue Eyes (Two Little Baby Shoes)
3/08 Byron G. Harlan
7/08 Billy Murray

13/38 **Two Bouquets** ... Guy Lombardo

Two Cigarettes In The Dark
2/34 Johnny Green
5/34 Bing Crosby
6/34 Jerry Johnson
6/34 Frank Parker
10/34 Glen Gray

12/38 **Two Dreams Got Together** ... Larry Clinton

Two Dreams Met
9/40 Mitchell Ayres
12/40 Tommy Dorsey
22/40 Eddy Duchin

5/03 **Two Eyes Of Blue** ... Harry Macdonough

10/10 **Two Gentlemen From Ireland** ... Billy Murray & Len Spencer

12/31 **Two Hearts In Waltz Time** ... Johnny Hamp

9/41 **Two In Love** ... Tommy Dorsey

1/93 **Two Little Girls In Blue** ... J.W. Myers

29/52 **Two Little Kisses** ... Four Aces

Two Little Love Bees
5/11 Reinald Werrenrath & Elizabeth Wheeler
5/12 Christie MacDonald & Reinald Werrenrath

Two Loves Have I
21/47 Frankie Laine
21/48 Perry Como

Two O'Clock Jump
19/43 Harry James
21/43 Muggsy Spanier
(also see: One O'Clock Jump)

20/54 **Two Purple Shadows** ... Jerry Vale

3/02 **Two Rubes In A Tavern** ... Frank Stanley & Byron G. Harlan

Two Sleepy People
1/38 Fats Waller
6/38 Sammy Kaye
7/38 Kay Kyser
11/38 Bob Crosby
13/38 Hoagy Carmichael & Ella Logan
13/38 Lawrence Welk
15/39 Bob Hope & Shirley Ross

21/53 **Typewriter, The** ... Leroy Anderson

Tzena, Tzena, Tzena
2/50 Weavers with Gordon Jenkins
3/50 Mitch Miller
6/50 Vic Damone
16/50 Ralph Flanagan

22/46 **Ugly Chile (You're Some Pretty Doll)** ... Johnny Mercer

6/25 **Ukelele Lady** ... Vaughn Deleath

Umbrella Man
1/39 Kay Kyser
12/39 Johnny Messner

24/44 **Umbriago** ... Jimmy Durante

26/54 **Unbelievable** ... Nat "King" Cole

2/91 **Uncle Jefferson** ... Billy Golden

7/07 **Uncle Josh And Aunt Nancy Go To Housekeeping** ... Cal Stewart with Haydn Quartet

9/05 **Uncle Josh And Aunt Nancy In The Subway** ... Cal Stewart

Uncle Josh And Aunt Nancy Put Up The Kitchen Stove
5/19 Ada Jones
5/19 Cal Stewart

4/03 **Uncle Josh And Aunt Nancy Smith On A Visit To New York** ... Cal Stewart

3/04 **Uncle Josh And The Insurance Company** ... Cal Stewart

3/99 **Uncle Josh And The Lightning Rod Agent** ... Cal Stewart

4/99 **Uncle Josh At A Baptizing At Hickory Corners Square** ... Cal Stewart

7/09 **Uncle Josh At A Baseball Game** ... Cal Stewart

2/99 **Uncle Josh At A Camp Meeting** ... Cal Stewart

9/07 **Uncle Josh At The Dentist's** ... Cal Stewart

2/98 **Uncle Josh At The Opera** ... Cal Stewart

4/05 **Uncle Josh At The White House** ... Cal Stewart

9/21 **Uncle Josh Buys A Victrola** ... Cal Stewart

601

16/40 **Vagabond Dreams** ... Glenn Miller
17/50 **Vagabond Shoes** ... Vic Damone
Valencia
1/26   Paul Whiteman
3/26   Ben Selvin
5/26   Revelers
12/26   Ross Gorman
14/26   Jesse Crawford
18/50   Tony Martin
Vamp, The
3/19   Joseph C. Smith's Orchestra
7/19   Waldorf-Astoria Dance Orchestra
9/52 **Vanessa** ... Hugo Winterhalter
Vanity
11/51   Don Cherry
18/51   Tony Martin
19/51   Sarah Vaughan
Varsity Drag
4/27   George Olsen
15/27   Cass Hagan
13/39 **Vas Vilst Du Gaily Star** ...
    Emery Deutsch
1/53 **Vaya Con Dios (May God Be With You)** ... Les Paul & Mary Ford
8/53 **Velvet Glove** ... Hugo Winterhalter
21/51 **Velvet Lips** ... Guy Lombardo
2/43 **Velvet Moon** ... Harry James
9/20 **Venetian Moon** ... Ben Selvin
30/54 **Veni-Vidi-Vici (I Came, I Saw, I Conquered)** ... Gaylords
29/54 **Venus De Milo** ... Bob Manning
9/13 **Venus On Earth Waltz** ...
    Sousa's Band
26/52 **Veradero** ... Camarata
Very Thought Of You
1/34   Ray Noble
11/34   Bing Crosby
19/44   Vaughn Monroe
Vesti La Giubla ... *see: I Pigliacci*
5/44 **Victory Polka** ...
    Bing Crosby & Andrews Sisters
29/49 **Vieni Su (Say You Love Me Too)** ...
    Vaughn Monroe
Vieni, Vieni
1/37   Rudy Vallee
4/37   Hoarce Heidt
9/37   Bert Block
17/37   Ted Fio Rito
18/37   Emery Deutsch
Vilia Song
3/08   Elise Stevenson
9/08   Helene Noldi

9/15 **Village Gossips** ...
    Cal Stewart & Byron G. Harlan
30/53 **Village In Peru** ... Vic Damone
14/47 **Violets** ... Ted Weems
Virginia Blues
4/22   Van & Schenck
7/22   Benson Orchestra Of Chicago
10/24 **Virginia (Don't Go Too Far)** ...
    Carl Fenton
4/15 **Virginia Lee** ... Peerless Quartet
10/32 **Voice In The Old Village Choir** ...
    Paul Whiteman
2/92 **Volunteers' March** ...
    Gilmore's Band
20/43 **Vos Zokt Eer** ... Baron Elliott

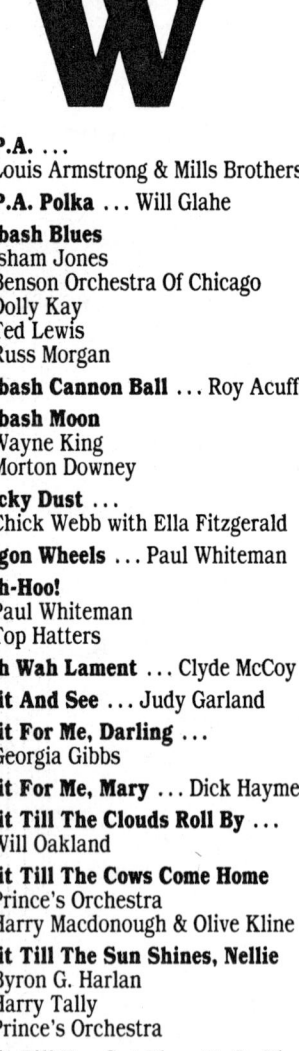

26/40 **W.P.A.** ...
    Louis Armstrong & Mills Brothers
11/39 **W.P.A. Polka** ... Will Glahe
Wabash Blues
1/21   Isham Jones
6/22   Benson Orchestra Of Chicago
13/22   Dolly Kay
16/30   Ted Lewis
17/39   Russ Morgan
12/38 **Wabash Cannon Ball** ... Roy Acuff
Wabash Moon
4/31   Wayne King
18/31   Morton Downey
13/38 **Wacky Dust** ...
    Chick Webb with Ella Fitzgerald
1/34 **Wagon Wheels** ... Paul Whiteman
Wah-Hoo!
9/36   Paul Whiteman
15/36   Top Hatters
12/33 **Wah Wah Lament** ... Clyde McCoy
24/45 **Wait And See** ... Judy Garland
24/54 **Wait For Me, Darling** ...
    Georgia Gibbs
6/43 **Wait For Me, Mary** ... Dick Haymes
5/10 **Wait Till The Clouds Roll By** ...
    Will Oakland
Wait Till The Cows Come Home
4/18   Prince's Orchestra
9/18   Harry Macdonough & Olive Kline
Wait Till The Sun Shines, Nellie
1/06   Byron G. Harlan
1/06   Harry Tally
5/06   Prince's Orchestra
7/20 **Wait Till You Get Them Up In The Air, Boys** ... Billy Murray

9/29	**Wait Till You See Ma Cherie** ...	
	Maurice Chevalier	
23/41	**Waiter And The Porter And The**	
	Upstairs Maid ... Bing Crosby, Mary	
	Martin & Jack Teagarden	
17/34	**Waitin' At The Gate For Katy** ...	
	Don Bestor	
	Waitin' For The Train To Come In	
4/45	Peggy Lee	
6/45	Harry James	
7/45	Johnny Long	
10/20	**Waiting** ... Charles Harrison	
	Waiting At The Church (My Wife Won't	
	Let Me)	
2/06	Ada Jones	
4/07	Vesta Victoria	
12/29	**Waiting At The End Of The Road** ...	
	Paul Whiteman	
14/29	**Waiting For A Train** ...	
	Jimmie Rodgers	
	Waiting For The Robert E. Lee	
1/12	Heidelberg Quintet	
3/12	Arthur Collins & Byron Harlan	
4/12	Dolly Connolly	
8/21	**Waiting For The Sun To Come Out** ...	
	Lambert Murphy	
2/16	**Wake Up, America!** ...	
	James F. Harrison	
	Wake Up And Live	
17/37	Cab Calloway	
17/37	Red Nichols	
18/37	Hudson-DeLange Orchestra	
15/36	**Wake Up And Sing** ... Bob Howard	
	Walkin' By The River	
14/41	Una Mae Carlisle	
16/41	Ginny Simms	
19/41	Hal Kemp	
29/52	Ella Fitzgerald	
	Walkin' My Baby Back Home	
8/31	Nick Lucas	
8/31	Ted Weems	
15/31	Charleston Chasers	
18/31	Lee Morse	
4/52	Johnnie Ray	
8/52	Nat "King" Cole	
11/52	**Walkin' To Missouri** ... Sammy Kaye	
10/45	**Walkin' With My Honey (Soon, Soon,**	
	Soon) ... Sammy Kaye	
23/41	**Walking The Floor Over You** ...	
	Ernest Tubb	
9/12	**Wallflower Sweet** ...	
	Charles Harrison & Grace Kerns	
16/36	**Waltz In Swing Time** ...	
	Johnny Green	
5/06	**Waltz Me Around Again, Willie** ...	
	Billy Murray & Haydn Quartet	
6/24	**Waltz Of Long Ago** ... Paul Specht	
9/18	**Waltz Of The Flowers** ...	
	Philharmonic Orchestra Of New York	

10/17	**Waltz Of The Hours** ...	
	Cincinnati Symphony Orchestra	
	Waltz You Saved For Me	
4/31	Wayne King	
18/34	Wayne King	
	Waltzing In A Dream	
6/32	Bing Crosby	
9/32	Guy Lombardo	
11/50	**Wanderin'** ... Sammy Kaye	
	Wang Wang Blues	
1/21	Paul Whiteman	
16/51	Ames Brothers	
28/51	Benny Goodman	
1/54	**Wanted** ... Perry Como	
5/15	**War Talk At Pun'kin Center** ...	
	Cal Stewart	
	Warsaw Concerto	
11/43	Freddy Martin	
26/48	Claude Thornhill	
27/53	Ralph Marterie	
	Was It A Dream?	
10/28	Jan Garber	
11/28	Fred Waring's Pennsylvanians	
11/37	**Was It Rain?** ... Frances Langford	
	Was That The Human Thing To Do?	
6/32	Bert Lown	
7/32	Boswell Sisters	
18/32	Benny Krueger	
10/20	**Was There Ever A Pal Like You?** ...	
	Henry Burr	
	Washboard Blues	
13/27	Red Nichols	
17/28	Paul Whiteman	
15/25	**Washington And Lee Swing** ...	
	Meyer Davis	
	Washington Post March	
1/90	U.S. Marine Band	
1/95	Sousa's Band	
5/09	Prince's Orchestra	
18/34	**Washington Squabble** ...	
	Claude Hopkins	
20/43	**Washington Whirligig** ...	
	Charlie Barnet	
23/41	**Wasn't It You?** ... Jimmy Dorsey	
21/52	**Water Can't Quench The Fire Of**	
	Love ... Helen O'Connell & Gisele	
	MacKenzie	
23/54	**Watermelon In December** ...	
	Artie Wayne	
	Watermelon Weather	
19/52	Perry Como & Eddie Fisher	
28/52	Bing Crosby & Peggy Lee	
19/46	**Wave To Me, My Lady** ... Elton Britt	
	Way Back Home	
6/35	Victor Young	
21/49	Bing Crosby with Fred Waring	
9/11	**Way Down East** ... Peerless Quartet	
9/25	**Way Down Home** ...	
	Gene Austin & Carson Robison	

7/17	**Way Down In Iowa, I'm Going To Hide Away** ... Irving Kaufman
1/02	**Way Down In Old Indiana** ... J.W. Myers
5/12	**'Way Down South** ... Heidelberg Quintet
17/37	**Way Down Upon The Swanee River** ... Erskine Hawkins

Way Down Yonder In New Orleans

9/22	Peerless Quartet
5/23	Blossom Seeley
5/23	Paul Whiteman
26/53	Frankie Laine & Jo Stafford
10/27	**Way Out Yonder In The Golden West** ... Avon Comedy Four
30/51	**Way Up In North Carolina** ... Belltones

Way You Look Tonight

1/36	Fred Astaire
3/36	Guy Lombardo
3/36	Teddy Wilson with Billie Holiday
21/42	Benny Goodman
22/42	**We Did It Before (And We Can Do It Again)** ... Dick Robertson

We Just Couldn't Say Goodbye

1/32	Guy Lombardo
3/32	Paul Whiteman
22/51	**We Kiss In A Shadow** ... Frank Sinatra
11/44	**We Might As Well Forget It** ... Bob Wills
21/42	**We Must Be Vigilant** ... Phil Spitalny
7/10	**We Parted On The Shore** ... Harry Lauder
15/36	**We Saw The Sea** ... Fred Astaire
10/10	**We Shall Meet Bye And Bye** ... Frank Stanley & Henry Burr

We Three (My Echo, My Shadow, And Me)

3/40	Tommy Dorsey
1/41	Ink Spots
1/94	**We Were Sweethearts, Nell And I** ... George J. Gaskin
30/54	**We'll Be Married In The Church In The Wildwood** ... Four Coins
22/50	**We'll Build A Bungalow** ... Johnny Long

We'll Build A Little Home In The U.S.A.

7/15	Irving Kaufman
2/16	James F. Harrison & James Reed
25/46	**We'll Gather Lilacs** ... Tommy Dorsey
8/34	**We'll Make Hay While The Sun Shines** ... Bing Crosby

We'll Meet Again

24/41	Kay Kyser
24/41	Guy Lombardo
16/42	Benny Goodman
29/54	Vera Lynn
3/18	**We're Going Over** ... Peerless Quartet
	We're In The Money ... *see: Gold Diggers' Song*
24/42	**We're The Couple In The Castle** ... Glenn Miller
8/39	**We've Come A Long Way Together** ... Sammy Kaye
7/33	**We've Got The Moon And Sixpence** ... Ray Noble

Weary River

2/29	Rudy Vallee
5/29	Gene Austin
11/35	**Weather Man** ... Adrian Rollini
20/29	**Web Of Love** ... Earl Burtnett
8/10	**Wedding Bells** ... American Quartet

Wedding Bells Are Breaking Up That Old Gang Of Mine

8/29	Gene Austin
21/48	Steve Gibson
22/54	Four Aces
30/49	**Wedding Bells Will Soon Be Ringing** ... Margaret Whiting & Jimmy Wakely
8/18	**Wedding Bells (Will They Ever Ring For Me?)** ... Al Jolson
4/12	**Wedding Glide** ... Ada Jones & Billy Murray
20/49	**Wedding Of Lili Marlene** ... Andrews Sisters

Wedding Of Reuben And The Maid

2/01	Arthur Collins & Byron Harlan
4/01	Harry Macdonough
10/08	**Wedding Of Sandy McNab** ... Harry Lauder

Wedding Of The Painted Doll

1/29	Leo Reisman
8/29	Charles King
10/29	Earl Burtnett
4/16	**Wedding Of The Sunshine And The Rose** ... Henry Burr & Albert Campbell

Wedding Of Uncle Josh And Aunt Nancy Smith

7/05	Cal Stewart
3/07	Cal Stewart

Wedding Samba

16/50	Edmundo Ros
23/50	Andrews Sisters & Carmen Miranda
28/50	Guy Lombardo
24/48	**Wedding Song** ... Irving Fields
10/38	**Weekend Of A Private Secretary** ... Red Norvo
17/33	**Weep No More, My Baby** ... Glen Gray

14/33	**When It's Lamp-Lightin' Time In The Valley** ... Wayne King
4/14	**When It's Moonlight On The Alamo** ... Peerless Quartet
22/42	**When It's Moonlight On The Blue Pacific** ... Alvino Rey
5/08	**When It's Moonlight On The Prairie** ... Haydn Quartet
6/14	**When It's Night Time Down In Burghandy** ... George MacFarlane
9/24	**When It's Night Time In Italy** ... Lew Holtz
6/15	**When It's Peach Picking Time In Delaware** ... Henry Burr & Albert Campbell

When It's Sleepy Time Down South
6/31	Paul Whiteman
19/52	Louis Armstrong

When It's Springtime In The Rockies
1/30	Hilo Hawaiian Orchestra
1/30	Ben Selvin
5/30	Ray Miller
14/30	Ford & Glenn

4/03	**When Kate And I Were Comin' Thro' The Rye** ... Harry Macdonough
4/24	**When Lights Are Low** ... Benson Orchestra Of Chicago
17/37	**When Love Is Young** ... Fats Waller
4/01	**When Mister Shakespeare Comes To Town** ... Dan Quinn
3/38	**When Mother Nature Sings Her Lullaby** ... Bing Crosby

When My Baby Smiles At Me
1/20	Ted Lewis
8/20	Billy Murray & Gladys Rice
11/20	Henry Burr
18/38	Ted Lewis

When My Dream Boat Comes Home
3/37	Guy Lombardo
10/37	Henry Allen
10/37	Shep Fields
18/53	Kay Starr

10/29	**When My Dreams Come True** ... Paul Whiteman
23/44	**When My Man Comes Home** ... Buddy Johnson
4/15	**When My Ship Comes In** ... Henry Burr & Albert Campbell

When My Sugar Walks Down The Street
3/25	Aileen Stanley & Gene Austin
14/25	Warner's Seven Aces
27/44	Ella Fitzgerald

5/20	**When Night Descends** ... John McCormack
7/16	**When Old Bill Bailey Plays The Ukelele** ... Peerless Quartet
9/38	**When Paw Was Courtin' Maw** ... Dick Todd

When Reuben Comes To Town
2/00	Dan Quinn
1/01	S.H. Dudley

4/10	**When Shadows Gather** ... John McCormack
12/22	**When Shall We Meet Again?** ... Prince's Orchestra
19/29	**When Summer Is Gone** ... Nat Shilkret
8/07	**When Summer Tells Autumn Good-Bye** ... Frank Stanley & Henry Burr
9/15	**When Sunday Comes To Town** ... Arthur Fields
6/08	**When Sweet Marie Was Sweet Sixteen** ... Harry Macdonough & John Bieling
23/41	**When That Man Is Dead And Gone** ... Glenn Miller

When The Angelus Is Ringing
3/14	Peerless Quartet
8/14	Lyric Quartet

7/30	**When The Bloom Is On The Sage** ... Beverly Hill Billies
9/19	**When The Boys Come Home** ... Louis Gravieure
5/07	**When The Flowers Bloom In The Springtime, Molly Dear** ... Haydn Quartet
8/15	**When The Grown-Up Ladies Act Like Babies (I've Got To Love 'Em, That's All)** ... Billy Murray

When The Harvest Days Are Over
2/01	Harry Macdonough
3/01	Byron G. Harlan

19/35	**When The Leaves Bid The Trees Goodbye** ... Enric Madriguera
11/23	**When The Leaves Come Tumbling Down** ... Paul Specht

When The Lights Go On Again (All Over The World)
1/43	Vaughn Monroe
12/43	Lucky Millinder
20/43	Lucky Millinder

6/30	**When The Little Red Roses Get The Blues** ... Al Jolson

When The Midnight Choo Choo Leaves For Alabam'
1/13	Arthur Collins & Byron Harlan
9/13	Victor Military Band

5/05	**When The Mists Have Rolled Away** ... Harry Anthony & James F. Harrison

When The Mocking Birds Are Singing In The Wildwood
6/06	Harry Macdonough
7/06	Frank Stanley

27/40	**When The Moon Comes Over Madison Square** ... Bing Crosby

When The Moon Comes Over The Mountain
1/31   Kate Smith
7/31   Nick Lucas
12/31   Leo Reisman
15/31   Radiolites

2/20   **When The Moon Shines On The Moonshine** ... Bert Williams

15/29   **When The Morning Glories Wake Up In The Morning (Then I'll Kiss Your Two Lips Goodbye)** ... Don Voorhees

7/25   **When The One You Love Loves You** ... Paul Whiteman

When The Organ Played "Oh Promise Me"
14/37   Guy Lombardo
19/37   Emery Deutsch
5/38   Bing Crosby

8/30   **When The Organ Played At Twilight** ... Ben Selvin

When The Poppies Bloom Again
8/37   Russ Morgan
15/37   George Hall

When The Red, Red Robin Comes Bob-Bob-Bobbin' Along
1/26   Al Jolson
7/26   Paul Whiteman
9/26   "Whispering" Jack Smith
12/26   Cliff Edwards
12/26   Ipana Troubadors
29/53   Doris Day

6/06   **When The Roll Is Called Up Yonder** ... Haydn Quartet

24/42   **When The Roses Bloom Again** ... Jimmy Dorsey

When The Saints Go Marching In
10/39   Louis Armstrong
27/51   Weavers
29/51   Percy Faith

When The Sun Goes Down In Dixie
5/17   Lewis James
5/17   George Wilson
6/17   Peerless Quartet

When The Swallows Come Back To Capistrano
2/40   Glenn Miller
4/40   Ink Spots

21/42   **When The White Azaleas Start Blooming** ... Bing Crosby

22/42   **When There's A Breeze On Lake Louise** ... Freddy Martin

4/44   **When They Ask About You** ... Jimmy Dorsey

When They Played The Polka
4/38   Sammy Kaye
14/38   Hoarce Heidt

12/34   **When Tomorrow Comes** ... Freddy Martin

13/37   **When Two Love Each Other (Just As You And I)** ... Shep Fields

2/12   **When Uncle Joe Plays A Rag On His Old Banjo** ... Arthur Collins

9/18   **When Uncle Joe Steps Into France** ... Arthur Collins & Byron Harlan

When We Are Dancing ...
see: I Get Ideas

1/08   **When We Are M-A-Double-R-I-E-D** ... Ada Jones & Billy Murray

When We Are Married
3/98   Estella Mann & John Havens
2/00   Harry Macdonough & Grace Spencer

28/55   **When We Come Of Age** ... Joni James

9/18   **When We Meet In The Sweet Bye And Bye** ... Sterling Trio

When We're Alone (Penthouse Serenade)
3/32   Arden-Ohman Orchestra
8/32   Ruth Etting
17/32   Tom Gerun

6/39   **When Winter Comes** ... Artie Shaw

8/18   **When Yankee Doodle Learns To Parlez Vous Francais** ... Arthur Fields

When You Ain't Got No More Money, Well, You Needn't Come Around
1/99   Arthur Collins
5/99   Len Spencer

11/25   **When You And I Were Seventeen** ... Marion Harris

When You And I Were Young, Maggie
4/05   Frank Stanley & Corrine Morgan
7/06   Richard Jose
7/08   Will Oakland
5/09   Henry Burr
5/23   Van & Schenck
8/51   Bing Crosby & Gary Crosby
20/51   Margaret Whiting & Jimmy Wakely

When You Come Back
4/19   John McCormack
9/19   Orpheus Quartet

7/18   **When You Come Home** ... Henry Burr

10/16   **When You Drop Off At Cairo, Illinois** ... Billy Murray

When You Look In The Heart Of A Rose
2/19   John McCormack
3/19   Charles Harrison

5/18   **When You Sang "Hush-A-Bye" To Me** ... Sterling Trio

When You Walked Out, Someone Else Walked Right In
4/23   Isham Jones
10/23   Frank Crumit

When You Were Sweet Sixteen
1/00   George J. Gaskin
1/00   Jere Mahoney
3/01   Harry Macdonough
3/01   J.W. Myers
2/47   Perry Como
15/47   Mills Brothers
17/47   Dick Jurgens

White Christmas

1/42	Bing Crosby
12/42	Charlie Spivak
15/42	Gordon Jenkins
24/42	Freddy Martin
5/44	Bing Crosby
6/44	Bing Crosby
7/44	Frank Sinatra
1/45	Bing Crosby
16/45	Freddy Martin
5/46	Frank Sinatra
6/46	Frank Sinatra
9/46	Jo Stafford
1/47	Bing Crosby
21/47	Eddy Howard
23/47	Perry Como
3/48	Bing Crosby
6/49	Bing Crosby
5/50	Bing Crosby
13/50	Bing Crosby
13/52	Bing Crosby
23/52	Mantovani
21/53	Bing Crosby
21/54	Bing Crosby

White Cliffs Of Dover ...
see: (There'll Be Bluebirds Over)

10/30 **White Dove** ... Lawrence Tibbett

20/33 **White Jazz** ... Glen Gray

White Sails (Beneath A Yellow Moon)

2/39	Ozzie Nelson
4/39	Sammy Kaye

Whither Thou Goest

10/54	Les Paul & Mary Ford
21/54	Laurie Loman
27/54	Marian Marlowe

19/31 **Who Am I?** ... Jacques Renard

9/12 **Who Are You With To-Night?** ...
Billy Murray

Who Blew Out The Flame?

6/38	Larry Clinton
8/38	Dolly Dawn
16/38	Ozzie Nelson

4/23 **Who Cares?** ... Al Jolson

9/23 **Who Did You Fool, After All?** ...
Nora Bayes

21/49 **Who Do You Know In Heaven (That Made You The Angel You Are?)** ...
Ink Spots

9/46 **Who Do You Love I Hope** ...
Elliot Lawrence

10/08 **Who Do You Love?** ...
Arthur Collins & Byron Harlan

23/53 **Who Kissed Me Last Night?** ...
Rosemary Clooney

4/36 **Who Loves You?** ...
Billie Holiday & Teddy Wilson

26/48 **Who Put That Dream In Your Eye?** ...
Mark Warnow

23/53 **Who Put The Devil In Evelyn's Eyes** ...
Mills Brothers

7/25 **Who Takes Care Of The Caretaker's Daughter?** ... Cliff Edwards

7/45 **Who Threw The Whiskey In The Well?** ... Lucky Millinder

15/39 **Who Told You I Cared?** ...
Ozzie Nelson

Who Told You That Lie?

15/46	Vaughn Monroe
22/46	Connee Boswell

15/34 **Who Walks In When I Walk Out?** ...
Ray Noble

20/28 **Who Wouldn't Be Blue?** ...
Ted Weems

20/29 **Who Wouldn't Be Jealous Of You?** ...
Ray Miller

1/42 **Who Wouldn't Love You** ...
Kay Kyser

Who'll Be The Next One (To Cry Over You)

6/21	Charles Harrison
24/49	Mills Brothers

11/20 **Who'll Take The Place Of Mary?** ...
Peerless Quartet

8/37 **Who's Afraid Of Love** ... Fats Waller

Who's Afraid Of The Big Bad Wolf?

2/33	Don Bestor
3/33	Victor Young
8/33	Ben Bernie

22/53 **Who's Gonna Pay The Check?** ...
Peggy Lee

Who's Sorry Now?

3/23	Isham Jones
5/23	Marion Harris
8/23	Original Memphis Five
11/23	Lewis James
11/23	Irving Kaufman
18/46	Harry James

Who's Yehoodi?

12/40	Kay Kyser
30/40	Jerry Colonna

Who?

12/25	Brox Sisters
1/26	George Olsen
5/37	Tommy Dorsey

Whole World Is Singing My Song

6/46	Les Brown
12/46	Jimmy Dorsey

10/20 **Whose Baby Are You?** ...
Joseph C. Smith's Orchestra

25/49 **Whose Girl Are You** ... Blue Barron

13/35 **Whose Honey Are You?** ...
Fats Waller

27/40 **Whose Theme Song?** ...
Richard Himber

Why

23/54	Karen Chandler
27/54	Nat "King" Cole

4/29 **Why Can't You?** ... Al Jolson

Why Couldn't It Be Poor Little Me?
8/25   Isham Jones
8/25   Ray Miller

(Why Couldn't It Last) Last Night
5/39   Glenn Miller
16/39   Bob Crosby

6/24   **Why Did I Kiss That Girl?** ...
        Paul Whiteman

Why Did You ...
see: (You Made Me Love You)

Why Do I Dream These Dreams?
8/34   Eddy Duchin
18/34   Bob Causer

9/28   **Why Do I Love You?** ... Nat Shilkret

9/26   **Why Do Ya Roll Those Eyes?** ...
        Paul Whiteman

22/46   **Why Does It Get So Late So Early** ...
        Helen Forrest & Dick Haymes

26/53   **Why Does It Have To Be Me?** ...
        Tony Bennett

Why Don't We Do This More Often?
8/41   Kay Kyser
14/41   Freddy Martin

Why Don't You Believe Me
1/52   Joni James
4/53   Patti Page
29/53   Margaret Whiting

4/43   **Why Don't You Do Right?** ...
        Benny Goodman

Why Don't You Fall In Love With Me?
21/42   Connee Boswell
3/43   Dinah Shore
4/43   Dick Jurgens
10/43   Johnny Long

22/49   **Why Don't You Haul Off And Love
        Me?** ... Wayne Raney

11/34   **Why Don't You Practice What You
        Preach?** ... Jan Garber

Why Should I Cry Over You?
3/22   Billy Jones
15/22   Virginians

25/54   **Why Should I Love You?** ...
        Harptones

8/31   **Why Shouldn't I?** ... Gus Arnheim

12/35   **Why Shouldn't I?** ... Johnny Green

Why Was I Born?
8/30   Helen Morgan
19/30   Libby Holman
20/49   Vic Damone

10/21   **Why Worry?** ... Nora Bayes

Why did You ...
see: (You Made Me Love You)

12/38   **Why'd Ya Make Me Fall In Love?** ...
        Benny Goodman

6/33   **Wild Goose Chase** ... Glen Gray

Wild Horses
6/53   Perry Como
28/53   Ray Anthony

15/27   **Wild Man Blues** ... Johnny Dodds

Wild Side Of Life
27/52   Hank Thompson
30/52   Burl Ives

18/38   **Wild, Wild Women (Are Making A Wild
        Man Of Me)** ... Freddie Fisher

22/47   **Wildest Gal In Town** ...
        Billy Eckstine

3/23   **Wildflower** ... Ben Bernie

3/28   **Wildwood Flower** ... Carter Family

10/36   **Will I Ever Know?** ... Jan Garber

18/34   **Will Love Find A Way?** ... Hal Kemp

10/24   **Will Rogers' First Political Speech** ...
        Will Rogers

13/23   **Will Rogers Tells Traffic Chiefs How
        To Direct Traffic** ... Will Rogers

Will The Circle Be Unbroken ...
see: Can The Circle Be Unbroken

**Will You Love Me In December As You
Do In May?**
2/06   Haydn Quartet
3/06   Albert Campbell

Will You Remember?
3/18   Olive Kline & Lambert Murphy
14/37   Victor Young

7/25   **Will You Remember Me?** ...
        Ben Selvin

7/38   **Will You Remember Tonight
        Tomorrow?** ... Russ Morgan

29/44   **Will You Still Be Mine?** ...
        Tommy Dorsey

William Tell Overture
3/01   Sousa's Band
9/20   Columbia Orchestra
6/48   Spike Jones

20/27   **Willie The Weeper** ... King Oliver

Willow Weep For Me
17/32   Ted Fio Rito
2/33   Paul Whiteman

14/52   **Wimoweh** ...
        Weavers with Gordon Jenkins

23/41   **Window Washer Man** ... Dick Kuhn

19/28   **Wings** ... Clicquot Club Eskimos

Winter
5/11   Lyric Quartet
23/53   Spike Jones

24/42   **Winter Weather** ... Benny Goodman

Winter Wonderland
2/34   Guy Lombardo
13/35   Ted Weems
10/46   Perry Como
22/46   Andrews Sisters
4/47   Johnny Mercer
27/52   Perry Como

Wise Old Owl
3/41   Al Donohue
18/41   Teddy Powell
22/41   Kay Kyser

THE
ACHIEVEMENTS

THE TOP 100 ARTISTS — 1890-1954

RANK	POINTS	RANK	POINTS
1. Bing Crosby	35,150	51. Henry Burr & Albert Campbell..	5,702
2. Paul Whiteman & His Orchestra	25,484	52. Artie Shaw & His Orchestra	5,637
3. Guy Lombardo & His Royal		53. George Olsen & His Orchestra...	5,637
Canadians	23,856	54. Hoarce Heidt & His Orchestra...	5,614
4. Tommy Dorsey & His Orchestra	20,439	55. Len Spencer	5,596
5. Billy Murray	19,772	56. Frankie Laine	5,455
6. Benny Goodman & His		57. Ada Jones & Billy Murray	5,265
Orchestra	17,280	58. Enrico Caruso	5,255
7. Glenn Miller & His Orchestra....	14,482	59. Woody Herman & His Orchestra	5,216
8. Henry Burr	13,607	60. Frank Stanley	5,185
9. Peerless Quartet	12,542		
10. Harry MacDonough	12,074	61. Marion Harris	5,099
		62. Cal Stewart	4,920
11. Ben Selvin & His Orchestra	11,751	63. Ink Spots	4,862
12. Ted Lewis & His Band	11,393	64. Eddy Howard & His Orchestra ..	4,853
13. Al Jolson	11,166	65. Ella Fitzgerald	4,797
14. Sammy Kaye & His Orchestra ...	11,144	66. Ben Bernie & His Orchestra	4,742
15. Arthur Collins & Byron Harlan .	10,601	67. Dick Haymes	4,691
16. Perry Como	10,589	68. Walter Van Brunt	4,618
17. Jimmy Dorsey & His Orchestra .	10,552	69. Patti Page	4,532
18. Frank Sinatra	10,251	70. Nora Bayes	4,478
19. Prince's Orchestra	9,492		
20. Andrews Sisters	9,173	71. Dan Quinn	4,392
		72. Eddie Fisher	4,356
21. Freddy Martin & His Orchestra.	8,884	73. Bob Crosby & His Orchestra	4,227
22. Kay Kyser & His Orchestra	8,743	74. Fred Astaire	4,216
23. John McCormack	8,616	75. Larry Clinton & His Orchestra..	4,201
24. Leo Reisman & His Orchestra ...	8,443	76. Cab Calloway & His Orchestra ..	4,154
25. Isham Jones & His Orchestra....	8,341	77. Shep Fields & His Rippling	
26. Rudy Vallee & His Connecticut		Rhythm Orchestra	4,151
Yankees	8,259	78. Margaret Whiting	4,121
27. Eddy Duchin & His Orchestra ...	8,256	79. George J. Gaskin	4,101
28. American Quartet	7,949	80. Charles Harrison	4,095
29. Dinah Shore	7,852		
30. Harry James & His Orchestra ...	7,770	81. Doris Day	4,079
		82. Bert Williams	4,063
31. Jo Stafford	7,616	83. Billie Holiday	4,024
32. Haydn Quartet	7,600	84. Teddy Wilson & His Orchestra ..	4,011
33. Ada Jones	7,496	85. Ozzie Nelson & His Orchestra ...	4,005
34. Duke Ellington & His Famous		86. J.W. Myers	3,950
Orchestra	7,052	87. Ted Weems & His Orchestra	3,842
35. Louis Armstrong	6,931	88. Wayne King & His Orchestra	3,780
36. Vaughn Monroe & His		89. Tony Martin	3,528
Orchestra	6,902	90. Vic Damone	3,498
37. Fats Waller	6,859		
38. Glen Gray & The Casa Loma		91. Lewis James	3,490
Orchestra	6,791	92. Frank Crumit	3,411
39. Jan Garber & His Orchestra	6,750	93. Peggy Lee	3,344
40. Hal Kemp & His Orchestra	6,747	94. Vincent Lopez & His Orchestra .	3,209
		95. Cliff Edwards	3,194
41. Mills Brothers	6,682	96. Sousa's Band	3,180
42. Ruth Etting	6,679	97. Vess Ossman	3,176
43. Byron G. Harlan	6,600	98. Connee Boswell	3,119
44. Gene Austin	6,296	99. Kay Starr	3,094
45. Ray Noble & His Orchestra	6,199	100. Johnny Mercer	3,090
46. Russ Morgan & His Orchestra ...	6,101		
47. Nat Shilkret & The Victor			
Orchestra	5,943		
48. Fred Waring's Pennsylvanians..	5,864		
49. Arthur Collins	5,846		
50. Nat 'King' Cole	5,765		

Artist's points are calculated using the following formula:

1. Each artist's charted singles are given points based on their highest charted position (#1=30; #2=29 points, etc.).

2. Bonus points are added to each single based on its highest charted position (#1=25; #2-5=20; #6-10=15; #11-20=5).

3. Total weeks charted are added in.

4. Total weeks a single held the #1 position are also added in.

THE TOP 100 ARTISTS — (A-Z)

THE TOP 10 ARTISTS BY DECADE

1890-1899

1. George J. Gaskin 3,577
2. Len Spencer 3,463
3. Dan Quinn 2,564
4. Cal Stewart............... 1,360
5. Russell Hunting........... 1,030
6. Vess Ossman 1,002
7. U.S. Marine Band......... 907
8. Steve Porter............... 891
9. Arthur Collins............. 811
10. Sousa's Band 785

1900-1909

1. Harry MacDonough 9,210
2. Billy Murray 8,853
3. Haydn Quartet 6,037
4. Byron G. Harlan 5,312
5. Arthur Collins & Byron
   Harlan...................... 4,515
6. Frank Stanley............. 4,329
7. Arthur Collins............. 3,410
8. J.W. Myers 3,181
9. Henry Burr 3,163
10. Ada Jones & Billy
    Murray.................... 3,045

1910-1919

1. Peerless Quartet......... 9,112
2. Billy Murray 7,749
3. Prince's Orchestra 7,482
4. American Quartet........ 7,301
5. Henry Burr 6,937
6. Arthur Collins & Byron
   Harlan...................... 6,086
7. John McCormack 6,036
8. Henry Burr & Albert
   Campbell 4,745
9. Ada Jones 4,737
10. Walter Van Brunt 4,496

1920-1929

1. Paul Whiteman & His
   Orchestra 18,772
2. Ben Selvin & His
   Orchestra 8,519
3. Ted Lewis & His Band .. 7,221
4. Al Jolson 6,816
5. Gene Austin................ 5,790
6. Isham Jones & His
   Orchestra 5,397
7. Nat Shilkret & The
   Victor Orchestra........ 5,260

1920-1929 — Cont'd

8. Fred Waring's
   Pennsylvanians 4,047
9. Ruth Etting................ 3,936
10. Marion Harris............. 3,683

1930-1939

1. Bing Crosby 17,906
2. Guy Lombardo & His
   Royal Canadians....... 14,516
3. Benny Goodman & His
   Orchestra 11,152
4. Tommy Dorsey & His
   Orchestra 10,473
5. Eddy Duchin & His
   Orchestra 6,780
6. Leo Reisman & His
   Orchestra 6,522
7. Fats Waller 6,487
8. Paul Whiteman & His
   Orchestra 6,472
9. Hal Kemp & His
   Orchestra 6,329
10. Rudy Vallee & His
    Connecticut Yankees. 6,262

1940-1949

1. Bing Crosby 13,864
2. Glenn Miller & His
   Orchestra 11,441
3. Tommy Dorsey & His
   Orchestra 9,881
4. Sammy Kaye & His
   Orchestra 7,762
5. Jimmy Dorsey & His
   Orchestra 7,610
6. Frank Sinatra 7,412
7. Harry James & His
   Orchestra 6,943
8. Andrews Sisters 6,739
9. Perry Como................ 6,198
10. Dinah Shore.............. 6,170

1950-1954

1. Perry Como................ 4,279
2. Eddie Fisher 4,225
3. Frankie Laine 4,208
4. Patti Page.................. 4,103
5. Nat 'King' Cole 3,581
6. Jo Stafford 3,397
7. Bing Crosby 3,380
8. Frank Sinatra 2,839
9. Kay Starr 2,797
10. Doris Day 2,636

TOP ARTIST ACHIEVEMENTS

MOST CHARTED SINGLES

1. BING CROSBY 317
2. PAUL WHITEMAN & HIS ORCHESTRA .220
3. GUY LOMBARDO & HIS ROYAL
   CANADIANS.................................218
4. TOMMY DORSEY & HIS ORCHESTRA ..186
5. BILLY MURRAY 169
6. BENNY GOODMAN & HIS ORCHESTRA 164
7. GLENN MILLER & HIS ORCHESTRA 129
8. HENRY BURR 116
9. PEERLESS QUARTET........................108
10. BEN SELVIN & HIS ORCHESTRA 107
11. SAMMY KAYE & HIS ORCHESTRA......103
12. TED LEWIS & HIS BAND...................102
13. FRANK SINATRA 102
14. PERRY COMO 100
15. JIMMY DORSEY & HIS ORCHESTRA ...100
16. HARRY MacDONOUGH 99
17. AL JOLSON..................................... 91
18. ANDREWS SISTERS.......................... 90
19. ARTHUR COLLINS & BYRON HARLAN . 89
20. FREDDY MARTIN & HIS ORCHESTRA .. 85

MOST #1 SINGLES

1. BING CROSBY 36
2. PAUL WHITEMAN & HIS ORCHESTRA .. 32
3. GUY LOMBARDO & HIS ROYAL
   CANADIANS................................. 26
4. GLENN MILLER & HIS ORCHESTRA 23
5. AL JOLSON..................................... 23
6. GEORGE J. GASKIN.......................... 19
7. BILLY MURRAY 18
8. TOMMY DORSEY & HIS ORCHESTRA ... 17
9. DAN QUINN.................................... 17
10. BENNY GOODMAN & HIS ORCHESTRA . 16
11. HENRY BURR 16
12. HARRY MacDONOUGH 15
13. LEN SPENCER 15
14. JIMMY DORSEY & HIS ORCHESTRA 12
15. ARTHUR COLLINS & BYRON HARLAN . 12
16. AMERICAN QUARTET 12
17. HAYDN QUARTET 12
18. BYRON G. HARLAN 12
19. ARTHUR COLLINS............................ 12
20. PERRY COMO 11
21. KAY KYSER & HIS ORCHESTRA 11

PRE-1955 ARTISTS WITH LONGEST CAREERS ON NATIONAL SINGLES CHARTS

RANK	YEARS	ARTIST
1.	40	**LOUIS ARMSTRONG** (1926-1966) (also 1924 with King Oliver)
2.	40	**FRANK SINATRA** (1940-1980)
3.	37	Mills Brothers (1931-68)
4.	36	Al Jolson (1912-48)
5.	35	Bing Crosby (1928-63) (1963 #2 Christmas hit - "Do You Hear What I Hear?")
6.	35	Perry Como (1939-74)
7.	35	Cab Calloway (1931-66) (only 2 hits from 1946-66)
8.	34	Paul Whiteman (1920-54)
9.	33	Eddie Cantor (1917-50) (no hits from 1935-50)
10.	32	Gene Austin (1925-57) (no hits from 1935-57)
11.	31	Fred Waring's Pennsylvanians (1923-54)
12.	31	Count Basie & His Orchestra (1937-68)
13.	29	Jimmy Dorsey (1928-57)
14.	28	Jan Garber & His Orchestra (1923-51)
15.	27	Guy Lombardo & His Royal Canadians (1927-54)
16.	27	Ella Fitzgerald (1937-64)
17.	27	Sammy Kaye & His Orchestra (1937-64)
18.	27	Lawrence Welk & His Orchestra (1938-65)
19.	27	Albert Campbell (1898-1925)
20.	27	Sophie Tucker (1910-37)
21.	26	Tommy Dorsey (1928-54) (not including 1958 Warren Covington hits)
22.	26	Duke Ellington & His Famous Orchestra (1927-53)
23.	26	Ted Weems & His Orchestra (1922-48)
24.	25	Benny Goodman & His Orchestra (1931-56)
25.	25	Henry Burr (1903-28)
26.	25	Al Martino (1952-77)

Only artists with 10 or more charted hits were included in this listing.
(George Burns' only two chart hits spanned 47 years (1933-80))

THE TOP 100 HITS — 1890-1954

YR	WKS	RANK	PEAK POS / PEAK WKS
			1 / 17
47	25	1.	**Near You** ... Francis Craig & His Orchestra
			1 / 14
42	63	2.	**White Cristmas** ... Bing Crosby
			1 / 13
40	30	3.	**Frenesi** ... Artie Shaw & His Orchestra
27	26	4.	**My Blue Heaven** ... Gene Austin
50	26	5.	**The Tennessee Waltz** ... Patti Page
43	25	6.	**I've Heard That Song Before** ... Harry James & His Orchestra
50	25	7.	**Goodnight, Irene** ... Weavers with Gordon Jenkins & His Orchestra
20	24	8.	**Dardanella** ... Ben Selvin & His Orchestra
46	23	9.	**The Gypsy** ... Ink Spots
47	20	10.	**Heartaches** ... Ted Weems & His Orchestra
			1 / 12
43	36	11.	**Paper Doll** ... Mills Brothers
26	32	12.	**The Prisoner's Song** ... Vernon Dalhart
40	31	13.	**In The Mood** ... Glenn Miller & His Orchestra
52	25	14.	**You Belong To Me** ... Jo Stafford
49	22	15.	**Riders In The Sky (A Cowboy Legend)** ... Vaughn Monroe & His Orchestra
40	20	16.	**I'll Never Smile Again** ... Tommy Dorsey & His Orchestra
28	19	17.	**Sonny Boy** ... Al Jolson
			1 / 11
53	31	18.	**Vaya Con Dios** ... Les Paul & Mary Ford
50	27	19.	**The Third Man Theme** ... Anton Karas
50	27	20.	**The Third Man Theme** ... Guy Lombardo & His Royal Canadians
51	27	21.	**Cry** ... Johnnie Ray
46	20	22.	**Oh! What It Seemed To Be** ... Frankie Carle & His Orchestra
20	20	23.	**Whispering** ... Paul Whiteman & His Orchestra
35	18	24.	**Cheek To Cheek** ... Fred Astaire
10	17	25.	**Casey Jones** ... Billy Murray & The American Quartet
09	17	26.	**Put On Your Old Gray Bonnet** ... Haydn Quartet
22	17	27.	**April Showers** ... Al Jolson
26	17	28.	**Valencia** ... Paul Whiteman & His Orchestra
07	16	29.	**School Days (When We Were A Couple Of Kids)** ... Byron G. Harlan
18	15	30.	**Just A Baby's Prayer At Twilight (For Her Daddy Over There)** ... Henry Burr
05	14	31.	**The Preacher And The Bear** ... Arthur Collins
02	14	32.	**Arkansaw Traveler** ... Len Spencer
			1 / 10
51	32	33.	**Because Of You** ... Tony Bennett
37	25	34.	**Sweet Leilani** ... Bing Crosby
48	25	35.	**Buttons And Bows** ... Dinah Shore
52	25	36.	**Wheel Of Fortune** ... Kay Starr
53	24	37.	**Song From "Moulin Rouge" (Where Is Your Heart)** ... Percy Faith & His Orchestra
32	22	38.	**In A Shanty In Old Shanty Town** ... Ted Lewis & His Band
47	22	39.	**Ballerina** ... Vaughn Monroe & His Orchestra
52	22	40.	**I Went To Your Wedding** ... Patti Page
30	21	41.	**Stein Song (University Of Maine)** ... Rudy Vallee & His Connecticut Yankees
45	20	42.	**Rum And Coca-Cola** ... Andrews Sisters
45	19	43.	**Till The End Of Time** ... Perry Como
38	19	44.	**A-Tisket, A-Tasket** ... Ella Fitzgerald with Chick Webb & His Orchestra
29	19	45.	**Tip Toe Through The Tulips** ... Nick Lucas
42	19	46.	**Moonlight Cocktail** ... Glenn Miller & His Orchestra
32	18	47.	**Night And Day** ... Fred Astaire with Leo Reisman & His Orchestra
11	17	48.	**Alexander's Ragtime Band** ... Arthur Collins & Byron Harlan

YR	WKS	RANK	PEAK POS / PEAK WKS
			1 / 10 — Cont'd
41	17	49.	Amapola . . . Jimmy Dorsey & His Orchestra
04	17	50.	Sweet Adeline (You're The Flower Of My Heart) . . . Haydn Quartet
50	16	51.	If I Knew You Were Comin' I'd've Baked A Cake . . . Eileen Barton
36	15	52.	Pennies From Heaven . . . Bing Crosby
06	15	53.	The Grand Old Rag . . . Billy Murray
98	13	54.	My Old New Hampshire Home . . . George J. Gaskin
07	13	55.	My Gal Sal . . . Byron G. Harlan
97	12	56.	On The Banks Of The Wabash . . . George J. Gaskin
93	10	57.	After The Ball . . . George J. Gaskin
91	10	58.	The Laughing Song . . . George Washington Johnson
95	10	59.	The Band Played On . . . Dan Quinn
			1 / 9
45	28	60.	Sentimental Journey . . . Les Brown & His Orchestra
44	28	61.	Swinging On A Star . . . Bing Crosby
54	26	62.	Little Things Mean A Lot . . . Kitty Kallen
41	25	63.	Chattanooga Choo Choo . . . Glenn Miller & His Orchestra
51	25	64.	How High The Moon . . . Les Paul & Mary Ford
33	24	65.	The Last Round-Up . . . George Olsen & His Orchestra
44	21	66.	Shoo-Shoo Baby . . . Andrews Sisters
48	21	67.	Manana (Is Soon Enough For Me) . . . Peggy Lee
52	21	68.	Auf Wiederseh'n Sweetheart . . . Vera Lynn
54	20	69.	Sh-Boom . . . Crew-Cuts
40	20	70.	Only Forever . . . Bing Crosby
40	19	71.	Tuxedo Junction . . . Glenn Miller & His Orchestra
17	18	72.	Over There . . . American Quartet
46	18	73.	Rumors Are Flying . . . Frankie Carle & His Orchestra
20	18	74.	Swanee . . . Al Jolson
06	17	75.	Wait Till The Sun Shines, Nellie . . . Byron G. Harlan
10	17	76.	By The Light Of The Silvery Moon . . . Billy Murray & The Haydn Quartet
19	15	77.	Till We Meet Again . . . Henry Burr & Albert Campbell
19	14	78.	Beautiful Ohio . . . Henry Burr
09	14	79.	Shine On, Harvest Moon . . . Harry MacDonough & "Miss Walton" (Elise Stevenson)
04	14	80.	Meet Me In St. Louis, Louis . . . Billy Murray
07	14	81.	Harrigan . . . Billy Murray
06	14	82.	Nobody . . . Bert Williams
39	13	83.	Deep Purple . . . Larry Clinton & His Orchestra
93	9	84.	Daisy Bell . . . Dan Quinn
95	9	85.	The Sidewalks Of New York . . . Dan Quinn
			1 / 8
43	34	86.	Pistol Packin' Mama . . . Al Dexter & His Troopers
48	32	87.	Twelfth Street Rag . . . Pee Wee Hunt & His Orchestra
53	31	88.	You You You . . . Ames Brothers
50	27	89.	Mona Lisa . . . Nat "King" Cole
47	26	90.	Peg O' My Heart . . . Harmonicats
53	25	91.	Rags To Riches . . . Tony Bennett
41	25	92.	Piano Concerto In B Flat . . . Freddy Martin & His Orchestra
51	24	93.	If . . . Perry Como
46	24	94.	To Each His Own . . . Eddy Howard & His Orchestra
51	24	95.	Sin (It's No Sin) . . . Eddy Howard & His Orchestra
54	22	96.	Wanted . . . Perry Como
49	22	97.	That Lucky Old Sun . . . Frankie Laine
44	21	98.	Don't Fence Me In . . . Bing Crosby & Andrews Sisters
46	21	99.	The Gypsy . . . Dinah Shore
53	20	100.	The Doggie In The Window . . . Patti Page

YR: Year of peak popularity
WKS: Total weeks charted
PEAK POS: Highest position attained
PEAK WKS: Total weeks record held peak position

Records are ranked in the following order:
1. Highest position attained
2. Total weeks record held peak position
3. Total weeks charted
4. Alphabetically by artist name

THE TOP 10 HITS BY DECADE

1890-1899

YR	WKS	RANK	PEAK POS / PEAK WKS
			1 / 10
98	13	1.	**My Old New Hampshire Home** ... George J. Gaskin
97	12	2.	**On The Banks Of The Wabash** ... George J. Gaskin
93	10	3.	**After The Ball** ... George J. Gaskin
91	10	4.	**The Laughing Song** ... George Washington Johnson
95	10	5.	**The Band Played On** ... Dan Quinn
			1 / 9
93	9	6.	**Daisy Bell** ... Dan Quinn
95	9	7.	**The Sidewalks Of New York** ... Dan Quinn
			1 / 8
97	15	8.	**Sweet Rosie O'Grady** ... George J. Gaskin
97	11	9.	**The Stars And Stripes Forever** ... Sousa's Band
93	8	10.	**O Promise Me** ... George J. Gaskin

1900-1909

YR	WKS	RANK	PEAK POS / PEAK WKS
			1 / 11
09	17	1.	**Put On Your Old Gray Bonnet** ... Haydn Quartet
07	16	2.	**School Days (When We Were A Couple Of Kids)** ... Byron G. Harlan
05	14	3.	**The Preacher And The Bear** ... Arthur Collins
02	14	4.	**Arkansaw Traveler** ... Len Spencer
			1 / 10
04	17	5.	**Sweet Adeline (You're The Flower Of My Heart)** ... Haydn Quartet
06	15	6.	**The Grand Old Rag** ... Billy Murray
07	13	7.	**My Gal Sal** ... Byron G. Harlan
			1 / 9
06	17	8.	**Wait Till The Sun Shines, Nellie** ... Byron G. Harlan
09	14	9.	**Shine On, Harvest Moon** ... Harry MacDonough & "Miss Walton" (Elise Stevenson)
04	14	10.	**Meet Me In St. Louis, Louis** ... Billy Murray

1910-1919

YR	WKS	RANK	PEAK POS / PEAK WKS
			1 / 11
10	17	1.	**Casey Jones** ... Billy Murray & The American Quartet
18	15	2.	**Just A Baby's Prayer At Twilight (For Her Daddy Over There)** ... Henry Burr
			1 / 10
11	17	3.	**Alexander's Ragtime Band** ... Arthur Collins & Byron Harlan
			1 / 9
17	18	4.	**Over There** ... American Quartet
10	17	5.	**By The Light Of The Silvery Moon** ... Billy Murray & The Haydn Quartet
19	15	6.	**Till We Meet Again** ... Henry Burr & Albert Campbell
19	14	7.	**Beautiful Ohio** ... Henry Burr
			1 / 8
12	16	8.	**Moonlight Bay** ... American Quartet
18	14	9.	**Rock-A-Bye Your Baby With A Dixie Melody** ... Al Jolson
15	13	10.	**It's A Long, Long Way To Tipperary** ... John McCormack

1920-1929

YR	WKS	RANK	PEAK POS / PEAK WKS
			1 / 13
27	26	1.	**My Blue Heaven** ... Gene Austin
20	24	2.	**Dardanella** ... Ben Selvin & His Orchestra
			1 / 12
26	32	3.	**The Prisoner's Song** ... Vernon Dalhart
28	19	4.	**Sonny Boy** ... Al Jolson
			1 / 11
20	20	5.	**Whispering** ... Paul Whiteman & His Orchestra
22	17	6.	**April Showers** ... Al Jolson
26	17	7.	**Valencia** ... Paul Whiteman & His Orchestra
			1 / 10
29	19	8.	**Tip Toe Through The Tulips** ... Nick Lucas
			1 / 9
20	18	9.	**Swanee** ... Al Jolson
			1 / 8
22	20	10.	**Three O'Clock In The Morning** ... Paul Whiteman & His Orchestra

1930-1939

YR	WKS	RANK	PEAK POS / PEAK WKS
			1 / 11
35	18	1.	**Cheek To Cheek** ... Fred Astaire
			1 / 10
37	25	2.	**Sweet Leilani** ... Bing Crosby
32	22	3.	**In A Shanty In Old Shanty Town** ... Ted Lewis & His Band
30	21	4.	**Stein Song (University Of Maine)** ... Rudy Vallee & His Connecticut Yankees
38	19	5.	**A-Tisket, A-Tasket** ... Ella Fitzgerald with Chick Webb & His Orchestra
32	18	6.	**Night And Day** ... Fred Astaire with Leo Reisman & His Orchestra
36	15	7.	**Pennies From Heaven** ... Bing Crosby
			1 / 9
33	24	8.	**The Last Round-Up** ... George Olsen & His Orchestra
39	13	9.	**Deep Purple** ... Larry Clinton & His Orchestra
			1 / 8
33	19	10.	**Stormy Weather** ... Leo Reisman & His Orchestra with Harold Arlen

1940-1949

YR	WKS	RANK	PEAK POS / PEAK WKS
			1 / 17
47	25	1.	**Near You** ... Francis Craig & His Orchestra
			1 / 14
42	47	2.	**White Christmas** ... Bing Crosby
			1 / 13
40	30	3.	**Frenesi** ... Artie Shaw & His Orchestra
43	25	4.	**I've Heard That Song Before** ... Harry James & His Orchestra
46	23	5.	**The Gypsy** ... Ink Spots
47	20	6.	**Heartaches** ... Ted Weems & His Orchestra
			1 / 12
43	36	7.	**Paper Doll** ... Mills Brothers
40	31	8.	**In The Mood** ... Glenn Miller & His Orchestra
49	22	9.	**Riders In The Sky (A Cowboy Legend)** ... Vaughn Monroe & His Orchestra
40	20	10.	**I'll Never Smile Again** ... Tommy Dorsey & His Orchestra

1950-1954

YR	WKS	RANK	PEAK POS / PEAK WKS
			1 / 13
50	26	1.	**The Tennessee Waltz** ... Patti Page
50	25	2.	**Goodnight, Irene** ... Weavers with Gordon Jenkins & His Orchestra
			1 / 12
52	25	3.	**You Belong To Me** ... Jo Stafford
			1 / 11
53	31	4.	**Vaya Con Dios** ... Les Paul & Mary Ford
50	27	5.	**The Third Man Theme** ... Anton Karas
50	27	6.	**The Third Man Theme** ... Guy Lombardo & His Royal Canadians
51	27	7.	**Cry** ... Johnnie Ray
			1 / 10
51	32	8.	**Because Of You** ... Tony Bennett
52	25	9.	**Wheel Of Fortune** ... Kay Starr
53	24	10.	**Song From "Moulin Rouge" (Where Is Your Heart)** ... Percy Faith & His Orchestra

THE BIGGEST-SELLING RECORDS
1890-1954

30 million+	1.	**WHITE CHRISTMAS** (1942) . . . Bing Crosby
8 million	2.	**RUDOLPH, THE RED-NOSED REINDEER** (1949) . . . Gene Autry
7 million	3.	**SILENT NIGHT** (1934) . . . Bing Crosby
7 million	4.	**THE PRISONER'S SONG** (1926) . . . Vernon Dalhart
6 million	5.	**PAPER DOLL** (1943) . . . Mills Brothers
6 million	6.	**THE TENNESSEE WALTZ** (1950) . . . Patti Page
5 million	7.	**MY BLUE HEAVEN** (1927) . . . Gene Austin
5 million	8.	**DARDANELLA** (1920) . . . Ben Selvin's Novelty Orchestra
3 million	9.	**MONA LISA** (1950) . . . Nat King Cole
3 million	10.	**THREE O'CLOCK IN THE MORNING** (1922) . . . Paul Whiteman & His Orchestra

2 Million:

Goodnight, Irene (1950) . . . The Weavers with Gordon Jenkins' Orchestra
Cry (1951) . . . Johnnie Ray
The Third Man Theme (1950) . . . Anton Karas
Near You (1947) . . . Francis Craig (vocal: Bob Lamm)
Smoke! Smoke! Smoke! (That Cigarette) (1947) . . . Tex Willliams' Western Caravan
Whispering (1920) . . . Paul Whiteman & His Orchestra
Be My Love (1951) . . . Mario Lanza
Wabash Cannon Ball (1938) . . . Roy Acuff
You Can't Be True, Dear (1948) . . . Ken Griffin (vocal: Jerry Wayne)
Heartaches (1947) . . . Ted Weems' Orchestra (featuring Elmo Tanner)
I Saw Mommy Kissing Santa Claus (1952) . . . Jimmy Boyd
Song From Moulin Rouge (1953) . . . Percy Faith's Orchestra (vocal: Felicia Sanders)
Blue Tango (1952) . . . Leroy Anderson & His Orchestra
Till The End Of Time (1945) . . . Perry Como
There! I've Said It Again (1945) . . . Vaughn Monroe
That Silver-Haired Daddy Of Mine (1934) . . . Gene Autry
The Preacher And The Bear (1905) . . . Arthur Collins
It Ain't Gonna Rain No Mo' (1924) . . . Wendell Hall
Casey Jones (1910) . . . Billy Murray & American Quartet

THE 100 MOST-RECORDED SONGS
1890-1954

During the pre-rock era, one of the most important indicators of a song's enduring musical greatness was the number of artists to record it. This list represents the most comprehensive survey ever made of the pre-1955 songs which have been recorded by the most artists (multiple versions by an artist do not count). It encompasses: Edison and Columbia cyclinders; all 78s in the extensive collections of the Library of Congress, the New York Public Library, and the Syracuse, Stanford and Yale University Libraries; and all new Recordaid listings from the 1950s to the present. Songs written before 1955 but most popular later, such as "Misty" and "Autumn Leaves", are not included. The year published and the songwriters are shown after the title.

1. **Silent Night** (1818) — Joseph Muhr & Franz Gruber
2. **St. Louis Blues** (1914) — W.C. Handy
3. **Star Dust** (1929) — Hoagy Carmichael & Mitchell Parish
4. **Body And Soul** (1930) — Johnny Green, Ed Heyman, Robert Sauer & Frank Eyton
5. **Summertime** (1935) — George Gershwin & Dubose Heyward
6. **The Old Folks At Home (Swanee River)** (1851) — Stephen Foster
7. **Tea For Two** (1925) — Vincent Youmans & Irving Caesar
8. **White Christmas** (1942) — Irving Berlin
9. **All The Things You Are** (1939) — Jerome Kern & Oscar Hammerstein II
10. **Night And Day** (1932) — Cole Porter

11. **Begin The Beguine** (1935) — Cole Porter
12. **Danny Boy** (1913) — Traditional, adapted by Fred Weatherly
13. **Sweet Georgia Brown** (1925) — Maceo Pinkard, Kenneth Casey & Ben Bernie
14. **The Man I Love** (1924) — George Gershwin & Ira Gershwin
15. **Over The Rainbow** (1939) — Harold Arlen & E.Y. Harburg
16. **Caravan** (1937) — Duke Ellington, Juan Tizol & Irving Mills
17. **After You've Gone** (1918) — Turner Layton & Harry Creamer
18. **Yesterdays** (1933) — Jerome Kern & Otto Harbach
19. **Ain't Misbehavin'** (1929) — Fats Waller, Harry Brooks & Andy Razaf
20. **Lover, Come Back To Me** (1928) — Sigmund Romberg & Oscar Hammerstein II

21. **What Is This Thing Called Love?** (1930) — Cole Porter
22. **I Can't Get Started** (1936) — Vernon Duke & Ira Gershwin
23. **Jingle Bells** (1857) — J.S. Pierpont
24. **I Can't Give You Anything But Love** (1928) — Jimmy McHugh & Dorothy Fields
25. **My Old Kentucky Home** (1853) — Stephen Foster
26. **When The Saints Go Marching In** (1896) — James Black & Katharine Purvis
27. **Tenderly** (1947) — Walter Gross & Jack Lawrence
28. **Blue Skies** (1927) — Irving Berlin
29. **September Song** (1938) — Kurt Weill & Maxwell Anderson
30. **My Blue Heaven** (1927) — Walter Donaldson & George Whiting

31. **Always** (1925) — Irving Berlin
32. **Tiger Rag** (1917) — Harry DeCosta & Original Dixieland Jazz Band
33. **The Rosary** (1898) — Ethelbert Nevins & Robert Cameron Rogers
34. **Home, Sweet Home** (1823) — Henry Bishop & John Howard Payne
35. **Smoke Gets In Your Eyes** (1933) — Jerome Kern & Otto Harbach
36. **These Foolish Things (Remind Me Of You)** (1936) — Jack Strachey, Harry Link & Holt Marvell
37. **Ol' Man River** (1928) — Jerome Kern & Oscar Hammerstein II
38. **Limehouse Blues** (1924) — Philip Braham & Douglas Furber
39. **Sheik Of Araby** (1923) — Ted Snyder, Harry B. Smith & Francis Wheeler
40. **Embraceable You** (1930) — George Gershwin & Ira Gershwin

41. **My Funny Valentine** (1937) — Richard Rodgers & Lorenz Hart
42. **Stormy Weather** (1933) — Harold Arlen & Ted Koehler
43. **12th Street Rag** (1914) — Euday L. Bowman
44. **Blue Moon** (1935) — Richard Rodgers & Lorenz Hart
45. **The Battle Hymn Of The Republic** (1863) — Julia Ward Howe & William Steffe

THE 100 MOST-RECORDED SONGS
1890-1954 — Cont'd

46. **My Melancholy Baby** (1913) — Ernie Burnett & George Norton
47. **I Got Rhythm** (1930) — George Gershwin & Ira Gershwin
48. **Honeysuckle Rose** (1929) — Fats Waller & Andy Razaf
49. **Love's Old Sweet Song** (1884) — G. Clifton Bingham & James Mulloy
50. **The Stars And Stripes Forever** (1896) — John Philip Sousa

51. **Where Or When** (1937) — Richard Rodgers & Lorenz Hart
52. **Laura** (1945) — David Raskin & Johnny Mercer
53. **Mood Indigo** (1931) — Duke Ellington, Barney Bigard & Irving Mills
54. **The Christmas Song** (1946) — Mel Torme & Robert Wells
55. **Love For Sale** (1930) — Cole Porter
56. **Georgia On My Mind** (1930) — Hoagy Carmichael & Stuart Gorrell
57. **San Antonio Rose** (1939) — Bob Wills
58. **How High The Moon** (1940) — Morgan Lewis & Nancy Hamilton
59. **Someone To Watch Over Me** (1926) — George Gershwin & Ira Gershwin
60. **I Only Have Eyes For You** (1934) — Harry Warren & Al Dubin

61. **Sweet Sue, Just You** (1928) — Victor Young & Will Harris
62. **The Darktown Strutters' Ball** (1917) — Shelton Brooks
63. **On The Sunny Side Of The Street** (1930) — Jimmy McHugh & Dorothy Fields
64. **Silver Threads Among The Gold** (1877) — Hart P. Danks & Eben Rexford
65. **I'm In The Mood For Love** (1935) — Jimmy McHugh & Dorothy Fields
66. **Deep Purple** (1939) — Peter DeRose & Mitchell Parish
67. **Sometimes I'm Happy** (1925) — Vincent Youmans & Irving Caesar
68. **I've Got You Under My Skin** (1934) — Cole Porter
69. **The Star-Spangled Banner** (1814) — Francis Scott Key
70. **Easy To Love** (1936) — Cole Porter

71. **Avalon** (1921) — B.G. DeSylva, Vincent Rose & Al Jolson
72. **Willow Weep For Me** (1932) — Ann Ronell
73. **Dinah** (1925) — Harry Akst, Sam Lewis & Joe Young
74. **Moonglow** (1934) — Will Hudson, Eddie DeLange & Irving Mills
75. **Auld Lang Syne** (1711) — adapted by Robert Burns
76. **Carry Me Back To Old Virginny** (1879) — James A. Bland
77. **Alexander's Ragtime Band** (1911) — Irving Berlin
78. **Santa Claus Is Comin' To Town** (1934) — J. Fred Coots & Haven Gillespie
79. **Basin Street Blues** (1929) — Spencer Williams
80. **Sweet Lorraine** (1935) — Clifford Burwell & Mitchell Parish

81. **I'll Remember April** (1942) — Don Raye, Gene DePaul & Patricia Johnston
82. **Rudolph, The Red-Nosed Reindeer** (1949) — Johnny Marks
83. **Solitude** (1934) — Duke Ellington
84. **Some Of These Days** (1910) — Shelton Brooks
85. **Stella By Starlight** (1947) — Victor Young & Ned Washington
86. **Maple Leaf Rag** (1899) — Scott Joplin
87. **Lover** (1933) — Richard Rodgers & Lorenz Hart
88. **The Way You Look Tonight** (1936) — Jerome Kern & Dorothy Fields
89. **Pennies From Heaven** (1936) — Arthur Johnston & John Burke
90. **Dancing In The Dark** (1931) — Howard Dietz & Arthur Schwartz

91. **Indiana** (1917) — James Hanley & Ballad MacDonald
92. **April In Paris** (1932) — Vernon Duke
93. **As Time Goes By** (1931) — Herman Hupfield
94. **Royal Garden Blues** (1923) — Spencer Williams & Clarence Williams
95. **The Very Thought Of You** (1934) — Ray Noble
96. **Lover Man** (1942) — Jimmy Davis, Roger Ramirez, & Jimmy Sherman
97. **'Round Midnight** (1947) — Thelonious Monk & Cootie Williams
98. **Perdido** (1942) — Juan Tizol, Ervin Drake & Hans Lengsfelder
99. **All Of Me** (1931) — Seymour Simons & Gerald Marks
100. **What's New?** (1939) — Johnny Burke & Robert Haggart

THE BEST-SELLING SHEET MUSIC SONGS
1890-1954

20 million+ 1. **THE OLD FOLKS AT HOME** (1851) — Stephen Foster
20 million 2. **LISTEN TO THE MOCKING BIRD** (1855) — Septimus Winner

6 million 3. **LET ME CALL YOU SWEETHEART** (1910) — Leo Friedman & Beth Slater Whitson
6 million 4. **DOWN BY THE OLD MILL STREAM** (1910) — Tell Taylor
5 million 5. **AFTER THE BALL** (1892) — Charles K. Harris
5 million 6. **TILL WE MEET AGAIN** (1918) — Richard Whiting & Raymond Egan
5 million 7. **BEAUTIFUL OHIO** (1918) — Robert A. King & Ballard MacDonald
5 million 8. **WHITE CHRISTMAS** (1942) — Irving Berlin
4 million 9. **POOR BUTTERFLY** (1916) — Raymond Hubbell & John Golden

3 Million:

Bedelia (1903) — Jean Schwartz & William Jerome
My Gal Sal (1905) — Paul Dresser
School Days (When We Were A Couple Of Kids) — Gus Edwards & Will Cobb
I Wonder Who's Kissing Her Now (1909) — Joe Howard, Harold Orlob, Frank Adams, & Will Hough
A Perfect Day (1910) — Carrie Jacobs Bond
The Missouri Waltz (1914) — Frederick K. Logan & James R. Shannon
For Me And My Gal (1917) — George Meyer, Edgar Leslie, & E. Ray Goetz
Goodbye Broadway, Hello France (1917) — Billy Baskette, C. Francis Reisner, & Benny Davis
Smiles (1918) — Lee Roberts & J. Will Callahan
Santa Claus Is Comin' To Town (1934) — J. Fred Coots & Haven Gillespie

THE ACADEMY AWARD-WINNING SONGS
1934-1954

Year	Best Song	Songwriters
1934	**THE CONTINENTAL**	Con Conrad & Herb Magidson
1935	**LULLABY OF BROADWAY**	Harry Warren & Al Dubin
1936	**THE WAY YOU LOOK TONIGHT**	Jerome Kern & Dorothy Fields
1937	**SWEET LEILANI**	Harry Owens
1938	**THANKS FOR THE MEMORY**	Ralph Rainger & Leo Robin
1939	**OVER THE RAINBOW**	Harold Arlen & E.Y. Harburg
1940	**WHEN YOU WISH UPON A STAR**	Leigh Harline & Ned Washington
1941	**THE LAST TIME I SAW PARIS**	Jerome Kern & Oscar Hammerstein II
1942	**WHITE CHRISTMAS**	Irving Berlin
1943	**YOU'LL NEVER KNOW**	Harry Warren & Mack Gordon
1944	**SWINGING ON A STAR**	Jimmy Van Heusen & Johnny Burke
1945	**IT MIGHT AS WELL BE SPRING**	Richard Rodgers & Oscar Hammerstein II
1946	**ON THE ATCHISON, TOPEKA & SANTA FE**	Harry Warren & Johnny Mercer
1947	**ZIP-A-DEE-DOO-DAH**	Allie Wrubel & Ray Gilbert
1948	**BUTTONS AND BOWS**	Jay Livingston & Ray Evans
1949	**BABY, IT'S COLD OUTSIDE**	Frank Loesser
1950	**MONA LISA**	Jay Livingston & Ray Evans
1951	**IN THE COOL COOL COOL OF THE EVENING**	Hoagy Carmichael & Johnny Mercer
1952	**HIGH NOON**	Dimitri Tiomkin & Ned Washington
1953	**SECRET LOVE**	Sammy Fain & Paul Francis Webster
1954	**THREE COINS IN THE FOUNTAIN**	Jule Styne & Sammy Cahn

NATIONAL ACADEMY OF RECORDING ARTS & SCIENCES HALL OF FAME

Every year since 1974, the National Academy of Recording Arts & Sciences (the Grammy Awards organization) has honored historic recordings made before the Grammies began in 1958, with the Hall of Fame awards. All the non-classical, pre-rock Hall of Fame selections are listed below, in chronological order from the year of recording or release. The eight original honorees are capitalized.

1. **Nobody** (1906) — Bert Williams
   (by Bert Williams & Alex Rogers)
2. **RHAPSODY IN BLUE** (1924) — Paul Whiteman's Concert Orchestra featuring George Gershwin
   (by George Gershwin)
3. **My Blue Heaven** (1927) — Gene Austin
   (by Walter Donaldson & George Whiting)
4. **Singin' The Blues** (1927) — Frankie Trumbauer featuring Bix Beiderbecke
   (by Sam Lewis, Joe Young, Con Conrad, & J. Russell Robinson)
5. **Mr. Jelly Lord** (1927) — Jelly Roll Morton's Red-Hot Peppers
   (by Jelly Roll Morton)
6. **In A Mist** (1927) — Bix Beiderbecke
7. **WEST END BLUES** (1928) — Louis Armstrong & His Hot Five
   (by Clarence Williams & Joe "King" Oliver)
8. **Black And Tan Fantasy** (1928) — Duke Ellington & His Orchestra
   (by Duke Ellington & Bubber Miley)
9. **Empty Bed Blues** (1928) — Bessie Smith
   (by J.C. Johnson)
10. **Blue Yodel (T For Texas)** (1928) — Jimmie Rodgers
    (by Jimmie Rodgers)
11. **Ain't Misbehavin'** (1929) — Fats Waller
    (by Fats Waller & Andy Razaf)
12. **Pine Top's Boogie Woogie** (1929) — Clarence "Pine Top" Smith
    (by Clarence "Pine Top" Smith)
13. **MOOD INDIGO** (1931) — Duke Ellington & His Orchestra
    (by Duke Ellington, Barney Bigard, & Irving Mills)
14. **One O'Clock Jump** (1937) — Count Basie & His Orchestra
    (by Count Basie)
15. **I CAN'T GET STARTED** (1938) — Bunny Berigan & His Orchestra
    (by Vernon Duke & Ira Gershwin)
16. **CARNEGIE HALL JAZZ CONCERT** (1938; album released 1950) — Benny Goodman & His Orchestra
17. **Sing, Sing, Sing (With A Swing)** (1938) — Benny Goodman & His Orchestra
    (by Louis Prima, with interpolation by Leon Berry)
18. **A-Tisket, A-Tasket** (1938) — Chick Webb & His Orchestra featuring Ella Fitzgerald
    (by Al Feldman & Ella Fitzgerald)
19. **Strange Fruit** (1939) — Billie Holiday
    (by Lewis Allen)
20. **Over The Rainbow** (1939) — Judy Garland
    (by Harold Arlen & E.Y. Harburg)
21. **In The Mood** (1939) — Glenn Miller & His Orchestra
    (by Joe Garland & Andy Razaf)
22. **September Song** (1939) — Walter Huston
    (by Kurt Weill & Maxwell Anderson)
23. **God Bless America** (1939) — Kate Smith
    (by Irving Berlin)
24. **Tea For Two** (1939) — Art Tatum
    (by Vincent Youmans & Irving Caesar)
25. **BODY AND SOUL** (1940) — Coleman Hawkins
    (by Johnny Green, Frank Eyton, Edward Heyman, Robert Sauer)
26. **I'll Never Smile Again** (1940) — Tommy Dorsey & His Orchestra featuring Frank Sinatra & Pied Pipers
    (by Ruth Lowe)
27. **Ballad For Americans** (1940) — Paul Robeson
    (by Earl Robinson & John La Touche)
28. **Take The "A" Train** (1941) — Duke Ellington & His Orchestra
    (by Billy Strayhorn)
29. **God Bless The Child** (1941) — Billie Holiday
    (by Billie Holiday)

30. **Cool Water** (1941) — Sons of the Pioneers
    (by Bob Nolan)
31. **WHITE CHRISTMAS** (1942) — Bing Crosby
    (by Irving Berlin)
32. **Oklahoma!** (1943) — Original Broadway Cast Recording, featuring Alfred Drake
    (by Richard Rodgers & Oscar Hammerstein II)
33. **Artistry In Rhythm** (1943) — Stan Kenton & His Orchestra
    (by Stan Kenton)
34. **THE CHRISTMAS SONG** (1946) — Nat "King" Cole with The King Cole Trio
    (by Robert Wells & Mel Torme)
35. **Rudolph, The Red-Nosed Reindeer** (1949) — Gene Autry
    (by Johnny Marks)
36. **Birth Of The Cool** (1949-50 recordings; album released 1957) — Miles Davis & His Orchestra
37. **How High The Moon** (1951) — Les Paul & Mary Ford
    (by Nancy Hamilton & Morgan Lewis)
38. **Porgy And Bess** (1951) — Carroll Gibbons & His Orchestra
    (by George Gershwin, Ira Gershwin, & Dubose Heyward)
39. **Your Cheatin' Heart** (1952) — Hank Williams
    (by Hank Williams)
40. **April In Paris** (1955) — Count Basie & His Orchestra
    (by Vernon Duke)

BILLBOARD DISC JOCKEY POLLS

BILLBOARD 1956 DISC JOCKEY POLL:
ALL-TIME FAVORITE RECORDS

In 1956 Billboard conducted a nationwide survey of disc jockeys on their favorite records of all time. The results constitute a representative cross-section of Big Band Era classics.

1. **Stardust** (1941) — Artie Shaw & His Orchestra
2. **Moonlight Serenade** (1939) — Glenn Miller & His Orchestra
3. **Begin The Beguine** (1938) — Artie Shaw & His Orchestra
4. **Stardust** (1941) — Glenn Miller & His Orchestra
5. **A String Of Pearls** (1941) — Glenn Miller & His Orchestra
6. **Tenderly** (1952) — Rosemary Clooney
7. **In The Mood** (1939) — Glenn Miller & His Orchestra
8. **Summit Ridge Drive** (1941) — Artie Shaw & His Gramercy Five
9. **Sing, Sing, Sing (With A Swing)** (1938) — Benny Goodman & His Orchestra
10. **I've Got My Love To Keep Me Warm** (1948) — Les Brown & His Orchestra

11. **I Can't Get Started** (1938) — Bunny Berigan & His Orchestra
12. **Opus One** (1945) — Tommy Dorsey & His Orchestra
13. **On The Sunny Side Of The Street** (1944) — Tommy Dorsey & His Orchestra
14. **September Song** (1939) — Walter Huston
15. **Frenesi** (1940) — Artie Shaw & His Orchestra
16. **Secret Love** (1954) — Doris Day
17. **Sophisticated Lady** (1933) — Duke Ellington & His Famous Orchestra
18. **Tuxedo Junction** (1940) — Glenn Miller & His Orchestra
19. **Don't Be That Way** (1938) — Benny Goodman & His Orchestra
20. **Blue Moon** (1949) — Mel Torme

21. **You Made Me Love You** (1941) — Harry James & His Orchestra
22. **Stardust** (1941) — Tommy Dorsey & His Orchestra featuring Frank Sinatra
23. **It's Magic** (1948) — Doris Day
24. **Sentimental Journey** (1945) — Les Brown & His Orchestra featuring Doris Day
25. **Dancing In The Dark** (1941) — Artie Shaw & His Orchestra
26. **Song From Moulin Rouge** (1953) — Percy Faith & His Orchestra featuring Felicia Sanders
27. **Let's Dance** (1935) — Benny Goodman & His Orchestra
28. **Marie** (1937) — Tommy Dorsey & His Orchestra featuring Jack Leonard
29. **Body And Soul** (1940) — Coleman Hawkins
30. **Take The "A" Train** (1941) — Duke Ellington & His Famous Orchestra

BILLBOARD DISC JOCKEY POLLS

BILLBOARD 1953 DISC JOCKEY POLL:
ALL-TIME FAVORITE SONGS

Billboard's 1953 national survey of disc jockeys offers another perspective on America's greatest popular songs.

1. **STARDUST** (1930) — Hoagy Carmichael & Mitchell Parish
2. **TENDERLY** (1947) — Walter Gross & Jack Lawrence
3. **BODY AND SOUL** (1930) — Johnny Green, Ed Heyman, Robert Sauer, & Frank Eyton
4. **DEEP PURPLE** (1939) — Peter DeRose & Mitchell Parish
5. **BEGIN THE BEGUINE** (1935) — Cole Porter
6. **LAURA** (1945) — David Raskin & Johnny Mercer
7. **APRIL IN PARIS** (1932) — Vernon Duke
8. **SEPTEMBER SONG** (1938) — Kurt Weill & Maxwell Anderson
9. **NIGHT AND DAY** (1932) — Cole Porter
10. **BLUE MOON** (1935) — Richard Rodgers & Lorenz Hart

11. **How High The Moon** (1940) — Morgan Lewis & Nancy Hamilton
12. **Lover** (1932) — Richard Rodgers & Lorenz Hart
13. **I Can't Get Started** (1936) — Vernon Duke & Ira Gershwin
14. **In The Mood** (1939) — Joe Garland & Andy Razaf
15. **That Old Black Magic** (1942) — Harold Arlen & Johnny Mercer
16. **Tea for Two** (1925) — Vincent Youmans & Irving Caesar
17. **I'm In The Mood For Love** (1935) — Jimmy McHugh & Dorothy Fields
18. **Lady Of Spain** (1931) — Robert Hargreaves, Tolchard Evans, Stanley Admerek, & Henry Tilsley
19. **Smoke Gets In Your Eyes** (1933) — Jerome Kern & Otto Harbach
20. **Embraceable You** (1930) — George Gershwin & Ira Gershwin

21. **Always** (1925) — Irving Berlin
22. **Just One Of Those Things** (1935) — Cole Porter
23. **Sophisticated Lady** (1933) — Duke Ellington, Mitchell Paris, & Irving Mills
24. **White Christmas** (1942) — Irving Berlin
25. **I Should Care** (1945) — Alex Stordahl, Paul Weston & Sammy Cahn
26. **On The Sunny Side Of The Street** (1930) — Jimmy McHugh & Dorothy Fields
27. **Penthouse Serenade (When We're Alone)** (1931) — Will Jason & Val Burton
28. **Yours (Quierme Mucho)** (1937) — Gonzalo Roig, Jack Sherr, & Albert Gamse
29. **St. Louis Blues** (1914) — W.C. Handy
30. **Jealousy** (1931) — Jacob Gade & Vera Bloom

BILLBOARD COLLEGE SURVEYS

FAVORITE BANDS

1938
1. **BENNY GOODMAN**
2. Tommy Dorsey
3. Hal Kemp
4. Guy Lombardo
5. Kay Kyser
6. Glen Gray
7. Hoarce Heidt
8. Sammy Kaye
9. Jimmie Lunceford
10. Wayne King

1939
1. **ARTIE SHAW**
2. Kay Kyser
3. Tommy Dorsey
4. Benny Goodman
5. Larry Clinton
6. Hal Kemp
7. Guy Lombardo
8. Hoarce Heidt
9. Glen Gray
10. Jimmy Dorsey

1940
1. **GLENN MILLER**
2. Kay Kyser
3. Tommy Dorsey
4. Benny Goodman
5. Orrin Tucker
6. Jan Savitt
7. Guy Lombardo
8. Sammy Kaye
9. Jimmy Dorsey
10. Artie Shaw

1941
1. **GLENN MILLER**
2. Tommy Dorsey
3. Kay Kyser
4. Artie Shaw
5. Benny Goodman
6. Jimmy Dorsey
7. Glen Gray
8. Jimmie Lunceford
9. Guy Lombardo
10. Will Bradley

1942
1. **GLENN MILLER**
2. Tommy Dorsey
3. Harry James
4. Benny Goodman
5. Jimmy Dorsey
6. Vaughn Monroe
7. Sammy Kaye
8. Kay Kyser
9. Charlie Spivak
10. Woody Herman

1943
1. **HARRY JAMES**
2. Tommy Dorsey
3. Glenn Miller
4. Benny Goodman
5. Jimmy Dorsey
6. Kay Kyser
7. Charlie Spivak
8. Fred Waring
9. Sammy Kaye
10. Vaughn Monroe

MOST POPULAR MALE BAND VOCALISTS

1939
1. **JACK LEONARD**
   (T. Dorsey)
2. Kenny Sargent (G. Gray)
3. Skinnay Ennis
4. Harry Babbitt (K. Kyser)
5. Perry Como (T. Weems)
6. Tommy Ryan (S. Kaye)
7. Bob Allen (H. Kemp)
8. Sully Mason (K. Kyser)
9. Bob Crosby
10. Pee Wee Hunt (G. Gray)

1940
1. **RAY EBERLE** (G. Miller)
2. Jack Leonard
3. Bob Eberly (J. Dorsey)
4. Harry Babbitt
5. Bon Bon (J. Savitt)
6. Eddy Howard
   (D. Jurgens)
7. Kenny Sargent
8. Sully Mason
9. Perry Como
10. Tommy Ryan

1941
1. **FRANK SINATRA**
   (T. Dorsey)
2. Ray Eberle
3. Bob Eberly
4. Harry Babbitt
5. Kenny Sargent
6. Bon Bon
7. Tommy Ryan
8. Bob Allen
9. Larry Cotton (H. Heidt)
10. Sully Mason

1942
1. **RAY EBERLE**
2. Frank Sinatra
3. Bob Eberly
4. Harry Babbitt
5. Vaughn Monroe
6. Tommy Ryan
7. Tex Beneke (G. Miller)
8. Woody Herman
9. Dick Haymes
   (B. Goodman)
10. Art Lund (B. Goodman)

1943
1. **FRANK SINATRA**
2. Bob Eberly
3. Ray Eberle
4. Harry Babbitt
5. Vaughn Monroe
6. Tommy Ryan
7. Dick Haymes
8. Skip Nelson (T. Dorsey)
9. Johnny McAfee
   (H. James)
10. Garry Stevens (C. Spivak)

Polls include only singers identified with bands

MOST POPULAR FEMALE BAND VOCALISTS

1939
1. **BEA WAIN** (L. Clinton)
2. Ella Fitzgerald (C. Webb)
3. Ginny Simms (K. Kyser)
4. Maxine Sullivan
   (C. Thornhill)
5. Martha Tilton
   (B. Goodman)
6. Mildred Bailey (R. Norvo)
7. Edythe Wright (T. Dorsey)
8. Judy Starr (H. Kemp)
9. Dolly Dawn (G. Hall)
10. Helen Forrest (A. Shaw)

1940
1. **BONNIE BAKER**
   (O. Tucker)
2. Ginny Simms
3. Ella Fitzgerald
4. Helen O'Connell
   (J. Dorsey)
5. Mildred Bailey
6. Bea Wain
7. Marion Hutton (G. Miller)
8. Helen Forrest (T. Dorsey)
9. Nan Wynn (H. Kemp)
10. Martha Tilton

1941
1. **GINNY SIMMS**
2. Helen O'Connell
3. Helen Forrest
4. Marion Hutton
5. Martha Tilton
6. Ella Fitzgerald
7. Bonnie Baker
8. Connie Haines (T. Dorsey)
9. Dorothy Claire (B. Byrne)
10. Paula Kelly (G. Miller)

1942
1. **HELEN O'CONNELL**
2. Marion Hutton
3. Ginny Simms
4. Helen Forrest
5. Peggy Lee (B. Goodman)
6. Anita O'Day (G. Krupa)
7. Ella Fitzgerald
8. Yvonne King (A. Rey)
9. Jo Stafford (T. Dorsey)
10. Connie Haines

1943
1. **HELEN FORREST**
2. Helen O'Connell
3. Peggy Lee
4. Marion Hutton
5. Anita O'Day
6. Donna Dae (F. Waring)
7. Peggy Mann (T. Powell)
8. Gracie Barrie
9. Betty Bradley (B. Chester)
10. Harriet Hilliard (O. Nelson)

Polls include only singers identified with bands

THE #1 HITS
(Listed Chronologically)
1890-1954

This section lists, chronologically, all 898 #1 hits from the 65 year era covered in this book. Because of the use of multiple charts for most of this era, you will find some dates are duplicated and the yearly total of weeks at #1 may not equal 52. The date shown is the earliest date that a record hit #1 on any of the charts. The total weeks at #1 is the highest total from any one of the charts. The totals are not combined from the different charts.

DATE: Date record first hit #1 position.
WKS: Total weeks record held #1 position.

Date Wks

1890
1. 8/02 6 **Semper Fidelis** ... U.S. Marine Band
2. 9/13 6 **Washington Post** ... U.S. Marine Band
3. 10/25 4 **The Thunderer** ... U.S. Marine Band

1891
1. 3/07 4 **Little 'Liza Loves You** ... Len Spencer
2. 4/04 10 **The Laughing Song** ... George Washington Johnson
3. 6/13 4 **Michael Casey As A Physician** ... Russell Hunting
4. 7/11 5 **The Whistling Coon** ... George Washington Johnson
5. 8/22 6 **The Mocking Bird** ... John Yorke Atlee
6. 9/19 4 **Pat Kelly As A Police Justice** ... Dan Kelly
7. 10/17 7 **Turkey In The Straw** ... Billy Golden
8. 12/05 5 **Drill, Ye Terriers, Drill** ... George J. Gaskin

1892
1. 1/09 3 **Slide, Kelly, Slide** ... George J. Gaskin
2. 1/30 8 **Ta-Ra-Ra-Boom Der E** ... Len Spencer
3. 3/26 6 **The Picture Turned Toward The Wall** ... Manhansett Quartette
4. 5/07 3 **Sally In Our Alley** ... Manhansett Quartette
5. 5/28 3 **The Song That Reached My Heart** ... Joe Natus
6. 6/18 3 **Throw Him Down, McCloskey** ... Charles Marsh
7. 7/09 5 **Michael Casey At The Telephone** ... Russell Hunting

8. 8/13 6 **The Old Folks At Home** ... Len Spencer
9. 9/24 2 **The Pretty Red Rose** ... Will Denny
10. 10/08 6 **Michael Casey Taking The Census** ... Russell Hunting
11. 11/19 2 **Near It** ... Len Spencer
12. 12/03 4 **Love's Old Sweet Song** ... Thomas Bott
13. 12/31 4 **Daddy Wouldn't Buy Me A Bow-Wow** ... Dan Quinn

1893
1. 1/28 5 **The Bowery** ... Dan Quinn
2. 3/04 8 **O Promise Me** ... George J. Gaskin
3. 4/29 10 **After The Ball** ... George J. Gaskin
4. 7/08 3 **My Country 'Tis Of Thee** ... Jules Levy
5. 7/29 3 **Mamie, Come And Kiss Your Honey Boy** ... Len Spencer
6. 8/19 4 **Two Little Girls In Blue** ... J.W. Myers
7. 9/16 9 **Daisy Bell** ... Dan Quinn
8. 11/18 8 **The Fatal Wedding** ... George J. Gaskin

1894
1. 1/13 3 **Casey As Insurance Agent** ... Russell Hunting
2. 2/03 5 **Sweeet Marie** ... George J. Gaskin
3. 3/10 5 **The Liberty Bell** ... U.S. Marine Band
4. 4/14 7 **Say Au Revoir, But Not Goodbye** ... Edward M. Favor
5. 6/02 4 **Yankee Doodle** ... Vess Ossman
6. 6/30 4 **Dem Golden Slippers** ... Silas Leachman
7. 7/28 3 **We Were Sweethearts, Nell And I** ... George J. Gaskin
8. 8/18 3 **Lindley, Does You Love Me?** ... Dan Quinn
9. 10/06 4 **My Pearl Is A Bowery Girl** ... Dan Quinn

1900 — Cont'd

4. 5/12   5   **A Bird In A Gilded Cage** ... Jere Mahoney
5. 6/16   6   **A Bird In A Gilded Cage** ... Steve Porter
6. 7/28   5   **Ma Tiger Lily** ... Len Spencer
7. 9/01   6   **Ma Tiger Lily** ... Arthur Collins
8. 10/13   4   **Because** ... Haydn Quartet
9. 11/10   8   **When You Were Sweet Sixteen** ... George J. Gaskin

1901

1. 1/05   7   **Ma Blushin' Rosie** ... Albert Campbell
2. 2/23   3   **The Stars And Stripes Forever** ... Sousa's Band
3. 3/16   3   **When Reuben Comes To Town** ... S.H. Dudley
4. 4/06   3   **Good-Bye, Dolly Gray** ... Big Four Quartet
5. 5/11   7   **Tell Me, Pretty Maiden** ... Harry MacDonough & Grace Spencer
6. 6/29   3   **Tell Me, Pretty Maiden** ... Byron G. Harlan, Joe Belmont, Frank Stanley, & Florodora Girls
7. 7/20   3   **Jim Lawson's Horse Trade With Deacon Witherspoon** ... Cal Stewart
8. 8/10   5   **Hello Central, Give Me Heaven** ... Byron G. Harlan
9. 9/14   1   **In The Shade Of The Palm** ... J.W. Myers
10. 9/21   3   **Uncle Josh's Huskin' Bee Dance** ... Cal Stewart
11. 10/12   4   **The Tale Of The Bumble Bee** ... Harry MacDonough
12. 11/09   3   **Absence Makes The Heart Grow Fonder** ... Harry MacDonough
13. 11/30   3   **Good Evening, Carrie** ... Dan Quinn
14. 12/21   4   **Any Old Place I Hang My Hat Is "Home, Sweet Home" To Me** ... Will Denny

1902

1. 1/18   5   **Good Morning, Carrie** ... Bert Williams & George Walker
2. 3/01   11   **Arkansaw Traveler** ... Len Spencer
3. 5/10   6   **On A Sunday Afternoon** ... J.W. Myers
4. 6/21   5   **Way Down In Old Indiana** ... J.W. Myers
5. 7/26   8   **Bill Bailey, Won't You Please Come Home** ... Arthur Collins
6. 9/20   3   **The Mansion Of Aching Hearts** ... Byron G. Harlan
7. 10/11   4   **The Mansion Of Aching Hearts** ... Harry MacDonough
8. 11/08   7   **In The Good Old Summer Time** ... J.W. Myers
9. 12/27   3   **Under The Bamboo Tree** ... Arthur Collins

1903

1. 1/17   5   **Down Where The Wurzburger Flows** ... Arthur Collins & Byron Harlan
2. 2/21   5   **Come Down, Ma Evening Star** ... Mina Hickman
3. 3/28   6   **In The Good Old Summer Time** ... Haydn Quartet
4. 5/09   4   **In The Good Old Summer Time** ... Sousa's Band
5. 6/06   4   **In The Sweet Bye And Bye** ... Harry MacDonough & John Bieling
6. 7/04   4   **Hiawatha** ... Harry MacDonough
7. 8/01   4   **Come Down, Ma Ev'ning Star** ... Henry Burr
8. 8/29   4   **Uncle Josh On An Automobile** ... Cal Stewart
9. 9/26   5   **Harrah For Baffin's Bay** ... Arthur Collins & Byron Harlan
10. 10/31   4   **Good-Bye, Eliza Jane** ... Arthur Collins
11. 12/05   5   **Any Rags?** ... Arthur Collins

1904

1. 1/09   7   **Bedelia** ... Harry MacDonough & Haydn Quartet
2. 2/27   3   **Bedelia** ... Billy Murray
3. 3/19   4   **Silver Threads Among The Gold** ... Richard Jose
4. 4/16   5   **Navajo** ... Billy Murray
5. 5/21   4   **Blue Bell** ... Frank Stanley & Byron G. Harlan
6. 6/18   3   **Blue Bell** ... Harry MacDonough & Haydn Quartet
7. 7/09   2   **Toyland** ... Corrine Morgan & Haydn Quartet
8. 7/23   9   **Meet Me In St. Louis, Louis** ... Billy Murray
9. 9/24   2   **All Aboard For Dreamland** ... Byron G. Harlan
10. 10/08   3   **Alexander** ... Billy Murray
11. 10/29   10   **Sweet Adeline (You're The Flower Of My Heart)** ... Haydn Quartet
12. 12/24   3   **You're The Flower Of My Heart, Sweet Adeline** ... Columbia Male Quartet (Peerless Quartet)

1905

1. 1/28 4 **Come Take A Trip In My Air-Ship** ... Billy Murray
2. 2/25 8 **Yankee Doodle Boy** ... Billy Murray
3. 4/22 7 **In The Shade Of The Old Apple Tree** ... Henry Burr
4. 6/10 11 **The Preacher And The Bear** ... Arthur Collins
5. 7/15 5 **Give My Regards To Broadway** ... Billy Murray
6. 9/30 2 **Dearie** ... Corrine Morgan & Haydn Quartet
7. 10/14 7 **In My Merry Oldsmobile** ... Billy Murray
8. 12/02 5 **Where The Morning Glories Twine Around The Door** ... Byron G. Harlan

1906

1. 1/06 3 **Everybody Works But Father** ... Billy Murray
2. 1/27 2 **How'd You Like To Spoon With Me?** ... Corrine Morgan & Haydn Quartet
3. 2/10 9 **Wait Till The Sun Shines, Nellie** ... Byron G. Harlan
4. 2/24 1 **Wait Till The Sun Shines, Nellie** ... Harry Tally
5. 4/21 3 **So Long, Mary** ... Corrine Morgan
6. 5/12 10 **The Grand Old Rag** ... Billy Murray
7. 7/21 9 **Nobody** ... Bert Williams
8. 9/22 4 **The Good Old U.S.A** ... Byron G. Harlan
9. 10/20 3 **Love Me And The World Is Mine** ... Albert Campbell
10. 11/10 7 **Love Me And The World Is Mine** ... Henry Burr
11. 12/29 2 **Let It Alone** ... Bert Williams

1907

1. 1/12 2 **Camp Meetin' Time** ... Arthur Collins & Byron Harlan
2. 1/26 2 **He's A Cousin Of Mine** ... Bert Williams
3. 2/12 10 **My Gal Sal** ... Byron G. Harlan
4. 4/20 2 **I Just Can't Make My Eyes Behave** ... Ada Jones
5. 5/04 2 **Because You're You** ... Harry MacDonough & Elise Stevenson

6. 5/18 11 **School Days (When We Were A Couple Of Kids)** ... Byron G. Harlan
7. 8/03 3 **Nobody's Little Girl** ... Byron G. Harlan
8. 8/24 4 **I Pagliacci - Vesti La Giubba (On With The Play)** ... Enrico Caruso
9. 9/21 9 **Harrigan** ... Billy Murray
10. 11/23 6 **Let's Take An Old-Fashioned Walk** ... Ada Jones & Billy Murray

1908

1. 1/04 5 **My Dear** ... Harry MacDonough
2. 2/08 6 **Under Any Old Flag At All** ... Billy Murray
3. 3/21 6 **As Long As The World Rolls On** ... Alan Turner
4. 5/02 3 **Wouldn't You Like To Have Me For A Sweetheart?** ... Ada Jones & Billy Murray
5. 5/23 5 **The Glow-Worm** ... Victor Orchestra
6. 6/27 5 **The Glow-Worm** ... Lucy Isabelle Marsh
7. 8/01 4 **Are You Sincere?** ... Elise Stevenson
8. 8/29 4 **When We Are M-A-Double-R-I-E-D** ... Ada Jones & Billy Murray
9. 9/26 5 **Cuddle Up A Little Closer, Lovey Mine** ... Ada Jones & Billy Murray
10. 10/31 7 **Take Me Out To The Ball Game** ... Billy Murray & Haydn Quartet
11. 12/12 5 **Sunbonnet Sue** ... Harry MacDonough & Haydn Quartet

1909

1. 1/23 5 **Good Evening, Caroline** ... Frank Stanley & Elise Stevenson
2. 2/27 6 **The Right Church, But The Wrong Pew** ... Arthur Collins & Byron Harlan
3. 4/10 9 **Shine On, Harvest Moon** ... Harry MacDonough & "Miss Walton" (Elise Stevenson)

Date Wks

4. 6/12 5 **Shine On, Harvest Moon** ... Ada Jones & Billy Murray

5. 7/13 3 **To The End Of The World With You** ... Henry Burr

6. 8/07 5 **The Yama Yama Man** ... Ada Jones & Victor Light Opera Co.

7. 9/11 8 **I Wonder Who's Kissing Her Now** ... Henry Burr

8. 11/06 2 **I've Got Rings On My Fingers** ... Blanche Ring

9. 11/20 4 **I've Got Rings On My Fingers** ... Ada Jones

10. 12/18 11 **Put On Your Old Gray Bonnet** ... Haydn Quartet

1910

1. 2/26 2 **Carrie (Carrie Marry Harry)** ... Billy Murray

2. 3/12 6 **Where The River Shannon Flows** ... Harry MacDonough

3. 4/23 9 **By The Light Of The Silvery Moon** ... Billy Murray & Haydn Quartet

4. 7/02 11 **Casey Jones** ... Billy Murray & American Quartet

5. 9/10 4 **Call Me Up Some Rainy Afternoon** ... Ada Jones, Billy Murray & American Quartet

6. 10/08 4 **Every Little Movement** ... Harry MacDonough & Lucy Isabelle Marsh

7. 11/12 1 **Tramp! Tramp! Tramp!** ... Frank Stanley & Byron G. Harlan

8. 11/19 2 **In The Valley Of Yesterday** ... Harry MacDonough

9. 12/10 4 **Meet Me To-Night In Dreamland** ... Henry Burr

10. 12/31 6 **Play That Barber-Shop Chord** ... Bert Williams

1911

1. 2/11 5 **Under The Yum Yum Tree** ... Arthur Collins & Byron Harlan

2. 3/18 2 **Mother Machree** ... Will Oakland

3. 4/01 5 **Put Your Arms Around Me, Honey** ... Arthur Collins & Byron Harlan

4. 5/06 2 **I Love The Name Of Mary** ... Will Oakland

5. 5/20 2 **Come, Josephine, In My Flying Machine** ... Blanche Ring

6. 6/03 3 **Come, Josephine, In My Flying Machine** ... Ada Jones, Billy Murray & American Quartet

7. 6/24 7 **I'm Falling In Love With Someone** ... John McCormack

8. 8/12 5 **Mother Machree** ... John McCormack

9. 9/16 10 **Alexander's Ragtime Band** ... Arthur Collins & Byron Harlan

10. 11/25 1 **Down By The Old Mill Stream** ... Arthur Clough & Brunswick Quartet

11. 12/02 7 **Let Me Call You Sweetheart** ... Columbia Male Quartet (Peerless Quartet)

1912

1. 1/20 7 **Down By The Old Mill Stream** ... Harry MacDonough

2. 2/03 1 **Oh, You Beautiful Doll** . . Billy Murray & American Quartet

3. 3/16 8 **Moonlight Bay** ... American Quartet

4. 5/11 2 **That Haunting Melody** ... Al Jolson

5. 5/25 4 **When I Was Twenty-One And You Were Sweet Sixteen** ... Henry Burr & Albert Campbell

6. 6/22 3 **Love Is Mine** ... Enrico Caruso

7. 7/13 5 **Ragging The Baby To Sleep** ... Al Jolson

8. 8/24 6 **Ragtime Cowboy Joe** ... Bob Roberts

9. 9/28 2 **I Love You Truly** ... Elsie Baker

10. 10/12 6 **Waiting For The Robert E. Lee** ... Heidelberg Quintet

11. 11/23 5 **Be My Little Baby Bumble Bee** ... Ada Jones & Billy Murray

12. 12/28 1 **Everybody Two-Step** ... American Quartet

1913

1. 1/04 3 **Till The Sands Of The Desert Grow Cold** ... Alan Turner

2. 1/25 3 **Row! Row! Row!** ... Ada Jones

3. 2/15 6 **When The Midnight Choo Choo Leaves For Alabam'** ... Arthur Collins & Byron Harlan

4. 3/29 2 **Sympathy** ... Walter Van Brunt & Helen Clark

5. 4/12 7 **When I Lost You** ... Henry Burr

6. 5/31 5 **The Spaniard That Blighted My Life** ... Al Jolson

7. 7/05 3 **The Trail Of The Lonesome Pine** ... Henry Burr & Albert Campbell

8. 7/26 7 **When Irish Eyes Are Smiling** ... Chauncey Olcott

1913 — Cont'd

9. 9/13 6 **Last Night Was The End Of The World** ... Henry Burr

10. 10/04 7 **You Made Me Love You, I Didn't Want To Do It** ... Al Jolson

11. 12/12 7 **Peg O' My Heart** ... Charles Harrison

1914

1. 1/31 4 **Too-Ra-Loo-Ra-Loo-Ral (That's An Irish Lullaby)** ... Chauncey Olcott

2. 2/28 6 **I'm On My Way To Mandalay** ... Henry Burr, Albert Campbell & Will Oakland

3. 4/11 6 **Rebecca Of Sunny-brook Farm** ... American Quartet

4. 5/23 3 **I Love The Ladies** ... Arthur Collins & Byron Harlan

5. 6/13 7 **The Song That Stole My Heart Away** ... Henry Burr

6. 8/01 6 **By The Beautiful Sea** ... Heidelberg Quintet

7. 9/12 5 **Cohen On The Telephone** ... Joe Hayman

8. 9/26 2 **By The Beautiful Sea** ... Ada Jones & Billy Watkins

9. 10/31 3 **Ballin' The Jack** ... Prince's Orchestra

10. 11/21 2 **The Aba Daba Honeymoon** ... Arthur Collins & Byron Harlan

11. 12/05 7 **It's A Long, Long Way To Tipperary** ... American Quartet

1915

1. 1/23 8 **It's A Long, Long Way To Tipperary** ... John McCormack

2. 3/20 2 **Chinatown, My Chinatown** ... American Quartet

3. 4/03 5 **Carry Me Back To Old Virginny** ... Alma Gluck

4. 4/24 3 **I Didn't Raise My Boy To Be A Soldier** ... Morton Harvey

5. 5/29 4 **I Didn't Raise My Boy To Be A Soldier** ... Peerless Quartet

6. 6/26 5 **A Little Bit Of Heaven ("Shure, They Call It Ireland")** ... George MacFarlane

7. 7/31 2 **Home, Sweet Home** ... Alice Nielsen

8. 8/14 4 **My Bird Of Paradise** ... Peerless Quartet

9. 9/11 2 **My Little Dream Girl** ... James F. Harrison & James Reed

10. 9/25 6 **Hello, Frisco!** ... Olive Kline & Reinald Werrenrath

11. 11/06 2 **Close To My Heart** ... Henry Burr & Albert Campbell

12. 11/20 7 **They Didn't Believe Me** ... Harry MacDonough & Olive Kline

1916

1. 1/08 2 **Keep The Home Fires Burning (Till The Boys Come Home)** ... Frederick J. Wheeler

2. 1/22 3 **There's A Long, Long Trail** ... James F. Harrison & James Reed

3. 2/12 2 **Somewhere A Voice Is Calling** ... John McCormack

4. 2/26 6 **M-O-T-H-E-R (A Word That Means The World To Me)** ... Henry Burr

5. 4/08 2 **The Lights Of My Home Town** ... Peerless Quartet

6. 4/22 5 **Hello, Hawaii, How Are You?** ... Prince's Orchestra

7. 5/06 1 **I Love A Piano** ... Billy Murray

8. 5/13 3 **The Girl On The Magazine** ... Harry MacDonough

9. 6/17 6 **Good-Bye, Good Luck, God Bless You (Is All That I Can Say)** ... Henry Burr

10. 7/29 3 **There's A Quaker Down In Quaker Town** ... Henry Burr & Albert Campbell

11. 8/19 2 **The Star-Spangled Banner** ... Prince's Orchestra

12. 9/02 2 **America** ... Columbia Mixed Double Quartet

13. 9/16 3 **I Sent My Wife To The Thousand Isles** ... Al Jolson

14. 10/07 3 **If I Knock The 'L' Out Of Kelly (It Would Still Be Kelly To Me)** ... Marguerite Farrell

15. 10/28 1 **Pretty Baby** ... Billy Murray

16. 11/04 3 **Ireland Must Be Heaven, For My Mother Came From There** ... Charles Harrison

17. 11/25 2 **Oh How She Could Yacki Hacki Wicki Wachi Woo (That's Love In Hawaii)** ... Arthur Collins & Byron Harlan

18. 12/09 3 **Turn Back The Universe And Give Me Yester Day** ... Harry MacDonough & Orpheus Quartet

19. 12/30 4 **The Sunshine Of Your Smile** ... John McCormack

Date Wks

1917

1. 1/27 4 **My Own Iona** ... Hoarce Wright & Rene Dietrich
2. 2/24 6 **Poor Butterfly** ... Victor Military Band
3. 4/07 4 **Hush-A-Bye Ma Baby (The Missouri Waltz)** ... Elsie Baker
4. 5/05 5 **Pack Up Your Troubles In Your Old Kit Bag (And Smile, Smile, Smile)** ... Knickerbocker Quartet
5. 6/09 3 **The Star-Spangled Banner** ... John McCormack
6. 6/30 3 **For Me And My Gal** ... Van & Schenck
7. 7/21 3 **Oh Johnny, Oh Johnny, Oh!** ... American Quartet
8. 8/11 2 **Lookout Mountain** ... Henry Burr & Albert Campbell
9. 8/25 6 **Till The Clouds Roll By** ... Anna Wheaton & James Harrod
10. 10/06 1 **Good-Bye Broadway, Hello France** ... American Quartet
11. 10/13 9 **Over There** ... American Quartet
12. 11/03 2 **Over There** ... Peerless Quartet
13. 12/01 3 **Over There** ... Nora Bayes

1918

1. 1/19 4 **Send Me Away With A Smile** ... John McCormack
2. 2/16 2 **I Don't Know Where I'm Going But I'm On My Way** ... Peerless Quartet
3. 3/02 1 **The Battle Hymn Of The Republic** ... Charles Harrison & Columbia Stellar Quartet
4. 3/09 4 **Hail! Hail! The Gang's All Here** ... Irving Kaufman & Columbia Quartet
5. 4/06 3 **I'm All Bound Round With The Mason Dixon Line** ... Al Jolson
6. 4/13 1 **Dark Town Strutters' Ball** ... Arthur Collins & Byron Harlan
7. 4/27 11 **Just A Baby's Prayer At Twilight (For Her Daddy Over There)** ... Henry Burr
8. 7/13 2 **I'm Sorry I Made You Cry** ... Henry Burr
9. 7/20 3 **Hello Central, Give Me No Man's Land** ... Al Jolson
10. 8/17 8 **Rock-A-Bye Your Baby With A Dixie Melody** ... Al Jolson
11. 9/07 1 **Smiles** ... Joseph C. Smith's Orchestra
12. 10/26 3 **Over There** ... Enrico Caruso

13. 11/12 2 **Tiger Rag** ... Original Dixieland Jazz Band
14. 11/16 4 **Oh, How I Hate To Get Up In The Morning** ... Arthur Fields
15. 12/14 5 **I'm Always Chasing Rainbows** ... Charles Harrison

1919

1. 1/18 2 **O Death, Where Is Thy Sting?** ... Bert Williams
2. 2/01 3 **After You've Gone** ... Marion Harris
3. 2/22 9 **Till We Meet Again** ... Henry Burr & Albert Campbell
4. 3/15 1 **Till We Meet Again** ... Lewis James & Charles Hart
5. 5/03 2 **Till We Meet Again** ... Nicholas Orlando's Orchestra
6. 5/17 1 **Beautiful Ohio** ... Waldorf-Astoria Dance Orchestra
7. 5/24 9 **Beautiful Ohio** ... Henry Burr
8. 7/12 2 **I'm Forever Blowing Bubbles** ... Henry Burr & Albert Campbell
9. 8/09 6 **I'll Say She Does** ... Al Jolson
10. 9/20 2 **It's Nobody's Business But My Own** ... Bert Williams
11. 10/04 5 **A Pretty Girl Is Like A Melody** ... John Steel
12. 10/25 4 **I'm Forever Blowing Bubbles** ... Ben Selvin's Novelty Orchestra
13. 12/05 6 **Oh! What A Pal Was Mary** ... Henry Burr

1920

1. 1/17 2 **I've Got My Captain Working For Me Now** ... Al Jolson
2. 1/31 13 **Dardanella** ... Ben Selvin's Novelty Orchestra
3. 5/01 1 **Alice Blue Gown** ... Edith Day
4. 5/08 9 **Swanee** ... Al Jolson
5. 7/03 7 **When My Baby Smiles At Me** ... Ted Lewis & His Band
6. 8/07 3 **Hold Me** ... Art Hickman
7. 9/18 4 **The Love Nest** ... John Steel
8. 9/25 3 **St. Louis Blues** ... Marion Harris
9. 10/16 2 **The Love Nest** ... Art Hickman
10. 10/30 11 **Whispering** ... Paul Whiteman
11. 12/11 2 **The Japanese Sandman** ... Paul Whiteman

Date Wks

1921

1.	1/29	6	**Wang Wang Blues** ... Paul Whiteman
2.	3/12	5	**Margie** ... Eddie Cantor
13.	4/16	4	**O-H-I-O (O-My! O!)** ... Al Jolson
4.	5/14	3	**Look For The Silver Lining** ... Marion Harris
5.	6/04	5	**My Mammy** ... Paul Whiteman
6.	7/08	3	**Make Believe** ... Nora Bayes
7.	7/30	6	**Cherie** ... Paul Whiteman
8.	9/10	2	**Ain't We Got Fun?** ... Van & Schenck
9.	9/24	5	**Song Of India** ... Paul Whiteman
10.	10/22	4	**All By Myself** ... Ted Lewis
11.	11/26	5	**Say It With Music** ... Paul Whiteman
12.	12/31	6	**Wabash Blues** . Isham Jones

1922

1.	2/11	11	**April Showers** ... Al Jolson
2.	3/25	1	**My Man** ... Fanny Brice
3.	5/06	5	**Angel Child** ... Al Jolson
4.	6/10	4	**On The Alamo** ... Isham Jones
5.	7/08	2	**Do It Again** ... Paul Whiteman
6.	7/22	6	**Stumbling** ... Paul Whiteman
7.	9/02	2	**Mr. Gallagher And Mr. Shean** ... Ernest Hare & Billy Jones
8.	9/16	6	**Hot Lips** ... Paul Whiteman
9.	10/28	6	**Mr. Gallagher And Mr. Shean** ... Gallagher & Shean
10.	12/09	1	**My Buddy** ... Henry Burr
11.	12/16	8	**Three O'Clock In The Morning** ... Paul Whiteman

1923

1.	1/06	1	**I'll Build A Stairway To Paradise** ... Paul Whiteman
2.	1/13	4	**Toot Toot Tootsie (Goo'bye)** ... Al Jolson
3.	3/10	3	**Carolina In The Morning** ... Van & Schenck
4.	4/07	7	**Parade Of The Wooden Soldiers** ... Paul Whiteman
5.	5/26	3	**Love Sends A Little Gift Of Roses** ... Carl Fenton
6.	6/16	1	**Bambalina** ... Paul Whiteman
7.	6/23	3	**Dreamy Melody** ... Art Landry
8.	7/14	4	**Down Hearted Blues** ... Bessie Smith
9.	8/11	6	**Swingin' Down The Lane** ... Isham Jones
10.	9/01	5	**Yes! We Have No Bananas** ... Billy Jones
11.	10/27	2	**Yes! We Have No Bananas** ... Ben Selvin
12.	11/10	6	**That Old Gang Of Mine** ... Billy Murray & Ed Smalle
13.	12/22	2	**No, No, Nora** ... Eddie Cantor

1924

1.	1/05	5	**Sleep** ... Fred Waring's Pennsylvanians
2.	1/26	1	**Charleston** ... Arthur Gibbs
3.	2/16	6	**It Ain't Gonna Rain No Mo'** ... Wendell Hall
4.	3/01	4	**Linger Awhile** ... Paul Whiteman
5.	3/29	5	**Somebody Stole My Gal** ... Ted Weems
6.	5/24	6	**California, Here I Come!** ... Al Jolson
7.	7/19	2	**Spain** ... Isham Jones
8.	8/02	5	**What'll I Do?** ... Paul Whiteman
9.	9/06	5	**It Had To Be You** ... Isham Jones
10.	10/11	5	**Memory Lane** ... Fred Waring's Pennsylvanians
11.	11/15	3	**I Wonder What's Become Of Sally?** ... Al Jolson
12.	12/06	5	**Somebody Loves Me** ... Paul Whiteman

1925

1.	1/10	5	**All Alone** ... Al Jolson
2.	2/07	3	**All Alone** ... Paul Whiteman
3.	2/28	3	**Tea For Two** ... Marion Harris
4.	3/21	2	**All Alone** ... John McCormack
5.	4/04	7	**I'll See You In My Dreams** ... Isham Jones with Ray Miller's Orchestra
6.	5/23	1	**O! Katharina** ... Ted Lewis
7.	5/30	5	**The Prisoner's Song** ... Vernon Dalhart (see #14 below)
8.	7/04	5	**Sweet Georgia Brown** ... Ben Bernie
9.	8/01	5	**If You Knew Susie** ... Eddie Cantor
10.	9/12	7	**Yes Sir! That's My Baby** ... Gene Austin
11.	10/31	3	**Oh, How I Miss You Tonight** ... Ben Selvin (Cavaliers)
12.	11/21	4	**Manhattan** ... Ben Selvin (Knickerbockers)
13.	12/19	1	**Remember** ... Isham Jones
14.	12/26	7	**The Prisoner's Song** ... Vernon Dalhart (total: 12 weeks at #1)

1926

1.	2/13	6	**Who?** ... George Olsen
2.	3/27	4	**Sleepy Time Gal** ... Ben Bernie
3.	4/17	2	**I'm Sitting On Top Of The World** ... Al Jolson

1926 — Cont'd

4. 5/08 3 **Always** ... George Olsen
5. 5/22 1 **Five Foot Two, Eyes Of Blue** ... Gene Austin
6. 6/05 2 **Always** ... Vincent Lopez
7. 6/19 2 **Gimme A Lil' Kiss, Will Ya, Huh?** ... "Whispering" Jack Smith
8. 7/03 11 **Valencia** ... Paul Whiteman
9. 9/04 3 **Bye Bye, Blackbird** ... Gene Austin
10. 10/02 2 **When The Red, Red Robin Comes Bob-Bob-Bobbin' Along** ... Al Jolson
11. 10/16 6 **Baby Face** ... Jan Garber
12. 11/27 2 **Breezin' Along With The Breeze** ... Johnny Marvin
13. 12/11 4 **The Birth Of The Blues** ... Paul Whiteman

1927

1. 1/08 8 **In A Little Spanish Town** ... Paul Whiteman
2. 3/05 5 **Some Of These Days** ... Sophie Tucker with Ted Lewis & His Band
3. 4/09 3 **Tonight You Belong To Me** ... Gene Austin
4. 4/30 2 **Blue Skies** ... Ben Selvin
5. 5/14 4 **Ain't She Sweet?** ... Ben Bernie
6. 6/11 3 **At Sundown (When Love Is Calling Me Home)** ... George Olsen
7. 7/02 5 **Two Black Crows-Parts 1 & 2 (The Early Bird Catches The Worm)** ... Moran & Mack
8. 8/06 1 **Forgive Me** ... Gene Austin
9. 8/13 4 **Me And My Shadow** ... "Whispering" Jack Smith
10. 9/10 3 **Russian Lullaby** ... Roger Wolfe Kahn
11. 10/01 7 **Charmaine!** ... Guy Lombardo
12. 11/19 1 **My Blue Heaven** ... Paul Whiteman
13. 11/26 3 **Ida, Sweet As Apple Cider** ... Red Nichols
14. 12/17 13 **My Blue Heaven** ... Gene Austin

1928

1. 3/17 4 **Among My Souvenirs** ... Paul Whiteman
2. 4/14 2 **Together** ... Paul Whiteman
3. 4/28 1 **Ol' Man River** ... Paul Whiteman
4. 5/05 3 **Ramona** ... Paul Whiteman
5. 5/26 8 **Ramona** ... Gene Austin
6. 7/21 1 **Laugh, Clown, Laugh!** ... Fred Waring's Pennsylvanians
7. 7/28 6 **My Angel** ... Paul Whiteman
8. 9/08 5 **Jeannine (I Dream Of Lilac Time)** ... Gene Austin

9. 10/13 1 **I Can't Give You Anything But Love** ... Cliff Edwards ("Ukelele Ike")
10. 10/20 12 **Sonny Boy** ... Al Jolson
11. 12/01 2 **There's A Rainbow Round My Shoulder** ... Al Jolson

1929

1. 1/26 3 **Sweethearts On Parade** ... Guy Lombardo
2. 2/16 7 **Carolina Moon** ... Gene Austin
3. 3/23 2 **A Precious Little Thing Called Love** ... George Olsen
4. 4/20 8 **Honey** ... Rudy Vallee
5. 6/15 4 **The Wedding Of The Painted Doll** ... Leo Reisman
6. 7/13 4 **Pagan Love Song** ... Copley Plaza Orchestra (Bob Haring)
7. 8/10 3 **Singin' In The Rain** ... Cliff Edwards ("Ukelele Ike")
8. 8/31 5 **Little Pal** ... Al Jolson
9. 10/05 2 **Am I Blue?** ... Ethel Waters
10. 10/19 10 **Tip Toe Through The Tulips** ... Nick Lucas
11. 12/28 2 **Great Day** ... Paul Whiteman

1930

1. 1/11 3 **Chant Of The Jungle** ... Roy Ingraham
2. 2/01 1 **The Man From The South** ... Ted Weems
3. 2/08 3 **Happy Days Are Here Again** ... Benny Meroff
4. 3/01 1 **Puttin' On The Ritz** ... Harry Richman
5. 3/08 2 **Happy Days Are Here Again** ... Ben Selvin
6. 3/22 10 **Stein Song (University Of Maine)** ... Rudy Vallee
7. 5/31 2 **When It's Springtime In The Rockies** ... Hilo Hawaiian Orchestra
8. 6/14 3 **When It's Springtime In The Rockies** ... Ben Selvin
9. 7/05 7 **Dancing With Tears In My Eyes** ... Nat Shilkret
10. 8/23 6 **Little White Lies** ... Fred Waring's Pennsylvanians
11. 9/20 2 **If I Could Be With You One Hour Tonight** ... McKinney's Cotton Pickers
12. 10/18 6 **Body And Soul** ... Paul Whiteman
13. 11/29 3 **Three Little Words** ... Duke Ellington
14. 12/20 4 **You're Driving Me Crazy! (What Did I Do?)** ... Guy Lombardo

1931

1. 1/17 7 **The Peanut Vendor** ... Don Azpiazu
2. 2/14 2 **Just A Gigolo** ... Ted Lewis
3. 3/21 3 **By The River St. Marie** ... Guy Lombardo
4. 4/04 1 **Minnie The Moocher** ... Cab Calloway
5. 4/18 1 **Star Dust** ... Isham Jones
6. 4/25 4 **Dream A Little Dream Of Me** ... Wayne King
7. 5/16 3 **Out Of Nowhere** ... Bing Crosby
8. 6/06 3 **(There Ought To Be A) Moonlight Saving Time** ... Guy Lombardo
9. 6/27 2 **Just One More Chance** ... Bing Crosby
10. 7/11 3 **I Found A Million-Dollar Baby (In A Five-And-Ten-Cent Store)** ... Fred Waring's Pennsylvanians
11. 8/08 3 **At Your Command** ... Bing Crosby
12. 8/22 6 **Sweet And Lovely** ... Gus Arnheim
13. 10/03 2 **When The Moon Comes Over The Mountain** ... Kate Smith
14. 10/17 7 **Good Night, Sweetheart** ... Wayne King
15. 12/05 2 **Goodnight, Sweetheart** ... Guy Lombardo
16. 12/19 4 **Tiger Rag** ... Mills Brothers

1932

1. 1/16 2 **River, Stay 'Way From My Door** ... Kate Smith with Guy Lombardo
2. 1/30 2 **Dinah** ... Bing Crosby & Mills Brothers
3. 2/13 3 **All Of Me** ... Paul Whiteman
4. 3/05 2 **All Of Me** ... Louis Armstrong
5. 3/19 2 **Too Many Tears** ... Guy Lombardo
6. 4/02 6 **Paradise** ... Leo Reisman
7. 5/14 3 **Paradise** ... Guy Lombardo
8. 6/04 2 **Lullaby Of The Leaves** ... George Olsen
9. 6/18 10 **In A Shanty In Old Shanty Town** ... Ted Lewis
10. 8/27 5 **We Just Couldn't Say Goodbye** ... Guy Lombardo
11. 10/01 2 **Say It Isn't So** ... George Olsen
12. 10/15 6 **Please** ... Bing Crosby
13. 11/26 2 **Brother, Can You Spare A Dime?** ... Bing Crosby
14. 12/10 2 **Brother, Can You Spare A Dime?** ... Rudy Vallee
15. 12/24 10 **Night And Day** ... Fred Astaire with Leo Reisman

1933

1. 3/04 4 **You're Getting To Be A Habit With Me** ... Bing Crosby
2. 4/01 3 **Forty-Second Street** ... Don Bestor
3. 4/22 8 **Stormy Weather** ... Leo Reisman featuring Harold Arlen
4. 6/17 3 **Stormy Weather** ... Ethel Waters
5. 7/08 2 **Shadow Waltz** ... Bing Crosby
6. 7/22 4 **Lazybones** ... Ted Lewis
7. 8/19 5 **Love Is The Sweetest Thing** ... Ray Noble
8. 9/23 9 **The Last Round-Up** ... George Olsen
9. 11/04 3 **The Last Round-Up** ... Guy Lombardo
10. 12/16 3 **Did You Ever See A Dream Walking?** ... Eddy Duchin

1934

1. 1/06 3 **The Old Spinning Wheel** ... Ray Noble
2. 1/20 6 **Smoke Gets In Your Eyes** ... Paul Whiteman
3. 2/24 5 **Let's Fall In Love** ... Eddy Duchin
4. 3/03 1 **My Little Grass Shack In Kealakekua, Hawaii** ... Ted Fio Rito
5. 3/31 2 **The Carioca** ... Enric Madriguera
6. 4/07 1 **Wagon Wheels** ... Paul Whiteman
7. 4/14 5 **Little Dutch Mill** ... Bing Crosby
8. 5/12 5 **Cocktails For Two** ... Duke Ellington
9. 6/09 5 **I'll String Along With You** ... Ted Fio Rito
10. 7/07 1 **Moon Glow** ... Benny Goodman
11. 7/14 5 **The Very Thought Of You** ... Ray Noble
12. 7/14 2 **All I Do Is Dream Of You** ... Jan Garber
13. 8/18 6 **Love In Bloom** ... Bing Crosby
14. 9/15 4 **I Saw Stars** ... Freddy Martin
15. 10/20 4 **One Night Of Love** ... Grace Moore
16. 10/27 2 **The Continental (You Kiss While You're Dancing)** ... Leo Reisman
17. 11/10 4 **Stars Fell On Alabama** ... Guy Lombardo
18. 12/08 7 **June In January** ... Bing Crosby
19. 12/08 3 **Stay As Sweet As You Are** ... Jimmie Grier
20. 12/29 2 **The Object Of My Affection** ... Jimmie Grier

1935

1. 1/12 7 **Isle Of Capri** ... Ray Noble
2. 1/26 3 **Blue Moon** ... Glen Gray
3. 1/26 2 **The Object Of My Affection** ... Boswell Sisters
4. 3/23 4 **Lovely To Look At** ... Eddy Duchin
5. 4/13 2 **It's Easy To Remember** ... Bing Crosby
6. 4/20 1 **Soon** ... Bing Crosby
7. 5/04 3 **I Won't Dance** ... Eddy Duchin
8. 5/04 2 **Lullaby Of Broadway** ... Dorsey Brothers Orchestra
9. 5/18 2 **What's The Reason (I'm Not Pleasin' You)** ... Guy Lombardo
10. 6/01 2 **Life Is A Song** ... Ruth Etting
11. 6/15 4 **When I Grow Too Old To Dream** ... Glen Gray
12. 6/22 4 **She's A Latin From Manhattan** ... Victor Young
13. 6/29 3 **Chasing Shadows** ... Dorsey Brothers Orchestra
14. 7/13 3 **In A Little Gypsy Tea Room** ... Bob Crosby
15. 7/20 2 **Let's Swing It** ... Ray Noble
16. 8/03 1 **Rhythm Is Our Business** ... Jimmie Lunceford
17. 8/10 11 **Cheek To Cheek** ... Fred Astaire
18. 8/10 1 **Paris In The Spring** ... Ray Noble
19. 8/17 1 **And Then Some** ... Ozzie Nelson
20. 8/24 2 **East Of The Sun (And West Of The Moon)** ... Tom Coakley
21. 9/07 3 **I'm In The Mood For Love** ... Little Jack Little
22. 10/19 3 **Truckin'** ... Fats Waller
23. 11/02 3 **You Are My Lucky Star** ... Eddy Duchin
24. 11/30 4 **Red Sails In The Sunset** ... Guy Lombardo
25. 12/21 2 **Red Sails In The Sunset** ... Bing Crosby
26. 12/21 1 **On Treasure Island** ... Tommy Dorsey
27. 12/28 2 **A Little Bit Independent** ... Fats Waller

1936

1. 1/04 5 **The Music Goes Round And Round** ... Tommy Dorsey
2. 1/04 3 **The Music Goes Round And Round** ... Riley-Farley Orchestra
3. 2/01 3 **Moon Over Miami** ... Eddy Duchin
4. 2/08 6 **Alone** ... Tommy Dorsey
5. 2/29 2 **A Beautiful Lady In Blue** ... Jan Garber

6. 3/14 6 **Goody-Goody** ... Benny Goodman
7. 3/21 1 **Lights Out** ... Eddy Duchin
8. 4/04 1 **I'm Putting All My Eggs In One Basket** ... Fred Astaire
9. 4/11 2 **It's Been So Long** ... Benny Goodman
10. 5/02 2 **Lost** ... Guy Lombardo
11. 5/09 3 **A Melody From The Sky** ... Jan Garber
12. 5/23 1 **You** ... Tommy Dorsey
13. 5/30 6 **The Glory Of Love** ... Benny Goodman
14. 6/06 4 **Is It True What They Say About Dixie?** ... Jimmy Dorsey
15. 6/06 1 **All My Life** ... Fats Waller
16. 7/11 2 **There's A Small Hotel** ... Hal Kemp
17. 7/18 2 **Take My Heart** ... Eddy Duchin
18. 7/25 4 **It's A Sin To Tell A Lie** ... Fats Waller
19. 8/01 2 **These Foolish Things Remind Me Of You** ... Benny Goodman
20. 8/15 2 **When I'm With You** ... Hal Kemp
21. 8/22 2 **Until The Real Thing Comes Along** ... Andy Kirk
22. 8/29 4 **Did I Remember?** ... Shep Fields
23. 9/05 5 **A Fine Romance** ... Fred Astaire
24. 10/03 6 **The Way You Look To-night** ... Fred Astaire
25. 10/10 2 **When Did You Leave Heaven?** ... Guy Lombardo
26. 11/14 2 **You Turned The Tables On Me** ... Benny Goodman
27. 11/28 10 **Pennies From Heaven** ... Bing Crosby
28. 12/05 1 **I'll Sing You A Thousand Love Songs** ... Eddy Duchin
29. 12/12 2 **In The Chapel In The Moonlight** ... Shep Fields

1937

1. 1/02 2 **It's De-Lovely** ... Eddy Duchin
2. 2/06 4 **Goodnight, My Love** ... Benny Goodman
3. 2/20 4 **This Year's Kisses** ... Hal Kemp
4. 2/20 1 **With Plenty Of Money And You** ... Henry Busse
5. 2/27 3 **This Year's Kisses** ... Benny Goodman
6. 3/27 2 **Marie** ... Tommy Dorsey
7. 4/03 5 **Boo Hoo** ... Guy Lombardo
8. 4/17 10 **Sweet Leilani** ... Bing Crosby
9. 4/24 1 **Too Marvelous For Words** ... Bing Crosby

1937 — Cont'd

10.	5/01	1	**They Can't Take That Away From Me** ... Fred Astaire
11.	5/15	3	**Carelessly** ... Teddy Wilson featuring Billie Holiday
12.	6/05	4	**September In The Rain** ... Guy Lombardo
13.	7/03	5	**It Looks Like Rain In Cherry Blossom Lane** ... Guy Lombardo
14.	7/03	2	**The Merry-Go-Round Broke Down** ... Russ Morgan
15.	7/17	2	**The Merry-Go-Round Broke Down** ... Shep Fields
16.	7/24	1	**Where Or When** ... Hal Kemp
17.	7/31	2	**Smarty** ... Fats Waller
18.	7/31	1	**Gone With The Wind** ... Hoarce Heidt
19.	8/07	3	**A Sailboat In The Moonlight** ... Guy Lombardo
20.	8/21	3	**Satan Takes A Holiday** ... Tommy Dorsey
21.	9/04	4	**Whispers In The Dark** ... Bob Crosby
22.	9/11	2	**The Big Apple** ... Tommy Dorsey's Clam Bake Seven
23.	9/11	1	**So Rare** ... Guy Lombardo
24.	9/25	4	**The Moon Got In My Eyes** ... Bing Crosby
25.	10/09	4	**That Old Feeling** ... Shep Fields
26.	10/16	2	**You Can't Stop Me From Dreaming** ... Teddy Wilson
27.	11/06	3	**Remember Me?** ... Bing Crosby
28.	11/20	1	**Vieni, Vieni** ... Rudy Vallee
29.	11/27	7	**Once In A While** ... Tommy Dorsey
30.	11/27	6	**The Dipsy Doodle** ... Tommy Dorsey
31.	12/11	1	**Bob White (Whatcha Gonna Swing Tonight?)** ... Bing Crosby & Connee Boswell

1938

1.	1/01	1	**Nice Work If You Can Get It** ... Fred Astaire
2.	1/15	2	**Rosalie** ... Sammy Kaye
3.	1/22	5	**Bei Mir Bist Du Schoen** ... Andrews Sisters
4.	1/29	1	**You're A Sweetheart** ... Dolly Dawn
5.	2/26	4	**Thanks For The Memory** ... Shep Fields
6.	3/19	6	**Ti-Pi-Tin** ... Hoarce Heidt
7.	3/19	5	**Don't Be That Way** ... Benny Goodman
8.	4/23	3	**I Let A Song Go Out Of My Heart** ... Duke Ellington
9.	5/07	2	**Please Be Kind** ... Red Norvo
10.	5/14	3	**Love Walked In** ... Sammy Kaye
11.	5/21	4	**Cry, Baby, Cry** ... Larry Clinton

12.	5/28	3	**Cathedral In The Pines** ... Shep Fields
13.	6/11	1	**I Let A Song Go Out Of My Heart** ... Benny Goodman
14.	6/18	4	**Says My Heart** ... Red Norvo
15.	6/25	10	**A-Tisket, A-Tasket** ... Ella Fitzgerald with Chick Webb
16.	7/16	6	**Music, Maestro, Please** ... Tommy Dorsey
17.	9/17	2	**Change Partners** ... Fred Astaire
18.	9/24	2	**Alexander's Ragtime Band** ... Bing Crosby & Connee Boswell
19.	10/01	8	**My Reverie** ... Larry Clinton
20.	10/01	4	**I've Got A Pocketful Of Dreams** ... Bing Crosby
21.	10/15	2	**Change Partners** ... Jimmy Dorsey
22.	10/29	2	**I've Got A Pocketful Of Dreams** ... Russ Morgan
23.	10/29	1	**Heart And Soul** ... Larry Clinton
24.	11/05	6	**Begin The Beguine** ... Artie Shaw
25.	12/17	2	**Two Sleepy People** ... Fats Waller
26.	12/31	2	**You Must Have Been A Beautiful Baby** ... Bing Crosby
27.	12/31	2	**I Won't Tell A Soul (I Love You)** ... Andy Kirk

1939

1.	1/07	2	**They Say** ... Artie Shaw
2.	1/14	5	**Jeepers Creepers** ... Al Donohue
3.	1/14	1	**Thanks For Ev'rything** ... Artie Shaw
4.	2/04	1	**The Umbrella Man** ... Kay Kyser
5.	2/11	9	**Deep Purple** ... Larry Clinton
6.	3/18	1	**Penny Serenade** ... Guy Lombardo
7.	4/22	2	**Heaven Can Wait** ... Glen Gray
8.	5/06	1	**Our Love** ... Tommy Dorsey
9.	5/13	5	**And The Angels Sing** ... Benny Goodman
10.	5/20	2	**Three Little Fishies** ... Kay Kyser
11.	6/03	4	**Beer Barrel Polka** ... Will Glahe
12.	6/10	4	**Wishing (Will Make It So)** ... Glenn Miller
13.	7/08	4	**Stairway To The Stars** ... Glenn Miller
14.	8/12	4	**Moon Love** ... Glenn Miller
15.	8/12	2	**Sunrise Serenade** ... Glen Gray
16.	9/09	7	**Over The Rainbow** ... Glenn Miller
17.	9/09	3	**The Man With The Mandolin** ... Glenn Miller

1939 — Cont'd

18. 9/30 1 **Blue Orchids** ... Glenn Miller
19. 10/21 1 **Day In, Day Out** ... Bob Crosby
20. 11/04 5 **South Of The Border (Down Mexico Way)** ... Shep Fields
21. 11/11 1 **Address Unknown** ... Ink Spots
22. 11/25 8 **Scatter-Brain** ... Frankie Masters

1940

1. 1/27 2 **All The Things You Are** ... Tommy Dorsey
2. 2/03 5 **Careless** ... Glenn Miller
3. 2/10 12 **In The Mood** ... Glenn Miller
4. 2/24 1 **Indian Summer** ... Tommy Dorsey
5. 3/16 1 **Darn That Dream** ... Benny Goodman
6. 3/30 5 **When You Wish Upon A Star** ... Glenn Miller
7. 5/04 9 **Tuxedo Junction** ... Glenn Miller
8. 5/04 7 **The Woodpecker Song** ... Glenn Miller
9. 6/22 3 **Imagination** ... Glenn Miller
10. 7/10 2 **Make-Believe Island** ... Mitchell Ayres
11. 7/20 1 **Fools Rush In (Where Angels Fear To Tread)** ... Glenn Miller
12. 7/27 12 **I'll Never Smile Again** ... Tommy Dorsey
13. 8/24 2 **Where Was I?** ... Charlie Barnet
14. 9/07 1 **The Breeze And I** ... Jimmy Dorsey
15. 9/14 4 **Sierra Sue** ... Bing Crosby
16. 10/19 9 **Only Forever** ... Bing Crosby
17. 11/23 1 **Blueberry Hill** ... Glenn Miller
18. 11/28 3 **Ferryboat Serenade** ... Andrews Sisters
19. 11/30 4 **Trade Winds** ... Bing Crosby
20. 12/21 13 **Frenesi** ... Artie Shaw

1941

1. 1/18 3 **We Three (My Echo, My Shadow, And Me)** ... Ink Spots
2. 2/08 3 **There I Go** ... Vaughn Monroe
3. 3/01 1 **Dream Valley** ... Sammy Kaye
4. 3/15 1 **Song Of The Volga Boatmen** ... Glenn Miller
5. 3/29 10 **Amapola** ... Jimmy Dorsey
6. 4/05 2 **I Hear A Rhapsody** ... Jimmy Dorsey
7. 4/19 4 **There'll Be Some Changes Made** ... Benny Goodman
8. 4/19 2 **High On A Windy Hill** ... Jimmy Dorsey

9. 6/07 2 **My Sister And I** ... Jimmy Dorsey
10. 6/14 6 **Maria Elena** ... Jimmy Dorsey
11. 6/21 8 **Daddy** ... Sammy Kaye
12. 6/28 1 **Dolores** ... Tommy Dorsey
13. 7/05 2 **The Band Played On** ... Guy Lombardo
14. 8/02 1 **Intermezzo (Souvenir De Vienne)** ... Guy Lombardo
15. 8/30 4 **Green Eyes** ... Jimmy Dorsey
16. 9/27 1 **Blue Champagne** ... Jimmy Dorsey
17. 10/04 8 **Piano Concerto In B Flat** ... Freddy Martin
18. 10/25 2 **(Lights Out) 'Til Reveille** ... Kay Kyser
19. 11/08 5 **You And I** ... Glenn Miller
20. 11/29 9 **Chattanooga Choo Choo** ... Glenn Miller
21. 12/13 3 **I Don't Want To Set The World On Fire** ... Hoarce Heidt
22. 12/20 1 **Elmer's Tune** ... Glenn Miller

1942

1. 2/07 2 **A String Of Pearls** ... Glenn Miller
2. 2/14 4 **Blues In The Night** ... Woody Herman
3. 2/28 10 **Moonlight Cocktail** ... Glenn Miller
4. 3/14 1 **(There'll Be Bluebirds Over) The White Cliffs Of Dover** ... Kay Kyser
5. 3/21 2 **Rose O'Day (The Filla-Da-Gusha Song)** ... Freddy Martin
6. 5/02 1 **Deep In The Heart Of Texas** ... Alvino Rey
7. 5/09 6 **Tangerine** ... Jimmy Dorsey
8. 5/09 2 **I Don't Want To Walk Without You** ... Harry James
9. 6/06 3 **Somebody Else Is Taking My Place** ... Benny Goodman
10. 6/13 4 **Jersey Bounce** ... Benny Goodman
11. 6/20 4 **Sleepy Lagoon** ... Harry James
12. 7/18 8 **Jingle, Jangle, Jingle** ... Kay Kyser
13. 7/25   **Don't Sit Under The Apple Tree (With Anyone Else But Me)** ... Glenn Miller
14. 8/29 2 **Who Wouldn't Love You** ... Kay Kyser
15. 9/26 4 **He Wears A Pair Of Silver Wings** ... Kay Kyser
16. 10/24 8 **(I've Got A Gal In) Kalamazoo** ... Glenn Miller

1942 — Cont'd

17. 10/31 11 **White Christmas** ... Bing Crosby
18. 12/19 1 **My Devotion** ... Vaughn Monroe
19. 12/26 2 **Strip Polka** ... Kay Kyser

1943

1. 1/09 3 **Praise The Lord And Pass The Ammunition!** ... Kay Kyser
2. 1/16 6 **There Are Such Things** ... Tommy Dorsey
3. 1/30 2 **Mister Five By Five** ... Harry James
4. 2/13 3 **When The Lights Go On Again (All Over The World)** ... Vaughn Monroe
5. 2/13 2 **I Had The Craziest Dream** ... Harry James
6. 3/06 13 **I've Heard That Song Before** ... Harry James
7. 4/17 2 **Moonlight Becomes You** ... Bing Crosby
8. 5/29 1 **That Old Black Magic** ... Glenn Miller
9. 6/12 3 **Taking A Chance On Love** ... Benny Goodman
10. 6/26 4 **As Time Goes By** ... Rudy Vallee
11. 7/03 3 **Comin' In On A Wing And A Prayer** ... Song Spinners
12. 7/24 7 **You'll Never Know** ... Dick Haymes
13. 7/24 3 **Let's Get Lost** ... Vaughn Monroe
14. 8/21 3 **In The Blue Of The Evening** ... Tommy Dorsey
15. 9/04 1 **It Can't Be Wrong** ... Dick Haymes
16. 9/11 7 **Sunday, Monday, Or Always** ... Bing Crosby
17. 9/11 2 **All Or Nothing At All** ... Frank Sinatra With Harry James
18. 10/30 8 **Pistol Packin' Mama** ... Al Dexter
19. 11/06 12 **Paper Doll** ... Mills Brothers

1944

1. 1/15 9 **Shoo-Shoo Baby** ... Andrews Sisters
2. 1/29 5 **My Heart Tells Me** ... Glen Gray
3. 3/04 7 **Besame Mucho** ... Jimmy Dorsey
4. 3/18 5 **Mairzy Doats** ... Merry Macs
5. 4/22 5 **San Fernando Valley** ... Bing Crosby
6. 4/22 2 **It's Love-Love-Love** ... Guy Lombardo
7. 5/06 5 **I Love You** ... Bing Crosby
8. 6/10 6 **I'll Get By (As Long As I Have You)** ... Harry James
9. 7/01 4 **I'll Be Seeing You** ... Bing Crosby

10. 8/05 9 **Swinging On A Star** ... Bing Crosby
11. 8/05 2 **G.I. Jive** ... Louis Jordan
12. 10/07 5 **You Always Hurt The One You Love** ... Mills Brothers
13. 10/14 6 **A Hot Time In The Town Of Berlin** ... Bing Crosby & Andrews Sisters
14. 10/14 4 **I'll Walk Alone** ... Dinah Shore
15. 12/02 2 **Into Each Life Some Rain Must Fall** ... Ella Fitzgerald & Ink Spots
16. 12/09 2 **I'm Making Believe** ... Ella Fitzgerald & Ink Spots
17. 12/16 8 **Don't Fence Me In** ... Bing Crosby & Andrews Sisters

1945

1. 2/10 10 **Rum And Coca-Cola** ... Andrews Sisters
2. 3/17 2 **Ac-Cent-Tchu-Ate The Positive** ... Johnny Mercer
3. 3/31 7 **My Dreams Are Getting Better All The Time** ... Les Brown
4. 3/31 1 **Candy** ... Johnny Mercer, Jo Stafford & Pied Pipers
5. 4/14 2 **I'm Beginning To See The Light** ... Harry James
6. 5/05 1 **Dream** ... Pied Pipers
7. 5/12 6 **There! I've Said It Again** ... Vaughn Monroe
8. 5/26 9 **Sentimental Journey** ... Les Brown
9. 7/28 8 **On The Atchison, Topeka, And The Santa Fe** ... Johnny Mercer
10. 9/15 10 **Till The End Of Time** ... Perry Como
11. 11/17 4 **Chickery Chick** ... Sammy Kaye
12. 11/24 3 **It's Been A Long, Long Time** ... Harry James
13. 12/08 2 **It's Been A Long, Long Time** ... Bing Crosby with Les Brown
14. 12/15 6 **I Can't Begin To Tell You** ... Bing Crosby
15. 12/29 2 **White Christmas** ... Bing Crosby

1946

1. 1/05 2 **Symphony** ... Freddy Martin
2. 1/26 5 **Let It Snow! Let It Snow! Let It Snow!** ... Vaughn Monroe
3. 2/09 2 **Doctor, Lawyer, Indian Chief** ... Betty Hutton
4. 3/02 2 **Personality** ... Johnny Mercer
5. 3/16 11 **Oh! What It Seemed To Be** ... Frankie Carle
6. 3/23 8 **Oh! What It Seemed To Be** ... Frank Sinatra

	Date	Wks	
			1946 — Cont'd
7.	4/27	1	**I'm A Big Girl Now** ... Sammy Kaye
8.	5/04	3	**Prisoner Of Love** ... Perry Como
9.	5/18	8	**The Gypsy** ... Dinah Shore
10.	5/25	13	**The Gypsy** ... Ink Spots
11.	8/03	8	**To Each His Own** ... Eddy Howard
12.	8/03	1	**Surrender** ... Perry Como
13.	8/31	2	**To Each His Own** ... Freddy Martin
14.	9/14	4	**Five Minutes More** ... Frank Sinatra
15.	9/21	1	**To Each His Own** ... Ink Spots
16.	10/19	9	**Rumors Are Flying** ... Frankie Carle
17.	12/14	2	**Ole Buttermilk Sky** ... Kay Kyser
18.	12/28	7	**The Old Lamp-Lighter** ... Sammy Kaye
19.	12/28	6	**(I Love You) For Sentimental Reasons** ... Nat "King" Cole
			1947
1.	1/04	1	**White Christmas** ... Bing Crosby
2.	2/08	2	**Huggin' And Chalkin'** ... Hoagy Carmichael
3.	2/22	3	**Managua, Nicaragua** ... Freddy Martin
4.	2/22	1	**Open The Door, Richard!** ... Count Basie
5.	3/01	1	**Open The Door, Richard!** ... Three Flames
6.	3/08	2	**Anniversary Song** ... Dinah Shore
7.	3/15	13	**Heartaches** ... Ted Weems
8.	3/15	1	**Managua, Nicaragua** ... Guy Lombardo
9.	5/10	2	**Linda** ... Ray Noble featuring Buddy Clark
10.	5/31	1	**Mam'selle** ... Frank Sinatra
11.	6/07	2	**Mam'selle** ... Art Lund
12.	6/21	8	**Peg O' My Heart** ... Harmonicats
13.	6/28	3	**Chi-Baba, Chi-Baba (My Bambino Go To Sleep)** ... Perry Como
14.	6/28	1	**Temptation (Tim-Tayshun)** ... Red Ingle
15.	7/05	6	**Peg O' My Heart** ... Buddy Clark
16.	8/09	6	**Smoke! Smoke! Smoke! (That Cigarette)** ... Tex Williams
17.	8/09	4	**Peg O' My Heart** ... Three Suns
18.	8/30	17	**Near You** ... Francis Craig
19.	12/13	10	**Ballerina** ... Vaughn Monroe
			1948
1.	2/21	5	**I'm Looking Over A Four-Leaf Clover** ... Art Mooney
2.	3/13	9	**Manana (Is Soon Enough For Me)** ... Peggy Lee
3.	4/24	3	**Now Is The Hour** ... Bing Crosby
4.	5/08	8	**Nature Boy** ... Nat "King" Cole
5.	5/22	7	**You Can't Be True, Dear** ... Ken Griffin
6.	7/03	6	**Woody Woodpecker** ... Kay Kyser
7.	8/14	6	**You Call Everybody Darlin'** ... Al Trace
8.	8/14	5	**Love Somebody** ... Doris Day & Buddy Clark
9.	8/28	8	**Twelfth Street Rag** ... Pee Wee Hunt
10.	10/09	5	**A Tree In The Meadow** ... Margaret Whiting
11.	11/06	10	**Buttons And Bows** ... Dinah Shore
12.	12/25	3	**All I Want For Christmas (Is My Two Front Teeth)** ... Spike Jones
			1949
1.	1/15	7	**A Little Bird Told Me** ... Evelyn Knight
2.	1/15	1	**My Darling, My Darling** ... Jo Stafford & Gordon Macrae
3.	3/05	1	**I've Got My Love To Keep Me Warm** ... Les Brown
4.	3/05	1	**Powder Your Face With Sunshine** ... Evelyn Knight
5.	3/12	7	**Cruising Down The River** ... Blue Barron
6.	3/26	7	**Cruising Down The River** ... Russ Morgan
7.	4/30	1	**Careless Hands** ... Mel Torme
8.	5/07	2	**"A" - You're Adorable** ... Perry Como
9.	5/14	12	**Riders In The Sky (A Cowboy Legend)** ... Vaughn Monroe
10.	5/14	3	**Forever And Ever** ... Russ Morgan
11.	7/30	5	**Some Enchanted Evening** ... Perry Como
12.	9/03	4	**You're Breaking My Heart** ... Vic Damone
13.	9/10	2	**Someday** ... Vaughn Monroe
14.	10/01	8	**That Lucky Old Sun** ... Frankie Laine
15.	11/12	3	**Slippin' Around** ... Margaret Whiting & Jimmy Wakely
16.	11/26	6	**Mule Train** ... Frankie Laine

1950

1. 1/07 1 **Rudolph, The Red-Nosed Reindeer** ... Gene Autry
2. 1/14 5 **I Can Dream, Can't I?** ... Andrews Sisters
3. 2/11 8 **Chattanoogie Shoe Shine Boy** ... Red Foley
4. 2/11 2 **Rag Mop** ... Ames Brothers
5. 3/11 2 **The Cry Of The Wild Goose** ... Frankie Laine
6. 3/18 4 **Music! Music! Music!** ... Teresa Brewer
7. 3/25 10 **If I Knew You Were Comin' I'd've Baked A Cake** ... Eileen Barton
8. 4/29 11 **The Third Man Theme** ... Anton Karas
9. 5/06 11 **The Third Man Theme** ... Guy Lombardo
10. 6/03 2 **Hoop-Dee-Doo** ... Perry Como with Fontane Sisters
11. 6/10 1 **Sentimental Me** ... Ames Brothers
12. 6/24 2 **I Wanna Be Loved** ... Andrews Sisters
13. 7/08 8 **Mona Lisa** ... Nat "King" Cole
14. 8/19 13 **Goodnight, Irene** ... Weavers with Gordon Jenkins
15. 10/28 5 **All My Love** ... Patti Page
16. 11/18 4 **Harbor Lights** ... Sammy Kaye
17. 12/02 5 **The Thing** ... Phil Harris
18. 12/16 13 **The Tennessee Waltz** ... Patti Page

1951

1. 3/03 8 **If** ... Perry Como
2. 3/10 1 **Be My Love** ... Mario Lanza
3. 4/21 9 **How High The Moon** ... Les Paul & Mary Ford
4. 6/23 5 **Too Young** ... Nat "King" Cole
5. 7/28 8 **Come On-A My House** ... Rosemary Clooney
6. 9/08 10 **Because Of You** ... Tony Bennett
7. 11/03 6 **Cold, Cold Heart** ... Tony Bennett
8. 11/17 8 **Sin (It's No Sin)** ... Eddy Howard
9. 12/29 11 **Cry** ... Johnnie Ray

1952

1. 1/05 3 **Slow Poke** ... Pee Wee King
2. 3/15 10 **Wheel Of Fortune** ... Kay Starr
3. 5/17 7 **Kiss Of Fire** ... Georgia Gibbs
4. 5/17 5 **Blue Tango** ... Leroy Anderson
5. 5/24 1 **A Guy Is A Guy** ... Doris Day
6. 6/07 3 **Here In My Heart** ... Al Martino

7. 7/05 1 **Delicado** ... Percy Faith
8. 7/12 9 **Auf Wiederseh'n Sweetheart** ... Vera Lynn
9. 7/26 3 **Half As Much** ... Rosemary Clooney
10. 9/06 1 **Wish You Were Here** ... Eddie Fisher
11. 9/13 12 **You Belong To Me** ... Jo Stafford
12. 9/27 10 **I Went To Your Wedding** ... Patti Page
13. 11/22 2 **It's In The Book** ... Johnny Standley
14. 11/29 6 **Why Don't You Believe Me** ... Joni James
15. 12/06 3 **The Glow-Worm** ... Mills Brothers
16. 12/27 2 **I Saw Mommy Kissing Santa Claus** ... Jimmy Boyd

1953

1. 1/10 5 **Don't Let The Stars Get In Your Eyes** ... Perry Como
2. 2/14 7 **Till I Waltz Again With You** ... Teresa Brewer
3. 3/21 8 **The Doggie In The Window** ... Patti Page
4. 5/16 10 **Song From "Moulin Rouge" (Where Is Your Heart)** ... Percy Faith
5. 7/04 7 **I'm Walking Behind You** ... Eddie Fisher
6. 8/08 11 **Vaya Con Dios (May God Be With You)** ... Les Paul & Mary Ford
7. 8/15 4 **No Other Love** ... Perry Como
8. 9/26 8 **You You You** ... Ames Brothers
9. 10/10 4 **St. George And The Dragonet** ... Stan Freberg
10. 11/21 8 **Rags To Riches** ... Tony Bennett

1954

1. 1/02 8 **Oh! My Pa-Pa** ... Eddie Fisher
2. 2/27 4 **Secret Love** ... Doris Day
3. 3/13 7 **Make Love To Me!** ... Jo Stafford
4. 4/10 8 **Wanted** ... Perry Como
5. 6/05 9 **Little Things Mean A Lot** ... Kitty Kallen
6. 7/24 1 **Three Coins In The Fountain** ... Four Aces
7. 8/07 9 **Sh-Boom** ... Crew-Cuts
8. 9/25 6 **Hey There** ... Rosemary Clooney
9. 11/06 3 **This Ole House** ... Rosemary Clooney
10. 11/13 3 **I Need You Now** ... Eddie Fisher
11. 12/04 7 **Mr. Sandman** ... Chordettes

OUT THESE
EARCH HITS!

Billboard's
MUSIC YEARBOOK
1985

The complete story of 1985's charted music in one concise volume. Covers 11 major Billboard charts. Updates all previous Record Research books and includes data on the exciting new "Top Pop Compact Disks" chart.
240 pages. Softcover $25.00

Billboard's
MUSIC YEARBOOK 1983 —
MUSIC YEARBOOK 1984

Two comprehensive books listing complete chart data on each of the records to appear on the 14 major Billboard charts in 1983 and 1984. Updates all previous Record Research books, plus complete data on 6 additional charts.
Softcover — $25.00 each
(1983 edition: 276 pages / 1984 edition: 264 pages.)

Joel Whitburn's
BUBBLING UNDER THE HOT 100
1959-1981

Lists over 4,000 hits that never made the "Hot 100". The only reference book of its kind.
240 pages. Softcover $25.00

UP AND COMING on next page

UP AND COMING!

BILLBOARD'S TOP VIDEOCASSETTES 1979-1986

Our first venture into the movie industry. The over one thousand hottest videos from the past 8 years, researched and ranked for the first time.

TOP BLACK 1942-1986

We've gone back further than ever before! Our research has been expanded to not only include every single to hit Billboard's Top 100 "Hot R&B (Black) Singles" chart, but also their "Best Selling," "Disc Jockey," and "Juke Box" R&B charts. The book will include well over a thousand artist biographies, and for the very first time, the complete history of every album to ever hit Billboard's "Top R&B (Black) Albums" chart.

TOP COUNTRY 1944-1986

Here's the revision you've been waiting for — featuring numerous artist biographies, title trivia and greatly expanded research. This book will begin with the first "Most Played Juke Box Folk Records" chart in 1944 and will list every single to ever hit Billboard's "Best Selling," "Disc Jockey," "Juke Box," and Top 100 "Hot Country Singles" charts. Also, for the very first time, the complete history of every album to ever hit Billboard's "Top Country Albums" chart.